15

Contemporary Social Problems

contributors

John A. Clausen *University of California, Berkeley*
Albert K. Cohen *University of Connecticut*
James S. Coleman *The Johns Hopkins University*
Donald R. Cressey *University of California, Santa Barbara*
Kingsley Davis *University of California, Berkeley*
Amitai Etzioni *Columbia University*
Jack P. Gibbs *University of Texas at Austin*
William J. Goode *Columbia University*
Edwin Harwood *Rice University*
Seymour M. Lipset *Harvard University*
David Matza *University of California, Berkeley*
Thomas F. Pettigrew *Harvard University*
David Riesman *Harvard University*
James F. Short, Jr. *Washington State University*
Robert Straus *University of Kentucky*
Robert S. Weiss *Harvard Medical School*

Contemporary
Social Problems

THIRD EDITION

edited by

ROBERT K. MERTON
Columbia University

and

ROBERT NISBET
University of California, Riverside

HARCOURT BRACE JOVANOVICH, INC.
New York   Chicago   San Francisco   Atlanta

COVER: Detail of photo by Hans Waldmann,
F. Hoffman-La Roche & Co., Switzerland.

ISBN: 0-15-513790-5

Library of Congress Catalog Card Number: 75-152586

PRINTED IN THE UNITED STATES OF AMERICA

Preface

Three central ideas govern the scope and character of this book. *First,* the growth of sociological knowledge has led to increasing specialization within the "field" of social problems; *second,* a comprehensive theory of social problems does not yet exist, although it may be in the making; and *third,* the student can best come to an understanding of social problems by focusing on the problems of a complex, industrial society. A few words about each of these ideas will introduce the reader to the plan and rationale of the book.

In sociology, as in other disciplines, specialization increases as knowledge accumulates through the combined efforts of scholars and scientists. The sociologist of a generation or two ago could acquire a thoroughgoing knowledge of almost everything that was then known about social problems, for, compared with today, relatively few sociologists were investigating these problems. With increased research, however, it has become a formidable task to keep up with the work done on even a few of these problems and almost impossible to keep thoroughly informed of the work going forward on all of them. Studies of population and mental health, for example, are developing at such a pace that the sociologist who would remain abreast of either subject recognizes that he cannot be equally informed in the fields, say, of ethnic relations or of community disorganization.

As sociologists generally realize, this development has led to splitting the study of social problems into a set of associated sociological specialties:

specialties dealing with forms of deviant behavior expressed, for example, in crime and juvenile delinquency, mental illness and drug addiction, suicide and prostitution; and specialties dealing with forms of social disorganization such as those found in relations between racial and ethnic collectivities, in various patterns of population change, in the organization of work, in the home, and in the local community. One way of acquainting the student with detailed knowledge of these subjects is to have a curriculum of specialized courses, each devoted to a single subject. This is what many departments of sociology actually do. But most undergraduates do not go on to these advanced courses. Moreover, there is added value in introducing the student, whether he continues his sociological studies or not, to an overview of social problems in a single course. This helps him see the many interconnections between problems and the ways in which general sociological ideas bring some understanding of seemingly disparate problems.

One way, then, of providing a comprehensive and authoritative overview of the associated special subjects is to have the essentials of each subject distilled by specialists. This affords the student an introduction to each subject under the guidance of a sociologist who knows that subject in depth. The specialist can inform the student of what is currently known in a particular field and, no less important, give him a sense of ongoing sociological inquiry by authoritatively indicating the limits of current knowledge in that field. This is one of the assumptions underlying *Contemporary Social Problems.*

From the outset, the editors and contributors to the book foresaw the difficulty that might arise from having each specialist deal with a separate social problem: The student may receive a suitable introduction to each subject *seriatim* but be left, in the end, with an assortment of disconnected sociological information. This point brings us to our second governing idea. Sociologists today generally recognize that there is no single, comprehensive, and tight-knit sociological theory of social problems, in the sense of a logically articulated set of precisely formulated propositions from which many empirical uniformities are rigorously derived. Instead, the condition is similar to the one often found when a discipline is still in its early phases of development: the presence of a good many confirmed hypotheses of fairly limited scope. In the study of social problems, however, a theoretical *orientation* of much broader scope has also been emerging, and has been found useful in guiding the observations of many sociologists at work in the different specialties encompassed by the subject. This theoretical orientation, rather than a comprehensive theory, unifies the chapters of this book.

The reader will identify this general orientation for himself in the following pages, but it may nevertheless be useful to summarize its principal components here.

1. The same social structure and culture that make for conforming and organized behavior also generate tendencies toward distinctive kinds of deviant behavior and potentials of social disorganization. In this sense, the problems current in a society reflect the social costs of a particular organization of social life.

2. From this premise, it can be seen that the sociological orientation rejects as demonstrably inadequate the commonly held doctrine that "evil is the cause of evil" in society. Instead, it alerts us to search out the ways in which socially prized arrangements and values in society can produce socially condemned results.

3. It also follows that, to a substantial extent, social problems are the un-willed, largely indirect, and often unanticipated consequences of insti-tutionalized patterns of social behavior.

4. From the preceding, it further follows that in order to study and under-stand disorganization in particular departments of social life, it is neces-sary to study and understand the social framework of their organization. The two—disorganization and organization, seemingly at odds in the commonsense view—are theoretically inseparable.

5. From these related ideas, it can be concluded that each social structure will have its distinctive social problems.

6. Another major premise in our theoretical orientation asserts that social structures are variously differentiated into social statuses, roles, and strata, having their distinctive as well as their shared values and inter-ests. This premise directs us to the differing pressures upon people dif-ferently located in a given structure to engage in certain forms of deviant behavior and be diversely subject to the consequences of social disorgani-zation. People in different social positions are variously exposed to the hazards of aberrant behavior and are variously vulnerable to these hazards.

7. The preceding two premises—#5 and #6—lead us to anticipate that people occupying different positions in the social structure will ordinarily differ in their appraisal of the same social situations and view them dif-ferently as problems requiring social action. Only in the exceptional and limiting case do people in all groups, social strata, organizations, com-munities, and regions in a complex society agree that particular condi-tions are social problems requiring solution.

8. Since, as was noted in premise #7, people variously located in the social structure differ in their appraisal of a particular situation as a social prob-lem, we should be prepared to find (and in fact we do find) that the "solu-tions" proposed for coping with these problems also differ; these too are limited and partly shaped by the social structure. As a result, the changes represented by the proposed solutions will accord with the interests and

values of some and run counter to the interests and values of others. It is, therefore, often difficult to develop and put into effect public policies designed to solve social problems.

9. Owing to the systemic interdependence among the parts of a social structure, efforts to do away with one social problem will often introduce other (either more or less damaging) problems. Sociologists have long noted this tendency; all that we can now say is that the image of a problem-free society, in which all is as all men would wish it to be, must be regarded as fantasy. But it does not follow that public policy cannot result in the progressive curbing of particular social problems and be the better prepared to cope with the new ones coming along.

It is not the function of a textbook to set out new theoretical systems with which the authors are currently experimenting. The orientation that pervades this book is not peculiar to it; the theoretical position has emerged from the collective efforts made by sociologists over a number of generations. It is held in common by the various "schools of sociology," differing somewhat in other respects but not, we believe, in the main substance of the premises we have just sketched out.

The third idea governing the plan of the book has to do with its scope and with the particular problems selected for examination. As will become apparent to the reader, the book focuses on contemporary social problems in the United States, considered as an instance of a complex, industrial society. However, even though the greater part of the factual evidence has been drawn from American society, the book is by no means confined to it. The chapter on the world's population crisis, of course, presents comparative materials drawn from various types of society, but so do many of the others — always with an eye to clarifying American social problems by comparison with problems found elsewhere.

The particular subjects selected are for the most part those kinds of deviant behavior and social disorganization that have long been at the center of sociological research on social problems. Once again, this decision was largely dictated by our plan for a textbook rather than a specialized monograph.

This collaborative effort, then, is designed to introduce the student to the sociology of social problems by giving him an overview of forms of deviant behavior and social disorganization and by showing him how sociologists identify, acquire, and interpret the evidence in order to arrive at what is now known about the subject.

.   .   .

The third edition retains the basic structure and governing ideas of the two preceding editions, but its content has been substantially changed to take account of new developments in the field and new areas of concern in American society. These changes are chiefly of three kinds: (1) Statistical and quantitative data have been updated as much as possible in all chapters; (2) most of the chapters have been considerably revised to include recent sociological research and analysis; (3) an entirely new chapter on youth and politics has been added to the book; (4) two chapters from earlier editions have been completely rewritten. The present chapter on race relations is wholly new and provides a systematic analysis of black-white relations in contemporary America. The chapter on war and disarmament has been replaced by a discussion of the phenomenon of violence and some of its implications. As was the first edition in its day, the present edition is directed to the most pressing problems facing our society.

We are greatly indebted to the following college and university instructors for their detailed suggestions and comments, which have been invaluable to us in planning the third edition: Richard A. Schermerhorn, Case Western Reserve University, Edward Tiryakian, Duke University, Mervin F. White, Washington State University, Stephen Schafer, Northeastern University, Jack C. Ross, Memorial University of Newfoundland, Dallas J. Reed, University of Nevada, Ervin Hummel, Portland Community College, Jane G. Herzog, City College of San Francisco, Joseph E. Kivlin, Bowling Green State University, R. E. Hilbert, University of Oklahoma, Charles Browning, Whittier College, Frank Burtner, Clemson University, Richard H. Hall, University of Minnesota, J. S. Heiss, University of Connecticut, James Hansen, West Valley Joint Junior College, Mark O. Rousseau, University of North Carolina at Chapel Hill.

ROBERT K. MERTON
Columbia University

ROBERT NISBET
University of California

Contents

xi

part two **Social Disorganization**

introduction

The Study
of Social Problems

ROBERT NISBET

WHAT IS A SOCIAL PROBLEM?

A social problem is a way of behavior that is regarded by a substantial part of a social order as being in violation of one or more generally accepted or approved norms. We will start with that definition. True, it presents certain difficulties. But it is the considered judgment of the editors of this book that it is not possible to provide comprehensive and rigorous definition of a social problem until the student has been exposed to some of the empirical details of social problems, as he will be in each of the 15 chapters of the book. Hence in the final chapter, the Epilogue, Robert Merton deals fully and in detail with the several dimensions involved in any effort to define or describe a social problem.

The above definition is designed merely to get us off to a beginning. Observe in the definition that there is an *objective* aspect of a social problem; this is the way of behavior itself. There is also a *subjective* aspect. No mode of human behavior can be considered a *social* problem, no matter how repugnant it may be to any given individual or small group, unless it is regarded as a morally objectionable deviance from some accepted norm, or norms, by a substantial and determining number of persons in the surrounding social order.

1

Consider poverty. Even in Western civilization poverty, as a condition affecting large numbers of persons, was not regarded as a social problem until perhaps a century and a half ago. Poverty was regarded as a built-in, inevitable, and ineffaceable part of the human condition. There are still persons in the West who appear to regard poverty in this light. And in the world at large today it is safe to generalize that the overwhelming majority of people, including, tragically, the poor themselves, regard poverty in this light. But, for reasons I shall come to shortly, poverty is widely regarded today by Americans, and by others in the world who have been affected by Western norms of the past century or two, as being in the first place "wrong" and in the second place a condition about which something should be and can be done. Thus poverty has become a social problem. So have mental disorder, alcoholism, family disorganization (all of which are very old in human annals) become only fairly recently defined as social problems.

Fifteen major social problems are considered in this book: drug use, mental disorders, delinquency, organized crime, alcohol abuse, suicide, sexual deviance, population increase, race relations, family disorganization, work and automation, urban conflict, poverty, violence, and youth revolution. Clearly a very wide range of behavior is represented by this list. Many different contexts and motivations as well as effects are involved. What do they have in common? Each is a mode of behavior that is widely regarded today in American society as being in violation of, or almost in violation of norms that are widely held in the current social order.

It may well be asked why these problems have been chosen by the editors for treatment by individual experts; why not others that for some persons at least might be regarded as even more pressing to national policy. The answer is that this is a textbook in sociology. Sociology is a special science characterized by concepts and conclusions, which are based on analysis and research, yielding in turn perspectives on society and its central problems. For many decades now, sociologists have worked carefully and patiently on these problems. In other words, this book is concerned not only with the presentation of major social problems but with the scientific concepts and procedures by which these problems have been, and continue to be, studied.

THE RELATIVITY OF SOCIAL PROBLEMS

In the tentative definition just given, the subjective element of social problems was stressed. That is, a social *problem* cannot be said to exist until it is defined as one. The way of behavior involved may be fixed and may be found among many peoples. But unless the way of behavior is defined as a violation of some norm, unless it is regarded by large numbers of people as being repugnant to moral consciousness, it cannot be termed a social problem; not, that is, within the social order concerned. In our society, if head-hunting or cannibalism were suddenly to be practiced by a small but continuing minority of persons both activities would no doubt be termed social problems. In those few societies, however, where either of these practices has fallen within the norms, that is, where head-hunting or cannibalism, within duly prescribed limits, has been approved, there is, plainly, no social problem.

One cannot study either history or comparative sociology without becoming strongly aware of the relativity of social problems, of what is pronounced as deviant behavior or immorality. Incest is regarded as deviant behavior and as both legally and morally wrong in our society. In other societies, such as ancient Egypt and pre-Christian Hawaii, incest, at least within families of high lineage, was considered proper.

In a famous phrase the American sociologist William Graham Sumner wrote: *The mores make right.* Sumner meant that conceptions of right and wrong, good and evil, are relative to the prevailing norms, to folkways which are possessed of sacred significance, in a given social order. And, as the evidence of both history and comparative sociology makes vividly clear, there is a vast diversity of such norms, folkways, and mores in mankind.

One may, if he chooses, believe that, such evidence notwithstanding, there is such a thing as absolute good or absolute evil. Certain philosophers, among them Immanuel Kant, and nearly all founders of religions, have so believed. They may be correct; possibly there is an absolute good or an absolute evil. But from the vantage point of the sociologist, of the social scientist, no such view can be taken. No matter what our own individual preferences and repugnances may be, no matter how devoted we may be to a given value, such as ethnic equality, or how repelled by violations of this norm in the society around us, we are still obliged, as sociologists, to recognize that social problems are inseparably joined to subjective awareness of a particular set of norms.

This highlights the whole matter of *moral consciousness* in society. Just as there is a reciprocal relation between individual thought, properly called, and the recognition of cognitive problems, so is there a reciprocal relation between moral consciousness in a society and the perceived existence of social problems. We may cite here Émile Durkheim's famous thesis of the "functional necessity of crime" in which he argued that a certain amount of crime is necessary to the stability of a moral order because without occasional violations there would be no occasions on which society could reaffirm the essential tenets of its moral code. Durkheim's thesis doubtless says more than most of us would care to conclude, but we may extract from it the important and paradoxical truth that while moral consciousness indeed underlies perception of social problems, it is only the recognition of, and response to, social problems that creates or reinforces the moral consciousness of any age. When a society pronounces narcotics addiction, poverty, or mental illness a social problem, it is saying something about, and *doing something for,* its level of moral regard. The gin-ridden slums of eighteenth-century London that William Hogarth sketched did not seem a social problem to the average Englishman of that day, any more than did the generally appalling lives of the indigent, the delinquent, and the mentally ill. This is not to say that the eighteenth century was without moral consciousness but only that such conditions, wretched though they seem to us in retrospect, had not yet seriously entered the province of moral consciousness, except in the minds of a very few.

While it would be presumptuous to claim for ourselves a higher level of morality than that of two centuries ago in England, we are certainly justified in saying that for more and more of us today these conditions have disturbing impact. Making all allowance for lethargy and for the hypocrisy and the parochially selective character of much of our response to poverty, narcotics addiction, alcoholism, juvenile delinquency, and prostitution, these have become active moral, and therefore social, problems for us in a way that they were not in the earlier age.

To be sure, we do not have to go back to the eighteenth century for negative examples of this point. After all, for how long can discrimination in civil rights be said to have existed in the domain of active moral consciousness and considered as one of America's social problems? There are curious fluctuations of moral regard for some problems: poverty, for instance. Once it was a staple of every textbook on the social ills of America. Then for two or three decades it largely disappeared, only to return to active attention in the 1960's, surrounded (as the chapter on poverty makes arrestingly evident) by a plethora of issues — moral, semantic and political — that complicate even its study.

Another fluctuation of moral attitude has been occurring with respect to fertility. Traditionally fertility has been a positive value — sanctified by religious dogma and attested to by folk rituals. Today, however, we are in the presence of what can only be called a confrontation between the traditional religious ethic on fertility and a new ethic, that of control of fertility, born of scientific understanding. Here are two conflicting activations of moral consciousness: one in the ranks of those for whom defense of the ancient ethic of fertility is urgent — for whom birth *control* is the social problem; the other in the ranks of those for whom the unrestrained increase of population ranks as perhaps the greatest single problem faced by mankind.

THE MODERN RECOGNITION
OF SOCIAL PROBLEMS

In our study of social problems, we must consider not only their intrinsic cognitive, moral, and social elements, but the historical currents through which social problems have gained the status of popular recognition in modern Western society.[1] Two historical currents are of greatest significance: *secular rationalism* and *humanitarianism*.

The essence of secular rationalism in modern Europe has been its conversion of problems and conditions from the ancient theological contexts of good and evil to the rationalist contexts of analytical understanding and control. Control is the essential element. If we did not think there was something that could be *done* about social problems, if we regarded them—as some of those in this book were once universally regarded—as unalterable elements of the human condition, we probably would not have included them in our contemporary lexicon of social problems. We would not define them, nor indeed even see them, as social problems. It is no accident that serious awareness of social problems in western Europe first entered the European mind during the Enlightenment, an age when reason, extolled by earlier philosophers such as Bacon and Descartes on behalf of the control or "reform" of *nature,* was now extolled on behalf of the control or reform of *society.* This was the age when, for the first time in many centuries—since, perhaps, the age of Socrates—men were inspired by the possibilities of putting reason in the service of man's earthly estate and happiness. And, given this new vision of reason and its potentialities, it was not strange that social conditions that had heretofore been regarded by even the most humane minds as, at best, distressing and regrettable aspects of man's sojourn on earth began to be noticed as "problems."

After the Enlightenment, the condition of the working class, poverty, crime, family disorganization, and similar conditions would be regarded by an ever widening public as matters about which something should and could be done. All too often, then as now, what was proposed as a cure could be worse than the ill—as in some of Jeremy Bentham's well-meant, scrupu-

---

[1] See the Epilogue (pp. 799–818) for an analysis of the sociological criteria for the recognition of social problems.

lously rational, but nevertheless merciless projects for the care of the indigent, delinquent, and mentally disturbed. His celebrated Panopticon (an ingenious mode of concentric architecture in which a centrally placed overseer could keep the delinquent or indigent inmates under constant and relentless eye, at little cost) was, as Disraeli later observed, the unlovable issue of a marriage between reason and inhumanity.[2]

It does not matter. Even if, as more than one student of the utilitarians has been led to conclude, it was the illogicality rather than the moral degradation or inhumanity of social conditions that spurred Bentham and his followers; the central point is that through their unrelenting effort one of the two essential conditions of the modern recognition of social problems was fulfilled: that is, the intellectual conversion of the "timeless and inevitable" into concrete problems that not only should, but *could* be met by human reason.

The second historical condition, also an emergent of the early nineteenth century, is humanitarianism. We may define humanitarianism as the gradual widening and institutionalization of compassion. Compassion is an individual sentiment, but its sway is largely established by socially prescribed channels and boundaries. There is, it is worth emphasizing, a history and a sociology of compassion just as there is a history and sociology of jealousy, affection, and other emotions that, though assuredly individual, nevertheless manifest themselves in ways largely prescribed by social norms. Compassion is a timeless and universal human sentiment, but its objects and intensity vary from age to age. In the same way that certain social conditions became, at the beginning of the nineteenth century, objects of rationalist regard, conceived as intellectual problems, they became also objects of moral regard, conceived as moral problems. Sudden reflections of this growing compassion are to be seen in the literature of the age, notably in the English social novel, where such problems were effectively brought to the attention of society.

Histories of modern European humanitarianism sometimes interpret this widening of compassion as the consequence of a humanization of the upper classes. While there may be something in this, the major reason lies, as Alexis de Tocqueville saw so vividly, in the tendency toward equalization of social ranks that followed the American and French revolutions. One of the by-products of the age of democratic revolution was a widening of the social area within which human compassion tended to operate. Tocqueville's illus-

---

[2] For an account of Bentham's Panopticon principle see Gertrude Himmelfarb's "The Haunted House of Jeremy Bentham" in *Ideas in History: Essays in Honor of Louis Gottschalk* (Durham, N. C.: Duke University Press, 1965).

trations of his thesis are vivid, and since the sociological elements remain as relevant today as then, they are worth repeating. He cites the following passage from a letter written in 1675 by a gentlewoman, Madame de Sévigné, to a friend about the brutal civil repression that followed an abortive tax revolt by the hard-pressed peasants of her area of Brittany:

> You talk very pleasantly about our miseries, but we are no longer so jaded with capital punishments; only one a week now, just to keep up appearances. It is true that hanging now seems to me quite a cooling entertainment. I have got a wholly new idea of justice since I have been in this region. Your galley slaves seem to me a society of good people who have retired from the world in order to lead a quiet life.[3]

These lines were written, as Tocqueville notes, not by a selfish and cruel, much less a sadistic, person, but by a woman passionately attached to her children, always ready to sympathize with the sorrows of her friends, and notably indulgent to servants and retainers. "But," writes Tocqueville, "Madame de Sévigné *had no clear notion of suffering in anyone who was not a person of quality*" (italics added). It was not a want of compassion that produced the cruel irony of Madame de Sévigné's words; it was the existence of a *social limit* of compassion that, try as she might have, she could not have gone beyond.

Why, Tocqueville asks, would such a letter from a person widely regarded as cultivated and humane be inconceivable in Tocqueville's own day? Not, he concludes, because of any intrinsic elevation of upper-class character, but instead because of a fundamental change in the relation of the ranks of society to one another, a change produced by the tides of political and civil democracy that were beginning to engulf social parochialisms and insensitivities that neither Christianity nor Renaissance humanism had had any marked effect upon. The widening of political democracy has had, Tocqueville suggests, the effect of widening the effective social field of recognition of suffering.

> When all the ranks of a community are nearly equal, as all men then think and feel in nearly the same manner, each of them may judge in a moment the sensations of all the others; he casts a rapid glance upon himself, and that is enough. There is no wretchedness into which he cannot readily enter, and a secret instinct reveals to him its extent. It signifies that not strangers or foes are the sufferers; imagination puts him in their place; something like a personal feeling is mingled with

---

[3] Alexis de Tocqueville, *Democracy in America* (New York: Knopf, 1945). This passage and those which follow are contained in Volume II, Book III, Chapter 1.

his pity and makes himself suffer while the body of his fellow creature is in torture.

Tocqueville offers a positive and a negative demonstration of his thesis, each highly germane to a chapter in this book. In the first, drawn from penology, Tocqueville adduces "the model system of criminal justice" that existed in the early nineteenth century in the United States (and was indeed the prime reason for Tocqueville's visit to this country, as it was of the visits of some other Europeans). "In no country is criminal justice administered with more mildness than in the United States. . . . North America is, I think, the only country upon earth in which the life of not one citizen has been taken for a political offense in the course of the last fifty years." And the reason for this, Tocqueville thought, was that Americans, by and large, could see those charged with criminal offenses as of like social class and, therefore, perceivable within the social limits of their compassion.

He draws the second, and negative, demonstration of his equalitarian thesis from the treatment of black slaves. Tocqueville, like other visitors to the South at that time, was appalled by the "frightful misery" and the "cruel punishments" inflicted on the blacks by Southern whites who were, in many instances, like Madame de Sévigné, notably kind and generous in their own circles. The black was, however, even farther outside the pale of social compassion than was the French peasant in the seventeenth century. He and his sufferings were, so to speak, invisible.

"Thus," Tocqueville concludes, "the same man who is full of humanity toward his fellow creatures when they are at the same time his equals becomes insensible of their afflictions as soon as that equality decreases. His mildness should therefore be attributed to the equality of conditions rather than to civilization and education."

Two further conclusions might be added, neither of which Tocqueville lived long enough to draw, but both of which add cognate illumination to his thesis. In penology, the mid-nineteenth-century beginnings of the deterioration of the "model system of criminal justice" that had so impressed Tocqueville coincided almost exactly with the changing composition of the American prison population. As the number of impoverished, lower-class Irish, Italians, and, then, eastern Europeans in the prison population increased — a consequence of the sudden increase of these nationalities in the larger population — the capacity of the middle-class American to conceive their plight compassionately declined notably. The results are written in a system of justice and prison administration that, by the late nineteenth century, brought few if any admiring European visitors.

The other illustration is the twentieth-century history of blacks in

America. What has manifestly been required to alter the position of blacks in American society is exactly what was required in early nineteenth-century Europe to alter the position of peasants: an extension of, first, political and civil equality and then, gradually, equality in economic and social areas. And if it be true that the French Revolution was required for the elevation of the status of European peasants, it is equally true that the contemporary "civil rights revolution" is required in the case of blacks.

THE CULTURAL BASE OF SOCIAL PROBLEMS

In the popular view, largely as the result of our religious and moral heritage, there is a common tendency to think of social problems as the consequences of "antisocial" behavior, as the embodiment of patently evil elements. For many centuries, Western ethics rested upon the view that, as only good can come from good, so the causes of evil must be located in the residually evil. If there is crime, it is because there are evil persons, evil groups, evil values.

Yet, as every chapter of this book makes clear, the crucial contexts of social problems are, in many cases, accepted by society as unobjectionable, even good. Thus the social *problem* of alcohol in American culture is largely inseparable from the social *function* that alcohol holds in literally scores of cherished contexts of association, ranging from the family cocktail before dinner through religious ceremonies to the indispensable diplomatic reception. Similarly, there is a close relation between certain social problems and urbanism. Apart from city life, whose cultural values attract people in large numbers,[4] many of the ills would not exist. The same is true of the difficulties presented by population growth. Obviously, there is nothing intrinsically evil in having large families; an entire morality rests upon the Biblical injunction to be fruitful and multiply. For thousands of years high birth rates were necessary and functional for the preservation of society. But today, in many areas, as the result of sharply lowered death rates, the growth of population has become one of society's most formidable problems.

In crime, suicide, and family disorganization, we often discover processes of behavior that, if not necessarily beneficent, are at least normal to human

---

[4] See Edward Banfield, *The Unheavenly City* (Boston: Little, Brown, 1970) for an informed, often brilliant presentation of the thesis that the urban scene, for all its difficulties, is yet superior to settings from which the migrants-to-cities have generally come. As Professor Banfield demonstrates too, much of the "crisis of the city," as it is often called, proceeds not so much from conditions themselves, bad as these can often be, as from the *higher levels of expectation* that life in the city has encouraged.

endeavor in our society. This is not said in moral exoneration. Stealing is wrong, and it can constitute a serious problem to any community that prizes its own maintenance and integrity. Sociologists interested in the causal conditions of types of crime, however, cannot overlook their effective contexts: the incentives, goals, status drives, and role needs that characterize the society. We may deplore our rates of suicide and of divorce – as measured in lives taken, in broken homes, and in personalities set adrift – but we cannot isolate these rates from a culture that sets high value upon individualism, secularism, and contractual ties.

Too often the popular view of social problems likens them to cancers: for most citizens, the image of society and its problems is that of an essentially healthy organism invaded by alien substances. The legislator, or the policeman, is thought of as a kind of physician, bound to remove the cyst, destroy the virus, but not alter the character of the organism itself.

Such an analogy seriously distorts social reality. We shall discover in the chapters of this book that social problems, even the worst of them, often have a functional relationship to the institutions and values by which we live. We cannot divorce racial and ethnic discrimination from the complex of customs that have sometimes given discrimination a wide variety of functions in our economic, political, domestic, and recreational life. We cannot separate many of the discontents of work from our own development of more cultivated standards of existence and of leisure values that we properly cherish. Even prostitution exists only as a dark reflection of the value we place on the monogamous family and the sanctity of marriage.

This is not to argue that social problems are so closely or so organically related to all parts of their social framework that the only possibility of their solution is a total change of society. This view, to be sure, has been taken by many a moral prophet and philosopher of history. We see it in revolutionary Marxism and in other doctrines which contend that social evils and corruptions are so inextricably embedded in the central character of a given society that until this central character has itself been purified by the fire of revolt against the entire social order specific and particular evils are bound to remain. The attractiveness of this total, chiliastic or revolutionary, approach is evident enough. In his fine historical study, *The Pursuit of the Millennium*,[5] Norman Cohn has shown how, from the late Middle Ages on, European society has been recurrently seized by messianic movements, from those of the fifteenth century that drew their eschatological inspiration from the Book of Daniel or the Sybilline Oracles to those of the twentieth century that

---

[5] Norman Cohn, *The Pursuit of the Millennium,* 2nd ed. (New York: Harper, 1961), especially the Conclusion.

have drawn inspiration instead from the writings of Marx, Lenin, Hitler, or Mao. The eschatological or revolutionary view is inevitably attractive, especially in ages of profound crisis such as our own. And, in purely intellectual terms, it is much easier to replace the manifest diversity and variety of social problems by some single, totally encompassing, all-pervading morbidity or pathology of which the diverse, particular, social problems are seen as mere reflections. Everyone familiar with the history of the West knows the extent to which such monolithic and millennialist interpretations have served as bases of social action. And, reflecting for a moment on the immense influence exerted in the history of thought by minds such as Plato, St. Augustine, Rousseau, and Marx, all of whom made some variation of this type of view the basis of either eschatological vision or of revolutionary prescription, it is well to bear in mind the continuing possibilities of such views and interpretations in our own day and in the foreseeable future. Either in religious or in political terms, the eschatological view of man and society is a powerful one; far more likely to arouse mass movements than the strictly scientific view and, sometimes, to effect signal changes in entire societies.

But although the social scientist cannot afford to overlook social millennialism, nor to be unmindful of the extent to which millennialism and revolution can often quicken the attention of both scientists and public in general to specific kinds of problems, it must be emphasized that there is no place for millennialist views in science as such. Those who choose to repudiate the scientific approach are entitled to say, "so much the worse for science." But those who, surveying the remarkable changes that have been effected in man's mind, man's culture, and man's command of the physical world by pursuit of the scientific ideal – an ideal nowhere better expressed than by Francis Bacon's famous statement that knowledge is power – will respond differently.

Modern sociology – as exemplified in the chapters of this book – maintains that social behavior, whether "moral" or "immoral," "legal" or "illegal," can be understood only in light of the values that give such behavior meaning and the institutions that provide channels for the achievement of these values. The values and the institutions may be (by whatever standards of moral and political assessment), evil or lacking in capacity to sustain a civilized social order. It does not matter. They must still be understood or else their renunciation, their control, is destined to be a matter of impotent ideal rather than effective determination. We observe repeatedly in deviant behavior the pursuit of the same values that are applauded by dominant elements of the social order, but through channels or by means that tend to be condemned by these dominant elements. As Robert Merton has observed, ". . . when a system of cultural values extols, virtually above all else, cer-

tain common success goals for the population at large while the social structure rigorously restricts or completely closes access to approved modes of
reaching these goals for a considerable part of the population, deviant behavior ensues on a large scale." [6]

Social problems are distinguished from other problems by their close
relation to institutional and normative contexts. They are social in that they
pertain to human relationships and to the value contexts in which human
relationships exist. They are problems in the sense that they represent inter-
ruptions in the socially expected, of the morally desired, scheme of things.
Bear in mind, as emphasized at the beginning of this chapter, that there is
the subjective as well as the objective dimension to any social problem. No
social problem exists for any people unless it has been *defined* as a social
problem. The subjective element is inescapable. If, as is entirely possible, the
smoking of marijuana ceases to be *defined* as deviant behavior by a determining number of the American people, the smoking of marijuana may increase
to the proportions of current smoking of ordinary tobacco and still not be
regarded, as it now tends to be among many Americans, as a social problem,
a manifestation of deviance.

Something should be said here about the ways whereby a given mode of
behavior is defined in a social order as being "deviant," "disorganized," or
"wrong." Robert Merton will deal with this in greater detail in the Epilogue.
For the moment it is sufficient to note that such definition often derives
from the set of norms held by a dominant group. A generation ago, the sociologist C. Wright Mills, in a now classic essay, demonstrated how norms acquired by social workers and others from the ascendant WASP (White,
Anglo-Saxon, Protestant) element in America were the bases of definition
as pathological of behavior patterns deeply entrenched, and were regarded
as both normal and proper, in ethnic groups such as the Irish, Italian, Polish,
Black, Chicano, Catholic, Jewish minorities in America. Behavior that
could seem disorganized and even bordering on the criminal to WASPs in
this country (themselves now a minority) was no more than behavior
governed by standards which were, within the ethnic group involved, fully
as "moral" or as "right" as the standards which were the points of reference
for the dominant WASP minority. There is, in short, an ethnic variability
to be seen in what is defined as social problems or deviant behavior. So is
there a variability accounted for by social class, as a large number of sociological studies have demonstrated. Behavior taken for granted in a lower

---

[6] Robert K. Merton, *Social Theory and Social Structure,* rev. ed. (New York: Free
Press, 1957), p. 146.

socioeconomic stratum of the population may be regarded as virtually pathological in a higher stratum (and vice versa).

So is there a historical variability of social problems. It is not necessary to repeat what was said above regarding the role of humanitarianism, of institutionalized compassion, in the recognition of social problems and in the decision by dominant elements of a society to do something about these problems. But it is useful to note that a given people, or a given ethnic group, can become nearly transformed within short periods of time, not only in the surrounding society's perception of them but also in the group's perception of itself. Consider the following statement, found in the United Hebrew Charities Annual Report for 1901:

> A condition of chronic poverty is developing in the Jewish community of New York that is appalling in its immensity. Forty-five percent of our applicants, representing between twenty and twenty-five thousand human beings, have been in the United States over five years; have been given the opportunities for economic and industrial improvement which this country affords; yet, notwithstanding all this, have not managed to reach a position of economic independence.[7]

For anyone even remotely acquainted with the extraordinary efflorescence of the Jews in the twentieth century—one that has been intellectual and cultural, as well as economic and political—comment on that passage would be superfluous.

There is nothing unique in the sociological perspective revealed by the historical experience of the Jews. From one point of view the whole of human history is a series of fluctuations in the economic, political, and cultural positions of the innumerable ethnic aggregates which have existed on the earth from the beginning of *homo sapiens* and which, presumably, will always exist. The histories of the Greeks, the Romans, the Germanic peoples, the Chinese, and others are histories of variations in political and economic position, in cultural achievement, *and also in specific types of social problems.* Had we the kinds of documentation in the realm of social problems for such peoples that we do have in the realms of political, economic, and cultural history, there is little doubt that we would find the same kind of variability in both the nature of social problems and also in the perceptions or recognitions of social problems that is so conspicuous a feature of American history during the past century.

Consider the Poles as an ethnic group in the United States today. At the

---

[7] Quoted by Edward Banfield, *The Unheavenly City,* p. 114.

present time, as a number of studies indicate, the Polish people, especially in the area of Chicago and its environs, reveal a substantial concern with the protection of jobs, residential values, schools, and other manifestations of achieved middle-class status from a perceived threat to this status, and to the civil order that surrounds it, by other ethnic minorities, chiefly black, who have recently come into the area. One may, of course, sympathize with the motivations involved, for they tend to be those of middle-class America, generally. But it is worth recalling that a bare half-century ago delinquency rates were high enough among the Poles in and around Chicago to furnish the point of departure of one of the classic studies in the history of American sociology: *The Polish Peasant* by William I. Thomas and Florian Znaniecki. Then it was the Poles who were regarded by a great many in the area as an ethnic threat to law and order, as well as to the fundamental values of middle-class society. Historical variability is, plainly, an indispensable perspective for our understanding of patterns of social problems. So, too, the comparative framework is indispensable for such understanding.

THE COMPARATIVE STUDY
OF SOCIAL PROBLEMS

It is one of the merits of the chapters in this book that they place American social problems against the background of other peoples — historic and contemporary, non-Western and Western. No society, however simple and stable, is altogether free of social dislocations and deviations, but the comparative study of human behavior makes it clear that both types and intensities of social problems differ widely from culture to culture, from age to age. In part this is the consequence, as we have just noted, of contrasting states of moral consciousness. It is also the result of contrasting standards of living and patterns of social authority, function, and membership.

Nonliterate and folk societies, largely organized in terms of kinship and other close personal ties, tend to have few, if any, of the social problems we consider in this book. For these societies other problems, chiefly those of adjustment to the physical environment — the need for food, shelter, physical security — loom much larger. When the basic problems of physical survival dominate a society's attention, there is less likelihood of those breakdowns in social relationships and deviations from social codes that are the stuff of social problems in present-day America. The raw challenge of physical environment has something of the same integrating effect upon social organization that catastrophe and disaster can have. In time of disaster and physical calamity, as has often been noted, crimes, suicides, divorces, and community conflicts tend to diminish in number. The very mobilization of human energies elicited by a harsh physical environment or threat of a catastrophe has a tonic effect upon human relationships, resulting in a stronger moral consensus and a more integrated social system.

In America today we live in what some call an affluent society. It is a society characterized by an impressive command of physical resources, high standards of private consumption, freedom from most of the uncertainties of life that plagued our ancestors, and relatively high levels of humanitarianism. There are also, of course, squalid slums, both urban and rural; occasional epidemics of disease; sudden eruptions of violence or bigotry, even in the most civilized of communities; people for whom the struggle for food and shelter yet remains obsessing and precarious. Thus, we are not free of social problems, and some of them seem to grow almost in direct proportion to our affluence. That there may indeed be a fundamental conflict between material welfare and social or moral consensus has crossed the minds of thinkers from Hesiod to Schweitzer. Such thinkers have argued that in the process of developing wealth and power a society must draw upon personal qualities—avarice, ambition, egoism, and others—which are the very antithesis of the qualities upon which social harmony and moral consensus rest.

Whether so fundamental a conflict in civilization exists is not, however, one of the questions dealt with by this book. However fascinating it may be as a problem in social ethics, it is not a question easily amenable to the concepts and methods of social science. It remains in the realm of moral philosophy, always interesting, always provocative, but basically unanswerable in the terms with which the sociologist seeks to clarify the social environment.

What we do know as social scientists emphasizes that there is no paradox in a civilization of high order containing certain social problems in greater number and intensity than are to be found in the kind of simple society that some philosophers have thought to be nearer man's essential nature. There is no paradox in relatively high rates of crimes against property in an advanced society that sets a high premium upon worldly goods and quick access to them. There is no paradox in the presence of racial and ethnic tensions in a society that, on the one hand, fosters equality through its constitution and laws but, on the other, maintains, through processes of use and wont, enclaves of discrimination and differential privilege.

Nor is there any paradox involved in the other problems that flourish (as this book makes plain) amid the opulence and aspirations of present-day America. Poverty, population tensions, social discontents in work, community conflicts, and divorce all have, in the form in which we know them, a close relation to the social patterns and values that we prize as elements of an advanced and free society. This does not mean that the problems are therefore ineradicable. Slavery and epidemic disease, once thought to be inextinguishable features of the human scene, have today largely disappeared. We therefore have every right to believe that our other problems are similarly subject to solution, given increasing knowledge and the will to use it.

APPROACHES TO SOCIAL PROBLEMS

It will help clarify our understanding of the distinctiveness of the sociological approach to social problems if we examine briefly four other possible approaches: religion, law, journalism, and art. Let us begin with one of the oldest and most deeply revered: religion.

RELIGION—For thousands of years religious and legal codes have been the major perspectives through which social problems have been defined and acted upon. And, as we shall have repeated occasion to note, one of the major difficulties experienced by the contemporary social scientist in his own approach to social problems is the ancient and insistent tendency of the human mind to foreclose consideration of matters like juvenile delinquency and alcoholism by simply pronouncing them illegal or evil.

Whatever else religion is, it is an alembic of social experience: It distills and also composes the data of experience. It is not what religion says *about* social problems that is crucial; it is the way religion perceives, identifies, and relates these problems that gives it powerful sway. Religion identifies the transcendental essence in the mundane. The realm of the sacred, Durkheim emphasized, was the most powerful realm in the early development of human consciousness. From it and from the differentiation made between it and the profane or the merely utilitarian arose many of our moral and even metaphysical concepts. It is hardly strange, therefore, that social problems should still, for most persons, be subjects in the sovereign realm of the sacred — the realm, that is, of good and evil, of right and wrong.

From a theological point of view, many of the problems treated in this book are, first and last, violations of a divinely sanctioned moral order. As such they are often considered to be manifestations of evil, of original sin. The theologian will concede readily that such acts as murder, adultery, and theft are susceptible in part to nonreligious explanations, to influences of environment, and, if he is engaged in pastoral work, he will not hesitate to avail himself of the help of legal and social agencies. But, as a theologian, he will probably choose to see the final explanation of these acts in religious terms, as violations of God's commandments, as sin. And, like the explanation, the ultimate solution is put by the theologian in religious terms: expiation through prayer and penance.

LAW — There is both a logical and historical relationship between the religious and the legal approaches to social problems. In law, as in religious morality, such acts as murder and theft are conceived, fundamentally, as violations of a normative order — in this instance, the duly constituted and sanctioned law of the society concerned. From a strictly juridical point of view, the only reality that a social problem has is its legal reality as a crime, tort, or other breach of the legal order. A murder is not something for either study or redemptive prayer; it is the signal for mobilization of the whole retributive apparatus of the state, a mobilization that does not end until judicial determination of guilt is concluded. To be sure, the modern legal process increasingly avails itself of the resources of medicine, psychiatry, and the social sciences. A case that begins as a hard and fast legal matter — with apprehension, prosecution, and punishment the sole ends in view — may, in some of the more enlightened halls of justice today, end therapeutically rather than retributively. The borrowed objective is cure rather than punishment. And that social prevention of crime, rather than repression alone, has become more widely accepted in many communities is a mark both of rising recognition of the practical contributions of the social sciences and of more humane objectives of law-enforcement agencies. Nevertheless, with all allowance for its liaisons with therapeutic and scientific disciplines, the sovereign end of the legal process remains that of enforcement and, where necessary, punishment for violations. There remains for most persons a strongly religious element in law and its relation to crime. The guilty person, we are prone to say, must pay his debt to society — that is, do penance — through various expiatory means, ranging from fines through imprisonment to execution.

JOURNALISM — A very different approach to social problems is the journalistic approach. Ever since the eighteenth century, newspapers and magazines have been notable organs of exposure of and protest against exploitation, corruption, and degradation in society. Not infrequently has honest and accurate exposure been the real basis of charges of sensationalism and yellow journalism in this country and elsewhere in the world. In the United States, early in this century, it was the writings of the so-called Muckrakers — a group of courageous and perceptive journalists that included Lincoln

Steffens, Ida Tarbell, and Upton Sinclair, working for such publishers as E. H. Scripps and Frank Munsey—that, perhaps above any other single force, first shocked the American public into awareness of social problems, particularly those of the burgeoning cities, and helped force public agencies into action. Today, the newspaper and the magazine remain valuable instruments for awakening popular response to narcotics, poverty, slums, prostitution, delinquency, and other ills that all too easily take refuge behind public lethargy or official incompetence. Modern thought as well as modern life would be the poorer but for the arts of cartoonists, the denunciations of editors, and the often brilliant exposures by newspaper reporters.

In such journalism, the primary intent is to shock or shame the public into awareness of violations of the legal or moral order. Exposure is the overriding aim; all else—whether understanding, prevention, cure, or punishment—is secondary. The method is consequently impressionistic and rarely contextual.

ART—A fourth approach to social problems, that of the artist, is to be seen in all spheres of art, painting, drama, poetry, but nowhere so compellingly as in the social novel. Some of the most celebrated literary works of the past century have been conceived by their authors in hatred of poverty, injustice, and inequality. In the nineteenth century, the mordant depictions of lower-class misery under the impact of the new industrialism contained in the works of Mrs. Gaskell, Charles Kingsley, Charles Dickens, and Émile Zola were, for many millions of readers, the indispensable means of perceiving what actually lay around them. So too, in a later period, did the works of Henrik Ibsen, H. G. Wells, Samuel Butler, George Bernard Shaw, and John Galsworthy bring to attention the cankering social and moral problems that had lain long concealed behind the thick folds of Victorian respectability. In Europe, the social novel and play attained, in the late nineteenth and early twentieth centuries, much of the appeal to popular taste that the picaresque or romantic novel had held earlier. It was therefore an effective vehicle of the development of humanitarianism.

In America, the social novel has been a conspicuous part of the literary tradition throughout the present century. The novels of David Graham Phillips, Upton Sinclair, Theodore Dreiser, John Steinbeck, James Farrell, Charles Jackson, Nelson Algren, Ralph Ellison, and many others have laid bare, often hauntingly, sometimes with genius, the essential human elements of social problems dealt with in this book. Merely to list such titles as *Susan Lenox, The Jungle, An American Tragedy, The Grapes of Wrath, Studs Lonigan, The Lost Weekend, The Man with the Golden Arm,* and *Invisible Man* is to be reminded of novels that, quite apart from their varying worth as imaginative literature, have had enormous impact in their illumination of prostitution, poverty, crime, job and family dislocation, juvenile delinquency, alcoholism, narcotics, ethnic segregation, and other social problems. At their best these works have conveyed to their readers a sense of poignant immediacy, of vicarious experience, that is always the test and essence of art. Nor should we overlook the powerful impact of music when it comes to awareness of social problems. Leaving aside earlier manifestations of such awareness in the history of the world's ballads and folk songs, so often directed by their composers to the plight of the oppressed and the miserable, we need but look at some of the contemporary songs highlighted by the genius of Bob Dylan, Simon and Garfunkel, and many others in our day. Consider only the beautiful and moving "The Boxer" by Simon and Garfunkel with its reminder of the world of the impoverished and the rootless. Or the very recent Crosby, Stills, Nash, and Young, *Déjà Vu,* which is folkrock music of high order in itself and that, as in the powerful "Teach Your Children," is a plea for understanding between generations in a world that none of us made. Nor, by any light, should one overlook the songs of the Beatles and their pioneering efforts to fuse the character of rock with illumination of the political and social setting. Music is today, as it always has been, one of the most important avenues to awareness of, and action on, social problems.

What all four of these approaches to social problems—religious, legal, journalistic, and artistic—have in common is their moral commitment. By their very nature they are caught up in, and are inseparable from ethical codes or ethical intent: in the case of religion or law, the governing end is that of inducing conformity to the moral or legal order, and in the case of the journalist or novelist, the end is that of arousing moral sympathy.

SOCIOLOGY AND SOCIAL PROBLEMS

Very different from the four approaches just discussed is the sociological approach to social problems. Here the objective is not dramatization, exposure, condemnation, or repression. The primary objective of the sociologist is to uncover the causes of the problems, to seek their determining contexts and their relation to other areas of social behavior. The sociologist is interested in understanding pathological social actions in exactly the same way that he is interested in understanding the normal and the good. In his strict role of scientist, as seeker of knowledge, he cannot be interested in exhortation or repressive sanctions except insofar as these responses are themselves involved in the nature of the social problems he is concerned with. What the scientist, as scientist, seeks is knowledge of the conditions involved, how the problems have come to be as we find them, and what the crucial factors are in their incidence. It is not action that the scientist seeks but hypothesis — clear, verifiable, and valid statements of causation.

Nothing could be more false than the occasional charge that sociologists are indifferent to moral standards; that for them one form of behavior is as good or bad as the next; that relativism is the moral code by which men should live. It would be as false as suggesting that the medical scientist is indifferent to the agonies of cancer because, instead of relying simply upon prayer or anesthetics, he insists upon the long-run study of this disease, upon approaching it in the same way that he would approach benign or normal aspects of organic functioning.

The social scientist is interested in making the protection of society his first responsibility, in seeing society reach higher levels of moral decency, and, when necessary, in promoting such legal actions as are necessary in the short run for protection or decency. But, as a scientist, it is his professional responsibility to deal with such matters as crime, suicide, narcotics, and ethnic tensions exactly in the manner in which he deals with other forms of human behavior.

Concern with social problems — including those treated in this book — has been an integral part of the main tradition of sociology. Emphasis on this point is valuable at the present time when, as Robert Merton suggests in the Epilogue, an ambivalence exists toward the sociology of social problems and toward applied social science in general. Let it be emphasized, therefore, that modern systematic sociology was born in the practical interests of its titans quite as much as in their theoretical interests. Two classic works, each immensely influential on the subsequent course of sociological theory, admirably illustrate this: *Suicide* by Émile Durkheim and *The Polish Peasant* by William I. Thomas and Florian Znaniecki, the first published in France in 1896, the second in the United States in 1918–1920. Durkheim took as his point of departure the social problem posed by the rising rate of suicide in European society; Thomas and Znaniecki began with the reported high incidence of delinquency and crime among the Polish population of Chicago. That we tend today to think of each of these momentous studies as falling in the main tradition of sociology, rather than in the literature of social problems, is tribute, of course, to the overriding scientific intent of their authors. The essential point, however, for our purposes is that each work, in the process of illuminating the nature of a widely recognized social problem (and also, be it emphasized, of seeking a practical answer to the problem), was led to theoretical analyses of the social order, of personality, social interaction, and social norms that were to have quite as much effect upon the subsequent study of social organization as of disorganization, of theory as well as practice. It is perhaps the crowning merit of each work that it lifted its problem from the simple and sterile perspectives in which it had previously lain — perspectives of "pathology," "evil," and the like — and related it significantly to some of the main currents and contexts of modern Western society: individualism, secularism, urbanism, and industrialism.

All of this is not to suggest that social problems — of the kind represented in this book — are the constitutive problems of sociology as a science. Such a suggestion would be wide of reality. For sociology, like any other analytical science, is built around a different type of problem: that which emerges from theoretical reflection and dispassionate observations. Even if we lived in a social order miraculously exempt from all the problems dealt with in this book, man — blessed (or cursed) by what William James called the "divine itch of curiosity" — would still be interested in his own nature and society, and, therefore, in problems of social structure, social interaction, social change, and the others that give distinctive identity to sociology as a basic science. The itch of curiosity has generally had more to do with the history of science than has the spur of moral conscience.

So much is incontestable. But having said this, two conclusions remain vital: First, in the actual history of modern sociology, it was the attention, as much moral as theoretical or analytical, that such pioneers as Le Play, Durkheim, Weber, Thomas, and Cooley paid to social problems like family disorganization, suicide, and delinquency that provided much of the base on which the relevance to society of sociology's *theoretical* problems and conclusions was first established. The major figures in the history of sociology have never been constrained by methodological or theoretical fastidiousness from dealing directly with social problems. After all, as John Dewey tirelessly emphasized, it is method, not subject, that identifies a science.

The second conclusion, no more than an extension of the first, is that even today, when sociology has built up an imposing body of empirical fact, method, and verified conclusion that separates it as clearly from social work and reform as modern physiology is separated from medicine and public health, sociologists continue to find in their studies of crime, narcotics, alcohol, delinquency, and other social problems insights into the nature of human behavior with implications that reach far beyond the empirical area from which they are drawn. It is hardly possible to read the chapters of this book and not realize frequently, and sometimes poignantly, the applicability of their main concepts to nondeviant behavior.

SOCIAL POLICY AND SOCIAL ACTION [8]

Throughout this book, in each of the chapters that follow, the reader will find concern with the all-important question: What is to be done? Plainly, we live in a world in which much needs to be done, and as quickly as knowledge and resources permit. It is all very well to say that in the long run social problems tend to become solved, or at least reduced in intensity, through normal human adaptation. We live, however, in the short run. And the pages of history are clear enough that societies and civilizations in the past have become extinct, or rendered impotent and lethargic, through the presence of problems no greater than those which are to be found in American society, and in the world at large, today.

What do we do? At every hand today there is the cry for knowledge that is *relevant*. And, there is no doubt about it, knowledge — that is, scientific knowledge — should be relevant: relevant to the urgencies of the human condition as we find them the world over. But what do we mean by "relevant?" The dictionary tells us that the word means "bearing upon, or connected with, the matter at hand — applicable, germaine, apposite." Well and good. But what *is* the matter at hand? Are we to limit reference solely to those surface aspects that are within the reach of everyone, even the small child? Or do we mean instead the matter at hand as it really is — complex, closely involved in other matters, some visible, some invisible save to the trained eye, and of a depth that ordinary, uninformed vision cannot hope to reach?

This book has been written in the belief that it is the second sense that is meant when the plea for relevance is made. Knowledge that is genuinely relevant — the kind of knowledge that has enabled us to accomplish such remarkable gains in the world of physical things and of human health — does not, cannot, limit itself to the surface or the fringes of a given condition. The kind of knowledge that is to be found in this book, in however tentative a form in many instances, is concerned with the forces and elements that are often out of sight for the ordinary, uninstructed mind, but which can frequently prove to be decisive in reform and revolution.

To the impatient or frightened suburban householder demanding that

[8] This final section is in considerable part an adaptation of the Epilogue of my *The Social Bond: An Introduction to the Study of Society*. (New York: Alfred A. Knopf, 1970), pp. 395–402.

"something be done immediately" about law and order, or to the militant and often intensely idealistic worker for civil rights and other forms of social improvement, the social scientist's stress upon research, careful evaluation of results, and upon knowledge generally, may often seem dreadfully time-consuming and futile. But what is the alternative?

We may say that *action*, in whatever form, direct or legislative or administrative, is the alternative. But no one, surely, would espouse blind or ignorant action, no matter how noble the precipitating ideal or goal. Even the most radical and action-oriented of groups are obliged to distinguish between informed action and uninformed, ignorant action. We may wish to point to some of the great reformers and revolutionists of history, those whom we are prone to call the *doers* rather than the thinkers: Moses, Cleisthenes, Buddha, and Jesus in the ancient world; all the way down to such remarkable individuals as Abraham Lincoln, Louis Brandeis, and Martin Luther King in the modern world. *Doers,* these men were indeed, but what they did was based upon intellectual insight, upon quite extraordinary powers of understanding of the objective scene that very few of us can properly lay claim to. No curtain was drawn by any of these remarkable individuals between action and knowledge. One may confidently assume that each of them, for all his individual gifts, must have wished for even more knowledge than was available to him.

The worst mistake that can be made is to assume that there is a gulf between the study of social problems and action leading to the eradication of social problems. This way lies not merely madness but utter futility. When pellagra, typhoid fever, and smallpox took their once crippling toll of mankind there were doubtless many who looked in amused wonder or disgust at those scientists who in due time began patiently seeking, through research and knowledge, the causes and cures of these epidemic diseases. What a Pasteur did must have seemed profoundly irrelevant to many who were looking for—indeed who in many instances thought they had already found—quick answer to the suffering associated with these diseases. Who at one time could have guessed that behind the ravages of pellagra among millions of Americans lay nothing more than a deficiency of niacin in diet? The literature of a century ago is filled with references to the "shiftlessness," the "squalor," the "heredity" of those suffering the effects of pellagra. But from knowledge of the cause came, within a remarkably short time, relief that has made this once dread disease almost unknown today.

To be sure, as was emphasized above, social problems are very different from biological and medical problems. It cannot be stressed too often that in dealing with social problems—those of the magnitude, say, of explosive population increase, or of mental disorders, crime, ethnic discord, and urban violence — we cannot expect sudden and dramatic breakthroughs that will overnight free the social order from the effects of these social problems. As each of the following studies makes vividly clear, a large part of the difficulty involved in each of our major social problems comes from the fact that the problem itself has contexts which include a great deal of behavior we are prone to regard as proper or normal. Drug use that reaches self-destructive or crippling proportions is, after all, associated with currents of behavior in our society in which the use of many kinds of drugs is deemed acceptable or even beneficial. Even population increase, which threatens to consume our physical, and possibly social, environment, is, obviously, related to reproductive desires that are regarded the world over as normal and rightful.

Nevertheless, there is ample evidence of the fact that knowledge gained and used can be as valuable in our approaches to social problems as to those of physical environment and to human health. Social problems may be more difficult, and far more complex in their details, than other kinds of problems. Knowledge about these social problems may be scantier at the moment. Willingness to use such knowledge as we possess may be sluggish, given vested interests and sheer human inertia in social matters. But there is nothing to suggest for a moment that these social problems have not already been aided in some degree by action based upon knowledge, or that the same problems will not be even more greatly aided in the near future by continued seeking of knowledge.

The worst mistake that could be made is to suppose that some kind of fatal contradiction exists between desire for knowledge and desire for action — action now, in light of the best available knowledge and in accord with the highest ideals. On what possible ground can anyone believe that the choice must be made between science — that is, the search for verifiable knowledge — and the kind of action we take as citizens? Is it not clear that there is both room and necessity for both: for science that looks toward ever more informed action; and for action now that is based upon the best available knowledge?

No matter what kind of society we are to have, no matter what the ruling values of society are to be (even those achieved by the most revolutionary forces in the social order at present), there will always be the necessity of some kind of government, some kind of organized approach to problems that are, in some degree, made inevitable by the sheer presence of human beings. There were those, a half-century ago in Soviet Russia, just after the great events that had brought the revolutionary Bolsheviks to power, who naively thought that the revolution itself was enough; that merely eliminating the hated bourgeoisie, the aristocracy, and others would ensure nearly effortless progress toward the classless, humane, and just society that had been for many decades the ideal of socialists and Communists. But within five years it had become clear to Lenin and others that no such easy passage into the future was possible. No matter how pure the zeal in behalf of justice and knowledge, detailed knowledge was indispensable. And it became also apparent that not a few of the social problems which had existed in pre-Communist Russia continued to exist, with new ones added as the consequence of unforeseen factors.

There are two major challenges, then, faced by sociology and by all the social sciences concerned in any way with the problems dealt with in this book. There is the challenge of social action, which we desperately need in many areas; and there is the challenge of social policy at all levels of government and society, the kind of policy that is itself, or should be, the context of action. Neither can be evaded or cynically ignored. There is every reason for action now, the kind of action that reflects the best knowledge available. There is every reason too for continued seeking of wise and effective policy.

But neither of these challenges in any way runs counter to the kind of challenge that exists within science: the challenge to learn more and more about the problems of our society and their contexts.

part one

Deviant
Behavior

1

Mental Disorders

JOHN A. CLAUSEN

Everyone suffers from physical ailments at one time or another. Most of us spend several days in a hospital at least once or twice in our lifetime. It is probably safe to say that most suffer from emotional upsets at one time or another, though most of us would balk at referring to them as "mental illness." Many of us may be surprised, nevertheless, to learn that approximately 500,000 adults are confined in the mental hospitals of the United States on any given day and that according to current estimates one person in twelve will spend some time in a mental hospital before he dies. It is probably not erroneous to say that almost all of us will at some time witness severe mental illness in a relative or close friend. Further, while mental diseases do not usually kill, they tend to be persistent, often resulting in long periods of incapacity.

We do not usually think of illness as a form of deviant behavior, although we commonly recognize the disruptive effect that illness of a key person can have in any organization. We also commonly recognize that illness is often related to life patterns and to unusual stresses upon the body. But for the diagnosis and treatment of most organic diseases, we have clearly relevant medical resources that are available to most of the population in the United States. Therefore, we generally regard physical illness not as a major social problem but as a medical problem with important economic and social consequences. This is scarcely true, however, of mental illness.

It appears that the mentally ill have always been regarded primarily as deviants rather than as ill persons. In biblical days, the mentally disordered were described as persons possessed by demons or devils. In colonial America, they were often regarded as witches, persecuted, and even executed; at best they were designated as "lunatics" or "madmen" and confined in jails or locked in well-barred rooms. In recent decades, however, there has been a significant social movement committed to the view that mental disorders are truly illnesses, no more to be stigmatized than any other illness. This view has had adherents at least since the rise of medicine in ancient Greece, but it has only recently received even token acceptance by a significant segment of the general public.

Now that mental disorders are officially recognized as a health problem, is there any reason to regard them as a social problem beyond the fact that many persons are incapacitated and that public facilities must be provided for the patients? The question is best answered by considering a brief case description (from the author's files).

Lorraine B. was 40 years old when she was first admitted to a mental hospital. Married for seven years to Fred B., a meagerly educated but hard-working and steady laborer, she was the mother of a five-year-old daughter and a three-year-old son. She had been married previously and had had two children who died in infancy. Her mother had been hospitalized with the diagnosis "schizophrenia" in 1943, staying in the hospital about six months.

Mrs. B. was committed to the hospital on certification by two physicians that she was insane. Questioned by the admitting psychiatrist as to why she was sent to the hospital, she blamed her husband. She said he was frequently drunk, sexually demanding, and running around with other women. Further, her family didn't want her to read the Bible and preach. On questioning, she acknowledged that she had seen God in the clouds and had been hearing noises which she was unable to identify. The provisional diagnosis was *schizophrenia, paranoid type.*

The B.'s lived in a small basement apartment in a metropolitan suburb. The apartment was somewhat sparsely and simply furnished. The rental was high for Mr. B.'s income, but they enjoyed the pleasant suburban neighborhood with its lawns and trees. They did not have a telephone; a television set was the one "luxury item" in their home. Mr. B. did not have a car but had the regular use of a small pick-up truck owned by his employer.

As part of a study of the impact of mental illness on the family, Mr. B. was interviewed at home soon after his wife's admission to the hospital. What had happened prior to her admission? When had he first felt that something might be wrong? Fred B. was not a highly verbal person. His education went only to the fifth grade in rural North Carolina. His answers were brief, direct, concrete — and, the interviewer felt, sincere. His wife had become violently distrustful of him, especially in the past 18 months, but the first indication had come nearly five years ago. He recalled: "It was when Sue [the daughter] was about three months old. My wife was jealous if I played with the baby. She resented it."

From this time, Mr. B. thought of his wife as having "a nasty streak in her that made her act jealous." She was frequently accusatory and he was frequently angry with her, especially when she falsely accused him of running around with other women. Still, she was a good mother to the children and when she flew off the handle, he would go out for a walk to avoid further conflict.

Had there been any other signs? "Yes, her drawing pictures." Mr. B. pointed to a crayon portrait of Christ thumbtacked to the wall. It was striking in coloring and expression. He mused, "It just beats me. She never had no training at drawing but that's a good picture. Don't you think so? She would read the Bible and then just sit there and stare and then she'd draw. It was like she didn't know there was anyone in the room with her. Even if the kids came in and spoke to her, she just didn't notice."

When had he first thought that the problem might be serious? [We did not use the term mental illness, since we wanted his words.] It was the night, about three months before she went to the hospital, when she said someone had "done something" to the alarm clock to change its shape. Her husband had tried to reason with her, but it wasn't any more possible to get her to listen than it had been when he tried to convince her he wasn't running around with other women. "Then," he said, "I thought she wasn't right in the head."

She began to restrict the children's play. When a neighbor came to see how Mrs. B. was, she ordered her former friend out of the house, waving a butcher knife. Lorraine B. moved out of her husband's bed, but frequently kept him awake much of the night while she prowled the house to "protect her papers and books."

A neighbor spoke to Mr. B., suggesting that his wife needed to see a doctor. Fred went to see the family doctor and asked him to drop by the apartment to see Mrs. B. The doctor did so. He prescribed some "nerve pills," which she threw away. Mrs. B. then "ran away" to a friend's home in another state, staying for several weeks; the friend finally called Mr. B. and asked him to take his wife home.

During the final week before hospitalization, Lorraine smashed the radio because it was making sounds even when it was turned off. When the children were invited to a friend's birthday party and went without their mother's consent, she went after them, denounced the neighbor who had invited them and screamed obscenities which aroused the whole neighborhood. Then she became mute and completely withdrawn.

Mr. B. went back to the doctor, who said he had known she was "off" when he saw her a month previously, though he hadn't told her husband then. The doctor filled out commitment papers and said Mr. B. would have to go to the county seat to arrange for taking Mrs. B.

to the hospital. Mr. B. asked a police lieutenant for information about procedures. He was told to swear out a warrant so the police could transport Mrs. B. to the hospital. He did so. The police then dispatched a car to pick up Mrs. B. and take her to the county jail overnight. The next day she was transported to the mental hospital, confused and enraged. She felt that she had been betrayed by her husband and rejected by everyone else.

The research interviewer asked Mr. B., "Looking back over this period, what would you say caused the greatest difficulty in trying to deal with your wife's problem?" His reply: "Not being able to get her to understand."

While their mother was in the hospital, the children were taken to North Carolina to stay with their paternal grandparents on the small farm where their father had grown up.

Mrs. B. was hospitalized for approximately three months. At first she did not wish to see her husband when he came to the hospital to visit; she was alternately seclusive and hostile toward others. She was started on a course of treatment using a strong tranquilizing drug and was transferred to a "chronic" ward. In the view of the examining physician, Mrs. B. had obviously been ill for a considerable time and was unlikely to respond to therapy. Quite soon thereafter, however, she was put in the care of a physician to whom she almost immediately responded positively. It was impossible to say why, but she became cooperative and in a few days was helping other patients and participating in cleaning and kitchen work. She reported no more delusions. After she had maintained apparently normal behavior for several weeks she was permitted to go home for a weekend. Her husband was wary but glad that she could visit. After a few more weeks she went home to stay. Her husband said she had not been "so easy to live with" since before Sue was born. The one thing she was still bitter about was that she had been arrested and thrown in jail overnight before going into the hospital. Mrs. B. was eager to have the children home with her; the family was reconstituted with the children's return a week after hers.

Mrs. B.'s period of hospitalization was about the average for patients with a diagnosis of schizophrenia but obviously longer than would be required for most physical ailments. Her symptoms were perhaps somewhat more violently manifest than those of most patients but were not by any means atypical. The difficulty that her husband had in assessing what was wrong and what could be done about the problem attests to the lack of clearly apparent patterns for dealing with mental illness. The indignity of a night in jail affords further testimony to a persisting difference between mental illnesses and other illnesses. For patient and family, then, and for the community as a whole, mental illness is a puzzling, disruptive phenomenon, a problem whose social aspects are not adequately encompassed within the medical context. (See Chapter 10, page 517.)

THE NATURE AND VARIETIES
OF MENTAL DISORDERS

Mental disorders vary in kind and in degree, just as physical illnesses do. Some mental illnesses result from organic lesions (e.g., disorders caused by syphilis of the central nervous system); others appear to have their roots in psychological experiences and to be quite different in quality from most somatic diseases. Indeed, there is some question as to whether certain mental disorders can really be considered illnesses. The psychiatrist Thomas Szasz has written of the "myth of mental illness,"[1] maintaining that all mental disorders are simply defective strategies for handling difficult life situations.

Few psychiatrists are disposed to agree with Szasz that even severe mental disorders are not to be considered illnesses. It is clear, however, that the general public does not tend to react to the mentally ill as it does to the physically ill, nor does the disordered person tend to see himself as ill, even though he may be desperately miserable. Ironically, the more serious the mental illness, the less likely the patient is to recognize that he is ill. Perhaps it is this aspect of mental illness — the patient's inability to realize that he is sick and needs help — along with the fact that mental illness disrupts interpersonal relationships, that has set off mental patients, not as ill persons, but as insane, "crazy," alienated.

As with other forms of illness, only the most severely impaired or acutely distressed mentally ill persons are in hospitals. Despite this fact, nearly four in ten of the hospital beds in the United States are occupied by mental patients. Some of these patients have been hospitalized continuously, not merely for years but for decades. Contrary to popular belief, however, most persons who become patients in our mental hospitals do not stay there. Most are returned home within a matter of months, depending, of course, on the nature of the particular disorder, the home environment of the patient, and the administrative and therapeutic policies and practices of the hospital. We shall return to a consideration of the nature of mental disorder from a sociological perspective after we have examined both the psychiatric perspective and popular beliefs about mental illness. To begin, let us briefly consider the kinds of disorders or diseases recognized by psychiatry and the bases for their classification.

From the physician's perspective, the first step in attempting to deal with

---

[1] Thomas S. Szasz, *The Myth of Mental Illness* (New York: Harper, 1961).

an illness is to identify what illness he is confronted with. A fever resulting from malaria calls for a different response than one resulting from typhoid. Systems of disease classification (*nosology*) are attempts to group together closely related disorders and to specify the bases for recognizing them and differentiating them from unrelated disorders. Ideally, a system of classification should be based upon adequate theories of the nature of the diseases or disorders, and should deal with such features as etiology, pathological processes, course, and outcome. Unfortunately, adequate theories of causation exist for only a few mental disorders. To a large extent the nomenclature of psychiatric disorders is based on symptomatology, and despite recent advances the system leaves much to be desired.

Until very recently, psychiatric classification varied from country to country, and usage varied even from state to state within the United States. Although the International Classification of Diseases has been used for several decades throughout the civilized world for compiling data on physical diseases, each country has tended to follow the current trends in its own schools of psychiatry for mental disorders. In the United States, it was not until 1968 that the standard nomenclature relating to mental disorders was brought into agreement with the International Classification of Diseases.[2] Even with the revision in nomenclature, there still are major differences among nations and schools of psychiatry in diagnostic practice and in criteria used for deciding among alternative diagnoses. This presents great problems for research workers who want to compare the frequency of particular disorders within different populations.

Social scientists are often impatient with psychiatric classification and sometimes suggest that because of its shortcomings it should be ignored. For all the inadequacies of the present system of classification of mental disorders, however, it incorporates the most sophisticated knowledge of those who have studied mental disorder intensively, and it increasingly incorporates research evidence regarding the correlates and courses of the various disorders that have been distinguished. To the extent that one can differentiate among disorders that will in time prove to differ in etiology, course, or outcome, one can ask questions about the nature of etiological and pathological processes. Conversely, if one can identify a specific etiologi-

---

[2] The standard nomenclature used in the United States is published as *Diagnostic and Statistical Manual of Mental Disorders* by the American Psychiatric Association. The second (revised) edition was issued in 1968. A detailed consideration of the purposes and problems of psychiatric classification, a wide range of research bearing upon such problems, and alternative ways of dealing with them are discussed in Martin M. Katz et al., eds., *The Role and Methodology of Classification in Psychiatry and Psychopathology* (Washington, D. C.: U. S. Government Printing Office, 1968).

cal factor underlying a form of mental disorder, it becomes possible to distinguish that form of disorder from others with similar symptomatology. This was the case, for example, with *paresis,* or syphilis of the central nervous system. Before the presence of the syphilitic spirochete could be established by blood tests, it was not possible to make an unequivocal diagnosis of paresis, and a good many patients suffering from this disorder were classified as having other mental disorders.

When no physical disorder exists, classification of mental disorders is likely to depend upon manifest symptomatology, life-history features, and the age and sex of the patient. The difficulties of classification are greatly magnified by the fact that the symptoms of mental disorder are largely ideational and behavioral. They reflect cultural emphases as well as disease processes. Many symptoms cannot be adequately interpreted without a knowledge of the norms of the subculture to which the individual belongs.

Forewarned of the complexity of the problem of classification, we can now consider the major categories of mental illness recognized by modern psychiatry. We may note that the recent changes in the classification of the psychoses largely represent a systematization and revision of the basic classifications of severe mental disorder developed by the German psychiatrist Emil Kraepelin at the close of the last century.

As a starting point, we may note the traditional breakdown of mental disorders into three major classes: the *psychoses,* which entail a gross derangement of mental processes and inability to evaluate external reality correctly; the *neuroses,* which entail emotional discomfort and impairment of functioning, often in a limited realm of behavior, but entail no sharp break with reality; and the *psychosomatic disorders,* which entail very real organic symptoms and malfunctions caused at least in part by psychological processes.

The present psychiatric classification also includes several other broad categories of mental disorder, of which the most important are the personality disorders and the behavior disorders of childhood and adolescence. The former are characterized by "deeply ingrained maladaptive patterns of behavior" and may be marked by difficulties in interpersonal relationships or by various forms of deviance, such as sexual deviation, alcoholism, and drug dependence. Since most of these forms of deviance are dealt with elsewhere in this book, we shall not further discuss this category in the present chapter.

The term "insane"—which has legal meaning but no technical status in psychiatry—is most often applicable to persons suffering from the acute or chronic phases of psychosis. However, a recurrent legal problem is posed by the fact that the boundary between sane and insane is not the same as that between psychotic and nonpsychotic. Of the several classes of psychoses, we shall be most concerned with the functional psychoses, especially schizophrenia, and with psychoses associated with organic brain damage, especially the mental disorders of old age. These are the most incapacitating mental disorders.

Our knowledge of the prevalence of each of the various categories of mental illness is limited to cases that come into treatment. Intensive studies made to ascertain the true prevalence of mental illnesses have demonstrated that only a small proportion of neurotic and psychosomatic ailments are diagnosed and treated. It may be assumed, however, that in Western society the majority of persons who show continuing symptoms of psychosis are at some time hospitalized or brought into some other type of treatment or confinement.

An idea of the relative frequency of treatment for mental disorders in the United States is given by Figure 1, which shows the number of individuals, per 100,000 population of each age group, who were treated in psychiatric facilities in a given year.[3] It will be apparent that very few persons are hospitalized prior to age 15, although a substantial number of children are treated in outpatient facilities. Rates of hospitalization in mental hospitals or in general hospitals with psychiatric facilities increase sharply to roughly age 40, then taper off somewhat to age 60, and then again begin a steep climb. Outpatient treatment is largely reserved for the mental disorders of youth and those of the middle years.

The actual number of episodes of psychiatric treatment – that is, the number of patients who were under treatment at some time during the year – was more than two and one-half million. In general, patients with psychotic disorders or organic brain syndromes are much more likely to be hospitalized than are persons with psychoneurotic or personality disorders. As we shall see, however, it is often not the seriousness of the disorder but the ease with which the patient can be cared for in the home that determines whether or not he is hospitalized.

---

[3] Data on the number and characteristics of patients are published annually in a series of reports (*Mental Health Facilities Reports*) prepared by the Office of Biometry, National Institute of Mental Health, Department of Health, Education, and Welfare. Included in the series are reports on state and county, Veterans' Administration and private mental hospitals, mental health clinics, and so on. The data to be presented on the number, characteristics, and diagnoses of patients in various facilities have been drawn primarily from one of the reports in this series, "Patients in State and County Mental Hospitals, 1967" (Public Health Service Publication No. 1921, Washington, D. C.: U. S. Government Printing Office, 1969).

FIGURE 1
Number of Patient Care Episodes Per 100,000 Population
in Psychiatric Facilities by Type of Facility,
by Age, United States, 1966

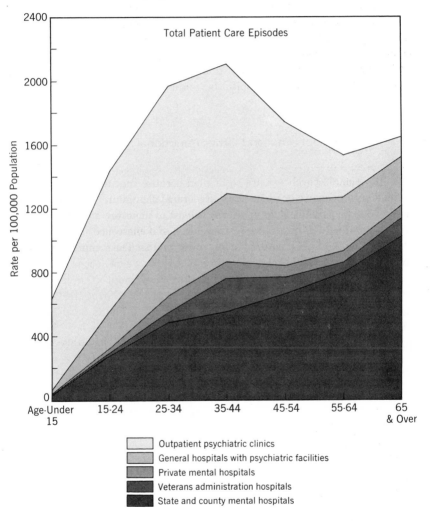

Source: Public Health Service Publication No. 1921.

Table 1 shows the distribution of disorders among new admissions to state and county hospitals during the year 1967 and among patients who were resident in those hospitals at the end of the year. It is in the resident-patient category that we find the group of chronic patients who are least likely to leave the hospital. It will be apparent that persons with certain types of disorders—the organic brain syndromes and schizophrenia, in particular—tend to remain in the hospital as chronic patients. Since most of the patients with organic brain syndromes are elderly, their life expectancy is not great, but neither is their expectancy of being returned to the community. Schizophrenics, on the other hand, tend to enter the hospital while they are relatively young, and *if they are not soon released,* they are likely to remain in the hospital for many years or decades.

Schizophrenia and Other Functional Psychoses

The "functional" psychoses are so labeled because they are without clearly defined organic cause or identifiable structural change in the brain and are assumed to be psychological in origin, at least to some degree. Schizophrenia was first called *dementia praecox* (psychosis of adolescence) because of the frequency with which it occurs among young adults. The symptomatic manifestations that are labeled schizophrenia may, however, occur at any age

TABLE I
New Admissions to State and County Mental Hospitals During 1967 and Resident Patients at End of Year by Disorder

Disorder	New Admissions	Resident Patients
Total	**164,219**	**426,309**
Organic Brain Syndromes	43,483	110,022
Psychotic Disorders (Schizophrenia, etc.)	39,799	242,008
Psychoneurotic Disorders	17,697	7,636
Personality Disorders [a]	41,380	16,845
Mental Deficiency [b]	4,241	35,949
Other and Undiagnosed	17,619	13,849

[a] Including alcoholism.
[b] These are patients in mental hospitals, exclusive of institutions for the mentally retarded.

level from childhood to senescence. Although schizophrenia is popularly referred to as "split personality," it is doubtful that this term will connote the basic symptoms of the disorder to most persons. The "split" refers to the separation of emotion from cognition or intellectual functioning. But what is most impressive about schizophrenia is the combination of psychological withdrawal from others with a wide variety of distortions or derangements of thought processes — delusions, bizarre associations, flights of ideas, and so on.

The major subtypes of schizophrenia — paranoid, hebephrenic, catatonic — are diagnosed on the basis of dominant symptomatology and course of illness, but these diagnoses are woefully unreliable over time. Many psychiatrists now believe that schizophrenia is not a single disease but a family of disorders. Be that as it may, more than one-fourth of the patients who enter a mental hospital before the age of forty receive this diagnosis in the United States. Many return home within a matter of months to live useful and happy lives. Others show a degree of symptomatology that may impair their relationships in day-to-day life in the community; they may return to the mental hospital for months or years at a time over several decades. A few patients fail ever to leave the hospital, becoming chronic or deteriorated to such a degree that they tend to be relegated to the "back wards."

Included with schizophrenia among the functional psychotic disorders are *manic-depressive reactions* and *involutional melancholia,* both of which tend to occur in middle life. In theory, the manic-depressive patient shows alternations of periods of extreme excitement and euphoria with periods of extreme depression and despair. In fact, however, the manic phase is relatively rare. Manic-depressive psychosis tends to be episodic. Patients given this diagnosis are more likely to recover completely than are those diagnosed as schizophrenic, but recurrences of the illness are quite usual.

The diagnosis of involutional psychosis tends to be given by psychiatrists if the patient is near the phase of physical change of life. The symptoms are very difficult to distinguish from those of the depressed type of manic-depressive patient. Whether there is a valid distinction between these affective states or whether they represent a psychiatric "folkway" cannot be definitely answered at the present time.

It should be noted that paranoid symptoms such as delusions of grandeur or of persecution may be found in manic-depressive and involutional states, and in the mental disorders of old age, as well as in schizophrenia. *Paranoia* used to be considered a specific mental disease; now it is more generally regarded as a common type of symptomatology occurring in a number of different disorders.

Mental Disorders of Old Age

As the bulk of the population has shifted from farms and small rural communities to the cities, and as life expectancy has been increased by medical science and public health programs, the mental disorders of old age — primarily *senile dementia* and *psychosis with cerebral arteriosclerosis* — have become both more prevalent and more difficult to cope with. These disorders involve a variety of symptoms, such as confusion, suspiciousness, loss of memory, lack of concern for amenities, and sometimes loss of control of bodily functions. To a considerable degree, the symptoms are accentuations of characteristics widely found among older persons, especially those who feel that they no longer have any real purpose or function in life.

In the past 50 years, hospitalization of persons suffering from the mental disorders of old age has increased tremendously; patients with these disorders now make up one-fourth of all first admissions to mental hospitals and a substantial proportion of the population of nursing homes. Surveys of older persons in the community suggest that from 4 to 7 percent of persons over 65 are severely impaired by mental disorders, and perhaps another 10 percent are appreciably impaired.[4] The longer one lives, the more likely he is to become mentally impaired.

The mental disorders of old age must not, however, be thought of as representing a steady or inevitable decline in the organism. Although it is true that many older patients go to mental hospitals to die there, a substantial number may be able to function with reasonable adequacy in a somewhat sheltered environment where they feel they have a secure place and some degree of usefulness. Moreover, symptoms often fluctuate with life circumstances, so that persons who are markedly impaired one month may be much more effective the next.

Grouped with the mental disorders of old age in the category now labeled "chronic brain syndrome" are the psychoses stemming from syphilis of the brain (*dementia paralytica* or *paresis*), those resulting from chronic alcoholism, and those resulting from long-continued trauma to the brain such as is received not infrequently by professional boxers. It is of interest to note that few cases of paresis have occurred since the advent of antibiotic treatment for syphilis, yet the proportion of cases now found in our mental

---

[4] For a review of several studies, see Marjorie Lowenthal *et al., Aging and Mental Disorder in San Francisco* (San Francisco: Jossey-Bass, 1967).

hospitals is greater than in the past. The explanation is simply the greater life expectancy of patients already hospitalized. Thus our present paretic patients are a heritage from the days before effective treatment for syphilis. In another few decades, however, this form of mental disease should be relatively infrequent.

The Psychoneuroses

The terms "neurosis" and "neurotic" have achieved a wide currency in contemporary life. They call various images to mind: the complaining, never satisfied housewife; the sensitive, tortured artist who cannot accept man's inhumanity to man; the businessman obsessed with the quest for wealth and power and unable to enjoy anything else to the full. Sometimes the terms are used with a note of approbation, sometimes as derogatory epithets. Sometimes it is even suggested that we are all a bit neurotic. If this statement is intended to indicate that at times we all behave in ways that deviate from objectively sensible or fruitful behavior, it can hardly be challenged.

Just where the line between normality and psychoneurosis should be drawn, for purposes of classifying people, is a matter of opinion, because psychoneurotic reactions are disturbances in the functioning of personalities, not diseases as usually understood. The chief characteristic of these disorders is *anxiety,* which may be directly felt and expressed or which may be unconsciously and automatically controlled by the utilization of various psychological defense mechanisms. When the intensity of anxiety is so great that it produces symptoms that markedly impair the individual's ability to carry out normal activities with his fellow men, it is appropriate to label the resulting state a neurosis.

The form that the neurosis takes – that is, the kinds of symptoms that will be manifest – will depend on the way the person has learned (whether consciously or not) to handle his anxiety. In the form called simply *anxiety reaction,* the anxiety is diffuse and uncontrolled. In *conversion reactions,* the anxiety is "converted" into organic dysfunctions – paralysis, tics, and so on. In *phobic reactions,* the anxiety is expressed symbolically as fear of some specific idea, object, or situation. In *obsessive-compulsive reactions,* the anxiety is associated with the persistence of unwanted ideas and of repetitive impulses to perform acts that may be considered morbid or unreasonable by the patient. In *depressive reactions,* which are often associated with a feeling of guilt for past failures or deeds, the anxiety may be allayed and hence partially relieved by the symptoms of depression and self-deprecation.

The prevalence of psychoneurosis obviously depends upon where one draws the dividing line between normal and pathological. During World War II more than half a million men were rejected by the Selective Service because of psychoneurotic tendencies; in addition, over 300,000 were discharged from the services for psychoneurosis.[5] In a recent study of a rural county, the Leightons found that over one-half the population had at some time exhibited psychoneurotic symptoms to a significant degree.[6] The Leightons suggest that many people have a number of the symptoms of psychoneurosis most of the time, but that the degree of impairment caused by such symptoms is variable, depending upon life experiences and pressures. In any event, most psychoneurosis goes undiagnosed and untreated, accounting for a large measure of unhappiness and ineffectiveness but not for the sharp social disruptions found with psychosis.

Psychosomatic or Psychophysiological Disorders

Closely akin to the psychoneuroses are those responses to emotional stress that take the form of physiological malfunction. In mild cases they may be nothing more than a headache, an occasional attack of diarrhea, or a transitory skin rash during or after periods of tension. More severe cases, such as *ulcerative colitis, hypertension,* or *anorexia nervosa* (severe loss of appetite and vomiting), sometimes produce structural changes that may threaten life.

These disorders are readily defined as belonging in the medical context, and need not further concern us as to their dynamics or treatment. There is, however, much evidence to suggest that these disorders are related to the kinds of demands placed upon persons in various social roles. Indeed, treatment programs often combine medication with prescribed changes in the life regime (or with psychotherapy) to relieve the stresses that produced the disorder.

The psychophysiological disorders appear to be the most prevalent manifestation of emotional disorder. The Leightons found that 77 percent of their study population reported reactions of this type, and it is quite likely that

---

[5] R. H. Felix and Morton Kramer, "Extent of the Problem of Mental Disorders," *Annals of the American Academy of Political and Social Science,* Vol. 286 (March, 1953), p. 8. See also Norman Q. Brill and Gilbert Beebe, *A Follow-up Study of War Neuroses* (Washington, D. C.: Veterans' Administration, 1955), p. 28.

[6] Dorothea C. Leighton *et al., The Character of Danger* (New York: Basic Books, 1964).

everyone at some time experiences such reactions without necessarily being aware of the cause. Whether these reactions should be regarded primarily as one of the prices we pay for our form of civilization, or whether they are rather the price that man pays for his highly developed nervous system, we cannot at present say.

Mental Deficiency

The phenomena representing mental deficiency differ significantly from those of mental illness, but like the latter term, mental deficiency encompasses a number of conditions brought about in distinctly different ways. The central circumstance is, of course, a defect of intelligence such that the person is not capable of performing normal mental tasks appropriate to his age and environment. The most extreme forms of mental deficiency — idiocy and imbecility — represent gross organic defects that not only impair the development of intelligence but markedly reduce life expectancy. The great majority of individuals so afflicted are institutionalized early in life and remain institutionalized, except for those in the upper ranges of the category called "imbeciles." As of 1970, nearly 200,000 persons are confined in public institutions for mental defectives in the United States. Their maintenance entails a direct cost of over $400,000,000 per year.[7]

This chapter does not attempt to assess mental deficiency as a social problem; it merely calls attention to it. Until quite recently, mental deficiency was a topic that aroused little interest in the general public or even among physicians and psychologists. For a long time the stigma of mental deficiency led families to conceal the existence of a mentally defective or retarded child. In recent decades, however, a number of prominent persons who are parents or relatives of severely retarded children have spoken out on the need for more adequate care for such children and for research into the causes of mental deficiency. Parent organizations and professional organizations focused on dealing with mental retardation have been formed, and, especially with the impetus given by the interest of President Kennedy, there has been a great increase in support and expansion of research in this field.[8]

---

[7] These data are from the National Clearing House for Mental Health Information (Bethesda, Md.).

[8] See, for example, the report of the President's Advisory Panel on Mental Retardation. See also Richard Masland, Seymour Sarason, and Thomas Gladwin, *Mental Subnormality* (New York: Basic Books, 1958); and Herbert G. Birch *et al., Mental Subnormality in the Community* (New York: Williams and Wilkins, 1970).

Although most severe mental deficiency has its origins in brain injury or organic defect, a substantial part of mental subnormality represents simply the lower end of the range of intellectual potentiality coupled with cultural and intellectual deprivation. Children from the poorest, most culturally deprived segments of the population fail to develop in the preschool years the language skills necessary for inclusion into the regular school system. This problem was tackled for the first time on a large scale under the Poverty Program of President Johnson. Efforts to provide intellectual stimulus to the deprived will probably make relatively little difference in the number of individuals who have to be institutionalized because of mental deficiency, but they may substantially decrease the much larger number of individuals who are ineffective in modern society because of mental retardation deriving from cultural deprivation.

THE PUBLIC IMAGE OF MENTAL DISORDER

Few members of the general public share the psychiatrist's perspective with reference to the nature and varieties of mental disorder. "Mental illness" is not the term most commonly used to refer to persons who are incapacitated by mental disorders, but it is certainly more current today than it was a generation ago. The first surveys of popular attitudes toward mental disorder, undertaken soon after World War II, revealed that only the most bizarre and threatening symptoms—those that connoted legal insanity and the need for hospitalization—came to mind when people were asked about mental illness.[9] Lesser symptoms of mental disorder were often regarded as "quirks," "bad habits," or signs of meanness or weakness rather than as manifestations of such mental disorders as psychoneurosis or personality disorders. More recent studies suggest that there is now a greater tendency to regard as mental illness conditions that do not require hospitalization but that do impair effective functioning.[10]

It is likely that public sophistication has increased after several decades

---

[9] The most ambitious of the studies of public attitudes toward mental illness was directed by Shirley Star for the National Opinion Research Center. The basic interview developed by Star was employed in several other studies. See, for example, John and Elaine Cumming, *Closed Ranks* (Harvard University Press, 1957).

[10] For a discussion of more recent developments see Paul V. Lemkau, "Evaluation of the Effect of Changes in Environmental Factors, with Special Attention to Public Attitudes toward Mental Health and Illness" in Joseph Zubin and F. Freyhan, *Social Psychiatry* (New York: Grune & Stratton, 1968).

of bombardment by the mass media with information about mental illness and psychiatry. Nevertheless, portrayals in the mass media designed to convey correct information about mental illness are far outweighed by presentations in which psychiatry and the mentally ill are pictured in stereotyped, distorted ways.[11] The bizarre symptoms of mental disorder are overemphasized. The occurrence of mental disorder is naively attributed to environmental pressures. The homespun philosopher of the "soap opera," with his trite homilies, becomes the expert on emotional problems. In a way, then, the mass media lag behind public attitudes toward mental illness rather than help to create informed attitudes.

Terms like "neurosis" now appear frequently in the press and in everyday speech, but they are used without anything approaching precise meaning. People who tend to complain a lot are called "neurotic" far more often than are those who are immobilized by anxiety. Moreover, the connotations of terms like "mentally ill" or "neurotic" are clearly negative, even though bizarre symptoms are not always entailed. Mental disorder still bears a stigma. Many persons will deny that they themselves look negatively upon the mentally ill, but they ascribe negative views to others.

The changes that have taken place in popular attitudes toward mental illness may not be due as much to the educational effects of the mass media as to changes in our public policies. Two decades ago the great bulk of patients in American mental hospitals were committed there against their wishes. Today, not only are there fewer patients in such hospitals, but four times as many persons now receive treatment for mental or emotional problems in the community. The message is that mental patients do not necessarily have to be locked up, that most are not dangerous to themselves or to others. Even without any deep understanding of the nature of mental disorder, then, people have come to perceive it as less threatening. It should be noted, though, that such changing practices and attitudes have not by any means brought acceptance of psychiatric help in the way that other medical treatment is accepted.[12] A person known to have sought help from a psychiatrist for a particular problem is in general less favorably viewed than one known to have gone to a clergyman for assistance with the same problem. Moreover, the ethic of "self-help" remains strong in our society. Most admired is the man who can stand up in the face of adversity without complaint, manifest anxiety, or psychosomatic symptoms. Such a man has no need for psychiatry

---

[11] Jum C. Nunnally, *Popular Conceptions of Mental Health* (New York: Holt, 1961).

[12] See, for example, Derek L. Phillips, "Rejection: A Possible Consequence of Seeking Help for Mental Disorders," *American Sociological Review,* Vol. 28 (December, 1963), pp. 963–73.

or for tranquilizers. Only among a relatively small group of intellectuals is it wholly accepted to seek psychiatric help in attempting to deal more effectively with life problems or to understand oneself better. Even here, the frequent reference to one's psychiatrist as his "shrink" indicates more than a little ambivalence.

Ignorance about mental disorders and distrust of psychiatry are found even among some members of the medical profession. Prior to World War II, mental disorders and psychiatry received little attention in the curricula of most medical schools. Although medical students now receive far more adequate orientation regarding mental illness and psychiatry, few have occasion to become really well informed about mental health facilities in the community. The family physician is the first professional to whom many people with an emotional problem turn for help, but it would appear that only a minority of physicians are adequately prepared to assess and assist those with mental disorders.

Confronting Mental Illness

It is one thing to be asked how one would define certain kinds of personal problems and how one would feel about consulting a psychiatrist. It is quite another thing to confront mental illness first-hand in the family. As we have already noted, mental illness is manifest primarily in behavior. The person with a mental disorder may be manifestly miserable, depressed, or frightened, or he may be irritable, argumentative, or overtly hostile. Since most of us vary in our moods and can at times be irritable as well as pleasant, it is not surprising that the first marked symptoms of mental disorder are seldom recognized as such.

In a study of the impact of mental illness on the family, it was found that early symptoms of mental illness were responded to within the normal frame of reference held by family members for one another.[13] As in the case described in the beginning of this chapter, the problem tends to be seen as physical illness or fatigue, as meanness or weakness of character, or as a natural response to crisis or other stress. Since the patient can seldom be reasoned with, conflict and hurt feelings take precedence over rational assessment of the nature of his problem.

If the husband's symptomatic behavior was complicated by physical illness, the wife frequently turned or urged her husband to turn to

---

[13] John A. Clausen and Marian R. Yarrow, eds., "The Impact of Mental Illness on the Family," *Journal of Social Issues*, Vol. 11, No. 4 (1955), p. 18.

the family doctor or another physician for treatment, or at least for diagnosis. If, on the other hand, it was seen as evidence of meanness or weak character, the wife often attempted over long periods to argue with her husband, to moralize, recriminate. Self-help tended to be stressed, though a few wives urged their husbands to talk with a clergyman. Several wives turned the husband over to his parents, suggesting that they try to do something about him. In part, this action seems to have been linked with an attitude of blaming the parents for the husband's behavior, but in some instances it appears also that the wife felt the husband's parents might be able to convince him of his need to get help. Where there was much aggression by the husband, a few wives invoked the police for protection; others temporarily escaped to the homes of friends or relatives. Typically, then, there were both professionals and non-professional associates of the family who entered into the process of trying to deal with the husband's mental illness.[14]

Until the past decade or so, very few communities had facilities for helping the acutely upset person. Relatively few persons could afford treatment from a private psychiatrist, and the small number of community mental health clinics had long waiting lists and seldom accepted patients in need of immediate help. Most communities have long had hospital emergency rooms ready to deal with accident victims or acutely ill persons in a matter of minutes, regardless of the time of day, but they are just beginning to acquire comparable facilities for dealing with emotional crises. Until recently, formal commitment to a mental hospital was the dominant mode of responding to the needs of the acutely distressed patient. Although the number of voluntary admissions to hospitals has increased, involuntary commitment, depriving the individual of liberty and of other basic rights and privileges, still takes place in a high proportion of cases. It will probably be a necessary last resort for a long time to come.

The meaning of mental illness is, then, not so much a matter of definition of terms as it is an inherent part of the response to persons who manifest mental illness. This has implications not only for psychiatry and social policy but for the patient himself.

Mental Illness as a Social Role

The labels "crazy," "insane," and "mentally ill" all connote in our culture a kind of thinking and behaving that is uncontrolled, senseless, and frighten-

---

[14] *Ibid.,* p. 28. Similar findings are reported from England by Enid Mills, *Living with Mental Illness* (London: Routledge, 1962).

ing. Except for rare institutionalized occasions, all societies place a high value on the individual's ability to control his behavior, if not his thoughts. In mental illness, the individual loses such control. This not only poses a problem for others; it poses a persisting problem for the individual himself. Once one is labeled a "madman," others expect him to behave in nonrational ways. Whatever the reason for his original loss of control or manifestation of other symptoms, being considered mentally ill by others puts him on precarious ground. Indeed, the sociologist Thomas Scheff has suggested that many persons may unconsciously take on the stereotyped role of the insane once someone has suggested that they are mentally ill.[15] Scheff observes that a great many people deviate from social norms without necessarily receiving any particular label thereby. If, however, this "residual deviance" is challenged and labeled mental illness by others, the disturbed individual may tend to let himself go and behave according to the stereotyped notion of mental illness.

It is unlikely that any substantial number of persons become mentally ill by virtue of being so labeled, but it does appear that calling a person mentally ill frequently intensifies his symptoms. Community mental health studies support Scheff's observation that there is a very high frequency of "residual deviance" or symptomatic behavior in the population. If the general public were to use psychiatrists' ratings as the basis for classifying their colleagues and relatives, it might be very difficult to maintain the stability of our society.

The social and personal consequences of being considered mentally ill are thus very different from the consequences of physical illness. This poses a very real dilemma for those who deal with emotionally upset or confused persons. The early provision of meaningful help will frequently minimize the person's distress and prevent more severe disorder. On the other hand, actions that brand the person as mentally ill may carry the connotation that he is no longer expected to behave responsibly. Much careful study of this problem is needed in order to assess its effects on the cause and course of mental disorders and its implications for attempts to provide help to disturbed persons.

It is apparent that mental disorders disrupt social functioning. The question to which we shall now turn is whether the conditions of life in society are themselves implicated in the etiology of mental disorder.

[15] Thomas Scheff, *Being Mentally Ill: A Sociological Theory* (Chicago: Aldine, 1966).

SOCIAL CORRELATES OF MENTAL DISORDER

To the extent that mental disorders are not manifestations of organic disease as such, they may be regarded primarily as disorders of cognitive processes, as distortions of the personality, or as faulty strategies in interpersonal relationships. The personality is itself, at any given time, the resultant of a complex interaction between constitutional potentialities and proclivities and the sociocultural environment as mediated through the family and other agents of socialization and influence. The human organism is not only reactive to its environment; it acts upon it and, beyond early childhood, to a considerable degree selects its local environment. This enormously complicates the task of establishing causal links between aspects of personality and aspects of the social and cultural order. Even the etiology of bacterial diseases turns out to be much more complex than had been assumed at the time that germ theory was evolved by Koch and Lister.[16] When one is dealing with reaction tendencies of highly differentiated personality systems, the complexities are such that the concept of cause may be inappropriate. Almost no one doubts that mental disorders are explicable in naturalistic terms; the question is whether they are explicable in terms of a relatively small number of influences whose effects can be specified with some precision.

The study of the distribution and course of disease in large populations is known as *epidemiology.*[17] Although originally developed as a methodology for studying the spread of epidemics, the epidemiological approach can be used to study the distribution of any form of disease or disability. The epidemiologist seeks to establish the characteristics that differentiate persons who are ill from those who are not. The first step in seeking to establish that any given characteristic or life circumstance is related to mental illness is to ascertain whether persons with this characteristic or subject to this circumstance have a higher rate of illness. The most frequently used approximation or index of severe mental illness is hospitalization, but we now have a good deal of evidence that many factors other than degree of illness influence whether or not one is hospitalized. For example, more people are hospitalized in communities near mental hospitals than in more remote com-

---

[16] See René Dubos, *The Mirage of Health* (New York: Harper, 1959), for a discussion of the complexities of disease causation.
[17] An excellent, relatively nontechnical treatment of this topic is contained in Donald D. Reid, *Epidemiological Methods in the Study of Mental Disorders* (Geneva, Switzerland: World Health Organization, 1960).

munities. Moreover, some families may attempt to take care of a markedly disturbed person in the home, while others will send him to a mental hospital. It is quite probable, then, that differences in rates of hospitalization among various population groups primarily reflect different attitudes and values toward mental illness and mental hospitals rather than different amounts of mental illness.

Similar considerations apply to data on other types of treatment as indexes of the amount of mental illness in any population group; private psychiatric care is probably a better reflection of income level than it is of need for treatment. Moreover, except for a very small proportion of mental disorders there is no technique, simple or complex, by which the presence of mental illness can be detected. All attempts to establish the frequency of mental illness rest, in the last analysis, upon an assessment of behavior by a qualified psychiatrist.

Periodic psychiatric examination of all members of the population might seem to be the most satisfactory basis for assessing mental health status, but it is not likely to be feasible for a long time to come. The cost and difficulty of recruiting and training a psychiatric staff that could examine sufficiently large samples of the population to yield stable rates of serious mental illness would be tremendous, requiring vastly more than the funds currently available for research. Further, there are attitudinal barriers to such an approach. Relatively few psychiatrists feel comfortable about examining persons who have not sought help and to whom services are not to be offered even if, in the psychiatrist's opinion, they are needed. Public attitudes toward seeking or accepting a proffered psychiatric examination pose an even more serious difficulty. Most people regard mental quirks in themselves or members of their family as something to be concealed, not exposed. Consequently, those persons who are most likely to be designated as "cases" are often the most reluctant to undergo psychiatric examination. Small-scale efforts to examine specified samples suggest that the refusal rate sometimes runs as high as 40 percent. In attempts to locate cases of severe mental illness—a phenomenon that occurs in a very small proportion of persons in a year—even a 10 percent refusal rate would make systematic estimation of the total amount of mental illness virtually impossible.

There is another side of the problem that further complicates classification through psychiatric examination or screening. Every community has some members who are regarded by their fellow citizens as "queer," "mean," "shy," "offensive," and the like. Many of these persons would be diagnosed by a psychiatrist as neurotic and some as psychotic, even though other community members may not regard them as mentally ill. Moreover, persons whose social backgrounds are grossly divergent from that of the psychiatrist (e.g., lower-class persons) tend to be seen by him as sicker than those whose attitudes and behaviors are closer to his own outlook. Unless and until there are valid tests for the diagnosis of schizophrenia and other mental illnesses, studies of so-called true prevalence must deal with biases in clinical classification due to subcultural perspectives, just as studies of treated prevalence must deal with biases in community and professional response. With these considerations in mind, let us examine what has been learned from research — most of it of quite recent origin — on the distribution of mental illness in time and space.

Mental Illness and Modern Urban Society

One frequently hears that the hectic pace of modern life has resulted in a great increase in mental disorders. Until quite recently, the population of our mental hospitals was increasing more rapidly than the rate of growth of the total population, which might seem to support the notion that more people are mentally ill at present than were in the past. Certainly more people now receive psychiatric care or enter mental hospitals than did previously. Present experience suggests that about one person in twelve in urban America will be hospitalized for mental illness sometime during his life. The proportion is higher, of course, for persons who live much beyond age 70. Although this expectancy of hospitalization is higher than in the past, it does not appear that the likelihood of becoming mentally ill prior to or during the prime of life has increased. For example, statistics relating to the number of mentally ill persons confined in jails, almshouses, and other institutions in Massachusetts between 1840 and 1850 suggest that, for all but the aged, rates of severe mental illness (psychotic states) were at least as high then as they are at present.[18]

Massachusetts was a highly urbanized state even in 1840. It is likely that many of the disorganizing effects of urbanization and industrialization had already taken place. The existence of value conflicts, the segmentalization of relationships, and the lack of stable occupational expectations — all concomitants of social change and of urbanization — might be expected to contribute stresses leading to an increase in mental breakdown. One might ask, then, whether a proportionally lower amount of mental illness would be expected in a population with high consensus as to values, a relatively homogeneous

---

[18] Herbert Goldhamer and Andrew Marshall, *Psychosis and Civilization* (New York: Free Press, 1953).

set of occupational and familial expectations, and close integration of the individual into the network of community relations. The Hutterite communities of Montana and the Dakotas, settled in the latter half of the nineteenth century by Anabaptist immigrants from central Europe, approximate this ideal type of homogeneous and highly integrated community. These rural villages have managed to maintain a surprising degree of resistance against the encroachments of the competitive, hedonistic emphasis in American life. Yet a careful check of Hutterite communities to locate mentally ill persons by a research team that included a psychiatrist, a psychologist, and a sociologist disclosed that the occurrence of episodes of severe mental illness among the Hutterites was roughly comparable to the occurrence of hospitalization for mental illness in New York State.[19] Among the Hutterites, however, patients were cared for at home rather than in mental hospitals. Moreover, both the duration and patterning of the symptoms manifested by members of the Hutterite communities differed somewhat from those of patients from the larger American society.

From time to time, anthropologists, travelers, and workers in nonliterate cultures have proclaimed the people of a particular society to be essentially without mental disorder. Unfortunately, in every instance in which more thorough study has been undertaken, the original reports have been found to be untrue. No one person's experience is likely to be an adequate basis for an estimate of the frequency of mental disorder unless systematic observations have been recorded for defined populations. Few of those who have made pronouncements in this area have been adequately trained in either psychiatry or statistics, and almost none have been adequately trained in both. The major forms of mental disorder are almost certainly found among all peoples, regardless of their way of life.[20]

Social Status and Mental Health

The social status of one's family influences to a considerable degree the relative ease or discomfort of one's physical existence, the values that one learns early in life, the opportunities that become available, and the attitudes that are expressed toward one by other persons. Social status does in-

---

[19] Joseph W. Eaton and Robert J. Weil, *Culture and Mental Disorders* (New York: Free Press, 1955).

[20] For a thorough analysis of the intricate relationships between the patterings of mental disorder and cultural orientations, see Marvin Opler, *Culture and Social Psychiatry,* rev. ed. (New York: Atherton, 1967).

fluence personality development. However, since one can move up or down the status hierarchy, the status of one's family is not in any sense determinative of personality. To what extent do mental disorders vary by social status? In seeking to answer this question, investigators have used a number of indexes of social status as well as a variety of indexes of mental disorder.

One of the most influential studies of the distribution of mental disorder was Faris and Dunham's *Mental Disorders in Urban Areas*.[21] These researchers plotted the residential distribution of all patients from the city of Chicago admitted to public and private mental hospitals and computed rates of hospital admission for the various diagnostic categories of illness by area. The study conclusively demonstrated that hospitalized mental illness was not randomly distributed through the city. The highest rates were found near the center of the city in areas of high population mobility and heterogeneity and low socioeconomic status. Conversely, the lowest rates were found in the stable residential areas of higher socioeconomic status.

In part, this overall distribution was influenced by the concentration of organic psychoses due to syphilis and alcohol in those "skid row" or "flophouse" areas where the homeless and workless males of any metropolis tend to collect. But Faris and Dunham found that the rate distribution of schizophrenia also tended to be much higher in these same areas of high population mobility and heterogeneity and low socioeconomic status than in stable residential areas. It did not seem likely that schizophrenics had simply drifted to these areas.

Nearly two decades after the study by Faris and Dunham, Hollingshead and Redlich [22] set out to establish whether there were significant differences in the prevalence and incidence of mental illness among the social classes in New Haven. Data were secured not only from hospitals and clinics but from private psychiatrists as well. For hospitalized mental illness, Hollingshead and Redlich found the same general pattern that Faris and Dunham had found, with highest rates in the lower social strata and substantially lower rates in the upper strata. The New Haven study contributed further evidence that schizophrenia, insofar as it results in psychiatric treatment, tends to be more prevalent in the lower social strata. On the other hand, most of the differential between classes resulted from the much greater duration of hospitalization for lower-class patients. Once they came into treatment or care, they were more likely to remain there, but the frequency with

[21] Robert E. L. Faris and H. Warren Dunham, *Mental Disorders in Urban Areas* (Chicago: University of Chicago Press, 1939).

[22] A. B. Hollingshead and F. Redlich, *Social Class and Mental Illness* (New York: Wiley, 1958).

which they initially became ill was only slightly greater than that of higher-status patients.

The New Haven study for the first time presented evidence on the distribution of persons receiving outpatient treatment, either in clinics or from private psychiatrists. Here the picture tended to be almost the reverse of that shown for hospitalized patients—the highest rates were in the upper social strata. Hollingshead and Redlich were able to demonstrate conclusively that the way in which persons came into treatment, the kind of treatment received, and the duration of treatment all varied greatly by social class. Their study was exceedingly valuable in giving an understanding of the way in which treatment services operate; by the same token it clearly demonstrated that data on treated cases of mental illness could not be used as a basis for estimating the true prevalence of illness within the population.

The most conclusive study to date of the actual distribution of symptoms in an urban population is the Midtown Manhattan study. Its psychiatric classifications were based upon interviews of a cross section of nearly 1700 persons in an area of New York City. The interview was designed to get at such matters as the respondent's having had a "nervous breakdown" or having sought psychotherapy; the presence of somatic disorders that frequently have a psychogenic basis; acknowledgment of nervousness, restlessness, and other psychophysiological manifestations of emotional disturbance; indications of memory difficulties; acknowledgment of difficulties in interpersonal relations; and indications of emotional disturbance given by the respondent's behavior in the interview situation.[23] Information from each of these areas of the interview was abstracted and given to a team of psychiatrists who rated the respondent as to the degree of psychiatric symptomatology, if any, and the apparent amount of impairment of functioning as a result of such symptomatology. The data provided by such a survey are generally not adequate for affixing a diagnostic label, even in instances of considerable symptomatology. On the other hand, as we shall see, such studies help with the interpretation of findings relating to hospitalized or treated mental illness.

Perhaps the most startling finding of the Midtown study was the very high proportion of the population rated "impaired" by psychiatric symptoms —23.4 percent.[24] This proportion varied considerably by socioeconomic

---

[23] For a full description of the methodology see Leo Srole *et al., Mental Health in the Metropolis* (New York: McGraw-Hill, 1962), Chapter 3.

[24] The impaired group is made up of three categories: marked symptom formation (13.2 percent); severe symptom formation (7.5 percent); incapacitated (2.7 percent). *Ibid.,* p. 138.

status. In the lowest economic stratum, nearly one-half of all those interviewed were rated "impaired," while in the highest stratum, only about one person in eight was so rated. Also striking was the finding that at the upper status levels, fully one-fifth of those persons who had been rated "impaired" were currently receiving outpatient therapy and more than one-half had at one time or another been psychiatric patients, mostly outpatients.[25] At the lower status levels, on the other hand, only one percent of the persons rated "impaired" were currently receiving psychiatric treatment and another 20 percent had previously been patients (almost all in mental hospitals). Thus more of the poor had serious symptoms, yet fewer of those with symptoms ever received treatment.

In light of the evidence of the Midtown Manhattan study and other similar surveys conducted in recent years, it can no longer be doubted that the frequency of emotional upset and other symptoms of mental distress is greater among the poor and deprived segments of the population than among those more highly advantaged. The Midtown Manhattan study also found that among persons who have moved from one social class position to another, the occurrence of symptoms of mental disorder is more highly related to social status as an adult than to social status as a child. People who move down in social status show considerably greater symptomatology than do their childhood peers who stayed at the same level. Conversely, those who move upward in social status show less symptomatology than do their peers who remained at the initial level.[26]

Receiving a rating of "impaired" as a result of one's responses to an intensive interview is not, of course, the same thing as being diagnosed mentally ill. The surveys used in epidemiological studies of mental illness have focused upon symptoms and have tended to ignore strengths. Moreover, many of the symptoms may be primarily reflections of physical illness or of objective problems of living. Nevertheless, an examination of the interview responses of persons classified as "impaired" leaves one with little doubt that most of them have emotional problems quite comparable to those of many persons who seek psychiatric help. Indeed, the finding that more than half of the upper-status impaired group had sought such help indicates something of the potential demand for psychiatric service if everyone with emotional problems were to seek it.

---

[25] *Ibid.*, p. 246.

[26] This generalization may not apply to all populations. Parker and Kleiner report that Negro men who have moved to the highest levels of status have a higher rate of disorder than those who remained at the initial level. See Seymour Parker and Robert Kleiner, *Mental Illness in the Urban Negro Community* (New York: Free Press, 1966).

Very similar in approach to the Midtown Manhattan study but much more intensive in its collection of data on psychiatric status is the Stirling County study of the Leightons.[27] For over 20 years a team of psychiatrists and social scientists has worked in a rural county of maritime Canada, using a wide variety of approaches but basing primary classifications of psychiatric status on a survey interview somewhat similar to that of the Midtown study. In general, the Leightons found that the prevalence of symptoms increased as social status declined, though perhaps not to the same degree as in the Midtown study. They noted substantially higher rates of symptomatology in communities that were poorly integrated or even disorganized.[28] A high proportion of the residents of such communities were employed in low-status occupations such as wage work in agriculture, fishing, and forestry. But it is quite possible that something more is involved. It has been suggested by some that working-class life is more stressful than that of the middle class. The notion of stress is itself worthy of some consideration.[29]

Social Stress and Mental Illness

The concept of stress is a convenient means of designating the notion that external pressures or loads can lead to internal deformations or strains. There are many problems, however, in applying the concept of stress to the human personality. Certain types of experiences are probably "stressful" to everyone—experiences such as the loss of a loved one. Aside from situations in which continuing physical strain and extreme personal danger are involved, however, it appears that the psychological stressfulness of any situation depends largely upon the meaning that it derives from the individual's life history. To the extent that any given situation or event is a threat to a person's image of himself or to the values that he has incorporated into his personality, it is likely to be experienced as stressful. On the other

---

[27] This research has been published in three volumes, of which the first, Alexander H. Leighton et al., *My Name is Legion* (New York: Basic Books, 1959), and the last, Dorothea C. Leighton et al., *The Character of Danger* (New York: Basic Books, 1963), are of primary importance.

[28] *Ibid.*, p. 348.

[29] A particularly interesting analysis is afforded in the second volume reporting the findings of the Midtown Manhattan study. See Thomas S. Langer and Stanley T. Michael, *Life Stress and Mental Health* (New York: Free Press, 1963).

hand, discomfort or even extremely unpleasant emotions do not necessarily impair or threaten the psychological functioning of the individual. For
example, it might be assumed that under the wartime stress of bombing,
civilian populations would show a very high incidence of mental breakdown. However, such is not the case. In a thorough review of wartime experience, Donald Reid concludes that "there was no evidence that the priva-
tions and anxieties of the War, either in the United Kingdom or in enemy-
occupied countries like Denmark, had produced any major increase in serious
psychosis." [30] Reid goes on to note that on the basis of data from the records
of general medical practice in London, there was some evidence of a slight
increase in the frequency of patients reporting sick with neurotic complaints
often a week or ten days after heavy bombing. Most of these complainants
had suffered from such illnesses in the past. Data on combatants themselves do, of course, indicate that the combination of extreme fatigue, terror,
and guilt can lead to a high incidence of breakdown in any group. In general,
however, we can say that instances of personal failure that lead to feelings
of inadequacy and call for a reevaluation of who and what one is appear to
be far more traumatic than is exposure to noxious stimuli as such.

There are many indications that the most significant social influences
upon the likelihood of one's developing a mental illness are those that occur during the early life experiences of the individual and that lead him to
have low self-esteem or deviant orientations. While the personality is by no
means totally formed during the early years in the family, those years are
of great significance. Maternal deprivation, parental rejection, conflicts between parents for the allegiance of the child, overly protective maternal care
— these and many other aspects of family relationships can render the
child insecure or vulnerable in the sense that certain types of life situations
subsequently encountered will produce a great deal of anxiety.[31] Some of
the most interesting research on family relations and psychopathology has
been carried out with the families of schizophrenic patients. We shall concentrate on research in this area as an illustration of the intricacy of the
problem.

---

[30] Donald D. Reid, "Precipitating Proximal Factors in the Occurrence of Mental
Disorders: Epidemiological Evidence," *Causes of Mental Disorders: A Review of Epidemiological Knowledge, 1959* (New York: Milbank Memorial Fund, 1961).

[31] See, for example, Leon Yarrow, "Separation from Parents During Early Child-
hood," in Martin L. Hoffman and Lois W. Hoffman, eds., *Review of Child Development
Research* (New York: Russell Sage Foundation, 1964). See also John H. Cumming,
"The Family and Mental Disorder: An Incomplete Essay," *Causes of Mental Disorders:
A Review of Epidemiological Knowledge, 1959.*

Social Relations and Schizophrenia

Each scientific discipline that has been involved in research on schizophrenia has tended to hypothesize that the causes of this most perplexing of mental disorders lie within that discipline's conceptual realm. Sociologists have proposed social isolation and the effects of status deprivation as causes; geneticists have presented strong evidence for hereditary influence, if not complete determinism; psychoanalysts have advanced theories of failure of ego differentiation largely as a result of deficient mothering; and biochemists, neuropathologists, and other scientists studying the nervous system have from time to time reported findings that showed differences between study groups of schizophrenic patients and samples of the normal population.

Thus far, none of the studies that have found a biochemical difference between schizophrenics and normal persons can be regarded as conclusive, since results have not been consistent; nor do biochemists agree on the nature of the biochemical processes that may be involved. Nevertheless, there is now overwhelming evidence for a genetic element or predisposition in schizophrenia. This comes not only from studies of twins, which show that identical (single-egg) twins are much more likely to be concordant for schizophrenia than are fraternal (two-egg) twins, but also from studies of adopted children born of schizophrenic mothers.[32] Thus, one study compared the life-history experiences of two groups of individuals adopted very early in life by normal parents — one group born to women hospitalized for schizophrenia and the other to nonschizophrenic mothers. Although the adoptive families differed little, schizophrenia and a variety of problematic behaviors were found far more often among those individuals whose mothers had been schizophrenic, despite the fact that both groups of infants were removed from their mothers at birth.[33]

The evidence for a genetic component in the etiology of schizophrenia does not rule out the possibility that social and psychological influences are also

---

[32] The most influential of the early genetic studies was that of Franz Kallman, *Genetics of Schizophrenia* (Locust Valley, N. Y.: Augustin, 1938). An excellent overview of more recent work is contained in David Rosenthal and Seymour Kety, eds., *The Transmission of Schizophrenia* (London: Pergammon, 1969). See especially Part II, Genetic Studies.

[33] See Leonard I. Heston, "Psychiatric Disorders of Foster-Home-Reared Children of Schizophrenic Mothers," *British Journal of Psychiatry*, Vol. 12 (1966), pp. 819–25.

involved. Only about 10 percent of the children of one schizophrenic parent and 40 to 50 percent of the offspring of two schizophrenic parents develop schizophrenia. Even among identical twins, only about one-half the co-twins of individuals diagnosed as schizophrenic are themselves afflicted by the disorder. It appears that various behavior disorders and other forms of deviance are possible outcomes of the same genetic linkage, and it would not be surprising if the overt manifestations were a resultant of interaction between experiential and genetic components.

With a few exceptions, studies of the backgrounds of mental patients who receive a diagnosis of schizophrenia show that the lower status segment of the population is overrepresented.[34] Some difference of opinion exists as to whether there is an even gradation of increasing rates as one descends the socioeconomic ladder or a marked increase toward the very bottom.[35] The higher prevalence and incidence of schizophrenia at the lower status levels appears to be due in part to the tendency of persons rendered ineffective by virtue of schizophrenia to drift downward in socioeconomic status, but more largely it is due to the failure of an appreciable proportion of persons who become schizophrenic to move upward (in keeping with patterns of inter-generational mobility for the population at large).[36] The greater stresses and personal devaluation often encountered at the lower status levels cannot be ruled out as a causal influence, but the evidence is not nearly as convincing as that for a genetic effect.

Family socialization and communication patterns may also have some effect in precipitating schizophrenia in vulnerable persons. In recent years, intensive psychiatric studies of the families of schizophrenic patients have suggested that the dynamics of family relationships in those families differs significantly from the patterns found in "normal" families.[37] The parents

---

[34] An excellent overview of this research is provided by Melvin Kohn, "Social Class and Schizophrenia: A Critical Review," in David Rosenthal and Seymour Kety, eds., *The Transmission of Schizophrenia,* pp. 155–74.

[35] See William Rushing, "Two Patterns in the Relationship between Social Class and Mental Hospitalization," *American Sociological Review,* Vol. 34 (August, 1969), pp. 533–41.

[36] The most thorough study is that of Turner and Wagenfield, "Occupational Mobility and Schizophrenia: An Assessment of the Social Causation and Social Selection Hypotheses," *American Sociological Review,* Vol. 32 (February, 1967), pp. 104–13.

[37] The work of Bateson, Lidz, and Wynne and Singer is especially noteworthy. For an overview of this research, see Mischler and Waxler, "Family Interaction Process and Schizophrenia: A Review of Current Theories," *Merrill-Palmer Quarterly,* Vol. 2 (October, 1965), pp. 269–316. Also the papers on family relations and schizophrenia in David Rosenthal and Seymour Kety, eds., *The Transmission of Schizophrenia,* pp. 175–266.

often seem impervious to the needs of the child for autonomy and self-respect. Their behavior toward the schizophrenic may communicate the opposite message from that conveyed verbally, thereby putting him in a "double bind." Intergenerational boundaries may be so obscured that the child is confused as to what his own role should be. The net effect of most of the family patterns noted is that they make it difficult for the child to achieve an identity of his own and to develop competence and self-reliance.

A major limitation on the inferences that can be drawn from such research, however, derives from the fact that the families can be identified and studied only after the schizophrenia has become manifest. In living with a schizophrenic child, the families are confronting one of the most devastating stresses that can be imagined, and parents may well develop behavioral patterns different from those that had characterized the family before.

Certainly the most tenable hypothesis as to the etiology of schizophrenia at this time is that various combinations of hereditary vulnerability and environmental stress (either in early childhood or in later life) may lead to overt manifestation of the disorder. It seems likely that hereditary vulnerability rests not on a single gene but on combinations of genes, and that the incidence of these combinations is much more widespread than is the incidence of schizophrenia. In families in which the infant does not receive affection and emotional sustenance and the child does not have security in his relationships with those who are most significant to his care, vulnerable personalities may be generated. If such vulnerability is coupled with even a small degree of genetic vulnerability, schizophrenia may result. On the other hand, given a favorable family environment, a child with the same genetic potential may never manifest any of the symptoms or signs of schizophrenia. But again, a child with a strong genetic predisposition may well develop schizophrenia even under very favorable circumstances. This formulation is conjectural, but is in keeping with the evidence available from various sources in 1970. (See Chapter 10, pages 520–22.)

Social Roles and the Mental Disorders of Old Age

Some persons perform well on psychological tests and function very well in social relationships even when they show considerable arteriosclerotic brain damage, while other persons show the symptoms of senility while manifesting little evidence of brain damage.[38] An increasing literature on

---

[38] See James E. Birren *et al., Human Aging* (Washington, D. C.: U. S. Government Printing Office, 1963). Also, Alexander Simon and Leon Epstein, eds., *Aging in Modern Society* (Washington, D. C.: American Psychiatric Association, 1968).

social adjustment in old age attests to the importance of continued involvement in meaningful activities and relationships. The impairment of physical and mental capacities in old age poses a problem for the older person in terms of changed activities, relationships, and self-conception. Whether or not extreme symptomatology (either neurotic or psychotic) results may depend, then, not so much on the physiological changes that have occurred as on the ways that physical aging is handled, both by the older person and by those in his environment.

There is no question that our contemporary urban society fails to provide meaningful and satisfying roles for a large number of the aged. A much higher proportion of persons survive beyond the age of 70 than even a generation ago, but the structure of occupational opportunities for older persons has not expanded. Indeed, industrial operations place a high premium on youth. Retirement programs and social security afford a greater measure of economic security than was hitherto available, but the transition to retirement often seems to entail a feeling of loss of purpose. The yielding of the occupational role is not compensated by other prestige-giving or satisfying functions. Moreover, as a consequence of the trend away from three-generation households to the nuclear family of husband, wife, and children, associated both with high population mobility and with the small dwelling units of the modern city, the aged are increasingly isolated from kin. Some grandparents may still enjoy the possibility of serving as built-in "baby-sitters," but perhaps more often the modern grandparent must be content with an occasional visit to or from children and grandchildren. (See Chapter 10, page 485.)

A recent study of the circumstances attending the hospitalization of more than 500 persons over 60 years of age in San Francisco suggests that the mental disorders of old age as such seldom lead immediately to hospitalization.[39] Most of these older people had gradually developed a wide variety of symptoms — mental, behavioral, and physical — well before they were hospitalized. Most frequently they were characterized as "confused," "mind-wandering," or "disoriented." Their families and other close relatives frequently tried a number of alternative ways of dealing with the annoyances and disruptions caused by the senile person. In one-third of the cases, this went on for five or more years before hospitalization. In the last analysis, it was the disruptiveness and potential self-destructiveness of most of these older persons that led to hospitalization. Thus, the mental disorders of old age are quite different from those of the middle years. Even though many of the same symptoms may be manifest — suspiciousness, disorientation, even

---

[39] See Marjorie Fiske Lowenthal, *Lives in Distress: The Paths of the Elderly to the Psychiatric Ward* (New York: Basic Books, 1964).

hallucinations — these symptoms are not maintained with the same intensity, nor do they evoke the same intensity of reaction from others.

The Etiology of Neuroses

There is much greater agreement as to the crucial role of psychosocial factors in the etiology of neuroses than in that of the functional psychoses or the psychoses of old age. In the United States, at least, the psychoanalytic theory of the neuroses, or some variant of it, is held by most psychiatrists. Without attempting to present this theory in detailed or technical terms, we may say that it rests upon the concept of unconscious motivation and upon the needs, vulnerabilities, and conflicts that are unconsciously internalized as a result of life experience, especially in early childhood. The biological organism, with its drives for physical gratification and its needs for nurturing, is entirely dependent upon others for security in the satisfaction of those needs. But for a variety of reasons, such security may not be achieved. Biological needs are channeled and "disciplined"; infant strivings are often frustrated. Kubie has characterized the human child as "one helpless Lilliputian among hordes of brutal rival Lilliputians in a Brobdingnagian world of giants who are always giving too much protection or too little." [40] In attempting to ward off anxiety stemming from inevitable frustrations and frightening experiences, the child evolves various modes of psychological defense. These "defense mechanisms," which everyone uses to some extent, may permit the channeling of anxiety into relatively harmless or at times quite useful practices. Unfortunately, they may also lead to stereotyped ways of meeting situations, often quite inappropriate to the requirements of the situation. And being unaware of the reason for his stereotyped behavior, the potential neurotic is unable to modify it. When defenses patently lead to inappropriate responses or when for some reason they break down, full-blown neurosis, in one form or another, results.

Classical psychoanalytic theory placed the roots of neurosis in early life experience by postulating an inevitable conflict between man's biological nature and the demands placed on that nature by civilization.[41] Neo-

---

[40] Lawrence S. Kubie, "Social Forces and the Neurotic Process," in Alexander H. Leighton, John A. Clausen, and Robert N. Wilson, eds., *Explorations in Social Psychiatry* (New York: Basic Books, 1957), p. 90.

[41] The classic statement was, of course, that of Freud in *Civilization and Its Discontents*.

Freudians, such as Erich Fromm, Karen Horney, and Harry Stack Sullivan, however, have pointed out that Freud mistook the characteristics of middle-class Austria in the late nineteenth century for the immutable characteristics of "civilization." As a consequence, he was unaware of the enormous role played by culture in patterning interaction within the family and in setting life goals. He seems also to have underestimated the importance of later childhood and subsequent experiences in generating neurotic conflicts.

In *The Neurotic Personality of Our Time,* Horney points out that our modern era is characterized by a highly individualistic, competitive striving for achievement and social status.[42] As a consequence, interpersonal relationships are suffused by hostile tension and insecurity. It is the fear of failure and the fear of one's own aggressive tendencies toward others that, according to Horney, account for the neurotic anxiety that is so prevalent today. Whereas Freud emphasized the frustration of libidinal (essentially sexual) needs by civilization, Horney emphasizes those conflicts contained in Western culture itself that are internalized by its bearers: the conflict between competitive striving and brotherly love; the conflict between materialistic aspirations and the possibility of their fulfillment; and the conflict between the ideal of individual freedom and the reality of regimentation. This last conflict is the theme of a cogent analysis by Erich Fromm that extends consideration far beyond the realm of neurosis into that of the political dilemma of modern man.[43]

Whether or not specific cultural themes and specific aspects of social organization today have produced a demonstrable increase in neurotic breakdown, there seems to be little question that the sociocultural heritage is implicated in neurotic conflicts and in psychophysiological disorders. We cannot, however, assume that the elimination of specific cultural themes (if this were possible) would automatically reduce pathology, any more than we can predict the psychological stress value of a specific situation without knowing the whole context in which it is embedded.

SOCIAL POLICY AND MENTAL DISORDER

Given the prevalence and distribution of mental disorders, and the nature of the difficulties posed by such disorders in modern industrial society, how does our society mobilize its resources to deal with this particular social

---

[42] Karen Horney, *The Neurotic Personality of Our Time* (New York: Norton, 1937).
[43] Erich Fromm, *Escape from Freedom* (New York: Rinehart, 1941).

problem? We have already noted that in recent years there have been major changes in the legal and medical techniques by which we deal with mental illness, and these have gone hand in hand with changes in our basic social policy in the period since World War II. In the past few decades we have shifted from a basic policy of confining the mentally ill to one of maintaining in the community those mental patients who are not regarded as a serious threat to themselves or to others. Mental health has become the concern of federal and local governments, not merely of state governments that maintain institutions for the mentally ill. To understand the magnitude of the changes that have taken place, a brief historical review seems in order.

Treatment of the Mentally Ill—A Historical Review

Knowledge of the nature, causes, and treatment of mental illness developed very little between the flowering of the Greek city-states and the founding of the Republic of the United States. Through the centuries, markedly variant views of the nature of mental illness and of the best ways of dealing with it have been expressed by physicians, philosophers, and priests. Until the modern era, however, the mentally ill did not occupy a special status. In the Middle Ages, many of the mentally disordered were thought to be witches; the Church prescribed the means of identifying them and the means of disposing of them, often by torture and death.

At the beginning of the Renaissance, mental illness in its most extreme form—"madness"—held a peculiar fascination for artists of all kinds.[44] With the overthrow of traditional modes of thought and the resulting instability of conceptions of truth, the madman was often pictured as the only one in touch with ultimate reality. The "fools" in so many of Shakespeare's plays and figures like Don Quixote exemplify this fascination. But the lot of the indigent madman was in general a desperate one and apparently became more desperate as cities grew.

In the sixteenth and seventeenth centuries, the plight of the indigent, especially the physically and mentally ill, became acute in many cities. Families could not care for their sick members. Begging and stealing became

---

[44] For a detailed account of how the mentally ill became differentiated and were defined and dealt with from the beginnings of the modern era, see Michel Foucault, *Madness and Civilization* (New York: Pantheon Books, 1965). The following discussion on conditions in Europe is based on this source. See also George Rosen, *Madness in Society* (Chicago: University of Chicago Press, 1968).

widespread. Many of the indigent were driven from the cities and roamed the countryside. Others were thrown into jail. As the problems of the cities became more acute, large "hospitals" and prisons were built to house the indigent and put them to work.

In colonial America, with its small and relatively dispersed population, there were no special provisions for the mentally ill until just before the Revolution. There was no need for asylums as long as communities were small and charitable provisions could be made for support of the poor. Mentally disordered persons were treated according to their social level and the nature of their deviance. If they came from relatively well-to-do families, they could be cared for at home. If they were indigent, but seemed harmless, they were likely to be referred to as "distracted" and given charity. If they were troublesome and their behavior was offensive, they were likely to be confined in jails or in any securely locked quarters that could be found.[45]

The first great "modern" reform to improve the lot of the mentally ill came with the French Revolution, when the physician Pinel was given responsibility for the operation of the great asylums in which hundreds of the mentally ill were confined along with the physically ill and with many criminals. Severely regressed patients were chained in their cells with no sanitary provisions and often no clothing. Pinel had their chains struck off and demonstrated that the mentally ill responded to humanitarian treatment. He sought to gain the patient's confidence and instill in him a sense of hope. His approach became known as "moral treatment" and was very similar to present-day efforts to create a "therapeutic milieu."

The brutal treatment of mental patients everywhere became a cause of concern. In England during the 1790's a group of Quakers led by William Tuke established the York Retreat, where three generations of Tukes provided humane care and moral treatment for the mentally ill. Word of these developments reached the new United States, and a number of asylums were created specifically for mental patients. As the population grew, however, the facilities for mental patients failed to keep abreast of the need.

A century ago, Dorothea Lynde Dix's work in mental illness became a national rallying point for efforts to build hospitals for the mentally ill, most of whom were still lodged in jails and poorhouses. She mobilized first the elite of New England and then a very large part of the nation, persuading political leaders to introduce bills into state legislatures for the building of

---

[45] For the history of the care of the mentally ill in America see Albert Deutsch, *The Mentally Ill in America* (New York: Columbia University Press, 1949). See also Gerald N. Grob, *The State and the Mentally Ill* (Chapel Hill, N. C.: University of North Carolina Press, 1966). These are the primary sources from which the following history is derived.

mental hospitals. As a result of her efforts, a bill was introduced into Congress in the late 1840's providing for federal land grants that would finance state hospital operation. After being rejected several times by either the House or the Senate, the bill was passed in 1854 by both houses of Congress but vetoed by President Pierce. In his veto message the President argued that he felt it a duty

> to provide for those who, in the mysterious order of Providence, are subject to want and to disease of body or mind, but I cannot find any authority in the Constitution for making the Federal Government the great almoner of public charity throughout the United States.[46]

Nearly a century was to pass before the federal government would assist the states in providing for the mentally ill. Increasingly the states did build hospitals, but as new waves of immigrants arrived in the cities and contributed what appeared to be more than their share of indigent insane, the state hospitals came to be regarded as repositories for the troublesome, not as settings for moral treatment. Public policy was to keep expenses down by building large institutions whose operation could be routinized. There was seldom any communication between the hospital and the community from which the patient came. Thus was the pattern of "isolation and denial" institutionalized.

Although governmental programs did little to improve the lot of the mentally ill until nearly one-half of the twentieth century had passed, there were individuals and groups working for reform. Among the most important of these were groups involved in the mental hygiene movement.

The Mental Hygiene Movement

Clifford Beers's psychosis came a few years after his graduation from Yale at the start of the present century. He must have been a difficult patient, combining paranoid symptomatology with a fierce demand for his rights and decent treatment. As a consequence, he called down upon himself the most punitive responses in the attendant staffs at the private and public hospitals in which he spent three years. He was beaten, choked, spat upon, and often imprisoned for days in straitjacket and padded cell. His determination to do something to change the lot of the mentally ill came well before his

---

[46] *Congressional Globe*, 33rd Cong., 1st Sess., Vol. 2, p. 1061.

return to the community. Impressed with the success of *Uncle Tom's Cabin* more than a generation before in arousing America to the fight against slavery, he resolved to make his own life story not merely an indictment of the mental hospital but an instrument for social change. He was convinced that mental disease was not only curable but preventable. In his autobiography, *A Mind That Found Itself,* he outlined a plan for establishing a national society that would undertake mental hospital reforms, public education about mental illness, research into the causes, nature, and treatment of mental disease, and the creation of services directed toward the prevention of these diseases. Beers was able to enlist the support of some of the leading psychiatrists of the period, and in 1909 the National Committee for Mental Hygiene was founded. Since then, it has played a major role in seeking more adequate public support for mental health services.

World War I gave impetus to the movement by calling attention to the high rate of disability from nervous and mental disorders among soldiers. Especially dramatic were the severe psychoneurotic reactions, which were at the time labeled "shell shock" and which had been reported from other armies well before our entrance into the war. Psychiatry was incorporated into the American Army, and the language of psychiatry received greater currency.

At about the same time, the emergence of social casework as an occupational specialty, requiring graduate training in theory and technique, brought into being a new profession that quickly became devoted to the ideals of mental hygiene. Delinquency and a wide variety of behavior problems and family difficulties were seen as reflecting individual maladjustment and therefore as requiring individual casework for their solution. The development of child guidance clinics in the 1920's was a direct reflection of this new orientation, supported by great enthusiasm based on the belief that a means of preventing both delinquency and mental illness was near at hand. The ensuing decades, however, have shown that neither delinquency nor mental illness is so easily dealt with.

Social movements have their origins in the disorganization or disruption of societal functioning or in manifest conflict between values and prevailing practices. Thus the mental hygiene movement had its roots in the conflict between the value placed upon human dignity and worth in the Judeo-Christian ethic and the manifest maltreatment of mental patients (once mental disorder could be regarded as illness and not as the manifestation of sin). Those most drawn to the mental hygiene movement were persons of high ethical commitment. Many were less concerned with the treatment of the mentally ill than they were with the possibility of increasing human happiness and improving mental health generally. Moreover, they were unequivocally middle class in the goals they equated with mental health.[47] Normal or healthy behavior was equated with "adjustment," and adjustment was equated with striving for occupational and social success in an individualistic, competitive society. There was no recognition that success was not equally within the reach of all individuals, as a consequence of inequalities of access to physical and emotional security in childhood, to education, to health facilities in time of need. In a way, then, the movement came to represent a strong force in behalf of conformity with middle-class aspirations and ethics.

The great depression of the 1930's served to counterbalance this bias to a considerable degree. It became impossible to maintain the comfortable view that men out of work were basically lazy or "psychopathic." Not individual maladjustment, but a basic societal maladjustment had to be recognized. As a consequence, there seems to have been a decline in emphasis on psychiatric services and facilities during the 1930's but at the same time a beginning of systematic inquiry into the social correlates of mental illness. Within the realm of psychiatric theory, perhaps the most influential development in the United States derived from the view, expressed by Harry Stack Sullivan and his followers, that mental illness is basically a disturbance in interpersonal relationships.[48] Its roots, Sullivan believed, lay in the realm of the social. Social and psychological were not, then, to be opposed; they were to be viewed as interacting.

With World War II, and its demand for dependable manpower, emphasis shifted to the assessment of individual capacities and vulnerabilities — capacities for specialized training, for functioning in the highly regimented social systems of the military services; vulnerabilities to breakdown under the routines of garrison life or under the stress of combat and isolation. The psychiatric disabilities of World War II took a different form from those of World War I. Their relationship to anxiety and fatigue was more clearly manifest, for they were seldom masked by the kinds of physical symptoms that led to the label "shell shock" in World War I.

Psychiatry played a more substantial role in World War II than it had in the previous conflict. It was given major responsibility for "screening" out those selectees who were likely to break down psychologically and major responsibility for returning to combat effectiveness or recommending for

---

[47] The consequences of the middle-class orientation of the leaders of the mental hygiene movement have been analyzed by Kingsley Davis, "Mental Hygiene and the Class Structure," *Psychiatry*, Vol. 1 (February, 1938), pp. 55–65.

[48] Harry Stack Sullivan, *Conceptions of Modern Psychiatry* (Washington, D. C.: William Alanson White Psychiatric Foundation, 1947).

other dispositions those who had become ineffective by virtue of psychological impairment. But almost certainly the chief impact of the war on the development of psychiatry and on services for the mentally ill was an indirect one: World War II called attention as nothing else had to the magnitude of the problem of psychoneurosis and the enormous loss of productivity to which it led. Not long after the end of the war, the issue of mental illness was posed to Congress as a major public health problem, on a par with any problem in the realm of physical illness. In 1946, after extensive hearings, Congress passed the National Mental Health Act, which established the National Institute of Mental Health within the United States Public Health Service.[49]

Enter the Federal Government

The establishment of a national mental health program within the public health field, with its traditional emphasis on prevention and control of disease, served as a powerful impetus to consideration of the mass aspects of mental disorder. Moreover, federal expenditures for mental health served to markedly stimulate state expenditures as well. Federal funds have gone primarily into research, the training of professional personnel, and grants to states for partial support of community services. State funds have gone largely into improvement and staffing of the mental hospitals.

In 1955, Congress passed the Mental Health Study Act, which provided funds for a Joint Commission on Mental Health and Illness to analyze and evaluate the needs and resources of the mentally ill in the United States and to make recommendations for new program developments. A number of excellent monographs were produced for or by the Joint Commission reviewing the current status of the field of mental health as of the late 1950's.[50] The final report of the Commission, entitled *Action for Mental Health,* strongly emphasized the need for more adequate facilities for immediate care of acutely disturbed persons and for substantial federal contributions toward the establishment of community mental health centers.

---

[49] For a description of the background and implications of this act see James V. Lowry, "Public Mental Health Agencies, State and National," *Annals of the American Academy of Political and Social Science,* Vol. 286 (March, 1953), p. 103.

[50] Of particular interest are Marie Jahoda, *Current Concepts of Positive Mental Health* and Rashi Fein, *Economics of Mental Illness* (New York: Basic Books, 1958); Gerald Gurin, Joseph Veroff, and Sheila Feld, *Americans View Their Mental Health;* Reginald Robinson, David DeMarche, and Mildred Wagle, *Community Resources in Mental Health* (New York: Basic Books, 1960); and the final summary report of the Commission, *Action for Mental Health* (New York: Basic Books, 1961).

Largely as a consequence of the work of the Joint Commission, Congress enacted the Community Mental Health Centers Act of 1963, which authorized federal funding for the construction of comprehensive community mental health centers throughout the nation. Two years later the act was amended to authorize funds for the staffing of the centers. The ultimate objective of this program is

> the establishment of a network of comprehensive community mental health center programs throughout the Nation which will integrate and coordinate the elements of comprehensive services at the local level so as to maintain patients close to their own environment and to protect their links with family and community. The five essential elements of service to be provided by every center include: (1) inpatient services providing 24-hour care for treatment of acute disorder; (2) outpatient services; (3) partial hospitalization services, such as day care, night care, weekend care; (4) emergency services 24 hours per day, which must be available within at least one of the first three services listed above; (5) consultation and education services available to community agencies and professional personnel. To reach the goal of comprehensive services, five additional services will be needed: (6) diagnostic services; (7) rehabilitative services, including vocational and educational programs; (8) precare and aftercare services in the community, including foster home placement, home visiting, and halfway houses; (9) training; and (10) research and evaluation.[51]

Thus, a century and a decade after President Pierce found no basis for providing federal aid to the states in their efforts to deal with mental illness, the federal government has to a large degree taken over the basic responsibility for seeing that adequate care is available. Let us now briefly note the nature of present facilities for caring for the mentally ill.

FACILITIES FOR THE CARE
OF THE MENTALLY ILL

The primary resource for diagnosing and treating the mentally ill in modern society is of course the psychiatric profession, together with the systems of services for which it is responsible. The plural, *systems,* is used advisedly, for until very recently (with the advent of mental health centers) there has been very little coordination or integration of mental health services. The

---

[51] Office of Biometry, National Institute of Mental Health, "Patients in State and County Mental Hospitals, 1967," *Mental Health Facility Reports,* p. 6.

TABLE 2

Patient Care Episodes in Various Facilities
for Mental Patients in the United States, 1966

	Total	Males	Females
All Facilities	**2,687,424**	**1,417,418**	**1,270,006**
Mental Hospitals: Total	1,035,182	519,336	455,846
State and County	(805,602)	(414,753)	(390,849)
Veterans Administration	(125,607)	(125,607)	
Private	(103,973)	(38,976)	(64,997)
General Hospitals with Psychiatric Services	466,242	186,963	279,279
Outpatient Psychiatric Clinics	1,186,000	651,119	534,081

Source: Mental Health Facilities Reports, Public Health Service Publication No. 1921, 1969.

basic responsibility for caring for mental patients who are most severely ill has been borne by the states, and two-fifths of the cost of mental patient care is still borne by the state governments.[52] Local governments contribute one-sixth and the federal government now contributes somewhat more than one-tenth of the three billion dollars spent annually for maintaining mental health facilities other than those provided within general hospital psychiatric services.

An indication of the level of services provided by various mental health facilities is given by Table 2, which shows for 1966 (the last year for which data have been published) the distribution of patient care episodes in each type of facility during the year. The mid-1960's mark the first time in our history that more patients were seen in outpatient psychiatric clinics than were treated in mental hospitals. Nevertheless, state and county mental hospitals remain by a wide margin the primary resource for treating the most severely mentally disordered. Nearly two of every three dollars spent for mental health care go to the maintenance of state and county hospitals. As of 1970, there are roughly 300 such hospitals, and as previously noted, on any given day approximately 400,000 persons are resident in them. As can be noted from Table 2, this figure comprises roughly half the patients served by state and county hospitals in a given year. The other half is made up of persons admitted to a mental hospital for the first time and a somewhat greater number of persons who have previously been hospitalized

---

[52] Provisional data provided by the Office of Biometry, National Institute of Mental Health.

and returned to the community and who again appear to require hospital care. Readmissions of patients with psychotic disorders are frequent.

As can be seen from Table 2, private mental hospitals accommodate only a small proportion of mental patients. In addition, the cost of maintaining a patient in a private mental hospital is beyond the means of any but the wealthiest families, so that most patients stay in such hospitals only a relatively short time. However, the influence of private mental hospitals on psychiatric theory and practice is great, for they provide valuable facilities for training and for research.

In addition to state and county hospitals providing prolonged care of mental patients, an increasing number of general hospitals are providing psychiatric wards for short-term care. Although the number of patients accommodated at any given time is not large, over the course of the year nearly half a million patients are admitted and discharged from the psychiatric services of general hospitals. Many of these patients would have gone to a state hospital a decade or so ago; one-third of them are diagnosed as having functional psychoses and another one-fourth as suffering from psychoneuroses. Because of policy and costs at a general hospital, mental patients seldom stay more than a few weeks. For many patients, this period is long enough to regain their equilibrium so that they may again function in the community. Moreover, by virtue of remaining in the community and not being stigmatized by hospitalization in an "insane asylum," these patients are likely to be better able to fit back into their normal social roles. Often, of course, they will receive subsequent treatment at an outpatient clinic.

The Mental Hospital

The mental hospital is charged not only with medical but with legal responsibility for many of its patients. This is true primarily of patients in state and county hospitals, many of whom are committed under legal provisions and procedures that vary from state to state.[53] In many states commitment may be arranged by filing a certificate signed by two physicians who have examined the prospective patient and who can attest to his being "insane," or by otherwise meeting the legal requirements that permit depriving a person of his liberty without a trial. In other states formal hear-

---

[53] See Ruth Roemer, "Mental Health Legislation Affecting Patient Care," *American Journal of Public Health,* Vol. 52 (1962), pp. 592–99.

ings are required to evaluate the problematic person. Such procedures are designed to protect persons who are not mentally ill from being "railroaded" into the mental hospital.

It is doubtful that commitment of well persons has ever accounted for any substantial proportion of hospital patients, but there is an ever present danger that the nonconformist or the person with extreme idiosyncracies will be committed unjustly, especially if he lacks power. Recent studies indicate that patients committed after formal hearings often do not manifest any behaviors that would legally justify hospitalization; rather, they are committed on the basis of hearsay and summary judgments that are based on complaints by family members, co-workers, and so on.[54] Such commitments occur infrequently, however, if the person being examined is represented by counsel. Of those represented at commitment proceedings by their own lawyers, most are released; among those *equally symptomatic* but not represented by counsel, most are committed. One recent study found, for example, that among persons appearing at sanity hearings but not exhibiting behaviors that met legal criteria for commitment, none of those having legal counsel were committed to the hospital but two-thirds of those without counsel were ordered hospitalized.[55]

Once in the mental hospital, the patient becomes primarily a medical responsibility. He is usually assigned to an admission or receiving ward, where he can be given close attention and, depending on available staff, such medical, psychiatric, and psychological examinations as will aid in diagnosis and the planning of treatment.

Our mental hospitals are, for the most part, understaffed and inadequately supported. Yet they must somehow cope with the anxiety-provoking propensities of the patients, provide what treatment can be managed, maintain livable quarters and physical facilities, schedule food preparation and serving, afford a program of activities for the patients, and at the same time decide when any given patient is ready to be released to the community. If they do less than a perfect job, we might well consider in what other realm of human activity we ask for such exacting performance with so little in the way of resources and support.

Because at one time the emphasis in mental hospital construction was upon building (usually in somewhat remote sites) a few extremely large in-

---

[54] See Thomas Scheff, "The Societal Reaction to Deviance: Ascriptive Elements in the Psychiatric Screening of Mental Patients in a Mid-Western State," *Social Problems,* Vol. 11 (Spring, 1964), pp. 401–13.

[55] See Dennis L. Wenger and C. R. Fletcher, "The Effect of Legal Counsel on Admissions to a Mental Hospital: A Confrontation of Professions," *Health and Social Behavior,* Vol. 10 (March, 1969), pp. 66–72.

stitutions where a great many patients could be confined at low per-person cost, the older hospitals tend to be unnecessarily prisonlike in appearance. In other respects, too, mental hospitals are quite different from the usual hospital to which we take our physical ailments. First of all, most mentally ill patients do not need to be in bed except for normal sleep requirements. Then, because of the mental hospital's legal responsibility and the nature of the symptomatic behavior of many patients at one time or another (but only a small minority at any given time), much attention is given to matters of security. More and more hospitals are managing to open—that is, to un-lock—many of their wards or buildings, but in most public mental hospitals in the United States locked wards are considered a virtual necessity. Where greater freedom is accorded the patients, greater staff vigilance and availability to patients is required to prevent "elopements" or interpersonal complications of one sort or another. In most hospitals, then, such freedom as "ground privileges" or visits in the community are accorded only to those patients who are judged to be well enough to take personal responsibility.

As a social organization designed to help mentally ill or emotionally disturbed persons achieve mental health and take up normal social roles in the community, the traditional mental hospital has many defects. Limited staff and resources, coupled with large size and isolation from the community, make many mental hospitals little more than repositories for custodial care of involuntary inmates. From the standpoint of the patient, herded as a member of a collectivity with little attention given to his personal needs or desires, such hospitals are not very different from prisons and concentration camps. Goffman has characterized such organizations as "total institutions" and has noted the ways in which staff and inmates interact and work out adjustments in such establishments.[56] Although supervision of the wards and decisions relating to patient care and release from the hospital are the responsibilities of the medical personnel, the limited number of psychiatrists and other physicians available in most public hospitals precludes any substantial amount of contact between doctor and patient. The doctors and even the graduate nurses must spend most of their time maintaining records and handling problems of patient disposition. As a consequence, in many hospitals it is the attendants who control the operations of the wards, largely by

---

[56] See Erving Goffman, *Asylums* (New York: Doubleday, 1961). Other influential studies of mental hospitals include the following: Ivan Belknap, *Human Problems of a State Mental Hospital* (New York: McGraw-Hill, 1956); William Caudill, *The Mental Hospital as a Small Society* (Cambridge, Mass.: Harvard University Press, 1958); H. Warren Dunham and S. K. Weinberg, *The Culture of a State Mental Hospital* (Detroit: Wayne State University Press, 1960); and Alfred Stanton and Morris Schwartz, *The Mental Hospital* (New York: Basic Books, 1954).

their control of access of patients to physicians and of physicians to information about patients. Patients are to be fitted to the demands of the system, not the system to the needs of patients. The distressed and often disoriented patient is usually deprived of his personal possessions, denied the privileges that self-respecting adults take for granted, and, in short, treated in such a way as to be deprived of all the trappings of self-respect.

Large, poorly supported public mental hospitals are likely to retain the objectionable characteristics of "total institutions," but there is now at least an awareness of the problem and an increasing disposition to seek other ways of dealing with mental illness. Recent research on the effects of the hospital social structure on the rehabilitative potential of patients, together with increasing support in many states for smaller, more adequately staffed hospitals, suggests that there is a decided trend away from custodial and toward therapeutic patient care. To this topic we shall return later in the chapter.

Outpatient Services

"Outpatient services" are those agencies and facilities that provide therapy or counseling to persons whose mental illness or emotional distress is not so acute or severe as to require their hospitalization. Available outpatient services include a wide variety of community clinics, counseling services, private psychiatrists, emergency services, psychiatric consultants to social agencies, and clinics or therapy groups maintained by mental hospitals for former patients. The expansion of mental health services within the community has been the most significant single development in efforts to deal with mental illness in recent decades. Prior to World War II there were fewer than 350 mental health clinics in the United States. By 1963 there were nearly 2300 such outpatient clinics, which provided diagnostic or treatment services to an estimated 1,500,000 persons.[57]

The psychiatric clinic is most often a team operation, usually involving psychiatrists, psychiatric social workers, and clinical psychologists. The psychiatrists are the chief therapists and also supervise and coordinate the work of other staff members. Psychiatric social workers screen applicants for service and often provide counseling or therapy to mothers of child pa-

---

[57] Office of Biometry, National Institute of Mental Health, "Provisional Patient Movement Data, Outpatient Psychiatric Clinics, July 1, 1967 – June 30, 1968," *Mental Health Facility Reports* (Washington, D. C.: U. S. Government Printing Office, 1969).

tients or to other members of the family. Psychologists may also provide treatment but their special contribution in most clinics is to provide systematic assessments of personality and intelligence as an aid to diagnosis and evaluation.

The primary therapeutic technique of outpatient services for the mentally ill is "psychotherapy," though drugs are also frequently employed to relieve anxiety. The aim of psychotherapy is to assist the distressed person in examining and hopefully understanding his ways of acting, thinking, and feeling. Clinic services have been most highly utilized by middle-class families who have a degree of familiarity with psychiatric thinking. By and large, persons with a working-class background seem less disposed to verbalize their feelings or to examine them introspectively.[58] For this reason, many working-class persons in need of help find psychotherapy unacceptable or unrewarding. Group therapy is being used increasingly in many community clinics, both because it enables the clinic to serve a larger number of patients and because the presence of the more verbal members in a group often facilitates communication by those not used to verbalizing their feelings.

As noted above, until quite recently most mental health clinics had long lists of persons waiting for diagnosis or treatment. An emotionally upset person in need of immediate help seldom could be seen the day he presented himself; often he could not be seen for weeks. With the enormous increase in community mental health facilities this picture has changed markedly in many states and communities, though not in all by any means. Many general hospitals now maintain emergency services for the mentally ill, just as they maintain them for persons injured in accidents or for those with acute problems of physical illness. A few communities are even experimenting with first-aid services for the mentally ill, with workers ready to go out into the community to assess acute problems of emotional disturbance in the social settings in which they become manifest.[59]

As mental health services have become more closely linked with the field of public health, and particularly with the establishment of mental health centers, a variety of new forms of treatment services and aids for those who suffer from chronic forms of mental illness have been developed. In some com-

---

[58] Jerome Myers and Leslie Schaffer, "Social Stratification and Psychiatric Practice: A Study of an Outpatient Clinic," *American Sociological Review,* Vol. 19 (June, 1954), pp. 307–10.

[59] A general discussion of recent developments in outpatient care as well as in other aspects of patient care is given in Morris and Charlotte Schwartz, *Social Approaches to Mental Patient Care* (New York: Columbia University Press, 1964). See also Leigh Roberts *et al., Community Psychiatry* (Madison, Wis.: University of Wisconsin Press, 1966).

munities "day-hospitals" serve acutely distressed patients who can play some role in family life but who need the emotional support of the hospital staff on a regular basis. There are also "night-hospitals" (often in the same physical facilities) for patients who are able to hold a job during the day but who require a measure of support when they are not at work. In general, the aim of recently developed programs has been to keep the patient in the community and functioning in at least some of his normal roles to the maximum extent possible.

From the above description of institutional resources, it might appear that professional resources are to be found primarily in mental hospitals, clinics, and other public or privately organized facilities for the mentally ill. However, more than half of the trained psychiatrists in the United States are engaged full or part time in the private practice of psychiatry. Psychiatrists in full-time private practice see about four-fifths of their patients in their own offices and the other fifth in general or private mental hospitals. About one-half of the patients served by private psychiatrists are diagnosed as psychoneurotic and one-fourth as psychotic, with the latter group comprising a substantial proportion of those seen in hospitals.[60] It has been estimated that private psychiatrists serve roughly 750,000 persons in a given year in the United States, but systematic statistics on such services are unavailable. In general, their clientele is white and relatively well-to-do. Most community clinics and emergency services refer to private psychiatrists those applicants who can afford to pay for private care.

Mental Health Personnel

In general, facilities and services for the mentally ill are directed by psychiatrists. Like other medical specialists, the fully qualified psychiatrist must meet stringent requirements as to training, experience, and knowledge before he is certified. To qualify for examination and certification by the American Board of Psychiatry and Neurology, a medical school graduate must serve his year of internship and two or three years of residency training in an approved institution (including both course work and supervised experience in treating a variety of patients) and secure an additional two years of relevant experience. An even longer period of training and experience is required for

---

[60] These estimates are from a small survey and must be regarded as very approximate. See Anita Bahn *et al.,* "Survey of Private Psychiatric Practice," *Archives of General Psychiatry,* Vol. 12 (1965), pp. 295–302.

psychiatrists who wish to be fully qualified as psychoanalysts. Formal psychoanalytic training is, in general, open only to physicians who have had at least a year of full-time psychiatric training and usually entails another three or more years. In addition to course work, the student must complete a personal psychoanalysis and must carry out a supervised psychoanalysis of one or more patients. Despite the relatively small number of psychoanalysts in the United States – about 1000 – psychoanalytic thinking has been a major influence in American psychiatry.

Although the development of psychiatry in the United States originated in the mental hospitals, only a small fraction of American psychiatrists are staff members of mental hospitals. Psychiatry moved out of the mental hospital in response to a number of influences in the early decades of the twentieth century: the influence of psychoanalytic theory and practice, leading to greater interest in the neuroses and in the private practice of intensive psychotherapy; the markedly greater financial rewards of private practice in an affluent society; the demands for a military psychiatry that could cope with emotional disturbances brought about by the stress of combat; the development of concern with preventive psychiatry through early treatment and through child guidance work. As a consequence of these developments, it is estimated that less than one-third of American psychiatrists are now engaged primarily in providing services for the severely mentally ill.[61] For Board-certified psychiatrists the proportion is almost certainly lower.

The tremendous increase in the number of outpatient facilities in recent years was possible only because of the vast expansion of training facilities and subsidized training for professional personnel.[62] In addition to their work in clinics, psychiatric social workers and clinical psychologists provide therapy or counseling and psychological assessment through a variety of community organizations (family service, child welfare, and other health and welfare agencies, and the schools). Within the mental hospital, psychiatric nurses constitute the largest single group of professionally trained workers. And in recent decades another category of nurse is being trained in increasing numbers – the public health nurse with mental health training. Such nurses, working largely on the staffs of local health departments, are in especially strategic positions to bring mental health services to large segments of the population.

A survey of staffed positions in all mental health facilities in the United

---

[61] This estimate was arrived at by pooling available data from a variety of sources.

[62] Descriptions of the qualifications of each of these categories of personnel and of trends in their training are given in George W. Albee, *Mental Health Manpower Trends* (New York: Basic Books, 1959).

States as of January 1968 revealed that there were then 302,546 full-time employees and 34,670 part-time employees. The great majority were in mental hospitals. Although the proportion of professionals in such facilities has nearly doubled in the past decade, it is still less than one-fifth. Indeed, only about 2 percent of the full-time personnel in mental hospitals and other mental health facilities are psychiatrists, though they comprise one-fifth of the part-time personnel. Nurses and social workers make up one-half of the full-time professionals. The largest single category of personnel, accounting for more than two-fifths of all full-time mental health workers, is comprised of nursing aides or "attendants" who provide the basic care of patients. Less than half of these nursing aides have completed even a high school education. A recent study of nursing aides revealed that only 8 percent had any relevant training prior to employment in the mental hospital where they were working.[63] Yet, as we have seen, studies of the operation of public mental hospitals have revealed that the attendants frequently control the patient's access to professional personnel and set the norms for patient care.[64] Only as hospital systems come to reward the nursing assistant or attendant with an adequate salary and provide thorough training and firm but supportive supervision will the transition from custodial to therapeutic care become a reality.

SOME RECENT TRENDS IN PATIENT CARE

We have seen that the support of mental health research, training, and facilities by the federal government has led to substantial changes in the treatment of mental patients, especially in the past two or three decades. The most striking change has been the decline in the number of patients in mental hospitals, despite substantial increases in our total population.

Until the mid-1950's mental hospitals were crowded and new construction could not keep up with the demands for additional beds. The number of resident patients in long-term mental hospitals increased every year until 1955. Since 1955, each year has seen a decline in the number of resident patients, despite the fact that the number of new admissions to long-term hospitals has continued to rise. The decline has resulted from the fact that newly admitted patients are, on the average, not staying as long as before.

---

[63] See *The Psychiatric Aide in State Mental Hospitals,* Public Health Service Publication No. 1286 (Washington, D. C.: U. S. Government Printing Office, 1965).

[64] See, for example, Ivan Belknap, *Human Problems of a State Mental Hospital.*

Far fewer patients now become victims of "hospitalitis," in which the patient loses all hope and all sense of personal responsibility as a consequence of his utter powerlessness and the depersonalizing experience of being on a ward for chronic patients. The number of newly admitted patients who now stay on indefinitely is substantially less than the number of deaths and discharges of patients who were already resident in long-term mental hospitals.

From the previous discussion of the shift from hospitalization to outpatient services, it will be apparent that the decline in mental hospital population does not reflect any decrease in the prevalence of mental illness. Rather, it reflects changes in policy and changes in facilities and technique. Both types of changes were unquestionably hastened by the critical evaluation of our mental hospitals and the great increase in trained personnel that came with the establishment of the National Institute of Mental Health.

Knowledge of the Effects of Long-Term Hospitalization

Only in the past two decades has conclusive evidence been secured on the effects of long-term hospitalization. Those effects were particularly devastating for persons who received a diagnosis of schizophrenia. Most psychiatrists believed that schizophrenia was a deteriorating disease. They could point to the average length of stay of resident patients in state mental hospitals as evidence for their belief. In turn, they were likely to decide that patients who did not show progress in the early stages of hospitalization were schizophrenic and to assign them to "back wards" where they would receive almost no personalized attention from professional personnel. Thereafter, the probability of such patients coming to attention as candidates for return to the community was very slight. The assignment of the label "schizophrenic" to a patient was, then, often a self-fulfilling prophecy that the patient would not be returned to the community.

As long as mental hospital statistics were compiled primarily on the basis of patients resident in hospitals at the beginning and end of the year, they failed to reveal a most significant fact, namely that most of the patients discharged in a given period are drawn from among those most recently admitted. In general, newly admitted patients are the focus of the most intensive treatment efforts. Initial diagnoses are usually regarded as tentative; being subject to change, they are not likely to determine the patient's course in the hospital. Patients who respond positively to the care or treatment provided in the early weeks of hospitalization are candidates for future discharge. Those who do not respond positively tend to be placed in wards where fewer services are available.

Knowledge of the dynamics of mental hospital population movement is not entirely new but has been widely understood since the early 1950's, when large-scale studies of *cohorts* of mental patients were first published and well publicized. A "cohort" of patients is a group of consecutive admissions whose status is continuously recorded for a period of months or years from the time of admission. At any given time within this period, one can establish what proportion of patients remain in the hospital, what proportion have been released to the community, and what proportion have died. The use of cohort studies by Kramer and others in the early 1950's clearly revealed that for four successive cohorts of patients hospitalized from 1916 to 1950, the chances of being released from the hospital were far greater in the first six months than at any subsequent time.[65] Once a patient had remained in the hospital continuously for as long as two years, his chances of ever being released were very slight.

One of the most depressing aspects of the whole mental health area — the stockpiling of "deteriorated" patients regarded as hopeless — appears, then, to have been created by the hospital itself. The dismal effects of long-term isolation of patients in large, poorly staffed, custodial institutions had been recognized by a number of psychiatrists since the early days of "moral treatment" (see p. 65), and it had been stressed by spokesmen for the mental hygiene movement and by journalists for several decades. Indeed, some hospital administrators were already moving to combat the effects of long-term hospitalization well before those effects had been systematically documented. Most state hospital personnel, however, attributed the patient's length of stay to his illness and not to the fact that hospital practices relegated many patients to a life without hope. The documentation of the negative consequences of indefinitely keeping patients in the hospital added impetus to efforts to provide better care and make the hospital environment more therapeutic. These efforts were markedly advanced by the introduction of the tranquilizing drugs, which also took place in the early 1950's.

The Tranquilizing Drugs

The tranquilizing drugs have unquestionably been the most exciting therapeutic innovation of the century for chronic and acute psychotic patients. These drugs do not appear to cure mental illness; rather they diminish the

---

[65] See Morton Kramer *et al.*, "A Historical Study of the Disposition of First Admissions to a State Mental Hospital," Public Health Monograph 32 (Washington, D. C.: U. S. Government Printing Office, 1955).

severity of certain types of symptoms (agitation, aggressive tendencies) [66] and thereby render the patient more comfortable, more socially acceptable, and also possibly more accessible to social relationships and psychotherapy. Thus the use of tranquilizers has greatly reduced the stresses upon staff members charged with the care of chronic patients and has permitted a more relaxed and therapeutic environment, including a much more hopeful attitude on the part of the hospital personnel. Although the downward trend in resident populations in prolonged-care public mental hospitals cannot be wholly attributed to the effects of the tranquilizers and other recently synthesized drugs, they have certainly played a significant role. Much current research is devoted to investigating the mode of drug action, not only to permit the production of even more effective pharmacological agents but also to illuminate the physiological dynamics of mental illness.

Improvements in Hospital Climates

The earlier return of patients to the community also reflects a growing awareness of the dangers associated with prolonged hospitalization. The enduring loss of normal social roles, coupled with adaptation to the hospital, tends to make the chronic patient unfit for any other mode of life. Part of the increased rate of return of patients is probably attributable also to the very real improvements in the staffing and patterns of patient care in our mental hospitals. Many hospitals are still far from adequate, but fewer can now be characterized as "snake pits." One of the major consequences of research on the mental hospital has been greater attention to its social climate.

Even in the time of Pinel there was some recognition that a brief stay in a protected, warm, accepting environment could restore many patients to more-or-less normal functioning. This was the essence of "moral treatment" and it is the essence of modern milieu therapy, though during the period of emphasis on the large public hospital this concept of patient care dropped out of sight. There are many different conceptions of the ideal nature of a therapeutic milieu,[67] but one indispensable aspect is that, if the patient is to achieve any self-respect, he must be treated as a person worthy of the respect of others. The rigid, hierarchical structure of the large mental hospital would

---

[66] Jonathan O. Cole and Ralph W. Gerard, *Pharmacotherapy: Problems in Evaluation* (Washington, D. C.: National Academy of Sciences, 1959).

[67] For an excellent general discussion, see Morris and Charlotte Schwartz, *Social Approaches to Mental Patient Care,* Chapter 11.

seem to preclude its being a therapeutic milieu. Only when all categories of staff who have dealings with patients are involved in the objective of providing a therapeutic atmosphere and when patients have a considerable voice in the conduct of hospital affairs does the desired pattern of relationships begin to emerge. Especially influential in improving the climate of hospitals have been efforts to develop "therapeutic communities," both in the United States and in Britain.[68] The first efforts along these lines came with attempts to assist long-time prisoners of war to make the difficult transition back to civilian life. Special "transitional communities" were established, in which the members were given an opportunity to redevelop and practice social skills and to acquire again the ability to make decisions for themselves.

Even an ideal therapeutic community is not, however, a viable pattern of adult life.[69] Institutional processes are inevitably different from family life. Further transitional stages seem called for, and there is currently much experimentation with halfway houses and other patterns that permit gradual reintegration of the patient who is not able to take on full adult responsibilities.

Recent research suggests that there are wide differences in the range of tolerance that former patients tend to receive in various living arrangements after hospitalization.[70] Patients who return to live with husband or wife are, in general, expected to perform adequately their normal roles as adults — spouse, parent, worker, neighbor, and the like. Much less is expected of those who return to the household of their parents, even if they are adults. As a consequence, former patients living in these two settings show substantial differences in degree of impairment and in the likelihood of being returned to the hospital if they become somewhat upset.

Some patients return from the mental hospital or emerge from outpatient treatment without any appreciable psychological impairment. They are effective, happy persons. Others show more or less marked impairment or unhappiness. Some had been, and again become, well integrated into a network of intimate relationships. Others had been and continue to be somewhat marginal in their social relationships. Here again, the difference between mental disorders and physical illnesses is great. The former mental patient not only has to cope with whatever degree of impairment his mental

---

[68] See especially Maxwell Jones, *The Therapeutic Community* (New York: Basic Books, 1953).

[69] In *Community as Doctor: New Perspectives on a Therapeutic Community* (London: Tavistock Publications, 1960), Robert N. Rapoport analyzes the objectives, procedures, and problems of one of the best-known therapeutic communities.

[70] See, for example, Howard E. Freeman and Ozzie G. Simmons, *The Mental Patient Comes Home* (New York: Wiley, 1963).

illness has entailed; he must also cope with the altered expectations of others. The recognition of this fact puts added stress on the desirability of attempting to prevent mental illness or at least hospitalization.

Maintaining Patients in the Community

In the past decade outpatient services have increasingly been addressed to the task of maintaining as many patients as possible—even psychotic patients—in the community. The use of tranquilizing drugs has made this more feasible by relieving the anxiety of the patient and making him less likely to act aggressively or disruptively. One carefully controlled experiment demonstrated that most patients admitted to a mental hospital with a diagnosis of schizophrenia could actually be treated at home with drugs, at far less cost than if they had remained in the hospital.[71] The patients were examined soon after their admission to the hospital and then (after those relatively few who seemed potentially homicidal or suicidal were eliminated) assigned randomly to one of three groups. One group, the "controls," stayed in the hospital and received standard care. The other two groups were returned to their homes, where they received medication and weekly visits from public health nurses. For one experimental group the medication given was a potent tranquilizer. For the other it was a *placebo*—that is, an inert pill having no chemical effect. Three-fourths of the patients receiving drug therapy and a third of those receiving only a placebo were able to remain in the community for the duration of the study (which ranged from six to thirty months, depending on when the patient first entered the hospital). Some patients subsequently had to be hospitalized, but most did not. The savings in cost of hospital care were substantial and the patients were not subjected to the trauma of hospitalization.

But there are, of course, other factors to be considered. A patient may be maintained in the home at the expense of the emotional well-being of other family members. If the patient is not able to work, his being at home may require other family members to stay away from work or school to care for him. Family routines and social activities are often disrupted. The patient's demands for attention may place an intolerable burden of concern and physical strain on other family members.[72]

---

[71] See Benjamin Passamanick *et al., Schizophrenics in the Community: An Experimental Study in the Prevention of Hospitalization* (New York: Appleton, 1967).

[72] *Ibid.,* pp. 124, 433. Also see Jacqueline Grad, "A Two-Year Follow-Up" in Richard H. Williams and Lucy D. Ozarin, *Community Mental Health: An International Perspective* (San Francisco: Jossey-Bass, 1968), pp. 429–54.

The development of comprehensive community mental health centers should help to give psychiatrists a flexible range of alternatives in deciding on treatment needs and weighing their costs. Many problems remain, but our recent policy of greatly increasing expenditures for mental health at all governmental levels seems to be paying off in human welfare.[73]

CAN MENTAL ILLNESS BE PREVENTED?[74]

Certain types of mental illness can definitely be prevented and, indeed, are now being prevented. Reference has been made to the effective treatment of general paresis by the use of drug therapy. Since paresis results only as a very late stage in the course of syphilis, the cure of syphilis in earlier stages prevents the development of the psychotic state. Psychoses associated with pellagra – once a common cause of admission to mental hospitals in the South, where dietary deficiencies were widespread – are now very rare. The provision of nicotinic acid in the diet was all that was required.

When we consider the functional psychoses and the mental disorders of old age, it is more difficult to apply our knowledge of etiology to preventive programs. For one thing, our knowledge of etiology is still very meager and would afford at best only partial control. For another, it would entail public education and social change in areas remarkably resistant to change, such as patterns of family life and even of mate selection. What public health workers call "secondary prevention" may for some time be more feasible. This entails the early recognition of illness and maladjustment and the provision of ameliorative services or environmental change to limit the severity and duration of disease. School counseling services and community clinics have been organized to serve this function, but the present pattern of clinic services cannot meet the demand for help; new, more flexible programs need to be developed.

Insofar as further research supports or disproves the hypothesis that high incidence of the functional psychoses and the neuroses is linked with the social deprivation and the conflict of values confronting families and individuals at the lowest socioeconomic levels, the implications for preventive programs will be similar to those for programs oriented toward limiting

---

[73] An excellent discussion of many of the issues that remain to be dealt with is given by David Mechanic, *Mental Health and Social Policy* (Englewood Cliffs, N. J.: Prentice-Hall, 1969).

[74] An influential presentation of the psychiatric approach to preventive and community psychiatry is Gerald Caplan, *Principles of Preventive Psychiatry* (New York: Basic Books, 1964).

the incidence of some of the other social problems that are discussed in this book. If, on the other hand, organic factors should be linked with severe mental illnesses in such a way that gross symptomatology can be prevented by drugs or other modes of biological control, preventive programs will be primarily a medical problem and responsibility. Even in this instance, however, it is likely that major issues of social policy will have to be dealt with. For the present, it appears that more adequate knowledge, through rigorous research that explores all possible leads, is our primary hope for preventing mental illness in the future.

PERSONAL DISORGANIZATION AND SOCIAL DISORGANIZATION

This chapter has been concerned with diagnosable mental disorder as a social problem. It has indicated some of the evidence pointing to the involvement of social factors in the complex etiology of a number of mental illnesses, but it has been more concerned with the problems of societal response and social organization for dealing with such illnesses than with the thesis that mental disorders are primarily reflections of social change and social disorganization. It will conclude by taking a more general perspective toward the relationship between social disorganization and personality development.

Personality may be conceived of as the organized totality of those aspects of behavior and tendencies to behavior that give meaning to an individual in society—his characteristic ways of acting, thinking, dealing with emergencies, relating to persons of the same or different age, sex, or social status, his view of himself, and his way of communicating that view to others. Our knowledge of the relationships of personality development to such variables as social-class status, family structure, and particular parental child-rearing practices is far from complete but does very clearly demonstrate that social and cultural patterns have a manifest influence.

Gross inconsistencies in the values and behaviors to which the child is exposed, or pervasive derogation or neglect of the child, are reflected in vulnerabilities that may subsequently lead to personality disorders. These vulnerabilities and disorders may come to the attention of mental health specialists, or they may be expressed in various forms of deviance and rebellious behavior. Whether or not one wants to call such problems mental illness will depend largely on philosophical grounds or on professional orientation. Much deviant behavior can legitimately be labeled as the manifestation of neurotic tendencies; however, as the other chapters in this section make clear, such labeling may well obscure underlying social causes. At the same time, personality dynamics cannot be ignored in trying to understand the relationship between social disorganization and forms of deviant behavior. Very little attention has been given in this chapter to the effects of mental illness and personal disorganization upon the functioning of the larger society. Our knowledge of this area tends to be of the anecdotal sort. That is, we can all cite instances of the disruptive influence of disturbed persons upon collective enterprises. The rabble-rousing demagogue whose appeal is addressed to the insecure and the frustrated is a case in point. Such persons have, for example, greatly increased the difficulties attendant upon the securing of civil rights for blacks in the southern states. In the realm of international relations, the threat to world peace that would be posed by mental illness in any one of a dozen political leaders is frightening to consider.

Many of us will have direct experience with mental illness. Persons on whom we depend will at one time or another seem unpredictable, angry, out of sorts. Usually these will be transitory deviations, but occasionally they will violate all our expectations and defy all our efforts to repair relationships. At such times we will become most acutely aware of the nature of the personal and social problems posed by mental illness.

To the extent that a person's ties with others are already tenuous when overt symptomatology occurs, mental illness is likely to go unrecognized and hence untreated until it has taken a high toll from the sick person and from his environment. To the extent that he is integrated into the social fabric — family, community, work group — there is hope for early, and not merely punitive, response to the disturbed deviant, and the consequences of the illness, difficult as they may be for those nearest to the patient, can often be limited.

2

Crime
and Juvenile Delinquency

ALBERT K. COHEN and JAMES F. SHORT, JR.

The study of crime and delinquency, vast as it is, deals with a special case of a general set of problems. Wherever people do business with one another — in families, in gangs, in offices, in schools, in factories — they develop rules, break the rules, and do something about people who break the rules. How rules come to be, who breaks them, how they come to break them, and what people do about rule-breaking vary enormously, even within the same class of social system — say, families or businesses. A rule may arise almost imperceptibly in the course of living, working, or playing together, so that, although no one can say just how or when it came to be, "everybody knows" that it is the rule. There may be, at the other extreme, elaborate and well-defined procedures, entailing a complex division of labor whereby rules are proposed, debated, amended, and, finally, at a point in time that can be precisely defined, "passed" and put into effect. Although rule-breaking is universal, every system shows its own pattern of rule-breaking: what rules are broken; how frequently they are broken; who breaks them; and how rule-breaking varies according to time, place, and circumstance. What people do about rule-breaking, like the making of rules, may be socially regulated in very different ways. In some groups, responsibility is widely diffused; almost everybody participates to some degree in policing, judging, penalizing, or correcting his fellows. In other groups, there is again an elaborate division of labor, different members being assigned very different and highly specialized responsibilities. Even within the same group, violations of different rules may be handled quite differently, some by a relatively formal, differentiated, specialized machinery, and some by the informal, unspecialized activities of the members at large.

THE CONCEPT OF CRIME

When we speak of crime and delinquency in this chapter, we take the perspective of a particular social system, which we call the "state," and the system of rules, which we call the "law," that is backed up by the authority of the state. One subdivision of the law is the criminal law. This is a body of rules specifying, with greater or less precision, certain kinds of acts as "crimes" and prescribing for those acts certain *punishments* to be administered by agents of the state in the name and on behalf of the politically organized community. Another subdivision of the law is the law of torts, which specifies certain kinds of acts as civil wrongs—that is to say, offenses against particular citizens of the state—for which the offended party is entitled to *compensation.* The state, in this instance, acts as an arbiter between private disputants, and for self-redress substitutes a procedure supervised, administered, and enforced by the state. A given action may constitute both a crime and a tort; it may be the one or the other; or it may be generally regarded by the community at large as bad or wicked, although it may be neither a crime nor a tort. An act may also be criminal, as defined above, and not be regarded as wrong—or at least not "seriously" wrong—by the general population.

Crime is, in a very real sense, a creation of the law. What crimes have in common is not that they are regarded as wrong or wicked (because they are not necessarily so regarded), but that people who commit them are liable to be arrested, tried, pronounced guilty in a solemn public ceremonial, and then punished and degraded by being deprived of their lives, liberty, or property; they are liable, in short, to be caught up in an elaborate social machinery called the criminal-justice system and to suffer the pain and humiliation this system is authorized to inflict. It makes a consequential difference whether a person is "sued" by a private citizen in a civil court and ordered to pay him damages for injuries sustained in an automobile accident, or indicted by a grand jury for willfully and with malice aforethought committing a crime against the peace and dignity of the state, found blameworthy by a jury of his peers, and led away in handcuffs. Where the state does not exist—and it is not universal—there will be some customary arrangements, perhaps the feud or vendetta, for the resolution of conflicts and obtainment of vengeance or compensation, but there will be no "crime" in our sense of the word. Even where the state does exist, what we call crime may still be scarcely, if at all, distinguishable from tort. The laws of the Anglo-Saxon kings, for example, set forth elaborate schedules listing offenses ranging from seizing a man by the hair or punching him on the nose to killing him, and for each offense specifying a compensation (*wergild*) to be paid to the victim or his kin.[1]

Where the criminal-justice system is clearly differentiated from other instrumentalities of social control, just what will be considered crime cannot be taken for granted but will be determined by social and historical circumstances. Take, for example, the crime of embezzlement, which consists of turning to one's own use that which is not his but which has come into his possession by virtue of a relation of trust to its proper owner—the pocketing, for example, of company funds by the custodian of the cash box. In the history of English law embezzlement was, for many centuries, no crime, although it was surely regarded as reprehensible, and it took a long series of legislative enactments, completed only in the nineteenth century, to bring all the varieties of embezzlement under the jurisdiction of the criminal-justice system. This does not mean that there were no other ways of obtaining redress and of making things unpleasant for the embezzler, both within the law and apart from it; but the embezzler could truly say, "I have committed no crime."[2]

Although the terms "criminal law" and "crimes" are ordinarily understood to refer to the criminal-justice system of the state, there are close analogues in other forms of human association. For example, a social club, a trade union, or a university may have, alongside other arrangements for social control and conflict resolution, a special set of rules spelled out and written down like the criminal law; formal procedures for bringing charges and determining guilt; and punishments administered in the name of the collectivity. The theoretical problems posed by such systems of rules and infractions thereof are very much like those posed by the criminal-justice system.

THE CONCEPT OF JUVENILE DELINQUENCY

Just as crime is a creation of the criminal law, so juvenile delinquency is a creation of the statutes establishing the juvenile courts. Until the end of the nineteenth century, young offenders in the United States were either subject

[1] Frederick L. Attenborough, *Laws of the Earliest English Kings* (Cambridge, Eng.: Cambridge University Press, 1922).
[2] Jerome Hall, *Theft, Law, and Society* (Boston: Little, Brown, 1935), pp. 3–36.

to the criminal law or were beyond the reach of the law. Our laws governing
the treatment of young offenders were based on the ancient common law of
England, which took age into account only in the following respect: Children
under seven were "irrebuttably presumed" to be incapable of having the
"criminal intent" that is a necessary ingredient of a criminal act. Children
from seven to fourteen were generally presumed to be capable of criminal
intent, but this presumption could be rebutted by evidence of their im-
maturity. If not capable of criminal intent, a child was not capable of crime.
His misconduct might be a matter for his parents or kinsmen, master or
priest, but it was not a matter for the criminal courts. If, on the other hand,
he were capable of criminal intent, he might be subject to the same law, the
same courts, the same procedures, and the same penalties as an adult.

During the nineteenth century a number of American courts developed
procedures for dealing with young offenders who deviated from this criminal
law model. An 1899 act of the Illinois legislature, establishing the juvenile
court of Cook County, embodied these changes and was widely imitated.
Within a generation practically every state in the United States had enacted
statutes establishing juvenile courts or their equivalent. These laws created
a new kind of machinery, outside the criminal law, for handling young
offenders, and therefore a new category of persons: young people subject to
handling by this machinery. The "delinquent child" — the legal term for a
child subject to the jurisdiction of the juvenile court — was, in a sense, a
nineteenth-century invention.[3]

The chief manifest function — that is, the acknowledged and intended
function — of the criminal courts is to administer "justice," to see that people
get their deserts, that offenders pay for their crimes. The chief manifest
function of the juvenile courts is to "help children in trouble," to "do what is in
the child's best interests," to "rehabilitate." The official language of the
juvenile court carefully avoids the terminology of the criminal process; it
speaks of "petition on behalf of the child" rather than "indictment," of "hearing" rather than "trial," of "disposition" rather than "sentence," of "training
school" rather than "prison," and so on. The statutes vary somewhat from
state to state, but they all set an upper age-limit — generally 16 to 18 — to
juvenile court jurisdiction. They also enumerate the kinds of behavior that
may bring a child under this jurisdiction, and here the contrast with the criminal law is striking. A crime is defined in more or less precise language. For
example, the legal definition of the crime of burglary included the following
elements: *breaking* and *entering* a *dwelling-house at night* with the *intent to*

---

[3] Anthony M. Platt, *The Child Savers: The Invention of Delinquency* (Chicago:
University of Chicago Press, 1969).

commit a felony. An act had to fit every part of this definition to qualify as the crime of burglary, and the court had to be satisfied by competent evidence on each point. Furthermore, the procedures of the criminal court are designed to provide the defendant an opportunity to confront his accusers, challenge their interpretation of the law, and rebut their testimony. The juvenile court statutes generally start out by defining a delinquent child as one who has committed any act which, if it were committed by an adult, would be a crime. Typically, however, they go on to name other actions and patterns of conduct that would not be crimes if committed by adults and are described in loose, vague language that would not be acceptable in the criminal law. Examples of such offenses and language include "is guilty of immoral or indecent language," "is growing up in idleness and crime," "is incorrigible," "habitually uses vile, indecent, or obscene language." Also in contrast to the criminal-justice system, the statutes typically do not prescribe procedures to be followed in the courtroom in order to insure "due process of law." The net — and intended — effect is to throw on the judge great discretion with respect to the conduct of juvenile proceedings and to the determination of whether a child falls under the definition of "delinquent child." This is consistent with what has come to be known as the juvenile court philosophy, the idea that the juvenile court, unlike the criminal court, is not concerned with exacting payment for a crime; that its job, like that of a loving parent or a physician, is to help the child; and that, if it is to do this, it must be free to take into consideration anything about the child's personality and the circumstances it considers relevant, and must not be hamstrung by minutely detailed rules of procedure. By the same logic, the statutes do not prescribe, as the criminal law does, that certain offenses shall be dealt with in specified ways — e.g., "three to ten years in a state prison." The presumption is that the needs of the child, not the seriousness of his offense, should determine the disposition. If, then, a child is committed to an institution, the time of release is not set by statute (except for an upper age-limit, which could be as high as 21) or by decision of the judge at the time of commitment, but is determined by the institutional authorities on the basis of their judgment as to the child's need for their further ministrations.

In point of fact, the dispositions of the juvenile court, ranging from probation to institutionalization, are deprivations of freedom and are experienced by the child as punishment. Furthermore, neither the court nor anyone else knows so much about the causes and treatment of delinquent behavior that it is possible to diagnose and prescribe treatment with confidence that the disposition will in fact prove rehabilitative. This amounts to saying that, regardless of the rhetoric or intentions of the juvenile court, it administers punishment like the criminal court but, unlike the criminal court, it is not constrained by procedural rules to insure justice to the child. During the 1950's and 1960's disillusionment with the juvenile courts mounted, culminating in 1967 in the United States Supreme Court's decision in the Gault case. The Court looked behind the rhetoric to the practical consequences of the juvenile courts and ruled that henceforth, in the interests of due process of law, children in juvenile courts are entitled, like defendants in criminal courts, to representation by counsel, timely notice of the charges against them, and the rights to confront and cross-examine the witnesses against them and to refuse to testify against themselves. It is still too early to state what the ultimate impact of this decision on juvenile justice will be, but it will surely curtail the discretion of the officers of the court and will arm the juvenile with rights that he did not previously have.[4]

THE CRIMINAL-JUSTICE SYSTEM AND THE EXTRALEGAL ORDER

We have distinguished the criminal-justice and juvenile-justice systems from the mechanisms of social control operative in other sectors of society. Their operations and effects, however, are not independent of the rest of society, but affect and respond to the other sectors in various ways.

1. Most of the behavior regulated by the legal system is also regulated by other institutions. Even police systems as we know them in the United States and England were established as recently as the first half of the nineteenth century. This means that rates of crime and delinquency are only to a small extent dependent upon the magnitude and the effectiveness of governmentally operated institutions of social control. They depend much more on the social conditions that create the incentives to crime and delinquency and the formal and informal mechanisms of control operating in the community at large.

2. The impact of the law upon behavior depends on what we shall call the moral status of the law. By this we mean the extent to which the rules

---

[4] On the juvenile court see Anthony M. Platt, *The Child Savers: The Invention of Delinquency,* Paul W. Tappan, *Juvenile Delinquency* (New York: McGraw-Hill, 1959); David Matza, *Delinquency and Drift* (New York: Wiley, 1964), Chapter 4; The President's Commission on Law Enforcement and Administration of Justice, *Task Force Report: Juvenile Delinquency and Youth Crime* (Washington, D. C.: U. S. Government Printing Office, 1967); *Indiana Law Journal* 43 (Spring, 1968), a special issue devoted to the Gault case. The text of the Gault case may be found in the *Task Force Report* (*supra,* this note).

of the legal system agree or disagree with the values and norms of the people to whom those rules apply, and the respect and legitimacy that are attributed to the police, the courts, and other agencies of the institutions of justice. Consider, for example, how differently the public regards abortion, drunken driving, forcible rape, armed robbery, the use of marijuana, misleading labeling of food products, and off-track betting – all of them crimes in most states. Even with respect to the same crimes, attitudes may vary from general consensus to bitter dissensus. There are laws whose necessity is universally conceded; there are others that are supported by some part of the public and denounced as intolerable infringements of liberty or privacy by others; and there are still others which, if enforced, would create furor and indignation in most quarters of the citizenry. Apart from their attitudes to particular laws, segments of the public may see the police and the courts as helpful, benign, and vested with unquestioned authority, or as instruments of oppression. Police and courts, at every stage of their operations, depend for their effectiveness on the cooperation of their publics: cooperation that depends on the moral status of the police and the courts and of the laws they enforce.

3. Laws sometimes have effects extending beyond the behavior they directly proscribe. They may, for example, be used to control or punish behavior that is not in fact illegal but is offensive to the law-enforcement agencies or to some influential segment of the public. There are few people who could not be arrested for violating some building code, fire department or sanitary regulation, licensing ordinance, or curfew, or for vagrancy or disturbing the peace. Most such laws are only infrequently and sporadically enforced, but they are available and are used to harass people whom other people consider unsightly, immoral, radical, or otherwise obnoxious in ways that are not actually illegal. The use of the law in this manner may, however, have the side effects of undermining belief in the disinterestedness and impartiality of the law and of increasing hostility to the agencies of law enforcement.

4. Attempts to regulate behavior – especially the so-called vices and the consumption of goods and services for which there is a widespread demand – may generate other forms of crime to make possible the forbidden activity under conditions of illegality. When the Volstead Act made alcoholic beverages illegal, the demand for these products was not extinguished. Instead a vast industry sprang up outside the law to satisfy the demand. It is a commonplace that the criminalization of the narcotics traffic has made this traffic disreputable and hazardous; has tended to drive the trade into the hands of professional criminals; and has created an intricate black market in which many different individuals get their "cut" – which includes compen-

sation for unusual risks—and which has made narcotic drugs enormously expensive to the ultimate consumers. Drugs that otherwise would cost very little to produce have been made so expensive that addicts, who find it difficult to manage without their drugs, turn in great numbers to theft and other forms of criminality in order to finance their habits.[5]

5. The consequences of being convicted of a crime or of being found delinquent by a juvenile court depend on the stigma that attaches to such labeling in the world outside the courts. The penalties and deprivations that the court itself directly inflicts may be only part, and often the lesser part, of the punishment that the offender experiences. The words "criminal" and "delinquent" are also terms for social roles of everyday life.[6] To a person who bears such a label there may be attributed a whole bundle of deviant attributes. Along with his label he may acquire a stereotyped and packaged, so to speak, social personality. People may place him and organize their behavior toward him on the basis of this imputed personality. The label, initially assigned by the court, may result in a transformation of his whole social world outside the court: through how other people see him and how they feel toward him, through their willingness to associate with him, and through the activities, jobs, and opportunities that are open to him. The criminal or delinquent role may so narrow his opportunities for the rewards and gratifications of conventional behavior that he may find illegal alternatives more, rather than less attractive. However, the social role of criminal or delinquent is not automatically acquired by virtue of an adjudication. People who have been convicted of tax irregularities or of "white-collar crimes"—i.e., violations of criminal statutes regulating the conduct of business and trade—are not likely to pick up the label "criminal" in their everyday world. By contrast, people who have been arrested, even if not convicted, for "ordinary" crimes are much more likely to be saddled with at least some of the burden of a criminal identity. The propensity to stigmatize and stereotype on the basis of "trouble with the law" also varies among different groups in the community; therefore the fearsomeness and deterrent effect of a potential arrest and conviction varies according to the reactions one anticipates from those who matter *to him* in *his* workaday world.

---

[5] This point, and the further effects upon the corruption of law-enforcement agencies, is discussed in Chapter 3, on organized crime. See also James S. Campbell, Joseph R. Sahid, and David P. Stang, *Law and Order Reconsidered: Report of the Task Force on Law and Law Enforcement to the National Commission on the Causes and Prevention of Violence* (Washington, D. C.: U. S. Government Printing Office, 1969), Chapter 23.

[6] See Frank Tannenbaum, *Crime and the Community* (New York: Ginn, 1938).

THE EFFECTS OF CRIME
ON THE CRIMINAL-JUSTICE SYSTEM

We have dealt at some length with the effects of the criminal-justice system upon the behavior it is designed to regulate, noting that these range from defining the behavior as criminal in the first place to producing the behavior that it defines as criminal. But crime, in turn, has important effects on the criminal-justice system. How the laws are written and how they are administered is responsive to how they are broken and on what scale. The criminal-justice system is not a machine that is programed once and forever after operates accordingly. Crime, like law enforcement, is intelligent, motivated behavior in which people may have high stakes. Sometimes it is cynical and self-interested, sometimes principled and idealistic. It is not extinguished readily and it sometimes grows in the face of efforts to suppress it, sometimes in consequence of those efforts. It is of many kinds, some of them invisible except to the participants, some obvious; some easy to prove in a court of law, some hard; some easily discouraged, some—to use the language of the economists—inelastic, since the demand for forbidden fruits does not decline in proportion to the increasing costs and risks. The criminal-justice system, like any set of social arrangements, changes as it runs into problems; it is shaped by the material it works on. When the material is obdurate and resistant, it may respond in various ways. (Which way it *should* respond often becomes a "social problem," a subject of social controversy and political conflict.) Laws may be sharpened, loopholes eliminated, penalties increased. Additional resources may be pumped into the system, or existing ones diverted from efforts to control some other crime that does not, at the moment, enjoy as high a priority. If the pressure to suppress, or at least to bring in convictions, is great, law-enforcement people may try to increase their efficiency by violating laws that restrict their freedom of operation—for example, those relating to arrest or illegal search and seizure. On the other hand, if the costs of enforcement become increasingly burdensome but the forbidden behavior continues to thrive, efforts to enforce the law may simply be abandoned, or, as sometimes happens, the law may be changed and the behavior legalized; instead of the law extinguishing the crime, the crime extinguishes the law and, in the process, ceases to be a crime.

Traditionally, criminology has taken as its subject matter the violation of law. It has treated the criminal law and the criminal-justice system as givens, as things to be taken into account in order to explain crime but not in themselves calling for explanation by criminologists. We have seen, however, that they are to some extent determined by the very behavior they regulate. The criminal law, the machinery of criminal justice, informal processes of social control outside the legal system, and criminal behavior — each influences the others, each transforms, so to speak, its environment, and in turn responds to changes in its environment. Criminologists are just beginning to grope for theoretical approaches that can deal simultaneously with all these sectors and their interaction.

CRIME AND SOCIAL PROBLEMS

Suppose that by a social problem we mean a situation that has become a public issue, one that makes people talk and tempers rise. It is not enough that a great many people find the situation distressing or obnoxious. If all are agreed that nothing can be done about it or, on the other hand, that the situation is being handled correctly, then there is little to argue about. It becomes a subject of controversy and therefore a social problem to the extent that people cannot agree that there is anything wrong that needs remedying, or, if they agree that there is something wrong, to the extent that they cannot agree on what to do about it. At the time of this writing marijuana use and "crime in the streets" are "serious" social problems in this sense, whereas tax-evasion and violations of the Sherman Anti-Trust Act and motor-vehicle speed laws are not so "serious." The violation of criminal statutes regulating the disposal of wastes is becoming a social problem as the public becomes alarmed about pollution of the environment and begins to debate the proper ways to deal with it. In the course of their crime-fighting activities police themselves often violate the law and abuse the citizens whom they arrest; this too has only recently become a social problem, although it is debatable whether the misconduct in question has increased in frequency. Social problems in the area of crime and delinquency arise when people argue strongly about whether some form of behavior should be made criminal or some criminal behavior should be legalized; about which laws should be enforced more vigorously and which less; about the proper penalty for, say, murder or drug use; or about the techniques of law enforcement (e.g., "police brutality" vs. "shackling the police").

To some extent the study of the social problems relating to crime is separable from the study of crime itself. Social problems may be differently defined by different segments of a population. To some, the need to suppress certain kinds of criminality is the problem; to others, the criminality is a minor issue, and the conduct of the police or the puritanical zeal of the legislature is the problem. A social problem can become a major social issue and then subside, without the situation it concerns having undergone any significant change.[7] Many situations have become problems today and others have ceased to be problems because the values in terms of which these situations are assessed have changed, or because a value consensus that once prevailed has broken down. As groups that formerly did not participate actively in the political process acquire political power, their voices come to be heard in the law-making and law-enforcing processes. To some degree this has happened to young people, black people, and poor people in the United States. As their power grows, they become more articulate and demanding, their distinct interests and perspectives are registered in the public forums, and situations that were previously not the subject of public controversy become lively social problems.

OUTPUTS OF CRIMINAL-JUSTICE SYSTEMS

If we are interested in what criminal-justice systems (or any other human organizations) *do*, we must, of course, consider what they are *for*—that is, their manifest functions, the purposes that bring them into being and in terms of which they justify their existence. But even the most rationally designed organization is much more than a mechanism for accomplishing a preconceived purpose. Police departments, courts, and prisons consist of people working at more or less full-time jobs. With these jobs they make their livings, support their families, pursue their careers, establish their social identities, earn their status, make friends and enemies, get along and get into trouble, have fun, accumulate worries, and grow gray. Like people in any organization, they seek to regularize, routinize, and simplify their lives; and to reduce insecurity, make themselves comfortable, and get along with the people they have to work with—especially those who can make trouble for them. They tend over time to develop understandings and relationships—that is, a subculture—that will serve these ends. These include understandings about their respective tasks, the lines of authority, and the distribution of responsibility, what constitutes a fair day's work,

---

[7] For example, witchcraft became a major social problem in Massachusetts in the second half of the seventeenth century, although the population of authenticated witches did not significantly rise. See Kai T. Erikson, *Wayward Puritans* (New York: Wiley, 1966).

mutual aid, and solidarity vis-à-vis "outsiders." What people actually do and what they produce is partly shaped by these understandings. But people do not have complete freedom to tailor the structure and their work to their own comfort and convenience. The organization as a whole is evaluated by its public or publics, from whom it receives legitimacy, support, resources, cooperation, and recognition—contingent, however, upon a favorable appraisal. Grumbling, denigration, or criticism may lead to withdrawal of support and may threaten the interests, the status, and the security of its members. Therefore the organization tends also to be adapted to the demands of the supporting environment: to produce, or appear to produce, what the environment demands; to call upon the members to cooperate in the promotion of a favorable public image, which includes the concealment of what is publicly discreditable; and to persuade its publics that they are getting what they are paying for.

This means that the actual activities of policemen, prosecutors, judges, probation officers, and corrections personnel are determined by a host of considerations over and above the manifest content of the criminal law and the official purpose of each agency. In any case, with resources that are invariably limited, each agency would be unable to do everything it is in principle supposed to do. It must somehow, deliberately or otherwise, develop priorities and concentrate on doing some things while scanting others. Furthermore, no matter how detailed the organization's mandate, it always leaves wide room for the exercise of judgment and discretion.

And so, by way of example, how the police and courts allocate their resources to the repression and prosecution of different offenses will depend in part on the feedback they get from different parts of their publics, which are likely to have different interests in the suppression of different kinds of crime or, to put it differently, "keep score" on the police and courts by different rules. These different publics will also have different power to help or hurt the various agencies, so that each agency will be more sensitive to the feedback from some than from others. The relative power of the different publics may itself change over time, and the agency's policy will be altered in response. And even for the same public, concern and alarm over some particular offense may vary over time, and with it the pressure on the agency to do something, or to appear to be doing something, about that particular offense.

We distinguish between "doing" and "appear to be doing" because publics may sometimes be mollified by bursts of activity that are not, in fact, highly productive. For example, the dramatic solution of one or two conspicuous and well-publicized crimes may produce large rewards for the agencies, although they may be achieved at the expense of solving many less well-publicized crimes. More generally, there is a tendency on the part of police to concentrate on areas of criminal activity that, for a given expenditure of resources, are likely to yield the greatest number of "good pinches," and for prosecutors to concentrate on offenses that are likely to pay off in successful prosecutions, although the same energies, distributed otherwise, might have a larger impact on the volume of crime. Police, in order to get "good pinches," will sometimes temporize with or even collude in other offenses. For example, successful police work depends upon information, and in some areas of police work the information necessary to make a "good pinch" can only or most easily be obtained from members of the offender group. (Drug law enforcement is a case in point.) If the pressure to bring in convictions is great, police may trade immunity for some offenders for information against others. On the court level, prosecutors, in order to obtain convictions with the least expenditure of time and manpower, may consent to waive or reduce charges against the defendant if he, in turn, consents to plead guilty to a lesser charge.

Farther up the line, in the correctional system—which comprises the systems of parole and probation and operation of jails, prisons, and juvenile training schools—what is actually done in the name of prevention, punishment, or rehabilitation is shaped by a variety of considerations, many of which are only remotely, if at all, related to these ends. One reason that other considerations weigh so heavily in this sector is that our measures of success in accomplishing these goals are poor at best, and where we do have useful measures, we know very little about how to achieve the desired results (except in the case of punishment, about which we know a good deal). The tendency, then, is to be guided on the one hand by intuitive but unsubstantiated ideas about what works, and on the other hand by considerations of administrative convenience, harmony among the staff, and the avoidance of public scandal and outrage. So, for example, in most prisons the most important single consideration in determining design of the physical plant, surveillance, staff-inmate relations, inmate autonomy and responsibility, and in fact almost every aspect of the program, is the prevention of escape, which has little to do with either crime prevention, punishment, or rehabilitation, but has a great deal to do with avoiding bad publicity, an alarmed public, and legislative investigations. Although the number of inmates prone to attempt escape may be small, the effort to contain that number determines in considerable measure what the prison experience will be like for the staff and the body of inmates as a whole. To take a very different sort of example, efforts to experiment with new types of programs in a correctional institution may entail a redistribution of power, changes in the value placed on various kinds of knowledge and skills, and new kinds of relationships among staff members and between staff and inmates. These changes may, in turn, be threatening to the security, status, and comfort of the staff, and their resistance may effectively thwart the attempt at innovation.

THE MEANINGS AND LIMITATIONS OF OFFICIAL STATISTICS

The statistics compiled by official agencies are commonly taken as measures of the distribution of crime and delinquency. Like other outputs of official agencies, they are shaped by a variety of influences. An appreciation of these influences is necessary for understanding the uses and abuses of these statistics.

Official statistics are the bookkeeping records of business transacted by official agencies. They tell us something about complaints received, crimes known to the police, the numbers of persons arrested or prosecuted for various crimes, the outcomes in court, and the size of institutional populations. They are kept for a variety of purposes: for internal use, for the preparation of budget requests, and for presentation to such audiences as "city hall," the mass media, and taxpayers' groups. They are direct descriptions of the behavior of officials rather than offenders. (An increase in the arrest rate, for example, tells us that the police are making more arrests; it does not necessarily mean that there are more crimes or criminals.) They are useful for the study of agency activities and the ways in which citizens who are caught up in the criminal-justice systems are moved and processed within those systems.

They are also useful as indicators of criminal behavior because such behavior is *one* of the influences on official behavior. It must be emphasized, however, that official statistics are neither a census nor a scientific sampling of the universe of crime or of criminals. Much crime and delinquency is not discovered; if discovered, it is not reported; if reported, it is not recorded. Different kinds of delinquents and delinquencies, criminals and crimes, have different but largely unknown probabilities of becoming officially known and of reaching any given stage in the law-enforcement process. Official statistics may be used as *indexes* of crime, but they are indexes of unknown validity because the phenomena they are supposed to indicate are of unknown dimensions.

A further limitation of official statistics is that they are not routinely compiled for all crimes, and, for some crimes, great secrecy surrounds the information that is collected. Examples include white-collar crime and organized crime. Many crimes committed by persons of upper socioeconomic status in the course of business are handled by quasi-judicial bodies, such as the Federal Trade Commission, partly in order to avoid stigmatizing businessmen as criminals, and are not recorded in the bookkeeping records of the criminal-justice system. Differences in the handling of various types of criminal and delinquent behavior also arise from technical problems having to do with the nature of the behavior over which control is sought. For example, local police departments are handicapped in their ability to deal with organized criminal activities that cross municipal and state boundaries. For another example, the legal technicalities of local business regulations require expertise beyond the resources available to police. As a result, systematic information about crime and delinquency is generated by widely scattered and sometimes overlapping agencies, and a good deal of crime goes unchecked by any agency. Coverage of different types of offenses varies enormously, as does the extent to which such information is publicly available. Furthermore, official statistics provide very meager information about the characteristics of offenders and the offenses that they record, although such information is vital to the understanding of the phenomena and to their control.[8]

To compensate for the limitations of official statistics, students of crime and delinquency have experimented with many other sources of data and methods of study. These include large numbers of clinical reports [9] and intensive case studies,[10] surveys of self-reported behavior [11] and of victimization,[12] "participant observation" and other types of field observation,[13] and other kinds of nonpublic data.[14] The methodological ingenuity of researchers into crime and delinquency has been considerable. However, our information continues to be uneven, sketchy, and, in many instances, of unknown repre-

[8] For further discussion, see Donald R. Cressey, "The State of Criminal Statistics," *National Probation and Parole Association Journal,* Vol. 3 (July, 1957), pp. 230–41, and other references in this section.

[9] See, for example, Lester E. Hewitt and Richard L. Jenkins, *Fundamental Patterns of Maladjustment: The Dynamics of Their Origin* (Springfield: State of Illinois, 1947).

[10] Such as Clifford R. Shaw, *The Jack-Roller: A Delinquent Boy's Own Story* (Chicago: University of Chicago Press, 1930, 1966).

[11] See Robert H. Hardt and George E. Bodme, *Development of Self-Reporting Instruments in Delinquency Research: A Conference Report* (Syracuse University Press, 1965).

[12] Phillip H. Ennis, "Crime, Victims, and the Police," *Trans-Action* (June, 1967), pp. 36–44.

[13] For a sharp critique of most other methods of studying criminals and delinquents and a defense of field observation, see Ned Polsky, "Research Method, Morality, and Criminology," Chapter 3 in *Hustlers, Beats and Others* (Chicago: Aldine, 1967).

[14] For example, the use of records of department-store detectives by Mary Owen Cameron, *The Booster and the Snitch* (New York: Free Press, 1965).

sentativeness and relevance to particular aspects of "the crime problem." As a result, much of what is "known" about crime is of questionable validity.

For many types of research, statistics serve as the social scientist's laboratory, allowing him to test the relationships of various behavioral phenomena to social conditions in a manner similar to the way laboratory experiments are used by other scientists. Present reporting systems are inadequate. However, imaginative attempts to refine and elaborate on data from official sources show promise of improving the usefulness of such data for administrative and scientific purposes.[15] Insofar as possible, the following discussion of variations in rates of crime and delinquency is based on repeatedly established relationships that cannot be readily "explained away" in terms of the inadequacy of available statistics.

TRENDS

It is impossible to state unequivocally how much crime and delinquency there is in the United States or whether such behavior has been increasing or decreasing over the past several decades. On the basis of both Children's Bureau and FBI data, it is widely believed that both phenomena rose to all-time high levels in the late 1960's, with no prospect of immediate decline. Both agencies reported startling rises since the period immediately following World War II: the Children's Bureau, of alleged delinquents known to juvenile courts; and the FBI, of crimes known to the police and of persons arrested. Crimes known to the police probably most reliably reflect the actual volume of serious crimes of a public nature, but no existing source is adequate as a measure of such phenomena as white-collar crime, gang delinquency, organized crime, and the vast amount of less serious, "ordinary" crime that is hidden from official view. In any case, it is important to note that roughly 2 percent of all children aged 10 through 17 were involved in court cases each year after 1954, and that by the end of the decade this figure had reached nearly 2.5 percent, in contrast to approximately 1 percent in the pre–World War II period. The risk that a citizen would be the victim of a serious crime, as reported by police agencies to the FBI, rose to more than 2 per 100 persons by the late 1960's. For all types of criminal victimization, a

---

[15] As, for example, the careful use of police descriptions of delinquency events to study delinquency by Thorsten Sellin and Marvin Wolfgang and their students. See Thorsten Sellin and Marvin Wolfgang, eds., *Delinquency: Selected Studies* (New York: Wiley, 1969).

study of a carefully drawn national sample of 10,000 households discovered roughly 2,100 verified incidents; that is, more than 20 percent of the households surveyed reported some type of criminal victimization during the preceding year.[16] All agree that these rates are high, but it is not at all clear that they are high relative to the rates of earlier times. Rates of crime and delinquency may be "very high" today only when compared to the "very low" rates of the 1930's, when national statistics began to be collected. This possibility is difficult to test, but it is supported by several studies, including a survey of delinquency in Cuyahoga County (Cleveland), Ohio, for the years 1918-1957,[17] another for Cook County, Illinois, for the years 1900-1959,[18] and studies of crime in individual urban areas extending in one case (Boston) as far back as the early years of the nineteenth century.[19] Studies of past historical eras, in the United States and other countries, chronicle the existence of a great deal of violence, theft, and other crimes. Although comparable data are virtually nonexistent, such studies provide strong evidence that present levels of crime and public concern have been equaled and exceeded in other countries and in our own past.

THE DISTRIBUTION OF CRIME AND DELINQUENCY

Variation By Age

Statistical evidence of so many kinds, in so many jurisdictions, over so many years, is so consistent on this score, that it may be reasonably assumed that older adolescents and young adults have higher crime rates than other age groups. Relevant data are presented in Table 1. Statistics are likely to ex-

---

[16] President's Commission on Law Enforcement and Administration of Justice, *The Challenge of Crime in a Free Society* (Washington, D. C.: U. S. Government Printing Office, 1967); see, also, Phillip H. Ennis, "Crime, Victims, and the Police," *Trans-Action*.

[17] Negley K. Teeters and David Matza, "The Extent of Delinquency in the United States," *The Journal of Negro Education*, Vol. 28 (Summer, 1959), pp. 210–11.

[18] Unpublished data collected by Henry McKay of the Institute for Juvenile Research, Chicago, Illinois.

[19] Data and references are discussed in Roger Lane, "Urbanization and Criminal Violence in the 19th Century: Massachusetts as a Test Case," Chapter 12 in Hugh Davis Graham and Ted Robert Gurr, eds., *Violence in America: Historical and Comparative Perspectives* (Washington, D. C.: U. S. Government Printing Office, 1969), pp. 359–70.

TABLE 1

Arrests for Major Crimes in the United States, 1968, by Age and Sex *

Offense Charged	Number of Persons Arrested	Percentage of Those Arrested	
		Under 18	Male
CLASS I OFFENSES			
Larceny—theft	463,928	54.0	75.6
Burglary—breaking or entering	256,216	54.7	95.8
Auto theft	125,263	60.7	95.1
Aggravated assault	106,475	16.5	87.6
Robbery	69,115	33.1	94.4
Forcible rape	12,685	20.2	100.0
Criminal homicide:			
(a) Murder and nonnegligent manslaughter	10,394	9.9	83.9
(b) Manslaughter by negligence	3,144	7.8	89.8
CLASS II OFFENSES			
Drunkenness	1,415,961	2.6	93.0
All other offenses (except traffic)	643,404	31.8	85.1
Disorderly conduct	593,104	21.7	86.6
Driving under the influence of alcohol	307,231	1.0	93.6
Other assaults	239,918	17.6	88.6
Liquor-law violations	215,376	31.8	88.1
Narcotic-drug-law violations	162,177	26.6	85.1
Running away	149,052	100.0	50.6
Vandalism	110,182	75.2	93.4
Vagrancy	99,147	11.1	89.8
Curfew-and-loitering-law violations	98,230	100.0	80.6
Suspicion	89,986	24.5	84.2
Weapons: carrying, possessing, etc.	83,721	17.8	93.7
Gambling	76,909	2.6	91.7
Fraud	56,710	4.5	76.0
Offenses against family and children	51,319	1.2	91.2
Sex offenses (except forcible rape and prostitution)	47,573	23.9	88.1
Prostitution and commercialized vice	42,338	2.1	21.7
Stolen property: buying, receiving, possessing	37,769	34.6	92.3
Forgery and counterfeiting	34,497	12.0	78.2
Arson	9,121	62.8	91.9
Embezzlement	5,894	4.2	80.4

* *Source:* Federal Bureau of Investigation, *Crime in the United States, Uniform Crime Reports, 1968* (Washington, D. C.: U. S. Government Printing Office, 1969), adapted from pp. 117–18.

aggerate offense rates of these age groups as compared with rates of other age groups,[20] but there appear to be real differences. In 1968, persons 16 years of age comprised the largest number of persons arrested for all crimes, with youngsters of 17 second, followed by 15- and 18-year-olds in almost equal numbers. It appears also that rates of serious crimes committed by young people have risen more rapidly than have these rates for older persons.

While they are not as likely as older persons to be involved in white-collar crime, professional theft, or organized crime, young people come to the attention of the police primarily for property crimes, for vandalism, and for specifically juvenile offenses such as running away and curfew violation. With the exception of embezzlement, fraud, forgery, and counterfeiting, which require greater finesse and higher social position, a large percentage of all property-offense arrests is accounted for by juveniles.

Variations by Sex

If an investigator were asked to use a single trait to predict which persons in any given town would become criminals, he would make the fewest mistakes if he simply chose sex status and predicted criminality for the males and noncriminality for the females. Most of the males, to be sure, would *not* become criminals, and a few of the females *would,* but he would be wrong in more cases if he used any other single trait, such as age, race, family background, or a personality characteristic.

Crime and delinquency rates for males are greatly in excess of rates for females: in all nations, all communities within a nation, all age groups, all periods of history for which organized statistics are available, and for all types of crime except for a few peculiar to women, such as prostitution, infanticide, and abortion. Ratios vary greatly by offense, however, as is clear from Table 1. Girls are typically brought before the court for sex offenses, as are their adult counterparts, and for "running away," "incorrigibility," and "delinquent tendencies," which often are euphemisms for problems related to sexual behavior.

In recent years the ratio of boys to girls appearing before juvenile courts

---

[20] Children and younger adolescents are less likely to be arrested and more likely to be turned over to their parents than are older adolescents, and older people are more likely to possess either the skills or the "clout" necessary to avoid arrest. Much juvenile auto theft, for example, in contrast to that of adults, consists of "joy riding," which attracts the attention of police and therefore is more likely to lead to detection and apprehension.

in the United States has dropped to about 4 to 1, probably the lowest ratio of any country. The figure represents a considerable decrease from the 50- to 60-to-1 ratios which obtained in this country around the turn of the century. The ratio in England and Wales is about 8 to 1, also a declining figure in recent years. Adult ratios tend to be higher than juvenile ratios, about 10 to 1 in the United States and 15 to 1 in England and Wales.[21] These figures appear to have changed less than have those for juveniles.

The extent to which male rates exceed those for females varies greatly from one cultural setting to another. In some traditional societies, such as those of Ceylon, Algeria, Tunis, and Japan before World War II, male criminals and delinquents came to official attention 3000 to 4000 times as frequently as females.[22] However, in Japan and Turkey, where women recently have become more nearly equal to men, as is the case in the United States and in Western Europe, marked increases in the proportion of female offenders have been noted.

"Crime is a young man's business," even in modern western countries, as is apparent from inspection of the data presented in Table 1. That criminal offenders are predominantly young and male is supported by data from self-reports and by studies conducted in other countries. And the case appears to be the same for most types of professional crime, except prostitution and abortion, in which larger proportions of women are engaged as professionals. In some countries, women commit higher proportions of theft-related offenses than in the United States, although men predominate even in these cases. Also, almost by definition, youth is less closely associated with *careers* in crime, and older men are more extensively involved in white-collar and organized crime.[23]

Race and Ethnicity

Racial and ethnic groups in the United States have widely varying rates of crime and delinquency. The rates for blacks, for example, are exceptionally high,[24] estimates range from about twice to about five times as many of-

---

[21] F. H. McClintock and N. Howard Avison, in collaboration with G. N. G. Rose, *Crime in England and Wales* (London: Heinemann, 1968), p. 26.

[22] E. Hacker, *Kriminalstatistische und Kriminalaetiologische Berichte* (Miskolc, Hungary: Ludwig, 1941).

[23] See, for example, F. H. McClintock and N. Howard Avison, *Crime in England and Wales, passim.*

[24] *The Journal of Negro Education,* Vol. 28 (Summer, 1959) is devoted to "Juvenile Delinquency Among Negroes in the United States."

fenders as would be expected on the basis of the proportion of blacks in the total population. Puerto Ricans, Mexicans, and American Indians likewise have especially high rates, whereas Orientals and Jews usually have strikingly low rates.

Differences such as these may be misleading, for numerous studies have found greater variation within these groups than between them. Furthermore, such intergroup comparisons are to some degree suspect because all the foregoing statements are based on *official* data, subject to all the qualifications of official data discussed earlier. Axelrad, for example, has found that black children were committed at younger ages, for less serious crimes, and with fewer prior court appearances and institutional commitments than were white children.[25] Other studies have found that blacks are more likely to be arrested, indicted, and convicted than are whites who commit the same offenses, and that blacks have less chance than whites to be placed on probation, to be granted parole or a suspended sentence, or to be pardoned or have a death sentence commuted.[26] When blacks are victims of crime, however, as they are in the vast majority of offenses committed by other blacks, official reaction has been shown to be less prompt and efficient in giving protection to the citizen.[27] Still other studies find that blacks are much less positive in their evaluation of the effectiveness, honesty, and respect for citizens on the part of police, and in their attitudes concerning the efficacy of the system of law enforcement and the administration of justice.[28] Fear and distrust of the police by many black Americans has been a prominent theme in the literature concerning recent ghetto riots and related types of criminality.[29]

---

[25] Sidney Axelrad, "Negro and White Male Institutionalized Delinquents," *American Journal of Sociology,* Vol. 57 (May, 1952), pp. 569–74. See also Don C. Gibbons and Manzer J. Griswold, "Sex Differences Among Juvenile Court Referrals," *Sociology and Social Research,* Vol. 42 (November–December, 1957), pp. 106–10.

[26] See, for example, Edwin M. Lemert and Judy Rosberg, "The Administration of Justice to Minority Groups in Los Angeles County," *University of California Publications in Culture and Society,* Vol. 2, No. 1 (1948), pp. 1–28; Thorsten Sellin, "Race Prejudice in the Administration of Justice," *American Journal of Sociology,* Vol. 41 (September, 1935), pp. 212–17.

[27] Guy B. Johnson, "The Negro and Crime," *Annals of the American Academy of Political and Social Science,* Vol. 217 (September, 1941), pp. 93–104. James D. Turner, "Differential Punishment in a Bi-racial Community," unpublished M.A. dissertation, Indiana University, 1948. James D. Turner, "Dynamics of Criminal Law Administration in a Bi-racial Community of the Deep South," unpublished Ph.D. dissertation, Indiana University, 1956.

[28] See Ennis, "Crime, Victims, and the Police," *Trans-Action.* See, also, *Report of the National Advisory Commission on Civil Disorders* (Washington, D. C.: U. S. Government Printing Office, 1968).

[29] See, for example, Sheldon G. Levy, "Attitudes Toward Political Violence," in

Ethnic variations present a striking picture of change over time, reflecting very closely the flow of immigration to this country. As recently as 1930, for example, shortly after the sharp restrictions imposed on immigration in the mid-1920's, about one-half of the children coming to the attention of the courts were of foreign-born parentage.[30] This is no longer the case, and recent studies indicate that neither the foreign born nor their children contribute disproportionately to delinquency rates.[31]

The high rates of some racial and ethnic groups must not be interpreted as a function of societal and administrative bias alone. The juvenile court philosophy is consistent with earlier intervention of the state in the case of groups living under such conditions as poverty, family and community disorganization. Where family and community resources are meager or questionable, this philosophy prescribes earlier official action and action with respect to less serious offenses which, when committed by persons belonging to more favored groups in society, might be handled by the family or the community or both. Furthermore, the high crime rates among blacks and certain other groups are in part attributable to the disproportion of concentration of these groups in the lower socioeconomic strata of large cities — a situation that produces disproportionately high rates among persons of native white stock as well.

Social Class and Delinquency

Many studies indicate that lower-class individuals run greater risks of becoming officially defined as criminal or delinquent. Studies based on self-reported behavior, however, reveal a great deal of "hidden" crime and delinquency on the part of persons of all social classes.[32]

James F. Kirkham, Sheldon G. Levy, and William J. Crotty, *Assassination and Political Violence: A Report of the National Commission on the Causes and Prevention of Violence* (Washington, D. C.: U. S. Government Printing Office, 1969), pp. 383–417; and David O. Sears and John P. McConahay, "Participation in the Los Angeles Riot," *Social Problems,* Vol. 17 (Summer, 1969), pp. 3–20.

[30] Donald R. Taft, "Nationality and Crime," *American Sociological Review,* Vol. 1 (October, 1936), pp. 724–36; and C. C. Van Vechten, "The Criminality of the Foreign-Born," *Journal of Criminal Law and Criminology,* Vol. 32 (July–August, 1941), pp. 139–47.

[31] See Roland J. Chilton, "Delinquency Area Research in Baltimore, Detroit and Indianapolis," *American Sociological Review,* Vol. 29 (February, 1964), pp. 71–83.

[32] See, e.g., Austin Porterfield, "Delinquency and Its Outcome in Court and College,"

Self-report studies in several small nonindustrial cities and towns in the United States do not support the higher rates of delinquency recorded for lower-class children.[33] While greater involvement by lower-class youngsters is found by studies conducted in a small industrial city and in large cities, differences are much smaller than those indicated by official statistics.[34] On the other hand, observational data from lower-class, large city areas with high rates of official delinquency demonstrate that the incidence of hidden delinquency in these areas is also very high.[35]

In sum, a considerable literature suggests that social-class differences in delinquency involvement vary according to the social setting — cities, towns, rural areas, etc. — but the evidence is conflicting and confused. Because social class occupies such an important position in etiological theories of delinquency, systematic, objective, and relevant data on the matter are of the greatest importance.

Ecological Differences

Probably the best-established patterns of variation in official crime and delinquency are of an ecological nature. Statistics from many countries and from many different times indicate that urban areas have higher rates of crime and delinquency than do rural areas; and that, in the United States at least, suburban and "semiurban" areas fall between these extremes. The chief caution in interpreting these findings is concerned with differences in resources for handling cases. It seems likely that in rural areas less serious

American Journal of Sociology, Vol. 49 (1943), pp. 199–204; J. S. Wallerstein and C. J. Syle, "Our Law-abiding Lawbreakers," *Probation,* Vol. 25 (March–April, 1947), pp. 107–12.

[33] See, e.g., F. Ivan Nye, James F. Short, Jr., and V. J. Olson, "Socio-economic Status and Delinquent Behavior," *American Journal of Sociology,* Vol. 63 (January, 1958), pp. 381–89; and Lamar T. Empey and Maynard L. Erickson, "Hidden Delinquency and Social Status," *Social Forces,* Vol. 44 (June, 1966), pp. 546–54.

[34] Robert H. Hardt, "Delinquency and Social Class: Bad Kids or Good Cops," in Irwin Deutscher and Elizabeth J. Thompson (eds.), *Among the People: Encounters with the Poor* (New York: Basic Books, 1968), pp. 132–45.

[35] See James F. Short, Jr. and Fred L. Strodtbeck, *Group Process and Gang Delinquency* (Chicago: University of Chicago Press, 1965), Chapters 4, 5, and 7; Walter B. Miller, Hildred S. Geertz, and Henry S. G. Cutter, "Aggression in a Boys' Street-Corner Group," *Psychiatry,* Vol. 24 (1961), pp. 283–98; John M. Wise, *A Comparison of Sources of Data as Indexes of Delinquent Behavior,* unpublished Masters thesis, University of Chicago, 1962.

offenses tend to be handled outside the court, by friends and neighbors, parents, ministers, teachers, and others; whereas in urban areas, where official resources are more fully developed and legal controls more relied upon, similar offenses are more likely to find their way into the courts. But the relationship between urban and rural crime rates holds for more serious offenses also, so it cannot be accounted for solely in these terms.

The classic works of Shaw and McKay and more recent studies reveal wide variations in the spatial concentration of crime and delinquency within the cities.[36] Though the details vary in different cities, the general nature of these patterns is remarkably consistent. Rates of crime and delinquency and of recidivism are highest in the inner-city areas characterized by physical deterioration and the concentration of other social ills, such as poverty, suicide, mental illness, and certain diseases. As one moves away from these "delinquency areas," rates go down fairly regularly. When studied over time these ecological distributions change little, despite changes in the racial and ethnic composition of the areas studied. These generalizations are based on studies of American cities and must be qualified for cities that have exhibited a different pattern of growth.[37]

Even in such "delinquency areas" delinquency rates are considerably below 100 percent. A delinquency rate of 25 percent (a very high rate) of all age-eligible boys in the area does not mean, however, that only 25 percent of these boys engage in delinquent behavior. The incidence of hidden delinquency is very large. Additionally, recent studies indicate that the percentage of youngsters who appear before the court at some time during their period of "eligibility" is several times the *annual* rate.

Sellin and Wolfgang, for example, found that of a cohort of approximately 10,000 boys born in 1945 and residing in Philadelphia from age 10 through 17,[38] 35 percent had at least one officially recorded police contact during this

[36] Clifford R. Shaw et al., Delinquency Areas (Chicago: University of Chicago Press, 1929); Clifford Shaw and Henry McKay, Juvenile Delinquency and Urban Areas (Chicago: University of Chicago Press, 1942 and 1969); and Robert A. Gordon, "Issues in the Ecological Study of Delinquency," American Sociological Review (December, 1967), pp. 927–44.

[37] See Lois B. DeFleur, "Ecological Variables in the Cross-Cultural Study of Delinquency," Social Forces (June, 1967), pp. 556–70.

[38] Thorsten Sellin and Marvin Wolfgang, Delinquency in a Birth Cohort (forthcoming); cf., John C. Ball, Alan Ross, and Alice Simpson, "Incidence and Estimated Prevalence of Recorded Delinquency in a Metropolitan Area," American Sociological Review, Vol. 29 (February, 1964), pp. 90–93; Thomas P. Monahan, "On the Incidence of Delinquency," Social Forces, Vol. 39 (October, 1960), pp. 66–72; and Leonard Savitz, "Delinquency and Migration," in Marvin Wolfgang, Leonard Savitz, and Norman Johnston, eds., The Sociology of Crime and Delinquency (New York: Wiley, 1962), p. 205.

eight-year period; of these, 55 percent had more than one police contact; a smaller group of 627 "chronic offenders" (5 or more recorded offenses) — 6.3 percent of the entire cohort — accounted for more than half of all delinquencies recorded, including 53 percent of the personal attacks, 62 percent of the property offenses, and 71 percent of the robberies attributed to the cohort. All of these measures of delinquency involvement tended to be concentrated in the blighted slum areas of the city. The concentration was greatest, however, for the most seriously involved boys. Thus delinquency areas not only have higher occurrence rates of delinquents, but also of the more serious types of delinquency, as well as the most seriously involved delinquents.

While trends in delinquency rates suggest that most communities are remarkably stable in this respect, rapid increases are found in a few communities and rapid decreases in others. McKay's analysis of trends in Chicago communities finds that the population in both types of areas in that city is predominantly black.[39] Communities with the most pronounced upward trends in delinquency rates are areas that were most recently settled by blacks, while communities with the most pronounced downward trends have been predominantly black since the beginning of the series studied. The findings are consistent with those concerning other racial and ethnic groups. Under the disorganizing impact of residential shift from an "invading" socially and economically disadvantaged population, communities lose their ability to control behavior defined as delinquent. Conventional institutions break down and social problems in great variety increase. In time, however, these institutions become reestablished and other forms of social control also become more effective.

Conclusion

All of these "categoric risks"[40] of crime and delinquency interact with and, in significant ways, influence one another. To the extent that these categoric risks are reliable, they provide important clues to causation; they constitute facts for which theories must account; and they are important in interpreting other statistics of crime. Ferdinand has demonstrated, for example, that when the migration of people from rural areas to cities is taken

---

[39] See Henry McKay's discussion of these findings in Clifford R. Shaw and Henry McKay, *Juvenile Delinquency and Urban Areas,* rev. edition (Chicago: University of Chicago Press, 1969).

[40] We employ Walter Reckless' felicitous phrasing. See *The Crime Problem* (New York: Appleton, 1955).

into account, approximately one-fifth of the increase in serious crime (FBI Class I offenses; see Table 1) in this country between 1950 and 1965 can be attributed to urbanization.[41] In addition, more than one-tenth of the arrests for these crimes in 1965 represented changes in the age structure during this period (that is, expansion of the 10-to-24 age group). The extent of influence of such demographic shifts varies for different offenses, with fully one-fourth of the recorded rise in robberies and auto thefts, but only 8 percent of criminal homicides, attributable to increased urbanization. Forty-seven percent of the increase in arrests for forcible rape, but much smaller percentages of other serious crimes, may be attributed to the increased proportion of the population in the 10-to-24 age group.

AN INTERACTIONAL FRAMEWORK FOR CRIMINOLOGICAL THEORY

It is customary to think of crime as if it consisted of a collection of actions, each produced by a particular person. The problem of explaining crime then becomes one of explaining why these people did these things. As is clear from the preceding discussion, however, this procedure is artificially simple. All social actions are episodes in some ongoing activity that has a history of some duration. To this activity different individual actors make different contributions at various stages of its evolution. What happens at any particular stage is the product of the history of an interaction process. As an illustration, if we want to know why a baseball player behaves in a particular way — let us say he bunts — we must first know that it was in fact an event in a baseball game. But, for full understanding of the event — for predictive or control purposes, for example — we must know more: the stage of the game, the general situation in terms of the score and the count, the disposition of players on the field, how the game has been going (the fielding, the pitching, the batting), and, closer to the event itself, the kind of pitch the pitcher delivers and the signals the batter is getting from his coach. Obviously, the batter has something to do with all this. If somebody else had been at bat (and just who happens to be at bat is itself a product of the history of the game to that point; turns at bat are rigidly controlled by the rules of the game), or if the batter had missed his attempted bunt, or if the pitcher had "pitched out," there might not have been a bunt. The process that produced

---

[41] Theodore N. Ferdinand, "Demographic Shifts and Criminality: An Inquiry," *British Journal of Criminology* (April, 1970), pp. 169–75.

the bunt was a very complex affair in which the batter was a significant participant but only one of many. To say that *this* man did *this* thing (bunted) is not to say that he produced the event or that he alone is responsible for it. Rather, it is to call attention to his role in a process in which he is a participant.

In important respects the situation described is not peculiar to baseball or even to games. It applies to social actions generally, in the sense that people behave according to rules or understandings, in interaction with other people, on the basis of past experience and the characteristics of the present situation, and with an eye to the future. The purchase of a used car (or the sale, which is the same event from the point of view of a different participant), the writing of a book, the selection of a meal in a restaurant, or enrolling in Eastern Establishment Junior College can be fully understood only if such information is taken into account; so, also, behavior defined as criminal or delinquent—cheating on an examination, larceny of sandwiches from the college dining hall, statutory rape, pickpocketing, false advertising, robbery of a filling station, vandalism of a school building, a criminal abortion, or a fight between two drunks. "Victims" may contribute as importantly to the development of the criminal act as "offenders" (there cannot be a fight between one drunk).

From this perspective, three kinds of questions can be asked about the "causation" of crime:

1. The question we have been asking is: How did this event occur? What was the interaction situation (the game) of which the criminal event was a product, and how did it evolve? This is a question in the "microsociology" of crime. *This question has been the least asked and the least is known about it.* The general theoretical question would be: What general propositions can we formulate about the structure and the development of interaction situations that produce criminal actions?

2. Why did *this* individual commit *this* crime? How is his involvement related to his personal characteristics, his background, or the roles he plays? It should be clear that no personality characteristics, no background, nor any particular configuration of roles can produce a crime of itself. It is reasonable to ask, however, whether we can identify kinds of persons who have a high *probability* of committing crimes; under what particular conditions they are likely to commit crimes; and how they became that way. These are "psychological" questions. From one point of view, an action can be seen as part of the biography of an individual—something he did or contributed to in some way. A variant form of the same question asks: What sorts of differences among the personalities and histories of individuals make what sorts of differences in the probability of involvement in criminal actions?

3. Criminal events are located not only in the biographies of individuals, but in social systems as well. Thus we ask also: What is it about the social systems in which events occur that helps to explain their occurrence? Rates of criminal events and of offenders can be enumerated and their characteristic distributions in social systems and time studied. For a variety of reasons, some criminal phenomena cannot be enumerated in this way. For example, the Mafia, or Cosa Nostra, the social organization of syndicated gambling in the United States; the organization of the market and the distribution network of marijuana compared to that of heroin; social organization among business firms and businessmen for illegal purposes—these phenomena do not lend themselves to study of rates. The chapter that follows treats these matters at greater length. Both types of phenomena can be understood in part in terms of their relations to the organization and culture of the community of which they are a part. This is the perspective of "macrosociology."

When we approach crime and delinquency from these different perspectives, we arrive at different explanations, but not necessarily competing or conflicting explanations. They are different because they are answers to different questions: They are explaining different things. Therefore, arguments to the effect that "psychological" explanations are superior to "sociological" explanations or vice versa are largely pointless. On the other hand, these different perspectives have mutual implications: Any theory about the ways in which the organization of society determines crime rates makes *some* assumptions about the nature of the human actor and what moves him to crime.

Most writers on crime and delinquency do not adhere strictly to one or another of the three levels of discourse that we have distinguished, and there is no reason why they should. It is important, however, to bear the distinctions in mind, so that we always understand when they are talking about one question or another.

Multiple-Factor Theories

We saw in an earlier section that crime and delinquency are statistically associated with many different conditions. So-called multiple-factor theories assume that such associations signify causation, the importance of each factor depending upon the strength of the association. According to multiple-factor theories, the presence of one of these factors constitutes a push in the direction of crime; the addition of a second factor increases the strength of the push; a third factor increases it still more, and so one. One person is said to become a criminal because of the influence of three or four factors present in his case, another because of three or four others.

Advocates of such theories often take pride in their broad-mindedness and their appreciation of the complexity of crime causation. However, their "theories" are not theories and their "explanations" do not explain. A statistical association means only that some factor occurs in connection with some phenomenon more frequently than would be expected by chance. It does not necessarily mean that one causes the other—that trousers, for example, cause maleness, or that maleness causes crime; or, to round out the absurdity, that trousers cause crime. Furthermore, as we have already suggested, no single circumstance is in itself a push in the direction of crime. Criminal events are the product of the *interaction* of some set of circumstances, and not their mere summation. Poverty in combination with one set of circumstances may indeed conduce to crime; in combination with another set of circumstances, it may conduce to honest toil. When we explain something—falling bodies, the price of corn, or a criminal act—we do two things: We point out some set of circumstances associated with the event; and we demonstrate that this set of circumstances conforms to some pattern or general rule that fits and makes sense, not only concerning the event in question, but all events of that class.

Such a rule (or, more often, a set of rules) is formulated in terms of abstract categories or "variables," each of which may take on various "values." The specific, concrete circumstances or "factors" that contribute to the event must be translatable into values of these variables. A great variety of situations, each consisting of a unique configuration of specific factors, may be equivalent when translated into the variables specified by the rule. The general rules by which we explain things are "theories." They are hard to come by. The best theories are those that make sense out of the most facts and leave the fewest threads dangling. Statistical relationships are not theories; they are descriptive statements of observed tendencies of the joint occurrence of certain events. They do not explain; they require explanation. Such explanation is the office of theory.

It is characteristic also of the multiple-factor approach, though not peculiar to it, that things we do not like (e.g., delinquency) must have antecedents we do not like (alcoholism, psychopathic personality, biological inferiority, lack of love by parents, overprotection by parents, etc.). This is the fallacy that "evil causes evil." Explanations of social problems in these terms are likely to be statements attributing causal power to a list of ugly and sordid conditions which any "decent citizen" deplores. It is very difficult to reason that crime, an evil, does not necessarily result from something also considered evil, but instead might result from something which most persons hold to be good. "Good things" like rising standards of living, an open class system, freedom, or individualism can have unanticipated consequences, including crime and delinquency. (It does not follow, of course, that all "bad things" are caused by "good things," or that any "bad thing" is always caused by a "good thing.") We tend to seek the "causes" of crime and delinquency in evil antecedents because doing so enables us to denounce crime without having to consider the necessity of changing conditions that we hold dear.

THE PSYCHOLOGICAL LEVEL OF EXPLANATION

Psychobiological Theories [42]

We speak here of theories according to which the independent variables in the determination of crime and delinquency are some observable or hypothetical aspect of the biological structure of the person. In the more extreme versions of such theories, variations in the situation are largely ignored, as variables in both the learning process and the motivational processes. Behavior becomes a direct manifestation of some underlying condition in the glands, the nervous system, or, more vaguely, "the constitution." These bodily characteristics are, in turn, ascribed to a defective heredity and the causation of crime becomes reduced to the formula: Heredity determines criminality.

The prototype of such theories is Cesare Lombroso's theory of the born criminal. Lombroso's conception of the born criminal was sharply criticized in his own day, and in his later work Lombroso greatly qualified himself,[43] but the general idea of a "criminal type," recognizable by his bestial or otherwise unlovely stigmata, has attracted many scholars. The American anthropologist E. A. Hooton claimed, on the basis of his comparison of criminals and noncriminals, that criminals showed various traits of biological inferi-

---

[42] For an excellent survey of this class of theories, see William McCord, "The Biological Basis of Juvenile Delinquency," in Joseph S. Roucek, ed., *Juvenile Delinquency* (New York: Philosophical Library, 1958), pp. 59–78.

[43] See the introduction to Gina Lombroso-Ferrero, *Criminal Man According to the Classifications of Cesare Lombroso* (New York: Putnam, 1911), pp. xiv–xv.

ority and degeneration and that criminality was the behavioral manifestation of such biological inadequacy.[44]

Quite different conclusions are reached by William H. Sheldon, the developer of a system for describing the varieties of human physiques.[45] To one such
variety, the mesomorph, characterized by a sturdy and muscular athletic
frame, he ascribes an unusual propensity to delinquency. "Mesomorphs" are
not regarded as inherently or specifically delinquent, however. The mesomorphic physique is associated with a distinctive type of temperament,
somatotonia, characterized by such traits as assertiveness of posture and
movement, love of physical adventure, abounding and restless energy, need
for and enjoyment of exercise. This temperament does not of itself produce
delinquency. Mesomorphy and its attendant somatotonia rather produce
aggressive, energetic, daring types of people; it is the stuff of which generals,
athletes, and politicians, as well as delinquents, are often made. All are
callings that are suited to the somatotonic temperament.

Sheldon's research has been the subject of devastating criticism,[46] but
his ideas have been given a new lease on life by the more recent work of
Sheldon and Eleanor Glueck.[47] Although their work has also been subject
to criticism, it is, of all the research in the field of the relationship between
physique and delinquency, methodologically the most scrupulous and respectable. Samples of delinquents and nondelinquents studied have been more
carefully drawn, statistical analysis is more cautious, and conclusions more
limited and guarded. It seems probable that the mesomorphic physique is
disproportionately common in officially delinquent populations, although it
is far from being the hallmark by which delinquents may be identified. (Even
in the Glueck research, 40 percent of their delinquents *were not* predominantly mesomorphic, and 30 percent of their nondelinquents *were*.) Whether
this is so because the temperament of the mesomorph, rooted in an inherited
biological constitution, has an inherent propensity for danger, violence,
and predatory behavior, or because the strenuous and active life of the lower-
class, street-dwelling delinquent tends to harden the body into a mesomorphic contour, or whether boys with the strength and energy of the meso-

---

[44] E. A. Hooton, *Crime and the Man* (Cambridge, Mass.: Harvard University Press,
1939). See also Robert K. Merton and M. F. Ashley-Montagu, "Crime and the Anthropologist," *American Anthropologist,* Vol. 42 (1940), pp. 384–468.

[45] William H. Sheldon, *Varieties of Delinquent Youth* (New York: Harper, 1949).

[46] Albert K. Cohen, Alfred R. Lindesmith, and Karl F. Schuessler, eds., *The Sutherland Papers* (Bloomington: Indiana University Press, 1956), pp. 279–90.

[47] Sheldon and Eleanor Glueck, *Physique and Delinquency* (New York: Harper,
1956).

morph find it easier than their scrawnier or more corpulent peers to gain status through the kinds of accomplishments that are rewarded in the delinquent gang, is uncertain.

Other attempts to establish the inherited basis of crime have included the detailing of family histories of degeneracy, such as Dugdale's *The Jukes*, published in 1877, and Goddard's investigation of *The Kallikak Family*, published in 1912.[48] In the history of attempts to relate crime and delinquency to biological phenomena, a large number of biological processes have been examined. Thus, the criminality of siblings, including one- and two-egg twins, has been examined in an effort to establish a hereditary basis for crime; organically related mental deficiency has been investigated in hundreds of studies; endocrine imbalance was for a time very popular as an "explanation" of crime; and there was proposed the concept—reminiscent of Lombroso's "born criminal"—of a constitutional psychopathic personality, an individual devoid of moral sense and feeling for others as a result of some underlying, but unspecified, defect of brain or nervous system. All these theories have been unconvincing to sociologists and biologists alike, however, and for a variety of reasons. The research on which they are based has typically used poor or inadequate controls; the measuring instruments have been inadequate or unskillfully applied; and the biological connection with delinquency has been so vague and undefined as to be unfit for scientific investigation. Furthermore, if we consider that the criminality of an act is culturally relative, we should not expect to find any consistent relationship between specific biological traits and criminal behavior. Certainly, biology has something to do with the way we act: it affects our temperaments and appetites; it affects our capacities; and, like our skin color and sexual characteristics, it affects those we interact with and therefore our own destinies. An adequate theory of crime, as of human behavior generally, must find ways of taking such things into account, but that is a rather different thing from making crime a simple function of biological structure.

Psychometric Approaches [49]

The interest of various disciplines in crime and delinquency has often been stimulated by technical developments in the testing and measurement of

---

[48] Richard Louis Dugdale, *The Jukes, A Study in Crime, Pauperism, Disease, and Heredity* (New York: Putnam, 1877); Henry H. Goddard, *The Kallikak Family, A Study in the Heredity of Feeblemindedness* (New York: Macmillan, 1912).

[49] A recent assessment of this class of theories is found in Herbert C. Quay, ed., *Juvenile Delinquency* (New York: Van Nostrand, 1965).

human capacities and characteristics. This has been particularly true of intelligence and personality characteristics.

Immediately before and after World War I, when intelligence testing began to come into vogue, the newly devised tests were applied to delinquents and criminals, and feeble-mindedness began to be regarded as an important cause of crime by an increasing number of scholars. In 1912, H. H. Goddard, one of the most enthusiastic early advocates of feeble-mindedness as the principal cause of crime, estimated that at least 25 percent of adult criminals were feeble-minded and hence unable to avoid involvement in crime; by 1914 Goddard estimated that the rate was at least 50 percent [50]; and by 1920 "nearly all" criminals and delinquents were regarded as of low-grade mentality.[51]

Writing in 1931, Sutherland analyzed about 350 reports on mental tests of criminals, and noted that the proportion of delinquents diagnosed as feeble-minded declined steadily from the early 1910–1914 period to 1928–1929. Sutherland concluded that the delinquent population closely resembles the general population in intelligence scores and that feeble-minded persons in the community at large do not show excessive rates of delinquency. These conclusions are consistent with other analyses and represent an almost complete retraction of the earlier conclusions that mentally defective persons are overrepresented in groups having high crime rates.[52]

Psychologists and others have used dozens of tests, rating scales, and other measuring devices to study the relationship between crime and delinquency and a host of psychological traits such as mechanical aptitude, aggressiveness, speed of decision, emotional instability, caution, self-assurance, excitability, and motor inhibition. Generally speaking, the work in this area has been fragmentary in character, in the sense that studies are made without reference to a systematically developed theory of crime.

Although individual studies do show correlations between personality traits and crime and delinquency, the correlations tend to be weak and the results of different studies to be inconsistent.[53] Certainly there is no criminal or delinquent "personality type," if by this is meant a distinguishable pat-

[50] Henry H. Goddard, *Feeblemindedness, Its Causes and Consequences* (New York: Macmillan, 1912).

[51] Henry H. Goddard, *Human Efficiency and Levels of Intelligence* (New Jersey: Princeton University Press, 1920), pp. 73–74.

[52] Carl Murchison, *Criminal Intelligence* (Worcester, Mass.: Clark University Press, 1926), and Samuel H. Tulchin, *Intelligence and Crime* (Chicago: University of Chicago Press, 1939).

[53] Karl F. Schuessler and Donald R. Cressey, "Personality Characteristics of Criminals," *American Journal of Sociology*, Vol. 55 (March, 1950), pp. 476–84.

tern of personality characteristics that results always or even usually in criminal or delinquent behavior. We cannot conclude that the study of personality traits is irrelevant to our subject; like biological traits, one's personality influences the major variables of a general theory of crime or delinquency.

Psychiatric Theories

Psychiatric perspectives on crime and delinquency rest heavily on conceptions of motivation and personality derived from psychoanalytic theory. According to this theory, behavior is motivated by impulses and "drive energy" of a fundamentally biological nature (the "Id"), and modified by socialization experiences, which provide the individual with the capacity for thought and rational assessment (the "Ego"), and internal restraints in the form of conscience (the "Superego").[54]

In the classic statement of this position, delinquent behavior results when the restraining forces are too weak to curb inherent aggressive and destructive tendencies. Such tendencies are universal to the species. We are all, in this view, born criminals. We do not learn to become criminals; rather some of us learn to control the criminality with which all are afflicted, while some do not.

While holding to the insight that "Every man has within him the capacity to commit the most objectionable antisocial acts, no matter how civilized or sophisticated his social training has made him,"[55] modern psychiatry has moved considerably beyond the simple determinism implied in the earlier model. Halleck observes that "While some aggressive and some sexual activity is often correlated with a weakening of control mechanisms . . . the act of law violation is often a deliberate, planned and complicated operation which may require a great deal of ego strength."[56]

Halleck and many other psychiatrists see behavior as adaptive, as problem solving. Specifically, crime is seen as "an adaptation to stress . . . best understood in terms of the manner in which the individual experiences the biological, psychological and socially determined situations of his existence."[57]

---

[54] For a review of this position and its modification, see Franz Alexander and Hugo Staub, *The Criminal, the Judge, and the Public* (New York: Free Press, 1956).

[55] Seymour Halleck, *Psychiatry and the Dilemmas of Crime* (New York: Harper, 1967), p. 60.

[56] *Ibid.*, p. 61.

[57] *Ibid.*, p. 63.

Psychiatric perspectives on crime and delinquency lean heavily on assumptions concerning unconscious mental and emotional problems and processes that do not easily admit to empirical inquiry. Psychiatric writing largely consists of detailed case histories of patients in treatment; it is not typically the product of systematic research aimed at generalized knowledge. Proceeding in this manner from case to case, and consisting largely of interpretations based on theory and on the author's clinical intuition, such writing does not often yield general propositions of a testable character. Investigators often probe psychic processes until an emotional problem is located, whereupon they announce that the problem is responsible for the delinquency, with little attempt to connect the two in a logical or empirical way. One cannot easily quarrel with the notion that human behavior is typically concerned with solving problems, whether these problems are conceived in biological, psychiatric, or sociological terms. All theories that attempt to account for crime or delinquency as ways of coping with such problems must deal with the necessity of explaining why some people solve their problems in these ways while others do not. Psychiatric theories do not often meet this test successfully, but the failing is not peculiar to them.

Sociological Perspectives on Motivation

A great deal of what sociologists have written about crime and delinquency deals with what we have called psychological questions. Elements of an emerging sociological perspective on motivation may be summarized as follows:

1. *Behavior is oriented to the maintenance and enhancement of the self.* The expression "the self" stands for an interrelated set of beliefs and attitudes of the actor. It has three major components. The first may be referred to as the self-image. It is what the actor believes about himself, how he describes himself to himself. The second component is self-demands, what the actor aspires to be, what he expects of himself. The third component is self-judgment, the result of comparisons between self-image and self-demands. It may involve pride or guilt, self-acceptance or rejection, self-satisfaction or hatred.

The general formula for motivation would be this: In any given situation, the actor tends to select, from the possibilities open to him, that mode of action that is most likely to reduce the discrepancy between his self-image and his self-demands, and thereby to maintain or enhance a satisfactory self-judgment.

2. *The self is largely defined in role terms.* People classify themselves and one another in terms of labels embedded in the language of their milieu. These labels evoke socially standardized expectations that we may fittingly call "role demands." Role demands define the full-fledged and adequate incumbent of the respective role and provide the standards in terms of which we judge him. What we have called self-demands consist largely of roles with which the individual identifies or to which he aspires, and the corresponding demands. Therefore, how a person reacts to his self-image, what he wants to preserve in himself and what he wants to change in himself, depends on how he labels himself in role terms ("tough guy," "law-abiding citizen," "friend," "member of the Golden Dragons," "husband," "playboy") and on the expectations that attach to these roles in his cultural setting.

In an effort to establish or validate a self or identity, one may act in a certain way because it directly signifies or fulfills the expectations of the roles of which that self is constructed, in which case the behavior is "role-expressive." Or one may act in a way which makes possible or facilitates behavior that is directly expressive of those roles, in which case it is "role-supportive." Grosser's [58] interpretation of the differences between the characteristic stealing behavior of boys and girls illustrates the application of these concepts to motivational analysis. Grosser observed that stealing by boys typically seemed to be directed to no practical end, that they seemed to steal all sorts of things for "fun," as it were, or for "kicks." Girls seemed to steal in a more "rational" way, to take things that they could use—typically, clothing, jewelry, and cosmetics.

Stealing, like "badness" in general, has connotations of masculinity in our society. The boy who is "bad" is, nevertheless, "all boy." For the young male, stealing may be one way of proving to himself something of great importance: that he is authentically and indubitably masculine. It is role-expressive. Stealing, destructiveness, and generally defiant behavior do not, on the other hand, have the same expressive significance for the female role. This behavior is likely to damage rather than to enhance a girl's self-conception *as a girl.* She is likely to be judged, and to judge herself, rather on the basis of her attractiveness, her "charm," her "sex appeal." Fulfillment of the demands of her role is facilitated by the right kind of clothing, cosmetics, and accessories. One way of getting these things is by stealing them. To steal these things, then, is *supportive* of the female role, although stealing *as such* is not a way of validating a claim to femininity.

These concepts lend themselves to very broad application. While fight-

---

[58] George Grosser, "Juvenile Delinquency and Contemporary American Sex Roles," unpublished Ph.D. dissertation, Harvard University, 1952.

ing and having sexual experiences are expressive of the male role, and therefore help to validate one's masculinity, behavior expressive of and compatible with the role of a boy or a "kid" may be inconsistent with the demands of a more adult role. The boy who breaks windows and steals hubcaps may, a few years later, abandon such behavior because it is defined as "kid stuff."

3. *The value and meaning of the self are influenced by one's reference groups.* What does it *mean* to be a boy, a girl, a "real man," a solid citizen? What must a person, such as I claim to be, do in order to make that claim stick? These meanings are not given in the nature of things. They are taken from the cultures of the groups around us. But these groups may disagree in small ways and large, and for each individual the judgments of some groups are more authoritative than those of others. Those whose authority carries the most weight are called "normative reference groups." More broadly, they are the groups whose culture provides the standards against which we check the correctness of our own beliefs. They are especially important when we are morally ambivalent—for example, when we are disposed to participate in an act of "civil disobedience" and at the same time have moral doubts about it. Is it "really all right" or is it not? The formulas by which we justify or "rationalize" decisions are convincing largely to the extent that they are shared by others whose opinions we value.

We seek from others not only confirmation of our judgments but also acceptance, respect, and status. We may call groups from whom we desire such acceptance our "status reference groups." The value that we place upon a particular identity—say, being "hip" or "tough" or "militant" or "Christian"—depends largely on how these identities are esteemed and rewarded by our status reference groups. Normative and status reference groups are likely to be identical, but they are not necessarily so. At some point in our development some group—say our parents—may lose its importance as a normative reference group but remain effective as a status reference group. In any case, how we choose a course of action entails a complex calculation in which reference group considerations of both kinds play an important role.

In general, sociological perspectives emphasize that most of what we do, we do with other people with an eye to what it will mean to them and how it will affect our relationships with them. They tend also to account for behavior that is criminal and behavior that is not criminal in terms of the same underlying motivational processes, whereas the other theories that we have discussed tend to seek their explanations in terms of personal qualities and characteristics that differentiate criminals from noncriminals.

Differential Association

The learning theories of sociologists may be characterized as cultural-transmission theories; they share the ideas that the values and beliefs that favor delinquent and criminal behavior are originally part of our cultural milieus and that they are taken over in the same way that antidelinquent and anticriminal values and beliefs are taken over. The most systematic statement of a cultural-transmission view is Edwin H. Sutherland's theory of differential association.[59]

Differential association emphasizes that criminal behavior is learned in interaction with other persons in a process of communication. Such learning includes the specific direction of values, attitudes, motives, drives, and rationalizations relative to criminality, as well as techniques of committing crime. Most importantly, however, definitions favorable and unfavorable to violation of law are communicated, and "a person becomes delinquent because of an excess of definitions favorable to violation of law over definitions unfavorable to violation of law."

This is probably the most powerful theory in the field of criminology — that is to say, it makes sense of the greatest range of facts about crime. As a theory of learning, its strength is enhanced by the addition of a central theme of identity theory: The impact of exposure to a definition — how effective it will be as a learning experience — depends upon its relevance to the kind of self we are trying to construct or maintain. Things that will help us in accomplishing our projects — and building a self is a most important project — are more quickly perceived and leave a deeper and more lasting impression.

Attempts have been made to translate differential association theory into the language of reinforcement learning theory.[60] Grossly oversimplified, the basic idea of reinforcement theory is that learning is a function of reward (positive reinforcement) and punishment (negative reinforcement). For example, in translation, Sutherland's statement, "The principle part of the learning of criminal behavior occurs within intimate personal groups,"

---

[59] Edwin H. Sutherland and Donald R. Cressey, *Principles of Criminology,* 6th ed. (Chicago: Lippincott, 1960).

[60] Robert L. Burgess and Ronald L. Akers, "A Differential Association — Reinforcement Theory of Criminal Behavior," *Social Problems,* Vol. 14, No. 2 (Fall, 1966), pp. 128–47. This reinformulation is based on principles largely associated with B. F. Skinner, *Science and Human Behavior* (New York: Macmillan, 1953).

becomes "The principal part of the learning of criminal behavior occurs in those groups which comprise the individual's major source of reinforcements."[61] If the reader will look back at the last sentence of the preceding paragraph, he will see that the notion of reinforcement or reward is implicit also in identity theory. The sentence might be restated, "We learn what is rewarding, and what is rewarding is what helps us to build a valued identity." It is likely that the future growth of criminological theory will come largely through attempts to integrate into a single, more powerful formulation the partial insights of a number of different theories.

MACROSOCIOLOGICAL THEORIES

Anomie Theory

According to this theory,[62] people's aspirations, and therefore their definitions of success and failure, are to a large extent determined by goals set for them by their culture. Success in American society is defined largely in terms of material success and a high style of living, and this definition of success is more or less the same for all groups. However, different racial, class, and ethnic groupings are radically unequal in their ability to realize their aspirations by those means that the culture defines as legitimate. Where the "disjunction" between "culture goals" and "institutionalized means" for their achievement is great, a condition of "anomie" prevails — that is, a breakdown of the regulative norms — and people have recourse to whatever means will "work." Where anomie prevails, we are likely to find high rates of crime and delinquency. In societies where different classes of people are indoctrinated with aspirations more in keeping with the means available to them, the sense of deprivation is not so acute, anomie is less likely to occur, and rates of deviant behavior are not so high.

This theory treats variations in rates of deviance both within and between societies as products of culture and social structure. It identifies several different possible responses to a disjunction between goals and means, including perseveration in conforming behavior even though it is not rewarded, but it does not specify the conditions that determine choices among the pos-

---

[61] *Ibid.*, pp. 553–54.
[62] Robert K. Merton, *Social Theory and Social Structure,* rev. ed. (New York: Free Press, 1957).

sible responses. Note also that a great deal of crime and delinquency does not readily make sense as alternative, albeit illegal, means to the acquisition of wordly goods. Examples would be gang violence and juvenile vandalism, on the one hand, and the illegal tactics employed by students and other groups today as part of "confrontation politics," on the other.

Differential Social Organization

"Differential association" states that the chances that an individual will engage in criminal behavior depend on the balance between his procriminal and anticriminal associations. It would follow that the *rate* of criminal behavior in a given social category or group depends on the way in which society is organized to promote or prevent exposure of members of that group to procriminal and anticriminal associations.[63] For example, to the extent that the family system and occupational systems restrict freedom of movement of females as compared with males, and consequently reduce the likelihood that they will be exposed to association with procriminal patterns, we would expect the female crime rate to be lower than the male crime rate. Starting from the premise that there exist in the society conflicting cultural definitions of criminal conduct, the concept of differential social organization adds the important idea that the organization of social relationships affects the chances of association with these different definitions. Note that this theory does not try to explain why variant cultural definitions exist; it deals only with the structural determinants of differential exposure and transmission.

Subcultural Theory

Cohen's theory of the delinquent subculture [64] seeks to explain only male, working-class delinquency, but the logic of the theory has implications for culturally supported deviance in general. Like Merton's theory it assumes that delinquency is in some way related to a discrepancy between culture goals and the availability of legitimate opportunities for achieving them. It assumes that in American society males of all social levels are to a great degree judged by the same set of standards, and that their self-respect and

---

[63] Albert K. Cohen, Alfred R. Lindesmith, and Karl F. Schuessler, eds., *The Sutherland Papers* (Bloomington: Indiana University Press, 1956).

[64] Albert K. Cohen, *Delinquent Boys* (New York: Free Press, 1955).

sense of adequacy are largely determined by their performance in terms of those standards, especially when they move out of the home situation and find themselves in competition with other youth in school and occupational settings. Cohen called these standards the middle-class criteria of status because they are most consistently applied by those segments of the population that control the gateways to success, such as teachers, business and professional people, ministers, and civic leaders. They include such things as a high level of ambition, an ability to defer gratification of immediate needs in the interest of achieving long-term goals, self-discipline, the possession of skills of potential academic, occupational, and economic value, and so on. Growing up in working-class homes is less likely to produce young people with the ability to perform well in terms of these criteria. The American ethos allows and even encourages working-class children to "better themselves" and to compete for status with middle-class children, and holds out some prospect of upward mobility if they are "deserving." By the same token, however, those who fail to demonstrate these attributes are "losers," as measured by middle-class standards. Thus, working-class children are systematically disadvantaged in the competitive pursuit of status and are likely to find themselves "at the bottom of the heap" with their self-respect damaged.

The working boy's problem of adjustment is one of status and self-respect. One way of resolving this problem is to draw together with others having the same problems — and they are many — and, through sympathetic interaction, to develop new social systems with new rules and criteria of status. These constitute a new subculture, one that is fully intelligible only as a reaction to the conventional status system. Virtue comes to consist in flouting and defying middle-class morality. Orderliness, amenability to adult supervision and guidance, respect for property, polite speech and manners, the derogation of violence — these are contemptuously spurned by the delinquent subculture. It is a "contraculture," an active "put-down" of the culture at whose hands working-class children have suffered. This conception of delinquency as behavior in accordance with a subculture makes sense only as a "group response." It depends upon the conditions that make possible the sympathetic interaction of a plurality of individuals with like problems. The part played by such interaction in the shaping of responses to problems of adjustment is a consideration that is lacking in the earlier formulations of anomie theory.

Subcultural theory has met with a number of criticisms. Sykes and Matza,[65] for example, dispute the very existence of a distinctive delinquent

---

[65] Gresham M. Sykes and David Matza, "Techniques of Neutralization: A Theory of Delinquency," *American Sociological Review,* Vol. 24, No. 2 (April 1959), pp. 208–15.

subculture. They argue that delinquents not only act on the basis of values that are widespread in all sectors of American society, but even justify their delinquency in terms of familiar rationalizations or "techniques of neutralization" that are part of the common American cultural stock. On the other hand, Walter Miller's theory, to be discussed below, rejects Cohen's explanation on very different grounds.

Cohen and Short [66] have identified and offered explanations of several delinquent subcultures. However, the most systematic effort to account for varieties of delinquent subcultures is Cloward's and Ohlin's.[67] Like Cohen, these authors assume that delinquent subcultures are jointly contrived solutions to problems arising out of thwarted aspirations. Like Merton, they conceive these problems as disjunctions between culture goals and the structure of legitimate opportunities. To Merton's scheme they add, however, an important element: Not only does the social structure provide differential access to legitimate opportunities, it also provides differential access to *illegitimate* opportunities, and the availability of illegitimate opportunities is an important determinant of the solutions that people will adopt. Their theory also incorporates the essential element of the cultural transmission school, in that they conceptualize the illegitimate opportunity structure in terms of models and support available for learning, practicing, and performing delinquent roles. In areas characterized by organized and professional crime, successful adult criminals prove attractive role-models, and criminal organizations hold forth the prospects of lucrative jobs. Here delinquent behavior is a kind of rehearsal for forms of adult crime. Because unnecessary violence, bloodshed, and impetuous or irresponsible behavior are frowned upon by professional criminals, delinquency takes on a relatively restrained and disciplined quality. In areas where neither conventional nor criminal elements are well organized, and adult crime is individual or amateurish and relatively unrewarding, opportunities to identify with successful and attractive role-models or to learn appropriate skills are absent. Here there are no effective controls on young people from any part of the adult population. These areas typically produce conflict-oriented subcultures, characterized by more violent and untrammeled forms of gang activity. Lastly, there are those individuals who, by reason of internalized moral inhibitions, the lack of necessary skills, or the objective unavailability of either criminal or violent opportunity structures, can make use of neither of these patterns.

---

[66] Albert K. Cohen and James F. Short, Jr., "Research in Delinquent Subcultures," *Journal of Social Issues,* Vol. 14, No. 3 (1958), pp. 20–37.

[67] Richard A. Cloward and Lloyd E. Ohlin, *Delinquency and Opportunity* (New York: Free Press, 1960).

Such individuals, "double failures," so to speak, tend to form their own "retreatist" subcultures, centering around the use of drugs, alcohol, or some other "kick."

There is evidence that the differences among delinquent groups and between delinquent and nondelinquent groups are in fact related to differences in their opportunity structures. However, most delinquent gangs have been found to be engaged in a wide variety of delinquent behavior, rather than to be "specialized" as implied by the theory.[68] However, the potential value of the idea of opportunity structures, legitimate and illegitimate, does not solely hinge on the validity of this typology. It is an idea with very broad implications. For example, theories that relate organized crime to the existence of markets for their products make use of this idea even if they do not use this terminology.

Lower-Class Culture and Focal Concerns

Walter Miller[69] also sees delinquent behavior as conformity to a culture pattern. He denies, however, that specifically delinquent subcultures are formed by lower-class children in reaction against cultural patterns and status criteria of the middle-class world. It is the lower-class culture itself, acquired through socialization in lower-class settings, that generates delinquent behavior. The culture attaches value to such personal qualities and experience as "trouble, toughness, smartness, excitement, fate, or luck, and autonomy." These "focal concerns," as Miller calls them, are not inherently and necessarily delinquent. However, their pursuit is highly conducive to delinquent behavior. The argument can easily be extended to provide an explanation of lower-class adult crime. Miller's description of the focal concerns is generally regarded as an excellent statement of the main concerns of lower-class street corner gangs. His theory has been criticized, however, on the grounds that it fails to explain why some lower-class groups are highly delinquent and others are not (for they are all supposed to share the same focal concerns). His assumption that these focal concerns are attributes of a very widespread "lower-class culture" unaffected by contact with middle-class culture has also been much disputed.

---

[68] See, e.g., James F. Short, Jr. and Fred L. Strodtbeck, *Group Process and Gang Delinquency* (Chicago: University of Chicago Press, 1965).

[69] Walter B. Miller, "Lower-Class Culture as a Generating Milieu of Gang Delinquency," *Journal of Social Issues,* Vol. 14, No. 3 (1958), pp. 5–19.

This treatment of macrosociological theories has dealt mostly with theories of delinquency and slighted the large literature focusing on adult crime. We have proceeded in this way because the major contributions on the macrosociological level in recent years have dealt with delinquency, and because the principal concepts, arguments, and theoretical issues contained in these contributions are relevant to crime in general and are not peculiar to delinquency.

THE MICROSOCIOLOGICAL PERSPECTIVE

The central concern of microsociological inquiry is the interactive processes that produce criminal actions, rather than the biographies that produce criminal offenders. The literature of the microsociology of crime is still comparatively modest and there have not yet been any ambitious attempts at theoretical synthesis. However, we do have some empirical studies that are rich with implication for theory.

One line of investigation shifts the spotlight from the offender — that is, the individual who eventually becomes socially or legally defined as "the offender" — to the relationship between the offender and his "victim." Consider the following quotation, summarizing the circumstances of a homicide, taken from Wolfgang's study of homicide in Philadelphia:

> Two friends became involved in an argument in a taproom over the nationality of the offender, an Italian, with uncomplimentary remarks being made by the victim about "dagos." This led to the accusation by the victim that the offender had stolen money from him. After they left the taproom, the victim threatened the offender with a broken beer bottle, whereupon the offender broke a piece of wood from a nearby fruit stand and beat the victim severely about the head.[70]

Note several things about this description, which is typical of a great many homicides. (1) The parties are "two friends," and it was friendship that provided the occasion for the interaction that eventually led to homicide. (2) Neither party had homicide in mind at the beginning of the interaction; the "state of mind" of both parties was built up and transformed by the interaction process itself. (3) The act of murder was the culmination of a continu-

---

[70] Marvin Wolfgang, *Patterns in Criminal Homicide* (New York: Wiley, 1966), p. 227.

ous process that moved through several stages. It is quite conceivable that, at any stage, the process could have veered off in some other direction, and the outcome been different, if the circumstances at that point had only been slightly different. (4) Up to the point of the lethal attack with a piece of wood, the victim was the more aggressive and provocative of the two, and in a real sense shaped the actions of the offender. This provides an excellent example of the type of case in which "it is probably only chance which results in one becoming a victim and the other an offender." [71] However, although Wolfgang provides us with much interesting data on the relationships between homicide offenders and their victims, he has little to say on a more theoretical level about the circumstances that determine how the interaction will develop and what the outcome will be.[72]

The latter type of question is addressed somewhat more systematically in several recent studies of gang delinquency.[73] Not only do particular episodes have their interactional history; the gang itself may alternate between relatively delinquent and relatively nondelinquent, "club" phases. Both types of development have been found to be related to interaction with organizations and institutions of the larger society (e.g., schools, police, social agents and agencies, places of employment) and the local community (e.g., other gangs, neighborhood events, hangouts), and also to processes *within* the group.

Who acts violently and who does not may be determined by factors peculiar to the immediate situation and even to a specific moment in time: a boy's status in the group; the role he has come to play in the group; where he stands in relation to the particular action in progress; who, at a particular moment, happens to be holding a gun that is being passed from one member of the group to another; who among the members of the group has the most face to lose by not rising to a particular challenge. Some members—e.g., a

---

[71] *Ibid.,* p. 265.

[72] William J. Goode has suggested that the culmination of intimacy which is involved in kinship, friendship, and in sexual relationships "is at the same time likely to be a culmination of grievance," and in extreme cases to lead to aggravated assault or homicide. William J. Goode, "Violence Among Intimates," in Donald Mulvihill and Melvin Tumin, with the assistance of Lynn C. Curtis, *Violent Crime: A Task Force Report to the National Commission on the Causes and Prevention of Violence* (Washington, D. C.: U. S. Government Printing Office, 1970), pp. 941–77.

[73] See, especially, James F. Short, Jr. and Fred L. Strodtbeck, *Group Process and Gang Delinquency*; Leon R. Jansyn, Jr., "Solidarity and Delinquency in a Street Corner Group," *American Sociological Review* (October, 1966), pp. 600–14; and articles in and referred to in the January, 1967 issue of *Journal of Research in Crime and Delinquency.*

"war counselor" — may be under greater pressure to be "warlike" than are other members of a group. They may be reluctant and fearful, but if "the other side" makes a provocative move, other members of the group may look to them for an aggressive response. During phases of declining solidarity and incipient group disintegration, group members may initiate delinquent episodes to rally the group around common pursuits and to restore its "rep"; some, including leaders, may be carried along reluctantly or face losing status in the group; others may drop out altogether. We have only the beginnings, however, of a body of theory that integrates the events of the moment, the more extended episode in which the events are incidents, and the group history of which the episode is a part.[74]

SOCIAL CONTROL

The study of social control of crime and delinquency deals with a number of interrelated questions. First, what do we in fact do about crime and delinquency and why do we do it? Earlier in this chapter we touched upon questions of this order.

A rather different set of questions has to do with *the effects* of activities performed in the name of doing something about crime and delinquency. These need not be limited to their effects on crime and delinquency but may extend far beyond their ostensible objectives. Insofar as we are concerned with investigating the extent to which the activities in fact succeed in achieving this or that particular objective, we are dealing with the question of *effectiveness.* This, of course, depends on what we take to be the objectives; for example, a system that is more effective than another in terms of discovering and punishing offenders might be less effective in terms of preventing crime or rehabilitating offenders. A related question is that of *efficiency,* which is concerned with the relationship between effects achieved and costs incurred. It might be possible, for example, to achieve comparable reductions in recidivism by commitment to a certain kind of institution or by a certain kind of parole program; in cost-accounting terms, however, one might be more efficient than the other.

Still a third type of question has to do with social policy — that is to say, "What shall we *do?*" Obviously the answers to such questions take into

---

[74] See, especially, James F. Short, Jr. and Fred L. Strodtbeck, *Group Process and Gang Delinquency.*

account knowledge and notions, sound and unsound, about the workings of social control structures and programs, their effectiveness, and their efficiency. But they cannot be resolved on such grounds alone. Whenever we deal with questions of social policy we also take into account, explicitly or unwittingly, notions about what is worth doing, what price is worth paying, who shall pay the price, and what objectives are worth slighting in order to achieve other objectives. Some of these costs are not easily reduced to dollars and cents. We have come to take for granted, for example, that the control of crime entails restraint on our mobility, proof of identity, surveillance by police, undercover investigation of private lives, and police power to detain, interrogate, and embarrass people, some of whom eventually turn out to be innocent. How much are we willing to pay in these terms for a given reduction of crime? Or, stating it differently, how much crime will we put up with rather than make further payments in terms of freedom and privacy? Turning now from the costs of social control to the objectives, suppose that it were established that the liberal use of the death penalty had no significant effect upon the murder rate (and the evidence suggests, in fact, that this is so). From this some of us might infer that we might as well abolish the death penalty. But what shall we say to those who insist that, whether the death penalty is an effective deterrent or not, a man who wantonly takes another's life deserves to pay for it with his own? Even should "all the facts be in," the resolution of questions of public policy still involves a weighing of values in which men may differ, sometimes passionately. Such issues cannot be resolved by the accumulation of still more facts or the expert counsel of a scientific criminology. They are settled, if at all, by persuasion, by appeals to sentiment and interests, and by superior power.

We debate, criticize, and justify what we do—or advocate doing—about crime and delinquency in terms of motives, slogans, and formulas that are currently respectable. This "rhetoric of control" imposes real constraints on what we do, or at least on what we can do with a clear conscience, but it is a very imperfect indicator of the considerations that actually determine our conduct. We may act for reasons of which we are not fully aware, or which we are reluctant to acknowledge publicly. Very different policies, which we advocate for all sorts of obscure reasons, can be plausibly defended in terms of the same rhetoric, and the same policy can be defended in terms of different rhetorics. For example, in our culture it is highly respectable to couch one's advocacy in terms of "rehabilitation"; it is not nearly so respectable to invoke "an eye for an eye and a tooth for a tooth." At other times the situation has been reversed. But what we actually do and the reasons for which we do it may change less—or more—than the rhetoric in terms of which we defend it.

The Functions of Social Control

We have distinguished, in this chapter, between the things that people try to accomplish through social control policies, the values and interests they acknowledge or claim in debating these policies, and the actual effects, intended or unintended, upon individuals severally or on the state of the social system generally. "Functions" in the sense of values and interests acknowledged in the rhetoric are easy to determine; we listen to what people say. The other two "functions" are not so easy to determine. The imputation of motives, on the one hand, and the assessment of actual effects, on the other, must be inferred from a much broader range of evidence; they entail a lot more speculation, and they are harder to prove.

The functions that have figured most in the literature and popular discussion are retribution, deterrence, and rehabilitation. There can be no doubt that any one of these may figure as motives, as justification, and as effects. By retribution we mean the infliction of pain or deprivation for reasons of vengeance or satisfaction of a sense of justice. By deterrence we mean the discouragement of the offender from repeated offenses or the discouragement of others by the example of what happens to offenders. By rehabilitation we mean efforts to retrain the offender or somehow alter his personality or other circumstances of his life so that he will no longer want to commit offenses. In the current rhetoric of control, retribution is under a cloud, but is more admissible as a motive in dealing with adult criminals than with juvenile offenders, who are regarded as less "responsible" and more entitled to rehabilitative "help." Deterrence is justified pragmatically as a measure of "social defense," and a good deal of debate is couched in terms of alleged deterrent effects.

Punishment—the infliction of pain or deprivation generally—is not synonymous with retribution because retribution includes the intention of vengeance or justice. On the other hand, we do not list it separately as coordinate with the other three, because it is better thought of as a policy or practice that is itself in turn justified by its supposed contribution to retribution, deterrence, or rehabilitation. Consider, for example, the dispositions of juvenile courts, including commitments to institutions. They are certainly punishing—i.e., painful and depriving—in their effect. How *effective* they are in terms of deterrence and rehabilitation is variable, uncertain, and always debatable. The *intent* of the court (and this, of course, will vary with the court) is surely retributive much of the time, deterrent or rehabilitative some of the time. But the dispositions are usually *justified* in terms of re-habilitation, sometimes in terms of deterrence, and only rarely in terms of retribution, which is a bad word in the rhetoric of juvenile justice. Students of social control have also considered other possible functions of social control. One may be to help define the "moral boundaries" of the collectivity.

Let us assume that the members of a political community have a stake in projecting a certain image of that community, a set of claims about its distinctive virtues that set it off from other communities. Branding certain kinds of behavior as crimes and conspicuous efforts at repressing them may serve the purpose of publicly dramatizing the devotion and commitment of the community to these virtues. It is not necessary that the efforts be effective, because what is important is the message carried by the busy display of enforcement activity. If necessary, crime may even be invented in order to justify the enforcement; the prosecution of witches in seventeenth-century Massachusetts is a case-in-point.[75]

It is sometimes argued, although difficult to prove, that an important function of social control is to bolster the defenses of the controllers against their own unacceptable impulses to do the very things they are trying to repress. The reasoning is that all people, although some more than others, have unconscious urges to behave in ways that they cannot acknowledge in themselves. To seek out and punish wickedness in others is a way of denying their own impulses and reassuring themselves of their own innocence.

A very different way of interpreting changing practices in social control of crime is in terms of their costs and utility to influential social groups. According to this type of interpretation, for example, the transportation of prisoners for forced labor in the colonies was discontinued, and the renting out of inmate labor (as in the chain-gang system of the American South) and the use of inmate labor in prison industries declined in response to changes in conditions that made these practices unprofitable, or in response to the interests of powerful groups in the free community — e.g., labor unions — who were adversely affected by the competition of cheap prison labor. It is quite clear that the practical interests of powerful groups do play an important and sometimes a decisive part in shaping control policy but, as we have seen, such considerations operate alongside many others. The sociology of control systems is very complex, and our understanding of the circumstances that shape them and the way they work is still fairly elementary.

One implication of what we have been saying is that the things we do in the name of social control seldom succeed in accomplishing their alleged objectives; they are often contradictory and cancel one another out. This is

[75] Kai T. Erikson, *Wayward Puritans.*

not necessarily a commentary on the irrationality of human behavior. It is a commentary on the fact that any human institution responds to a variety of demands, many of them conflicting, and is therefore compromised, sometimes doing well none of the things that it is supposed to do, and sometimes even doing what nobody wants it to do. For example, we have discussed earlier the ways in which processing by the machinery of criminal and juvenile justice may reduce opportunities for lawful behavior and, through its effects upon the self-conception, strengthen one's commitment to unlawful behavior. We do not know how general this effect is but, taking "function" in the sense of practical consequences, we may state paradoxically that the production of criminal behavior is sometimes a function of social control.

One way of classifying specific programs and strategies of crime and delinquency control is by what we will call "levels of intervention."

1. *Individual treatment*. What distinguishes this level is not the control agent, for he might be a teacher, a minister, a Big Brother, a psychiatrist, or a probation officer; nor is it the methods he employs, for these might vary from fatherly advice to prolonged psychoanalysis. It is the fact that the control agent selects, or is assigned to, a particular target individual thought to be in need of treatment, and that the source of change in the target individual's behavior is supposed to lie somewhere in the interaction between him and the agent.

2. *Group treatment*. Group treatment, like individual treatment, may vary in many ways. What distinguishes this level is that the control agent works with a group of persons, either a natural group like a boys' gang or a group contrived and assembled for this purpose like many "therapy groups" in prisons, and the hoped-for change is expected to arise from the interaction of the worker and the group and the members of the group with one another.

3. *Institutionalization*. This means bringing together a number of target individuals in a self-contained and administratively controlled environment, segregated from the "inmates'" natural, everyday environment. Institutions vary from a small forestry camp for delinquent youngsters to a maximum security prison containing thousands of adult felons. The program, the discipline, the atmosphere, and the treatment philosophy can vary in numerous ways, and the institutional program could include various approaches to individual or group treatment. Although certain aspects of the program will, in the minds of the administrators, be thought of as "treatment" and others simply as "housekeeping," "management," and so on, institutionalization represents a transformation of the total experience-world of the inmate, any aspect of which might make a contribution, intended or not, to his subsequent behavior.

4. *Structural change*. Structural change in the community rests on one or

both of the following assumptions. (a) The aspects of the experience-world that most decisively affect a person's behavior cannot be reached by focusing solely on individuals, groups, or institutional populations defined as criminal or delinquent. The assumption is, rather, that the most relevant and important parts of their worlds are those they share with other people in the open community, like the school system, the system of race relations, and the job market. Therefore, what must be changed, in limited or in radical ways, is some aspect or aspects of the social structure of the community itself. (b) The approaches we have already considered, even if they are effective with offenders who have been identified by and processed through the machinery of social work or of juvenile or criminal justice, can only touch a small fraction of the iceberg of crime and delinquency. To achieve a broader impact we must concentrate on social changes that will transform the conditions of life for great numbers of people, not just for a selected and laboriously isolated few. The essence of structural change, then, is that it is directed at a population, or a segment of a population, from which offenders come – that is, a "population-at-risk" – rather than at particular, identified target individuals or groups.

Needless to say, even if we accept both of the foregoing assumptions, the question remains: What sorts of structural changes will be effective in reducing crime and delinquency in the population-at-risk? And behind this question are questions of a different kind: What will be the material and moral costs of such changes; are they worth it; who will pay them; and who should decide?

Control Strategies and Behavior Theories

On any level of intervention it is possible to proceed in many different ways. One way of approaching these differences is to consider the different theories about the origin and transformation of delinquent and criminal behavior and the kinds of procedures for effecting behavior change that seem to follow from them.

BIOLOGICAL THEORIES – If one assumes that the behavior in question stems from genetic or acquired biological defects – e.g., brain damage – then the alternatives seem to be fairly limited. Surgical or other biological intervention, if the defect can be reached in this manner, is a possibility. Special training of a compensatory nature is another. If one believes that the defects are transmitted by known mechanisms of heredity, one might advocate selective sterilization to reduce the incidence of the defect in the population. All these methods have been advocated and all have been tried, sometimes at great cost in terms of personal freedom. However, there is little evidence that biological theories account for any significant fraction of the great bulk of delinquency and crime and therefore little reason to think that such forms of intervention will contribute significantly to their reduction.

PSYCHIATRIC THEORIES—We deal with theories that interpret crime and delinquency as failures to control instinctual drives, mechanisms of defense, symptoms of unconscious neurotic conflicts, and the like. Although the theories vary greatly they have in common an explanation in terms of some defect or pathology of the personality; treatment must correct that defect. However, there is no single, obvious conclusion about how such changes are to be effected. Different psychiatric conceptions of etiology suggest different treatment strategies. For example, if the theory emphasizes the importance of long-buried and festering unconscious traumas or unresolved Oedipal complexes, treatment theory might emphasize techniques of making the unconscious conscious. On the other hand, if the theory emphasizes early learning experiences that have created unrealistically threatening and hostile images of the human environment, the treatment might seek to provide experiences that will result in a more realistic and discriminating view of the world.

Generally speaking, psychiatry has favored intervention at the level of individual treatment, in which a therapist meets periodically with a patient and, by manipulating the interaction in one way or another, tries to bring to light unconscious materials so that they can then be dealt with in a rational and constructive way; or to provide learning experiences that will undo the effects of earlier damaging and unrealistic learning. In recent years, however, psychiatrists have turned increasingly to *group therapeutic* techniques, with a view to utilizing the interaction among the members of the group to accomplish the same results.

OPPORTUNITY STRUCTURE THEORIES—The common element of these theories is the assumption that people resort to crime and delinquency because their opportunities to satisfy their wants in legitimate ways are restricted, either in consequence of a poverty of opportunity in their environments or of personal qualities, or by learning deficits that make it difficult for them to take advantage of such opportunities. Again, the implications for intervention that can be derived from such theories are various, depending in part on what aspects of the opportunity structure are seen as crucial and what techniques of changing it are believed to be effective. A Big Brother helping

a boy with reading or academic skills on the assumption that it will help
him to get along better in school and reduce the attractiveness of an out-of-
school delinquent style of life; a parole officer helping his parolee find
legitimate and rewarding work; and a psychiatrist helping a patient overcome fearfulness in social relations so that he can make and enjoy normal
friendships instead of filling the void in his emotional life by some sort of
"retreatist" drug experience, are all attempting to alter some aspect of the
opportunity structure thought to be relevant to the deviance in question.
These examples focus on individual targets, but an opportunity-structure
approach has implications for intervention on all levels. "Detached work,"
that is, working with natural street-corner groups on their own home ground,
can be seen as a set of techniques for opening up legitimate opportunities.[76]
To the extent that the worker concentrates on counseling with individual
boys, teaching them useful skills, trying to find them jobs, and so on, he is
really dealing with the group as a collection of individuals. On the other
hand, to the extent that he concentrates on providing them with knowledge,
skills, equipment that will make it possible for them to function more
successfully and command more respect *as a group*—as an athletic team,
a social club, a service organization—he is trying to enlarge the legitimate
opportunity structure on the group level of intervention. Many of the
activities in correctional institutions have as their object, and possibly as
their effect, an enlargement of legitimate opportunity, especially by impart-
ing habits and skills that will enable the inmates to take advantage of jobs
and other resources in the larger community. Finally, there are those programs that seek to transform opportunity structures by means of structural
changes that alter the conditions of life not only for identified individuals
and groups but for a population-at-risk. A program that seeks to create new
jobs, to break down ethnic and other barriers to employment in existing
jobs, or to provide training and experience to qualify people for successful
performance in these jobs is making an effort to expand legitimate opportunities for all those satisfactions that are dependent on income and occupation. Recent years have seen an increasing number of such programs, usually
funded by the federal government.

CULTURAL-TRANSMISSION AND SUBCULTURAL THEORIES—To the extent that
crime and delinquency are ways of conforming to the style of life called for
by a particular culture, behavior modification might be sought either by
(1) redirecting associations so that people are more exposed to law-abiding

---

[76] Irving Spergel, *Street Gang Work: Theory and Practice* (Reading, Mass.: Addison-
Wesley, 1966).

and anticriminal cultural patterns or (2) changing cultures so that they are more supportive of law-abiding behavior. Examples of programs with the first type of intention would be placement in foster homes, requiring probationers to avoid "bad associates" as a condition of probation, and transfer to institutional settings where the inmates will be insulated from the delinquent and criminal cultures of the larger community. (The paradox of the last device is that it brings together in intimate association a collection of people who have in common a history of illegal behavior and trouble with the law; on the basis of differential association theory this situation might be interpreted as rescuing people from the frying pan by dumping them into the fire.)

Suppose, however, that one takes his groups as he finds them, or even creates groups of people with similar histories of crime or delinquency, and seeks to change their culture. In recent years there have been a number of experiments along these lines, some of them initiated and under the control of courts, probation departments, and institutions, and others initiated and run by the subjects themselves. They include a form of group therapy called guided group interaction [77]; attempts to engage the total population of an institution in a collective effort to create an anticriminal culture, an approach known as the "therapeutic community" [78]; and Synanon,[79] which is a program for dealing with drug addiction based on principles applicable to other kinds of behavior as well, and which (along with Alcoholics Anonymous) is one of the best-known programs controlled and administered by the participants in the program. They also include detached work, if its objective is somehow to foster transformation of the group's culture. Although they differ in important ways, they have in common certain characteristics. The rewards and punishments for behavior and attitude change come from the group members, the people with whom one lives, works, and plays, and they come in the form of status and security in the group. The members of the group are people with similar "problems," so that each can speak with a certain expertise and authority that the others can respect; the force of no one's example or exhortations is weakened by the accusation that "he has

---

[77] See, for example, Lloyd W. McCorkle, Albert Elias, and F. Lovell Bixby, *The Highfields Story: An Experimental Treatment Project for Youthful Offenders* (New York: Holt, 1958).

[78] Maxwell Jones, *Social Psychiatry in the Community, in Hospitals, and in Prisons* (Springfield, Ill.: Charles C Thomas, 1962).

[79] Rita Volkman and Donald R. Cressey, "Differential Association and the Rehabilitation of Drug Addicts," *American Journal of Sociology,* Vol. 69 (September, 1963), pp. 129–42; Lewis Yablonsky, *The Tunnel Back: Synanon* (New York: Macmillan, 1965).

not been through it" and "does not know what it is like." The sought-for transformations of behavior are not seen as ways of placating or satisfying somebody in authority outside the group and with whom the members of the group do not identify, but as contributions to the group's own goals. Specifically, one makes his contribution to the group, and enhances his position in the group by an active effort, if he is a novice, to learn and practice the new culture, and by providing support, encouragement, and example if he is a veteran. In brief, one finds fulfillment of his own social needs and aspirations by taking over, making his own, supporting and maintaining, and converting others to a new way of life.

Opportunity structure theory can be seen, as it is in the work of Ohlin and Cloward, as an aspect of subcultural theory rather than a contrasting or rival theory. That is, subcultures may be understood as systems of norms and criteria of status that groups evolve to legitimize and make more rewarding a style of life that is itself an accommodation to the opportunity structure. Programs that emphasize structural change may envision as their long-range objective a change in the culture itself. The theory is that opening up new opportunities makes it possible for people to discover, explore, and practice new possibilities of action; to enhance their confidence in their power to accomplish what before seemed beyond their grasp and therefore not worth seeking; to develop new aspirations adjusted to the new conceptions of what is possible; and to evolve new, collectively supported values, beliefs, and standards to support a new style of life.

IDENTITY THEORY—The basic principle of identity theory is that most of what we do, whether it is deviant or conforming, is a way of persuading ourselves and others that we are the kind of person we claim to be. It follows, then, that what we do depends on (1) our identities, (2) the kinds of claims and expectations that go with those identities, and (3) the alternative courses of action, legitimate and illegitimate, open to us for fulfilling these claims and expectations. It follows further that efforts to change behavior will be successful if we can (1) change people's identities, or make some components of their identity more central and important and others less so; (2) change the meaning—that is, the claims and expectations—that goes with their identities; or (3) change the relative availability and costs of different ways of fulfilling those claims and expectations.

It becomes impossible to further pursue the implications of identity theory without talking at the same time about the ways it ties in with other theories. Consider, for example, the reference above to alternative ways of fulfilling the claims and expectations attached to an identity. Clearly we are speaking here of opportunity structure, but in relation to the question,

Opportunity for what? We are not contrasting identity theory with opportunity structure theory; we are emphasizing that the opportunities that make a difference, that can move people to action, and that are strategic for social control, are those that help them to realize the identities they claim or aspire to. Nor are we contrasting identity theory with subcultural theory; we are saying that, according to identity theory, what is critical about a culture is the kinds of identities it recognizes, the value it places upon them, and the meaning it gives to them. If we want to change behavior by changing the culture, these are the things about the culture that are important.

In similar fashion we might discuss the relationship of identity theory to other theories. On whatever level we intervene and by whatever techniques, those forms of intervention will be effective that reduce the utility of crime and delinquency and enhance the utility of law-abiding behavior as ways of achieving a valued identity.

MICROSOCIOLOGICAL PERSPECTIVE—According to the microsociological perspective, criminal and delinquent events have histories, and movement from one stage to another is dependent upon a host of situational facts and contingencies of the moment. This suggests that, where a control agent—e.g., a detached worker—can establish a close relationship with a group, he can be most effective in curbing delinquent behavior by being present on the street, continuously monitoring the flow of events, and by tactical intervention at critical points, altering or counterbalancing the contingencies that shape that flow. He may, for example, direct the attention of the group to circumstances that have been overlooked in the heat of momentary passions; he may do something to enhance the status of a particular member and thereby reduce his propensity to improve his position in the group by provocative actions; he may provide face-saving ways out of dangerous conflict situations where other members of the group could not do so without appearing "chicken." In fact, there is evidence that, as far as the detached worker is effective, he is so by this kind of intervention rather than by changing stubborn opportunity structures or bringing about fundamental changes in the personalities or values of the boys.[80]

A LEGAL APPROACH—One method of reducing crime and delinquency that might seem like a deceptive play on words is to change the law so that some

---

[80] See James F. Short, Jr. and Fred L. Strodtbeck, *Group Process and Gang Delinquency*; and Malcolm Klein, "Violence in American Juvenile Gangs: Causes, Prevalence, and Control," in *Violent Crime: A Task Force Report to the National Commission on the Causes and Prevention of Violence,* pp. 1427–60.

things cease to be criminal or delinquent. The proposal, however, is a serious one. Definitions of illegality and immorality are always historically determined and subject to change, and even when something is defined as immoral and a problem for social control, it does not follow that the heavy artillery of the criminal and juvenile-justice systems are the most effective weapons. In some cases it has been plausibly argued that attempts to control behavior by means of prohibitive laws may increase the very behavior the laws are intended to reduce.[81]

CONCLUSIONS

Our knowledge about the effectiveness of specific techniques of social control and behavior change is still rudimentary. However we do know that rates of recidivism are high under all systems of control that have been closely studied. We know that crime and delinquency continue to climb in the face of a multitude of programs, traditional and experimental, designed to cope with them. Perhaps we should not expect any particular technique for effecting behavioral change to produce dramatic and massive successes. One might even wish to argue that we should not want a society in which it were possible to stamp out crime and delinquency, on the grounds that this would require a concentration of control over people's lives that we would, or should find intolerable. It may be that the only measures of control that are compatible with a high degree of individual autonomy and respect for personality are those that can be expected to yield only moderate reductions in overall crime and delinquency.

Be that as it may, we do not even have much tested knowledge of the *relative* effectiveness of the methods that have been tried. But we do have theoretical grounds and some evidence for a few conclusions.

1. Attempts to modify behavior are most likely to be successful when the people concerned see those changes as instrumental to the fulfillment of their own aspirations, which means the validation of their identities and more satisfying relationships with people who are important to them. They are most successful when the *effort* to change (as in Synanon and Alcoholics Anonymous), as distinct from the final result, is itself rewarded by one's "significant others" and thereby sustained. They are most successful when the people concerned see themselves making choices of their own free will,

---

[81] See, for example, the discussion of laws restricting teen-age drinking in Chapter 5 of this text.

rather than merely complying with somebody else's instructions, whether he be a probation officer or a physician. We are not just throwing in a good word for autonomy and freedom of action because it is always safe to speak well of them. The point is that people feel more *responsible* for choices that are perceived as *their* choices and feel more committed to carrying through the corresponding course of action. It follows that those methods have the greatest promise that enlist the voluntary participation of the members of groups in collective efforts to effect changes in their own culture and style of life, changes that they see as contributing to their own dignity and their own aspirations.

2. Certainly people will continue to want to identify and do something about those individuals and groups that make life insecure and hazardous for others. However, piecemeal and narrowly focused efforts directed at identified lawbreakers, or even at the "hard core" of persistent recidivists,[82] are not likely to be very successful in effecting substantial reductions in overall levels of crime and delinquency. We have seen that there is much crime that cannot be traced to identified offenders; we have reviewed the argument that it is difficult to effect significant changes even in the behavior of identified offenders without changing the conditions of life that they share with the larger populations from which they come; and in any case, measures directed to identified offenders are measures taken in consequence of the crimes they have already committed. It is probable that substantial overall reductions can be accomplished only by structural changes (in which the people themselves participate) aimed at changing the conditions of life for an entire community or population-at-risk.

---

[82] It has been shown that a relatively small number of boys account for a disproportionately large percentage of all offenses — and especially of serious offenses — committed by juvenile lawbreakers. See Thorsten Sellin and Marvin Wolfgang, *Delinquency in a Birth Cohort* (forthcoming).

3

Delinquent and Criminal Structures

DONALD R. CRESSEY

There is a broad range of informal and formal organization among delinquents and criminals. Delinquent gangs, working groups of pickpockets, and criminal syndicates are all forms of criminal organization. Each of these units consists of a set of positions designed to achieve continuity and efficiency in delinquent and criminal endeavors. Thus each is an expression of rational, careful concern for efficient law-breaking operations.[1]

There is some degree of organization even in a group of two middle-class boys engaged in the casual shoplifting of a toy from a variety store. There is a greater degree of organization in high-school groups and college dormitory

---

[1] Any delinquent or criminal organization might provide nondelinquent and noncriminal services to its members. For example, gangs and other illegitimate groups might accord prestige to persons who have had difficulty achieving prestige in legitimate systems. This chapter, however, will focus on ways organizations serve the delinquent and criminal interests of their members. Parts of the chapter are adapted from Donald R. Cressey, *Theft of the Nation: The Structure and Operations of Organized Crime in America* (New York: Harper, 1969); Donald R. Cressey, "The Functions and Structure of Criminal Syndicates," President's Commission on Law Enforcement and Administration of Justice, *Task Force Report: Organized Crime* (Washington, D. C.: U. S. Government Printing Office, 1967), Appendix A, pp. 25–60; Edwin H. Sutherland and Donald R. Cressey, *Principles of Criminology,* 8th ed. (Philadelphia: Lippincott, 1970); and Donald R. Cressey and David A. Ward, *Delinquency, Crime and Social Process* (New York: Harper, 1969).

groups of friends who associate with each other frequently and who occasionally commit collective crimes, but who do not have specific delinquent or criminal goals. Delinquent gangs are more rational in their delinquent and criminal operations than friendship groups that engage in stealing on occasion: their divisions of labor are sometimes based on the requirements of specific team operations in crime. Small working groups of robbers, check passers, and automobile thieves, in turn, are more organized than delinquent gangs; and "professional" working groups of pickpockets, confidence men, and shoplifters are more organized than nonprofessional working groups. Further, criminal syndicates such as the Cosa Nostra are more organized than working groups of professional criminals in the sense that their organization more rationally provides for efficient law-violation.

An organization is an ongoing system whose existence is independent of its current membership. Any delinquent or criminal organization worthy of the name has been designed in such a way that it continues to violate the law even when its membership changes. Thus friendship groups are not necessarily delinquent or criminal organizations even if the members occasionally cooperate in a delinquency or a crime. But if two boys practice team shoplifting, with each boy having responsibility for part of the operation, then there is a delinquent organization. Each boy would be lost without the other, and if one boy quits the organization his position would be vacant. Street corner groups—often called delinquent gangs—are, at most, "informal" organizations. This kind of organization is simply a stabilized pattern of interaction based on similarities of interests and attitudes and, occasionally, on mutual aid. Interaction patterns have become routinized to a degree that it can be said that there is a "structure," a cluster of role-relationships, but the structure is not necessarily perceived as serving collective purposes. The organization has not been made very rational—it is not carefully designed for the purpose of making profits, conferring status, committing crime, or anything else. Street corner groups and other cliques have their own standards, attitudes, and opinions, as well as an effective system of communication and common defenses against "outsiders." Some of the members might have shared the danger of arrest or the pains of incarceration. But street corner groups barely possess the degree of rationality that characterizes more "formal" organizations.

Unlike the structures of street corner groups and other informal organizations, the structures of formal organizations allocate certain tasks to certain members, limit entrance, and influence the rules established for their own maintenance and survival. As structures of informal criminal organizations take on the rationality essential to creating a criminal division of labor—what in criminal law is called a "continuing criminal conspiracy"—

they become formal organizations, but the line dividing the two kinds of organizations is not sharp.

Formal organizations, criminal or otherwise, have three characteristics that indicate rationality. *First,* a division of labor is present. There is occupational specialization, and each specialty fits into the set of occupations. *Second,* the activities of each person in the system are coordinated with the activities of other members by rules, agreements, understandings, and codes that support the division of labor. *Third,* the entire enterprise is purposively designed to achieve announced objectives.[2] All these features are matters of degree, so it might properly be said that some organizations are more "formal" and thus more "organized" than others. It is in this sense that criminal syndicates are located further along on an organizational continuum of rationality than are delinquent gangs and working groups of criminals.

Among criminal organizations, the degree to which these features are present affects the character of the crimes perpetrated. There is, for example, the shoplifting team of two or more boys, each of whom has vaguely come to see a set of role-relationships as serving express criminal purposes. Then there is the professional pickpocket team that has a rather precise division of labor and rather careful coordination of the occupational activities of each member, but only loose control of each member's life style. Further along the continuum there is the criminal syndicate in which members' activities are tightly coordinated by the definitions of the position that each member occupies in the division of labor, and where further control is exercised by enforcement of a criminal code that governs most of the interpersonal relationships of members even when they are "off the job."

JUVENILE GANGS

The term "informal organization" appropriately describes role-relationships that have more to do with social life and life styles than with occupational specialization. Some so-called delinquent gangs barely qualify as even informal organizations, but others move up the ladder and qualify as formal organizations because the labor is quite precisely divided. The latter probably should be called working groups rather than gangs, but a careful

---

[2] *Cf.* Stanley H. Udy, Jr., "The Comparative Analysis of Organizations," in James G. March, ed., *Handbook of Organizations* (Chicago: Rand McNally, 1965), Chapter 16, pp. 678, 687–88.

distinction between the two kinds of juvenile organizations is rarely drawn.

Most juvenile gangs do not engage in delinquency. Accordingly, they are not delinquent organizations. Almost all boys, and many girls, are members of groups that they call "gangs," but the activities of these groups—even their mild rowdyism—are quite harmless. Bloch and Niederhoffer attribute groupings of this kind to the problems arising in the transition from the status of child to the status of adult, and they find "gang behavior" in many cultures.[3] In some neighborhoods, these childhood cliques assume the form of street clubs with rather vague and rapidly changing leadership. A member of a Los Angeles street club, the Rebel Rousers, described his group's social activities as follows:

> When the club first got started, we didn't have no specific activities, you know, like every day we'd go over to the park and lay down and talk and drink all day. Not many 12-year-old boys go around drinking wine; but 'cause everybody else did it, I did it too. Maybe on weekends, everybody goin' to a swimmin' pool or somethin'. We usually stayed at one another's house, and stayed together most of the time, play cards, something like that. We'd go down to the park and talk. At night, them that was goin' to school they'd come down to the park.[4]

Street clubs, in turn, sometimes join together in loose confederations. Frequently a portion of the neighborhood boys of about the same age and with similar attitudes toward delinquency have a common meeting place and engage in many delinquent activities without any formal organization. A stranger would not be permitted to associate with the members of these street clubs and federations of clubs, and certain boys might be ostracized, but the groups are not organized for delinquency. In some areas of high delinquency, all the cliques of boys who live on one street, or the cliques of boys with membership in the same ethnic group, join together for purposes of fights and are known by a common name. Spergel has shown that gangs oriented to "bopping" and defending the "turf" have elements of a hierarchical structure of the kind characterizing formal organizations. There are organizational positions for, at least, a president, a vice president, a war chief, and an armorer.[5] The activities of these fighting gangs are systematic

---

[3] Herbert A. Bloch and Arthur Niederhoffer, *The Gang: A Study in Adolescent Behavior* (New York: Philosophical Library, 1958).

[4] R. E. Rice and R. B. Christensen, *The Juvenile Gang: Its Structure, Function, and Treatment* (Los Angeles: Los Angeles County Probation Department Research Report No. 24, 1965), p. 21. See also Edward Eldefonso, *Law Enforcement and the Youthful Offender: Juvenile Procedures* (New York: Wiley, 1967), pp. 247–66.

[5] Irving Spergel, *Racketville, Slumtown, Haulburg: An Exploratory Study of Delinquent Subcultures* (Chicago: University of Chicago Press, 1964), pp. 42–45.

and ritualized, but their goals are neither clear nor precise. Accordingly, their structure is not tightly integrated. Short and Strodtbeck have stressed the nonutilitarian, expressive character of such gangs as follows:

> . . . we may describe our conflict-oriented gangs as *invested in their reputation for fighting vis-a-vis certain other gangs.* This investment gives the boys a group identity which provides incentive for conflict involvement and a basis for "threats" to leadership and to group status. The structure of these groups provides another clue to their orientation. Unlike other gangs, *they create roles expressive of their conflict orientation,* e.g., war counselor and armorer. Competition for those roles was observed among members of several gangs. This is not to say that the duties and privileges of such offices were clearly defined or performed. Instead of such formal role specifications and expectations, these roles tended to be the focus of ceremonial deference within the group. The existence of such roles provided yet another basis for individual status and group identity which were conflict oriented.[6]

One analysis suggested that street clubs and loose confederations are not even groups, let alone delinquent organizations. They were called "near groups," and the argument underlying this characterization is that these gangs are merely loose associations of individual boys who are trying to work out their own emotional problems in group activities.[7] There is little consensus, little identification with the group, and unstable leadership. Thrasher observed the unorganized character of Chicago delinquent gangs in the 1920's.[8] Even gangs that are "organized" for the achievement of some objective such as protection of turf from invaders, and that have senior, junior, and midget sections, do not have a precise division of labor. Such gangs often disintegrate if a leader is arrested or moves out of the neighborhood—there is no organizational position to be filled by another boy. In 1962, the staff of a research project in two areas of high delinquency in Chicago had contact with 35 groups, all of which had names such as Aristocrats, Dukes, Top Boys. Fifteen months later, in 1963, the staff had contact with 44 such groups, but only 15 were continued by name from 1962; 20 of the 1962 names had disappeared from the list, and 29 new names had appeared.[9]

[6] James F. Short, Jr. and Fred L. Strodtbeck, *Group Process and Gang Delinquency* (Chicago: University of Chicago Press, 1965), p. 200. See also Malcolm W. Klein and Lois Y. Crawford, "Groups, Gangs, and Cohesiveness," *Journal of Research in Crime and Delinquency,* Vol. 4 (January, 1967), pp. 63–75.

[7] Lewis Yablonsky, "The Delinquent Gang as a Near-Group," *Social Problems,* Vol. 7 (Fall, 1959), pp. 108–17.

[8] Frederic M. Thrasher, *The Gang* (Chicago: University of Chicago Press, 1927), pp. 35–37.

[9] Hans W. Mattick and Nathan S. Caplan, *The Chicago Youth Development Project*

Clearly, street clubs are ephemeral, as had been suggested. But while it may be true that the members of these gangs are trying to work out their emotional problems, it is not at all certain that emotionally disturbed boys are attracted to them in a disproportionate degree. A Chicago study found only 10 percent of the members of street clubs were emotionally disturbed enough to be referred to a casework agency.[10]

A little further along the continuum of rationality are so-called retreatist gangs of drug users.[11] Studies of the group activities of "cool cats" and "righteous dope fiends" have suggested that street addicts are neither "retreatist" nor organized gangs.[12] The structure of role-relationships in such groups has more to do with life styles than with occupational specialization. Most street addicts participate in ongoing social structures with distinctive styles of language, clothing, and definitions of appropriate behavior, but the activities are not organized around a rationally planned and coordinated effort to achieve specific goals. The main features of the world of the "cat" and the "righteous dope fiend" are the "hustle" and the "kick." The former involves the person's activities as a pimp; the latter involves relationships relevant to drug use. Drug users are not even organized to secure a constant and safe source of drugs. The distribution and sale of drugs is left to formally organized criminal groups; those who use drugs are not necessarily members.

Delinquent gangs engaging in theft, fraud, robbery, and extortion clearly represent the meeting ground of informal and formal criminal organizations. Some of them are merely informally organized street groups that engage in thefts occasionally even if not oriented to this kind of activity. Others are like bopping gangs, more formally organized, with names, leaders, passwords, slogans, and a rudimentary division of labor.[13] They

---

(Ann Arbor: University of Michigan Institute for Social Research, 1964), pp. 96, 104. Cited by Ruth Shonle Cavan, *Juvenile Delinquency,* 2nd ed. (Philadelphia: Lippincott, 1969), p. 262.

[10] Charles H. Shireman, *The Hyde Park Youth Project, May 1955 – May 1958* (Chicago: Welfare Council of Metropolitan Chicago, undated), p. 147.

[11] See Richard A. Cloward and Lloyd E. Ohlin, *Delinquency and Opportunity: A Theory of Delinquent Gangs* (New York: Free Press, 1960), pp. 111–24, 161–86.

[12] Harold Finestone, "Cats, Kicks, and Color," *Social Problems,* Vol. 5 (July, 1957), pp. 3–13; Alan G. Sutter, "Worlds of Drug Use on the Street Scene," in Donald R. Cressey and David A. Ward, *Delinquency, Crime and Social Process,* pp. 802–29.

[13] The distinction between gangs oriented to drug use, to bopping and defense of turf, and to theft is difficult to maintain in practice. Although criminal activity is found in nearly all street corner groups and conflict gangs, criminally oriented gangs (as distinct from working groups of juvenile thieves) are difficult to find. See James F. Short, Jr. and Fred L. Strodtbeck, *Group Process and Gang Delinquency,* pp. 11–13. This research failed to locate a "full-blown" delinquent gang oriented to theft.

may persist for decades with changing personnel. Such a delinquent gang "is a means of disseminating techniques of delinquency, or training in delinquency, or protecting members engaged in delinquency, and of maintaining continuity in delinquency." [14] It is not necessary that there be bad boys inducing good boys to commit offenses. It is generally a mutual stimulation, as a result of which each boy commits delinquencies he would not commit alone. [15] The gang educates each member in the ways of theft, but it is not purposively designed to do so. Yet the fact that there is a rudimentary division of labor—for "leaders" and "planners," if nothing else—suggests that the delinquencies of each boy are necessarily coordinated with the delinquencies of others.

But an *organized* delinquent gang, in the formal sense, is devoted to theft rather than merely oriented to it. Gangs of this kind are, as indicated, working groups of juvenile thieves whose criminal activities are rationally planned and coordinated. Assignments to perform specific tasks related to theft are given to individuals. In a boys' working group organized for robbery, for example, one boy drives the car, a second carries a gun and acts as lookout, while a third carries a gun, does the talking, and collects the cash. The assignment of tasks, of course, varies with the offense to be committed. Each man rehearses his role, whether it be that of wiring the ignition of the automobile to be stolen, distracting a store clerk, or picking the "burglar-proof" locks on houses.

Short and Strodtbeck found such juvenile working groups of thieves to be organized *within* larger conflict gangs, street clubs, and confederations:

> None of our gangs is properly characterized as a "criminal subculture," or a carrier of such a subculture. No clear separation between criminal and conflict emphases is apparent from the factor analysis or from observational data. The latter suggests, however, that various criminal activities may characterize *cliques of conflict gangs.* Data from a large, white street-corner group *without discernible delinquency specialization* . . . also suggest that "criminal cliques" may develop within such groups. In the observed case a clique of eight boys formed exclusively around rationally directed theft activities—auto stripping, burglary, shoplifting, etc. This clique did not hang together on the corner, but met in one another's homes. When on the corner they hung with other members of the larger group. They participated in the general hanging and drinking patterns, and in occasional altercations with various adults as part of this larger group, but not as a distinguishable

---

[14] John B. Mays, "A Study of a Delinquent Community," *British Journal of Delinquency,* Vol. 3 (July, 1952), pp. 5–19.

[15] See Albert K. Cohen, *Delinquent Boys: The Culture of the Gang* (New York: Free Press, 1955), pp. 59–61.

clique. *Only in their pattern of theft activities were they a clique.* For at least two years they were reasonably successful in these activities, in terms of money and goods acquired, in fending or selling directly to customers, and in avoiding arrest or "fixing" arrests when they were apprehended.[16]

But even when this level of formal organization is present, the ultimate ambition of members of the working group is likely to be that of moving out of the clique and into a career as a professional thief or a syndicated criminal. The members do not view their criminal specialization as their occupation, and they are only vaguely governed by a code relating to their activities. Nevertheless, thefts by cliques of boys clearly show the transition from generalized social activity involving delinquency to specialized occupational careers requiring rational planning, and, consequently, the establishment of formally organized structures.

Members of both street clubs and organized gangs are committed to a set of norms in opposition to those held by law-abiding groups of the larger society. They have "withdrawn their attribution of legitimacy to certain of the norms maintained by law-abiding groups of the larger society and have given it, instead, to new patterns of conduct which are defined as illegitimate by representatives of official agencies." [17] The activities of delinquent groups follow the rules that make up the delinquent subcultures of the specific neighborhoods where their members reside. American society has become organized in such a way that a premium has been placed on both perpetrating crime and refraining from crime. A boy living in this society may be a member of a neighborhood group organized for criminal behavior and, at the same time, a member of another group organized against criminal behavior. Under such conditions of differential group organization, one would expect delinquency rates to be relatively high, for there are "rules for delinquency" as well as "rules against delinquency." The various "rules for delinquency" constitute delinquent subcultures. Although new sets of values ("rules for delinquency") that make delinquency "all right," even if illegal, are invented from time to time, most apparent inventions are merely variations on old themes, invented long ago.[18]

---

[16] James F. Short, Jr. and Fred L. Strodtbeck, *Group Process and Gang Delinquency,* p. 98.

[17] Richard A. Cloward and Lloyd E. Ohlin, *Delinquency and Opportunity: A Theory of Delinquent Gangs,* p. 19.

[18] David J. Bordua, "Delinquent Subcultures: Sociological Interpretations of Gang Delinquency," *Annals of the American Academy of Political and Social Science,* Vol. 338 (November, 1961), pp. 119–36.

Various types of delinquent subcultures have arisen and thrive at different locations in the social structure. The evidence is fragmentary, impressionistic, and uncoordinated, but it seems to indicate that some types of delinquent and criminal subcultures have developed in large metropolitan centers, particularly in those areas of cities that are characterized by poverty; other types have arisen among middle-class persons and in rural areas. Because the sets of delinquent values are located in different parts of the social structure, they are not equally available for adoption by all segments of the society.[19] Working-class persons living in the slum areas of large cities come into contact with a different kind of delinquent subculture than do upper-class persons. And even within slum areas, alternative kinds of delinquent values are available, with the result that juvenile groups in these areas are not all organized for the achievement of the same ends.

Cloward and Ohlin, among others, have attempted to account for the invention of delinquent subcultures. Following the leads provided by Durkheim and Merton, they conclude that different types of delinquent subcultures have been invented as a response to a clash between values that promote unlimited aspirations and a social structure that restricts accomplishment of those aspirations.[20] They observe that among some segments of the population the possibilities of legitimately achieving even *limited* success goals are restricted, and they find three types of delinquent subcultures in these areas of poor opportunity. Two of these subcultures provide illegal avenues to success goals: the "criminal subculture," which contains rules for the pursuit of material gain by such means as theft; and the "conflict subculture," which contains rules for achieving status through the manipulation of force or the threat of force. The other subculture, the "retreatist subculture," contains rules favoring the consumption of drugs. The basic notion here is that the subcultures are invented when aspirations are frustrated and when the frustration is diagnosed as due to the conditions of

---

[19] John P. Clark and Eugene P. Wenninger, "Socio-Economic Class and Area as Correlates of Illegal Behavior Among Juveniles," *American Sociological Review,* Vol. 27 (December, 1962), pp. 826–34; Edmund W. Vaz, "Middle-Class Adolescents: Self-Reported Delinquency and Youth Culture Activities," *Canadian Review of Sociology and Anthropology,* Vol. 2 (February, 1965), pp. 52–70; and Kenneth Polk and David S. Halferty, "Adolescence, Commitment, and Delinquency," *Journal of Research in Crime and Delinquency,* Vol. 3 (July, 1966), pp. 82–96.

[20] Robert K. Merton, "Social Structure and Anomie," *American Sociological Review,* Vol. 3 (October, 1938), pp. 677–82. (This article has been revised and enlarged, and it now appears in Robert K. Merton, *Social Theory and Social Structure,* rev. ed. (New York: Free Press, 1957), pp. 161–94). Émile Durkheim, *Suicide: A Study in Sociology,* translated by George Simpson (New York: Free Press, 1951), pp. 246–57. (This book was first published in Paris in 1897.)

the social order rather than to personal attributes of the interacting but frustrated population.[21]

Delinquent street corner groups and delinquent gangs are, above all, important agencies for maintaining and diffusing the values that make up delinquent subcultures. In groups engaging in theft, a boy's social position in the group can be maintained if he can "score" now and then, and if he can exhibit the behavior patterns of a "real man" or a "thief."[22] In street groups engaging in fighting and violence, a member's social position depends upon frequent exhibitions of "heart" and skill in the use of violence. Fighting groups are almost constantly involved in negotiations with each other, and, as demonstrations of strength, many agreements, alliances, and contracts are made. "These are generally pseudobargains, which serve as means for gang members to flex muscles they are unsure they have."[23] In groups engaging in drug use, the individual can lay claim to "rep" by displaying his ability to obtain drugs and to increase the experience of the "kick."

Spergel has shown that the degree of rationality characterizing a delinquent group varies with the subculture and social organization of the social area supporting the group. His study of three neighborhoods—"Slumtown," "Haulburg," and "Racketville"—showed, for example, that bopping and defending the turf were the principal gang activities in Slumtown. Two-thirds of the residents of this neighborhood were Puerto Rican; 24 percent were black. Ten percent of the male working force was listed as unemployed. The neighborhood was poorly integrated, delinquents were principally oriented to standards of legitimate or conventional culture, and relationships between offenders of differing age levels were tenuous. Consistently, the delinquent gangs were engaged principally in fighting each other. A considerable number of delinquent groups were in varying states of "peace" and "war." "The typical fighting group of young delinquents was as much estranged from the adult criminal system as from the adult conventional system."[24]

Gang fighting occurred less frequently in Haulburg, a neighborhood that on the surface appeared to be sedate, respectable, and cosmopolitan. A dis-

---

[21] Richard A. Cloward and Lloyd E. Ohlin, *Delinquency and Opportunity: A Theory of Delinquent Gangs,* pp. 111–24.

[22] See John Irwin and Donald R. Cressey, "Thieves, Convicts and the Inmate Culture," *Social Problems,* Vol. 10 (Fall, 1962), pp. 142–55.

[23] Lewis Yablonsky, *The Violent Gang* (New York: Macmillan, 1962), p. 157. See also Walter B. Miller, "Violent Crime in Street Gangs," *Annals of the American Academy of Political and Social Science,* Vol. 343 (March, 1966), pp. 97–112.

[24] Irving Spergel, *Racketville, Slumtown, Haulburg: An Exploratory Study of Delinquent Subcultures,* p. 20.

tinctly middle-class atmosphere permeated its streets. Stealing was the most pervasive activity among delinquents, but the boys were not organized for stealing. Their thefts as a rule were not carefully planned or executed. Nine out of ten delinquents admitted frequent participation in car theft — the median involvement was 30 instances. "In Haulburg car theft appeared to have a function similar to gang fighting in Slumtown or being a 'tough guy' in Racketville. In each neighborhood, delinquent behavior was a way of demonstrating conformity with the model of 'big shot' or 'important guy.' " [25] While "the burglary or theft pattern represented a more systematic and purposeful orientation in Haulburg than in other areas," [26] the delinquents rarely formed into continuing working groups of thieves. The boys who were engaged in apartment burglary knew who the neighborhood fences were, and they sometimes arranged to sell stolen items to a fence even before the goods had been stolen. Further evidence of rationality and organization appeared in the fact that some boys were highly skilled at picking locks and disposing of stolen goods. But while the organization of a deliberate income-producing theft pattern was most developed among the boys of Haulburg, most of the stealing, even in this neighborhood, was for "fun."

Racketville was the most affluent of the three neighborhoods, as measured by median income. Over 42 percent of its residents were of Italian origin and mainly of the first American-born generation; 25 percent were Puerto Ricans. Syndicated criminals were the standard-bearers of this neighborhood, and the boys were oriented to their style of life. Older boys carefully instructed younger boys in proper attitudes, dress, and demeanor. Seniority and influence of the next older generation appeared to be inviolate:

> Little Augie, Monk, and Freddie were excited by the presence of the younger fellows. They acted as big brothers and bosses. They told them to straighten their collars, to be wary of "fags," or homosexuals, to talk straight. Monk said that the fellows had better look nice so that if they ever got into a fight and the cops picked them up, they, the cops, would be baffled and would probably conclude, "These fellows are too well dressed and too nice; they couldn't be involved," and they would be released.[27]

While upper-echelon positions in the criminal syndicate were not available to Racketville delinquents, they aspired to membership in this organization. A few were given opportunities to prepare for roles in the rackets. Some participated in illegal lottery operations ("numbers"), primarily

---

[25] *Ibid.,* p. 48.
[26] *Ibid.,* p. 52.
[27] *Ibid.,* p. 23.

through family connections. For example, one boy drove his uncle's Cadillac to pick up the receipts from a numbers seller. Another boy was elated when a man he said was "big" in the numbers racket asked him to perform a minor errand. He said this might be a "break" for him, that this "big shot" might give him a job paying "a couple hundred dollars a week for hardly doing nothing," that he would be able to arise late in the morning, have girls, and go to nightclubs. The boys themselves engaged in usurious moneylending (loan-sharking), and during the course of Spergel's study two boys were arrested for systematic loan-sharking while still attending school.

The delinquent boys in Racketville developed a keen business sense, which was not characteristic of the boys in the other two areas, and were also more "criminally oriented." The influence of syndicated crime in this area was further reflected in the fact that the delinquents in the neighborhood believed, to a greater degree than the boys in the other two areas, that having "connections" (as opposed to having "ability," "luck," or "education") was the most important quality for getting ahead. On the other hand, drug use and gang fighting were not regarded as commensurate with the cool, rational approach to life demanded of organized criminals, and these activities occurred in Racketville less frequently than in either Slumtown or Haulburg.

WORKING GROUPS

Small groups, each organized for the execution of a particular type of crime, have existed for centuries. The small criminal groups that operated in England in the Elizabethan period have been described in some detail.[28] Similar groups exist today for the purpose of burglary, robbery, shoplifting, confidence games, pocket-picking, passing worthless checks, and stealing automobiles. Some, but not all of these groups differ from specialized juvenile gangs involved in the same kinds of activities principally in that their members have become "professionalized." This means, essentially, that they operate more rationally than do the juvenile groups, or even amateur or transitory groups of adult criminals.

Sutherland pointed out years ago that the term "professional" when applied to a criminal refers to the following things: pursuit of crime as a regular, day-by-day occupation; development and use of skilled techniques in

---

[28] A. V. Judges, *The Elizabethan Underworld* (London: Routledge, 1930); Frank Aydelotte, *Elizabethan Rogues and Vagabonds* (Oxford: Clarendon Press, 1913).

that occupation; certain shared understandings, agreements, and attitudes; high status among criminals; and identification of self as a thief.[29] Thus professional criminals include the "loner" who uses his skills to commit his own burglaries or robberies; and he commits them outside any working organization. Usually, however, professional criminals subordinate their individual activities and skills to the collective interests of two or three other professional criminals. When this occurs, there is organized professional theft: the formal division of labor calls for several specialized occupational skills that when coordinated, increase efficiency.

The principal occupations of professional thieves are confidence games, shoplifting, and pocket-picking. The organization of a working group of professional criminals varies with the specific goal being sought, and the positions and roles making up a team of confidence men are different from those making up a team of pickpockets. The techniques, skills, and divisions of labor characterizing these groups are often ancient, having been developed over a period of centuries. Codes of behavior, *esprit de corps,* understandings, attitudes, and consensus about criteria of high and low status extend beyond the boundaries of any working group; they are characteristics of the profession. Professional criminals carefully select their teammates and other colleagues. They associate with each other and rarely associate with nonprofessionals on the same basis, even if the outsiders are other criminals. They tend to look down on amateur thieves and juvenile delinquents, referring to them as "neurotic kids" because their poorly planned crimes arouse the police and the public, making the serious practice of theft more difficult and less profitable.

The consistently dishonest bond salesman is not a professional; neither is the Cosa Nostra member who runs an illegal gambling game. Men engaged in these occupations work regularly at crime, possess technical skills, and sometimes perform roles in working groups. But they do not identify themselves as thieves and do not have high status among thieves. Even the men or boys playing roles in organized working groups of burglars and automobile thieves are not necessarily professionals in this sense. Juveniles operating in working groups view their activities as recreation or as training for better things, not as professional activities. Similarly, few adult burglars regard themselves as professionals, or even as burglars, and few are so regarded by other criminals. Although a working group of armed robbers can have all the characteristics of a professional group, and although a robber or extortionist can be professional, professional thieves working in confidence

---

[29] Edwin H. Sutherland, *The Professional Thief* (Chicago: University of Chicago Press, 1937), pp. 3–5, 197–215.

games, shoplifting, and pocket-picking tend to look down on robbers, just as they look down on bopping gangs of juveniles. These thieves use the non-violent techniques of the salesman and the actor to manipulate the interests, attention, and behavior of the victim, and consider a criminal who relies on force or the threat of force crude and quite unskilled. Most professional confidence men are proud of the fact that they, unlike the robber, almost always give the victim a chance to say "No." Robbers, in turn, are likely to view confidence men as swindlers of widows and orphans, and to view pickpockets and shoplifters as spineless crooks who do not dare stage a hold-up.

Certain types of crimes can be committed without previous experience in crime. Murder by shooting, for example, can be committed by a person with no experience in murder and, for that matter, with very little experience in shooting. But most crimes require training. Boys residing in high delinquency areas are taught how to commit thefts of various kinds. If a ten-year-old boy moves into some areas of New York, Chicago, or any other large city, he has to learn many criminal techniques and attitudes to keep his new-found friends. The members of his street club or clique show him how to steal articles from department stores, how to steal from a truck, how to steal an automobile, how to roll a drunk. The training extends to knowledge about effective behavior when caught. He learns when to cry and when not to cry, and what kinds of lies to tell parents, police, and court officials. The criminal sophistication of such a boy is much greater than that of adult episodic offenders such as murderers, embezzlers, and rapists, even if the boy is not playing a specialist role in a delinquent gang.

Professional crime is a rational extension of this training. But the rationality of a working group of professional criminals extends beyond acquisition of the manual and social skills necessary for executing the crime itself. It includes planning, prior location of target areas and victims, and prior preparation for avoiding punishment in case of detection. Arrangements are made in advance for bail, legal services, and fixing the case. The rational system for making these arrangements, as well as the use of technical skills, among other things, distinguishes professional thieves from ordinary thieves. Yet in professional crime the rationality does not extend to the point where a syndicate is developed, as in what is traditionally called "organized crime."

Sutherland observed the rationality behind the operations of working groups of criminals in three different contexts, all of them concerned with continuing safe and profitable operations as well as with a specialized division of labor.[30] First, the division of labor is such that all incumbents must be skilled in the use of specific techniques that in combination make the

---

[30] *Ibid.*, pp. 217–18.

whole group's work safe and therefore profitable. They develop these skills through tutelage and practice. "Skills" include organizational talent such as employing one man to maneuver a victim so that another can pick his pocket; or utilizing one member of a shoplifting team to distract attention from another by kicking a child or otherwise creating a commotion; or employing an "outside man" ("roper," "steerer," "catchman") to put a likely confidence-game victim in touch with the "inside man" ("spieler," "lickman").[31] An extensive study of pickpockets indicated that the fundamental form of organization in the occupation is the "tribe," "mob," "troupe" or "team" of two, three, or four members. The relationships among the men occupying the positions in the team's division of labor are "loose, ephemeral, and highly insecure,"[32] but there is organization nevertheless. The duties and responsibilities constituting each position are finely detailed. There is a position for a man (a "stall" or "steer") whose duty is to locate the prospective victim (the "mark") and distract his attention. Another position calls for a specialist who is skilled in removing the wallet from the victim's pocket ("hook," "tool," "wire," "mechanic"). A third position (also a "stall") requires skills in receiving the wallet from the man who took it, and in concealing it.

A very high degree of individual skill is necessary for filling such specialized roles. Many of the pickpockets whose job it is to remove a victim's belongings from his person have sufficient dexterity to steal a victim's watch from his wrist or his belt from his trousers. Confidence men playing an old game called "pigeon drop" must have the sleight-of-hand essential to exchanging pieces of cut-up newspaper for money. And professional shoplifters must have enough ingenuity to utilize shoplifting devices such as innocent-looking boxes with false bottoms, trousers with hidden pockets and liners, false arms, and rubber suction cups attached to strings and elastic bands.[33] The rational development of such skills helps make professional theft safer and more profitable than ordinary theft.

Second, Sutherland observed that the crimes committed by teams of criminals tend to be those whose nature makes it difficult to apprehend and successfully prosecute the perpetrators. Picking pockets is relatively safe because the legal rules of evidence require direct evidence that the thief with-

---

[31] Robert Louis Gasser, "The Confidence Game," *Federal Probation,* Vol. 27 (December, 1963), pp. 47–54.

[32] David W. Maurer, *Whiz Mob: A Correlation of the Technical Argot of Pickpockets with Their Behavior Pattern* (Florida: American Dialect Society Publication No. 24, 1955), p. 84.

[33] Mary Owen Cameron, *The Booster and the Snitch: Department Store Shoplifting* (New York: Free Press, 1964), pp. 45–49.

drew the item from the pocket, and such evidence is difficult to obtain. Shoplifting is relatively safe because store employees do not want to run the risk of accusing legitimate customers of stealing, and of making themselves liable for false arrest suits. Confidence games are relatively safe because the victim often agrees to participate in a dishonest transaction, and when he finds that he is the victim he cannot make a public complaint without disgracing himself.[34] For example, in the confidence game called "the rag" a victim joins a group of thieves in what he thinks is a conspiracy to defraud the holders of worthless stock. He believes the confidence men when they tell him they have dishonestly obtained "inside" information regarding the great value of the stock, but when he puts up the necessary capital he learns that the stock is indeed worthless. Some confidence games do not depend upon the victim's willingness to do something dishonest, but even these games are quite safe, principally because the victim does not discover that he has been cheated until long after the transaction has been completed. For example, in "pigeon drop" an old lady is persuaded to withdraw her life's savings from a bank on some pretext, watches while the confidence men put her money in a suitcase, holds the suitcase for a specified period such as a week or two, then discovers that the "money" she saw go into the suitcase was in fact pieces of newspaper.[35]

Third, in some groups of working criminals, including all groups of professional criminals, rational organization for safety and profit involves the establishment of at least one organizational position for "corrupter" and one or more positions for "corruptees." The corruptee position is occupied by a public official who, for a fee, insures that the group can operate with relative immunity from the penal process. It is as much a part of the criminal organization as is any other position. The professional criminal expects that every case will be fixed. He rarely bribes a store detective, policeman, prosecutor, or judge himself. He relies upon his corrupter, who sometimes needs only to promise the victim that his stolen property will be returned, sometimes with a bonus, if he will refuse to press charges or if he will testify in a way that will not damage the thief. Sometimes the corrupter employs policemen to help persuade victims to accept restitution. If these corrupting devices fail, a policeman may be bribed not to file a complaint, or, if a complaint is filed, not to testify truthfully. The prosecutor may be induced to drop the charge against the thief or, if prosecution is inevitable, to bungle the case.

---

[34] Edwin M. Schur, "Sociological Analysis of Confidence Swindling," *Journal of Criminal Law, Criminology, and Police Science,* Vol. 48 (October, 1957), pp. 296–304; and David W. Maurer, *The Big Con* (Indianapolis: Bobbs-Merrill, 1940).

[35] See Julian B. Roebuck and Ronald C. Johnson, "The Short Con Man," *Crime and Delinquency,* Vol. 10 (July, 1964), pp. 237–45.

As a last resort, the judge may be bribed to find the thief not guilty or to impose a minor penalty.

As Maurer has said about pickpockets, "The dominant culture could control the predatory cultures without difficulty, and what is more, it could exterminate them, for no criminal subculture can operate continuously and professionally without the connivance of the law." [36] The President's Commission on Law Enforcement and Administration of Justice agrees, saying, "Professional crime would not exist except for two essential relationships with legitimate society: the 'fence' and the 'fix.' " [37] Professional theft exists because some persons are willing to steal, but also because the rest of the society has created a place for professional theft in its total organizational structure.

Professional criminals display a certain lack of concern and sympathy when dealing with the public, and especially in dealing with victims. This is a part of the attitude that goes with professionalism. Just as a businessman operates on the principle that "business is business," the professional criminal operates on the principle that "crime is crime." There is no place for sentiment in either case. Yet professional criminals are not "wanton criminals." Amateur criminals, not professionals, stir up the police and public by displays of toughness, violence, and bravado. A group of young criminals recently made a successful daylight robbery of a liquor store across the street from a police station, and as they drove away they shot out a station window. Another criminal, on trial in a courtroom filled with policemen, bailiffs, and spectators, secured a gun and tried to shoot his way out of the room. Such acts might give the criminal status in his group, but not in the profession of theft. Professionals avoid "heat." Professional pickpocket teams, for example, could easily pick the pockets of policemen and judges, but they deliberately try to avoid doing so because this behavior would antagonize those who have the power to put restraints on the pocket-picking profession. Professionals are rationally motivated.

SYNDICATED CRIME

Although there is a wide range and variety of criminal organization, the term "organized crime" is customarily used to refer only to a system based

---

[36] David W. Maurer, *Whiz Mob: A Correlation of the Technical Argot of Pickpockets with Their Behavior Pattern*, p. 129.

[37] President's Commission on Law Enforcement and Administration of Justice, *The Challenge of Crime in a Free Society* (Washington, D. C.: U. S. Government Printing Office, 1967), p. 46.

on an extension of the rational design of working groups of professional criminals; that is, "organized crime" is used as a synonym for syndicated crime, not for the varieties of criminal organization. At the core of American syndicated crime is a membership organization, "La Cosa Nostra," sometimes called "The Mafia." The organizational base of "organized crime" or "syndicated crime" can be understood by studying Cosa Nostra, but it should be understood that this organization is only part of a larger whole.

While it is true that the division of labor in Cosa Nostra has been designed for the perpetration of crimes that cannot be perpetrated profitably by small working groups of criminals, let alone by criminals working outside an organization, the critical difference is not merely a difference in size. Small firms selling illicit goods and services such as illegal bets, usurious loans, and nonunion labor must, if they are to capitalize on the great demand for their wares, expand by establishing a division of labor that includes positions for financiers, purchasing agents, supervisors, transportation specialists, lawyers, accountants, and employee-training specialists. The next rational move is consolidation and integration of separate divisions of labor into a cartel designed to minimize competition and maximize profits. Such a monopolistic move is, of course, a rational decision for peace. As such, it necessarily involves governmental considerations and positions as well as business considerations and positions. Cosa Nostra's contemporary division of labor reflects the fact that it is at once an illegal, monopolistic cartel and an illegal, unofficial government.

The Cosa Nostra syndicate grew out of the working groups organized to meet the demand for illicit alcohol during the period of national prohibition. Almost from the first, the manufacture, distribution, and sale of prohibited alcohol was in the hands of organized groups, rather than of isolated, individual criminals. There were many such groups, at first organized on a neighborhood or ethnic basis. With increasing competition, violent warfare broke out; some of the smaller units were fused into larger units, and these larger units were fused into loosely organized regional syndicates.[38] The process was exactly the same as in legitimate business, though the methods inclined more to violence and less to fraud than in legitimate business. While the syndicates were using warnings, destruction of property, and murder as means of stifling competition in the illicit business, law-enforcement agents, acting under orders from political leaders, were harassing new

---

[38] See Donald R. Cressey, *Theft of the Nation: The Structure and Operations of Organized Crime in America*, pp. 59–63; and Henry B. Chamberlin, "Some Observations Concerning Organized Crime," *Journal of Criminal Law and Criminology*, Vol. 22 (January, 1932), pp. 652–70.

manufacturers or dealers who tried to enter the illegal liquor business. Nevertheless, the syndicated criminal organizations were never secure, and a true nationwide alliance never developed. Subordinates were ambitious, and some of the gangs were rebellious. Since the entire business was illegal, control depended finally on violence.

Near the end of the prohibition period, the basic framework of the current structure of syndicated crime was established as the final product of a series of gangland wars in which an alliance of Italians and Sicilians first conquered other groups, then fought each other. A decision for peaceful coexistence was made in 1931, and that decision, which amounted to a peace treaty, has determined the shape of American syndicated crime ever since. When the period of national prohibition ended, the new alliance of Sicilians and Italians, now called "Mafia" or Cosa Nostra, moved into other illicit fields.

Members of Cosa Nostra currently control all but a tiny part of the illegal gambling in the United States. They are the principal usurers (loan sharks), and the principal importers and wholesalers of narcotics. They have infiltrated certain labor unions, where they extort money from the employers and, at the same time, cheat the members of the union. The Cosa Nostra has a virtual monopoly on some legitimate enterprises, such as cigarette vending machines and jukeboxes, and it owns a wide variety of legitimate retail firms, restaurants and bars, hotels, trucking companies, food companies, linen-supply houses, garbage collection routes, and factories. It has corrupted officials in the legislative, executive, and judicial branches of government at the local, state, and federal levels. Measured by amount of profit, Cosa Nostra is one of America's largest business enterprises. The President's Commission estimated that syndicated crime costs Americans almost $9 billion—more than all other types of crime combined, and just about double the amount spent annually in the United States for all police, court, and correctional work.[39]

Extensive investigations and studies of the structure of the Cosa Nostra justify the conclusion that it is indeed an organization, with both formal and informal aspects. When there are specialized but integrated positions for a board of directors, presidents, vice presidents, staff specialists, works managers, foremen, and workers, there is an economic organization. When there are specialized but integrated positions for legislators, judges, and administrators of criminal justice, there is a political organization. Like the large legitimate corporations that it resembles, Cosa Nostra has both

---

[39] President's Commission on Law Enforcement and Administration of Justice, *The Challenge of Crime in a Free Society,* p. 33.

kinds of positions, making it both a business organization and a government. Further, the Cosa Nostra exists independently of its current personnel, as does any big business or government. No man is indispensable. If a president, vice president, or some other functionary resigns or dies, another person is recruited to fill the vacant position. Organization, or "structure," not persons, gives Cosa Nostra its self-perpetuating character.

The highest ruling body in the confederation is the "commission." This body serves as a combination board of business directors, legislature, supreme court, and arbitration board, but most of its functions are judicial. Members look to the commission as the ultimate authority on organizational disputes. It is made up of the rulers of the most powerful of the 24 Cosa Nostra "families," the name given to a geographical unit of the organization.[40] From nine to twelve men usually sit on the commission. The commission is not a representative body, and its members do not regard each other as equals.

Beneath the commission are the 24 "families," each with its "boss." The "family" is the most significant level of organization and the largest unit of criminal organization in which allegiance is owed to one man, the boss. (Italian words are often used interchangeably with each of the English words designating a position in the division of labor. Rather than "boss," the words *il capo, don,* and *rappresentante* are used.) The boss's primary function is to maintain order while at the same time maximizing profits. Subject to the possibility of being overruled by the commission, his authority is absolute. He is the final arbiter in all matters relating to his branch of the confederation.

Beneath each boss of at least the larger "families" is an "underboss" or *sottocapo.* This position is essentially that of vice president and deputy director of the "family" unit. The man occupying the position often collects information for the boss; he relays messages to him; and he passes his orders down to the men occupying positions below him in the hierarchy. He acts as boss in the absence of the boss.

On the same level as the underboss there is a position for a "counselor" or adviser. Such members are referred to as *consiglieri* or *consulieri.* The person occupying this position is a staff officer rather than a line officer. He is likely to be an elder member who is partially retired after a career in which he did not quite succeed in becoming a boss. He gives advice to "family" members, including the boss and underboss, and therefore enjoys considerable influence and power.

Also at about the same level as the underboss is a "buffer" position. The

---

[40] Because the "families" are fictive, in the sense that the members are not all relatives, it is necessary to refer to them in quotation marks.

top members of the "family" hierarchy, particularly the boss, avoid direct communication with the lower-echelon personnel, the workers. They are insulated from the police. To obtain this insulation, all commands, information, money, and complaints generally flow back and forth through the buffer, who is a trusted and clever go-between. However, the buffer does not make decisions or assume any of the authority of his boss, as the underboss does.

To reach the working level, a boss usually goes through channels. For example, a boss's decision on the settlement of a dispute involving the activities of the "runners" (ticket sellers) in a particular numbers game, passes first to his buffer, then to the next level of rank, the "lieutenant" or *capodecina* or *caporegima*. This position, considered from a business standpoint, is analogous to works manager or sales manager. The person occupying it is the chief of an operating unit. The term "lieutenant" gives the position a military and governmental flavor. Although *capodecina* is translated as "head of ten," there apparently is no settled number of men supervised by any given lieutenant. The number of such leaders in an organization varies with the size of the organization and with the specialized activities in that organization. The lieutenant usually has one or two associates who work closely with him, serving as messengers and buffers. They carry orders, information, and money back and forth between the lieutenant and the men in his regime, they do not share his administrative power.

Beneath the lieutenants there might be one or more "section chiefs." Messages and orders received from the boss's buffer by the lieutenant or his buffer are passed on to a section chief, who also may have a buffer. A section chief may be deputy lieutenant in charge of a section of the lieutenant's operations. In smaller "families," the positions of lieutenant and section chief are combined. In general, the larger the regime, the greater the power of the section chief. Since it is against the law to consort for criminal purposes, it is advantageous to reduce the number of individuals who are directly responsible to any given line supervisor.

About five "soldiers" (also called "buttons," or just "members" or "people") report to each section chief or, if there is no section chief position, to a lieutenant. The number of soldiers in a "family" varies; some "families" have as many as 600 members, some as few as 20. A soldier might operate an illicit enterprise for a boss, on a commission basis, or he might "own" the enterprise and give a percentage of the profits to the boss for "protection," the right to operate. Partnerships between two or more soldiers, and between soldiers and men higher up in the hierarchy, including bosses, are common. An "enterprise" could be a usury operation, a dice game, a lottery, a bookmaking operation, a smuggling operation, or a resort hotel. Some soldiers and most upper-echelon "family" members have interests in more than one business.

The authority structure sketched out above constitutes the "organizational chart" of Cosa Nostra as it is described by its members. Three things are missing. *First,* there is no description of the many organizational positions necessary to actual street-level operation of illicit enterprises such as bookmaking establishments and lotteries. Many of the positions in such enterprises are occupied by persons who are not Cosa Nostra members. *Second,* and more important, the structure described is primarily only the "official" organization, such as that which might be described by the organizational chart of a legitimate corporation. Cosa Nostra informants have not described (probably because they have not been asked to do so) the many "unofficial" positions any organization must contain. To put the matter in another way, there is no description of the many functional roles performed by the men occupying the formally established positions making up the organization. *Third,* the structure as described by members is the structure of membership roles, not of the relationships between members and indispensable outsiders like street-level workers, attorneys, accountants, tax experts, and corrupt public officials.[41]

Although Cosa Nostra functions as an illegal and almost invisible government, its political objective is not in competition with the established agencies of legitimate government. It is not interested in political and economic reform. Its political objective is a negative one: nullification of government.

Nullification is sought at two different levels. At the lower level are the agencies for law enforcement and the administration of criminal justice. When a Cosa Nostra soldier bribes a policeman, a police chief, a prosecutor, a judge, or a license administrator, he does so in an attempt to nullify the law-enforcement process. At the upper level are legislative agencies, including federal and state legislatures as well as city councils and county boards of supervisors. When a "family" boss supports a candidate for political office, he does so in an attempt to deprive honest citizens of their democratic voice, thus nullifying the democratic process.

The two levels are not discrete. If an elected official can be persuaded not to represent the honest citizens of his district on matters pertaining to the interests of organized criminals, he is, at the same time, persuaded that he should help insure that some laws are not enforced, or are enforced selectively. When the political "representative" of a district works to prevent the passing of laws that would damage the Cosa Nostra but help honest citizens, the political process has been nullified. But when the same "representative"

[41] For these details, see Donald R. Cressey, *Theft of the Nation: The Structure and Operations of Organized Crime in America,* pp. 126–85.

is paid by criminals to block appropriations for law-enforcement agencies that would fight organized crime, to block the promotion of policemen who create "embarrassing incidents" by enforcing antigambling statutes, and to use his political position to insure that dishonest or stupid administrators of criminal justice are appointed, he is being paid to nullify the law-enforcement process. The American Bar Association's *Report on Organized Crime* concluded, "The largest single factor in the breakdown of law enforcement dealing with organized crime is the corruption and connivance of many public officials." [42] Similarly, the President's Commission concluded, "All available data indicate that organized crime flourishes only where it has corrupted local officials." [43]

The operations of organized crime should never be referred to as the operations of the "underworld." The activities of Cosa Nostra members are so interwoven with the activities of "respectable" businessmen and government officials that such a reference directs attention to the wrong places. Lindesmith long ago warned, "It is a mistake to regard the underworld as a separate detached organization. It is rather an integral part of our total culture." He pointed out that syndicated crime flourishes in the culture characterizing most large American cities:

> An individualistic predatory philosophy of success, indifference to public affairs, general disregard for law, the profit motive, decentralized government, laissez-faire economics, and political practice which is often as openly predatory as the rackets, have produced in our great cities a fertile breeding ground for organized crime. [44]

Every Cosa Nostra "family," like every working group of professional criminals, has in its division of labor at least one position for a "corrupter." The person occupying this position bribes, buys, intimidates, threatens, negotiates, and sweet-talks himself into a relationship with police, public officials, and anyone else who might help "family" members maintain immunity from arrest, prosecution, and punishment. The corrupter is not depicted on the "organizational chart" that informants and others have sketched out as they have described Cosa Nostra's hierarchy from commissioner to soldier.

---

[42] American Bar Association, *Report on Organized Crime and Law Enforcement* (New York: American Bar Association, 1952), p. 16.

[43] President's Commission on Law Enforcement and Administration of Justice, *Task Force Report: Organized Crime,* p. 6.

[44] Alfred R. Lindesmith, "Organized Crime," *Annals of the American Academy of Political and Social Science,* Vol. 217 (September, 1941), pp. 76–83. See also Daniel Bell, "Crime as an American Way of Life," *Antioch Review,* Vol. 13 (June, 1953), pp. 131–54.

It is an essential, but "unofficial," functional position, like that of buffer, and might be occupied by a soldier, a lieutenant, an underboss, or even a boss. Most frequently, the position of corrupter is occupied by the *consiglieri,* or counselor.

For every corrupter, there must be at least one corruptee. Most corrupt policemen and public officials have been sought out and wooed to the position of corruptee. Men must be recruited and selected for this position just as they must be recruited and selected for a position such as bookmaker or lieutenant. Occasionally, a corrupter does not have to recruit a public official to a corruptee position because the corrupter's "family" has, with the help of the corrupter, recruited him in advance and put him in office. In 1962 a member of a city council who was "owned" by the Cosa Nostra resigned after a meeting with the boss, giving "ill health" as the reason. The boss then picked one of his relatives for the job, but this man withdrew from candidacy when his association with the boss was publicized by alert newspapermen. Another man was later selected by the boss, and this one won the election, despite the fact that he did not meet the residence requirements. This deficiency was discovered, and the man resigned about sixty days after he was elected. The boss then gave the seat to a man who was the partner of a well-known usurer. In the same district, also in 1962, a United States congressman who employed the son-in-law of the boss as his assistant fell out with the boss, who told him to resign. He did so immediately, giving "health of wife" as his reason. The boss selected another man to assume the congressional seat, and his son-in-law stayed on as the new congressman's assistant. In this district, Cosa Nostra also controls judges and the officials who assign criminal cases to judges. About 90 percent of the organized-crime defendants appear before the same few judges. It may properly be said that the entire political district is "owned" by a Cosa Nostra boss. Both law enforcement and democracy have been nullified.

We have suggested that the owners and managers of the large American enterprise selling illicit goods and services must be governors as well as business executives. The illegal character of the crime cartel turns the cartel into a confederation, a governmental organization as well as a commercial organization. The authority structure of Cosa Nostra "families" and of the relationship among the "families" and their bosses, is the structure of a government as well as a business. The governmental structure of Cosa Nostra is superimposed on the operations of any specific illegal business owned or operated by Cosa Nostra, often with drastic results. For example, a soldier who operates a numbers game must produce profits, but he also must obey his superiors. Should he disobey the boss, he is likely to be punished or murdered, even if his disobedience brings in greater profits.

The fundamental basis of any government, legal or illegal, is a code of conduct. Governmental structure is always closely associated with some code of behavior that its members are expected to follow. The legislative and judicial processes of government are concerned with the specification and enforcement of this code, whether or not it is clearly set down in rules precise enough to be called "law." A behavioral code, such as the Ten Commandments, becomes "law" only when it is officially adopted by a state. Yet the distinction between a state and other types of organization, such as a church, an extended family, or a trade union, is quite arbitrary. The distinction is most difficult to maintain in the case of societies where patriarchal power is found.[45] The problem can be illustrated by gypsies, who have no territorial organization and no written law, but who do have customs, taboos, and a semijudicial council that makes decisions about the propriety of behavior and, on the basis of these decisions, assesses damages and imposes penalties. The problem also can be illustrated by Cosa Nostra "families" and the confederation between them. Behavior in these "families" is controlled by a government that is a substitute for the state, even if the code being enforced can in no sense be considered "criminal law" or "civil law."

Cosa Nostra members, professional thieves, and sophisticated juvenile delinquents all follow specialized codes of behavior. The codes are not the same for all types of crime or all types of criminals. There are, however, two very general rules. One is a prohibition against informing. "Be a stand-up guy," "Keep your eyes and ears open and your mouth shut," and "Don't sell out" are variations on this theme. The second is a prohibition against dishonesty. "Don't burn your partner," "Don't interfere with each other's interests," "Be loyal to the mob," and "Be a man of honor," are some of the variations. A less general rule, but one that characterizes both professional theft and syndicated crime, demands a certain degree of aloofness and sophistication. "Have class," "Know your way around the world," and "Be independent" are variations of it. Even less general is a Cosa Nostra rule demanding the corporate rationality necessary to conducting illicit businesses in a quiet, safe, and profitable manner. "Be sharp," "Don't engage in battle if you can't win," and "Be a member of the team" express this idea. The last rule means that violence involving other Cosa Nostra members and stealing from members are to be avoided. The directive extends to personal life. It means, for example, that neither a soldier nor any other member is to use narcotics, to be drunk on duty, to get into fights, to have an affair with another member's wife or (if married) with the sister or daughter of a member, or to do much of anything without first checking with his superiors.

Unquestionably, these commandments are violated frequently. On the

---

[45] See E. J. Hobsbawm, *Primitive Rebels: Studies in Archaic Forms of Social Movement in the 19th and 20th Centuries* (New York: Norton, 1965).

other hand, it is sometimes surprising how much punishment a syndicated criminal will endure rather than inform on other criminals. In Cosa Nostra, the commandments are enforced by direct, violent punishment. The table of organization provides for "enforcers" and "executioners." These positions, like others, are not to be confused with the persons occupying them. The positions are more often unoccupied than occupied. The man who moves into an enforcer or executioner position and behaves in terms of its duties and obligations might occupy it for only a few days and then never occupy it again.

Any person occupying the position of enforcer makes arrangements for injuring or killing other members and, occasionally, nonmembers. The person occupying the position does not himself injure or kill anyone. He performs functions analogous to those performed by a prison warden or the prison official who makes the arrangements for imposing the death penalty. This means that the position must necessarily be integrated with a number of others, including a position for the person actually doing the killing or maiming (executioner), and a position for the person (boss, underboss, or commissioner) giving orders to and participating in "understandings" with the person occupying the enforcer position. Moreover, since these positions, like the enforcer's functions, are political, they must necessarily be coordinated with other governmental positions and functions of a legislative, adjudicative, or law-enforcement character. The enforcer position is necessarily one of a subset of positions existing within a broader division of labor designed to maximize organizational integration by means of "just" infliction of punishment on code violators. The presence of an enforcer position in a criminal organization must, in other words, be taken as evidence of the presence of complementary governmental positions, the epitome of organizational rationality.

The rationality of working groups of criminals, as compared with that of juvenile street clubs, is suggested by the provision for the corrupter and corruptee positions. The further rationality of the Cosa Nostra is indicated by the existence of these two positions plus the enforcer position. The members of organizations such as pickpocket troupes, check-passing rings, and juvenile gangs are likely to take punitive action against any member who holds out more than his share of the spoils, or who betrays the group to the police. But unlike Cosa Nostra, these organizations have not been rationally organized in advance to enforce specific rules prohibiting organizational dishonesty and disloyalty. They do not, among other things, recruit or train persons for a well-established enforcer position. They are not governments. The members of a gypsy band that engages in a wide variety of criminal activities are likely to censure, condemn, and in other ways punish a participant who cheats his fellows or informs the police about their crimes. Gypsy organization probably includes an enforcer position. It is clear, however, that gypsies do not have positions for corrupters and corruptees. Thus their structure is not the structure of the Cosa Nostra.

Cosa Nostra, its allies, and its subsidiaries thrive in the United States because a large minority of citizens demand the illicit goods and services they have for sale. As Walter Lippmann observed at the end of the prohibition era, the basic distinction between ordinary criminals and organized criminals in the United States turns on the fact that the ordinary criminal is wholly predatory, while the man participating in crime on a rational, systematic basis offers a return to the respectable members of society.[46] If all burglars were miraculously abolished, they would be missed by only a few persons to whose income or employment they contribute directly—burglary insurance companies, manufacturers of locks and other security devices, police, prison personnel, and a few others. But if the confederation of men employed in illicit businesses were suddenly abolished, it would be sorely missed because it performs services that are in great public demand. By definition, the syndicated criminal occupies a position in a social system, an organization, that has been rationally designed to maximize profits by performing illegal services and providing legally forbidden products demanded by the members of the broader society in which he lives. Just as society has made a place for the confederation by demanding illicit gambling, alcohol and narcotics, usurious loans, and a cheap supply of labor, the confederation has made places, in an integrated set of positions, for the use of the skills of a wide variety of specialists who furnish these goods and services.

It is true, of course, that criminals who do not occupy positions in any large-scale organization also supply the same kinds of illicit goods and services supplied by the confederation. A gray-haired old lady who accepts a few horse-racing bets from the patrons of her neighborhood grocery store performs an illegal service for those patrons, as does the factory worker who sells his own brand of whisky to friends at the plant. Law violators of this kind do not seem very dangerous, and, if treated in isolation, such persons cannot be perceived as much of a threat to the social order. Accordingly, they tend to be protected in various ways by their society: The policeman is inclined to overlook the bookmaker's offenses or merely to insist that they not occur in his precinct; the judge is likely to invoke the mildest punishment the legislature has established; and the jailer is likely to differentiate such offenders from "real criminals."

But such providers of illegal services cannot be individual entrepreneurs

[46] Walter Lippmann, "Underworld: Our Secret Servant," and "The Underworld: A Stultified Conscience," *Forum*, Vol. 85 (January and February, 1931), pp. 1–4 and 65–69.

for long. The nature of the illegal lottery and bookmaking business is such that bookmakers must join hands with others in the same business. Bookmakers and lottery operators are organized to insure that *making* bets is gambling but *taking* bets is not. Other illicit businesses have the same character. Free enterprise does not exist in the field of illicit services and goods — any small illicit business must soon take in, voluntarily or involuntarily, a Cosa Nostra member as a partner.

By joining hands, the suppliers of illicit goods and services (1) cut costs, improve their markets, and pool capital; (2) gain monopolies either on certain illicit services or on all of the illicit services provided in a specific geographic area, whether it be a neighborhood or a large city; (3) centralize the procedures for stimulating the agencies of law enforcement and administration of justice to overlook the illegal operations; and (4) accumulate vast wealth, which can be used to attain even wider monopolies on illicit activities, and on legal businesses as well. The demand in America for illicit goods and services produces huge Cosa Nostra profits, which are then invested in legitimate enterprises in politics. Robert F. Kennedy made the following statement while he was attorney general of the United States: "What is at least disturbing — and for me insidious — is the increasing encroachment of the big businessmen of the rackets into legitimate business." [47] Cosa Nostra members have been, and are, acquiring and operating legitimate enterprises, ranging from Las Vegas casinos to huge corporations. Moreover, some of them have deposited huge sums in Swiss banks, and they draw on these fruits of crime whenever they want to buy or corrupt another segment of America.

In the long run, then, the "small operation" corrupts the traditional economic and political procedures designed to insure that citizens need not pay tribute to a criminal in order to conduct a legitimate business. The demand and the profits are too great to be left in the hands of small operators. As the Kefauver Committee reported about the demand for gambling services, "The creeping paralysis of law enforcement which results from a failure to enforce gambling laws contributes to a breakdown in connection with other fields of crime." [48] Organization, not gambling or usury or narcotics distribution or labor racketeering or extortion or murder, is the phenomenon to worry about.

The principal operations of organized criminals are not independent of

---

[47] *Hearings Before the Permanent Subcommittee on Investigations of the Senate Committee on Governmental Operations,* 88th Congress, 1st Session, 1963, p. 12.

[48] Special Committee to Investigate Crime in Interstate Commerce (Kefauver Committee), *Third Interim Report* (U. S. Senate Report No. 307, 82nd Congress, 1st Session, 1951), p. 37.

each other. Bet-taking, usury, narcotics distribution, labor fraud and extortion, corruption of government, and control of legitimate businesses all go together. Legitimate interests serve as an outlet for the vast amounts of money acquired illegitimately and also provide a tax cover. With the aid of lawyers and accountants, some of whom have done tours of duty as employees of the Internal Revenue Service, members of Cosa Nostra now claim that it is extremely difficult to catch them in income-tax evasion. Ownership of legitimate enterprises creates an aura of respectability. Moreover, by investing the profits of illicit businesses in legitimate businesses, the member is able to earn more money, which is the fruit of crime and therefore contraband. When contraband money is invested in legitimate businesses, it is almost impossible to trace it to its criminal source.

SYNDICATED CRIME AND DELINQUENCY

Although syndicated crime touches every American, the direct victims are the citizens living in the deteriorated areas of our large cities. The economic base of organized crime's multibillion dollar investments in legitimate business and in politics is the precious money of the urban poor. The War on Poverty has not been a smashing success at least in part because government money poured into ghettos goes immediately from the pockets of the poor to the pockets of syndicated criminals. From there, the money goes toward nullification of the very economic and political processes that make the War on Poverty possible in the first place.

Numbers games and bookmaking businesses thrive on the dollars of unskilled blacks and other inner-city residents, not on bets placed by the rich, the educated, the well-housed, the well-employed. Similarly, the American drug addict is likely to be poorly educated and unskilled, a resident of a central-city area, and a member of a disadvantaged ethnic minority group. And it is the factory worker, the marginal businessman, and the urban welfare recipient, not the suburbanite, who frequently is so desperate for a loan that he seeks out a loan shark.

Cosa Nostra is a membership organization, and "family" membership ends at the soldier level. About 5000 men of Italian and Sicilian descent are now members, view themselves as members, and take special cognizance of other members. But not all the persons making a living from syndicated crime are members of Cosa Nostra. For example, very few of the public officials corrupted by Cosa Nostra are members, yet the services they provide are essential to the continuing operations of the organization. Accordingly, the corruptee is part of syndicated crime even if he is excluded from membership in the core organization.

Similarly, the persons occupying the lowest levels of the division of labor constituting syndicated crime ordinarily are not Cosa Nostra members. These are the "street men" involved in the retailing of Cosa Nostra's illicit goods and services, such as narcotics and bet-taking. They also fill the organization's needs for personnel to provide low-level services such as driving trucks and cars, delivering messages, running errands, picking up illegal betting slips, and answering the thousands of telephones utilized by bookmakers. They have no buffers or other forms of insulation from the police. In the ghetto areas of large cities, much of the street work is done by blacks. These street-level workers are employed by Cosa Nostra in much the same way corruptees are employed. That is, they may be part-time employees paid on a piece-work basis, or full-time salaried employees, or commissioned agents.

Commissioned agents are the most affluent street-level syndicated criminals. Some of them solicit bets for centrally located bookmakers who have title to a neighborhood. Others sell illegal lottery tickets. Still others are considered the "owners" or "bankers" of illegal lotteries. These last men are likely to be called "independents" because they are not members of Cosa Nostra. But they are not independent. Each of them must give a percentage of his gross to a Cosa Nostra member for the privilege of doing business in his territory.

The street-level commissioned agents working in black ghettos ordinarily are black men. All of them—and especially the "independent" numbers bankers—have high status in their neighborhoods. They are the "hustlers" with the ready bank roll, the Cadillac, the Omega watch, the $85 alligator shoes, and other symbols of affluence. Despite the fact that discriminatory practices prevent black commissioned agents from moving up into the echelons of Cosa Nostra where the *real* money is, these organized criminals are the idols of young ghetto residents. They are men who have made it.[49]

The National Advisory Commission on Civil Disorders recently noted that poverty, violence, and syndicated crime activities combine to produce great cynicism about the idea that success is to be achieved by legitimate means. The Commission succinctly stated what many other persons and agencies have observed:

---

[49] See Victor Eisner, *The Delinquency Label: The Epidemiology of Juvenile Delinquency* (New York: Random House, 1969), p. 94; and Charles Keil, *Urban Blues* (Chicago: University of Chicago Press, 1966), p. 20.

With the father absent and the mother working, many ghetto children spend the bulk of their time on the streets — the streets of a crime-ridden, violence-prone and poverty-stricken world. The image of success in this world is not that of the "solid citizen," the responsible husband and father, but rather that of the "hustler" who takes care of himself by exploiting others. The dope sellers and the numbers runners are the "successful" men because their earnings far outstrip those men who try to climb the economic ladder in honest ways.

Young people in the ghetto are acutely conscious of a system which appears to offer rewards to those who illegally exploit others, and failure to those who struggle under traditional responsibilities. Under these circumstances, many adopt exploitation and the "hustle" as a way of life, disclaiming both work and marriage in favor of casual and temporary liaisons. This pattern reinforces itself from one generation to the next, creating a "culture of poverty" and an ingrained cynicism about society and its institutions.[50]

As far as urban ghettos are concerned, Cosa Nostra is comparable to an invading army. Its troops have conquered territory and, with the assistance of the local traitors who serve them, have made a certain peace with the residents, including law-enforcement agents. The alliances of syndicated criminals operating in inner-city areas contribute to more general crime and delinquency rates in three interrelated ways. *First,* by their opulence the persons engaged in organized crime demonstrate to the people, and especially to the young, that crime does pay. *Second,* by their very presence, organized criminals demonstrate the existence of a rich vein of corruption in political and law-enforcement organizations, making it difficult for parents and others to convince children that people get ahead in the world by good, hard, honest labor. *Third,* the presence of organized crime in a neighborhood lowers the status of the people in the district, just as do conditions of squalor, with the result that anticriminal admonitions lose their effectiveness because the people have less to lose if convicted of crime.

If an organization is to survive, it must have an institutional process for enlisting new members and inculcating them with organizational values and ways of behaving. But the most successful recruitment processes are those which do not appear to be recruiting techniques at all. These are the processes by which membership becomes highly desirable because of the rewards and benefits prospective members believe it confers on them. These, also, are the processes that enable inner-city youth to find niches in the world of crime.

---

[50] National Advisory Commission on Civil Disorders, *Report* (New York: Bantam, 1968), p. 262.

Some boys grow up knowing that it is a "good thing" to be a banker, to belong to a certain club, to attend a certain university. They know these are "good things" because men they emulate have done them. Other boys—those in the central areas of our large cities—grow up knowing that it is a "good thing" to be a street-level syndicated criminal, to have the respect of established criminals, and to be given the opportunity to learn the skills and attitudes necessary to bookmaking or numbers selling. Still other slum boys—like those in Spergel's "Racketville"—grow up knowing that if they have the right qualifications and connections they might be admitted to membership in Cosa Nostra itself, thus becoming eligible for a share of the billions of dollars Cosa Nostra makes annually from the illegal bets placed with the street-level workers who are employed by Cosa Nostra.

Many slum boys grow up in social situations in which the desire for participation in syndicated crime comes naturally and painlessly. The former assistant chief of Brooklyn South Detectives has reported that in some Brooklyn neighborhoods, boys grow up under two "flags."[51] One is the flag of the United States, symbolizing middle-class institutions, tradition, and culture. The other is the flag of syndicated crime, symbolizing criminal society. Stated in more general terms, the principle is this: Persons growing up in some geographic and social areas have a good chance to come into contact with norms and values that support legitimate activities (in contrast to criminal activities); while for those growing up in other areas the reverse is true. In many inner-city areas, alternative educational processes are in operation, so that a child may be educated in either conventional or criminal means of achieving success.[52]

Boys growing up in areas where the "syndicate flag" is flying learn that success comes to "real men," to "stand-up guys" who violate the law with impunity. Accordingly, they train themselves in skills and attitudes that they believe will be as valuable to their success as they have been in the careers of the men they admire. Spergel's study suggested that these especially include personal values about silence, honor, and loyalty—values that make the boys controllable by the adult criminals about whom they are silent, to whom they behave honorably, and to whom they are loyal.[53] Spergel concluded, however, that it is more important for someone aspiring

---

[51] Raymond V. Martin, *Revolt in the Mafia* (New York: Duell, Sloan and Pearce, 1963), p. 60.

[52] Henry D. McKay, "The Neighborhood and Child Conduct," *Annals of the American Academy of Political and Social Science,* Vol. 261 (January, 1949), pp. 32–42.

[53] Irving Spergel, *Racketville, Slumtown, Haulburg: An Exploratory Study of Delinquent Subcultures,* pp. 35–36.

to syndicated crime to display evidence that he is a "stand-up guy" than to learn specific criminal skills. A "stand-up guy" shows courage and "heart." He does not whine or complain in the face of adversity, including arrest, interrogation, and punishment. He has learned to rate criminals higher than noncriminals.

> Racketeers placed a premium on smooth and unobtrusive operation of their employees. The undisciplined, trouble-making young "punk" was not acceptable. The primary condition for admission to the racket organization was not necessarily involvement in delinquent acts but training in attitudes and beliefs which would facilitate the smooth operation of the criminal organization. Prior development of specific skills and experiences seemed less necessary than the learning of an underlying illegitimate orientation or point of view conducive to the development of organized crime.[54]

The following transcript of a bugged conversation between a New York Cosa Nostra soldier and his lieutenant indicates that this "underlying illegitimate orientation" is sought in neighborhoods other than Racketville. The speaker is praising the qualities of his lieutenant's regime by telling him his members have the desired criminal attitudes. They are "stand-up kids." The conversation refers to an FBI investigation.

> They are telling them everything. Who's Cosa Nostra. What's the picture here. Who the bosses are. Who's the bosses? These are kids that don't know nothing. They are schooling them. They are telling them up and down the line what everything is here. They are actually exposing the whole . . . thing to innocent kids. [*Inaudible.*] Innocent kids. Exposing the whole thing. "He's a captain." [*Inaudible.*] And so forth, I said. Good. *Your kids, now, you know, are stand-up kids . . . They are going to tell them not a word.*[55]

Spergel asked the delinquents in his study, "What is the occupation of the adult in your neighborhood whom you most want to be like ten years from now?" Racketville boys did not name bankers, or policemen, or scientists, or teachers, or businessmen, or skilled workers. Eight out of ten responded to the question by naming some aspect of syndicated crime. There is an important lesson here for administrators of programs designed to encourage inner-city youth to remain in school and "get a good education" so they can

---

[54] *Ibid.*

[55] *The Voices of Organized Crime,* an educational tape prepared by the New York State Joint Legislative Committee on Crime: Its Causes, Control and Effect on Society, 1968.

contribute to their own welfare and the welfare of the nation. This message does not fit the reality of daily street experiences in ghettos. By watching the part of syndicated crime available for them to see—the street operations—inner-city boys learn that men who take the illegitimate route to success fare much better than those taking the legitimate route. The same experiences also convince them that it is who you know, not what you know, that counts.

Slum boys who think this way are factually incorrect, even with reference to syndicated crime. The orientation sought by inner-city boys—the attitudes of the "stand-up guy"—helps prepare them for street crime like burglary and robbery, and for street-level involvement in syndicated crime. But positions of leadership in syndicated crime, like positions of leadership everywhere in this day and age, increasingly require skills learned in colleges and universities, not on the streets. Moreover, being a "stand-up guy" might get a boy a position as a bookmaker or a numbers seller if he has good connections, but to become a Cosa Nostra member he must have better connections than this. And if he is to advance in Cosa Nostra he now must have the skills of a purchasing agent, an accountant, a lawyer, an executive. Spergel found, in fact, that significant upper-echelon opportunities in organized crime were not even open to the youth of Racketville. Some delinquents, he says, eventually become racketeers "without necessarily starting at the bottom."[56]

Occasionally, even honest government officials inadvertently contribute to the glory of syndicated criminals and, thus, to a more general illegitimate orientation among slum youth. For example, in the summer of 1966 the director of New York City's Youth Board asked two Cosa Nostra soldiers, Albert and Lawrence Gallo, to help halt racial violence in the East New York section of Brooklyn. The implication, probably correct, was that Cosa Nostra men could keep order where the police and social workers could not. But another implication, also correct, was that boys who want to be neighborhood leaders should go into syndicated crime. John J. Cassesse, then President of the New York Patrolmen's Benevolent Association, commented that the use of the two organized criminals by city officials both sapped the morale of the police force and made "tin gods" of the organized criminals involved:

> I can just see what will happen. It's this way. When a police officer goes up to some juveniles who have been misbehaving and tells them to quiet down and move along, what will they say to him? "You're not the boss around here, Mr. Gallo is." When you single people out like that you make them tin gods in the neighborhood—people known for their habitual lawlessness.[57]

---

[56] Irving Spergel, *Racketville, Slumtown, Haulburg: An Exploratory Study of Delinquent Subcultures*, p. 31.

[57] *The New York Times*, August 15, 1966.

The fact that syndicated crime activities float on a swamp of corruption teaches an insidious lesson to those inner-city youth who, in order to survive, must be astute observers of the facts of life: "The government is for sale; lawlessness is the road to wealth; honesty is a pitfall and morality is a trap for suckers."[58] The most eloquent evangelists and best-trained school teachers combined could not teach this lesson as effectively as it is taught by the everyday experiences of central-city youth.

The areas of high delinquency and crime in American cities are also the areas of low socioeconomic status and poverty. However, it is not correct to conclude from this fact that poverty is the direct cause of delinquency and crime. Rather, it should be concluded that in some areas of poverty lawlessness has become traditional. It is not poverty that causes ghetto youth to admire the professional criminal and the syndicated criminal more than the policeman, the banker, or the preacher. It is not poverty that transmits criminal techniques, codes, and standards from older to younger offenders, and from criminals in city hall to criminals on the street. It is not poverty that teaches boys the techniques of "fixing," intimidating witnesses, telling plausible lies in court, or appealing to sympathy. The fact is that in areas of poverty, the values, norms, and behavior patterns most favorable to crime and delinquency are strong and constant. And the dominant purveyors of these illicit values, norms, and behavior patterns are adult criminals.

Respectable residents of affluent neighborhoods can protect themselves from the direct corrupting effects of syndicated crime. Respectable but politically weaker inner-city residents cannot. In every community there are interests in morality, efficiency, and law enforcement. But in every community there are also interests in immorality, political jobs and favors, and evasion of the law. The first set of interests is reflected when we pass laws and ordinances against syndicated crime activities. The second set becomes manifest when we argue that any policy that does not tolerate syndicated crime activities — despite what the law says — is bad for business, especially for the "convention business." Just as inner-city residents buy organized crime's services because they hope to "get rich quick," more affluent businessmen demand these services because they hope they will help business.

But the "respectable" persons who, in effect, argue that syndicated crime is "not all bad" do not want organized crime in their areas of residence or even in their business areas. Their solution is to pressure the police and other officials to insure that syndicated crime activities take place in neighborhoods populated by the powerless. This means that political corruption — at

---

[58] President's Commission on Law Enforcement and Administration of Justice, *Task Force Report: Organized Crime*, p. 24.

least the corruption of indifference – in large American cities drives crime into ghettos, especially black ghettos.

The Reverend Martin Luther King, Jr., was keenly aware of this fundamental fact. Because the tendency to let syndicated crime flourish in ghettos is so pervasive, he called syndicated crime "permissive crime":

> Permissive crime in ghettos is the nightmare of the slum family. Permissive crime is the name for organized crime that flourishes in the ghettos – designed, directed, and cultivated by the white national crime syndicates operating numbers, narcotics, and prostitution rackets freely in the protected sanctuaries of the ghettos. Because no one, including the police, cares particularly about ghetto crime, it pervades every area of life.[59]

The principle noted by King has not changed much since 1912 – over a half century ago – when the Chicago chief of police warned prostitutes that so long as they confined their residence to districts west of Wabash Avenue and east of Wentworth Avenue, they would not be disturbed.[60] At that time this area contained the largest concentration of blacks in the city. The accuracy of the principle was reaffirmed in 1922, when a Chicago Commission on Race Relations published the following statement:

> That many Negroes live near vice districts is not due to their choice, nor to low moral standards, but to three causes: (1) Negroes are unwelcome in desirable white residence localities; (2) small incomes compel them to live in the least expensive places regardless of surroundings; while premises rented for immoral purposes bring notoriously high rentals, they make the neighborhood undesirable and the rent of other living quarters there abnormally low; and (3) Negroes lack sufficient influence and power to protest effectively against the encroachments of vice.[61]

The practice of keeping crime out of affluent areas but tolerating it in less affluent areas is, together with the corruption that supports the practice, a great contributor to the traditions of delinquency and crime characterizing inner-city areas. Because crime is driven into the slums, the residents of these areas – even the respectable residents – know better the details of any graft or dishonesty in their city's politics than do most members of the middle

---

[59] Martin Luther King, Jr., "Beyond the Los Angeles Riots: Next Stop: The North," *Saturday Review*, Vol. 48 (November 13, 1965), p. 34.

[60] Chicago Commission on Race Relations, *A Study of Race Relations and a Race Riot* (Chicago: Commission on Race Relations, 1922), p. 343.

[61] *Ibid.*, pp. 343–44.

and upper classes. The American culture they see is a culture of competition, corruption, deceit, graft, delinquency, crime, and immorality. They see practically nothing of the culture of cooperation, decency, beauty, and lawfulness in which some Americans are immersed from infancy, and in which middle-class people are now telling them to participate. Instead, they come into intimate and frequent contact with a rather lawless neighborhood and the rather lawless public culture of America.

At the same time, antidelinquency and anticriminal influences are few in the poverty pockets of America. Ghetto dwellers are isolated from the predominantly law-abiding culture (as far as street crime is concerned) of the American middle-class population. Moreover, in inner-city areas, organized opposition to delinquency and crime is weak. Because the population is poor, mobile, and heterogeneous, it is unable to act in concert when dealing with its own problems. Schools, businesses, social work agencies, and even churches are administered by people who reside elsewhere. Accordingly, these agencies are for the most part simply formal and external appendages to the life of the neighborhood. "Society" and "community" are meaningless, except as they refer to ethnic identity, and even "neighborhood" is likely to refer to delinquent or criminal turf of some kind. Under such conditions people are not likely to react to arrest, conviction, and incarceration with feelings of guilt or shame; they do not have very much to lose.

But while poverty and delinquency coexist in our inner-city ghettos, the "poverty problem" and the "delinquency problem" are not identical. In fact, many persons residing in areas of low income or poverty are not delinquents or criminals. Some persons live under the same conditions of housing and low income as do the delinquents and criminals of inner-city areas, yet do not get into serious trouble with the law. Either they are somehow isolated from behavior patterns favorable to delinquency—including those patterns inexorably accompanying syndicated crime activities—or they are in contact with anticriminal influences that somehow offset those favorable to delinquency. We can reduce the incidence of inner-city delinquency by eradicating the kind of behavior patterns diffused by adult criminals. We can reduce the incidence even further by discovering and then maximizing those anticriminal behavior patterns that somehow keep many inner-city children out of trouble, even in syndicated crime areas.

4

Drug Use

JOHN A. CLAUSEN

Drug use illustrates, perhaps better than any other form of deviance, the extent to which the existence of a social problem depends on definitions made within a given society at a given time. The use of drugs to achieve relaxation and pleasurable states of mind is as ancient as the use of drugs to treat illness. In fact, until the start of the present century, the most widely used drugs in the pharmacopoeia of Western medicine were opium and its derivatives—potently addictive drugs. Yet drug addiction has not been regarded as a major social problem in most countries and was not so regarded even in Western society until a century or so ago. The opiates were commonly dispensed in patent medicines until shortly before World War I, and the number of persons in the United States who were physically addicted to opiates at the turn of the century was much larger than it is at present. After the problem of addiction had been widely publicized, however, control over drug distribution was instituted by state and federal governments, and for half a century drug addiction has been a matter of great public concern.

When the first edition of *Contemporary Social Problems* was published in 1961, LSD had been available only as an experimental drug, and its use was largely confined to therapy with mental patients or to experiments on changes in psychic state. Marijuana was widely used in urban slum areas, especially in cities with a Mexican-American population; its use was also common among jazz musicians, but comparatively rare among college students. Drug control laws were aimed primarily at the opiates, cocaine, and marijuana. "Drug addiction" implied opiate addiction, and it was primarily to the problem of opiate addiction that we addressed most of our attention. Then the "psychedelic revolution" occurred in the mid-1960's. One casualty of that revolution was the chapter of the second edition of this book entitled "Drug Addiction." The present chapter surveys a much broader area, one in which there is far less consensus as to the nature of the problem and the means of dealing with it.

Our task will be to examine the various facets of drug use and dependence in American society and the changing attitudes and policies that have marked efforts to deal with drug use. First we shall consider the respects in which drug use is believed to be a social problem. Then we shall turn to what is known and what is popularly believed about various drugs now proscribed by law except when the drugs are medically prescribed. We shall touch upon the physiological and psychological effects of these drugs and upon such matters as addiction, tolerance, habituation, and craving. A knowledge of drug effects tells us very little about how drugs will be used but is a necessary step toward analysis of use. Next we shall consider the nature and amount of illegal drug use and the historical and social patterns of such use. Since drug use is learned within social contexts and cannot be understood without consideration of its meanings in particular groups and relationships, we shall be dealing with a variety of practices among a variety of groups and not with a single phenomenon. We shall examine, for certain of these groups, the symbolic significance of drugs, how drug use begins, how it is sustained, and, insofar as is known, the psychological and social consequences of using various drugs in various ways. Social policy toward drug use will then be reviewed in historical perspective and in the light of comparative data from other societies. Finally, we shall examine some of the assumptions underlying our legal definitions of drug use and the practical problems of implementing our drug laws.

DRUG USE AS A SOCIAL PROBLEM

In what ways is drug use a social problem? The answer depends on one's point of view and personal experience. For most members of our society, certain drugs have been regarded as a problem because they are said to impair the individual's ability to mobilize himself and direct his life. Some drugs are believed to undermine moral restraints and to lead to criminality and violence. Perhaps the most feared drugs are the opiates, because of the physiological dependence attaching to opiate use and the consequent psychological dependence on these drugs.

We are just emerging from a period in which the image of the "drug fiend" was foisted upon the American people in order to secure public support for enforcement of narcotics laws.[1] If most members of the public are now somewhat less ready than their parents were to believe horror stories about drugs — largely because alternative evidence is available — the consensus of expert opinion is that drug use entails dangers and negative features for many users. In any event, persons who use mind-altering drugs for pleasure, escape, or mystical experience (and especially those who are "dependent" on drugs) are stigmatized in most segments of American society.

Drug use is regarded as a social problem by other members of our society because certain drugs have become part of a life style whose values are the antithesis of such conventional middle-class values as the pursuit of wealth and occupational success. Drug use, like long hair and unconventional dress, is interpreted as a symbol of an ominous threat to the American way of life. Even if the drugs are not seriously harmful, their use is opposed by those who feel it tends to flout basic moral values.

Recently, an increasing number of people have taken a very different perspective, maintaining that it is not so much the use of drugs but the laws that have been erected against such use that create the primary social problem at the present time. Early in this century, according to the best estimates available, there were between 200,000 and 500,000 opiate addicts in the United States, most of them addicted to patent medicines that were available at any drugstore.[2] Their addiction was basically a medical problem, and in many instances, it did not seriously interfere with their personal effectiveness. But by legislation that made opiates unavailable except through illegal channels, and by subsequent vilification of the drug-user, addicts were transformed into criminals.

The laws against marijuana use are at present especially problematical. Millions of Americans, most of them under 30 years of age, use marijuana at

---

[1] See, for example, the annual reports of the Commissioner, Bureau of Narcotics, U. S. Treasury Department, during the 1930's, 1940's, and 1950's; and Harry J. Anslinger and William S. Tompkins, *The Traffic in Narcotics* (New York: Funk and Wagnalls, 1953). For more than 30 years, Anslinger, as Commissioner, promulgated a fantastically distorted view of drugs and drug users.

[2] See Charles E. Terry and Mildred Pellens, *The Opium Problem* (New York: Committee on Drug Addiction, 1928), for a thorough analysis of the nature and extent of drug use in the United States prior to federal control of opium and its derivatives. The various estimates of the number of opiate addicts (some ran as high as one million) were derived primarily from state and local surveys of pharmacists and physicians.

least occasionally. At any time, these individuals may be defined as felons if they are arrested with marijuana in their possession. The penalties for violation of drug laws are in many states more severe than those for armed robbery or attempted murder.[3] Widespread use of marijuana in the face of current drug laws has accentuated lack of respect for the law and has resulted in nonenforcement or in differential enforcement of the law, depending upon the whims of law enforcement officers.

When drug laws *are* enforced, this enforcement leads to the piling up of both addicts and casual users in our prisons and jails. To some observers of American society, our efforts to deal with drug use have produced a far greater problem than have drugs themselves, similar to that brought about by Prohibition 50 years ago. Few events in American history did more to undermine the authority of the law and to encourage the development of organized crime than did the passing of a Constitutional amendment to prohibit the manufacture, sale, and transport of alcohol as a beverage.

Drug use may also be viewed as an aspect or manifestation of a much more general social problem. If substantial numbers of people find it necessary to use drugs in order to feel comfortable, or if their lives are lacking in meaning and they therefore turn to drugs in their quest for meaning, the problem is less in the drugs than in the way of life that has been offered them. Although drugs can serve many functions for the individual, they can also undermine the individual's motivation to deal more effectively with his problems and to work for social reforms that will attack the causes of those problems.

There are, then, several senses in which drugs pose a problem in contemporary society. Experts are not unanimous as to what our public policy should be, but almost all informed persons except enforcement personnel seem to agree that our current punitive laws make little sense.

DRUGS AND THEIR EFFECTS

Social definitions are, as we have noted, of crucial importance in understanding the "problem" of drug use. It may be helpful, then, to start by examining our terms of reference. First of all, what is a "drug"? A standard textbook on therapeutic pharmacology defines a drug as "any chemical agent which affects living protoplasm," and goes on to note that few substances would

---

[3] See Neil L. Chayet, "Legal Aspects of Drug Abuse," in J. R. Wittenborn *et al.*, eds., *Drugs and Youth* (Springfield, Ill.: Charles C Thomas, 1969), pp. 236–49.

escape this definition.[4] A substance may be known as a food in one century and a drug in the next, or vice versa. Drugs may be used to fight disease; to avoid or minimize pain, fatigue, or anxiety; or to achieve a level of euphoria. In most societies, there is approval of at least occasional use of stimulants, narcotics, or other drugs to help achieve these objectives. When such use is not *disapproved,* the substances are most often no longer referred to as drugs. Thus, in contemporary America as in much of the world, alcohol is the drug most widely used to produce pleasurable states of mind, yet most drinkers do not regard their indulgence as drug use.

Similarly, tobacco and coffee are widely used for their drug effects (those of nicotine and caffeine), and there was a time when both were proscribed drugs. It is rather startling to read treatises written by leading physicians and lawmakers just a century or two ago, describing the moral depravity and physical debilitation that followed the use of coffee or of tobacco.[5] The smoking of tobacco was at one time or another punishable by death in Russia, Persia, Turkey, and parts of Germany. In England, a little more than two centuries ago, efforts to stamp out the use of tobacco included penalties as extreme as splitting or cutting off the nose of the offender. Ironically, tobacco use became respectable, and ultimately the most common form of such use was in cigarettes. Today we know that heavy use of cigarettes starting early in adolescence can reduce life expectancy by as much as eight years, yet tobacco use is not yet markedly devalued in the United States.[6] Smokers are not called drug-users or drug addicts, despite the fact that many heavy smokers meet all of the criteria that would define "classical" addiction (see below). Few people would brand cigarette advertisers as "merchants of death," yet those who sell illegal drugs that may have less serious consequences for health have been so branded.

When we talk of drug use in our society as a social problem, then, we shall be talking primarily about legally outlawed or markedly devalued forms of drug use. Custom and law, not science or logic, are the definers. We shall be primarily concerned with the use of opiates, the hallucinogens, the barbiturates, and the amphetamines, but we shall occasionally touch on other forms of drug use, including prescription drugs, since attitudes toward one form of

---

[4] Louis S. Goodman and Alfred Gilman, eds., *The Pharmacological Basis of Therapeutics,* 3rd ed. (New York: Macmillan, 1965), p. 1.

[5] Louis Lewin, *Phantastica: Narcotic and Stimulating Drugs, Their Use and Abuse,* trans. from 2nd German ed. by P. H. A. Wirth (New York: Dutton, 1964).

[6] See James L. Hedrick, "Smoking, Tobacco and Health," *Public Health Service Publication Number 1931* (Washington, D. C.: U. S. Government Printing Office, 1969).

drug use may influence attitudes toward other forms, and customs and laws are themselves subject to change as a consequence of such influence.

Addiction, Dependency, and Abuse

The Expert Committee on Addiction-Producing Drugs of the World Health Organization attempted in the 1950's and early 1960's to formulate a definition of addiction. At one time they distinguished between drug "addiction" and drug "habituation." "Addiction" was characterized by (1) a compulsion to use the drug, (2) a tendency to increase the dose, (3) psychic and physical dependence, and (4) detrimental effects on the individual and on society. "Habituation," on the other hand, entailed (1) desire but not compulsion, (2) little tendency to increase the dose, (3) no physical dependence, and (4) detrimental effects primarily on the individual. But these attributes do not go neatly together, either for drugs or for individuals, and the Committee has abandoned its efforts to make such a distinction.[7]

Currently, various substitute terms such as "drug dependency" or "drug abuse" are widely used by experts, but even these terms are unsatisfactory, for, if physical dependence is not involved, the matter of dependency or abuse is very often a value judgment. We shall use the term "addiction" to refer to use of drugs that produce physical dependence and "drug use" when other drugs are involved, leaving for empirical determination the extent to which psychic dependence or craving is entailed.

What we might call the "classical" concept of drug addiction involves both the generation of such pleasant effects as to make the drug a source of preoccupation and craving and the development of physiological dependence on the drug after it has been used for some time. The opiates epitomize addicting power based on initial euphoria and subsequent physical dependence. This dependence is closely linked with "tolerance," the ability of the body to adapt to progressive increases in the amount of the drug that can safely be taken. Such increases are not only tolerable, however; they are required if the drug is to have an effect. Physiological processes eventually adjust to high doses, and once stabilization is reached, an acute illness known as the "abstinence syndrome" results from the absence of the drug.

Certain types of drugs induce tolerance and physical dependence as well

---

[7] For a discussion of some of the issues, unfortunately not adequately resolved, see Nathan B. Eddy *et al.,* "Drug Dependence: Its Significance and Characteristics," *Bulletin of the World Health Organization,* Vol. 32 (1965), pp. 721–33.

as psychological craving; others produce tolerance without physical dependence or craving without tolerance; and still others produce neither physical dependence nor craving, yet may be sought for their psychic effects. The characteristics of drug action depend on the chemical structure of the drug, on the amount of drug administered (and sometimes on the route of administration—e.g., oral, subcutaneous, or intravenous), and on the social definitions and the circumstances of the situation in which the drug is used. In large enough doses, chemical effects tend to override the influence of social circumstances. Even for relatively modest doses, drugs differ in their effects, but the differences are often quite subtle.

The Opiates

The opium poppy has been the source of sleep-inducing drugs and soothing beverages since antiquity. Eventually it was learned that the ingredients responsible for the soporific properties were contained in the juice that exudes from the ripe poppy head when it is lanced. This juice, collected and dried, is opium. Early in the nineteenth century, the two major components (alkaloids) of opium, morphine and codeine, were first identified. They are distinct though related in drug action. From morphine are derived heroin, dilaudid, and a number of other drugs that produce similar effects. Comparable drugs such as methadone are synthetically produced.

Opium and its derivatives were inexpensive drugs and were used with almost no limitations for a wide variety of human ills until the early twentieth century.[8] The bold use of opium appears to have been the basis for the reputations of a number of famous physicians of earlier times. If the drug was used intermittently, tolerance was not built up and addiction was not recognized. The regular user developed tolerance, but as long as he had a steady, inexpensive supply available, he was unlikely to recognize the extent of his physical dependence. Indeed, it was not until the 1830's that the phenomenon of physical dependency was described in medical literature and that physicians began to warn against the dangers of opiate addiction.

When a person has been taking one of the opiates steadily for a period of

---

[8] The history of narcotics use and addiction is treated in some detail in Charles E. Terry and Mildred Pellens, *The Opium Problem,* Chapter 2. See also Glenn Sonnedecker, "Emergence and Concept of the Problems of Addiction," in Robert B. Livingston, ed., *Narcotic Drug Addiction Problems* (Washington, D. C.: U. S. Government Printing Office, 1963).

several weeks (orally, subcutaneously, or intravenously), his body comes to require the drug in order to feel normal. If he is then deprived of the drug he will experience a train of symptoms, varying somewhat in intensity and course depending upon the particular drug, the length of time he has used it, and the amount of the drug he has been taking. For example, some six hours after morphine or heroin is suddenly and completely withdrawn, an addict begins to feel tense. A little later his eyes begin to water, his nose runs, and he sweats and yawns. Restlessness and nervousness become progressively worse as the hours go by. Within 24 hours of the last dose of the drug, most patients are acutely miserable, complaining of chilly sensations and cramps in the muscles of the back and extremities. Recurring waves of goose flesh appear. Restlessness is accompanied by almost constant twitching of the arms, legs, and feet.

The abstinent addict becomes nauseated; through vomiting and diarrhea he may lose five to fifteen pounds in 24 hours. Peak intensity of the illness occurs in the second and third days, with symptoms then declining until at the end of a week the only remaining complaints are likely to be nervousness, insomnia, and weakness; however, these may not disappear for several months. The abstinence syndrome reaches peak intensity earlier and subsides more rapidly for heroin than for morphine. It is much less acute for methadone, which is therefore frequently used for helping the addict make the transition from drug use to abstinence.

Perhaps the most startling aspect of the bodily reaction of an addict deprived of an opiate is that at any time during the acute abstinence period, a single dose of the drug (or any closely related opiate or synthetic) will produce a prompt and pronounced reduction of intensity of the disturbances mentioned. The drug becomes, then, both a source of euphoria and the means of avoiding the acute illness of withdrawal.

We have noted that as long as persons physically tolerant of high doses of an opiate are able to continue taking the drug regularly they will not experience the abstinence syndrome and they will have no reason to regard themselves as addicted. Lindesmith has postulated that the essential feature of addiction is that the addict recognizes that the tortures of abstinence can be warded off by the drug.[9] While most psychiatrists and pharmacologists express reservations about this formulation, few would deny that a person's labeling of himself as dependent on the drug is a highly significant part of the process of becoming an addict. Although it does not entirely explain craving for the drug long beyond the period of abstinence symptoms, the process

---

[9] Alfred R. Lindesmith, *Opiate Addiction* (Evanston, Ill.: Principia Press, 1947).

of labeling has important consequences for identity. The addict knows the extent to which his future comfort depends on the drug; he knows he is hooked. Before he has experienced the abstinence syndrome, he may assume that he can stop using the drug at any time, though he may not choose to do so. Once he is hooked, only inability to get the drug will permit him to stop using it. Consequently, when he realizes he is hooked, he is ripe for assimilation into the culture of the addict, where assurance of drug supply becomes a primary goal in life.

Marijuana

Marijuana is a crude preparation of the flowering tops, leaves, seeds, and stems of female plants of Indian hemp (*Cannabis sativa*).[10] In the United States it is usually smoked in cigarettes ("joints," "reefers") rolled by the user. The active drug ingredient is found in the sticky resin exuded by the tops of the plants. When the tops and leaves are used, the resin is not highly concentrated. The resin itself may be used for smoking or eating; it is best known as hashish. *Cannabis* use has long been widespread in the Orient and has taken various forms, though only in the past 50 years has it come to the United States.

Although Indian hemp grows throughout the world, its pharmacological activity depends to a large extent on the amount of sunshine the plants receive and other conditions under which they are grown. Most marijuana grown in the United States is of low strength and is acceptable to smokers only if no other grade is available. Considerably better grades of marijuana originate in Mexico, and the highest grades come from the Orient.

There are few topics on which opinions are as sharply divided as are those on marijuana and its effects. Moreover, the divergency of opinions is unlikely to be resolved by scientific evidence; it is based on ideological commitments and grossly differing premises as to what is good, right, or desirable.[11] Research evidence on the long-term effects of moderate marijuana use is simply nonexistent, but the short-term effects have been studied in the laboratory, and of course, both short- and longer-range effects have been observed by millions of users. Therefore, it is hardly correct to say, as some

---

[10] For a good factual description of marijuana and its marketing in the United States in the 1960's, and for an examination of markedly different perspectives toward marijuana, see Erich Goode, *Marijuana* (New York: Atherton Press, 1969).

[11] On this point see Erich Goode, "Marijuana and the Politics of Reality," *Journal of Health and Social Behavior*, Vol. 10 (June, 1969), pp. 83–94.

writers do, that we know almost nothing about the effects of marijuana. We know a good deal, but what we make of this knowledge depends on what we choose to emphasize.

During the 1930's, the former head of the Bureau of Narcotics, Harry J. Anslinger, became committed to the proposition that marijuana was a major menace to the nation. In propagandizing against the drug, he asserted that use of *cannabis* has drastic consequences:

> In the earliest stages of intoxication the will power is destroyed and inhibitions and restraints are released; moral barricades are broken down and often debauchery and sexuality result. Where mental instability is inherent, behavior is generally violent.[12]

Careful studies of the effects of marijuana give no support whatsoever to such assertions. Pharmacological and psychological studies reveal changes in perception and in the flow of ideas but no increased tendency to excitement or violence. Reviewing the evidence, one research worker states:

> There seems to be a growing agreement within the medical community, at least, that marihuana does not directly cause criminal behavior, juvenile delinquency, sexual excitement, or addiction. Therefore, while attempts to limit its use are appropriate, the hazards of use should not be exaggerated.[13]

The most carefully controlled study of the effects of marijuana smoking, by Weil and his associates, led to several surprising findings. The effects of marijuana on regular users were compared with those on naive subjects who had never before tried the drug.[14] The latter had to be trained to inhale deeply, since effects of smoking marijuana are produced by absorption of the active ingredients in the lungs. Training was done with tobacco cigarettes. The only adverse reactions in the entire study came from inhaling the tobacco cigarettes in the initial training phase, which produced acute nicotine reactions in five of the subjects.

Weil and his team administered cigarettes of marijuana judged by regular users to be of good quality. They found that young adult males who had not previously used marijuana did not have strong subjective experiences after

---

[12] Harry J. Anslinger and W. S. Tompkins, *The Traffic in Narcotics* (New York: Funk & Wagnalls), pp. 21–22, quoted from Erich Goode, *Marijuana.*

[13] Jerome H. Jaffe, "Drug Addiction and Drug Abuse," in Louis S. Goodman and Alfred Gilman, eds., *The Pharmacological Basis of Therapeutics,* pp. 300–01.

[14] Andrew T. Weil *et al.,* "Clinical and Psychological Effects of Marihuana in Man," *Science,* Vol. 162 (December 13, 1968), pp. 1235–38.

smoking either low or high doses of the drug. On the other hand, regular users of marijuana, smoking comparable cigarettes of the same strength, all achieved "highs." Despite their lack of strong subjective experiences, the naive subjects showed impaired performance on simple intellectual and psychomotor tests after smoking marijuana. By contrast, regular users of marijuana, despite feeling high, showed no impairment of performance; indeed, some showed slight improvement of performance. The observable effects of marijuana were maximum about 15 minutes after smoking, diminished between 30 minutes and one hour, and were largely dissipated by three hours after the end of smoking. The conclusion of this research team, based on all the evidence of their very carefully conducted laboratory study, is that "marijuana appears to be a relatively mild intoxicant."

The primary source of drug action in marijuana is a chemical labeled *tetrahydrocannabinol,* commonly known as THC. THC has recently been synthesized and has been administered orally to subjects in laboratory experiments. Its effects are much more striking than are those of marijuana cigarettes and have certain similarities with the effects of LSD.[15] Because of variations in drug dosage when marijuana is smoked, some pharmacologists and other research scientists argue that the only defensible studies of drug effects are those produced by oral administration of a carefully predetermined drug dosage. Such predetermination is almost impossible when marijuana is smoked, for the technique of smoking as well as the chemical composition of the marijuana will influence the amount of dosage received. Nevertheless, if one is interested in the effects of marijuana as it is actually used in a given population, those effects can hardly be assessed by techniques that have nothing to do with the normal use of the drug. Generalizations based upon administration of tetrahydrocannabinol in the laboratory cannot in any sense be equated with the smoking of marijuana cigarettes.

LSD and Other Hallucinogens

LSD—lysergic acid diethylamide—was first synthesized in 1938.[16] Its capacity to produce hallucinations and emotional changes was not discovered

---

[15] See Leo E. Hollister and H. K. Gillespie, "Similarities and Differences between the Effects of LSD and Tetrahydrocannabinol in Man," in J. R. Wittenborn *et al.,* eds., *Drugs and Youth,* pp. 208–12.

[16] The pharmacological properties of LSD and its behavioral effects, as well as many aspects of LSD use are discussed in Richard C. DeBold and R. C. Leaf, *LSD, Man and Society* (Middletown, Conn.: Wesleyan University Press, 1967).

until five years later, and it was used only for experimental studies and limited therapeutic trials until well into the 1950's. Its effects were thought to provide a temporary model of psychosis, and hence psychiatrists originally called it a *psychotomimetic* drug. Some psychiatrists used it to gain access to chronically withdrawn patients and found that it enabled patients to verbalize suppressed components of their conflicts. Others used it, in small quantities, as an aid to psychotherapy, especially with neurotic and alcoholic patients. Discovery of the intensity and depth of perceptual and emotional experience released by the drug made it attractive to many persons interested in esthetic and mystical experience as well as to those seeking to transcend the normal range of consciousness. The psychotomimetic label was dropped; in its place came "psychedelic" ("mind-manifesting").

The psychic effects of LSD — the "trip" — begin approximately 30 minutes after the ingestion of a tiny quantity (150 micrograms), and are often preceded by transitory physical symptoms such as nausea, headache, chills, and sweating. Emotions are markedly heightened, but whether the individual will be happy or miserable is likely to depend on the social situation. Sensitivity to sensory input is enormously enhanced. Tactile and visual distortions and "hallucinations" occur, flooding the senses. The altered subjective experience presents a startling contrast to ordinary reality. Portentous meanings attach to the most banal objects and impressions. Drug-related activity lasts for eight to twelve hours, but the most intensive changes in mood and perception occur in the first four hours or so, after which the person usually becomes introspective, dwelling on the experience he has just been through. Similar to LSD in chemical structure and in psychic effects are psilocybin and mescaline (which have been used to achieve psychic effects for a much longer time), and more recent preparations like STP (an illegally produced experimental drug).

The dangers of LSD and related hallucinogens appear to be of three types: (1) those associated with "bad trips" or panic states, especially when the drug is used without proper safeguards and by persons who have severe neuroses or "hang-ups"; (2) the tendency of many users to become so preoccupied with subjective experiences and sensations as to become disengaged from normal social roles and activities (Freedman refers to this as the danger of too many "good trips"); and (3) the danger that such drugs may cause damage to the organism, either with respect to brain function or in effects on the genetic apparatus (chromosome breakage).[17] Research findings regarding organic damage are conflicting.

---

[17] See Daniel X. Freedman, "Drug Abuse — Comments on the Current Scene," in J. R. Wittenborn *et al.,* eds., *Drugs and Youth,* pp. 345–61.

Unfortunately, no research on long-term effects of the hallucinogens has been conducted using an adequate sample of persons studied before and after prolonged use of such drugs.[18] LSD users are frequently convinced that they have greater understanding of themselves as a consequence of having taken the drug; most nonusers who have intimately known a person who has taken a number of trips cannot share this perception. What is most striking, perhaps, is the extent to which many heavy users seem to lose critical judgment and the ability to mobilize their efforts. Of course, if one believes that turning on and dropping out are behaviors that make good sense, one will not be dismayed at such changes and indeed may argue that the assessment of "critical judgment" is itself a value judgment.

Tolerance to high doses of LSD and other hallucinogens develops rapidly, but there is no evidence of physical dependence, nor do most persons who have tried LSD experimentally develop any craving to use it subsequently.

The Amphetamines

The amphetamines are stimulant drugs that have been widely prescribed in recent decades to control weight (through reduction of appetite) and to offset fatigue and feelings of depression. The acute effects of these drugs also include wakefulness and nervousness. With continued use, tolerance develops with respect to the euphoric effects — that is, it takes more of the drug to produce the same "high" — but insomnia is produced without increasing dosage. Performance on a wide variety of tasks that require alertness is improved by low dosages of these drugs. This effect has long made the amphetamines popular with students cramming for examinations, truck drivers desiring to overcome sleepiness, and individuals having difficulty in getting going.[19] Higher dosage levels lead to tension and the "jitters" and to loss of reflective judgment.

In general, the amphetamines are taken orally, but in recent years members of some drug-using groups have taken to injecting methamphetamine (known as "crystal" or "speed") intravenously. This produces a "flash" or

---

[18] William McGlothlin has followed up a group of early users and finds few evidences of personality changes apart from subjective feelings. His research report, not yet published, was presented at the Conference on Drug Usage and Drug Subcultures, Asilomar, California, February 12, 1970.

[19] See Chauncey Leake, *The Amphetamines: Their Actions and Uses* (Springfield, Ill.: Charles C Thomas, 1958); and J. R. Russo, ed., *Amphetamine Abuse* (Springfield, Ill.: Charles C Thomas, 1968).

"rush" of feeling not unlike that derived from the injection of heroin, but the subsequent effects are almost exactly the opposite – the user becomes talkative and hyperactive rather than drowsy and reflective. Injections may be repeated every few hours for several days, during which period the user is continuously awake, does not eat, and tends to become disorganized. Physical debilitation is severe, with extreme weight loss. At the end of the "run," the user falls into a deep sleep that may last more than 24 hours. Apathy and feelings of depression may persist for weeks or months after such a run.[20]

Paranoid symptomatology is a common occurence among heavy users of amphetamines. In general, the amphetamines show effects similar to those produced by cocaine, once a widely used drug but now relatively unimportant among populations having access to amphetamines.

The Barbiturates

The barbiturates and hypnotics (nembutal, seconal, and the like) are drugs used medically for calming and slowing down the patient, helping him to sleep soundly, and so forth. They have a disinhibiting effect not unlike that of alcohol and hence can be used to attain "highs" as well as relaxation.[21] Barbiturates are sometimes used by opiate addicts as a substitute for an opiate but more commonly are paired with other drugs to enhance or offset their effects, depending on circumstances. Because of easy availability, they are widely used by youth experimenting with drug effects.

Barbiturates are characterized by tolerance and physical dependence. The abstinence syndrome following heavy barbiturate use is extremely severe, often involving convulsions. Barbiturate action is in several respects similar to that of alcohol, and the latter may be used to attenuate withdrawal effects of barbiturates.

---

[20] See J. C. Kramer *et al.*, "Amphetamine Abuse," *Journal of the American Medical Association,* Vol. 201 (July 31, 1967), pp. 305–10; and J. T. Carey and J. Mandel, "A San Francisco Bay Area 'Speed' Scene," *Journal of Health and Social Behavior,* Vol. 9 (June, 1968), pp. 164–74.

[21] See Nathan B. Eddy *et al.*, "Drug Dependence: Its Significance and Characteristics," pp. 725–26; and Committee on Alcoholism and Addiction, "Dependence on Barbiturates and Other Sedative Drugs," *Journal of the American Medical Association,* Vol. 193 (August 23, 1965), pp. 107–11.

EXTENT AND DISTRIBUTION OF DRUG USE

American society was long characterized by a valuing of asceticism and of rational practicality. The use of drugs is not consonant with such values. It is not surprising that a high proportion of the persons addicted to opiates in the period before drug control were middle-class women whose "female disorders" could serve as an excuse for their reliance on patent medicines. Apart from such members of conventional society, heavy drug use has until recently been largely confined to members of subgroups whose behaviors were seriously deviant in other respects. Criminals and prostitutes, who by and large have lived dreary lives, full of anxiety and misery, have long tended to use drugs. This is one reason for the belief that drugs cause crime; there has been an undeniable association between the two.

In recent years, the ethic against drug use has grown less strong. Esthetic and mystical experiences have been increasingly valued among American intellectuals, especially in the past decade or two. At the same time, there has been a great increase in the discovery and use of a wide variety of drugs for treating all manner of human ailments. As we have noted, these have included a number of drugs with effects on mood and psychic functioning, such as the amphetamines and the tranquilizers. Sale of such psychoactive or psychotropic drugs on medical prescription has reached extremely high levels in recent years. For example, in 1965 some 58 million new prescriptions were written and 108 million refills obtained for psychotropic drugs; they accounted for 14 percent of all prescriptions in the United States in that year.[22]

Legal Use of Psychotropic Drugs

Recent studies suggest that perhaps one-fourth of the adult population of the United States uses, in a given year, one or more of the psychotropic drugs, including many of the drugs that are controlled by federal and state

---

[22] See Hugh S. Parry, "Use of Psychotropic Drugs by U. S. Adults," *Public Health Reports,* Vol. 83 (October, 1968), p. 799. The widespread advertising and prescription of psychoactive drugs to ease life stresses that are in no sense medical problems entails serious dangers. See Henry L. Lennard *et al.,* "Hazards Implicit in Prescribing Psychoactive Drugs," *Science,* Vol. 169 (July 31, 1970), pp. 438–41.

laws on the grounds that they are subject to "abuse." [23] Most frequently used are stimulants (largely amphetamines), hypnotics (nembutal, seconal, and the like), mild tranquilizers (Librium, Miltown) and sedatives (such as phenobarbital). Most adults obtain such drugs by prescription, but the same drugs are widely available through illegal channels, as is well known to many high school and college students, especially in metropolitan areas. Prescription drugs are most readily available to middle-class persons who have a relationship with a private physician. In addition, there are a number of widely advertised "over-the-counter" drugs that purportedly help the nervous, tense, or apathetic person get through the day without losing his temper or falling asleep. Such drug use is neither illegal nor devalued to any significant degree by most adults.

At least three-fourths of the adult males and two-thirds of the adult females in the United States drink alcoholic beverages (see Chapter 5). Slightly smaller proportions smoke cigarettes. Except in a few counties where alcoholic beverages may not be sold because of local laws, among religious groups that oppose smoking and drinking, and more recently, among medical circles in which cigarette smoking is now devalued, it is both legal and morally acceptable for adults to smoke and drink. These aspects of the contemporary legal and only minimally controlled use of various substances in the United States are relevant to an understanding of beliefs and attitudes regarding the illegal use of various drugs.

Illegal Drug Use

Estimates of the extent of illegal drug use are at best crude. In general, a user becomes known to agencies that compile statistics on drug use and addiction only if he is arrested or seeks treatment. Most persons who are arrested for drug possession are users, but drug possession as such tells nothing about the extent of the individual's drug use.

In recent years, survey research has been utilized to assess the frequency of drug use in the population at large and among students and other institutional populations. Drug use varies with characteristics of personality, demography, social structure, and culture. Willingness to admit drug use to an unknown interviewer likewise varies. If most of his associates and the members of various groups to which he belongs are also drug-users, and if

---

[23] *Ibid.,* p. 800.

this fact is widely known, an individual is much more likely to be willing to acknowledge his drug use than if very few of his associates are users. Even in the former instance, however, acknowledgment of drug use will certainly depend upon the kind of agency conducting the survey and the characteristics of the interviewer himself. In general, we would expect surveys to understate the amount of drug use except in groups where drug use is valued as a sign of sophistication and maturity (as would seem to be the case among some adolescents).

Most forms of drug use are more prevalent among the young than among the old, among persons living in or near large cities than among those in small towns, among the unconventional than among the conventional. Drug use is overwhelmingly *social* behavior; it is a group activity. Like any other form of social behavior, drug use means different things to different individuals; its functions for the individual depend upon both his personal history and the way that drug use is defined behaviorally in those groups that mean most to him. Knowledge of such meanings is difficult to assess unless one can freely observe the drug-user among his friends or at least come to know thoroughly how members of the group think and feel about drug use for themselves and their peers. Different drugs may be used, or the same drug may have very different meanings, in different social worlds.[24] One frequently hears the term "the drug scene," but there are many drug scenes and they are played to different scenarios.

Estimates of the number of persons who have used or are using any given drug reveal little about the nature of drug use; they give no basis, for example, for determining the significance of drug use in the life of the individual. On the other hand, it is certainly desirable to know the relative magnitude of the problem of drug use, and any adequate analysis of drug use as a social phenomenon requires some knowledge of the distribution of various forms of drug use in different parts of the population. We shall therefore briefly review available statistical data before turning to a more detailed examination of patterns of drug use.

MARIJUANA—Marijuana is undoubtedly the most frequently used illegal drug and has been for some decades. Its use has increased enormously since 1960, especially among middle-class adolescents and young adults. Studies of marijuana use in high schools and colleges around the country show much regional variation but suggest that a high proportion of young people (from

---

[24] For an excellent statement of the importance of collective interpretations, see Herbert Blumer *et al.*, "The World of Youthful Drug Use," mimeographed (Berkeley, California: School of Criminology, January, 1967).

one-fifth to one-half in many colleges) have tried marijuana a few times, and that perhaps one-third of those who have tried it continue to use it occasionally or on a regular basis.

Despite the high prevalence of drug use in some student populations, age rather than student status seems to be the primary factor. A survey conducted among a cross section of the adult residents in two San Francisco Bay Area counties in 1968 and 1969 revealed highest rates of having tried marijuana or currently using it among persons under 25 years of age and a marked dropping off of both rates for persons over 35.[25] Roughly one-half of the men and one-third of the women aged 18–24 had tried marijuana and one-fourth of the men in this age group had smoked it 50 or more times. Male students in this study were slightly less likely to smoke marijuana than were nonstudents the same age, while the reverse was true of women. Occasional or regular marijuana use (as contrasted with merely having tried it once or twice) was much more frequent among women who had been to college and especially among those currently in college than among other women of the same age.

Although an accurate estimate of the number of persons who have tried marijuana is very difficult to arrive at, the various sample surveys in different parts of the country suggest that a figure of ten million is not unreasonable.[26] Perhaps half of these persons have merely tried marijuana once or twice; others use it on an occasional basis, and perhaps not more than one-fifth use it fairly regularly. This would still mean that perhaps two million Americans are fairly regular smokers of marijuana. Even among regular users, except for groups organized very largely around drug use, we have no idea of how many are preoccupied with drug use to the extent that it poses serious problems other than their being subject to arrest.

Young men and women who smoke tobacco are more than twice as likely

---

[25] The data are from interviews with a cross section of persons 18 years and over in San Francisco and in a suburban county and were reported by Dean Manheimer in "Marijuana Use Among Adults in Two San Francisco Bay Area Locales," a paper presented at the Conference on Drug Use and Drug Subcultures, Asilomar, California, February 12, 1970 (mimeographed, p. 15). For a preliminary report, see Dean I. Manheimer *et al.,* "Marijuana Use Among Urban Adults," *Science,* Vol. 166 (December 19, 1969), pp. 1544–45. The study, conducted under a Public Health Service grant, was primarily concerned with use of prescription drugs and only incidentally contained questions related to marijuana and LSD usage.

[26] A governmental task force "conservatively" estimated that five million Americans had tried marijuana, while the Director of the National Institute of Mental Health put the total between 12 and 20 million. See "Pop Drugs: The High as a Way of Life," *Time* (September 26, 1969), p. 69.

to use marijuana as are nonsmokers.[27] Although some marijuana users feel negatively about alcohol and are less likely than nonusers to drink alcoholic beverages, it appears than in general marijuana users are also more likely to be at least occasional drinkers. More importantly, studies in diverse groups of users suggest that there is a strong negative relationship between attitudes arising from personality rigidity, conventionality, or conformity and the use of marijuana; this statistical relationship accounts for many of the behavioral correlates of such use. In this sense, marijuana is a symbol of the rejection of conventional, "uptight" morality. As Suchman has noted, marijuana use goes with the "hang-loose" ethic, which (in the words of Simmons and Winograd),

> repudiates or at least questions such convictions of conventional society as Christianity, "my country right or wrong," the sanctity of marriage and premarital chastity, civil obedience, the accumulation of wealth, the right and even competence of parents, the schools and the government to head and make decisions for everyone—in sum, the Establishment.[28]

LSD—Illicit LSD use appears to be much more highly concentrated in student, "hippie," and intellectual circles than is marijuana use, though this may simply reflect greater publicity attending use among students. Practically all persons who try LSD have at least tried marijuana, but it is only in the under-25 age group that a substantial proportion of marijuana users have also taken LSD. Over all, the Manheimer study of drug use in the San Francisco Bay Area suggests that between 2 and 3 percent of the adult population of the counties studied had tried LSD. In the under-25 age group, on the other hand, between one-sixth and one-fourth said they had tried LSD. This is considerably higher than the proportion reporting LSD use in most studies of college samples, which have usually yielded estimates in the range of 2 to 7 percent.[29] The San Francisco area is, without question, one of the major centers of drug use, drawing recruits from all over the United States.

---

[27] Dean I. Manheimer, "Marijuana Use Among Adults in Two San Francisco Bay Area Locales," 1970, p. 10.

[28] Edward A. Suchman, "The Hang-Loose Ethic and the Spirit of Drug Use," *Journal of Health and Social Behavior,* Vol. 9 (June, 1968), pp. 146–55. The quotation cited by Suchman is from Jerry L. Simmons and Barry Winograd, *It's Happening: A Portrait of the Youth Scene Today* (Santa Barbara, Calif.: Marc-Laird Publications, 1966), p. 12.

[29] Estimates compiled from various surveys were summarized in a mimeographed report, "Extent of Illicit Drug Use," by the Division of Drug Science, Bureau of Narcotics and Dangerous Drugs (Washington, D. C.: Department of Justice, May, 1969).

Data on the frequency of LSD use by those who have tried the drug are less adequate still. The nature of drug effects and the ends sought by users are such that relatively few persons use LSD with any frequency; but on the other hand, if the initial experience is not excessively frightening, many persons apparently wish to repeat it. At least this appeared to be the case in a period between 1966 and 1968, when LSD use was apparently at a peak. The high proportion of psychiatric casualties from indiscriminate use of LSD, coupled with indications that the drug might produce genetic damage, apparently has led to a decline in LSD use since 1968.

AMPHETAMINES — School and campus studies have generally found amphetamines to be more widely used than any other drug except marijuana. At some high schools and many colleges, drugs of this group have been used by more than one student in five.[30] Perhaps more important than the proportion who have taken amphetamines is the evidence that these drugs are often (again, second only to marijuana) the younger person's introduction to drug effects. Amphetamines appeal especially to the young (whereas barbiturates are used much more heavily by older persons), and are easily obtained in most communities. Again, the use of amphetamines is by no means peculiarly concentrated among students; it is apparently a part of nearly all of the scenes where drug use is an accepted part of life.

Methedrine or "speed" is, however, used largely by persons who have become detached from conventional society. Systematic evidence on the characteristics of "speed-freaks" or "meth-heads" is lacking, but even in circles where a good deal of drug experimentation is accepted, the "speed-freak" tends to be derogated.[31]

HEROIN — The distribution of heroin use is much less diffuse, though some users may be found in most deviant subcultures. In recent decades, heroin use has been most heavily concentrated in the larger metropolitan centers, and within these centers it has been most prevalent in areas where the most economically deprived members of the population live.[32] Several states and the Federal Bureau of Narcotics and Dangerous Drugs maintain "registers"

---

[30] For a summary of available evidence see Louise C. Richards, "Patterns and Extent of Abuse (Drugs of the Amphetamine and Barbiturate Tranquilizer Types)," in J. R. Wittenborn *et al.*, eds., *Drugs and Youth*, pp. 141–47.

[31] See, for example, Fred Davis and Laura Muñoz, "Heads and Freaks: Patterns and Meanings of Drug Use Among Hippies," *Journal of Health and Social Behavior,* Vol. 9 (June, 1968), pp. 156–64.

[32] The most thorough study of the distribution and correlates of heroin use remains *The Road to H* by Isidor Chein *et al.* (New York: Basic Books, 1964).

or lists of known opiate addicts. In addition, various treatment facilities from time to time analyze the characteristics of persons treated for addiction. If one assumes that most *addicts* eventually get into trouble with the law, and that most of those persons arrested for heroin sales are addicted to the drug, it would appear that between 100,000 and 200,000 persons are addicted to heroin in the United States at the present time.

When we consider that there are an estimated five million alcoholics in the United States (see Chapter 5), the frequency of heroin addiction is not great. On the other hand, no other Western nation has anywhere near this number of addicts. Great Britain, France, and the Scandinavian countries report only a few hundred addicts each. There was some increase in opiate use in England in the 1960's, but the total number of addicts remained under 1,000 toward the end of the decade.[33] (Somewhat ironically, the British have seemed more concerned about *cannabis* use than about the opiates, perhaps because marijuana has been a recent import and is chiefly used by immigrants from West Africa or the West Indies.) West Germany has a somewhat greater number of addicts (somewhat over 4,000), but they are to a large extent older persons who became addicted to synthetic counterparts of the opiates as a result of prolonged medicinal use.[34] Thus heroin addiction is a peculiarly American problem at this time.

Most young heroin users have previously smoked marijuana and tried other drugs. Again, however, it must be stressed that most marijuana users do not try heroin. There are striking differences between heroin addicts from the southeastern states (largely older men) and those from the rest of the country with respect to their prior use of marijuana. Most addicts from the Southeast did not first use marijuana but were directly inducted into opiate use.[35] In general, it appears that linkages between drugs and the sequence in which various drugs are tried, if they are tried at all, depend on the availability of drugs and on the beliefs and practices prevalent among the peer groups to which any individual belongs.

---

[33] See T. H. Bewley, "Recent Changes in the Pattern of Drug Abuse in London and the United Kingdom," in C. W. M. Wilson, ed., *The Pharmacological and Epidemiological Aspects of Adolescent Drug Dependence* (London: Pergamon Press, 1968), pp. 197–220.

[34] Information relating to many aspects of narcotics production and abuse is published annually by the Commission on Narcotic Drugs of the United Nations Economic and Social Council. See its *Summary of the Annual Reports of Governments Relating to Opium and Other Dangerous Drugs,* 1962, p. 27.

[35] John C. Ball *et al.,* "The Association of Marihuana Smoking with Opiate Addiction in the United States," *Journal of Criminal Law, Criminology and Police Science,* Vol. 59 (June, 1968), pp. 171–82.

INDUCTION INTO DRUG USE

How does one explain the high prevalence of drug use in American society at the present time? One view is that importers and peddlers of drugs, out to make fortunes at the expense of ruined lives, push drugs upon the young, the innocent, and the weak members of the larger society. Another is that persons who are maladjusted or unable to face up to the realities of life seek escape in drug use. A third view, more widely accepted by social scientists, is that various forms of drug use are patterns of learned behavior that are congenial to persons sharing certain values and views of society and of themselves, and that group memberships and identifications are more important as explanations of drug use than are personality factors or the mere availability of drugs.

Let us start by considering the circumstances under which young people are introduced to marijuana and other drugs in school and neighborhood settings in the United States today. Overwhelmingly, it appears that they are introduced to drugs by friends, either in social gatherings or in intimate relationships. Nearly 20 years ago, when marijuana use was much less general than at present, Howard S. Becker described the process of becoming a marijuana user.[36] Even then, as he noted, the number of persons using marijuana was quite large, despite the fact that such use was both illegal and disapproved. Unless they had already been exposed to a good deal of evidence to the contrary, most persons faced with an opportunity to try marijuana had some qualms about doing so. Many had to some degree accepted traditional views that defined any drug use as a sign of moral degradation. As Becker noted, becoming a regular marijuana user entails learning to disengage oneself from the controls exerted by such beliefs and attitudes, as well as learning the proper techniques and definitions to insure positive pleasure from the drug experience.

Marijuana use is now so widespread and has received so much publicity that much of the mythology that previously served to deter persons from trying a "joint" has been dispelled. Nevertheless, becoming a regular marijuana user still entails learning to enjoy the drug, to arrange for supplies,

---

[36] Howard S. Becker, "Becoming a Marihuana User," *American Journal of Sociology,* Vol. 59 (November, 1953), pp. 235–42. See also "Marihuana Use and Social Control," *Social Problems,* Vol. 3 (July, 1955), pp. 35–44. Both papers are contained in Becker's book, *Outsiders* (New York: Free Press, 1963).

and the like. Becker noted that the novice does not ordinarily get high the first time he smokes marijuana — a finding clearly confirmed by Weil's research (see page 195). To get maximum effect, one must first learn to inhale deeply, and hold the smoke in his lungs long enough to allow for absorption of the drug into the blood stream. Even with training in the technique of inhaling, one must learn to recognize and label the effects, which are quite subtle. Further, the novice may not feel high, even though his performance of intellectual tasks is appreciably impaired, whereas the experienced smoker of marijuana may feel high without showing any decrement in performance of the same tasks.

As we have noted, marijuana is most often first experienced by an individual because it has been made available either by a close friend or, in a group setting, by a member who has access to a source of supply. In fact, the use of marijuana tends at first to be primarily a function of availability; the occasional user can become a regular user only by finding a stable source. He must get to know sellers, but this is not usually difficult, since most regular users tend to become sellers at one time or another.

Initially, the neophyte is likely to be concerned with keeping the fact of his marijuana use a secret and confining that use to times and places where friends or relatives who disapprove will not be likely to see him. As he participates more with other users, however, he tends either to give up ties with those who strongly disapprove or to learn to control the expression of his "highs" so that nonusers will not be aware of them. When Becker first described the process of becoming a marijuana user, most members of the general public accepted the horror stories that had been associated with marijuana use. Therefore, becoming a regular user was likely to affect one's close social ties and self-concept to a greater degree than at the present time. Even now, however, direct experience with marijuana is likely to lead to a restructuring of beliefs about drug use and some restructuring of one's social ties.[37] In the process of becoming a marijuana user, one set of norms and controls is discarded in favor of another.

People who find pleasure in smoking marijuana at social occasions have an added bond, and those who are uncomfortable in such situations tend to steer clear of them. Whether or not one uses a wide variety of other drugs along with marijuana is likely to depend both upon one's personality and upon the dominant values, interests, and activities of the group in which one has his primary identification. Goode notes:

---

[37] This has been dramatically documented by Erich Goode, "Multiple Drug Use among Marijuana Smokers," *Social Problems,* Vol. 17 (Summer, 1969), pp. 48–64.

The fact that one has friends who smoke further increases the likelihood that one will smoke more, and the fact that one smokes implicates one in relationships with those who also smoke.[38]

The greater the proportion of one's friends who are regular marijuana smokers, the greater is the likelihood that one smokes marijuana frequently and that one has tried drugs other than marijuana.

Goode found the relationship between levels of use and whether or not one has bought or sold marijuana to be nicely in accord with Becker's earlier formulation.[39] The great majority of those who used marijuana more than once a month had bought marijuana, but less than one-third of occasional users had directly purchased their marijuana. Relatively few of Goode's respondents who smoked marijuana less than once a week had ever sold it, but among those who smoked several times a week, the vast majority had themselves dealt in selling marijuana. Those who had bought or sold marijuana were very likely to have tried a number of other drugs. The group of subjects studied by Goode included a much higher proportion of heavy users than one would find in a cross section of those who have tried marijuana, however, and he notes that most individuals do not progress to using marijuana several times a week, as more than half of his subjects did. Nevertheless, his study makes clear that persons assimilated to groups in which regular drug use is the rule are by that assimilation inducted into practices that sustain and enlarge their use of drugs.

DRUG SUBCULTURES

The use of drugs by young people takes many forms and serves a variety of functions, but such drug use is pervasively social. Middle-aged people, especially in the middle class, may use amphetamines for weight control or to combat depression, or may use barbiturates to help them sleep or tranquilizers to overcome their anxieties, but they do so largely in private. Only in the use of alcohol do they occasionally acknowledge their pleasure in getting "high" in the presence of others. There is, then, a real generational gap in the way drugs are used, a gap that makes it especially difficult for older persons to realize that much of the drug use of their children is more akin to their own cocktail drinking than to their use of amphetamines, barbiturates,

---

[38] *Ibid.,* p. 56.
[39] *Ibid.,* p. 57.

and tranquilizers. The function served may in a sense be related to personal needs in both instances, but certainly not in the same sense. Most young people do not initially take drugs because they feel they have to have them; they take them because they are curious and expect to like the effects. Of course there are some who, by virtue of personality needs, become heavily dependent on drugs. The heroin addict, in particular, appears often to have had acute difficulties in his personal functioning, but this tendency is by no means universal.

Major studies of subcultural variants of drug use have focused on college communities, hippie enclaves, and slum communities. Only within the hippie enclaves does one find drug use almost universal; indeed, interest in drugs appears to have been a primary basis for recruitment and incorporation into the hippie life. In other settings where drug use is prevalent, one finds considerable variation in levels of use and in the meanings attaching to such use. In all these settings the inhabitants have their own labels for the social types that make up the community and their own constellation of values and activities that make particular drugs attractive to members.

Marijuana was first widely used in the United States by minority-group youths in the "street-corner society" of the urban slums. Marijuana and sometimes heroin and other drugs were incorporated into peer group activity that occasionally involved delinquency but most especially was directed toward the search for and exploitation of "kicks." The norms and values of street-corner society tend to be inconsistent or in conflict with those of the larger society. Yet they *are* norms and values; consequently, they constrain or dictate certain types of behavior and help bind the peer group together and enhance feelings of adequacy and power in the face of dismal living conditions and family relationships.

In a group seeking "kicks," prestige comes from willingness to experiment and let oneself go, whether in delinquent acts, in the use of intoxicants or stimulants, or in other forms of behavior that are intrinsically exhilarating, involve an element of risk, or defy convention and conformity.[40] In the language of the "cats" — originally derived from the argot of the older drug addict and from that of the jazz musician — adherence to conventional norms is for the "squares." The culture of the "cats" and the pursuit of "kicks" are much more widespread than is the use of narcotics. Even in the areas of highest drug use, it appears that only a minority of young people experiment with

---

[40] See Harold Finestone, "Cats, Kicks, and Color," *Social Problems,* Vol. 5 (July, 1957), pp. 3–13. For a more recent but consonant description, see Harvey W. Feldman, "Ideological Supports to Becoming and Remaining a Heroin Addict," *Health and Social Behavior,* Vol. 9 (June, 1968), pp. 131–39.

heroin or other opiates, though most of them have incorporated the norms and values of street-corner society. Most have also incorporated many of the norms of conventional society.

Blumer and his associates have recently delineated the patterns of drug use and characterizations of social types among underprivileged minority-group members in an area of Oakland, California.[41] Occasional users — "mellow dudes" — appear to be in the majority. For the most part, these youths use drugs to enhance enjoyment of sex and music but do not regularly maintain drug supplies and do not deal for profit. For them, "pot" is a fine addition to partying but not an end in itself. LSD, amphetamines or speed may be used occasionally but not to the extent that one ceases to be "cool." "Pot heads" tend to limit themselves to marijuana, with which they are constantly supplied. Again they value coolness, but they tend to deal in marijuana and their lives rotate much more around the drug. In this setting they dress neatly and inconspicuously (in marked contrast to hippie "heads") and, apart from dealing, engage in conventional activities. Quite different are the "rowdy dudes," whose drug use is often indiscriminate but who tend to prefer alcohol. This type tends to be aggressive, wild, and more likely to engage in violent forms of delinquent behavior. The rowdy type is not seen by his peers as trustworthy where drugs are concerned, for his "uncool" behavior draws unfavorable attention and therefore may lead to arrest. Nevertheless, it is only among the rowdies that heroin use is not strongly devalued, and they are far more likely to become addicts than are any of the other types.

Within drug scenes generally, the "head" is the user whose life tends to revolve around drugs. In a study of drug use in Berkeley, Carey describes three orientations toward drugs. He contrasts the experimenters, who tried marijuana but did not proceed to regular use; the recreational users, who find marijuana a pleasant adjunct to many social situations but who use it with discretion and are concerned not to become overly dependent on it; and the "heads," whose use is more open, frequent, and central to their life styles.[42] Very similar is Keniston's characterization of "tasters," "seekers," and "heads" among college users.[43] Keniston's seekers are occasional users who "seek in drug use some way of intensifying experience, expanding awareness, breaking out of deadness and flatness or overcoming depression." The

---

[41] Herbert Blumer *et al.,* "The World of Youthful Drug Use."

[42] James J. Carey, *The College Drug Scene* (Englewood Cliffs, N. J.: Prentice-Hall, 1968).

[43] Kenneth Keniston, "Heads and Seekers: Drugs on Campus, Counter Cultures and American Society," *The American Scholar,* Vol. 38 (Winter, 1968–69), p. 100.

heads, whether pot-heads or acid-heads, are the committed users, who share the "turned-on" ideology of the hippie subculture even though they retain at least some relationship to the campus community.

Recreational users or seekers in the college scene are often average or better than average students, intellectually curious, and not vocationally oriented in their studies. They are more often found among students in the humanities and social sciences than among students in the "hard" sciences or in professional schools. They often have good work habits and a genuine interest in academic work but are not overly grade conscious. They may or may not be alienated from American society, but most are critical of the materialistic, militaristic, and racist tendencies they see in American life.

Heads, on the other hand, tend to be disengaged from conventional ties and to be much more sharply alienated from most of the dominant values in American society. Perhaps most alienated are those heads who become members of hippie enclaves or communes. Here one's whole way of life expresses estrangement from the institutions and fashions of conventional society. Shoulder-length hair and flowing beards for men, striking clothes (most of which may be shared communally), and manifest contempt for amenities and for material comforts serve both as disclaimers of membership in the larger society and as elements in a new identity.[44]

The characterization of types is more defensible as a descriptive aid than as a model of reality. While it is useful to know what distinctions are being made within groups of drug-users themselves, most individuals do not conform to the stereotypes. Tasters may become seekers and seekers may become heads. And even long-term heads may decide that the drug scene is at best a bad trip. In addition to the flux across type lines, there is considerable variation in the combination of backgrounds, motives, and activities of users, as well as in the mixture of drugs used. Unhappy, unstable, and amoral individuals tend to gravitate into drug scenes. One cannot explain most drug use on the basis of motives, but it would be absurd to suggest that the personality of the user is irrelevant to an understanding of his use of drugs.

Personality Characteristics and Drug Use

Psychiatrists who have specialized in the treatment of drug addicts are in substantial agreement that most addicts are not "normal" personalities. Few

---

[44] This is not to suggest that such attributes are all there is (or once was) to hippie life. For a description of positive themes in the hippie way of life, see Fred Davis, "Why All of Us May Be Hippies Someday," *Trans-action,* Vol. 5 (December, 1967), pp. 10–18.

would make the same assertion about recreational drug-users. Social scientists are more inclined to hold the view that both addicts and nonaddicted drug-users are the products of particular types of environments and the occupants of particular social roles — that is, that the patterns of behavior and attitude characteristic of drug subcultures are learned by a high proportion of persons who share a given milieu. These patterns are learned from role models just as skills in sports are learned from older youth by boys growing up in middle-class suburbs.

But there is no necessary conflict between the view of the addict as a deviant personality and the view of the addict as a social type. Undoubtedly the addiction of some persons is to be understood primarily as the expression of personal unhappiness or even of severe psychopathology. The addiction of others has come about as a result of subjection to environmental pressures too strong to resist — as is the case, for example, with children whose older siblings or peers made drugs available to them. But personality is not independent of environmental influences, and, by and large, the influences that permit heroin to be available to a teen-ager and permit a high proportion of adolescents to become members of street-corner society also create psychological needs and vulnerabilities that enhance the value of narcotics to the individual.

Psychopathology is both more frequent and more severe among young drug-users than among nonusers growing up in the same environment. Chein and his associates provide convincing evidence that the personality attributes of young heroin users are not merely a reflection of their deviance and social role but derive from family experiences that have been found generally to contribute to the development of psychopathology. As compared with nonusers from the same neighborhoods, drug-users far more often came from homes characterized by the absence of a positive relationship between the boy and an adult male role model:

> In almost all the addict families (97 percent), there was a disturbed relationship between parents, as evidenced by separation, divorce, open hostility, or lack of warmth and mutual interest. In these conditions, the mother usually became the most important parent figure in the life of the youngster. But, whatever the vicissitudes of the relationship between the boy and his mother, one theme was almost invariably the same — the absence of a warm relationship with a father figure with whom the boy could identify.[45]

We may say, then, that among the younger group of addicts whose early life was spent in the milieu of drug use, family relationships, psychodynamics, and prevailing social attitudes all played a part in leading the

---

[45] Isidor Chein *et al., The Road to H,* pp. 273–74.

adolescent or young adult to experimentation with drugs and incorporation into the culture of narcotics use.

Marijuana users and users of what have come to be called "soft" (i.e., nonaddicting) drugs do not present a comparable picture of psychopathology. Nevertheless, many heavy users began to experiment with drugs during periods of stress or upset that made them less responsive to relationships and controls that had previously been influential. Thus, among members of the East Village drug scene who were asked about their life circumstances at the time they began to use drugs, nearly half reported emotional problems, and almost as many reported that they were in conflict with their families (41%) or felt at odds with society (38%).[46] Detachment from society, purposelessness, and lack of direction in life were almost universally felt in substantial degrees in this group. It would appear, then, that persons who become most fully committed to regular drug use are likely to have had personal problems that led them to be deeply alienated and to find in drugs a sense of solidarity with others. Nearly all the East Village hippies interviewed reported that they had felt like "outsiders" from early childhood, and 95 percent said they tended to be "loners." Yet they were living in the most intimate of social relationships with people who had shortly before been strangers to them. We do not, of course, know what proportion of well-educated young people in the population at large would voice similar feelings about themselves and their society. Nevertheless, what evidence we have regarding recreational users suggests that they were much less influenced by personal problems and alienation in their early drug use.

Many users decide, after a time, that drugs are unduly complicating their lives. Some give up drugs for the same social reasons that led to turning on in the first place. That is, they become attached to new groups where drug use is not in vogue, or they fall in love with someone who has strong feelings against drug use. Others find that life crises are more difficult to handle with drugs than without them. To date, we have just the beginnings of research on this topic, but much more attention needs to be addressed to it. It is, of course, easiest for the occasional or recreational user to turn his back on drugs. For "heads" to do so, particularly when their drug use has been part of a quest for meaning, there must typically be both a crisis that precipitates the decision and an alternative code for governing their lives.[47]

---

[46] Douglas Holmes, "Selected Characteristics of 'Hippies' in New York City: An Overview," paper presented at the Conference on Drug Use and Drug Subcultures, Asilomar, California, February 12, 1970.

[47] Patrick Biernacki and Fred Davis, "Turning Off: A Study of Ex-Marihuana Users," paper presented at the Conference on Drug Use and Drug Subcultures, Asilomar, California, February 12, 1970.

Quite often fundamentalist religious sects or Eastern religious cults provide this alternative for heavy users of marijuana and other psychedelic drugs.

HEROIN ADDICTION AS A SPECIAL PROBLEM

Heroin and other opiates pose a special problem because of the nature of the physiological dependence that these drugs entail. When it was first produced in Germany in 1898, heroin was heralded as being free from addiction-producing properties, possessing all the virtues but none of the dangers of morphine. Its widespread use for producing euphoria initially took place in the underworld, long before physicians became aware of the dangers of the drug. Heroin's potency and the ease with which the pure drug could be diluted with lactose (sugar of milk) made it a convenient drug for regular use even when it could be freely purchased. These characteristics made it an ideal opiate for illicit use after federal control of narcotics had been established.

The process by which individuals become heroin users is, on the whole, quite similar to that described for marijuana users. That is, they are first introduced to the drug in a group or in an intimate, personal relationship, and the drug is freely provided by a friend. Since heroin is more widely devalued than marijuana, however, members of the groups in which it is used are for the most part already deviant in a number of other respects. Prior to World War II, heroin use was most frequent among persons in the entertainment world and in service occupations where individuals had extremely heterogeneous contacts. Following World War II, it became to a large extent a phenomenon of the urban slums, especially in the largest metropolitan areas. Nearly half of the known addicts in the United States live in New York City, and perhaps another one-quarter live in the Chicago and Los Angeles areas.[48]

Whether or not they participated in delinquency or crime prior to turning to heroin, the overwhelming majority of heroin addicts support their habits through various forms of theft.[49] The addict who is without drugs will go to any length to obtain drugs to ward off the abstinence syndrome. Thus the importance of narcotics as a cause of crime is due not to the direct effect of the drug but rather to the addict's need for it. Whereas the addicted pharmacist or physician generally commits no crime beyond his illegitimate use

---

[48] See John A. O'Donnell and John C. Ball, eds., *Narcotic Addiction* (New York: Harper, 1966), pp. 6–10.

[49] Harold Finestone, "Narcotics and Criminality," *Law and Contemporary Problems,* Vol. 22 (Winter, 1957), pp. 76–77.

of drugs to which he has access, the young minority-group addict in an urban slum has to commit many crimes to maintain his addiction. Contrary to popular belief, violent offenses against the person—sex offenses such as rape and various forms of assault—are much less frequent among addicts than among other criminal offenders.[50] Studies of the behavior of adolescent gangs in which a substantial number of members begin to use heroin reveals a decrease in such activity as gangfights and assaults after heroin use is widespread in the gang.[51]

Not everyone who experiments with heroin becomes addicted. Once an individual becomes addicted, however, the opiate habit is extremely difficult to break. Even after long periods of enforced abstinence, the addict tends to return to the drug, at least during his younger years. It has been suggested that this is partly a consequence of the intravenous technique of taking heroin. Until the late 1920's, it appears that relatively few addicts injected heroin directly into the vein; most either sniffed it as a powder or administered it by hypodermic needle subcutaneously. In the late 1920's, however, it was discovered that intravenous administration—"mainlining" the drug—gave a much more potent pleasure; as a consequence, use of the intravenous technique became widespread, especially among urban and minority-group users.[52] There is some reason to believe that the effects of an intravenous shot provide a kind of psychological reinforcement to the drug-taking habit that is peculiarly difficult to overcome.

In the 1930's, two federal narcotics hospitals were established within the Public Health Service for the treatment of addicts and for research on opiate addiction. Subsequently additional hospitals were established in several communities or states having high rates of opiate addiction. Uniformly, it has been found that addicts treated in these programs and returned to the community without supervision revert to the use of drugs in overwhelming proportion, usually in a very short period of time. However, when former addicts are followed up over a period of a decade or more, a significant proportion of them manage to remain abstinent.[53] Although the average addict remained addicted for a decade or more, by the age of 42 only about one-quarter of a sample of addicts studied by Vaillant were still using narcotics.

---

[50] *Ibid.,* p. 71.

[51] Isidor Chein *et al., The Road to H,* p. 166.

[52] See John A. O'Donnell and Judith P. Jones, "Diffusion of the Intravenous Technique Among Narcotic Addicts in the United States," *Journal of Health and Social Behavior,* Vol. 9 (June, 1968), pp. 120–30.

[53] See George E. Vaillant, "Twelve Year Follow-Up of New York Narcotic Addicts: II, The Natural History of a Chronic Disease," *New England Journal of Medicine,* Vol. 275 (December 8, 1966), pp. 1282–88.

The tendency of addicts to give up heroin as they get older is also evident from one of the few studies of drug use in a normal population. Robins and Murphy followed up 235 black males who had attended elementary school in St. Louis 26 to 30 years previously.[54] Slightly more than half of this group had tried drugs at some period of their lives. Almost all who tried any drug at all had smoked marijuana—49 percent of the total. One in eight had tried heroin, and all who tried it six or more times had become addicts. When these men were followed up in their mid-30's, most of the former heroin addicts were no longer addicted, though half of them were still using marijuana.

One aspect of heroin addiction that must be mentioned is the high mortality of addicts. In Vaillant's 12-year follow-up, addict mortality was two to five times that which would be normally expected for the age group. In New York City in 1969, 900 heroin-related deaths were recorded, and the number has roughly run 80 per month during the first half of 1970. Most of these deaths were a consequence of overdoses through use of heroin of unknown strength. Hepatitis is, of course, a frequent disease among addicts who use the intravenous technique (as it is with users of "speed"). Many addicts also experience extreme debilitation due to poor nutrition and self-neglect. Thus there are unique problems posed by the opiates and by drugs injected intravenously that make these drugs especially dangerous.

THE DRUG TRAFFIC

When a much-wanted substance is prohibited by law, it can be obtained only through illegal channels such as smuggling or clandestine manufacture. These procedures entail high risks, which will be undertaken only if there is sufficient demand to make possible high profits from dealing in the substance. It is, of course, extremely difficult to obtain an accurate picture of drug distribution channels. Drug-users may be quite willing to talk about their activities and their feelings about drugs, but they are much more wary of discussing where they obtain their supplies. Until recently, when the subcultures of drug use were clearly separated from conventional society, our knowledge of drug distribution was largely limited to the picture obtained from small-time user-pushers who are the principal retailers, and

---

[54] Lee N. Robins and G. E. Murphy, "Drug Use in a Normal Population of Young Negro Men," *American Journal of Public Health,* Vol. 57 (September, 1967), pp. 1580–96.

information obtained from the occasional arrests of large operators. In the last few years, the great expansion of drug distribution into circles to which research workers have access has made possible a fuller description of the whole apparatus.[55]

Characterizations of the social organization of drug dealing make fascinating reading, but for our purposes we need only be aware of the major features that have implications for efforts to control the illegal use of drugs. A number of myths about the drug traffic are prevalent, perhaps the most important of which relates to the enormous profits involved. It is true that the total amount spent on drugs by consumers in the community is enormous, but except at the highest levels of drug production and distribution, profits have been greatly exaggerated. Particularly as regards the marijuana traffic, the profit margin at each stage of distribution (smuggling, supplying large dealers, subdividing and supplying smaller dealers and street pushers) tends to be modest for the amount of time actually spent in the process. As Carey points out, there is much wasted time and motion in arranging for purchases and for delivery and there are inevitable "burns" (drugs of poor quality, or even inert substitutes supplied as potent drugs), aborted transactions, and arrests.[56]

Profits may be somewhat higher in dealing in LSD, amphetamines, and heroin, but again there are many middlemen and much lost time and motion in the process of distributing drugs. Moreover, the drug market even in heroin is much more loosely organized than it apparently was a decade or two ago.[57] The traffic is not tightly organized by criminal syndicates, though such syndicates may provide financing for certain major dealers. Perhaps the most important aspect of the psychedelic market is the diffuseness of sources of supply and the availability of alternative drugs which, coupled with high demand for these various drugs, insure competition from many sources. Further, almost all lower-level dealers and pushers are themselves drug-users who keep themselves supplied by buying in some quantity and selling only a portion. There are no direct ties between high-level dealers and the street pushers and, indeed, it would appear that even within the system of distribution most persons know only a few individuals one level above them or one level below them.

Addict pushers are, of course, frequently arrested and alternately under

[55] See, for example, Erich Goode, "The Marijuana Market," *Columbia Forum,* Vol. 12 (Winter, 1969), pp. 4–8; and James J. Carey, *The College Drug Scene,* Chapters 4 and 5.

[56] James J. Carey, *The College Drug Scene,* pp. 68–121.

[57] Michael Stern, "Heroin Traffickers Here Tell How $219 Million Trade Works," *New York Times,* April 20, 1970, pp. 1, 30.

pressure to inform on their sources of supply or to pay off police. Because of the relatively large amounts of money involved, payoffs may be extremely lucrative when a higher-level dealer is involved, and periodically there are charges of police corruption. In general such corruption appears more likely to occur at the local level than among federal enforcement agents, though it is not unknown in all branches of enforcement.

The large numbers of persons involved, the looseness of organization of the distribution apparatus, and the very large demand for drugs make it virtually impossible to eliminate drugs from the environment. At the same time, effective control efforts keep the price of drugs up and make drugs less readily available to the uninitiated.

PUBLIC POLICY AND DRUGS

By and large, public policy relating to drugs has been a product of fear and ignorance. It has received expression in laws designed to stamp out traffic in drugs and to imprison drug peddlers and drug-users. Legislation at the local and state levels occurred well before any federal legislation in this field, and state and local laws have continued to be a "patchwork of poorly drafted statutes and unfortunate amendments erected upon a structure of erroneous medical and psychological premises." [58] Since 1932, the states have received guidance in the preparation of drug acts from the federal government, but until recently that guidance has been based primarily upon the views of law enforcement officers and not upon sophisticated understanding of either the drugs or their effects.

The Harrison Act and Subsequent Legislation

The first federal legislation relating to addictive drugs was not an outgrowth of concern with addiction in the United States; rather it derived from concern with opium smoking in Far Eastern territories. [59] Early in the nineteenth century, British trading companies had introduced opium into China, against the wishes of the then powerless Chinese government. After the

---

[58] Neil L. Chayet, "Legal Aspects of Drug Abuse," in J. R. Wittenborn et al., *Drugs and Youth*, p. 236.

[59] See Glenn Sonnedecker, "Emergence and Concept of the Problems of Addiction."

pattern of opium smoking had spread widely, international conferences were held to consider the control of traffic in opium and other addictive drugs. As an expression of our adherence to the Hague Opium Convention of 1912, Congress in 1914 passed the Harrison Act to control the domestic sale, use, and transfer of opium and coca products. The Harrison Act provided for close control of the distribution of addicting drugs and prohibited possession except for "legitimate medical purposes." It also provided for an excise tax on such products; as a consequence, enforcement was lodged in the Treasury Department.

As previously noted, prior to the imposition of controls under the Harrison Act, there were at least 200,000 persons, and possibly as many as 1,000,000 persons addicted to opiates in the United States, many of them respected members of society. Up to that time, such persons could apply to any member of the medical profession for help in cutting down their drug use, or they could purchase drugs directly from any supplier at moderate prices. The Harrison Act cut off sources of direct drug supply and left the question of medical dosage open to legal interpretation. Officials of the Narcotics Division of the Treasury Department decided that "legitimate medical purposes" did not include administering opiates to addicted persons. As the former chairman of the Committee on Narcotics and Alcohol of the American Bar Association has noted, the Narcotics Division then "launched a reign of terror" against addicts and the physicians who treated them.[60] Doctors were bullied and threatened; addicted persons were portrayed as moral degenerates and criminals who should be locked up. Although the Supreme Court in 1925 rejected the interpretation that physicians were prohibited by the Harrison Act from treating addicts by prescribing drugs, the medical profession had by this time abandoned the field to the illicit drug peddler.

In 1937, marijuana was added to the list of drugs controlled under the Harrison Act. States were urged to pass similar legislation and all of them subsequently did, often without any more adequate knowledge of what they were legislating against than the assertions of personnel from the Federal Bureau of Narcotics. Since the use of drugs was characterized as leading inevitably to moral degeneracy, legislators hurried to express their aversion to degeneracy by increasing penalties for those found to have drugs in their possession.

The Massachusetts state law is a good example of the extent to which

---

[60] See Rufus King, "Narcotic Drug Laws and Enforcement Policies," *Law and Contemporary Problems,* Vol. 22 (Winter, 1957), p. 122. The effect of drug laws on the moral status of the drug-user is discussed in Troy Duster, *The Legislation of Morality: Law, Drugs and Moral Judgment* (New York: Free Press, 1970).

panicky thinking has characterized some state legislatures. To offer another person a marijuana cigarette and to have that person accept it carries a penalty of 10 to 25 years in state prison for the first offense and 20 to 50 years for a second offense. Even more fantastic is that the Massachusetts law provides: "Whoever is present where a narcotic drug is illegally kept or deposited or whoever is in the company of a person knowing that said person is illegally in possession of a narcotic drug . . . may be arrested without a warrant and may be punished by imprisonment in the state prison for not more than five years." [61] In other words, a person visiting in the apartment of a friend may be charged and convicted of a felony punishable by up to five years in a state prison if that friend has a marijuana cigarette hidden somewhere in his apartment. As Chayet notes, this section of the Massachusetts law is defended by supporters because it makes enforcement of the law much easier, since many persons can be arrested in a raid without evidence having to be collected against them individually.

By the mid-1960's it was apparent that many drugs other than marijuana and heroin were being obtained and used without prescription; Congress reacted by passing the Drug Abuse Control Amendments of 1965. The new laws were initially aimed at preventing abuse of stimulant and depressant drugs; however, they left up to the head of the Federal Drug Administration the designation of specific drugs to be controlled. Subsequently, LSD and other psychedelic drugs were readily brought under control without additional legislation. The primary concern of the new law soon became the prevention of careless or illegal distribution of drugs that are subject to abuse because of their psychedelic effects. The goal was not to arrest and imprison drug-users but to exercise greater control over the flow of dangerous drugs from the manufacturer to the consumer and to provide penalties for illegal sale of such drugs. Law enforcement personnel were added to the staff of the FDA, but simultaneously attention was given to furthering research on drug use and to educational programs that would provide more accurate information about drug effects and consequences.

This left our federal program of drug control divided between two agencies, the Department of the Treasury and the Department of Health, Education and Welfare. In 1968, both programs were removed from the departments in which they had been lodged and were combined in the Department of Justice. While the Department of Justice would seem a more sensible setting for law enforcement than the Treasury Department, the

---

[61] Massachusetts General Laws Annotated, Chapter 94, 213 A (Supplements, 1966), quoted by Neil L. Chayet in J. R. Wittenborn *et al., Drugs and Youth,* p. 237.

former has neither medical staff nor staff and facilities to develop education and research in the field of drug abuse. The consequences were clearly manifest when, in late summer of 1969, Attorney General Mitchell introduced into Congress a bill designed to replace all previous federal legislation dealing with addictive and dangerous drugs.

The advice of scientific panels was almost totally disregarded in the framing of the bill. As originally introduced, the bill was narrowly concerned with the control of drugs and with penalties for those who violated the control features. No provision was made for treatment of drug offenders but only for their imprisonment. The bill would have given the Attorney General control over the circumstances under which research on drug effects could be carried out and would have been a marked deterrent to such research.

Although it received prompt approval in committee and was strongly endorsed by advocates of "law and order," the Administration's new law was opposed almost unanimously by members of the scientific community concerned with drug legislation. Concerted opposition to the original bill brought about a number of significant modifications before the Comprehensive Drug Abuse Prevention and Control Act of 1970 (H.R. 18583) was finally passed by both Houses of Congress in October, 1970.[62] As enacted, the law provides for federal support of community treatment facilities for drug-dependent individuals and gives the Secretary of Health, Education and Welfare rather than the Attorney General authority over medical and scientific matters relating to drug abuse. The penalties for drug possession have been greatly reduced and judges are now allowed a wider measure of discretion in dealing with first offenders. Penalties for drug sale are, however, extremely severe; the law again ignores the economic and social realities that make most regular drug-users sellers at one time or another. Marijuana remains in the same control category as heroin, but the law provides for the establishment of a commission to make further recommendations with reference to the status of marijuana. In sum, the new law repre-

---

[62] Early in 1970, a group of physicians, scientists, and lawyers organized The Committee for Effective Drug Abuse Legislation to coordinate efforts to inform the members of Congress and the public generally about appropriate governmental action to deal with problems of drug abuse. The substantial measure of success that was achieved in modifying the bill originally proposed by the administration is due largely to the efforts of this group. Congress did not, however, accept the recommendations of the scientific community with reference to the classification of drugs to be controlled nor would it abandon the "no-knock" provisions that authorize narcotics agents with a warrant to batter down doors of suspected sellers or to intrude unannounced into a physician's office when he is with a patient.

sents some improvement over the previous hodgepodge of federal legislation but still puts primary emphasis on the punitive approach that has so consistently failed to halt drug abuse in the United States.

Consequences of the Punitive Approach

During the period when laws against drug use have multiplied and penalties have become more severe, drug use has increased enormously. While the punitive approach has not ended the traffic in drugs or cut down drug use, it has had other consequences.

One consequence of the increasing severity of penalties for narcotics offenses is that drug offenders have come to make up a considerable portion of all federal and state prisoners. In the past decade, the bulk of narcotics arrests and prosecutions were made by local enforcement agencies operating under state laws.[63] Yet despite the declining proportion of federal prosecutions, the number and proportion of drug offenders in federal prisons had more than doubled between 1950 and the early 1960's. The average length of sentences served by these prisoners increased roughly fourfold in the same period.

Another consequence of inflexible, severe sentences for drug possession is that the penalties frequently seem so senseless to judges and juries that the rate of conviction drops markedly. In Michigan, for example, where the penalty for the first offense of selling is a minimum of 20 years, without possibility of suspension or probation, only 3 percent of the persons charged as narcotics peddlers have been convicted on this charge. A study by the American Bar Foundation reported that juries were unwilling to convict persons of sale of narcotics when the penalty was set so high.[64]

Recognition of the hopelessness of solving the addiction problem by locking addicts in state and federal prisons led many states, in the early 1960's, to develop "civil commitment" programs. In essence, civil commitment laws provide for suspension of criminal proceedings against addicts who have committed crimes in order to supply their drug habit. These addicts are then committed not to prisons but to rehabilitation programs where they pre-

---

[63] Alfred R. Lindesmith, in *The Addict and the Law* (Bloomington, Ind.: Indiana University Press, 1965), pp. 106–07, summarizes data from several sources that suggest that at least 95 percent of all narcotics prosecutions in the early 1960's were nonfederal.

[64] See William B. Eldridge, *Narcotics and the Law* (New York: American Bar Foundation, 1962), pp. 88–89.

sumably receive therapy and useful training, following which they are returned to the community and receive close supervision for a substantial period.

Civil commitment programs are not a panacea. Civil commitment sometimes represents little more than a change of name for imprisonment; the rights of the individual to due process of the law may actually be infringed. Although "civil" commitment technically avoids the label of "criminal," the individual may in fact be as strongly stigmatized as if he had been imprisoned for a criminal charge, especially if he is committed to facilities that also house convicted felons, as is the case in California. On the other hand, the development of specialized programs for drug-users and the provision of close supervision in the community offer some promise that more effective rehabilitation methods will be developed. In any case, the New York and California programs have produced some valuable information about the addict after his return to the community.

Perhaps the most serious consequence of the punitive approach that has characterized efforts to deal with drug use and addiction in the United States is that deriving from the educational impact of such laws and their enforcement or nonenforcement. On the one hand, laws that are based on false conceptions of the dangers of drugs mislead members of the general public who have no first-hand knowledge of drug effects. In order to justify passage of such laws, distorted pictures of the drug-user are created, reducing his chances for acceptance by others and making his reincorporation into conventional society much more difficult. On the other hand, young persons who are aware of the falsity of some of the "evidence" cited as reasons for harsh penalties may be led to discount the very real dangers inherent in much drug use. Not only is respect for the law undermined, but valid information is rendered suspect.

Attitudes Toward Drug Use

Some schools and colleges have taken the same punitive stand toward the drug-user as have legislators. Students who use drugs are often suspended or put on probation. One unfortunate consequence is that those whose drug use is really problematical, because of either their personal problems or their bad trips, are prevented from seeking professional help by the threat posed to their status as students.

Many older, conventional Americans seem to be more concerned about drugs than about almost any other topic. Even the financial pages of our newspapers now contain articles about how to cope with employees who "use drugs." "If you are typical," writes financial columnist Sylvia Porter, "you wouldn't hire an addict or try to reform one if you found him in your employ." [65] Unfortunately, "addict" seems to mean anyone who uses drugs. The policies of companies that have considered the problem are reported as follows:

> When someone admits he uses drugs, they refer him to a mental health clinic immediately. If medical prognosis is poor, they dismiss him; if it is good, each company follows the employee's progress to be sure that he continues treatment and stays off drugs. If the user rejects treatment or continues to use drugs, all companies fire him.[66]

Again, in June 1970, a bill was introduced into the California legislature that provided for a mandatory course of education on drug abuse for any young persons caught using marijuana.

To suggest that marijuana users as a group can be educated out of their drug use or that smoking an occasional joint is an indication for "treatment" is as absurd as suggesting that all social drinkers ought to have therapy. The basic difference between the social drinker and the marijuana smoker is that the former consumes a socially acceptable drug while the latter is violating state and federal laws. This is not a negligible difference. It is very difficult for most adults in their middle years — especially if they are conventional members of the middle class — to understand how a bright and responsible adolescent or young adult would be willing to risk a felony charge for a casual pleasure. Nevertheless, the fact that a very substantial proportion of bright, responsible young people do precisely that seems a clear indication that we are dealing with a gross conflict of values and very different perceptions of relevant group norms. Such problems are not resolved by therapy or by education that merely states a different set of personal preferences.

There are, of course, many drug-users — especially addicts — who need medical and psychiatric treatment. In the confines of the present chapter it has not been possible to deal with such recent developments in the treatment of addiction as methadone maintenance for addicts on outpatient status or with such programs as that of Synanon.[67] In general, incarceration,

---

[65] Sylvia Porter, "Employers and Drug Use," *San Francisco Chronicle,* June 5, 1970, p. 60.

[66] *Ibid.*

[67] Descriptions of Synanon are given in Daniel Casriel, *So Fair a House: The Story of Synanon* (Englewood Cliffs, N. J.: Prentice-Hall, 1963); Rita Volkman and Donald R. Cressey, "Differential Association and the Rehabilitation of Drug Addicts," *Ameri-*

forced education, and compulsory treatment do not seem to be appropriate
ways of dealing with the alienation that frequently underlies drug use; nor
are they appropriate responses to levels of recreational drug use that do not
interfere with the individual's ability to manage his affairs. So long as the
drug-user is isolated, rejected, and punished, he is likely to become more
alienated and more deviant. There comes a point, of course, where enforced
isolation of deviants may be necessary. Too often we seem to push drug-
users to that point.

Should Marijuana Be Legalized?

If the traffic in marijuana is unlikely to be shut off and if young people continue to smoke the drug despite the threat of harsh penalties, would it be
more sensible to legalize marijuana than to continue present policies? Experts differ sharply in their views on this topic but most are opposed to complete legalization. So is most of the public. A Gallup Poll, taken in October
1969, found only 14 percent of American men and 10 percent of American
women favoring legalization. The chief reasons stated by the respondents
for their opposition to legal pot were that it "harms the mind" and that it
frequently leads to the use of other drugs. As might be expected, support for
legal marijuana came very largely from persons in the age group 21–30 and
from persons with a college education, roughly one-fourth of each of these
groups expressing the view that marijuana should be made legal.

Whether or not marijuana is harmful to physical or mental health, it is
an intoxicant that can lead to poor judgment and contribute to accidents if
used to excess or at inappropriate times. In this respect it is similar to alcohol, which is *not* legally available to persons below certain age levels. It
would seem that some measure of control would be desirable for marijuana,
even if it were to be made legally available to adults; yet, paradoxically,
such controls would prohibit use by the very group most heavily involved with
marijuana at the present time. On the other hand, just as it appears good
educational practice for older adolescents to learn to use alcohol with discrimination in the family setting, one might envision families enjoying
smoking marijuana together.

The main arguments for a measure of legalization would seem to be the

can Journal of Sociology, Vol. 69 (September, 1963), pp. 129–42; Lewis Yablonsky,
The Tunnel Back: Synanon (New York: Macmillan, 1965); and Guy Endore, *Synanon*
(New York: Doubleday, 1968).

evidence (not yet conclusive) that marijuana is *not* more harmful than alcohol and tobacco, that it is widely used, and that making its use a serious crime has entailed high costs, economically, morally, and psychologically. Most persons using marijuana are never arrested. Of those arrested for possession, two-thirds are released, dismissed, or acquitted.[68] But the marijuana laws are differentially enforced; they afford a means of harassing persons whose appearances and social views are unpopular. Such differential treatment contributes to the further alienation of those already disadvantaged and discriminated against. But if the laws were to be more strictly enforced, the entire police and judicial systems would quickly be inundated and rendered ineffective for any other purpose. As it is, the courts are struggling under the heavy burden of dealing with drug arrests.

Of course, it is possible that marijuana smoking may, like cigarette smoking, be found to increase the probability of contracting a chronic respiratory disorder. Many years of heavy smoking by millions of persons were required before the statistics on lung cancer and other diseases associated with cigarette smoking had made blatantly evident to everyone but the tobacco industry that cigarettes shorten life. The same may be true of other forms of smoking. Moreover, long-term use may have other deleterious effects. If marijuana were to be legalized, careful long-term monitoring of physical effects would seem desirable.

In the last analysis, legislation will require substantial changes in public opinion. However, in little more than a decade, the views of educated Americans toward abortion underwent an almost complete turnabout, and views on marijuana may well change as radically in the next ten to fifteen years, as today's pot users become an increasingly large proportion of the electorate. Although for the present some lessening of the severity of penalties is the only change that seems to have a fair degree of support among the informed public, as one commentator notes, "If the public *generally* begins to regard marijuana as 'not that bad' or desirable and that attitude is translated into demands for legislation by groups that possess or come to possess the ability to have their views enacted into law, legalization of marijuana would be in order."[69] If and when this occurs, the nature of the "drug problem" in the United States will itself have markedly changed.

---

[68] John Kaplan, "What the Legislator Should Consider," in J. R. Wittenborn *et al.*, *Drugs and Youth,* p. 257.

[69] Michael P. Rosenthal, "Marihuana: Some Alternatives," in J. R. Wittenborn *et al., Drugs and Youth,* p. 263.

5

Alcohol
and Alcoholism

ROBERT STRAUS

Alcohol has been described as a substance that, together with its uses and effects, "permeates, pleases and yet plagues most of the world."[1] Certainly the problems associated with the use of alcohol affect, directly or indirectly, a large segment of mankind. Often, they occur in association with other problems of human well-being and are part of a malignant clustering of destructive personal and social pathologies. Man has used alcohol since before the beginnings of recorded history and in most parts of the world. The nature and extent of alcohol use has varied considerably according to cultural context and historical period, as have the problems associated with alcohol and the measures taken to control or prevent them. The troubles caused by alcohol have been "so massive that many governments and religions have tried suppressing its use totally,"[2] yet the attractions of alcohol have been so compelling that such prohibitions have been repealed, circumvented, or defied.

An essential dilemma that has complicated the task of those who would invent social policy designed to deal with alcohol problems stems from the

---

[1] Mark Keller in M. Keller and M. McCormick, *A Dictionary of Words About Alcohol* (New Brunswick, N. J.: Rutgers Center of Alcohol Studies, 1968), p. xv.

[2] *Ibid.,* p. xvi.

fact that alcohol is both functional and dysfunctional. Under certain circumstances alcohol has great capacity for alleviating pain; relieving tension and worry; providing a pleasurable sense of warmth, well-being, and relaxation; and heightening a sense of conviviality and good will toward one's fellow men. For these reasons the use of alcohol has been regarded as functional in many societies, and man has clung tenaciously to his right to drink. Alcohol has been enshrined with positive religious symbolism, associated with good health and nutrition, and used commonly in the sanctification of birth, puberty, marriage, and death. Alcohol has been an important element in the economy of many nations, supporting international commerce, creating employment, and providing revenue from heavy taxation.

A few societies have been able to enjoy the benefits of alcohol and avoid its severe liabilities. However, for most of the world where its use has been common, alcohol has also brought serious consequences. Essentially these stem from its intoxicating properties, which can affect any user, by which many become temporarily incapacitated, and to which some become addicted. In societies having high rates of alcohol abuse, concerns about drunkenness and alcoholism have increased as urbanization and industrialization have brought into sharper focus the perceived threat that the intoxicated person or the alcoholic poses to the well-being of others. Today, the recognized problems of alcohol throughout much of the world include, in addition to drunkenness and alcoholism, accidents caused by driving vehicles while under the influence of alcohol; industrial accidents, absenteeism, and loss of production attributable to alcohol abuse; the special threat that some societies perceive in drinking by the young and "uninitiated"; and the relationship of alcohol use to such problems as poverty, physical and mental illnesses, family instability, crime, and suicide.

Efforts to understand the phenomena associated with alcohol have frequently been limited by a tendency to cast the consideration within a single conceptual model, to think exclusively within the frame of reference of morality or medicine or the law, instead of recognizing that drinking behavior has broad social implications affecting in some way almost every aspect of social life. Alcohol problems also transcend the lines of traditional disciplines devoted to the study of human behavior.

The nature and severity of alcohol problems found in a particular society or at a particular time depend on the customs of drinking that prevail in that society. However, the relationship between drinking customs and drinking problems can be understood only if consideration is given to the nature of alcohol and its impact on the human body and human behavior.

THE ACTION OF ALCOHOL ON MAN

To understand the relationship between drinking customs and drinking problems we require a conceptual model that considers the functional relationship, continuing interaction, and fundamental interdependence among the basic components of drinking behavior.[3] These include the pharmacological properties of alcohol; man's physiological, biochemical, and psychological reactions to alcohol; the varieties of alcoholic beverages; drinking customs and beliefs about alcohol; the relationship of drinking practices and attitudes to the family, religious, economic, political, medical, and recreation systems of a society; and the impact of drinking customs on personal experiences of drinking.

The Nature of Alcohol: Physiological Effects [4]

Alcoholic beverages [5] vary widely in their alcohol content depending on the natural products from which, and the processes by which, they are derived. Wines, produced by fermentation of fruit juices, have a natural alcohol content of from 9 to 14 percent. Some wines are "reinforced" or "fortified" by the addition of alcohol to bring their content up to about 20 percent. Brewed

---

[3] In a discussion of the relevance of biological variables to the understanding of deviant behavior, R. L. Means cited the sociological literature on alcoholism as an example of the tendency of sociologists to neglect the consideration of biological factors in their studies and analyses of social problems. R. L. Means, "Sociology, Biology and the Analysis of Social Problems," *Social Problems,* Vol. 15 (Fall, 1967), pp. 200–12.

[4] For a more complete discussion see Leon Greenberg, "Alcohol in the Body," in R. G. McCarthy, ed., *Drinking and Intoxication* (New York: Free Press, 1959), pp. 7–13; and Leonard Goldberg, "The Metabolism of Alcohol," in S. P. Lucia, ed., *Alcohol and Civilization* (New York: McGraw-Hill, 1963), pp. 23–42.

[5] Beverage alcohol—technically, ethyl alcohol—is only one of numerous forms of alcohol. Unlike other alcohols, ethyl alcohol can be rapidly oxidized in the human body. A variety of nonpotable alcohols are used in industrial processes and in such common substances as automobile antifreeze, cleaning fluids, fuels, liniments, and numerous other readily available items. The ingestion of these poisonous alcohols can, and frequently does, lead to blindness, permanent nerve disorder, or death. The occasional use of nonbeverage alcohols for human consumption, either by accident or in desperation by alcoholics, poses an additional social problem of alcohol, one which is not considered in this chapter.

beverages, derived from various cereals, usually have an alcohol content of from 3 to 6 percent, depending on local custom or law. Stronger beverages such as whiskies and brandies are manufactured by distilling fermented or brewed products and recovering liquids with an alcohol content of from 35 to 50 percent.

The major impact of alcohol on human behavior depends on the action of its pharmacological properties, which include those of an anesthetic and a depressant, on the central nervous system. The degree of effect depends on the concentration of alcohol in the blood when it reaches the brain. Since alcohol, once absorbed by the blood, is subject to oxidation, by which it is eventually reduced to carbon dioxide and water, significant intoxication will be experienced only when the conditions of drinking are such that the rate of absorption is sufficiently greater than the rate of oxidation. Significant drinking conditions include the type and alcoholic strength of the beverage, the rate of ingestion, the presence or absence of foods in the stomach that impede the rate of absorption, and the amount consumed in relation to the body weight of the drinker.

A man of average weight consuming a pint of whisky gradually over a 24-hour period would probably experience no marked effect, while the same man consuming the same amount of whisky in the space of an hour would suffer extreme intoxication. A man weighing 120 pounds will feel a much greater effect from the same amount and rate of drinking than a man weighing 240 pounds. Ten ounces of 50 percent whisky should produce a greater effect than 100 ounces of 5 percent beer.[6] The effect of drinking on an empty stomach greatly exceeds the effect produced by drinking the same amount after a heavy meal.

Roughly speaking, a man of moderate weight (155–165 pounds) who consumes an ounce of whisky or a bottle of beer might achieve an alcohol concentration in the blood of no more than 0.02 percent. However, were he to consume 5 or 6 ounces of whisky rather quickly, he would achieve a concentration of about 0.1 percent.

The effect on behavior of a concentration of 0.02 percent is negligible for most people. But a concentration of 0.1 percent produces definite depression of sensory and motor functions (slight staggering, fumbling, and tripping of the tongue over even familiar words). Despite a reduction in digital dexterity, auditory and visual discrimination, tactile perception, and the speed of motor responses, many drinkers at this level have the illusion that their reactions, perception, and discrimination are better than normal. A concentration of

---

[6] This is so because the 5 ounces of absolute alcohol in the whisky can be consumed and would be absorbed much more quickly than the same amount of alcohol in the beer.

0.2 percent of alcohol incapacitates most drinkers both physically and emotionally. At 0.3 percent the drinker is stuporous; a concentration above 0.4 percent leads to coma. A concentration of 0.6 or 0.7 percent would affect the ability to breathe and cause death.[7]

The Psychological Effects of Alcohol

The psychological effects of alcohol have been classified into two distinct but related categories.[8] First are effects on *overt* behavior, such as "sensation, perception, reaction time, the performance of motor tasks and skills and processes of learning, remembering, thinking, reasoning, and solving problems." [9] Second are the effects on *emotional* behavior, such as fear, anxiety, tension, hostility, or the feelings of being "on edge" or of euphoria.

Numerous studies have clearly found that alcohol, even in small amounts, does have a deleterious influence on task performance. The effect of given amounts of alcohol on skilled performance increases with the complexity of the task, the unfamiliarity of the task to the performer, and the inexperience of the performer with drinking. Even small amounts of alcohol may affect simple tasks if the performer is inexperienced both in drinking and in carrying out the task at hand. The inexperienced drinker, moreover, is apt to overreact to the sensations of alcohol. He may merely be fulfilling what he perceives to be the socially expected behavior in response to drinking. Such a reaction is commonly seen in groups of young people who behave as if hilariously intoxicated under the influence of very small amounts of alcohol (and sometimes without alcohol at all). Some drinking novices are so unaccustomed to even the mild sensations of a little alcohol that it may actually impede their task performance beyond the normal expectation for their level of blood alcohol concentration. This phenomenon contributes to a special concern over drinking combined with driving in young people who are neither experienced drinkers nor experienced drivers.

Some experienced drinkers, on the other hand, appear to learn how to compensate psychologically for the sensations produced by alcohol, so that they can present the outward manifestations of sobriety and can sometimes even satisfactorily perform complex tasks with which they are familiar, despite the handicap of alcohol's effect.

---

[7] Leon Greenberg, "Alcohol in the Body," pp. 11–12.

[8] Edith S. Lisansky, "Psychological Effects of Alcohol," in McCarthy, ed., *Drinking and Intoxication*, pp. 18–25.

[9] *Ibid.,* p. 18.

The detrimental effect of alcohol on task performance may be counteracted by its effect on emotional behavior. For those individuals whose ability to perform effectively is often seriously limited by their tension or anxiety, alcohol, which serves as a kind of sedative, may provide enough relief to permit more effective performance. In situations where "effective performance" does not demand a special skill, such as social gatherings, alcohol can produce the desired feeling of well-being and relaxation. However, where some degree of efficiency is required, the relaxing qualities of alcohol may be dangerously misleading, for, as E. M. Jellinek has noted, "the properties of alcohol that are conducive to sedation or relaxation are by no means conducive to task efficiency." [10]

This paradox leaves unresolved the question of how helpful or damaging the use of alcohol may be for particular individuals faced with particular tasks.[11] As a general rule drinking does not enhance task performance; however, for some individuals, especially very tense, experienced drinkers performing familiar tasks, the relaxing qualities of alcohol may override its deleterious effects in terms of overall performance.

There is, of course, a fundamental relationship between man's physiological and psychological responses to alcohol. For example, psychological conditions can either promote or retard stomach motility, thereby increasing or decreasing the rate of alcohol absorption and directly influencing the level of effect resulting from a given amount of alcohol. The intensity of psychological effect is directly related to physiological effect. Also, some individuals appear to be psychologically more sensitive to alcohol when they are fatigued.

The Impact of Drinking Customs

The impact of alcohol on man is also related to differences in customary beliefs and patterns of use. Conditions that favor the rapid absorption of sufficient alcohol to affect behavior are associated with higher rates of intoxication and increased exposure to alcoholism. Such conditions are generally found in societies where most drinking is done on an empty stomach and involves beverages with a high alcohol content in relatively undiluted form.

---

[10] E. M. Jellinek, *How Alcohol Affects Psychological Behavior* (New Haven: *Quarterly Journal of Studies on Alcohol,* Lay Supplement No. 11, 1944), p. 12.

[11] For a critical review of relevant literature since 1940, see John A. Carpenter, "The Effects of Alcohol on Some Psychological Processes," *Quarterly Journal of Studies on Alcohol,* Vol. 23 (June, 1962), pp. 274–314.

Not only is the buffering effect of food missing, but people tend to drink more rapidly when they are not eating, and when they are standing rather than seated.

Low rates of alcohol pathology tend to be found where customs favor drinking of beers or low-alcohol wines and where the conditions of drinking impede rapid ingestion or absorption. People who consume alcohol primarily because they believe in its medicinal efficacy are apt to space their drinking regularly over time or use it only when a specific need arises. People who consider alcohol to be a form of food and who customarily drink only with meals rarely achieve a high level of alcohol concentration. Food provides a competing substance for ingestion and impedes the absorption of alcohol in the stomach.

Historically, variations in types of alcoholic beverages and patterns of drinking have been related to geographical factors such as soil, climate, and terrain. For example, the geographic conditions of southern Europe have favored the growth of succulent grapes and thus have supported wine technology and wine-drinking customs. Brewing technology and customs favoring beer consumption have their origins in areas where barley and other suitable grains have been plentiful. However, technological advances in agriculture, transportation, and manufacturing have reduced the barriers that distinguished drinking customs of different societies and permitted the development of more heterogeneous drinking practices. This process is illustrated by the history of drinking in the United States.

AMERICAN DRINKING CUSTOMS
IN HISTORICAL PERSPECTIVE [12]

The drinking customs and attitudes of the American population reflect a configuration of practices, beliefs, and attitudes that have come from many parts of the world and represent many cultures.[13] Over the years, there have been significant changes.

---

[12] This section draws primarily from the following sources: H. W. Haggard and E. M. Jellinek, *Alcohol Explored* (New York: Doubleday, 1945), pp. 3–85; R. G. McCarthy and E. M. Douglass, *Alcohol and Social Responsibility* (New York: Crowell, 1949), p. 34; R. Straus and S. D. Bacon, "Drinking Customs and Attitudes in American Society," Chapter 2, *Drinking in College* (New Haven: Yale University Press, 1953), pp. 20–35.

[13] For pertinent references to cultural variations in drinking patterns see R. Sadoun, G. Lolli, and M. Silverman, *Drinking in French Culture* (New Brunswick, N. J.: Rutgers Center of Alcohol Studies, 1965); G. Lolli, W. Serianni, G. Golder, and

The colonists who came to America from England brought with them well-established habits and attitudes about the use of alcohol. Alcoholic beverages had important religious, medical, and dietary significance; they were well integrated into family life and community recreational practices and quickly became a prominent component of commerce and of the colonial economy. At first, most drinking was of beer and wine. However, by the end of the eighteenth century about 90 percent of the alcohol consumed in this country was in the form of distilled spirits.

Prior to 1700, drinking appears to have been primarily a family-centered and family-controlled activity. Religious sanctions were directed against drunkenness and its concomitants. The significance of distilled spirits grew coincidentally with the immigration of numbers of unattached males, whose drinking was unrelated to family sanctions and may have served to compensate for the absence of the gratifications, responsibilities, and stability of family living. The frequent use of alcohol to produce intoxication became particularly characteristic of life on the ever expanding frontier and among the less stable segments of communities during the several decades following the Revolutionary War.

Perhaps in reaction to the excesses of drinking on the frontier and in its urban counterpart, the practice of family drinking appears to have diminished by the early nineteenth century, when frequent heavy consumption of distilled spirits, much of it by unattached men, became the dominant drinking practice. This type of drinking, which was often accompanied by wild, destructive behavior, became a major social concern. Intoxication was seen as a threat to the personal well-being and property of peaceful citizens, and the loss of productive manpower through drunkenness was seen as a threat to the national economy and vitality.

At the beginning of the nineteenth century, when the use of distilled spirits dominated American drinking, 90 percent of the white population was of British heritage. After about 1820, waves of immigrants from other nations significantly altered the ethnic composition of this country. In the next century, more than 20 million people migrated from southern, central, and eastern Europe, where the predominant alcoholic beverages were either beers or wines. By about 1840, the change in the ethnic composition of the

P. Luzzatto-Fegiz, *Alcohol in Italian Culture* (New York: Free Press, 1958); R. G. McCarthy, ed., *Drinking and Intoxication;* David J. Pittman and Charles R. Snyder, eds., *Society, Culture, and Drinking Patterns* (New York: Wiley, 1962); S. P. Lucia, ed., *Alcohol and Civilization* (New York: McGraw-Hill, 1963); and the files of the *Quarterly Journal of Studies on Alcohol,* Vols. 1–31 (1940–1970).

population began to be reflected in patterns of alcohol consumption. From 1850 to 1960, alcohol consumed in the form of distilled spirits fell from roughly 90 percent to 41 percent of the total alcohol consumed. During the same period, alcohol consumed in the form of beer rose from 6 to 48 percent of the total, while that in the form of wine rose from 4 to 11 percent. From 1850 to 1960 the total annual per capita (persons 15 years of age and over) consumption of absolute alcohol in all beverage forms remained virtually unchanged at just over 2 gallons. However, during the last decade a steady rise has been recorded from 2.07 gallons of absolute alcohol consumed in 1960 to 2.45 gallons in 1968.[14]

Changes in the types of alcoholic beverages consumed naturally reflect changes in drinking customs. E. M. Jellinek has noted that "a large consumption of distilled spirits and a small consumption of beer is generally an indication that the users are relatively few in number but individually heavy consumers. A large consumption of beer, on the other hand, is indicative of wide use and relatively small individual consumption."[15] Data on consumption from 1750 to 1850 suggest that there were relatively few moderate drinkers and that most people were either heavy drinkers or abstainers. During the last century there has been a gradual rise in the relative number of users. It is currently estimated that about 70 percent of the adult population use alcohol compared with under 50 percent in 1850. This increase reflects the emergence of a dominant pattern of relatively moderate drinking. The sharp increase in beer consumption has further implications in terms of effects on behavior. Whereas a person drinking whisky could easily consume a pint of alcohol in the course of a day by drinking a quart of whisky, a beer drinker would have to drink 10 quarts to take in the same amount of alcohol.

---

[14] Personal communication from Mark Keller, Director, Documentation Division, Rutgers Center of Alcohol Studies, February, 1970. These data are based on sales of legally manufactured alcohol. Although further research is needed to explain this phenomenon, Keller believes that changes since 1960, which include a 28 percent rise in the consumption of distilled spirits from 0.86 to 1.10 gallons of absolute alcohol per capita, probably reflect a recent decline in the illegal manufacture and distribution of distilled spirits and a switch in consumption from illegal (unrecorded) to legal (recorded) beverages, rather than a real or significant rise in the consumption of distilled spirits. During the same period, the long-time trend in beer consumption continued with a 10 percent rise from 0.99 to 1.09 gallons.

[15] E. M. Jellinek, "Recent Trends in Alcoholism and in Alcohol Consumption," *Quarterly Journal of Studies on Alcohol,* Vol. 8 (June, 1947), p. 9. This observation does not exclude beer as the beverage of choice of the majority of those people who drink heavily in predominantly beer-drinking areas such as Czechoslovakia, Denmark, and Bavaria.

From our knowledge of the absorption, metabolism, and impact of alcohol in the human body, it is quite obvious that the intoxicating effects of beer drinking are quite different from those of drinking that involves primarily whisky.

CONTEMPORARY DRINKING CUSTOMS

We have yet to examine the prevalence of drinking in contemporary society. Although it may seem to be a simple matter, measurements in this field are as difficult to come by as those in fields of mental illness, crime, delinquency, poverty, and the other social problems reviewed in this book. The problem of measurement is complicated by wide variations in the interpretation of just what constitutes being a drinker or an abstainer.

How frequently in a month, a year, or a lifetime, or how much does one have to drink in order to be considered or to consider himself a "drinker"? Some people who take beverage alcohol daily think of themselves as abstainers because they believe they are drinking for reasons of health. Others who have used alcohol only on infrequent social occasions during their lifetime may classify themselves as users. Neither the general public nor the various investigators who have tried to measure the prevalence of drinking have so far agreed on criteria.

Recent studies show that between 63 and 71 percent of the adult population (age 21 and above) in the United States drink some form of alcoholic beverages.[16] Although this figure represents about 85 million American

---

[16] D. Cahalan, I. M. Crisin and H. M. Crossley reported in 1969 that 68 percent of those interviewed in a national probability sample said that they drink at least once a year. See *American Drinking Practices: A National Study of Drinking Behavior and Attitudes* (New Brunswick, N. J.: Publications Division, Rutgers Center of Alcohol Studies, 1969), p. 19. Harold A. Mulford reported a figure of 71 percent, based on modified random sampling conducted by the National Opinion Research Center in 1963. See "Drinking and Deviant Drinking in the U. S. A., 1963," *Quarterly Journal of Studies on Alcohol,* Vol. 25 (December, 1964), pp. 634–50. Mulford's findings compare with 63 percent reported in 1964 and 65 percent in 1966 by the American Institute of Public Opinion (cited in Cahalan *et al.,* p. 20). Both studies used the same basic question on prevalence, "Do you ever have occasion to use alcoholic beverages such as liquor, wine, or beer, or are you a total abstainer?" In 1946, a survey based on a sample comparable to Mulford's reported a drinking prevalence rate of 65 percent for American adults. J. W. Riley, Jr. and C. F. Marden, "The Social Pattern of Alcoholic Drinking," *Quarterly Journal of Studies on Alcohol,* Vol. 8 (September, 1947), pp. 265–73. Also in 1946, the American Institute of Public Opinion reported that 67 percent of American adults used alcohol.

adults, it grossly underestimates the prevalence of drinking since it omits drinkers under 21 years of age. Several studies of teen-age alcohol use in various parts of the United States between 1953 and 1963 found that most high school graduates have had some exposure to drinking.[17] A 1953 study of the drinking practices of 16,300 students in 27 American colleges throughout the country found that 74 percent reported some use of alcoholic beverages beyond experimental, joking, or ceremonial use in childhood or isolated experiences.[18]

These various studies of the prevalence of drinking in high-school and college age groups provide a basis for estimating that about 12 million young people in the age range of 16 to 20 drink alcoholic beverages beyond the extent of isolated incidents. Added to the estimates for the adult population, this suggests that close to 100 million Americans above the age of 15 can be considered users of alcoholic beverages.

Some Social Correlates of Drinking

Gross data on the prevalence of drinking in a total population may be quite misleading. All the studies of adult drinking just cited have reported greater use by men than by women (men 75 to 79 percent; women 56 to 63 percent), although the prevalence of users among women is rising more rapidly than among men. Several studies have also reported that the prevalence of drinkers tends to be greater for persons with more education, for those living in large urban centers, and for those of the Jewish and Catholic faiths. There is also a decreasing prevalence of drinking with advancing age past 35.

---

[17] See E. A. Shepherd and Mary R. Barber, *Teen-Age Alcohol Use* (Hartford, Conn.: Connecticut Department of Mental Health, Alcoholism Division, 1965). It was reported in 1953 that about 90 percent of the students 16 years and older in Nassau County, New York, drink on some occasions. See Hofstra College Research Bureau, *Use of the Alcoholic Beverages Among High School Students* (New York: Sheppard Foundation, 1953). A study of 2000 Michigan high school students found, however, that although 92 percent had tasted alcohol at some time, only 23 percent drank in any continuing pattern. See G. L. Maddox and B. C. McCall, *Drinking Among Teen-Agers* (New Brunswick, N. J.: Rutgers Center of Alcohol Studies, 1964). Another study, conducted in Kansas, suggested that about one-half of the high school youths in that state use alcohol, with the prevalence of use increasing gradually as they progress through school. See University of Kansas, Department of Sociology and Anthropology, *Attitudes of High School Students Toward Alcoholic Beverages* (New York: Sheppard Foundation, 1956).

[18] R. Straus and S. D. Bacon, *Drinking in College.*

Prevalence varies with other factors, including geographical region (highest prevalence in New England and the Middle Atlantic states, lowest in East South Central states); denomination among Protestants; annual income (decreasing prevalence with decreasing income); and occupational and marital status.

Straus and Bacon found similar variations among college students. There were nearly twice as many abstainers among the women (39 percent) as among the men (20 percent); more users in private than in public colleges; more users among students from higher-income families and among Jewish and Catholic students; more users among Jews and Catholics who were *frequent* participants in religious activity, but more users among Protestants — especially Mormons — who were *infrequent* churchgoers; and many more users among those whose parents were both users.

Even more striking relationships between drinking customs and the sociocultural characteristics of both adults and students have been found in such matters as the types of beverages used, the quantity and frequency of drinking, usual drinking companions, the occasions or settings in which drinking normally takes place, and the stated reasons for drinking. Consistently, drinking patterns reflect the practices and sanctions of significant reference groups — parents, close friends, and persons with similar regional, ethnic, and educational backgrounds. These data clearly identify reference-group behavior as a primary determinant of an individual's participation or non-participation in the customs of drinking as well as the nature of drinking patterns that may be followed. It is also clear that certain kinds of social groups attract or repel members in part because of their reputation for heavy or moderate drinking or for abstaining.

Another important social variable, that of race, has only recently been investigated.[19] On the basis of their study of a national probability sample, Cahalan *et al.* reported similar rates of alcohol use among white and black men (77 percent and 79 percent) but much higher rates of use for white than for black women (61 percent and 49 percent). Among male drinkers there

---

[19] G. L. Maddox and E. Borinski reported ("Drinking Behavior of Negro Collegians," *Quarterly Journal of Studies on Alcohol,* Vol. 25 [December, 1964], pp. 651–68) that in reviewing the literature they found only 17 items in the *Classified Abstract Archives of the Alcohol Literature* and only six additional occasional references. From their own study they concluded primarily that drinking is at least as prevalent among blacks as among other Americans and that drinking among blacks is associated with a higher incidence of personal and social complications. This conclusion was supported by the findings of Maddox and J. R. Williams in a study of 262 black college freshmen in North Carolina ("Drinking Behavior of Negro Collegians," *Quarterly Journal of Studies on Alcohol,* Vol. 29 [March, 1968], pp. 117–29).

were relatively more white than black "heavy" drinkers (29 percent and 24 percent) but fewer white "heavy-escape" drinkers (13 percent and 20 percent). Among women users, blacks were more likely than whites to be both "heavy" drinkers (22 percent and 7 percent) and "heavy-escape" drinkers (16 percent and 4 percent).[20] The drinking behavior of 235 black men in their 30's, as reported by Robins *et al.*, reveals much higher rates of heavy drinking and associated problems than in a comparable white population, and that "excessive drinking, poor parental performance and childhood behavior problems appear to be connected in a vicious circle." [21] The relative paucity of significant data on the drinking practices of the largest ethnic minority in the United States has been a glaring gap in the sociological study of alcohol problems.[22]

ALCOHOL AND YOUTH

A major social problem associated with alcoholic beverages revolves around drinking by young people. The onset of drinking for most people usually occurs before adulthood, and the goal of preventing the use of alcohol by children and youth has received high priority from both temperance societies and lawmakers. The laws of every state in this country have required instruction in the public schools about the "evils" of alcohol. Social concern about drinking in youth has been both reflected in and created by a tendency of the mass media for many years to assume that almost any untoward behavior involving young people resulted from their drinking. Such assump-

---

[20] D. Cahalan *et al., American Drinking Practices,* p. 48 and D. Cahalan and I. H. Cisin, "American Drinking Practices: Summary of Findings from a National Probability Sample," *Quarterly Journal of Studies on Alcohol,* Vol. 29 (March, 1968), pp. 130–51. The term "heavy-escape" was applied to drinkers whose use of alcohol was "heavy" according to an index which incorporated the quantity and frequency of drinking, the types of beverages used, and factors of variability in drinking patterns, and who also acknowledged at least two personal or "escape" (as compared with social) reasons for drinking from an 11-item index of reasons. Rates of use among male black and white college students reported in 1953 were also similar, and there were also significantly fewer users among black than white female students (R. Straus and S. D. Bacon, *Drinking in College,* p. 53).

[21] L. N. Robins, G. E. Murphy, and M. B. Breckenridge, "Drinking Behavior of Young Urban Negro Men," *Quarterly Journal of Studies on Alcohol,* Vol. 29 (September, 1968), pp. 657–84.

[22] A study by Muriel W. Sterne and David J. Pittman of drinking patterns in the black ghetto of St. Louis is in process.

tions were sometimes made in the face of clear evidence to the contrary.[23] This tendency to equate disturbing behavior in young people with drinking has been overshadowed in the late 1960's by social concern about the use of LSD, marijuana, and other drugs, as well as anxiety on the part of adults over the many ways in which young people are expressing their disenchantment with the values and social priorities of adults. Simplistic explanations for juvenile behavior regarded as deviant still prevail, and however focused, they tend to neglect multiple causation and to exaggerate the role of alcohol or marijuana in that behavior.

Adult attitudes toward teen-age drinking often confuse drinking with alcohol pathology, although there is no evidence to show that particular patterns of teen-age drinking are especially linked with alcoholism. Like many other social problems, the question of teen-age drinking elicits a wide variety of ineffectual social responses. Some people exaggerate the problem; others deny that it even exists. Parents, schools, and law-enforcement agencies tend to place responsibility on each other, and churches frequently blame all three.

Available data indicate that the majority of high-school students who drink at all do not drink very often, nor do they consume very much at a time. In the college age group of 18 to 21, however, the prevalence of drinking equals, and the quantity and frequency may exceed, that of the general population. Intoxication is a special problem for teen-agers, perhaps because their reactions to alcohol are complicated by their lack of experience in coping with the effects of alcohol. When adolescents do become intoxicated they are therefore likely to get involved in other difficulties and so become highly visible. As noted earlier, some adolescents may give the illusion of intoxication when they have consumed only a single drink. Such behavior undoubtedly has contributed to a stereotype among adults of the excesses of teen-age drinking.

Most adolescent drinking has reflected the practices and sanctions of family, friends, and other reference groups.[24] For some adolescents, however, drinking involves breaking with family or religious convictions. The mere act of drinking, or the effects of drinking, or the behavior of drinking companions may evoke feelings of personal conflict or guilt. Or drinking may be

---

[23] For example, a news item about vandalism that occurred during a college outing noted in its headline and lead paragraph that the incident was undoubtedly the result of drinking by students, while buried in the rest of the article was a police report that exonerated the students altogether.

[24] G. L. Maddox, "High School Drinking Behavior: Incidental Information from Two National Surveys," *Quarterly Journal of Studies on Alcohol,* Vol. 25 (June, 1964), pp. 339–47.

associated with sexual behavior, which evokes similar kinds of conflict. The reaction of students to the anxiety associated with drinking is complicated by the fact that pharmacological properties of alcohol can provide temporary relief for the drinker from the very anxiety that his concern about drinking has created. This is a "solace" denied to the young person who may be equally anxious because he has decided not to drink despite pressures from his peers. The dilemma of those who abstain in the face of pressures to drink should not be omitted from an inventory of alcohol problems.

The confusion prevailing in American society with respect to drinking by young people is compounded by a gross inconsistency between custom and law. Most states prohibit the use of distilled spirits by anyone under the age of 21. Only New York and Louisiana set the legal age at 18. Five states permit the use of wine, and 14 the use of beer, before age 21, but six of the latter make the exception only for beer containing no more than 3.2 percent alcohol.[25] Kentucky and Georgia permit voting at age 18, but not drinking. From the standpoint of the law, drinking is clearly defined as an adult behavior. Two states waive the age limit if the drinker is married (an adult status), and one state exempts members of the armed services (another potentially adult status).

As we have seen, the realities of drinking by high-school and college youth exhibit widespread disregard of legal sanctions. It has been found, in fact, that the quantity and frequency of drinking among college users appears to increase with age up to about 21, after which there is a slight decline.[26] There is a hint that once drinking becomes legally permissible it becomes somewhat less interesting.

The college drinking survey also found a distinct correlation between formal prohibitions on drinking in colleges and the excesses displayed by student drinkers. Although colleges with formal prohibitions had relatively fewer drinkers than those with no restrictions or only token prohibition, the students at "restricted" schools who broke the formal code by drinking generally drank more frequently, more heavily, and were more often involved in drinking-related problems than the drinking students at more "liberal" colleges. As one student put it, "When you go to the trouble of driving fifty miles to get a drink, you don't have just two drinks." [27]

The tendency to use alcohol as a way of flouting authority is not restricted

---

[25] R. G. McCarthy, ed., *Alcohol Education for Classroom and Community* (New York: McGraw-Hill, 1964), p. 26; and Cooperative Commission on the Study of Alcoholism, *Alcohol Problems: A Report to the Nation,* prepared by Thomas F. A. Plaut (New York: Oxford University Press, 1967), pp. 148–49.

[26] R. Straus and S. D. Bacon, *Drinking in College,* p. 106.

[27] *Ibid.,* p. 69.

242 Alcohol and Alcoholism

to adolescents. It is reminiscent of adult drinking practices under Prohibition. Yet, in the 1960's, this pattern may provide a key to the special significance of drinking for adolescents.

Adolescents are faced with many discontinuities and inconsistencies. They are expected to assume certain "adult" roles and responsibilities, while many "adult" rights and privileges are withheld. Much adolescent behavior that is culturally sanctioned does little to prepare the adolescent for the roles required of an adult. Adolescence is a time of transition from dependence on a parental family to independence in marriage, employment, and community status. In our culture, it is a period during which social and psychological maturity frequently lags behind physical maturity. Restrictions on adolescents lead many of them to develop doubts about their own manliness or womanliness. For some young men, drinking behavior provides a symbolic proof of manliness. For both sexes, alcohol can help remove inhibitions to demonstrating sexual attraction or prowess.

Rapid social change enlarges the barriers between the roles and values of parents and those of their adolescent children. The greater the rate of change, the less meaningful are adults as role models and the less security they can provide.[28]

In the face of conflict, insecurity, and confusion, adolescents have developed a distinctive subculture. They seek a self-identity. They tend to press for adult status and to reject symbols of authority as repressive. Drinking behavior provides an apt symbol of having achieved adult status since it is defined legally as an adult privilege. At the same time, restrictions against teen-age drinking provide the symbolic "red flag" for rejection of authority. Thus, many efforts to control or moderate the drinking of young people, although charged with good intent, simply serve to enhance the attractiveness and status of drinking. Drinking that is an expression of personal conflict or social rebellion is more likely to involve conditions conducive to intoxication—large amounts of alcohol, distilled spirits rather than beer, quick consumption, no food, and often the specific purpose of becoming high, tight, or drunk.

Studies have documented the long-recognized anachronism of most legally prescribed age limits on drinking as compared with the realities of

---

[28] For a fuller discussion see R. Straus, "Drinking in College in the Perspective of Social Change," in G. L. Maddox, ed., *The Domesticated Drug: Drinking Among Collegians* (New Haven: College and University Press, 1970), pp. 27–44. The dilemma of adolescents in contemporary society is discussed in James S. Coleman, *The Adolescent Society* (New York: Free Press, 1961), pp. 1–57; Paul Goodman, *Growing Up Absurd* (New York: Random House, 1960); and Kenneth Keniston, *The Uncommitted: Alienated Youth in American Society* (New York: Harcourt Brace Jovanovich, 1965).

adolescent drinking.[29] Since existing laws do not deter teen-agers from drinking, it has been recommended that states adopt uniform laws to lower the legal age for purchasing and consuming alcoholic beverages to 18.[30] A special problem in this respect is found in the states bordering New York, whose young people drive into New York to take advantage of the lower legal age for purchasing alcohol. This practice, which welds driving and drinking into a single pattern, has dramatized the need for uniformity of state laws.

Statutes requiring alcohol education that emphasizes the evils of alcohol or employs a psychology of fear are equally outdated. Modern educational approaches focus on instruction about the physiological and psychological effects of alcohol in an effort to promote more responsible drinking practices on the part of those who drink and to provide peer group understanding and acceptance for those who abstain.[31]

A major question, unanswered at this time, concerns the relationship of drinking to the waves of experimentation with LSD, amphetamines, and other powerful hallucinogenic and stimulant drugs, and the apparent sharp rise in the use of marijuana by young people. Serious users of other powerful drugs would find it physiologically impossible to tolerate alcohol at the same time. It may be that these drugs have replaced alcohol for some highly disturbed students. With respect to marijuana, while evidence suggests that "pot" parties have sometimes replaced drinking parties, there is yet no evidence that a rise in the use of marijuana has been accompanied by any marked diminution in alcohol use. Although many loose comparisons are made between alcohol and marijuana, it is significant that these drugs are very different pharmacologically, and their symbolic use also seems quite different. Alcohol, as noted, has served as a symbol of asserting adulthood and being like adults—its use by adolescents is often patterned after that of their parents. Marijuana, on the other hand, seems to have special appeal for today's youth because it is their "own thing," and smoking "pot" is a symbol of emancipation from the values and customs of the adult society. It will be interesting to see whether, among those engaged in youth protest, alcohol is significantly displaced by marijuana or other substances that youth perceive as their own, and whether the use of such substances is carried over by today's youth into their adult life.

---

[29] For example, Muriel W. Sterne, David J. Pittman, and T. Coe, "Teen-agers, Drinking and the Law," *Crime and Delinquency,* Vol. 11 (January, 1965), pp. 78–85.

[30] Cooperative Commission on the Study of Alcoholism, *Alcohol Problems: A Report to the Nation,* pp. 149–52.

[31] See R. G. McCarthy, ed., *Alcohol Education for Classroom and Community.*

DRINKING AND DRIVING [32]

Throughout the world wherever men drive automobiles or fly aircraft, there is increasing social concern about the role of alcohol in vehicular accidents. Many countries are assembling an increasing body of data from blood-alcohol measurements of drivers in support of the claim that alcohol is the major factor in driver-caused traffic accidents.[33]

In 1968, the Secretary of Transportation reported that the use of alcohol by drivers and pedestrians in the United States leads to about 25,000 deaths and at least 800,000 accidents each year with much loss of life, limb, and property involving innocent others.[34] Not only does alcohol contribute to a high proportion of all automobile accidents, but such accidents tend to be more severe both in property damage and in personal injury than accidents unrelated to alcohol.[35]

Reports based on pilot toxicology examinations have also identified alcohol involvement in a significant portion of fatal crashes of small aircraft.[36] The Advisory Committee on Traffic Safety to the Secretary of Health, Education and Welfare has described this problem as "one of the most costly aftermaths of the introduction of technology in modern society."[37]

A great deal of research has been concerned with the impact of various levels of alcohol in the body on psychosensory and psychomotor behavior. Numerous chemical tests have been developed for quantifying alcohol levels in blood reaching the brain by analyzing breath or samples of urine or

---

[32] For comprehensive reviews of this topic see S. D. Bacon, ed., *Studies of Driving and Drinking (Quarterly Journal of Studies on Alcohol,* Supplement No. 4, 1968) and B. H. Fox and J. H. Fox, eds., *Alcohol and Traffic Safety,* Public Health Service Publication No. 1043 (Washington, D. C.: U. S. Government Printing Office, 1963).

[33] "European Police Crack Down on the Drinking Driver," *Military Police Journal,* Vol. 16, No. 5 (1966), pp. 7–10.

[34] *Alcohol and Highway Safety,* A Report to the Congress from the Secretary of Transportation (Washington, D. C.: U. S. Dept. of Transportation, 1968).

[35] J. A. Waller, "Alcohol Ingestion, Alcoholism and Traffic Accidents," in *The Legal Issues in Alcoholism and Alcohol Usage* (Boston: Boston University Law-Medicine Institute, 1965).

[36] H. L. Gibbons, J. W. Ellis, Jr., and J. L. Plechus reported alcohol implication in 31 percent of autopsied pilots involved in fatal accidents in 1965. "Analysis of Medical Factors in Fatal Accidents in 1965," *Texas Medicine,* Vol. 63 (January, 1967), pp. 64–68.

[37] *Report of the Secretary's Advisory Committee on Traffic Safety,* Dept. of Health, Education and Welfare (Washington, D. C.: U. S. Government Printing Office, 1968), p. xi.

capillary blood. In the 1930's, several "packaged laboratories" were developed for use by police departments in order to obtain quick measurements of the blood-alcohol concentration of drivers from samples of blood or breath that could be obtained at the scene of an accident.[38] In 1938, a committee of the National Safety Council recommended a uniform code for designating legal evidence of intoxication. It was suggested that a blood-alcohol concentration of 0.05 percent or less be recognized as evidence that alcohol influence was not sufficient to impair driving ability; levels between 0.05 and 0.15 percent were designated as relevant but not conclusive evidence of intoxication; and levels of 0.15 percent or more, as evidence of intoxication sufficient to impair driving ability.[39] The code was formulated in an effort to provide a precise basis for nationwide standardization of statutes regarding drinking and driving and also to provide law-enforcement agencies with a basis for obtaining indisputable evidence that would stand up in court.

There has been anything but uniformity in the application of the National Safety Council's uniform code. States have varied widely both in their statutes and interpretations of the law regarding the obtaining and use of evidence from breath or blood samples, particularly if evidence is provided involuntarily. Doubts have been expressed about the limits of alcohol concentration permitted by the code, suggesting that they may be much too liberal. There is strong evidence to suggest that a level of 0.1 percent involves some risk for most drivers, and that even levels of alcohol below 0.05 percent may impair the driving of some individuals, especially poor drivers or young people who are both inexperienced drinkers and inexperienced drivers. Even mild sensations produced by alcohol, if they come at a time when the novice drinker-driver is called upon to respond to an unusual traffic situation, might "cause" an accident. For poor-risk drinkers and poor-risk drivers, the implication of a "safe level" can provide a dangerous justification of driving after drinking.

It has also been demonstrated that there are wide variations in the curve of blood-alcohol concentration so that some drivers who might test within "safe" limits shortly after an accident could have experienced a peak within the dangerous limits of alcohol concentration at the time of the accident. Such relatively precipitous but brief peaks of alcohol effect may be particularly common in persons who are driving from a late afternoon cocktail party where they have been drinking moderately but hastily and on an empty stomach.

---

[38] R. F. Borkenstein, H. J. Trubitt, and R. J. Lease, "Problems of Enforcement and Prosecution," in B. H. Fox and J. H. Fox, eds., *Alcohol and Traffic Safety.*

[39] Compare these levels with the discussion of effects on behavior of various levels of alcohol concentration on pages 230–31 of this chapter.

Recent studies have identified *alcoholics* as responsible for a disproportionately high number of alcohol-related accidents.[40] The particularly high risk of alcoholic drivers can be attributed to the frequency and intensity of their intoxication, the false sense of security and omnipotence that many alcoholics develop, and their high incidence of emotional instability with possible suicidal tendencies.

In several countries, notably Great Britain and the Scandinavian nations, efforts have been made to reduce the prevalence of drinking and driving through legislation imposing both loss of license and imprisonment on persons convicted of driving while intoxicated. In Norway, for example, 46.5 percent of all prison sentences in 1962 were imposed for drunken driving.[41] Public opinion seems to support such sanctions and there have been some modifications of social custom to provide alcohol-free drivers for persons who plan to drink away from home. Yet traffic-accident rates remain high and the involvement of alcohol in such accidents remains significant. In both Great Britain and Scandinavia, it is clear that efforts to control drinking and driving have had the least effect on the two highest-risk groups — alcoholics and youths. The very condition of alcoholism makes alcoholics less likely to be deterred by sanctions, blood tests, or punishment. In the second case, for many young drivers, severe sanctions may offer a special challenge that becomes an incentive for drinking or an attractive way of expressing bravado and rejecting authority felt to be oppressive.

In the United States, while the interests of public safety clearly support a broad social movement to discourage drinking prior to driving, laws requiring drivers in accidents to submit to blood-alcohol tests and prescribing penalties for conviction have been generally ineffective. Efforts to modify drinking-and-driving customs have met with abysmal failure, despite daily dramatic evidence of the impact of drinking combined with driving on innocent victims. Public resistance seems rooted in the strong mores that have protected the "right to drink" against legal prohibitions, and in the equally strong mores that have developed around the "right to drive." Supported perhaps by an illusion of individual omnipotence or invulnerability, public sentiment in the United States has generally resisted efforts to protect the public safety that involve increasingly stringent control on the right to drive. There has been resistance to reexamining drivers, to inspecting

---

[40] J. A. Waller and H. W. Turkel, "Alcoholism and Traffic Deaths," *New England Journal of Medicine,* Vol. 275, No. 10 (September 8, 1966), pp. 532–36; and M. L. Selzer, "Alcohol Impairment, Alcoholism and Traffic Accidents," *University of Michigan Medical Center Journal,* Vol. 32 (September–October, 1966), pp. 238–41.

[41] Nils Christie, "Scandinavian Experience In Legislation and Control," in *The Legal Issues in Alcoholism and Alcohol Usage,* pp. 101–22.

vehicles, and to imposing penalties on chronic traffic law violators, as well as to efforts to control driving while intoxicated. At this time, prevailing mores in America appear to place a higher value on the right to drink and drive than on protection from the drinking driver. A mass-media educational campaign was initiated in 1969 by the insurance industry in an effort to sway American public opinion to support legal sanctions against the drinking driver.

ALCOHOLISM

Most people, when they speak of the problems of alcohol, are thinking primarily of alcoholism. The term "alcoholism" is an elusive one that defies clear-cut, generally acceptable definition. As more and more is understood about the causes and forms of pathological drinking, it is apparent that the term "alcoholism" encompasses pathological behavioral syndromes associated with alcohol use. If it were not semantically awkward, it would be more appropriate to speak of alcoholisms [42] rather than alcoholism, for it has become recognized that the term "alcoholism" has been used to describe a number of quite distinct disorders whose major common characteristic is the pathological seeking for and reacting to the effects of alcohol on the nervous system.

For purposes of clarification, the typology of alcoholism will be considered in terms of addictive and nonaddictive pathological drinking.[43] Alcoholism, or pathological drinking, can be defined operationally as the use of alcoholic beverages to the extent that it repeatedly "exceeds customary dietary use or ordinary compliance with the social drinking of the community, and interferes with the drinker's health, interpersonal relations, or economic functioning." [44] Associated with this condition is a state of stress, discontent, or inner tension, the origin of which may be physiological, psychological, or

---

[42] This thesis is detailed by E. M. Jellinek, *The Disease Concept of Alcoholism* (New Haven: Hillhouse Press, 1960). Jellinek describes five primary types of alcoholism, which he designates *alpha, beta, gamma, delta,* and *epsilon*. The typology discussed here reflects the influence of Jellinek and of Mark Keller and John R. Seeley's disciplined considerations in *The Alcohol Language* (Toronto: University of Toronto Press, 1958) along with a thesis developed by the author in collaboration with R. G. McCarthy.

[43] R. Straus and R. G. McCarthy, "Nonaddictive Pathological Drinking Patterns of Homeless Men," *Quarterly Journal of Studies on Alcohol,* Vol. 12 (December, 1951), pp. 601–11.

[44] From a definition of alcoholism in Mark Keller and John R. Seeley, *The Alcohol Language,* p. 19.

social, or a blending of all three. Alcohol is used to relieve these discomforts.

For some alcoholics, the recourse to alcohol is accompanied by characteristics of an addiction. The addictive drinker has lost control over his drinking. Once he starts, he seems impelled to continue drinking until he has reached peak intensity of intoxication. Yet an essential criterion of addiction is insatiability — a persistent seeking for the unattainable. If alcohol becomes unavailable before a drinking spree has run its course, there are severe withdrawal reactions expressed in various physical forms, such as rapid heartbeat, profuse sweating, severe nausea, and uncontrollable trembling. In some addictive drinkers, loss of control over drinking becomes generalized, and they are unable to abstain for even a day without suffering withdrawal symptoms.

Alcohol addiction may be defined as a condition in which the drinking of alcoholic beverages becomes persistent, repetitive, uncontrollable, and progressively destructive of the psychological, social, and sometimes physiological functioning of the individual. It runs its episodic course with complete indifference to the logic or reality of the normal life situation or basic social responsibilities. For most addictive drinkers, the condition develops only after years of exposure to relatively high levels of alcohol concentration. It may be surmised that at some point there develops a kind of conditioned response to alcohol such that reaching a given concentration releases an impulsive drive to attain a peak intensity of effect.

Addictive drinking, as characterized here, represents the most commonly recognized form of alcoholism in the United States. An important variation, and indeed the predominant type of alcoholism in much of France, is characterized by the drinker's inability to abstain for even a day or two without the manifestation of withdrawal symptoms. Yet the ability to control the amount of intake on any given occasion remains intact.[45] This type of alcoholism is related to social acceptance of high alcohol intake, which facilitates progressively increasing tolerance and the development of physical dependency. Such alcoholics less frequently manifest prealcoholic psychological vulnerability and there is little apparent social or psychological damage, but they suffer high vulnerability to physical damage and a shortened lifespan.[46]

Obviously, all addictive drinkers can be classified as alcoholics. But not every alcoholic is an alcohol addict. There are several categories of alcoholics whose drinking repeatedly interferes with health or personal relations or

---

[45] E. M. Jellinek, *The Disease Concept of Alcoholism,* pp. 38–39. See also R. Sadoun, G. Lolli, and M. Silverman, *Drinking in French Culture,* pp. 110–12.

[46] Mark Keller and M. McCormick, *A Dictionary of Words About Alcohol,* p. 18.

reduces efficiency and dependability, but who never experience the symptoms of alcohol addiction such as insatiability, loss of control over drinking, or withdrawal symptoms.

The nonaddictive alcoholic seems to be primarily concerned with achieving a limited level of alcohol-induced oblivion from reality and often with maintaining a state of alcohol-induced euphoria for a convenient period of time. The addictive alcoholic strives for a *peak* intensity of effect from alcohol; the nonaddictive alcoholic, on the other hand, seeks a *plateau* at much lower levels of alcohol concentration. The nonaddictive alcoholic not only can control his drinking, but often he will plan it quite carefully in order to attain the most desirable combination of effect and duration within the limits of resources for drinking and available time. He is also able to adapt his drinking practices – apparently without severe difficulty – to variations in his living conditions.

Nonaddictive alcoholism is common among men who frequent skid row areas, and jails and other public institutions. Although there is also a high proportion of alcohol addicts in this population, many homeless men have a routine of living dominated by the use of alcohol to attain relief from discomfort or escape from reality as often as possible and to maintain that state as long as convenient. They may demonstrate considerable foresight in allocating their major funds for alcoholic beverages and in planning their drinking. For many, their drinking seems to be associated with unmet needs to be dependent, psychologically or socially, on other people to help them obtain such basic requirements as food and shelter, to make decisions for them, and to prescribe their routine of living. When deprived of alcohol under conditions where their particular dependency needs are fulfilled, such as in a jail or a hospital, they manifest no particular urgency to drink.[47]

Other nonaddictive drinkers may plan their drinking to dull the experience of unpleasant situations. These include men who function quite successfully at work but seek an alcohol-induced escape from their marital responsibilities on evenings and weekends. Increasingly, nonaddictive alcoholism

---

[47] See R. Straus, "Alcohol and the Homeless Man," *Quarterly Journal of Studies on Alcohol,* Vol. 7 (December, 1946), pp. 360–404; R. Straus and R. G. McCarthy, "Nonaddictive Pathological Drinking Patterns of Homeless Men"; Joan K. Jackson and R. Connor, "The Skid Road Alcoholic," *Quarterly Journal of Studies on Alcohol,* Vol. 14 (September, 1953), pp. 468–86; E. Rubington, "The Chronic Drunkenness Offender," *Annals of the American Academy of Political and Social Science,* Vol. 315 (January, 1958), pp. 65–72; Donald J. Bogue, *Skid Row in American Cities* (Chicago: Community and Family Study Center, University of Chicago, 1963); Samuel E. Wallace, *Skid Row as a Way of Life* (Totowa, N. J.: Bedminster Press, 1965); H. M. Bahr and S. J. Langfur, "Social Attachment and Drinking in Skid-Row Life Histories," *Social Problems,* Vol. 14 (Spring, 1967), pp. 464–72.

occurs among women who have failed to fulfill their self-expectations in their routine roles as housewives and mothers. Such alcoholics may never experience real intoxication, but their daylong sipping will be sufficient to render them chronically ineffective and inefficient.

As might be expected, there are significant differences in the types of alcoholic beverages used by addictive and nonaddictive alcoholics. Addictive drinkers usually seek distilled beverages with the highest alcohol content available, for their goal is intensity of effect. Nonaddictive drinkers, however, particularly if their funds are limited, will usually drink beer or wine, which is much more suited to their goal of maintaining a limited effect from alcohol for some planned duration of time. Sherry, for example, is a common beverage for the housewife who is a continuous sipper.

Depending on the relation of drinking to his life pattern and on physiological variables that are not fully understood, the alcoholic may or may not develop such physical complications of alcohol as cirrhosis of the liver, polyneuropathy, gastritis, or a nutritional disease. Such complications may develop in either addictive or nonaddictive drinkers.

Theories of Etiology

The understanding of alcoholism has until quite recently been clouded by a persistent groping for unilateral theories of etiology. Much research and many efforts to explain alcoholism have been restricted by the blinders of single academic disciplines. Various theories have been based on consideration of such important factors as liver metabolism, the function of the central nervous system, hormonal imbalances, vitamin and nutritional deficiencies, personality deviations, and the forces of culture and of social pathology.

There is enough evidence today to suggest that alcoholism in its various forms is a manifestation of one or more of several underlying stress-producing conditions. It is difficult to identify primary etiological factors because the pathological use of alcohol in connection with primary forms of stress invariably results in generating additional stress-producing conditions. These ultimately become an integral part of the overall syndrome. Harold Kalant has emphasized the problem of sorting out specific processes from the viewpoint of a biological scientist:

> With the expansion of knowledge on functional interrelations, it has become clear that the metabolism of the liver affects the function of the central nervous system, that psychological and peripheral sensory stimuli acting on the central nervous system affect the release of vari-

ous hormonal factors, that the resulting hormonal imbalances affect the metabolic behavior of the liver and of all other tissues, including the brain and so on and on. Because of this, it has become very difficult indeed to pick out those effects of alcohol which are primary, and those which are secondary and nonspecific consequences of the disturbance resulting from alcohol.[48]

The social scientist faces the same kind of dilemma in his effort to understand alcoholism. Most types of alcoholism are found in association with some form or forms of social pathology. Marital discord, job instability, social alienation, economic strain, and chronic ill health can contribute to and be supported by an alcoholic drinking pattern, and each of these problems tends to interact with the others in a complex clustering of social, psychological, and biological pathology.

There are no completely satisfactory theories about the causes of various types of pathological drinking. Although no specific physiological or biochemical factors have yet been satisfactorily identified as causing alcoholism, the existence of some biological deficiencies or sensitivities as possible contributing factors cannot be ruled out.

A number of psychological traits have commonly been identified in individuals who drink excessively, and much has been written about the "alcoholic personality."[49] Alcoholics have been characterized as suffering from extreme feelings of inadequacy and chronic anxiety and as being excessively dependent on emotional support from others. Yet similar traits can be found in users of narcotics, individuals with various kinds of psychosomatic diseases, persons addicted to food, as well as in many men and women who appear to function quite effectively within normal ranges of physical health and socially acceptable behavior. Knowledge about the psychological effects of alcohol in alleviating anxiety and providing a sense of well-being helps explain why alcohol is attractive to and functional for persons with deep feelings of emotional insecurity. But psychological theory cannot tell us why, of the people with a so-called alcoholic personality, some become alcoholics, while others do not.

Sociologists have approached the study of alcoholism in part by considering the customs of drinking. Obviously alcoholism occurs only in persons who participate in drinking customs. And differences in the prevalence and ty-

---

[48] Harold Kalant, "Some Recent Physiological and Biochemical Investigations on Alcohol and Alcoholism," *Quarterly Journal of Studies on Alcohol,* Vol. 23 (March, 1962), p. 53.

[49] For a summary, see John D. Armstrong, "The Search for the Alcoholic Personality," *Annals of the American Academy of Political and Social Science,* Vol. 315 (January, 1958), pp. 40–47.

pology of pathological drinking have been identified with variations both in the overt customs of drinking and in the beliefs, attitudes, and values about alcohol that mold reference-group sanctions on drinking.

A conceptual approach to the study of cultural differences in rates of alcoholism was provided by R. F. Bales, based in part on his own observations of the striking differences between drinking customs and rates of alcoholism among Irish and Orthodox Jews in the United States.[50]

Studies of the *prevalence* of drinking in the United States consistently place those who identify themselves as Jewish, along with Italians, at the top of a religious-ethnic scale. In both groups, a majority of adults use alcohol and report having done so since childhood. In contrast, persons of Irish background are somewhat less likely to drink as adults and much less likely to have experienced drinking in childhood.[51] When rates of drinking are compared with rates of alcoholism for these cultural groups, an inverse relationship is found. Studies of *alcohol pathology* in the United States consistently place the rates of alcoholism among the Irish at the top of the ethnic scale, many times greater than rates for either Italians or Jews, both of which are strikingly low. It is also noteworthy that rates of alcoholism among women in most societies are much lower than those for men, a difference that is generally much greater than the sex differences in prevalence of drinking. The negative correlation between prevalence of drinking and alcoholism might be easily explained if it could be demonstrated that societies with high prevalence rates were all characterized by patterns of moderate consumption. However, numerous studies of drinking have shown that there are cultures, both primitive and advanced, that combine high prevalence with high rates of consumption.

Bales [52] has suggested three general ways in which culture and social organization may influence rates of alcoholism: First are factors that operate to create inner tension, such as culturally induced anxiety, guilt, conflict, suppressed hostility, and sexual tension. Second are culturally supported attitudes toward drinking and intoxication that determine whether drinking is an acceptable means of relieving inner tension or whether the thought of

---

[50] Robert Freed Bales, "Cultural Differences in Rates of Alcoholism," *Quarterly Journal of Studies on Alcohol,* Vol. 6 (March, 1946), pp. 480–99.

[51] R. Straus and S. D. Bacon, *Drinking in College,* found that students who reported drinking in childhood included 80 percent of those who identified themselves as Jewish and 86 percent of the Italians, compared with 45 percent of the Irish.

[52] Robert Freed Bales, "Cultural Differences in Rates of Alcoholism," and "Attitudes Toward Drinking in Irish Culture," in David J. Pittman and Charles R. Snyder, eds., *Society, Culture and Drinking Patterns,* pp. 157–87.

drinking for this purpose is in itself sufficiently anxiety-provoking to preclude its use. Third are the alternate methods for resolving tension provided by the culture.

Bales then describes how the nineteenth-century culture in Ireland, at the time many Irish emigrated to the United States, supported the development of intensive inner frustration, hostility, and unrelieved sexual tension in the large numbers of males who were retained in the social status of "boy" throughout their adulthood.[53] As a form of social control for the potentially explosive force created by enforced dependency, especially mother-son dependency, and sexual deprivation, the culture supported the frequent excessive use of alcohol by single males, thus providing a relatively "safe" outlet for tension and hostility through a kind of institutionalized intoxication. In addition, Bales noted, there was a tendency to substitute drinking for eating since food was often in short supply. After emigrating to the United States, the Irish found themselves at the bottom of the socioeconomic scale. There was much in their situation that perpetuated the anxieties of the old country; moreover, finding themselves suddenly in a new culture, subject especially to new expectations regarding the independence of the adult male, served to deepen their anxiety. Because they brought with them supportive practices and attitudes for the use of alcohol to the point of intoxication to deal with tension, Irish males have experienced a greater exposure to frequent intoxication than most other Americans.

C. R. Snyder[54] tested Bales' concepts in an extensive study of the use of alcohol by Jews in the United States. Particularly among the more orthodox Jews, Snyder found that drinking was an integral part of the socialization process, repeatedly experienced as a part of religious ritualism and thoroughly compatible with moral symbolism. Even though alcohol use was extensive, sobriety was maintained as a norm; the experience of intoxication was limited to culturally sanctioned, symbolically meaningful situations, and alcoholism was virtually nonexistent. Snyder found that with decreasing orthodoxy among Jews, the disruption of the traditional rites with which drinking had been integrated, the dissociation of drinking experiences from the normal socialization process, and the introduction of drinking in social contexts where its use for the purpose of achieving an individual effect from alcohol was stressed, were all associated with an increase in the rates of alcohol pathology.

---

[53] See the classic study by Conrad M. Arensberg, *The Irish Countryman* (New York: Macmillan, 1937).

[54] Charles R. Snyder, *Alcohol and the Jews* (New York: Free Press, 1958).

Several studies of the drinking practices of Italians in both Italy and the United States [55] have identified alcohol as an integral part of dietary beliefs and practices. Drinking and eating are inseparable activities. Drinking usually involves wine (with low alcohol content), and excessive drinking usually occurs in the context of excessive eating. Even when large amounts of alcohol are consumed, they are taken slowly and interspaced with food, which impedes the rate of absorption. Intoxication, when it does occur, is in the context of social conviviality and is considered in the same light as indigestion or other concomitants of gluttony. Alcoholism is rare. As in the case of the Jews, studies of Italian drinking reveal marked changes in drinking patterns according to generation and degree of acculturation in the United States. As alienation from the original Italian culture takes place, drinking occurs apart from the context of meals, involves beverages other than wine or beer, and occurs in settings where Italian group sanctions do not prevail. Under such conditions, drinking for the sake of drinking becomes more common, intoxication more frequent, and alcoholism begins to appear.

From all this it should not be conjectured that Italians or Jews have less inner tension or fewer problems of adjustment; on the contrary, both groups appear to have their expected share of various forms of mental illness, with Jews perhaps exceeding most other religious groups.[56] Both groups seem to include more than their share of individuals who eat to the point of gross obesity in an apparent effort to deal with stress.[57]

The studies cited here and many others that have considered the relationship between cultural norms and pathological drinking add convincing support to the inclusion of cultural factors in a holistic theory of the causes of alcoholism.[58] We have seen that alcoholism becomes a response to stress primarily in those cultures where drinking customs create exposure to frequent intoxication, where intoxication is a means of fulfilling individual

---

[55] See especially G. Lolli et al., *Alcohol in Italian Culture.*

[56] See, for example, A. B. Hollingshead and F. C. Redlich, *Social Class and Mental Illness* (New York: Wiley, 1958), pp. 204–05; see also Robert Freed Bales, "Cultural Differences in Rates of Alcoholism," p. 490.

[57] Charles R. Snyder, *Alcohol and the Jews,* pp. 9–10; G. Lolli et al., "The Use of Wine and Other Alcoholic Beverages by a Group of Italians and Americans of Italian Extraction," *Quarterly Journal of Studies on Alcohol,* Vol. 13 (March, 1952), pp. 27–48.

[58] In another relevant study, R. Jessor et al. examined varying rates of alcoholism and other forms of deviance in about 3000 inhabitants of a small triethnic (Anglo-American, Spanish-American, American Indian) community in southwestern Colorado. Varying rates of pathology were found to be associated with the degree of culture-conflict with Anglo values. R. Jessor, T. D. Graves, R. C. Hanson and S. L. Jessor, *Society, Personality and Deviant Behavior* (New York: Holt, 1968).

rather than group functions, and where there are no culture-approved alternative modes of dealing with stress.

Most theories of alcoholism emphasize the role of stress as a precondition of alcoholism. Stress may originate in a physiological condition, personality characteristics, adaptation to the social setting, or in a combination of these sources.

Although temperance writings for a century equated drinking and alcoholism, the role of drinking has generally been discounted as the cause of alcoholism. It is pointed out that most people who drink do not become alcoholics, and that the behavior of the alcoholic in using alcohol is very different from that of the average person who drinks.[59] However, the normative drinking practices of a society cannot be dismissed as insignificant factors in determining the exposure of an individual to alcoholism. In some areas of France, the particular patterns of drinking that are supported by the culture appear to contribute significantly to high rates of alcoholism, just as quite different cultural patterns of drinking are associated with low rates of alcoholism in Italy.

It is particularly important to distinguish drinking from alcoholism because of the many misunderstandings about phenomena generally associated with alcohol. There are perhaps some people for whom drinking violates such strong social norms that they come to rely on the effects of alcohol to alleviate their feelings of guilt over drinking, thus experiencing a self-perpetuating syndrome. Clinicians have identified deep-seated guilt about alcoholism as a serious barrier to effective therapy; Jews and Italians whose alcoholism represented alienation from their cultural background were found to be particularly recalcitrant patients. In the study of college drinking practices and attitudes it was found that Mormon students and those from fundamentalist colleges who violated their religious and cultural norms by drinking had become intoxicated, experienced social complications, and displayed some early signs of pathological drinking more frequently than other student drinkers.[60]

Magnitude of the Problem

It has been very difficult to count the number of alcoholics, not only because there is no universally accepted definition of alcoholism, but also because

---

[59] See S. D. Bacon, "Alcoholics Do Not Drink," *Annals of the American Academy of Political and Social Science,* Vol. 315 (January, 1958), pp. 55–64.

[60] R. Straus and S. D. Bacon, *Drinking in College,* Chapters 10 and 12.

the condition is still shrouded in stigma and therefore frequently denied or hidden.[61] Optimism for more accurate counting in the future has recently been provided by the National Health Survey in the United States. A pilot household survey found that members of the general population will discuss their drinking behavior with interviewers and apparently are not offended or disturbed by inquiries about even the most extreme deviant forms of drinking.[62] It has been estimated that there were 5,200,000 alcoholics in the United States in 1968. These comprise 4.2 percent of the population aged 20 and over or about one alcoholic for every 20 persons who customarily drink alcoholic beverages. Men outnumber women alcoholics by about five to one.[63, 64]

Variations in methods of estimation, reporting and recording of index variables, and definitions of alcoholism make comparisons of prevalence rates between countries so tentative as to be virtually meaningless. Moreover, estimates of prevalence reveal wide variations in rates within many countries. For example, the rate in central and western France is assumed to be several times greater than in France's beer-drinking districts of the Northeast. Within the United States, rates in Connecticut or Massachusetts are two or three times greater than those in most of the East South Central states.

The magnitude of alcoholism involves much more than a count of individuals who are alcoholics. Much of the behavior associated with alcoholism is social behavior. A primary consequence of alcoholism is the inability of the alcoholic to function effectively in a variety of social roles and to carry

---

[61] Most estimates rely on a formula devised by E. M. Jellinek that is based on projections made from reported deaths due to cirrhosis of the liver attributable to alcoholism. See World Health Organization, Expert Committee on Mental Health, *Report on the First Session of the Alcoholism Subcommittee* (WHO Technical Report Series, No. 42, 1951), pp. 21–24.

[62] National Center for Health Statistics, "Identifying Problem Drinkers in a Household Health Survey," Series 2, Number 16, Public Health Service Publication No. 1000 (Washington, D. C.: U. S. Government Printing Office, May, 1966).

[63] Personal communication, Mark Keller, Documentation Division, Rutgers Center of Alcohol Studies, February, 1970.

[64] A rise in reported death rates from alcoholic disorders in the United States from 5.5 per 100,000 in 1950–1951 to 8.7 per 100,000 in 1963–1964 has been reported, with the rate of rise for women more than twice that for men, and for nonwhite men, three times that for white men. Death rates for nonwhites, men and women, were more than twice those for whites, with the greatest discrepancies in the age groups below 40. See Metropolitan Life Insurance Company, "Alcoholism: A Growing Medical-Social Problem," *Statistical Bulletin,* Vol. 48, No. 4 (April, 1967), pp. 7–10. We do not know to what extent these differences reflect changes in reporting practices between 1950 and 1964.

out social responsibilities. The millions of wives, husbands, children, or parents who live in the same households with alcoholics are directly affected by their behavior. Most alcoholics hold jobs, and the magnitude of alcoholism should also be measured in terms of lost manpower, accidents, industrial waste, and inefficiency. Alcoholics drive cars and usually involve others when accidents occur. Alcoholics also have higher rates of most kinds of sickness than other people and place a heavy demand on already taxed medical facilities and personnel. Social consequences also include the considerable investment of public funds that communities spend on their police, courts, jails, hospitals, and other institutional responses to the problems of chronic intoxication.[65]

THE PROBLEMS OF ALCOHOL
AND MAJOR SOCIAL SYSTEMS

The various forms of alcoholism, and the other problems associated with drinking customs, are reflected in and affected by the behavior and functions of every major social system. Bare mention of these may be enough to indicate the complex interdependence.

The national economy reflects the great size of the alcoholic-beverage industry as an employer, and as a user of natural products and of such major services as transportation, advertising, and retail sales. For example, expenditures by the alcoholic-beverage industries for national advertising in newspapers, magazines, and on television in 1968 amounted to almost 250 million dollars, or 5 percent of the total advertising revenue of these media.[66] Personal-consumption expenditures for packaged alcoholic beverages in the United States in 1967 amounted to 14.5 billion dollars, or 3 percent of all personal expenditures.[67]

The alcoholic-beverage industry is a significant source of tax revenue for

---

[65] The clustering of problems around alcoholism has been described in a report from the U.S.S.R. submitted for publication in the United States by the U.S.S.R. embassy in Washington. Noting that "heavy drinking and alcoholism are usually held accountable for many-faced tragedies," the report cites figures provided by the Ministry of Protection of Social Order that associate alcohol use with crime, divorce, delinquency, retardation, and traffic accidents. Elena Korenevskaya, "Combatting Alcoholism in the U.S.S.R.," *Quarterly Journal of Studies on Alcohol,* Vol. 27 (March, 1966), pp. 97–102.

[66] *Statistical Abstract of the United States, 1969* (Washington, D. C.: U. S. Government Printing Office, 1969), pp. 776–77.

[67] *Ibid.,* p. 314.

local, state, and federal government. Federal taxes on alcoholic beverages in 1968 came to 4.3 billion dollars, and the states collected an additional billion. Together these sources accounted for nearly 2.5 percent of all federal and state tax revenue.[68]

The Problem Drinking Employee

Employers in many fields are coming to recognize the costs of alcohol problems in terms of absenteeism, accidents and injuries, job turnover, wasted time, and spoiled goods. Although concrete cost estimates are not available, the sick time of alcoholic employees has been reported as significantly greater than that of other employees.[69] Many major industrial concerns have been reexamining their policies with respect to employees who have a drinking problem, and a few have established programs of education, detection, and treatment of alcoholism among their employees.[70]

The Family

It is within the family that the questions of drinking and problems of alcohol are most intimately experienced. Most people are first exposed to the values, beliefs, and customs of drinking or abstaining within the context of their family. Several studies have found that the family is the most frequent setting and family members the most frequent companions at the time of earliest exposure to alcohol, and that about half of those who drink report some experiment or taste by the age of 10. The importance of the family in the transmission of drinking customs is further demonstrated by high correlations between young people and their parents in regard to the types of beverages used, frequency of drinking, and amounts consumed. The significance of the family for adolescent drinking is also seen in those cases where use of alcohol does not conform to family norms but appears rather as a symbol of rejecting the authority of parents and others. It is within the family that most individuals acquire the sense of security or inadequacy that may

---

[68] *Ibid.*, pp. 385, 419.

[69] Harrison M. Trice, "The Job Behavior of Problem Drinkers," in David J. Pittman and Charles R. Snyder, eds., *Society, Culture, and Drinking Patterns,* pp. 493–510.

[70] *The Wall Street Journal,* October 2, 1969, pp. 1, 15.

influence the psychological meaning of alcohol for them and their future motivations for drinking.

The family's role in the generation of a "personality" prone to alcoholism has been the subject of much debate. The life histories of alcoholics usually present clear evidence that family stress or unresolved conflicts over ambivalent feelings toward parents are contributing factors, especially in families that generated conflict or guilt about the use of alcohol or that provided role-models for the use of alcohol as a way of acting out conflict or dealing with stress. Although there is no evidence of the genetic inheritance of alcoholism, the fact that children of alcoholic parents are more prone to alcoholism suggests that the family environment may contribute to its occurrence.

In turn, alcoholism clearly contributes to family stress and instability. Alcoholics are more frequently divorced or separated than nonalcoholics, and the wives, husbands, and children of alcoholics have relatively high rates of physical, emotional, and psychosomatic illness. Alcoholics usually over-demand emotional support from others but provide little or no such support for them in turn. Also, because of the preoccupation with alcohol, or because of personality traits associated with alcoholism, or merely because of the impotence resulting from the sedative impact of alcohol, alcoholics are often unsatisfying sexual partners. Additional stress for families of alcoholics stems from the economic burdens often associated with the relatively high cost of alcohol or the loss of income resulting from alcohol pathology.

Some studies that have found certain personality traits to be fairly characteristic of the wives of alcoholics have led to the suggestion that there is a kind of mutual selection process in marriages involving known alcoholics or alcoholism-prone individuals, or that the experience of marriage to an alcoholic leads to the development of a unique pattern of social and psychological adjustment.[71] The possibility that alcoholism, despite its considerable stress-producing potential, may provide compensations as well, is supported by the fact that a large segment of the alcoholic population does maintain family stability [72] and by the further fact that some marriages collapse only after the alcoholic has ceased drinking.

The significance of the family as an important stabilizing factor must not be overlooked. Statistics reveal that persons who have never married or whose marriages have been disrupted do not live as long and have higher

---

[71] Joan K. Jackson, "The Adjustment of the Family to the Crisis of Alcoholism," *Quarterly Journal of Studies on Alcohol,* Vol. 15 (December, 1954), pp. 562–86.

[72] Margaret B. Bailey, "Alcoholism and Marriage," *Quarterly Journal of Studies on Alcohol,* Vol. 22 (March, 1961), pp. 80–94; Margaret B. Bailey, P. Haberman, and H. Alksne, "Outcomes of Alcoholic Marriages," *Quarterly Journal of Studies on Alcohol,* Vol. 23 (December, 1962), pp. 610–23.

rates of disease than those living within families. Studies of homeless men suggest that, while alcoholism and its underlying causes undoubtedly contribute to homelessness, the stress associated with alienation or isolation from a family clearly supports patterns of pathological drinking.[73]

Medicine

In recent years, medical, psychiatric, public health, and hospital resources have been under increasing pressure to assume greater responsibility for treating or preventing alcoholism. There has been a calculated effort to create a public health or medical model, in place of a moralistic model, for conceptualizing the problems of alcoholism and for mobilizing social responses. This movement has involved citizens' voluntary committees on alcoholism, public agencies, recovered alcoholics, and some educational and research organizations. In order to encourage alcoholics to seek treatment, to create a more sympathetic public image of alcoholism, and to develop support for research and treatment resources, alcoholism has been defined as a "disease" and the alcoholic as a "sick person."

Ironically, the medical model has probably had less impact on medical institutions and personnel than it has had on other segments of society. The health professions, although long involved in treating alcoholics suffering from cirrhosis of the liver, nutritional deficiency, and other specific diseases or injuries, still try to avoid responsibility for treating alcoholism. Although several studies have identified alcoholism in a significant segment of patients under treatment in general hospitals, most hospitals resist or forbid accepting patients specifically for the treatment of alcoholism. Therefore, only rarely are alcoholics recognized as such by hospital personnel. As a result, the treatment of the illnesses for which they are hospitalized is often compromised.[74] This has prompted an observation that hospitals which have removed the usual discriminatory practices from their admission policies still discriminate against the victims of a particular disease.[75] Discrim-

---

[73] R. Straus, "Alcohol and the Homeless Man," pp. 360–404.

[74] See R. Barchha, M. A. Stewart, and S. B. Guze, "The Prevalence of Alcoholism Among General Hospital Ward Patients," *American Journal of Psychiatry*, Vol. 125, No. 5 (November, 1968), pp. 681–84.

[75] R. Straus, "Social Factors in General Hospital Patient Care," *American Journal of Psychiatry*, Vol. 124 (June, 1968), pp. 1663–68.

inatory practices have also been identified in the variable treatment of alcoholics according to social class.[76]

While the substitution of a medical model for a moralistic model appears to have been somewhat effective in modifying public attitudes, it perpetuates the oversimplification of a complex problem.[77] The problems of alcohol, including alcoholism, certainly have medical ramifications, but they continue to be moral problems as well, and they continue to involve government, religion, law, and education. Like most serious medical problems, they have significant implications for family and employment.

SOCIAL RESPONSES TO ALCOHOL PROBLEMS

Up to about 1940, public provision for alcoholics was found only in jails, asylums, public infirmaries, or shelters. It was assumed that most alcoholics were men, alienated from their families, unemployed or unemployable, highly unstable, and socially irresponsible.[78] Chronic inebriates who belonged to families, who held jobs, who were relatively stable members of the community, or who happened to be women, were not usually labeled as alcoholics. They did not fit the stereotype, and their condition was generally hidden or denied by relatives and close friends.

The following statement from a Finnish report on social policy typifies the situation that has prevailed in many parts of the world:

> So far, the care of alcoholics . . . has carried the stamp of sanitary services of a kind . . . but the alcoholics . . . hardly felt themselves to be the favorite children of the agencies concerned. . . . That an individual is expressly labeled antisocial will hardly promote his adjustment. . . . In depriving a citizen of his freedom, society also pursues goals other than the adjustment of the individual. . . . The primary

---

[76] W. Schmidt, R. G. Smart, and M. K. Moss, *Social Class and the Treatment of Alcoholism* (Toronto: University of Toronto Press, 1968).

[77] See John R. Seeley, "Alcoholism Is a Disease: Implications for Social Policy," in David J. Pittman and Charles R. Snyder, eds., *Society, Culture, and Drinking Patterns,* pp. 586–93.

[78] These characteristics did describe the more conspicuous categories of alcoholics. See S. D. Bacon, "Inebriety, Social Integration, and Marriage," *Quarterly Journal of Studies on Alcohol,* Vol. 5 (June, 1944), pp. 86–125, (September, 1944), pp. 303–39; David J. Pittman and C. W. Gordon, *Revolving Door* (New York: Free Press, 1958).

purpose of detention is not to help the individual adjust to his environment, but to guard the public against the offender.[79]

The Public Health Approach

Important changes in social response to alcoholism and alcohol problems began to take place in the early 1940's. A modest volume of scientific research involving numerous disciplines began to explore long-neglected questions.[80] The *Quarterly Journal of Studies on Alcohol* has provided a means for disseminating information and stimulating investigation. Pilot outpatient clinics were established to offer a combination of medical, psychological, and social work therapies for alcoholics. By providing both help and hope, these community-based programs began to attract the formerly hidden alcoholic for treatment, making possible a better understanding of the alcoholic's social assets and liabilities. They brought into visibility patients with relative stability in marriage, employment, and community. This helped to alter the then prevailing stereotypes that tended to equate alcoholism with skid row living or severe psychopathology.[81] Coincidentally, in the 1940's, the organization known as Alcoholics Anonymous emerged into prominence. The Alcoholics Anonymous program is structured around reliance on personal faith and the support and insight gained from others with similar experiences and needs.[82] Its essential therapeutic element

---

[79] Pekka Kuusi, *Social Policy for the Sixties* (Helsinki: Finnish Social Policy Association, 1964), p. 266.

[80] Prominent organizations that have been specifically engaged in research on alcohol problems include the Rutgers (formerly Yale) Center of Alcohol Studies in the U. S. A.; the Finnish Foundation for Alcohol Studies in Helsinki; and the Alcoholism and Drug Addiction Research Foundation in Toronto, Canada.

[81] See R. Straus and S. D. Bacon, "Alcoholism and Social Stability," *Quarterly Journal of Studies on Alcohol,* Vol. 12 (June, 1951), pp. 231–60, for an analysis of the characteristics of 2000 male patients seen in nine of the first outpatient clinics established in the United States during the 1940's.

[82] Several sociologists have studied the phenomenon of Alcoholics Anonymous. See Robert Freed Bales, "The Therapeutic Role of Alcoholics Anonymous as Seen by a Sociologist," *Quarterly Journal of Studies on Alcohol,* Vol. 5 (September, 1944), pp. 267–78; O. W. Ritchie, "A Sociohistorical Survey of Alcoholics Anonymous," *Quarterly Journal of Studies on Alcohol,* Vol. 9 (June, 1948), pp. 119–56; Milton A. Maxwell, "Alcoholics Anonymous: An Interpretation," in David J. Pittman and Charles R. Snyder, eds., *Society, Culture, and Drinking Patterns,* pp. 577–85; and Harrison M. Trice, "Alcoholics Anonymous," *Annals of the American Academy of Political and Social Science,* Vol. 315 (January, 1958), pp. 108–16.

appears to be the provision of a meaningful reference group concerned with maintaining sobriety. The social impact of Alcoholics Anonymous lies in its contribution to the reduction of the stigma of alcoholism and thus to a better understanding of and sympathy for, the alcoholic. The movement has demonstrated more dramatically than formal treatment programs that alcoholics are drawn from all walks of life and that they can be reclaimed as useful, productive, and respectable members of the community.

Along with their families, members of Alcoholics Anonymous and other victims of alcoholism have provided much of the drive behind efforts to focus attention and understanding on the long-neglected problems of alcohol, develop effective social mechanisms for coping with these problems, and stimulate the assumption of responsibility by governments at all levels. Constructive provisions for alcoholics have been built into the health and welfare systems of several countries designed to "induce people in difficulty to seek help and to aid them in leading socially acceptable lives."[83]

In the United States, a substantial public health movement has developed encompassing the voluntary National Council on Alcoholism, community-based voluntary health groups in many major cities, state tax-supported programs for education about and treatment of alcoholism, and, quite recently, significant developments at the level of the federal government.[84] During the 1960's a federal grant supported the Cooperative Commission on the Study of Alcoholism, which was created to conduct a five-year study leading to recommendations for long term federal policy.[85] Based partly on the Commission's recommendations, a National Center for the Control and Prevention of Alcoholism was established in the National Institute of Mental Health in 1966, and, in response to a Presidential directive, a National Advisory Committee on Alcoholism was appointed, also in 1966.[86] In the meantime, numerous agencies of the federal government began to examine their responsibility with respect to specific alcohol problems.[87]

---

[83] P. Kuusi, *Social Policy for the Sixties,* p. 269. See also Orla Jensen, *Social Welfare in Denmark* (Copenhagen: Det Danske Selskab, 1964), p. 69; *Social Benefits in Sweden* (Stockholm: The Swedish Institute, 1968), p. 30; and *Alcoholics: Health Services for Their Treatment and Rehabilitation* (Edinburgh: Her Majesty's Stationery Office, 1965).

[84] Jay N. Cross, *Guide to the Community Control of Alcoholism* (New York: American Public Health Association, 1963).

[85] Cooperative Commission on the Study of Alcoholism, *Alcohol Problems: A Report to the Nation,* prepared by Thomas F. A. Plaut (New York: Oxford University Press, 1967).

[86] *An Interim Report of the National Advisory Committee on Alcoholism* was issued in December, 1968 (Washington, D. C.: U. S. Government Printing Office, 1969).

[87] These included the Department of Transportation with respect to alcohol and

Evaluating Change in Social Responses

In spite of increased activity at various levels of government, there is as yet no consistent social response to alcohol problems in the United States. Many discriminatory or ineffective policies still prevail. Proposals for prohibition, in varying forms, are still introduced and occasionally adopted. Jails and mental hospitals are still relied on to deal with chronic public intoxication. The force of public opinion continues to make laws against drinking and driving a mockery. Many hospitals, social agencies, and health and welfare personnel still try to justify rejecting responsibility for treating the victims of alcoholism. Many employers summarily dismiss alcoholic employees upon detection. In relation to the magnitude and severity of these problems, the funds invested in research, education, treatment, and prevention are pitifully small.

Yet the past 30 years have seen encouraging change. The stigma of alcoholism has been moderated. The alcoholic is less likely to be held morally responsible for his problem and more likely to be depicted as the victim of a disease. He is now more likely also to admit that he has a problem and to seek help.

Several different kinds of alcoholism have been identified and concepts of multiple causation have emerged, although there is as yet no generally acceptable theory of etiology. Numerous treatment resources have been developed and a variety of drugs have been found to help the alcoholic maintain sobriety, although they do not cure his alcoholism. Some clinics, hospitals, and specially designated beds in general hospitals have become available to alcoholics, and a few physicians are specializing in the treatment of alcoholism. Alcoholics Anonymous has had a significant, if unmeasurable,

---

highway safety; the Social Service and Rehabilitation Service, the Office of Education, the Civil Service Commission, and the Department of Defense with respect to alcoholic employees and servicemen; the Office of Economic Opportunity with respect to alcoholism and poverty; and the President's Commission on Law Enforcement and the Administration of Justice with respect to the chronic public drunkenness offender. See *Alcohol and Highway Safety,* A Report to the Congress from the Secretary of Transportation, August 1968; *Report of the Secretary's Advisory Committee on Traffic Safety,* U. S. Department of Health, Education and Welfare, 1968; *Social, Psychological and Economic Aspects of Alcoholism,* Welfare Research Report 3, Department of Health, Education and Welfare (Washington, D. C.: U. S. Government Printing Office, 1966); and the President's Commission on Law Enforcement and Administration of Justice, *Task Force Report: Drunkenness* (Washington, D. C.: U. S. Government Printing Office, 1967).

impact. Although these growing resources serve only a small portion of the population of alcoholics and must operate within the limits of available knowledge, they are proving effective. Generally, those approaches to treatment that combine medical, psychological, and social intervention have had the greatest degree of success.

A growing awareness of public responsibility for the problems of alcoholism has been reflected in the increasing support provided for treatment services at the local and state levels of government and for research by the federal government. After much resistance, major employers and insurance companies are also beginning to give some attention to these problems. But as yet there are no sure cures and no known ways of preventing alcoholism. Nor does there appear to be any measurable reduction in the incidence or prevalence of alcoholism in the United States.

SOCIAL POLICY

Because the problems of alcoholism are so vast and generally occur only in association with other serious problems of health and life adjustment, the National Advisory Committee on Alcoholism has recommended that future "Federal policy should stress the inclusion of adequate attention to problems of alcohol abuse in the planning and development of all Federally supported comprehensive programs for health and human well-being." [88] Such a policy would reverse the long-time trend of approaching specific problems on a categorical basis. It would include treatment and education on alcoholism in comprehensive community mental health programs, incorporate provisions for alcoholism control into the nation's attack on poverty, revise the policies of government as an employer toward its alcoholic employees, encourage general hospitals to assume their proper role in the spectrum of resources available to cope with alcoholism, develop national guidelines for prepayment and insurance coverage to treat alcoholism, and develop effective strategies for alcohol education. Finally, this policy would increase significantly the resources available for research, manpower training, and demonstration projects designed to enhance the nation's technical and personnel resources available to cope with alcoholism and its many ramifications. Many of these recommendations were incorporated in the Comprehensive Alcohol Abuse and Alcoholism Prevention and Rehabilitation Act passed by the Congress in December, 1970. This legislation also created a National Institute on Alcohol Abuse and Alcoholism.

---

[88] *Interim Report of the National Advisory Committee on Alcoholism*, p. 9.

Many countries have been modifying their approach to education about alcohol by replacing generally ineffective antialcohol propaganda, based on a psychology of fear, with a factually based appeal to reason and intelligence designed to inspire both responsible alcohol use on the part of those who choose to drink and respect for the nonuser. The National Advisory Committee on Alcoholism in the United States has noted "considerable evidence to suggest that existing laws and policies designed to restrict drinking by young people have contributed to exactly the opposite effect than that intended; and that changes in existing laws may be indicated as a step toward the prevention and control of alcohol problems." [89] The Cooperative Commission on the Study of Alcoholism was quite specific in recommending a uniform reduction of the legal age for drinking to 18 in all states.[90]

The Chronic Public Inebriate

A special problem involves the response of most societies to chronic public intoxication. For centuries, the public drunkard has been the object of both fear and disdain. Public intoxication inspired the rise of the temperance movement in the late eighteenth century, and characteristics of the public drunkard molded the stereotype of the alcoholic. Most societies have relied on their police and jails to protect them from the perceived dangers or discomforts imposed by drunkards in their midst. A substantial portion of society's investment in police, courts, and jails is absorbed by the "crimes" of drunkenness and related offenses. The futility of incarceration for these men who are repeatedly arrested, convicted, sentenced, and released was brought into sharp focus and its legality challenged by several court cases in the late 1960's. These culminated in a review by the Supreme Court of the case of Powell v. Texas. The conviction of Mr. Powell, a chronic inebriate with a long history of arrests, was challenged on the grounds that criminal punishment of an alcoholic for public intoxication was "cruel and unusual" and in violation of the Eighth and Fourteenth amendments to the Constitution. Although the Supreme Court, by a split vote, did not reverse the conviction,[91] this case served to crystallize the need for change in both law and policy. The Court observed that its decision was based in part on the

---

[89] *Interim Report of the National Advisory Committee on Alcoholism*, p. 28.

[90] *Alcohol Problems, A Report to the Nation*, pp. 148–52.

[91] Supreme Court of the United States, No. 405: October Term, 1967, Leroy Powell, Appellant, v. State of Texas (June 17, 1968).

absence of well-developed social alternatives to jail as a device for protecting society from the public inebriate and the inebriate from himself.

A recommendation for establishing community "detoxification" centers throughout the country was made by the President's Commission on Law Enforcement and Administration of Justice in 1967,[92] and by other advisory bodies. A model "Alcoholism and Intoxication Treatment Act," [93] prepared for the National Institute of Mental Health in 1969, provides in explicit detail recommended legislation that would enable the states to effect such a change in policy and procedure. Several demonstration projects, notably in Maryland and Washington, D. C., are now testing the practicality of initiating continuing treatment and rehabilitation for the chronic public inebriate, while providing more humane and effective alternatives to the drunk tank of local jails.

Social Policy and Normative Behavior

Laws or regulations necessary to invoke change in social policy are often in conflict with the forces of normative behavior. This poses a dilemma for many societies today, as it has for generations, with respect to social policy on alcohol. In most societies where a large majority of the adult population attaches some importance to the right to drink, governments have accepted a responsibility to facilitate accessibility of alcohol and have capitalized on an opportunity for a considerable source of tax revenue. At the same time, governments have a fundamental responsibility to protect the individual and society from the many threats that alcohol abuse poses to the public health and well-being.

The most common type of governmental intervention — prohibition — has been invoked for the purpose of protecting the public but at the expense of both accessibility and tax revenue. Prohibition has generally failed because it has violated prevailing norms that demanded accessibility of alcohol. Recently, a new policy was instituted in Poland and proposed in Ontario, Canada, to raise the price of alcohol relative to disposable income. This is an attempt to reduce problems by decreasing the consumption of alcohol while retaining the "right" to accessibility and maintaining government

---

[92] President's Commission on Law Enforcement and Administration of Justice, *Task Force Report: Drunkenness* (1967), p. 506.

[93] Prepared by the Legislative Drafting Research Fund of Columbia University, final draft dated July 18, 1969, mimeographed.

revenue. It has been reasoned that this policy could succeed, even though it would limit accessibility for many people, if adequate attention were given to intensive education aimed at changing prevailing norms.[94]

In the United States, conflicts between mores and laws continue to characterize many aspects of drinking behavior. The phrase "vote dry and drink wet" is an apt description not merely of behavior associated with prohibition laws, but also of the predominant response to most other legal restrictions associated with drinking customs: the legal-age laws, drinking-and-driving codes, laws regulating the hours of sale and other aspects of distribution, and laws covering manufacturing and taxation. Many people will strongly support alcohol control laws in principle but will violate them freely and, unless a violation has involved personal and direct damage to themselves, will condone their violation by others.

Experience in the United States and elsewhere in the world has clearly indicated that efforts to cope with problems of alcohol by legislating change will prove ineffective unless laws can be made that reflect normative forces of behavior. Yet, in the United States, the heterogeneous nature of the population makes the task of delineating a single normative pattern of drinking behavior impossible. Drinking customs and attitudes and drinking problems in American society reflect the practices, beliefs, and values of many national, regional, ethnic, and social groups. The absence of homogeneity in drinking norms itself contributes to an additional problem of alcohol—the problem of conceptualization, which has been a recurring though as yet unidentified theme of this chapter.

THE PROBLEM OF CONCEPTUALIZING ALCOHOL PROBLEMS

The many diverse problems of alcohol affect all segments of the population, although in very different ways, and they involve all major social institutions. They interrelate with other major social problems—poverty, crime,

---

[94] This recommendation has been made to the Ontario Provincial Government by the Alcoholism and Drug Addiction Research Foundation. It is based on an ecological analysis of worldwide statistical data over many years, which revealed a constant relationship between rates of alcohol abuse and rates of absolute alcohol consumption. The prevailing cost of alcohol in relation to prevailing income was identified as the only factor consistently associated with rates of use and abuse. Personal communication from Mr. H. David Archibald, Executive Director, Alcoholism and Drug Addiction Foundation of Ontario, December 5, 1969.

the abuse of narcotics, hallucinogens, and other dangerous drugs, accidents, disease, suicide, family instability. They include both deviant behavior, such as alcoholism and intoxication, and social disorganization, such as the consequences of prohibition and the conflicts between mores and laws.

More than any other factor, the existence of many conflicting conceptual models, each with their own limited dimensions, has restricted the understanding of alcohol problems and the development of effective social responses to them. Too often, references to alcohol problems have tended to confuse drinking with alcoholism, while references to alcoholism have tended to overlook the many different forms of pathological drinking. Much of the study of alcohol problems has been restricted by the boundaries of traditional academic disciplines. A conceptualization that takes into account the interaction of biological, psychological, social, and cultural components and the reciprocal relationship between the action of alcohol on the human organism and the customs of drinking is fundamental to the development of effective social policy for the prevention and control of alcohol problems.

6

Suicide

JACK P. GIBBS

Like any other form of death, suicide carries with it the idea of tragedy. Unlike other forms, however, it is considered in most societies as not only tragic but also avoidable, and this avoidability stamps it as a social problem.

SOME ASPECTS OF SUICIDE AS A SOCIAL PROBLEM

Cases of voluntary death are experienced by the victim's associates as a personal loss, but they also represent a societal loss. Beyond personal and ethical valuations, a person's worth can be assessed in terms of his contribution to society — as a producer, as a parent, as a soldier, and so on. Suicide is thus a social problem independent of personal grief because it represents a measurable loss to society.

This loss is greater than one might suspect. Consider, for example, the number of suicides in each of five countries in one year (Table 1).

Suicide is generally believed to be of little quantitative importance in comparison to other causes of death. The fact is, however, that it constitutes a major cause of death, at least in some societies. This is seen from Table 2, which lists the rank of suicide among causes of death in four countries.

TABLE 1
Number of Suicides in Selected Countries

Country	Year	Number of Suicides
United States	1966	21,281
Japan	1965	14,444
West Germany	1965	11,779
France	1965	7,352
United Kingdom	1966	5,489

Source: Demographic Yearbook, 1967 (New York: United Nations, 1968), Table 24.

If we judge contributions to society in terms of status, then married persons between 15 and 64 years of age warrant a high position. If only the nonproductive members of a society (e.g., the extremely aged) took their lives, the collective loss would be negligible; but this is not the case. In the United States, for example, approximately one-half of the suicides are married persons between 15 and 64 years of age. Thus, suicide represents a substantial social loss, both quantitatively and qualitatively.

Suicide and Social Disorganization

Although social disorganization is subject to various definitions, the failure of groups or individuals to conform to social norms is often viewed as indicative of disorganization, on the grounds that such behavior is not in accord with the expectations of others. On the other hand, nonconformity may be construed as evidence of a conflict in values, which in itself constitutes social disorganization.[1] However social disorganization is defined, it is generally thought to be linked to deviant behavior, and in this context suicide is a social problem beyond collective and personal loss.

In all Christian and Moslem nations, and in Israel, self-destruction violates normative expectations. It is, in fact, treated as a crime in some countries; but the moral evaluation now accorded the act is by no means as severe as it once was. In European history there are numerous instances of violent opposition to voluntary death—the victim's body was subject to abuse, religious services were denied, and his property was confiscated.[2]

[1] See Ralph H. Turner, "Value Conflict in Social Disorganization," *Sociology and Social Research,* Vol. 38 (May–June, 1954), pp. 301–08.

[2] Émile Durkheim, *Suicide: A Study in Sociology,* trans. by John A. Spaulding and George Simpson (New York: Free Press, 1951), pp. 326–38.

TABLE 2

Rank of Suicide as a Cause of Death, Selected Countries

Country and Year	Rank of Suicide as One of 50 Major Causes of Death	Suicides as a Percentage of All Deaths
Finland, 1966	9	2.0
Hungary, 1966	6	3.0
Austria, 1966	11	1.8
United States, 1966	14	1.1

Source: Demographic Yearbook, 1967, Table 24.

Where suicide is opposed by the mores, by the law, or by both, its occurrence is evidence of weak social norms. This is true for deviant acts generally, but it is all the more accentuated by the very nature of voluntary death—the individual not only defies collective authority but renounces his membership in the collectivity as well. (This was perhaps sensed by the citizens of Greek city-states when they demanded that the prospective victim petition for the right to take his life.) The seriousness to society of this renunciation is pointed up by its military illustration whereby treason and desertion in time of war are considered the gravest of crimes.

That suicide may reflect weak social norms is indicated by studies that have found it to be most prevalent in areas of a city that abound with other deviations, such as mental illness, drug addiction, and prostitution.[3] This association suggests that where some people readily renounce their membership in society, others are not prone to respect the norms that govern the living.

In addition to the distinctly sociological correlates of suicide, the act is believed to be associated with emotional disorders and mental illness.[4] From the psychological point of view, frequent suicides may be taken as

[3] See Ruth S. Cavan, *Suicide* (Chicago: University of Chicago Press, 1928), pp. 81–105; Calvin F. Schmid, "Suicides in Seattle, 1914–1925: An Ecological and Behavioristic Study," *University of Washington Publications in the Social Sciences,* Vol. 5 (October, 1928), pp. 4–23; Calvin F. Schmid, *A Social Saga of Two Cities; An Ecological and Statistical Study of Social Trends in Minneapolis and St. Paul* (Minneapolis: Minneapolis Council of Social Agencies, Bureau of Social Research, 1937), pp. 370–80; Ernest R. Mowrer, *Disorganization: Personal and Social* (Philadelphia: Lippincott, 1942); Peter Sainsbury, *Suicide in London: An Ecological Study* (New York: Basic Books, 1956).

[4] See Karl A. Menninger, *Man Against Himself* (New York: Harcourt Brace Jovanovich, 1938) and Simpson's observations in Durkheim, *Suicide,* pp. 20–25.

evidence of marked psychopathology in the population, and sociological studies in urban areas have produced findings that support the idea.[5] As we shall see, however, the relationship between suicide and its alleged psychological and sociological correlates is subject to debate; nevertheless, there are reasons for regarding suicide as a form of deviant behavior reflecting conditions that constitute serious social problems.[6]

The Prevention of Suicide

Most social problems are believed to be subject to remedial action. In this context suicide is unique, in that it is difficult to imagine any course of action that would substantially reduce its incidence. There have been arguments for more severe prison sentences for drug addicts, curfew laws for juveniles, and so on; but whatever their merits as preventives of other deviant acts, such repressive devices are clearly not applicable to suicide. Punishment holds little fear for the would-be victim. Confiscation of property and punishment of relatives might act to deter self-destruction, but the public would almost certainly reject such measures. The long and short of the matter is that suicide is not subject to conventional means of control; consequently, it is all the more a social problem.

As an alternative to "repressive" measures, suicide prevention may be attempted by therapeutic programs (e.g., counseling, psychiatric treatment, and custodial care). In the United States and other countries, various programs have been initiated, some of which have been organized as suicide-prevention centers. Ultimately, of course, the success of such a program depends on the type of therapy, and no particular type has been demonstrated as effective. Hence, the focus in suicide prevention will be on the development of new forms of therapy. But no therapy can reduce the incidence of suicide without first giving attention to several problems and questions. As an obvious example, unless potential victims seek the aid of therapists or otherwise come to their notice, no prevention program will be effective. So regardless of the type of therapy contemplated, there are two questions. First, what kind of program will induce potential victims to seek the aid of therapists? Second, apart from seeking aid, what are the symptoms of impending suicide? The literature clearly reveals that at present there is

---

[5] See Peter Sainsbury, *Suicide in London,* pp. 84–87.

[6] For related observations, see Erich Fromm, *The Sane Society* (New York: Rinehart, 1955), pp. 3–11.

no satisfactory answer to either question,[7] and for that reason conventional basic research takes on special significance, especially in connection with the second question. Diverse "warnings" of suicide are mentioned in the literature—e.g., ostensible attempts, threats, depression, expression of despair, accident proneness—but the relation among these commonly recognized symptoms and actual suicide is most problematic. The difficulty is not just that victims differ as to presuicidal symptoms (which is true enough), but also that millions of individuals probably manifest a commonly recognized symptom and yet never even attempt suicide. Of course, the significance of "false warnings" should not be overlooked, for no prevention program will have the resources to respond to just any commonly recognized symptom of impending suicide. Until more reliable symptoms can be identified, it is difficult to imagine an effective prevention program. Basic research on that subject need not be confined to the study of individual cases. An adequate sociological theory on variation in the suicide rate would be of value if only to identify the social characteristics of individuals who are serious "risks."

SUICIDE AS A SOCIOLOGICAL PROBLEM

Few *specific* forms of deviant behavior have claimed the attention of as many scholars in a variety of fields as has suicide. Dahlgren estimates that as of 1945 there were approximately 4000 published works on the subject.[8] Sociologists have been among those drawn to the subject, and this poses a question: Why should a discipline concerned with the study of society be interested in an individual and ostensibly asocial act? The question deserves an answer, if only to show that an inclination for the morbid is not an occupational prerequisite for sociologists.

For an answer, we turn to Émile Durkheim, who established the basic rationale for the sociological analysis of suicide. This rationale takes the form of a working postulate: The volume of suicide reflects something basic in the characteristics of social entities independent of the individual victims. We can best understand this postulate by analyzing everyday experience.

It is obvious that some statuses and social groups are quite different from others, and these differences are reflected both in norms and in actual behavior. True, we may be unable to specify the exact nature of such differ-

---

[7] World Health Organization, *Prevention of Suicide* (Geneva: 1968).
[8] Karl Gustav Dahlgren, *On Suicide and Attempted Suicide* (Lund, Sweden: Hakan Ohlssons Boktryskeri, 1945), p. 1.

ences. But this does not alter the fact that social contrasts exist between men and women, the old and the young, the married and the single, blacks and whites in the South, bankers and laborers, Catholics and Unitarians, and so on. Differences among whole societies cannot readily be experienced at first hand, but it does not require a social scientist to appreciate a variety of contrasts between, for example, Denmark and Ceylon.

The importance of these contrasts lies in the consistency with which social entities otherwise deemed dissimilar also have vastly different suicide rates.[9] Thus we find a sharp difference between rates for men and women, the old and the young, the married and the single, blacks and whites in the South, and Denmark and Ceylon. Such differences were known to exist before Durkheim's research, but it was he who first showed that the suicide rate reflects something basic in the social characteristics of a population.

Note, however, that Durkheim's argument may apply to practically all forms of deviant behavior. Why, then, has suicide been selected for extensive study? Primarily because sociology has a particular ax to grind: to demonstrate the social influences upon all manner of human behavior. And what better way is there to add to the efficacy of the argument for social causation than to show that it extends even to such a personal and desperate act as suicide?

Durkheim's approach has greatly influenced later studies of suicide by setting the central problem—the explanation of differences in suicide rates. Why, for example, was Sweden's 1961 suicide rate more than twice that of Norway; and why did Finland's rate increase from 6.1 in 1901 to 22.1 in 1962?[10]

Concern with suicide rates has created still another problem for sociological research—the question of the reliability of official suicide statistics. Following Durkheim, suicide may be defined formally as "death resulting directly or indirectly from a positive or negative act of the victim himself, which he knows will produce this result."[11] But this may not be applied by persons who compile official mortality statistics. The author finds that officials (e.g., coroners) who make such decisions are not governed by a formal

---

[9] A suicide rate is usually computed by the formula: $r = (S/P)100,000$, where S is the number of suicides occurring in a given year, or the average number per year, and P is the mean number of people in the population over the year or years. Thus r represents the annual number or mean annual number of suicides per 100,000 population during a year or period of years.

[10] World Health Organization, *Epidemiological and Vital Statistics Report,* Vol. 9, Table 2 and p. 251; and *Demographic Yearbook, 1963* (New York: United Nations, 1964), Table 25.

[11] Émile Durkheim, *Suicide,* p. 44.

definition of this kind. Thus the use of official suicide statistics in research rests on the assumptions that the commonly held conception of the act (1) corresponds to the research definition, (2) does not vary from one population to the next, and (3) is applied consistently to all cases of death. Many observers rightly question these assumptions and thereby cast doubts on the use of official statistics. Zilboorg, for instance, argues that

statistical data on suicide as they are compiled today deserve little if any credence; it has been repeatedly pointed out by scientific students of the problem that suicide cannot be subject to statistical evaluation.[12]

But Zilboorg's evaluation of official statistics as unreliable is purely intuitive. Thus he cites as a "scientific student" of the problem, of all people, Durkheim, who made extensive use of official suicide statistics. Simpson's rejection of official data is equally dubious. He rests his judgment in part on the failure of persons to agree as to whether suicide increases or decreases with civilization.[13] He also questions official statistics because they indicate that suicide is rare among children, whereas Zilboorg considered suicide among children significant enough for a study of it.[14]

All things considered, present knowledge precludes an adequate evaluation of official statistics. Probably they are not very accurate, but the amount of error is another question. Moreover, reliability probably varies not only by place and time but also according to the source of official statistics. Gargas reports that in the Netherlands during 1900–1925 suicide rates based on criminal statistics were generally 32 percent higher than those based on the statistics of the registrar's office.[15] This is one of the few studies that have offered concrete evidence of the questionable reliability of suicide rates based on official data. Other research, however, suggests that some rates are more reliable than is generally assumed. This conclusion was reached by the author after applying Durkheim's definition of self-destruction to each cor-

---

[12] Gregory Zilboorg, "Suicide Among Civilized and Primitive Races," *American Journal of Psychiatry,* Vol. 92 (May, 1936), p. 1350.

[13] George Simpson, "Methodological Problems in Determining the Aetiology of Suicide," *American Sociological Review,* Vol. 15 (October, 1950), p. 660.

[14] *Ibid.,* p. 660. Simpson fails to report that Zilboorg presents no evidence to show that suicide is actually common among children. See Gregory Zilboorg, "Considerations on Suicide, with Particular Reference to That of the Young," *American Journal of Orthopsychiatry,* Vol. 7 (January, 1937), pp. 15–31.

[15] S. Gargas, "Suicide in the Netherlands," *American Journal of Sociology,* Vol. 37 (March, 1932), p. 699. The figures provided by Gargas suggest that the discrepancy between the two sets of rates over the years indicated is on the average far less than 32 percent.

oner's report of a death in New Zealand during the period 1946–1951. Inspection of these records produced an estimate of 955 cases of suicide over the six years,[16] as compared with 1036 cases reported in official statistics.[17] The rates computed on the basis of the two figures differ very little. More noteworthy, perhaps, is that the officially reported number exceeds the count reached by careful inspection of all coroner reports. This contradicts the often expressed belief that official figures always seriously underestimate the amount of suicide, but it does not prove that all suicide rates are reliable, any more than Gargas' findings demonstrate that the reverse is true. We can conclude only that the question of the reliability of suicide statistics remains unsolved. (See Chapter 3.)

Jack Douglas has articulated the most sweeping condemnation of the use of official suicide statistics, and the evidence he presents indicates that some rates are grossly unreliable.[18] Douglas deserves credit for bringing the issue to the forefront, but his argument is not convincing. As Douglas himself admits, there is very little systematic evidence on the subject, certainly not enough to justify sweeping conclusions. Even if it could be known with certainty that some official rates are grossly unreliable, it would be questionable to generalize this fact to all rates. Also, the crucial consideration is not absolute reliability but relative reliability—specifically, the extent to which the proportion of cases are officially reported as such. Douglas ignores the distinction, and he appears indifferent to the reason sociologists use official statistics—there is no feasible alternative. Above all, Douglas' epistemology negates the very notion of a "reliable" rate.

> Suicides are not something of a set nature waiting to be correctly or incorrectly categorized by officials. The very nature of the "thing" is itself problematic so that "suicides" cannot correctly be said to exist . . . until a categorization has been made. Moreover, since there exists great disagreement between interested parties in the categorization of real-world cases, "suicides" can generally be said to exist and not to exist at the same time . . . .[19]

So from Douglas' perspective there are as many suicides in a population as there are divergent categorizations of deaths, and hence no rate is any more

---

[16] This research was made possible by a Fulbright grant and the cooperation of New Zealand's Department of Justice.

[17] *New Zealand Official Year-Book, 1947–49, 1950, 1951–52,* and *1954,* Census and Statistics Dept. (Wellington: Government Printer).

[18] Jack D. Douglas, *The Social Meanings of Suicide* (Princeton, N. J.: Princeton University Press, 1967).

[19] *Ibid.,* p. 106.

or less reliable than another. Indeed, the very notion of a reliable rate is alien to his perspective. Now the true incidence of suicide is unknown and unknowable, but it can be considered inferentially. For example, suppose that, working independently, several investigators gather data and compute a suicide rate for the same population. If those rates correspond closely, there is reason to regard each as fairly reliable. Douglas has no conception of a "true" rate, and he asserts that "great disagreement" exists among officials, investigators, and laymen (surely they are "interested parties") in categorizing deaths as suicide. But he presents no systematic evidence on the question, and that is precisely the kind of research we need.

VIEWPOINTS AND INTERESTS
OF THE VARIOUS DISCIPLINES

The foremost concern in this survey is with differences in suicide rates as a sociological problem. However, the study of suicide is not the exclusive property of any particular field; hence the viewpoints and interests of several disciplines warrant attention.

Psychological Studies and Observations

Understandably, psychological and psychiatric studies of suicide have focused on explaining the individual case. Several types of inquiries have sought this explanation. One type is based on all cases (or a sample taken as representative) occurring in a population over a specified period.[20] Such studies may consider the social characteristics of victims and the epidemiology of suicide, but as a rule they focus on possible motives or reasons for the act and the psychological or psychiatric classification of the victim. At least three serious difficulties confront this type of research. *First,* the ascription of motives or reasons is likely to be arbitrary. *Second,* the victims cannot be classified psychologically on the basis of direct observation. And, *third,* even when particular motives or psychological-psychiatric types are known to have prevailed among the cases, they can seldom be evaluated because the prevalence of these factors in the total population is generally

---

[20] A number of these studies are cited in William A. Rushing, "Individual Behavior and Suicide," in Jack P. Gibbs, ed., *Suicide* (New York: Harper, 1968), pp. 96–121.

unknown. Accordingly, such studies can at best isolate only the necessary and not the sufficient conditions for suicide.[21]

These psychological-psychiatric studies suggest that completed or attempted suicides often are persons with some mental or emotional disorder; however, the proportion so diagnosed has been in some instances as small as 15 percent, and it varies considerably from one population to the next. Although depressive psychotics are particularly prone to take their own lives, suicide occurs among persons with almost any type of psychiatric disorder.[22]

A second type of inquiry employs control groups. One such investigation compared four groups of persons with psychiatric histories: persons (1) who had committed suicide, (2) with a history of attempted suicide, (3) with a history of having threatened suicide, and (4) without a history of suicidal behavior. The investigators found that a potentially suicidal person could not be reliably distinguished on the basis of details in his case history.[23] No significant differences were detected among the four groups other than that a disproportionate number of actual suicides had been diagnosed previously as suffering from either reactive depression or paranoid schizophrenia and had one or more relatives with a history of mental hospitalization.

A third type of inquiry, the psychoanalytic approach, relies on random case-history data and clinical experience. Typically, it is guided by one of two major ideas. The first is that the "suicidal person is the victim of strong aggressive impulses which he fails to express outwardly and which he, as a result, turns inward, i.e., on himself.[24] Whatever its merits, this conception clearly does not adequately explain the act, because nothing is said concerning the conditions that generate aggression and determine the direction of its expression. The second idea suggests a death instinct as underlying suicide.[25] But this view is subject to the following objection:

> Valid as they are, one must nevertheless remark that the psychological speculations built around the death instinct as a pivotal point explain comparatively little since they are essentially restatements of the observation that, under certain known and mostly unknown cir-

---

[21] The first and third problems apply to some extent to studies of attempted suicide. See Margarethe von Andics, *Suicide and the Meaning of Life* (London: Hodge, 1947); and other studies cited in Weiss, "Suicide," pp. 250–52.

[22] Peter Sainsbury, *Suicide in London,* pp. 84–86. Weiss, "Suicide," p. 236. Zilboorg, "Considerations on Suicide." Gregory Zilboorg, "Differential Diagnostic Types of Suicide," *Archives of Neurology and Psychiatry,* Vol. 35 (January, 1936), pp. 270–91.

[23] Edwin S. Shneidman and Norman L. Farberow, "Clues to Suicide," *Public Health Reports,* Vol. 71 (February, 1956), pp. 109–14.

[24] Gregory Zilboorg, "Differential Diagnostic Types of Suicide," p. 272.

[25] See Karl A. Menninger, *Man Against Himself.*

cumstances, the impulse to die becomes greater than the impulse to live, at which time man will injure or kill himself. To say that the death instinct gains the upper hand over the life instinct is merely an elaborate way of stating that man does die or kill himself.[26]

Thus, with regard to explaining why some individuals kill themselves and others do not, the results of the three types of psychological-psychiatric inquiries appear generally inconclusive.

Anthropological Observations

Observations on suicide appear occasionally in anthropological literature, usually in a larger report on a particular culture. These observations (and a few special studies) generally deal with three aspects of suicide in a society—alleged typical motives or reasons, incidence, and societal reaction.

Accounts of ritual suicide suggest a peculiarity and a homogeneity of motives or reasons for suicide among some non-European peoples. The fact is, however, that suicide occurs among non-Europeans in a variety of situations and probably has widely diverse motives. Consider the following list of typical reasons or motives given for suicide in various populations: among the natives of Dobu—domestic quarrels; among the Iroquois—for the females, mistreatment in love and marriage and, for the males, the desire to escape apprehension for a violent crime; among the Mohave—longing for the dead; among the Lepchas of Sikkim—disgrace by public reproof; among the Eskimos of St. Lawrence Island—sickness, suffering, and a feeling of uselessness; and among the Chukchee—quarrels, suffering, longing for the dead, or a feeling of *taedium vitae*.[27] These and other reports confirm the earlier findings of Steinmetz and Westermarck,[28] both of whom reached the conclu-

---

[26] Gregory Zilboorg, "Considerations on Suicide," p. 17.

[27] R. F. Fortune, *Sorcerers of Dobu* (New York: Dutton, 1932), pp. 2–21. William N. Fenton, "Iroquois Suicide: A Study of the Stability of a Cultural Pattern," *Anthropological Papers,* No. 14, U. S. Bureau of American Ethnology, Bulletin No. 128 (Washington, D. C., 1941), p. 90 and pp. 130–34. George Devereux, "Mohave Soul Concepts," *American Anthropologist,* Vol. 39 (New Series, 1937), p. 422. Geoffrey Gorer, *Himalayan Village* (London: Joseph, 1938), p. 269. Alexander Leighton and Charles C. Hughes, "Notes on Eskimo Patterns of Suicide," *Southwestern Journal of Anthropology,* Vol. 11 (Winter, 1955), pp. 327–28. Waldemar Bogoras, "The Chukchee," American Museum of Natural History, *Memoirs* (New York: Stechert, 1904), Vol. 11, Pt. 3, pp. 560–68.

[28] S. R. Steinmetz, "Suicide Among Primitive People," *American Anthropologist,* Vol. 7 (January, 1894), pp. 53–60. Edward Westermarck, *Origin and Development of Moral Ideas* (London: Macmillan, 1908), Vol. 2, pp. 229–64.

sion that a wide variety of motives or reasons are ascribed to suicides among nonliterates.

One thing is clear. Whatever their relevance to etiological inquiry, the alleged motives among nonliterates and other non-Europeans appear to be much more akin to those among Europeans than the presence of ritual suicide in some non-European societies might suggest.[29]

Anthropological observations on the incidence of suicide are difficult to interpret, and the inferences drawn from them are hazardous at best. The reason this is so should be clear from the observations cited in Table 3.

These reports are not without value, but some of them treat incidence of suicide so impressionistically that they are inadequate for systematic comparisons. Only a rate of suicide is suited for comparisons, and descriptions of the act as "common," "rare," and so on, are poor substitutes. These accounts report neither the probable rate of suicide nor the basis for the observer's vague estimate. One danger is that a few exotic cases may give the impression that suicide is rampant in the society. For example, reports on ritual suicide and on the special case of *suttee* (a ceremony in which the wife kills herself on the death of her husband)[30] suggest that suicide was once rampant in India. But was this the case? We do not have the historical statistics needed to provide the answer. But it has been estimated that the rate for the whole of India in 1907 was only about 4.8, with a high of 8.1 in the Central Provinces, as compared, for example, with a rate of 32.6 for Saxony during 1906–1910.[31]

The case of Japan serves as another warning against confusing the occurrence of ritual self-destruction with a high rate of suicide. Ceremonial self-destruction, known as *hara-kiri*, has long prevailed in the country; however, Japan's suicide rate during 1881–1885 may have been less than that of the United States for 1906–1915, and it appears that only since the turn of the century has the suicide rate in Japan substantially exceeded that in the United States.[32]

Until such time as we have something other than impressionistic accounts

---

[29] The similarity of motives for suicide in different types of societies is stressed in Louis I. Dublin and Bessie Bunzel, *To Be or Not To Be* (New York: Harrison Smith and Robert Haas, 1933), p. 142. Revised version: Louis I. Dublin, *Suicide: A Sociological and Statistical Study* (New York: Ronald Press, 1963).

[30] R. V. Russell and Rai Bahadur Hira Lal, *The Tribes and Castes of the Central Provinces of India* (London: Macmillan, 1916), Vol. 2, pp. 259–67. N. M. Penzer, *The Ocean of Story* (London: Sawyer, 1925), Vol. 4, pp. 255–72.

[31] John Rice Miner, "Suicide and Its Relation to Climatic and Other Factors," *American Journal of Hygiene,* Monographic Series No. 2 (July, 1922), pp. 2–3 and 17.

[32] *Ibid.,* p. 3.

TABLE 3
Incidence of Suicide in Some Non-European Populations

Population	Observations on the Incidence of Suicide
Mohave [1]	"The conflict between longing for the dead and the impossibility of catching up with them should one live too long after they died leads to an appalling number of suicides. . . ."
Kwakiutl [2]	"In practice suicide was comparatively common."
Tanaina [3]	"Suicide is more common now, when old men live to see the last of their sons die."
Havasupai [4]	"Suicides, like the insane, are rare. The practice is referred to in myths and funeral speeches, and is credited to the Walapai, yet there have been no instances for a generation."
Lepchas of Sikkim [5]	"Considering the size of the community suicide is fairly frequent among the Lepchas. There have been six suicides in Lingthem and the neighbouring smaller villages in the last twenty years. . . ."
Indians of the Southwestern U. S. and Northern Mexico [6]	"Suicides occur among most of the tribes visited, but on the whole they are rare, especially among women."
White Mountain Apache [7]	". . . one or more cases of self-destruction occur every year."
Southern Ute [8]	"No instance of death by suicide was learned of. . . ."
Papago [9]	". . . suicide is seldom heard of."
Puma [10]	". . . suicide is rare."

Sources:

[1] Devereux, "Mohave Soul Concepts," *American Anthropologist,* Vol. 39, p. 422.

[2] Benedict, *Patterns of Culture* (Boston: Houghton Mifflin, 1934), p. 219.

[3] Osgood, *American Anthropologist,* Vol. 35, p. 714.

[4] Spier, American Museum of Natural History, *Anthropological Papers,* Vol. 29, Part 3, p. 343.

[5] Gorer, *Himalayan Village,* p. 269.

[6,7,8,9,10] Hrdlicka, U. S. Bureau of American Ethnology, Bulletin No. 34, p. 171.

of suicide in nonliterate and other non-European societies any cross-cultural generalization is suspect. For the time being one tentative conclusion is that the suicide rates of nonliterate peoples are probably low on the average, but also that the rates for some of them now exceed or have exceeded those of several European countries.

On the whole, anthropologists have devoted little attention to accounting for cross-cultural variation in the incidence of suicide. This probably reflects the primary interest of individual anthropologists in a particular culture and a strong bias against generalization in the discipline. This may also underlie the preference for clearly *ad hoc* or parochial explanations. As an example, it is said that the suicide rate of the Bison-horn Maria is higher than that of the neighboring Muria because Maria children do not grow up in a village dormitory.[33] The village dormitory is held to be pertinent because it supposedly fosters respect for cultural values and discipline and discourages individualistic attachment to personal property and jealousy. Benedict, as another example, attributes the allegedly high frequency of suicide among the Kwakiutl to a value system that extolled rivalry and envy.[34] These and similar explanations are stated as though their validity is not contingent on how well they apply to other cultures.

We have previously noted marked historical changes in societal reaction to self-destruction. Anthropological reports suggest that pronounced variation also occurs cross-culturally. Among the Pueblos, for example:

> The taking of one's life, however, is entirely outlawed. Suicide is too violent an act, even in its most casual forms, for the Pueblos to contemplate. They have no idea what it could be.[35]

But a quite different reaction prevailed among the Chukchee.

> That voluntary death is considered praiseworthy, may be seen also from the fact that, in descriptions of the other world, those who have died in this way are given one of the best dwelling places. They dwell on the red blaze of the aurora borealis, and pass their time playing ball with a walrus skull.[36]

These and other observations [37] indicate clearly that societal reaction to voluntary death varies, both historically and cross-culturally, from glorification through moral indifference to severe condemnation. However, these variations remain unexplained.

Sociological Studies

Sociologists have tended to follow Durkheim's lead in considering variation in suicide rates as the major problem. This has produced three types of studies: those concerned primarily with the fact of variation,[38] those that

---

[33] Verrier Elwin, *Maria Murder and Suicide* (London: Oxford University Press, 1950), pp. xxi–xxii.

[34] Ruth Benedict, *Patterns of Culture* (Boston: Houghton Mifflin, 1934), pp. 189–222.

[35] *Ibid.,* p. 117.

[36] Waldemar Bogoras, "The Chukchee," pp. 562–63.

[37] See Edward Westermarck, *Origin and Development of Moral Ideas,* pp. 236–54.

[38] See, for example, Walter A. Lunden, "Suicides in France, 1910–1943," *American*

represent an extension of Durkheim's theories and concepts,[39] and those that rest on theories not derived from Durkheim's work.

As suggested earlier, sociologists have all but ignored the reliability of suicide statistics as a problem. This is inderstandable, considering the obstacles posed by the task of verification and its unrewarding nature, but it is nevertheless, for obvious reasons, most unfortunate. Less understandable is the sociologists' lack of concern with variation in societal reaction to suicide.[40] An adequate explanation of such variation is, of course, a sociological goal in itself, but it is doubly important because of a possible relationship between societal reaction and the incidence of suicide.

The remaining problem – accounting for individual cases of suicide – has received spotty treatment at the hands of sociologists, though it has by no means been ignored. Numerous studies have analyzed the case histories of individual victims,[41] but the results have been uniformly poor. Analyses of alleged motives or reasons have proved to be fruitless, and attempts to find purely sociological characteristics that consistently differentiate victims have been unsuccessful.[42] True, we can speak of certain statuses (such as being divorced or being of a certain age) as representing a greater suicide "risk" than others, but virtually no status provides absolute immunity. Accordingly, the "risk" approach is not adequate.

A far more sophisticated approach looks to conditions that do not influence all individuals in the same way, but that, at the same time, prevail more in some statuses and societies than in others.[43] The isolation of such conditions and the demonstration that they are linked to suicide would be a great achievement, solving two theoretical problems – differentiating persons who commit suicide from those who do not and predicting the magnitude of suicide rates.

Two recent studies that have moved in this direction will be considered. Powell, in line with Durkheim, points to anomie as a crucial factor in the etiology of suicide:

When the ends of action become contradictory, unaccessible or insignificant, a condition of anomie arises. Characterized by general loss

---

Journal of Sociology, Vol. 52 (January, 1947), pp. 321–34; S. Gargas, "Suicide in the Netherlands."

[39] See Maurice Halbwachs, *Les Causes du Suicide* (Paris: Alcan, 1930).

[40] One notable recent exception: Austin L. Porterfield, "The Problem of Suicide," in Jack P. Gibbs, *Suicide.*

[41] See, for example, Ruth S. Cavan, *Suicide.*

[42] See William A. Rushing, "Individual Behavior and Suicide."

[43] See *ibid.*

of orientation and accompanied by feelings of "emptiness" and apathy, anomie can be simply conceived as meaninglessness.[44]

Having so described anomie, Powell judged its prevalence in various occupational categories and sought confirmation through inspection of the suicide rates of the categories.[45] Unfortunately, he did not state the operations by which the prevalence of anomie may be gauged; his procedure seemed completely intuitive. Because the conditions that constitute or give rise to anomie are not described in strictly empirical terms, the theory cannot be subjected to a systematic test on either individual cases or suicide rates.

Far more empirical is Porterfield's analysis of rifts in social relations as factors in suicide.[46] He distinguishes between rifts in *Gesellschaft* relations (e.g., a loss of economic position) and rifts in *Gemeinschaft* relations (e.g., divorce) and considers each of these types to be more important in some cases than in others. Porterfield's findings suggest that rifts of both types occur with surprising frequency in cases of voluntary death, but there are some obvious problems that confront an explanation of suicide in such terms. *First,* the conditions that determine the relative importance of one type of relational rift over the other are not clearly specified. *Second,* there are numerous instances in which self-destruction is not preceded by a relational rift of either type. *Third,* it is probably true that the vast majority of disruptions in social relations are not followed by suicide. Despite these problems, Porterfield's approach has merit in that it attempts to achieve a synthesis of the explanation of individual cases and several theories of the incidence of suicide.

VARIATION IN AMOUNT OF SUICIDE

A general theory of the incidence of suicide must account for variation among all types of populations. Accordingly, before considering some general theories, let us examine some further detailed evidence of the kinds of differences in suicide rates.

---

[44] Elwin H. Powell, "Occupation, Status, and Suicide: Toward a Redefinition of Anomie," *American Sociological Review,* Vol. 23 (April, 1958), p. 132.

[45] Here Powell is concerned with suicide rates and not individual cases, but otherwise his observations suggest that the theory applies to both levels.

[46] Austin L. Porterfield, "Suicide and Crime in the Social Structure of an Urban Setting: Fort Worth, 1930–50," *American Sociological Review,* Vol. 17 (June, 1952), pp. 341–49. In a more recent work, disruption of social relations is treated as the major factor in suicide. See Jack P. Gibbs, *Suicide.*

TABLE 4

Suicide Rates for 43 Countries, *circa* 1966

Country	Suicide Rate per 100,000 Population	Year	Country	Suicide Rate per 100,000 Population	Year
Australia	14.1	1966	Japan	14.7	1965
Austria	23.1	1966	Jordan	0.1	1966
Belgium	15.0	1965	Luxembourg	11.0	1964
Bulgaria	9.9	1966	Mexico	1.6	1966
Canada	8.6	1966	Netherlands	7.1	1966
Ceylon	12.2	1963	New Zealand	9.2	1966
Colombia	5.9	1966	Nicaragua	1.2	1965
Costa Rica	3.2	1966	Norway	7.7	1965
Cuba	11.3	1964	Panama	6.1	1966
Czechoslovakia	21.5	1965	Philippines	0.5	1965
Denmark	19.3	1965	Poland	9.0	1965
Ecuador	0.6	1965	Portugal	9.4	1966
Finland	19.2	1966	South Africa	16.9 *a*	1962
France	15.0	1965	Spain	4.9	1963
Germany, West	20.0	1965	Sweden	20.1	1966
Greece	3.2	1966	Switzerland	18.1	1965
Guatemala	2.4	1965	Taiwan	9.4	1966
Hungary	29.6	1966	United Kingdom	10.4 *b*	1966
Iceland	18.9	1966	United States	10.9	1966
Ireland	2.4	1966	Uruguay	8.7	1964
Israel	6.0	1966	Venezuela	6.9	1966
Italy	5.4	1965			

Source: Demographic Yearbook, 1967, Table 24.
Qualifications: *a* "White population only." *b* Rate based on 1961 population.

Variation by Political Units

For more than a century it has been known that rates of suicide differ among nations [47]; this continues to the present, as can be seen in Table 4. It is not at all unusual to find a suicide rate in one country that is more than five times the rate in another. General observations do not suggest a close relation between the suicide rate and either climatic factors or any apparent cultural characteristics. True, the majority of high rates are found far north of the equator, but sharp differences between Finland, Sweden, and Norway

[47] See Henry Morselli, *Suicide: An Essay on Comparative Moral Statistics* (New York: Appleton, 1882), pp. 1–35, for a detailed study of European suicide rates in the nineteenth century.

TABLE 5

Suicide Rate of Some Political Divisions
of the United States, 1960

Political Divisions	Suicide Rate per 100,000 Population
States	
California	16.0
Texas	8.8
Cities	
Los Angeles, California	20.4
San Jose, California	19.1
Midland, Texas	14.4
Waco, Texas	5.1

Source: Rates computed from suicide data in *Vital Statistics of the United States, 1960,* Vol. II, Pt. B, Table 9-9.

suggest that this is not a matter of climatic factors. The six countries with the highest rates of suicide are technologically advanced, but the rates for the United Kingdom, the United States, Australia, New Zealand, and Canada are clearly deviant cases in this regard. Also, the fact that the predominantly Catholic countries generally have very low suicide rates does not, of course, explain the comparative rates of Japan, Ceylon, and Jordan. Moreover, Austria, a predominantly Catholic nation with a high suicide rate, is a crucial negative case.

A general theory of the incidence of suicide must also deal with variations within nations. Evidence indicates that suicide rates for political divisions of a nation are never uniform; they vary to a degree approaching that of differences between nations, as can be seen from Table 5. The suicide rate of one state (California) is nearly twice that of another (Texas), and the cities exhibit an even wider range of differences.[48]

Differences by Sex

As is generally known, women enjoy greater immunity to suicide than men. Less widely known is the great variation in the suicide rates of women, as attested by Table 6. This variation suggests that a biological explanation of differences in the suicide rates of males and females is untenable.

[48] For an extensive compilation of suicide statistics by states and some other territorial divisions of the United States, see National Center for Health Statistics, *Suicide in the United States, 1950–1964* (Washington, D. C.: U. S. Government Printing Office, 1967).

TABLE 6
Male and Female Suicide Rates by Countries, *circa* 1966

Country and Year	Suicide Rate per 100,000 Population		Ratio of Male to Female Rate	Excess of Male Rate
	Male	Female		
Australia, 1966	17.5	10.6	1.7	6.9
Austria, 1966	32.9	14.5	2.3	18.4
Belgium, 1965	20.7	9.6	2.2	11.1
Bulgaria, 1966	13.7	6.1	2.2	7.6
Canada, 1966	12.8	4.3	3.0	8.5
Colombia, 1966	7.2	4.5	1.6	2.7
Costa Rica, 1966	5.8	0.7	8.3	5.1
Cuba, 1964	14.4	8.2	1.8	6.2
Czechoslovakia, 1965	31.2	12.5	2.5	18.7
Denmark, 1965	24.0	14.7	1.6	9.3
Ecuador, 1965	1.1	0.1	11.0	1.0
England and Wales, 1966	12.1	8.8	1.4	3.3
Finland, 1966	30.1	9.1	3.3	21.0
France, 1965	23.0	7.5	3.1	15.5
Germany, West, 1965	26.8	13.8	1.9	13.0
Greece, 1966	4.1	2.3	1.8	1.8
Hungary, 1966	42.0	18.0	2.3	24.0
Iceland, 1966	31.4	6.2	5.1	25.2
Ireland, 1966	3.6	1.2	3.0	2.4
Israel, 1966	7.5	4.4	1.7	3.1
Italy, 1965	7.8	3.1	2.5	4.7
Japan, 1965	17.3	12.2	1.4	5.1
Luxembourg, 1964	11.0	10.3	1.1	0.7
Mexico, 1966	2.4	0.9	2.7	1.5
Netherlands, 1966	8.9	5.3	1.7	3.6
New Zealand, 1966	11.6	6.7	1.7	4.9
Nicaragua, 1965	2.3	0.1	23.0	2.2
Norway, 1965	11.8	3.6	3.3	8.2
Panama, 1966	7.6	4.0	1.9	3.6
Philippines, 1965	0.7	0.3	2.3	0.4
Poland, 1965	14.9	3.4	4.4	11.5
Portugal, 1966	14.8	4.3	3.4	11.5
South Africa, 1962 [a]	26.8	7.1	3.8	19.7
Spain, 1963	7.4	2.6	2.8	4.8
Sweden, 1966	29.4	10.8	2.7	18.6
Switzerland, 1965	27.2	9.5	2.9	17.7
Taiwan, 1966	18.3	12.8	1.4	5.5
United States, 1966	16.1	5.9	2.7	10.2
Venezuela, 1966	10.7	4.2	2.5	6.5

Source: Demographic Yearbook, 1967, Table 24.
Qualifications: [a] White population only.

In the Philippines, the male suicide rate exceeds the female rate by only 0.4, while the difference in the case of Iceland is 25.2. Viewed another way, the extreme cases are Nicaragua and Luxembourg, with the male rate 23.0 times the female rate in the former country but only 1.1 in the latter. The varying character of female immunity is further reflected by the fact that the female suicide rate in Hungary exceeds that of males in 26 of the countries listed in Table 6.

That in all countries listed women are less prone to commit suicide is not as instructive as the variation in the rates, which is so wide that we might expect to find cases where the usual male excess does not obtain. This was found in Bengal, where in 1907 there were 177 female suicides reported for every 100 male suicides.[49]

Variation by Age

Suicide rates in the United States vary consistently by age. In 1960, for example, the rate (per 100,000 population) was 0.3 for persons 5–14 and increased somewhat regularly from one age group to the next up to 27.9 for persons 75–84 and then declined slightly to 26.0 for the 85-and-over category. This pattern is often found in European nations but the relationship between suicide rates and age varies tremendously, as is illustrated in Figure 1.

The data illustrate both common and uncommon patterns. American males exhibit the frequently found direct relation between suicide and age, while American females exhibit another common pattern – a decrease in the suicide rate beyond a certain age.[50] The pattern in Japan is most unusual: The rate increases rapidly up to age 24, then plunges to a low between 30 and 50, and then rises again with advancing age. These and other patterns indicate that there is nothing biologically inherent in aging that produces self-destruction.

Racial Differences

Our knowledge of suicide rates by race is clearly inadequate because it is restricted to rates in a small number of countries, and some relevant obser-

---

[49] John Rice Miner, "Suicide and Its Relation to Climatic and Other Factors," p. 31.

[50] A decrease beyond a certain age is also characteristic of the male suicide rate in some countries.

FIGURE 1

Suicide Rates by Age and Sex in the United States and Japan, 1956–1958

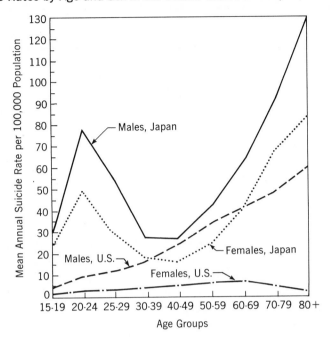

Source: World Health Organization, *Epidemiological and Vital Statistics Report,* Vol. 14, No. 5 (1961), Table 1.4.

vations are not comparable. For example, in the United States blacks have a low suicide rate, but it is reported that suicide is "rather common" among certain Negro tribes in Africa.[51]

The evidence permits only one general conclusion: the immunity of any race to suicide is extremely variable. This conclusion is suggested by data in Table 7. Here we find that in the United States Negroes have a suicide rate much lower than that of Caucasians, but instances of a higher Negro rate can be found. Compare the Negro rate in Seattle, Washington, with the Caucasian rate in Mississippi.

It is perhaps surprising to find that during the period 1949–1951 Orientals in the United States had a suicide rate higher than Caucasians. There are, however, instances where the Caucasian rate exceeds the Oriental rate.

---

[51] Adolph Frenay, *The Suicide Problem in the United States* (Boston: Gorham, 1927), pp. 150–52.

TABLE 7
Suicide Rates by Race: A Variety of Cases

Race	Location	Years	Suicide Rate per 100,000 Population
Oriental (Chinese)	United States	1960	22.3
Caucasian [a]	United States	1938–40	15.7 [b]
Oriental [c]	United States	1949–51	14.6 [b]
Caucasian [a]	United States	1960	11.4
Oriental [c]	United States	1960	11.1
Negro	Seattle, Washington	1948–52	10.2 [b]
Caucasian [b]	Mississippi	1949–51	9.7 [b]
Negro	United States	1960	3.9

Sources: *Vital Statistics, Special Reports*, Vol. 43, No. 30, p. 471; *Vital Statistics of The United States* (1949, 1950, 1951); *American Sociological Review*, Vol. 20, p. 279; *Vital Statistics of The United States, 1960*, Vol. II, Pt. A, Tables 5–8.
Qualifications: [a] White. [b] Average annual rate. [c] Identified racially as other than Negro or white.

In the period 1948–1952, the suicide rate for whites in Seattle was nearly twice the Japanese rate and nearly three times the Chinese rate.[52] Finally, while the 1960 suicide rates for Caucasians and Orientals in the United States are virtually identical, both are much lower than the 1960 rate for Chinese (a segment of the Oriental population), which clearly suggests that ethnicity is much more important than race.

The Rural-Urban Difference

During the nineteenth century, the urban suicide rate exceeded the rural rate in virtually all countries and provinces.[53] Yet, during recent decades the rural-urban difference in rates has changed sharply in some countries. For example, during the period 1904–1913, the urban suicide rate in the United States Registration States was 17.7, while the rural rate was only 12.2.[54] Over the decades the rural-urban difference has declined, and as shown in

---

[52] Calvin F. Schmid and Maurice D. Van Arsdol, Jr., "Completed and Attempted Suicides: A Comparative Analysis," *American Sociological Review*, Vol. 20 (June, 1955), p. 279.

[53] Pitirim Sorokin and Carl C. Zimmerman, *Principles of Rural-Urban Sociology* (New York: Holt, 1929), Chapter 7.

[54] Frederick L. Hoffman, *Suicide Problems* (Newark, N. J.: Prudential Press, 1927), p. 182.

TABLE 8

Rural and Urban Suicide Rates, United States, 1960

Territorial Categories	Suicide Rate per 100,000 Population
Metropolitan counties	10.6
Urban	10.7
Rural	10.4
Nonmetropolitan counties	10.7
Urban	10.1
Rural	11.0
Total urban	10.5
Total rural	10.8

Source and qualification: Rates computed from suicide data in *Vital Statistics of The United States, 1960,* Vol. II, Pt. B, Table 9-9. Census figures for the urban and rural populations have been adjusted (in the way of estimates) to make them correspond to the urban-rural distinction employed in gathering and reporting vital statistics. For all practical purposes, the urban population is restricted to persons residing in incorporated places of 2500 or more inhabitants, which is a much more narrow definition of urban than that employed in the 1960 population census.

Table 8, by 1960 the rural rate was actually slightly higher.[55] What is truly remarkable about the data in Table 8 is the minute variation in the suicide rate from one territorial category to the next, and it is all the more remarkable when one considers that such small differences could be due to minor errors in the vital statistics and/or in the population estimates employed to compute the rates. However, granted the possibility of errors, it is perhaps significant that a higher suicide rate for rural males has been reported previously.[56]

Some Occupational Differences

Official statistics on suicide rates by occupation are reported in only a few countries, and the occupations considered are seldom strictly comparable.

---

[55] Exceptions to the relation between urbanization and suicide are not peculiar to the United States; it was the situation in the Netherlands as early as 1911–1920. See S. Gargas, "Suicide in the Netherlands," p. 700. Note, however, that the spread of urban population beyond the political limits of cities may produce higher rates for administrative rural areas. This is particularly true for the U. S., where urban suicides are reported only for incorporated places. The rural-urban difference consequently remains subject to question.

[56] W. Widwick Schroeder and J. Allan Beegle, "Suicide: An Instance of High Rural Rates," *Rural Sociology,* Vol. 18 (March, 1953), pp. 45–52.

Consequently, observations on the subject are sketchy and questionable. What little is known on the subject suggests extreme variation in the suicide rates of different occupations. An example of this is provided by Powell's study in Tulsa County, in which he found the rate for pharmacists to be 24 times that of carpenters.[57] Such contrasts are peculiar neither to Tulsa, the United States, nor the twentieth century. In Italy, during 1866–1876, the suicide rate was 61.8 for persons engaged in "letters and science," as compared to a rate of only 2.5 for persons engaged in "production of raw materials" and one of only 6.8 for "domestic servants." [58]

Extremely high suicide rates generally prevail in occupations at the extremes—those with either very high income and prestige or very low income and prestige. For example, high rates are often found in both the professional-managerial category and the category of unskilled laborers, with occupations ranking midway between these two in status having lower rates.[59] The high rate that typically prevails among the unemployed and retired appears to fit the low-income—low-prestige pattern.

Again, there are exceptions to the general rule. In some countries, several occupations in both the professional-managerial and the unskilled categories do not have high suicide rates. Also to be noted are data for England and Wales during 1921–1923, which show that the highest and lowest rates among five major occupational groups (designated as social classes) vary from one age group to the next.[60] Moreover, the suicide rate of an occupational category may increase or decrease considerably without any apparent corresponding change in income or prestige. For example, the rate for the professional-managerial category in Tulsa County dropped from 63.0 in 1937–1941 to 21.2 in 1947–1951; in the latter period the rate was lower than that for all other occupations combined.[61]

---

[57] Elwin H. Powell, "Occupation, Status, and Suicide," p. 136. For statistics on occupation and suicide for the United States, see National Office of Vital Statistics, *Vital Statistics—Special Reports*, Vol. 53, Nos. 1–5 (June, 1961–September, 1963). Certain questions concerning reliability preclude an analysis of these data.

[58] Henry Morselli, *Suicide*, p. 244.

[59] See Elwin H. Powell, "Occupation, Status, and Suicide," p. 137; *The Registrar General's Decennial Supplement, England and Wales, 1951, Occupational Mortality*, Pt. 1 (London: H.M.S.O., 1954), p. 11; and Sanford Labovitz, "Variation in Suicide Rates," in Jack P. Gibbs, *Suicide*, pp. 57–73. Labovitz (p. 69) stresses two important considerations: (1) two occupations at approximately the same prestige level may have quite different suicide rates and (2) the suicide rate of an occupation varies enormously from place to place and time to time.

[60] See Louis I. Dublin and Bessie Bunzel, *To Be or Not To Be*, pp. 95, 96, 108–09, and 399.

[61] Elwin H. Powell, "Occupation, Status, and Suicide," p. 135. For some statistics

TABLE 9
Suicide Rates by Religion: Selected Cases

Religious Group	Location	Mean Annual Suicide Rate per 100,000 Population	Years
Jewish	Netherlands	23.3 [1]	1900–10
Protestant	Prussia	18.7 [2]	1869–72
Protestant	Netherlands	17.1 [1]	1900–10
Congregational	New Zealand	15.1 [3]	1946–51
Methodist	New Zealand	12.9 [3]	1946–51
Catholic	Toronto	11.0 [4]	1928–35
Church of England	New Zealand	9.7 [3]	1946–51
Jewish	Prussia	9.6 [2]	1869–72
Baptist	New Zealand	9.5 [3]	1946–51
Presbyterian	New Zealand	9.5 [3]	1946–51
Protestant	Austria	8.0 [2]	1852–59
Catholic	New Zealand	7.3 [3]	1946–51
Catholic	Netherlands	7.0 [1]	1900–10
Catholic	Prussia	6.9 [2]	1869–72
Church of Christ	New Zealand	6.9 [3]	1946–51
Ringatu and Ratana [a]	New Zealand	6.6 [3]	1946–51
Jewish	Toronto	5.6 [4]	1928–35
Catholic	Austria	5.1 [2]	1852–59
Protestant	Toronto	4.5 [4]	1928–35
Jewish	Austria	2.1 [2]	1852–59

Sources:

[1] S. Gargas, "Suicide in the Netherlands," *American Journal of Sociology,* Vol. 37 (March, 1932), p. 709.

[2] Émile Durkheim, *Suicide: A Study in Sociology,* translated by John A. Spaulding and George Simpson (New York: Free Press, 1951), p. 154.

[3] From records of New Zealand's Registrar-General (Wellington).

[4] Cited by James M. A. Weiss, "Suicide: An Epidemiologic Analysis," *The Psychiatric Quarterly,* Vol. 28, p. 235.

[a] Predominantly Maori faiths.

Differences by Religion

A series of studies have shown that Catholics and Jews are much less prone to take their lives than Protestants are. In most cases this is true, but Table 9 shows that the immunity enjoyed by Jews and Catholics is clearly relative to place and time.

Of religious groups in 20 different locations and periods the Jews have both the highest and the lowest suicide rate. The highest Catholic rate

and theoretical observations on the relation between occupational mobility and suicide, see Warren Breed, "Occupational Mobility and Suicide Among White Males," *American Sociological Review,* Vol. 28 (April, 1963), pp. 179–88.

exceeds Protestant rates in seven cases. On occasion, either the Jewish rate or the Catholic rate exceeds the Protestant rate in the same location and period. Finally, as the New Zealand data show, the suicide rates of various Protestant denominations are by no means uniform.

Some of the rates shown in Table 9 doubtless represent unusual cases, but more systematic data lead to the same conclusion.[62] For example, the suicide rate of Jews in Prussia was 4.6 during the period 1849–1855, or about one-third the Protestant rate; but by the period 1901–1907 it had increased to 29.4, at which point it exceeded the Protestant rate by some 17 percent; and by 1925 it had reached 53.0, nearly twice the Protestant rate.

Variation by Marital Status

It is generally but not universally true that married persons are less prone to suicide than the widowed, divorced, or single. For one thing, when age is ignored the single have the lowest suicide rate. Even if we consider the population above 14 years of age, the single may have the lowest rate. For instance, the average annual rates (per 100,000 population) in the United States during the period 1959–1961 are single, 12.1; married, 13.6; widowed, 24.3; and divorced, 48.0.

Only within particular age groups, as shown in Figure 2, is the greater immunity of the married evident. But note the exceptions. In the age group 15–19 the suicide rates of the married and the single are equal, and in the age groups above 80 the widowed have a lower suicide rate than the married.

Instances in which the suicide rate of the single or the widowed corresponds closely to, or is less than that of the married in certain age groups are not peculiar to the United States; they have been noted in other countries.[63]

Relativity of Suicide Rates

Throughout we have noted that the rate of suicide in a particular status (or social category) varies from place to place and time to time. This should always be recognized in attempts to explain differences in suicide rates, if only to avoid the dubious assumption that there is something inherent in each status that generates a certain rate. Thus, more than one investigator

---

[62] Louis I. Dublin and Bessie Bunzel, *To Be or Not To Be,* pp. 117–18.

[63] See Émile Durkheim, *Suicide,* pp. 175–80.

FIGURE 2

Average Annual Suicide Rates by Marital Status
in the United States, 1956–61

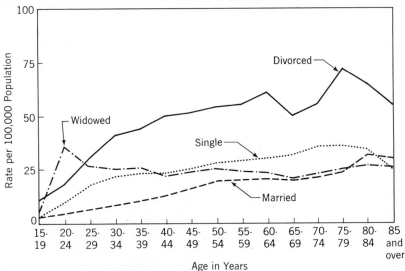

Source: National Center for Health Statistics, *Suicide in the United States, 1950–1964* (Washington, D. C.: U. S. Government Printing Office, 1967), p. 7.

has noted increasing suicide with advancing age in a particular country and explained it by postulating something suicidal in the aging process, without recognizing that some elderly populations actually have very low rates.

The universal picture is one of extreme contrast in the suicide rates of different statuses. This suggests that status is in some way linked to the incidence of suicide, but beyond this little can be said. Any doubts as to the relative character of the immunity provided by a particular status should be resolved by the data presented in Table 10.

Temporal Variation

Cases of a suicide rate remaining stable over an extended period have been noted and stressed by earlier investigators, particularly Durkheim.[64] There are recent instances of such constancy over the short run, as, for example, the suicide rate in Canada: 1956, 7.6; 1957, 7.5; 1958, 7.5; 1959, 7.4; 1960, 7.6.[65]

---

[64] Émile Durkheim, *Suicide,* pp. 46–53.

[65] *Demographic Yearbook, 1961* (New York: United Nations, 1962), Table 17.

Table 10

Suicide Rates Per 100,000 Population by Status: Selected Extreme Cases

Status	Lowest Suicide Rate Noted and Conditions	Highest Suicide Rate Noted and Conditions
Male	Nonwhite, single, under 20 years of age, United States, 1949–51 Rate: 0.4	White, divorced, over 75 years of age, United States, 1949–51 Rate: 139.1
Female	Nonwhite, single, under 20 years of age, United States, 1949–51 Rate: 0.3	70 years of age and over, Japan, 1947–49 Rate: 74.3
Young (20–24)	Female, Ireland, 1945–54 Rate: 0.3	Male, Japan, 1952–54 Rate: 60.0
Old (70+)	Female, Chile, 1947–49 Rate: 0.4	White, divorced, male, 70–74 years of age, United States, 1949–51 Rate: 124.4
White	Single, female, under 20 years of age, United States, 1949–51 Rate: 0.3	Divorced, male, over 75 years of age, United States, 1949–51 Rate: 139.1
Nonwhite	Single, female, under 20 years of age, United States, 1949–51 Rate: 0.3	Male, single, 70–74 years of age, United States, 1949–51 Rate: 56.7
Married	Nonwhite, female, under 20 years of age, United States, 1949–51 Rate: 1.0	White, male, over 75 years of age, United States, 1949–51 Rate: 40.8
Divorced	Nonwhite, female, 35–44 years of age, United States, 1949–51 Rate: 0.7	White, male, over 75 years of age, United States, 1949–51 Rate: 139.1

But generally there have been marked changes in suicide rates during recent decades.

The course of the suicide rate in six countries between 1901 and 1960 is shown in Figure 3. Of the six, only Ireland has exhibited a remarkably constant rate over the 60 years. The changes in the rates of the other five countries are not purely random fluctuations; several long-range trends appear. The United States rate climbed somewhat regularly from 10.4 in 1901 to 16.2 in 1915, and after a decline it again moved up almost continually from 10.2 in 1920 to 17.4 in 1932. Finland provides an even better example of a trend; its rate increased fairly consistently from 10.6 in 1920 to 23.4 in 1931.

Figure 3 also reveals an association between suicide trends and periods

FIGURE 3

Trends in the Suicide Rates of Finland, Ireland, Japan, Norway, Sweden, and the United States, 1901–60

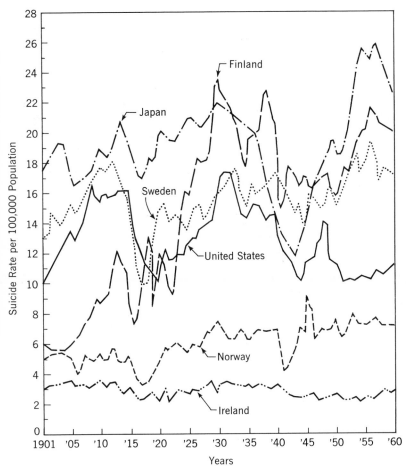

Sources: World Health Organization, *Epidemiological and Vital Statistics Report,* Vol. 9, No. 4 (1956), Table 2, and Vol. 15, No. 10 (1962), Table 2; *Demographic Yearbook, 1957* (New York: United Nations, 1958), Table 14; *Demographic Yearbook, 1961,* Table 17.

of war and depression. In most cases, wars are associated with decreases in suicide rates, while economic depressions are accompanied by increases. These patterns often have been noted,[66] but wars and economic depressions in themselves do not provide an adequate explanation of suicide trends. Obviously, there are numerous instances of definite decreasing or increasing trends in rates without wars or depressions. Moreover, any explanation of temporal variation should be set forth in the context of a general theory, in which explaining why wars and depressions are associated with change in the suicide rate (and why they are not in some cases) is a special case of a more general problem.

PARTICULAR THEORIES
ON VARIATION IN SUICIDE RATES

The data in the previous section point out the general character of variation in suicide rates. In this section we will consider several theories on the subject and, in doing so, rely heavily on the predictive power of each theory as a criterion of its explanatory adequacy. This criterion cannot be applied rigorously, however, since most theories are far from systematic and the operations necessary for empirical tests often are not specified.

Psychopathology and the Suicide Rate

Running through much speculation on the subject is the suggestion that the suicide rate varies directly with the prevalence or incidence of psychopathology. This hypothesized relationship is apparently not the product of a formal theory; it appears, rather, to stem from the common belief that any individual who commits suicide is mentally ill. Whatever the source of the hypothesized relationship, it is not possible to subject it to a definitive test, primarily because of the problem of obtaining reliable statistics on the incidence of mental disorders.[67]

---

[66] See Adolph Frenay, *The Suicide Problem,* Chapters 2 and 8; Émile Durkheim, *Suicide,* pp. 202–08 and 241–46; Maurice Halbwachs, *Les Causes du Suicide,* Chapters 11 and 12.

[67] For a discussion of the problems as they relate to United States data, see U. S. Federal Security Agency, *Patients in Mental Institutions, 1949* (Washington, D. C., 1952), p. 9.

Granting that the negative results may be due to deficiencies in the data, we must nevertheless recognize that some careful investigations have not found evidence to support the assertion of a direct relationship between the incidence of psychopathology and suicide. Some 70 years ago, Durkheim found no close relationship between the number of institutionalized "insane" and the number of suicides by age, sex, religious affiliation, provinces, and countries in Europe. Using a wide variety of data, a more recent investigation [68] found no close direct relationship between any of four measures of the incidence or prevalence of mental disorder and suicide rates by states in the United States.

It may be that a particular type of psychopathology holds the key to variation in suicide rates; this possibility remains to be investigated thoroughly. However, at least in the United States, only rates for total mental disorders exhibit a uniform increase with advancing age that corresponds to a similar increase in the suicide rate, but this type of mental-disorder rate bears no close relationship to variation in suicide rates by states. Moreover, there is no evidence to show that mental disorder varies by race and sex in a manner corresponding to the suicide rate.

Societal Reaction to Suicide

Concern with societal reaction to voluntary death has produced a candidate for a general theory of variation in suicide rates.

> Where custom and tradition accept or condone it, many persons will take their own lives; where it is sternly condemned by the rules of the Church and State, suicide will be an unusual occurrence.[69]

This idea can be formally restated: The suicide rate varies inversely with the degree of societal condemnation of suicide.

In terms of general cross-cultural and historical observation, this proposition is not without some support.[70] However, apart from its seemingly self-evident character, the thesis requires a more exacting measure, or at least classification, of the degree of societal condemnation.

Even before a formal measure is devised, we can anticipate cases in which

---

[68] Jack P. Gibbs, "A Sociological Study of Suicide," Ph.D. dissertation, University of Oregon, 1957, pp. 363–75.

[69] Louis I. Dublin and Bessie Bunzel, *To Be or Not To Be,* p. 15.

[70] *Ibid.,* Pt. 4.

the predictive power of the proposition might well be negligible. It is unlikely that the range of reaction to suicide among the different statuses in a society (age, sex, race, marital status, occupation, etc.) is as wide as differences in their suicide rates. For example, there is no reason to suppose that suicide is more severely disapproved among blacks and females in the United States than it is among whites and males. There is no evidence that all increases or decreases in the suicide rates of countries reflect corresponding changes in the norms pertaining to suicide, and this would seem particularly true for the recent decrease of the rate in the United States.

Social Disorganization

Studies of suicide in the United States and in England have been largely oriented toward the concept of social disorganization. These studies suggest a general proposition: The suicide rate varies directly with the extent of social disorganization.

The major problem in evaluating this proposition is to distinguish between social disorganization and its alleged effects. The treatment of the concept at the hands of Mowrer, Elliott and Merrill, Faris, and Cavan [71] does not provide an adequate distinction; on the contrary, it often appears that the concept simply means a lack of conformity to social norms, and, accordingly, the relationship between social disorganization and deviant behavior is essentially tautological. [72] More recent treatments of the concept make a better distinction between social disorganization and its alleged effects, [73] but they do not clearly specify the operations by which the prevalence of social disorganization is to be gauged.

---

[71] Ernest R. Mowrer, *Disorganization*; Mabel A. Elliott and Francis E. Merrill, *Social Disorganization* (New York: Harper, 1941); Robert E. L. Faris, *Social Disorganization* (New York: Ronald Press, 1948); Ruth S. Cavan, *Suicide*.

[72] Ernest R. Mowrer, for example, refers to suicide as "a form" of social disorganization (*Disorganization*, p. 19); Ruth S. Cavan (*Suicide*, p. 330) states that social disorganization is the loss of control of the mores over the members of a group, which suggests that the concept is defined in terms of deviant behavior.

[73] Arnold M. Rose, *Theory and Methods in the Social Sciences* (Minneapolis: University of Minnesota Press, 1954), pp. 3–24; Ralph H. Turner, "Value Conflict"; Albert K. Cohen, "The Study of Social Disorganization and Deviant Behavior," in Robert K. Merton *et al.*, eds., *Sociology Today* (New York: Basic Books, 1959), pp. 461–84.

As a consequence of the nebulous character of the concept, the alleged relation between social disorganization and suicide does not rest on direct empirical confirmation; it rests instead on correlations between suicide and other alleged effects of social disorganization. As previously noted, it has been found in some American cities that suicide occurs most frequently in urban areas that abound with other forms of deviant behavior. But there are contradictory observations. Porterfield has shown that rates of suicide may be *unrelated to or actually vary inversely with* other alleged effects of social disorganization (e.g., crime).[74]

It is of course methodologically indefensible to ignore cases in which suicide rates do not correlate directly with other alleged effects of social disorganization. Sainsbury, for example, in testing the hypothesis, found suicide rates in the boroughs of London to be fairly closely related to rates of divorce and illegitimacy but not to the rate of juvenile delinquency.[75] He accepted these findings as support for the hypothesis by suggesting that juvenile delinquency is not after all indicative of social disorganization in London.[76] This suggests that the only valid indicators of social disorganization are those that vary directly with the suicide rate, which makes the relation between the two tautological.

Schmid has attempted to substantiate the social disorganization theory more directly. After designating population mobility as indicative of social disorganization, he demonstrated a fairly high correlation (+.60) in American cities between a measure of mobility and suicide rates.[77] A similar relation has been reported for the boroughs of London.[78]

Measures of population mobility may produce correct predictions of territorial variation in the suicide rate, but this does not extend to statuses and social categories. In the United States during 1949–1951, the least mobile age groups had the highest suicide rates; that is, the suicide rate varied inversely by age groups with each of six measures of mobility.[79]

---

[74] Austin L. Porterfield, "Suicide and Crime in the Social Structure of an Urban Setting: Fort Worth, 1930–1950" and "Indices of Suicide and Homicide by States and Cities," p. 489.

[75] Peter Sainsbury, *Suicide in London,* p. 41.

[76] *Ibid.,* pp. 78–79.

[77] Calvin F. Schmid, "Suicides in Seattle, 1914–1925: An Ecological and Behavioristic Study," p. 12, and "Suicide in Minneapolis, Minnesota: 1928–32," *American Journal of Sociology,* Vol. 39 (July, 1933), p. 30.

[78] Peter Sainsbury, *Suicide in London,* p. 41.

[79] Jack P. Gibbs, "A Sociological Study of Suicide," p. 354.

304 Suicide

Secularization and Suicide

Porterfield's observations on the incidence of suicide by types of society suggest a general proposition: The suicide rate varies directly with the degree of secularization. In tests of the proposition on states in the United States, Porterfield found a fairly close relationship between an index of secularization (based on the degree of urbanization, industrialization, membership in churches, and non-nativity) and the suicide rate.[80]

Two points should be noted in evaluating the proposition. First, even if we assume that it applies only to differences among societies, secularization does not seem to account for the moderate suicide rates of the United States, the United Kingdom, New Zealand, Canada, and Australia, all of which are, presumably, highly "secularized." Second, the proposition does not generate predictions of differences in suicide rates by age, sex, and marital status. The same may be said for any theory that links the incidence of suicide to civilization, modernization, urbanization, and so on. (See Chapter 1, page 51.)

Social Integration and Suicide

The most influential sociological theory of suicide was advanced by Durkheim at the end of the nineteenth century. Having produced an impressive body of evidence to refute explanations of variations in suicide rates in terms of extrasocial variables (psychopathy, race, heredity, climate, and imitation), he turned to the nature of social life for an answer.

Durkheim's inspection of nineteenth-century European data led him to postulate three major types of suicide. High suicide rates for Protestants, the unmarried, and married couples without children suggested the *egoistic* type: the suicide that stems from excessive individualism, or, put another way, a lack of social integration. On the other hand, insufficient individuation, or excessive social integration, produces the *altruistic* type of suicide. This type was suggested to Durkheim by reports that suicide (particularly

---

[80] Austin L. Porterfield, "Suicide and Crime in Folk and Secular Society," *American Journal of Sociology,* Vol. 57 (January, 1952), pp. 331–38.

the ritual form) was common in "lower" societies and by high suicide rates for the military, especially among elite troops. Finally, the connection between the incidence of suicide and economic crisis, divorce, and certain business occupations suggested to Durkheim a third type of suicide—the *anomic*—which is produced by insufficient social regulation of the individual.[81]

Most discussions of Durkheim's study center on his conceptions of egoistic, altruistic, and anomic suicide; and only rarely is it recognized that the translation of his observations on the three types into a theory of variation in suicide rates is fraught with difficulties. At first glance it might appear that any test of his theory would necessarily have to be based on separate rates for egoistic, altruistic, and anomic suicide. But since the three types are defined in terms of their causes, and only vaguely so, it is doubtful if individual cases can be classified as either egoistic, altruistic, or anomic; Durkheim certainly did not apply his typology to all cases of suicide in a population, nor did he compute a rate for each of the three types. Even if separate rates could be established, there would still remain the problem of distinguishing the cause of variation in one of the rates from the causes of variation in the other two. Durkheim distinguished between *altruistic* and *egoistic* suicides by designating the former as a product of excessive social integration and the latter as a product of insufficient social integration. But his distinction between the causes of *anomic* and *egoistic* suicide is by no means clear, and it is doubtful whether an adequate distinction can be drawn even on the conceptual level, much less in strictly empirical terms.[82] In the face of no clear-cut empirical distinction between the causes of anomic and egoistic suicide, we can only resort to what appears to be the most general and certainly the least ambiguous statement of Durkheim's theory:

> So we reach the general conclusion: suicide varies inversely with the degree of integration of the social groups of which the individual forms a part.[83]

---

[81] Émile Durkheim, *Suicide,* pp. 152–216, 217–40, and 241–76.

[82] Peter Sainsbury (*Suicide in London,* p. 22) has voiced a similar opinion, as have Martin and Johnson. See Walter T. Martin, "Theories of Variation in the Suicide Rate," in Jack P. Gibbs, *Suicide,* pp. 74–96; and Barclay D. Johnson, "Durkheim's One Cause of Suicide," *American Sociological Review,* Vol. 30 (December, 1965), pp. 875–86. For a statement of a contrary position (i.e., Durkheim's concepts can be distinguished), see Bruce P. Dohrenwend, "Egoism, Altruism, Anomie, and Fatalism: A Conceptual Analysis of Durkheim's Types," *American Sociological Review,* Vol. 24 (August, 1959), pp. 466–73.

[83] Émile Durkheim, *Suicide,* p. 209.

This general statement should perhaps be qualified by noting that Durkheim's observations on altruism suggest that beyond a certain point an increase in social integration results in more suicide.[84]

What can be said in support of Durkheim's general theory that suicide rates vary inversely with the degree of social integration? Relatively little, because Durkheim did not conduct a series of rigorous tests. There is not one instance in which he correlates a measure of integration with suicide rates. Moreover, at no time does he provide either a real or a nominal definition of social integration, much less an operational one. It is not even made clear whether social integration relates to consensus in values or whether it is found in actual behavior (e.g., the frequency, duration, and regularity of social interaction).

The support for the theory lies not in its demonstrated predictive power but rather in Durkheim's forceful argument. As long as no universal measure of integration was involved, he could argue from knowledge of suicide rates and ascribe degrees of integration to each population accordingly. Perhaps we can sense that Catholics, Jews, and married persons with children are highly integrated (i.e., enveloped in binding social relations), but sensing that something is true and demonstrating it are two different things. Moreover, what is the appropriate conclusion when the usual differences in suicide rates no longer prevail? One can say that the usual degree of integration has also changed, but this is merely arguing backward from knowledge of suicide rates. Interpretation and *ex post facto* explanations are a poor substitute for predictions. Durkheim provided no basis for predictions, and consequently his theory cannot be subjected to any rigorous test. Nonetheless, his achievement was not a small one, for his basic ideas have guided numerous subsequent investigations.

Status and Suicide

Durkheim's influence is particularly marked in a theory advanced by Henry and Short.[85] Their theory rests on three postulates: (1) The suicide rate of a population varies inversely with the strength of the relational systems of the members, (2) the strength of the relational systems of the members of

[84] Little can be said for this side of Durkheim's theory; he uncritically accepted reports of ritual suicide in supposedly highly integrated societies as evidence of a high suicide rate and attempted to account for such cases by invoking altruism.

[85] Andrew F. Henry and James F. Short, Jr., *Suicide and Homicide* (New York: Free Press, 1954).

a population varies directly with the external restraints placed on their behavior, and (3) the external restraints placed on the behavior of the members varies inversely with their status (position in the prestige hierarchy).

Since Henry and Short do not specify the operations necessary for gauging either the strength of relational systems or the extent of external restraints,[86] we must be content to consider the proposition that the suicide rate of a population varies directly with the status of its members, a relation which can be derived from the three postulates above.

Even in the case of status there are no actual measures provided; it is only described conceptually in terms of achievement, possession, authority, and power. Rather than use actual measures in testing hypotheses, Henry and Short assume that in terms of status in the United States the whites exceed blacks, males exceed females, high-income groups exceed low-income groups, the young and the middle-aged exceed those past the age of 65, and army officers exceed enlisted men.

These assumptions appear to be sound, but certain problems come to mind. For one thing, how are predictions to be made in cultures where status cannot be determined on an intuitive basis? Of equal importance, how does the proposition apply to countries and political units?

Apart from these two crucial questions, there appear to be cases in which the status of certain segments of the United States population is not in line with the suicide rates. The suicide rate of Orientals in the United States is typically higher than that of whites. Note also that in the United States the rate for persons over 65 exceeds that of persons 15–64, yet the older segment of the population supposedly has less status. This discrepancy is recognized by Henry and Short, but they appear to shift ground in attempting to account for it. They suggest that the strength of the relational system decreases with age; and this contradicts their suggestion that status and the strength of the relational system vary inversely. Another inconsistency is found in their treatment of the lower suicide rate of the married. The low rate can hardly be attributed to low status, so it is described as the product of external restraints and strong relational systems. Even here, however, there is no real basis for anticipating the close correspondence between the suicide rates of the married and the widowed in the older age groups. Finally, we should note again that high suicide rates have been known to prevail among occupations on the lower end of the status hierarchy.

---

[86] Henry and Short define the strength of a relational system as the degree of involvement in cathectic relations with other persons, and they define the strength of external restraints as the degree to which behavior is required to conform to the demands and expectations of other persons.

Status Integration and Suicide

Running throughout Durkheim's observations is the suggestion that the suicide rate varies inversely with the stability and durability of social relations. This suggestion served as a point of departure for a recent theory that links the suicide rate to a particular *pattern* of status occupancy.[87] Through a series of postulates and assumptions it is deduced that in populations where the occupancy of one particular status tends to be closely associated with the occupancy of certain other statuses, the members are less subject to role conflict, more capable of conforming to the demands and expectations of others, more capable of maintaining stable and durable social relations, and consequently less prone to suicide.[88] The extent of association in the occupancy of statuses is referred to as the degree of *status integration,* which is at a maximum in a society or other population where knowledge of all but one of an individual's statuses enables an observer to predict correctly the remaining undisclosed status of the individual (e.g., all of the persons with a certain occupation, age, sex, race, and religion are married).

The major theorem is: *The suicide rate varies inversely with the degree of status integration in the population.* This theorem applies both to societies and to different segments of any one society. Those societies characterized by a high degree of status integration would be expected to have low suicide rates. *Within* a society those status configurations (i.e., clusters of statuses, such as a particular age, sex, race, marital status, etc.) that are infrequently occupied would be expected to have a high suicide rate. Consider, as an illustration, data on marital status by age in the United States. In 1960, of white males 60–64 years of age, 83.5 percent were married, 7.6 percent were single, 6 percent were widowed, and 2.9 percent were divorced. The average annual suicide rates during 1959–1961 for the four marital statuses in the age group (per 100,000 population) are as follows: divorced, 118.8; widowed, 82.5; single, 57.4; and married, 32.9. Consistent with the major theorem, there is a perfect inverse relation between the proportion in a marital status and the suicide rate of the status. The prediction of such a relation (and all other predictions generated by the theory) rests on the assumption that the relative frequency with which a cluster of statuses is actually occupied re-

---

[87] Jack P. Gibbs and Walter T. Martin, *Status Integration and Suicide: A Sociological Study* (Eugene, Oregon: University of Oregon Books, 1964).

[88] *Ibid.,* Chapter 2.

flects the extent of role conflict among the statuses, with infrequently occupied clusters assumed to be characterized by role conflict and, consequently, weak social relations.

Because status integration can be measured, the major theorem can be subjected to systematic tests. An initial series of tests has produced positive results,[89] but an adequate evaluation of the theory must await further tests and judgment by impartial critics.[90]

NEEDS AND PROSPECTS

After more than six decades we still lack an adequate treatment of suicide as a social and sociological problem. It behooves us, then, to look more to the future than to the past.

Future Sociological Investigations

One problem that will confront future studies is the idea of multiple causation, the notion that populations may have high or low suicide rates for different reasons—as, for example, when the difference between the suicide rates of men and women is explained in one way, while the difference between the rates of the old and the young is explained in another way.

However real the case for multiple causation may appear, the very idea defeats the quest for a truly general theory through a search for a common denominator that underlies all instances of high rates. This quest carries on the tradition of Durkheim's approach. But future investigations must not slavishly follow Durkheim, if only because the search must go beyond the generation of indefinite concepts. Little is accomplished by suggesting that the common denominator is "anomie," or some other equally vague term. Future investigations must not only locate a common denominator and describe it conceptually; they must also specify the operations necessary for assessment of its prevalence in populations.

As we have seen, the concern of sociologists with individual cases of self-destruction has yielded very little. Future studies must thus choose among a

---

[89] *Ibid.* See also Jack P. Gibbs, "Marital Status and Suicide in the United States: A Special Test of the Status Integration Theory," *American Journal of Sociology,* Vol. 74 (March, 1969), pp. 521–33.

[90] The present author hardly qualifies as an impartial critic in this instance.

wide variety of possible approaches, one of which is suggested by George Simpson in his plea for a greater integration of sociological and psychoanalytic views on suicide.[91] It is not clear, however, just how the observations of two fields with quite different, if not opposing, perspectives are to be integrated. In the author's opinion the opportunities for a distinctly sociological contribution lie not in a forced marriage with psychoanalysis but rather in cross-cultural investigations of the characteristics of suicide cases and in the analysis of the sociological past of victims.

In regard to the sociological past of victims, it has become a truism that purely social conditions cannot explain the individual suicide because persons react differently to apparently identical conditions. This is true, but that which is purely social is a part of each person's past as well as the present, and the former may be of greater importance than the latter in the etiology of suicide. We remain largely ignorant of the influence of the sociological past on behavior, but an investigation of past statuses of suicide victims and the timing of their status changes could serve as a point of departure.

Suicide as a Social Problem

There is general agreement that current efforts to prevent suicide are not effective. In this case, however, it is senseless to call for an aroused citizenry to demand action, for the brutal truth is that no existing program appears capable of substantially reducing the incidence of suicide.

Practically all attempts to prevent suicide focus on individuals who have shown symptoms of self-destructive tendencies. In the case of attempted suicide the would-be victim may be directed by the court, the police, or relatives to the care of a physician, a psychiatrist, a clinic, a mental institution, or a special antisuicide organization.[92] Persons who are contemplating suicide or who have in some way exhibited self-destructive symptoms may also be brought to the attention of these agencies.

However humane or helpful the program that focuses on individual cases may be, it has some definite limitations in reducing the incidence of suicide.

---

[91] Editor's Introduction to Émile Durkheim, *Suicide,* pp. 20–25.

[92] For a discussion of antisuicide organizations see Louis I. Dublin and Bessie Bunzel, *To Be or Not To Be,* pp. 321–25; and World Health Organization, *Prevention of Suicide.* For references to more recent suicide prevention programs and a relevant theory see Arthur L. Kobler and Ezra Stotland, *The End of Hope* (New York: Free Press, 1964), particularly Chapters I and IX.

Such a program could be effective only if those who are about to commit suicide show definite signs of their intentions. The author's study of all cases of suicide in New Zealand during 1946–1951 indicates that suicidal symptoms are by no means always conspicuous. Judging from the testimony of witnesses before the investigating coroner, a previous attempt was reported for only 7 percent of the 955 cases. This represents the minimum number, of course, since some previous attempts may have gone undetected or unreported. The figure does agree somewhat closely, however, with Sainsbury's findings in London, where a previous attempt was reported for 9 percent of the victims.[93] Moreover, it appears that the majority of the New Zealand victims did not suggest, directly or indirectly, that they were contemplating suicide; judging from testimony some 26 percent of them did so. Once again this represents the minimum because of the difficulties of assessing indications and because witnesses are probably reluctant to report that the victim's behavior suggested suicide and that they did not prevent it. Reports of intensive studies of suicide cases indicate that as many as 83 percent of the victims "communicated" their intent,[94] but the problem is that the typical layman may not (1) recognize at the time the communications of intent that are detected later by trained investigators in the reconstruction of cases, or (2) take effective action even if a suicidal intent is communicated and if he recognizes it as such.

Finally, there is a widespread belief that suicide is preceded by mental disorder and that signs of this disorder can be used to detect and predict attempts at suicide. An analysis of the New Zealand cases indicates that 34 percent of the victims may have suffered from some form of mental disorder (neuroses or psychoses), a number almost identical with an average of 33 percent reported in 16 studies of completed and attempted suicide.[95] We have noted the difficulty of judging psychopathology, particularly on the basis of testimony rather than observation, and therefore know that these figures represent only rough estimates. But it does seem that symptoms of psychopathology are not adequate for identifying potential suicides.

The foregoing observations bear directly on social policy concerning suicide. If any theory on the suicide rate is valid, then conceivably the volume

---

[93] Peter Sainsbury, *Suicide in London,* p. 92. Note, however, that other studies of suicide have reported that between 14 and 33 percent of the victims had made previous attempts. See Arthur L. Kobler and Ezra Stotland, *The End of Hope,* p. 5. Nonetheless, there appears to be general agreement that a previous attempt is not a reliable indicator of a potential suicide victim.

[94] For references to and summaries of these studies, see *ibid.,* Chapter I, particularly p. 8.

[95] Peter Sainsbury, *Suicide in London,* p. 85.

of suicide could be reduced substantially by deliberate social change. However, most theories deal with such basic structural components of society that few policymakers would contemplate attempting changes, let alone succeed. Further, neither policymakers nor the public is likely to view the "cost" of suicide as sufficiently great to justify undertaking any major remedial action. So in the final analysis, there appears to be only one way to reduce the incidence of suicide, and that is by instituting prevention programs that focus on individual cases. But even here a policy issue is posed. As suggested previously, there is no sufficiently reliable criterion or method for identifying the potential suicide victim, and the argument is that basic research on the problem should receive as much support as do prevention programs.

7

Sexual Behavior

KINGSLEY DAVIS

How much control should society exercise over sexual behavior? Conflicting views range from a purely authoritarian position at one extreme to an utterly individualistic or anarchic position at the other. The extremes are interesting, not because they are persuasive or widely held, but because they bring the logic of the issue into sharp focus.

The extreme authoritarian point of view claims that sexual problems would disappear if the sexual mores were observed. The mores, it explains, have been tried out during thousands of years and therefore reflect the wisdom of cumulative human experience. The anarchic position holds that sex is natural and private; hence attempts to regulate it are contrary to nature and an invasion of privacy. Worse yet, according to this view, the effort to suppress and control sexual expression creates hypocrisy, subjects individuals to the risk of public disgrace, and often leads to excessive guilt and neurosis.

The authoritarian argument obviously begs the question. If the problem is violation of the rules, then conformity is a "solution" only in a tautological sense (the cure for a disease is recovery). An effective solution would require a change in the *causes* of violation. These may lie in the mores themselves under changed conditions, or in a breakdown of enforcement machinery; but, wherever found, the causes must be effectively dealt with if the problem is to be solved. Admonition to conform is futile.

The anarchic position also begs the question. If sex is purely natural and its regulation harmful, how does it happen that human societies always and everywhere have rules governing sexual conduct? To dismiss the rules as "prejudice" or "superstition" is merely to restate the question, because these are terms for the sentiments or beliefs constituting the mores themselves. There must be some explanation of why people are so widely and similarly prejudiced. Perhaps the rules accomplish something; perhaps their abolition would have undesirable consequences. If rules are "outmoded," new ones may be needed, not the absence of all rules.

Seldom do people espouse either extreme. Virtually no one maintains that *all* sexual mores should be obeyed or that *none* should be. Some rules are inconsistent, others anachronistic or quixotic; it would be difficult to observe them all. On the other hand, even the most rabid nonconformists tend to take for granted certain regulations – such as those against rape and incest. The debate over sexual regulation thus boils down in practice to a quarrel between "liberal" and "conservative" points of view, neither of which represents an absolute position. The liberal approach is to condemn *certain* of the existing norms and advocate their modification or replacement by "more enlightened" ones. The conservative's reply is to point out that the particular norms being criticized *are* the most enlightened and should be retained and obeyed or at most be only slightly modified. With the debate thus focusing on particular rules, there is a large area of unspoken, if somewhat nebulous, agreement. It is this common ground that allows liberals and conservatives to coexist in the same society.

Our aim is to deal solely with the causes and consequences of sexual behavior in human societies. A logical first step is to explain why sexual norms exist, and the next is to explain why violations occur. If these two foundations in sociological theory are laid, the third task is easier – an understanding of how changing conditions in modern society have affected observance and violation of sex norms. Sometimes a social problem is defined as deviation, but frequently it is defined rather as a consequence of deviation or else as an unforeseen and undesired consequence of conformity.

THE THEORY OF SEXUAL NORMS

The basic answer to why sex norms exist is given in terms of what they *do* for human societies. Broadly speaking, what they do is what norms in general do; but beyond that the sex norms make a special contribution arising from the particular characteristics and unique potentialities of sexual behavior. Accordingly, in this section I shall first analyze what norms in general do, then delineate significant features of the sex drive and sexual behavior, and finally describe how these features are utilized in viable societies.

Norms in General [1]

Norms exist because human behavior is mainly learned from others by symbolic communication and example. The life of a society is consequently not organized solely by instinct but also by patterns received from and enforced by other members of the society. Competition between societies as well as with other species forces the invention and spread of new patterns. Those that prove advantageous survive, the others die out. Through thousands of years of evolution, man has become so dependent on acquired patterns that he cannot live without them.

Conformity to patterns does not occur automatically. It is induced by rewards and penalties. The very existence of regulation implies something that needs regulating. This something is by no means confined to organic drives or appetites; it is also composed of interests, emotions, and desires generated by social interaction itself. Violation may occur because the individual cannot help himself (as in an acquired drug addiction), because the norms themselves are in conflict, or because the risk is less than the potential gain. A man who successfully embezzles a million dollars reaps a big reward for nonconformity, just as a wife does who secretly murders her rich but unloved husband. The factors making for nonconformity are so powerful, and so much a part of society itself, that the battle for social control is never-ending. Understandably, then, the mechanisms by which conformity is induced are complex. Much of the enforcement is informal and personal. If an individual disappoints the expectations of others, they retaliate by disappointing *his* expectations.

Like other forms of behavior, sexual activity must be learned. Without socialization, human beings would not even know how to copulate. The sex norms are like other norms in that they help get the business of society accomplished. As a powerful drive, sex can be utilized to motivate people to per-

---

[1] For a more complete presentation of the theory of norms, with citations to the literature, see Judith Blake and Kingsley Davis, "Norms, Values, and Sanctions," in Robert E. L. Faris, ed., *Handbook of Modern Sociology* (Chicago: Rand McNally, 1964), Chapter 13.

form in ways that benefit the community at large, while lack of regulation may bring conflict and disruption.

The Sex Drive as an Object of Regulation

The sex drive has more scope for social articulation than most other drives. The fact that it is dormant during childhood and tapers off in old age permits social roles to rest on sexual readiness or maturity. Further, although sexual gratification cannot be entirely suppressed after puberty,[2] it is not required for individual survival, as is release from hunger, thirst, or fatigue.[3] Again, the sex drive is capable of an extraordinary amount of both situational and emotional conditioning. This gives the sex norms an amazing variety of possible behaviors to regulate.

The capacity for conditioning *allows* the sex drive to be enmeshed in a web of social relations; another feature forces it to be so enmeshed — namely, the physiological appropriateness and stimulating effect of direct intimate cooperation of another person for gratification. This feature makes sexual motives an integral part of roles based on age and sex, brings erotic interests into interpersonal relations, and connects eroticism with affection, trust, dependence, esteem, aggression, distrust, jealousy, and envy. The complexities thus introduced into sexual control can be readily grasped. In satisfying any desire for which the means are scarce, people compete with

---

[2] Kinsey and his associates found only about one-third of one percent of physiologically normal males to have a "low" sex drive. They found none with no drive at all and concluded that "sublimation" is a myth. See Alfred C. Kinsey *et al., Sexual Behavior in the Human Male* (Philadelphia: Saunders, 1948), pp. 205–13. They found about 2 percent of females to evince no sexual impulse. See *Sexual Behavior in the Human Female* (Philadelphia: Saunders, 1953), pp. 512, 526–27. W. S. Taylor, studying a small sample of males in various walks of life, concluded that there are no males without a sexual outlet. See *A Critique of Sublimation in Males,* Genetic Psychology Monographs, Vol. 13 (1933) and Hugo G. Beigel, "Abstinence," *Encyclopedia of Sexual Behavior* (New York: Hawthorn Books, 1961).

[3] There is of course one kind of necessity connected with sex that cannot be denied — the necessity of reproduction; but this is a communal rather than an individual requirement. The communal requirement of population replacement is an important aspect of sex regulation, as discussed below. However, this need can now be met with only a tiny fraction of the energy of the sex drive. Under maximum conditions, a couple could have intercourse only three times and have three children; with artificial insemination, a woman could have no intercourse and have fifteen children. Even with normal relations, the low mortality of modern society would permit replacement of the population by only one-fourth to one-third of the women of each generation.

one another. An orderly society, by definition, keeps competition from degenerating into force or fraud. In the case of sexual desire, however, the objects of gratification are themselves persons. This makes the assignment of rights to the means of satisfaction much more difficult than when the means are economic objects like land or inventions. As a scarce means, sexual access can be deliberately withheld or made available by an attractive person. Sexual desirability is thus an asset that can be traded for economic and social advantage. Conversely, sexual unattractiveness is a liability that can be overcome by nonsexual means. The development and maintenance of a stable competitive order with respect to sex is extremely difficult, because sexual desire itself is inherently unstable and anarchic. Erotic relations are subject to constant danger—a change of whim, a loss of interest, a third party, a misunderstanding. Competition for the same sexual object inflames passions and stirs conflicts; failure injures one's self-esteem. The intertwining of sex and society is a fertile ground for paranoia, for homicide, and suicide.[4]

The Problem of Enforcement

Given these characteristics of the sex drive, we can understand why the enforcement of sexual norms is difficult. Not only is the drive strong and yet capable of release in a brief and clandestine encounter, but it is so subject to conditioning and social involvement that the stimuli to prurient arousal are almost limitless in variety. Of necessity, sex regulation must be versatile in coverage and sanctions, running the gamut from the most informal mechanisms to the most awesome rewards and penalties.

The role of informal and personal enforcement—by gossip, loss of face, resentment, retaliation—is often overlooked. A girl may refrain from suggestive behavior because friends might talk or males become aggressive. In Java, husbands and wives are suspicious of any outside contact. They interpret minute deviations of behavior as indications of possible infidelity. When asked the meaning of *tjemburu* (jealousy, suspicion), they give examples showing "an almost paranoid watchfulness between spouses." If violation occurs, anger and reprisal are certain.[5] In all societies such informal control probably bears the major share of sex regulation; but giving

---

[4] In the writer's book, *Human Society* (New York: Macmillan, 1948), Chapter 7, "Jealousy and Sexual Property."

[5] Hildred Geertz, *The Javanese Family* (New York: Free Press, 1961), pp. 128–33.

it support are more formal enforcement mechanisms, the heroic quality of which suggests the difficulty of the task. One such mechanism is the elevation of the sex mores to the sacred realm, where they are surrounded with mystery and imbued with deep moral significance. For instance, of the six Old Testament Commandments dealing with human relationships, two are concerned with sex. Placing sex control under supernatural auspices makes punishment for transgression seem inescapable, because God sees everything. A related mechanism is ignorance and silence. Women and children are particularly protected from "the facts of life." Under such circumstances, "sin" tends to be contemplated with deep fear. In addition, certain social conventions, such as chaperonage and female seclusion, limit the opportunities for indiscretion. Finally, law adds its weight to control by enabling individuals to retaliate in court when their sexual interests have been injured or by enabling officials to prosecute when public morals have been offended.

The Gradation of Sex Norms

What has just been said suggests that sex norms come in "layers," so to speak. At the top are the official crystallized statements, often dating from long ago and often unrelated to current conditions. These presumably embody the highest ideals, publicly professed. Below these are secondary norms, which often conflict with the crystallized official ideals but nevertheless regulate behavior because conformity to them is rewarded and deviation punished. Beneath these are tertiary norms, and so on down the scale of respectability and rightness until one gets to the "countermores," which define certain kinds of conduct as good precisely because, in respectable circles, they are defined as bad.

Further, the norms apply differentially to people in different roles. By a strict interpretation, absolute celibacy is the highest Catholic ideal; but in practice it applies only to the clergy, lay celibacy being looked at askance by Catholics as well as others. Many practices of the young are disapproved by the general public but nevertheless expected and ignored. Among youth a "real man" may be one adept at seducing girls, a "real sport" may be a girl willing to be seduced. People usually favor more license for themselves than for others. Much depends on *whose* behavior is being judged, and *who* is doing the judging.

What Sex Regulation Does: Two Keys to Sex Norms

With these features before us, we can answer the question we started with — why sex regulation? The answer lies in two facts: *First,* sexual intercourse has the potential of creating a new human being. What the normative system does is to link coitus with the institutional mechanisms that guarantee the bearing and rearing of children. This causes sexual norms and reproductive norms to become intertwined; it adds to illicit intercourse the possibility of illegitimate parenthood. *Second,* a person's desirability as a sex object is a valuable but scarce and perishable good. This being the case, the normative system provides for an orderly distribution of rights in the use of this good. Of necessity, the regulation of rights and obligations with respect to this good must be integrated with the regulation of rights and obligations with respect to other goods. In sum, then, the sex norms contribute to the replacement of people in society and to the maintenance of an orderly system of production and distribution.

These facts give us two keys to the nature of sex regulation. The first is this: Sex rules are subordinate to the family, in the sense that they either support the formation and continuance of families or at least do not interfere with them; the second is that the departures from the familial character of sex norms derive mainly from the system of political and economic differentiation in the society. Let us consider each one in turn.

THE PRIMACY OF MARRIAGE AND THE FAMILY — The primacy of marriage and the family in sex regulation accounts for the relative force and universality of certain well-known sex mores. It explains, for instance, the principle of legitimacy (which establishes a family), the incest taboo (which eliminates overt sexual rivalry from the nuclear family), and the rule that coitus is *obligatory* within marriage (the only universal positive sex rule). The primacy of the family also accounts for the widespread preoccupation in sex regulation with *premarital* relationships and the universal fact that sex norms are different for men and women. It further enables us to account for the inequality of certain roles, or statuses, within societies. Family roles generally have more prestige than other roles in which sexual relations play a part. For a woman, for example, the status of being a wife has more economic and legal security, and more respectability, than any other status involving sexual relations. A concubine has a lower position than a wife even when concubinage is customary. In all societies the "single woman" — that

is, one who has remained unmarried past the customary age of marriage —
has done nothing illegal, yet she is punished by her inability to be a "legitimate" mother and by her exclusion from other advantages (economic and
social) accruing to wives. She is assumed to be single by necessity rather than
by choice.

Sex rules that are variables from one society to another are those that
either interfere least with family formation and continuance, or that fit the
special features of family structure in different kinds of societies. For example, although the incest taboo essential for the structure of the nuclear
family is found everywhere and is always strongly sanctioned, premarital
intercourse is treated quite differently from one normative system to another, being outlawed in some groups, abetted in others. The reason for this
variability is that premarital relations do not necessarily interfere with
marriage; when controlled in certain ways, they may *lead to* marriage.
Again, extended incest taboos vary from one society to another, because the
number and kinds of kinsmen outside the nuclear family who are socially
important to the individual are different in different societies.

ECONOMIC EXCHANGE AND SEX BARGAINING — The second key to sex norms explains most of the rules that cannot be explained by the first principle.
Societies are not merely under the necessity of biologically engendering
the next generation; they are also under the necessity of supplying the goods
and services that the present and next generations need. These must be
exchanged as well as produced, hence in the division of labor that characterizes human societies there is an incentive system (normatively regulated)
through which goods are produced and exchanged. Since sexual desirability
is itself a good, sexual access can be exchanged for economic or political
advantage. The distribution of sexual favors thus gets involved with the
distribution of political and economic goods. There are, of course, limits to
treating sex as an exchangeable commodity. These limits are precisely the
norms already referred to, for they regulate the exchange of sex in favor of
the family. Within the limits, rules governing the exchange of sex favors
tend to resemble those governing human services in general. The basic principle is that in entering into an agreement, each person be a free agent, not
subject to force or fraud. Thus the sex rules protect minors against sexual
exploitation, bar the use of force in gaining sexual submission, protect the
public from nuisances and health hazards, condemn sexual blackmail, limit
third-party profiting from sexual relations (as in pandering), and hold the
individual responsible for the consequences of his sexual acts. The tenor
of the rules, whether by law or custom, is to guarantee fair bargaining in
sexual matters.

It happens that both sexual desirability and economic capacity are age-linked, but the two scales are at variance. Sexual attractiveness is greatest in youth whereas economic and political advantage (other things equal) are greater in middle or late age. Also, there is a division of labor by sex, the man's sphere being primarily economic and the woman's primarily familial. Hence the normal outcome is that, in competing for attractive younger women, men partially compensate economically and politically for what they may lack in youth and handsomeness.

CONFLICT BETWEEN THE TWO PRINCIPLES — Inevitably, some conflict arises between the "exchange" and the "family" side of sexual regulation. For instance, since the rights and duties of marriage are economic as well as sexual, a major consideration in sexual bargaining is commitment or noncommitment to marriage. In most societies a woman sexually involved with a man married to someone else is not only violating a norm but is also, in the absence of compensating advantages, making a bad bargain. However, the man may be able to offer advantages that compensate for his unmarriageability. This possibility has a class aspect. Ordinarily, children are born into the social class of their parents and given the attitudes of that class, with the result that different social strata in the same society have contrasting norms. The differences are not random, but are often complementary and mutually reinforcing. Since both sexes are present in each social class, every class must regulate sex relations among its *own* members; but, by the same token, the members of any stratum also have the possibility of sex relations with members of *other* strata. Accordingly, members of the higher classes can use their economic advantage to gain sexual favors from people of lesser means. Except in societies permitting plural mating, this trading tends to be extrafamilial rather than familial. Commitment to marriage is not part of the bargain, both because it does not have to be and because marriage itself tends to be class endogamous. Unlike wealth, sexual desirability is approximately equally distributed among the social classes. For this reason, the trading of economic means for sexual favors would be a powerful equalizer *if it involved commitment to marriage;* but the more rigidly a society is organized along inherited status lines, the stronger are the barriers to interclass marriages.[6]

---

[6] This is particularly true of strata that are racially defined, because in that case the offspring of mixed unions blur the biological as well as the sociocultural basis of distinction. Even if the society is not rigidly stratified by inheritance, there are strong incentives to marry equals. See K. Davis, "Intermarriage in Caste Societies," *American Anthropologist,* Vol. 43 (July–September, 1941), pp. 376–95; "American Society and Its Group Structure," *Contemporary Civilization,* Vol. 2 (Chicago: Scott, 1961), pp. 171–86. On the general tendency of marriages to be class endogamous, see pp. 553–58 and 645–56 in *Handbook of Marriage and the Family* (Chicago: Rand McNally, 1964).

On the other hand, the barriers against interclass sexual relations are at most only as strong as those against extramarital relations generally. Given differences in class norms, it is possible for members of a higher stratum (usually males) to command the favors of the lower stratum (usually females), each side acting in conformity with the norms of its class *in regard to that kind of exchange.* Although such an exchange may not reflect the "highest" mores of the society, it may nevertheless be customary and subject to normative expectations in its own right.

The conflict between the familial and the exchange sides of sex regulation sometimes confuses the distinction between conformity and violation. However, most societies manage to reconcile the two fairly well. They prevent family domination from turning the society into an economically unproductive breeding system and they prevent economic domination from subordinating all sex to money, status, and pleasure. There is no perfect solution to the dilemmas of sexual regulation.

ALTERNATIVE SCHEMES OF SEX REGULATION

In comparing societies with respect to sex regulation, we have no single criterion, or scale, that can be used. The rules of each society are too many and too varied for that, as can be seen by examining the most common yardstick ("strictness") used in single-axis comparisons.

Are Some Societies "Stricter" Than Others?

Certain societies (those least known to the author) are claimed to regulate sex hardly at all. "There are cultures," says Kinsey, "which more freely accept sexual activities as matters of everyday physiology, while maintaining extensive rituals and establishing taboos around feeding activities." [7] By implication, sexual control is merely a matter of prejudice, and "our" so-

---

[7] Alfred C. Kinsey *et al., Sexual Behavior in the Human Male,* p. 4. The sole evidence given is a reference to Bronislaw Malinowski, *The Sexual Life of Savages in Northwestern Melanesia* (New York: Halcyon, 1929), but this account of the Trobriand Islanders gives abundant evidence of sexual control. For instance, women of a man's own clan (roughly one-fourth of the women in the society) are forbidden as sexual objects; adultery by either husband or wife is forbidden; "many things which we regard as natural, proper, and moral are anathema to the Trobriander."

ciety is abnormal and sadistic with its "rigid" controls. Such comparisons usually focus on only one aspect of sexual regulation, forgetting the other aspects. Courtship in Norway is seen to be uninhibited, and so Norway is said to have more sexual freedom than, say, Mexico; but the greater license of a large class of females and of all males in the latter country is overlooked. Sometimes the gradation of norms is ignored, the "highest" norms of one society being compared with the everyday ones of another. "Our own culture," says Murdock, "includes . . . an over-all prohibition of all sexual intercourse outside of the marital relationship"[8]; but surveys disprove this. In Catholic Belgium 49.1 percent of 1674 adult respondents in 1965 said that sexual relations between engaged persons were either advisable or inevitable.[9] In the United States, according to a national survey in 1963, 19.5 percent of adults approved of premarital intercourse for males and 16.9 percent approved of it for females. The percentages were much higher among some groups – 43.2 percent of blacks approved for men and 40.3 percent for women; among white New York college students in a companion study, the proportion approving for males was 78.3, and for females, 74.3 percent.[10] A majority of Americans favor premarital "petting," a practice that would strike hundreds of millions of Hindus and Muslims as immoral. A society strict in one sphere will not necessarily be strict in another.

Who Are the Sex Partners?

Comparison should be made on some basis more fundamental than strictness. Among all the rules by which the sex drive is harnessed, the most important are those defining the proper partners. As we have seen, one of these rules – that coitus is obligatory within marriage – universally links sex regulation to the family. Given that rule, the only variation possible among societies concerns coitus *outside* of marriage.

Here we encounter one of man's major moral dilemmas. Should sexual expression be confined to marriage? If not, to what degree, under what circum-

---

[8] George P. Murdock, *Social Structure* (New York: Macmillan, 1949), p. 263.

[9] Claude Henryon and Edmond Lambrechts, *Le Mariage en Belgique* (Bruxelles: Evo, 1968), p. 118.

[10] Ira L. Reiss, "The Scaling of Premarital Sexual Permissiveness," *Journal of Marriage and the Family,* Vol. 26 (May, 1964), pp. 188–98. This article also contains references to other research on American attitudes toward sexual behavior. Also see the same author's *The Social Context of Premarital Sexual Permissiveness* (New York: Holt, 1967).

stances, and for whom should it be permitted? There is no satisfactory solution. As literature throughout history demonstrates, the issue involves emotional and often tragic conflicts that cannot be reconciled. This is why different societies have different rules about it, and why the rules, whatever they are, are subject to criticism and violation.

Two Imaginary Types of Society

Let us imagine two extreme types of society. One of these would be a society in which *all* sex expression is confined by law to marriage. The other would be a society in which there is *no restriction whatever* on sex outside of marriage. What would the consequences of each type be?

For the first type, the consequences would depend on how the society defined marriage. If it defined marriage as we traditionally would—that is, as a durable bond protected by law and custom—an attempt to confine all sexual expression to marriage would be a straitjacket that many would find intolerable. To begin with, if the customary age at marriage were late enough for newlyweds to be socially mature, sexual expression would have to be postponed during the very period when the sex drive is strongest; if, on the other hand, people married at puberty, the lack of maturity would militate against durable unions. Wedlock, moreover, regardless of its start, has features which tend to militate against perpetual sexual interest. The same partner becomes old hat; a couple is associated in other contexts that produce tension and conflict; and the partners themselves change. The cute girl at 19 years of age becomes fat and frowsy, the dashing young man becomes flabby. A normative system cannot immunize people against the effects of time and dissension. Appetites and emotions cannot be determined by will or fiat; they can be concealed or kept from manifesting themselves in certain ways, but not banished or denied any expression whatever. Accordingly, it appears impossible to require that marriage be both a durable bond and the sole sexual relationship for everybody. No society has enforced such a system, despite occasional lip service to the ideal.

The only way to confine sex expression to wedlock would be to make marriage dependent on sexual interest. But then marriage would become highly unstable, because sexual desire in and of itself is anarchic and fickle. A couple who slept together one night would *ipso facto* be married; and if they took other partners the next night they would instantaneously be "divorced" and "remarried." This strikes us as a *reductio ad absurdam* because the norms of every society show an intent to make the marital bond a durable one, primarily for the security of children. Viewed in this light, marriage is not for intercourse, but intercourse is for marriage.

We now see why a society that confines all sex expression to wedlock must be imaginary. No real society can induce everybody *first* to abjure sexual activity until a durable marriage is established and *second* to confine it entirely to that union thereafter. And no real society will degrade marriage to a sexual interlude. But what about the opposite — the society that puts no restraint whatever on sex outside of marriage? Must it be imaginary too?

The answer is yes. In fact, this case is exactly the same as the second variant of the first case — the degradation of marriage to mere sexual impulse. Absolute sexual freedom would wind up by making marriage dependent on sex, rather than vice versa. Our thinking about this matter is clouded by the tendency to interpret social control as solely a matter of law. As noted above, most control of sex behavior is a function not of law but of opinion and reprisal. Complete sex freedom outside of marriage would mean that nobody cared beyond the mere act itself. There would be no expectation as to the future, because such expectation by another person restricts one's freedom. There would be no incentive or reward for fidelity, because that would call for the disciplining of impulse. If it is argued that some people would choose to "get married" because they want to have children, the answer is that this would be meaningless. Under a regime of total license with respect to sexual partners, a couple could live together as long as they felt so inclined, but there would be no expectation that they would continue to do so the next day, and no expectation that the children would be those of the couple. Women would have children whenever they wished, by whomever they chose. Men would have little interest in children, for they could count on no personal connection with a particular child or with the particular child's mother. In such a regime "marriage" would not exist as a sexual relationship implying permanence and parenthood. It would be reduced to a sexual contact implying only momentary gratification. This kind of society is difficult to imagine, because it is so remote from known societies.

Real Societies: Old and Modern

Real societies settle for some kind of compromise. They have a moral preference for durable marriage and esteem marital fidelity as a virtue, especially for the wife. They differ in what is expected prior to marriage, and they differ in the ease of divorce and remarriage; but they manage somehow to give priority to the marital bond.

Most of the world's people live in societies that have a "double standard" of sexual morality — double in two ways: Respectable women are held to very strict rules, while respectable men are free to philander; and women are divided into two categories, reputable and disreputable, the disreputable being the ones who make male freedom possible. Such a system accentuates the woman's family role and usually supports marital permanence. The husband, once married, is theoretically bound to the woman for life. In return he is given sexual freedom both before and after marriage, and he is given reasonable assurance that the offspring will be his own. The wife, chaperoned before marriage and jealously watched afterwards, has little opportunity for sexual experience apart from marriage. In other ways as well, the feminine sphere is sharply demarcated from the masculine, thus reinforcing the double standard.

A recent survey in Chile illustrates the system.[11] Of married men, 25 percent in the rural sample, 49 percent of the lower-class urban sample, and 61 percent of the middle and upper-class urban sample, admitted extramarital intercourse during the three months preceding the interview. Among unmarried men, the proportion reporting intercourse was 84 percent for the rural and 93 percent for the urban sample. No question on extramarital intercourse was asked of married women, but unmarried women were asked about use of contraception. Only six percent reported such use, although 45 percent of the unmarried men did so.

In such a system the women available for extramarital coitus (prostitutes, concubines, mistresses, servants, and pickups) come predominantly from the lower classes. The distinction between them and respectable women is sometimes so pronounced that sexual relations for enjoyment are felt to be almost inappropriate for a married couple. Puerto Rican husbands, for instance, "draw a sharp distinction between prostitutes, easy women, and their wives. The former are women to be enjoyed because they are evil. The wife, on the other hand, is like one's mother — holy, pure, and saintly. . . . Husbands seem concerned about the fidelity of their wives and the chastity of the daughters to an almost phobic extent."[12]

Under urban-industrial conditions, the double standard does not disappear; it becomes attenuated as surveillance by neighbors and relatives diminishes. As female economic independence grows with outside employ-

---

[11] M.-Francoise Hall, "Male Use of Contraception and Attitudes toward Abortion, Santiago, Chile, 1968," *Milbank Memorial Fund Quarterly,* Vol. 48 (April, 1970), pp. 145–66.

[12] J. Mayone Stycos and Reuben Hill, "The Prospects of Birth Control in Puerto Rico," *Annals of the American Academy of Political and Social Science,* Vol. 285 (January, 1953), p. 141.

ment, as contraception separates coitus more surely from pregnancy, women have less to fear from sexual indiscretion. Within wedlock, sexual love and daily companionship gain greater importance. Marriage comes to depend more on mutual affection; divorce is more by mutual consent and easier to obtain. Inevitably the rules of sexual behavior grow more similar for the two sexes. Adultery becomes less acceptable for husbands, premarital coitus more acceptable for women. The double standard changes from a difference of kind to one of degree.

Admittedly, the tendency to base marriage on mutual affection leads to considerable instability. There are several ways, however, in which marital instability is mitigated. For instance, intimate courtship encourages selection on the basis of compatibility and starts marriages with an already established personal bond. Premarital intercourse — either socially sanctioned, as in Scandinavian countries,[13] or reluctantly tolerated, as in the United States — allows courtship to approximate a trial marriage. Marital stability is further encouraged by a convergence of male and female interests. Women study, work, travel, and pursue interests, much like men. Education and birth control help to keep the home from completely dominating the wife's existence. Nevertheless, although the reduction of role differentiation makes marriages more companionable it also gives them less support.

Social Change and Sex in Advanced Societies

Although it is clear that contemporary industrial societies are shifting from the old standards, it is not clear where they are headed. While the underdeveloped countries are at an earlier stage of the shift and so have familiar problems, the industrial countries are moving in unprecedented directions and experiencing unparalleled problems. One development is a rising skepticism and dissension concerning the sex rules themselves. Premarital intercourse is viewed by some as an evil, by others as a good. Pornography is widely condemned but, because of solicitude for press freedom, not suppressed. Nudity is regarded by some as obscene and by others as wholesome. Abortion is seen both as the solution of a problem and as a problem in itself. Without consensus on what the problems are, arguments over the means of solving them are pointless.

---

[13] Harold T. Christensen, "Cultural Relativism and Premarital Sex Norms," *American Sociological Review,* Vol. 25 (February, 1960), pp. 31–39; and "Scandinavian and American Sex Norms: Some Comparisons, with Sociological Implications," *Journal of Social Issues,* Vol. 22 (April, 1966), pp. 60–75. Thomas D. Eliot and Arthur Hillman, eds., *Norway's Families* (Philadelphia: University of Pennsylvania Press, 1960).

In the relatively stable agricultural societies where the old mores were formed, one of the main problems was how to bear and rear enough children to survive high death rates. The sex rules encouraged, or at least did not interfere with, marriage and reproduction. Supernatural sanctions for these rules were taken literally by people steeped in religion and magic, and small villages facilitated consensus and surveillance. Now, however, with death rates lowered to an unprecedented level, the old rules tying sex to reproduction and the family have become obsolete. Not only that, but industrial societies have grown to massive proportions, embracing people of diverse cultural and educational levels. Skeptical and cloaked in urban anonymity, they violate sexual rules with relative impunity. Criticism of the rules is hailed as "open-mindedness"; advocacy of enforcement is condemned as "authoritarianism." Groups arise who express their hostilities and psychic insecurities by attacking the validity of whatever rules restrict their freedom.

Sex regulation, however, does not become completely paralyzed. Industrial societies are, after all, societies. Violations bring efforts to restore order; personal injury brings retaliation. Individuals have a stake in sexual bargaining, and since they cannot always protect their interests, the community at large helps them. Children and youth are particularly vulnerable to sexual aggression. For such reasons, some consensus on sex regulation exists.

There is majority agreement, for instance, on the desirability of minimizing certain by-products of sexual activity. Illegal abortion, venereal disease, illegitimate birth, forced marriage, child marriage, and organized procuring are widely regarded as evils. Dispute is mainly confined to means of combatting them. One side argues that a major cause of the evils is illicit coitus, while the other side argues that this is not the cause but rather that something else is. *If* contraception is efficiently practiced, coitus will *not* lead to an abortion or an illegitimate birth; nor will it lead to venereal disease *if* prophylactic precautions are taken. "Why, then," ask the libertarians, "try to cure obvious evils by the difficult route of limiting sexual pleasure? Why not simply teach people contraception and prophylaxis? Why not recognize that problems are caused by oppressive sex rules themselves? Abortion is dangerous *because* it is illegal, not vice versa."[14] As noted

---

[14] In nations that freely permit and provide facilities for abortion, as many do today, the operation is not dangerous. The Soviet Union, Japan, Scandinavian countries, and satellite countries in eastern Europe (except Albania and East Germany) have all permitted abortion and made facilities available. Studies of the outcomes of abortion in those countries show that it is a safe operation when performed properly. In Den-

earlier, if this approach were applied consistently to condemn all sex rules, it would be an extreme anarchic, or libertarian view, but the ordinary liberal is not so consistent. He tends to overlook other sex rules that limit coital freedom—rules against rape, incest, and female adultery.[15]

The familiar conflict over sex norms is then not a simple division between a view that sexual pleasure is always sinful and a notion that it is always desirable. The questions being debated are limited. The argument against regulation is generally that the behavior in question does no harm—a proposition hard to refute because the harm is assumed away by unconsciously positing that other elements in the situation are favorable. Prostitution does no harm *if* there is protection against disease, *if* the woman is of age and *if* she is a free agent; adultery does no harm *if* the spouse approves. Further, insofar as the antiregulation argument attributes psychological harm to sex rules themselves, it is hard to refute, because any rule, if violated, has the possibility of causing guilt feelings and therefore, presumably, psychological malaise.

Conflict over sex norms for youth is especially intense, because in youth the sex drive reaches its peak simultaneously with emancipation from authority and the making of lifetime decisions. It is the younger generation whose sex problems are most intensified by changing social conditions. The adults mainly responsible for youth—parents, school officials, group leaders —are too demoralized by radical criticism to give firm guidance. By default, the operating norms come to be those spontaneously arising among young people themselves. These have strong countermoral and egocentric components that cripple the individual's capacity to perform as an adult. James Coleman shows, for instance, that the American high school fails to instill either a desire to learn or a capacity for adult adjustment.

---

mark and Sweden, for example, there were only six or seven deaths per 10,000 legal abortions during 1953–57. See Christopher Tietze, "The Current Status of Fertility Control," *Law and Contemporary Problems,* Vol. 25 (Summer, 1960), p. 442; "Legal Abortion in Eastern Europe," *Journal of the American Medical Association,* Vol. 175 (April, 1961), pp. 1149–54; "Abortion," *Scientific American,* Vol. 220, pp. 3–9. Gunnar K. af Geijerstam, ed., *An Annotated Bibliography of Induced Abortion* (Ann Arbor: Center for Population Planning, 1969).

[15] It is interesting to ask why liberals criticize certain sex norms and not others. Why do they attack popular views on homosexuality but not those on adultery and incest? One might expect them to favor incest (harmful genetic effects being avoided by contraception), but instead they seem hardly to think of it, even though it occurs with some frequency. See S. Kirson Weinberg, *Incest Behavior* (New York: Citadel Press, 1963), Chapters 1–3. Similarly they do not defend rape, child molestation, or the sale of girls into prostitution.

The dichotomy . . . between "life-adjustment" and "academic emphasis" is a false one, for it forgets that most of the teen-ager's energy is not directed toward either of these goals. Instead the relevant dichotomy is cars and the cruel jungle of rating and dating versus school activities.[16]

To an unusual degree, each young person must fend for himself by a costly process of trial and error.[17] This is doubtless the reason that the Group for Advancement of Psychiatry in their report *Sex and the College Student*[18] recommends that "if a college has certain expectations about sexual conduct on the campus, it has a responsibility to clarify them."

PREMARITAL SEX RELATIONS

Of the various kinds of sexual deviation, the most debated in contemporary societies is premarital intercourse. This preoccupation is due not only to the fact that youth are primarily implicated, but also to the fact that the issue is sociologically unimportant. Premarital sex is widely debated because its regulation is less fundamental than the regulation of many other aspects of sexual life. In other words, the premarital rules are marginal; they can be one way or the other without altering the character of the society. This conclusion may deflate young people who are preoccupied with their own premarital sex problems or with "sex freedom," but the evidence seems convincing.

The first thing to note is that premarital norms are rules about proper sex partners. Among the negative partner rules, the strongest are those pertaining to pairs *for whom marriage is forbidden* (near kin, already married, too young, same sex, celibate orders, or wrong castes). This rationale, however, does not pertain to premarital relations per se. If a young couple are both of age and free to marry, their coitus does not interfere with marriage but may, under certain rules, facilitate it. This is why premarital intercourse can be permitted in many societies, and why, if not permitted, it is usually punished less severely than other infractions of the partner rules.

Then why is premarital intercourse ever forbidden at all? The answer is

---

[16] James S. Coleman, *The Adolescent Society* (New York: Free Press, 1961), p. 51.

[17] Physical force and misuse of advantage are often unchallenged because no one wants to cause scandal. See Clifford Kirkpatrick and Eugene Kanin, "Male Sex Aggression on a University Campus," *American Sociological Review,* Vol. 22 (1957), pp. 52–58.

[18] Group for the Advancement of Psychiatry, *Sex and the College Student* (New York: Mental Health Materials Center, Inc., 1965), p. 16.

that societies thus seek to avoid illegitimacy. If so, why is premarital intercourse often permitted or only mildly sanctioned? The answer is that the unmarried are generally young and sexually at their peak. A ban on intercourse among them is difficult to enforce, especially for males; anyway, there is always a possibility that coitus will not result in childbirth, or that, if it does, the couple will get married.

Variations in Premarital Regulation

Faced with this dilemma in social organization, societies have unconsciously evolved different solutions. I have already cited the widespread system that strictly forbids premarital coitus for respectable women but permits it for respectable men and a limited class of disreputable women. In Egypt, for example, each family bases its reputation on the sexual purity of its women. Each household exerts the utmost vigilance to prevent the unmarried girls from committing any sexual indiscretion. For village boys and girls

> any conversation about sex is taboo . . . Chastity as a moral and religious ideal implies the avoidance of any stimulating pleasurable influence from the opposite sex. . . . Sexual pleasure of any kind outside the marriage tie is condemned by the Koran, . . . Manifestations of this excessive repression and fear of sex are obvious in the veiling of adolescent girls and women and the hiding of the breast contours with extra pieces of cloth, . . .
>
> In this community I heard of no cases of adultery or illegitimate children for the last thirty years, though cases of homosexuality and jokes about sexual pleasure from animals are not uncommon among the adolescents and young men.[19]

In contrast, some peasant societies have allowed freedom of intercourse on condition that the couple marry if pregnancy ensues. In preindustrial Scandinavia, the girl's pregnancy demonstrated that the union would be fertile and that therefore marriage was in order. Such a custom, in effect a "trial marriage," required a rural society where everybody knew who was "keeping company," and where, accordingly, expected behavior could be enforced even when the male was reluctant to marry. In a highly developed society, although the identification of the father is technologically feasible (with blood tests, lie detectors, monitoring devices, and sworn witnesses), it is

---

[19] Hamed Ammar, *Growing Up in an Egyptian Village* (London: Routledge, 1954), pp. 185–92.

socially repugnant and is used mainly in legal proceedings in which the pregnant woman's goal is not marriage but money.

A different kind of arrangement is one that can be called the "promiscuous peer-group system." It permits intercourse freely among young unmarried people but condemns unmarried reproduction. Obviously requiring abortion or contraception, it is often found in primitive societies that emphasize age classes. Chagga boys, after puberty but prior to marriage, were "instructed to practice interfemoral intercourse or coitus interruptus unless the girl places a pad in the vagina to avoid conception." [20] A somewhat similar pattern was observed among American college students in the 1920's to 1940's. Kinsey found "petting to climax" to be a major "outlet." Among males aged 21, it had occurred in 12.3 percent of those with a grade-school education, 23.7 percent of those with a high-school education, and 50.1 percent of those with college education.[21] By age 20, 10 percent of the women who were born before 1900 had petted to climax, while almost 28 percent of those born during 1920–1929 had done so; and by age 25, the two percentages were 14 and 43.[22]

The Rise of Premarital Intercourse

Petting to climax was evidently a transitional stage in the changing American pattern. Former restraints on unmarried girls were giving way to indulgence in intercourse, but during the interim heavy petting was a compromise. It prevented pregnancy and maintained "technical virginity." As condoms, diaphragms, spermicidal jellies, and steroid pills became increasingly available to teenagers, full coitus became more frequent. A 1960 survey among students at four Peoples' colleges in Sweden found that 40 percent of the girls had experienced intercourse; a 1965 survey of the same colleges found that 64 percent had done so. A recent study of 497 students (average

---

[20] Clellan S. Ford and Frank A. Beach, *Patterns of Sexual Behavior* (New York: Harper, 1951), p. 182. Among the Zulu, "intercourse *intra crura* by youngsters was allowed. If an unmarried girl became pregnant by a young warrior, both they and their families were liable to be killed." See Max Gluckman, "Kinship and Marriage among the Lozi of Northern Rhodesia and the Zulu of Natal" in A. R. Radcliffe-Brown and Daryll Forde, eds., *African Systems of Kinship and Marriage* (London: Oxford University Press, 1950), p. 181.

[21] Alfred C. Kinsey *et al., Sexual Behavior in the Human Male*, p. 56.

[22] Alfred C. Kinsey *et al., Sexual Behavior in the Human Female*, p. 275.

age 17) at two schools in Örebro found that 46 percent had had intercourse.[23] In the United States, Kinsey found that the proportion having intercourse prior to marriage was much less for women born prior to 1900 than for those born afterwards. The percentage of women in each cohort who had had premarital intercourse by a given age was as follows: [24]

	Women Born		
	Before 1900	1900–1909	1910–1929
By age 15	2	2	4
By age 20	8	18	22
By age 25	14	36	39

Furthermore, among those who had premarital coitus, promiscuity was increasing. The percentage having the stated number of partners was as follows: [25]

	Women with Premarital Experience		
	Born Before 1900	Born 1900–1909	Born 1910–1919
One partner only	56	55	48
2–5 partners	33	31	38
6 or more partners	11	14	14

These trends are all the more striking in view of the fact that the age at marriage was falling after 1900, thus offering less chance for girls to have premarital experience.

Somewhat similar trends appear in other advanced countries. A French survey in the 1950's found that 17 percent of the married women born in 1900–1915 had experienced premarital coitus, while 38 percent of those born after 1920 had had it.[26]

---

[23] Gustav Jonsson, "Sexualvanor hos svensk ungdom," in SOU, 1951, p. 41. Cited in Birgitta Linnér, *Sex and Society in Sweden* (New York: Random House, 1967), pp. 18–20.

[24] Alfred C. Kinsey *et al., Sexual Behavior in the Human Female,* p. 339. I have combined the data for the cohorts born in 1910–1919 and 1920–1929.

[25] *Ibid.,* p. 336

[26] French Institute of Public Opinion, *Patterns of Sex and Love* (New York: Crown Publishers, 1961), p. 109. Cited in Robert R. Bell, *Premarital Sex in a Changing Society* (Englewood Cliffs, N. J.: Prentice-Hall, 1966), p. 61. For Britain, see Eustace Chesser, *The Sexual, Marital and Family Relations of the English Woman* (New York: Ray Publishers, 1957), p. 311.

The rise in premarital coitus is often attributed to *a change in moral standards,* but one can argue just as well that it is due to a *breakdown* of standards, and that until new ones arise, the situation is one of disorganization rather than reorganization. If reorganization does occur, it will doubtless be because of the problems created by the present condition. Let us look at some of these.

Anomie and Conflict in Courtship

Formerly in northwest European society a respectable woman gave her sexual favors only in return for the promise of a stable relationship and economic support. The man was drawn into the bargain by his sexual interest. If he obtained coitus under false pretenses, he risked retaliation by the girl's relatives and loss of face. The girl could thus use her relatively short period of maximum attractiveness to settle her future in the best way possible—by marriage. This is still the bargain that many girls in contemporary society would like to make, and some of them do; but their bargaining position has been undermined by the growing loss of family and community controls. As a consequence, girls increasingly give their favors for nothing. This is described, ironically, as female "emancipation." In some circles a girl now feels that she must be willing to indulge in intercourse even to enjoy male company. As a student nurse put it,

> Whether you like it or not, you have to go along with them, at least some of the time. Otherwise, you get left out and sitting in the dorm all the time.[27]

Given an absence of sanctions against males and the intense desire of females to get married, girls are easily exploited.

> One nursing student reported she became acquainted with an intern, . . . became sexually intimate and eventually very serious about him, only to discover he was already married; the whole charade was carried out with the knowledgeable aid of the intern's friends and cohorts.[28]

In the United States, at the age-specific rates of 1965, each thousand women living from age 10 to age 50 would experience approximately 48

---

[27] James K. Skipper, Jr. and Gilbert Nass, "Dating Behavior: A Framework for Analysis and an Illustration," *Journal of Marriage and the Family,* Vol. 28 (November, 1966), p. 417.

[28] *Ibid.,* p. 419.

rapes.[29] However, this amazing rate is no adequate measure of the amount of force and intimidation used by males to gain sexual access. Many rapes and attempted rapes are not reported, still less other forms of sexual coercion. In a study of girls at Ohio State University, Kirkpatrick and Kanin found that 56 percent of 291 girl respondents had been offended at least once during the preceding academic year by sexual aggression.

21 percent were offended by forceful attempts at intercourse and 6 percent by . . . attempts . . . in the course of which menacing threats or coercive infliction of physical pain were employed.[30]

One-fourth of the offenses occurred on the *first* date![31] The offended girls usually felt it would injure their own reputation if they reported the offense.[32]

The girl of today must walk a slender tightrope. Expected to be "a good sport"—that is, comply—she is, on the other hand, in danger of a bad reputation if she does. With the logical consistency of emperors, males do not wish to marry the females whom they have "passed around."[33]

In quest of a stable relationship, a girl often does more than perform the normal duties of a wife. In many cases she interrupts her own education and takes a dead-end job in order to support the young man while he pursues his education. She may do this without the compensation of marriage—that is, with no legal commitment whatever. Even if married, the girl may find herself later divorced, in favor of a younger and more eager competitor. Whereas it formerly was the man who was obligated to practice birth control with the condom or withdrawal, the burden has gradually been shifted to the woman. It is she, not he, who makes intercourse safe by having an intrauterine device inserted, taking a dangerous pill, or having an "unrestricted" abortion performed on her. It is she who has to bear the responsibility for

---

[29] A rapist's chance of avoiding a penalty is excellent. In 1967, in the cities reporting crimes, only 57.6 percent of the rapes reported resulted in an arrest, only 42.9 percent resulted in charges, and only 14.7 percent received any penalty. *Ibid.,* p. 141. For an account of 646 rape cases reported in Philadelphia in 1958, see Monachem Amir, "Forcible Rape," *Federal Probation,* Vol. 21 (March, 1967), pp. 51–58, reprinted in Simon Dinitz, Russell R. Dynes, and Alfred C. Clarke, eds., *Deviance* (New York: Oxford University Press, 1969), pp. 67–74.

[30] Clifford Kirkpatrick and Eugene Kanin, "Male Sex Aggression on a University Campus," *American Sociological Review,* Vol. 22 (February, 1957), p. 53.

[31] Eugene Kanin, "Male Aggression in Dating-Courtship Relationships," *American Journal of Sociology,* Vol. 62 (September, 1957), p. 200.

[32] *Ibid.,* p. 203.

[33] In the lower class in Britain, premarital intercourse appears to be taken for granted; yet a girl runs the danger of injuring her marriage prospects if she gets a reputation for promiscuity. See Mary Morse, *The Unattached* (Baltimore: Penguin Books, 1965), pp. 116, 164–65, 172–73.

any illegitimate children born of her sexual hospitality. In its rush to "abolish" illegitimacy, contemporary society has mainly succeeded in abolishing the old and equitable custom of holding the male financially responsible.

Problems Associated with Premarital Coitus

Unmarried coitus can have one or more of several outcomes: nothing at all beyond the act itself, venereal disease, an illicit pregnancy ending in abortion, a forced marriage, or an illegitimate child. In view of the diffusion of contraceptive and prophylactic techniques during the so-called sexual revolution, it is strange that the undesired sequelae have tended to rise rather than fall.

ILLICIT PREGNANCY—Nobody knows how many illicit impregnations there are. An estimate can be obtained by adding a conjectural number of spontaneous and induced abortions occurring to unmarried women to the number of illegitimate births and other premarital conceptions. In the United States in 1965, for example, my estimate is that approximately 1,324,000 illicit pregnancies occurred. The calculation has no claim to accuracy because the largest component (induced abortions) is unknown, but as a conservative guess it suggests that one-fourth or more of all pregnancies in 1965 were of unmarried women.

In 1965 the illegitimate births were officially estimated to be 291,200, yielding a birth rate of 23.5 per 1000 unmarried women aged 15–44, as compared to a rate of 131.1 for married women. The illegitimate fertility was more than three times as high as it was in 1940, when it was 7.1 per 1000 unmarried women. Similar rises have occurred in other industrial countries, despite the increasing availability of contraception and sexual knowledge. In Australia, the 1966 illegitimate fertility rate was four and one-half times that of 1940; in England and Wales the 1964 rate was three and one-half times that of 1938.

Illegitimate births result either from an unsuccessful effort to trap a man into marriage, from sheer indifference, or from an inability to find a reliable and/or cheap abortionist. Among a sample of 1062 unwed mothers studied in California in 1954, only 55 percent claimed that the child was conceived in a friendship or love relationship.[34] Worse motives for the creation of new human beings could hardly be imagined, and the meager information available on the child's subsequent history shows the consequence. Infant mortal-

---

[34] Clark Vincent, *Unmarried Mothers* (New York: Free Press, 1961), p. 83.

ity among illegitimate children is generally from one-and-one-half to two times that for legitimate children, the birth weight is substantially less, and the proportion of premature births is much higher.[35] If the child survives, he usually has no father or lives with adopted or foster parents.[36] For her part, the mother goes through the onerous and hazardous experience of pregnancy either for a small welfare pittance or an adoption fee, or for the dubious privilege of caring for a child by herself. The rapid rise in illegitimacy hardly exalts the "emancipation" of women.

FORCED MARRIAGES—Illicit pregnancies almost as often lead to marriage as to illegitimate births. In 1965 the number of marriages in which the bride was pregnant was approximately 250,000. Since in a high proportion of these marriages, the original sex relations were casual and the couple immature, the marriage is usually ill-advised. In the period 1964–1966 in the United States, 65 percent of all premaritally conceived but legitimate first births were to girls *under 20 when the child was born,* whereas among all legitimately conceived births only 24 percent were to such young mothers.[37] As is well known, young marriages are highly unstable.[38] The marriages in which the bride is not only young but pregnant are the least stable of all. Insofar as premarital pregnancy leads to forced marriages, it leads to tragedy.

ABORTIONS—Since contraception is readily available to anyone who wants it in nearly any advanced nation, illicit pregnancy today is due mainly to carelessness. Once conception has occurred, however, further troubles are due not solely to further carelessness but also to laws which, in many countries, still make abortion illegal and therefore dangerous and expensive. After World War II Japan and some Scandinavian and East European countries

---

[35] See *Trends in Illegitimacy, United States, 1940–65,* Series 21, No. 15 (Washington, D. C.: National Center for Health Statistics, February, 1968), pp. 17–21; also the National Center's studies of infant mortality in Denmark, Norway, and Great Britain, Series 3.

[36] Among the illegitimate children born in Minnesota in 1952, 53 percent were adopted and 11 percent legitimized by age 10. Cited in *Trends in Illegitimacy, United States, 1940–65,* p. 21. Clark Vincent, *Unmarried Mothers,* pp. 186–87, found that more of his unwed mothers wanted to give up the child than keep it.

[37] Computed from "Interval Between First Marriage and Legitimate First Birth, United States, 1964–66," *Monthly Vital Statistics Report,* Vol. 18, No. 12 (Washington, D. C.: National Center for Health Statistics, supplement, March 27, 1970).

[38] In 1965, 49 percent of American women getting divorces were married at ages under 20, whereas during the eight preceding years (when most of those getting divorced were married) only 39 percent of all brides were under that age. See "Divorce Statistics Analysis, United States, 1964 and 1965," Series 21, No. 17 (Washington, D. C.: National Center for Health Statistics), p. 31.

enacted legislation allowing abortion on liberal grounds. The change doubt-less dampened the otherwise rising trend in illegitimacy. In Japan, for ex-ample, the decline in illegitimacy after liberalization of the abortion laws was spectacular: The ratio dropped from 3.8 percent of all births in 1947 to 1.0 percent in 1964. In Norway and Sweden, where abortion laws were liberalized, the rise in illegitimacy after 1940 was much less than in the United States or Britain, where liberalization did not begin until the late 1960's. In the United States, Colorado led off in 1967 by allowing abortion in case of rape or incest or when the mother's health or the child's heredity is at risk. By 1970 some 14 states had enacted similar legislation, and three of them — Alaska, Hawaii, and New York — had gone even further to make abortion in the first months of pregnancy a matter to be determined by a woman and her doctor. In addition, appellate courts tended to treat as un-constitutional the old laws forbidding abortion, since they in effect force women to have children against their will. The greatest resort to abortion comes, however, when the costs are reduced as well as the grounds liber-alized. By 1970 in the United States the costs had not been reduced suffi-ciently to enable the women of the poorer classes to obtain the operation readily. When abortion is made legal, safe, and virtually free, it effectively helps to prevent illegitimate births and forced marriages, regardless of the extent of premarital coitus or the effectiveness of the available contraceptives.

VENEREAL DISEASE — Another problem associated with sex freedom — venereal disease — is underestimated for two reasons: *first,* the underreporting of the well-known venereal diseases, and *second,* the public unawareness of other venereal diseases. With respect to syphilis, gonorrhea, and chancroid, phy-sicians often refuse to report cases even though required to do so by law. In addition, chronic gonorrhea is difficult to diagnose, particularly in women. As a consequence, all statistics on V.D. are undercounts, and trends are affected to an unknown degree by changes in the extent of reporting. How-ever, even the reported figures are sizable, the trends generally upward. The frequency is ironic, because modern prevention and treatment could either eliminate or greatly reduce these diseases.

Almost all countries reporting to the World Health Organization showed a high incidence of gonorrhea soon after World War II. There was then a decline that reached a trough about 1951–1952 and remained there for three to five years, and next a sharp rise again in most countries.[39] "Viewed

---

[39] R. S. Morton, *Venereal Diseases* (Baltimore: Penguin Books, 1966), p. 33. In the United States the number of reported civilian cases was 313,363 in 1945, fell to 236,197 in 1955, and rose again to 404,836 in 1967. See *Statistical Abstract of the United States* (Washington, D. C.: U. S. Department of Commerce, 1969), p. 77.

globally," says one authority, "we find something of a general paradox, in that the more highly developed countries, with the best arrangements, seem to have the highest incidences." [40] The ratio of male to female cases varies between 2:1 and 6:1, not because males have more gonorrhea than females, but because "most females infected are asymptomatic carriers" who less often get diagnosed and reported unless a special effort is made to find them as contacts of male cases.[41] Despite underreporting, gonorrhea is now becoming the most commonly reported infectious disease in advanced countries. It is by far the most important cause of sterility.[42] In about 10 percent of women who have the disease, inflammation of the Fallopian tubes (salpingitis) occurs, and approximately 20 percent of such cases result in permanent infecundity. Sometimes, chronic arthritis also results from the disease, and if the gonococci infect the eyes of a baby at parturition, blindness is likely to occur without treatment.

The statistical record for syphilis looks better. In England and Wales, infectious syphilis rose sharply to a peak in 1946 (immediately after World War II), declined thereafter, and did not rise again, and then by not much, until about 1959.[43] In the United States the drop after 1945 in cases reported was less spectacular, but a brief upturn in the 1950's was not sustained, the number of cases in 1967 being lower than in any year since World War II.[44] Although deaths attributable to syphilis have declined sharply, the disease

---

[40] R. S. Morton, *Venereal Diseases*, p. 35.

[41] *Ibid.,* p. 36.

[42] In groups with high rates of venereal infection, childlessness is correspondingly high unless there is a thorough system of V.D. detection and treatment. In the United States in 1960, for example, nonwhite women in large cities had an extremely high rate of childlessness. Of those aged 40–44 ever married, more than 29 percent reported never bearing a child. See United States Census of Population, 1960, *Women by Number of Children Ever Born* (Final Report PC(2)-3A), p. 18 and Wilson H. Grabill and Paul C. Glick, "Demographic and Social Aspects of Childlessness: Census Data," *Milbank Memorial Fund Quarterly,* Vol. 37 (1959), pp. 1–27.

[43] R. S. Morton, *Venereal Diseases*, p. 40.

[44]	REPORTED CIVILIAN CASES		DEATHS FROM SYPHILIS (Per 100,000 Population)
	Gonorrhea	Syphilis	
1940			14.4
1945	313,363	351,767	10.6
1950	286,746	217,558	5.0
1955	236,197	122,392	2.3
1960	258,933	122,003	1.6
1965	324,925	112,842	1.3
1967	404,836	102,581	1.2

Sources: *Vital Statistics of the United States, 1940–1960* (Washington, D. C.: National Center for Health Statistics), p. 388; and *Statistical Abstract of the United States, 1969,* pp. 58, 77.

still kills more people in the United States than do complications associated with pregnancy and childbirth. Also, the decline is due to improved treatment, not to a drop in *new* cases. In fact, the number of new cases has tended to rise in the United States, as in England, since around 1955. Then the reported incidence of primary and secondary syphilis was 6516 cases (6.1 per 100,000 population); by 1966 it was 22,473 cases (11.6 per 100,000).[45]

Antibiotics in the late 1930's and early 1940's led to the belief that V.D. would be eliminated, if attitudes would change. "We could eliminate venereal diseases in a couple of years at the cost of one or two battleships, but we are not doing so," [46] said a physician in 1943. He attributed the failure to puritanical attitudes in "middle class countries." [47] Three decades later, however, after a great relaxation of sexual restrictions, V.D. was epidemic. The gonococcus and spirochete had evolved strains resistant to penicillin and other widely used antibiotics.[48] Furthermore, rising promiscuity, especially among teen-agers, and the apparently growing contribution of homosexual contacts, had increased the number of undetected carriers.

Among all types of bodily contact, sexual intercourse is the most intimate, moist, and prolonged — an ideal means for the transmission of disease. Not surprising, then, is the recent discovery that other diseases are transmitted in this way. One of these, nonspecific urethritis in the male, may be the cause of Reiter's syndrome, involving arthritis and inflammation of the eyes.[49] A common female disease apparently transmitted by coitus is trichomonal vaginitis.[50] But more disturbing is the discovery that cervical cancer is spread venereally. Women who start coitus early and have numerous sex partners, and wives whose husbands are promiscuous, appear more susceptible than others.[51]

All told, the hazards of premarital intercourse are not slight. For the woman, they seem to outweigh the advantages. At least under the old system there was a sense of a fair bargain. Under contemporary conditions, there is hardly any system of premarital conduct; it is each for himself. Many get hurt. Let us now turn to another problem.

---

[45] Ward L. Oliver and George M. Warner, "The Resurgence of Venereal Disease: The Syphilis Problem Today," *Health News,* Vol. 40 (June, 1963), p. 10; and United States Public Health Service, *Venereal Disease Fact Sheet, 1966.*

[46] Henry E. Sigerist, *Civilization and Disease* (Ithaca, N. Y.: Cornell University Press, 1943), p. 238.

[47] *Ibid.,* p. 78.

[48] See T. Guthe, "Failure to Control Gonorrhoea," *Bulletin of the World Health Organization,* Vol. 24 (1961), pp. 297–306.

[49] R. S. Morton, *Venereal Diseases,* p. 98.

[50] *Ibid.,* pp. 100–07.

[51] *American Journal of Public Health,* Vol. 57 (May, 1967), pp. 803–29, 840–47.

PROSTITUTION

Among the types of extramarital coitus, prostitution is noteworthy for the ambivalence it evokes. Often officially condemned, it is nevertheless defended as an escape valve for pent-up sexual energy. Although the prostitute enjoys the closest intimacy with men in all walks of life, she is not exalted but is rather disesteemed. Frequent attempts to outlaw and limit prostitution are failures, because the institution thrives whether banned or not.

How are we to explain the ambivalence? It cannot be explained in terms of consequences. If prostitution has bad effects, these are the result, not the cause, of the attitude toward it. Its effect in spreading venereal disease is as much because of carelessness as because of prostitution itself. Its close association with organized crime and neighborhood deterioration is explained by its social ostracism, not by prostitution per se. It must be, then, that popular disapproval of prostitution occurs precisely because it has no consequences. It is regarded as a vice—something intrinsically evil—and is approved only when it is made to serve socially desired goals. Why societies maintain an institution that they simultaneously condemn is an interesting question.

The present discussion will focus on female prostitution, with only occasional references to male prostitution.[52] Necessarily, we must get beyond the superficial view either that prostitution can be readily abolished or that its persistence is due simply to "human nature." We must seek to understand the ways in which prostitution is bound to other institutions, particularly those involving sexual relations.

Why the Attitudes Toward Prostitution?

Prostitution is officially condemned in contemporary industrial societies mainly because it fulfills no recognized goal.[53] The norms of every society

---

[52] A chapter on homosexual prostitution, with numerous references, can be found in Harry Benjamin and R. E. L. Masters, *Prostitution and Morality* (New York: Julian Press, 1964).

[53] Defense of prostitution was common in the 1930's when reformers aiming to stamp it out, or at least get rid of "red light districts," were most active. See, for ex-

tend to link the sexual act to some stable, or potentially stable, social relationship. This is hard to do, but for this very reason, the moral condemnation of promiscuity is strong. Men consider women as sexual property to be prohibited to other males. They therefore find promiscuity on the part of women repugnant. Since one woman can satisfy many men, the prostitute is more promiscuous than her customers. Her extreme promiscuity brings her into disrepute.

Her willingness to *sell* her favors and her feeling of *emotional indifference* are also condemned, but, from a moral point of view, there is nothing wrong with either of these. A wife who submits dutifully but reluctantly to intercourse is often considered virtuous for that reason, although she is expected to cherish her husband in a spiritual sense. The trading of sexual favors for a consideration is what is done in marriage, for in consenting to get married a woman exchanges her sexual favors for economic support. As long as the bargain struck is one that achieves a stable relationship, especially a marriage, the mores offer praise rather than condemnation for the trade. The prostitute's affront is that she trades promiscuously.[54]

Both prostitution and the prostitute herself rise in social esteem insofar as one or more of three conditions are present: (1) The promiscuity is lessened by some basis of choice; (2) the earnings of prostitution are used for a goal considered socially desirable; (3) the prostitute combines other roles with that of sexual gratification.

---

ample, T. Swann Harding, "The Endless War on 'Vice,'" *Medical Record,* April 20, 1938. Since that time, the reformist zeal and the liberal's defense both seem to have ebbed. Prostitution seems less a public issue than it was from 1910 to 1940.

Although hounded by the police, the streetwalker is not necessarily felt to be objectionable by the public at large. A survey conducted by *McCalls Magazine* and reported there in February, 1965, found that only 7 percent of the persons questioned said they would bother to clear the streets of prostitutes if they had the chance. Conducted in New York City and Newark, New Jersey, the survey found that 67 percent said they would not clear the streets of prostitution if they could, and another 26 percent gave no opinion, leaving only 7 percent who would definitely take action.

A readable account of the history of organized prostitution and organized reform movements in New York City is to be found in John M. Murtagh and Sara Harris, *Cast the First Stone* (New York: McGraw-Hill, 1957).

[54] An opinion survey in Britain in 1949 showed that "Marriage is still regarded as the vitally important center of sex relationship, and only one person in six condones prostitution. But . . . there is a fairly widespread belief that many cases of extramarital and premarital relationships have a good justification, and often people who are living together without being married are cited as providing a better 'example' than the married." L. R. England, "Little Kinsey: An Outline of Sex Attitudes in Britain" in Jerome Himelhoch and Sylvia Fleis Fava, eds., *Sexual Behavior in American Society* (New York: Norton, 1955), p. 350.

In ancient Greece, the lowest were those who practiced in brothels. The brothels were open to anybody who had the price, which was not high, and were concentrated mainly in the neighborhood of docks and markets. In many ways they resembled the houses in the red light districts of the United States a few decades ago. Ranking almost as low were the streetwalkers, but far above both were the *hetairae,* who were distinguished by being educated in the arts, by being available only to the wealthy and powerful, and by providing entertainment and intellectual companionship as well as sexual gratification. The hetairae were a focus of Greek cultural and literary interests. Their portrait statues appeared in public buildings alongside those of the great men. They were the heroines of plays and poems,[55] even influential in public affairs. Aspasia, daughter of the most celebrated of the Greek hetairae, became Pericles' concubine, supplanting his wife. Her house became the center of Athenian literary and philosophical society, frequented by no less a person than Socrates. The hetairae, drawn from the alien population, were providers of entertainment and intellectual companionship because respectable wives and daughters (that is, women of Greek citizen families) were not permitted to entertain, get outside the home, or acquire an education. Often cited in this connection is a statement attributed to Demosthenes: "Man has the hetairae for erotic enjoyments, concubines for daily use, and wives of equal rank to bring up children and to be faithful housewives." [56] Yet the *hetairae* were not respectable. They had a reputation for being faithless, avaricious, vain, and shrewd.[57]

Similarly, Japan until recently had three classes of women outside of respectable family life—the *joro* in brothels; the *jogoku,* or unlicensed prostitutes on the streets or in bath houses; and the *geisha,* or dancing girls. The last-named were taken as little girls, often by arrangement with their parents and sometimes through adoption by the proprietors of the *geisha ya.* Trained in dancing, singing, samisen playing, and other methods of entertaining guests in tea houses, geisha girls were an indispensable adjunct at every Japanese entertainment. Not all of them were open to prostitution; and even if they were, they were selective as to type of customer. They were usually available as concubines, and some of them married.

Witty, quick at repartee, pretty, and always well dressed, — the geisha has proved a formidable rival for the demure, quiet maiden of good

---

[55] Hans Licht, *Sexual Life in Ancient Greece* (London: Routledge, 1932), pp. 332–63, 395–410.

[56] Cited in *ibid.,* p. 399. See also Alfred Zimmern, *The Greek Commonwealth* (Oxford: Clarendon Press, 1931), pp. 341–44.

[57] Hans Licht, *Sexual Life in Ancient Greece,* pp. 354–56, 358–63.

family, who can only give her husband an unsullied name, silent obedience, and faithful service all her life.[58]

Prostitution may also enjoy social esteem by association with religion. Throughout much of the ancient world, including Greece apart from Athens,[59] prostitutes were associated with religious temples and took part in religious and liturgical ceremonies. In India until recently the temples contained dancing girls. The Abbé Dubois, describing southern India as he saw it during the years 1792 to 1823, had this to say:

> The courtesans or dancing-girls attached to each temple . . . are called *deva-dasis* (servants or slaves of the gods), but the public call them by the more vulgar name of prostitutes. . . .
> The courtesans are the only women in India who enjoy the privilege of learning to read, to dance, and to sing. A well-bred and respectable woman would for this reason blush to acquire any one of these accomplishments.[60]

Religious prostitution differs from commercial prostitution because the woman is a religious ministrant, the money given her can be used for religious purposes, and the act of intercourse itself can be viewed as religious ritual.[61] Similar considerations apply to the type of prostitution in which the girl obtains a dowry for her subsequent marriage.[62]

In modern society all that is left of the types of prostitution is the purely commercial form in which both parties use sex for a purpose not socially acceptable, the one for pleasure, the other for money. To tie intercourse to sheer pleasure is to divorce it both from reproduction and from any sentimental social relationship. To tie it simply to money does the same. Purely commercial prostitution and the women who practice it will be denigrated in any society.

---

[58] Alice Bacon, *Japanese Girls and Women,* rev. and enl. ed. (Boston: Houghton Mifflin, 1919), first published in 1891, pp. 286–87, 288–89.

[59] Hans Licht, *Sexual Life in Ancient Greece,* pp. 388–95.

[60] Abbé J. A. Dubois, *Hindu Manners, Customs, and Ceremonies,* 3rd ed. (Oxford: Clarendon Press, 1906), pp. 584–86.

[61] Edward Westermarck, *Origin and Development of Moral Ideas* (London: Macmillan, 1908), Vol. 1, p. 224: "In Morocco supernatural benefits are to this day expected not only from heterosexual but also from homosexual intercourse with a holy person."

[62] Havelock Ellis, *Studies in the Psychology of Sex* (Philadelphia: Davis, 1913), Vol. 6, p. 233.

The "Causes" of Prostitution

Why is it that an occupation so disrespected should find recruits? Under the influence of the great Depression and Marxism, the "cause" of prostitution was frequently said to be economic. Since prostitution is defined as selling sexual favors, the fact that it has economic causes should hardly occasion surprise. One might as well say, with equal perspicacity, that retail merchandising has economic causes. The assumption is often made that the sole question concerns the factors leading women to enter the business. Actually, there are at least five separable questions: (1) the causes of the *existence of prostitution;* (2) the causes of the *different forms or types* of prostitution; (3) the causes of the *rate or amount* of prostitution; (4) the causes leading *some women to enter* and others not to enter the profession; and (5) the causes leading *some men to patronize,* and others not to patronize, the prostitute. Let us keep these separate questions in mind.

On the physical side, it is to be noted that the human female has no *season* of sexual dormancy. This introduces sex as a permanent element in social life and insures constant association of the two sexes. Further, sexual behavior is not simply automatic but is linked with numerous nonsexual stimuli. The sexual response may thus be used not only (or not at all) for the individual's own erotic gratification, but as a means to some ulterior purpose. This being true, the next question is why it should be used for money or other valuable favors. Here the roles of the family and social stratification are relevant. The demand for the prostitute's services arises out of the strictly limited liability of the relationship. Regardless of the situation giving rise to the customer's erotic desire, he can obtain satisfaction if he has the money, with no further obligations. He does not become enmeshed in "courtship," "friendship," or "marriage." Every male finds himself at one time or another in circumstances where release through more reputable channels is impossible. Furthermore the division of labor by sex inevitably makes women dependent to some extent on their sexual attractiveness and puts men in control of economic means. Since the economic means are distributed unequally between classes but female attractiveness is not, some women of lower economic means can exploit their attractiveness for economic gain.

For these reasons the demand for prostitution is broadly based and inextinguishable. This is why, when prostitution is outlawed, it falls into a category of crime that is notoriously hard to control — the type in which one of the guilty parties is the ordinary law-abiding citizen, who is receiving an illicit service. It is economically and politically foolish to punish a large number of a society's productive and otherwise orderly members. To throw good citizens into jail for a vice that injures no one, would cause more social disruption than correcting the alleged crime would be worth.

> The professional prostitute being a social outcast may be periodically punished without disturbing the usual course of society; no one misses her while she is serving out her turn—no one, at least, about whom society has any concern. The man, however, is something more than partner in an immoral act: he discharges important social and business relations, is as father or brother responsible for the maintenance of others, has commercial or industrial duties to meet. He cannot be imprisoned without deranging society.[63]

However, not all males visit prostitutes, nor do those who do necessarily depend on them for a major share of their sexual outlet. In Kinsey's sample of white American males, about 30 percent never have any contact with these women at all. Of the rest, many "never have more than a single experience or two, and not more than 15 or 20 percent of them ever have such relations more often than a few times a year, over as much as a five-year period in their lives." [64] This still leaves a substantial portion of the adult male population. For them, what does prostitution provide that other outlets do not provide?

One advantage of prostitution is precisely its impartiality and impersonality. The exacting requirements of attracting and persuading a female, or perhaps getting entangled with her in courtship or even marriage, are unnecessary. All that is needed is the cash. Kinsey states that before World War II the average cost of intercourse with a prostitute "was less than the cost of a single supper date with a girl who was not a prostitute." [65] By its very effort to make the sex drive part of a meaningful and enduring social relationship, society creates advantages for prostitution. For instance, the impersonality of prostitution makes it particularly suited to strangers. The man away from his wife or the circle of girls that he knows, cannot in a short time count on seducing a respectable woman in the place he happens to be. Also, by defining certain coital techniques as immoral and hence out of bounds for wives and sweethearts, the moral order gives an advantage to the prostitute. Further, the man who is in a stable relationship with a woman and who theoretically should have ample opportunity for more legitimate sexual expression, may nevertheless find such expression thwarted by the vicissitudes of interpersonal relations. "The common and ignorant assump-

---

[63] Abraham Flexner, *Prostitution in Europe* (New York: Century, 1920), p. 108.
[64] Alfred C. Kinsey *et al., Sexual Behavior in the Human Male,* p. 597.
[65] *Ibid.,* p. 607.

tion that prostitution exists to satisfy the gross sensuality of the young un-married man, and that if he is taught to bridle gross sexual impulse or induced to marry early, the prostitute must be idle, is altogether incorrect." [66]

Seen in this light, the demand for prostitution will not be eliminated or seriously altered by a change in the economic system. The underlying basis for the demand is inherent in human society and therefore not subject to change by economic reform alone.

The economic thesis is scarcely more satisfactory on the supply side. It used to be said that prostitution could be abolished or seriously curtailed if the salaries of working girls were raised, or that it could be abolished by getting rid of the capitalist system. Such a view rests on the assumption that girls enter the profession because of economic necessity – a view that can most easily be seen to be false if we assume it to be true. Why, for example, should a girl enter prostitution only when she is forced to by financial need? Is the occupation so arduous? On the contrary, we often speak as if harlots "would rather prostitute themselves than work." [67] The interesting question is not why so many women become prostitutes, but why so few of them do.

The answer of course is that the return is not primarily a reward for labor, skill, or capital, but a reward for loss of social standing. The prostitute loses esteem because the moral system – especially when prostitution is purely commercial – condemns her. If, then, she refuses to take up the profession until forced by sheer want, the basic cause of her hesitation is not economic but moral.

The wages of prostitution are far above the wages of ordinary women's work. "No practicable rise in the rate of wages paid to women in ordinary industries can possibly compete with the wages which fairly attractive women of quite ordinary ability can earn by prostitution." [68]

---

[66] Havelock Ellis, *Studies in the Psychology of Sex*, pp. 295–96. Kinsey's sample, *Sexual Behavior in the Human Male*, p. 288, shows that, age for age, a greater proportion of the unmarried male's sexual expression is with prostitutes than is that of the married man. (At age 21–25 the ratio is 5.4 to 1; at age 26–30, it is 7.5 to 1; at age 31–35, it is 11.5 to 1.) Above age 25, however, the number of married men is so much greater than the number of single men that the clientele of prostitutes is mostly composed of married men, despite the fact that less of the married man's sexual experience is with such women.

[67] W. L. George's novel, *Bed of Roses*, vividly contrasts the hard life of the working girl with the easy life of the prostitute. The novel by Caroline Slade, *Sterile Sun*, does not depict the work as particularly arduous. The economic justification is a rationalization. The title of Sheila Cousins' autobiographical account, *To Beg I Am Ashamed*, illustrates the self-exculpation.

[68] Havelock Ellis, *Studies in the Psychology of Sex*, p. 263. "There are call-girls who earn between fifty and a hundred thousand dollars a year." John M. Murtagh and Sara Harris, *Cast the First Stone*, p. 2.

In a book, *Red Virtue*,[69] published in 1933, when the Soviet Union was regarded as utopia, there was a chapter entitled "Ending Prostitution," at the head of which stood a quotation from a Soviet physician: "Soviet life does not permit of prostitution." Widely accepted in the 1930's, this belief was used as evidence that capitalism is the basic cause of prostitution. In 1959, a reporter who had just completed a long stay in Russia had this to say:

> A stroller in the central Moscow streets of an early evening is apt to be approached near big hotels. The women are strange sights — heavily rouged, gaunt-faced and costumed as in sketches by Hogarth.
> Around the Hotel Astoria in Leningrad prostitutes may also be seen. Typically, the Leningrad women are smartly attired, affect high heels and pony-tail hairdos.[70]

It will take more than communism to eliminate the world's oldest profession. The changes the Russians tried to make are in fact much like the changes all industrial countries try to make. They all combat the organized aspects of prostitution, legislating against third parties — pimps, madams, landlords, bookers — who abet and profit from prostitution. The reason is clear. A vice to which large sections of the public are addicted is potentially profitable to those who organize it. If not officially organized, it will be run by private entrepreneurs, and if banned it will be run by criminal syndicates. Pandering to forbidden pleasures can become big business, as shown by bootlegging in India and the United States under prohibition and by black-market operations under wartime trading controls. If illegal big business were allowed to operate with no official harassment, control of the vice in question would be nullified. Any government that undertakes to restrict a vice must be prepared to make war on the organizations that inevitably spring up to cater to it.

In the case of prostitution, the vice syndicates did a fabulous business in the United States earlier in the century, when they were linked to bootlegging. In 1927 William Hale Thompson was returned to office as mayor of Chicago with the help of a fund, alleged to be $5,000,000, which organized vice and crime had paid his machine. The following year, two thousand vice establishments were reported to be spending $100 to $750 per week for police protection. The only threat to vice kings such as Al Capone, Dan Jackson, and Jack Zuta was murder by competitors or prosecution by federal tax authorities. Al Capone's delinquent taxes for the years 1924–1929 were

---

[69] Ella Winter, *Red Virtue* (New York: Harcourt Brace Jovanovich, 1933).
[70] Harrison Salisbury, *The New York Times,* Sept. 10, 1959, p. 10.

originally estimated to be $1,038,654, but in the course of his trial they were scaled down to $266,000.[71] In 1936, "Motzie" Di Nicola, overlord of a chain of Connecticut vice resorts, was sentenced to seven years in a federal penitentiary for income-tax evasion. His business in prostitution yielded approximately $2,500,000 annually.[72]

Organized crime continued to find prostitution profitable, but the link with bootlegging was replaced by labor-union racketeering, coin-machine control, record pirating, and pornographic activity. In 1954, two underworld figures from Seattle worked out a scheme to take over vice operations in Portland, Oregon. With top officials of the Teamsters Union, they elected a district attorney who then worked with them to set up facilities for pinball, punchboard, and card-room operations, off-track betting, and prostitution. The Teamsters Union threatened to stop deliveries to restaurants, cafeterias, and bars that refused to use the syndicate's equipment.[73] Such underworld activities show that legislation against third parties in prostitution [74] has only partial success. Commercial sex has a chameleon-like adaptability, fitting itself to whatever conditions prevail at the time. By 1970 the expansion of drug abuse and the consequent demand for narcotics brought a new phase to organized prostitution.

Mary is only 15. Until a couple of weeks ago, she worked as a prostitute . . . to support her "old man," an 18-year-old heroin addict.

. . . prostitution and heroin addiction [among residents of Potrero Hill, a section of San Francisco] are spreading to the very young at a startling rate. . . .

A girl hustling on the streets can make up to $400 or more a night, depending on where she works. Territories are strictly enforced. . . .

At Everett Junior High it was said that groups of ninth grade boys often deal in narcotics and prostitution, with seventh and eighth grade girls "turning tricks." . . .[75]

---

[71] Walter C. Reckless, *Vice in Chicago* (Chicago: University of Chicago Press, 1933), Chapter 3.

[72] *The New York Times,* November 11, 1936. See also John M. Murtagh and Sara Harris, *Cast the First Stone,* Chapters 12–13.

[73] Robert F. Kennedy, *The Enemy Within* (New York: Popular Library, 1960), pp. 245–50.

[74] See United Nations, "The Suppression of the Traffic in Persons and of the Exploitation of the Prostitution of Others," Document E/CN.5/338 (New York: United Nations, March 26, 1959).

[75] *San Francisco Chronicle,* March 10, 1970, p. 4.

Prostitution and Sexual Freedom

With the rise of sex freedom among single, widowed, and divorced women, the role of prostitution has necessarily declined. Kinsey found that his males of recent generations were down to two-thirds to one-half the frequencies of contact with prostitutes recorded by the older generation.[76] "The frequencies of coitus with females who were not prostitutes had increased to an extent which largely compensated for the decreased frequencies with prostitutes." [77]

If we reverse the proposition that increased sex freedom among women of all classes reduces the role of prostitution, we find ourselves admitting that increased prostitution can reduce the sexual irregularities of respectable women. This, in fact, has been the ancient justification for tolerated prostitution — that it "protected" the family and kept the wives and daughters of the respectable citizenry pure.[78] Such a view seems paradoxical, because in popular thought an evil such as prostitution cannot cause a good such as feminine virtue, or vice versa. Yet, as our analysis has implied throughout, there is a close connection between prostitution and the structure of the family.

In practice, the contemporary attitude toward prostitution is one of tolerance for the thing itself as a necessary evil, but intolerance of its open manifestation; pity for the prostitute, and loathing of the pimp. Hence the fight to eliminate third parties and open manifestations. In Britain, for example, prostitution itself is not illegal, and the Wolfenden report recommended against making it so.[79] But the laws are being tightened to penalize street solicitation, the maintenance of a brothel, the willful taking of rent derived from habitual prostitution in the premises, and so forth. People do not wish to see streetwalkers or to live in a building or a block where men in large numbers are seen visiting women. As long as people do not see it, they can forget about prostitution.

---

[76] Alfred C. Kinsey *et al., Sexual Behavior in the Human Male,* p. 411. He gives additional references substantiating this change.

[77] Alfred C. Kinsey *et al., Sexual Behavior in the Human Female,* p. 300.

[78] W. E. H. Lecky, *History of European Morals,* 3rd ed. rev. (London: Longmans, 1877), Vol. 2, pp. 282–83.

[79] *Report of the Committee on Homosexual Offences and Prostitution* (London: Her Majesty's Stationery Office, 1957, Cmnd. 247), p. 79. It is not illegal in the United States either under common law, but is made so by statute in many states.

Why modern societies pursue the path of female premarital sex freedom instead of the path of companionate prostitution has already been answered. It is a function of the social mobility and anonymity inevitably associated with an urban-industrial system. The difference between an educated prostitute and a citizen wife in a small town like Athens was known to everyone. In Paris, New York, or Moscow the case is different. There the girls capable of being high-class prostitutes will enter marriage by preference, and movement in and out of the profession will make status distinctions difficult and pointless. In other words, in a complex mobile society any sexual status except marriage is a temporary and anonymous one for a woman. Prostitution is seldom a permanent occupation; it is pursued at the age when it is most lucrative and then abandoned.

The most persistent form of prostitution is the pure commercial form. Whether in brothels or in the streets, under bridges or in automobiles, this form is practiced everywhere and remains at the bottom of the social scale. Although its scope may be reduced by sex freedom and "amateur competition," the practice itself is not likely to be displaced. Not only will there always be a system of social dominance that gives a motive for selling sexual favors, and a scale of attractiveness that creates the need for buying them, but this form of prostitution is, in the last analysis, economical. Enabling a small number of women to take care of the needs of a large number of men, it is the most convenient sexual outlet for armies and for the legions of strangers, perverts, and physically repulsive in our midst. It performs a role which apparently no other institution fully performs.

HOMOSEXUAL BEHAVIOR

To understand the attitudes toward homosexuality, we must recall that some of the strongest sexual norms are those defining permissible partners. Masturbation involves no partner at all; adultery, a partner other than one's spouse; homosexuality, a partner of the same sex. Yet the community's view depends to some extent on other considerations as well. It depends, for example, on whether the homosexual relation is emotionally indifferent (the partner being merely a substitute for the opposite sex) or is sentimental, and whether the individual's behavior is exclusively or merely occasionally homosexual.

How Widely Is Homosexuality Disapproved?

Critics of our society often imply that we rigidly taboo homosexuality and that this attitude is abnormal. The public, it is said, needs to be "educated to accept" sexual deviancy. The facts are different. To be sure, the public disapproves of obligate homosexuality and stigmatizes those who openly manifest it, but this is far from being an absolute "taboo." Unable to stop the practice, people tolerate it to a considerable extent and, in effect, refuse to treat homosexuality per se as a crime. Even the laws do not ban homosexuality as such; they confine themselves to specific sexual acts usual in homosexual relations, to public indecency, and to corruption of minors. Lesbianism is usually not legislated against at all.[80]

The search for societies that approve of homosexuality yields little. In all complex civilizations there are those who engage in homosexual practices and intellectuals who apologize for them. Accordingly, for historical civilizations, literary evidence can always be cited as documents of approval or toleration, but when one tries to assess the general public attitude, evidence is scarce. A picture of the ancient Greeks as idealizing homosexuality has been painted by Hans Licht, citing art and literature. There can be no doubt that beginning with the fifth century B.C. the love of juveniles was idealized by the literati and that male prostitution was practiced,[81] but Athens was a small city and its people were suspicious of the intellectuals. Anaxagoras was condemned and exiled for impiety; Protagoras was expelled from the city and his books burned; Socrates was condemned to death. These men were charged with "corruption of youth," which probably meant disrespect for Athenian institutions. In reaction, Greek parents of the citizen class put great care into the education of their sons.

> Far from casting out their sons into public schools, with the full knowledge that they will there lose all their simplicity and innocence, Greek parents of the better sort kept their sons constantly under the eye of a slave tutor or pedagogue, . . . who never let them out of their sight.[82]

---

[80] See Morris Ploscowe, *Sex and the Law* (Englewoods Cliffs, N. J.: Prentice-Hall, 1951), Chapter 7; Robert V. Sherwin, "Laws on Sex Crimes," *Encyclopedia of Sexual Behavior* (New York: Hawthorn Books, 1961), pp. 626–27; *Report of the Committee on Homosexual Offences and Prostitution,* pp. 149–51.

[81] Hans Licht, *Sexual Life in Ancient Greece.*

[82] J. P. Mahaffy, *Social Life in Greece,* 5th ed. (London: Macmillan, 1883), p. 331. H. D. Kitto argues that the ordinary male citizen of Athens took a deep interest in his family. See *The Greeks* (Baltimore: Penguin Books, 1951), pp. 219–36.

Actual public opinion concerning homosexual relations in the various periods of ancient Greece will never be known. The hypothesis of general approval seems unproved. The Romans, after losing their early rustic morality, evidently tolerated a considerable amount of homosexuality, and the poets of the empire adopted a matter-of-fact attitude toward it.[83] However, ascetic and stoic philosophy was also strong in Rome, and again it seems difficult to document actual public opinion in this matter. The Hebrew moral code strongly condemned homosexuality, as did that of classical Hinduism, but without preventing homosexual behavior or homosexual prostitution.[84] In sum, highly complex societies seem to tolerate a certain amount of homosexual behavior (and literary praise of it) without giving it respect.[85] The law may be permissive even when public attitudes are negative. The British royal commission's report in 1957 recommended "that homosexual behavior between consenting adults in private be no longer a criminal offense." [86] Eventually enacted into law, this did not mean that the British public favored homosexuality. A Gallup Poll taken shortly after the report was issued showed 38 percent favoring legalization, 47 percent against, and 15 percent uncertain.[87] One can favor legalization and still detest the behavior.

---

[83] Otto Kiefer, *Sexual Life in Rome* (New York: Dutton, 1935), Chapter 5.

[84] Robert Wood, "Sex Life in Ancient Civilizations," *Encyclopedia of Sexual Behavior,* pp. 130–31; and Jelal M. Shah, "Sex Life in India and Pakistan," *ibid.,* pp. 533–34.

[85] Primitive societies furnish some examples of accepted but not esteemed homosexuality under restricted circumstances. "Nearly all societies," says George P. Murdock, "seek to confine marriage and sex relations to persons of complementary sex. Some permit homosexuality in specifically delimited contexts, and a very few manifest wide latitude in this respect." [George P. Murdock, *Social Structure,* p. 317.] Ford and Beach list, in a total of 77 societies, 49 (all primitive) in which "homosexual activities of one sort or another are considered normal and socially acceptable for certain members of the community." [Clellan S. Ford and Frank A. Beach, *Patterns of Sexual Behavior* (New York: Harper, 1951), p. 130.] Most of these cases represent acceptance of the berdache or transvestite. "The berdache is a male who dresses like a woman, performs woman's tasks, and adopts some aspects of the feminine role in sexual behavior with male partners." [*Ibid.*] The reversal of roles is rare in those societies and is not approved for men generally. The Chukchee shaman assuming the female role was "believed to have been involuntarily transformed by supernatural power and some men fear being thus changed. . . ." [*Ibid.,* p. 131.] Among the Lango of Uganda, the men who assumed the feminine role were "believed to be impotent and to have been afflicted by some supernatural agency." [*Ibid.*] In other words, the existence of institutionalized homosexuality does not necessarily mean that it has high standing in the scale of desirability or that it is widely practiced.

[86] *Report of the Committee on Homosexual Offences and Prostitution,* p. 115.

[87] J. E. Hall Williams, "Sex Offenses: The British Experience," *Law and Contemporary Problems,* Vol. 25 (Spring, 1960), pp. 354–55.

Why the Disapproval?

Homosexual intercourse is obviously incompatible with the family and the sexual bargaining system. The norms and attitudes required to support these institutions as a means of getting the business of reproduction and sexual allocation accomplished tend to downgrade homosexuality. In one sense, the threat to the main system of sex relations is least when homosexuality is purely instrumental—that is, when it is simply a means of sexual release; but in another sense, this conflicts with the seriousness of sexual matters. When boys indulge in sexual play among themselves as a passing sport in the absence of girls, or when prisoners are forced into it by their isolation, it carries little or no implication of a "homosexual way of life," and for that reason is only mildly censured. Nevertheless, it is denigrated because it treats sex as a purely organic release, whereas the intent of the rules is somehow to "civilize" the sex impulse by linking it with acceptable social relations and sentiments. Similarly, purely transitory homosexual encounters such as those that take place in public lavatories are considered degrading,[88] whereas durable homosexual relations involving affection are thought of as "elevating" sex to an emotional plane.[89] Homosexual devotion, however, directly competes with male-female relationships; it may even mimic heterosexual love, as when the pair pretend to be "married," set up "housekeeping" together, demand mutual fidelity, and distinguish between the dominant (masculine) and the subordinate (feminine) mate.[90]

---

[88] These are described in graphic detail by a minister-sociologist in Laud Humphreys, *Tearoom Trade: Impersonal Sex in Public Places* (Chicago: Aldine, 1970).

[89] Homosexual idealism, like the heterosexual kind, can be carried to the point of excluding physical consummation. Plato, for example, built his ideas of beauty and immortality around the idea of male friendship but frowned on the idea of physical contact, the "black horse" of the *Phaedrus*. One can see in such idealism the influence of the sexual norms that, in part, deprecate the purely organic part of sexual expression.

[90] If sex roles are assumed, the public in general and homosexuals themselves hold in low esteem the one who takes the physiologically inappropriate role. This is evidently due not only to the anatomical inappropriateness but also to the greater difficulty of resuming the normal heterosexual role. In prison populations it is most often the partner who has kept his regular sex role (the "femme" in lesbian and the "wolf" in homosexual relations) who returns to heterosexual conduct after release. Many of the dominant homosexuals in a women's prison prefer to remain fully dressed while they stimulate their subordinate partners—the reason apparently being that they hate to

One may object that this theory takes no account of changed conditions. Today the problem is not how to keep the birth rate high enough to top a high death rate, but how to keep the birth rate low enough to compensate for the low death rate. No longer are women categorically subordinate to men, and no longer is heterosexual behavior restricted by old fetters. Why should homosexuality continue to be denigrated?

Insofar as the question refers to the future, it is unanswerable because nobody knows the future. For the present, family ties seem to be particularly valued in industrial societies because they are virtually the only ones left that are both personal and enduring. People are married in higher proportion today than they were a century ago, and more couples have children than had them then. The complementarity of sex roles shows a surprising persistence. In contrast, homosexual relationships are notoriously unstable, in part because they are not reinforced by other bonds. As yet, there is no evidence that public opinion is abandoning its antipathy to the dedicated homosexual.

Why Homosexual Behavior?

If the public attitude is hostile, why does homosexual behavior occur? Kinsey found 37 percent of his white males and 13 percent of his white females had at some time or other had an overt homosexual experience, and 4 percent of the males and 1 percent of the females had been exclusively homosexual.[91]

These figures are suprisingly low; if accurate, they demonstrate the power of normative control. In regulating heterosexual behavior, each society inadvertently facilitates homosexual contacts. Boys are encouraged to be with boys, girls with girls, in dormitories, jails, and camps. Under such arrangements virtually every adolescent has opportunities for same-sex stimulation of the *faute de mieux* sort. Such incidents are not "homosexual" in an emotional or exclusive sense, and are generally not taken seriously, although their role in habit formation, if engaged in often, is undeniable. What deters young people from becoming emotionally committed to this

---

reveal to the partner the inescapable feminine character of their anatomy, which otherwise can be somewhat hidden by masculine clothing, hair style, and mannerisms. See David A. Ward and Gene G. Kassebaum, *Women's Prison: Sex and Social Structure* (Chicago: Aldine, 1965), pp. 179, 194.

[91] Alfred C. Kinsey, *Sexual Behavior in the Human Male,* pp. 650–51; and *Sexual Behavior in the Human Female,* pp. 474–75.

form of release is doubtless the negative evaluation of the homosexual by their peers and the fact that personal rewards are contingent on normal heterosexual relations. The few who turn into "true" homosexuals are presumably like the few drinkers who turn into confirmed alcoholics: They do so because they cannot make the normal adjustments in life. Relations between men and women tend to involve obligations and performance; they are caught up in a network of institutionalized expectations. To some persons, as a consequence, heterosexual satisfactions seem almost unattainable, or attainable at too high a price. By contrast, homosexual relations are less institutionalized; they seem less complicated and thus provide an escape from the demands of male-female involvement. The homosexual's problem "is not so much that he is attracted to males, but that he is in flight from females." [92] Once the homosexual habit is fixed by the reinforcement of frequent gratification, it becomes extraordinarily difficult to break.

That some homosexuals seek sentimental and emotional satisfaction as well as organic release is comprehensible. Sex is woven into social relations. One's self-image, one's motives and emotions, depend not on sheer physical gratification (which in itself has little more significance than defecation) but on the meaning of sexual activity as an expression of companionship and affection. It happens that in most aspects of life, one shares one's emotions with others of the same as well as different sex. It is a complex process for the growing individual to learn to discriminate between who is suitable for erotic feelings and who is not, especially since erotic motivation is often subtle and unrecognized as such. A relatively slight derangement in the mechanics of personal-social development—caused either by prolonged homosexual practice itself or by neurotic problems—may cause a failure in this discrimination.

A sociological theory of homosexual behavior does not preclude biological influence, but the main biological contribution appears to lie in the human capacity for conditioning. Beyond that, genetic determinism seems unlikely. Since homosexuals have a low rate of reproduction, any hereditary homosexual trait would be rapidly bred out of the population; only a frequently recurring homosexual mutation of some sort (say, a hormone abnormality) could counter such a trend. Possibly, genetic traits conducive to general personality weakness or neuroticism contribute to an exclusive homosexual adjustment, but the hypothesis awaits evidence.

That social factors play a role is demonstrated by differences in the amount and style of homosexual behavior from one society or group to

---

[92] Donald Webster Cory, "Homosexuality," *Encyclopedia of Sexual Behavior,* p. 492.

another. David A. Ward and Gene Kassebaum, two sociologists, began their study of a women's prison in California with the idea of analyzing personality types. They found lesbianism so prevalent (with at least 50 percent of the inmates participating) and so important in inmate social organization that they concentrated on that subject instead; this is why they entitled their book *Women's Prison: Sex and Social Structure*.[93] Donald Clemmer estimated that of 2300 adult male prisoners he studied, 30 percent were partly homosexual and 10 percent "true homosexuals." [94] Experiments show that homosexual behavior can be induced in rats. By supplying ample food and water to caged rats, allowing them to breed until very high population densities were reached, Calhoun observed homosexual as well as other pathological forms of behavior. "The general level of activity of these [homosexual] animals was only moderate. They were frequently attacked by their dominant associates, but they very rarely contended for status." [95]

Ward and Kassebaum describe how new prisoners are skillfully brought into lesbian activities by techniques of persuasion and compulsion.[96] In some primitive societies there is no homosexuality at all [97]; in most civilized societies there is a good deal of it. In some societies boys are reared to be homosexual prostitutes, and in still others *everybody* must temporarily engage in homosexual behavior as a sort of *rite de passage*.[98] "Observations of this nature emphasize the tremendous importance of early experience and social conditioning upon human sexuality." [99]

One might expect that homosexual behavior, like prostitution, would diminish in contemporary urban-industrial societies as heterosexual coitus becomes easier. In fact, however, the opposite seems true. The reasons may

---

[93] David A. Ward and Gene G. Kassebaum, *Women's Prison: Sex and Social Structure,* p. 92.

[94] Donald Clemmer, *The Prison Community* (New York: Rinehart, 1958), pp. 257–64, cited by David A. Ward and Gene G. Kassebaum, *Ibid.,* p. 94.

[95] John B. Calhoun, "Population Density and Social Pathology," *Scientific American,* Vol. 206 (February, 1962), p. 146.

[96] David A. Ward and Gene G. Kassebaum, *Women's Prison: Sex and Social Structure,* Chapter 6. See also Clellan S. Ford and Frank A. Beach, *Patterns of Sexual Behavior,* p. 126.

[97] In the Trobriand Islands, homosexuality "was known to exist in other tribes and regarded as a filthy and ridiculous practice. It cropped up in the Trobriands only with the influence of white man. . . . The boys and girls on a Mission Station, penned in separate and strictly isolated houses, cooped up together, had to help themselves out as best they could . . ." Bronislaw Malinowski, *Sex and Repression in Savage Society* (London: Kegan Paul, 1927), p. 90.

[98] Clellan S. Ford and Frank A. Beach, *Patterns of Sexual Behavior,* pp. 131–32. Jelal M. Shah, "Sex Life in India and Pakistan," pp. 533–34.

[99] Clellan S. Ford and Frank A. Beach, *Ibid.,* p. 134, citing Havelock Ellis.

be as follows: The rise of heterosexual freedom is in part a function of social disorganization rather than reorganization; if so, it gives rise to personal anomie and encourages retreat into homosexual relations, promiscuous as well as durable. Also, to the extent that heterosexual relations are reduced to a free basis, they lose their novelty and become boring, whereas homosexual relations, still held in contempt by popular opinion, retain something of the risqué and are therefore erotically stimulating. Finally, modern societies are increasingly beset with large groups hostile to existing standards and impatient of all official authority; these flaunt homosexuality as an expression of rebellion.

Problems of Homosexual Behavior

Whatever its causes, homosexual behavior gives rise to problems considered serious in modern times. Among these, homosexual prostitution, venereal disease, crime, and youth corruption are the most important.

Homosexual prostitution by males in their teens and early twenties is widespread in many countries. It is "probably much more prevalent in the United States than ever before. . . ." [100] Young boys are often inducted or forced into "hustling" by older gang members. They do not consider themselves homosexuals but are out to make easy money and satisfy gang leaders. For some gangs, "the practice becomes one of 'queer-baiting,' to roll the 'queer' for his money, since he fears legal recourse. . . ." [101] Since the service often involves orgasm by the boy, the end result of his prostitution is frequently that he himself, despite his intentions, becomes a confirmed homosexual. The customers' eagerness for youthful partners is such that the career of the homosexual prostitute is usually ended by age 25; a premium is placed on youths from 12 to 20.[102]

In the 1920's homosexual behavior was subordinate as a source of venereal infection, but by the late 1960's it had become a major factor, with countries reporting anywhere from 10 to 90 percent of venereal cases as homosexual in origin.[103] In surveys in Los Angeles from 1959 to 1961, from 50 to

---

[100] Harry Benjamin and R. E. L. Masters, *Prostitution and Morality,* p. 290.

[101] Albert J. Reiss, "Sex Offenses: The Marginal Status of the Adolescent," *Law and Contemporary Problems,* Vol. 25 (Spring, 1960), p. 323.

[102] Harry Benjamin and R. E. L. Masters, *Prostitution and Morality,* pp. 294–95, 299–302.

[103] World Health Organization, "V.D. Around the World," *Today's V.D. Control Problems,* 1968.

77 percent of infected males named purely homosexual contacts; in some districts the percentage reached as high as 86 percent.[104] Not surprisingly, over the same period, the young age groups showed greater rises in V.D. rates than older groups.[105]

Apart from robbery and violence associated with male prostitution, the main hazards of homosexual conduct are blackmail, homicidal jealousy, and marital fraud. Any homosexual of wealth or prominence runs the risk of public exposure; and given the instability and promiscuity of homosexual relationships, the risk is great. No one knows how many murders occur in homosexual quarrels, but the circumstances in newspaper accounts suggest that they are fairly frequent. Another kind of wrong associated with homosexuality is marriage. Homosexual men, like others, often wish to have a legitimate home and family. They sometimes marry without telling the bride of their habits, with tragic consequences for her.

Will the "Homosexual Community" Be Recognized?

Among the avant-garde it is fashionable to speak of homosexuals as being a "minority" in society and to demand that they be allowed to practice their own beliefs "just like any other minority." An organization in San Francisco called the Council on Religion and the Homosexual has actively promoted "a continuing dialogue . . . between the religious community, other segments of San Francisco life, and the homophile community." The "San Francisco homosexual minority," it claims, is "the second largest—following the Negro minority." [106] The *San Francisco Chronicle* (December 30, 1969) headlined a West Coast all-gay symposium as "Gays Seeking a 'Community.'"

Although the future is unpredictable, an examination of the assumptions in the "gay liberation" movement makes its success appear questionable. One assumption is that the opposition to homosexuality is due to prejudice, and that the "gay community" will gain recognition if the public is merely educated about homosexuality. Our analysis has shown, on the other hand, that sexual norms reflect sociological requirements. Only if those requirements change drastically can the prejudices be expected to disappear.

---

[104] Evelyn Hooker, "Male Homosexual Life Styles and Venereal Disease," in *Proceedings of the World Forum on Syphilis* (U. S. Public Health Service, 1964).

[105] One major American city tried the experiment of giving a badge to each homosexual medically determined to be free of infection. The badge was greatly appreciated, because it facilitated contact among homosexuals.

[106] From a letter (undated) addressed to Dear Fellow Citizens.

Further, a "minority" or "community," in the sociological sense, is ordinarily one in which membership is acquired by birth, each person being socialized from infancy in the customs and symbols of the group. The homosexual group, instead, is preeminently one in which membership is by recruitment (seduction), and it will die out without it. Here, inevitably, is a source of tension with nonhomosexuals. The Wolfenden Report commended "the steps taken by the Ministry of Education and the Scottish Education Department to ensure that men guilty of homosexual offences are not allowed to continue in the teaching profession," [107] but it admitted that detection was difficult. There is also the assumption that if homosexuality were made respectable, this would be the only change made. However, support by norms means regulation. Homosexual behavior, if institutionalized and given the same normative status as heterosexual behavior, would involve obligations and conformity to stipulated patterns. The distribution of that scarce resource — youthful homosexual attractiveness — would be subject to systematic rules, and sexual bargaining would be linked with economic and social rights and obligations in much the same way as heterosexual bargaining. Under such a regime, the nature and role of homosexual intercourse in personal life would be fundamentally altered. It would no longer constitute an avenue of neurotic escape, an expression of social hostility, a means of protest. It would no longer enjoy the stimulating status of being illicit. Under such circumstances would many choose the "homosexual way of life" as against the normal heterosexual way?

---

[107] *Report of the Committee on Homosexual Offences and Prostitution,* p. 78.

part two

Social
Disorganization

8

The World's Population Crisis

KINGSLEY DAVIS

The demographic condition most often viewed as a social problem is the growth of the number of people. The world's population (3.63 billion in 1970) is growing so fast that a continuance of the same rate would double the figure every 37 years. Within 200 years, for example, the earth's population would be 157 billion, or 41 times the 1970 total. Some countries have even more bizarre increases ahead if the present trend continues. Mexico's population, for instance, is growing at more than twice the world's rate. If the current rate keeps up, it will grow from 51 million in 1970 to some 154 million by the end of the century, and to 2.2 billion in 100 years.

Few experts believe that such a frightening human multiplication will actually occur. But the fact that the current trend would lead to impossibly high figures demonstrates that the trend must stop. *How* it is to be stopped, and the possible consequences *before* it is halted, pose a social problem of the first magnitude.

The spectacular character of the present rate of increase should not blind us, however, to the fact that there are other population problems, some of them independent of the question of growth in total numbers. For example, there are problems that arise from high fertility regardless of whether the population is growing or not. There are also problems that arise from very low fertility. Of the latter, one problem that is very much in the public eye is an aging population; low birth rates result in aged populations.

In the present chapter we shall deal with several major population problems, starting with the question of world population growth. In trying to understand the causes and consequences of this growth, we must necessarily discuss changes in death rates, birth rates, and the age structure. This will enable us to see how the various population problems are interrelated, all connected with a fundamental transition that has been, and still is, occurring in human society. An examination of the differences in population growth around the world will quickly show that the situation in the industrial countries is different from that in the peasant-agrarian countries. Consequently, once the world view is sketched, our consideration of the major problems will be divided into two sections, the one dealing with the less developed and the other with the more advanced nations.

ACCELERATING GROWTH
AND ITS WORLD DISTRIBUTION

The unprecedented speed and magnitude of increase in the world's population in recent decades have earned the name "population explosion," a metaphor that sums up the situation in a single phrase. During hundreds

TABLE 1
Growth of the Human Population

	Estimated Population (Millions)	Percent Average Yearly Growth in Prior Period	Number of Years in Which Population Will Double at Given Growth Rate
400,000 BC	0.5	—	—
8000 BC	5	.001	59,007
1 AD	300	.05	1,354
1750	791	.06	1,250
1800	978	.43	163
1850	1,262	.51	136
1900	1,650	.54	129
1950	2,517	.85	82
1970	3,625	1.84	38

Sources: The first figure is conjectural but conservative, because Homo sapiens may have originated one-half million to one million years ago. The estimates for the period 8000 BC to 1900 AD are from John D. Durand, "The Modern Expansion of World Population," *Proceedings of the American Philosophical Society*, Vol. 3 (June, 1967), p. 137; the 1950 estimate is from the *Demographic Yearbook, 1968* (New York: United Nations, 1969); the final estimate is the author's.

of millennia — in fact, during at least 97 percent of man's existence — the species expanded with infinite slowness, multiplying temporarily in some areas, declining in others, but remaining sparse everywhere. If the first period shown in Table 1 is even remotely correct, the population did not double itself any oftener than about every 60,000 years on the average. But around 8000 BC, something happened. The invention and spread of agriculture, animal husbandry, pottery, and eventually metallurgy immensely speeded up the rate of population growth. After that there was little change in the rate until 1750, when the Industrial Revolution got under way. Finally, after World War II, when the international diffusion of advanced technology became worldwide, the rate reached an even higher level. Thus there have been at least three escalations in human increase: one around 8000 BC, another around 1750, and a third about 1945. The following figures, derived from Table 1, show the approximate magnitudes of the shifts:

	Percent Average Yearly Increase [a]	Ratio to Prior Rate
400,000–8000 BC	.001	—
8000 BC–1750 AD	.058	58:1
1750–1950	.580	10:1
1950–1970	1.841	3:1

[a] The use of averages over long periods tends to exaggerate the shifts, but the jumps are nevertheless so large as to be impressive.

Not only has the rate of population growth risen but the absolute base has become larger. As a consequence, the recent rise in human numbers is staggering. The gain in 50 years from 1920 to 1970 almost equals the population of the entire earth in 1920. Fifty-six percent of that gain occurred in the last 20 years. If during the next 20 years the earth's people increase at the *same rate* as they did in the 1950–1970 period, the number added will be nearly 500 million greater than it was during the earlier period.

Is this unprecedented population growth a social problem? Some leaders and intellectuals deny that it is, but an expanding majority — including nearly all demographers and sociologists, most economists, many Roman Catholics, and some communists — say "yes." They do not believe that rapid population growth is an inherent evil apart from its consequences, but simply that the consequences are regrettable. If we define as a social problem any condition or threatened condition that is regarded by a substantial portion of the citizenry as bad in itself or in its consequences, then the extremely rapid population growth of today is such a problem. However, before analyzing the precise reasons usually given for viewing it or not viewing it as a problem, let us try to understand the actual situation. There is clearly a large body of reliable information about population which makes possible a scientific analysis, quite apart from the evaluations, sentiments, and taboos that people bring to the facts.

Shift of Population Growth to Less Developed Countries

One of the salient facts is that population is growing faster in the poorer countries than in the richer ones. This trend is recent, dating from sometime around 1920. Prior to World War I, the most rapid numerical gains occurred in the more successful nations — in those that were expanding economically and raising their standard of living. As a consequence the northwest Europeans, both in Europe and overseas, multiplied more rapidly than the rest of the world's people. In a little more than two and one-half centuries the proportion of Europeans in the world nearly doubled, rising from about 18 percent in 1650 to approximately 35 percent in 1920. Since 1920, as Table 2 shows, the underdeveloped countries (overwhelmingly non-European in race and culture) have exhibited the more rapid growth, and their advantage has been accelerating. If we take the gain in the underdeveloped regions as a ratio to the gain in the developed ones, the following results emerge:

Period	Ratio
1900–1920	0.5
1920–1930	1.1
1930–1940	1.7
1940–1950	3.0
1950–1960	1.5
1960–1970	1.9

From 1920 to 1930, the underdeveloped regions still had high death rates which virtually wiped out their advantage in birth rates. From 1940 to 1950, on the other hand, the industrial nations were caught in a world war which increased their death rates and reduced their immigration, whereas the non-industrial countries lowered their death rates precipitously and continued their high reproductive rates. In the 1950–1960 decade, the industrial countries maintained their steady gain in mortality, maintained fairly well their postwar high plateau in fertility, and gained in immigration from agrarian countries. By 1970, however, their birth rates had generally dropped, and their population growth was expected to fall further behind the backward countries.

TABLE 2

Population Increase in Developed and Less Developed
Countries in Each Decade from 1900 to 1970

| | Population (Millions) | |
	Developed	Less Developed
1900	251	1,399
1920	309	1,551
% Increase	**11.0**	**5.3**
1920	317	1,543
1930	349	1,721
% Increase	**10.1**	**11.5**
1930	528	1,542
1940	565	1,730
% Increase	**7.0**	**12.2**
1940	649	1,646
1950	674	1,843
% Increase	**3.9**	**11.8**
1950	741	1,776
1960	845	2,160
% Increase	**14.0**	**21.6**
1960	959	2,046
1970	1,078	2,536
% Increase	**12.4**	**23.9**

Note: For each period, the countries in each category are the same, but between one period and the next certain countries are switched from "less developed" to "developed" as their progress justifies. Percent increase is *per decade.* Data chiefly from John D. Durand, "The Modern Expansion of World Population," and *Demographic Yearbook* (1960, 1962, and 1968).

That the poorer countries are increasing their populations almost twice as fast as the richer ones is one of the most tragic circumstances of the modern demographic situation, for it is these countries that have the least need for, and that can least afford, inflated numbers of human beings. Some of the countries are already extremely overcrowded. It is at least fortunate that, among the underdeveloped regions, Latin America, on the whole less crowded and less impoverished than Asia or Africa, is exhibiting the fastest population increase.[1] But on whichever underdeveloped continent one looks, one finds exceedingly poor countries struggling to take care of an ever rising tide of humanity. El Salvador, a poor Central American country whose population density is one and two-thirds times that of France, has a human increment of approximately 3.4 percent per year. Egypt, another agrarian

---

[1] See *World Population Prospects as Assessed in 1963* (New York: United Nations, 1966), pp. 15–16. Latin America is predicted to increase in population by 32 percent between 1970 and 1980; Africa by 31 percent, and South Asia by 26 percent.

country whose poverty is notorious and whose density in settled areas is four times that of the highly industrial United Kingdom, has an annual increase of 2.5 percent, also four times that of the United Kingdom. Ceylon, an Asian country whose economy is in the doldrums and whose politics is chaotic, nevertheless has a population that is gaining at the incongruous rate of 2.4 percent per year. Other crowded agrarian countries with annual population increments of between 2.5 and 3.5 percent are Mexico, Taiwan, Lebanon, Albania, Rwanda, Sudan, Trinidad, and South Korea. Among others that could probably be put in this class if we had the data are Nigeria, Ghana, the Dominican Republic, and Thailand.

It must be remembered that a population increasing at 3 percent per year will double in 23 years and will multiply 10 times in 77 years; a population increasing at 2 percent per year will double in 35 years and increase 10 times in 116 years.

Why the Rapid Population Growth?

In explaining modern population growth we are faced with two questions: Why has the world's population as a whole increased at an accelerating pace? Why has the fastest growth shifted from the more advanced to the less advanced nations? Although the two questions are interrelated, the answer to the first does not suffice to answer the second.

In strictly demographic terms, the explanation of the great wave of population growth in the last two centuries is the decline in the death rate, not a rise in the birth rate. The long-run trend of the birth rate, taking the world as a whole, has been generally downward, but it has not fallen as fast, or as consistently and widely, as the death rate.

The standard explanation of why the death rate has declined has been economic. At first the decline was limited to those countries experiencing real economic progress. It began gradually but gained momentum as the Industrial Revolution proceeded. The Western gains in agriculture, transportation, and commerce during the eighteenth and nineteenth centuries made better diets possible; the gains in industrial manufacturing made clothing, housing, and other amenities more widely available; the rise in real income facilitated the growth of public sanitation, medical science, and popular education. "It is no disparagement of medical science and practice," said Warren Thompson in 1953, "to recognize that the great decline in the death rate that has taken place during the last two centuries in the West is due, basically, to improvement in production and economic conditions."[2]

This traditional explanation of the death-rate decline seems correct as an interpretation of Western history. But when it is applied to contemporary underdeveloped areas, it is substantially wrong. These areas, since 1920, have benefited from a much faster drop in death rates than the northwest European peoples ever experienced, and they have had this experience without a comparable rate of economic development — in some cases without any visible gain in per capita income at all. Death rates have been brought down with revolutionary speed in the economically backward countries because the latest medical discoveries, made and financed in the industrial nations, can be immediately applied everywhere. Historically in the West, medical advances had to be slowly invented and diffused, with the result that death rates were lowered gradually. Recently, however, the nonindustrial nations have suddenly been getting the benefit of these accumulated inventions and such new ones as are produced each year, with the result that their death rates have been declining almost miraculously. The most important source of death being eliminated is infectious disease. Such diseases are being conquered through the transfer of medical techniques and personnel and funds from the industrial nations, especially under the auspices of international agencies like the World Health Organization, Pan American Health Organization, UNICEF, FAO, and the like. It has been demonstrated in country after country that widespread diseases such as malaria, yellow fever, yaws, syphilis, trachoma, cholera, plague, typhoid, smallpox, tuberculosis, and dysentery can be controlled on a mass basis at low cost. Most of the discoveries making this possible are recent: insecticides like DDT, antibiotics like penicillin, vaccines like BCG, drugs like sulfanilamide, better instruments like portable X-ray machines, and rationalized public health campaigns and statistical reporting. Preventive public health measures, instituted and organized by the government and employing only a handful of specialists, can save millions of lives at costs ranging from a few cents to a few dollars per person per year.

An illustrative case is that of Ceylon. A country suffering from chronic malaria, it had a crude death rate averaging 26.9 per 1000 population during 1920–1929 and 24.5 during 1930–1939. In 1946 the rate was still 20.3, but in 1947 it was 14.3, a 43 percent decline in one year! By 1954 it was down to 10.4. The main cause of this unexampled drop was the use of DDT as a residual spray to control malaria. This measure not only greatly reduced malarial

---

[2] Warren S. Thompson, *Population Problems,* 4th ed. (New York: McGraw-Hill, 1953), p. 77.

infection but it also lowered mortality from other causes. The costs were negligible (less than $2.00 annually per head for all medical services), but even these were partly met from WHO funds; the DDT, first invented in Switzerland, was imported; the experts involved either originated or were trained outside the country. Furthermore, nothing was required of the Ceylonese themselves. Their houses were sprayed *for* them. They were not required to change their habits or institutions, to acquire a knowledge of malaria, or to take any initiative. We can see, then, how the spectacular decline in the death rate of the island came about through no basic economic development or change in the institutional structure.

Similar developments have occurred in other underdeveloped countries. The World Health Organization reported in 1965 that antimalarial efforts since World War II had rid 815 million people of the threat of this disease.[3] Numerous other causes of death have also been conquered. Between 1940 and 1964, the recorded death rate fell by 61 percent in Puerto Rico, 71 percent in Taiwan, and 81 percent in Cyprus.[4] As the developing countries approach a modern level of mortality, the rate of decline in age-specific death rates slackens, but the crude death rate (deaths per 1000 persons of *all* ages) keeps on falling rapidly. The reason for this is that a swift fall in mortality, coupled with high fertility, makes the age structure abnormally young. Since the greatest saving of lives comes at young ages, the drop in mortality acts like an increase in fertility. Thus, in underdeveloped countries nearly everybody is under age 40. But under modern mortality conditions practically nobody dies under age 40; in the United States, for example, the life-table for 1967 shows that over 93 percent of persons born live to age 40. With very few people dying before age 40, and with the bulk of its population under that age, the average underdeveloped country today has an extremely low crude death rate. The following comparison between Costa Rica and Denmark illustrates the situation:

---

[3] *The New York Times,* March 26, 1965. Malaria has been almost entirely eliminated in many countries, including such formerly afflicted areas as Corsica, Barbados, Cyprus, and Ukraine.

[4] For fuller analysis and references on the spectacular declines in death rates, see George J. Stolnitz, "A Century of International Mortality Trends," *Population Studies,* Vol. 9 (July, 1955), pp. 24–55; Vol. 10 (July, 1956), pp. 17–42; Kingsley Davis, "The Amazing Decline of Mortality in Underdeveloped Areas," *Journal of the American Economic Association,* Vol. 46 (May, 1956), pp. 305–18; Eduardo E. Arriaga, *Mortality Decline and Its Demographic Effects in Latin America* (Berkeley: Institute of International Studies, 1970); and the *Proceedings of the World Population Conference* (Belgrade: 1965).

	Percent of Population under Age 40 (1963–1964)	Percent of Those Born Surviving to Age 40 (1963–1964)	Crude Death Rate (1968)
Costa Rica	82.4	83.6	6.5
Denmark	58.6	95.0	9.7

The mortality conditions of Denmark are better than those of Costa Rica, but because Costa Rica has so many people at young ages, it has a lower crude death rate.[5]

Since recent disease control has not rested on basic changes in social institutions, birth rates have remained high in nonindustrial regions. They were higher to begin with in most of these regions than they ever were in northwestern Europe, and at first they tended to rise slightly as a result of mortality improvement.[6] In the most progressive countries of the underdeveloped world, the crude birth rates have been declining during some part or all of the 1960's, but so far this is due almost as much to an increasingly youthful age structure as to a drop in fertility per se. (Since the crude birth rate is obtained by dividing births by the *total* population, a rise in the proportion of people too young to reproduce will lower the rate even if the births per adult woman remain the same.) Whereas the presently industrial countries began lowering their birth rates *before* their sharpest declines in mortality, the backward areas of today are doing so, if at all, long *after* their mortality has reached a modern low level. It is this dual fact—the unprecedented conquest of mortality and the postponement of fertility decline—that explains the extraordinarily fast population growth in the two-thirds of the world that still remains underdeveloped. Along with the postwar baby boom and continued gradual lowering of mortality in industrial nations, this fast growth accounts for the latest explosion of the world's entire population.

CONSEQUENCES OF POPULATION CHANGE: THE AGRARIAN COUNTRIES

With this explanation of how the modern upsurge in population has come about, we can more clearly understand the consequences. If, for example,

---

[5] See Kingsley Davis, "The Changing Balance of Births and Deaths," *Proceedings of Conference on Technological Change and Population Growth* (California Institute of Technology, May, 1970).

[6] O. Andrew Collver, *Birth Rates in Latin America: New Estimates of Historical Trends and Fluctuations* (Berkeley: Institute of International Studies, 1965).

the most rapid multiplication is occurring in the underdeveloped countries, and if this is attributable to causes other than economic development, we can see at once that the human increase may be retarding the rise in level of living or thwarting it altogether. For this to happen, the country does not have to be densely settled already. An area may be sparsely settled, e.g., Brazil, and still have too fast a population growth from an economic point of view. Furthermore, a country may be prosperous, even heavily industrialized, and still have too fast an increase and other population problems. Let us consider the agrarian nations.

Rising Numbers, Poverty, and Economic Development

Strictly speaking, economic development does not mean simply a gain in total national income. It means a gain in *per capita* income. This requires that capital be added to production faster than labor, which in turn means that the rate of investment must be adequate. With a constant population, a rate of investment of 3 to 5 percent of national income is required to produce a one percent increase in per capita income; whereas, with a population growing at 3 percent per year, an investment of between 12 and 20 percent of the national income is required. A poor country finds it extremely difficult to invest even 10 percent of its national income in economic development. Since most underdeveloped countries now have a rate of population growth that is between 2 and 3.5 percent, we can see that they have come dangerously close to making genuine economic development impossible for themselves. Even if they achieve such development, it will be at a slower rate than would be the case with a less climactic population growth. For instance, in 1960–1965 Latin America's gross investment was 16.8 percent of its total product.[7] Had there been no population growth, this high investment coefficient would have increased per capita income by 4 to 5 percent per year, but since the population grew at an annual rate of 2.9 percent, the yearly rise in per capita income was only 1.6 percent.[8] In short, two-thirds of Latin America's economic expansion was used simply to accommodate more people.[9]

---

[7] *Economic Bulletin for Latin America,* Vol. 11 (April, 1966), p. 8.

[8] Theodore Morgan and George W. Betz, *Economic Development: Readings in Theory and Practice* (Belmont, California: Wadsworth, 1970), p. 19.

[9] For analyses of the relation of population growth to economic development, see Goran Ohlin, *Population Control and Economic Development* (Paris: Organization for Economic Cooperation and Development, 1967); Ansley J. Coale and Edgar M. Hoover, *Population Growth and Economic Development in Low-Income Countries* (Princeton,

A graphic appreciation of the population burden can be obtained by looking at particular countries. We have seen how Ceylon's death rate plummeted after 1946. As a result, its population nearly doubled in 24 years, rising from 6.9 million in 1946 to 12.5 million in 1970. This phenomenal increase in a poor and already crowded agrarian island did not come from prosperity, nor did it bring wealth; instead it helped to bring economic stagnation.

> The main problem of Ceylonese economic growth [is] the difficulty of developing a large enough volume of saving and investment. . . . The pressure of population growth, causing increments in national income to be used for consumption rather than investment . . . , shows no sign of abating.[10]

From 1950 to 1960 the real income per capita rose by about one percent per year [11]; from 1960 to 1965, by about one-half percent.[12] Faced by mounting deficits, the government instituted ever more drastic economic controls, causing the level of consumption, especially that of the middle class, to decline.[13] Ceylon's main economic activity is agriculture, accounting for 45 percent of the GNP in 1960 as against 5 percent for manufacturing. As a result of planned development, arable land has expanded, but so has the agricultural labor force. There has thus been very little reduction in the island's high agricultural density, which in 1950 stood at 178 males in agriculture per square mile of arable land, and in 1960 at 173. Ceylon is thus a poor country in which population growth nearly cancels the national economic success achieved by ever more drastic government control. There are now twice as many poor people on the island as there were 25 years ago.

Egypt's situation is worse. Its already dense population increased from 14.2 million in 1927 to 33.3 million in 1970, mainly as a result of a falling death rate; the death rate was 26.9 per 1000 population in 1935–1939, but only 15.1 in 1965–1968. In contrast, the birth rate showed little change; it was 43.8 in 1950–1954 and 40.0 in 1965–1968 — extremely high, considering that the birth registration is officially said to be only about 80 percent com-

---

N. J.: Princeton University Press, 1958); Stephen Enke, *Economics for Development* (Englewood Cliffs, N. J.: Prentice-Hall, 1963); Alfred Sauvy, *General Theory of Population* (New York: Basic Books, 1969).

[10] Donald R. Snodgrass, *Ceylon: An Export Economy in Transition* (Homewood, Ill.: Richard D. Irwin, 1966), p. 232.

[11] Computed from *ibid.*, p. 271.

[12] Ceylon Ministry of Planning and Economic Affairs, *Development Programme, 1966–67* (Colombo: Government Publications Bureau, July, 1966), p. 5.

[13] Donald R. Snodgrass, *Ceylon: An Export Economy in Transition*, p. 223.

plete. Since Egypt is mostly desert, its population is squeezed into an area comprising only 3.6 percent of the national territory. This makes Egypt one of the world's most crowded countries. In the settled area, there are, on the average, 2424 persons per square mile. In Belgium, another crowded country, the density is 828 per square mile. Unlike Belgium, however, Egypt is agricultural and therefore has to rely mainly on its arable land, almost all of which is irrigated. The government has made great efforts to expand the area under cultivation, to improve agricultural techniques, and to equalize the size of holdings. All of these efforts have met with success, but their effect on the level of living of the average Egyptian has been almost nil because of the rapid population growth. The Aswan Dam was relied on to increase the area under cultivation by 10 to 20 percent, but it took ten years to build the dam, during which time the *total* population grew by 28 percent and the *rural* population by 16 percent. Long before the dam was started it was foreseen that population growth would "eat up" the area added by the dam.[14] As for the redistribution of large holdings, some 1.5 million people were in families given land between 1952 and 1962 [15]; during that time the rural population increased by approximately 2.2 million. In 1950 the number of males engaged in agriculture for each square mile of arable land was 358; by 1961–1962 it was up to 381. Despite strenuous governmental effort to develop the economy—an effort which has led to considerable control over economic life—the nation is still impoverished. It derives less than 5 percent of its food calories from meat; its children commonly suffer from rickets and anemia; its per capita GNP ($189 in 1966) is below that of most agrarian countries. The nation's economic gains have been used overwhelmingly to support more people poorly rather than fewer people better.

In many other agrarian countries—India, Indonesia, Philippines, Haiti, Morocco, Uganda, to mention only a few—per capita income has risen little if at all, despite a rise in national income. An economist who worked in Ceylon had this to say:

> The issue is plain: Any check to population growth will make economic progress more likely or speed it up. Continued or accelerated population growth will make progress slow down or stop. In one meeting of government officials I attended, the problem of development was put as that of keeping the standard of living from falling—not of raising it.[16]

---

[14] National Population Commission, *The Population Problem in Egypt* (Cairo: Permanent Council of Public Services, 1955), pp. 22–23.

[15] United Nations, *Economic Survey of Africa,* Vol. 2, *North African Subregion* (New York: 1968), p. 41.

[16] Theodore Morgan, "The Economic Development of Ceylon," *Annals of the American Academy of Political and Social Science,* Vol. 305 (May, 1956), p. 94.

Youthful Populations, Unemployment, and Political Instability

Further problems in underdeveloped countries arise from changes in the age structure. When mortality is reduced rapidly with little or no change in fertility, the population gets more youthful; because the greatest gains in saving lives are made in infancy and early childhood. Many of these countries now have the youngest populations the world has ever known. The contrast between an agrarian country and an industrialized one can be seen in Figure 1, which shows two age pyramids. Costa Rica, whose death rate dropped 62 percent in 20 years but whose birth rate has remained high (in fact, during the period of 1965–1969 the average birth rate was 5.4 times the average death rate), has 127 children under 15 years of age for each 100 adults aged 20 to 59. Denmark, on the other hand, being a country that has long had both a low death rate and a low birth rate, has only 46 children per 100 adults in their prime (see Table 3). Such young populations mean that the underdeveloped countries are struggling not only with the problem of rapidly rising numbers of people but also with the problem of a burdensome child-dependency ratio. To an unusual degree, adults work for the purpose of supporting large numbers of children rather than of producing the long-run basis for economic improvement. Furthermore, the women are so burdened with constant childbearing and child rearing that they cannot participate in economic production beyond the traditional and usually inefficient tasks of the home and garden. As if to compensate for the heavy child-dependency drag, the agrarian countries tend to start children to work at an early age. Child labor, however, is neither efficient in the short run nor conducive to economic development in the long run. What is required for social and economic development is the acquisition of skills by the population, which means careful and systematic education of children. When children are kept out of school in order to work, the work is normally unskilled and inefficient. Furthermore, especially in an agrarian economy, a failure to educate children in schools deprives them of their main chance of acquiring ideas and attitudes conducive to social change rather than traditionalism. Underdeveloped countries have a hard enough time getting sufficient funds for education, despite heroic proportions of the national budget spent for this purpose. The massive waves of children coming as a result of demographic changes make the problem all the worse.

The problem is not solely the swollen ranks of children. It is also the engorged contingents of youth. It can be seen from Table 3 that Costa Rica, for example, has 26 young people aged 15–19 for each 100 adults aged 20–59;

FIGURE 1 Age Pyramids for Costa Rica and Denmark

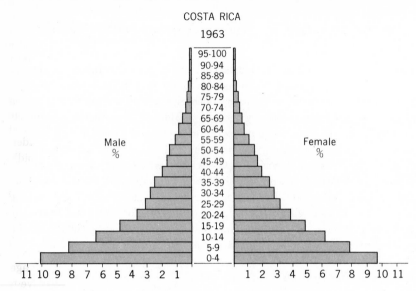

COSTA RICA

1963

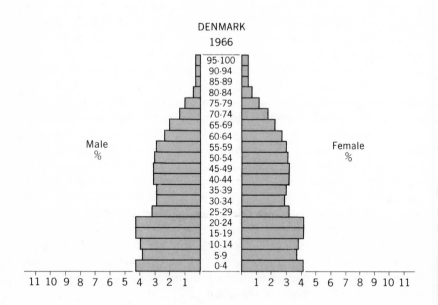

DENMARK

1966

Source: Demographic Yearbook (1968), Table 5.

TABLE 3
Indices of the Age Structure in Selected Countries

	Ratio of Given Age Group to Adults 20–59		
	Children under 15	Youths 15–19	Oldsters 60+
Underdeveloped Countries			
Costa Rica, 1963	127	26	14
Mauritius, 1967	111	30	14
Taiwan, 1967	106	27	11
Ceylon, 1963	98	23	14
Industrial Countries			
Old World			
Belgium, 1966	48	15	37
Denmark, 1966	46	16	32
France, 1966	50	18	37
New World			
United States, 1969	61	19	28
New Zealand, 1967	70	20	26
Life-Table Populations			
U. S. white female (1967)			
with life expectancy of 75	39	13	47
Hypothetical future U. S.			
with life expectancy of 83	38	13	60

Sources: Demographic Yearbook, 1968, Table 5; U. S. Bureau of the Census, Current Population Reports, Series P-25, No. 441 (Washington, D.C.: March 19, 1970), pp. 12–13; U. S. National Center for Health Statistics, *Vital Statistics of the United States,* Vol. 2, Section 5 (1967), pp. 5–7; hypothetical U. S. life-table population made by the author, unpublished. A life-table population is the one that would result from the age-specific death rates of a given period, assuming a birth rate equal to the death rate.

whereas in Belgium the ratio is only 15 to each 100. With ever larger waves of youths entering the labor market each year, an underdeveloped country must have a very rapid economic development to absorb them all. If it falters, large numbers of youths become unemployed. They may go to school, but this may merely succeed in making them a class of "educated unemployed." Possessed of youthful energy and idealism, having no stake in the existing situation, being extremely numerous in relation to the adult population, these youths are politically explosive, often ready to follow any leader who promises the quickest and most violent solution. Their role in making and breaking dictators has often been demonstrated in backward countries, whether in Latin America or the Middle East. Their fiery impatience makes it hard for a ruler to follow a policy of basic economic development, for that seems too slow and too prosaic. It is easier for the ruler to satisfy the youthful rabble by threatening war, casting out the foreign devils, seizing property, and insulting the enemy—all in the name of sacred nationalistic sentiment and holy religious or communist beliefs.

Functionless Fertility and the Family

The dilemmas of rapid population growth can be seen not only in nations but also, on a minute scale, in families. As the head of the household in an agrarian country often sees it, the problem is how to get enough land. This is why a scheme of land distribution will generally receive popular support, regardless of how uneconomic it may be. But, as the cases of Ceylon and Egypt show, there may not be any more land to be had, at least without large-scale collective investment. Failing additional land, the peasant finds it hard to maintain his children, much less educate them. His aspirations for his children may be high, because he sees the lack of opportunity in the village and he knows of schools and urban employment, but he cannot meet these aspirations. His wife, on the other hand, is burdened with the same round of childbearing that her ancestors experienced, but with one difference—a far greater proportion of the children remain alive. With a larger family than normal, child care is a more constant burden, the available land is even more inadequate, the aspirations even more unreachable.

The Geographical Shift of People

Another problem plagues the underdeveloped country growing rapidly in population, especially when the peasantry is already densely settled on the land. This is the necessity of moving something like 60 percent of the people from the country to the cities. It is a problem so formidable that few governments seem willing to face it realistically; yet, if rapid economic development is to be achieved, the territorial shift must take place rapidly.

The necessity of rural-urban migration arises from the fact that an agrarian population is all located in the wrong places for purposes of an industrial economy. The chief instrument of agriculture is land. When the level of technology is low, as it is in peasant farming, it takes a great deal of labor in ratio to land to produce the crops. For this reason, the population tends to be spread out thickly over the land, and it is generally most numerous where the land is fertile unless the pattern of land ownership interferes. In industrial societies, on the other hand, the character of agriculture is transformed by the substitution of technology for labor on the farms. The people are emptied off the farm land; they go to the cities where occupations in manufacturing and services are opening up. The growth of urban economic activity contributes to the technological revolution on farms both by furnishing the science, engineering, education, and machinery for better agriculture and by increasing the demand for agricultural products. The superior productivity of urban enterprise pulls labor from the farms by offering higher wages and at the same time fosters farm capitalization by increasing demand. As a consequence, the loss of labor to the cities does not lower farm production but raises it; the few farmers who remain make a much better living than did their more numerous predecessors.

The magnitude of the transformation can be seen from data for the United States (see Table 4). During the period 1940 to 1960, the average annual net migration from American farms was 3.7 percent of the farm population at the start of each year. Since the average natural increase was 1.2 percent, the net migration was large enough not only to cancel the natural increase but also to reduce the farm population at an average rate of 1.5 percent each year. After 1910 the farm population, despite the rapid growth of the total United States population, showed no increase. By 1917 the farm population began to decline, at first gradually and then rapidly.

Farm Population

1917	32,236,000
1959	21,172,000
1969	10,307,000

The effect of rapid population growth in a still underdeveloped country is to aggravate the problem of rural-urban migration. For this there are two

TABLE 4
Shift of Population Out of Agriculture
in the United States

| Year | Percentage of Population | |
	On Farms	Not on Farms
1820	72 [a]	28
1969	5 [b]	95

[a] U. S. Bureau of the Census, *Historical Statistics of the United States, Colonial Times to 1957* (Washington, D.C.: 1960), p. 74. This is the percentage of *gainful workers* engaged in agriculture. We do not have data on the farm population for 1820, but its proportion of the total population should not differ much from the proportion of farmers among gainful workers.
[b] Departments of Commerce and Agriculture, *Farm Population,* Current Population Reports, Series Census-ERS, P-27, No. 41 (June 18, 1970).

reasons: *First,* the size of the annual increments to the population is such that the economy, if it is to achieve gains in per capita income, must grow at a rate more rapid than that experienced by industrial countries during their history. From 1820 to 1900, the population of the United States grew at an average rate of 2.8 percent per year. This very fast rate was achieved only because it was helped along by massive immigration from overseas and by expansion of territory. However, as we have seen, many of today's under-developed countries, without either immigration or territorial expansion, are eclipsing this rate by their own natural increase. They must therefore find a way to achieve a rate of economic development (i.e., an industrial revolution) more rapid than that experienced by the United States, and this means that the geographic redistribution of their people must be achieved more quickly. *Second,* rapid population growth in an agrarian country today causes cities to grow rapidly too and thereby multiplies urban problems, and yet it does not succeed in removing the surplus population from the country-side. An analysis of data for 170 underdeveloped countries between 1950 and 1970 shows that their urban population grew at an average rate of 4.5 percent per year. This figure is virtually equal to the rate of urban popula- tion growth (4.6 percent) in 18 industrialized countries *when they were at the peak of their urban population growth.*[17]

The main factor explaining the rapid city growth in the underdeveloped countries today is not rural-urban migration but sheer population growth. As a consequence, their rural populations are also growing rapidly and are piling up on the land, especially in the more backward agrarian regions. In the early history of the now industrial countries, the growth of cities, modest as it was, took the surplus population from the countryside and thus helped in the modernization of agriculture. In those days, the cities had low birth rates and high death rates compared to the rural areas. Today in the under-developed nations the cities often have lower death rates than the farm areas and birth rates that are as high or nearly as high. As a result, the city populations are skyrocketing simply by their own natural increase. It is the rapid city growth, engendered mainly by the high rates of natural increase, that is causing the great squatter problem in the cities throughout the under-developed parts of the world. In all of these cities there are thousands of people living in self-built shacks in thickly settled shantytowns without sanitary facilities. They settle in parks, schoolgrounds, vacant lots. It is said that in the metropolitan areas of Peru there were nearly a million

---

[17] Kingsley Davis, "The Changing Demography of World Urbanization," unpub-lished paper. See also the author's *World Urbanization,* Vol. II (Berkeley: Institute of International Studies, 1971).

squatters in 1960; in Manila the number of squatters is expected to reach 800,000 by 1980; in Caracas squatters make up over 35 percent of the city's population; in Ankara, nearly 50 percent. Under such circumstances, rapid city growth is not solving the agricultural problem and is creating urban crises on an unprecedented scale.[18]

The governments of nonindustrial countries often harbor a well-founded suspicion of their growing urban masses. They know that city growth brings problems of frightening dimensions – problems of housing, sanitation, education, public order. They know that swollen city populations tend to become unruly and that they easily resort to violence if the political leaders do not satisfy them. The danger of urban mobs is all the greater in view of the fact that the city populations are bulging with youth. As noted already, a population with recently and drastically reduced mortality and a continuing high fertility is young, and in cities this feature is magnified by the added migration of young adults from the rural areas.

It is thus for good reason that governments are suspicious of growing urban masses, but they are generally mistaken as to the chief cause of the growth. They think of rural-urban migration as the chief culprit and sometimes advocate a policy of preventing such movement. Since World War II, however, the main factor in city growth in the underdeveloped areas has increasingly become sheer population growth.

CONSEQUENCES OF POPULATION CHANGE: THE INDUSTRIALIZED COUNTRIES

One should not assume that rapid population growth is confined to the poorer countries or that it has deleterious effects only in them. The advanced countries of the world, although showing less growth than the poorer ones, are nevertheless characterized by soaring populations. As a whole, their populations increased, as shown in Table 5, by 12.4 percent between 1960 and 1970. It is interesting that, among the advanced areas, the ones showing the most rapid growth are the newer and less crowded ones. Europe's growth is less than one-half of the Soviet Union's rate. The newer industrial countries are showing the greater growth because their postwar baby boom was

---

[18] For further analysis, see Kingsley Davis, "The Urbanization of the Human Population," *Scientific American,* Vol. 213 (September, 1965), pp. 40–53. This entire issue is devoted to "Cities"; the data on squatters are taken from the article by Charles Abrams, "The Uses of Land in Cities," p. 152.

TABLE 5
Population Growth in Advanced Regions, 1960 to 1970

	Millions		Percent Gain
	1960	1970	1960–1970
Asia [a]	95	106	11
Australia – New Zealand	13	15	21
Europe (developed) [b]	379	411	8
Latin America (developed) [c]	41	50	23
Northern America [d]	199	227	14
South Africa	16	20	26
U. S. S. R.	214	243	13

Sources: 1960 data, *Demographic Yearbook, 1968,* pp. 112–19; 1970 data extrapolated from 1966–1968 data. (Percentage gain calculated on basis of less-rounded numbers than those shown.)
[a] Israel, Japan.
[b] Northern and western Europe, Czechoslovakia, Germany, Hungary, Italy, Poland, Spain, Yugoslavia.
[c] Argentina, Chile, Puerto Rico, Uruguay, Venezuela.
[d] Bermuda, Canada, Greenland, St. Pierre and Miquelon, U. S. A.

more extreme and has lasted longer, and because some of them – particularly Australia, Canada, and the United States – are receiving huge numbers of immigrants. The United States, for example, has a higher birth rate than most industrial countries and regularly receives more immigrants (counting both the legal and illegal ones) than any country in the world. Its population is still growing at a rate that will, if continued, double the number in 70 years, although the postwar growth was reduced after 1960 (see Table 6).

Paradoxically, the prosperous countries find rapid population growth troublesome precisely because of their prosperity. As the goods and services used by each individual mount, and as the number of individuals multiplies, the complications become fantastic. The United States, for example, increased its consumption of energy by 39 percent in eight years, from 1960 to 1968. In the latter year each man, woman, and child consumed on the average an amount of commercially produced energy equal to 12 short tons of coal. This was approximately one hundred times the amount of such energy consumed per person in Ceylon. Also, the congestion of people and their material possessions causes an increasing proportion of effort and resources to be used simply to mitigate the effects of congestion. As we have seen, the attainment of high living standards is accompanied by concentration of people in cities. In the advanced countries 55 to 70 percent of the inhabitants live in urbanized areas of more than 100,000. The New York metropolitan region contains about 16 million people, the Buenos Aires and Los Angeles agglomerations around 8 million. As these giant urban aggregates grow

TABLE 6
Growth Rate of United States and Canadian Populations

| | Percent Increase per Decade | |
Decade	U. S.[a]	Canada[b]
1850–1860	35.6	32.6
1860–1870	26.6	14.2
1870–1880	26.0	17.2
1880–1890	25.5	11.8
1890–1900	20.7	11.1
1900–1910	21.0	34.2
1910–1920	14.9	21.9
1920–1930	16.1	18.9
1930–1940	7.2	11.4
1940–1950	14.5	17.4
1950–1960	18.7	30.4
1960–1970	13.7	19.5

[a] Computed from U. S. Bureau of the Census, *Historical Statistics of the United States, Colonial Times to 1957*, p. 8; and Current Population Reports, Series P-25, No. 446 (June, 1970).
[b] Computed from *Demographic Yearbook, 1955*, p. 132, and (1968), p. 114; and *Population and Vital Statistics Report* (New York: United Nations, April 1, 1970).

more populous and the per capita apparatus more complex, the resulting congestion becomes ever more costly. Automobiles, radios, television antennas, boats, houses, freezers, and myriad other possessions multiply much faster than the population, which itself is multiplying. To acquire room to enjoy and store their goods, city families move to the suburbs where a house, yard, and garage can be obtained. The cost of this gain in space is, of course, a longer and more expensive commuting trip for the head of the family. Not only is it burdensome for him but it is also costly to the entire economy, because elaborate throughways and transportation networks have to be built. In addition, utility lines have to be extended, water mains laid, schools built. But the problems of urban crowding cannot be permanently solved by metropolitan deconcentration, because more people each year are trying to find space in each expanding metropolis.

Ultimately the combined human and material multiplication is self-defeating. The effort to escape mounting congestion simply creates more congestion. Every economic activity seeks more space: Retailers want one-floor supermarkets and acres for parking; manufacturers want one-floor factories and parklike grounds; commuters and truckers want eight-lane highways and cloverleaf turns. In addition, municipalities want parks and unpolluted watersheds, and families want ranch homes on half-acre plots.

As the urban population grows, as each new area fills up, the quest for space takes the suburbs farther out and multiplies the connecting links. The home that was once "in the country" or "in a pleasant little suburb" is presently a dot in a continuous sea of housing developments and shopping centers. The throughway that was so spacious and convenient when it was finished soon becomes an exasperating trap at rush hours. Also, the industries that supply the material wealth, the automobiles and buses that travel ever greater distances between home and work, the dumps where the mounting refuse is burned — all combine to create a social disease of the twentieth century, smog. This air pollution is extending far beyond the cities themselves; in California, for example, it is beginning to affect the crops in the Central Valley, the richest agricultural region in the world. The movement to the suburbs winds up not as an escape from the city but as an extension of the city outward in space, with smog, traffic congestion, and crowds appearing all over again. The urban sprawl may cover 20 to 40 miles today; it will cover 40 to 60, or even 100, tomorrow.

The cost of all this becomes staggering. Not only is land increasingly removed from agricultural use, not only do freeways and transit lines cost billions, but the individual himself pays dearly. The man who commutes 45 minutes to reach his job, the family that maintains a summer home some scores or hundreds of miles from its regular home, the woman who abandons her career because she is stuck deep in the suburbs — all are paying a heavy price for what is in the end a fruitless search for escape from the city. As time goes by, as the population doubles or triples and material possessions get more numerous, the additional costs will mount until they cancel the gains in wealth.[19]

When the level of living is measured as per capita income or per capita GNP, it is a summary index of all economic transactions, not an index of human welfare or satisfaction. Many economic transactions are deleterious for the community at large or even for the parties directly involved, and many are remedial or compensatory for the ill effects of other transactions.

---

[19] For a further analysis of the ways in which the multiplication of people and possessions is impinging on human adjustment, see R. A. Piddington, *The Limits of Mankind* (Bristol: Wright, 1956) and Paul R. and Anne H. Ehrlich, *Population, Resources, Environment* (San Francisco: W. H. Freeman, 1970). For analyses of urban problems, see Wilfred Owen, *Cities in the Motor Age* (New York: Viking, 1959); Robert C. Wood, *Suburbia* (New York: Houghton Mifflin, 1958); Morroe Berger, ed., *The New Metropolis in the Arab World* (New York: Allied, 1963); *Scientific American* (September, 1965), entire issue; Richard B. Andrews, *Urban Growth and Development* (New York: Simmons-Boardman, 1962); Charles Abrams, *The City Is the Frontier* (New York: Harper, 1965).

For example, when millions of dollars are spent in research to find a way of reducing the smog emissions of autos, this "investment" is included in the national income; yet its sole purpose is to mitigate an evil that an affluent mode of life has itself created. Similarly, money and labor used in hauling garbage from cities to open spaces hundreds of miles away is counted in the national income, but it produces nothing except escape from a noxious consequence of a burgeoning population and a rising per capita consumption.

PROPOSED SOLUTIONS AND PUBLIC CONTROVERSY

The demographic facts given above are seldom disputed, at least in general outline. More controversial are the social and economic consequences alluded to, and there is accordingly no universal agreement that a "population problem" exists. Interestingly enough, however, the greatest overt controversy arises among those who ostensibly agree that there is such a problem, because they disagree on the proper means of reaching a solution. Let us begin with the debate over the problem itself and then consider the proposed solutions.

The Debate over the Existence of a Population Problem

The contention that there is at bottom no population problem at all has been maintained more consistently by Soviet spokesmen than by anyone else. As repeatedly expressed in the United Nations, this Marx-Leninist line regards, or rather regarded, overpopulation as a myth invented by capitalist apologists for the purpose of distracting attention from the real problem, capitalism itself. Such evils as poverty, unemployment, war, or hunger, according to this view, cannot be attributed to the number of people or their rate of increase, but only to the particular social order. In the words of the former Soviet member of the United Nations Population Commission:

> Under the conditions of a capitalistic mode of production a certain part of the population systematically becomes relatively superfluous [because] as a result of the very process of capitalistic production a part of working power (and consequently still greater part of population) is found to be superfluous for the purposes of production. Here lies the root of unemployment, an incurable chronic disease of capitalism. . . .

> In socialist society where the immediate purpose of production is satisfaction of the requirements of society but not the gaining of maximum profits, the problem of excessive population no longer arises.[20]

However, the facts of world population growth, increasingly evident in the 1950's and 1960's, could not be indefinitely ignored. Since 1965, a debate has gone on in the Soviet Union between a group who call for official population policies in developing countries and a group who still cling to the old doctrine (but in softer tones).[21] Although still claiming to abhor Malthusianism and to adhere to Marxist philosophy, the first group maintains, in effect, that although social and economic improvement may ultimately bring down birth rates, it is necessary to work on population directly, with family planning programs, because population growth, if left alone, can slow down or possibly prevent economic improvement.

> The developing countries . . . inherited from colonialism a backward economy. . . . Under these conditions, and with an acute lack of capital and skilled workers, the rate of population growth began to exceed the rate of increase in production, particularly in agriculture. Due to the high birthrate the labor force is swollen with youths, as a rule much more than the demand for labor. Furthermore, the increasing demands for residential quarters, schools, and hospitals cannot be satisfactorily met.[22]

The other side argues that the population problem, if it exists at all, is only incidental.

> Methods of artificially reducing the birth rate . . . can play a certain role as a transitory measure, but only when the population has attained the necessary cultural level.[23]

---

[20] T. V. Ryabushkin, "Social Aspects of Population Structure and Movement," *Papers of the World Population Conference, 1954,* Vol. 5 (New York: United Nations, 1955), pp. 1032–33.

[21] James W. Brackett, "The Evolution of Marxist Theories of Population: Marxism Recognizes the Population Problem," *Demography,* Vol. 5 (1968), pp. 158–73. The debate was apparently brought to a head by the World Population Conference in Belgrade, 1965, sponsored jointly by the United Nations and the International Union for the Scientific Study of Population. See *Proceedings of the World Population Conference, 1965* (New York: United Nations, 1967), in which Soviet writers gave recognition to population problems.

[22] Quoted in *ibid.,* p. 166, from Ya Guzevaty, "What Is the Population Explosion?" *Literaturnaya gazeta* (Nov. 30, 1965).

[23] Quoted in James W. Brackett, "The Evolution of Marxist Theories of Population: Marxism Recognizes the Population Problem," p. 168, from Peter Podyachikh, *Literaturnaya gazeta* (Feb. 22, 1966).

The official Soviet position at international meetings in the late 1960's was one of quiet caution. It did not oppose family planning programs, so long as they were desired by the governments concerned and were not used as a substitute for economic and social measures.

Logically, what is at issue here is the question of causation. The original Soviet spokesmen did not deny that unemployment, poverty, or economic stagnation exists in some places and times; they simply said that the causation of these evils is to be found in the social system, never in the demographic sphere. Obviously, the kind of system at fault could not be a truly communist one, because communism, as the greatest good, cannot cause any evil. The cause of the aforesaid evils, therefore, must lie in the even greater evil, capitalism, either as the official system now present or as an influence from former times.

A different basis for saying that there is no population problem, that "overpopulation" is therefore a myth, is advanced by some communists and noncommunists alike. They hold that science *will* or *can keep ahead* of population growth, no matter how rapid this growth may be. In statements to this effect, one should keep an eye out for the small unobtrusive words. If the view is that science *will* do something, the speaker is presumably resting his case on a notion of automatic or inevitable change; yet others maintain that science depends on human activity and volition, and that its accomplishments are anything but automatic. If instead the statement holds that science *can* do something, then the important question is "under what conditions"? Also, a little phrase like "keep ahead" may contain significant ambiguities. Does it mean merely feeding the population, or does it mean giving people a better life? Finally, does the speaker set a time limit on how long he thinks that science will automatically, or can possibly, keep ahead of population growth? Unless some time limit is set, the position becomes absurd, because the world's population, if it continued the growth exhibited from 1950 to 1970, would weigh as much as the entire earth within approximately 1750 years. In other words, the earth would be entirely absorbed in human beings, leaving no "resources" for science to utilize.

On the other hand, many observers believe that there *is* a population problem in the sense that certain evils are caused by too high a population density and/or too rapid a rate of increase. They do not all agree on which evils, or when or where, but they do agree that overpopulation can have deleterious consequences. The most common view is that overpopulation is responsible for hunger and famine in various parts of the world.[24] In fact,

---

[24] Works concerned with population and the food supply are legion. Some examples are Michel Cépède *et al., Population and Food* (New York: Sheed, 1964); William and

this conception has dominated the thinking about population ever since Malthus' day, perhaps as a result of his inspiration but also partly as a result of an untutored impulse to visualize the population problem in terms of mere physical survival. More subtle is the idea that, under certain conditions, rapid population growth may prevent or reduce economic development.[25] Sometimes this view is challenged on the ground that a gain in per capita income "is not the highest goal." The objection is valid, as noted above, but in so far as technological means are involved in the level of living, they are necessary for a wide variety of purposes — better education and health, more security and leisure, finer arts and churches, and stronger defense and public order. Any damper on genuine economic development is therefore a threat to many goals.

Fundamentally, in order to see the disadvantages of population growth, one has to ask what it is that people want. It turns out that they do not want just enough to eat or an ever more complicated technology. They want freedom from close external authority, release from crowding, escape from ugly surroundings, freedom from pollution. It is no accident that the most emphatic and widest public support for population control policies has come with the realization that population growth is degrading the "quality of life" or the "quality of the environment." Such degrading occurs in the most pronounced fashion at a *high* level of living, with plenty of food and without much poverty. The conditions that people object to, and to which population growth contributes, include air and water pollution, destruction of natural beauty, elimination of animal life (except for man's domesticated beasts and parasites), traffic congestion, crowding, noise, and incessant human contact. Sometimes such arguments are pilloried as being misanthropic. William Vogt, for example, was accused by *Time* magazine of preferring birds to men because he pointed out in his famous book, *Road to Survival,*[26] that many species of birds are becoming extinct as the earth's human population burgeons. But the disappearance of wildlife is a distinct loss to man-

Paul Paddock, *Famine 1975!* (Boston: Little, Brown, 1967); George Borgstrom, *The Hungry Planet,* rev. ed. (New York: Collier Books, 1967), and *Too Many* (New York: Macmillan, 1969); National Academy of Sciences, *Resources and Man* (San Francisco: W. H. Freeman, 1969), Chapters 1–5.

[25] For a history of population theory, see *The Determinants and Consequences of Population Trends* (New York: United Nations, 1953), Chapter 3. This volume also contains chapters on the effects of population growth on economic development. Also, D. E. C. Eversley, *Social Theories of Fertility and the Malthusian Debate* (Oxford: Clarendon, 1959); and Joseph J. Spengler and Otis Dudley Duncan, eds., *Population Theory and Policy* (New York: Free Press, 1956).

[26] New York: Sloane, 1948.

kind, and it is hardly misanthropic to feel that three billion people on earth with the enjoyment of wildlife and with other enjoyments is better than six or ten billion without them. As time goes by, we shall hear population increasingly discussed from the standpoint of the sociological, esthetic, and psychic problems involved.

The Debate over the Means

If there is a population problem, it requires a demographic solution. The evils said to flow from too many people or too fast a rate of increase are real enough, but they do not constitute a population problem unless they in fact do flow from such causes. The older Soviet theorists held the view that, since the evils are due to capitalism, it makes no sense to try to deal with them by demographic measures. The super-scientists, or "cornucopians," hold the view that the problem is not population but scientific inadequacy; hence the means of solving the problem is more science. Often people are inconsistent. Roman Catholics, for example, sometimes maintain that there is a population problem but refuse to admit any demographic solution.[27] Actually, there are only three possible *demographic* solutions: a rise in the death rate, a drop in the birth rate, or migration. If we are thinking of the entire world, migration is not a solution.[28]

A CHANGE IN THE DEATH RATE — Practically no one wants to see a rise in the death rate, and certainly such a rise is not likely to be adopted as a policy. In the past, death has frequently been used as a population control measure: sometimes by killing the aged or other incapacitated persons, but more often by infanticide.[29] In wars, the death of enemy soldiers is necessarily pursued, and there are instances of genocide attempted against whole groups. In modern eyes, however, keeping people alive is generally viewed as a supreme value; a policy of deliberately destroying life is so tabooed that capital punishment for even the most heinous crimes is outlawed in some countries. Indeed, the genius of modern civilization in keeping people alive

---

[27] See the discussion of economic development below.

[28] Except, of course, for the possibility of travel away from the earth — a possibility we shall show in a moment is remote indeed.

[29] See Herbert Aptheker, *Anjea* (New York: Godwin, 1931), Chapter 7; Knud Rasmussen, *The Netsilik Eskimos* (Copenhagen, 1931), pp. 139–40; Olga Lang, *Chinese Family and Society* (New Haven: Yale University Press, 1946), p. 150; Raymond Firth, *We, the Tikopia,* 2nd ed. (London: Allen & Unwin, 1957).

has been, as we have seen, the major factor in creating the fantastic population increase of recent times.

Still, even though it is not adopted as a population policy, a rise in the death rate may prove to be an unintended and unwanted solution. There is no guarantee that the mounting population pressure will not ultimately give rise, directly or indirectly, to catastrophic rises in mortality. Warfare alone could decimate hundreds of millions, especially if fought with thermonuclear weapons. The Russians are estimated to have lost 25,000,000 through deaths caused by World War II.[30] It must be remembered that there is no inherent limit to the death rate. Entire populations can be wiped out, and with modern weapons the attackers could succeed in killing themselves as well as their enemies. In other words, as is usually the case, destruction can be more rapid than construction. Populations can be destroyed much faster than they can be built up by reproduction. The threat of mortality as a terrible solution to the population problem is one of the dangers that drives people to try to find other solutions.

REDUCTION OF THE BIRTH RATE—In industrial countries the rate of population growth has been greatly reduced by a long-run decline in the birth rate. For instance, in four countries of northwest Europe, the average annual births per 1000 population were as shown by the figures in Table 7. In the first half-century, the rate of natural increase was held down by a high death rate, whereas in the last period the birth rate had dropped faster than mortality. This reduction came primarily from the use of contraception and abortion within marriage, but it was helped along, especially at first, by postponement or abnegation of marriage.

The thought has naturally arisen, then, that birth rates could be further reduced in industrial countries (to the point where, on the average, they match the low death rates and the population does not grow) and that they could be drastically reduced in the underdeveloped countries (to begin to catch up with the spectacular declines in mortality).

This solution, however, encounters opposition from those who cling to the rules and sentiments that prevailed when death rates were high. At that time—say, during the Middle Ages in Europe—the problem was not too many babies but too few, because, since the death rate was high, a prolific rate of reproduction was required merely to replace the population. The modern fall in the death rate, which has more than doubled the average

---

[30] Warren W. Eason, "The Soviet Population Today," *Foreign Affairs,* Vol. 37 (July, 1959), pp. 600–02.

TABLE 7

History of Crude Birth, Death, and Natural Increase Rates,
Advanced European Countries

Period	Birth Rate	Death Rate	Natural Increase Rate
1731–1749	31.9	28.9	3.0
1750–1799	32.6	26.9	5.7
1800–1849	31.5	22.5	9.0
1850–1899	31.5	18.9	12.6
1900–1949	21.0	12.5	8.5
1950–1968	16.7	10.0	6.7

Sources: (Until 1841, the average is for three countries – Denmark, Norway, and Sweden; after 1841, England–Wales is added.) Computed from H. Gille, "Demographic History of the Northern European Countries in the Eighteenth Century," *Population Studies*, Vol. 3 (June, 1949), p. 63; *Demographic Yearbook* (1953, '54, '57, '63, '68); *Population and Vital Statistics Report; Statistisk Aarbok* (Denmark: 1922, 1954); the Registrar General's *Statistical Review of England and Wales* (1941, 1950).

lifetime, eliminated the need for prolific reproduction but did not immediately alter the old religious and moral rules supporting it. Eventually, in Western countries, individual couples took matters in their own hands, using contraception and abortion to reduce their offspring. Although all religious groups opposed such practices at first, some of them – e.g., Methodists, Lutherans, Presbyterians, Episcopalians, Reformed Jews – changed their views to conform to the changed conditions, holding that the limitation and spacing of births are morally obligatory. The Roman Catholic Church, perhaps because of its celibate clergy, which can be expected to take a negative attitude toward sexual enjoyment, remained more strongly opposed to birth control; but when the notion of the "safe period" was announced in the early 1930's (coincident with the onset of the great economic depression), the Catholic clergy declared this method to be morally acceptable under certain circumstances and thus left itself opposed only to what it called "artificial" methods. Some Protestant sects and Orthodox Judaism have remained opposed to birth control, but not with the vehemence or influence that characterized the Catholic attack on "artificial" methods. In the 1960's, however, with the continued acceleration of world population growth and with growing interest in family planning, public opinion strongly favored birth control. According to a Gallup survey in 1965, 84 percent of Americans generally, and 81 percent of Catholics, favored making information about birth control "easily available to any *married* person who wants it"; and 50 percent of Americans and 43 percent of Catholics favored doing so for

392 The World's Population Crisis

single persons.[31] In addition, another survey in 1965 showed that among Catholic women using some method of birth control, only 36 percent were relying on "rhythm," the only method sanctioned by the church (the proportion was 54 percent in 1955).[32] Various studies indicate that American Catholics do not desire large families, despite the praise of them in parochial textbooks.[33] With such lay intransigence, it is no wonder that in 1963 Pope John XXIII appointed a Commission for the Study of Population, Family and Birth, a body subsequently enlarged by Pope Paul VI. Many Catholics expected this commission to revise the church's official position on birth control, and a secret report of the commission, released without authorization by the *National Catholic Reporter* in early 1967, indicated that a majority of the commission did oppose the church's ban on birth control. However, in 1968 Pope Paul issued the encyclical *Humanae Vitae,* which rejected the commission's findings. The doctrine of Pope Pius XI in 1930 forbade

> every action which, either in anticipation of the conjugal act, or in its accomplishment, or in the development of its natural consequences, proposes, whether as an end or as a means, to render procreation impossible.

The only means of birth control left open to pious Catholics was abstinence or the rhythm method. A survey in 1969 showed that only 16.3 percent of Catholic women in the United States agreed with the Pope; 60.2 percent definitely disagreed, and the rest were ambivalent or nonresponsive.[34]

---

[31] Population Council, "American Attitudes on Population Policy," *Studies in Family Planning,* No. 9 (January, 1966), pp. 6–7; for earlier poll results, see *National Catholic Reporter* (December 2, 1964), p. 10.

[32] Charles F. Westoff, "United States: Methods of Fertility Control, 1955, 1960, and 1965," *Population Studies,* No. 17 (February, 1967), p. 3; and Pascal K. Whelpton, Arthur A. Campbell and John E. Patterson, *Fertility and Family Planning in the United States* (Princeton, N. J.: Princeton University Press, 1966), p. 284.

[33] Judith Blake, "The Americanization of Catholic Reproductive Ideals," *Population Studies,* Vol. 20 (July, 1966), pp. 27–43. Catholics in the United States have somewhat larger families than Protestants and Jews. For instance, in the 1960 survey, the number of children born to Catholic women aged 35–39 was 3.0; to Protestant women, 2.7. The difference in fertility is less than usually supposed. Some Catholic countries, such as Belgium and Italy, have very low birth rates—lower than some Protestant countries such as Australia and New Zealand and much lower than Muslim, Hindu, and Buddhist countries.

[34] Charles F. Westoff, "United States: Methods of Fertility Control, 1955, 1960, and 1965," p. 6. For further history and discussion of public attitudes, see Alvah W. Sulloway, *Birth Control and Catholic Doctrine* (Boston: Beacon, 1959); John P. Murphy and John D. Laux, *The Rhythm Way to Family Happiness* (Ithaca, N. Y.: Practical Publishers, 1955); Kingsley Davis and Judith Blake, "Birth Control and Public Policy," *Commen-*

It seems likely, if civilization continues, that use of modern birth control devices will eventually become an established practice everywhere in the world. There is no guarantee, however, that it will come soon enough or be practiced thoroughly enough to solve the worsening problems of runaway population growth. What is being proposed as a demographic solution, by most policy leaders today, is not a passive waiting for contraceptive practice to spread, but a deliberate attempt to speed its diffusion. Otherwise, it is feared, the interim population growth will be so enormous that it will interfere with economic development and civilized progress. Also, there are reasons for family planning that are independent of the question of population growth. The proper spacing and limitation of births are held to be good for the health and welfare of both parents and children and to be advantageous for the education and employment of youth. The proponents of family planning, therefore, wish to have efficient contraceptive methods and materials made available as soon as possible to all people, in lower as well as in upper classes and in agrarian as well as in industrial countries. They believe that in peasant countries the governments can play a crucial role in speeding this availability, and that international aid should be expended not just to reduce deaths and finance economic projects, but also to reduce births. Only in this way, the proponents of family planning say, can the heavy burdens of functionless fertility among the poorer peoples of the world be reduced.

Of course, if one maintains the view that there is no population problem, then no demographic amelioration of such problems can be admitted. For instance, at the 1947 meeting of the United Nations Population Commission, the Ukrainian representative, Vasil Rjabichko, stated: "We consider as barbarous all propositions formulated in this commission in favor of the limitation of marriages or the limitation of births within marriage." [35] This view was softened by later Soviet writers, as world population growth accelerated. Meanwhile, the governments of underdeveloped countries—the ones most exposed to the evils of abnormal increase—did not wait for the theoreticians in Moscow or Rome to decide whether birth limitation is correct or not. They inaugurated national policies aimed at reducing the birth rate. Whether these policies are succeeding is an important question. The chief measure has been "family planning," the adequacy of which we shall examine.

---

tary, Vol. 29 (February, 1960), pp. 115–21; John T. Noonan, Jr., *Contraception* (Cambridge, Mass.: Harvard University Press, 1965); Carl Reiterman, "Birth Control and Catholics," *Journal for the Scientific Study of Religion,* Vol. 4 (Spring, 1965), pp. 213–33.

[35] Cited by Alfred Sauvy, *De Malthus à Mao Tsé-toung* (Paris: Denoël, 1958), p. 257.

INTERNATIONAL MIGRATION AS A SOLUTION — Migration generally has a favorable connotation among "liberals," because it is seen as an escape valve for political dissidents. It is therefore sometimes suggested as a solution to population problems in preference to limiting fertility. Obviously, if one is thinking of the world's population as a whole, migration offers no help. It is at best a local aid, and in some cases — for example, Puerto Rico after World War II, Ireland after the famine of the 1840's, Palestine at the creation of the Israeli state, and Norway, Sweden, and Switzerland in the latter nineteenth century — migration can bring substantial if temporary relief from population pressure. But such local relief is ephemeral unless accompanied by a decline in the birth rate. China sent out millions of emigrants over the world, as did India, with no lessening of population growth, because the gap left by migration was quickly filled by the continuing high birth rate. In fact, what migration seems to do in many cases is to postpone the reduction of the birth rate, as can be shown by analysis of European demographic history. In any case, migration is exceedingly costly, because the migrants, mainly in the young working ages, have been reared and educated, if educated at all, at the expense of the sending country. This cost is compensated for to some extent, but usually not sufficiently, by remittances received from the emigrants. Often it is the more skilled people who leave, thus depriving the sending country of human resources for which it has paid and for which it has a need. The tendency of scientific and technological manpower to gravitate from underdeveloped to highly developed countries and, among the developed countries, from the poorer to the wealthier (such as the United States), has been characterized as the "brain drain" and considered so undesirable that efforts have been made to mitigate it.[36]

Migration can also have disadvantages from the standpoint of the receiving country. Unless the migrants are similar in culture to the people whose country they enter, they are not assimilated. Thus, the Irish in the United States kept their own religion by going to parochial schools where this religion was reinforced, marrying among their own co-religionists, advocat-

---

[36] In 1968 the United States admitted 3110 scientists and 9313 engineers as immigrants. The first figure was nearly equal to one-third of the doctorates conferred in science in that year, and the second was more than one-fourth of all engineering degrees granted. The drain comes in two ways — from foreign students remaining after they complete their education, and from foreign professionals coming after their education. See *Statistical Abstract of the United States, 1969,* pp. 129, 530–31; *Hearings* of Subcommittee on Government Operations, House of Representatives, 90th Cong., 2nd Sess. (January 23, 1968); F. Bechhofer, ed., *Population Growth and the Brain Drain* (Edinburgh: Edinburgh University Press, 1969), pp. 1–71.

ing laws for the entire community based on their own religious principles, and so forth. The Indians in South Africa, Malaya, Fiji, and Burma remained a separate community, as did the Chinese in Indonesia, Malaya, Borneo, Thailand, and many other places where they went. When assimilation does not occur, friction develops between the immigrant minority or majority and the rest of the population. Some observers therefore maintain that migration often creates greater problems than it solves. This would seem to be the case with the Arab refugees from Palestine, with the Chinese in Indonesia, with the Indians in Burma, with the West Indian and West African Negroes in Britain. In time of war or international tension, unassimilated bodies of immigrants — e.g., the Japanese and Germans in Brazil, the Turkish Muslims in communist Bulgaria, the French in Algeria, the Tamils in Ceylon — are sometimes more loyal to a country other than the local one, or else are feared to be. Furthermore, various groups in a country are economically injured, or feel injured, by immigration. Employers often want immigrants for precisely the same reason that labor unions do not want them — their cheap labor. Religious groups do not want immigrants who have sinful customs, and political groups do not want those of opposite political persuasion. A democratic country is hardly likely to welcome communists or fascists as immigrants, and vice versa.[37]

There is little wonder, then, that each nation jealously guards its right to determine whom it will admit and whom it will exclude. Some nations, such as Japan and Russia, have been extremely exclusionist in policy, whereas others such as the United States and Australia have been extremely liberal; but in the last analysis the record of past migration, in which whole continents were conquered by people from overseas, is not likely to be repeated. The very fact that the fastest growth of population is now occurring in the poorer rather than the wealthier lands indicates the immensity of the migration that would have to take place to make a dent in regional problems. The nonindustrial countries contain about two-thirds of the world's people. Their rate of growth is such that they will add approximately one billion to their population between 1970 and 1985, or an average of 65 million per year.

---

[37] For a skeptical but penetrating analysis of migration as a solution of population problems, see William Petersen, *Planned Migration* (Berkeley: University of California Press, 1955) and W. D. Forsyth, *The Myth of Open Spaces* (Melbourne: Melbourne University Press, 1942). Also see Julius Isaac, *Economics of Migration* (New York: Oxford University Press, 1947). The objection of the British public to continued Negro and Asian immigration is said to be one of the reasons for the victory of the Conservative Party over the incumbent Labor Party in 1970.

Merely to relieve these areas of their natural increase would therefore require a volume of migration which *in a single year* would exceed the total intercontinental migration estimated for the world *during the 83 years* from 1846 to 1932.[38] In other words, the volume of migration would have to be some 80 times what it was during the heyday of international migration in the nineteenth and early twentieth centuries. It seems inconceivable that the countries to which migrants are attracted would admit such an enormous influx, or that the ships and money for it could be found in any case.

As for interplanetary travel, is there any heavenly body that would be both accessible and livable? Would anybody want to go there? If not, how would the interplanetary migrants (victims) be chosen? What would be the costs? Merely to remove the earth's natural increase, approximately 185,000 persons would, at present, have to be shot into space *each day*. It is expensive to move people from one country to another on *this* globe; to move them through space in any number is prohibitive. During the 1965–1969 period the United States federal government spent some 17.3 billion dollars on manned space flight alone (not counting all the other expenses indirectly contributory to the flights). With this expenditure, four men actually landed on the moon, but they stayed only a few hours because the moon is uninhabitable. The task of sending even a few people to other (more distant) heavenly bodies is stupendous, and the idea of sending many millions is nonsensical. The striking thing about this proposed solution to the world's population problem is not its impracticality but the strange phobia that compels people to suggest it. Evidently some people are so afraid of human fertility control that they will seize upon any alternative, no matter how improbable.

ECONOMIC DEVELOPMENT AS A SOLUTION — The Ukrainian representative, in a statement already cited, said, "Overpopulation is nothing but the fruit of capitalism; with an adequate social regime, it is possible to face any growth of population. It is the economy that must be adapted to the population, not the reverse." This notion has been echoed time and again. In 1959, for example, the Roman Catholic bishops of the United States declared:

> United States Catholics do not wish to ignore or minimize the problem of population pressure, but they do deplore the studious omission of adequate reference to the role of modern agriculture in food production. The "population explosion" alarmists do not place in proper focus

[38] A. M. Carr-Saunders, *World Population* (Oxford: Clarendon, 1936), p. 49, estimates the total intercontinental *em*igration during 1846–1932 at 53.45 million, and the total *im*migration during 1821–1932 at 59.19 million.

the idea of increasing the acreage yield to meet the food demands of an increasing population. . . . It seems never to dawn on them that in a chronic condition where we have more people than food, the logical answer would be, not to decrease the number of people but to increase the food supply which is almost unlimited in potential.[39]

At first, these statements may seem plausible. But let us ask again, what is the problem? Apparently the problem posed is poverty—a low level of living. Now, if the sole solution proposed is economic development, then we have to ask, once again, what "economic development" is. It is a *rise* in the level of living—that is, a movement away from poverty. By definition, obviously, to the extent that we have economic development we will not have poverty. But this is merely a play on words, not an intelligent proposal for solving a problem. It is like telling a man who has pneumonia that the remedy is simple, what he needs to do is get rid of the pneumonia. The solution for poverty is economic development, that is, getting rid of poverty.

The question still remains, how to get economic development (i.e., release from poverty). What the demographers and many economists are proposing is that, along with specific economic measures such as the use of international funds and domestic savings for the financing of factories, highways, research laboratories, irrigation schemes, public health programs, and so forth, attention should also be given to bringing down the birth rate and thus relieving the mounting pressure for consumer goods and the mounting costs of schooling and other immediate services for children. In other words, the *demographic* measure is proposed as an aid to, not a substitute for, economic development. It is like saying that the pneumonia patient should have both medicine and rest.

SCIENCE AS THE SOLUTION—As noted already, to claim that science will take care of any population growth is to deny that there is a population problem. Logically, therefore, such a claim offers no "solution"; and when it is offered as a solution, it has certain inherent contradictions. Many who advance the claim think in "food supply" terms, the idea being that if science can produce ever more food, the population can keep ever growing. But if science is to become continually more profound, the population cannot be at a subsistence level, because science is not advanced by people at that level; it is maintained and advanced only by people having the means to acquire university educa-

---

[39] From the text of the statement appearing in *The New York Times* (November 25, 1959).

tion and technical skills, to support research laboratories and research personnel, to finance libraries and technical journals, and to reward scientific and academic achievement. A really large world population can therefore be supported only at a very high, not at a subsistent, standard of living. Yet a high standard of living means that the earth's resources are used not simply to support more people but to support fewer people better.

The paradoxical character of the "miraculous science" solution becomes particularly clear if we ask again what the problem is. The problem depends on the goal. Is the goal simply to have more people on the earth? Colin Clark, a British economist who was a member of the Pope's population commission, has estimated that the world has enough land to feed 47 billion people "on an American type diet" and 157 billion on a Japanese type diet.[40]

A Soviet writer, not to be outdone, has predicted that science will enable us to capture 10 percent of the solar energy reaching the earth, and that it will then be possible "to obtain food for 10,000 people per square kilometer" [26,000 per square mile] and to support 933 billion on the earth's entire cultivable land area.[41]

What kind of people would be, on the one hand, so brilliant that they could develop science and technology far beyond present attainment and, on the other hand, so stupid that they would occupy the earth's land at an average density of 26,000 per square mile? The scramble of present-day men to escape crowded central cities does not suggest that they would use all their science simply to increase their population density. But as long as the goal is assumed to be more people, then the uses to which science can be put are limitless. For instance, one drawback to population increase is the size of human beings. Science could therefore breed smaller ones — say human beings weighing only five pounds. Even this would be too big. More human beings could inhabit the earth if they were the size of ants.

In view of the present poverty, pollution, illiteracy, and conflict in much of the world, the burden of proof is on those who believe that science makes population growth no problem. Instead, it appears that science has helped to create the problem. The application of science is out of balance; it is being applied with remarkable success to the control of deaths, but not to a compensatory control of births. It *can* be applied, and with equal success (even at far less cost), to the control of births; and if this is done, population pressure will be removed as a major obstacle to scientific development.

---

[40] Colin Clark, *Population Growth and Land Use* (London: Macmillan, 1967), pp. 142–53.

[41] K. Malin, "Food Resources of the Earth," *Proceedings of the World Population Conference, 1965,* Vol. 3, pp. 385–87.

NATIONAL POPULATION POLICIES

The assumption that skyrocketing population growth will not hinder economic development and other goals is so dubious that many governments have abandoned it. Instead, they are undertaking to introduce some fertility control in order to insure or hasten material progress. Since the purpose is widely approved, people have tended to praise the effort uncritically; but the question remains as to whether the measures taken are adequate. What are the measures?

THE FAMILY PLANNING EMPHASIS—It turns out, upon examination, that national population-control policies rely almost exclusively on "family planning," which means furnishing couples with contraceptives. In the 1950's and most of the 1960's it was automatically and unconsciously assumed that this was *the* way to solve the population problem, and governments were strongly urged to set up programs designed to improve contraceptive methods and diffuse them to the public. India, in 1952, was the first independent country to inaugurate such a program, but soon others followed, such as Pakistan, South Korea, Turkey, and Singapore. By 1970 over 20 countries had some form of governmental family planning program. However, by 1967, questions were raised concerning the adequacy of this approach, both on empirical and on theoretical grounds.[42] A lively debate ensued after that, but for various reasons—the power of the organized family planning movement, the millions invested in existing programs, and political expediency—government policies did not change. In order to delineate the issues as clearly as possible, let us look at a concrete program—that of the Republic of Singapore.

In 1965 the Singapore government set forth its population policy in a White Paper, the essentials of which are as follows:

> Singapore's present population is over 1.8 million . . . Our annual crude birth rate of over 30 per thousand is too high . . . There is too much unnecessary human misery . . . this can be effectively stopped through a determined effort on the part of Government to provide Family Planning on a mass basis. This we propose to do.

> It is the intention of the Singapore Government, under its Second 5-Year Development Plan (1966–70), to bring the message to every mar-

---

[42] See Kingsley Davis, "Population Policy: Will Current Programs Succeed?" *Science,* Vol. 158 (November 10, 1967), pp. 730–39.

ried woman . . . that Family Planning brings her immeasurable benefits. And, at her request, to advise her on the best available methods of
Family Planning which will be simple, inexpensive, and safe.

It is proposed to establish a Family Planning and Population Board.

Each FP [Family Planning] clinic is expected to deal up to 12,500 IUCD
[Intra-uterine Contraceptive Device] insertions per annum.

From 1970, when the Plan is over, 12 Centres with 14 FP clinics will
continue to service all cases.[43]

To lower the birth rate, a *government program* devoted to *family planning* is
assumed to be both necessary and sufficient. Family planning itself is viewed
as a *medical* matter, requiring *clinics* and *a near perfect, medically supervised
method.* Further, it is only for *married women* and is *entirely voluntary.* These
features are typical of virtually all national efforts purporting to lower fertility.

The basic difficulty with this exclusive reliance on family planning is that
it misconstrues the population problem. Overpopulation or too rapid growth
is a condition of the society as a whole, not an individual predicament. The
family planning movement stresses as its motto that every couple should
have the number of children they want, but the number of children couples
want is not necessarily the number that the society should have. The "planning" is only *family* planning, whereas "population control" involves *national*
planning. We do not construe planning by each businessman as national economic planning, nor do we regard freedom to use drugs as drug control.

Implicitly, the family planning approach assumes that the sole cause of
the population problem is *unwanted* babies. It says, in effect, that if couples
plan all their offspring there will be no unwanted babies and *hence* no population problem. Unfortunately, as surveys indicate, people can want many children as well as few. In the advanced countries the desired number exceeds
the actual number, despite the fact that populations are growing rapidly.
In the underdeveloped countries, both rural and urban couples want a sizable
family. In South Korea, where a national family planning program began in
1964, a survey in 1967 found no change in ideal family size. "Almost every
respondent says she wants two or three sons, with one or two daughters." [44]

---

[43] Singapore, *White Paper on Family Planning,* Cmd. 22 (1965), pp. 1, 12, 13. Quoted
at greater length in Population Council, "Government Policy Statements on Population: An Inventory," *Reports on Population Family Planning* (February, 1970), p. 10.

[44] "Korea: Trends in Four National KAP Surveys, 1964–67," *Studies in Family
Planning,* No. 43 (June, 1969), p. 7. In Ghana 94 percent of women in an urban sample,
and 98 percent in a rural sample, wanted four or more children. D. I. Pool, "Ghana: A
Survey on Fertility and Attitudes towards Family Limitation," *ibid.,* No. 25 (December, 1967), p. 11.

Under some conditions women will want many children, and under other conditions they will want few. It is the conditions, not the availability of contraception, which determine the number couples want. Given certain conditions, they will lower their fertility with or without a government program. The long decline of the birth rate in advanced countries from 1870 to 1932 took place in the teeth of governmental, religious, and medical opposition to birth control. It occurred because people wished to rise or to avoid falling in relative social status by taking advantage of the new opportunities unfolding in a developing society—opportunities that early marriage and prolific reproduction obstructed. They used whatever means were available—late marriage, nonmarriage, illegal abortion, coitus interruptus, nonvaginal coitus, condoms, douches, diaphragms, sponges, foam tablets, safe periods.[45] Some of these methods, such as nonvaginal coitus and abortion, were close to 100 percent effective as birth control devices, others were imperfect; but it is a mistake to think that fertility cannot be greatly reduced with imperfect methods. Many couples have had the number of children they wanted with an imperfect contraceptive; they simply used it all the time, the occasional failures being the number of children desired. During the Depression, without the IUD or the "pill," the people of the advanced nations reduced their fertility to such a point that, had it continued at that level, the populations would have declined. In the case of Japan, whose birth rate fell later, the most rapid decline was accomplished mainly by postponed marriage and abortion.

Clearly if the conditions are such that few children are wanted, people are not so stupid as to be unable to find the means. If, on the other hand, conditions are such that they want many, no contraceptive, no matter how perfect, will stop them from having them.

It follows that a national policy that confines itself to furnishing contraceptives cannot provide population control. The only contribution it can make is perhaps, in the transition from a peasant-agrarian to an urban-industrial type of society, to facilitate the adjustment of reproductive behavior to the new conditions. In this transition, the individual's ability to adjust means to new conditions is not perfect, and furnishing the means may speed the adjustment.

Although there is thus no inherent disadvantage to furnishing contraceptives, the tendency to rely on this alone has distinct disadvantages for population control. In the first place, it deflects attention from making those social changes that would motivate people to reduce their offspring. These changes

---

[45] See Kingsley Davis, "The Theory of Change and Response in Modern Demographic History," *Population Index,* Vol. 29 (October, 1963), pp. 345–66. Reprinted in Bobbs–Merrill Reprint Series in the Social Sciences, No. S–568.

would necessarily be unorthodox, because they would go against the pronatalist institutions and values built into the structure of all preindustrial societies. An exclusive emphasis on family planning deludes people into believing the population problem is being solved painlessly. In the second place, even within its own sphere, the family planning movement has been restrictive. Until recently when the abortion movement became popular, it opposed legalizing abortion — in fact, it justified contraception as a way of combatting "the abortion problem." By concerning itself with *married* women and *family* planning, by stressing its sterility treatment as well as its contraceptive role, and by linking its services with *maternal* health, the movement reinforced familistic ideology. It viewed women as having childbearing as their sole concern. By declaring family planning to be a "health" service, and by promoting contraceptive techniques that require medical attention, the movement constricted contraceptive programs to the scope permitted by the scarcity of medical personnel, a scarcity particularly acute in underdeveloped countries. Women seeking contraception were "patients," although they certainly were not "sick." The population problem, which is an economic and social problem, was given to physicians to solve, although they are not trained in economics and demography but in the skills that created the problem in the first place — saving lives and bringing babies into the world.

Social Change and Population Control

Proponents of current policies reply that family planning is a "first step," that it has the advantage of being "acceptable," and that its program is "voluntary" whereas other measures are "compulsory." [46] The critics reply that if various steps are needed, taking one and not the others will delay the possibility of controlling population. They say, in fact, that this defense confirms the criticism that family planning is a means of avoiding effective measures. As for acceptability, the critics point out that, since the older mores are pronatalist, effective measures will of course be unacceptable until an effort is made to redefine the institutional patterns. Finally, the "compulsory" accu-

[46] See the debate between the present author and William McElroy, "Will Family Planning Solve the Population Problem?" *Victor-Bostrom Fund, Report No. 10 (Fa* 1968), pp. 16–17, 30–31. The most systematic attempt to answer the critics is that by Bernard Berelson, "Beyond Family Planning," *Science,* Vol. 163 (February 7, 1969), pp. 533–43. Berelson is president of the Population Council, an organization which has invested millions of dollars of Ford, Rockefeller, and government funds in family planning programs around the world.

sation is turned against the family planners themselves, because in accepting the restrictions of the older mores in all but contraception itself, they are perpetuating the strong sanctions and role definitions that still compel people to reproduce in abundance. They are permitting children to be forced into early marriage in India and many other agrarian countries; they are permitting the seclusion of women in the home and their exclusion from economic and professional opportunities; and they are perpetuating old sexual taboos whose function was to maximize reproduction. Further, in treating the couple's desire for children as sacred, the family planners are confusing the issue, according to the critics. In the main, social control is not achieved by resorting to sheer force; it is achieved indirectly by altering the conditions under which people make their decisions. The interest rate, for example, is not regulated by laws compelling individuals to pay a certain rate, but rather by regulation of the money supply. Releasing people from old compulsions will do more to lower fertility than furnishing contraceptives, say the critics.

In general, the most effective social changes would be those that offer opportunities and goals that compete with family roles. For instance, giving advantages in housing, taxes, scholarships, and recreation to single as compared to married people, would discourage early marriage. Giving special educational and employment opportunities to women would foster career interests and therefore lessen motherhood as a woman's sole commitment. Structuring recreational life around the place of work rather than the home, and in the peer group rather than the family, would further discourage family formation. Discontinuing the custom of family names, giving more complete control over children to nursery and elementary schools while holding parents responsible for the costs, and releasing children from all responsibility for parents would tend to break down the ego-identity which plays a strong role in parental motivation. Also, giving young people a realistic, as opposed to a moralistic, education about sexual relations, family life, the position of women, population problems, and individual achievement would help release them from old taboos and role definitions that guaranteed a high rate of reproduction. As for methods of birth control, including abortion, these could be provided free of charge; those requiring no medical attention could be supplied through ordinary social and commercial channels.

The measures for keeping the birth rate low are not mysterious, and they do not require a "revolution of the whole society." There are countries today, notably those in Eastern Europe and Scandinavia, where the birth rate is at or near the replacement level. The problem is not lack of knowledge but lack of agreement. Until population control is given a priority so high that people will accept unorthodox social measures and unaccustomed self-discipline, no amount of "research" or "technical assistance" will suffice.

FUTURE DEVELOPMENTS IN WORLD POPULATION

It seems unlikely that human societies will achieve deliberate population control within the lifetime of those now adults. The chief obstacles are not ignorance or even old attitudes, but the economic and social interests bound up with reproduction. Surveys everywhere show that women do not want as many children as "nature" and low mortality can give them, but they do want more than just enough to replace the population. The reason is that the family is uniquely important in modern society. It is the only personal group to which one belongs regardless of what one is or does. To reduce its young members to only one or two children is risky, because if one child turns out badly, the loss is great. Also, since parents now live to an advanced age (the average American woman now bears her last child at age 30, then lives another 47 years!), further shrinkage of the nuclear family would deprive adults of the company of children during most of their existence. Institutional supports of the family will not be easily removed, because families strengthen other groups with which people identify. The groups commanding the most loyalty – nations, religions, races, ethnic communities, linguistic groups – tend to be those to which people belong because their parents belonged. Their members acquire the group's attitudes and practices and distinctive genetic traits (if any) from their parents. Other things equal, the role of the group in the larger society is proportional to its size, particularly in a democracy where each person has a vote. Demographic competition is thus built into social organization throughout the world. As all groups achieve low mortality, differential fertility becomes a powerful weapon in intergroup competition. Of course, the advantages of sheer numerical aggrandizement are limited, because group success depends on skills as well as bodies, but in either case – in producing talents as well as bodies – the family is crucial and thus not likely to be deliberately undermined.

If deliberate control of fertility for society's benefit fails to occur, the already painful consequences of population growth will become worse. Some of the consequences, however, have a feedback character likely to decrease or reverse the growth by raising mortality. For instance, as more billions with ever higher levels of consumption struggle for the earth's scarce space and resources, all-out warfare seems inescapable. Compared to past wars, however, a new world war could be far more deadly, simply because of technological advances. Not only would a thermonuclear war cause direct casualties of an unprecedented magnitude, but it would cause indirect ones as well – in star-

vation due to the destruction of crops and transport facilities, in disease due
to the loss of nutrition, shelter, and medicines, and in fetal deaths due to ir-
radiation. The genetic damage could be so great among the survivors that
a licensing system for parenthood would be adopted, only those persons least
likely to transmit defects being allowed to reproduce.[47] In that case, the social
control of reproduction would be a reality, and when the number of people
again became oppressive, effective population control could be instituted.

The argument is not that solving the population problem will end warfare,
but that ending warfare will be impossible if population growth is left uncontrolled. The population problem is an underlying and long-run irritant
that people overlook because they are impressed by the short-run symptomatic events that "cause" wars or by the "motives" of those who "make"
wars. They also seize upon the fact that the more technologically advanced
underdeveloped countries—like Hong Kong, Singapore, Taiwan, Chile, and
Costa Rica—are now showing declines in fertility as they shift from a preindustrial to an industrial level. Yet the pressure is now on a scale hitherto unknown. The increase in the world's inhabitants in the last ten years—some
600 million—*exceeds the entire population of the Western Hemisphere* by 27
percent. The ten-year increase in the developed countries themselves, where
fertility is already at an industrial level, was 119 million, equal to one-half
the population of the Soviet Union. Since at the same time people are making
their "demands," the population explosion seems bound to set off a political
explosion, regardless of what or who lights the fuse.

---

[47] See the author's "Sociological Aspects of Genetic Control" in John D. Roslansky,
ed., *Genetics and the Future of Man* (New York: Appleton-Century-Crofts, 1965), pp.
173–204.

9

Race
Relations

THOMAS F. PETTIGREW

American race relations often appear as a blurred series of violent newspaper headlines. We read of racial law suits, protest demonstrations, ghetto riots, Black Panther incidents, police brutality, and the assassinations of black leaders.

These events are important indicators of the process of racial change in the United States. They expose the bitter resistance to change of some white Americans and the desperate insistence on it of some black Americans. Yet sensational episodes highlighted by the glare of mass-media attention cannot in themselves provide the broad sociological view necessary for a full understanding of the sweeping changes underway on the American racial scene. This chapter, then, endeavors to go behind the headlines and to suggest a broader perspective on this critical social problem. It focuses almost entirely on black-white relations in the United States. Serious social problems also exist in other racial contexts both inside and outside of America, of course; but we shall allude to them only by way of comparisons with our central concern—the most pervasive and profound of our nation's intergroup conflicts.

SIX BASIC APPROACHES TO THE PROBLEM

All relations between groups are conditioned by six interconnected factors, each forming a different but necessary approach: They are discussed under the rubrics, *historical, sociocultural, situational, personality, phenomenological,* and *stimulus-object*.[1] "There is no master key," wrote Gordon Allport, the originator of this eclectic scheme. "Rather, what we have at our disposal is a ring of keys, each of which opens one gate of understanding."[2] As shown in Figure 1, the six approaches form a lens model that focuses down from the broadest approach, the historical, to the main stimulus-object of the process, in this case, black Americans. While this scheme helps to order our thinking about race relations, one should not be misled by Figure 1 into thinking that the six sets of factors do not overlap or that there is no interaction between such diverse sets as the sociocultural and personality factors. The force of these qualifications becomes clearer when we review what each approach entails.

THE HISTORICAL APPROACH — How did black-white relations in North America begin? Why have blacks been singled out as objects of prejudice and discrimination? How was slavery different in the American colonies from slavery elsewhere and what are the consequences of these differences today? And how did the past shape the particular patterns of racial segregation that have characterized the United States in this century? Only history can supply the answers.

As illustrated in Figure 1, history offers the broadest context of any of the six approaches. In bold strokes, historical considerations outline the scope and direction of the process; but, like any one of the approaches, these considerations are incomplete in themselves. For instance, history does not spell out how particular social forces, once begun, eventually structure diverse racial patterns in similar localities, or how one white American develops a hatred of blacks while another does not. In short, to utilize fully the general insights that history provides, it is necessary to trace these insights through a series of more specific approaches.

---

[1] This scheme is adapted from one proposed for prejudice in Gordon W. Allport, *The Nature of Prejudice* (Cambridge: Addison-Wesley, 1954), pp. 206–18.

[2] *Ibid.,* p. 208.

FIGURE 1

Six Approaches to the Study of Race Relations [a]

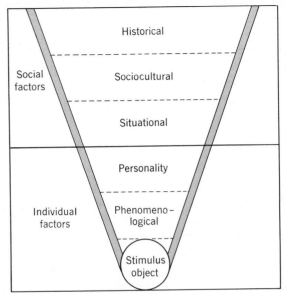

[a] Source: adapted from Gordon W. Allport, *The Nature of Prejudice* (Cambridge: Addison-Wesley, 1954), Figure 11, p. 207.

THE SOCIOCULTURAL APPROACH—This second category includes the many cultural and institutional factors which form the sociocultural setting within which race relations take place. A new group of relevant questions are now posed: How have black Americans changed demographically, politically, and economically in this century? What is the significance for black-white relations of the dominant social trends in American society? Together with situational factors, sociocultural considerations constitute the basic contribution of sociology to the understanding of this contemporary social problem.

THE SITUATIONAL APPROACH—Narrowing the analysis down to the third of the social approaches, the situational perspective considers the specific context in which the races actually meet face to face. It is here that the historical and sociocultural factors, on the one hand, and the individual factors, on the other, come to a focus and, conditioned by particular circumstances, produce "race relations" as such. Throughout this chapter, we shall stress the critical importance of interracial contact and the conditions under which it occurs. This is at the heart of the situational approach, and it is central to the design of effective remedies. Indeed we shall contend that *efforts at improving American race relations are successful to the extent that they further black-white contact under optimal conditions.*

But such a contention raises a series of key questions: What are the conditions for "optimal" contact? How do legal decisions affect "the hearts and minds of men?" How are racial attitudes altered by new interracial experiences? Research in sociology and social psychology provides interesting answers to these queries.

THE PERSONALITY APPROACH—The initial three approaches explain the social climate within which racial interaction occurs. But what about the individuals who live and act in this climate? Beginning with personality considerations, the remaining three approaches are concerned with individual factors.

Do white Americans need, for various psychological reasons, antiblack bigotry? This is no mere academic issue for psychologists to ponder; the answer is vital to the future of American race relations. If the answer is "yes," then the modification of the country's racial patterns faces stern difficulties, and strategies for change might strive largely to contain the prejudice while minimizing discrimination. But if the answer is essentially "no," then the reformer can set his sights higher and work for an interracial society where racial prejudice and discrimination are minor social problems at worst. We need, then, to sift carefully through the available evidence on this and related personality issues.

THE PHENOMENOLOGICAL APPROACH—This approach refers to how white Americans view their nation's race relations and their own interracial contact and experiences. After all, it is what men think is true, whether or not it is indeed true, that actually guides their behavior. Here we check on the racial stereotypes which are prevalent in the United States, and how these capsule images of a whole race have influenced our thinking less in recent years.

THE STIMULUS-OBJECT APPROACH—Finally, we look at the focus of the issue, the black American himself—not just as a victim of prejudice and discrimination, but as a reactor to this pattern of oppression.

Let us now discuss America's racial problems, their causes, and their potential remedies in terms of this multiple-causation model.

THE HISTORICAL APPROACH
TO RACE RELATIONS [3]

Slavery

Blacks have been an integral part of American society ever since their arrival at Jamestown, Virginia on a Dutch frigate in August, 1619. It is erroneous to think of Negroes as merely transplanted Africans or as a group with a culture totally divorced from the larger society, for these conceptions miss a vital historical point. After 14 generations, black Americans truly belong in the United States; not even white racists question their "belongingness." [4] They are Americans in every conceivable sense. And this fact ironically poses the problem: Although an integral part of the American nation, blacks have for three and one-half centuries been denied their full rights as citizens.

The roots of the problem can be traced back to slavery. The first "twenty and odd Negroes" who landed at Jamestown were apparently not slaves. The peculiar institution was not established by law in Virginia until 1661; and it placed upon Negroes, alone of all American minorities, a stigma of assumed inferiority which is only now being erased. This raises an important question: Why did slavery in the United States leave such a deep and lasting scar while other areas of the world, such as Brazil, which had the institution longer, more successfully threw off its effects?

The answer lies in the peculiar nature of slavery under English law. The historian, Frank Tannenbaum, points out that the Iberian countries of Spain and Portugal, unlike England, had centuries of experience with slavery prior

---

[3] For an authoritative, one-volume history of the Negro in America see John Hope Franklin, *From Slavery to Freedom: A History of American Negroes,* 2nd ed. (New York: Knopf, 1961).

[4] This contrasts with the difficulty that colored peoples in England have in being accepted as "English." Landis notes that "belongingness" of blacks is typically not found in Europe or South Africa, but is throughout the New World. She suggests that this may be because no New World group, save perhaps Indian Americans, feel their roots are so deep that they can safely question the belongingness of others. Ruth Landis, "Biracialism in American Society: A Comparative View," *American Anthropologist,* Vol. 57 (December, 1955), pp. 1253–63.

to the founding of the New World.[5] Hence under Iberian law there evolved a special category for the slave as a human being. But English law, unfamiliar with the institution, had no such special category and treated the slave as merely dehumanized property—no different legally from a house, a barn, or an animal. Consequently, Latin America, emulating Iberian law, never developed the totally dehumanizing stigma surrounding slavery that the American colonies did, following English law. This is not to say that slavery was not also cruel in Latin America or that there are no race problems there at present; but it is to say that the Latin American definition of slavery left it without the stigmata of a legally dehumanized people.[6] Incidentally, Tannenbaum's thesis receives comparative support from the history of South Africa, for slavery began in South Africa under Dutch law, which, like English law, placed the slave in the same category as property.[7]

Slavery expanded rapidly once it was seized upon as a solution to the labor shortage in the colonies. There were, for example, 400 times as many blacks in Virginia in 1756 (120,000) as there were in 1650 (300).[8] This phenomenal growth soon led to white fears of slave revolts. Consequently, the colonial slave codes became firmly established by the early 1700's, codes that severely restricted the slave's movements and provided further legal support for slavery as a dehumanizing institution. Slavery varied considerably among the colonies. Large slave holdings were economically feasible only in warm areas with vast, flat, agricultural lands. Thus Maryland, Virginia, and South Carolina had the most slaves and the harshest codes, while New England had the fewest slaves and the mildest codes.

Three antislavery forces combined during the late eighteenth century to spawn the first strong movement against the peculiar institution: the liberal philosophy of the American Revolution, the struggle for the slave's allegiance during the Revolution, and the declining utility of slavery. This led to its gradual abolition in all of the Northern states by the early nineteenth century, and to a provision in the Northwest Ordinance that outlawed it in what became Ohio, Indiana, Illinois, Michigan, and Wisconsin. The movement almost succeeded in ending slavery even in the South, as agriculture there fell on bad times.

---

[5] Frank Tannenbaum, *Slave and Citizen: The Negro in the Americas* (New York: Knopf, 1947). For later validation, see H. S. Klein, *Slavery in the Americas: A Comparative Study of Cuba and Virginia* (Chicago: University of Chicago Press, 1967).

[6] Stanley Elkins, *Slavery* (Chicago: University of Chicago Press, 1959).

[7] For a sociological analysis of racial conflict in South Africa, see Pierre L. van den Berghe, *South Africa, A Study in Conflict* (Middletown, Conn.: Wesleyan University Press, 1965).

[8] John Hope Franklin, *From Slavery to Freedom: A History of American Negroes*, p. 72.

But just as southern slavery was teetering, a series of history-making inventions appeared that not only revived the institution, but expanded it as never before. In England, radically new spinning and weaving machinery made possible mass production of cotton textiles, leading to a voracious demand for cotton. The South, however, could not greatly expand its modest cotton production until an efficient method for removing seeds was devised. Never was an invention so eagerly sought. Soon a visiting young Yankee schoolteacher, Eli Whitney, developed a satisfactory gin. Because he could not secure a monopoly patent, moderately priced copies became widely available. Cotton now became the ruling passion of the region. Production soared. The amount grown in the South in 1830 was almost double that grown in 1820; by 1840 it had doubled again; and by 1860 it had more than tripled again.[9] The abolitionist trends were snuffed out. Slavery now had a firm economic base and vastly increased. From less than one million slaves in the entire nation in 1800, the number rose to two million by 1830 and to almost four million by 1860.[10] Slavery's deep roots required the bloody Civil War to end it.

But how could slaveholders treat human beings as mere property and also believe in the high American ideals of human equality? The answer is that many of them never did rest easily with this glaring contradiction, though they tried as best they could to rationalize the conflict. Into the nineteenth century, believers in slavery generally employed religious justifications. Slavery was an effective method, some claimed, to introduce Christianity to African heathens. God had willed that the black man serve the white man, claimed others who loosely interpreted selected passages of the Old Testament while ignoring the New Testament. In time, these rationalizations lost their potency. For one thing, blacks were increasingly becoming Christian themselves.

But just as the religious reasons were losing their force, new biological ideas were being introduced, for the nineteenth century was the age of Darwin and biological thinking. Almost desperately, many white Americans seized the racist theories from Europe and accepted the divisive and dangerous concepts of race and racial superiority.[11] And the new feature of modern slavery—its limitation to one group—could be explained away without invoking religious considerations. Negroes were slaves of Caucasians, so the reasoning had it, simply because they were a lower order of human

---

[9] Rayford W. Logan, *The Negro in the United States: A Brief History* (Princeton, N. J.: Van Nostrand, 1957), p. 13.

[10] United States Bureau of the Census, *Negro Population: 1790–1915* (Washington, D. C.: U. S. Government Printing Office, 1918), p. 53.

[11] William Stanton, *The Leopard's Spots: Scientific Attitudes Toward Race in America, 1815–59* (Chicago: University of Chicago Press, 1960).

development in a Darwinian sense. Naive and vicious as this seems today in the light of the vast advances in biology of recent generations, this racist explanation seemed logical to all but the thoughtful. For all one had to do was look around him. Were not slaves obviously inferior to their masters in intelligence and manners? And were they not happy and childlike in their behavior? And if such things are all biologically determined, is this not proof that whites are racially superior to Negroes? Such was the argument, for the sweeping importance of environment and opportunity were not understood at this time.

The Ostensibly "Free Negro"

The defenders of slavery sought to strengthen their case by pointing to the lowly condition of the free Negro. Though technically free, these blacks in the South were restricted in almost every conceivable manner. The haunting fear was that they would lead slave revolts. Most southern states kept their free Negroes from voting, denied their right to assemble, granted them no equality in the courts, circumscribed their movements, and attempted to withhold education from them. Consequently, many free Negroes slipped below the living standards of even the slaves, who at least enjoyed a modicum of paternalistic benefits in their status as property. Though again a repressive environment led directly to their desperate plight, the free Negroes of the South were often cited as proof that blacks were just children and needed the protection of slavery.

By 1860, there were almost one-half million free Negroes in the nation, and about one-half of them were in the North.[12] But they fared little better in the North prior to the Civil War.[13] Violent anti-Negro riots flared up in Providence, Cincinnati, New York, Pittsburgh, Philadelphia and other northern cities in the 1830's and 1840's. Most northern states either denied or restricted black suffrage, five did not allow Negroes to testify in court, two outlawed interracial marriage, and one, Oregon, even made it illegal for Negroes to hold real estate or make contracts. Many northern cities established separate Negro schools. Indeed even Massachusetts did not abolish *de jure* segregated schools until 1855.

The importance of this nationwide discrimination against the free Negro

---

[12] United States Bureau of the Census, *Negro Population: 1790–1915*, p. 53.

[13] For a treatment of the status of the freedman in the North, see Leon F. Litwack, *North of Slavery* (Chicago: University of Chicago Press, 1961).

prior to the Civil War was that it furnished a convenient and dangerous precedent for handling the emancipated blacks after the Civil War.[14] For example, the ink was barely dry at Appomattox before North Carolina had legislatively extended to the new freedmen the same restrictions, burdens, and disabilities that had formerly applied to free Negroes in that state. Other southern states passed similar statutes. In short, the full fruits of the most dramatic action in black American history — the 1863 Emancipation Proclamation — were being denied by the South as soon as the Civil War ended.

The Roots of Modern Segregation

Then the Reconstruction era began. The victorious Union retained its military occupation of the South and set up Reconstruction state governments. Today segregationists liken Reconstruction to the depths of the Dark Ages; but we must not forget that this period witnessed the repeal of anti-Negro laws and the passage of antidiscrimination laws throughout the South. Many blacks assumed important public office, and those with education proved capable. Mississippi, for instance, was ably represented by a Negro Senator who was a graduate of Oberlin College. The great tragedy of this period, however, is that measures were not employed to strengthen the South's sagging economy and thus make more permanent these sweeping improvements in race relations.

It is wrong to assume that the South reverted immediately to white supremacy when the Reconstruction era drew to a close in the 1870's. C. Vann Woodward has shown that segregation did *not* rush in as a system until very late in the nineteenth century.[15] Segregationists are fond of saying that segregation of the races has *always* been traditional in the South; but they ignore this interesting ten- to fifteen-year period after Reconstruction when formal discrimination and separation did not exist. It was not until the North tired of race relations problems and the South was faced with state political crises that legalized racism returned. Throughout the South, state government scandals and a powerful agrarian movement made it expedient to use the Negro once again as a scapegoat. White men had to stick together, argued the conservative politicians who feared a class coalition between Negro and poor white voters. Other whites joined them out of fear that uneducated Negroes would sell their votes to wealthy politicians.

---

[14] H. S. Klein, *Slavery in the Americas: A Comparative Study of Cuba and Virginia.*
[15] C. Vann Woodward, *The Strange Career of Jim Crow,* 2nd rev. ed. (New York: Oxford University Press, 1966).

By the turn of the century, southern states, one by one, were disfranchising the Negro. And between 1890 and 1910 the whole complex of so-called "Jim Crow" laws were enacted—separate railroad cars, separate lunch counters, separate doorways, separate toilets, and separate waiting rooms. Indeed no detail was too minute: Oklahoma later required separate telephone booths, Arkansas required separate gambling tables, and many courts began to use separate Bibles to be sworn upon.

This period marked the very nadir of Negro American fortunes in the 100 years since Abraham Lincoln's Emancipation Proclamation. It was the period of mass lynchings of blacks as well as an attack upon their legal rights and sense of human dignity. But with relentless determination, black Americans have step by step succeeded in this century to write Jim Crow's epitaph. This is a story we all know much better than the events of the nineteenth century: the mass migration of the Negro out of the rural South; the black community's ever-increasing political and economic power; the historic May, 1954 ruling of the United States Supreme Court against *de jure* segregation of public schools; and always the Negro's constant reminder to white America that racial discrimination betrays the nation's highest national ideals. It is to these institutional trends that we now turn.

THE SOCIOCULTURAL APPROACH TO RACE RELATIONS

Trends in six different areas provide a sociocultural perspective on race relations: *laws, demography, politics, housing, economics,* and *education.* Each area contributes understanding of one part of the problem; and proposed remedies within each of these fields supply part of the answer for future national goals.

Legal Trends [16]

THE SEGREGATION ERA, 1876–1910—We have seen how the black American's legal status in America began as mere property and seldom included the

---

[16] For legal histories of American race relations, see Jack Greenberg, *Race Relations and American Law* (New York: Columbia University Press, 1959); Albert P. Blaustein and Clarence C. Ferguson, Jr., *Desegregation and the Law* (New Brunswick, N. J.: Rutgers University Press, 1957); Robert J. Harris, *The Quest for Equality* (Baton Rouge: University of Louisiana Press, 1960); and Rayford W. Logan, "The United States Supreme Court and the Segregation Issue," *The Annals of the American Academy of Political and Social Science,* Vol. 304 (March, 1956), pp. 10–16.

elementary rights and privileges which white Americans took for granted. But the Civil War and Reconstruction periods promised a sharp departure from this sad history. In particular, the Thirteenth, Fourteenth, and Fifteenth Amendments to the Constitution forcefully spelled out this new direction. Witness the key passage of the Fourteenth Amendment:

> No state shall make or enforce any law which shall abridge the privileges or immunities of citizens of the United States; nor shall any state deprive any person of life, liberty, or property, without due process of law; nor deny to any person within its jurisdiction the equal protection to the laws . . .

Yet even this straightforward guarantee was narrowed and distorted for one-third of a century by the country's highest tribunal. The segregationist era of the United States Supreme Court began in 1876 with Chief Justice Morrison Waite presiding. Repeatedly, the Waite Court ruled both state and federal antidiscrimination laws as unconstitutional.[17] The most famous of these cases were the Civil Rights Cases of 1883.[18] The High Court found an 1875 federal statute requiring no discrimination in public accommodations to be unconstitutional on the grounds that neither the Thirteenth nor Fourteenth Amendments gave Congress the right to pass laws against individuals. Such rulings of the Waite Court tempted parts of the white South into setting up the first forms of legalized segregation. Under the next Chief Justice, Melville Fuller, this temptation to the South became an open invitation. While Waite's Court had typically denied the constitutionality of desegregation legislation, the Fuller Court from 1888 through 1910 typically found constitutional a series of early southern state laws requiring segregation.[19] "Although the South had lost the war," writes one legal historian, "it had conquered constitutional law." [20]

The Fuller Court's most important race decision was *Plessy v. Ferguson*

---

[17] Examples include *U. S. v. Cruikshank,* 92 U. S. 542 (1876); *U. S. v. Reese,* 92 U. S. 214 (1876); *Hall v. DeCuir,* 95 U. S. 485 (1878); and *U. S. v. Harris,* 106 U. S. 629 (1883). Exceptions to this trend denied states the right to exclude qualified Negroes from jury panels: *Ex parte Virginia,* 100 U. S. 339 (1880); *Stauder v. West Virginia,* 100 U. S. 303 (1880); *Neal v. Delaware,* 103 U. S. 70 (1881); and *Bush v. Kentucky,* 107 U. S. 100 (1883).

[18] *Civil Rights Cases,* 190 U. S. 3 (1883).

[19] For example, *Louisville, New Orleans, and Texas Railroad v. Mississippi,* 133 U. S. 587 (1890). Later cases include *Cumming v. County Board of Education,* 175 U. S. 528 (1899); *Giles v. Harris,* 189 U. S. 475 (1903); *Giles v. Teasley,* 193 U. S. 146 (1904); and *Berea College v. Kentucky,* 211 U. S. 45 (1908).

[20] Robert J. Harris, *The Quest for Equality,* p. 108.

in 1896.[21] Homer Plessy, one-eighth Negro by birth, had been arrested for riding in a rail car reserved for whites under a new Louisiana law. Plessy went to court and claimed among other things that the Louisiana statute was unconstitutional. Affirming the earlier rulings of state courts, the Supreme Court denied Plessy's plea. Only Justice John Harlan, a former slaveholder from Kentucky, dissented by maintaining that "our constitution is color-blind." The majority opinion interestingly ventured into the realms of psychology and sociology. Its contention that "legislation is powerless to eradicate racial instincts" and overcome "natural affinities" was merely a restatement of the then-current sociological dictum that *stateways* cannot change *folkways.*[22] And its concepts of "racial instincts" and "natural affinities" are not legal terms but are lifted directly from the Social Darwinism then in vogue in social science. The *Plessy* ruling set up the segregationist formula of "separate but equal"—that is, separate racial facilities may be required by state law providing that the facilities are equal.[23] The South, of course, was too poor to have even one set of adequate public facilities, so the precise legal formula in practice lapsed into separate but very unequal.

THE PREPARATORY ERA, 1911–1930—In the *Plessy* opinion, the High Court was merely accentuating the trend of the times, not manufacturing it. By 1910, however, the climate was changing, and the Supreme Court changed with it. From 1909–1911, four justices died and a fifth resigned. A new Supreme Court period was beginning, a transitional era that prepared the ground for the desegregation decisions of recent years. Interestingly, this preparatory era began with a southern-born Chief Justice and ended with an ex-President as Chief Justice. Edward White was a Louisiana sugar planter who had fought in the Confederate Army; and he was followed in 1921 by ex-President William Taft. Under their leadership the Court struck down an Alabama law that enforced peonage,[24] attempted to protect the Negro's right to vote by holding both the infamous "grandfather clauses" and white-only primaries to be unconstitutional,[25] ruled against municipal ordinances re-

---

[21] *Plessy v. Ferguson,* 163 U. S. 537 (1896).

[22] Using the situational approach, we shall see that modern social science data and theory point to a sharply different conclusion today.

[23] This phrase was not actually employed in the *Plessy* opinion, but it soon came into common usage in lower courts attempting to implement the ruling.

[24] *Bailey v. Alabama,* 219 U. S. 219 (1911).

[25] *Guinn v. United States,* 238 U. S. 347 (1915); *Myers et al. v. Anderson,* 238 U. S. 368 (1915); *U. S. v. Mosley,* 238 U. S. 383 (1915); and *Nixon v. Herndon,* 273 U. S. 536 (1927). "Grandfather clauses" refer to attempts by southern states to restrict black

quiring residential segregation,[26] and overruled a "legal lynching" verdict by insisting that an accused man must have a trial free from mob domination.[27] Among the minor exceptions to this preparatory trend,[28] only *Gong Lum v. Rice* in 1927 is of special interest. Gong Lum was a Chinese-American who challenged the right of Mississippi to assign his daughter to a Negro school. The Supreme Court rejected his plea; and, though the case is only peripherally related to segregation laws, it marked the last time in our national history when unequal and *de jure* segregated education was supported by our highest tribunal.

On the legislative front, however, there is little about the years 1911–1930 that can be described as "preparatory" for desegregation. The federal government and northern states ignored racial discrimination. Southern states continued to pass segregation statutes concerned with every facet of life in the vein of the 1890–1910 period. Affirmative legislative action would have to await the post-World War II years.

THE DESEGREGATION ERA, 1930–1969 — The third Supreme Court period began in 1930 when Charles Evans Hughes returned to the High Bench as Chief Justice. The Hughes Court, and later the Stone and Vinson Courts, whittled away at the "separate but equal" doctrine by applying increasingly more rigorous definitions of "equal." Progress was slow, but the corner had been turned.

The Negro made gains early in this era in six key areas. In *due process* cases, for example, the Court consistently ruled that the exclusion of blacks and other minorities from juries is presumptive evidence of discrimination.[29] In the *employment* area, the Court agreed that states have the power under the Fourteenth Amendment to prohibit racial discrimination by labor unions.[30] In a series of *public accommodations* cases, the Court held that interstate segregation is an unconstitutional burden on interstate commerce

---

voting by eliminating all potential voters whose relatives (i.e., "grandfathers") could not vote in 1866 — when blacks were still kept from most voting rolls.

[26] *Buchanan v. Warley*, 245 U. S. 60 (1917); and *Harmon v. Tyler*, 273 U. S. 668 (1927).

[27] *Moore v. Dempsey*, 261 U. S. 86 (1923).

[28] *Butts v. Merchants and Miners Transportation Co.*, 230 U. S. 126 (1913); *South Covington and Cincinnati St. Railway v. Kentucky*, 252 U. S. 299 (1920); *Corrigan v. Buckley*, 271 U. S. 323 (1926); and *Gong Lum v. Rice*, 275 U. S. 78 (1927).

[29] *Norris v. Alabama*, 294 U. S. 587 (1935); *Pierre v. Louisiana*, 306 U. S. 354 (1939); *Smith v. Texas*, 311 U. S. 128 (1940); *Patton v. Mississippi*, 332 U. S. 463 (1967); *Cassell v. Texas*, 239 U. S. 282 (1950); and *Reece v. Georgia*, 350 U. S. 85 (1955).

[30] *Railway Mail Association v. Corsi*, 326 U. S. 88 (1945).

and that blacks cannot be rightfully denied an unoccupied Pullman seat or an unoccupied dining car seat.[31] In two cases in 1948 and 1953, the Court ruled that racially restrictive *housing* covenants could not be supported by state court action.[32] The major legal breakthrough on *voting* came in 1944, when the High Court reversed itself and declared that state political conventions and party memberships were state actions and hence, under the Fourteenth Amendment, could not discriminate against Negro citizens.[33] For those who are skeptical about the ability of High Court decisions to influence the white South, it is worthwhile pointing out that the number of blacks registered to vote in the South more than tripled from 1940 to 1946, largely because of the 1944 Supreme Court decision.[34]

In addition, continuous legal advances were made in the field of *education*. The unanimous decision on May 17, 1954 against *de jure* racial segregation in public schools finally destroyed the "separate but equal" doctrine by ruling that "separate educational facilities are inherently unequal." [35] A year later, the Supreme Court handed down a weak enforcement order with the vague standard of "with all deliberate speed." [36] As predicted in advance by social scientists, this weak standard proved to be a serious mistake.[37] It encouraged white segregationists to resist racial desegregation, and it necessitated an almost endless flow of implementation cases in the crowded lower courts. Only after a decade and one-half of delay did the High Bench grow impatient and call for greater speed in elimination of *de jure* segregation in public schools.

The historic 1954 ruling set the course for the Warren Court's final 15 years. The new "separate cannot be equal" doctrine was extended to public

---

[31] *Mitchell v. U. S.,* 313 U. S. 80 (1941); and *Henderson v. U. S.,* 339 U. S. 816 (1950).

[32] *Shelley v. Kraemer,* 334 U. S. 1 (1948); and *Barrows v. Jackson,* 346 U. S. 249 (1953).

[33] *Smith v. Allwright,* 321 U. S. 649 (1944). Later attempts to restrict black suffrage were also struck down: *Terry v. Adams,* 345 U. S. 461 (1953).

[34] Negro voting registrants in the South went from about 150,000 in 1940 to about 595,000 in 1946; see Luther P. Jackson, "Race and Suffrage in the South Since 1940," *New South,* Vol. 3 (June–July, 1948), p. 4.

[35] *Brown v. Board of Education,* 347 U. S. 483 (1954).

[36] *Brown v. Board of Education,* 349 U. S. 294 (1955).

[37] Clark had noted two years earlier that firm leadership, rather than vague standards, was the single most important ingredient in achieving successful desegregation without conflict. Kenneth B. Clark, "Desegregation: An Appraisal of the Evidence," *Journal of Social Issues,* Vol. 9 (1953), pp. 1–76. Hugo L. Black, one of the nine 1954 justices, was inclined to agree 14 years later. In a public statement, Black thought that the call for "all deliberate speed" had probably "delayed the process of outlawing segregation." "'All deliberate speed' was unwise policy, Black feels," *The Washington Post* (December 4, 1968), p. A28, Col. 1.

pools, beaches, golf courses, and amphitheaters.[38] Further gains were made in due process, employment, and voting; state laws banning interracial marriage were struck down in 1967.[39]

Belatedly, civil rights legislation outlawing racial discrimination in public accommodations began to be enacted in the late 1940's in such states as New York and Massachusetts. Similar state statutes in employment and then housing followed until today a large number of states boast an array of antidiscrimination legislation on their books. In 1957 and 1960 the first federal civil rights legislation since 1875 managed to survive southern filibusters in Congress and plugged some of the gaping holes in the federal legislative armor against voting discrimination. The 1957 Act also established the first United States Civil Rights Commission. But the important breakthrough occurred with the passage of the Civil Rights Act of 1964. This sweeping federal legislation contained, among other items, provisions to combat discrimination in public accommodations and employment, to establish training institutes in educational desegregation, and to withdraw federal funds from localities and institutions that practice racial discrimination. In 1965 a well-designed Voting Rights Act was enacted, and in 1968 the first federal statute against housing discrimination was passed.

To date, the practical results of this spate of civil rights laws are not impressive. The reasons for this are not difficult to uncover. Typically the enforcement agencies are grossly understaffed and narrowly circumscribed; enforcement is often limited to processing complaints on an inefficient case-by-case basis. Leon Mayhew, in an illuminating sociological analysis,[40] finds that the typical complaints of employment discrimination are nonstrategic. Thus they are generally lodged against the firms which discriminate least, while complaints against notoriously unfair employers seldom arise. This situation comes about because complaints often concern such on-the-job matters as promotion, and these cannot be raised obviously until blacks are employed by the firm. Moreover, firms with discriminatory hiring policies get to be known as such in the black community, causing Negroes

---

[38] For example, *Baltimore v. Dawson,* 350 U. S. 877 (1955); and *Holmes v. Atlanta,* 350 U. S. 879 (1955). For a summary of the many lower federal court decisions, see Jack Greenberg, *Race Relations and American Law,* pp. 92–96.

[39] *Fikes v. Alabama,* 352 U. S. 191 (1957); *Syres v. Oil Workers International Union,* 223 F. 2d 739 (5th Cir. 1955), *rev'd per curiam,* 350 U. S. 892 (1955); *Cowley v. Gibson,* 355 U. S. 41 (1957); and *Gomillion v. Lightfoot,* 362 U. S. 916 (1960). For a human interest account of this last voting case, see Bernard Taber, *Gomillion v. Lightfoot* (New York: McGraw-Hill, 1962). The intermarriage decision citation is *Loving et ux. v. Virginia,* 388 U. S. 1 (1966).

[40] Leon Mayhew, *Law and Equal Opportunity: A Study of the Massachusetts Commission Against Discrimination* (Cambridge: Harvard University Press, 1968).

to avoid seeking employment with them. In short, racial discrimination is patterned, and only patterned enforcement not dependent upon nonstrategic complaints can be effective.

THE POST-WARREN ERA, 1970–ON – The retirement of Chief Justice Earl Warren in 1969 and the series of conservatives nominated for the Supreme Court by the Nixon Administration signal a new era. The character of this new period is as yet unclear, though it appears that the Court will surrender its role of leadership in civil rights. Its first decisions on the racial issue suggest that the Burger Court will uphold the basic positions of the Warren Court, but will act to restrict some forms of protest and will be reluctant to enter upon new legal ground.

A more conservative stance of the Supreme Court, however, will not dispel mounting civil rights pressures. One concept in particular will come up increasingly for judicial review. So-called *de facto* segregation, that is, racial separation presumably not created by state action in the sense of the Fourteenth Amendment, will have to be faced directly as an issue in the 1970's. The Warren Court struck down *de jure* segregation, that is, racial separation required by governmental action. Yet, as we shall shortly note, most separation of blacks and whites in the United States is not the result of blatant state laws; nevertheless, *de facto* segregation has many of the same negative effects of *de jure* segregation.

Three complementary lines of argument against *de facto* segregation are available. The first is to question the very existence of the phenomenon. When traced to its origins, what appears initially as *de facto* separation invariably turns out to be, at least in part, the consequence of governmental action. The governmental action is seldom a state law as in the South; nevertheless, it appears to be "state action" in the Fourteenth Amendment sense. Examples include city zoning ordinances, boundary determinations, and local decisions as to the placement of public facilities. To the extent that these facts can be convincingly demonstrated in court, the distinction between *de facto* and *de jure* segregation melts away and virtually all racial separation could come under the Warren Court dicta.

A second line of reasoning follows the political reapportionment decision and makes the state the defendant rather than local districts. In the reapportionment case, *Baker v. Carr* (1962),[41] the state of Tennessee was held responsible for not changing voting district boundaries for six decades in order to equate the ballots of an urbanizing population. By analogy, it can

---

[41] *Baker v. Carr,* 369 U. S. 186 (1962).

be maintained that states should not allow city and school district boundaries to remain stable when such lines create increasing degrees of racial segregation and inequality of services. The third argument would maintain that racially integrated classrooms, for instance, are essential for securing "equality of educational opportunity"; and the right to such equality might be abstracted from the equal protection clause of the Fourteenth Amendment. Combinations of these three compatible arguments typify briefs that have already been presented to state and federal courts. As with the initial assaults against obvious *de jure* segregation, these first cases against *de facto* segregation are likely to receive evasive treatment from cautious judges. But pressures will rapidly develop during the 1970's for judicial action against so-called *de facto* racial segregation.

Two antidiscrimination legislative goals commend themselves for the 1970's. State and local legislation are needed in the southern and Rocky Mountain states on basic civil rights protections not coverable in federal legislation. And a general strengthening of enforcement procedures and strategies is required for the civil rights legislation already enacted by both federal and state governmemts. Such strengthening could include: strategic and patterned enforcement with specific goals, rather than case-by-case complaint procedures; greatly enlarged enforcement staffs; and more publicity given offenders who are found in violation of the legislation.

Demographic Trends [42]

MIGRATION TO THE CITY—In this century the Negro has become an urbanite. Three out of every four black Americans today reside in cities, while only one in four did so as recently as 1910. This shift represents a process of massive migration involving many millions of uprooted people. Significant black migration to the city began during World War I. European hostilities simultaneously provided large war orders for American industry and stemmed the vast tide of immigrant labor, thereby opening up new employment opportunities for those blacks willing to migrate. Labor recruiters encouraged the process, and young Negroes in vast numbers began what one demographer

---

[42] For a useful description of Negro American demography, see Karl E. Taeuber and Alma Taeuber, "The Negro Population in the United States," in John P. Davis, ed., *The American Negro Reference Book* (Englewood Cliffs, N. J.: Prentice-Hall, 1966), pp. 96–160. Parts of this section are drawn from Thomas F. Pettigrew, *Racially Separate or Together?* (New York: McGraw-Hill, 1971).

describes as "the greatest and most significant sociological event of our country's recent history." [43]

Not all of this human surge was stimulated by the attractive pull of new jobs; there were significant "push" factors as well. The high birth rate among rural southerners, the mechanization of southern agriculture, the boll weevil, government programs limiting agricultural production, and, finally, the shift of cotton cultivation to the Southwest and West—these factors literally almost starved the Negro off the southern farm. And there was always the motivation to escape from the South's oppressive racial system.

The migration increased to enormous proportions in the 1920's. The pace slowed during the Depression, but accelerated with America's entry into World War II and continued to be heavy during the 1950's and 1960's. Between 1950 and 1969, over two and one-third million black southerners broke their home ties and left the region, and the total Negro population gains in the North and West reached almost six million. [44] Negroes in the North and West are now so numerous that natural increase rather than migration provides the greater part of black growth. This wider distribution of black Americans throughout the nation has made absurd the time-honored segregationist claim that race relations are a southern problem and should be left exclusively to the South to solve. Now that more Negroes live outside the ex-Confederacy than in it, race relations are clearly a national concern.

It is a national concern, however, with a strongly urban cast. Today the black American is more urban than the white American and is especially concentrated in the largest metropolitan centers. The twelve biggest central cities now contain over two-thirds of the Negro population outside the South and one-third of the total Negro population. Since 1950 the Negro population in Chicago, Boston, Seattle, Detroit, Cleveland, St. Louis, Milwaukee, Minneapolis, San Francisco, Buffalo, Denver, New York, and Los Angeles at least doubled. By 1968, eleven central cities were almost one-third Negro and Washington, D. C. was over two-thirds Negro. [45] Today more Negroes live in the New York metropolitan area than in any single southern state, more in metropolitan Chicago than in the entire state of Mississippi, and more in

---

[43] Horace C. Hamilton, "The Negro Leaves the South," *Demography,* Vol. 1 (1964), p. 294. Thus the five deep South states—South Carolina, Georgia, Alabama, Mississippi, and Louisiana—lost 400,000 Negroes through "out-migration" from 1910 to 1920.

[44] U. S. Departments of Labor and Commerce, *The Social and Economic Status of Negroes in the United States, 1969* (Washington, D. C.: U. S. Government Printing Office, 1969), pp. 3, 5; and *U. S. Riot Commission Report* (New York: Bantam, 1968), pp. 241–42.

[45] *Ibid.,* p. 243; and U. S. Departments of Labor and Commerce, *The Social and Economic Status of Negroes in the United States, 1969,* p. 9.

metropolitan Philadelphia than in the entire states of Arkansas and Kentucky combined.

Dramatic as these data are, they systematically understate the mass movement of the Negro American over the past two generations by showing merely the net result of those moving to cities minus those few who move back to rural America. There is, in addition, considerable movement back and forth between cities that does not appear in these figures but which accounts for an increasing proportion of "in-migrants." Consequently, if the old stereotype of the Negro sharecropper is outdated, so, too, is the only slightly less dated stereotype of the urban Negro as a raw migrant fresh from the hinterland. The typical pattern is for Negroes to come to a northern city from a southern city rather than from the farm. They tend to be the better-educated black southerners, though their educational level is still below that of the typical black northerner.[46] In addition, Negroes who migrate from one northern city to another are often especially skilled and well educated.

The raw migrant stereotype particularly neglects the growing number of blacks who were born and raised in cities and have never experienced rural living. The urban-born black American, especially in the North, is young and somewhat better educated and skilled, far more militant, and less religious than his parents. We return to a consideration of him at the close of the chapter.

PROJECTIONS OF THE FUTURE—In 1969, Negro Americans numbered 22.3 million people and constituted 11 percent of the nation's population; by 1984, they will probably number between 30 and 33 million people and constitute about 12 percent of the nation's population. Most of this expansion will be absorbed by our largest metropolitan centers in the North and West, followed by continued growth of metropolitan centers in the South. The demographer C. Horace Hamilton predicts, "Ultimately, if present migration trends continue, from 75 to 85 percent of the Negro population will live outside of the South."[47] This expansion will mean black majorities in many central cities. Cleveland, Detroit, Baltimore, St. Louis, and Philadelphia in the North,

---

[46] This process has the unusual effect of depressing the median Negro education levels of both the places of origin and destination.

[47] Horace C. Hamilton, "The Negro Leaves the South," *Demography,* p. 294. Rates of Negro out-migration from the South in the 1960's have declined from those of the 1950's. Nevertheless, percentages of nonwhites in southern metropolitan areas of less than one-half million have started to decline, in direct contradiction with metropolitan areas of all sizes in the rest of the nation. Leo Schnore and Harry Sharp, "Racial Changes in Metropolitan Areas, 1950–1960," *Social Forces,* Vol. 41 (March, 1963), pp. 247–53.

and Atlanta, New Orleans, Richmond, and Memphis in the South may soon join Washington, Gary, and Newark, where Negro majorities already exist.

Another important projection is the age profile of the black population. With a median age of only 21, Negroes constitute a young group, and the unusually high Negro birth rates from 1948 on, rates that did not level off until 1957, mean that twelve to twenty-one-year-old blacks will be especially numerous from 1969 to 1978. Since riots are often sparked by this age segment, the potential for urban racial disturbances will remain high for some years to come. The young Negro age profile also demonstrates the urgent need for expanded civic services and opportunities, for more public schools, recreational facilities, welfare programs, housing, and for a larger labor market. The need far exceeds present plans for expansion in most of our major urban areas largely because of costs. Yet these are the social costs incurred by any rapidly growing and migrating group, costs which the central city cannot be expected to bear alone. Federal funding at an order of magnitude not yet envisioned will be absolutely essential. Equally important, this funding must require metropolitan involvement in order to be successful.

From a national perspective, the Negro's move to the city should not be viewed exclusively in cost terms, for it contains many positive features. It has prevented an uneconomic piling up of near-peasant blacks in the South's depressed agricultural areas. The South, it is true, loses its investment in young migrants who go North, but at the same time the nonsouthern metropolis adds to its young, productive labor force. In addition, the shift from farm to city has been more responsible for Negro gains in income, education, health, and housing during the past generation than has the concurrent reduction in racial discrimination.[48] Finally, urbanization has created a more sophisticated people capable of effective protest, a people more cognizant of what discrimination over the years has denied them and more eager to benefit from the full privileges of American citizenship.

These national advantages would probably outweigh the local disadvantages were it not for the enforced segregation of blacks into central-city ghettos. Concentrated into blighted and underserviced areas, all of the problems of rapid growth are multiplied for both the Negro and the city. It is this embedded pattern of racial separation that provides the backdrop for the remaining sociocultural areas: politics, housing, economics, and education.

---

[48] Thomas F. Pettigrew, *A Profile of the Negro American* (Princeton, N. J.: Van Nostrand, 1964), pp. 180–81.

Political Trends

The political power of black America has increased enormously in recent decades, partly because of the demographic trends just outlined. This increase is visible nationally, statewide, and locally among both voters and candidates. Thus in the presidential election of 1968, the overwhelming support of Negroes for Hubert Humphrey meant that black ballots constituted one-fifth of his total votes. Similarly, a black and labor coalition in Virginia put into office in 1969 the first Republican governor in Virginia since Reconstruction. And local political races, south as well as north, are now crucially determined by black voters in many areas.

Together with growing political sophistication and discipline, this new power is fueled by a vast increase in blacks who are registered to vote. This trend is especially pronounced in the South. Recall that black registration in the South totaled only 150,000 in 1940; thanks to the 1944 Supreme Court ruling in *Smith v. Allwright,* this figure had risen to 600,000 in 1946. By 1958, it had reached about 1.4 million or 27 percent of the Negro voting age population; by 1961, about 32 percent.[49] But by 1968 it had reached three and two-thirds million voters and constituted 62 percent of the black voting age population in the South.[50] The greatest gains of recent years occurred in those states covered by the Voting Rights Act of 1965, an act extended in 1970 for five additional years. Thus under the Act, Negro registration in Alabama had more than doubled by 1968, and significant gains were made in Louisiana, Georgia, South Carolina, and Virginia. Yet the most dramatic results of the Act are to be found in Mississippi, where the registered percentage of voting age black citizens climbed from a low of 8 percent in 1964 to almost 60 percent by 1968.[51]

Another significant factor in encouraging Negro registration is the availability of popular Negro candidates for office. When one white segregationist ran against another in a rural southern county, it was understandably difficult for blacks to become enthusiastic about the election. But serious black candidates have become commonplace throughout the South as Negro

---

[49] Donald Matthews and James W. Prothro, *Negroes and the New Southern Politics* (New York: Harcourt Brace Jovanovich, 1966), pp. 112–13.

[50] U. S. Departments of Labor and Commerce, *The Social and Economic Status of Negroes in the United States, 1969,* p. 88; and Vernon E. Jordan, Jr., "New Forces of Urban Political Power," *New South,* Vol. 23 (Spring, 1968), pp. 46–51.

[51] *Ibid.*

registration rose. Their entry into the electoral races has stimulated further Negro registration. Daniel provides vivid evidence for this effect and that of the Voting Rights Act for Alabama counties in 1966.[52] For counties with both Negro candidates and the presence of federal examiners under the Act, the median black registration percentage was 78; for counties with one or the other, the median was 68; and for counties with neither, the median was only 48.

The effects of this southern increase in black registration have been partly countered by a sharp rise in white registration, especially among poorer whites. Yet the counterincrease in the white electorate has not totally canceled out the new power of black Southerners at the ballot box. As early as 1964, for example, the black vote more than made the difference in five southern states for Lyndon Johnson in his successful bid for the presidency. And it has been the major factor in the election in 1968 of over 400 Negro officials throughout the South: from 57 southern state legislators to 22 mayors of southern towns and small cities.[53]

Less dramatic, perhaps, but equally significant has been increasing registration and organization in black communities in the North. Typically the problem in northern cities has not been in restrictions against registering as in the black-belt South, but in unifying the community and getting out the vote. Many black communities in the North have only recently become highly organized and politicized. And the results became apparent in the election of Negro mayors in Gary and Cleveland in 1967 and Newark, New Jersey in 1970.

The new era of black mayors actually began in 1965 when Carl Stokes, then an Ohio state legislator, ran as an independent for mayor of Cleveland.[54]

---

[52] Johnnie Daniel, "Negro Political Behavior and Community Political and Socioeconomic Structural Factors," *Social Forces,* Vol. 47 (March, 1969), pp. 274–80. Moreover, Daniel shows that the Voting Rights Act shifted the signs of the census predictors of Negro registration in Alabama. Hence in 1960 the typical county with a high registration percentage was a relatively prosperous area with manufacturing and a small percentage of Negroes; but in 1966 the typical county with a high registration percentage was a poor area with considerable tenant farming and a high percentage of Negroes.

[53] U. S. Departments of Labor and Commerce, *The Social and Economic Status of Negroes in the United States, 1969,* p. 90. For interviews with 19 recent Negro political candidates in the South, see Julian Bond, *Black Candidates: Southern Campaign Experiences* (Atlanta: Southern Regional Council, 1969).

[54] The data on candidates are taken from Thomas F. Pettigrew, Robert T. Riley, and J. M. Ross, *The Process of Racial Change: Research in American Race Relations* (Cambridge: Harvard University Press, in press). In the total North and West in 1968, there were 81 Negro state legislators and 14 Negro mayors (U.S. Departments of Labor and Commerce, *The Social and Economic Status of Negroes in the United States, 1969,* p. 90).

Though backed strongly by the blacks, who constitute nearly two-fifths of the city's electorate, he was unsuccessful and garnered only about 11 percent of the white vote. In 1967, however, he won the Democratic party primary over the entrenched incumbent, Ralph Locher; then went on to win Cleveland's highest office over Republican Seth Taft by capturing a solid Negro vote together with about 19 percent of the white vote. In 1969, Stokes won reelection with another solid Negro vote and about 22 percent of the white vote.

The same election night in November of 1967 which saw Carl Stokes become mayor of Cleveland saw another black become mayor of Gary, Indiana. Richard Hatcher, an experienced city councilor, managed an equally narrow victory over his Republican opponent with a large Negro turnout and roughly 15 to 17 percent of the white ballots. His victory followed an unusually bitter contest that involved open opposition from his own party organization and required federal intervention to insure a fair election. A year later, however, Hatcher's support among white registrants in a survey had increased to 27 percent.

Los Angeles and Detroit were the scenes for narrow defeats of black candidates for mayor in 1969. Thomas Bradley ran a well-conducted campaign in Los Angeles and came in first in the nonpartisan first race. But he lost a heated run-off race to incumbent Samuel Yorty despite receiving the solid backing of the relatively small black community and roughly one-third of the white vote. In Detroit, Richard Austin lost an equally close nonpartisan election. In June of 1970, however, Kenneth Gibson in Newark won a resounding victory over the incumbent mayor Hugh Addonisio, who was then under a federal indictment for corruption. Gibson, too, put together about 16 percent of the white vote and about 96 percent of the black vote, the latter constituting approximately 47 percent of the registered electorate.

On the federal level, Edward Brooke, a state attorney general, became in 1966 the first Negro Senator of the twentieth century. Brooke attracted 62 percent of the voters in Massachusetts where less than 3 percent of the electorate is black. Moreover, black members of the House of Representatives nearly doubled in the 1960's, with all of the new additions coming from overwhelmingly black districts in north central cities. However, in 1970 the three new black members of the House of Representatives all came from predominately white districts in Berkeley, California, metropolitan Chicago, and metropolitan Baltimore.

Nevertheless, Negro Americans remain grossly underrepresented at all levels of the country's political system. The 1970's, however, promise a continuing trend toward correcting this inequity. On demographic grounds alone, it can be projected that by the early 1980's there will probably be about 25 Negro mayors of major central cities and 30 Negro members of the United

States House of Representatives from all regions. Perhaps, too, there will be a few additional Negro senators and even a black vice-president.

Housing Trends

THE DEGREE OF HOUSING SEGREGATION—Racial trends in housing appear as bleak as trends in politics appear encouraging. Strict racial separation is the rule within both metropolitan areas and cities, and present trends threaten to exacerbate the problem further. White population growth in the suburbs in recent decades has been as dramatic as the black population growth in the central cities. By 1965, three out of every five whites in the nation's 212 standard metropolitan statistical areas (S.M.S.A.'s) resided in suburbs, while four out of every five nonwhites in S.M.S.A.'s resided in central cities.[55] And since the racial separation by residence is even more extreme for whites and blacks of childbearing age, natural increase alone is likely to heighten this situation during the 1970's.[56]

Even these striking contrasts between suburban rings and central cities grossly understate racial segregation in housing, for within both suburbs and central cities the Negro is still further segregated into particular neighborhoods. According to the Taeubers,[57] the median central city in the United States in 1960 would require 88 percent of its black households to move from Negro blocks to predominantly white blocks to achieve racially random residential patterns. From 1940 to 1950, this index of housing segregation increased throughout the nation; from 1950 to 1960, it continued to rise in the South and decreased slightly in other regions[58]; and in the 1960's, it

---

[55] T. Clemence, "Residential Segregation in the Mid-Sixties," *Demography,* Vol. 4 (1967), p. 563.

[56] The meaning of such trends has been calculated for metropolitan Philadelphia by George Schermer. He notes that a yearly outflow of 8,000 Negro households to white areas would be required just to keep Negro areas from expanding further. To reverse the trend and spread the Negro population evenly throughout metropolitan Philadelphia by the year 2000 would require at a minimum the entry of 9,700 Negro households annually into presently white areas and the reciprocal movement of 3,700 white households into presently Negro areas. The absence of such shifts and the continued growth of central cities means that these minimal estimates will progressively increase. Quoted in E. and G. Grier, "Equality and Beyond: Housing Segregation in the Great Society," in T. Parsons and Kenneth B. Clark, eds., *The Negro American* (Boston: Houghton Mifflin, 1966), p. 535.

[57] K. E. Taeuber and A. F. Taeuber, *Negroes in Cities* (Chicago: Aldine, 1965).

[58] *Ibid.*

appears to have generally increased again with a leveling off in the late years of the decade.[59] In addition, the relatively few blacks who reside in suburbs are generally segregated, too.[60]

THE CAUSES OF HOUSING SEGREGATION—The Taeubers have also demonstrated that "economic factors cannot account for more than a small portion of observed levels of racial residential segregation."[61] Five other causes are more important: federal housing policies, blatant racial discrimination, the tight supply of low-income housing, suburban zoning barriers, and binding ties within the black community.

Federal housing policy has been one of the largest contributors to the present state of extreme racial separation.[62] From the first National Housing Act in 1935 until 1950, the federal government actively enforced segregation for the over 11 million units built during these critical years. From 1950 to 1962, federal housing policy was officially neutral but actually segregationist. Not until President Kennedy's limited antidiscrimination executive order in 1962 and the 1968 Fair Housing Act did it turn integrationist, though it has been largely ineffective to date. The discriminatory mechanisms over three decades were blatant. The Federal Housing Administration's manual for years openly advocated racial and social class segregation; and its mortgage insurance program, together with the Veterans Administration's mortgage program, encouraged suburban home ownership with more liberal terms and generally discriminated economically and racially against blacks. As those efforts encouraged whites to leave the central city, public housing developments, urban renewal programs, and urban highway construction further concentrated and segregated Negroes within the central city. Newer housing efforts, such as the Model Cities programs, improve on these earlier and disastrous policies but offer little hope for sweeping remedial measures.

Blatant racial discrimination in the private market has achieved further separation. Public referenda against discrimination in housing have lost by two-to-one majorities in Akron, Seattle, Detroit, and California. We now

[59] T. Clemence, "Residential Segregation in the Mid-Sixties," *Demography;* and National Advisory Commission on Civil Disorders, *Report* (Washington, D. C.: U. S. Government Printing Office, 1968), p. 467.

[60] Karl E. Taeuber and Alma Taeuber, in John P. Davis, ed., *The American Negro Reference Book*, pp. 132–36; and Taeuber and Taeuber, *Negroes in Cities*, pp. 55–62.

[61] *Ibid.*, p. 2.

[62] Charles Abrams, "The Housing Problem and the Negro," and E. Grier and G. Grier, "Equality and Beyond: Housing Segregation in the Great Society," in T. Parsons and Kenneth B. Clark, eds., *The Negro American*, pp. 512–24, 535; E. Grier and G. Grier, *Privately Developed Interracial Housing* (Berkeley: University of California Press, 1960), Chapter 8.

have produced essentially two separate housing markets, with the Negro market guaranteeing overcrowding, inferior facilities, and inflated rents. True, home ownership and intact housing have been increasing among black households; but these trends have not kept pace with white advances nor have they eroded the dual markets. They result from migration to the cities and the acquisition by middle-class Negroes of older homes left behind by suburban-bound whites, rather than any relaxation of discrimination. And during the 1950's, the number of nonwhites living in substandard housing actually increased from 1.4 to 1.8 million people, and this trend continued during the 1960's in New York City and other cities.[63]

The problem is made worse by the generally short supply of low- and medium-income housing, a supply that in recent years has not been increasing fast enough to meet the needs of the expanding population much less to replace aging housing stock. In addition, suburban zoning barriers not only act to keep blacks in the central city but also serve to confine low-income housing in general to the tax-weak central cities. Charles Abrams called these restrictive zoning regulations the new "Mason-Dixon lines of America." Such restrictive policies as minimum lot sizes and dwelling costs result in part from the suburb's eagerness to attract residents who will contribute more to local taxes than they require in services.[64]

Such practices nourish racial fears and prejudices.[65] Both racial groups are now so adapted to dual housing markets that whites easily come to think that their security is dependent upon separation and relatively few middle-class Negroes challenge the exclusion even when circumstances are favorable.[66] Equally important, residents of the black community develop binding ties of friendship and status which they are reluctant to give up. The black separatist ideology, to be discussed later, adds further impetus to this phenomenon.

HOUSING REMEDIES — Detailed strategies for achieving residential integration can only evolve over time, but we must begin now. The goal is not to eliminate the black neighborhood, but to convert it from an isolated racial prison

---

[63] National Advisory Commission on Civil Disorders, *Report,* p. 467.

[64] B. J. Frieden, "Toward Equality of Urban Opportunity," *Journal of the American Institute of Planners,* Vol. 31 (1965), pp. 320–30.

[65] Unscrupulous segments of the real estate industry exacerbate and perpetuate these fears. For empirical evidence that the widely believed notion that Negro neighbors lower property values is not valid, see Luigi Laurenti, *Property Values and Race* (Berkeley and Los Angeles: University of California Press, 1960).

[66] L. G. Watts, H. E. Freeman, H. Hughes, R. Morris, and T. F. Pettigrew, *The Middle-Income Negro Family Faces Urban Renewal* (Boston: Massachusetts Department of Commerce and Development, 1965), p. 79.

to an ethnic area of *choice*. This effort must be projected for entire metropolitan areas; it must be systemic, closely intermeshed with such components as mass transit, education, and employment; and it must foster the type of optimal interracial contact to be discussed in the situational approach. Many promising ideas are now available toward these ends.

Public housing authorities require responsibility for entire metropolitan areas; and area-wide "land banks" together with state-initiated housing development corporations modeled after industrial development groups would promote the spread of modest-income housing.[67] Suburban zoning practices could be countered by court challenges. It could also be reversed through legislation that granted zoning authority to counties and metropolitan planning commissions only, and by extra state and federal aid allocated to communities with low-income families so that the present economic incentives to exclude the poor could be offset.[68]

A bolder use of Title VI of the 1964 Civil Rights Act in cutting off funds from discriminatory communities is the ultimate weapon. Short of this, considerable progress could be made if future federal urban grants: (1) were metropolitan in character and required cooperation between central cities and suburbs; (2) provided not only housing aid but a coordinated package for the entire urban system; and (3) gave priority and incentive funds to areas with previous metropolitan cooperation. A number of current programs offer a forerunner of this approach by requiring metropolitan planning commissions to review proposals; and the Model Cities strategy offers a more systematic attack than bulldozer demolition, but does not require metropolitan involvement.

Systemic approaches must also attempt to upgrade current substandard housing. Here state involvement in local housing-code enforcement and in guaranteeing rehabilitation-loan funds would help. So, too, would strengthened judicial powers, including court-administered withholding of rent to force basic repairs, the use of a court housing investigator analogous to the probation officer, and new procedures for the disposition of abandoned buildings.[69] Related possibilities include funding for long-overdue research in

---

[67] White House Conference, *To Fulfill These Rights* (Washington, D. C.: U. S. Government Printing Office, 1966).

[68] B. J. Frieden, "Toward Equality of Urban Opportunity," *Journal of the American Institute of Planners*. A Pennsylvania court decision against the four-acre-per-home zoning requirement of Easttown township may prove a landmark challenge to suburban restrictions. Neil Ulman, "States Move to Trim Local Zoning Autonomy as Criticisms Increase," *Wall Street Journal* (August 15, 1966), pp. 1, 12.

[69] Special State Commission on Low-Income Housing, *Decent Housing for All* (Boston: Commonwealth of Massachusetts, March, 1965).

low-cost housing and the establishment of a National Housing Corporation that would combine public and private interests in the manner of the Communications Satellite Corporation.[70]

Together with metropolitan and systemic concerns, racial housing remedies must also foster positive black-white interaction. The 1968 federal Fair Housing Act was a first step in the direction of eliminating housing discrimination and the dual markets, but realistic enforcement is needed. Nondiscriminatory practices should also be a stern requirement in state licensing of real estate agents. The imaginative but inadequately-supported federal rent supplement program is a more direct attempt at achieving optimal contact across caste and class. Heretofore, public housing has segregated the poor, Negroes and others, in a latter-day version of the poorhouse. Such separation insures the evolution of deviant norms and values by limiting contact with other Americans. Rent supplements mark an important break with these past mistakes by promoting vitally needed equal-status contact between advantaged and disadvantaged. To be effective, however, its funding must be substantially increased and the veto power local jurisdictions now have to keep the program out must be eliminated. The rent supplement concept also suggests similar measures for subsidizing home ownership among the poor. Some argue, in the American tradition of giving land to homesteaders, low-income families should be given housing without cost if they maintain it. Others stress the need for providing incentives and technical assistance to a variety of cooperative efforts.[71]

The nation, then, faces related crises in racial segregation by residence and the scarcity of low-cost housing. It cannot afford to avoid these situations any longer and to continue allowing both of them to fester and grow worse.

Economic Trends

THE PROBLEM—The key economic concern, employment, presents only a slightly brighter outlook than housing. To be sure, the upgrading of Negro

---

[70] The National Housing Corporation could establish revolving funds to purchase, for resale or rental on a desegregated basis, strategically located existing structures as they become available. James Tobin, "On Improving the Economic Status of the Negro," in T. Parsons and Kenneth B. Clark, *The Negro American,* p. 461.

[71] Below-market interest programs (e.g., 221 (d) (3) housing) for nonprofit groups are noteworthy examples of this approach, though these efforts as yet constitute a bare fraction of the low-cost housing needed. Among the more interesting cooperating groups are the Foundation for Cooperative Housing in Stamford, Conn.; Action Housing, Inc., in Pittsburgh; Community Resources Corporation in New York City; and the Housing Development Corporation in Washington, D. C.

employment has not kept pace with the upgrading created by automation; nor has it significantly narrowed the gap with white employment. Yet definite gains were made during the 1960's, and economic predictions for the 1970's indicate the potential for substantial improvement.

In 1966, for the first time, over one-half of nonwhite workers had white-collar, craftsmen, or operative jobs. Their employment in these jobs increased 67 percent between 1960 and 1969, compared with a 22 percent increase for whites. The percentage of nonwhites employed as professionals or technicians increased over these years by 109 percent, clerical workers by 114 percent, and craftsmen and foremen by 70 percent. Consequently, the median Negro family income, which had remained at or below 54 percent that of whites until 1964, shot up in the late 1960's to reach 60 percent of whites by 1968.[72]

But unemployment rates for both Negro adults and youths have remained roughly twice those of white unemployment since the Korean War. Even the tight labor market of 1968 with its total unemployment rate reduced to below 4 percent, still witnessed a Negro adult unemployment rate of roughly 7 percent. Among youths, rates soared as high as 25–30 percent for out-of-school Negroes aged 16 to 19 and at least 19 percent for the larger 16-to-21 age group.[73] With rising unemployment in a year such as 1970, these unemployment rates tend to increase at twice the pace of those of whites. Rashi Fein sums up the problem: "What is recession for the white (say, an unemployment rate of 6 percent) is prosperity for the nonwhite. . . . Therefore, perhaps, it is appropriate to say that whites fluctuate between prosperity and recession but Negroes fluctuate between depression and great depression."[74] Four factors cause even these grim data to underestimate the problem. *First,* even black jobholders are more often underemployed and less frequently hold jobs commensurate with their education than white jobholders. *Second,* Negroes typically do not earn as much as whites in comparable jobs.[75] Indeed nonwhite families with an employed head of household

---

[72] U. S. Departments of Labor and Commerce, *The Social and Economic Status of Negroes in the United States, 1969,* pp. 14, 40–41. The size of these percentages is somewhat deceptive, for they represent increments over small base numbers in the past. Consequently, gains in absolute numbers are less dramatic. Thus by 1967 the nonwhite increases in these three key occupational areas was only two million workers. See Harold L. Sheppard, *The Nature of the Job Problem and the Role of New Public Service Employment* (Kalamazoo, Mich.: The W. E. Upjohn Institute for Employment Research, 1969), p. 4.

[73] White House Conference, *To Fulfill These Rights,* pp. 5–6.

[74] Rashi Fein, "An Economic and Social Profile of the Negro American," in T. Parsons and Kenneth B. Clark, eds., *The Negro American,* pp. 114–15.

[75] *Ibid.,* p. 231. Among males in 1960, for example, the median income of nonwhite

have in some years a lower median family income than white families with an unemployed head.[76] *Third,* a disproportionately high percentage of working-age Negroes withdraw from the labor force in despair and are not officially recorded as unemployed. *Finally,* most of these economic data are for "nonwhites," a strangely negative census category that includes prosperous Japanese- and Chinese-Americans and inflates "nonwhite" conditions above those of Negro Americans.[77]

Economic and social data reveal an ominous trend that is masked by aggregate statistics: Some Negroes are making significant gains, while many others are slipping further behind the increasing prosperity of the most affluent country on earth.[78] Those Negroes less scarred by past deprivations are in a position to take advantage of current racial adjustments. These are the Negro Americans who in 15 years will be truly integrated into "the affluent society."[79] There is, however, another black America that is less fortunate. Now constituting at least two-thirds of all Negroes, this group has not been significantly touched by racial change. Its hopes were raised in the 1950's,[80] but now it cannot even rationalize personal failure entirely in racial terms, for *Ebony* bulges each month with evidence that "affluent Negro America" is making rapid strides. Basic progress in improving the economic position of blacks depends upon reaching "the other Negro America."

---

professionals was only 69 percent that of white professionals; among salesmen, 57 percent; among craftsmen, 66 percent; and among operatives, 71 percent. The only reversal to this pattern, interestingly, is among private household workers, where for both sexes nonwhites earn slightly more than whites.

[76] Daniel Patrick Moynihan, "Employment, Income, and the Negro Family," in T. Parsons and Kenneth B. Clark, eds., *The Negro American,* pp. 148–49.

[77] *Ibid.,* p. 143. Moynihan points out that in 1960 there were only 192,000 nonwhite managers, officials, and proprietors; over one-fourth of these were Asian Americans.

[78] Andrew Brimmer, "The Negro in the National Economy," in John P. Davis, ed., *The American Negro Reference Book,* pp. 261–71, provides the economic confirmation for this income differentiation. The bottom two-fifths of nonwhite families in terms of income accounted for 15 percent of total nonwhite income in 1947, but only 13.5 percent in 1960; the top two-fifths garnered 69.3 percent of total nonwhite income in 1947 and 70.1 percent in 1960. These figures reveal a sharper income differentiation than among whites, for in 1960 the bottom two-fifths of white families acquired 17.4 percent and the top two-fifths 64.7 percent of total white income.

[79] Progress for "the affluent Negro America" is, of course, not inconsequential. Successful middle-class Negroes offer needed achievement models for the black community; they effectively obliterate racial barriers by being "the first of the race" in previously all-white situations; they help eliminate the Negro stigma by providing a constant contradiction between class and caste; and they furnish the great majority of protest leaders. But middle-class Negroes remain only a minority of the group.

[80] Thomas F. Pettigrew, *A Profile of the Negro American,* pp. 184–85.

Although blatant racial discrimination is an obvious cause of the other Negro America's economic plight, it is not the sole one. Relative to whites, blacks more often reside in the South, have received fewer years and a poorer quality of education, and form a younger segment of the labor force, all characteristics apart from race which contribute to economic marginality. Moreover, the central cities of the North and West, where blacks are concentrated in increasing numbers, are actually losing manufacturing jobs.[81] Implicit in these factors are forms of indirect economic discrimination. For instance, the inability of most Negroes to move to the suburbs puts them at a disadvantage in following the manufacturing jobs from central city to outer ring. Similarly, educational discrimination indirectly fosters economic discrimination.

Nevertheless, direct and obvious job discrimination by both employers and unions remains the major barrier, for the economic position of "the other Negro America" still lags dangerously behind the rest of the country even after these indirect factors are taken into account. Attacks upon blatant discrimination in employment also offer far more hope for short-term effects than the slower, though ultimately necessary, alterations in these indirect contributors.[82]

The urgency for both short-term and long-term remedial action becomes clear when we survey the consequences of the dire poverty of the other Negro America. At the national level, the gross national product (GNP) would be lifted annually by five billion dollars if Negro unemployment were lowered to the 1966 white rate; an additional GNP gain of 22 billion dollars would result if the Negro labor force's productivity equaled that of the white; and gains beyond this annual 27 billion dollars would result if Negroes obtained jobs commensurate with their abilities and training.[83] Some further investment would be necessary, of course, to achieve these GNP increments.

More important, however, are the social consequences of black poverty. The statistics themselves suggest the dire results of the unemployment pattern, particularly among the young. Early unemployment means that Negro youths are less likely to secure the on-the-job training necessary for the more stable, skilled work; thus condemning them as adults to join the ranks of the

---

[81] Daniel Patrick Moynihan, "Employment, Income, and the Negro Family," in T. Parsons and K. B. Clark, eds., *The Negro American,* p. 142.

[82] Rashi Fein, "An Economic and Social Profile of the Negro American," in *ibid.,* pp. 112, 119–21.

[83] White House Conference, *To Fulfill These Rights,* p. 6. Twenty-seven billion dollars represents roughly 3 percent of the total GNP, approximately the real gain annually during the 1960's. The degree of investment required is difficult to estimate but would probably not be substantial relative to the long-term gain.

hard-core unemployed. It is these factors which account for much of the grossly higher rate of unemployment of Negro adults.[84]

ECONOMIC REMEDIES — All affirmative measures in the economic area must take place within a context of vigorous growth for the nation. A tight labor market is essential, even if "creeping inflation" is one of its costs.[85] Following the recession of 1970, the American economy is expected to expand rapidly. But much of this expansion will come in the professional, technical, and white collar sectors of the labor market.[86] This is helpful for affluent Negro America, but what about the more serious plight of the poorly educated other Negro America? There will be substantial increases in occupations requiring less training, increases which must be made still greater by legislation. Between 1965 and 1975, urban reconstruction and service work are both expected to increase markedly. In 1966 the Commission on Technology, Automation and Economic Progress estimated that 5.3 million new public service jobs should be created.[87] This would not involve degrading "make-work" employment; rather, these jobs are urgently needed now to upgrade public services in health, education, welfare and home care, protection, beautification, and sanitation. The first proposed remedy, then, is for legislation to create public service employment at local, state, and national levels of government.

A second legislative direction entails effective antidiscrimination statutes in employment. Title VII of the 1964 Civil Rights Act is directed to this problem; but it has not proven generally effective for the reasons cited earlier — understaffed enforcement based largely on a complaint strategy. The necessity of broad, patterned enforcement points up again the systemic nature of racial problems in America. This suggests further remedies: the creation of metropolitan job councils which combine business, labor, and government interests for whole metropolitan areas in order "to plan, coordinate and implement local programs to increase jobs"; the federalization of public employment services, which are now ineffectively operated by states on federal funds; and the design of new mass transit systems so that black workers have

---

[84] They do not account for all of the higher rate, however. Negro unemployment rates remain higher at each level on the occupational scale. Ginzberg and Hiestand, "Employment Patterns of Negro Men and Women," in John P. Davis, ed., *The American Negro Reference Book,* pp. 205–50.

[85] James Tobin, "On Improving the Economic Status of the Negro," in T. Parsons and Kenneth B. Clark, eds., *The Negro American,* pp. 451–71.

[86] Harold L. Sheppard, *The Nature of the Job Problem and the Role of New Public Service Employment.*

[87] *Ibid.,* pp. 14–15.

direct access to the increasingly suburban centers of metropolitan employment.

Two further directions commend themselves for action: retraining and guaranteed income levels. The Manpower Retraining Act needs to be revised to lower its entrance requirements (it has often rejected those applicants who need it most) and to furnish relocation funds so that the retrained can move to where the jobs are. Also the job training potential of the Armed Forces is typically unavailable to those who need the training and interracial experience the most. Lower entrance standards in peacetime are indicated. A start in this direction has been made in the United States Army's Project One-Hundred-Thousand.

The present patchwork of welfare programs has clearly failed, with blacks prominent among its victims. This has understandably led to nationwide guaranteed income plans, the most promising of which is the "negative income tax plan." [88] All Americans would file an annual income tax statement, but those falling below stated poverty levels would receive graduated funds from the federal government. An equitable negative income tax system can encourage employment, thrift, and intact families, all of which are discouraged by present welfare programs. The negative income tax can also be simpler than the welfare programs to administer, avoiding the indignities of many present procedures, and including all segments of the poor. The plan is being tested in a number of New Jersey communities. Together with local and better-designed welfare programs, the negative income tax plan promises to be an important step toward the elimination of poverty in the world's richest country. This would, of course, disproportionately benefit Negroes, though white Americans still constitute a majority of the nation's poor.

Educational Trends

No institution is more central to the full inclusion of blacks into American society than public education. Yet problems mount faster than progress in this area. While formal education for Negroes as well as their percentages in school at each age level are rising,[89] black education is in serious trouble

---

[88] James Tobin, "On Improving the Economic Status of the Negro," in T. Parsons and Kenneth B. Clark, eds., *The Negro American.*

[89] U. S. Departments of Labor and Commerce, *The Social and Economic Status of Negroes in the United States,* 1969, pp. 48, 50–53.

and so-called "compensatory education" is not an answer.[90] At the root of the trouble is the racial segregation of schools.

THE EXTENT AND CAUSES OF SEGREGATED EDUCATION — America's public schools are widely segregated by race. Thus in the fall of 1965, 87 percent of all black pupils in the first grade of public schools and 66 percent in the twelfth grade were enrolled in predominantly Negro schools. White children are even more segregated. In 1965, 80 percent of white public school pupils in both the first and twelfth grades were in 90 to 100 percent white schools.[91] Worse, this pervasive pattern of educational separation is increasing, especially in the large central cities where black Americans are concentrated in greatest numbers.[92]

There are four major causes for the trend toward greater segregation: (1) trends in racial demography, (2) the antimetropolitan nature of school-district organization, (3) the effects of private schools, and (4) intentional segregation comparable to earlier school segregation in the South.[93] The first two of these causes become apparent as soon as we compare school-district organization with the demographic shifts already discussed. There are over 25,000 school districts in America which typically cut suburbs sharply off from central cities; yet suburbs, as we noted, are growing evermore white while central cities are growing evermore black. And we have seen that housing trends offer no hope for substantial relief from this pattern in the 1970's. Thus America would face an enormous problem of so-called *de facto* school segregation even if there were no intradistrict separation by race.

But, of course, there is also rigorous racial separation within school dis-

---

[90] U. S. Commission on Civil Rights, *Racial Isolation in the Public Schools,* Vols. 1 and 2 (Washington, D. C.: U. S. Government Printing Office, 1967).

[91] James S. Coleman et al., *Equality of Educational Opportunity* (Washington, D. C.: U. S. Government Printing Office, 1966), pp. 3–7.

[92] Higher education presents a brighter picture, offering another indication of the increasing polarity between "the affluent Negro America" and "the other Negro America." Total Negro college enrollment expanded 85 percent from 1964 to 1968, and Negro enrollment in predominantly white colleges expanded 144 percent. Thus by 1968 about 36 percent of all Negro college students were attending predominantly Negro institutions as opposed to 51 percent in 1964 (U. S. Departments of Labor and Commerce, *The Social and Economic Status of Negroes in the United States, 1969,* p. 53). One informed observer has challenged the magnitude of these increases estimated by the census, though he believes, too, that increases in total Negro college enrollment and in predominately white colleges have occurred in recent years. John Egerton, "Negro College Enrollment — Growing or Guessing?" *Reporter News Supplement* (Race Relations Information Center, July 1, 1970).

[93] For a detailed discussion of these causes, see U. S. Commission on Civil Rights, *Racial Isolation in the Public Schools.*

tricts. Central city segregation is heightened by the absorption of many white school children into private schools. For example, in cities with large Roman Catholic parochial school systems the numbers of white children in the public system often become too small to desegregate the schools adequately.[94] However, much of the intradistrict segregation is due to explicit and cynical manipulation by politicians and school administrators. As mentioned previously, what is misleadingly labeled *de facto* school segregation turns out on closer inspection to be blatantly *de jure* in its origins and maintenance.

THE EFFECTS OF SEGREGATED EDUCATION [95] — Considerable recent research reveals the negative consequences of racially segregated schools for both black and white children. In broad terms, this new work indicates that black children tend to achieve better in predominantly white schools than they do in predominantly Negro ones, while white children tend to achieve as well in predominantly white schools as they do in all-white schools. What are the processes which underlie these general results? The large 1966 study of the United States Office of Education suggests that they derived largely from the fact that predominantly white schools usually afford their students a more middle-class climate, one characterized by high aspirations and expectations.[96] And the 1967 report of the United States Commission on Civil Rights suggests that in addition to this "social class climate" factor there are also aspects of optimal interracial interaction that facilitate achievement.[97] A number of studies support these interpretations and point to some of the specific psychological processes which are probably operating.[98]

The benefits of interracial schools are not limited to academic achieve-

---

[94] In Boston and St. Louis, roughly two out of every five central city white school-aged children go to private schools; while in Philadelphia three out of five do so. Few Negroes attend parochial schools, since only about six percent are Roman Catholic (N. Glenn, "Negro Religion and Negro Status in the United States," in L. Schneider, ed., *Religion, Culture, and Society* [New York: Wiley, 1964], pp. 623–39).

[95] For an extended treatment of this topic, see Thomas F. Pettigrew, "The Negro and Education: Problems and Proposals," in Irwin Katz and Patricia Gurin, eds., *Race and the Social Sciences* (New York: Basic Books, 1969), pp. 49–112.

[96] James S. Coleman et al., *Equality of Educational Opportunity.*

[97] U. S. Commission on Civil Rights, *Racial Isolation in the Public Schools.*

[98] Thomas F. Pettigrew, "Race and Equal Educational Opportunity," *Harvard Educational Review,* Vol. 38 (Winter, 1968), pp. 66–76; and "Social Evaluation Theory: Convergences and Applications," in D. Levine, ed., *Nebraska Symposium on Motivation, 1967* (Lincoln: University of Nebraska Press, 1967), pp. 241–311; Irwin Katz, "Review of Evidence Relating to Effects of Desegregation on the Performance of Negroes," *American Psychologist,* Vol. 19 (June, 1964), pp. 381–99; and "The Socialization of Academic Motivation in Minority Group Children," in D. Levine, ed., *Nebraska Symposium on Motivation,* pp. 133–91.

ment. Interracial attitudes and behavior are improved among both Negro and white students by positive contact. Thus white students who attend public schools with blacks are the least likely to prefer all-white classrooms and all-white "close friends." [99] Surveys of urban adults find that these trends continue into adulthood and are extended to other social areas. Negro adults who themselves attended interracial schools as children tend to send their children to such schools more than comparable Negro adults who attended only segregated schools as children. [100] Similarly, white adults with desegregated schooling differ from comparable whites in their greater willingness to reside in an interracial neighborhood, to have their children attend interracial schools, and to have Negro friends. [101] Desegregated schools appear to prepare their products for an interracial world; segregated schools, white and black, do not.

Three practical caveats must be made concerning this research. *First,* these demonstrated benefits of interracial schools are strongest for the early grades, where actual desegregation occurs least. *Second,* a distinction must be made between merely "desegregated" and truly "integrated" schools. The former involve merely mixed student bodies and faculties; while the latter are mixed, too, but also involve crossracial acceptance and the optimal contact conditions to be discussed under the situational approach. Not surprisingly, the benefits of interracial schools are minimized in desegregated schools, maximized in integrated schools. *Third,* there is an urgent need for further social research in this area both to enlarge our understanding and to guide future educational policy.

EDUCATIONAL REMEDIES — To counter segregationist trends, a clear differentiation must be made between small and large ghetto situations. The small ghetto involves a city in which black students are less than one-seventh of the public school population. The high schools and often the junior high schools are naturally desegregated. But the city's elementary schools, the most critical level for racial contact, are generally segregated. With good faith, small ghettos can be totally desegregated within their districts by

[99] James S. Coleman *et al., Equality of Educational Opportunity,* p. 133. Consistent with these findings are data from Louisville, Kentucky on Negro pupils. In an open-choice situation, Negro children are far more likely to select predominantly white high schools if they are currently attending predominantly white junior high schools. (U. S. Commission on Civil Rights, *Civil Rights U. S. A.: Public Schools, Southern States, 1962* [Washington, D. C.: U. S. Government Printing Office, 1963], p. 55).

[100] U. S. Commission on Civil Rights, *Racial Isolation in the Public Schools,* Vol. I, pp. 111–13.

[101] *Ibid.*

applying a combination of proven techniques: (1) district-wide redrawing of school lines to maximize racial balance; (2) the pairing of white and black schools along the borders of the Negro ghetto; and (3) a priority for and careful placement of new and typically larger schools outside of the ghetto. Two additional devices serve to desegregate the junior and senior high levels: (4) the alteration of "feeder" arrangements from elementary grades to higher grades in order to maximize racial balance; and (5) the conversion of schools into district-wide specialized institutions.

The real problems occur for the large ghetto situation, where small ghetto techniques are mere band-aids at best. It is here that careful consideration of the four major causes of central city school segregation just enumerated is necessary to establish criteria for effective remedies. Thus desegregation measures in school systems with large ghettos must be metropolitan in scope in order to break out of demographic and school organization barriers to interracial education; they must encourage cooperation not only between central city and suburban school systems but between public and private systems as well; and they must have such wide appeal that they can override such resisting shibboleths as "the neighborhood school" and "antibusing." [102]

A number of ideas have been presented that meet these criteria, but let's discuss one as illustrative. *The Metropolitan Educational Park* would establish campus-like centers on spokes of the new mass transit systems.[103] Aided by federal building funds, it might include two high, four-to-six junior high, and 14-to-20 elementary schools serving about 15,000 students drawn from a pie slice that is narrow in the dense central city and broad in the less dense suburbs. It could be operated jointly by two or more school systems and placed on racially "neutral turf" that is seen neither as "white" nor "black" territory.

Designed imaginatively, the Metropolitan Educational Park could not only meet our desegregation criteria but many other problems starkly confronting public education today. Capital and operating cost efficiency, educational innovations, more individualized instruction, wider course offerings,

---

[102] While these shibboleths are not entirely inspired by segregationist sentiment, they become suspect when we realize that: Only a small minority of America's school children attend truly neighborhood schools; about one-half of the nation's school children are "bused" to school each day; the country's school buses travel about two billion miles annually; and little concern is voiced about these aspects of our educational system until race and integration enter as issues.

[103] For a more complete description of this concept, see Thomas F. Pettigrew, "The Negro and Education: Problems and Proposals," in Irwin Katz and Patricia Gurin, eds., *Race and the Social Sciences.*

special facilities, and easier coordination with universities and private schools — all of these advantages of the well-planned Metropolitan Educational Park are features that parents, white and black, would welcome.[104] This is politically crucial, for desegregation efforts have seldom come as intrinsic parts of a larger package promising an across-the-board improvement for *all* children.

As with housing and economics, the educational remedies suggested here are not sufficient in themselves to meet all of the racial problems involved. But they have been sketched out to indicate the nature and viability of first steps that would set our nation in the direction toward solution as opposed to the present and ominous trends toward furthering "a nation divisible by race."

THE SITUATIONAL APPROACH
TO RACE RELATIONS

Intergroup Contact

It is often naively believed that mere contact between two groups will improve relations between them. But consider the South where for 350 years the greatest amount of sheer contact between black and white Americans has occurred without conspicuous development of interracial acceptance. Similar observations could be made of Indian-white contact in the Midwest or African-European contact in South Africa. It almost appears as if the more two groups get together, the more prejudice and conflict is generated. Yet this conclusion, too, would be fallacious. The crucial questions concern the nature of the contact between two groups. What types of contact lead to

---

[104] Three major objections have been raised to the Park concept: excessive capital costs, the problem of impersonalization in large complexes, and the loss of neighborhood involvement in the school. The Park as outlined is expensive and substantial federal funding is necessary. It is considerably cheaper than building the same schools on single sites, however, and federal building monies to consortia of central city and suburbs would be productive, to single districts counterproductive, for desegregation. The impersonalization, or "Kafka," problem is already present for education as single schools are built increasingly larger for economic reasons. A well-planned Park would make it feasible to construct smaller units, each with its own privacy and individuation. Finally, good planning, adult use of facilities, and innovations such as a Park School Board made up of elected parents could generate community interest and pride in the Metropolitan Educational Park that might easily exceed that which is typical today of isolated schools.

greater tolerance and trust? And what types lead to greater prejudice and distrust?

THE CONDITIONS OF OPTIMAL CONTACT—Allport reviewed the considerable evidence on the point and concluded that four situational factors are of crucial significance.[105] Prejudice is reduced and conflict minimized when the two groups (1) possess equal status in the situation, (2) seek common goals, (3) are cooperatively dependent upon each other rather than in competition, and (4) interact with the positive support of authorities, law, or custom. Allport's principles are seen in operation in racially integrated situations. For example, in the late 1940's President Harry Truman ordered all American merchant ships to end racial segregation and discrimination. Soon after, one study showed that white American seamen tended to hold racial attitudes in direct relation to how many voyages they had taken with equal-status Negro American seamen—the more desegregated voyages, the more positive their attitudes.[106] Similarly, a study of the police force of the city of Philadelphia found that those white policemen who had personally worked with black policemen were far more favorable toward the further desegregation of the force than other white policemen.[107]

Such interracial bonds built through optimal contact situations can even withstand severe crises. For instance, while Negro and white mobs raged in the streets of Detroit during that city's race riot of 1943, desegregated coworkers, university students, and neighbors of long standing carried on their interracial lives side by side.[108]

Mention of neighborhood desegregation introduces the most solid research evidence available. Repeated investigations have found that racially desegregated living in public housing developments which meet all four of Allport's contact criteria sharply reduces intergroup prejudice among both black and white neighbors.[109] Similarly, the same investigations demon-

---

[105] Gordon W. Allport, *The Nature of Prejudice,* Chapter 16.

[106] I. N. Brophy, "The Luxury of Anti-Negro Prejudice," *Public Opinion Quarterly,* Vol. 9 (Winter, 1945–1946), pp. 456–66. An alternative explanation for the results of this and similar studies is that the people who were least prejudiced to begin with sought out interracial contact. Many of these studies, however, rule out the operation of this self-selection factor.

[107] W. M. Kephart, *Racial Factors and Urban Law Enforcement* (Philadelphia: University of Pennsylvania Press, 1957), pp. 188–89.

[108] A. M. Lee and N. D. Humphrey, *Race Riot* (New York: Octagon, 1943), pp. 97, 130, 140.

[109] M. Deutsch and Mary Collins, *Interracial Housing: A Psychological Evaluation of a Social Experiment* (Minneapolis: University of Minnesota Press, 1951); Marie Jahoda

446 Race Relations

strate that living in segregated, but otherwise identical, housing developments tends to structure interracial contact in such a manner that, if anything, intergroup bitterness is enhanced.

Another example comes from World War II.[110] Late in the war in Europe
when the fighting in the Battle of the Bulge became severe, a number of
black infantry platoons were attached to previously all-white companies
and fought side by side with white platoons until the completion of the war.
Note this situation meets all four prerequisites for favorable attitude change.
For one of the few times in our national history, Negro and white soldiers
were on equal-status terms. Furthermore, they had common goals — namely,
to stay alive and win the battle. And they emphatically were not competing
along racial lines. Finally, the contact had the sanction of top authority,
having been ordered by the Army's high command. The effects of this contact
were dramatic. When questioned later, the vast majority of white soldiers
who had fought beside Negroes had radically changed their ideas about the
black American as a combat soldier. Regardless of whether the white respondent was an officer or an enlisted man, or whether he was from the South
or North, he typically believed the Negro troops to be as good or better than
white troops.

LIMITATIONS OF THE EFFECTS OF OPTIMAL CONTACT—This wartime study also
reveals another important aspect of the effects of contact. Despite the fact
that their opinions about the Negro soldier as a fighting man had sharply
changed, the white soldiers did not alter their attitudes toward segregated
post-exchanges back of the lines. In a parallel situation, another study found
that white steelworkers in the northern United States generally approved
of the racial desegregation of their union to the point of sharing all union
facilities with blacks and electing blacks to high office, yet they also sternly
opposed the desegregation of their all-white neighborhoods.[111] In this case,

and Patricia West, "Race Relations in Public Housing," *Journal of Social Issues,* Vol. 7,
Nos. 1 and 2 (1951), pp. 132–39; D. M. Wilner, Rosabelle Walkley, and S. W. Cook,
Human Relations in Interracial Housing: A Study of the Contact Hypothesis (Minneapolis: University of Minnesota Press, 1955); and E. Works, "The Prejudice-Inter-
action Hypothesis from the Point of View of the Negro Minority Group," *American
Journal of Sociology,* Vol. 67 (July, 1961), pp. 47–52. This last study is interesting,
for it indicates that the contact conditions apply with equal force for Negro attitudes
toward whites.

[110] S. A. Stouffer et al., *Studies in Social Psychology in World War II,* Vol. 1, *The
American Soldier: Adjustment During Army Life* (Princeton, N. J.: Princeton University Press, 1949), Chapter 10.

[111] J. D. Lohman and D. C. Reitzes, "Note on Race Relations in Mass Society," *American Journal of Sociology,* Vol. 58 (November, 1952), pp. 240–46; J. D. Lohman and

as in many others, institutional structures limited the contact effects. Interracial attitudes and behavior had changed in the work situation with the support of the union organization; but these changes had not generalized to the neighborhood situation where a community organization resisted desegregation.

In other words, intergroup contact first affects attitudes that are specifically involved in the new situation itself. But such contact does not generally mean that a person's whole attitudinal structure will crumble without other situations changing, too. Most of us, indeed, are adept, in Allport's word, at "re-fencing" our prejudices and stereotypes.[112] These limitations of the effects of even optimal contact are a result of the depth and complexity with which racism and segregation have snarled the vital fabric of American life — indeed we have already traced their depth and complexity in the historical and sociocultural approaches. Untying one knot will not prove a solution; but should integration in many realms of American life become a reality, there could be more generalization from one situation to another.

Discriminatory Behavior

THE POWER OF SITUATIONAL NORMS — Intergroup contact meeting Allport's four conditions, then, can sharply modify prejudiced attitudes, especially those directly related to the contact situation. Yet modifying prejudiced attitudes is only a beginning, for the elimination of discriminatory behavior is the central problem. And attitudes and discrimination should not be confused. To be sure, individual prejudice often lies behind discriminatory behavior. But the power of situational norms makes it common to find social circumstances where bigoted individuals do not discriminate and other circumstances where unbigoted individuals do.

The sociological literature contains many examples of the power of situational norms in race relations. For example, in Panama there is a divided street, one side of which is in the United States Canal Zone and the other side is in Panama. For many years, the facilities on the Canal Zone side were tightly segregated by race, while no segregation was practiced on the Panamanian side.[113] Yet customers conducting their business managed to adjust

---

D. C. Reitzes, "Deliberately Organized Groups and Racial Behavior," *American Sociological Review,* Vol. 19 (June, 1954), pp. 342–44; and D. C. Reitzes, "The Role of Organizational Structures: Union vs. Neighborhood in a Tension Situation," *Journal of Social Issues,* Vol. 9, No. 1 (1953), pp. 37–44.

[112] Gordon W. Allport, *The Nature of Prejudice,* p. 23.

[113] J. Biesanz and L. M. Smith, "Race Relations of Panama and the Canal Zone," *American Journal of Sociology,* Vol. 57 (July, 1951), pp. 7–14.

their behavior easily as they crossed first to one **side** of the street and then to the other. Similarly, in the coal mining county of McDowell, West Virginia, Negro and white miners at one time followed a traditional pattern of desegregation below the ground and almost complete segregation above the ground.[114] Obviously, the Canal Zone residents did not shift their racial views each time they crossed and recrossed the business street. Nor did the West Virginian miners change their racial attitudes each time they went below the ground and came above it. Attitudes and behavior need not always be congruent; particular situations can structure how most people behave in spite of the attitudes they may harbor.

Sociologists were first alerted to this by a 1934 study of verbal versus actual discrimination.[115] A Chinese couple traveled widely over the United States, stopping at 250 sleeping and eating establishments. They were refused service only once. Later, the same places received inquiries by mail as to whether or not they served "members of the Chinese race." About one-half did not reply; of those which did, over 90 percent announced they did not accommodate Chinese guests. A control sample of comparable, unvisited establishments yielded similar results.

This phenomenon was repeated during the early 1950's in 11 restaurants in a northeastern suburban community.[116] Three women, two white and one Negro, went to the establishments, encountered no difficulty, and in each received exemplary service. Two weeks later, requests were sent to the restaurants for reservations for a similar group. Ten of the letters went unanswered, and follow-up phone calls met great resistance. Control calls for all-white parties led to ten reservations. It is more difficult to reject another human being face to face than through impersonal letters and phone calls.

The power of specific situational norms to shape racial patterns of behavior is dramatized by the difficulties which arise when there are no such norms. One ingenious project studied New York State facilities unaccustomed to Negro patronage.[117] Negro researchers would enter a tavern, seek service, and later record their experiences, while white researchers would

---

[114] R. D. Minard, "Race Relations in the Pocahontas Coal Field," *Journal of Social Issues,* Vol. 8, No. 1 (1952), pp. 29–44.

[115] R. T. LaPiere, "Attitudes versus Actions," *Social Forces,* Vol. 13 (December, 1934), pp. 230–37.

[116] B. Kutner, Caroll Wilkins, and Penny R. Yarrow, "Verbal Attitudes and Overt Behavior Involving Racial Prejudice," *Journal of Abnormal and Social Psychology,* Vol. 47 (July, 1952), pp. 649–52.

[117] M. L. Kohn and R. M. Williams, Jr., "Situational Patterning in Intergroup Relations," *American Sociological Review,* Vol. 21 (April, 1956), pp. 164–74.

observe the same situation and record their impressions for comparison. Typically the first reaction of waitresses and bartenders was to turn to the owner or others in authority for guidance. When this was unavailable, the slightest behavioral cue from anyone in the situation was utilized as a gauge of what was expected of them. And if there were no such cues, confusion often continued until somehow the threatening situation had been structured.

LAWS CAN CHANGE THE HEARTS AND MINDS OF MEN—Within this perspective, a reappraisal can be made of the old saw—"Laws cannot change the hearts and minds of men." A case in point is the 1945 antidiscrimination employment legislation enacted by New York State. This law led to the initial hiring of blacks as sales clerks in New York City department stores. Two investigators conducted separate tests of the effects of this law-induced desegregation. One study of white sales personnel revealed that those who had experienced the new equal-status job contact with Negroes held more favorable attitudes toward interracial interaction in the work situation.[118] Once again, however, the initial effects of this contact did not extend beyond the immediate situation; equal-status clerks were not more accepting of Negroes in eating and residential situations. The other investigation questioned customers.[119] Their responses showed widespread acceptance of this legally required racial change. They were concerned largely with shopping conveniently and efficiently; many hesitated to challenge the *fait accompli* established by the law; and for many the new pattern was consistent with their belief in the American creed of equal opportunity for all.[120]

Contrary to the old adage, then, laws *can* change the hearts and minds of men. They do so through a vital intermediate step. Laws first act to modify behavior, and this modified behavior in turn changes the participants' attitudes. Notice that this is precisely the opposite sequence commonly believed to be the most effective method of attitude change. When people are convinced that they should be less prejudiced as a result of informational and good-will campaigns, conventional reasoning asserts, then they will discriminate less. To be sure, this sequence is sometimes effective, but the preponderance of social psychological evidence attests to the greater efficacy of

---

[118] J. Harding and R. Hogrefe, "Attitudes of White Department Store Employees Toward Negro Co-Workers," *Journal of Social Issues*, Vol. 8, No. 1 (1952), pp. 18–28.

[119] G. Saenger and Emily Gilbert, "Customer Reactions to the Integration of Negro Sales Personnnel," *International Journal of Opinion and Attitude Research*, Vol. 4 (Spring, 1950), pp. 57–76.

[120] Prohibition provides an interesting contrast. It apparently failed because it was neither enforced nor, despite its moral overtones for some Protestants, did it articulate with national traditions or ease the consciences of many Americans.

the opposite approach.[121] Behaving differently is more often the precursor to thinking differently.

THE PERSONALITY APPROACH
TO RACE RELATIONS

The Three Functions of Prejudice

Attitudes of any sort serve three vital personality functions.[122] First, there is the *object appraisal* function, that is, attitudes aid in understanding "reality" as it is defined by the culture. As societies and cultures change, the social consensus as to what constitutes "reality" shifts and attitudes shift accordingly. This is one of the psychological processes underlying the individual adaptations to the sweeping social alterations, such as those considered under previous approaches. Another, and somewhat similar, psychological process is involved in the second function of attitudes, that of *social adjustment*. Attitudes aid socially by contributing to the individual's identification with, or differentiation from, various "reference groups."[123] They can help him conform to what is expected of him. Finally, attitudes can reduce anxiety by serving an expressive or *externalization* function. This occurs when an individual senses an analogy between a perceived event and some unresolved inner problem; he then adopts an attitude toward the event which is a transformed version of his way of dealing with his inner difficulty. In short, he externalizes his personality problems by projecting them onto the world through particular attitudes. Thus if he has sexual problems, he may come to regard blacks as dangerously hypersexed. The most fashionable psycho-

---

[121] M. Sherif et al., *Intergroup Conflict and Cooperation: The Robbers Cave Experiment* (Norman, Oklahoma: Institute of Group Relations, 1961).

[122] M. B. Smith, J. S. Bruner, and R. W. White, *Opinion and Personality* (New York: Wiley, 1956).

[123] "Reference group" is an important social psychological concept needed to relate the social and personality systems. A reference group supplies standards which an individual may use to guide his own behavior and with which he may compare his own position in life. Note that a reference group is not necessarily a membership group. See H. H. Hyman and Eleanor Singer, *Readings in Reference Group Theory and Research* (New York: Free Press, 1968); Robert K. Merton, *Social Theory and Social Structure* (New York: Free Press, 1968), Chapters 10 and 11; and Thomas F. Pettigrew, "Social Evaluation Theory: Convergences and Applications," in D. Levine, ed., *Nebraska Symposium on Motivation,* 1967.

logical explanations of prejudice—frustration-aggression, psychoanalytic, and authoritarianism theories—all deal chiefly with the externalization process. The last of these, authoritarianism, has received massive research emphasis and deserves our special attention.[124]

The Bigoted Personality

THE AUTHORITARIAN PERSONALITY—Motivated by a need to understand the Nazi movement in Germany, a group of personality specialists at the University of California at Berkeley intensively studied the personality dynamics of anti-Semites in the United States during the 1940's. They found a syndrome of personality traits, which was labeled "authoritarianism," that consistently differentiated many highly anti-Semitic and ethnocentric individuals from others. Central to the syndrome is anti-intraception, the refusal to look inside of yourself and a general lack of insight into one's own behavior and feelings. Probably deriving from early childhood training, the authoritarian refuses to accept his own emotions and tries hard to deny them. For instance, as a child the authoritarian may have frequently been punished by a stern father and in turn felt intense hatred for him. But unable to express his feelings for fear of further punishment, the authoritarian found these aggressive emotions threatening and unacceptable, denied them, and instead began to project them onto others. If he felt hatred for his father, he saw hatred not in himself but in the dangerous outside world.

Consequently, the authoritarian typically conveys an idealized picture of his parents as absolutely perfect and loving. Generalizing this unrealistic view to other authorities, the authoritarian comes to view the world in good-bad, up-and-down power terms. He is generally outwardly submissive toward those he sees as authorities with power over him. Similarly, he is

---

[124] The basic work was reported in T. W. Adorno, Else Frenkel-Brunswik, D. J. Levinson, and R. N. Sanford, *The Authoritarian Personality* (New York: Harper, 1950). Valuable critiques of the original work together with reviews of the extensive research inspired by it are found in Roger Brown, *Social Psychology* (New York: Free Press, 1965), Chapter 10; R. Christie and Marie Jahoda, eds., *Studies in the Scope and Method of "The Authoritarian Personality"* (New York: Free Press, 1954); R. Christie and Peggy Cook, "A Guide to Published Literature Relating to the Authoritarian Personality Through 1956," *Journal of Psychology,* Vol. 45 (1958), pp. 171–99; H. E. Titus and E. P. Hollander, "The California F. Scale in Psychological Research: 1950–1955," *Psychological Bulletin,* Vol. 54 (January, 1957), pp. 47–64; and J. W. Kirscht and R. C. Dillehay, *Dimensions of Authoritarianism: A Review of Research and Theory* (Lexington: University of Kentucky Press, 1967).

aggressive toward those he sees as being beneath him in status. This hierarchical view of authority led to the label of "authoritarian personality," a term referring to a personality syndrome that produces prejudice against minority groups; indeed prejudice becomes for individuals possessing this personality "a crutch" upon which to limp through life. Lacking insight into their inner feelings, they project their own unacceptable impulses on the minorities whom they regard as being beneath them.[125] One study demonstrated that such persons will often reject on a questionnaire groups which do not even exist.[126]

THE CONFORMING PERSONALITY—The psychoanalytically inspired theory of the authoritarian personality is a valuable contribution to an understanding of race relations in America. But the almost exclusive attention given the externalization function of prejudice has caused a lack of attention to the equally important function of social adjustment. By no means do all white Americans who hold anti-Negro opinions and participate in discriminatory actions exhibit the authoritarian personality syndrome. For many, antiblack views and behavior are not nearly so expressive as they are socially adaptive in a racist society. In sharp contrast to the deeply rooted bigotry of authoritarianism, the bigotry of "conformity" requires prejudice as a social entrance ticket. The conformity bigot wants to be liked and accepted by people important to him; and if these people are antiblack, he reflects their attitudes.

Notice the two significant differences between the crutch and conformity varieties of intolerance. Those who are anti-Negro for largely conformity reasons have antipathy only for those groups that it is fashionable to dislike; their prejudice does not spread to out-groups in general as does that of authoritarians. They follow the path of least social resistance, for they need to be liked rather than to hate. More important, conformity prejudice is not so deeply rooted in childhood socialization, but is only an attempt to "live down" to what associates expect. Thus as social expectations are altered, conforming bigots shed their bigotry with relative ease. They continue to

---

[125] We shall explore this point further under the phenomenological approach. But note that this description fits only the authoritarian of the political right. Authoritarians are also found on the political left; with equal dogmatism, they reject all authorities and attempt a strangely condescending identification with minorities. The politics of the two authoritarian types may be polar opposites, but the personality style remains strikingly the same. The first statement on this point was provided by E. A. Shils, "Authoritarianism: 'Right' and 'Left,'" in R. Christie and Marie Jahoda, eds., *Studies in the Scope and Method of "The Authoritarian Personality,"* pp. 24–49.

[126] Eugene L. Hartley, *Problems in Prejudice* (New York: Kings Crown, 1946).

conform, but the customs and norms that guide their beliefs and actions change. Obviously, conformity prejudice makes possible at the individual level the power of situational norms to determine racial attitudes and behavior at the social level.

THE PREVALENCE OF PREJUDICE TYPES—Hence under the personality approach, it becomes important to inquire about the distributions of crutch-type and conformity-type bigots across the United States. Do most white Americans *need*, in a deep authoritarian personality sense, antiblack prejudice? Or do most white Americans who harbor anti-Negro attitudes do so largely in order to follow racist dictates and expectations? As observed earlier, the answers to these questions are of considerable importance for public policy and the future of American race relations.

First, it must be realized that the two types of prejudice that were described are ideal types. In practice, the two are seldom seen in pure form; more typically, antiblack prejudice weaves together elements of both types. Yet it is still possible to ascertain roughly the prevalence of persons who are relatively authoritarian in their orientation against Negroes in contrast to those who are relatively more conforming.

After a close inspection of the relevant data in 1953, Allport estimated that roughly "four-fifths of the American population harbors enough antagonism toward minority groups to influence their daily conduct." [127] This crude figure varies widely, of course, across regional, age, and social class groupings; and it varies widely, too, according to the research question and method employed. Yet Allport's estimate continues to receive support from divergent data sources. Furthermore, the unprejudiced one-fifth noted by Allport appears to be matched by a prejudiced one-fifth motivated largely by authoritarian personality needs. These are the citizens who place their racial beliefs so high in their value structure that they will follow them even when they conflict with their other values. They can be counted on to vote against any civil rights legislation; to favor political candidates who run on openly anti-Negro platforms [128]; and to answer most survey questions on minority groups in general with bigoted responses. [129]

---

[127] Gordon W. Allport, *The Nature of Prejudice,* p. 78.

[128] Thus at his high point in national opinion surveys, George Wallace received support from 22 percent (25 percent of whites) in his 1968 third-party candidacy for the presidency and secured almost 14 percent (or 16 percent of whites) of the total vote (Thomas F. Pettigrew, *Racially Separate or Together?,* Chapter 11).

[129] Thus 18 percent believed in December of 1963 that "white people should have the first chance at any kind of job"—the most extreme item in Sheatsley's pro-integration scale. At the other extreme, only 27 percent disagreed that "Negroes shouldn't push

Roughly speaking, then, three-fifths of white Americans may well be conforming bigots. On racial issues that face considerable societal disapproval, such as the "busing" of children to interracial schools, most of these citizens will join the crutch-types in forming a majority resistant to change. On racial issues that win wide societal approval, such as the 1964 Civil Rights Act after the assassination of President John F. Kennedy, most of these citizens will join the unprejudiced in forming a majority favorable to change. It is they, then, who are primarily responsible for the breathtaking swings in the national mood on racial change, swings from the high of 1964 to the low of 1970.

Crude as these ratios must necessarily be, they are accurate enough to order and render understandable a great mass of relevant race relations data of recent years.[130] Such an analysis suggests that persons who approximate the conformity-type bigots probably outnumber those who believe and act

---

themselves where they're not wanted." Paul B. Sheatsley, "White Attitudes Toward the Negro," in T. Parsons and Kenneth B. Clark, eds., *The Negro American,* pp. 303–24. Similarly, the Harris national survey for *Newsweek* in 1966 found on its four most extreme anti-Negro items only "the authoritarian fifth" objecting "to using the same restrooms as Negroes" (22 percent), "to sitting next to a Negro in a movie" (21 percent), "to sitting next to a Negro on a bus" (16 percent), and "to sitting next to a Negro in a restaurant" (16 percent). William Brink and Louis Harris, *Black and White: A Study of U. S. Racial Attitudes Today* (New York: Simon and Schuster, 1967), p. 136. Finally, the "tolerant fifth" reveals itself sharply in four questions asked in a Gallup national survey of May, 1968. When queries as to whether "white people or Negroes themselves" were more to blame for the present conditions of Negroes, only 23 percent of the whites cited "white people" with 19 percent holding "no opinion." Similarly, only 17 percent of whites (10 percent "no opinion") thought Negroes were being treated in their communities either "badly" or "not very well"; only 18 percent (14 percent "no opinion") thought businesses in their area discriminated against Negroes in hiring; and only 17 percent (31 percent "no opinion") thought labor unions in their area discriminated against Negroes in their membership practices. Hazel Erskine, "The Polls: Recent Opinion on Racial Problems," *Public Opinion Quarterly,* Vol. 32 (Winter, 1968–1969), pp. 696–703.

[130] Compilations of relevant survey data on race relations include Hazel Erskine, "The Polls: Recent Opinion on Racial Problems," *Public Opinion Quarterly;* "The Polls: Race Relations," *Public Opinion Quarterly,* Vol. 26 (Spring, 1962), pp. 137–48; "The Polls: Negro Housing," *Public Opinion Quarterly,* Vol. 31 (Fall, 1967), pp. 482–98; "The Polls: Demonstrations and Race Riots," *Public Opinion Quarterly,* Vol. 31 (Winter, 1967–1968), pp. 655–77; "The Polls: Negro Employment," *Public Opinion Quarterly,* Vol. 32 (Spring, 1968), pp. 132–53; "The Polls: Speed of Racial Integration," *Public Opinion Quarterly,* Vol. 32 (Fall, 1968), pp. 513–24; J. M. Fenton, *In Your Opinion* (Boston: Little, Brown, 1960); William Brink and Louis Harris, *The Negro Revolution in America* (New York: Simon and Schuster, 1964); and William Brink and Louis Harris, *Black and White: A Study of U. S. Racial Attitudes Today.*

consistently on race, including both those who approximate crutch-type bigots and those who are not anti-Negro. Even for the South, there is considerable evidence suggesting that conformity prejudice against blacks is considerably more common than authoritarian prejudice.[131]

Two practical implications flow from this personality analysis. On the one hand, it suggests that white American racial opinion is more flexible than it might at first appear. If major sociocultural changes create optimal conditions for increased interracial contact, attitudes toward Negroes and racial change could continue to improve as they have since 1944.[132] Reform efforts for the needed structural changes specified earlier should not be deterred by initial opposition of a majority of white Americans. On the other hand, the strong possibility of antiblack sentiments of about one-fifth of white America reflecting in varying measure deep externalizing functions should give us pause. Twenty million adult citizens who approximate crutch-types form a critical mass for societal conflict and make it likely the Wallace phenomenon of 1968 will be repeated throughout the seventies.

THE PHENOMENOLOGICAL APPROACH TO RACE RELATIONS

The tendency for deeply rooted bigots to externalize their inner problems and project them upon minority groups shapes the stereotypes of out-groups having wide currency in societies throughout the world. In broad psychoanalytic terms, two contrasting phenomenologies emerge. One type is rooted in superego concerns, with the out-group stereotyped as shrewd, mercenary, pushy, ambitious, sly, and clannish. The other type is rooted in id concerns, with the out-group stereotyped as superstitious, lazy, happy-go-lucky, ignorant, dirty, irresponsible, and sexually uninhibited. In the United States, the prejudiced person typically personifies his own superego sins of ambition, deceit, and egotism in the Jew and his own id sins of the flesh in the Negro.[133]

The psychoanalytic distinction between superego and id stereotypes is applicable to a variety of crosscultural situations. Thus out-groups assigned

---

[131] Thomas F. Pettigrew, "Social Psychology and Desegregation Research," *American Psychologist,* Vol. 16 (1961), pp. 105–12.

[132] H. H. Hyman and P. B. Sheatsley, "Attitudes Toward Desegregation," *Scientific American,* Vol. 211 (July, 1964), pp. 16–23; and Thomas F. Pettigrew, *Racially Separate or Together?,* Chapter 8.

[133] T. W. Adorno et al., *The Authoritarian Personality,* and Bruno Bettelheim and Morris Janowitz, *Social Change and Prejudice* (New York: Harper, 1964).

a superego stigma are usually merchants who are not native to an area, middlemen caught between the landed and the laboring classes as were the European Jews in the Middle Ages.[134] Nor are the people who invoke the superego stereotype unaware of this similarity, for the Chinese merchants of Malaysia and Indonesia are often called the "Jews of Asia" and the Muslim Indian merchants of East and South Africa the "Jews of Africa." In somewhat the same fashion, the id stigma is invoked in many parts of the world for groups that are usually found on the bottom of the social structure; in Europe, Gypsies and southern Italians are often the targets.[135] Yet the black American inherits the id stigma with special force. Not only is he typically confined by class barriers at the bottom of the social structure, but he is also condemned by caste barriers as the degrading legacy of three centuries of slavery and segregation.

The id stigma branded upon the black American is only now beginning to recede. Compared with the results of a study in the early 1930's, a follow-up study of Princeton University undergraduates in 1950 found that the Negro stereotype, like other stereotypes, had lost some of its salience. The percentage of students regarding the Negro American as "superstitious" had declined from 84 to 41 percent, as "lazy" from 75 to 31 percent, as "happy-go-lucky" from 38 to 17 percent, and as "ignorant" from 38 to 24 percent.[136] Evidence of a similar trend for the entire adult population comes from repeated surveys of the National Opinion Research Center asking, "In general, do you think Negroes are as intelligent as white people—that is, can they learn just as well if they are given the same education and training?" The percentage among the white respondents answering "yes" in 1942 was only 42, by 1946 this figure had risen to 52, by 1956 it had climbed to 77, and in

---

[134] The superego out-group pattern also typically involves a middleman minority which is separatist in an expanding nationalist state which emphasizes unity. Thus the Huguenots of England and Ireland were not separatist, nor was India an expanding nationalist state when it received the Parsis—and neither the Huguenots nor the Parsis triggered the superego pattern (S. Stryker, "Social Structure and Prejudice," *Social Problems,* Vol. 6 [Spring, 1959], pp. 340–54).

[135] Direct parallels between the American stereotype of the Negro and the northern Italian stereotype of the southern Italian are demonstrated in M. W. Battacchi, *Meridionali e Settentrionali nella Struttura del Pregiudizio Ethnico in Italia* [Southerners and Northerners in the Structure of Ethnic Prejudice in Italy] (Bologna, Italia: Societa Editrice Il Mulino, 1959).

[136] D. Katz and K. W. Braly, "Racial Stereotypes of 100 College Students," *Journal of Abnormal and Social Psychology,* Vol. 28 (October–November, 1933), pp. 280–90; and G. M. Gilbert, "Stereotype Persistence and Change Among College Students," *Journal of Abnormal and Social Psychology,* Vol. 46 (April, 1951), pp. 245–54.

1963 it still remained at 77.[137] Even among white southerners, 59 percent said "yes" to the query by 1963.

For striking evidence of how this shift is reflected in the mass media, one need only compare contemporary materials with the early issues of *Life* magazine.[138] While occasionally portraying Negroes neutrally or as "credits to their race," *Life* in the late 1930's overwhelmingly presented Negroes as either musical, primitive, amusing, or religious, or as violent and criminal; occupationally, they were pictured as either servants, athletes, entertainers, or as unemployed. Pictures included a Negro choir at a graveside funeral, an all-Negro chain gang, and Negro W.P.A. workers beating a drum "in tribal fashion" at a W.P.A. circus. Dialect was common: to the question of who was Father Divine's father, "Mrs. Mayfield cackled, 'Lawd chile, that been so long ago, I done fergit.'" Descriptions of Negroes dancing included such terms as "barbaric," "jungle," and "native gusto." Today the mass media would not consider such material.

This is not to imply by any means that the id stereotype of Negroes has faded completely. The two Harris national surveys for *Newsweek* in 1963 and 1966 found that the bedrock racist beliefs of the inferiority of Negroes still persisted not only among "the authoritarian fifth" but also among many of those more approximating conformity prejudice.[139] Thus in 1966, Harris found that 56 percent of white Americans still believed that Negroes "laugh a lot" (down from 68 percent in 1963), 52 percent believed that they "smell different" (down from 60 percent in 1963), 50 percent that they "have looser morals" (down from 55 percent in 1963), and 43 percent that they "want to live off the handout" (up from 41 percent in 1963).

Nevertheless, all of these studies reveal that the id stereotype of the Negro is slowly, sometimes almost imperceptibly, receding. And as the stereotyped racial beliefs fade, so, too, do the white attitudes which favor the maintenance of racial discrimination and segregation. Table 1 provides survey evidence on this point for attitudes toward desegregated schools. Observe the marked shift since 1942 in response to the first question. Note, too, the remarkable attitude changes recorded among white southerners on both ques-

---

[137] H. H. Hyman and P. B. Sheatsley, "Attitudes Toward Desegregation," *Scientific American,* Vol. 195 (December, 1956), pp. 35–39 and Vol. 211 (July, 1964), pp. 16–23.

[138] The author is indebted to Dr. Patricia Pajonas Gadbon, formerly of Harvard University, for her analysis of all racial material appearing in 34 issues of *Life* sampled from November, 1936 through March, 1938.

[139] William Brink and Louis Harris, *The Negro Revolution in America,* pp. 140–41; and W. Brink and L. Harris, *Black and White: A Study of U. S. Racial Attitudes Today,* p. 136.

TABLE 1

Changing White Attitudes Toward School Desegregation

"Do you think white students and Negro students should go to the same schools or to separate schools?" [a]

Percentage answering "same schools"

	1942	April, June, Sept. Average, 1956	June, Nov., Dec. Average, 1963	1965
White Northerners	40	61	74	78
White Southerners	2	14	32	36
Total Whites	30	49	63	67

"Would you, yourself, have any objection to sending your children to a school where a few of the children are colored?" [b]

Percentage answering "No, would not object"

	1963	1965	1966	1969	1970
White Northern Parents	87	91	93	93	93
White Southern Parents	38	62	74	78	83

". . . where half of the children are colored?"

	1963	1965	1966	1969	1970
White Northern Parents	56	65	64	69	70
White Southern Parents	17	27	44	47	52

". . . where more than half of the children are colored?"

	1963	1965	1966	1969	1970
White Northern Parents	31	37	32	39	38
White Southern Parents	6	16	27	26	26

Sources:
[a] H. H. Hyman and P. B. Sheatsley, "Attitudes Toward Desegregation," *Scientific American,* Vol. 195 (December, 1956), and Vol. 211 (July, 1964); Paul B. Sheatsley, "White Attitudes Toward the Negro," in T. Parsons and Kenneth B. Clark, eds., *The Negro American* (Boston: Houghton, Mifflin, 1966).
[b] AIPO releases (May 22, 1965 and May 3, 1970); Roper Public Research Center, Williamstown, Massachusetts supplied the 1966 data; *Integrated Education,* Vol. 7 (November–December, 1969), pp. 51–52.

tions. Indeed, the swing from only 38 percent of southern parents in 1963 not objecting to sending their children to a school with a few Negro children to 83 percent not objecting in 1970 is of a magnitude rarely recorded in public opinion research. Furthermore, H. H. Hyman and P. B. Sheatsley have found that white attitude change on racial matters in the South typically comes after there has been school and other types of desegregation in the community. This *fait accompli* effect, as it is called, follows from the previous analysis of attitude change under the situational approach.[140]

The historical and sociocultural trends reviewed earlier simply force a realignment in the views of blacks held by white Americans. The new black legal status, the increase in black political power, the upgrading of the black labor force, the rising levels of black income and education, and the marked improvement of mass-media racial content all combine with the assertive resourcefulness of black protest itself to spell the gradual abolition of the centuries-old racist stigma. It will continue to recede from view in direct relation to how dysfunctional it is for American society. But this process will require a number of generations before the most entrenched aspects of the stereotype are essentially eradicated.

THE STIMULUS-OBJECT APPROACH TO RACE RELATIONS

Now we turn to the focus of the issue, the black American himself. Other chapters in this volume discuss aspects of the black community that touch upon other contemporary social problems of American society. But here, within the context supplied by the previous five approaches, we shall look at the black American, first, as a victim of prejudice and discrimination and, next, as a protesting reactor to oppression.

The "Negro" Role

Recall that prejudice recedes when contact between two groups involves equal status, common goals, interdependence, and authority sanction. Most of the interaction between white and Negro Americans down through the years has not involved these optimal contact conditions. Rather, black-white contact in the United States has generally been characterized by a rigid inferior- and superior-status differentiation; and such contact has reinforced racial stereotypes and mediated the oppressive racial system effects upon individual blacks. One useful way to conceptualize such racial interaction and its effects is to describe them in role-theory terms.[141] Discrimi-

---

[140] H. H. Hyman and P. B. Sheatsley, "Attitudes Toward Desegregation," *Scientific American,* Vol. 211 (July, 1964).

[141] Thomas F. Pettigrew, *A Profile of the Negro American* (Princeton, N. J.: Van Nostrand, 1964).

natory encounters between whites and blacks require that both parties "play the game." The white must act out the role of the "superior"; by direct action or subtle cue, he must convey the expectation that he will be treated with deference. For his part, the Negro must, if traditional norms are to be obeyed, act out the role of the "inferior"; he must play the social role of "Negro." And should he refuse to play the game, he would be judged by many whites as "not knowing his place," and harsh sanctions could follow.[142]

The socially stigmatized role of "Negro" is the critical feature of having dark skin in the United States. At the personality level, such enforced role adoption divides each individual Negro both from other human beings and from himself. Of course, all social roles, necessary as they are, hinder to some extent forthright, uninhibited social interaction. An employer and employee, for example, may never begin to understand each other as complete human beings unless they break through the formality and constraints of their role relationships. Similarly, whites and blacks can never communicate as equals unless they break through the role barriers. As long as racial roles are maintained, both parties find it difficult to perceive the humanity behind the façade. Many whites unthinkingly confuse the role of "Negro" with the people who must play this role. "That's just the way Negroes are," goes the phrase. Conversely, many Negroes confuse the role of "white man" with whites. "Whites are just like that, they are born thinking they should be boss."

Intimately associated with this impairment of human relatedness is an impairment of the individual's acceptance and understanding of himself. Both whites and blacks can confuse their own roles as being an essential part of themselves. Whites can easily flatter themselves into believing that they are in fact "superior"; after all, does not the deferent behavior of the role-playing Negro confirm this "superiority"? And Negroes in turn often accept much of the mythology; for does not the imperious behavior of the role-playing white confirm this "inferiority"?

These ideas are supported by a large body of social psychological research. This research convincingly demonstrates the power of role playing to change deeply held attitudes, values, and even self-conceptions.[143] Moreover, these remarkable changes have been rendered experimentally by temporary role adoptions of an exceedingly trivial nature when compared to the lifelong role of "Negro." Imagine, then, the depth of the effects of having to play a role

---

[142] The terror such a subordinate role can have for a white person, inexperienced in its subtleties, is revealed in John Griffin, *Black Like Me* (Boston: Houghton Mifflin, 1961).

[143] Thomas F. Pettigrew, *A Profile of the Negro American.*

which has such vast personal and social significance that it affects virtually all realms of daily living. In short, racial roles have profound and direct psychological as well as behavioral effects upon their adopters.

Relative Deprivation and Black Unrest of the 1960's [144]

The deferent nature of the deeply established "Negro" role raises interesting questions about the assertive protest behavior which Negroes in large numbers began exhibiting in the 1960's. Why did black unrest come to a boil in the 1960's and not in the 1980's or in the depth of the Depression of the 1930's? And how were the young in particular so able to break through the constraints of the accommodating "Negro" role?

Answers to these questions are suggested by the already detailed sociocultural changes black Americans have been undergoing as a people. As noted earlier, the latest product of this dramatic transformation from southern peasant to northern urbanite is a second- and third-generation northern-born youth. The most significant fact about this "newest new Negro" is that he is relatively released from the principal social controls recognized by his parents and grandparents, from the restraints of an extended kinship system, a conservative religion and an acceptance of the inevitability of white supremacy. Consider the experience of a young black today. If he were born in 1950: He was four years old when the highest court in the land decreed against *de jure* public school segregation; he was only seven years old at the time of the Little Rock, Arkansas desegregation confrontation; he was ten years old when the student-organized sit-ins began at segregated lunch counters throughout the South; and he was 13 when the dramatic March-on-Washington took place; and 15 when the climactic Selma march occurred. He has literally witnessed during his short life the initial dismantling of the formal structure of white supremacy. Conventional wisdom holds that such an experience should lead to a highly satisfied generation of young Negro Americans. Newspaper headlines and social-psychological theory tell us precisely the opposite is closer to the truth.

The past three decades of black American history constitute an almost classic case for relative deprivation theory.[145] Mass unrest has reoccurred

---

[144] For more thorough coverage of this subject, see: Thomas F. Pettigrew, *Racially Separate or Together?*, Chapter 7.

[145] *Ibid.;* Thomas F. Pettigrew, *A Profile of the Negro American,* Chapter 8; and T. F. Pettigrew, "Social Evaluation Theory: Convergences and Applications," in D. Levine, ed., *Nebraska Symposium on Motivation, 1969.*

throughout history after long periods of improvement followed by abrupt periods of reversal.[146] This pattern derives from four revolt-stirring conditions triggered by long-term improvements: (1) Living conditions of the dominant group typically advance faster than those of the subordinate group; (2) the aspirations of the subordinate group climb far more rapidly than actual changes; (3) status inconsistencies among subordinate group members increase sharply; and (4) a broadening of comparative reference groups occurs for the subordinate group.[147]

Each of these four conditions typifies the Negro American situation today.[148] (1) Though the past few decades have witnessed the most rapid gains in Negro American history, these gains have generally not kept pace with those of white America during these same prosperous years. (2) Public opinion surveys document the swiftly rising aspirations of black Americans, especially since 1954. Moreover, (3) status inconsistency has been increasing among Negroes, particularly among the young whose educational level typically exceeds the low status employment offered them. Finally, (4) Negro Americans have greatly expanded their relevant reference groups in recent years; affluent referents in the richest country on earth are now routinely adopted as the appropriate standard with which to judge one's condition. The second component of unrest involving a sudden reversal has been supplied, too, by the Vietnam War. Little wonder, then, that America's racial crisis reached the combustible point in the late 1960's.

A FUTURE DIRECTION
FOR AMERICAN RACE RELATIONS

Armed with the perspective of the six different approaches to the problem we can now contemplate the future of American race relations. In the early 1960's, there seemed little question as to the future: Achieve full-scaled institutional integration and the problem will be solved. But the unwanted Vietnam War, widespread race rioting, and the rise of a much-publicized but little-understood ideology of "black separatism" in the middle and late

---

[146] J. C. Davies, "Towards a Theory of Revolution," *American Sociological Review,* Vol. 27 (February, 1962), pp. 5–19.

[147] Thomas F. Pettigrew, "Social Evaluation Theory: Convergences and Applications," in D. Levine, ed., *Nebraska Symposium on Motivation, 1969.*

[148] *Ibid.;* and J. A. Geschwender, "Social Structure and the Negro Revolt: An Examination of Some Hypotheses," *Social Forces,* Vol. 43 (December, 1964), pp. 248–56.

1960's has brought on a new mood and a confusion over goals. The nation hesitates. It seems unsure as to even the direction in which a solution lies or even if a solution is possible. Yet our review suggests that if the earlier consensus on "integration" was too simple, so, too, is the pessimism which prevails as the country enters the last one-third of the twentieth century.

Recall the vital sociocultural trends. Extrapolating from our earlier discussions, the outlines of the situation in the 1970's are these: (1) Widespread integration is possible everywhere in the United States save in the largest central cities; (2) it will not come unless present trends are reversed and considerable resources are provided for the process; (3) big central cities will continue to have significant Negro concentrations even with successful metropolitan dispersal; (4) large Negro ghettos are presently in need of intensive enrichment; and (5) some ghetto enrichment programs run the clear and present danger of embalming the ghetto further.

A Mixed Integration-Enrichment Strategy

Given this situation and the considerations of this chapter, a mixed strategy for the future would contain the following elements:

1. A major effort toward racial integration must be mounted in order to provide genuine choice to all black Americans in all areas of life. This effort should envisage by the late 1970's complete attainment of the goal in smaller communities and cities and a halting of segregationist trends in major central cities with a movement toward metropolitan cooperation.
2. A simultaneous effort is required to enrich the vast central city ghettos of the nation, to change them structurally, and to make life in them more viable. In order to avoid embalming them, however, strict criteria must be applied to proposed enrichment programs to insure that they are productive for later dispersal and integration. Restructuring the economics of the ghetto, especially the development of urban cooperatives, offers a fine example of productive enrichment. The building of enormous public housing developments within the ghetto presents a good illustration of counterproductive enrichment. Some programs, such as the decentralization of huge public school systems or the encouragement of Negro business ownership, can be either productive or counterproductive, depending upon how they are implemented. An urban decentralization plan of many homogeneous school districts is clearly counterproductive for later integration; a plan of a relatively small number of heterogeneous school districts could well be productive. Further, black

entrepreneurs encouraged to open small shops and expected to prosper with an all-Negro clientele are not only counterproductive but are probably committing economic suicide. Black businessmen encouraged to pool resources to establish somewhat larger operations and to appeal to white as well as Negro customers on major traffic arteries running through the ghetto could be productive.

Black Support

Survey results strongly suggest that such a mixed strategy would meet with widespread Negro approval. On the basis of their extensive 1968 survey of black residents in 15 major cities, Angus Campbell and Howard Schuman conclude:

> Separatism appeals to from five to eighteen per cent of the Negro sample, depending on the question, with the largest appeal involving black ownership of stores and black administration of schools in Negro neighborhoods, and the smallest appeal the rejection of whites as friends or in other informal contacts. Even on questions having the largest appeal, however, more than three-quarters of the Negro sample indicate a clear preference for integration. Moreover, the reasons given by respondents for their choices suggest that the desire for integration is not simply a practical wish for better material facilities, but represents a commitment to principles of nondiscrimination and racial harmony.[149]

But if separatism draws little favorable response even in the most politicized ghettos, positive aspects of cultural pluralism attract wide interest. For example, 42 percent endorse the statement that "Negro school children should study an African language." And this interest seems rather general across age, sex, and education categories. Campbell and Schuman regard this as evidence of a broadly supported attempt ". . . to emphasize black consciousness *without* rejection of whites. . . . A substantial number of Negroes want *both* integration and black identity." [150] This is not a new position for Negro Americans, for their dominant response to Marcus Garvey's movement in the 1920's was essentially the same. Garvey stressed the beauty of

---

[149] Angus Campbell and Howard Schuman, "Racial Attitudes in Fifteen American Cities," in The National Advisory Commission on Civil Disorders, *Supplementary Studies* (Washington, D. C.: U. S. Government Printing Office, 1968), p. 5.
[150] *Ibid.,* p. 6.

blackness and pride in Africa and mounted a mass movement in the urban ghettos of the day, but his "back to Africa" separatist appeals were largely ignored.

The Campbell and Schuman data indicate little if any change from the pro-integration results of earlier Negro surveys.[151] And they are consistent with the results of surveys in Detroit, Miami, New York City, and other cities.[152] Data from Bedford-Stuyvesant in Brooklyn are especially significant, for here separatist ideology and a full-scale enrichment program are in full view. Yet when asked if they would prefer to live on a block with people of the same race or of every race, 80 percent of the Negro respondents chose an interracial block.[153] Interestingly, the largest Negro segment choosing integration — 88 percent — consisted of residents of public housing where a modest amount of interracial tenancy still prevails.

A final study from Watts links these surveys to the analysis of this paper.[154] It found that Negro willingness to use violence was closely and positively related to a sense of powerlessness, feelings of racial dissatisfaction, and limited contact with whites. Respondents who indicated that they had no social contact with white people, "like going to the movies together or visiting each others' homes," were significantly more likely to feel powerless and express racial dissatisfaction as well as to report greater willingness to use violence. The personal, group, and national costs of racial separatism are great.

Together with the specific remedies mentioned previously, the mixed strategy of integration efforts combined with productive ghetto enrichment offers a promising future direction for American race relations. The basic question, then, becomes: How long will it be before we initiate a broad-scale program of *both* enrichment and integration? Or put differently, how much damage will the United States inflict upon itself before it realizes its own dream of equality?

[151] William Brink and Louis Harris, *The Negro Revolution in America* and *Black and White: A Study of U. S. Racial Attitudes Today.* Nor is sharp change evident in 1969 data; see Peter Goldman, *Report from Black America* (New York: Simon and Schuster, 1970), pp. 244, 266–70.

[152] Philip Meyer, *A Survey of Attitudes of Detroit Negroes After the Riot of 1967* (Detroit: Detroit Urban League, 1968); *Miami Negroes: A Study in Depth* (Miami: The Miami Herald, 1968); and The Center for Urban Education, "Survey of the Residents of Bedford-Stuyvesant" (Unpublished Paper, 1968).

[153] *Ibid.*

[154] H. E. Ransford, "Isolation, Powerlessness, and Violence: A Study of Attitudes and Participation in the Watts Riot," *American Journal of Sociology,* Vol. 73 (March, 1968), pp. 581–91.

10

Family Disorganization

WILLIAM J. GOODE

For the past several hundred years – if we are to believe eyewitnesses – the family has been in a state of constant decline. This assertion applies even more strongly to the American family. Commentators, observers, philosophers, prophets and preachers, political leaders, and social analysts, both in their private letters and diaries and in their public statements, have all attested to this breakdown over generation after generation. They have recorded their beliefs that in *their* generation, parental authority was breaking down, people were no longer obeying the old sexual taboos, husbands and wives did not trust one another, and wives were rebelling against their husbands; all in contrast to the period of their grandfathers, when the old customs were followed and the family seemed vigorous and strong.

We must conclude, therefore, that the family is both fragile and tough: fragile because it is constantly breaking down; and tough because, manifestly, it has not disappeared. Perhaps we should conclude instead that all these observers were wrong, that they were merely sentimentalizing the state of family relations in their grandparents' generation and expressing no more than their own dissatisfaction with contemporary family life. Or we might consider, alternatively, another interpretation: that all such state-

I wish to acknowledge the help of Nicholas Tavuchis, Joel Telles, and Cynthia Fuchs Epstein in the various revisions of this chapter.

ments, in past generations and in our own, are no more than the complaints of moralists everywhere and in all times that people are not living up to the ideals of the society.

Perhaps a more fruitful interpretation would be that disorganization is *endemic* to the family, that our supercilious laughter at radio and television soap operas has been in error, for they represent the more normal patterns of daily family life, that is, recurring sets of dissolving pressures, with a repeated and often stumbling reassertion of old patterns. If this is indeed the case, then to speak of family disorganization is not so much to single out peculiarities and strange deviations from some widely accepted and typical set of norms, but rather to look at expectable processes that are at least potential in any family unit and observable in at least a substantial minority of all families. Indeed, if we had some way of measuring all the social patterns that people view as deviant in some way, it is not at all certain that the total number of "deviants" would be a minority.

More simply put, marriages, like lives, must end. Some marriages are dissolved by divorce, some by death, and some gradually come apart, to exist for years as a mere formality. Since family life is suffused with emotion, those who are unhappy in their family relationships usually learn that this kind of misery, like a toothache, cannot easily be set apart, compartmentalized, or controlled by an effort of will. It affects much of their lives. Almost everyone will eventually experience one or another of the various forms of family disorganization at some time in their lives.

TYPES OF FAMILY DISORGANIZATION

If family disorganization may be defined as the breakup of a family unit, the dissolution or fracture of a structure of social roles when one or more members fail to perform adequately their role obligations, then several modes of disorganization may be analyzed separately. Such an examination need not confine itself to the contemporary United States and may properly extend to the consideration of larger social structures in which family processes take place.

In the sections that follow, certain major forms of family disorganization will be sketched first. Data from other societies will be used at times, especially in the analyses of illegitimacy and divorce, to throw light on certain broader aspects of family systems. Considerable space will be given to divorce, because so many other types of family disorganization are likely to end this way, because it is the focus of so much moral concern on the part of the public, and because changes in the divorce rate are usually an index of changes in other elements in the family patterns of any society.

As a foundation for the later analysis of these forms, a general view of their meaning for social structures will first be outlined.

The major forms of family disorganization may be classified as follows:

1. The uncompleted family unit: *illegitimacy*. Although the family unit may not be said to "dissolve" if it never existed, illegitimacy may nevertheless be viewed as one form of family disorganization for two reasons: (a) the potential "father-husband" conspicuously fails in his role-obligations as these are defined by the society, mother, and child; and (b) the role failure of members of the families of both mother and father, especially with regard to social control, is a major indirect cause of illegitimacy.

2. Family dissolution by virtue of the voluntary departure of one spouse: *annulment, separation, divorce, desertion. Job desertion* may also be included here when the individual uses the excuse of a job to stay away from home for a long period.

3. Alterations in role-definition resulting from differential impact of cultural changes: These may effect relations between husband and wife — but the major result is a *parent-youth conflict.*

4. The "empty shell" family, in which individuals live together, but have minimal communication and contact with one another, failing especially in the obligation to give emotional support to one another.

5. The family crisis caused by "external" events, such as the temporary or permanent involuntary absence of one of the spouses because of death or incarceration in jail or because of such impersonal catastrophes as flood, war, and depression.

6. Internal catastrophes that cause involuntary major role failures through mental, emotional, or physical pathologies: severe mental retardation of the child, psychosis of the child or spouse, or chronic and incurable physical conditions.

Such a rough classification emphasizes that the family is, like other institutional patterns, an organization of roles, and that a continuing pattern of role performances is necessary if a particular family is to continue to exist.[1] In addition, the classification anticipates one theme we shall discuss later: that the larger kinship structure or society is concerned about certain forms of family dissolution more than others (the family of the deserter, for

---

[1] Obviously, other modes of measurement or classification might also be useful. Among recent suggestions, see those of L. L. Geismar, Michael A. LaSorte, and Beverly Ayres, "Measuring Family Disorganization," *Marriage and Family Living,* Vol. 25 (November, 1963), pp. 479–81; and Alice L. Voiland and Bradley Bull, "A Classification of Disordered Family Types," *Social Work,* Vol. 6 (October, 1961), pp. 3–11.

example, receives more sympathy than that of the prisoner); that the society furnishes social patterns for certain participants, but not others, to follow (death, although more tragic than divorce is more acceptable in some circles); that it avoids any inquiry into some forms which may nevertheless be emotionally important to the participants (the "empty shell" family, or the family adjusting to the strain of the severe pathology of one of its members); and that even when the society does concern itself with the problem, it may focus on only one of the participants (the deserter or the illegitimate father), not on the entire family.

FAMILY DISORGANIZATION
AND THE LARGER SOCIETY

These various forms of family disorganization may best be understood after a consideration of their meaning for the larger social structure. They are found in all societies, but the *rates* of family dissolution from different causes will vary from one society to another. The way individuals adjust to these forms will also vary.

Because family relations are emotional and involve much of the individual's life and because each individual is unique, family members are likely to see any disorganizing experience as highly particular, different from the experiences of other families. A child feels the death of *his* mother is different from that of any other mother, and the divorcing husband looks back on a series of conflicts which seem to him to be different from those of any other divorcing husband. Each event is, of course, unique, if viewed in all its particularity and detail. However, in this as in other areas of social action, when researchers inquire systematically into a large aggregate of cases, common patterns are usually uncovered. Often people are unaware that they are adjusting in ways which are similar to those of others who have had similar disorganizing experiences, but the observer may nevertheless chart the similarities. Even if research is scanty, so that knowledge about the area is as yet neither systematic nor certain, sociology can be expected to locate some regularities in these forms of family disorganization and to suggest where others might be found. Thus order and pattern emerge even in social events which are experienced as unique.

A distinction must also be maintained between the disorganization of a family *unit* and that of the family *system* in a particular society, and both of these must be distinguished from *change* in a family system. All enduring marriages inevitably end with the death of one or both spouses, but the family *system* which is common throughout that society is not thereby affected. The family customs of the society may continue without change, and indeed they contain provisions for the contingency of death. A society may also have a high divorce rate, but the family *system* may remain unchanged. It is likely, for example, that high divorce rates have been part of Arab family systems for many generations, as they are now. We can ask whether the family system contains provisions for coping with the problems generated by the dissolution of particular family units, but no data exist to show that if the answer is negative the system as a whole will dissolve.

Wherever the world's population is experiencing industrialization, family systems are also undergoing some changes, though not all these are being recorded. This means that at least some of the elements of the old family patterns, such as arranged marriages in China, are dissolving. Of course, if a family *system* is undergoing change, the rates of occurrence of certain forms of disorganization, such as divorce, separation, illegitimacy, or desertion, may change.

The new system may have *lower* rates of occurrence of certain forms of disorganization. For example, the divorce rates in Arab Algeria and in Japan have been *declining,* though somewhat erratically at times, for half a century. In several Latin-American countries, the rate of illegitimacy has apparently been decreasing. The improved techniques for prolonging life in industrialized countries have meant that fewer children must face life as orphans. Aside from these facts, the main structure of a family system may be altered only slightly by such changes in rates. Finally, though the old set of patterns is in part dissolved, it is usually replaced by a new set of patterns that is just as determinate and controlling as the old one.

Despite the importance of these forms of family disorganization for the individuals in the family, and thus for the society, the legal and formal structures of society reflect little concern with these problems. If a couple in the United States decides to separate, no agency of the society acts, or is even empowered to find out that a separation occurred, unless the wife seeks financial support. There are few customs to guide the illegitimate mother or father, and once again the state moves only in narrowly defined circumstances (e.g., if the mother wants to get on the relief rolls). If a wife becomes schizophrenic or a child is born an idiot, few customs exist to help guide the family members, and the formal agencies of the society do not act unless asked to do so.

This relative autonomy of the family simply expresses the fact that no one outside the family has any "rights" in its deliberations and decisions. Which kin may be included varies from one family system to another, but in general the *state* may interfere only where (1) family members themselves initiate state action, or (2) someone in the family is officially reported to be receiving inadequate physical care. In a modern industrial society, where the network of relatives in close interaction is likely to be small, the breakup of a particular family unit is more likely (than in prior centuries, or in other family systems) to leave one or more members without anyone who feels any responsibility for even their physical care. Consequently, state initiative in these matters continues to increase in importance.

The analysis of family disorganization of any kind must also keep in view the extent to which the pressures and structures of the *society itself* help to *create* the problems which family units, or at times some agency of the society, must solve, such as illegitimacy, incarceration, war, or divorce.

THE UNCOMPLETED FAMILY: ILLEGITIMACY

A generation ago, Bronislaw Malinowski formulated the Rule of Legitimacy, which asserts that every society has a rule that each child should have a legitimate father to act as its protector, guardian, and representative in the society.[2] Like all other rules, this one is violated, and those who violate the rule are punished in some way. Where the rule is strongly enforced, the illegitimacy rate is low, and individuals who do not conform, together with their illegitimate children, suffer more severe sanctions. The regulations that form and sustain the family system function to move eligible young men and women toward marriage, to place the child in a definite position in a unit within the kinship and social structure, and to fix responsibility for its maintenance and socialization on that specific family unit. These regulations define "legitimacy" in the society, and thereby "illegitimacy" as well. In a much quoted statement, Crane Brinton has epitomized the close relation between legitimacy and illegitimacy:

> Bastardy and marriage in this world are quite supplementary — you cannot have one without the other. In another world, you may indeed separate the two institutions and eliminate one of them, either by having marriage so perfect — in various senses — that no one will ever commit fornication or adultery, or by having fornication so perfect that no one will ever commit marriage.[3]

---

[2] One such statement is to be found in his "Parenthood, the Basis of Social Structure," in V. F. Calverton and Samuel D. Schmalhausen, eds., *The New Generation* (New York: Macaulay, 1930), pp. 137–38.

[3] Crane Brinton, *French Revolutionary Legislation on Illegitimacy, 1789–1804* (Cambridge: Harvard University Press, 1936), pp. 82–83.

Such a view of illegitimacy has important implications. One is that the humanitarian notion that the "problem" of illegitimacy will be "solved" if the law defines all children as legitimate, or if the birth certificate omits any information about illegitimacy (as of 1967, such information was not available without a court order in 36 states) is incorrect. As long as no family unit has been established according to the norms of the society, the child's status is unchanged, and there will be considerable ambiguity as to the father's, mother's, and blood relatives' role-obligations toward him or her.

The answer to the questions, "Why illegitimacy?" and "Why legitimacy?" is the same—the maintenance of the social structure requires that the obligation to create the next generation biologically and socially be assigned to a socially-approved unit, the family.

Let us pursue this question further. In the United States and in Western society generally, illegitimacy is condemned partly because it is evidence of sexual relations outside marriage. However, this connection is not usual, for some degree of premarital sexual license is found in about 70 percent of the societies about which we have information,[4] but childbirth outside marriage is not approved in those societies. This suggests that most societies are more concerned with illegitimacy than with sexual intercourse outside marriage. Public opinion in the United States condemns illegitimacy more strongly than a simple violation of the norms of sexual conduct.[5] Indeed, the disapproval of sex relations outside marriage is less strong when a marriage between the couple is imminent than when it is unlikely or even impossible.

Thus the question posed by Kingsley Davis must be asked: Why does society not "solve" the problem by requiring the use of contraceptive methods and, when these fail, abortion?[6] His answer is that to break the normative relations between sexuality and the family, so that adults would as a matter of course decide rationally whether they would enjoy sex within or outside the family, would also reduce the strength of the motive to marry and found a family. The radical changes necessary to eliminate illegitimacy almost completely would very likely come close to eliminating the family system too.

But though societies generally condemn illegitimacy, the intensity of this disapproval, the strength of the sanctions visited on the child and parents, and the place in the social structure which the child is permitted to oc-

---

[4] George P. Murdock, *Social Structure* (New York: Macmillan, 1949), p. 265.

[5] For different reactions to different types of illegitimacy, see Kingsley Davis, "The Forms of Illegitimacy," *Social Forces,* Vol. 18 (October, 1939), pp. 77–89.

[6] Kingsley Davis, "Illegitimacy and the Social Structure," *American Journal of Sociology,* Vol. 45 (September, 1939), pp. 221–22, 231–33. Davis also "proposes," not seriously, that some penalties be provided for violation.

cupy vary. In different class strata of a society, too, illegitimacy arouses different responses. If the sociological view sketched so far is correct, illegitimacy rates are low where family norms are upheld vigorously. It should then be useful to compare societies having high illegitimacy rates with those having low rates.

Although numerical data are not available for all these societies, the lowest illegitimacy rates are likely to be in the Arab countries, where the rate is about 1 to 2 percent of live births, and in India. Most African societies prior to industrialization had low rates. In these societies, marriages were arranged, for the most part, when the girl was still in her teens. In India and the Arab countries, social contact between a nubile girl and a man occurred, if at all, only under the close supervision of her relatives, and often his as well. African tribes varied greatly in this respect, but great value was set on children and a marriage could be arranged before childbirth.

In western Europe, numerical data are more exact than in other cultural areas (except Japan). For recent rates, see Table 1.

A slight downward trend in these rates has occurred over the past half a century. Although the sexual freedom of young adults has increased greatly, social pressures to enter marriage before childbirth have evidently not decreased.

One northwestern European rural pattern, now disappearing, throws some light on the effect of social controls on illegitimacy rates. In the Scandinavian countries and in parts of Germany, adolescent children of farmers were permitted considerable sexual freedom. This created high illegitimacy rates in some regions (e.g., 17 to 28 percent in certain Swedish departments in the years 1921–1925); however, the courtships were publicly known, and the couples were guided by both peer group and adult norms. The father was likely to be known in cases of pregnancy, and by that stage in the relation-

TABLE 1
Illegitimacy Rates in Selected Countries

Country	Percent Illegitimate of All Live Births
United States (1968)	9.7
Sweden (1967)	15.1
Italy (1967)	2.0
England and Wales (1968)	8.5
Japan (1967)	0.9
Israel (1960)	0.3

Source: Personal Communication with U.N. Division (October, 1970).

ship, both families had at least tentatively approved the match as well. The legal fact that the child might be born out of wedlock was important to Church and State, but of little concern to the local community; the marriage was a "settled matter" and would take place at the convenience of the couple's parents.

Evidence from the United States suggests that one out of five marriages is preceded by conception.[7] A comparison with Denmark shows that its rate is even higher — more than one in three.[8] However, because the Danes have greater tolerance of sexual intercourse between engaged couples, there are no great pressures to rush into marriage. Thus the modal time of conception for these cases is 5 months prior to marriage. In the United States sample, it is 2 months. A recent comparison with Belgium not only shows premarital conception rates comparable with those in the United States, but also indicates that these rates vary inversely with occupational rank.[9] In both the United States and Denmark, the likelihood of divorce is greater for couples who conceive premaritally than for couples who do not, but the difference between the former and the latter is smaller in Denmark. Here, the premarital pregnancy is more likely than in Scandinavia to happen to a couple who had, up to that point, no intention of marrying. Thus the forced marriage which forestalls an illegitimate birth takes place between a young man and woman who have not adjusted to one another, or even to the idea of being married.

The New World south of the Rio Grande offers an instructive contrast to both the United States and Europe generally. Illegitimacy rates there are higher than anywhere else on record, except for urbanized slums in sub-Saharan Africa. Some of these rates are presented in Table 2.

Here, as so often in analyzing a social pattern, two questions must be considered: (1) Are there recurring decision-situations in which the elements

---

[7] The evidence for the U. S. data is derived from a study of counties in Indiana and Utah in which the sociologist traced each birth for a given period to the specific date of the couple's marriage. See Harold T. Christensen, "The Method of Record Linkage Applied to Family Date," *Marriage and Family Living,* Vol. 20 (February, 1958), pp. 38–43; and his "Cultural Relativism and Premarital Sex Norms," *American Sociological Review,* Vol. 25 (February, 1960), pp. 31–39. Cf. Sidney G. Croog, "Aspects of the Cultural Background of Premarital Pregnancy in Denmark," *Social Forces,* Vol. 30 (December, 1951), pp. 215–19.

[8] The U. S. cases were drawn from records in selected years between 1905 and 1941, the Danish cases from 1948. A recent HEW survey found that 33 percent of all first births were conceived out of marriage, and 19 percent of the total were finally legitimated by marriage (*The New York Times,* April 8, 1970).

[9] Gilbert Dooghie, "Premarital Conception with Married Couples According to Socio-Professional Status," *Journal of Marriage and the Family,* Vol. 30 (May, 1968), pp. 324–28.

TABLE 2

Selected New World Illegitimacy Rates

Country	Percent Illegitimate of All Live Births
Mexico (1968)	22.5
Argentina (1966)	26.4
Peru (1965)	48.9
Paraguay (1968)	43.0
Guatemala (1965)	67.4
Venezuela (1967)	53.2
Jamaica (1964)	74.1
Panama (1967)	70.1

Source: Personal communication with United Nations Statistical Division (October, 1970).

important for the decision are similar? and (2) are there larger social struc-tures which permit or cause that type of decision-situation to occur fre-quently?

These high rates are not a product of "Indian" or "transplanted African" cultures, in which "illegitimacy in the white man's sense" has no social value. Descriptions of the older Indian and African family systems show that they did not approve of illegitimacy. Moreover, the New World nations are Western in culture, and only here and there can one find pockets of "natives" who have maintained any great part of their Indian or African culture (the land of the Bush Negroes in the Guianas, the northwestern highlands of Gua-temala, and the Andean highlands of Peru, Ecuador, and Bolivia). Finally, every study of a specific community, even in the countries with the highest rates, proves that illegitimacy is not approved and that the ideal is child-birth within wedlock.[10]

On the other hand, where a high proportion of the people in a given area or social stratum are illegitimate themselves, no one can be singled out for much punishment or reward for deviation from or conformity to the norm. More central, however, is the immediate decision-situation faced by the young woman. Courtship is anonymous or is without supervision by either adult kin or adolescent peers. Illegitimacy occurs primarily in lower-class families, which are themselves unstable and have little family honor to lose,

---

[10] The best study of this point may be found in Judith Blake, *Family Structure in Jamaica* (New York: Free Press, 1961). See also William J. Goode, "Illegitimacy in the Caribbean Social Structure," *American Sociological Review,* Vol. 25 (February, 1960), pp. 21–30.

so that motivation to control courtship is not high. Consequently, the young girl establishes, essentially, an individual role-bargain with a male. Unless she has outstanding personal qualities, she is in a poor bargaining position. She must be willing to accept the risk of childbirth out of wedlock if she is to have a chance at marriage. These "consensual" unions are less stable than legal ones, but a stable relationship may emerge. Eventually, most people do marry.

This pattern of individual courtship outside family controls results from cultural and social disorganization in New World countries comparable to the dissolution of immigrant social and cultural patterns in the United States and the disintegration of African patterns during the slavery era in the United States and, in modern times, during African industrialization. The courtship structure just noted has, in fact, not entirely disappeared among the black population of the South, where illegitimacy rates now range from 18 to 32 percent.

Public outcry with reference to this problem has been far more strident than the facts suggest. The striking change in the United States over the past generation is that illegitimacy has changed from a personal or family problem to a *social* problem, in the sense that the state and private agencies are far more concerned with the fate of the illegitimate child and mother, believe that they should be helped, and are in fact contributing to their support. This very transformation has, however, created strong sentiments against "helping mothers to have more illegitimate children," or against "paying to increase the illegitimacy rate."

In fact, however, contrary to the apparent trend, black illegitimacy rates have certainly dropped over the past half a century or more and, without question, will drop further in the future. In the post-Civil War period, a large majority of black parents were not legally married. In most southern states, no serious effort was made to collect accurate data on black births, illegitimate or legitimate. Some part of the recent rise (since 1938) is attributable to improved record keeping, rather than to a change in family patterns. Indeed, our illegitimacy records even now come from only 35 states, and, in earlier periods, they were even scantier. It is not at all clear that there has been a genuine rise in illegitimacy rates, white or black, and it is unlikely that the rise has been sharp.[11] Over the period 1940–1960, the illegitimacy rate for whites based on such data rose from about 4 percent to 4.8 percent.

---

[11] On these points, see Elizabeth Herzog, "Unmarried Mothers: Some Questions to Be Answered and Some Answers to Be Questioned," *Child Welfare,* Vol. 41 (October, 1962), pp. 341 ff.

Since much of the public outcry has centered on the behavior of teen-agers, it is important to comment that teen-age girls are the *one* age group for which the *rate* of illegitimate births has not increased in recent years. The trend since 1938 is even more striking: In 1938, the rate for teen-agers was higher than that for any age group except those 20 to 24 years old. Now, the rate for this younger group is lower than for any age group under 35.[12]

The black revolution of the 1960's demonstrates the extent to which the black population is actually entering the mainstream of United States society. Far from being an index of disorganization, it is evidence of a major step toward integration, and presages, in fact, a substantial decrease in the illegitimacy rate among black citizens.

In American society, the unwed mother has a difficult personal adjustment to make. There is little toleration for the young mother who wishes to keep her child as her own. Some families try to deny the connection of the child with the mother and say that it belongs to a relative. More often, the preferred solution is to have the girl bear the child in a nursing home run for this purpose and to leave it there for adoption. The economic problems and the problem of parental control are likely to be too great to handle when there is no father available, and no community support (other than economic) is forthcoming. The mother may undergo much emotional suffering, because of the social disapproval to which she is exposed and because she may develop a strong love for her child when it is born. For these reasons, the modern nursing home may enlist the services of social workers whose aim it is to help the young mother adjust.

No simple moral or technical solution exists for these problems. The mechanical process of marriage does not automatically create a family relationship, though it may confer the status of legitimacy on the child. Illegitimacy in the United States most often occurs precisely among those who are not deeply involved with one another emotionally and who have shared mainly a sexual experience. Often, the pregnancy occurred partly because of carelessness on both sides and partly because the father has little feeling of responsibility about the relationship, the girl, or the consequences. Marriage would "give a name," but not a father, to the child. Fundamental changes in the social structure would be required to give full social rights to the illegitimate child, and these are not likely to take place in the next few generations.

---

[12] For these and other relevant facts of illegitimacy, see "Illegitimate Births: Fact Sheet" (Washington, D. C.: National Office of Vital Statistics, April 15, 1960); and Joseph Schachter and Mary McCarthy, *Illegitimate Births: United States, 1938–1957* (Washington, D. C.: National Office of Vital Statistics, 1960).

Moreover, this situation applies, although somewhat less harshly, to all the Communist countries in which illegitimacy has been "abolished" by law.

VOLUNTARY DEPARTURES: SEPARATION, DIVORCE, ANNULMENT, AND DESERTION

The legal differences among separation, annulment, desertion, and divorce may not be ignored, but they should not obscure the similarity of conflict behavior in this large category of marital dissolution. Focusing mainly on divorce patterns in the succeeding sections simplifies the exposition without distorting reality, if available data on the other subtypes are also used where they are relevant.

The Western reader tends to view divorce as a misfortune or a tragedy, and high divorce rates as evidence that the family system is not working well. This attitude is part of our religious heritage that made divorce a rare event until the early part of the present century, although various Protestant sects asserted the right to divorce as early as the sixteenth century and Milton's famous plea for this right was written in the seventeenth century.[13] Our Western bias in favor of romantic love also views marriage as based on love, and divorce as failure.

All marriage systems require that at least two people, with individual desires, needs, and values, live together; and all systems create some tensions and unhappiness. In this basic sense, then, marriage "causes" divorce, annulment, separation, or desertion. But though a social pattern must be able to survive even when many individuals in it are unsatisfied, it will also contain various mechanisms for keeping interpersonal hostilities within certain limits. Some family systems prevent the development of severe marital strains, but offer few solutions if they do develop. Two main patterns of prevention are discernible. One is to *lower the expectations* about what the individual may expect from marriage. For example, the Chinese praised family life as the most important institution, but taught their children that they were not to expect romance or happiness from it. At best, they might achieve contentment or peace.

A second pattern, widespread in preindustrial societies and also found among the Chinese, is to value the kinship network more than the relation between husband and wife. Elders direct the affairs of the family, arrange

---

[13] *The Doctrine and Discipline of Divorce* was first published in 1643.

the marriages of the young, and intervene in quarrels between husband and wife. The success of the marriage is rated not so much by the intimate emotional harmony of husband and wife as by the contribution of the couple to the lineage or extended kin. Consequently, tensions between husband and wife are less likely to build up to an unbearable level.

In addition, there are some social patterns in all groups by which marital tensions may be *avoided*. One pattern is to consider certain disagreements as trivial. For example, individuals in the United States are told that disagreement on the relative values of bowling and bridge is not important. Another pattern is to suppress some irritations. As individuals become adult, they are increasingly forced to control their anger, unless the problem is serious. Still another pattern is to train children and adolescents to expect similar things in marriage, so that what one spouse does is in harmony with the demands of the other.

Societies vary in their definitions of what is a *bearable* level of dissension between husband and wife, as well as in their *solutions* for marital difficulties. It seems likely that public opinion in the United States during the nineteenth century considered bearable a degree of disharmony that modern couples would not tolerate. People took for granted that spouses who no longer loved one another and who found life together distasteful should at least live together in public amity for the sake of their children and their standing in the community.

Ideas as to what should be done about an unsatisfying marriage vary considerably, even among Western countries. Spain, Ireland, Italy, and Brazil permit only legal separations, which are common in the last two of these four countries.[14] In Chile, marriages are dissolved mostly by annulment.[15] In societies with extended kinship networks, but without divorce as an alternative, husband and wife may continue their daily tasks but confine their contacts to a minimum. In a polygynous society, a man may refuse to spend any time with one of his wives if their relationship is an unhappy one. Under the family systems of Manchu China and Tokugawa Japan, a man (but not a woman) could bring a concubine into his house. In China, a dissatisfied husband, if he was unable to afford a concubine, might instead stay away from his home for long periods of time, going to visit distant relatives or going on business trips — a form of separation.

These devices to avoid trouble, to divert dissension, to train individuals to put up with difficulties, or to seek alternative relationships to ease the

---

[14] Paul H. Jacobson, *American Marriage and Divorce* (New York: Rinehart, 1959), p. 97.

[15] In 1970, Italy passed a bill that permits divorce under some circumstances.

the burden of marriage show that societies generally do not value divorce highly. In no society, with the possible exception of the American Indian, has divorce been an ideal mode of marital behavior. The reasons for this are easily seen. Divorce grows out of dissension but creates additional conflict between both sides of the family lines. Prior marriage agreements are broken, and prior harmonious relationships among in-laws are disrupted. There are problems of custody, child support, and remarriage, which will be analyzed in more detail later on.

In no society, however, are the mechanisms for avoiding or reducing marital conflict enough to make all couples able to tolerate their marriage. Divorce is, then, one of the safety valves for the inevitable tensions of married life. At present we cannot say why a particular society adopts the pattern of divorce rather than that of separation, or of living together but enlarging the household to take in additional wives, but divorce is clearly a widespread solution for the problems of marital living. Moreover, the alternative solutions that various societies offer are only a variation on the pattern of divorce.

Divorce differs from these variations principally in that it permits both partners to remarry. In societies without divorce, ordinarily only the man can enter a new union, even if it is not entirely a legal one. For example, in in the past in India a man might take an additional wife or, in China or Japan, a concubine, but no such possibility was open to the woman who was dissatisfied with her marriage. In a polygynous society, a man might marry additional wives in order to have a tolerable marital life, but the woman whom he disliked was not permitted additional husbands. In Western nations where separation is permitted, but not divorce, the attitudes opposing a wife's entering into an unsanctioned public union are very strong, but the husband is usually permitted to have a mistress outside his household.

It is not correct to speak of divorce as a more extreme solution than some of the other patterns already described. Whether divorce creates more unhappiness, for example, than the introduction of a concubine into the household, is unknown. Whether it is more extreme to divorce or to bear the misery of an unhappy marriage is not measurable, and in any event is partly a matter of personal or social evaluation.

Countries with High Divorce Rates

The United States has the highest divorce rate among Western nations. Nevertheless, various countries in the past have had higher rates than the

United States; e.g., Israel (1935–1944), Egypt (1935–1954), Japan (1887–1919), and Algeria (1887–1940). It is perhaps useful to look at some of these countries briefly in order to understand better the relationship between divorce and the family system. In Table 3, various divorce rates are presented for comparison.

Westerners tend to think of Japan as having a stable society. It is therefore instructive to consider that in 1887 there were 320 divorces per 1000 marriages and that this level of marital instability continued until the late 1890's, when certain changes in the marriage law were made. Indeed, not until the 1920's did Japan's divorce rate begin to fall below that of the United States, although the present rate is considerably lower. Yet there is no evidence to suggest that the higher degree of marital instability in the past has, in any way, undermined the Japanese social structure.

TABLE 3
Divorces per 1000 Marriages in Selected Countries, 1890–1965

Country	Year 1890	1900	1910	1920	1930	1940	1950	1965
U. S.	55.6	75.3	87.4	133.3	173.9	165.3	231.7	258 (1965)
Germany		17.6	29.9	40.7	72.4	125.7	145.8	112 (1965)
England & Wales				8.0	11.1	16.5	86.1	91 (1965)
France	24.3	26.1	46.3	49.4	68.6	80.3	106.9	101 (1965)
Sweden		12.9	18.4	30.5	50.6	65.1	147.7	168 (1966)
Egypt					269 (1935)	273	273	216 (1963)
Japan	335	184	131	100	98	76	100	81 (1965)
Algeria	370 (1897)	352	288	396	286	292	a	54 (1963)

Sources:
All figures calculated from governmental sources and from *Demographic Yearbook,* 19th Issue (New York: United Nations, 1967).
a 1950 Algerian figures are not used, because in that year over 200,000 marriages from previous years were registered civilly, for the first time, thus reducing the true level of divorce rates. How much this under-registration in previous years inflated the divorce rate is not known. Decennial years are used in the table, but in a few cases the true year is one year off. The 1963 figure may be very inaccurate.
A better measure of divorce frequency is the number of divorces per 1000 *existing* marriages, but the latter figure is not often available. The above rate compares marriages in a given year, with divorces occurring to marriages from *previous* years. However, changes from one year to another, or differences among countries, may be seen just as clearly by this procedure.

The high Japanese divorce rate during the early years of the Meiji Restoration is based on data from family registers, rather than on the modern system of registration of vital statistics. Consequently, the exact figures may be questioned. Nevertheless, known sources of error could not have inflated the rate substantially; indeed, since a divorce was unlikely to be registered unless the marriage had been registered, and many unstable marriages were never registered at all, the correct figure might be higher still.

Why was the Japanese rate so high? In Japan, as in China, marriages were arranged by the elders of the two families through a go-between. The young man and woman themselves took little part in these negotiations, although both were likely to be adults. Child marriage was not an ideal in Japan, and at the turn of the century the average age of recorded first marriages was 27 for men and 23 for women.[16] The couple were, however, likely to be younger if the family had wealth and position, since they were not expected to live independently; if the groom was the eldest son, he would ordinarily not set up a separate household.

The negotiations took account of such matters as good health, social position, wealth, and good temper, but after marriage the matter of prime importance was whether the young bride would or could adjust well to her elder in-laws. She was under a stern obligation to pay great respect to them, to defer to their wishes, and to obey them even against the opposed wishes of her husband. If she could not obtain or retain the approval of her in-laws, she would be sent back to her parents with little regard to whether she and her husband got along well. The "divorce" in Japan was then a repudiation of the bride by her in-laws.

There is reason to suppose that (as in most societies) the divorce rate was lower in the upper social strata than in the lower strata, in part because the Japanese noble could adjust to marital problems by obtaining a concubine. His wife's position was secure enough if she obtained the favor of her in-laws and bore sons for the family. The average man could not afford an additional wife or concubine, and if his family did not accept his wife, she would simply have to be returned. And, since marriage among the nobility was often a family alliance, a divorce would be more likely to cause conflict between the two families.

Changes in the Japanese family system have been extensive over the past 50 years and cannot be analyzed in detail here. For our purposes, however, the most important fact is the decline of the divorce rate since the 1890's, as

---

[16] The actual date used is 1910. Irene Taeuber, *The Population of Japan* (Princeton, N. J.: Princeton University Press, 1958), p. 227.

shown in Table 3. One important shift has been toward an increasing proportion of marriages based either on personal choice or on personal preferences which are then approved by parents. As a consequence, the young wife has only to adjust to her husband's needs, not to the needs of a group of elders. Industrialization and urban living have meant that more families are small and are housed in small dwelling units, so that fewer young brides now live with their in-laws. At the same time, although the Japanese are the most industrialized of all Eastern countries, the culture remains family-centered to a considerable degree.

Divorce rates are also high in Arab countries, where divorce and remarriage have been described as the "poor man's polygyny." In all polygynous societies, except those in which a large proportion of men are killed in war, men must generally marry late while women marry early, or extra women must be obtained by capture or purchase. Even where females marry early and men late, so that there are more "female years in marriage," most men must be content with only one wife at a time. This general observation also holds in Arab countries, and divorce has always been easy. Traditionally, a man could divorce a woman with only the formality of saying, "I divorce thee." If he said this three times, the divorce was final, and they could not remarry each other until the wife married, cohabited with, and divorced another man. Even said once, however, the phrase betokened a divorce. The financial consequences of divorce were not serious for the man. Remarriage was easy, especially for the man, and both divorcees and children were able to return to their parental circle.

Changes in Divorce Rates as Indices of Other Social Changes

Changes in the rate of divorce in various countries need not indicate that these societies are becoming disorganized, but they do provide an index of change within the family system and an index of change in the larger social structure. Clearly, the industrialization under way in most countries does not imply an increase in divorce rates. In Japan, the divorce rate has been dropping for well over half a century, and the recorded drop in the Arab-Algerian rate suggests that the rate in other Arab countries may eventually decline as well. By contrast, divorce rates have risen in every western European country where divorce is possible and at a faster *rate* than in the United States. For example, the divorce rate in England a generation ago was about 6 percent, and is now 35 percent, that of the United States. In the industrializing areas of sub-Saharan Africa and in Communist China, divorce rates are rising. Since 1955, when the Indian Marriage Act extended the privilege of divorce to the entire Indian population, the divorce rate has risen there.

Both these opposite developments are the result of a stronger emphasis in all these family systems on the independent conjugal family unit. This new type of system has a relatively high divorce rate, but the rate may be lower than in the system which it replaces. Let us look at this conjugal system briefly.

Under the fully developed conjugal pattern, as in the United States, people have greater freedom of action and the right to choose their own mates. Under industrialization, people can begin their marriages on the basis of the jobs to be had in the new occupations, in factories or offices; they no longer require land in order to make a living. They depend less upon their older relatives, feel fewer obligations to take care of their elders, and, of course, receive less aid from them. Correlatively, the social controls on both sides are less exacting and effective.

This type of family system, characteristic of the West for several generations, requires that husband and wife obtain most of their emotional solace within the small family unit made up of husband, wife, and children; the extended kin network no longer serves as a buffer against the outside world. The conjugal family unit carries a heavier emotional burden when it exists independently than when it is a small unit within a larger kin fabric. As a consequence, this unit is relatively fragile. When husband or wife fails to find emotional satisfaction within this unit, there are few other sources of satisfaction and few other bases for common living. The specialization of service in an industrialized economy permits the man to purchase many domestic services if he has no wife, and the woman is increasingly able to support herself, even if she has no property and no husband. For these reasons, the independent conjugal family is not highly stable. On the other hand, where the union under the earlier system was fragile because of the elders, as in Japan, or dependent on the whim of the man, as in the Arab countries, the new independence of the young couple, their emotional ties with one another, and the increased bargaining power of the woman may mean somewhat greater stability of the family unit.

Fluctuations and Trends in United States Divorce Rates

Divorce rates in the United States have fluctuated a good deal over the past century, but have shown a consistent upward trend. Table 4 presents this trend.

TABLE 4

Number of United States Divorces per 1000 Existing Marriages,
1860–1968 [a]

Year	Number
1860	1.2
1880	2.2
1900	4.0
1920	7.7
1940	8.7
1956	9.3
1960	258 divorces per 1000 marriage ceremonies [b]
1968	282 divorces per 1000 marriage ceremonies [b]

Sources:
[a] Paul H. Jacobson, *American Marriage and Divorce* (New York: Rinehart, 1959), p. 90. The data from 1920 on contain annulments, and all these data are partly estimated since not all states are included in the divorce registration system. The earlier rates are, of course, even more open to question than the later rates.
[b] Bureau of the Census, *Statistical Abstract of the United States: 1969,* 90th ed. (Washington, D. C., 1970), Tables 76, 78.

Both divorce and marriage tend to follow the business cycle, increasing during periods of prosperity and decreasing during periods of depression. Of course, people do not lead more contented family lives during depressions. It is rather that the cost of the divorce itself and the still greater cost of establishing new households prevent people from embarking on such a venture. The effect can be seen dramatically in the swift change after the stock market crash in 1929. Up to that point, "the divorce rate had climbed to a new peak of 7.9 per 1000 existing marriages. . . . In the deepening depression that ensued, the rate dropped more than one-fifth to a low of 6.1 per 1000 in 1932 and 1933." [17] The frequency of divorce declined for marriages of long duration as well as for those of short duration. However, the return of better economic conditions soon pushed divorce rates, once more, to a new high.

The effect of war on divorce rates is somewhat less clear, but after the Civil War and both World Wars the rate at first rose sharply and then fell off somewhat, only to resume its upward trend after a few years. [18] During the Civil War and World War I, there was at first a *drop* in the divorce rate. However, in World War II, the rate continued to *rise* during the war, and in the later period of the Civil War the rate also rose. It seems clear that both wartime marriages and unions immediately upon the return of soldiers are

[17] Paul H. Jacobson, *American Marriage and Divorce,* p. 95.
[18] *Ibid.,* p. 91.

less stable than marriages begun at other times. In addition, after World War II the returning soldier and his wife in many cases could not adjust to one another, so that a record total of 629,000 divorces and annulments took place in 1946.

In part, however, the higher number of divorces after a war is due to the increased number of marriages. There are more marriages exposed to the risk of divorce, and the risks are greater in the first years of marriage. After the first few months of marriage, the risk quickly rises, reaching a maximum during the third year. For example, in 1955, the rate per 1000 existing marriages was 18 during the first year, 25.1 in the second (i.e., less than two years), 25.4 during the third, and 22.1 during the fourth. Thus after the third year, the rate begins to drop.[19] In general, there has been a recent trend for divorces to occur somewhat later in the marriage.[20] At the turn of the century, divorce was most frequent among those married four years (during the fifth year). Consequently, some part of the decrease in the number of divorces during the 1950's can be ascribed to the drop in the number of marriages—which in turn was due to the low fertility of the 1930's and the resultant decrease in the number of young men and women of marriageable age.

An examination of the long-term trend in United States divorce rates poses the question, "What changes in the social structure have taken place in the last 100 years that have had an effect on the family system and thus on the divorce rate?"

Perhaps the most striking changes have occurred in the general *values* and *norms* relating to divorce. Certainly there has been no acceptance of a philosophy that divorce is good, a thing to be desired, but divorce is no longer viewed as a shameful episode that one must hide from others or as a sufficient reason for casting a person out of respectable social circles. It is an experience to be regretted, one which commands some sympathy, but it is not considered a violation of public decency. Whether the individual sins or is sinned against, divorce is generally accepted as one possible solution for family difficulties.

No public opinion surveys of this change of attitudes, which began during the last half of the nineteenth century, were made at that time but newspaper debates, the novelist's increasing use of divorce as a solution for bad marriages, and congressional debates in various states where new divorce

---

[19] *Ibid.*, pp. 144–47.
[20] *Summary of Marriage and Divorce Statistics, 1957,* Dept. of Health, Education and Welfare, National Office of Vital Statistics, National Summaries, Vol. 50, No. 18 (November 25, 1959), p. 48. The median duration of marriage in 1966 was 7.1 years.

legislation was being considered, all throw some light on the growing toleration of divorce.[21] It must not be supposed that public opinion, even 100 years ago, was unequivocally set against divorce. Churches and their leaders fulminated against it and most public figures drew freely on biblical sources to denounce it, but strong opponents of the indissolubility of marriage did not cease their attacks. The border and frontier states, with their shifting and rootless populations, seem not to have had rigid views against divorce, and Connecticut on the eastern seaboard had liberal laws.[22] The growing feminist movement sought freedom for women, especially from the disabilities imposed by existing family laws; and though feminist leaders could not muster compelling theological arguments, they were able to best their opponents on humanitarian grounds.[23]

It is not possible to state the "causes" of this basic change in attitude. It is merely one facet of a broader set of changes in Western society, called "secularization": patterns that were once weighed by strong moral norms have come to be evaluated by instrumental norms. Instead of asking, "Is this moral?" the individual is more likely to ask, "Is this a more useful or better procedure for my needs?" Sometimes the term "individualism" is applied to this change. Instead of asking whether his church or his community approves of divorce, the individual asks, "Is it the right thing for *me* to do?"

However, a change in values alone does not necessarily lead to a great change in action patterns; other elements are always involved. Certainly, one important change has been in the types of *social pressures* from kinfolk and friends when there is marital discord. A hundred years ago, these pressures were essentially unidirectional. The individual was told by everyone to adjust, to bear the burden, and to accept his fate. He was told that for the sake of the children it was necessary to remain with his spouse, and he recognized that a divorce would mean losing standing in his social circle. Although in contemporary society friends and kin do give advice to people who are involved in marital difficulties, and though it is safe to say that in the initial stages, at least, the advice is to stay together, especially when there are children, these pressures are not nearly so strong as they once were. They relax even more when those within the social circle recognize that the marriage cannot be mended.

---

[21] A good compilation of this material, concentrating on the novel, may be found in James H. Barnett, *Divorce and the American Divorce Novel, 1858–1937* (Philadelphia: University of Pennsylvania, 1939, privately printed), especially Chapters 3–5.

[22] *Ibid.,* p. 36.

[23] *Ibid.,* pp. 40 ff.

A substantial change has also taken place in the *alternatives* faced by the husband or wife considering a divorce. Formerly a man found it very difficult to get along from day to day unless he had a wife. This was especially true on the farm, where many activities were defined as "female," but it was true in urban areas as well. Women had almost no opportunities for employment, except as domestics. Few women were trained for any kind of technical job, and even when a woman's family had money, returning to her family was viewed as a shameful alternative to continuing her marriage. These alternatives have radically changed. A man can get along quite well without a wife, for he can purchase most of the services a wife would perform. Women's alternatives have, of course, expanded even more. Many more women are trained to handle jobs that pay substantial salaries. Finally, and most central in this change, is the fact that since being divorced is no longer a stigma, and since there are many people who have been either widowed or divorced, the person with marital difficulties can hope for another marriage as an alternative.

We should also consider some deeper factors that have influenced the continued rise in the divorce rate. The egalitarian ethos, which has spread throughout much of the Western culture complex during the past 150 years, has argued consistently for equality of rights for women. Men have fought a rear-guard action, winning this battle and losing that one, but in general retreating. This change has a philosophical basis, but it is also rooted in the demands of an industrialized system, which offers each person the opportunity to develop his skills as fully as possible and to utilize them in the economy. An industrial economy apparently requires the services of women as well as men, and only to a limited extent are these services defined by sex roles.

Men typically exaggerate when they assert that women have achieved equal rights. It seems fair to say that women demand a greater range of *rights* than men are willing to concede, just as men are willing to impose a few more *obligations* than women are willing to accept. In a period of great change in sex roles, there is necessarily considerable tension in the day-to-day interaction of husbands and wives. Love is likely to be the crystallizing element in the decision to marry, both in fact and ideally, and the assumption that the aim of married life is personal happiness has come to be widely accepted. The combination of these two factors with the tensions normal in sex roles means that there are bound to be more conflicts between husbands and wives now than there were a hundred years ago and that when such conflicts do arise, individuals feel that the *primary* aim of marriage has not been achieved. Since the only common enterprise is now the family itself, it is not surprising that when this fails to yield the expected personal satisfactions, the likelihood of divorce is greater than it was a century ago.

These pressures and patterns are not at all peculiar to the United States. The general rise in the divorce rate in Europe is not caused by the insidious influence of "bad" American customs, like Coca-Cola and chewing gum. Rather, the United States is in the vanguard of a process which is becoming worldwide. The European countries follow behind simply because they are going through similar phases at a later date. The same processes have been taking place in Communist China, Japan, and parts of Africa.[24]

Where will this process end? Will the ratio of divorces to marriages rise until there are as many divorces each year as marriages? The prediction of a future event is always dubious. We cannot simply extend the curve of the divorce rate indefinitely upward in the future, unless we are absolutely sure that (1) we have located the important factors in its rise, and (2) these factors will continue to increase in the future. It is, however, possible to make a guess, one which is worth some debate. The fertility pattern in the post-World War II epoch suggests that a change in family attitudes is taking place, especially in the middle and upper-middle strata, which seems to be at present the vanguard of new styles of life. This change may be summarized by saying that the style of life now held to be ideal is one that is centered around the home to a greater extent than a generation ago, that values children far more than the prior generation, and that seeks professional help when there are marital difficulties. Running counter to those forces, however, is the increasing freedom of sexual relations, the lessening social disapproval of divorce, and the increasing ability of wives to earn an adequate income by themselves. Thus, it is difficult to predict whether there will be a rise or a fall in divorce rates over the next two decades.

Divorce and Desertion in Different Segments of the United States Population

The similarities of people in the United States form the basis of national unity, but individuals in different positions *within* the social structure have

---

[24] For these data see William J. Goode, *World Revolution and Family Patterns* (New York: Free Press, 1963). For China, see especially C. K. Yang, *The Chinese Family in the Communist Revolution* (Cambridge: Harvard University Press, 1959) and Olga Lang, *Chinese Family and Society* (New Haven: Yale University Press, 1946). See also R. P. Dore, *City Life in Japan* (Berkeley: University of California Press, 1958) and Arthur Phillips, ed., *Survey of African Marriage and Family Life* (London: Oxford University Press, 1953).

different experiences since childhood from others in the society, interpret them differently, and are subjected to different social influences. Consequently, it is to be expected that differentials in divorce, annulment, and desertion might be found among people from different socioeconomic strata, religions, race, and rural-urban backgrounds. In the succeeding pages, some of these differentials are presented and analyzed.

Common sense has long suggested that economic factors may be of great significance in the breakup of marriages, while many family analyses have tried to show that differences over money matters often hide underlying bases of conflict, such as definitions of sex roles, personality differences, divergent life styles. Doubtless, both positions contain some truth. Although most married couples in the United States earn enough to "get by," surveys show that families feel they need 50 percent to 100 percent more money to be "comfortable,"[25] and believe that they really cannot get along on their income. Spouses tend to have separate ideals of proper economic behavior, different attitudes toward spending money on one thing rather than another, different measures of economic success, and so on. If husband and wife have temperamental incompatibilities and do not meet each other's *emotional* needs, they can express them in conflicts about economic matters, for economic problems pervade much of the family's life. Since economic difficulties are more severe in lower economic strata, divorces might be supposed to be more common there, contrary to popular opinion as expressed in editorials and fiction for well over a generation. In fact, divorce rates *are* higher in the lower socioeconomic strata. It is therefore useful to look at both the basis for popular opinion and the survey data which show that the upper strata are less prone to divorce.

Census and survey data cannot ascertain the class pattern of divorce in the last part of the nineteenth century. Probably it was mainly the rich who could afford divorce. This was unquestionably so from the early period of United States history until about the Civil War, for in some states divorce required, as in England, a special act of the legislature. But there is no reason to suppose that the marital *stability* of the lower strata was greater. The popular picture of lower-class family life as warm and inviting, with frequent exchange of kinship obligations and tightly knit against the outside world, was a literary stereotype, often used by authors who had never observed a lower-class family. Instability was probably expressed in separation and desertion, as it still is among the lowest strata in our population. In addition, divorces in middle and upper social strata were given much more publicity.

---

[25] Hadley Cantril and Mildred Strunk, *Public Opinion, 1935–1946* (Princeton, N. J.: Princeton University Press, 1951), p. 66.

TABLE 5

Proneness to Divorce by Urban Occupation, United States,
March, 1959

Occupation	Index of Proneness to Divorce
Professional, semiprofessional	69
Proprietors, managers, officials	65
Clerical, sales	99
Craftsmen, foremen	90
Operators (semiskilled)	107
Service workers	165
Laborers (except farm and mine)	131

Source: Calculated from *U. S. Census of Population, Marital Status,* Final Report PC (2) 4E (1960), Table 5,
p. 92, by dividing:

$$\frac{\text{\% of the divorced in a given category}}{\text{\% of those ``ever married'' in that category}} \times 100.$$

Data for 1949 will be found in William J. Goode, *After Divorce* (New York: Free Press, 1956), p. 46. If different
occupational categories are used, or collapsed differently, a somewhat different ranking will be obtained, but
the basic relationship between socioeconomic position and divorce remains the same.

At just what date the lower strata began to exceed the middle and upper
in turning to divorce cannot be determined, although the pattern was definite
by the 1920's.[26]

A 1965 summary of various research studies, sample surveys, and census
data clearly demonstrates this inverse relationship between socioeconomic
rank and the divorce rate.[27] Two tables from this summary, both calculated
from national data, show this relationship (see Tables 5 and 6).

The relationship between education and proneness to divorce is not
simple, in part because social pressures force most people to go through high

[26] J. H. S. Bossard uses data from the 1930 Census, and thus the results of family behavior of the 1920's, to show that divorced women were predominantly to be found in
the poorer census tracts of Philadelphia. "Spatial Distribution of Divorced Women,"
American Journal of Sociology, Vol. 40 (1935), especially pp. 503, 507. Clarence W.
Schroeder, in a more elaborate study, used 1930 Census data to corroborate this conclusion. *Divorce in a City of 100,000 Population* (Peoria, Ill.: Bradley Polytechnic
Institute Library, 1939), pp. 83, 84.

[27] William J. Goode, *Women in Divorce* (New York: Free Press, 1965), Chapters 4,
5. See also W. J. Goode, "Marital Satisfaction and Instability: A Crosscultural
Class Analysis of Divorce Rates," *International Social Science Journal,* Vol. 14, No. 3
(1962), pp. 507–26; and Karen G. Hillman, "Marital Instability and Its Relation to
Education, Income, and Occupation: An Analysis Based on Census Data," in Robert F.
Winch, Robert McGinnis, and Herbert R. Barringer, eds., *Selected Studies in Marriage
and the Family,* rev. ed. (New York: Holt, 1962), pp. 603–08.

William J. Goode **493**

TABLE 6

Proneness to Divorce Index by Income, 14 Years and Over,
United States, March, 1959

Income (1959)	Index
Without income or loss	291
$1 to $999	192
$1,000 to $2,999	132
$3,000 to $4,999	94
$5,000 to $6,999	69
$9,000 to $9,999	51
$10,000 or more	44

Source: *U. S. Census of Population, Marital Status,* Table 6, p. 108.

school, so that they share a similar *formal* educational experience, when in fact their social experiences and backgrounds are heterogeneous. Nevertheless, the connection is clear at the extremes of education. Americans with only an elementary school education or less are much more prone to divorce than those who have completed high school or attended college. The lowest rate is found among college graduates.

Interestingly, the relationship between education and proneness to divorce is more marked among blacks than whites, but reverses the pattern: the higher the level of education, the higher the divorce rate.[28] Detailed analysis of the data suggests that the divorce rate of blacks who actually *finish* college, however, is almost as low as that of those who have very little education. We cannot interpret these data satisfactorily. It is likely, however, that blacks with very little education, like similarly placed whites of more than a generation ago, simply do not use the divorce courts as much. Whether the higher rates for the segments with greater education are also an index of the tensions in middle-class black living, cannot be ascertained from these data.

What do such correlations mean? Husbands and wives do not ordinarily quarrel about their respective social or economic positions, or their education. It is rather that socioeconomic factors are among the social influences playing on the family, and thus indirectly affect many decisions within the family. For example, in our society most individuals come to want a wide range of material things that their limited incomes deny them. Individuals are not reared to accept *normative* limits on their economic goals, although of course many people realistically accept the limits of *fact;* that is to say, al-

[28] William J. Goode, *After Divorce,* p. 54.

though they know they cannot afford a fine car, a house, or a fur coat, they do not feel they have no right to these goods. As a consequence, most families feel that their income is insufficient. The responsibility for satisfying these desires rests primarily with the husband, and any failure is his failure. At the same time, almost every study of job satisfaction shows that men in jobs with greater responsibility and prestige enjoy those jobs more than men in lower-ranking jobs enjoy theirs. Thus, both job satisfaction and economic reward point to a similar possibility: that there is more socioeconomic dissatisfaction in the lower strata, and thus possibly more marital tension from this source. Just as personality problems can be displaced onto economic factors within a marriage, so too economic strains may be displaced onto noneconomic relationships, such as sex and marital adjustment.

Other factors varying with socioeconomic position also affect divorce rates. Upper and lower social strata contrast in these relevant ways: (1) More of the income in the upper strata is allotted to long-term investment expenditures, such as houses, insurance, and annuities, while more of the income in the lower strata is allocated to consumer goods such as food and clothing. One consequence is that the husband in the upper strata cannot as easily "walk out" on his obligations. (2) The difference between the potential earnings of the lower-class wife and her husband is smaller than between those of the wife and husband in the upper strata. Consequently, the wife's potential loss is much greater in the upper strata. (3) The network of both kin and friends is larger and more tightly knit among the upper strata than among the lower strata, so that the consequences of divorce are likely to be greater. It is easier for the lower-class husband simply to abandon his marital duties, either by separation or desertion. He cannot be so easily traced, and often loses little if he obtains an equal job in another city where he is unknown. Men are now more easily traceable than formerly, through social security, FBI, Veterans Administration, and other bureaucratic records, but a differential between upper and lower levels nevertheless remains.

We now see that even if tensions from economic factors were the same at all economic levels, the objective complexities and difficulties ensuing from divorce are greater for upper-strata marriages and result in the likelihood of couples staying together.

The foregoing analysis also applies to black and white divorce and desertion differentials. Divorce and desertion rates are higher among blacks and the poor than among whites and the well-to-do. Some attention to desertion as a specific, separate phenomenon throws some light on these divorce differentials. The amount of social research on desertion does not correspond to its importance as a type of family disorganization. No full-scale analysis of the problem has appeared since World War I.[29] Yet of the 2,600,000 children receiving Aid-to-Dependent-Children grants in 1955, 1,400,000 had fathers who were separated from their families.[30] In Pennsylvania, estrangement of the husband accounted for 52 percent of such cases in 1948, and in Philadelphia, there were twice as many new cases of nonsupport and desertion in the period 1920–1950 as divorces.[31] The number of divorces granted in the United States for desertion has increased during most of the decades for which data are available, reaching a peak of 112,000 in 1946 and falling (along with divorces from other causes) to about 68,000 in 1950.[32] Desertion has often been called the poor man's divorce, and certainly it has been a common solution for marital difficulties among southern blacks, black migrants to northern cities, and whites in the lowest occupational strata.[33]

One family analyst has asked, "How many days' absence constitutes desertion?"[34] thus suggesting that a "separation" cannot always be sharply distinguished from desertion. A separation presumably includes some agreement about the support of the family left behind, but this agreement may be violated, and even when there is no such agreement a husband may send money to the family and keep in indirect touch with the family. One of the older studies cited above found that 87 percent of deserters were "repeaters," leading to the notion that desertion is often a "holiday" from marital obligations.[35] This form of marital behavior violates central moral values of family life, so that it is most common in strata where social controls are weaker and the difficulties of family life are greater. However, desertion is also more

---

[29] See E. E. Eubank, *A Study of Family Desertions* (unpublished Ph.D. dissertation, University of Chicago, 1916); J. C. Colcord, *Broken Homes* (New York: Russell Sage Foundation, 1919). Perhaps E. R. Mowrer's study of desertion in Chicago should be added: *Family Disorganization* (Chicago: University of Chicago Press, 1927).

[30] Jessie Bernard, *Social Problems at Midcentury* (New York: Dryden, 1957), p. 383, from a report by the Social Security Commissioner.

[31] William M. Kephart and Thomas P. Monahan, "Desertion and Divorce in Philadelphia," *American Sociological Review,* Vol. 17 (December, 1952), pp. 719–20.

[32] Paul H. Jacobson, *American Marriage and Divorce,* p. 124. In 1960, desertion — including abandonment, absence, and combinations of desertion with other grounds — was the alleged ground in about one-quarter of the divorces granted in the Divorce Registration Area (18 states). The total was 24,943.

[33] For a good description of the older rural southern pattern, and the black adjustment to the northern slum, see E. Franklin Frazier, *The Negro Family in the United States,* rev. ed. (New York: Dryden, 1948), Chapters 7, 15.

[34] Thomas D. Eliot, "Handling Family Strains and Shocks," in Howard Becker and Reuben Hill, eds., *Family, Marriage, and Parenthood* (Boston: Heath, 1948), p. 623.

[35] J. C. Colcord, *Broken Homes,* pp. 7–8.

common among Catholics than Protestants, because of their objection to a formal divorce.[36]

Since many separations become desertions *or* divorces, and perhaps most desertions end in a return to the family, no firm estimate can be made of the number of desertions each year. There were 60 women whose husbands were absent and 43 women who were divorced, per 1000 married women aged 14 and over in the 1960 Census. For nonwhites the rates were 196 and 60 respectively. In 1950, the percentage of women separated was 2.0 for those with four years of college education, but 6.9 for women with 0–8 years of education.[37] The *recorded* desertions appear in three situations: the divorce courts, applications for compulsory support from the husband, and applications for Aid to Dependent Children. The apparent increase over the past decades in the number of desertions may actually be due to the present-day existence of machinery for giving help to the deserted family. Increasingly, too, as we noted before, it is possible to *find* the husband or wife who abandons his family, so that they are more likely to report this abandonment.[38]

To continue the analysis of divorce rate differentials, three broad patterns in black divorce rates are worthy of comment. One, noted previously, is that in contrast to whites, the higher the educational level of blacks, the higher the divorce rate, except for the small stratum of those who have *completed* college. A second is the apparently greater effect of depression and prosperity on the black divorce rate. The third is that as the black population has become more assimilated into the dominant white culture, both their marriage and divorce behavior has become much like that of whites.

The reason for the second pattern is that depression has, in the past, put blacks out of work earlier than whites, because blacks have had proportionately fewer white-collar jobs, where employment is steadier. During depressions, black women have been better able than men to get jobs (primarily as domestics). One study which illustrated this general divorce pattern found that during 1918–1928, for the most part a prosperous period, the

---

[36] Thomas P. Monahan and William M. Kephart, "Divorce and Desertion by Religious and Mixed-Religious Groups," *American Journal of Sociology,* Vol. 59 (March, 1954), pp. 462–65.

[37] Data for 1950 from Paul C. Glick, *American Families* (New York: Wiley, 1957), p. 154. 1960 data calculated from Bureau of the Census, *U. S. Census of Population, 1960,* Vol. 1, *Characteristics of the Population,* Part 1, United States Summary (Washington, D. C.: U. S. Government Printing Office, 1964), Table 176, p. 424.

[38] In 1955, the National Desertion Bureau changed its name to the Family Location Service, to emphasize its concern with reconciliation and rehabilitation, rather than merely tracking down the missing husband (Jessie Bernard, *Social Problems at Midcentury,* p. 383).

TABLE 7

Ratios of the Percentage of Nonwhites Divorced to the
Percentage of Whites Divorced, 1890–1960

	1890	1900	1910	1920	1930	1940	1950	1960 [a]
Ratios:	1.24	1.95	1.67	1.52	1.50	0.95	1.05	1.25

Source: Calculated from William J. Goode, After Divorce, p. 49. The original data refer to the population in the marital status of "divorced," and thus exclude those who have divorced but remarried. The table above, essentially, shows the extent to which the two population segments produce more or fewer divorces, relative to the size of their respective populations. The table on p. 51 of that book is in error, because it compares the black rate with the rate of the *total* U. S. population.
[a] Calculated from Bureau of the Census, *U. S. Census of Population: 1960*, Vol. 1, *Characteristics of the Population*, Part 1, United States Summary (Washington, D. C.: U. S. Government Printing Office, 1964), Table 48, p. 155.

black divorce rate in Virginia was higher than that of whites', but during 1929–1940 the black rate dropped below the white rate.[39] An even sharper relative change was recorded in Mississippi during the same period. The total black divorce rate in the United States also dropped below the white level during the 1930's, so that in the 1940 Census, for the first time since 1890, there was a lower percentage of black divorcees than of white divorcees.[40] These changes may be seen in Table 7.

The data show that in only one censual year, 1940, was the percentage of blacks divorced lower than the percentage of whites, the result of a lower divorce rate during the 1930's. However, we must examine the *meaning* of these figures. In 1890, most blacks were in the rural South; the major migration to northern cities did not occur until World War I. It is doubtful that blacks were in fact using southern divorce *courts* to a greater extent than whites. A substantial minority of blacks lived together without legally marrying, and in many southern communities they would have been laughed at had they attempted to obtain a formal divorce. When they gave the answer "divorced" to the census enumerator, they were merely saying that they were no longer living with their mates, who had probably deserted them. On the other hand, the figures do show that black marital *instability* was greater, whether it was legally recorded or not.

The table also suggests that the black and white rates are converging, especially if it can be assumed that since 1940 the census category "divorced"

[39] Paul H. Jacobson, *American Marriage and Divorce*, p. 174.
[40] For this reason, William M. Kephart and Thomas P. Monahan, "Desertion and Divorce in Philadelphia," p. 724, could report that the nonwhite divorce rate in Philadelphia was lower than the white: Their data were primarily from the 1930's.

has increasingly come to mean that a legal divorce actually did take place. As a higher proportion of blacks are assimilated into prevailing social patterns, it seems likely that they will resort to the courts more, but that their divorce rate will be about the same as that of whites.[41]

To ascertain divorce differentials by religion is especially difficult, since the United States Census has never asked about religion, the occasional Census of Religious Bodies uses only the reports made by churches, and the last published data from even this source were obtained in 1936. The religious beliefs of Catholic, Protestant, and Jewish churches generally stand in opposition to divorce but vary in the intensity of their disapproval. The Catholic Church takes the most extreme position, since it does not accept divorce at all (legal separation is permitted), and thus denies the right of a Catholic to remarry. Individual Catholics, of course, vary in their conformity to this proscription. The following statements summarize much of what we know about the relationship between marital dissolution and religion, although no technically adequate national study of this problem has been carried out:

> In two-thirds of the new desertion cases in Philadelphia, one or both parties were Catholic; some of these cases ended in divorce.[42]

> The proportion of Jews was about the same in the total population as in the divorce courts; i.e., they were not "overrepresented." [43] However, two studies (1938 and 1949) suggest that when both spouses are Jewish, the divorce rate is as low as when both are Catholic.[44]

> When both spouses are of the same religion, the divorce rate is low, and two studies have found that the Catholic-Catholic marriage is not more stable than the Jewish-Jewish or Protestant-Protestant.[45] However, most evidence suggests that the Catholic-Catholic rate of divorce is from one-half to two-thirds the Protestant-Protestant rate.[46]

---

[41] See E. Franklin Frazier, *The Negro Family in the United States,* Chapter 20, and also his *The Negro in the United States,* rev. ed. (New York: Macmillan, 1957), Chapter 13.

[42] Thomas P. Monahan and William M. Kephart, "Divorce and Desertion by Religious and Mixed-Religious Groups," p. 460.

[43] *Ibid.,* p. 461. William J. Goode, *After Divorce,* p. 35, found the same result for Detroit.

[44] Judson T. Landis, "Marriages of Mixed and Nonmixed Religious Faith," *American Sociological Review,* Vol. 14 (June, 1949), p. 403.

[45] *Ibid.*

[46] Loren E. Chancellor and Thomas P. Monahan, "Religious Preference and Interracial Mixture in Marriage and Divorce in Loua," *American Journal of Sociology,* Vol. 61 (November, 1955), pp. 238–39. Thomas P. Monahan and William M. Kephart, "Divorce and Desertion by Religious and Mixed-Religious Groups," pp. 460–61.

In general, the highest divorce rates are found among spouses with no religious affiliation, and the next highest among the mixed-faith marriages (Protestant-Catholic, Jewish-Catholic, Jewish-Protestant). Among the many combinations possible, the Catholic husband married to the Protestant wife is most prone to divorce. Mixed-faith marriages of Catholics are becoming more common, varying between 4% and 50% or more in different regions of the United States.[47]

This summary requires only little comment. Several general factors interact to produce these results: (1) Groups strongly opposing divorce do have lower divorce rates, but their total voluntary marital dissolution rate may be almost as high as that of other groups. (2) People who claim no church membership are less strongly opposed to divorce, but they may be deviant in other ways, too, so that their divorce rate is higher. (3) Interfaith marriages are less stable, partly because of other differences in social background to be found in such unions and partly because of religious conflict. However, in general, those who marry outside their church are less committed to its belief. (4) Mothers generally control the religious education of the children.[48] When a Catholic man marries a Protestant, however, he is likely to insist that his children become Catholics. Protestant fathers seem not to insist so strongly that their children become Protestants when the mother is Catholic. Consequently, the divorce rate is relatively high when the union involves a Catholic father and a Protestant mother. Note, too, that it is women who ordinarily initiate a divorce suit and the Catholic mother would probably tolerate more conflict than the Protestant mother before bringing suit. It is also possible, although no research has been done in this area, that when there are male children, the Jewish father–Christian mother combination is also less stable than the reverse combination because of similar processes at work.

Two final comments should be added here, (1) that most analysts of religious behavior argue that the differences among members of different churches have been declining over the past two decades, and (2) that the dif-

---

[47] Judson T. Landis, "Marriages of Mixed and Nonmixed Religious Faith," p. 403. Loren E. Chancellor and Thomas P. Monahan, "Religious Preference and Interracial Mixture in Marriage and Divorce in Loua," pp. 238–39. In general, the *larger* the percentage of Catholics in a city or region, the *lower* the proportion of out-marriages. See John L. Thomas, "The Factor of Religion in the Selection of Marriage Mates," *American Sociological Review,* Vol. 16 (August, 1951), pp. 487–91; Harvey J. Locke, Georges Sabagh, and Mary Margaret Thomas, "Interfaith Marriages," *Social Problems,* Vol. 4 April, 1957), pp. 329–33.

[48] Judson T. Landis, "Marriages of Mixed and Nonmixed Religious Faith," pp. 404–06.

ferences between nonattenders and those who attend church regularly are often greater than the differences among people affiliated with different churches.

The Meaning of Differences in Social Background

Our analysis of voluntary dissolutions of families has moved from a consideration of the broad institutional structures in which marital breakups occur to a focus on the differences in marital instability that arise among individuals in different parts of the social structure, as these dissolutions are determined by class, race, and religion. In the present section, we assess still more specific background traits of couples who marry. These experiences cannot be called "causes" of divorce, except in the sense that they help to generate (or lower) the tensions that may finally erupt in annulment, desertion, or divorce. Later, we shall analyze the specific complaints and countercharges of the divorcing couples.

To the extent that certain characteristics of social position and background experiences increase or decrease the likelihood of marital dissolution, it may almost be said that divorce "begins" before the first quarrel or before the couple even meet. It is not possible to review here all the factors which have been related to eventual marital breakup, but those which seem to be based on good evidence can be presented, together with their sociological meaning. These may be summarized and compared as follows:

BACKGROUND CHARACTERISTICS ASSOCIATED WITH A GREATER
OR LESSER PRONENESS TO DIVORCE

Greater Proneness	*Lesser Proneness*
Urban background	Rural background
Marriage at very young age (15–19 years)	Marriage at average age (males, 23; females, 20)
Short acquaintanceship before marriage	Acquaintanceship of 2 or more years prior to marriage
Short engagement, or none	Engagement of 6 months or more
Couples whose parents had unhappy marriages	Couples with happily married parents

Greater Proneness	Lesser Proneness
Couples who do not attend church, or are of different faiths	Couples who attend church regularly, are Catholic, or adhere to the same church
Kin and friends disapprove of the marriage	Kin and friends approve of the marriage
General *dis*similarity in background	Similarity ("homogamy") of background
Husband and wife have different definitions of their mutual role-obligations	Husband and wife agree as to their role-obligations

These findings are in conformity with common sense, but they also deserve sociological annotation. First, the evidence on which they are based varies considerably, for some (for example, the finding that the divorce rate of women 15 to 19 years of age is about 50 percent higher than that of older women) are derived from national samples or censuses of individuals, analyzed by marital status and other characteristics.[49] Other studies have taken small samples of people who are still married and have measured their *marital adjustment,* sometimes comparing a happily married sample with a sample of couples whose marriages ended in divorce.[50] The important sociological factors contributing to these and similar findings may be placed under four main headings:

1. Individual values. An individual from a particular background may be more strongly opposed to divorce than someone from another background.
2. Social pressures.
3. Mate-selection processes.
4. The ease of marital adjustment between people of similar social backgrounds.

Although a specific factor may play some part in more than one of these sets of processes, the general categories will help to clarify the exposition somewhat.

There is greater tolerance of divorce in the United States today than there

---

[49] Paul C. Glick, *American Families,* p. 154.
[50] Harvey J. Locke, *Predicting Adjustment in Marriage* (New York: Holt, 1951). William J. Goode's study, *After Divorce,* often compares divorced couples with the married population.

was a century ago, but many groups still oppose it strongly and view it as a nearly inconceivable alternative to even a bad marriage. Catholics are strongly against divorce, but many Protestant sects also oppose it. Rural populations are more strongly against divorce than residents of urban areas. It seems likely that those with less education are less tolerant of divorce (but more tolerant of unconventional marital arrangements) than those with more education. In general, people from a "conventional" background and circle feel more strongly opposed to divorce than those with a less conventional background.

These differences may not lessen the *possibility* of conflict, but they do lessen the likelihood that individuals strongly opposed to divorce will accept that solution for their marital difficulties. However, these differences in opposition to divorce have lessened in the United States. For example, rural-urban social differences are gradually being erased, as the population becomes more concentrated in large urban agglomerations and the remaining rural areas increasingly take on urban characteristics.

Values in opposition to divorce work to reinforce conventional morality. The individual who has such values is less likely to think of divorce in the first place.[51] He is also more likely to be involved in *circles* that are opposed to divorce and pressure him to attempt a reconciliation or some other adjustment to the conflict. For example, the individual who regularly attends church is also likely to belong to a social circle that focuses on divorce. When kinfolk and friends approve of a marriage, they are likely to advise the couple to adjust and not to take their conflict seriously. Since a divorce within any social network threatens to some extent the ties which bind it together, the members of the network have a personal stake in attempting to prevent the divorce of any couple.

Some of these background factors, especially the approval of kin or friends, also help an individual to find a congenial companion and to adjust to that person even before marriage. We should, therefore, think of the approval of kin and friends as having a double aspect. On the one hand it represents a kind of *prediction* that the engaged couple seem fitted for one another. Such circles know one or both of the individuals and judge whether they will fit together. On the other hand, the approval actually helps to bind them together, since it makes the interaction between the engaged or married couple easier and more pleasant. Similarly, the length of acquaintance and the

---

[51] Marriage demands a certain amount of repression from the partners, who must in a sense "not see" all each other's faults or all the ramifications of a quarrel. Cf. Willard Waller and Reuben Hill, *The Family* (New York: Dryden, 1952), pp. 516–17. An important phase in the dissolution process occurs when one or both spouses first consider divorce as a serious possibility.

length of engagement may be viewed as an *index* of their adjustment to one another, but there are also *periods* of shared experience, during which further adjustment or dissolution can take place.

The length of the engagement is in part, however, a reflection of still other factors. Often, for example, marriages which take place without any engagement at all are really forced marriages, and marriages based upon premarital conception are more likely to end in divorce. Next, short engagements seem to be much more characteristic of lower-strata families, and we have already seen that the divorce rate is higher in such strata. Thus, a short engagement may be either a cause or an effect. Finally, it seems likely that the length of engagement has a different social meaning in different strata. A very short engagement in a middle- or upper-class stratum is more likely to be a deviant union in some respects than it would be in the lower strata. It at least suggests that there may be background characteristics of the two couples that are incompatible.

Grounds for Divorce and Complaints and Conflicts

All states now permit both absolute divorce and annulment. Because domestic law is decided by the individual states, there are many variations in the grounds that are acceptable for divorce suit. The most popular is cruelty; almost three-fifths of all divorces are granted on these grounds. This type of complaint has been used in some jurisdictions for one hundred years, but its meaning has gradually changed in almost all of them. Formerly it meant physical cruelty, an attack upon the spouse's life, or unusual personal indignities. However, in most jurisdictions it has now come to mean little more than "incompatibility," and almost any complaint can be used in support of the charge.

The only other category of complaint that is used in any substantial number of divorces is desertion. In the 1880's, about 40 percent of all divorces granted were for desertion, but the proportion now is less than 18 percent.[52] The other most common complaints are adultery, drunkenness, and neglect to provide, none of which accounts for more than 5 percent of all divorces in the United States.

However, it is common knowledge that tabulations of divorces by grounds for complaint do not necessarily reflect the reality of the divorce conflict. Rather, they reflect the fact that our legal system requires the "innocent"

---

[52] Paul H. Jacobson, *American Marriage and Divorce,* p. 124. The total number of divorces on grounds of desertion was 68,000 in 1950.

party to prove that the other is "guilty" in his marital behavior. By the time the suit is filed, both husband and wife have usually agreed to obtain a divorce, and they simply utilize the grounds that are legally most effective and socially least accusatory. Of course, in those relatively rare cases where drunkenness or adultery is charged, the chances are greater that the accused party was in fact guilty and that the accusing party still feels resentful.

What then are the *real* complaints of husbands and wives against one another? Many studies have attempted to unravel the complex web of their charges and countercharges. Such listings of marital difficulties are worth examining, but they are not necessarily the "true" causes of marital disorganization. Such lists merely reflect the various areas of marital *interaction*. How much *weight* to give each of them is not known, even when a given wife or husband believes that a particular complaint was the most serious matter involved. A wife may complain that her husband has had an affair, but she does not probe into the meaning of that affair or inquire what failure on her part made an outside solace attractive to her husband. A husband may complain that sexual relations with his wife were always unsatisfactory, and never know that his own ineptitude was the major factor in her frigidity. Neither may make a complaint about financial matters, but both may have lived under great tension because of their economic problems.

We shall examine two such lists, one derived from a comparison of happily married couples with divorcees, one derived from a study of divorced women who have not remarried.[53] The first study asked each spouse or ex-spouse to check the items in a list of possible marital problems, if the item had in their opinion caused *serious* difficulties in their marriage.[54] The other study, however, asked the divorced woman to state in her own words what in her opinion was the *main* cause of the divorce. The differences in the questions created differences in the results; a check-list question will usually elicit more complaints than an open-ended question. Nevertheless, a study of the results helps us to understand these complaints (see Table 8).

One set of differences is created by sex roles. Fewer men than women complain about nonsupport, adultery, gambling, drunkenness, or desertion. On the other hand, both happily married and divorced men in Locke's study complained more than women about unsatisfactory sex relations, a difference which stems from the lesser importance of the sexual act itself to the woman's happiness. And men and women complained about equally in regard to purely affectional relations.

---

[53] See Harvey J. Locke, *Predicting Adjustment in Marriage*. See also William J. Goode, *After Divorce*.

[54] Harvey J. Locke, *Predicting Adjustment in Marriage*, pp. 75–76, 377–78.

TABLE 8

Common Complaints of Happily Married and Divorced Couples

	Locke Study ("Check . . . the following things which . . . have caused serious difficulties. . . .") [a]				Goode Study ("What was the main cause . . . ?") [b]
	Happily Married		**Divorced**		**Divorced**
	Men	Women	Men	Women	Women
Complaints	(Percent)		(Percent)		(Percent)
Affectional and Sex Relationships					
1. Mate paid attention to another person	3	6	66	74	
2. No longer in love	4	2	60	61	
3. Adultery	1	2	44	55	
4. Unsatisfying sex relations	8	6	46	33	
5. Triangle					16
6. Home life					25
Socially Disapproved Behavior					
1. Drunkenness	3	2	26	56	30
2. Gambling	3	3	6	26	
3. "Drinking, gambling, & helling around"					31
Nonsupport	0	0	7	49	33
Desertion	0	0	20	27	8
Relatives	17	20	53	30	4
Values					21
1. Religion	6	5	8	8	
2. Amusements	29	20	34	29	
Personality					29
Selfishness, Lack of Cooperation	6	12	22	30	
Husband's Attempt to Dominate					32

Sources:
[a] Harvey J. Locke, *Predicting Adjustment in Marriage,* pp. 75–76.
[b] William J. Goode, *After Divorce,* p. 123.

The table also shows how few areas there are in which the divorced couples do not remember having had serious difficulties. The happily married, by contrast, reported serious difficulties only with respect to in-laws, amusements, and "other difficulties over money" (men, 14 percent; women, 19 percent); while 39 percent of the men and 27 percent of the women reported "no difficulties at all." By the time of the divorce, most of the interaction between husband and wife has become unpleasant.

All such lists require some interpretation of what each item *meant* to the spouses. Some wives complain that their husbands are simply too "bossy," but others use a more sophisticated vocabulary and refer to the "personality problems" of their husbands. Lower-class wives may accept a degree of domination by their husbands that middle-class wives would find intolerable. A lower-class wife married to a middle-class husband may feel that their income level is adequate, while a middle-class wife married to a factory worker with the same income may feel that they have to scrimp too much. Finally, in all these studies, the specific *answers* of each spouse to the charges of the other are missing.[55]

This analysis has laid relatively little stress upon sexual factors in family disorganization. This is not because divorcees fail to complain that at times their sex relations in their former marriage were unsatisfactory (cf. Locke's figures of 46 percent for men, 33 percent for women). It is rather that this area of dissatisfaction is less likely than others to be crucial. Until about the time of World War II, many marital analysts and counselors were convinced, on the basis of psychodynamic speculations, that sexual dissatisfaction was at the root of much marital conflict. It is quite possible that marital dissatisfaction *was* greater a generation ago, particularly in the period after World War I, when sexual expectations became higher as a result of the general sexual emancipation of that time. By contrast, though the expectations of modern couples have doubtless dropped not at all, young people today are much better prepared for sex in marriage than their parents or grandparents were, and hence they probably experience less actual sexual dissatisfaction.

A change has also taken place with respect to the supposed *meaning* of sexual dissatisfaction. Family analysts have come increasingly to accept the view that great sexual dissatisfaction is a reflection of dissatisfaction in *other* areas of life. Neither husband nor wife is able to give emotional solace, tenderness, and sexual pleasure when conflicts are severe in other areas. Consequently, even though sexual dissatisfaction may be one focus of complaint, it is usually now viewed as no more than a symptom.[56]

In a deeper analysis of family disorganization, we must know not only exactly what the behavior was that caused the husband and wife to become dissatisfied with each other, but also the standards or *norms* by which that

---

[55] For further analyses of the kinds of complaints made by husbands and wives, see Judson T. Landis, "Social Correlates of Divorce or Nondivorce Among the Unhappily Married," *Marriage and Family Living,* Vol. 25 (May, 1963), pp. 178–80; and Howard E. Mitchell, James W. Bullard, and Emily H. Mudd, "Areas of Marital Conflict in Successfully and Unsuccessfully Functioning Families," *Journal of Health and Human Behavior,* Vol. 3 (Summer, 1962), pp. 88–93.

[56] Ernest W. Burgess and Harvey J. Locke, *The Family,* 2nd ed. (New York: American Book, 1953), pp. 524–25.

behavior was judged. Even casual observation of one's married acquaintances underlines the importance of this. Some husbands, for example, are fairly contented with wives who, even by the standards of their own group, seem to be poor housekeepers and relatively unaffectionate. What is needed is a more precise disentangling of the standards by which different people judge similar marital behavior and the responses they make to that behavior; the various patterns of behavior; and the words and phrases used to describe the behavior.

PATTERNS OF CONFLICT—Although divorce conflict is often depicted in dramatic terms in newspaper accounts, novels, and even in sociology textbooks, such accounts really telescope a long series of relatively minor maladjustments, difficulties, and disagreements, a recital of which would be extremely boring. Not many marriages end by the husband or wife simply storming out of the house in rage, or informing the other that he or she has found a new love. More often the period of conflict extends over years (in Goode's study [page 137], the median time from serious consideration to decree was two years) and is punctuated by relatively harmonious periods as well as by episodes of anger and disillusionment. Mostly, however, it is merely the slow dragging out of an increasingly unsatisfying life together. A curve of divorce conflict would not be a simple upward or downward line; rather, it would take the form of a spiral, in which the husband and wife come back again and again to points of disagreement, rehashing them interminably. An apparent agreement about some point is accepted for a while and then later rejected. A disagreement seems to be forgotten and then reappears. Sometimes even their friends do not know until late in the marriage that it is a failure, because they see them only under happy circumstances. Nevertheless, a full tape recording of their entire life together would make it evident that the marriage had become intolerable for one or both of them.

Two primary patterns are evident in the gradual intensification of conflict. First, husband and wife are wounded in a disagreement over some matter, and one or the other withdraws some of his emotion; the affectional commitment is decreased as a means of protection against further hurt. However, this very withdrawal is coupled with the second pattern, the requirement that they in fact cooperate, work together and live together, day by day. Husband and wife can give sympathy, understanding, and support precisely because they ordinarily do have affection for one another, but living together when that affection is diminished makes any further hurt or wound increasingly hard to bear. However, if the individual cannot obtain comfort from his spouse, there is no other place to go, unless eventually he leaves the marriage and establishes a new one.

At some point in this progressive withdrawal of affection and increasing discomfort in the relationship itself, there comes a time when one spouse decides that he no longer cares a great deal what the other does. The husband no longer hopes for improvement from his wife.[57] The wife looks from a great distance at the foibles and idiosyncrasies of her husband and no longer sees any reason why she should tolerate them at all. In a sense, the conflict proceeds to the point where they look at each other as strangers, and, after all, one need not tolerate the bad habits, the domineering qualities, the selfishness, or the nagging of strangers.

It often happens that one spouse either continues to love the partner who has withdrawn his affection, or is so embedded in a fabric of marital habits that any change is painful. One individual may be very dependent on the other, so that the conflict process itself will take a longer time. In order to drive his spouse out, the individual who has withdrawn his affection may have to show considerable hostility as well. He or she may commit some dramatic act such as moving out of the house or engaging in an affair with another, in order to crystallize the decision. It must be kept in mind, of course, that the mere withdrawal of affection is not a sufficient "cause" for divorce. Many couples, especially those who have been married a long time, have at best a mild affection for one another; but their habit systems are so meshed and their expectations are so closely geared to the actual performances of their spouses that living in the same social space is not at all a burden. It has the comfortable qualities of an old shoe. Marriages that have held together for a long time are not necessarily "better adjusted" as time goes on, but certainly their stability is greater.

It is this *reciprocality* of the conflict process, the contribution that *both* husband and wife make to the eventual divorce, that makes the legal theory of divorce so hollow. Legal procedure requires that the offended party bring suit against the offender and prove that the erring spouse has indeed broken the rules of marriage. The legal theory also assumes that there is no collusion between the spouses with respect to getting a divorce. Both these elements fail to reflect the facts. In every divorce, both parties are offenders, although one party may have offended more than the other; and in practically every divorce both husband and wife agree on the terms of the suit beforehand. Indeed one might claim that the tragedy of divorce is not so much the breakup of a marriage as it is the apparent destruction of two seemingly honest and decent people, to the point where they behave evilly toward one another. They may come to attack one another savagely for minor wrongs, while showing tolerance and sympathy to their acquaintances and friends for the same faults.

---

[57] For a fuller discussion of the process of alienation, see Willard Waller and Reuben Hill, *The Family,* Chapter 23.

In the United States, nearly three-fourths of all divorces are granted to wives. Presumably, women are not the innocent parties in three-fourths of divorces. Rather, the kinds of charges which can be brought without opprobrium are most easily brought against the husband. Even the charge of adultery damages a man's reputation less than it does a woman's. Cruelty is the most common charge, and the phrasing of legal grounds makes it easier to prove this charge against the husband.

One study has made the claim that the divorces are more frequently granted to wives because the husband more often wants to break up the marriage.[58] The general process it describes may be outlined as follows. In spite of the substantial change in the position of women in our society, men remain dominant in the family as in the occupational sphere. The socialization of the female is still primarily directed toward the ultimate assumption of the roles of wife, mother, and housekeeper. The male never makes a decision as to whether he will "take a job *or* stay home and take care of the children." Much of his attention, time, and energy are directed to things outside the home. He has a greater scope of activity and his choices are less restricted than those of his wife. Behavior that might be criticized as questionable for the wife is viewed as legitimate and innocent for the husband.

One consequence of these differences is that the husband is less likely than the wife to focus all his emotion on the home and is more likely to find pleasurable or exciting activities outside it, including some involving the opposite sex. Because the wife's commitment to the home remains dominant, and because in the twentieth century she increasingly applies an equalitarian standard to her husband's activity, she is likely to object to these interests. At least she will object to some of their consequences, such as the apparently lessened interest of the husband in the family, his willingness to spend money and time outside the home, his failure to appear for dinner on time, and so on. From the husband's viewpoint, many of his activities are perfectly innocent, in part because he is permitted by society to wander farther afield and in part because he does not at first intend to move away from his family.

It is no paradox, then, to assert that wives, more often than husbands, first suggest divorce and eventually get one, yet husbands more often are the first to lose interest in the marriage. Since the wife's commitment to the marriage is likely to be greater, and her potential loss through divorce is greater, the husband is more likely to create a situation in which his wife also wants to break the bond. Perhaps without intending to do so, he must eventually make himself so obnoxious that she is as eager to break up the marriage as he is. Since his position in society depends far less on his family behavior

---

[58] William J. Goode, *After Divorce,* Chapter 11.

than on his other activities, he may continue to be a congenial and effective co-worker or companion, all the while acting offensively toward his wife. One consequence of her initiative is that it frees him, at least to some extent, from feelings of guilt he might otherwise suffer because he set in motion the train of events leading to the divorce.

INTERNAL DISSOLUTION:
THE "EMPTY SHELL" FAMILY

The Bureau of the Census estimates that in 1966 about 104 million Americans 14 years and older had been married at some time in their lives.[59] This category of "ever-married" included those currently married (over four-fifths) as well as those who had been widowed, separated, or divorced. The state may ask many questions of the individual, but so far it has not dared to ask whether a supposedly intact family is in truth merely a physical location in which the individuals have no satisfying emotional connections with one another. There is no way by which sociologists and marital counselors can locate a reliable sample of such cases, although a few will turn up in almost any family study. This brief section, then, can present only a few unsystematic observations on this type of family dissolution, not a series of firm conclusions drawn from research studies.

As noted earlier, most families that divorce pass through a state — granted, sometimes *after* the divorce — in which husband and wife no longer feel bound to each other, cease to cooperate or share with each other, and look on one another as almost strangers. The "empty shell" family is in such a state, for its members no longer feel any strong commitment to many of their mutual role-obligations; but for various reasons the husband and wife do not separate or divorce.

Violent, open quarrels are not common in this family, but the atmosphere is without laughter or fun, and gloom pervades the household. Members do not discuss their problems or experiences with each other and communication is kept to a minimum. Parents and children fulfill their *instrumental* obligations, but not their expressive ones. The husband holds a job and provides for the family. The wife takes care of the house and meals and nurses those who become ill. The children go to school and, at home, do their chores. But any spontaneous expression of affection, or even of delight in a personal experience, is rebuffed by the others. Each tells the others whatever is neces-

---

[59] Bureau of the Census, *Current Population Reports*, P-25, No. 354, Table 4, p. 19.

sary to integrate their instrumental activities — when one will be home for a meal, how much school supplies cost, or what the next chore to be done is.

Usually, one or both of the spouses are strong personalities, at least passively. The rationalizations for avoiding divorce are, on the part of one or both, "sacrifice for the children," "neighborhood respectability," and a religious conviction that divorce is morally wrong. The first two of these are factually erroneous, since children in such a family unit are usually starved for love, embarrassed when friends visit them, and ashamed to be forced to "explain" their parents' behavior to others. The neighborhood always knows about the internal dissolution of the family, for the couple engage in few activities together, show no pleasure in one another's company, and exhibit innumerable, if tiny, differences from normal families.

The repression of emotion extends, naturally, to sex as well. This type of family is usually highly conventional with respect to sex roles, and considerably less liberal in its attitudes toward sex than other families in its neighborhood. The daughters are given less freedom than other girls their age and face more restrictions upon what types of activities they may engage in, places where they may go, and when they must be home. Sexual relations between husband and wife are rare and unsatisfactory. Adolescents keep their dating activities a secret, or lie about them, to escape punishment.

The hostility in such a home is great, but arguments focus on the small issues, not the large ones. Facing the latter would, of course, lead directly to separation or divorce, and the couple has decided that staying together overrides other values, including each other's happiness and the psychological health of their children. The casual visitor may believe that the members are cold, callous, and insensitive to each other's needs, but closer observation usually discloses that at certain levels they are sensitive: They prove that they do know each other's weaknesses and guilts by the way in which they manage frequently to hurt each other.

The members of such a family do not often live a full and satisfactory life outside the family, for they are not really independent of one another, and their relations with outsiders are crippled by their emotional experiences within the family. When the children grow up and begin to think of marriage, they often make their decision without informing their parents until shortly before the marriage, and frequently marry as an escape from their own family.

Until an adequate study of such families is made, these observations cannot be properly assessed. The nearly unrelieved bleakness of this picture may be erroneous, in that some possible rewards that members get from one another in such a unit may have been overlooked. It must at least be conceded that these people rarely violate any of the important mores of the society.

Finally, this type of family is less likely to occur when large family units live together as in other, non-Western cultures, since each member of such a nuclear family unit may enjoy satisfactory relations with other relatives, and the need for the sharing of direct emotional solace among parents and children is not so great as in the Western family system.

THE EXTERNALLY INDUCED CRISIS: DEPRESSION, WAR, SEPARATIONS, NATURAL CATASTROPHES, INCARCERATION, AND DEATH

This section focuses primarily on the family's *adjustment* to crises, since in this type of marital breakup the cause of the problem lies outside the family itself. Space does not permit a full examination of all those problems and, indeed, little research has been done in these areas. Because adjustment to death has often been related to post-divorce adjustment, we shall compare the two patterns, although divorce does not logically fall in this category of marital crises. Thereafter, brief attention is given to the adjustment to separations caused by war and to the crises caused by economic depressions.

Divorce and Bereavement

The main similarities between divorce and bereavement have to do with the basic sociological fact that a set of role-relationships has been disrupted, requiring a profound adjustment throughout the family network. Moreover, the old habit patterns tend to continue, making it difficult for an individual to find immediate substitutes or to fill his life with alternate satisfactions. In both events, the removal of the spouse means the cessation of sexual satisfaction. (In divorce cases, this often occurs before the divorce itself.) In both, emotional problems may be so intense that the sex drive temporarily diminishes. If the divorced or dead spouse is the husband, his initiative and leadership in the family are missing. Economic problems may become pressing. If the missing spouse is the wife, profound adjustments in household management are necessary. In either case emotional solace, friendship, and love are missing. Children of the same sex as the missing spouse no longer have an adult model to follow and the spouse remaining with the children is likely to find the problem of controlling and supervising them difficult and wearying. In both situations there are likely to be endless discussions with friends and kinfolk about the former spouse and the problems of the adjustment.

The institutionalized character of death contrasts it sharply with divorce.[60] In all societies, the rituals and customs of death are an important part of the social structure. The removal by death of one person from the social network weakens the social structure, and this threat is met by a set of observances that serve to rally the feeling of community, to alleviate sorrow, and to help the bereaved individuals adjust. We all accept intellectually the inevitability of death, but a particular death hurts us emotionally. It always calls forth the question, "Why did he have to die?" and a *satisfying* answer cannot be given in only biological terms. The death has to be invested with some kind of meaning. It must be placed somewhere in the total cosmos, and this meaning is usually drawn from religious beliefs, acted out in religious rituals. Even in a society as secular as our own, these customs remain strong. When the death is marked by nonreligious ceremonials, they still retain a quasi-religious character.

Unlike divorce, death formally requires kinfolk and friends to attend the bereaved person, to offer their services, to give support. They must be at the funeral if possible, and may offer financial help, even if it is insufficient. The bereaved person is not only permitted to express his grief, but is encouraged to do so. He is told, "Go ahead and cry it out." It is recognized that the crying itself helps alleviate the grief psychodynamically. The very fact that there is so much social support at this moment makes it possible to give way completely to grief.

The rituals and observances also give the bereaved person some definite tasks to carry out. These are not difficult, and may be no more than moving from one part of the funeral parlor to another, sitting in one place rather than another at the cemetery, greeting and talking with relatives and kin, and so on. The bereaved person is not permitted to grieve alone but is forced, almost mechanically, to go through various activities that serve to keep him within the social network. The funeral service itself expresses the finality of death; there is nothing in the sequence of steps toward divorce which has this character.

The bereaved person does not usually feel hostility toward the wife or husband who has died; on the contrary, there is a tendency to idealize the past relationship and the person. Both sides of the kin network are encouraged to praise the dead one, whereas in the case of divorce, both sides

---

[60] In this immediate section we shall draw upon the summary of Thomas D. Eliot, "Bereavement: Inevitable But Not Insurmountable," in Howard Becker and Reuben Hill, eds., *Family, Marriage, and Parenthood,* pp. 665–67. We also have utilized Willard Waller, *The Family* (New York: Dryden, 1938), pp. 480–522, and Waller and Hill, *The Family,* Chapter 22. See also the interesting observations in David Sudnow, *Passing On* (Englewood Cliffs, N. J.: Prentice-Hall, 1967).

tend to criticize their relative's former spouse. Wounded pride does not figure in death as it does in divorce, and of course the widower or widow is less likely to feel a sense of failure simply because the relationship has been broken.

Although the customs of mourning do not specify solutions for many of the problems of death, they do offer some solutions; divorce offers none, simply because the social responses to divorce are not deeply institutionalized. There is no set of agreed-upon rights and obligations concerning the divorced person. It is not entirely clear whether either kin line has any obligation to the divorced person, or to his or her children. The relationship of the ex-husband and ex-wife after the divorce is not spelled out either. Although the husband may have specific financial obligations toward his children, his obligations in regard to their supervision, socialization, and even emotional health are not stated by custom. Finally, the institutions of our society do not specify whether friends or kin should sympathize with the divorced person, congratulate him, or help him to search for a new mate. Although there is considerable similarity in the adjustment patterns of divorcees, these similarities are not so much results of specific social *customs* as they are of such common social *experiences* as the economic needs of a broken family unit, the loneliness of the divorced person, and the difficulty in our society of working out an easy life adjustment outside marriage.

Some of the structural differences between the situations of divorce and bereavement also make for differences in the emotional situation of the divorcee, as opposed to that of the widower or widow. The divorced person is likely to have gone through a long period, on the average about two years, during which his emotional attachment to the spouse was gradually undermined or destroyed. Consequently, some of the emotional "work of adjustment" is accomplished even before the divorce. Also, under most circumstances, the divorced spouse can give certain types of help, especially if there are children. The divorced person is unlikely to idealize the departed spouse and hence may find it easier to accept another. Divorce is not so irrevocable as death, and of course a much higher proportion of those who lose their spouses by death are older people, for whom the loss may be emotionally crushing.

The widow and widower, as noted, are guided more than the divorced by social customs. These customs include a period of mourning, in which the individual is supposed to avoid his relations with the opposite sex. It is a betrayal of the dead spouse to engage in a love affair too soon. There are always some who praise the widow who so reveres her dead husband that she never remarries, and this was the ideal in both China and India. The widow is less able than the widower to find a new spouse, in part because an older man is not criticized for marrying a considerably younger woman. Twice as many widowers as widows remarry during the first five years after the death of their spouses. On the other hand, both widows and widowers are now much more likely to remarry than a generation ago.[61]

War and Depression

Although war may remove a husband from the family and a depression may not, the existing analyses of the effects of these two social crises on marriage have focused on a common problem of role-impairment caused by an external event, and have shared a common perspective that the major variables in the continuing functioning of the family are (1) its internal integration and (2) its adaptability.[62] Although space does not permit a full discussion of the problems, or the solutions, a brief summary of certain research findings is possible.

A not surprising finding in these inquiries was that a considerable number of families seem to undergo no crisis at all. When the husband went away to war, either the family welcomed his departure as a relief or each member took on added duties with willingness and a renewed sense of devotion. At the height of the Great Depression, in 1932–1933, some 14 to 16 million people, about one out of four of the labor force, were unemployed; but many families with economic difficulties remained happy and united, adjusted easily to the new demands of the situation.

Families face a similar set of problems when the father goes away to war: The income is likely to be less, many household tasks defined as "male" must be taken over by others, the mother gets no relief from disciplining or nursing the children and administering the household, and the children both miss their father and lack an important role relationship in the socialization process. The adjustment to both his departure and his later return depends not alone on (1) the *difficulties* of the event itself, however, but equally on

---

[61] Willard Waller and Reuben Hill, *The Family*, p. 395.

[62] See Robert C. Angell, *The Family Encounters the Depression* (New York: Scribner, 1936), especially Chapter 13; E. Wight Bakke, *Citizens Without Work* (New Haven: Yale University Press, 1940); Mirra Komarovsky, *The Unemployed Man and His Family* (New York: Dryden, 1940); Reuben Hill, *Families Under Stress* (New York: Harper, 1949), especially Chapters 5, 6; Elise Boulding, "Family Adjustments to War Separation and Reunion," *Annals of the American Academy of Political and Social Science*, Vol. 272 (November, 1950), pp. 59–67. See also S. A. Stouffer and Paul F. Lazarsfeld, *Research Memorandum on the Family in the Depression* (New York: Social Science Research Council, 1937).

(2) the *resources* (both material and social) that the family commands and on (3) how the family *defines* the situation. The family that defines the departure or reunion as a catastrophe is more likely than others to respond in an uncoordinated and mutually unsatisfactory way.

The impact of the depression crisis is felt more slowly and many families face no real problems until late in the economic cycle. White-collar workers may suffer no loss of pay for a time, whereas manual laborers and skilled workers in the construction industry begin to lose their jobs early. The lower class generally is at an even greater disadvantage economically in a depression than in normal times, but it is not certain that their definition of the situation leads to less effective handling of the problems. Middle-class families work far more toward future goals, many of which have to do with status or prestige, so that even when they do not starve or become homeless, the emotional hurt of giving up club memberships, frequent dinners and parties, plans for college, and modish clothes or — and apparently this is among the most hurtful of experiences — accepting relief, may be as great as the lower-class anxiety from the difficulties of simple economic survival.[63] In addition, even in normal times many lower-class families exist close to a minimum standard of living, or lower still. The father is often without work and each member of the family is expected to contribute economically when he can. To accept relief is not pleasant; but it is not so degrading as it is for middle-class families that have never even considered that possibility.

The depression crisis has a greater impact on the husband's position, just as the war crisis affects the wife's position more. The role-obligations of family head, husband, father, and breadwinner are not ordinarily distinguished from one another by members of the family. The fact that the father is without a job for months, and the gradual understanding that a new job is unlikely to turn up, may therefore reveal weaknesses in the family that were not previously visible. Sometimes, for example, the family is tightly integrated, but is absolutely dependent on the father's leadership and unable to easily adapt when he loses his status as breadwinner.[64] Or the family has instead been held together only because everyone has been dependent on his earnings, while secretly they hate him. In all cases, however, some role-adjustments of family members are created by his job loss, especially as this continues over time. Many men are psychologically crushed by this loss, and some may desert their families because they are unable to adjust to the wife's taking a job and the children earning much of the family income.

---

[63] Ruth S. Cavan, *The American Family* (New York: Crowell, 1953), p. 538.

[64] See, for example, Robert C. Angell's type, highly integrated but unadaptable in *The Family Encounters the Depression*, p. 261.

Lip service, at least, is paid to the ideal of the "democratic" family, in which all members have an equal voice in important decisions, and public opinion seems to assert that such families are "more adaptable." The previously cited research on the crisis of wartime separations found that a majority of the families thought of themselves as "equalitarian," but slightly less than 7 percent were so in practice — and that though the *marital* adjustment scores of equalitarian families were higher than those of other types, their ability to adjust to the crisis of separation and reunion was *not* higher. Effective handling of this type of crisis was found among many different kinds of family, including the "old-fashioned patriarchal" type. [65] Effectiveness was greater when adaptability and integration were high, when affection among family members was strong, the marital adjustment (i.e., between husband and wife) was high, and when the family had previously experienced some success in handling similar crises.[66] These findings parallel the findings from the research on the response of families to the depression crisis.

THE INTERNAL SOCIAL CATASTROPHE: MAJOR, INVOLUNTARY ROLE-FAILURES DUE TO MENTAL, EMOTIONAL, OR PHYSICAL PATHOLOGIES

The philosophical question of "blame" seems remote from the kind of crises here discussed. In these types of problems, the individual may be physically present, but his pathology prevents him from effectively carrying out his role-obligations. Mental and physical illness are discussed elsewhere in this volume; the present context concerns only their impact on the family. As in the external crises which the family must face, the varieties of individual pathologies affecting role-behavior are so many that it is not possible here to deal with all of them. The onset of blindness or poliomyelitis may destroy a husband's earning capacity and transform a capable family head into a physical and psychological invalid. Schizophrenia may change an apparently healthy and happy mother into a suspicious and incoherent individual, bent on hurting everyone she once loved (see Chapter 1, pages 30–32).

The exposition will be simplified somewhat if we first call attention to certain aspects of adult mental illness in the family, and then discuss at greater length the problem of severe mental retardation in children, since in certain respects the effect of this problem is similar to that of mental illness.

---

[65] Reuben Hill, *Families Under Stress,* pp. 120–21.
[66] *Ibid.,* pp. 324, 326.

Of course, a high (but unknown) percentage of the mentally and emotionally ill and those with severe physical pathologies never marry because they cannot find a partner.[67] On the other hand, some do, and some individuals fall victims to these problems after marriage. Two stages of family adjustment to adult mental illness may be singled out here for attention: the onset of the disease and the return of the victim to his family for shorter or longer periods after therapy.

The most significant fact about the first behavioral symptoms of mental illness is that the members of the family are typically not competent to judge their meaning, unless the behavior is violent or "hysterical." [68] Role-failure is first viewed as some sort of moral problem, deliberate or careless, and the response to it is anger, scolding, withdrawal, or the advice to "get a grip on yourself." A man with a brain tumor may begin to be suspicious, moody, and distracted, and so may a person who is a paranoid schizophrenic, but everyone has at times had a friend or acquaintance who behaved similarly. The husband thinks of laziness, weakness of character, or even organic difficulties before he begins to guess that his wife may need psychiatric care. Often, the victim behaves normally in many respects, and perhaps (for a while) most of the time. Since the layman considers the acts of others as deliberate, the marriage may actually break up before the husband or wife understands that the problem is one of mental illness.

Once this possibility is faced, most families act to obtain professional help, whether tax-supported services or private psychotherapy. Only a few remain whose attitude is like that of a half-century ago, when a family was expected to "take care of its own" as long as there was no threat of violence. Most psychotherapy of a limited type is done by psychiatric social workers. Both clinical psychologists and psychiatrists – within mental institutions and on an outpatient basis – are engaged in deeper therapy. The layman, however loving and sensitive, cannot substitute for these services. Members of the family can contribute best by readjusting the family structure and shouldering the additional burdens.

These additional burdens are in some ways similar to those caused by desertion, divorce, or death, if the patient is hospitalized. However, the increasing use of drugs in psychotherapy, permitting the patient to function normally while (or, often, without) undergoing treatment, has meant that he

---

[67] For a review of this matter, see Aubrey Lewis, "Fertility and Mental Illness," *Eugenics Review,* Vol. 50 (July, 1958), pp. 91–105.

[68] For more detailed data on the family's response to mental illness, see Jerome K. Myers and Bertram H. Roberts, *Family and Class Dynamics in Mental Illness* (New York: Wiley, 1959), Chapter 8. See also Joan K. Jackson, "The Adjustment of the Family to Alcoholism," *Marriage and Family Living,* Vol. 18 (1956), pp. 361–69.

may return to his family for varying periods of time. Preliminary research has thrown some light on this adjustment. It is not entirely certain that a loving, permissive reception is most effective for continued rehabilitation. More important, patients who are not very effective in interpersonal relations after leaving a mental hospital are likely to have returned to a parental home where their relatives have strongly negative attitudes toward hospitalization and believe that the illness is inborn and that people who have once been mentally ill are never the same again. As a consequence, the family feels there is nothing they can do except accept the patient's quirks. By contrast, some patients return to families who seem to expect more from them. There is some evidence that these expectations may aid the patient in his rehabilitation.[69] Thus a diagnosis of the fit between the patient's needs and the structure of family relations may sometimes lead to a decision that he should not return to his family at first, but to other groups that will expect him to behave normally.[70]

Interesting work has been carried out in the area of the family adjustment to various problems of mental disease. This problem has come to be of special importance because of the greater use of drugs that permit the mental patient to function outside the walls of the asylum. These drugs do not cure, but they shorten the patient's stay in the hospital, and give him some promise of quasi-normality. The family, however, has new problems of adjustment. Several findings can be noted here.

One significant line of research focuses on what kind of family setting is most helpful for the returning mental patient, and what kinds of roles he can play.[71] For example, one of the more destructive family configurations

---

[69] James A. Davis, Howard E. Freeman, and Ozzie G. Simmons, "Rehospitalization and Performance Level among Former Mental Patients," *Social Problems,* Vol. 5 (July, 1957), pp. 37–44.

[70] For a good analysis of the extent to which there may be destructive tolerance in a family, see Lyman C. Wynne, Irving M. Ryckoff, Juliana Day, and Stanley I. Hirsch, "Pseudo-Mutuality in the Family Relations of Schizophrenics," in Norman W. Bell and Ezra F. Vogel, eds., *The Family* (New York: Free Press, 1960), especially pp. 579 ff.

[71] For both analyses and descriptive data on these problems, see James C. Baxter, Joseph Becker, and Walter Hooks, "Defensive Style in the Families of Schizophrenics and Controls," *Journal of Abnormal and Social Psychology,* Vol. 66 (May 5, 1963), pp. 512–18; Walter Kempler, Robert Iverson, and Arnold Beisser, "The Adult Schizophrenic and his Siblings," *Family Process,* Vol. 1 (September, 1962), pp. 224–35; Christian F. Midelfort, "Use of Members of the Family in the Treatment of Schizophrenia," *Family Process,* Vol. 1 (March, 1962), pp. 114–18; and Robert D. Towne, Sheldon L. Messinger, and Harold Sampson, "Schizophrenia and the Marital Family: Accommodations to Symbiosis," *Family Process,* Vol. 1 (September, 1962), pp. 304–18; and Paul H. Glasser, "Changes in Family Equilibrium During Psychotherapy," *ibid.,* pp. 245–64.

occurs when the *son* returns, especially if his family is lower class, precisely *because* of their greater tolerance of his "queerness." That is, they "accept" him "as he is," take care of him as well as they can, but make few demands on him.

A somewhat contrasting situation awaits the male breadwinner, for he is likely to return to an *over*demanding configuration. He is unlikely to be able to produce as much as when he was well, but there is no substitute for his services. Correlatively, his performance and prognosis are better if he returns to a large household in which there are *other adult males*. A somewhat less demanding environment is encountered by the wife who returns home from the mental hospital, since other members of the household can take over as many of her functions as she is unable to perform; by her failure and success they can easily gauge the challenge to her fitness.

What is evident from these and related findings is that though the onset of mental disease is a catastrophe that threatens the foundations of the family, thousands of families not only meet it adequately, but later develop a family situation in which the returning patient not only can perform reasonably well but can even sometimes be helped on the slow road back to health.

In most discussions of marital disorganization, the impact of marital problems on the emotional and mental health of the child is emphasized. The potentially destructive impact of children upon the marriage is usually ignored. Leaving aside the problem of the unwanted child who enters a marriage in which the mother and father are unprepared for parenthood, a more tragic set of cases is to be found when the child is severely mentally retarded, suffers a brain injury at birth, or becomes psychotic during his childhood. To a lesser extent, problems are also experienced when a child is severely neurotic without being psychotic.

Many families are nearly destroyed by the impact of such children upon them. When the child is born, both parents typically respond with considerable love and pleasure, even though all children are necessarily a burden upon both the family's energy and its pocketbook. Whether the child is viewed as a "doll" or as a young person, his first months are a period in which he gets considerable love and attention. He has no role-obligations, so that everything he does causes delight to those about him. In the earliest months, even an expert may find it difficult to tell that a retarded child will never become normal. In some instances the parents themselves are the last to know. Sometimes the pediatrician first ascertains the fact. The child may be brought to a doctor only for a physical illness; he undergoes no systematic tests to ascertain his normality, so that the question is never raised. Gradually it becomes apparent that the child is not normal in some way. He does not begin to sit up at the proper age. He does not fix his eyes properly or does not respond to people within the first six months. Neighbors may talk among themselves about the child, but do not let on their suspicions to the parents.

Gradually, however, the parents begin to suspect that something is wrong, and they are shocked when they find that others have long thought so. Then there begins a tragic series of journeys, complicated and more extensive among parents with money, but disheartening and frustrating for all parents. They take the child to medical or psychological clinics for testing and receive from each report a gloomy prognosis, but they do not easily give up. Instead, they continue to hope, sometimes for years, that a new drug, some form of therapy, or simple maturation will solve the problem.

The emotions of parents in such situations are complex. Aside from the sadness they feel, most of them also suffer from deep guilt feelings.[72] They feel that in some manner it was their fault. This is especially so when the child becomes psychotic, since nearly all parents know that there is likely to be some relationship between the child's social experiences and the development of the psychosis. Even when there is an injury to the brain at birth, parents feel guilty. They wish to assuage their guilt by finding a cure and are willing to bankrupt themselves in order to seek a solution. It is a rare couple who are able to put the child in an institution at an early stage in this process. Rather, they lavish love on the child and try desperately to compensate for his deficiencies. The child cannot dress himself or take care of himself, and the parents spend their energies in hovering over him. When there are other children, who suffer from the stigma of having such a child in their midst, considerable hostility may develop between the normal children and the parents. The strains on role-relationships become intense, and the hostilities and aggressions between husband and wife may grow severe.

A few of the findings from current research on the impact of the severely mentally retarded child on the family may be summarized here:

1. The initial emotional impact is greater on the wife than on the husband.
2. Initially, her reaction is about the same whether the child is a boy or girl, but the husband's is greater if the child is a boy.
3. Later on, the impact on the wife is greater if the child is a boy, primarily because of the impact on the husband.[73]
4. Families are more willing to place a boy in an institution than a girl;

---

[72] "Having a severely mentally retarded child frequently creates a situation of utter chaos." See Bernard Farber, *Family Organization and Crisis,* Society for Research in Child Development (Indiana), Serial No. 75, Vol. 25, No. 1 (1960), p. 5.

[73] *Ibid.,* p. 39.

and lower-class families are still more willing to do so than middle-class families.[74]

5. Institutionalization of the child especially relieves the pressures on a retarded child's sister.[75]
6. As a retarded boy grows older, he has a greater disruptive effect on the family; and placing him in an institution helps the family integration.[76]

The prognosis for the psychotic child is, however, somewhat less gloomy than it was a generation ago. Child psychiatry has improved considerably in recent decades, and some radical techniques have been developed in an effort to solve these problems; but all of them still require the separation of the child from the family for any degree of success.

ADJUSTMENT TO DIVORCE AND BEREAVEMENT: THE NEW COURTSHIP

Some quantitative data are available on the emotional impact of divorce upon mothers, but no correlative data exist for men. One interesting finding is that a higher proportion of these women experience more emotional difficulty at the time of *separation* than at any other time in the divorce process, from the time it is first considered to the final decree. Although the filing of the suit is a public act, it is not necessarily known to the social groups important to the wife or husband. The final separation, however, means a public acknowledgment of failure, and the onset of the first genuine impact of all the problems of post-divorce adjustment. By contrast, at the time of the final decree, which is sometimes not obtained until many months after the final separation, many of the first problems of adjustment have already been met.

As might be supposed, when the marriage is a long one, the impact of the divorce on the divorcée is greater; similarly, older wives are more affected by divorce than younger wives. The greatest degree of trauma is experienced when the divorce was suggested first by the husband, and the least when the divorce was suggested by both husband and wife at about the same time. In

---

[74] *Ibid.,* pp. 46–47.

[75] *Ibid.,* p. 58.

[76] Bernard Farber, *Effects of a Severely Mentally Retarded Child on Family Integration,* Society for Research in Child Development (Indiana), Serial No. 71, Vol. 24, No. 2 (1959), pp. 55–58. See also Bernard Farber, W. C. Jenne, Romolo Toigo, *Family Crisis and the Decision to Institutionalize the Retarded Child,* Institute for Research on Exceptional Children (1960).

general, the divorce is less likely to have much emotional impact if both the husband's and the wife's relatives and friends are relatively indifferent to it, rather than being highly disapproving or approving.

No matter how the family unit was ended, or how intense the emotional impact of death or divorce, those who remain must continue to meet their role-obligations. Although poetic literature contains many wails of despair about the loss of a beloved spouse, by death or divorce, old habits are insistent, and acquaintances cannot carry the individual's grief for him. Children demand attention, bills require payment, jobs must be completed, and in general the network of friends, acquaintances, and relatives soon show that whatever sympathies they may still feel, they nevertheless expect continued interaction and some fulfillment of obligations. Many husbands and wives feel that without their spouses they could not carry on, but in fact almost all of them do.

In China, and even more so in India, the ideal widow did not remarry. In our own society, by contrast, the social structure gently but firmly encourages the widowed or divorced person to reenter marriage as a mode of adjustment. Indeed, except for the youngest age groups, both widowed and divorced men and women have a higher marriage rate than single people of the same ages. Well over 90 percent of the men and women whose divorce or bereavement occur when they are in their twenties will eventually remarry.[77]

As noted earlier, Arab countries have had very high divorce rates, but these did not indicate any breakdown of the family *system:* It continued in this fashion for centuries. However, the divorce adjustment was eased by several factors. *First,* some part of the bride price was usually not paid by the husband at the marriage, but it was required when he divorced his wife. Thus, when she was sent home, she did not go empty-handed. *Second,* her share in her family's property was one-half that of her brothers, and although she seldom took it, she had at least a moral right to share in its fruits. Consequently, her family could not properly begrudge her reentrance into the household. *Third,* and most important, since divorce rates were high, husbands were likely to be available, and thus the family could actually look forward to another bride price in time. The rules regarding custody of the children were clear: At the early ages, children were taken care of by their mother, but without question they belonged to their father's line, and eventually they were returned to his home.

All this is not to imply that there were no heartaches in the Arab divorce system, but the fragility of the family unit in the early years of marriage did not create as many adjustmental difficulties in the woman's network of blood

---

[77] Paul H. Jacobson, *American Marriage and Divorce,* pp. 83–85.

kin relations; many matters were settled by custom and, therefore, with less argument over principle and right.[78]

It seems safe to say that there is no strong moral norm which asserts that people *should* remarry. It is rather that the institutional patterns of our society leave little room for the individual who wishes to "go it alone." This is of course especially true if there are children, but even if there are none the pressures are strong. Invitations among adults are typically from one couple to another. Adult conversations focus on families and children. Few adults are unmarried, and those who are unmarried are usually courting someone. Couples often view the widowed or divorced person, whether male or female, as a potential threat to existing marriages, and often try a bit of matchmaking to see to it that everyone moves back into the married state. When the individual has remarried, he no longer has to answer questions about his former marital experiences.

For the woman, and especially the mother, the pressures are even stronger. The common judgment is that children need both parents, and parents also need each other to handle children. Sexual problems also press the individual toward remarriage. Although in our era it is socially more acceptable than before to engage in sexual relations outside marriage, this adjustment is not easy on an extended basis. A man and woman who intend to continue a sexual relationship are likely to become involved in many awkward situations if it is not finally legitimated by marriage.

None of the above pressures is likely to be very strong, but they are recurrent. As a consequence, the pattern of adjustment that is followed by most widowed and divorced persons is eventually to establish a new marriage.

The beginning of courtship and the process of courtship interaction are both an *index* of gradual adjustment to divorce or bereavement and important causal factors in that adjustment. Successful dating indicates that the hurt pride or the sense of loss of the individual has diminished somewhat. At the same time, the date helps the process of adjustment by discouraging constant references to the former husband or wife. The spouse gradually begins to think of himself not as the "ex-spouse of — ," but as a date, friend, or sweetheart — in short, a person with a particular identity.

CHILDREN IN MARITAL DISORGANIZATION

Refined statistical calculations suggest that children have only a small effect on the maintenance of a marriage. In divorce cases involving children,

---

[78] For a more elaborate description of divorce in Arabic Islam, see William J. Goode, *World Revolution and Family Patterns* (New York: Free Press, 1963), pp. 115–61.

the average number of offspring has been slightly less than two for the past half-century. However, slightly more than one-half of all divorced couples have no children. Childless couples are more likely to divorce because couples with serious marital problems are less likely to have children. Nevertheless, the number of children involved in various forms of social disorganization is substantial. About 630,000 children were involved in divorce and annulment cases during 1965.[79] As of the year 1965 there were approximately 3,290,000 children 17 years of age and under in the United States who had been orphaned by the loss of one or both parents.[80] In 1960, there were 2,100,000 families with at least one child under 18 years of age headed by only one parent because the other parent was dead or divorced, or had simply left.[81]

It is difficult to measure exactly the impact of family disorganization upon children. Without question, children are more likely to grow up to be law-abiding, healthy, and happy if they spend their entire childhood in a happy family than if the family unit is broken by divorce or death. However, the family can be equally split by violent disagreements and by the unhappiness of either spouse within marriage. Keeping the marriage together "in spite of everything" does not necessarily make happier children.

The general association of broken homes with delinquency has been demonstrated by many studies. This association has been traced to two large sets of factors. One of these has to do with the fact that both divorce rates and mortality rates are higher in slum areas, where delinquency rates are also higher. To this extent, the association may be in part a spurious one. The other large set of factors has to do with the role-models that parents offer to their children and the social controls they impose upon them. If either parent is missing, the boy or girl may not have an adequate role-model to emulate and may not learn adequate patterns of behavior. It is also likely that the boy or girl needs a parent of the opposite sex as a *complementary* figure with whom to enact role-relations. More fundamentally, both parents are needed to control the children, simply because of the time and energy required to socialize them.

All this is true whether the marriage is broken by death or by divorce, and the relationship between broken homes and delinquency is not spurious. Even when the class position of parents is held constant, the delinquency rate of children is higher for broken than for unbroken homes. Similarly, the

---

[79] *Vital Statistics of the United States — 1965,* Table 2–9.

[80] Bureau of the Census, *Statistical Abstract of the United States: 1969,* 90th ed. (Washington, D. C., 1965), Table 471, p. 301.

[81] Bureau of the Census Population Series, 1960, *Families,* Final Report PC(2)-4A, Table 6.

rate of delinquency among boys and girls is higher for those whose parents are separated or divorced than it is for those who have lost a parent by death.[82]

Unfortunately for those who seek easy solutions for family disorganization, it also seems likely that a family in which there is continued marital conflict, or separation, is more likely to produce children with problems of personal adjustment than a family in which there is divorce or death.[83] In general, separation and continued conflict may have a greater disorganizing effect upon children than divorce, and divorce a greater effect than death, because the degree of intimate acceptance, love, support, and control given by the remaining parent or substitute parent is likely to be greater in that same order: separation and conflict, divorce, and death. It is the quality of the childhood experience, not the mere fact of divorce, which is crucial.

Parents in conflict, therefore, must face a critical choice: Of course, they cannot choose whether the marriage will end in death, but neither do they have a clear alternative in the matter of divorce and conflict. They can choose not to divorce, but they cannot by conscious decision create the happy home that would be the most healthful environment in which to rear their children. Their choice usually has to be between a continuing conflict or a divorce. And the evidence so far suggests that it is the *conflict of divorce,* not the divorce itself, that has the greater impact on children.[84]

Finally, we must keep in mind that most spouses who lose their husbands or wives will remarry, so that most of these children will eventually enter a new family relationship. The problems of adjustment in this new relationship have been insufficiently explored; we cannot now state just how much it improves the chances of emotional health in children who have gone through the experience of divorce or bereavement. There is at least some evidence that their adjustment is likely to be better with a stepfather than with a stepmother.[85] The reasons are not difficult to ascertain. It is the woman, after all, who must have the closest contact with the children, who must take their

---

[82] Myer F. Nimkoff, *Marriage and the Family* (Boston: Houghton Mifflin, 1947), p. 645. See also Sheldon and Eleanor Glueck, *Unraveling Juvenile Delinquency* (New York: Commonwealth Fund, 1951).

[83] Paul H. Landis, "The Broken Home in Teen-age Adjustments," *Rural Sociology Series on the Family,* No. 4 (Pullman, Wash.: Institute of Agricultural Sciences, State College of Washington, 1953), p. 10.

[84] For more recent findings on these points, see Judson T. Landis, "A Comparison of Children from Divorced and Nondivorced Unhappy Marriages," *Family Life Co-ordinator,* Vol. 11 (July, 1962), pp. 61–65; and Harry Pannor and Sylvia Schild, "Impact of Divorce on Children," *Child Welfare,* Vol. 39 (February, 1960), pp. 6–10.

[85] Jessie Bernard, *Remarriage,* pp. 220–21.

daily burdens on her shoulders, and who must pick up the pieces when there is breakage. It is then easier for the man to adjust to a set of children not his own than it is for the woman.

PARENT-YOUTH CONFLICT

No one who has witnessed the fighting capabilities of a three-year-old who seeks to resist parental authority can doubt that this type of interaction can be called "parent-youth conflict." However, the term refers more commonly to the adolescent period, when several social factors converge to create a qualitatively different type of conflict. Of course, at this time the child simply begins to be more competent at resisting authority. He or she is physically larger and is often bigger and stronger than the mother, who spends more time at social control than the father. An adolescent child is also fully as capable of reasoning well as the parent, and thus can often win an argument. Even in factual matters, he may be reasonably well-informed, especially in those areas which concern him. Adolescents spend much of their time outside the family, where they cannot be supervised easily; and of course, as their sexual development proceeds, they not only have a greater amount of energy and ease of energy recovery than the exhausted parent, but they begin to feel internal pushes and stresses that cause them to express their own will and seek their own goals with greater persistence.

The parent-youth conflict that is most widely discussed does not, however, center upon such matters as being neat, studying hard, or showing respect for elders. Rather, the conflict that is the center of both public attention and private discussion among parents relates to what might be called philosophical and political matters.

That is to say, youngsters begin to acquire different values and attitudes, to seek new goals, to express their preferences with respect to their present and future life styles, and, in short, to reject precisely the values that the parent has been trying for years to inculcate. Thus the day to day analyses of both public leaders and parents focus not so much on the kind of "deviation" that expresses itself in ordinary juvenile crime, or the unwillingness of a child to fulfill his usual family obligations of helping out with the housework, but upon fundamental values. Even when much of the argument centers upon the sexual behavior of the adolescent, the youngster is not merely disobeying old rules because of temptation. Rather, he or she is asserting the *right* to behave in that fashion; hence the conflict may be fierce and often breaks, either temporarily or permanently, the attachment of parents and children.

In explaining the widespread contemporary parent-youth conflict, analysts have pointed to such factors as the importance of the peer group in the life of the adolescent, the rise of numerous competing philosophies, the impossibility of isolating youngsters from a wide range of influences other than those of their parents, and the mass media; but a still more fundamental factor is simply the *speed of social change* in Western society. This can best be understood by reference to the life cycle. There is always some basic conflict between parents and children simply because they are in different age statuses. The 20-year-old father does not experience the same problems, conflicts, and emotions that his infant son of two does, and this discrepancy remains throughout much of the lifetime of both father and son. When the man is elderly, his son is mature, but once again their experiences, needs, friendships, and so forth are all different.

Nevertheless, although they are different, where the society does not change rapidly the parents can at least understand somewhat better the experiences of their child because the experiences are much like those they had in their own formative years. They played as a child in the same area, knew the same temptations and rebellions, and were pushed around by the same kind of adult authority figures. The child does not typically enjoy being told, "When you are as old as I am, you will understand." But a parent *is* likely to understand, if he has any wisdom at all, if he did indeed go through similar experiences.

The situation is fundamentally different in the rapidly changing society. The same age differences exist, with their inevitably different evaluations of what is urgent and unimportant, but the problem is exacerbated by the fact that the youngster now goes through experiences and acquires knowledge that the parents never had at all. Although many contemporary parents have indeed tried some of the outlawed drugs, especially marijuana, none has the experience of growing up in what must now be labeled a "drug culture," in which almost every child is subjected to the temptation of nonaddictive or addictive drugs. To compare this problem to the problem of drinking a generation ago is to miss the point, for drinking has a very long cultural history, and a wide range of assorted beliefs, practices, and ways of handling the problem exist.

There have always been contraceptives, but this is the first generation that has grown up with "the pill." The United States has, in almost every year of its history, been at war with one group or another, but only since World War II has it maintained a large standing army and an enormous military complex that constitutes a large part of the industrial system. The list could be lengthened, but the principle remains the same. Both parents and adolescents find it difficult to empathize or sympathize with the daily problems of the other, since many of the most profound experiences and thus the new values of the adolescent are so at variance with anything the parent knows or can understand.

The modern decade has witnessed an entirely new phenomenon, super-imposed upon the somewhat older pattern of parent-youth conflict, that is due to social change. The new patterns are more akin to those that occur during the most rapid kind of social change, that is, during a revolution. For in both revolutions and in the modern decade, youngsters not only affirm the irrelevance of their parents' philosophies and political attitudes and urge that they step down from their position of authority; typically, they also *organize*. Whether we consider the Chinese communists, the Soviet revolution, the changes in Cuban social life, or the Nazi period, we note that youngsters organize themselves, or are organized by the new leaders, into cadres, clubs, troops, or shifting bands, and voluntary associations designed to focus a maximum of their energy on specific objectives. Thus though the conflict is fundamentally one between parents and children, it becomes much more openly a conflict between *generations,* that is, between young people and parents generally, rather than between young people and their own parents. Children's sympathy and tolerance for gradual social improvement are very low, the time at their disposal is high, and their militancy is great precisely because they find supporters all about them.

Parent-youth conflict in this narrower sense of actively pressing for social change obviously overlaps with parent-youth conflict in the larger sense, in which the youngster simply presses for personal individual freedom from restrictions while retaining some of the advantages of the links with his parents. For any given person or any given epoch, it is difficult to know how much of the total parent-youth conflict is one or the other. Clearly, if an adolescent is trying to break the bonds that subordinate him to his parents, he has a handy weapon in the new ideologies, new leaders, and new data that support his position. Secondly, the youngster who feels only anger and resentment at his parents for their restrictions may actually be responding to nationwide social currents that he becomes aware of through listening to radio or television, reading magazines or newspapers, or talking over problems with his school friends.

The question is of some consequence, because it links the institutional area of the family with other institutions and raises the issue of whether the current parent-youth conflict in the United States represents, possibly, a watershed point, a qualitative alteration in the *direction* of national developments. That is, some analysts will argue that although most young people do not revolt seriously against their parents or against the established institutions, among those who do revolt are to be found many of the future leaders of the nation; that although their policies will not be fully implemented, they will not totally change their political philosophies when they take on positions of authority; and that as a consequence, the nation may indeed gradually reorder its priorities, de-emphasizing the importance of an ever-increasing Gross National Product and paying increasing attention to the human quality of social arrangements.

So radical a shift seems highly unlikely, but without question the present form of parent-youth conflict is unlike any that has previously been witnessed in the United States. It has linkages with the "younger generation" in the lower schools, increasingly obtains political support from people in a wide range of social statuses, and is likely to be supported in the future by a continuing rapid rate of social change, which will generate, as at present, a great amount of parent-youth conflict that will further encourage this type of national transformation.

Most societies in the past have been highly familistic, with the kinship network playing a more central role than in Western societies, so that the young person could not escape the controls of his family without catastrophe. The young woman would be a prey to other men with no one to protect her, and the young man could not even earn a living.

However, we should keep in mind that even in highly patriarchal societies such as classical China, the rebellious son was not simply the victim of a crude authoritarianism. Because their authority was so precious, fathers did not risk challenges to it unnecessarily. Like the boss or foreman who hesitates to give a particular order because he is afraid that a tough workman will refuse to carry it out, thus creating an awkward or embarrassing situation, the Manchu father would often overlook the behavior of his nearly adult son rather than press for a fight that would demonstrate to everyone his lack of real authority.

Such a mechanism is, of course, visible in any society. Another tactic, again characteristic of familistic societies in which the kin network is prominent, is simply to move the rebellious child from his own nuclear family to that of a relative. Sometimes this move can be glossed over by a face-saving explanation—by claiming that the kinsman's family needs the youngster's help, or that the visit is temporary. What is significant is that the extended kin network, both in traditional societies and in our own, does act at times as a kind of shock absorber to prevent the parent-youth conflict from (1) destroying the relationship between parents and a rebellious child and (2) undermining the other role-relations in the family.

Although it is likely that parents will be more or less on one side and the rebellious youngsters on the other, many other coalitions are possible. The mother may secretly side with the girl who wishes more personal freedom, because she remembers her own childhood battles about such matters, or she may give an adequate allowance to the rebellious son who has been thrown out by the father. A high percentage of parents fight with each other when a youngster rebels, if only in the process of trying to place the blame. The rebellious youngster may also generate battles among siblings and not just between parents.

It is obvious that any major *policy* to reduce (or even to increase) parent-youth conflict is unlikely to be successful. Both the sets of major variables, intrafamilial and societal, are not very amenable to intervention. There are few policies that could conceivably affect the socialization practices of individual parents in any reasonable length of time; and up to this point our ability to alter the massive, slow forces of social change in the nation as a whole seems quite limited.

The term "massive" as applied to intrafamilial elements should be emphasized because sociologists are inclined to think only of the great social forces like technology or war as massive. In addition, we are likely to think that familial forces can be changed rather easily, since so many thousands of experts constantly exhort us to alter our ways—to treat our children with love, give them security, participate with them in family activities, and so forth—as though all this were possible. (If it is not possible, then why preach to us?) Such advice corresponds also to our daily experience, for when we observe parent-youth conflicts among our acquaintances over time, we see quite easily how the parents could change their behavior to solve the problem.

Nevertheless one may perceive how massive these forces that generate parent-youth conflict within the family are simply by thinking of any habit that is difficult to break, from cigarette smoking or drinking to nagging one's loved ones. Experts are generally pro-child in attitude, and thus constantly emphasize how parents ought to behave. Unfortunately, almost no one can *will* himself to give love, not to react with anger to a violation of an important norm, not to feel exhausted and snappish at the end of the day, not to feel worried when an adolescent stays out all night without telling anyone of his plans, and so on. The child has his own personality, whether derived from his socialization or his biological heritage, but so has the parent, and whatever his wisdom he is less flexible than the child. Almost everyone *wishes* to be a good parent; perhaps most youngsters would like to be "good children," if only to earn the pat on the head that goes with it. But both are in the grip of rather large psychological and social forces, and others that stem from the day's events.

In any event, one need not even be cynical to predict that most cases of parent-youth conflict are not "solved." Children simply move out and drift away for a while; the problem is glossed over and avoided, and parents and children avoid seeing one another except for an occasional swift meal in silence. Marriage and the arrival of grandchildren may lessen some of the old conflicts and reveal some new areas of agreement. At this time in their lives many young adults begin to have mild twitches of sympathy for the problems of their own parents a generation before.

It should perhaps be equally emphasized that for all the bitterness and ferocity of parent-youth conflict the destinies of parents and children remain indissolubly linked in all but a few cases. Their lives and emotions remain intertwined not merely during the parents' lifetime, but for years after they have died. The battles lose their intensity and parents and children do not typically stay apart. Every study of visiting patterns among grown parents and their own parents shows frequent visiting, telephoning, exchanging or giving of gifts, and so forth, whether the locale is New York City (which has a peculiarly elaborate pattern of extended kin networks) or cities in Holland, France, England, or anywhere else in the world.

WOMEN'S LIBERATION: NEW ROLES IN THE FAMILY? [86]

Since every period of revolt cries for new attempts to redress the injustices of the society, and throughout the world the downtrodden are restive or rebellious against their masters, it cannot be surprising that women have also called for equality. The women's liberation movement, like most real revolutions, aims at altering the family structure. And, as in most other revolutions, those in power, whether colonial governors, southern or northern whites, parents, or men, plaintively ask, "What do they want? We've been so good to them."

It is not conceptually important for our analysis whether we use the extreme term "revolution," which always suggests violence, or the more diffuse term "social movement," but it is at least worthwhile to note further parallels between this revolutionary movement and others. One significant parallel, in addition to those noted above, is that the rulers are typically caught by

---

[86] Among the books already in print that elucidate one or another aspect of this topic, see: Cynthia Fuchs Epstein, *Woman's Place* (Berkeley: University of California Press, 1970); Jessie Bernard, *The Sex Game* (New York: Prentice-Hall, 1968); Kate Millet, *Sexual Politics* (Garden City, New York: Doubleday, 1970); Betty Friedan, *The Feminine Mystique* (New York: Norton, 1963); William L. O'Neill, *Everyone Was Brave: The Rise and Fall of Feminism in America* (Chicago: Quadrangle, 1969); and Caroline Bird, *Born Female* (New York: McKay, 1968).

surprise. That is, they had indeed heard or been aware of complaints and problems but they had not supposed that the dissent had reached such great proportions. They had not expected to confront a full-scale and organized program of action against the existing social arrangements. Furthermore, the hostility of those in revolt seems always to be greater than the rulers had believed possible. In their view, the relationship between subordinates and superordinates had been amicable. Those who were rulers felt that they had protected and worked for the present rebels, had listened to and solved many of their problems, and were owed some loyalty and affection in return. In the case of women, of course, this is even more true; husbands usually feel that they are "working hard" for their wives and families and that they enjoy no great advantages. Nevertheless, every report from the wide range of informal and formal women's organizations in this movement describes a considerable amount of resentment and anger.

Next, the outsider, and especially the ruler under stress, finds it difficult to ascertain precisely what the demands of the rebels are; hence the query, "What do they want?" is heard in every revolution. The demands generally include a wide range of conflicting proposals, programs, attacks, and lists of complaints, precisely because they grow from a *widespread* groundswell of bitterness and a deep sense of injustice. Because so many women from all classes and educational levels participate in the movement, no single and consistent set of programmatic suggestions can encompass all of its demands.

Correspondingly, the former rulers are typically surprised to find that some social customs, which they viewed as relatively minor and unimportant, rise to prominence as indexes of oppression, injustice, or denigration. Thus a professor may remark in a letter of recommendation that a female applicant for a job or fellowship is "attractive," but the candidate herself may feel that this intrudes the question of sex where only the question of competence is at issue. A young woman in a law class who is asked to comment on the woman's point of view with reference to a given legal issue may be angry that she has been singled out as a female, rather than as a law student. Parallel items can, of course, be found in the new frictions between whites and blacks in the United States.

Closely linked with the former process is the increased sensitivity of women to their condition. Women who had formerly considered themselves relatively contented have suddenly become aware of a deep reservoir of hostility and resentment at the deprecation, denigration, or oppression that they now feel they have suffered. Since men in interacting with women (even when they are trying to adjust to the new demands) have no well worked out system of new role-patterns to follow, and since they have not been socialized under such a system they may encounter frequent explosions of anger or hurt even when they feel their motives were relatively egalitarian. Women meeting in informal sessions to discuss their problems may bring each other to a high degree of awareness of how they were molded by society to fit a set of rules that they had never agreed to and had not even thought much about, but to which they now feel they strongly object.

As in other revolutions, the leaders are likely to be of higher social rank, have more education, and be more successful, even under the existing discriminations, than other women, but because all women (like all blacks) are in the same social situation to some degree, the movement attracts converts from many sources. Women who had formerly been relatively sensitive and militant may become more so, but those who accepted their subordinate role also furnish recruits. Professional women furnish most of the leadership, but both leaders and followers may come from other segments of the population as well.

We ought also to note that one major process in any revolution is an enormous release of *energy*. Once the new opportunities become real and tantalizing and the old social arrangements no longer seem changeable, when the submerged hostilities begin to rise to consciousness, those who begin to participate feel able to attack problems that they would have said were impossible to solve before and assume responsibilities that they would have said were impossible to take on, given their existing obligations. They are able and willing to work long hours and with great enthusiasm, and women frequently exhibit a persistence and daring of which they had formerly supposed themselves incapable.

Judged by the egalitarian canons of our official ideology as embodied in the Constitution and Bill of Rights, women can make an excellent case in every society; whatever tasks are defined as exciting, interesting, and challenging are labeled as appropriate for men only. In modern society, very few jobs from flying a combat plane to designing a building require muscular strength, but women are discouraged from even aspiring to such positions. Those at the top in any society typically attempt to erect and maintain an ideology which asserts that the excluded segments of the population are simply not *capable* of doing a wide range of tasks—from administering a feudal manor to directing a corporation. Since socialization and recruitment patterns follow that ideology, the disadvantaged segments of a society are prevented from acquiring the experiences and training that would enable them to at least test whether the assertion is true. Obviously, if blacks or women *cannot* adequately discharge the requirements of a given job, there is no point in having any discriminatory rules: they would fail anyway. All societies attempt to prevent the awkward situation that would arise were it learned that many of the people who were excluded could indeed do the work; however, they are not permitted to try.

Women are told that "because" they bear the children, they must stay home and take care of them. But this is an obvious failure in logic. Women do, in fact, menstruate, bear children, and give milk after birth, but these facts do not constitute an argument for keeping them at home to take care of children. All the evidence from thousands of investigations suggests that the overall differences in intelligence between the sexes are minor and that the differences in intellectual strength in different areas (space perception versus verbal facility) are small and so overlapping that many women are abler than many men in supposedly "male" areas. Moreover, these small differences seem clearly to be the result of differences in socialization. (Boys are urged to take courses in mechanical drawing, women to study literature or languages.) In any event, since the differences are so small, it would seem wise to encourage everyone to try his hand at whatever job attracts him, rather than perpetuating pressures toward a sexual division of labor.

If women do persist in demanding to be valued without regard to sex, they invariably find subtle or gross barriers of discrimination. They are likely to be paid less for the same type of work, to be rewarded less for the same level of achievement, and to be encouraged to abandon their self-development in order to stay in the home. A wide array of "women's activities," from bridge clubs to community service, are offered to them as substitutes.

Within the home, although the women's wishes are given some consideration, this and other societies (including all the Communist nations) assume that when there is conflict the woman should permit the man to make the final decision. If the man has a job opportunity in another area, it is generally expected that the woman should agree to a move, even if it is to her disadvantage. She is expected to be nurturant, to forego taking the initiative, to be much more chaste than her husband, and to enjoy housekeeping and childrearing — even if her personality is not suited to such tasks and even if a different arrangement would also suit her husband better.

The foregoing illustrations are not meant to be a complete list of the complaints that women make and they do not affirm that men have no corresponding complaints. Here we are simply trying to examine a social movement and to consider what conditions may have caused it. However, we ought not to overlook the broader social forces that have ushered this movement into a new phase — "new" because feminism in some form is at least relatively old in the English-speaking world and has continually cropped up in almost every revolutionary program. The present movement, however, seems much more likely to meet with some future success.

We may once again incorporate a suggestion from the literature on revolution and note that during the nineteenth century and the beginning of the twentieth, some small but real steps were taken toward *legal* liberation: women were given the right to retain custody of children in divorce cases, to engage independently in economic transactions and contracts, to sue for divorce, and ultimately to vote. Gradually, toward the end of the nineteenth century, women were able to get jobs and promotions without the intervention of husbands or fathers, so that, in effect, a higher percentage of women became economically independent. This furnished an economic base for social and individual bargaining that had been lacking up to that time. Of course during wartime more women entered the labor force and enjoyed this advantage, but most of them were dropped, or dropped out voluntarily, from the labor force at the war's end.

Nevertheless, it is possible to argue that the percentage of women in the traditional professions hardly increased from the turn of the century to midcentury, and even in these they were confined largely to "female specialties" such as family law, gynecology, obstetrics, and psychiatry. Women in corporate life were hired mainly for staff positions in which technical skill was important, rather than for line positions in which administrative authority was relevant.

More important, it is possible that in the past decade, and *possibly for several decades,* women have *not* been closing the gap between their opportunities and rewards and those of men.[87] Indeed a cogent case may be made for the opposite, that there was a distinct loss, as there was almost certainly among blacks relative to whites during the decade of the 1950's.

As every student of revolution knows, there is at least some evidence that a common prelude to revolt is a slow, steady improvement followed by a relatively sharp drop, or at least a substantial discrepancy between what was expected as part of the rising curve and the reality. Even if this pattern cannot be fully demonstrated for women, an additional process, which may be almost as powerful (and which again applies also to blacks), is demonstrable. Specifically, over the past several decades, the training and capacity of women have risen steadily. An increasing number of women have learned that they can do a wide range of jobs to which they have traditionally had little access. In universities and in training courses after college, and in specific positions within voluntary organizations and corporations, they found that their abilities and skills were high. They also learned, however, that rewards commensurate with these abilities and skills would not be forthcoming.

Not only have the economic rewards been less for both blacks and women, but (and this is a much subtler but perhaps an equally important failure)

---

[87] See the challenging data in Dean K. Knudsen, "The Declining Status of Women: Popular Myths and the Failure of Functionalist Thought," *Social Forces* (December, 1969), pp. 83–93.

men have failed to grant prestige, deference, and respect to women as persons and general esteem for their performances. The harsh experience of successful women is that when even they hold demanding and well-paid jobs, men still treat them as representatives of an inferior group, not as individuals. They are not acceptable socially, especially in informal interaction, except as women. To put it more subtly, men think of each other as "people" but of women as "females," a distinction that women have come more and more to resent. Men are still surprised that women have important positions and they do not pay them the respect they would pay to men in similar positions.

It is obvious that if the women's liberation movement gains momentum, family relations will be transformed and many of the existing role-patterns will be dissolved or weakened. Women will acquire full rights not merely to sexual enjoyment, but to sexual exploration outside of marriage. They will have the right to take the initiative in all matters relating to their occupation and family and will enjoy as much authority in family relations as men. Laws will distinguish less between men and women than they do now. The division of labor within the family will not be based on sex, and there will be considerably greater conflict as to who will do what. If, as now seems clear, all of us are mixtures of "male and female traits," then perhaps some liberated women will be able to find mates who complement their personalities well, although others may not. In any event, the decision as to who will do the housekeeping or take care of the children will not be based upon sex.

Similar changes will take place in the occupational world. Certainly men and women will wish to move toward more comprehensive day care centers, since at present there are few facilities for handling the problems that would be created by women's assertions of full equality. Whether society will go so far as to take most of the responsibility of child care from the parents, as in the Israeli kibbutz, cannot be prophesied at present. Some representatives of the women's liberation movement have also urged communal meals and entirely different housekeeping arrangements—perhaps something between a kibbutz and a hotel—to eliminate the problem of housekeeping. Certainly there will be greater pressure on women to use their talents and develop their potentialities. Under such a new dispensation, perhaps *both* men and women would ask themselves the question: "Do I want to take a job or stay home and take care of the children?" At present, only a woman can ask that question.

Although the safest prediction about such matters is that things will go on for a long while very much as they are now, it seems likely that neither blacks nor women will ever again accept the domination they once tolerated. The older generation has always shown great cleverness and tenacity in holding on to traditional arrangements, but the young have an advantage that is hard to match—they will eventually replace their elders. Of course, people also change as they assume new statuses and roles, and many women who now seek liberation will doubtless adjust to, and be relatively contented in, the traditional housekeeping role. Nevertheless, it seems likely that this social movement will gain considerable momentum, and may eventually substantially dissolve the current role-relations within the family.

AGING AND THE FAMILY

Philosophers have tried for millennia to persuade their listeners that age, like poverty, brings no necessary evils and some potential good, but their converts have been few. People have commonly believed that being rich and young is more desirable. At best, being poor and old gives one the opportunity to practice serenity and to exhibit strength in the face of adversity. Although the individual with personal courage, health, luck, and some money *can* manage very well when he becomes old, it is difficult to think of any *special* advantages of old age. Similarly, although most couples do keep their marriages together until they die and maintain good relations with their grown children, old age seems to bring no unequivocal solutions to old family problems, and may create a few new ones.

People who seem to be extreme in one trait are also likely to be somewhat extreme in others. Consequently, it is difficult to make many generalizations about the impact of old age upon family problems. Some 10 percent of the population is 65 years of age or older, and about one million of these people still live on farms. If we think only of *averages* or simple percentages, those who are older are more *likely* to be female, less educated than the young, living with others, without a private pension or adequate health insurance, in less than satisfactory health, and willing to do more but without enough opportunities.

On the other hand, it is clear that millions of older people do *not* fall into these categories. Consider the fact that one-fourth of the members of the United States Senate are also in the 65 and over age bracket.[88] It is obvious that as people age, their physical and mental capacities decline and it is known that the creative people in many fields do much of their best work

---

[88] Marvin R. Koller, *Social Gerontology* (New York: Random House, 1968), p. 94. See also Mathilda W. Riley and Anne Foner, eds., *Aging and Society,* Vol. I (New York: Russell Sage, 1968).

when they are relatively young—between about 25 and 40 years of age. On the other hand, if we consider only the creative people and look only at those who have lived to be relatively old, it is striking that their creativity does not decline much by the age of 60. Moreover, as is obvious from the biographies of such major figures in the arts and sciences as Titian or Michelangelo, Goethe or Gauss, Casals or Picasso, some men quite advanced in years continued to be productive. Almost everyone knows of some people in their sixties who seem "old" and others who seem vigorous and little impaired by the years. In short, at the end of the age curve, we observe so wide a range of life patterns that it is difficult to encompass all of them by any simple set of descriptions. Many old people are poor, chronically ill, incompetent, and a burden on their families and thus cannot discharge the ordinary role-obligations of family members; others may be leaders of an extended family clan almost until their deaths. Some elderly parents become such a nuisance to their grown children that they eventually have them placed in institutions, while other elderly couples maintain homes that are the centers of their grown children's lives.

How well an elderly person can discharge the role-obligations of a family member is, of course, in part a function of how well he has physically survived the attack of the years. Either by chance or good management, many older people remain vigorous, while others who apparently have paid as much attention to their health may be nearly helpless. The very way in which we look at the "problem" of aging casts light upon the position of older people in the family within our society. The emphasis upon role-obligations underlines the fact that our society typically does not pay much respect to the elderly unless they continue to "contribute." Neither in the modern industrial era nor in Western society generally has age ever been considered a virtue, a status to which respect is to be paid whether or not the individual continues to carry out important tasks. By contrast, in most primitive societies and in the East generally, life has been viewed more or less as a circle, each phase of which has specific pleasures and pains and each of which has its own value and merit. Old age brings with it a loss of function, but also an increase in prestige and honor. The West, and especially the industrial West, has seen life as the arc of a rocket in which it is man's obligation to rise and to strive as long as he can, until, ultimately, he reaches a peak and then begins a quick descent into uselessness and obsolescence. Some people do, of course, receive deference in their older years, but there is no norm and no social support for the notion that the elderly should be honored and listened to. Even the norm, now almost totally disappeared from the American scene, that young people should give up their seats in buses or subways to elderly men was an expression of solicitude for the helpless, rather than of deference.

As many analysts have noted, the elderly may have been given far more respect in nonindustrial societies simply because the old in such societies often had a considerable amount of useful knowledge. In an agricultural society that followed traditional modes of production, the elderly would naturally be the repositories of more useful knowledge than would the young. In addition, they were considered closer to the ancestors and the gods of their tribe or society, would soon be in direct contact with those spiritual beings, and usually had control over whatever magical and religious power the society believed anyone possessed. Consequently, they were viewed as important people, even if they were no longer young and vigorous.

Of course, the respect norms that we speak of are not only ideals — and in all societies ideals are violated — but, in addition, they are the ideals of the relatively affluent stratum of the society. It was much more possible for a wealthy Chinese landowner to gain respect from his sons and his sons' sons, simply because he was no great burden anyway, and he controlled the land. We cannot assume, on the other hand, that so much deference and honor would be given to the aged grandmother of a poverty-stricken peasant. It is not mere cynicism that suggests these qualifications. Rather, it is our awareness that in all social relations people do count the costs to some extent. In traditional societies, to offend the elderly might be dangerous and people were likely to ostracize the man who treated his aged parents badly. In societies where elderly people do not have such levers — magic, wealth, political influence, or the ability to contribute to the family resources — in their hands, one can predict considerably greater neglect.

In our own society, the position of the elderly has been complicated by a shift in these norms that perhaps began toward the end of the nineteenth century. It is not that our era is, as we so frequently hear, "the age of youth" in which youth is worshipped, served, and given power. We need only look at the ages of those in power — our political leaders, the chairmen and heads of departments in universities and corporations, the generals of our armies — to understand the error of that description. As Churchill once remarked, the young do not understand either the craftiness or the staying power of the old. Rather, the change is that in the modern era there are fewer specific stereotypes or role-expectations for the old.

This change may be seen in several dimensions. For example, it is no longer considered especially important for a man to "build an estate" for his children. Many men still do it, and advertising aims at creating or affirming such a norm, but in fact very few people view such a goal as other than a bit old-fashioned. Fathers who have money may set aside funds for their grandchildren, but this is simply a normal way of maintaining relations with their sons and daughters. Building an estate for a "family line" is not viewed as a goal for everyone. Instead, it is assumed that older people have a right to spend their money as they choose, within of course the limits of economic rationality. People may try to save for their own old age, and social support is given for that type of self-protection, rather than for starting a family fund. Similarly, people do not take seriously any longer the notion of a family property—a particular house and grounds. The family home is not given a name (as it may still be in England where the custom is partly supported by real estate pressures), and there is continuity of ownership. Families are not associated with particular properties and no one supposes that there is any point in attempting to create such an association.

Norms do not state that older people should sit on the front porch in their rocking chairs, but neither are they expected to ride to hounds. The fact is that the specific social definitions of what is proper behavior for an elderly person have become diffuse, poorly supported, and highly individual. The kinds of costumes that elderly men may wear in a resort area now would shock their grandparents. The old may still wear sober and sedate clothing, if they wish, but they may also wear youthful styles and attempt almost any range of physical activity that suits them. On the one hand, they are perhaps less protected by the young, but on the other, they are less pushed into stereotypical behavior appropriate to the physically or socially incompetent. If an elderly man is willing to try water-skiing he is applauded and his children are no longer embarrassed—except insofar as some children will always be a bit embarrassed by any sign of life from their older parents.

It is evident that such differences in the position of the elderly from one society to another and in the social definitions of appropriate behavior, are intimately linked with family patterns. It is difficult to create a specific family role for an elderly couple if, upon retirement, they simply move from their former neighborhood to Florida or California and establish a new social life. If the older generation has not been devoting much of its time, energy, or attention to building a family estate and has urged the children to establish themselves in life independently, it cannot come as a great surprise that the younger people do not expect either to live with their parents or to have their parents live with them. And indeed, public opinion surveys typically show that a majority of the public believes that the old should own their own home and keep their own households. For an elderly person to live with a child or relative is viewed by the American public as a very undesirable situation.[89]

It should also not come as a surprise that farmers, who have typically enjoyed far more freedom of decision, are more likely than other people to

[89] Mathilda W. Riley and Anne Foner, eds., *Aging and Society,* Vol. I, p. 182.

oppose the idea of moving in with their grown children. In harmony with this pattern is the growing tendency for old people to maintain their own household or to live with nonrelatives, and also a decline in the percentage of parents maintaining a household in which adult offspring live.

The increasing concern of Western societies with "the problem of the aged" does not necessarily have its roots in a growing awareness that the elderly population has been steadily increasing. It is true that the percentage of people 65 years of age and over has more than doubled since 1900, but few people now living were social observers in 1900, and very few people are aware that there are more older people now than 50 years ago. Indeed if all respondents in population surveys were to rely only upon their own memories, they would probably remember their childhood as being far more filled with elderly people than is their adulthood.

Western societies do have a higher percentage of the elderly, simply because more people live to be old once infant mortality has been reduced. Of course, this higher percentage does create a greater economic burden for a nation. And all Western nations have some type of social security plan for the aged, simply because relatives and children can no longer be counted upon to take care of older people. Is this evidence of a major change in family patterns?

It is the decline of the farm, rather than a decrease in concern about aged relatives, that has created this family-linked problem. In both hunting and agricultural societies the elderly remain useful. As long as they are not physically helpless, they can prepare skins or help in cooking or gathering wood for fires; if they are too weak to break new soil, they can at least help with the harvest or in the preservation of food. They can help in many small tasks that do not require great energy or strength. Moreover, it is only recently in the history of any society that people typically "retire," because in effect they are forced out of jobs once they reach a certain age. Thus there is not only a larger number of older people, but for the first time they have been left without essential tasks to perform. Moreover, one more mouth to feed on a farm is not usually a great burden. It becomes a larger burden when all the commodities and services of modern living must be purchased. Thus the increasing reluctance on the part of the younger generation to care for the elderly is in part based on their decreasing ability to do so adequately.

Finally, of course, with the advent of popular suffrage, the elderly have come to represent a substantial bloc of votes, which can be captured by developing plans for social security and medical service. The affluence of modern industrial society yields a large enough economic surplus to implement such programs. Even the United States, which has typically lagged far behind other developed nations in this respect, has created an array of programs designed, in effect, to take the burden of caring for the aged from individual families. Although the amounts are small and are tied to both previous and current earnings, at least at the lower income levels, an elderly person or couple may be able to contribute substantially to the family income through their pension.

We have commented more about the relations between elderly parents and grown children than the relations between elderly spouses, and in fact three-fourths of those over 65 years of age have a living child and almost 70 percent have grandchildren. Forty percent of these people even have great grandchildren. Moreover, some 60 percent either live in the same household as their children or are no more than ten minutes' journey from them, so that this relationship does loom large in the life of older people.

However, it should be kept in mind that most people over 65 years of age are married: 80 percent of the males in the 65–69 age bracket and 59 percent of the females. Since both sexes tend to live longer now than they have in the past, more husbands and wives have survived together through the middle years. Thus a greater number of elderly couples now exist. Relatively little research has been done on the relations of elderly people with their spouses, however; most research has focused on their relations with living adult children or on the general problems of living arrangements. Perhaps this neglect is in part a function of the pragmatic or ameliorative impulse in American sociology, although it is difficult to imagine any kind of counseling service or therapy that could help the interspousal relations of elderly people if they continue to be unhappy.

Earlier studies on marital adjustment suggest that, in general, as age approaches there is a decline in marital adjustment, not in the sense of increasingly sharp and bitter exchanges, but in the sense of a lesser emotional attachment to other people. It is perhaps erroneous to suppose that old people "accept" the traits they have always disliked in their spouses in the deep sense of coming to feel ultimately that they are really to be valued, but it is likely that they fight less about such traits and focus far more of their affect on their own adjustment to the day-to-day problems of living.

One change is occurring in husband-wife relations that will create tensions for a while, though perhaps ultimately these will lead to better, more satisfactory life patterns. Until recently, it is safe to say that most people, but especially wives, took it for granted that with the menopause they would decrease or even cease entirely their sexual activities. This pattern had the approval of the younger generation to whom sexual activities among older people seemed slightly ridiculous or obscene. In addition, the generally puritanical bent of Western society, which disapproved of sexual activities for pleasure alone, especially for women, made postmenopausal sex seem vaguely wrong. We do not know yet whether this pattern, which emphasized a greater decline in sexual activity for women than for men, increased the tension between husbands and wives.

In the past, studies of marital adjustment have suggested that far more men objected to a lack of sexual activity than women, and since the decline in sexual interest was greater among women, it may well be that even today there is greater tension between husbands and wives from this source in the postmenopausal years than at earlier stages of the marriage. On the other hand, an increasing number of studies have shown that sexual desire does not decrease sharply for either men or women, if we focus only on the biological factors. In the past, of course, the social factors have been predominant. Since these studies will be given increasing credence, and both laymen and professional counselors will approve continuing sexual activity as long as both husband and wife enjoy it, we can suppose that in the future more of the elderly will enjoy this aspect of their lives. In the meantime, as some spouses will be persuaded while their mates may not be, there may be an increasing amount of sexual tension for another decade or so.

This change may also herald an alteration in the pattern of marriage in the future. Women live longer than men; indeed the mortality rate for women is lower in every age group. Of course, one consequence is that there are more widows than widowers and thus a larger pool of "available" women. On the other hand, a man of 65 years of age is viewed as far more eligible for marriage than a woman of 65. Thus, as noted above, most men in the 65–69 age bracket are married, and 70 percent of all elderly men are married, while a much smaller percentage of elderly women are married. The pattern of widows not marrying has been socially supported in most Western countries. However, as women come to be less stereotyped, and less restricted by their role-obligations as homemakers and mothers, a high percentage of them may come to be viewed as sexually attractive even in their later years. This trend will be emphasized by the increasing awareness that older women are sexually responsive; thus a larger percentage of widows may remarry in the future than at present.

11

Work and Automation: Problems and Prospects

ROBERT S. WEISS, EDWIN HARWOOD, and DAVID RIESMAN *

Though it is claimed that the Germans and Swiss work harder than we Americans, it is doubtful that there are any other people on earth to whom work is as important to a man's sense of self.[1] Problems arise for us when work has too little meaning, when it conflicts with other areas of our lives, when there is too little work for us, or when the rewards of work are insufficient or its conditions oppressive. In a technologically dynamic economy like ours, in which jobs may change rapidly in content or gradually disappear, there are the additional problems of dislocation and unemployment. These problems arise from a number of causes, including automation, changes in demand for goods and services, and abandonment by industry of people in declining regions such as Appalachia and the western mining towns.

---

* We would like to acknowledge the very expert statistical assistance of Mrs. Claire C. Hodge, U. S. Bureau of Labor Statistics, and also the help provided by Miss Barbara Podratz, Mrs. Alana Whitlow, and Mr. Mun-woong Lee.

[1] It is true that in the pre-Civil War South, slavery put a curse on work in the plantation areas, but even so the gentlemanly code of the planter could never completely subdue the effect of Protestantism in making idleness suspect. In a mobile, democratic society people cannot readily coast on ancestral inheritance, and we have been a society which is inhospitable to playboys and which, even in its response to the dropouts from its schools or jobs, gives its respect to those who by hard work eventually come to realize themselves.

A generation ago, widespread unemployment due to economic recessions was the main concern of all industrial societies. Though unemployment is severely damaging to whoever experiences it, we will deal with it primarily in terms of its concentration within limited groups and occupations, and its relationship to automation and technological change. Strikes and lockouts also have a smaller place here than they would have had a generation ago, not because we have solved the problem of industrial conflict, but because we have learned to live with strikes, to reduce their violence, to settle by government mediation those that might damage the economy, and even at times to manipulate them as part of the process of balancing production and consumption. Yet in truth it is still possible for a prolonged strike in a critical industry to do serious damage to the workers, the industry, the public, and the economy. Here, as elsewhere, we have not so much solved the problem as learned to reduce some of its dangers and to live with those that remain.

It was once debated whether human beings naturally wanted to work and what the incentives needed to drive men to work would be if hunger and plain necessity were eliminated. Even in industrial societies, until recently, a large minority of the work force labored for a bare subsistence. Today we better understand our needs and recognize that we will continue to work, even when subsistence is not an issue, so long as we can find in our job a basis for self-esteem. Today the problem of giving workers the material incentives needed to compel effort is less important than that of learning how to make work more meaningful or how to enable men forced into involuntary idleness by early retirement or technological change to continue to contribute to society. Because of increased confidence that society offers both assured subsistence and almost unlimited opportunity for choice, the desire for self-realization seems to have increased. Today the young college graduate may ponder whether a managerial job will present him with as much challenge as did his undergraduate research project, whereas a generation ago he might have been much more interested in the job's chances for advancement.

The old problems of industrialization—job-related accidents and disease, dismally low wages, and sweatshop exploitation—have receded significantly thanks to strong unions and government regulations, which have introduced safety standards, accident and unemployment insurance, minimum wage laws, and the like. But the problems have not disappeared entirely. Many migrant agricultural laborers still lead a kind of life not too different from that of the Okies in John Steinbeck's *Grapes of Wrath*. And if violence is no longer an expected part of a strike, neither is it altogether unknown. Though no present government administration could tolerate the high unemployment levels caused by depressions 30 or more years ago, marginal wages and unemployment are still the lot of many Americans. Fifty years ago the government probably had little choice but to tolerate these ills. The economy produced too little money and the schools too few experts to deal with these problems, and the victims had too little political leverage. We have come some distance since then, but, as we shall suggest, we still have a way to go.

THE AMERICAN LABOR FORCE

From the Current Population Survey, undertaken monthly by the Bureau of the Census in collaboration with the Bureau of Labor Statistics, we can learn how many Americans hold jobs and how many do not. We can also learn how many Americans had full-time or part-time jobs, and whether those working part-time do so by choice or because their employers are unable to keep them fully employed. The CPS provides additional data, including breakdowns on the distribution of workers by type of job and industry.[2]

This monthly survey is our best source of current information on unemployment. If a person is in the labor force, he is classified by the CPS as either (1) holding a job during the week of interview (in which case he is "employed") or (2) having made specific efforts to find work during the four weeks preceding the survey and available to work during the week of the survey (in which case he is "unemployed"). Since definitions must simplify in order to make survey data manageable, some persons who have no serious economic problems are counted "unemployed," whereas others who do are not. Thus the middle-class housewife who reports that she is looking for just the right part-time secretarial job, one not too far from home and with hours that will allow her to drive her children to and from school, will be counted unemployed until she finds the job. By contrast, a discouraged Appalachian white or an unskilled southern black who has made no effort to look for a job because he believes no work exists will not be counted unemployed: He is not in the labor force.

Table 1 shows the extent to which age, sex, and color make a difference in the likelihood of holding a job or being out of one.

The table reveals that in 1968, black teen-age females had the highest unemployment rate. White males between 35 and 44 years of age had the lowest unemployment rate (1.4 percent). Unemployment rates drop sharply for both sexes and both color groups at age 20 and again at age 25. By this time most men have left school and must seek full-time work to support

---

[2] The CPS findings appear in the monthly U. S. Bureau of Labor Statistics publication, *Employment and Earnings.*

families, and most women have become housewives. Two other generalizations stand out clearly: *First,* except for older black men, both white and black males suffer less unemployment than their female counterparts; *second,* blacks have an average unemployment rate approximately twice that for whites, and this imbalance holds for most of the specific age-sex comparisons.

Table 1 does not give the reasons for the failure of persons "not in the

TABLE 1

Employment Status of the Civilian Noninstitutional Population [a] (1968)

| | Persons in the Labor Force | | | | Percentage of the Population in the Labor Force | |
| | Number in Thousands | | Percentage Unemployed | | | |
Age	White	Blacks and Other Races	White	Blacks and Other Races	White	Blacks and Other Races
			Men			
16 years and over	44,554	4,979	2.6	5.6	80	78
16–19	3,236	445	10.1	22.1	56	50
20–24	4,432	639	4.6	8.3	82	85
25–34	9,477	1,133	1.7	3.8	97	95
35–44	9,661	1,064	1.4	2.9	98	93
45–54	9,340	927	1.5	2.5	95	90
55–64	6,427	598	1.7	3.6	85	80
65+	1,980	174	2.8	4.0	27	27
			Women			
16 years and over	25,424	3,780	4.3	8.3	41	49
16–19	2,603	335	12.1	28.8	43	35
20–24	3,677	558	5.9	12.3	54	58
25–34	4,263	835	3.9	8.4	41	57
35–44	5,021	845	3.1	5.0	48	59
45–54	5,416	715	2.3	3.2	52	60
55–64	3,541	397	2.1	2.8	42	47
65+	903	96	2.7	2.4	9	12

Source: U. S. Bureau of Labor Statistics, *Employment and Earnings* (January, 1969), adapted from Tables A-1 and A-2, pp. 113–16. The percentages in the last column on the right have been rounded off.
[a] In the United States 92 percent of all nonwhites are blacks; on a national level, the labor force characteristics of blacks are adequately represented by statistics on "blacks and other races."

labor force" to look for jobs, though such data are reported in the Bureau of Labor Statistics' *Employment and Earnings,* where we find what we might suspect: (1) With increasing age, more persons leave the labor force because of poor health and retirement; (2) most teenagers are not in the labor force because they still attend school; and (3) after age 20 most adult women do not seek work because of housekeeping duties at home.

Over the past 70 years, the number of women in the labor force has increased significantly. In 1900 only 20 percent of all women worked, whereas over 40 percent are at work today. The proportion of men in the labor force has declined slightly over the same period. More men go to school and those who go stay longer; older men retire earlier because of Social Security, company pension plans, and retirement rules that require men to leave their work at some arbitrary age whether they want to or not. Though women also stay longer in school, and though as mothers they must meet the rising expectations of proper child care, their time has been partially freed from household drudgery by labor-saving kitchen appliances, precooked foods, perma-press clothing, diaper services, and day-care nurseries; thus even if women are not wholly free for an eight-hour day, they are able to take part-time sales and service jobs. Also the trend toward smaller households means fewer persons to cook, sew, and launder for, and with fewer children, spaced closer together in age, the modern woman finds herself with many more productive years remaining after the last child leaves home. If she has received college training, as many more women have been doing, she can return either part-time or full-time to professional work.[3]

Though the black male is somewhat less likely to be in the labor force than the white male, the participation rate is roughly similar for both groups as each moves through the life cycle. By contrast, black women have higher labor force participation rates than white women, and their rates of participation by age differ. As Table 1 suggests, white females tend to leave work between ages 25 and 44 to attend to their families, to reenter in force only later when their children are grown. Black women, on the other hand, sustain a higher rate of participation at all but the youngest ages, 16 to 19.

The data contradict the still widely held belief that black women fare better in the urban labor market than black men. As Table 1 indicates, black males have less unemployment than black females and are more actively involved in the labor force. This is true even in the very poor neighborhoods of the large cities surveyed by the government's new Urban Employ-

---

[3] For a discussion of the increased labor force participation of women, see Clarence D. Long, *The Labor Force Under Changing Income and Employment* (Princeton, N. J.: Princeton University Press, 1958), pp. 8–30.

ment Survey. Between 1968 and 1969 the survey found that among blacks, as among whites, males earned substantially more than females and had less unemployment.[4]

Trends in Jobs

A staggering number of different occupations exist in a mature industrial society. According to the Bureau of the Census' *Dictionary of Occupational Titles* (1965), our society has organized 22,000 different occupations into its complex network of economic exchange. These occupations may not all be found in every large American city, but probably most would be represented by at least a few workers in the largest cities, and common jobs like factory assembler and delivery and route salesman would be represented by many hundreds of workers in all cities. Of course there are differences among cities: New York had proportionately more of the country's 34,000 actors and entertainers in 1969, and many more of the nation's 49,000 authors, than neighboring Newark; yet it probably had very few of the nation's 500 to 1000 midwives (returned in the 1960 census) who no doubt were to be found where doctors were not.[5]

With so complex a division of labor it would be hard to find a human aptitude that is not put into play by some job somewhere. Though nostalgia for the past still weighs heavily in much contemporary criticism of the specialization an industrial society exacts, few can deny the greatly expanded range of opportunity open to American workers in relation to what men living in the peasant societies of the past or the present could expect.

It may be, as one critic claims, that the man who can say, "I am a peasant," has a stable job identity not shared by the individual who can say only, "I am an electroencephalograph technician."[6] However, such stability is pos-

---

[4] In two cities, Detroit and Houston, the weekly earnings of black males were twice those of females. In New York and Chicago, the wage differentials were less but still substantial. U. S. Bureau of Labor Statistics, *Employment Situation in Poverty Areas of Six Cities, July 1968–June 1969,* Report No. 370 (October, 1969), p. 19.

[5] Current Population Survey, 1969 annual averages.

[6] Peter L. Berger, "Some General Observations on the Problem of Work," in Peter L. Berger, ed., *The Human Shape of Work* (New York: Macmillan, 1964), pp. 214–16. We have too few records to know for sure what verdict the medieval peasant would have returned on the modern critic's brief. When not totally exhausted trying to keep abreast of the seasonal pace set by nature, which gave rest only when no work could be done, most had only an occasional fair, religious drama, or the foibles of their neighbors as sources of amusement.

sible only on the condition that there is little economic growth and little rise in living standards of the kind that regularly allows modern men to choose among jobs and to get the education needed for more creative skills. Moreover, it is doubtful that most technical jobs are so narrow and confining as this school of thought implies. Though specialization increases the number of jobs in our society, it does not necessarily decrease job complexity. Each specialized job can acquire a large variety of very complex tasks. Deadening routine, as Walker and Guest found in their study of automobile assemblers, is a part of many semiskilled factory jobs, but over the past century many engineering and technician jobs have been created midway between the assembly line and management. The technician, for example, helps with the drafting, design, construction, and testing of sophisticated machinery, and though he may lack the independence of the preindustrial artisan, he does retain much of the artisan's practical virtuosity, combining an esoteric knowledge of engineering principles with craft skills.[7] Many young men who formerly would have followed their fathers into the plant to work on the line now enter a community college or enroll in evening extension courses for two to four years' study that afterward will allow them to work in the research and development division of a major corporation. Electronic technicians, for example, have been one of the fastest growing occupational groups since World War II. In 1969, they numbered 164,000 and were projected to increase to almost one-half million by 1975.[8]

What power there is in the critic's charge that specialization degrades work by narrowing the content of jobs lies in the past history of industrialization, when most factories and much construction work needed only unskilled laborers and line or bench workers whose jobs were limited to a few simple and repetitive operations. Today, the backbreaking drudgery of much unskilled labor and the endless repetitiveness of many mass production jobs have been eliminated in some plants by the mechanization of material handling, and may be a fading characteristic of the work scene. Some of the criticism of the nature of work in the modern world is based on a highly romanticized view of alternatives. Work in agricultural societies is as hard, as repetitive, as little rewarding intellectually, as any factory work, and in addition members of these societies more often face the hazards of insufficient food and inadequate medicine.

---

[7] For information on the assembly line, see Charles R. Walker and Robert H. Guest, *The Man on the Assembly Line* (Cambridge, Mass.: Harvard University Press, 1952). For the technician, see William M. Evan, "On the Margin—The Engineering Technician," in Peter L. Berger, ed., *The Human Shape of Work.*

[8] See Leonard A. Lecht, *Manpower Needs for National Goals in the 1970's* (New York: Praeger, 1969), Table B-5, p. 150.

Because we know only a small fraction of the many types of jobs performed in our society, we tend to lump together many of the thousands of jobs represented in a single giant corporation, although the workers themselves make fierce distinctions among them. Factory studies have shown that workers are highly sensitive about small differences in pay and job content, even though from the outsider's point of view they all appear to occupy the same relative occupational status. For example, the furnacemen and smeltermen of an iron plant and the machine operators of a fabricating plant are all classified as semiskilled, blue-collar workers, but the status and pay differences between these jobs are of great importance to the men who hold them.[9]

The census, faced with the task of devising some way of grouping occupations to permit a manageable social accounting, emerged with 11 major occupational groupings (see Table 2). Verbal and conceptual skills tend to be more highly rewarded than manual skills; however, the census occupational groupings afford only a rough ranking of pay and prestige because of the considerable overlap both within and between the 11 categories. Some skilled craftsmen earn more than college-educated engineers and accountants just starting out. Many factory workers earn more than professionals. For example, in 1959 foremen in durable goods manufacture had a higher median income as a group than a majority of the occupations listed in the professional and technical category.

There is a wide range of incomes within each occupational category. For example, self-employed physicians and surgeons, who earned the highest median income in 1969 ($24,512), are included in the "professional, technical, and kindred" category along with primary and secondary school teachers whose median salary for 1969 was $8,241.[10] The "sales" category includes the department store clerk earning $2.00 an hour and the regional sales representative of a large firm earning $25,000 per year. The range across the labor force as a whole is enormous. The very top executives in the largest firms seldom earn less than six-figure salaries. Many service workers and most unskilled laborers and farm workers earn less than the poverty-level income of a few thousand dollars.

Table 2 compares the jobs men and women held in 1968. Though women are overrepresented in white-collar jobs, they are more apt to be office workers than managers and officials. They are underrepresented not only

---

[9] Often conflicts arise when management introduces new machinery that upsets previously established pay and status differences. See William Foote Whyte, *Money and Motivation* (New York: Harper, 1955), pp. 68–80.

[10] U. S. Bureau of the Census, *Current Population Reports,* Series P-60, No. 66 (December 23, 1969), Table 43, p. 103.

TABLE 2

Employed Persons (16 Years of Age and Over) by Major Occupation
Group and Sex
(1968 Annual Average)

	Percentage in labor force	
	Males	Females
1 Professionals and technical workers (accountants, authors, clergymen, engineers, lawyers, physicians, schoolteachers).	13.4	13.9
2 Managers, officials, and proprietors (government inspectors, corporation executives, retail tradesmen).	13.6	4.5
3 Clerical workers (bookkeepers, cashiers, secretaries, telephone operators).	7.1	33.8
4 Sales workers (insurance brokers, sales clerks).	5.7	6.9
5 Craftsmen and foremen (bankers, carpenters, machinists, plumbers, tool and die makers).	20.2	1.1
6 Operatives (factory assemblers, bus drivers, textile spinners, deliverymen, dry-cleaning operatives).	20.1	15.3
7 Nonfarm laborers (fishermen, stevedores, lumbermen).	7.1	0.5
8 Private household workers (cooks, ladies' maids, servants).	0.1	6.1
9 Other service workers (janitors, hairdressers, waiters, policemen, barbers).	6.8	15.8
10 Farmers and farm managers	3.8	0.3
11 Farm laborers and foremen	2.1	1.8
Total	**100.0**	**100.0**

Source: U. S. Bureau of Labor Statistics, *Employment and Earnings*, Vol. 16 (January, 1969), adapted from Table A-17, p. 125.

among the managers but also in heavy manual work (nonfarm laborers), in farming, in the skilled crafts, and in supervisory posts in production. In short, though women are spared the heaviest manual labor, they tend to be order-takers rather than order-givers in the economy.

Women earn appreciably less than men. Men do the heavy manual labor in our society, and they are compensated with higher pay. Earth moving, truck driving, durable goods assembly, and auto repair earn more than the clerical jobs in the front office. Table 2 shows that a high percentage of women are operatives, but they are more likely than men to be working in laundry and dry-cleaning establishments or in nondurable goods fabrication (food processing, textile, and apparel industries), which pay less than durable goods industries, such as automobile and appliance manufacturing. Almost all private household workers are women, and this work pays the least of all nonfarm occupations. And not only are women more likely to be hired for

TABLE 3

Some Major Occupations of Men and Women Listed
as "Professional, Technical, and Kindred"
Experienced Civilian Labor Force, April 1960

	Men	Women
	(in thousands)	
All professional, technical and kindred workers [a]	4,543	2,793
Engineers, technical	864	7
Clergymen	197	5
Lawyers and Judges	206	8
Draftsmen	206	12
Physicians and Surgeons	214	16
Accountants and Auditors	396	80
Nurses, except student	15	577
Teachers, except college	478	1,206

Source: U. S. Bureau of the Census, *Census of Population: 1960,* Vol. 1, Part 1, United States Summary, Table 201. Detailed Occupations of the Experienced Civilian Labor Force, by Sex, for the United States: 1960 and 1950, pp. 1–522.
[a] Only those professions in which a combined total of 200,000 men and women reported membership are listed in this table.

work that pays less well; they are also likely to be paid less than men for similar work, although subtle differences in job definition may make discrimination difficult to demonstrate.

The decennial *Census of Population* provides a more detailed occupational breakdown, which shows how particular occupations can be defined as either man's work or woman's work within each of the 11 major categories. Table 3 shows that within the professional and technical category jobs like medicine and engineering fall mostly to males, whereas jobs like teaching and nursing are held for the most part by women. In 1960, women constituted fewer than one percent of all engineers and 10 percent of all physicians but over 97 percent of all nurses and 70 percent of all primary and secondary school teachers. These differences are almost unchanged from 1950, and we believe that they will continue to be displayed in the 1970 census, except for some increase in the proportion of men teaching in both primary and secondary schools.

Table 4 shows the difference color makes in the distribution of jobs. In 1968, almost one-half the white labor force held white-collar jobs, as compared to only one-quarter of all black workers. Blacks were much more likely to be working in low-paying domestic and laboring jobs. Though heavily concentrated in blue-collar occupations, they had considerably fewer skilled craftsmen and foremen in comparison with the white labor force.

Robert S. Weiss, Edwin Harwood, and David Riesman **555**

TABLE 4

Employed Persons (16 Years of Age and Older)
by Major Occupation
Group and Race
(1968 Annual Average)

		Percentage in labor force	
		Whites	Blacks and Other Races
Professional and technical		14.3	7.8
Managers, officials, and proprietors		11.1	2.8
Clerical workers		17.5	11.8
Sales workers		6.6	1.9
Craftsmen and foremen		13.8	8.0
Operatives		17.7	23.6
Nonfarm laborers		4.0	10.7
Private household workers		1.4	9.5
Other service workers		9.0	18.8
Farmers and farm managers		2.7	1.2
Farm laborers and foremen		1.8	3.7
	Total	**100.0**	**100.0**

Source: U. S. Bureau of Labor Statistics, *Employment and Earnings,* Vol. 16 (January, 1969), adapted from Table A-17, p. 125.

Yet the 1960's show a trend toward better opportunities for younger blacks. In 1967 for the first time more blacks were in the better paying top six of the eleven occupational groups ("operatives" and above) than were in laboring, services, and farm work.[11]

It was argued in the early 1960's that automation would eliminate many semiskilled manual and office jobs that could be filled by black workers, with the consequence that blacks would face a declining market for their labor.[12] However, this prediction did not take into account the stimulus to production of rising demands for durable consumer goods and of an expanded land war in Asia, or the potential for change still present in our society even in its

---

[11] Between 1957 and 1967, there were 173,000 fewer black domestics and 100,000 fewer black laborers, although the number of blacks in the labor force increased from under six and one-half million to over eight million workers. See Claire C. Hodge, "The Negro Job Situation: Has It Improved?" Special Labor Force Report No. 102 (U. S. Bureau of Labor Statistics, January, 1969). For a balanced account of black progress in jobs and income since 1940, see Ben Wattenberg and Richard Scammon, *This USA* (Garden City, N. Y.: Doubleday, 1965), pp. 277–93.

[12] See, for example, Kenneth B. Clark, *Dark Ghetto: Dilemmas of Social Power* (New York: Harper, 1965), p. 36.

more sclerotic industrial sectors. In fact, what happened in the 1960's was that the number of black workers more than doubled in clerical jobs and tripled in the health professions, though in each case blacks were represented disproportionately in lower-level positions, becoming, for example, medical technicians more often than physicians. Improvement appeared in other occupational categories: Whereas in 1957 black laborers outnumbered black craftsmen almost three to one, by 1967 they were only one and one-half times as numerous as craftsmen.

The most recent statistics on job holding suggest a further closing of the gap between whites and blacks. Between 1967 and 1969 the number of black craftsmen and foremen increased by 92,000, and though a greater number of whites (255,000) were also entering these occupations, the proportion of those in the occupation who were black went up to 8 percent, whereas ten years earlier it had been less than 5 percent. If the black share of growth in the skilled blue-collar occupations continues at the present rate, eventually blacks will achieve parity—that is, a proportion in the crafts equal to their proportion in the labor force. Parity would require that about 11 percent of those in the occupational category be black.[13] There are understandable black demands for "parity now," but these demands must confront the obdurate demographic patterns and social injustices of the past. Before the gains of the younger and better-trained black workers can fully register in our accounting systems, the older, less well-trained men must retire from the labor force.[14] In addition, the important issue is not parity but rather an end to handicaps to individual mobility based on discrimination and past disadvantage. Different groups in our population—not only racial or ethnic groups but also sex and regional groups—may well have different interests and different representation in the labor force. Parity is at best an imperfect indicator of how far we have yet to go to achieve equality of opportunity.[15]

The American occupational structure has changed radically over the past 100 years as the nation moved from a predominantly agrarian society to an industrial one. Close to 40 percent of the working population worked on

---

[13] Data on craftsmen for 1969 are based on Current Population Survey findings for the first six months of the year. They were made available by the courtesy of the U. S. Bureau of Labor Statistics.

[14] As Ben Wattenberg and Richard Scammon point out in *This USA,* pp. 284–95.

[15] However, Walter Metzger argues that many blacks and their white supporters do not want simply equality of opportunity, and especially not if it can only be achieved in a slow-motion way; rather they want equality of outcomes, for the group rather than for the individual, sometimes using past deprivations as justification for the disruptions this would require. See his "The Crisis of Academic Authority," *Daedalus,* Vol. 99 (Summer, 1970), pp. 568–608.

farms in 1900, but by 1960 only 6 percent of the labor force were farmers or farm laborers.[16] The mechanization of farms – the installation of machinery for plowing, harvesting, and handling crops – scientific soil analysis, and the use of intensive fertilizers and scientific breeding rationalized farming and made it possible to produce more crops with fewer workers. Seemingly independent farmers were supplied by the government with a host of ancillary services, ranging from architectural advice on the building of barns to helicopters for the spraying of crops. As a result, a great part of the working population was no longer needed on the farm and turned to the new industries of the cities. But there too change took place. Mechanization increased the productivity of workers, thus allowing a larger proportion of the labor force to enter occupations other than manufacturing. By 1956, a majority of all American workers were either in white-collar or in service occupations.

Some social analysts have spoken of a postindustrial society in which a high standard of living will allow workers to spend more of their income on a variety of personal and professional services. The white-collar industries, such as banking, health, education, insurance, and government, are the fastest growing sectors, and professional, clerical, and service workers (private household workers excepted) are increasing in number at a much faster rate than blue-collar workers. In 1968 white-collar occupations accounted for over 80 percent of the total increase in employment in that year. At the same time, unskilled laborers declined not just as a proportion of the labor force but in absolute numbers as well.

What effect automation will have on our job mix is still a matter of debate. Not long ago many people believed that advanced technology would raise the educational and skill requirements of workers in all sectors of the economy. However, today most labor force experts believe that the high unemployment experienced by factory workers during the late 1950's was due not to the advent of automatic machinery but to inadequate aggregate demand for manufactured goods. It is possible that individual manufacturing corporations did introduce technological improvements that changed their requirements for semiskilled production workers, but in the aggregate automation did not appear to have a uniform effect on either raising or lowering skill requirements.[17] When aggregate demand for manufactured goods picked up in the 1960's, blue-collar workers were once again in great

---

[16] Irene B. Taeuber, *Population Trends in the United States, 1900–1960*, Technical Paper No. 10 (U. S. Bureau of the Census, 1964), p. 375.

[17] See James R. Bright, *Automation and Management* (Boston: Harvard Graduate School of Business Administration, 1958), Chapter 12. See also Howard R. Bowen and Garth L. Mangum, *Automation and Economic Progress* (Englewood Cliffs, N. J.: Prentice-Hall, 1966), pp. 17, 72.

demand, and their numbers were the highest they had been in the nation's history, the World War II years excepted.

Table 5 supports this argument by showing how the proportion of production workers—those thought most subject to technological dislocation—has changed since 1920 relative to (1) all workers in the economy outside of agriculture (column 4) and (2) all manufacturing workers, which includes the managers, salesmen, clerical staff, engineers, and technicians of corporations as well as the blue-collar work force (column 5). Column 4 shows that over the past half-century factory production workers have declined in importance relative to *all* American workers, a fact that is consistent with what we know about the expansion of the white-collar industries: Once comprising close to one-third of the nonfarm labor force, they are now only slightly more than one-fifth. Only in 1943, the peak year of wartime production, was this trend reversed. But if within the plant blue-collar workers were being displaced by white-collar technicians and automated machinery, then column 5 should show a decline in their number as a percentage of all manufacturing workers as drastic as column 4. But in fact the decrease shown in column 5 is modest and suggests that factory production workers were holding their own, against technological changes that were assumed to be replacing them.

Now at the start of the 1970's we are in the midst of a new rise in unemployment, as an unfortunate side effect of government policy aimed at checking inflation. By reducing the ease with which money can be borrowed, the government has reduced industry's ability to expand, and this in turn has slowed production and commerce throughout the economy. In addition the government has limited the level of increase in its own spending, and actually cut expenses in the previously sacred area of defense as well as in more vulnerable areas such as support for research and for the development of impoverished urban areas. And so once again many in our labor force are unemployed, especially among those formerly in the government-supported aerospace industries, and among the young and unskilled who have always been marginal everywhere except in the armed forces.

While some economists in and out of the government have believed that depressions can be avoided by proper regulation of interest rates and of the money supply (while others have believed that only wage and price controls will hold back inflation and limit business cycles) it would seem that our understanding of our national economics is not nearly good enough for us to predict with assurance what outcomes will result from given policies. A national economy can be influenced by a variety of developments at home and abroad, and we may have become overconfident in recent years of our ability to control the cyclical unemployment of booms and busts.

In the centuries before the urban-industrial revolution, though unemployment existed, business cycles were slower and of longer duration, and

TABLE 5

Production Workers in Manufacturing as a Proportion of
All U. S. Workers on Nonagricultural Payrolls and of All
Payroll Workers in Manufacturing
(numbers in thousands)

Year	(1) All Workers on Non- agricultural Payrolls	(2) All Payroll Workers in Manu- facturing	(3) Production Workers on Manu- facturing Payrolls	(4) Proportion of All Workers (3) ÷ (1)	(5) Proportion of Workers in Manu- facturing (3) ÷ (2)
1920	27,350	10,658	8,652	0.32	0.81
1925	28,778	9,939	8,061	.28	.81
1930	29,424	9,562	7,464	.25	.78
1935	27,053	9,069	7,374	.27	.81
1940	32,376	10,985	8,940	.28	.81
1943	42,452	17,602	15,147	.37	.86
1945	40,394	15,524	13,009	.32	.83
1950	45,222	15,241	12,523	.28	.82
1955	50,675	16,882	13,288	.26	.79
1960	54,234	17,796	12,586	.23	.75
1965	60,832	18,062	13,434	.22	.74
1969	70,139	20,121	14,736	.21	.73

Source: U. S. Bureau of Labor Statistics, *Employment and Earnings Statistics for the United States 1909–1968,*
Bulletin No. 1312-6 (August, 1968), pp. 2, 47–48.

their impact on a predominantly rural population was doubtless less severe. The landless agricultural laborer was poor in good times and poorer in bad, but when no work existed he could fall back on a garden plot or on the mercy of the local squire. England's agricultural revolution, which began as early as the sixteenth century, substituted pasture for arable farming on many large estates (creating the "paradox of sheep eating men"), and consolidated small tenant holdings into larger, more efficiently operated farms.[18] This structural unemployment created many destitute cottagers, and led finally to the passage of the Elizabethan poor laws. Each county parish was assessed a tax to support its indigenous poor and thereby keep them off the roads. Later, as towns began to grow, workhouses — or houses of correction, as they were sometimes called — put vagabonds and other sturdy poor into prisonlike garb and locked quarters to work with no pay and no future.[19]

[18] R. H. Tawney, *The Agrarian Problem in the 16th Century* (London: Longmans, 1912), pp. 262–80. Considerably fewer hands were needed for pasture farming, which required only a few men and a few sheep dogs.

[19] These workhouses lasted well into the twentieth century. For a vivid description of how the poor were degraded, see George Orwell's autobiographical essay, *Down and Out in Paris and London* (New York: Harper and Brothers, 1933), pp. 196–204.

Today's lineal descendants of the poor laws and workhouses, programs like Aid to Dependent Children and the federal food stamp and manpower training programs, are more generous and humane than anything that preceded them, although they too need improvement. They are administered differently in the different regions of the country, generally to the disadvantage of locally disparaged groups; their level of benefits is often inadequate; and they are sometimes used as means for controlling deviant politics or life styles. However, a hundred years ago there was often no relief at all for many of the poor. When depression struck, the industrial worker queued first at the pawnshop and then at the breadline. If the government was moved to help at all, it did so less from motives of compassion than fear of civil commotions, such as the angry massed gatherings that caused food riots in the late 1800's in England. America's urban riots in the 1960's, described by Morris Janowitz as "commodity riots," show continuity with the past but also progress: Not food but color TV's and other durable consumers goods were the targets of ghetto frenzy.[20]

In the 1930's the Great Depression struck with such force that many educated middle-class people were affected along with the blue-collar workers, who generally suffer most from cyclical swings. In the worst year, 1933, thirteen million workers, or close to 25 percent of the civilian labor force, were unemployed. The Wall Street apple vendor with beaver cap may have been caricature, yet a large number of wealthy people suddenly found themselves penniless. New college graduates worried about what they might do. Not only was one-fourth of the working force without jobs, but whole occupations were unemployed: There were no buildings for architects or engineers to plan, and few citizens were affluent enough to hire a lawyer or a music teacher, or to send their children to a dentist. College-trained people took jobs as post office clerks, and for millions there were simply no jobs at all.[21]

---

[20] Morris Janowitz, *Social Control of Escalated Riots* (Chicago: University of Chicago Press, 1968), Center for Policy Study. Just as we have a rising standard of living, we might also be said to have a rising standard of poverty.

[21] One of the authors (D. R.), while a law student in the 1930's, decided to test the belief of his prosperous New England friends that the unemployed were lazy and that "anybody who wants to work can get a job." He naively took off in workman's clothes for Detroit and Chicago in search of a job. After tramping the streets and lining up at plants he caught nothing except the flu and the only job he could find was a very temporary one, helping a street vendor sell fruit. In a short spell in a federal transient shelter, hastily constructed in Detroit when local relief gave out, he encountered destitute though surprisingly undesperate men who had worked for years as electricians, pattern-makers, miners, or farmers, and who had left their families (whose snapshots they still carried in their pockets) to mingle with hobos in a wandering and desultory search for nonexistent work.

Because so many people saw unemployment as the personal failure of the unemployed individual, the Great Depression brought with it psychological as well as economic catastrophe. As the depression deepened, the Roosevelt administration sought to assess the impact of joblessness on family life and community participation. Researchers found that many unemployed men blamed themselves for a situation not of their making. They often turned their bitterness at job loss into hostility toward their wives and children. Their authority at home, based on their status as breadwinner, was threatened by their loss of income. As the wife of a former factory worker told a government researcher: "My husband never used to get upset at anything, but since the shutdown he's been hell on me and on the kids." [22]

After America entered World War II, first as an arsenal for the allies and then as a co-belligerent, industry's renewed need for workers rapidly absorbed the pool of unemployed. The millions of men taken from the civilian labor force to serve in the military were replaced by hundreds of thousands of wives, daughters, and sisters. The wartime lesson was not lost on the government. Heavy spending for guns could equally well stimulate demand for butter, and by sustaining the demand for workers it could check the devastating effects of the business cycle.

TECHNOLOGICAL CHANGE AND AUTOMATION

Most industrial workers — and most Americans in general — have ambivalent feelings about automation. It promises to rid our society of monotonous and physically exhausting work, but it is also felt to threaten jobs and earnings. When the United States Steel Corporation opened the first continuous seamless pipe mill in Ohio 20 years ago, workers who were transferred there expressed satisfaction that the backbreaking physical labor of the old mill had been eliminated and that the new mill was also safer, cleaner, and better illuminated. Yet they noted too that they were fewer in number and were working in a plant with potentially three to four times the productive capacity of the old mill. They feared the company might eventually find *their* jobs unnecessary, and that by overproducing they would make layoffs unavoidable.[23] Concern with job security explains this ambivalence, as it does the

---

[22] Richard C. Wilcock and Walter H. Franke, *Unwanted Workers* (New York: Free Press, 1963), p. 85. See also Mirra Komarovsky, *The Unemployed Man and His Family* (New York: Dryden Press, 1940).

[23] Charles R. Walker, *Toward the Automatic Factory* (New Haven, Conn.: Yale University Press, 1957), pp. 100–02.

practice, uncovered by industrial researchers among factory work groups, of setting informal quotas on their members' output despite management assurances that overproduction would not cost workers their jobs.[24]

As far as we know, the term "automation" was first uttered by a Ford Vice President, D. S. Harder, in 1946. He used it to describe the work-feeding and material-handling machinery that Ford had started using on the assembly line. While reviewing plans for a new plant, he advised:

> Let's see some more mechanical handling between these transfer machines. Give us some more of that automatic business. . . . Some more of that—that "automation." [25]

It took ten years for "automation" to become widely used both as promise and threat, suggesting production without people, although what was taking place in the factories was only a further extension of mechanical processes long known. In eighteenth-century London, beer manufacturers had installed steam engines to replace horsedriven milling and pump machines and then found that the engines were equally well suited to taking over some of the heavy laboring jobs such as cask cleansing, hoisting, and mashing.[26] Nevertheless ten years ago congressional and union concern treated automation as an entirely unprecedented threat to the livelihoods of workers, whereas in reality the displacements of the 1950's were continuous with past trends: for example, the displacement of agricultural workers by the large combine or, in the 1920's, unskilled material handlers by the crane and trolley.[27] In numerical terms, the really sizable dislocations have occurred among unskilled rather than semiskilled workers in agriculture, mining, fishing, forestry, and to some extent manufacturing. But this decline

---

[24] Other factors, such as the degree of trust between workers and management, also figure in worker resistance to incentive bonus schemes for overproducing and hostility to "rate busters." William Foote Whyte, *Pattern for Industrial Peace* (New York: Harper and Brothers, 1951), pp. 188–97.

[25] This story and quote were taken from James R. Bright, *Automation and Management,* pp. 4–5. The "automation" referred to was an overhead trolley conveyor that "carried the engine through assembly, paint, bake, test, repair, and storage and into shipping. All this material handling was done without manually operated transfers and without rehandling or trucking between these basic production areas." *Ibid.,* p. 62.

[26] Peter Mathias, "The Entrepreneur in Brewing, 1700–1830," *The Entrepreneur,* Annual Conference of the Economic History Society at Cambridge, England (April, 1957), p. 35.

[27] These and other examples of the impact of conventional mechanization are cited by Howard R. Bowen and Garth L. Mangum, *Automation and Economic Progress,* pp. 66–70.

in the proportion of unskilled workers in our labor force has been steady since the turn of the century.

Many observers of the industrial scene have been highly selective in their criticisms of automation, focusing on the most radical innovations of the present without considering the equally drastic changes that occurred in very short periods in the past. For example, electrification can be considered a form of automation. When electric motors replaced the belt, shaft, and steam engine they abolished much exhausting labor that had gone into the handling of fossil fuels used for industrial power as well as in households. And like most forms of automation, electrification is a "continuous process" requiring very little human intervention en route.

The labor force scholars A. J. Jaffe and Joseph Froomkin have noted that in all periods when unemployment seemed to increase significantly, concerned legislators, union leaders, and social analysts blamed technological innovations.[28] Taking the longer view of history this cannot possibly have been the case, since the labor force has grown and continues to grow very rapidly along with progressive increases in labor productivity due to advanced mechanization. These scholars argue that the relatively high unemployment rate of ten years ago was due to the rapid increase in the number of younger labor force entrants, which in turn was the result of the war baby boom and a slackening of consumer demand for manufactured goods, as well as shifts in defense procurement from such conventional armaments as tanks whose manufacture requires proportionately greater numbers of factory workers, to more technologically innovative "weapons systems," which require many more scientists, technicians, and skilled craftsmen.

In general, the level of employment seems to depend less on the processes by which goods are made than on the forms taken by government spending and the nature of consumer demand. It is to these latter issues that attention seems now to be turning, with the possibility that a shift in national resources toward the production of urban housing and the provision of urban

---

[28] The contributions to the controversy of ten years ago are too numerous to cite in detail here. A very strong statement of the extent to which automation threatens the job structure was offered by "The Ad Hoc Committee on the Triple Revolution" and appears in the U. S. Congress, House Committee on Education and Labor, *Report of the National Commission on Technology, Automation, and Economic Progress* (Washington, D. C.: U. S. Government Printing Office, 1964), pp. 125–35. More recent research supporting the skeptical position can be found in A. J. Jaffe and Joseph Froomkin, *Technology and Jobs* (New York: Praeger, 1968); Howard R. Bowen and Garth L. Mangum, *Automation and Economic Progress*; and Charles E. Silverman and the editors of *Fortune, The Myths of Automation* (New York: Harper, 1967).

transport, along with a retraining of people for new kinds of jobs, may prevent a serious recession. Yet it is far from clear how social consensus can be won for new goals to replace the now questionable ones of defense, space, and highway building.[29]

However, no matter how prosperous the economy, the individual firm will still face the problem of dislocation for workers as it introduces new labor-saving machinery in both office and factory production. Companies have responded to this problem in very different ways; some have taken it seriously and responsibly, while others either have considered it not their business or have felt they could do nothing about it. When Bell Telephone, for example, consolidated its exchanges, it gave operators in small towns the option of leaving the firm or of moving to the consolidated exchange in the city.[30] Many large corporations provide job retraining programs and severance pay for workers, as well as numerous alternative jobs to cushion the impact of technological change. Large corporations also often engineer and supply their own innovations and thus have adequate lead time to prepare their work force for change. Smaller firms, on the other hand, often lack the resources to ready their workers for major changes. Thus, we cannot say that worker anxiety over laborsaving devices is a will-o'-the-wisp, of no interest to unions or government.

Despite our argument that automation is in fundamental respects simply a continuation of a long-standing trend toward mechanization and electrification, there is one respect in which it differs: the perspective of the plant designer. Professor James Bright says:

> Since automaticity in both machinery and control is evolutionary, what new thing is happening in "automated" factories? At just what point is automation "different"? There is the evidence of history to say that it is not different. *The contribution of "automation" is not in a new technical concept, but in creating a new design attitude: a conscious effort to synthesize a total mechanized production system.*[31]

The most recent developments in automaticity can be classified in four groups: office automation, production line, numerical-control machines, and continuous-processing systems.

OFFICE AUTOMATION — Computers store and process information involved in record-keeping, billing, and mathematical computations. Now, for example,

---

[29] Leonard A. Lecht, *Manpower Needs for National Goals in the 1970's,* pp. 47–49.

[30] For a description of how Bell Telephone faced its conversion problems see U. S. Bureau of Labor Statistics, *Manpower Planning for Technological Change, 1968,* Bulletin No. 1574, p. 6.

[31] James R. Bright, *Automation and Management,* p. 18. Italics are ours.

a bank teller with dates and sums in a savings passbook can give the customer an instant accounting of the compound interest he has earned. In the telephone industry, fewer than one-half the long-distance calls require an operator's intervention; the drudgery of writing down on a sheet the numbers of both caller and receiver, the time and charges, has been assumed by machines, which manage information faster and more accurately. Computers have also taken on tasks that previously had only been haphazardly dealt with by front office staffs. For example, computers may monitor the stock of raw materials and the inventory of finished goods and so help manufacturers cut waste and storage costs.

PRODUCTION LINE — Assembly lines are consolidated by automatic-transfer and material-handling machinery. Parts are now moved not from one manual station to another but from one machine to another. The tools operating on the parts are automatically positioned. An early effort to achieve continuous nonmanual movement through a fabricating process was the A. O. Smith Corporation's automobile frame line, built in the early 1920's. The line turned out 10,000 frames a day (or about one every ten seconds), with about 552 operations performed on each frame during a one-and-one-half-hour cycle.[32] The same concept was applied in more advanced form 30 years later to automobile engine blocks.

NUMERICAL-CONTROL MACHINES — Punched tape codes are inserted into electronic control devices that guide metalworking cutting tools through the drilling, milling, boring, and turning of parts. These devices have replaced much of the work of skilled machinists, who formerly worked from blueprints while guiding machine tools by hand. Numerical control developed because of the need for greater precision in the manufacture of intricate parts for jet aircraft. Though it was believed the job of the skilled metalworker would revert to that of an operative who would merely insert the workpiece into the machine, place the tape in the control mechanism, and push a button, this apparently has not happened. A government study reports that many firms using numerical control retrained their machinists for the new job of "part programmer" because, while it called for new knowledge of servo-mechanisms, it still demanded the skilled machinist's knowledge of the feed and cutting speeds of machines and the various uses of cutting tools and fixtures, as well as the ability to interpret the engineering specifications on blueprints.[33]

---

[32] James R. Bright, *Automation and Management,* p. 14.
[33] U. S. Bureau of Labor Statistics, *Outlook for Numerical Control of Machine Tools,* Bulletin No. 1437 (March, 1965).

CONTINUOUS-PROCESSING SYSTEM—The continuous-processing system was first developed in oil and chemical industries. It represents the closest approximation to full automation today. At Humble Oil's Texas fields, the largest computer in American private industry regulates both the extraction of oil and its shipment to processing stations without human intervention. Should a serious breakdown occur late at night, the computer even knows which executives to alert by phone.

A *fully* automatic factory would require cybernetic devices capable not only of controlling the routine process but also of sensing deviations and making the pertinent corrections. The feedback, or closed-loop principle, as it is also called, is the function of discretion supplied by all humans in all jobs simply by virtue of having a highly developed nervous and sensory system as well as skilled training in the narrow sense. It is the reason that full automation—if it ever arrives—is a long way in the future.

Mechanization increases productivity because men lack the strength of machines and also the ability to supply the same kind and degree of constraints in each successive fabrication, which is what standardized precision fabrication demands. But machines have nowhere made men unnecessary, because men have a flexibility no robot can duplicate. Men are needed to service and repair machines, as shown by the increased numbers of maintenance personnel in automated plants. In addition, the cost of machinery that can detect unanticipated changes and correct its own operations in response is prohibitive for many manufacturing concerns.[34]

The best material on the relation between automation and jobs comes from case studies of individual firms. These studies show that automation has no uniform impact but varies depending on the firm and the type of automation introduced. In the baking industry, continuous mixing units and improved ovens that bake the product while it moves along a conveyor have reduced the number of skilled bakers, and automatic slicing and packaging machines have reduced the need for semiskilled operatives. However, the increased volume of bakery sales required more truck drivers, and more clerical and sales workers. Total employment in this industry rose sharply between 1950 and 1960. Semiskilled workers became a higher proportion of the total bakery work force than in 1950 simply because the loss of production workers inside the bakery was offset by the gain in truck drivers. On the other hand, advances in automaticity in petroleum and electrical power

---

[34] A. J. Jaffe and Joseph Froomkin state that "closed-loop" production processes requiring "no human intervention between the time raw material is inserted into the machine to the time the finished product is stacked or stored at the end of the line" is still rare. Only the oil industry comes close. *Technology and Jobs,* p. 18.

plants appear to have increased the proportion of skilled maintenance men relative to operatives (extensively in the former, less so in the latter).[35]

In the case of office automation, computerized bookkeeping and magnetic ink character recognition did reduce the need for bookkeepers and clerks. However, it created new semiskilled clerical jobs that could easily be learned in a short period: reader-sorter operators, check encoders, control clerks, and keypunch operators. Tellers, secretaries, typists, and professional workers were not affected by the changeover. We do not know what happened to the women displaced as clerks. Possibly some found openings as tellers, replacing the men who, as mentioned earlier, have been leaving clerical jobs.[36] As already noted, opportunities for clerical workers at all skill levels grew steadily during the 1960's. Women displaced by computers in one firm or industry may well have found jobs in other firms.

Advanced mechanization does change the climate of work for the semi-skilled worker. As Charles Walker found, workers in the old pipe mill were able to learn their new duties in the automatic mill in a relatively short period of time. Yet many workers found that though they were free of the physically tiring chores of the old factory, they were psychologically fatigued by having to constantly watch for machine breakdowns that could cause serious damage if unattended to. Interviews with the workers revealed that

> . . . many emphasized that they had more levers, buttons, positioners, gauges, etc., than on the old mills and hence "more to think about" and "more to worry about." . . .
> Not all . . . exercised *greater* skills. But with the exception of one or two anachronistic jobs, the new mill called for skills *different in kind:* skills of the head rather than of the hand, of the logician rather than the craftsman; of nerve rather than muscle; of the pilot rather than the worker; of the maintenance man rather than the operator.[37]

In both an automobile engine plant and an advanced electrical power plant, operatives felt their new jobs required more responsibility; in the former, because they had to watch the machines constantly to avoid costly mal-

---

[35] Examples of the diverse impact of automation are given by Howard R. Bowen and Garth L. Mangum, *Automation and Economic Progress,* p. 68. Also, F. C. Mann and L. R. Hoffman, *Automation and the Worker* (New York: Henry Holt, 1960), pp. 52–53. These researchers found only one-half as many workers were needed to operate the new electric power plant as were needed in the older plants serving the region they studied. Workers were not displaced, however, because increased growth in the region kept demand up, and the old plants continued in operation.

[36] U. S. Bureau of the Budget, *Occupational Trends, 1960–1975,* pp. 20–21.

[37] Charles R. Walker, *Toward the Automatic Factory,* pp. 31–32, 195.

functions; in the latter, because operatives who before had worked at only one station, a boiler or turbine, now had to learn the entire energy conversion process. Job enlargement and job rotation occurred because the new technology combined boilers, turbines, and electrical switching into integrated units.[38]

The research to date suggests that the job fragmentation associated with earlier phases of the industrial revolution may become less pronounced as machines come to be integrated into an electronically synchronized fabrication process. Maintenance workers increase their proportions in the work force, and even for many semiskilled operatives, "watching" and maintenance tend to replace routine, repetitive work. Maintenance workers have more diverse tasks and challenges and this is one reason that they express higher levels of job satisfaction in interviews. They are not apt to yell "hurrah" when the assembly line breaks down, as Charles R. Walker and Robert H. Guest observed automobile workers do in the plant they studied. We might expect an eventual end to the fatiguing pace and tension of keeping up with the conveyor belt on the line. At the same time, the higher cost of equipment demands more responsibility from the worker, and this is for some a gain but for others a new burden.

Science fiction writers have described a society in which work becomes so scarce that it has to be reserved for a privileged few, leaving to the rest of the population the task of consuming an enormous product turned out (in sorcerer's apprentice fashion) by the automatic industrial plant. Some serious scholars of technology have come close to predicting the actual elimination of work.[39] Such a prediction, however, makes a radical assumption: that computers can acquire the abilities of perception and judgment that people have, and can be able to exercise discretion in regard to novel and rapid environmental change. Against this thesis it can be argued that too many jobs deal with what Herbert Simon has called "rough terrain." [40] The rough terrain of work consists of rapidly changing conditions that demand a high degree of flexibility in discerning and acting upon new data. The

---

[38] William A. Faunce, "Automation and the Automobile Worker," in Sigmund Nosow and William H. Form, eds., *Man, Work and Society* (New York: Basic Books, 1962), pp. 69–72; F. C. Mann and L. R. Hoffman, *Automation and the Worker,* pp. 70–74.

[39] E. R. F. W. Crossman predicted in 1964 that by the middle of the twenty-first century, information-processing would be done almost entirely by mechanical means, making nearly all human labor unnecessary. "European Experience with the Changing Nature of Jobs due to Automation," *The Requirements of Automated Jobs,* North American Joint Conference, Paris (December 8–10, 1964), pp. 164–65.

[40] See Herbert A. Simon's engaging work, *The Shape of Automation* (New York: Harper, 1965).

principles of remote control have been applied for years to toys, missiles, jet aircraft, and more recently to automobiles crashed purposely to test safety devices. They have not been applied to caterpillar bulldozers, trucks, or private automobiles on the open road. The rapid disappearance of the private household worker is certainly creating the need for a technological innovation—call it the mechanical maid—that can get efficiently and quietly into all the corners of every type of dwelling, apply just the right pressures to the cleaning of china as opposed to pans, know where the stairs begin and end, and detect differences in surface textures so that rugs will be vacuumed but wood surfaces polished. Clearly it is unlikely that such an automated marvel will ever be developed.

America is far from moving into an era when work will be scarce. Today rising incomes seem to be creating a growing demand for personal services of all kinds, from hair-styling to psychiatry, and this sector cannot easily raise its labor productivity as in the manufacturing sector. The flourishing state of the professions also reflects the widespread affluence of our society; in many professions—not only medicine but also the apparently more leisurely academic profession—the ubiquity of overwork reflects not a condition of too little pay but rather a condition of too much demand and the difficulty of turning customers away. The demand for expertise at conventions, conferences, and lecture programs often supplies more opportunities for talented scholars than they have the time for. Although the recession in business and the cutback in government support have hurt engineering, and other fields too have been affected by the 1970 economic chill, it continues to appear that in most of the professions there is more demand for services than there are people trained to provide them.

THE IMPORTANCE OF WORK

What underlies the fact that in our society almost all men between the ages of 25 and 55 who are capable of working are either employed or looking for work? The common-sense answer to the matter has been that men are brought to work by a combination of "carrot and stick," the "carrot" referring to the reward obtainable through work and the "stick" referring to the penalties of unemployment. But common sense is here misleading: There are some men who prefer to live as long as possible off their unemployment benefits, or to go on welfare, rather than work for very low wages at disagreeable jobs; but the fact is that few choose this alternative.

Money is still a very important incentive in our society whatever an individual's income level. Recent evidence suggests that rather than taking out gains in industrial productivity in the form of leisure, the American worker continues to prefer a full and even overtime workweek for the extra money it brings.[41] In the 1950's it was argued that the affluent society had arrived, and that large numbers of middle-class Americans were approaching satiation in their demand for goods. Since then we have come to realize that even the reasonably well-paid blue-collar worker can easily enlarge his schedule of wants to include costlier dental and medical services – and then move on to join his middle-class fellow citizens in a desire for patio extensions and sporting and other leisure equipment, as well as more and better education for his children.[42]

Yet the importance of work cannot be referred simply to financial need. As noted earlier, many people choose teaching and welfare work over a lucrative career in business for the satisfaction they get helping people; that is, they put economic success lower on their scale of values than service to the community. Others choose a career more for the moral approbation it confers than for the money it can ever bring. The man who chooses the Protestant ministry in a small farming community feels no shame at his poverty or at the fact that his parishioners help to meet his family's economic needs with occasional gifts in lieu of a fixed and dependable salary. Of course the minister's wife, who shares in the penalties of poverty, but not in the satisfaction of doing good, might view matters differently.

Among the better educated young, the older and simpler incentives of cash and class, whose achievement Thorstein Veblen saw expressed in the conspicuous consumption of the newly rich of his era, have lost their lure. Middle-class Americans are likely now to see careers more in terms of opportunities for interesting lives than as chances for moving into a desired social class. For some the goals defined by the career itself, of scientific or professional or entrepreneurial achievement, may be taken as ultimate ends, and they may look to their colleagues rather than to social arbiters for estimation of their worth. For others the pursuit of accomplishment itself seems a shallow goal except when they can see it as a contribution to the betterment of their society. Responding to this new ethos, some law firms

---

[41] Over the past 20 years, 90 percent of the gain in productivity has been taken in the form of increased income, in preference to more leisure. Howard R. Bowen and Garth L. Mangum, *Automation and Economic Progress,* p. 60. However, this gives no clue to the increased "leisure" appearing within the plant in the form of less pressure, longer breaks, and conveniences that introduce some of the amenities of home right into the firm.

[42] For a sharp criticism of the view that blue-collar workers have been affluent, see Stephan Thernstrom, "The Myth of American Affluence," *Commentary,* Vol. 48 (October, 1969), pp. 74–78.

now promise time off for public service in order to attract bright law graduates who might otherwise spurn them entirely for less well-paying jobs in
government or social agencies, and some aerospace firms offer in their ad-
vertisements for engineers an opportunity to contribute to plans for the
better organization of urban services. Still other young people find that the
generous aims of public service do not necessarily meet their desires for
self-realization and the ability to be spontaneous and impulsive. They
prefer to choose their life style first and then to look for work that will
support the life style, hopefully without too great an invasion of their time
and energy. However, the number of those who manage altogether to evade
competition for distinction, though growing, is small.

A measure of the general importance of work may be given by a study in
which a representative sample of American men was asked, "If by some
chance you inherited enough money to live comfortably without working,
do you think you would work anyway or not?" Eighty percent replied that
they would work anyway.[43] Their motives for wanting to continue to work
were not clear to themselves and were often explained in such terms as "In
order to keep occupied" or "I'd be nervous otherwise." They recognized that
work is functional, without understanding why this should be so.

A more recent study of male blue-collar workers found almost the same
proportion of interviewees (83 percent) claiming they would work even if
they had enough money to dispense with their jobs. It also revealed that most
working-class males rate their jobs in terms of the income it provides rather
than its status; most said they would prefer higher-paying manual jobs to
lower-paying white-collar jobs.[44]

This finding is consistent with what we know about automobile production workers from an earlier study. Charles Walker and Robert Guest found
that the monotony and fatigue of jobs on the assembly line, where the worker
had to keep up with a pace set by the conveyors, made these jobs intensely
disliked by almost all workers. Notwithstanding the negative reaction to
the line, the company had no trouble recruiting employees because the assembly jobs paid more than the previous jobs held by the workers in the
same area.[45] We can conclude that for working-class men, the pay of the job

---

[43] Nancy C. Morse and Robert S. Weiss, "The Function and Meaning of Work and
the Job," *American Sociological Review*, Vol. 20, No. 2 (April, 1955), pp. 191–98.

[44] Curt Tausky, "Meanings of Work Among Blue-Collar Men," *Pacific Sociological
Review*, Vol. 12 (Spring, 1969), pp. 49–55. Tausky notes that going on welfare remains
the stigma it has always been. To one forced-choice item on the questionnaire, almost
all who were interviewed said they would take a job washing cars that paid the same
as welfare before they would consider going on the welfare rolls.

[45] Charles R. Walker and Robert H. Guest, *The Man on the Assembly Line,* pp. 62–
87.

is the most important factor in choosing between jobs so long as the work done meets the standard set by other working-class friends and relatives, and is a "man's" job. This does not, however, fully guarantee satisfaction with the job's content.

Even older men, whom one might suppose would be eager to retire after many active years, have ambivalent feelings about leaving work. Retirement means lowered income for most. In addition, active employment may still be important because it provides continued participation in community life through social ties and responsibilities that support self-esteem. In interviews with retired executives Chad Gordon found that some men attempt to give clerical directives to their wives as they had been accustomed to doing for so long with their office secretaries.[46]

In their research on hotel and restaurant workers, William F. Whyte and his associates noted how a worker's past background could influence in crucial respects both the adjustment he made to a given job and the meaning he attached to it. Hotel service workers, many of whom came from broken homes and drifted about the country without establishing firm social attachments, obtained vicarious satisfactions from working in a flashy environment of luxury and "high living." Waitresses who were divorcees or downwardly mobile for other reasons often could not cope with the normal pressures of their job because of the overriding psychological preoccupations that their personal misfortune caused them. Such personal factors, when combined with the pressures of the job, meant that some girls were often overwhelmed to the point that they would break down and cry.[47]

It has long been recognized that men whose occupational history is filled with quittings and firings are likely to have personality traits objectionable to others if not to themselves. But even among the stable work force one can discern a partial sorting out of personalities by occupations. Night watchmen, for example, are more inclined to be both suspicious by nature and have less need for social interaction. Men raised on farms object less to isolated jobs with limited opportunities for sociability than individuals reared in cities, because farm work has accustomed them to long stretches of isolated activity.[48] Executives in high corporate positions are not just well-rounded men who have moved up because they knew the right people or had the right social backgrounds; more important to their success is the

---

[46] In personal communication to the authors.

[47] William Foote Whyte, *Human Relations in the Restaurant Industry* (New York: McGraw-Hill, 1948), pp. 112–28; and Whyte and Edith L. Hamilton, *Action Research for Management* (Homewood, Ill.: Dorsey Press, 1964), pp. 16–18, 69.

[48] These and other illustrations of the link between personality and work are to be found in studies cited by William Foote Whyte, *Organizational Behavior: Theory and Application* (Homewood, Ill.: Dorsey Press, 1969), pp. 98–100.

fact that they possess a capacity for coping with a multitude of tasks that extend over long spans of time and that expose them continuously to uncertainty about the decisions they must make each step of the way. Elliott Jaques describes the decisions involved and the nature of the stress they induce:

> Work may be described as a kind of investment behavior — investment in one's foresight, one's ability to foresee the consequences of one's actions. The bigger the job the bigger the problem of investment, in the sense that the longer is the series of decisions to be negotiated and the longer the periods of foresight required. *So also, the longer is the period of uncertainty about the wisdom of the investments being made.*
>
> Being weighted down by too much responsibility means, in these terms, being exposed to continuous uncertainty for such long periods as to induce insecurity, lack of sureness, and anxiety.[49]

Occupational attainment is also determined by one's ethnicity. Many first-generation immigrants took up their old world trades in the American setting, or learned new trades compatible with their past experience and present constraints. Jews peddled dry goods and notions to gain the capital to establish retail and department stores. Italian "bankers" and *padrones* channeled migrant laborers from southern Italy to the railroads. West Coast Chinese, barred by discrimination from many jobs, turned — after the railroads no longer needed their labor — to proprietorship by using the cheap labor of relatives and friends and loans from credit associations.[50]

On the other hand, the broadening reach of higher education, especially through the urban commuter colleges, is expanding recruitment from the old ethnic neighborhoods. The "melting pot" of the university, with its universalism of professional and technical careers, will diminish significantly the ethnic differences that remain. Moreover, careers today demand considerably more residential mobility than they did in a period when people might live out their lives in an ethnic enclave in the city. From the Chinatowns, little Sicilies, and other urban villages of America these new careers will draw the young into the white-collar industries and their residential sub-

---

[49] Elliott Jaques, *Measurement of Responsibility* (London: Tavistock Publications, 1962), pp. 92–93. See also Joseph A. Schumpeter, *The Theory of Economic Development* (New York: Oxford University Press, 1961), pp. 132–36. Schumpeter argued that certain qualities of personality, such as stamina and perseverance, perhaps biologically rooted, are crucial to the making of entrepreneurs, a view that departs from the frequently encountered sociological one that individual capacities hardly count.

[50] See Ivan Light, "Sociological Aspects of Self-Employment and Social Welfare among Chinese, Japanese and Negroes in the U. S." (unpublished Ph.D. dissertation, Department of Sociology, University of California, Berkeley, 1969).

urbs, much as the good jobs and bright lights of the city as a whole have taken the ambitious rural young away from the farms and small towns of America. These children of working and lower-middle-class Americans may finally complete a cultural emancipation denied their parents by taking skilled white-collar jobs that are first incentive and then reward for taking higher education seriously.

Yet, as we have noted, not all our young people are attracted by the rewards of occupational success: Many secure and affluent collegians seem to have made a permanent existence of downward mobility. We see this among students who find the off-campus life so attractive — perhaps especially when because of graduation or resignation they no longer need attend classes — that they remain in the university's host community as sales and service workers, taking jobs that less well-educated people once performed. Some seem to think more highly of the semipoverty of living and working as a postal clerk in Berkeley or as a member of a new agrarian settlement in Oregon than the potential self-alienation and the annoyances of insurance policies and the early-to-bed, early-to-rise life in middle-class Daly City. Just as some factory jobs have hidden "fringe benefits" for the workers because they permit daydreaming and casual banter, so unskilled jobs may be attractive for the educated dropout because they present fewer demands to be a particular kind of person, and what they do demand may seem more natural to him. Freed from preoccupations with achievement as it is ordinarily thought of, and from the anxiety aroused by concern that a final judgment of one's worth may be suspended for months or even years, these young people can find respect and recognition in a confined circle of like-minded peers who consider self-realization the most important of all achievements.

OCCUPATION AND SCHOOLING

Most American men work in jobs not too different in prestige from those their fathers held. There is a great deal of upward movement, but with the exception of those who are the first in their families to complete college, most men move upward for only a short distance. Because opportunities are expanding in occupations at the top of the prestige hierarchy and contracting in occupations at the bottom, the new generation as a whole is doing better, but only a bit better, than the old.[51]

---

[51] See Peter M. Blau and Otis Dudley Duncan, *The American Occupational Structure* (New York: Wiley, 1967), pp. 78–79. See also William Form, "Occupations and Careers," Vol. 16, *International Encyclopedia of the Social Sciences,* David Sills, ed. (New York: Macmillan, 1968), pp. 250–51.

The point at which a boy leaves the educational escalator is critical in determining his future occupational opportunities. In 1962 almost one-half the men who had completed college had gone a good deal further than their fathers occupationally. College — and even more decidedly graduate and professional schools — prepare young men for a life in one of the more prestigious middle-class occupations, although there are very large differences among colleges in just how well they place their graduates. In contrast, the boy who leaves high school before graduation is unlikely ever to do anything other than manual work, unless it is to have a fling at running a small business, such as a gas station or a TV repair shop.[52]

A number of studies have shown the pressures that impel even academically talented youths to withdraw from school in fact or feeling if they come from families that have little experience of education themselves, that suffer from inadequate income, that have several children competing for space in a crowded home, and that are headed by a single overburdened parent.[53] These disabilities are likely to cluster in the family life of the lower-class youth, and it is little wonder that such a youth finds the immediate rewards of a job — both spending money and the right to spend it — more attractive than the immediate irksomeness of school, and that he weighs the decision in favor of leaving school. Self-esteem too plays a role: Students with low self-esteem have been shown to come disproportionately from groups of lower socioeconomic status and to be less confident of their ability to succeed in a demanding enterprise.[54] In addition, the lower-class youth is less likely than the middle-class youth to see the relevance of education for his later occupational activity. He is more likely to see education as a task set by an arbitrary society, rather than as an opportunity to prepare for a gratifying adulthood. His understanding of the occupational world, and the way in which one aims for a definite niche in it, is in every way naive. It has been found that even in kindergarten, middle-class children are consistently more sophisticated than working-class children in their conceptions of the variety of jobs available and in their understanding of the instrumental value of education.[55]

Thus it is inevitable that school authorities will encounter many difficulties in communicating with working-class children. Even so, they are

---

[52] For the relationship of education to mobility see Peter M. Blau and Otis Dudley Duncan, *ibid.,* especially p. 499.

[53] See Beverly Duncan, *Family Factors and School Dropouts: 1920–1960* (Ann Arbor, Michigan: University of Michigan Press, 1965).

[54] See Morris Rosenberg, *Society and the Adolescent Self-Image* (Princeton, N. J.: Princeton University Press, 1965).

[55] Donald B. O'Dowd and David C. Beardslee, *College Student Images of Professions and Occupations* (Middletown, Conn.: Wesleyan University Press, 1960).

often in a quandary as to how to employ even their limited influence over the educational, and hence the occupational, future of their charges. Lacking sufficient resources, schools in the past have been under pressure to concentrate attention upon the students who are clearly middle-class because these were the students who seemed to fit best in the school, and whose parents were most likely to be concerned regarding their progress.[56] Yet the situation now seems to be changing, at least for black and Puerto Rican students in some of our cities, whose parents are increasingly mobilizing politically outside the home to put pressure on schools to prepare their children for advanced education while working within their homes to insure that their children will make use of their new opportunities.

The working-class boy who will eventually drop out of high school experiences a kind of progressive alienation from the high-school situation, sometimes initiated by a single difficult relationship with a teacher and sometimes by a complex of factors, including poor grades and close friends who share his view of the school as a hostile environment.[57] Nevertheless, a number of programs have had some success in inducing low-income youths to remain in high school until they receive their diploma. The vocational school movement, although it gave rise to schools that functioned for the most part as "aging vats," in which young people remained until they were old enough to enter the labor force, has provided a practical introduction to a trade for some youths who wanted training but not college. But most working-class youths who are determined to leave school at the first opportunity are not deterred by vocational programs, especially as they are currently organized, and would not be by even much better programs. For the most part, these youths are so alienated from the idea of schooling, though perhaps not from the idea of education, that they cannot conceive as relevant to themselves anything that happens in class.

With the same casualness and lack of perspective that characterize the

---

[56] For a somewhat outdated but still valuable discussion of these dilemmas of the school, see W. Lloyd Warner, Robert J. Havighurst, and Martin Loeb, *Who Shall Be Educated?* (New York: Harper, 1944); and see, in addition, for discussion of the forms of discrimination against working-class children in a middle-class school, August B. Hollingshead, *Elmtown's Youth* (New York: Wiley, 1949).

[57] The various reasons boys may have for dropping out of school are vividly described by S. M. Miller and Ira E. Harrison in "Types of Dropouts: 'The Unemployables,'" in Arthur B. Shostak and William Gomberg, eds., *Blue-Collar World* (Englewood Cliffs, N. J.: Prentice-Hall, 1964), pp. 469–84. The boy who gets a "bad reputation" in the school may find he is almost forced by teachers and fellow students into a role antagonistic to the school. See Robert B. Vinter and Rosemary C. Sarri, "Malperformance in the Public School: A Group Work Approach," *Social Work* (January, 1965), pp. 3–13.

act of dropping out of school, these young people enter the labor market, where some find jobs through random application or the recommendation of a friend or relative and many do not find jobs at all. In 1967, there were about two and one-half million youths who had completed their education with high school and about one-half million who had dropped out even before finishing high school. In October of that year, taking only the males, about nine and one-half percent of the high school graduates were unemployed, compared with 19 percent of the dropouts. In addition, about 12 percent of the dropouts reported that they were neither working nor looking for work. At least temporarily they had entirely rejected the work role.[58]

Many working-class youths will accept the first job that presents itself. They may feel, even in relatively good times, that jobs are scarce, that there is not much difference between jobs, and that there is a good deal to be said for just having something to do — although, as we have said, their reliability on the job may not be too high.[59] Some of these young people will have to work because their parents need their income, or because they have begun families of their own.

What follows for many of these youths is a series of shifts among jobs within the blue-collar world, before some job turns out to be relatively permanent.[60] In his novel *On the Line,* Harvey Swados describes how a number of men of very different origins, ambitions, and abilities came to an automobile assembly line. Many of these men took the job only temporarily and then found themselves stuck there, even though they resented the work; others left the line, sometimes precipitously, without great hope of finding anything more satisfying.[61]

In contrast with working-class youths, middle-class youths tend to find

---

[58] Herbert Bienstock, "The Transition to Work Here and Abroad: Do U. S. Youth Fare Worse?" *New Generation,* Vol. 51, No. 1 (Winter, 1969), pp. 2–5. Alvin L. Schorr estimates that at any given time one of five youths without a high school diploma is unemployed and at least as many dropouts are not even seeking work. See his *Poor Kids* (New York: Basic Books, 1966), p. 28.

[59] See Lloyd G. Reynolds and Joseph Shister, *Job Horizons* (New York: Harper, 1949). Also Lloyd G. Reynolds, *Wages and Labor Mobility in Theory and Practice* (New York: Harper, 1951).

[60] See, for discussion of the careers of blue-collar workers, William H. Form and Delbert C. Miller, "Occupational Career Pattern as a Sociological Instrument," in Sigmund Nosow and William H. Form, eds., *Man, Work and Society,* pp. 287–97. Among the conclusions of the authors is, "Once started on an occupational level, a worker tends to remain on that level."

[61] Harvey Swados, *On the Line* (Boston: Little, Brown, 1957). See also Gladys Palmer, "Epilogue: Social Values in Labor Mobility," *Labor, Mobility and Economic Opportunity* (New York: Wiley, 1954), pp. 47–67.

the school system less uncongenial than its alternatives, although many of them in talks with one another or in the increasingly widespread network of underground papers disparage the educational value of their high-school and even their college courses.[62] In some schools, acceptance by peers requires a willingness to take risks in drugs or demonstrations or dropping out which sometimes leads to a permanent separation from school and a probable limiting of development and of future choices. But it is only a small minority of the American middle class that becomes seriously disaffected. Most middle-class young people still characteristically see their vocational problem as one of deciding what they want to do. They are eager to assess their own talents and abilities as a means of establishing occupational goals, and their position in the social system gives them opportunity for insight into the occupational world. They are more apt than the lower-class youth to have a family member or family friend who is a member of the occupational group toward which they aim and from whom they can get a more intimate view of the work involved. The less fortunate youngster may have to depend on an occasional article in a popular magazine and on what can be picked up in school in the content of courses and in conversation with teachers for his image of his chosen work.[63]

The problem of the adolescent is intensified by the fact that while some fields, such as law and teaching, admit those who have decided to enter fairly late in life, other fields, including some branches of science and many of the skilled trades, require early career decisions by prospective entrants.[64] Thus, for example, those who want to become physicists must decide in high school to take the right kinds of science courses and enough mathematics to qualify for acceptance in the physics department of an undergraduate college, where they may then acquire the training adequate to prepare them for graduate school.[65]

Many college youths find themselves making career choices almost inadvertently as they elect one major rather than another or apply to graduate school in the absence of anything better to do. Some recognize the hazards

---

[62] For a discussion of the problems posed for universities by the increasing delegitimization of authority see Walter Metzger, "The Crisis of Academic Authority," *Daedalus,* Vol. 99, pp. 568–608.

[63] Eli Ginzberg *et al., Occupational Choice* (New York: Columbia University Press, 1951).

[64] For material on the decision to enter medicine, see Natalie Rogoff, "The Decision to Study Medicine," and Wagner Thielens, Jr., "Some Comparisons of Entrants to Medical and Law School," in Robert K. Merton, George G. Reader, and Patricia L. Kendall, eds., *The Student Physician* (Cambridge, Mass.: Harvard University Press, 1957), pp. 109–29, 131–52.

[65] Everett C. Hughes, *Men and Their Work* (New York: Free Press, 1958).

inherent in choosing one's lifework without adequate information about one-self, and take a year away from school to explore themselves and, perhaps less intensely, the occupational world. But too long a moratorium on choice brings trouble with the draft, discomfort for parents, and perhaps anxieties the young person himself cannot entirely suppress. The desire for independence may press the young person to choose, ready or not.

An evaluation of our system for bringing people and jobs together would have to consider a number of issues. We are very far from a system of equal opportunity: The children of poor families, especially if they are black, and to a lesser extent if they are from the South, have much less chance of gaining a high prestige job than do other young people. In this respect our society is defective, though there are signs that it is improving. However, the relative opportunities of disadvantaged young people, taken as a group, for moving into professional and managerial positions are probably greater here than in any other country, which suggests both the relative openness of our social classes and the less permeable boundaries maintained in other societies.[66]

From another standpoint, that of filling the jobs that need to be done, our system for matching individuals and jobs seems better, though imperfect. One of the areas of mismatch is in medicine: At this point it appears that there will be shortages of personnel in all the health occupations – physicians, dentists, nurses, occupational and physical therapists, and particularly the health administrators who must manage the growing health industry.[67]

American medicine has traditionally been concerned with cure rather than prevention, and to shift the emphasis away from caring for patients who are sick to taking care of whole societies so that people will remain well requires the development of new types of physician-managers and public health specialists who for a long time will be in short supply. While organized medicine has relaxed its once restrictive stance and has supported large increases in the number of medical schools and medical students, the problems of health care now lie less in the shortage of physicians than in the shortage of the others who make up the "medical team" and in the difficulty of persuading highly skilled people to live in sparsely settled or culturally disadvantaged areas. Few people foresaw in time the enormous increase in medical personnel of every kind that would be required to provide the level of medical care that we now increasingly feel to be the right of every citizen. There has been

[66] Peter M. Blau and Otis Dudley Duncan, *The American Occupational Structure*, p. 435.

[67] Neal H. Rosenthal and Janice Neiport Hedge, "Matching Sheepskins with Jobs," *Monthly Labor Review*, Vol. 91, No. 9 (November, 1968), pp. 9–15.

a considerable shift of resources toward the health sciences, but not nearly enough to meet the needs.

In other fields our cadres of trained personnel seem more nearly adequate, although we have had short-lived shortages in several fields in the past few years—notably in engineering, computer programming, and teaching. But even if we tried to avoid the occasional instance of undersupply or oversupply of individuals of particular training by changing to some form of centralized planning and guidance from our present system by which individuals choose their own jobs and fields, it is by no means certain that we could provide more effectively for the needs of both the individual and society. Occupations now in great demand may in the near future find their functions absorbed by new equipment or a new field. In ten years we may not need engineers or even automobile mechanics in anywhere near the number we require now. We have to develop our curricula to encourage young people to grow along with a field, and to be ready to start again in a new field if necessary, and we have to organize our training and placement facilities to support this kind of readiness for change.

If we compare the situation in the United States with that in other advanced industrial societies, it is evident that America offers many more chances for shifting one's field of study in the university and shifting again in later life, perhaps with some part-time college work or on-the-job training. Other societies restrict people much earlier to a definitive academic program and the corresponding level of careers. Thus, Americans have been able to respond to rapidly changing occupational demands and, on the whole, have not insisted that they were only prepared to accept one kind of job at one particular level of status. Yet even so, there are frictions in the linkage between the educational and the occupational structures, and we cannot be confident that in the future the society will have trained and motivated the people it will need. Young people in school and college need to discover their capabilities to learn new languages and skills. Learning how to learn becomes the most important ability in a world where there are few positions fixed for life. And for the adult worker already tied to a job, something akin to the sabbatical academics now enjoy might be attempted to give the mature worker in other fields greater flexibility.

LABOR AND THE WORKING-CLASS JOB

At the beginning of the Industrial Revolution, Adam Smith was so impressed with the stultifying nature of factory life that he could only hope that the hours away from work might somehow enable workers to maintain those qualities of character he regarded as essentially human. Marx went much further in seeing the factory as a place of brutishness, long hours, prison-like conditions, and virtual contempt for the well-being of the worker. For Marx, factory work was a job that "exhausts the nervous system to the uttermost, does away with the many-sided play of the muscles, and confiscates every atom of freedom, both in bodily and intellectual activity," which, in sum, makes the worker "a mere living appendage" to the machine.[68]

With hindsight, we can see that observers of the evils of factory life may have neglected the elements of passivity and boredom in the life of the peasant and yeoman prior to the coming of industry. And it is likely too that both the nineteenth-century and the contemporary observers who have commented on the factory have failed to see the elements of creativity, disguised in tricks of the trade or sabotage, by which seemingly oppressed workers maintain a certain amount of control over the conditions of work. Furthermore, small talk and "kidding around" can sometimes make bearable the most repetitive task.[69]

However, the sharpest criticism of the industrial job, made by Karl Marx and other nineteenth-century observers of factory life, was aimed not at the immediate discomfort produced by the job, but rather at a condition they characterized as "alienation." They argued that when men engage in activities that have no inner meanings for them as individuals but are merely a part of a productive process they become alienated from their own deepest passions. Work comes to be something "out there," its processes dwarfing the men who perform them, its products bearing no recognizable relationship to the individual effort of the individual worker. The workers' only awareness of the state of alienation may be the recognition that their work life is unrewarding: The possibility that work might become meaningful is beyond their vision.[70] Empirical study, however, does not support the assertions some-

---

[68] Karl Marx, *Capital* (New York: Modern Library, 1932), p. 462.

[69] The work of Donald Roy is particularly useful here. See "Quota Restrictions and Goldbricking in a Machine Shop," *American Journal of Sociology* (March, 1952), pp. 427–42; and "Banana Time," Warren G. Bennis, Edgar H. Schein, David E. Berlew, and Fred I. Steele, eds., *Interpersonal Dynamics* (Homewood, Ill.: Dorsey, 1964), pp. 583–99.

[70] See Karl Marx and Friedrich Engels, "On Alienation," in C. Wright Mills, ed., *Images of Man* (New York: Braziller, 1960), pp. 486–507. For a discussion of the Marxist and pre-Marxist use of the concept, see Daniel Bell, *The End of Ideology* (New York: Free Press, 1960), pp. 388–402. A compact review of the meanings the term carries in current sociological thought is given by Melvin Seeman, "On the Meaning of Alienation," *American Sociological Review*, Vol. 24 (December, 1959), pp. 783–91. For an empirical study of the relation between work and alienation see Robert Blauner, *Alienation and Freedom: The Factory Worker and His Industry* (Chicago: University of Chicago Press, 1964).

times made that alienation from one's work generalizes to alienation from oneself or society — though of course, alienation in any form is bad enough.[71]

The same demand for freedom from work pressures leads men not themselves close to retirement and thus not faced with its financial and psychological hazards to press for an ever earlier age of retirement, "so that a man can do all those things in life you can't do while you're working." Warner Bloomberg, Jr., a sociologist who worked in the Gary steel mills and elsewhere, reports that steelworkers from ages 25 to 55 almost unanimously advocate retirement commencing at age 55 or earlier. They blithely dismiss the inevitable economic questions with assertions that they will be able to "make out" based perhaps on a Micawber-like belief that something will turn up — possibly that better stipends for the retired are just around the political corner.[72]

Retirement, when it is in fact reached, sometimes turns out to be much less desirable than had been anticipated. For although the job itself may have been oppressive, the absence of work can in a different way be equally so. Much depends on whether a man can find something to do, and whether he has the freedom from financial worry that will enable him to do it.

In the working class, jobs are often so unsatisfactory that there is no social pressure to say that one enjoys one's work; it is socially permitted to regard work with dislike or at best detachment. The Morse-Weiss study, referred to earlier, shows that although the great majority of men would continue to work even if it were not economically required of them, only in the middle-class occupations would the majority continue in the same type of work (see Table 6). Less than one in six among unskilled workers and about one in three among the workers in service occupations or in the semiskilled occupations would continue at their present work.[73] It is in these groups that the social and personal function of working at any job, together with pure economic compulsion, serves to hold the individual to a job he does not really want.

One of the things wrong with the working-class job is simply that it is working-class. In a society in which the worth of a man is apt to be measured by how far he has gotten, the unskilled laborer or service worker, despite the pieties that may be uttered periodically about the dignity of labor, knows

---

[71] See Melvin Seeman, "Les conséquences de l'aliénation dans le travail," *Sociologie du Travail*, Vol. 9, No. 2 (April–June, 1967).

[72] Warren Peterson in a study of Kansas City school teachers also found this growing demand for early retirement, with teachers expressing boredom and defeatism about work as much as any specific desires for postwork activities. (Unpublished dissertation, Department of Sociology, University of Chicago, 1956).

[73] See also Curt Tausky, "Meanings of Work Among Blue-Collar Men."

Robert S. Weiss, Edwin Harwood, and David Riesman **583**

TABLE 6

Percentage of Respondents Who Would Continue
to Work and Percentage Who Would Continue
on the Same Job

	Would Continue to Work	Would Continue in Same Type of Work
Middle Class		
Professional	86	68
Manager	82	55
Sales	91	59
Working Class		
Trades	79	40
Operatives	78	32
Unskilled	58	16
Service	71	33

Source: Nancy C. Morse and Robert S. Weiss, "The Function and Meaning of Work and the Job," *American Sociological Review* (April, 1965).

that he has not gotten very far. His distress is due primarily, not to his inferior standing in the community, as might be a European worker's, but rather to his inability to provide as well for himself and his family as he believes he should. In most industries many workers do not want their children to wind up as they have. A black packing-house worker, for example, responded to an interviewer's question about getting his children into the plant to work by saying, "I wouldn't want a kid of mine to ever have a job like this." [74]

It is widely recognized that the modern factory offers virtually no opportunity for advancement from the blue-collar ranks, although a few firms have introduced education programs that might facilitate upward mobility for some workers. In one study, almost one-half of all factory workers in a large group of firms felt that there was no opportunity for promotion in their jobs: They believed that no matter how well they performed their jobs, they were stuck in them, unless seniority and the most exceptional good luck combined to give them a break. [75] Generally factory workers cannot move into highly skilled work, since entrance is controlled by the union and requires an apprenticeship that a man with a family can seldom afford. Nor would the unions in the skilled trades permit entry to all applicants: The electricians, like the physicians of a few years ago, have no desire to greatly increase the numbers of those licensed to compete for available work.

---

[74] Theodore V. Purcell, S.J., "The Hopes of Negro Workers for Their Children," in Arthur B. Shostak and William Gomberg, eds., *Blue-Collar World*, pp. 144–53.
[75] Robert Blauner, *Alienation and Freedom,* Table 45, p. 206.

In this situation of blocked mobility an emphasis develops on the small differences that make one job slightly better than another: a somewhat better machine, a better shift, a fractionally higher hourly wage, a little more freedom to move around on the job floor. These gradations are controlled by seniority, and seniority also determines what comes to be the most desirable job characteristic of all: job security in case of a reduction in the work force. "Getting ahead" does not entirely lose its meaning to working-class men; rather, it comes to be redefined in terms of their lives as consumers, not as producers. The better-paid workers can find some status in the plant by means of their extracurricular activities—extravagant hunting trips, a boat, expensive travels, or a new home in a pleasant suburb. And, of course, it is always possible for the worker to dream that he may one day be able to get out of the plant.[76]

Chinoy noted that "a dozen men spontaneously observed that 'almost everybody' talks about getting out of the shop," and reports an assembly-line tender as saying, "It makes the time go quicker and easier if I keep thinking about that turkey farm I'd like to buy." The small business is simply a daydream for most men. Some men try it, but many—if not most—fail; they lack capital, contacts, and experience in what is at best a hazardous undertaking.[77]

It must be remembered that even though blue-collar work has come to be associated with the factory, in fact only a minority of blue-collar workers tend assembly lines. A good many blue-collar jobs, particularly those that allow freedom of movement—such as a milk-route salesman, a telephone lineman, a trucker, a maintenance worker—do provide variety and a considerable amount of challenge and responsibility, and they give many who hold them a sense of achievement. Moreover, there are declining numbers of blue-collar jobs, such as high iron work, that give their practitioners a kind of elite standing because of their difficulty, danger, and the avoidance of that extreme subdivision of labor in which the worker repeats operations over and over through the day.

Extreme subdivision of work is the result of decades of engineering effort motivated by a belief that a total work process can be carried out most efficiently if it is broken down into many smaller processes, each of which is allocated to specific workers who specialize in its performance. Though the re-

---

[76] Ely Chinoy, "The Traditions of Opportunity and the Aspirations of Automobile Workers," *American Journal of Sociology,* Vol. 57, No. 5 (March, 1952), pp. 453–59.

[77] Mayer and Goldstein found that of 81 small business firms that began operating in the Providence, Rhode Island, area in the first part of 1958, 78 percent survived their first year in business, and 51 percent survived their second. See Kurt B. Mayer and Sidney Goldstein, *The First Two Years: Problems of Small Firm Growth and Survival* (Washington, D. C.: Small Business Administration, 1961).

petitive job can be justified by the logic of efficiency, its disagreeable qualities have long been recognized. Alexis de Tocqueville noted:

> When a workman is unceasingly and exclusively engaged in the fabrication of one thing, he ultimately does his work with singular dexterity; but at the same time he loses the general faculty of applying his mind to the direction of the work. He every day becomes more adroit and less industrious; so that it may be said of him that in proportion as the workman improves, the man is degraded.[78]

However, research on the effect of repetitive jobs has shown that worker response is more complicated than Tocqueville suggests. Some workers willingly perform monotonous jobs that strike them as important but will resist equally monotonous jobs that strike them as meaningless. In addition, individuals differ greatly in the extent to which they value work that provides a steady rhythm, as opposed to work that is continually presenting new problems.[79] Moreover, as has already been suggested, workers are not helpless cogs in a system. They often find ways of doing jobs a little more easily, of controlling their work pace, and of introducing variety into the day's routine. Still, most studies show that the assembly-line system reduces the freedom of the worker more than any other type of factory system. If the line is speeded up beyond the point that workers will accept, there may be sudden, almost spontaneous, refusal to work, or the line may mysteriously break down, or the number of defective parts greatly increase. Human beings have always been able to act in concert to control their environment, in a factory setting as well as anywhere else. Even in plants without formal union leadership factory workers manage to organize informally in work groups and cliques, to humanize the bleak impersonality of the plant but also to control the impact of managerial directives and technological innovations on their work—or simply to show their power to humiliate supervisors.[80]

Management tends to see these informal work groups as implacably hostile to company aims. Often enough it is right: By work restriction and other means, informal social groups do act to reduce the efficiency of the factory's operation. They may hoard work secrets and refuse them to newcomers until the newcomers are accepted into the group; they may insist that certain jobs be given only to men with high seniority and refuse to allow management to

---

[78] Alexis de Tocqueville, *Democracy in America,* Vol. 2 (New York: Vintage Books, 1959), p. 168.

[79] See Georges Friedmann, *Industrial Society,* especially the chapters on problems of monotony, rhythm of work, and assembly-line work.

[80] See, in this connection, Charles R. Walker and Robert H. Guest, *The Man on the Assembly Line.*

assign a new man to these jobs, no matter how competent his experience out-side the plant may have made him; they may by social pressure force an in-spector or a foreman to modify his insistence on a particular level of quality. They are not always antagonistic. Factory studies have often found that the most valued member of such a group is also the man who is valued most highly by the supervisory staff, and even though the group is likely to restrict its output to a level below that which management would consider optimal, it nevertheless tends to keep its output up to a level that seems to it fair [81] and may in fact set quite high levels of productivity where management is favorably regarded.

The Union

For many workers the union is a bulwark against a potentially oppressive management. A steelworker, asked what would happen if the union were to disappear, said:

> You'd lose everything. The company would really throw you around and put the pressure on. They'd be demanding, and high-pressuring everybody. They'd demote people any time they wanted to. There wouldn't be any seniority.[82]

Workers tend to be loyal to their unions; most join because they believe in what the unions stand for. Of course, in closed shops — which are outlawed in some states by "right-to-work" laws — a worker must join the union as a condition of employment, no matter what he believes, and even if a shop is open a worker may find that his unionized co-workers expect and at times in-sist that he join, saying, "We pay dues and get benefits and you should help pay the load too." [83] But it is wrong to think of workers as unwilling victims of exploitative unions: Most workers believe their unions to be their advo-cates in what would otherwise be a hopelessly unequal struggle with man-agement.

---

[81] See Stanley Seashore, *Group Cohesiveness and Industrial Work Group,* Publica-tion No. 14 (Ann Arbor, Michigan: University of Michigan, Institute for Social Re-search, Survey Research Center, 1955).

[82] Joel Seidman, "The Labor Union as an Organization," Arthur Kornhauser, Robert Dubin, and Arthur M. Ross, eds., *Industrial Conflict* (New York: McGraw-Hill, 1954), p. 112.

[83] Joel Seidman, Jack London, and Bernard Karsh, "Why Workers Join Unions," E. Wight Bakke, Clark Kerr, and Charles W. Anrod, eds., *Unions, Management, and the Public,* third ed. (New York: Harcourt Brace Jovanovich, 1967), pp. 92–96.

Despite the loyalty of its members, the union does not usually absorb a great deal of their time, energy, or concern. Rarely does a union member attend a meeting of his local, unless there is a strike vote scheduled or a contested election to be decided. In one study it was found that only one-half of one percent of the membership of a steelworkers' local attended a biweekly membership meeting.[84] Forty years ago, when the large industrial unions were beginning to establish themselves and when membership in a union was a hazardous undertaking that might well have resulted in loss of job and quite possibly in intimidation and violence, joining a union was a major decision in a worker's life. Today when violence and the threat of violence are relatively rare in labor relations, the union is much more likely to be accepted by both its members and their bosses as a part of the normal work environment and as therefore no longer an appropriate object for passion.

Criticism of unions has now become almost a standard feature of liberal and radical rhetoric, replacing the criticism that used to be heard from conservatives and the right wing. Unions are attacked as undemocratic because the leadership is unresponsive to the rank and file. Behind this criticism is the unquestioned belief that some version of participatory democracy should prevail in all subunits of society, whether unions, or universities, or churches. Sometimes critics of unions overlook the fact that the policies of the leadership of a union like the United Auto Workers on such issues as racial discrimination, education, or the war economy are far more enlightened than those of most of the rank and file; this is probably true even in such unions as the building trades, not noted for humaneness and vision, where leadership efforts to help at least a token number of blacks to make an entry into the skilled work force have been bitterly criticized by white workers who fear for their jobs and their chance to pass on opportunities to their children. Yet unions are rarely sufficiently undemocratic to allow the leadership great leeway and freedom from the judgments of the rank and file. This is true at the national level, where incumbent union presidents have now and then been defeated for reelection, and it is even more the case on the local level, where the rank and file can see much more clearly the relation between their local's policy and their own economic position and where would-be national leaders can try to get a start by representing their constituency in locals that are opposed to the national's policies. A leader of a local union can support

---

[84] Joel Seidman, "The Labor Union as an Organization." For further discussion see William Spinrad, "Correlates of Trade Union Participation: Summary of the Literature," *American Sociological Review,* Vol. 25 (April, 1960), pp. 237–44; and Arnold S. Tannenbaum and Robert L. Kahn, *Participation in Local Unions* (Evanston, Illinois: Row, Peterson, 1958).

wildcat strikes and so sabotage the efforts of the national leadership to reach a settlement with management and, if a settlement is reached, undermine it by charging that it is a sellout of the workers' claims.[85]

When at least in appearance, but very often in reality as well, "the bosses" exploited underpaid and overdriven workers, union organization excited the sympathy of liberals and radicals, and union leadership often responded by coupling trade union demands with progressive rhetoric. And, at various times and places, there have been radical unions among miners, seamen, longshoremen, electrical workers, and others, who wanted not only more of the pie, but a different recipe as well. But in general American unions have not been mobilized for radical politics, and union leaders have seldom been able to deliver a union vote, although in marginal elections their campaign chests can make a difference. Disappointment occurring because unions are now established, and their leaders seem more nearly bureaucrats than missionaries, and limit their demands to the well-being of their membership, has led many of their former friends to disparage their capacity to be forces for progress. Furthermore, continuing, though sporadic, evidence that union leaders sometimes exploit their positions for financial gain strengthens the image of the union as just another organization of self-interested individuals.

While racketeering does exist in unions, it is not nearly so common as one might assume from news stories. Racketeering can seldom persist without the toleration of management, or even its active cooperation, and so tends to occur primarily in such fields as trucking, building, and restaurant trades, where managements are small, decentralized, and beset by competitive pressures. In such situations, it is not unknown for a business agent of the union to make a deal with a management representative that is profitable for each, though costly to the members of the union. This should not suggest, however, that all such industrial situations give rise to union racketeering. In the garment industry, where firms are also small and highly competitive, the union has brought a certain measure of stability without racketeering. In fact, the International Ladies Garment Workers Union is representative

---

[85] See Jack Barbash, *American Unions: Structure, Government and Politics* (New York: Random House, 1967), p. 143. Incumbent presidents who have been defeated for reelection in recent years include McDonald of the Steelworkers and Carey of the International Union of Electrical, Radio and Machine Workers. (See his pp. 96–99.) See also Delbert C. Miller and William H. Form, "Power and Union Organization," in *Industrial Sociology* (New York: Harper, 1951), Chapter 8, pp. 288–325. For a discussion of an exceptional union, in which two competing parties provide alternative slates to the membership, see Seymour Lipset, Martin Trow, and James Coleman, *Union Democracy: The Internal Politics of the International Typographical Union* (New York: Free Press, 1956).

of the majority of unions in that it is led by honest, dedicated men. A former Secretary of Labor has said, "Despite some bad examples and a bad press, the fact is that most of organized labor is governed by a private democracy characterized by idealism, honesty, and responsiveness to the membership." [86]

Since the period between the two World Wars, when the union movement grew to a potent force in American economic life, unions have been successful in achieving most of their immediate objectives. Wages have been raised; welfare and security measures for workers are now normally in the union contract; managements are not so often able to act capriciously in layoffs and promotions. Yet economists disagree as to whether labor unions have succeeded in raising the real income of all workers. Some claim that they have raised the wage rates for all workers in the unionized industries, not just in the union shops but also in the nonunion shops,[87] but at the expense of workers in nonunionized industries, who must pay more for goods turned out by the better organized sectors of the economy.

Unions have at times been accused of making it difficult for members of some minority groups to work as craftsmen. For example, the building-trades locals maintain monopolistic control over the right to perform electrical work, plumbing, masonry, and the like. These craft unions typically restrict entrance to individuals who are acceptable to the membership and often to individuals who are relatives of those who are already members. In general, management is not discriminatory, but wants as large a labor pool as possible, and it is primarily the trade unions, rather than management, that keep blacks or Latin-Americans out of the construction industry. In many of these union groups, work gangs are small in size and have a team spirit, and as might be the case in a cohesive working-class neighborhood, they are not likely to welcome a member of an ethnic out-group. Members of building-trades unions are also likely to feel that access to the union represents the one resource they can control and make available to a son or other relative. Thus it becomes clear why plumbers or masons may feel that membership in their union belongs by right to their particular group. In addition they are apt to feel that they built the union during the years when work was

---

[86] W. Willard Wirtz, "Union Morals," in E. Wight Bakke, Clark Kerr, and Charles W. Anrod, eds., *Unions, Management, and the Public,* p. 682. For a different view see "Corruption in American Industrial Relations," by the European unionist, B. C. Roberts, in the same volume, pp. 672–77. Compared with trade unions of northern Europe, within which corruption is almost unknown, he finds the American scene astonishing. But it might be noted that there are many other sectors of American life which would prove equally astonishing to a visitor from another country.

[87] H. M. Douty, "Union and Nonunion Wages," in *Unions, Management, and the Public,* pp. 603–04.

scarce and pay was low and now that they have an organization which can insure them a reasonable livelihood the federal government in alliance with an affluent elite is trying to open it to blacks who had nothing to do with its nurturing. They may recognize the validity of the argument that prejudice and discrimination have put blacks everywhere at a disadvantage, but they may respond that they arrived in the United States long after the end of slavery and have no special obligation to deal with its long-run consequences.

As people become more "middle class" in life style and more distant from their immigrant background and its deprivations, these group distinctions may fade. In addition, the combined pressures of the whites who have achieved a solid middle-class position and of the blacks who want the chance to go at least a bit further toward it may be effective in modifying the policies of the craft unions. On the other hand, perhaps new recruits from impoverished groups will lack the perspective and confidence in the future to tolerate the long and poorly paying apprenticeship the building trades demand. But blacks and members of other out-groups understandably want a chance at these trades, and they want that chance now.

Even as the unions try to deal with their now traditional concerns of wages, fringe benefits, working conditions, and the like, new problems present themselves as consequences of the occupational changes in our society discussed earlier, such as the growth in the service industries. If the unions are to grow, they will have to expand into white-collar industries in which they have had little success in the past. The unions are finally reaching migrant farm workers and the underpaid employees of small firms far from industrial centers, but these successes, important as they are, are outside of the major sectors of economic growth.[88]

The Strike

Strikes are very much a part of the American industrial scene. Since the end of World War II there have been between 3500 and 5000 strikes each year; in recent years, perhaps because of inflation, the number has been at the high

---

[88] See Leo Troy, "Trade Union Growth in a Changing Economy," *Monthly Labor Review,* Vol. 92, No. 9 (September, 1969), pp. 3–7. There has been a substantial increase in the number of local government workers entering the ranks of organized labor in the past ten years, and now increasingly school and college teachers are beginning to organize as well.

end of this range.[89] Most of these strikes end in a few days, but those that result from conflict between a giant industry and equally large unions are liable to last much longer: In the years from 1957 to 1967 the average duration of the ten strikes that involved over 100,000 workers was 40 days.[90] This is long enough to use up the savings of many workers and to put some of them well into debt. The union supplies workers with funds from its treasury, but these barely cover a family's necessities. Some states permit workers on strike to draw unemployment benefits; others do not. In the long and bitter 1970 strike of General Electric workers, those who worked in the Schenectady, New York, plant, where they were eligible for benefits, fared much better than those who worked in the Lynn, Massachusetts, plant, where they were not.

In the great organizing drives in the 1930's, the strike was often a way in which a union created itself out of the sporadic and isolated discontents of clusters of workers. Today strikes are likely to result not so much from an unwillingness of management to recognize unions—though this still occurs in textiles, agriculture, and in some holdout firms in the more nearly unionized industries—as from disputes over the terms of a new contract or the interpretation of a current one. Though wages continue to be an issue, they may not be the only one or even the leading one, except possibly in times of inflation, when workers see previous gains defeated by rising prices. Fringe benefits, including pension plans and vacation pay, are likely to play more of a role, along with questions of management's authority, such as procedures for deciding when a worker may be laid off. Anything that affects the work life of a union member may become a matter for negotiation and eventually a strike. There have been instances in which the strike's aim was to change the organization's policies—notably the teachers' strike against the New York City Board of Education in 1968—although the assertion by employees of a right to veto their superiors' policy decisions, except in the areas of wages and manpower use, is still unusual.[91]

Violence is no longer an expected part of long and bitter strikes, though like other aspects of what one would like to consider the past history of labor

[89] "Current Labor Statistics," *Monthly Labor Review,* Vol. 92, No. 11 (November, 1969), p. 125. This represents about 2 percent of the total number of union-management contracts in existence. See Elizabeth Jager, "Why Strikes?" E. Wight Bakke, Clark Kerr, and Charles W. Anrod, eds., *Unions, Management, and the Public,* pp. 273–82.

[90] Howard N. Fullerton, "Major Strikes During 1967," *Monthly Labor Review,* Vol. 91, No. 4 (April, 1968), pp. 42–43.

[91] Howard N. Fullerton, *ibid.*

relations, it has not entirely disappeared. Violence is especially likely today when small operators confront unions that are weak locally, as in agriculture and, in the South, in textiles and to an extent in other industries. But there can also be violence resulting from intraunion disputes when management is caught between groups contending for control, or when a union appears to be losing a strike and may seek to maintain morale by a tactical escalation.

It is difficult to determine how costly a strike is to the local or national economy. Production may be stepped up in anticipation of a strike or may be increased in one locality because there is a strike in another. The end of a strike may be followed by greatly increased production, as manufacturers work to catch up with the backlog of orders. The strike may simply replace an otherwise inevitable layoff in an industry in which a full year's production would not be sold, as is reported to have been the case with many strikes in the coal fields. On the other hand, a strike can be extremely costly: It may cause the men involved to lose most of their savings; it may shut down plants that are not themselves involved in the strike but that use the materials made by a striking plant; it may force merchants in a strike area either to close or to extend unlimited credit; and it may strain the budget of public assistance agencies.

If the struck industry is one that serves the public, such as the postal service, the telephone company, or the newspaper companies, the strike may give rise to expanding pools of inconvenience. Irritation with a particular strike or with a wave of strikes sometimes leads to demands that strikes be eliminated. This has been accomplished in some Western countries by giving the government power to arbitrate all differences. Actually most union-management contracts call for arbitration of disputes during the life of the contract. But managements want a free hand to negotiate new contracts, and organized labor almost always opposes imposed arbitration, believing that the strike or the threat of a strike is its most effective weapon, and often its only effective weapon, in dealing with management. A report by a United States Senate subcommittee states "The threat of a strike, which must be exercised when necessary if it is to remain a threat, is the drive which gives continuous meaning and substance to collective bargaining." [92] But for the union the strike is very much a two-edged weapon, damaging not only to a firm but also to the workers and to their families.

---

[92] United States Senate, Subcommittee on Labor-Management Relations of the Committee on Labor and Public Welfare, *Factors in Successful Collective Bargaining,* 82nd Cong., 1st sess., quoted in E. Wight Bakke, Clark Kerr, and Charles W. Anrod, eds., *Unions, Management, and the Public,* p. 270.

MIDDLE MANAGEMENT AND WHITE-COLLAR JOBS

Some leaders of large industrial unions, as they contemplate the decreasing membership of their unions and the increasing number of nonunion technical, white-collar, and middle-management personnel—the clerical workers, draftsmen, accountants, salesmen, office managers, and junior executives—in the urban labor force, wonder if the future of unionization does not lie in the organization of these lower- and middle-level "mind workers." Yet, with the exception of government employees, such workers have been extremely difficult to unionize. The problem is that men and women in these ranks do not think of themselves as "workers" set off from management by opposing interests. Rather, they think of themselves as full-fledged members of their organization, and identify more with top management than with manual workers, though their income levels would place them with the latter.

They can be characterized, as foremen have been, as "men in the middle." Whereas the top executives and professional men have a good deal of freedom in terms of how and when they do their work, and the blue-collar workers have another kind of freedom in that their jobs do not depend on their maintaining an acceptable social reputation, those in most white-collar jobs have neither the freedom of the top nor that of the bottom. The psychoanalyst Erich Fromm has written about the emptiness of the lives of junior executives, salesmen, and other suburbanites in the United States today.[93] And C. Wright Mills has described how little scope for self-expression is permitted to many people in the middle and lower ranks of large organizations, where great emphasis is put on ability to work with others:

> In many strata of white-collar employment, such traits as courtesy, helpfulness, and kindness, once intimate, are now part of the impersonal means of livelihood. Self-alienation is thus an accompaniment of . . . alienated labor. . . . When white-collar people get jobs they sell not only their time and energy but their personalities as well.[94]

Mills, in his general indictment, neglects somewhat the concrete differences in the climate of organizations: One department store may demand a submissive conformity and amiability from all its employees, while another may welcome or permit a wider spectrum of behavior.

---

[93] Erich Fromm, *The Sane Society* (New York: Rinehart, 1955).

[94] C. Wright Mills, *White Collar* (New York: Oxford University Press, 1951), p. xvii.

Along with the general enlargement of permissiveness in American society, employers have unevenly followed suit, so that some technical companies may be proud of the fact that their employees wear beards and hold unconventional political as well as cultural views. Some companies, such as IBM, pride themselves on virtually never firing anybody, though they may, as IBM does, demote or otherwise penalize an executive who fails to deliver, while other companies, such as the automobile manufacturers, pride themselves on their toughness and woe to him who can be charged with failure.[95] Since some companies are headed by sales people, others by men whose background is in accounting, and still others by production people, and since companies differ enormously in the degree of hierarchy, the organizational climate varies greatly from firm to firm.

Many middle-level, white-collar employees are in positions that demand no special skill (except perhaps an amorphous administrative "know-how") and are sometimes hired for their personalities alone. Their tenure depends on getting the job done while still "getting along" with those above and around them in the organization and with the organization's customers. They are hired less because of a specific gift than because of a general social facility. Those who have scarce and specialized skills are held less accountable for their personalities—as Steinmetz is reputed to have been tolerated by General Electric—yet bookkeepers, cashiers, and many others who have definite and narrow responsibilities are expected not only to perform specific tasks but to be good members of their organization.

Outside his work group, the white-collar worker may have a variety of different stances toward the organization employing him. On the one hand, he may see the organization as "Them"—people who demand his allegiance to inexplicable directives but are beyond his counterinfluence and reach. Yet on the other hand, he may understand company policies but regard them as socially malicious or unjustifiable. Such a situation confronts many who work in advertising: They believe they must justify advertising as having importance to the economy or else become cynical about their worth to society. (Some few, however, may still take pleasure in their virtuosity, enjoying the exercise of creative talents regardless of their "real" economic importance.) More troubling questions may haunt the reflective workers in defense industries, especially those paid to invent and construct devices that may result in a contaminated, and in the long run, even uninhabitable world.

Compared to these questions concerning ultimate ends, the issue of conformity, salient in the last two decades, seems less important. William H.

[95] See Fred H. Goldner, "Demotion in Industrial Management," *American Sociological Review,* Vol. 30, No. 5 (October, 1965), pp. 714–25.

Whyte's *The Organization Man* helped give rise to the discussion of conformity, and probably helped lead to the elimination of some of its most obvious manifestations such as the choice of clothing or automobile on the basis of what the firm deemed suitable for a given level of the hierarchy. Whyte complained that the wives of management personnel must pass muster before their husbands could be promoted, but this is probably more true for college presidents and Protestant ministers than it is for businessmen. Michel Crozier makes what seems to us a better case when he contends that the most conforming members of an organization—in appearance at least—will be those in the highest ranks who must set the standard, and that much more independence is allowed their subordinates than Whyte contended.[96]

More important than the superficial issue of organizational etiquette is the question of the contradictory pressures Americans face in many different kinds of settings in order to get their work done. The egalitarian spirit of the United States and the dislike of hierarchy mean that informal ties based on mutual acceptance rather than lines of authority determine work behavior.[97] Some companies try to break down inhibitions of lower-level personnel through encouraging sensitivity training and encounter groups among all levels of the company. Yet because Americans want to be liked as well as accepted, they may exaggerate the degree of pleasing or conciliatory behavior that is necessary for them to do their work and then feel a strain between repressed hostility and outward friendliness.

There are other contradictions. Members of organizations may be required to delegate authority while retaining responsibility, to display initiative while following rules, and to rely on others in the organization while maintaining independence. They must resolve these and other conflicting pressures day in and day out.[98]

Professional men and executives have problems substantially different from those of an industrial worker whose day is spent at a disliked task in a subordinate position. They must make a very great personal commitment to their tasks because their self-esteem depends on accomplishment and its recognition, and baffled frustration awaits the man who achieves neither. In addition, there is strong pressure for an individual in these occupations to

---

[96] Michel Crozier, *The Bureaucratic Phenomenon* (Chicago: University of Chicago Press, 1964).

[97] There have been a great many case studies of American organizations. An extensive listing is given by Delbert C. Miller, in his "Industry and the Worker," Henry Borow, ed., *Man in a World at Work* (Boston: Houghton, 1964), pp. 107–09.

[98] For a discussion of the difficulties which may be encountered in organization life by individuals of different temperaments, see Robert L. Kahn *et al.*, *Organizational Stress: Studies in Role Conflict and Ambiguity* (New York: Wiley, 1964).

evaluate his success not only in terms of his job but also in terms of his career, and of where he is in an anticipated sequence of ever-increasing accomplishment and recognition.

There is some logic in discussing the managerial and professional occupations together, beyond the fact that they carry about the same social ranking and that members of each are likely to be concerned with the rise and fall of their career chances. The managerial occupation is becoming more and more professionalized. Such distinctively professional institutions as the graduate school and the professional journal have found their place in the business world. The modern manager is no longer a man who built the business he is running; instead, he is a paid employee whose stake in ownership is likely to be minimal (although stock-option plans give him a speculative stake in the profits). While he may receive a handsome salary and feel surrounded by the trappings of high rank, he can seldom afford to be autocratic; he must exercise his power with restraint and tact.[99] By the same token, the professional is becoming more and more an organization man. Everett Hughes has noted that both law and medicine, the model professions, are "far along the road to practice in organizations," and that other professions—teaching, for example—are almost entirely practiced within organizations.[100] The professional within organizations has some problems that he does not share with managers, often stemming from conflicting responsibilities to firm and to clients; but in his desire for achievement and recognition he is apt to be indistinguishable from the manager.

As we noted in an earlier section, both managers and professionals frequently pay for the stimulation their responsibilities give them by working 70-hour weeks with a good deal of their limited "leisure" devoted to their jobs. If asked their hobby, some businessmen would respond, "work," and would insist that not only do they work constantly but that it is only at work that they truly enjoy themselves.[101] Wilensky reports that only one-fifth of all lawyers and one-quarter of all professors work *fewer* than 45 hours per week.[102] When such men are forced to retire, they may have more than adequate financial resources, but they are often bereft of psychological ones. If

---

[99] See Wilbert E. Moore, *The Conduct of the Corporation* (New York: Random House, 1962), especially Chapter 1.

[100] Everett C. Hughes, "Professions," in *Daedalus,* Vol. 92 (Fall, 1963), pp. 655–68.

[101] See William H. Whyte, Jr., "How Hard Do Executives Work?" in Gerald D. Bell, ed., *Organizations and Human Behavior* (Englewood Cliffs, N. J.: Prentice-Hall, 1967), pp. 272–81.

[102] Harold L. Wilensky, "The Uneven Distribution of Leisure: The Impact of Economic Growth on 'Free Time,' " in Erwin O. Smigel, ed., *Work and Leisure* (New Haven, Conn.: College and University Press, 1963), pp. 107–45.

they have been successful enough in their business or profession to have the power to retire, they may phase their retirement gradually, always maintaining enough touch with affairs so that they can feel in the swim of things. A few retired businessmen have been able to spend their declining years in government or other public service, just as a few retired professors have become emeriti at universities that might not have been able to attract their services earlier in their careers.

The self-employed professional can often work as long as he cares to, since he does not belong to a bureaucracy that forces him to retire at a certain age. His job remains as long as patients, clients, or students continue to come to him. But America values youth and vigor more than age and wisdom, and a lawyer may well find himself losing clients before he begins losing cases. In fact, the dependence of the professional man on his customers or clients always has elements of tension in it, no matter how much these may be glossed over by friendliness and tact on both sides: The clients will judge the professional's competence without understanding how to do so, and the professional, though he may reject their conclusion, will prosper or fail according to it.[103]

The fact that the professions are freely chosen is by no means as advantageous as it might first appear. Just as in one's choice of husband or wife, one's choice of profession is sometimes misguided, and this is the more likely since the choice of profession, unlike that of future spouse, allows for a less adequate "getting acquainted" period and often requires a near-final decision on the basis mainly of public image. These images frequently prove false: Medicine, for example seems to provide unrivaled opportunity for service, but the medical student must in the course of training learn to see his patients as problems rather than persons, and to see himself as someone with a function rather than a mission.[104] Often the problems that will be met in the course of a professional career are not visible to its aspirants, whose models may be furnished by the most prominent "stars" of the career. Thus Lawrence Kubie, the late psychiatrist, argued that the scientific career and its hazards are little understood by the young people attracted to it: In particular, they underestimate the possibility that they may devote themselves to science without ever being able to make a noteworthy contribution to their

---

[103] Everett C. Hughes, "Work and the Self," in John H. Rohrer and Muzafer Sherif, eds., *Social Psychology at the Crossroads* (New York: Harper, 1951).

[104] See Howard S. Becker and Blanche Geer, "The Fate of Idealism in Medical School," *American Sociological Review*, Vol. 23, No. 1 (February, 1958), pp. 50–56. See also, for the extent to which psychiatry seems to promise intimate communication and then erects barriers, Allen Wheelis, *The Quest for Identity* (New York: Norton, 1958), Chapter 7.

field.[105] But we are led to wonder if possibly the growing disenchantment with creative callings stems more from the unrealistically high aspirations that young people, who are more aware of international standards today, set for themselves. The need to be at the very top—to be an Einstein rather than a good secondary school teacher of physics—exacts its toll from among the many who could do quite well in the middle ranges of a profession, and who a generation ago would have felt their accomplishment to be satisfactory even in the lower brackets.

In these top careers, the content of the job may turn out to be quite different from what the young man in training had pictured, but because of the time and money spent in training, he has no alternative but to stay with it. To be sure, in some professions it is possible to shift one's actual activities without a drastic change of occupational title. A physician, for example, may decide that he doesn't really like to have to deal directly with patients and may become a research man in a hospital or an anesthesiologist dealing with patients only when they are "out," or he may find a new career as a hospital administrator or as the editor of a medical journal. But these shifts always require that the professional find new colleagues and develop new skills, in the process hazarding whatever reputation he has already developed. As a man gets older, shifting becomes increasingly difficult.

Of course, it is not only in the professions that people are in effect frozen into their jobs by the contingencies of their careers. A machinist might want to try his hand at a business of his own but hesitate to lose his seniority at his present factory job. Many occupations in addition to the managerial and professional fields—such as entertainment and sales—require maintenance of a large number of "contacts," and the individual who leaves any of these fields for a time risks not being able to return.[106]

Each occupation within the managerial and professional group has its own distinct career line, and some of these are more likely to permit the realization of hopes for success than are others. Some career lines are marked by early rises and high plateaus, as is the case in many areas of government service. Others provide a relatively steady increase in responsibilities and rewards and a degree of advancement for all those who overcome the hurdles of entry, as in some parts of the academic profession in which there is a steady progression from fairly elevated floor to moderate ceiling. The academic profession also illustrates the divergence that may exist even within what to an

[105] Lawrence S. Kubie, "Psychoneurotic Problems of the American Scientist," *Chicago Review,* Vol. 8, No. 3 (1954), pp. 65–80.

[106] See, in this connection, Fred E. Katz, "Occupational Contact Networks," in Sigmund Nosow and William H. Form, eds., *Man, Work, and Society,* pp. 317–21.

outsider might appear to be a single occupation. In the sciences an unusually able and successful man may become a full professor, running an enormous operation, while in his early 30's; on the other hand, an equally able and equally well-regarded man teaching Greek may be unable to advance from a junior rank until an already occupied position is vacated by the death or retirement of the incumbent.

Executives and professionals tend to assess the progress of their careers by comparing how far they have come with the progress of others of the same age or length of time in their field. In addition, there may be some absolute standards: Executives, for example, sometimes say that the man who has not entered top management by the age of 40 will never enter it at all, and both physicists and mathematicians believe that if one is first-class, he will have made a significant contribution by thirty. As people age, their aspirations often shrink to meet the "reality" they have come to perceive, and this is as true of professionals and managers as it is of industrial workers. As a result, they may redefine success in terms of their personal relations with clients or their ability to support their family and lead a pleasant life away from work. Whether this maneuver brings satisfaction we cannot say: There has been little systematic attention given to the problems, if they exist, of the executive or professional of moderate achievement.[107]

It should be noted that a career consists of more than the reflected images of glory or of failure associated with having attained a certain outward status. This is certainly one aspect of the story, which shows up in a lack of attention to the work itself and to its potential challenges and exhilarations. This concern with images of glory or failure often results in excessive attention to the egocentric self engaged in doing the work — a misplaced focus that leads to boredom and anxiety. But a career is not only the graph line of one's journey through life, or a running record of places and statuses. It is also a way of providing coherence to one's changing responsibilities and so furnishing a rationale for one's life.

The professional and the managerial occupations are unique in that they permit the individual to hope that his efforts will be cumulative and will contribute to some end. Thus the priest hopes not only to become a bishop but also to give faith and courage; the doctor not only to "make good" in the conventional sense but also to save lives; and the business executive not only to "get to the top" but also to improve his society. Still, a great many priests would hate to become bishops, though they might want to be able to influence

---

[107] For evidence that the pursuit of the usual notion of intellectual success may frequently produce heartbreak see the account of failures along the tenure trail, by Ben Morreale, "Tales of Academe," *Encounter,* Vol. 33 (August, 1969), pp. 25–32.

bishops toward liberalization of the Church and the diminution of the power of bishops in the dioceses. Some men may want to be at the top to prove they can make it, but they still do not like those terrible responsibilities. Others, less insecure, may feel that there is the greatest room to put their talents to work just under the top where they are less visible but also less vulnerable. What might be termed the life cycle of institutions may not coincide with the life cycle of individuals, so that, for example, a man may become a college president just at the moment in history when such men are targets of student and faculty discontent and taxpayer backlash, or a man may indeed become a bishop at the very moment when he loses his faith.

Since we tend to know more about the frustrations of the literate and articulate, it is sometimes believed that the lure of opportunities for achievement causes men in professional and managerial occupations to lead lives that are particularly harried and full of tension. But the research clearly indicates that the chances for contentment and sense of self-realization are on the whole greater in these prestigious occupations.[108]

Many social critics contend that much if not most of the work in our society is unnecessary, reflecting a wasteful consumerism and international rivalry. Unquestionably, there is great waste. But it would be romantic to underestimate the amount of work required even in a more humane America to keep ourselves clothed and fed and reasonably healthy and mobile. Much of the world's work cannot possibly depend on the current fashionable aspiration for meaningfulness. Assuring that these jobs will continue to convey some sense of dignity may be our most important problem, for even the pressure of unemployment we have now (1971) will not compel men to take jobs or hold them if they consider them unworthy. In a society where the schedule of expectations for jobs, income, and leisure continues to be driven up, there is the danger that automation, far from displacing workers who still want their jobs, may not advance at the rate necessary to absorb the many other jobs that people today without the stick and with plenty of carrot are trying to escape.

---

[108] See, for example, the data quoted by Gerald Gurin, Joseph Veroff, and Sheila Feld in *America Looks at Its Mental Health* (New York: Basic Books, 1960), especially Chapter 6, "The Job."

12

Poverty
and Disrepute

DAVID MATZA

At its source, poverty is an economic matter. Especially in advanced industrial nations, its causes may be found in the existing arrangements of property and income; in the persistence of business cycles in capitalist economies, with the resultant periodic underemployment and unemployment; and in the prevailing system of public welfare that doles out approximately the demeaning assistance desired by the entrepreneurs of a disciplined and "productive" labor force. The manifestations and consequences of poverty, however, are to be found mainly among the poor themselves and — as the reader will shortly discover — poverty is not especially ennobling. This does not mean — as some readers of an earlier version of this essay apparently thought — that I believe the poor to be the "cause" of poverty or responsible for their own condition.[1] My actual view happens to be almost precisely the opposite: The only sense in which the poor themselves perpetuate their condition is by sometimes being so engulfed or demoralized by their situation as to be unable to effectively act against and overthrow existing arrangements or change them to their own advantage. That is a very minimal assignment of responsibility for one's own condition — roughly equivalent to that properly accorded the slave for his captivity or a people for their destruction.

---

[1] See Charles Valentine, *Culture and Poverty: Critique and Counter-Proposals* (Chicago: University of Chicago Press, 1968). For the author's response, see *Current Anthropology,* Vol. 10, No. 3 (April–June, 1969), pp. 192–94.

A corollary of this conception of the social whereabouts of the basic causes and consequences of poverty is a certain cynicism regarding the possibilities of any real or durable solution to the "social question" of poverty—as long as the current system of property and class relations prevails. This may surprise those readers who expect a social problem to have a solution that does not require a thorough reordering of key economic institutions. If there is a solution to the "social question," it has become increasingly difficult for me, at any rate, to visualize its emergence within the class and property system known as capitalism. To argue or "prove" that belief or assertion is beyond the scope of this essay. Besides, the basic argument as to why the "social question" cannot be resolved within the context of capitalism has already been made. For serious students—those who are truly interested in profound questions and, thus, difficult answers—a number of nineteenth-century classics might prove illuminating. Despite its minor errors and deficiencies, the classic argument as to why the "social question"—poverty—cannot be resolved within capitalism has been made by Marx. The student should first consult Karl Marx's *The Poverty of Philosophy: Answer to the Philosophy of Poverty,* by M. Proudhon. Though a moderately difficult book, it is often quite hilarious, thus making it relatively entertaining to read. (If the student is interested *only* in being amused, and cares nothing about being enlightened, he may also read the book by Proudhon, attacked by Marx, or for that matter anything else written by Proudhon, including his best work, *What Is Property?*) After reading the relatively easy *Philosophy of Poverty,* the student who still desires the more total argument must, of course, read Karl Marx's *Capital* (all three volumes). With regard to the solution to the "social question" that may begin as a "movement" within the very bowels of capitalism but cannot be realized until the system is transcended or "overthrown," the student could do considerably worse—and perhaps no better—than to consult Karl Marx's *Communist Manifesto.*

Thus, perhaps, the decision to ignore the so-called War on Poverty in the first edition of this essay appears vindicated; and the only thing worth noting in this revision is its obvious and predictable failure. It follows, of course, that by ignoring the much ballyhooed Moynihan-Nixon Family Assistance Plan too, I risk the same implicit prediction. It should be apparent that the risk inherent in ignoring the Nixon administration's device for eradicating poverty is minuscule.

Such a stance hardly denies that some improvements have occurred—technology, sanitation, and medicine alone have guaranteed that contemporary poor people will live longer, and at not so debased a level. Thus, it should go without saying—and without celebration—that contemporary, poor Americans are better off than their counterparts in Pakistan and China or their American predecessors in 1933 or 1872. Today, poor Americans may even purchase new cars, though the actual number who do so seemed for a time to be under considerable dispute.[2] Nonetheless, the categories of poverty — as well as the attendant disrepute — have easily survived, and for a very good and simple reason: The reality of poverty continues to plague a substantial minority of persons in the world's richest nation and the overwhelming majority of persons in the nations of the world.

The persistence of poverty and the cyclical nature of its specific magnitude must be stressed, even to understand the general data presented here. Between 1959 and 1966, there was a reduction in the level of poverty in the United States. But even as these data are reported (as they will be, since the last generally available compilation is for 1966), they take on a certain unreality. By the end of 1970, the official rate of unemployment reached 6 percent, substantially above what it was during the wartime boom in 1966, but probably still below the rate contemplated and planned for by the business-minded, anti-inflationary Nixon administration.[3]

What does a national unemployment rate of 6 percent mean with regard to the level of poverty? It has long been clear that such statistics are somewhat misleading because unemployment is concentrated in certain sections of the population and much additional unemployment, underemployment, and impoverished employment exist in the very same sections. We may gain some understanding of the concentrated poverty lying behind an average rate of national unemployment by briefly considering an excellent Department of Labor study conducted in 1966.[4]

Nineteen sixty-six was a prosperous year. The economy was doing well; the unemployment rate, 3.7 percent, was low, at least by American standards. The Labor Department study had two aims: to assess the unemployment rate, as usually defined, in selected slums and, for ten of those slums, to estimate the level of "sub-employment." What is the difference between unem-

---

[2] Fourteen percent, according to Irving Kristol, "The Lower Fifth," *The New Leader*, February 17, 1964; but less than 2 percent, according to Herman Miller, "The Dimensions of Poverty" in Ben Seligman, ed., *Poverty as a Public Issue* (New York: Free Press, 1965), p. 22. Alas, for Mr. Kristol, less than 2 percent as well according to the 1960 University of Michigan Survey Research Center Report erroneously reported by the same Mr. Kristol.

[3] For a good discussion and statistical analysis of the close relationship between a decline in the poverty-elimination rate, a rising rate of unemployment, and a lagging rate of economic growth, see Lowell Gallaway, "The Foundations of the War on Poverty," *American Economic Review* (March, 1965), pp. 122–30.

[4] U. S. Department of Labor, "A Sharper Look at Unemployment in U. S. Cities and Slums." No date of publication given.

ployment, as usually defined, and the Labor Department's conception of sub-employment? The study drew a clear distinction:

> This traditional unemployment measure counts as employed a person who is working only part-time, although he is trying to find full-time work; gives no consideration to the amount of earnings; omits those who are not "actively looking for work" — even though the reason for this is their conviction (whether right or wrong) that they can't find a job, at least the one they want; and omits the "under-count" factor — those who are known to be present in the community but who do not show up at all under present survey method. . . . A sub-employment index . . . covers the entire employment-hardship area . . . (1) those actively looking for work and unable to find it (2) part-time workers who are trying to get full-time work (3) heads of households under 65 who earn less than \$60/week and individuals under 65 who are not heads of households and earn less than \$50/week in a full-time job (4) half the number of "non-participants" (those not working and not looking for work) in the male 20–64 age groups (5) a conservative estimate of the male "undercount" group based on the assumption — indicated from the evidence — that the number of males in the area should approximate the number of females, and that half of the unfound males are sub-employed.[5]

The survey of the ten areas closely scrutinized revealed that in addition to almost 10 percent official unemployment,

> 6.9% of those listed as employed are working only part-time, although they are trying to find full-time work . . . 21% of those working full-time are earning less than \$60 a week. . . . A large number of persons . . . are not working and not looking for work. . . . This "non-participation" rate . . . is 11% among men in the 20–64 year age group. . . . Between a fifth and a third of the adult males expected . . . to be part of this slum area were unfound in the November survey. . . .[6]

Table 1 summarizes the findings of the Labor Department Study for 1966.

If behind the prosperity of 1966 lurks a concentrated poverty, what can be said of periods of recession? If inflation continues, there is no telling what level of recession and unemployment will be deemed "acceptable" by business and government as they jointly pursue price stability. And if the war in Vietnam continues, there is no telling whether price stability is in fact attainable at any level of recession. Irrespective, however, of whether a

---

[5] *Ibid.*
[6] *Ibid.*

TABLE 1

Unemployment and Subemployment in
Selected Slums, November 1966

Location	Official Unemployment Rate	Subemployment Rate
United States	3.7	
Boston (Roxbury)	6.9	24.2
Cleveland (Hough area)	15.6	
Detroit (Central Woodward area)	10.1	
Los Angeles (South L.A.)	12.0	
New Orleans (several areas)	10.0	45.3
New York (Harlem)	8.1	28.6
New York (E. Harlem)	9.0	33.1
New York (Bedford-Stuyvesant)	6.2	27.6
Oakland (Bayside)	13.0	
Philadelphia (N. Phila.)	11.0	34.2
Phoenix (Salt River Bed area)	13.2	41.7
St. Louis (North Side)	12.9	38.9
San Antonio (East and West Sides)	8.1	47.4
San Francisco (Mission-Filmore)	11.1	24.6
San Juan (El Fanguito)	15.8	
Areas surveyed in study	10.0	33.9

Source: Adapted from U. S. Department of Labor, "A Sharper Look at Unemployment in U. S. Cities and Slums."

recession continues, widespread though concentrated poverty will surely persist in America. The experience of 1966 assures that. Since there is no final solution to the social question in sight, we shall focus in the remainder of this chapter on the manifestations and consequences of poverty.

CIRCLES OF POVERTY

A discussion of the varieties of poverty is facilitated—though necessarily oversimplified—by conceiving of its victims as occupying concentric circles: The widest circle is composed of all the poor; an intermediary circle, considerably smaller, consists of those who are poor and on the welfare rolls; and the smallest circle, the disreputable poor, represents those who are poor, sporadically or permanently on welfare, and, additionally, suffer the especially demoralizing effects of the stigma of immorality.

Description and analysis of the disreputable poor is seriously hindered by several difficulties. These people are not only hard to reach, but also hard to identify or designate in any rigorous statistical fashion. Part of the problem is institutionally created, especially by the character of the Aid to Families with Dependent Children program—the largest single welfare program in America. Until very recently, this program was limited to families in which the father, from an official standpoint, was no longer in the home. One defect (there were many others) of this provision was that very little information regarding the males was officially collected. However, the more important difficulty is theoretical, and rooted in public sentiments of America and other Western nations. Attempts to clearly distinguish the disreputable poor from others who superficially resemble them are systematically frustrated because a certain element of disrepute attaches even to the poor who are deemed deserving and morally above reproach. Poverty itself is slightly disreputable, and being on welfare somewhat more so. The inner circle—the so-called hard core—is not alone in living in disrepute. That feature is shared to some extent by all who are poor or on welfare. But the hard core is further along on a range of disrepute. To the minor shortcoming of being poor is added the more substantial vice of requiring assistance and, finally, the major stigma of immorality. These last features are the special characteristics of the disreputable poor and distinguish them from portions of the population whose moral shortcomings are more limited and more tolerable.

The distinction between the poor, those on welfare, and the disreputable poor is further complicated by a public tendency, echoed by certain sociologists, to gratuitously extend the features of the inner circle—the hard core—to the wider but next-removed circle of the welfare poor, and then to the furthest removed circle of the poor altogether.[7] This tendency must be guarded against, partly for reasons of sociological precision, but more generally for the public purpose of avoiding defamation.

Despite these problems, the concept of the three concentric circles is useful in considering the extent and composition of the various populations under discussion, as a rough guide subject to the qualification that actual persons and families move from one circle to the other and even to social circles beyond the realm of poverty.[8]

---

[7] See, for instance, Walter Miller, "Lower-Class Culture as a Generating Milieu of Gang Delinquency," *Journal of Social Issues,* Vol. 14, No. 3 (1958), pp. 5–19.

[8] For related distinctions, see S. M. Miller, "The American Lower Classes: A Typological Approach," *Sociology and Social Research,* Vol. 48 (April, 1964), reprinted in Arthur Shostak and William Gomberg, eds., *Blue-Collar World* (Englewood Cliffs, N. J.: Prentice-Hall, 1964), pp. 12–13.

The Poor

In estimating the extent of poverty in America, one may choose between an absolute and a relative conception. The former defines poverty in terms of an arbitrary dividing line, usually a yearly dollar income which remains fixed over time. In Robert Lampman's definition, for instance, a "low-income person" is "one with an income equivalent to that of a four-person family with total income of not more than $2,500 in 1957 dollars." [9] Herman Miller, in a somewhat more recent study, used $3,000 as the dividing line. [10]

In the most recent studies, $3,000 continues as the poverty line, with a minor adjustment made for a rise in the cost of living. "As applied to 1966 incomes, the poverty level of nonfarm residents ranges from $1,560 for a woman 65 years or older living alone to $5,440 for a family of seven or more persons; it was $3,335 for a nonfarm family of four." [11] For readers unfamiliar with regard to what living in poverty means, it may help to learn that "according to the most recent Bureau of Labor Statistics expenditure survey, it would require an income of $9,200 for a family of four to achieve a modest but adequate standard of living in most of our large cities." [12]

Paradoxically, an absolute definition of poverty is highly useful in stressing the relative deprivation [13] experienced by various segments of society. Subjectively, making less than $3,000 means one thing in a setting where most others make no more and quite another where only a small

---

[9] Robert Lampman, "The Low-Income Population and Economic Growth," Study Paper No. 21 (Washington, D. C.: U. S. Congress Joint Economic Committee, 1959), p. 4.

[10] Herman Miller, *Trends in the Income of Families and Persons in the United States 1947-1960,* Technical Paper No. 8 (Washington, D. C.: U. S. Dept. of Commerce, Bureau of the Census).

[11] Current Population Reports, *Consumer Income,* "The Extent of Poverty in the United States 1959 to 1966," Series P-60, No. 54 (May 31, 1968), p. 1.

[12] *Ibid.,* p. 2.

[13] Relative deprivation refers to the idea that subjective feelings of deprivation depend on how one's own experiences compare to those close at hand, to what one has become accustomed to in the past, or to what one anticipates. Thus, profound degradation in an absolute sense may be tolerable or even pass unnoticed if others close at hand fare no better or if one never had reason to expect any better. A general discussion of relative deprivation may be found in Robert Merton, *Social Theory and Social Structure* (New York: Free Press, 1957), pp. 225-36.

minority earn so little. The point is that the possibilities of relative depriva-tion are most fully appreciated when we use an *absolute* or fixed conception of poverty. If the poverty line were allowed to float according to rising cus-tomary standards or needs, one aspect of relative deprivation would be obscured. There would be a tendency for the proportion of persons experi-encing poverty to remain relatively constant, and thus there would be little insight into the psychic significance of how many others are in the same boat. However, a fixed or absolute conception has shortcomings. The main dif-ficulty is that it ignores shifts in the customary definitions of an acceptable minimal standard of life. Rising aspirations, which are hardly limited to underdeveloped economies, not only refer to the highest possibilities; they also affect the minimal standards of life acceptable in a society. Each concep-tion of poverty has advantages and disadvantages. The relative conception reflects the plausible contention that those in the bottom one-fifth of an in-come distribution will feel deprived irrespective of their level of income. A key question when using this conception is whether important shifts have oc-

TABLE 2

Percentage Share of Aggregate Income in 1947, 1950, and 1955 to 1966, Received by Each One-Fifth of Families and Unrelated Individuals, Ranked by Income, for the United States

Income Rate	1966	1965	1964	1963	1962	1961
Families						
Total	**100.0**	**100.0**	**100.0**	**100.0**	**100.0**	**100.0**
Lowest fifth	5.4	5.3	5.2	5.1	5.1	4.8
Second fifth	12.4	12.2	12.0	12.0	12.0	11.7
Middle fifth	17.7	17.6	17.7	17.6	17.5	17.4
Fourth fifth	23.8	24.0	24.0	23.9	23.7	23.6
Highest fifth	40.7	40.9	41.1	41.4	41.7	42.6
Top 5 percent	14.8	15.2	15.7	16.0	16.3	17.1
Unrelated Individuals						
Total	**100.0**	**100.0**	**100.0**	**100.0**	**100.0**	**100.0**
Lowest fifth	2.9	3.1	2.4	2.4	3.0	2.6
Second fifth	7.6	7.3	7.1	7.3	7.4	7.0
Middle fifth	13.3	13.4	12.8	12.7	12.7	13.0
Fourth fifth	24.2	25.4	24.5	24.6	24.1	24.2
Highest fifth	52.0	50.9	53.1	53.0	52.8	53.3
Top 5 percent	21.8	20.2	22.6	21.2	21.1	22.7

curred in the percentage of aggregate income going to the poorest one-fifth. A doubling of the share of aggregate income going, say, to the poorest one-fifth in a population would represent a major improvement in their position. However, no such shift has occurred in recent American history. As indicated in Table 2, the share of aggregate income going to the poorest one-fifth (as well as every other segment of the population) remained virtually stable from 1947 to 1966.

A basic shortcoming of a relative conception of poverty — one, say, that considers the lowest one-fifth poor regardless of its actual income — is that it obscures the proportion of the population who share the lot of being poor. Obviously, the proportion poor cannot vary if the proportion is fixed, as it is in the relative conception; it can only vary if the dollar level of a poverty line is more or less fixed, a banal though, admittedly, cute point made by Irving Kristol in an otherwise banal though, admittedly, cute essay in *New Leader*. But, as we have noted, a fixed or absolute conception of poverty contains its own shortcoming. It ignores shifting definitions of a tolerable minimal

1960	1959	1958	1957	1956	1955	1950	1947
100.0	100.0	100.0	100.0	100.0	100.0	100.0	100.0
4.9	5.0	5.1	5.0	5.0	4.8	4.5	5.0
12.0	12.1	12.4	12.6	12.4	12.2	12.0	11.8
17.6	17.7	17.9	18.1	17.8	17.7	17.4	17.0
23.6	23.7	23.7	23.8	23.7	23.7	23.5	23.1
42.0	41.4	40.9	40.5	41.2	41.6	42.6	43.0
16.8	16.3	15.8	15.7	16.3	16.8	17.0	17.2
100.0	100.0	100.0	100.0	100.0	100.0	100.0	100.0
2.6	2.3	2.4	2.6	2.7	2.5	2.3	1.9
7.1	6.9	7.0	7.3	7.3	7.3	7.0	5.8
13.6	13.0	13.1	13.7	13.6	13.4	13.8	11.9
25.7	24.2	25.1	25.4	25.3	25.0	26.5	21.4
50.9	53.5	52.5	51.1	51.1	51.9	50.4	59.1
20.0	22.8	21.4	19.8	20.3	21.7	19.3	33.3

Source: Current Population Reports, *Consumer Income,* "Income in 1966 of Families and Persons in the United States," Series P-60, No. 53 (Dec. 28, 1967).

standard of life and thus tends to yield overly sanguine findings. Let us consider the recent shifts in the extent of poverty in America, keeping in mind two distinct possibilities: The situation today may not be as good as in the boom year of 1966; and the poverty line used in recent studies may bear little resemblance to customary conceptions of the minimal standard of life tolerable in a rich and mass-communicative nation.

The first half of the 1960's "witnessed a pronounced decline in the extent of poverty in the United States." [14] Using a poverty line of $3,335 for a non-farm family of four, the proportion considered poor fell from 22 percent in 1959 to about 15 percent in 1966. The number of persons accounted poor by this standard declined from about 39 to 30 million. [15] This improvement "was largely a result of increased job opportunities and higher earnings," and thus "those equipped to make the most of such possibilities fared best." [16]

But just as a national unemployment rate of 3.7 percent obscures a rate of 12.9 percent in the north side of St. Louis and a sub-employment rate there of 38.9 percent, so too a figure of 15 percent for those below the poverty line fails to convey the concentration of those 30 million Americans in certain sectors of the population.

There are two ways of visualizing the main contours of poverty in America. Although they are not tied to any particular ideology, these two views have come to represent rival political positions. The first stresses the persistence of racist institutions that, apparently, permanently relegate nonwhites (mainly blacks, but in some areas Mexican-Americans or American Indians) to the bottom of the economic pyramid. Thus it may be observed that "In 1966, after 6 consecutive years of economic expansion, 41 percent of the non-white population was poor as compared with 12 percent of the whites." [17] The second position, associated in the public mind with Daniel Moynihan, stresses the low earning capacity of families headed by women — where the male is divorced, has died, or deserted — or the plight of unrelated individuals who are aged or disabled. Thus, it can be observed that "By 1966, families of a woman with children, the aged and the households of the disabled accounted for about 3 million of the 6 million families counted poor." [18] The choice between the two positions is of course a false one. Not only may both

---

[14] Current Population Reports, *Consumer Income,* "The Extent of Poverty in the United States 1959 to 1966."

[15] *Ibid.;* see also, Molly Orshansky, "The Shape of Poverty in 1966," *Social Security Bulletin,* Vol. 3, No. 3 (March, 1968), p. 3.

[16] Molly Orshansky, *ibid.,* p. 4.

[17] Current Population Reports, *Consumer Income,* "The Extent of Poverty in the United States 1959 to 1966," p. 3.

[18] Molly Orshansky, "The Shape of Poverty in 1966," *Social Security Bulletin,* p. 4.

be operative; more important, perhaps, part of the social consequence of poverty is a constant pressure on the stability of the family, a higher likelihood of illness and disability, and the virtual certainty that the old will have neither ample savings nor retirement benefits. But if one must choose between the competing approaches, the stress on the persistence of institutional racism seems more warranted. In considering these rival theses, Molly Orshansky observes:

> The impression is widespread that nonwhite families are poor because of the absence of a male breadwinner and the presence of too many children. The statistics lend some support to these impressions, but the more important finding is that nonwhite families are far more likely to be in poverty whatever their composition. Within each sex of head and size of family group, the incidence of poverty among nonwhite families far exceeds that of white families. For families headed by men, the poverty rates for nonwhite families are about four times as high as for white families except at the extremes — two person families which include a high proportion of aged white units and seven-or-more person families where even the white rate gets fairly high. For families headed by women, there is a white-nonwhite difference of at least 20 percentage points in every category." [19]

In summary, the evidence indicates that broken families, a great many children, and the aging may worsen the economic situation of any household, but that the situation of nonwhites is poor even under ideal family conditions. Table 3 summarizes the relative economic position of whites and nonwhites according to whether the family is intact and according to the number of children.

A final indication of the racial concentration of poverty in America may be found in another aspect of the shift between 1959 and 1966. Though the nonwhite minorities in America have always suffered a disproportionate share of poverty, they have never made up a majority of the poor. Because whites are a majority in this country, most poor people have been white despite the fact that the proportion is low compared to the nonwhite population. That is still true, but between 1959 and 1966 it became significantly less true. The nonwhite minority now constitutes a more substantial segment of poor people in America than previously.

> The nonwhite population had not fared as well as the white during the 1959–1966 upswing, though by the end of the period it was making greater strides than at the beginning. To be sure, in 1966 it was 1 in

---

[19] *Ibid.*, p. 6.

TABLE 3
Percentage Poor by Race and Head of Household

Size of Family	Male Head		Female Head	
	White	Nonwhite	White	Nonwhite
Total	**8.2**	**27.0**	**27.7**	**60.2**
Two persons	11.3	21.7	21.2	42.6
Three persons	5.0	18.3	25.2	48.7
Four persons	4.6	19.9	36.6	62.1
Five persons	6.0	26.7	43.9	76.0
Six persons	8.4	34.7	50.9	83.8
Seven persons or more	18.3	47.6	62.3	83.9

Source: Current Population Reports, Consumer Income, "The Extent of Poverty in the United States 1959 to 1966," p. 6.

3 nonwhite families who were poor compared with 1 in 10 white families, and back in 1959 it was 1 in 2 nonwhite families and 1 in 7 white families who were poor. It is also a fact [however] that the nonwhite made up about a third of the nation's poor in 1966, compared with just over one-fourth in 1959 — a widening disadvantage explained only in small part by the greater population growth among the nonwhite.[20]

The Welfare Poor

The welfare poor correspond to the intermediary circle, considerably narrower than that comprising the poor, and considerably wider than that made up of the disreputable poor. The majority of those whose poverty is relieved — the welfare poor — suffer no disrepute beyond that implicit in their failure to be self-supporting. But, as suggested earlier, dependency itself emits a hint of disrepute in a nation whose official values stress independence, initiative, and capacity. Thus, a public stereotype tends — but only *tends* — to emerge in which the minimal disrepute inherent in the fact of dependency is coupled with the maximal disrepute implicit in demoralization. (Demoralization should be understood in the double sense of the withering of conscientious effort and the decline of moral standards.) The unrestrained tendency to couple dependency with demoralization would yield a public stereotype equating the welfare poor with the disreputable poor. But this

[20] *Ibid.*, p. 10.

tendency is partly offset by another tendency, also traditional. Certain forms of dependency are understood, tolerated, and subsequently exempted from the special stigma of demoralization. We have long regarded the disabled, the aged, the blind as occupying a special moral place in society—a place where the normally assumed relation between dependency and demoralization is either inoperative or irrelevant. These two tendencies operate simultaneously. A mechanism by which the public equates families "on welfare" with the disreputable poor is through a systematic forgetting—a collective repressing—of the composition of the publicly aided population.

The welfare poor are defined by the fact that they depend wholly or partly on some manner of public assistance for sustenance. Morgan and his associates, in a survey of consumption units, found that "less than one-fourth of the poor families received public assistance during 1959." [21] This estimate corresponds roughly with one derived from totaling the numbers assisted by the variety of aid programs in existence. There are five major aid programs in the United States. This does not—and should not—include Unemployment Insurance and Old-Age, Survivors, and Disability Insurance. Assistance programs are not insurance programs. They are a relief to the needy to which the recipient does not contribute. The major programs that relieve poverty are Old-Age Assistance, Aid to Families with Dependent Children, Aid to the Permanently and Total Disabled, Aid to the Blind, and General Assistance. All but the last are federally subsidized. General Assistance is locally financed and administered and is typically reserved for persons who are not covered by any of the other programs but are nonetheless deemed needy. In November of 1966, somewhat more than 7.9 million Americans received some kind of public welfare assistance. Of the total, about 2,079,000 received Old-Age Assistance; about 585,000 received Aid to the Permanently and Total Disabled; and about 84,000 received Aid to the Blind. Local General Assistance programs helped about 611,000 persons; and, finally, the largest group, about 4,568,000 persons—of whom 3,460,000 were children, the rest adults—received Aid to Families with Dependent Children. A rough notion of the magnitude of the relief provided can be derived from the average amount given recipients in the different programs. Though the averages obscure the considerable differences among states, listing them should squelch any illusions the reader may harbor about the generosity of the American dole. The average *monthly* payment ranged from about $86 to the blind to about $36 per recipient in Aid to Families with Dependent Children. Those on Old-Age Assistance received a little more than $67 per month,

---

[21] James Morgan, Martin David, Wilbur Cohen, and Harvey Brazer, *Income and Welfare in the United States* (New York: McGraw-Hill, 1962), p. 216.

TABLE 4

AFDC Recipient Rates by Place of Residence

Place of Residence	Recipient Rate
Standard metropolitan statistical areas	39
Central cities	63
Outside central cities	17
Outside standard metropolitan statistical areas	38
Urban places	39
Rural-nonfarm	41
Rural-farm	27
Total (excluding Puerto Rico and Virgin Islands)	**38**

Source: Robert Mugge, "Aid to Families with Dependent Children," *Social Security Bulletin,* Vol. 26, No. 3, p. 4.

while the disabled were given closer to $74. The average amount given in General Assistance programs was about $79 — but that was for each *case*, not each recipient. It is true that states like Mississippi bring down the average. However, it is also true that New York brings it up.[22]

Since Aid to Families with Dependent Children is the most important of the programs, some data on the composition of the recipients are available. Persons receiving this kind of aid are disproportionately nonwhite and are concentrated in the central city areas of the large metropolises. Robert Mugge summarizes the racial composition of AFDC recipients:

> Almost half the cases receiving Aid to Families with Dependent Children were reported to be white, two-fifths were reported as Negro, 2 percent American Indian, and 9 percent "other nonwhite and unknown." [The last category is so large because Puerto Rico and the Virgin Islands reported all cases as "race unknown," and New York state erroneously classified all cases of Puerto Rican origin as "other nonwhite."] It appears . . . reasonable . . . that at least half of the 9 percent . . . were actually white. Therefore, according to a rough estimate, about 54 percent of all cases were white, 44 percent Negro, and 2 percent Indian and other nonwhite.[23]

The concentration of AFDC recipients in central cities is evident in Table 4, which shows recipient rates for different types of areas. (A recipient rate is the number of child recipients per 1,000 children under age 18.)

---

[22] The figures in this section are from Health, Education and Welfare, *Indicators* (February, 1967), pp. s-24 and s-25.

[23] Robert Mugge, "Aid to Families with Dependent Children," *Social Security Bulletin,* Vol. 26, No. 3 (March, 1963), p. 3.

The Disreputable Poor

In the phrase, "the disreputable poor," the word "disreputable" is intended to distinguish a segment of the poor rather than to describe all those who are poor. Though there is considerable variation, at any given time only a portion of those who can reasonably be considered poor are disreputable. The term disreputable introduces no personal judgment but takes account of the judgments made by other members of society; to ignore the stigma that adheres to this special kind of poverty is to miss one of its key aspects.

The disreputable poor are the people who remain unemployed, or casually and irregularly employed, even during periods approaching full employment and prosperity; for that reason, and others, they live in disrepute. This group does not include the majority of those who are unemployed or irregularly employed during a period of mass unemployment. To locate the section of the able-bodied poor that remains unemployed or casually employed during periods of full employment is a difficult task, particularly in the American setting where the number unemployed is subject to frequent and relatively drastic fluctuations.[24] Consequently, the line separating those who are unemployed only during periods of depression or recession and those who are more permanently unoccupied is especially difficult to draw.

The search for the disreputable poor will, of necessity, yield extremely crude estimates subject to wide margins of error. This is due to four major obstacles. *First,* it is extremely difficult to obtain data on persons receiving General Assistance. States vary widely in the conditions of eligibility for that program, and persons awaiting placement in one of the federally subsidized programs are often in the state programs for short periods of time. Accordingly, the discussion will focus on persons relieved by the Aid to Families with Dependent Children Program. *Second,* the character of AFDC makes the males, who are associated with the women and children helped by the program, institutionally nonexistent. These men are not typically relieved by AFDC, but frequently they live in the same neighborhoods as those who are relieved, share and perhaps dominate the style of communal life in these neighborhoods, father many of the children, allegedly expend some of the monthly welfare payments, and in many other ways are part of the same

---

[24] Stanley Lebergott, "Economic Crises in the United States," in Special Committee on Unemployment Problems, *Readings in Unemployment* (Washington, D. C.: U. S. Government Printing Office, 1960), pp. 86–87.

social milieu. *Third,* the indicators used here to estimate the proportion of AFDC recipients who can reasonably be deemed disreputable by general community standards are, of necessity, extremely crude. *Fourth,* there are undoubtedly persons living in disreputable poverty who are for a variety of reasons temporarily—or perhaps even permanently—off the welfare rolls. For all these reasons, the reader is cautioned regarding the accuracy of the estimates. The main reason for proposing these estimates is the somewhat shaky belief that some statistically established estimates—however crude—are better than the half-conscious estimates, based on public stereotypes, that all of us carry in mind.

One indication of disrepute revolves around the question of a man's relationship with the children he has fathered and the women with whom he has cohabited. Bastardy, or illegitimacy, has been a persistent sign of disrepute despite the somewhat variable reaction to it by different social classes, races, and nations.[25] Even if illegitimacy is somewhat tolerated in neighborhoods where it is relatively prevalent, a person's status may be derogated by allusions to the questionable moral character of his mother and the dubious existence of his father.[26]

The reader will note in Table 5 that in 21.2 percent of the 910,000 families on AFDC at the time of collection of the data the man was not married to the mother.[27] A key, but unfortunately unanswerable, question in arriving at an estimate of the population living in disreputable poverty is: How many men have fathered the children in any given family?

Being imprisoned may be taken as another indicator of disrepute. Despite variable levels of tolerance toward criminality, there is typically some acknowledgment of official morality, and this minimal acknowledgment is reflected in the potentially stigmatic character of being or having been imprisoned.

One may add to these two indicators of disrepute—illegitimacy and im-

---

[25] For a more detailed discussion of this point, see William J. Goode, "Family Disorganization," in this volume; also see Judith Blake and Kingsley Davis, "Norms, Values, and Sanctions," in Robert Faris, ed., *Handbook of Modern Sociology* (Chicago: Rand McNally, 1964), Chapter 13.

[26] See, in this connection, the interesting discussion of ranking, the "dozens," and other forms of cutting, albeit playful, talk in Roger D. Abrahams, *Deep Down in the Jungle: Negro Narrative Folklore from the Streets of Philadelphia* (Hatboro, Pa.: Folklore Associates, 1964).

[27] For data bearing on a similar point, see Gordon Blackwell and Raymond Gould, *Future Citizens All* (Chicago: Public Welfare Association, 1952), pp. 8–9; and M. Elaine Burgess and Daniel Price, *An American Dependency Challenge* (Chicago: Public Welfare Association, 1963), p. 40.

TABLE 5

Status of the Father in AFDC Families

Father's Status	Percentage of 910,000 AFDC Families
Dead	7.7
Incapacitated	17.8
Absent from Home	67.2
Divorced or legally separated	14.3
Separated without court decree	8.3
Deserting	18.3
Not married to mother	21.2
Imprisoned	4.2
Other reason	0.6
Unemployed	5.1
Other Status	2.2

Source: These figures are reported in Robert Mugge, "Aid to Families with Dependent Children," *Social Security Bulletin*, Vol. 26, No. 3, p. 8.

prisonment—desertion and separation without court decree. But there we are on somewhat shakier grounds, especially with regard to acknowledged separation, even if the matter has not come to court. One may arrive at low and high estimates of the magnitude of disreputable poverty; illegitimacy and imprisonment can be used to derive low estimates, and desertion can be added to arrive at a high estimate.

Accordingly, a low estimate would be that about 25 percent of AFDC families may be regarded as disreputable by general community standards, and a high estimate would be that about 45 percent are so regarded.

The same general impression may be derived from additional data bearing on the usual occupation of the father officially associated with the AFDC family. Table 6 shows the usual occupation reported for such fathers and compares that distribution to that of employed men. An indicator of the proportion of men living in disrepute can be inferred from this table. Any sort of usual occupation confers a minimal legitimacy. Disrepute is most apt to follow from the absence of any occupation or the lack of public knowledge regarding an occupational pursuit. Thus, a crude estimate of the proportion living in disrepute may be derived from adding the last two categories— *occupation unknown* and *never had full-time employment.* This could be considered a low estimate, since some proportion of those doing unskilled work are apt to be relatively casual or irregular laborers.[28]

---

[28] The fact that the occupation of the father associated with an AFDC family is unknown can hardly be attributed to mere administrative oversight, since the question

TABLE 6

Usual Occupational Class of Fathers in Assistance Families
and That of Employed Men

Occupational Class	Percent AFDC Fathers	Percent Employed Men in General Population
Professional and semiprofessional	0.6	10.3
Farmowners, renters, and managers	1.5	5.5
Proprietors, managers, and officials	0.5	10.7
Clerical, sales, and kindred workers	2.3	13.8
Craftsmen, foremen, and kindred workers	6.6	19.9
Operatives and kindred semiskilled and skilled workers	13.9	19.9
Farm laborers, including sharecroppers	10.2	2.8
Service workers	5.6	6.1
Unskilled laborers	33.7	6.9
Never had full-time employment	3.1	—
Unknown	22.0	4.6

Source: Robert Mugge, "Aid to Families with Dependent Children," *Social Security Bulletin,* Vol. 26, No. 3, p. 10.

A final indication of the proportion living in disrepute is suggested by the common assumption that relief should be a *temporary* matter. Persons who maintain dependent status over a seemingly permanent period are suspect, unless they are aged or otherwise infirm. Thus, long-term dependency may be taken as another indicator of the proportion of AFDC families living in disrepute. Table 7 shows the distribution of AFDC families by length of time on assistance. By this indication, too, somewhere between 25 and 45 percent of AFDC families bear the onus of disrepute. Thus, we may hazard the guess that from one-quarter to about two-fifths of the families on AFDC, and the men who live in the same social circles, can be regarded as disreputable by general community standards.

WELFARE CHISELING—It is hardly possible to write on the subject of welfare and disrepute without considering the phenomenon of "welfare chiseling." This trait is often imputed to the welfare poor, and especially to the disreputable among them. This understandable—one might even say reasonable—response to being on the dole received considerable attention as a result of

---

of eligibility for AFDC turns on the earning capacity of the father. Welfare officials look into the matter carefully. That his occupation is unknown usually means that the alliance culminating in a child was so casual that the mother hardly knows the man's name or location—itself an indication of disrepute—or that the man has no known usual legitimate occupation.

TABLE 7
Length of Time on Assistance
for AFDC Families

Length of Time	Percent of AFDC Families
Less than 6 months	17
Six months but less than 1 year	15
One year but less than 2	17
Two years but less than 3	12
Three years but less than 5	16
Five years or more	24

Source: Robert Mugge, "Aid to Families with Dependent Children," *Social Security Bulletin,* Vol. 26, No. 3, p. 4.

the "Newburgh affair"[29] and subsequently achieved some prominence in the ill-fated Goldwater campaign of 1964.

Welfare chiseling may be defined as the receipt of assistance despite ineligibility or the receipt of more assistance than is legitimately warranted, given prevailing rules and rates. Needless to say, such illicit receipt should be *intentional* if it is to be regarded as chiseling. The beneficiaries of modest windfalls in an inefficient welfare system can hardly be regarded as chiselers unless they knowingly contrived toward that end.

There is little adequate knowledge of the number or proportion of chiselers among those who are assisted—no more, say, than exists for wealthy tax chiselers. What little research does exist has been limited to recipients of AFDC, and it is handicapped by the obvious fact that if welfare investigators can be defrauded, so can researchers.[30]

That some amount of welfare chiseling occurs is hardly disputable. This assumption receives support from a national study of the proportion of AFDC recipients who were ineligible but nonetheless received support. However, the main finding of the report is that a relatively small proportion of recipients engaged in apparent or detectable chiseling.

Despite the inconclusiveness of research in this area, some of the main findings of this national study are worth summarizing. The proportion of

[29] For a good review of the Newburgh affair, see Edgar May, *The Wasted Americans* (New York: Harper, 1964), Chapter 2.

[30] Studies dealing with this and related questions have included Greenleigh Associates, *Facts, Fallacies, and Future,* A Study of the Aid to Dependent Children Program of Cook County, Illinois (New York: 1960); and a National Study requested by the United States Senate Appropriations Committee, *Eligibility of Families Receiving Aid to Families with Dependent Children* (Department of Health, Education and Welfare, July, 1963).

ineligible families found to be receiving assistance under AFDC in 1963 varied considerably according to state of residence. Generally, southern states had relatively high proportions of unqualified persons on relief; northern and western states low proportions. In West Virginia, 19 percent of the families receiving AFDC assistance were found by special investigators to be wholly or partly ineligible; in Georgia, 17.9 percent; and in South Carolina, 16.8 percent. At the other extreme were Massachusetts, California, Montana, North Dakota, Idaho, Iowa, New Jersey, and Nebraska, where less than 2.5 percent of families receiving AFDC assistance were found to be

TABLE 8

Eligibility of Families Receiving Assistance
According to State Requirements Governing Eligibility, by State

State	Families Receiving AFDC in March 1963	Percent of Eligible Families			
		Total	All Persons in Family Eligible	Family Eligible, But Not All Members Eligible	Percent of Ineligible Families
Alabama	22,550	91.6	89.5	2.1	8.4
Alaska	1,245	92.0	89.1	2.9	8.0
Arizona	9,535	93.2	88.2	5.0	6.8
Arkansas	7,045	93.4	92.3	1.1	6.6
California	91,422	98.9	97.8	1.1	1.2
Colorado	9,656	98.1	97.1	1.0	1.9
Connecticut	12,712	89.0	87.1	1.9	11.0
Delaware	2,465	89.8	88.3	1.5	10.2
Florida	27,801	91.0	89.5	1.5	9.0
Georgia	17,146	83.7	82.2	1.5	16.4
Hawaii	3,239	93.8	92.8	1.0	6.2
Idaho	2,563	98.8	97.6	1.2	1.1
Illinois	59,212	95.1	92.6	2.5	4.9
Indiana	12,181	97.4	96.4	1.0	2.6
Iowa	10,652	98.5	97.4	1.1	1.5
Kansas	6,940	99.1	97.9	1.2	0.8
Kentucky	21,600	87.2	78.5	8.7	12.8
Louisiana	22,629	96.8	93.6	3.2	3.2
Maine	6,175	97.6	96.1	1.5	2.4
Maryland	14,183	97.4	96.5	0.9	2.6
Massachusetts	20,366	99.1	98.6	0.5	0.8
Michigan	33,376	94.2	94.0	0.2	5.8
Minnesota	11,725	97.9	96.5	1.4	2.1
Mississippi	20,463	88.5	84.0	4.5	11.6
Missouri	26,334	95.5	94.8	0.7	4.5
Montana	1,811	100.0	97.9	2.1	—

TABLE 8 (cont.)

State	Families Receiving AFDC in March 1963	Total	All Persons in Family Eligible	Family Eligible, But Not All Members Eligible	Percent of Ineligible Families
Nebraska	3,337	99.1	99.1	—	0.9
Nevada	1,310	87.6	84.8	2.8	12.4
New Hampshire	1,024	93.8	93.5	0.3	6.2
New Jersey	22,914	98.1	97.8	0.3	2.0
New Mexico	7,435	90.3	88.9	1.4	9.8
New York	100,473	96.5	94.4	2.1	3.7
North Carolina	28,660	96.6	94.6	2.0	3.5
North Dakota	1,726	100.0	100.0	—	—
Ohio	37,344	95.0	93.0	2.0	5.0
Oklahoma	18,275	98.3	97.1	1.2	1.7
Oregon	8,603	94.7	92.7	2.0	5.4
Pennsylvania	80,522	97.1	95.9	1.2	2.9
Rhode Island	5,464	96.8	95.1	1.7	3.3
South Carolina	8,540	86.7	83.3	3.4	13.4
South Dakota	2,818	96.9	94.4	2.5	3.1
Tennessee	21,485	85.7	83.8	1.9	14.3
Texas	18,317	90.5	89.4	1.1	9.6
Utah	4,597	99.1	97.2	1.9	0.9
Vermont	1,358	96.9	96.9	—	3.1
Virginia	10,736	95.5	91.0	4.5	4.5
Washington	12,072	95.4	91.7	3.7	4.6
West Virginia	31,018	82.7	81.0	1.7	17.3
Wisconsin	11,131	97.1	96.0	1.1	2.9
Wyoming	851	94.7	91.0	3.7	5.3

Percent of Eligible Families

Source: Eligibility of Families Receiving Aid to Families with Dependent Children (Department of Health, Education and Welfare, July, 1963).

wholly or partly ineligible.[31] The full range of the proportion of families found wholly or partly ineligible according to state of residence is shown in Table 8.

The reason that ineligible families receive assistance, however, may be rooted in agency oversights or administrative errors as well as in the recipient's deceitful or naive failure to report relevant information or a change in conditions. Though actual situations were highly complicated, the study attempted to assign the main responsibility to either the agency or the recipient. In West Virginia, for instance, where 19 percent of AFDC families were found to be wholly or partly ineligible, 13 percent of these cases, in the

[31] *Eligibility of Families Receiving Aid to Families with Dependent Children,* p. 11.

TABLE 9

Percent of AFDC Families in Which All or Some Members
Were Found Ineligible, Listed by State and by Principal
Reason That Ineligibility Was Not Previously Known
or Acted Upon by the Local Agency

| State | Total | Percent of Errors in Agency Practice | | | Percent of Change Not Reported by Recipient | | |
		Inadequate Determination of Initial or Continuing Eligibility	Agency Failure to Follow Up on Indicated or Known Changes in Family Circumstances	Staff Misinterpretations of Eligibility Policy and Administrative Errors	No Evidence of Intent to Conceal or Misrepresent Facts	Appears to Have Intentionally Concealed or Misrepresented Facts	Other Reasons [a]
Alabama	10.5	4.4	0.5	0.3	2.5	2.2	0.6
Alaska	10.9	1.4	2.9	1.8	3.1	–	1.6
Arizona	11.8	4.3	2.3	1.4	1.8	1.9	–
Arkansas	7.7	5.1	0.4	–	0.4	1.6	–
California	2.3	0.2	0.6	0.2	0.3	0.7	0.1
Colorado	2.9	1.6	0.3	0.9	0.1	–	–
Connecticut	12.9	3.4	1.1	1.2	2.0	4.5	0.8
Delaware	11.7	1.6	1.4	–	1.4	7.4	–
Florida	10.5	3.5	1.3	0.2	2.0	3.3	0.2
Georgia	17.9	9.3	0.3	1.1	3.8	2.1	1.3
Hawaii	7.2	3.3	–	0.9	–	2.0	1.0
Idaho	2.3	1.1	–	–	–	1.2	–
Illinois	7.4	2.2	1.6	0.4	1.0	1.6	0.5
Indiana	3.6	1.0	0.9	0.4	0.6	0.6	0.3
Iowa	2.6	1.8	0.4	0.1	–	0.2	–
Kansas	2.0	0.5	0.1	1.0	0.4	–	–
Kentucky	21.5	7.4	2.7	1.4	3.3	2.8	4.0
Louisiana	6.4	0.7	0.8	0.7	2.3	1.8	–
Maine	3.9	2.8	0.1	–	0.5	0.5	–
Maryland	3.5	0.8	–	0.5	0.5	1.8	–
Massachusetts	1.3	0.7	0.2	0.3	0.2	–	–
Michigan	6.0	0.4	–	0.1	0.5	3.6	1.4
Minnesota	3.5	0.8	0.4	0.5	1.6	0.3	–
Mississippi	16.1	7.7	3.0	0.2	2.8	1.1	1.2
Missouri	5.2	0.4	–	0.2	1.5	2.6	0.6
Montana	2.1	–	2.2	–	–	–	–
Nebraska	0.9	–	0.9	–	–	–	–
Nevada	15.2	4.8	–	1.5	1.5	7.4	–
New Hampshire	6.5	–	–	–	–	6.5	–
New Jersey	2.3	0.5	–	–	0.3	1.2	0.3
New Mexico	11.2	2.6	2.9	1.7	2.0	2.1	–
New York	5.8	2.2	1.0	0.4	0.8	1.3	0.1

TABLE 9 (cont.)

State	Total	Inadequate Determination of Initial or Continuing Eligibility	Agency Failure to Follow Up on Indicated or Known Changes in Family Circumstances	Staff Misinterpretations of Eligibility Policy and Administrative Errors	No Evidence of Intent to Conceal or Misrepresent Facts	Appears to Have Intentionally Concealed or Misrepresented Facts	Other Reasons [a]
		Percent of Errors in Agency Practice			*Percent of Change Not Reported by Recipient*		
North Carolina	5.5	2.4	0.5	—	1.0	1.6	—
North Dakota	0.0	—	—	—	—	—	—
Ohio	7.0	2.2	2.4	0.2	1.1	0.9	0.5
Oklahoma	2.9	0.5	—	—	1.2	0.6	0.5
Oregon	7.4	0.8	2.2	0.8	0.2	3.5	—
Pennsylvania	4.1	0.8	—	0.4	0.5	1.8	0.5
Rhode Island	5.0	3.6	0.4	0.2	—	0.8	—
South Carolina	16.8	8.6	2.4	1.2	2.4	1.8	0.4
South Dakota	5.6	1.5	1.2	—	2.8	—	—
Tennessee	16.2	4.4	1.0	4.3	2.0	3.8	0.6
Texas	10.7	4.4	0.5	0.3	3.7	1.8	—
Utah	2.8	0.2	0.7	—	—	1.8	—
Vermont	3.1	0.1	—	—	1.6	1.6	—
Virginia	9.0	2.4	1.3	3.2	0.8	0.8	0.4
Washington	8.3	2.9	1.1	1.0	0.9	2.6	—
West Virginia	19.0	7.6	4.8	0.5	4.5	1.5	—
Wisconsin	4.0	1.6	—	0.3	0.5	1.7	—
Wyoming	9.0	4.9	1.6	—	—	2.6	—

Source: Eligibility of Families Receiving Aid to Families with Dependent Children (Department of Health, Education and Welfare, July, 1963).
[a] The most frequently reported reasons in this column are: (1) recent changes in agency policy which were to be first applied in each case as it came up for periodic reinvestigation in 1963 (Connecticut and Kentucky); and (2) cases closed before any improper payments of assistance were made (Illinois, Missouri, Ohio).

assessment of the researchers, were due to agency errors or oversights, and 6 percent were due to changes not reported by the recipient.[32]

In almost all the states, the pattern is apparently the same: Agency errors or oversights exceed recipient culpability. Among the very few exceptions is Nevada where, perhaps for reasons of local custom, a kind of gaming relation-

---

[32] *Ibid.,* p. 16. Furthermore, the researchers in each state tried to assess whether the recipient's failure to report a relevant change was willful or not. Such an attempt seems idle. The variations in these assessments by state indicate the arbitrary charac-

ship between the citizenry and the state seems to maintain. At least that is one inference that can be drawn from the investigators' findings. In Nevada, where 15.2 percent of AFDC families were found wholly or partly ineligible, the researchers judged that 6.3 percent of these cases were due to agency errors and oversights and 8.9 percent were due to changes not reported by the recipient. The full range of the assessed responsibility for receipt of assistance despite ineligibility is shown by state in Table 9.

With this brief consideration of poverty, welfare, and disrepute, and the possible statistical bases for differentiation among them as background, we may proceed to focus on the nature of disreputable poverty itself. The oppressive and demoralizing consequences of poverty are illuminated by such a focus.

CONCEPTIONS OF DISREPUTABLE POVERTY

The historical continuity of disreputable poverty has been obscured by the obsessive shifting of terms. One predictable consequence has been the continual rediscovery of the poor—an example of what Pitirim Sorokin called the Columbus complex. The poor, it seems, are perennially hidden, and the enterprising publicists of each decade reiterate their previous invisibility and regularly proclaim the distinctive and special qualities of the "new poor." Dr. John Griscom, commenting on the wretchedness of slum life in the 1840's, said, "one half of the world does not know how the other half lives."[33] Griscom's language and viewpoint were echoed almost a half-century later by Jacob Riis,[34] and now, more than another half-century later, Michael Harrington[35] again rediscovers a heretofore invisible class of submerged poor and again stresses the novelty of their predicament. Actually,

---

ter of such imputations. The results in this regard from our two newest states will serve to illustrate my point. In Alaska, *nobody* among the 3.1 percent who failed to report a change "appears to have intentionally concealed or misrepresented the facts." In Hawaii, *everybody* among the 2 percent who failed to report a change "appears to have intentionally concealed or misrepresented the facts." Accordingly, it would seem best to treat these imputations with extreme skepticism, despite the fact that they are reproduced in Table 8. Else, we should be driven to rescind statehood for one or the other according to our moral preferences.

[33] Robert H. Bremner, *From the Depths* (New York: New York University Press, 1956), pp. 5–6.

[34] Jacob A. Riis, *How the Other Half Lives* (New York: Sagamore Press, 1957). (Originally published in 1890.)

[35] Michael Harrington, *The Other America* (New York: Macmillan, 1962).

the idea that this segment is "invisible" can be highly misleading. From time to time, it may be invisible to intellectuals, publicists, radicals, and the middle-class students who read their tracts, but it is highly and persistently exposed to two social perspectives that are more relevant for those who are themselves disreputably poor. As will be elaborated below, the disreputable poor are highly visible to welfare officials and to the respectable working classes. For the officials, they come close to living in a fishbowl. For the respectable working classes, they are part of what is seen and commented on when looking out through the lace curtain.

Disreputable poverty has gone under many names in the past two centuries. The major purpose of word substitution has been to reduce and remove the stigma, and perhaps the reason for this obsession with terminology is that the effort is fruitless. The stigma inheres mostly in the referent and not in the concept. In five years or so, if not already, the term "hard to reach" may be considered stigmatizing and may be relegated to the dead file of offensive labels. The culmination of this process is not hard to predict since it has already occurred in a discipline even more addicted to word substitution and mystification—the field of education. Perhaps we shall eventually refer to the poor as "exceptional families."

Each conception of disreputable poverty contains some insights and thus illuminates the referent; each makes us one-eyed and thus obscures it. Thus, a sample of conceptions of disreputable poverty may serve to introduce a consideration of its persistent features.

The current phrase "hard to reach" considers and defines the disreputable poor from the vantage point of the administrator of public welfare activities. Implicit in the concept is a view of the disreputable poor as human material that can be worked on, helped, and, hopefully, transformed.[36] Reasonably enough, this conception implies one crucial difficulty—that the material cannot be got hold of. It is hard to reach; to do so requires great expenditures of time and effort. Only a short step is required to transform the concept from one rooted in administrative problems to one suggesting an important insight. Surely, they are not hard to reach only because the welfare establishment is deficient. Rather, the elusiveness resides at least partially in the stratum itself. The disreputable poor are disaffiliated; they exist in the crevices or at the margins of modern society.

Beyond this, the concept "hard to reach" tells us little. We should not be discouraged, however, since finding one insight per concept is doing well.

---

[36] For a brief discussion of the administrative welfare perspective, see Thomas Gladwin, "The Anthropologist's View of Poverty," *The Social Welfare Forum* (New York: Columbia University Press, 1961), pp. 73–74.

Many concepts are completely nondescript, like the bland and neutral labels used by British and American sociologists who refer to segments of the population as Class 5 or Class E. There is nothing wrong with this. Indeed, from the viewpoint of science it is meritorious. Strictly speaking, concepts should not contain implicit theories, since this permits one to smuggle in hypotheses better left to empirical investigators. But concepts that imply specific theories are a boon, providing the theory is empirically sound rather than romantically foolish, like the theory of the "happy poor."

Almost nondescript, but not quite, is the phrase initiated by Warner and still fashionable among sociologists—the "lower-lower class." Since Warner's categories were ostensibly supplied by members of the community, it implies that, from their perspective, the distinction between two sections of the lower class is meaningful. The difference between lower-lowers and upper-lowers is chiefly a matter of reputation—the one is disreputable and the other reputable.

More suggestive is the British term "problem family." Implicit in this concept are two points. *First,* to refer to problem families is to observe with typical English understatement that the disreputable poor are a bit of a pain in the neck. They are bothersome and disproportionately costly in terms of the amount of care, welfare, and policing they get. *Second,* and more important, the term suggests that these families "collect" problems. They contribute far more than their share to the relief rolls, to crime and delinquency rates, to rates of alcoholism, to the list of unmarried mothers and thus illegitimate children, to divorces, desertions, and to the mentally ill. The idea of plural problems, reinforcing and nurturing each other in a vicious circle, was well stated and developed in the English notion. Thus, the American adaptation, "multiproblem family," is redundant. Moreover, it loses the *double-entendre* implicit in the British formulation.

The remaining concepts, unlike those already discussed, were not attempts to reduce the stigma of poverty, but, on the contrary, are decidedly offensive terms developed outside the circle of sociologists, social workers, and psychiatrists. The first term, *Lumpenproletariat,* which despite its wide usage among Marxists was never really clarified or developed systematically, refers to the dirt or scum that inhabits the lower orders, nearby, but not of, the working class. The *Lumpenproletariat,* according to Bukharin, was one of the "categories of persons outside the outlines of social labor" and barred from being a revolutionary class "chiefly by the circumstance that it performs no productive work." [37] For the Marxist, this stratum was fundamentally reactionary and, in the revolutionary situation, it would

---

[37] Nikolai Bukharin, *Historical Materialism* (New York: International, 1925), pp. 284, 290.

either remain apathetic or its members would become mercenaries in the service of the bourgeoisie. Bukharin maintains that in the *Lumpenproletariat* we find "shiftlessness, lack of discipline, hatred of the old, but impotence to construct or organize anything new, an individualistic declassed 'personality,' whose actions are based only on foolish caprices." [38]

Frequently, *Lumpenproletariat* was used as a derogatory term in the struggles for power among various revolutionaries. If an opponent could be associated with the *Lumpenproletariat,* his stature might be lessened. Despite frequent abuse, the term retained some of its original meaning and continued to be used to refer to the disreputable poor. Implicit in the Marxian conception are a number of suggestive insights regarding the character, background, and destiny of these people. The description of them given by Victor Chernov, a Russian social revolutionary, is typical: It is garbed in highly evaluative language, and is used to attack an opponent, in this case, Lenin.

> Besides the proletarian *"demos"* there exists in all capitalist countries a proletarian *"ochlos,"* the enormous mass of *déclassés,* chronic paupers *Lumpenproletariat,* what may be termed the "capitalistically superfluous industrial reserve army." Like the proletariat, it is a product of capitalist civilization, but it reflects the destructive, not the constructive aspects of capitalism. Exploited and down-trodden, it is full of bitterness and despair, but has none of the traditions and none of the potentialities of organization, of a new consciousness, a new law, and a new culture, which distinguish the genuine "hereditary" proletariat. In Russia the growth of capitalism has been strongest in its destructive, predatory aspects, while its constructive achievements have lagged. It was accompanied by a catastrophic growth of the *"ochlos,"* a tremendous mass of uprooted, drifting humanity. Wrongly idealized at times, as in Gorky's early works, this mob supplied the contingents for those sporadic mass outbursts, pogroms, anti-Jewish and others, for which old Russia was famous. During the war, "the personnel of industry had . . . been completely transformed. . . . The ranks of factory workers, severely depleted by indiscriminate mobilizations, were filled with whatever human material came to hand: peasants, small shopkeepers, clerks, janitors, porters, people of indeterminate trade. . . . The genuine proletariat was submerged in a motley crowd of *Lumpenproletarians* and *Lumpenbourgeois.*[39]

What may we infer from this description? First, the *Lumpenproletariat* differs in economic function from the proletariat. It is not an industrial work-

[38] *Ibid.,* p. 290.
[39] Victor Chernov, *The Great Russian Revolution* (New Haven: Yale University Press, 1936), pp. 414–15.

ing class; instead, it consists of a heterogeneous mass of casual and irregular laborers, farmworkers, artisans, tradesmen, service workers, and petty thieves. They work in traditional and increasingly obsolete jobs rather than, in the Marxian phrase, in the technologically advanced sectors of the economy. They are not of stable working-class stock, but include declassed persons of every stratum. Because of its background and character, the *Lumpenproletariat* is not easily amenable to organization for political and economic protest. It is apathetic. It has been "hard to reach" for agitators as well as for social workers, or at least so the Marxists thought. In point of fact, it has frequently been amenable to political organization, but as soon as it was organized, it was no longer *Lumpenproletariat,* at least not by Marxian standards.

Another idea worth exploring is one suggested by Thorstein Veblen: the concept of a spurious leisure class. It too was never fully developed. Veblen intimated that at the very bottom of the class system, as at the very top, there developed a stratum that lived in leisure and was given to predatory sentiments and behavior.[40] The resemblance between the genuine and spurious leisure class was also noted by George Dowling in 1893. He wrote in *Scribner's,* "The opulent who are not rich by the results of their own industry . . . suffer atrophy of virile and moral powers, and like paupers live on the world's surplus without adding to it or giving any fair equivalent for their maintenance." [41] The spurious leisure class, like Veblen's pecuniary masters of society, lived in industrial society but temperamentally and functionally were not part of it. Because they were not dedicated to the spirit of industrial workmanship, they never evinced the matter-of-fact, mechanistic, and sober frame of mind so admired by Veblen. Instead, this class, like the genuine leisure class, was parasitic and useless, barbaric and military-minded, and given to wasteful display and frequent excess. The major difference was that its leisure was bolstered by neither aristocratic right nor financial wherewithal.[42] Such a class, he reasoned, must be peculiarly embittered and resentful. It is dedicated to luxury without the necessary finances, and thus its members are given to posturing, pretense, and bluster. Veblen's caricature of these people is as harsh as anything he had to say

---

[40] Thorstein Veblen, *The Theory of the Leisure Class* (New York: Huebsch, 1919), Chapter 10.

[41] Robert H. Bremner, *From the Depths,* p. 22.

[42] In like manner, Boulding has referred to "poor aristocrats" who pass easily into the criminal and purely exploitative subcultures which survive on the "transfer of commodities and . . . produce very little." See Kenneth Boulding, "Reflections on Poverty," *The Social Welfare Forum* (New York: Columbia University Press, 1961), p. 52.

about the pecuniary captains of society, and though there is a ring of truth to it, there is just as surely distortion.

A final conception pertaining to disreputable poverty was that of the pauper. The distinction between paupers and the poor, maintained during the nineteenth and early twentieth centuries, is a useful one; and its demise was one of the major casualties of obsessive word substitution. Harriet Martineau, commenting on England in the early nineteenth century, observed that "Except for the distinction between sovereign and subject, there is no social difference . . . so wide as that between independent laborer and the pauper."[43] Paupers, as distinguished from the poor, were often characterized as apathetic regarding their condition. While they were not deemed happy, they were considered less miserable or unhappy than the poor. They had adapted to their poverty, and that was their distinctive feature. Robert Hunter said:

> Paupers are not, as a rule, unhappy. They are not ashamed; they are not keen to become independent; they are not bitter or discontented. They have passed over the line which separates poverty from pauperism. . . . This distinction between the poor and paupers may be seen everywhere. They are in all large cities in America and abroad, streets and courts and alleys where a class of people live who have lost all self-respect and ambition, who rarely, if ever, work, who are aimless and drifting, who like drink, who have no thought for their children, and who live more or less contentedly on rubbish and alms. Such districts are . . . in all cities everywhere. The lowest level of humanity is reached in these districts. . . . This is pauperism. There is no mental agony here; they do not work sore; there is no dread; they live miserably, but they do not care.[44]

Of all the conceptions reviewed, pauperism comes closest to what is conveyed by the term "disreputable poverty." Though there are differences,[45] many of the features of disreputable poverty are implicit in the conception of pauperism. It conveys the same ideas of disaffiliation and immobilization that, taken together, indicate the outcasting from modern society suggested by Thomas and Znaniecki. Pauperism, like vice, "declasses a man definitely,

---

[43] Cited in Karl Polanyi, *The Great Transformation* (New York: Rinehart, 1944), p. 100.

[44] Robert Hunter, *Poverty* (New York: Macmillan, 1912), pp. 3–4.

[45] For instance, a pauper, strictly speaking, depends on public or private charity for sustenance, while in my conception, the disreputable poor are sometime recipients of welfare. They also work casually or irregularly and occasionally engage in petty crime and other forms of hustling.

puts him outside both the old and new hierarchy. Beggars, tramps, criminals, prostitutes, have no place in the class hierarchy." [46]

Among laymen, the common conception of disreputable poverty has persisted, despite the changing theories of intellectuals, social scientists, and public welfare practitioners. This persistence is implicit in a lay conception of pauperism that, throughout, has insisted on a distinction between the deserving and undeserving poor. Ordinary members of society still maintain the views expressed in 1851 by Robert Harley, the founder of the New York Association for Improving the Condition of the Poor. The debased poor, he said, "love to clan together in some out-of-the-way place, are content to live in filth and disorder with a bare subsistence, provided they can drink, and smoke, and gossip, and enjoy their balls, and wakes, and frolics, without molestation." [47] One need not concur with Harley's sentiment, still pervasive today, that the debased poor do not deserve sympathy to concur with the wisdom in the common understanding of the differences between paupers and independent laborers. A distinction between the two, measured instead of radical, refined rather than obtuse, is a preface to understanding the working classes, and especially the unemployed among them. A similar point is made by S. M. Miller and Frank Riessman in their discussion of the implications of failing to distinguish between the working and lower class. They observe:

> This reluctance to make the distinction between "working class" and "lower class," despite useful discussions by Kahl and others . . . leads to errors. For example, the findings of Hollingshead and Redlich . . . have been interpreted as: The lower the class, the higher the rate of mental illness. Close examination of their data reveals, however, that the working class (Class IV) is closer to the upper and middle class (Classes I, II, and III) than to the lower class (Class V). Classes I through IV are similar, whereas Class V is quite dissimilar from all other classes, including the working class. [48]

THE SITUATION OF THE DISREPUTABLE POOR

To understand disreputable poverty, and to appreciate its complexity, one must distinguish among the various components of its milieu. Disreputable poverty and the tradition it sustains are a compote, blending together the distinctive contributions of each ingredient.

---

[46] William I. Thomas and Florian Znaniecki, *The Polish Peasant in America* (New York: Dover, reissued 1958), p. 136.

[47] Robert H. Bremner, *From the Depths*, p. 5.

[48] S. M. Miller and Frank Riessman, "The Working-Class Subculture: A New View," *Social Problems,* Vol. 9 (Summer, 1961), p. 26.

Dregs

The core of disreputable poor consists of dregs – persons spawned in poverty and belonging to families who have been left behind by otherwise mobile ethnic populations. In these families there is at least the beginning of some tradition of disreputable poverty.[49] In America, the primary examples include immobile descendants of Italian and Polish immigrants and of the remnants of even earlier arrivals – Germans, Irish, and Yankees and blacks who have already become habituated to the regions in which disreputable poverty flourishes. The situation of dregs is well described in a Russell Sage Foundation report on Hell's Kitchen in New York shortly before World War I.

> The district is like a spider's web. Of those who come to it very few, either by their own efforts or through outside agency, ever leave it. Usually those who come to live here find at first . . . that they cannot get out, and presently that they do not want to. . . . It is not [just] that conditions throughout the district are economically extreme, although greater misery and worse poverty cannot be found in other parts of New York. But there is something of the dullness of these West Side streets and the traditional apathy of their tenants that crushes the wish for anything better and kills the hope of change. It is as though decades of lawlessness and neglect have formed an atmospheric monster, beyond the power and understanding of its creators, overwhelming German and Irish alike.[50]

This description refers to the dregs of the mid-nineteenth-century Irish and German migrations, to those who did not advance along with their ethnic brethren. Only a small proportion of the Irish and Germans living in New York at the time were trapped in the "spider's web" of Hell's Kitchen. Putting Hell's Kitchen in its proper context, Handlin says:

> From 1870 onward the Irish and Germans were dynamically moving groups. . . . [However] some remained unskilled laborers. They stayed

---

[49] Kenneth Boulding suggests that there is perhaps some cause for alarm when "the dependent children who have been aided ask for aid for *their* dependent children." See his "Reflections on Poverty." Burgess and Price estimate that "more than 40 percent of the mothers and/or fathers [who were on AFDC] were raised in homes where some form of assistance had been received at some time." See M. Elaine Burgess and Daniel Price, *An American Dependency Challenge,* p. 21.

[50] *West Side Studies,* Vol. 1 (New York: Russell Sage Foundation, 1914), pp. 8–9; also see Richard O'Connor, *Hell's Kitchen* (Philadelphia: Lippincott, 1958), p. 176.

either downtown or in the middle West Side, beyond Eighth Avenue and between 23rd and 59th streets, where the other shanty towns were transformed into Hell's Kitchen, a teeming neighborhood that housed laborers from the docks and from the nearby . . . factories, and also a good portion of the city's vice and crime.[51]

Rural immigrants to urban areas in the United States and other nations usually entered the system at the very bottom, but in the course of a few generations — depending on the availability of new ethnic or regional replacements and numerous other factors — their descendants achieved conventional, reputable positions in society. But some proportion of each cohort, the majority of which advances to the reputable working class or the lower rungs of the middle class, remains behind. Each experience of ethnic mobility leaves a sediment that appears to be trapped in slum life, whether because some of those who come insist on maintaining traditional peasant values or as a result of family disorganization, limited opportunities for steady employment, or just plain misfortune. These are the dregs who settle into the milieu of disreputable poverty and perpetuate its distinctive characteristics.

An excellent description of this sort of area in England is provided by Josephine Klein in her summary account of "Branch Street":

Branch Street is a "residual area." All those who can get away from it have left. That includes not only those capable of achieving respectability under their own steam, but also those who, in the opinion of the housing authorities, are capable of doing better in more favorable circumstances. . . . Branch Street is also a "transitional area." Immigrants into the city come here, but they do not stay if they have any chance of going somewhere better. A large proportion of the inhabitants [during 1944–1949] are Irish.[52]

Neighborhoods in which this style of life flourishes possess diversified populations that, like the layers of a geological specimen, reflect their dim history. Handlin describes a single tenement in such an area.

The poor and the unsuccessful [of each ethnic group] were generally lost in the characterless enclaves scattered throughout the city, in part of the West Side, in Greenwich Village, in Brooklyn, and later in Queens where they were surrounded by communities of the foreign-born. The very poorest were left behind, immobilized by their failure,

---

[51] Oscar Handlin, *The Newcomers* (Cambridge, Mass.: Harvard University Press, 1959), p. 31.

[52] Josephine Klein, *Samples from English Cultures* (London: Routledge, 1965), pp. 3–4.

and swamped by successive waves of immigrants. In the notorious "Big Flat" tenement on Mott Street, for instance, lived 478 residents, of whom 368 were Jews and 31 Italians, who were just entering the neighborhood. But there were also 31 Irish, 30 Germans, and 4 natives, a kind of sediment left behind when their groups departed.[53]

Dregs are the key components of the milieu of disreputable poverty also because they link new groups entering the lowest level of society and the old ones leaving it. In the conflict between new and old ethnic arrivals, the unseemly traditions of disreputable poverty are transmitted from one to the other. These traditions are manifested in a style of life distinctive to disreputable poverty and apparently similar in different parts of the world.

What are the main features of this style?[54] Income in this stratum is obviously low, but "more important even than the size of income is its regularity."[55] Unemployment and underemployment are common. When work can be found it is unskilled or at best semiskilled. Jobs are available for relatively short periods; hiring is frequently on a day-to-day basis. Child labor lingers on,[56] and in many families, the wage earner, if there is one, is frequently ill and only intermittently employed. Saving, even for a very short time, is vitually unknown, and, as a result, small quantities of food may be bought many times a day as the need arises. Also evident is "the pawning of personal possessions, borrowing from local money lenders at usurious rates, and the use of secondhand clothing and furniture."[57] The Brock Committee in England indignantly observed that "an important feature of this group is

---

[53] Oscar Handlin, *The Newcomers*, p. 29.

[54] It should be reiterated that these characteristics pertain mostly to the disreputable poor and considerably less to categories like the welfare poor or the lower class. The latter two are broader categories that include the disreputable poor as a small segment. If one appreciates these distinctions, the skeptical and critical discussion of the thesis positing a close relationship between poverty and pathology by Barbara Wooten will not seem inconsistent with the view taken here. See the excellent summary of studies bearing on the presumed general relationship between poverty and pathology in Barbara Wooten, *Social Science and Social Pathology* (New York: Macmillan, 1959), Chapter 2, "Social Pathology and Social Hierarchy." For a more recent and more limited consideration, guided by the same skeptical spirit, see Henry Miller, "Characteristics of AFDC Families," *Social Service Review* (December, 1965), pp. 399–409.

[55] Tom Stephens, ed., *Problem Families* (London: Victor Gollancz, 1946), p. 3. The coincidence between the nature of work and style of life was succinctly and classically summarized by Charles Booth in 1896. He said: "The character of the men matched well with the character of the work and that of its remuneration. All alike were low and irregular."

[56] Oscar Lewis, *The Children of Sanchez* (New York: Random House, 1961), p. xxvi.

[57] *Ibid.*

misspending." "Misspending," the committee asserted, "is the visible expression of thriftlessness and improvidence." The Committee was impressed with the frequency with which "money is squandered on gambling, drinking, cigarettes, and unnecessary household luxuries when bare necessities are lacking." [58] Available resources are frequently mismanaged. "Rent is typically in arrears . . . and similar irresponsibility is shown towards bills and debts." [59]

To British investigators, the most obvious common feature of thse families is the disorder of family life.[60] People frequently resort to violence in training children and in settling quarrels; wifebeating, early initiation into sex, and free unions or consensual marriage are common, and the incidence of abandoned mothers and children is high.[61] "The children play outside until late in the evening . . . and are sent to bed, all ages at the same time, when the parents are tired. . . ." In many of these homes there is no clock, and "one may visit at ten in the morning to find the entire household asleep." [62] Relations between parents are often characterized by constant dissension and an absence of affection and mutual trust.[63] As a result, family dissolution is frequent, and there is a distinct pressure toward a mother-centered family — a rather disorganized version of what anthropologists call serial monogamy with a female-based household.[64] Although family solidarity is emphasized as an ideal, it is rarely even approximated.[65] The disposition to paternal authoritarianism is strong, but since paternal authority is frequently challenged, its implementation frequently requires a show of power or force. The discipline of children has been described as "a mixture of spoiling affection and impatient chastisement or mental and physical cruelty." [66] Moreover, the household is extremely complex. It may contain, "in addition to the joint offspring, children of diverse parentage." There may be children from

---

[58] Cited in C. P. Blacker, ed., *Problem Families: Five Inquiries* (London: Eugenics Society, 1952), p. 3.

[59] Tom Stephens, ed., *Problem Families,* p. 3.

[60] *Ibid.,* p. 4.

[61] Oscar Lewis, *The Children of Sanchez,* p. xxvi.

[62] Tom Stephens, ed., *Problem Families,* p. 4.

[63] *Ibid.,* p. 5.

[64] Some are so taken by the durability of this style that, straight-faced, they hold the adjective "disorganized" to be an unwarranted ethnocentric imputation. See *Delinquent Behavior: Culture and the Individual* (Washington, D. C.: National Education Association, 1959), pp. 94–97.

[65] Oscar Lewis, *The Children of Sanchez,* p. xxvi.

[66] Tom Stephens, ed., *Problem Families,* p. 5.

previous marriages, illegitimate children, and children of near-relatives and friends who have deserted, died, or been imprisoned.[67]

The disreputable poor are "the least educated group in the population and the least interested in education." [68] Returning to the Brock Committee report, we learn that this group suffers from "an intractable ineducability which expresses itself in a refusal, or else an incapacity, to make effective use of the technical advice available." [69] But the assumption that these families seem content with squalor obviously arises from a failure to distinguish between satisfaction and apathy.

The disreputable poor "react to their economic situation and to their degradation in the eyes of respectable people by becoming fatalistic; they feel that they are down and out, and that there is no point in trying to improve. . . ." [70] Their life is provincial and locally oriented. "Its members are only partly integrated into national institutions and are a marginal people even when they live in the heart of a great city." [71] Typically, they neither belong to trade unions nor support any political party.[72] They are immobilized in that they do not participate in the two responses to discontent characteristic of Western working classes—collective mobilization culminating in trade unions, ethnic federations, or political action, and familial mobilization culminating in individual mobility.

Thus, the style of disreputable poverty apparently transcends national boundaries, though it is perhaps most noticeable in nations with strong puritan traditions. Transmission of this style from one group to the next is a major contribution of dregs, but it is not the only one. Just as important, perhaps, is the unmistakable tone of embittered resentment emanating from their immobility. Dregs are immobile within a context of considerable mobility in their ethnic reference groups. Consequently, they are apt to see

---

[67] C. P. Blacker, *Problem Families: Five Inquiries,* p. 32; for a perceptive documentation, read Oscar Lewis, *The Children of Sanchez,* in its entirety.

[68] Joseph A. Kahl, *The American Class Structure* (New York: Rinehart, 1953), p. 211. In recent years, a theory stressing "stimulus deprivation" during the formative years has become fashionable in accounting for the relatively dull performance of poor children in school. See Martin P. Deutsch, "The Disadvantaged Child and the Learning Process," in Frank Riessman, Jerome Cohen, and Arthur Pearl, eds., *Mental Health and the Poor* (New York: Free Press, 1964), pp. 172–87.

[69] C. P. Blacker, *Problem Families: Five Inquiries,* p. 16.

[70] Joseph A. Kahl, *The American Class Structure,* p. 211.

[71] Oscar Lewis, *The Children of Sanchez,* p. xxvi.

[72] Genevieve Knupfer, "Portrait of the Underdog," *Public Opinion Quarterly* (Spring, 1947), pp. 103–14.

the good fortunes of their more successful ethnic brethren as desertion and obsequious ambition. Their view of those who have been successfully mobile is likely to be jaundiced and defensive. How else can they explain their own failure? What the reputable applaud as sobriety and effort must seem to those left behind an implicit, if not explicit, rejection of their way of life, and thus a rejection of themselves as persons.

This perspective, coupled with a peculiarly seamy view of law-enforcement agencies, gives slum denizens a cynical sense of superiority, based on the partially accurate belief that they are privy to guilty knowledge shared only by influential insiders. In a word, they are "hip," free of the delusions regarding ethics and propriety that guide the "square" citizenry. Thus, "hip" slum dwellers in New York knew or claimed to know of the incidents underlying the famous basketball scandals years before the public was shocked by exposés, just as "hip" slum dwellers in Chicago knew or claimed to know of the incidents underlying the police scandals in that city.

Newcomers

Recent arrivals are the second component of the disreputable poor. Not all newcomers gravitate to the slums or ghettos — mostly, those who come are without marketable skills or financial resources. Irish newcomers escaping to America, even before the great famine, settled in neighborhoods already infamous and disreputable. Robert Ernst describes one of the most notorious of these neighborhoods in New York:

> To live in the lower wards required some money. The penniless stranger, wholly without means, could not afford the relative luxury of a boardinghouse. His search for shelter led him to the sparsely populated sections north of the settled part of town. In the twenties and thirties Irish immigrants clustered around the "Five Points," a depressed and unhealthy area on the site of the filled-in Collect swamp in the old Sixth ward. Here, at little or no cost, the poorest of the Irish occupied dilapidated old dwellings and built flimsy shanties. . . . In the heart of the Five Points was the Old Brewery, erected in 1792. . . . Transformed into a dwelling in 1837, the Old Brewery came to house several hundred men, women, and children, almost equally divided between Irish and Negroes, including an assortment of "thieves, murderers, pickpockets, beggars, harlots, and degenerates of every type." . . . As early as 1830 the Sixth ward, and the Five Points in particular, had become notorious as a center of crime. . . . The criminality of the area was usually overemphasized, but poverty was wide-

spread, and thousands of law-abiding inhabitants led wretched lives in cellars and garrets.[73]

Numerically, newcomers are probably the largest component of the disreputable poor, but it is important to recall that except for a small proportion their collective destiny is eventually to enter reputable society. Thus, the new ethnics do not fully exhibit the features of disreputable poverty described above, nor do they manifest the embittered sense of defeat and resignation characteristic of dregs.[74] They are more apt to express a sort of naive optimism, especially since their new urban standard of life is, if anything, higher than the standard they previously experienced.

Newcomers contribute an exotic element, whether they are European, Latin American, or indigenously American as in the case of southern blacks. They season the melting pot of the streets with the spice of peasant tradition. It is this element that has excited the imagination of Bohemians and other intellectuals and led to the persistent romanticizing of life among the disreputable poor. Unfortunately, however, this exotic quality is double-edged, and one of the edges is considerably sharper than the other. Admiration from intellectuals was of little consequence for newly arrived ethnics compared with the persistent humiliation and degradation they underwent at the hands of resident ethnics.

A negative, degrading conception of newcomers seems a general feature of the attitude of older, established members of the community. The description of recent Appalachian migrants to the big city illustrates the stereotypical mold into which the agrarian newcomer is placed. William Powles reports the stereotype and comments on its validity.

The outside world claims that the people of Appalachia "look odd," "talk funny," "act stupid." They are lampooned as "Newfies," "Arkies," "brierhoppers," "hillbillies," "poor white trash," fit only for the hills or the slums. No doubt a minority may have gone under, stupefied, demoralized, debauched, debased, inbred, reverted over generations to the status of near-savages, without (so it is broadly hinted by their

[73] Robert Ernst, *Immigrant Life in New York City, 1825–1863* (New York: King's Crown Press, 1949), p. 39.
[74] For a discussion contrasting the ambition and optimism of new European migrants with the resignation and apathy of old Americans of Scotch-Irish descent, see Herman Lantz, "Resignation, Industrialization and the Problem of Social Change," in Arthur Shostak and William Gomberg, eds., *Blue-Collar World*, pp. 258–70. Also see Herman Lantz, *People of Coal Town* (New York: Columbia University Press, 1958).

detractors) even the incest-taboo of . . . respectable savages. But the majority, despite their lack of emphasis on formal learning and their shyness of the great, busy, city world, are warm, friendly, intelligent people, loving their land, creating a folk music both cheerful and sad, and, when transplanted to the city, coping with characteristic vigor with that forbidding world. Their misfortune is that the stable and successful evoke little notice. Only the minority come to the attention of social agencies, the law, and the press. In the city, this minority probably amounts to no more than 10 percent.[75]

The style of disreputable poverty was transmitted in a context of humiliation and victimization. In the folklore of slum tradition and, to a considerable degree, in reality, the newcomers are untutored in the ways of slum sophistication. "Greenhorns," "banana boaters," whatever they are called, they learn the style of disreputable poverty primarily through being victims of it. They learn not by doing but, initially, by "being had." This traditional pattern is neatly summarized in an older description of the environment of newcomers in American slums, a description refreshingly free of the contrived relativism that currently misleads some anthropologists and sociologists.

> The moral surroundings are . . . bad for them. In tenement districts the unsophisticated Italian peasant or the quiet, inoffensive Hebrew is thrown into contact with the degenerate remnants of former immigrant populations, who bring influence to bear to rob, persecute, and corrupt the newcomers.[76]

Why have the newly arrived ethnics been so persistently humiliated and degraded by the old ethnic remnants? At one level, the answer seems simple. Despite all their failings, those who were left behind could lord it over the new arrivals, for they at least were somewhat Americanized, though not sufficiently so to be confident. Embittered and resentful on the one hand, and anxious and uncertain about their Americanism on the other, the ethnic dregs suffered from the classic conditions which make groups seek out scapegoats.

Exposure to the life style of disreputable poverty in the context of humiliation and victimization helped to dampen the optimism which newcomers

---

[75] William E. Powles, "The Southern Appalachian Migrant: Country Boy Turned Blue-Collarite," in Arthur Shostak and William Gomberg, eds., *Blue-Collar World,* p. 272.

[76] *United States Industrial Commission on Immigration,* Volume 15 of the Commission's Report (Washington, D. C.: U. S. Government Printing Office, 1901), p. xlvii.

frequently felt and thus facilitated the adoption of a similar life style by a segment of them. Optimism and other cultural resistances were never completely obliterated, however, and only a small proportion were actually reduced to disreputable poverty. Ethnic groups entering America and other nations have varied considerably in their vulnerability to slum pressures,[77] but in each one at least a few families became dregs.

Skidders

Skidders are a third component in the milieu of disreputable poverty. These are men and women who have fallen from higher social niches. They include alcoholics, addicts, perverts, and otherwise disturbed individuals who come, after a long history of skidding, to live in the run-down sections of the metropolis.[78] To a slight extent, low-cost public housing has concealed skidders from immediate view, but it still serves only a small proportion of the poor and at any rate tends to be reserved for the deserving poor. Among the disreputable poor, the visibility of skidders remains high.

Occasionally, along with the skidders, one finds some especially hardy Bohemians who take their ideology seriously enough to live among their folk. But it is the skidders, rather than the Bohemians, who contribute importantly to the culture of disreputable poverty. Even when they live in these sections, Bohemians tend to be insulated, partially by their clannishness but primarily because they are ungratefully rejected by the authentic outsiders they romanticize.

Skidders contribute a tone of neuroticism and flagrant degradation to the life style of the slums. They are pathetic and dramatic symbols of the ultimate in disreputable poverty. Perhaps more important, they are visible evidence of the flimsy foundations of success and standing in society; they, as such, furnish yet another argument against sustained and conscientious effort. These are the fallen; they have achieved at least modest success and found it somehow lacking in worth. Skidders are important not because they are very numerous among the disreputable poor, but because they dramatically exemplify the worthlessness of effort. While their degradation may sometimes goad others, particularly the new ethnic, to conscientious efforts

---

[77] The reasons for this variability are complicated; some of them will be suggested in the final section of this essay, "The Process of Pauperization."

[78] For a recent empirical study of skidders in Chicago, see Donald Bogue, *Skid Row in American Cities* (Chicago: Community and Family Study Center, 1963).

to escape a similar fate, the old ethnic dregs take the skidder's fall as additional evidence of the meanness of social life and the whimsy of destiny. Such a view of life makes it almost impossible to maintain either ambition or morality.

The Infirm

The infirm are the fourth element in the milieu of disreputable poverty. Before age, injury, or illness made them infirm, these people belonged to other strata — especially in the reputable sections of the working class. Their downward shift may take the form of physically moving from a reputable to a disreputable neighborhood, but more frequently perhaps, the infirm stay put, and the neighborhood moves out from under them. Frequently, they belong to old ethnic groups, but not to the dregs, since they did achieve reputable status. They slipped because of some misfortune: aging being the most common.[79] Their contribution is, in part, similar to the skidders', but without the blatant elements of neuroticism and degradation. Like the skidders, they testify to the flimsy foundations of respectability, the worthlessness of sustained effort, and the whimsical nature of fate, or destiny. Like the skidders — even more so because they have done less to provoke their fate — they symbolize the "beat" conception of life among the disreputable poor.

But the infirm have a distinctive contribution to make. In a completely ineffective way, they oppose the tradition of disreputable poverty. Their cantankerous complaints and what is perceived as their nosy interference frequently precipitate a flagrant and vengeful show of license and sin. The infirm become a captive and powerless audience before whom the youth who inhabit this world can flaunt their freedom from restraint. Intruders in this world because they are of different stock, because they claim reputability, or because of both these reasons, they are simultaneously powerless and rejected. Those who claim reputability in a disreputable milieu inevitably give the appearance of taking on airs and are thus vulnerable to ridicule and sarcasm — the typical sanctions for that minor vice. Furthermore, their opposition is weakened because before long the law-enforcement

---

[79] For good reviews of the economic situation of the aged, see Charles Linninger, "Some Aspects of the Economic Situation of the Aged," and Lenore Epstein, "The Income Position of the Aged," both in Harold Orbach and Clark Tibbits, eds., *Aging and the Economy* (Ann Arbor, Mich.: University of Michigan Press, 1963), pp. 71–90 and 91–102.

agencies begin to view them as pests; the police cannot, after all, bother with their complaints if they are to attend to the serious violations that abound in these areas. The infirm are the one indigenous source of opposition, but their marginal status makes them powerless to effect change. Thus, their distinctive contribution is to demonstrate the pettiness of character and the incredible impotence of those who oppose disreputable poverty.

Functionaries

Functionaries occupy a special and persistent place in the lives of the disreputable poor. The regions these poor inhabit are inundated by a variety of agents and officials whose conventional purposes include regulation, control, and moral restoration.[80] "Branch Street," which may be regarded as typical of such regions, is notable for the fact that "social workers of all kinds are in and out of [the] houses continually."[81] Not only are the disreputable poor dependent—a feature they share with others—but they have deviated from conventional standards. For both reasons, their habits are seen as a suitable topic for inquiry, their paths as warranting redirection, and their lives as requiring intervention. The direct responsibility for these tasks falls to welfare functionaries.

Part of the job of welfare functionaries is to oversee the conduct of those who require assistance. Consequently, they are appropriately placed to pass judgment on the moral character of the welfare poor. The distinction between deserving and undeserving poor and the moral classification of persons as one or the other originate in the functionary perspective and continue to be a matter of special moment among those who share that perspective. Though welfare functionaries possess no monopoly either in making the distinction between reputable and disreputable poverty or in morally classifying persons within these categories, they claim and are accorded special competence in these endeavors. For welfare functionaries, these are not matters of idle gossip or spirited indignation but rather the substance of their profession. They are the duly authorized overseers of the assisted. Though they may think it, it is hard for recipients to utter the phrase, "It's none of your business," to welfare functionaries—a phrase regarded as legitimate when di-

---

[80] For a general discussion of the relations between the poor and officials, see Warren C. Haggstrom, "The Power of the Poor," in Frank Riessman, Jerome Cohen, and Arthur Pearl, eds., *Mental Health and the Poor,* pp. 212–13.

[81] Josephine Klein, *Samples from English Cultures,* pp. 4–5.

rected to those for whom moral judgment is a mere avocation. For welfare functionaries, moral classification is a vocation. In the strictest possible sense, it *is* their business.[82]

Moral classification is implicit in the work of functionaries because it is, first, necessary in determining eligibility for assistance, and, subsequently, part of what is taken into account in reviewing the advisability of continued assistance. Such classification must be based on systematic scrutiny. As a condition of assistance, the modern state (like private charities before it) requires that its agents become privy to matters that are otherwise regarded as private. Welfare functionaries possess a license to scrutinize. Many writers have suggested the stigmatizing consequences of such scrutiny. It is because the recipients of aid are subjected to extraordinary scrutiny and regulation that Lewis Coser goes so far as to suggest that public assistance is forthcoming "only at the price of . . . degradation."[83]

Though Coser's comments apply to the welfare poor generally, they have special meaning for the disreputable poor. Coser attributes the degradation of being assisted to the fact that recipients are obliged, as a condition of assistance, to partly forfeit their privacy and partly surrender key symbols of maturity. With regard to the partial forfeiture of privacy, he says:

> Members of nearly all status groups in society can make use of a variety of legitimate mechanisms to shield their behavior from observability by others; society recognizes a right to privacy, that is, the right to conceal parts of his role behavior from public observation. But this right is denied to the poor. At least in principle, facets of his behavior which ordinarily are not public are . . . under public control and are open to scrutiny by social workers and other investigators.[84]

And in connection with the partial surrender of key symbols of maturity, he observes:

---

[82] The observation that psychiatric or casework "diagnosis" frequently harbors moral judgments has been made many times. For a discussion of the transition from the explicit moral classification of the Charity Organization Societies to the implicit moral judgments of "casework diagnosis," see Roy Lubove, *The Professional Altruist* (Cambridge, Mass.: Harvard University Press, 1965). For more general discussions of the persistence of moral classification in "scientific" disciplines, see Kingsley Davis, "Mental Hygiene and the Class Structure," *Psychiatry,* Vol. 1 (February, 1938); C. W. Mills, "The Professional Ideology of Social Pathologists," *American Journal of Sociology* (September, 1943); and Erving Goffman, *Asylums* (New York: Doubleday [Anchor], 1961).

[83] Lewis Coser, "The Sociology of Poverty," *Social Problems,* Vol. 13, No. 2 (Fall, 1965), p. 144.

[84] *Ibid.,* p. 145.

When money is allocated to members of any other status group in society, they have the freedom to dispose of it in almost any way they
see fit. Here again, the treatment of the poor differs sharply. When
monies are allocated to them, they do not have free disposition over
their use. They must account to the donors for their expenses and the
donors decide whether the money is spent "wisely" or "foolishly."
. . . The poor are treated in this respect much like children who have
to account to their parents for the wise use of their pocket money; the
poor are infantilized through such procedures.[85]

Thus, Coser argues that degradation is implicit in the situation of assistance since the ordinarily conceived rights of privacy and maturity are partly
abrogated. This applies generally to the welfare poor. For the disreputable
poor, however, an additional degradation is implicit in the official scrutiny
to which they are subjected. They are reminded of their undeserving character; their disrepute is noted, commented on, and filed away. Irrespective of
whether sanctions are taken—the main sanction being the "holding of
checks"—the negative moral judgments of officials and the wider society they
represent are subtly implied, cued, or loudly proclaimed.[86] In either case,
the common conception of the disreputable poor as something less than human is apt to be confirmed and reinforced. It is in this light, perhaps, that the
piercing cry of a nameless black welfare recipient is best understood. "I'm
human! I'm human! I'm human! You dirty son of a bitch, can't you see I'm
human!"[87] And it is in their encounters with functionaries that the disreputable poor are most apt to be reminded of their dismal moral condition
and of their basic differences from the rest of humanity. Perhaps that is
why, as Julius Horwitz observed, "the cry of being human was the most commonplace cry in the service. I heard it daily."[88]

The various elements that coincidentally inhabit the regions of disreputable poverty conspire to perpetuate immobilization. Thus, part of the explanation for its anachronistic persistence lies in the relations among its

[85] *Ibid.* Also on the point of "infantilizing," see Charles Silberman, *Crisis in Black
and White* (New York: Random House, 1964), pp. 313–15. For a detailed and documented discussion of the special legal status and special penalties of the assisted that
bears directly on the partial forfeitures of privacy and maturity, see Jacobus TenBroek,
"California's Dual System of Family Law: Its Origin, Development, and Present
Status," *Stanford Law Review,* Vol. 16 (March, 1964), pp. 257–317; (July, 1964),
pp. 900–81; and Vol. 17 (April, 1965), pp. 614–82.

[86] For a journalistic description of checkholding and other matters relating to the
treatment of disreputable clients by welfare caseworkers, see Joseph P. Mullen, *Room
103* (Philadelphia: Dorrance, 1963).

[87] Julius Horwitz, *The Inhabitants* (Cleveland: World, 1960), p. 104.

[88] *Ibid.*

components. But at best this is a partial explanation, and at worst it begs the more basic questions. To understand how disreputable poverty is produced and maintained, we must examine the process of pauperization.

THE PROCESS OF PAUPERIZATION

Although disreputable poverty has always existed, we do not yet know how the ranks of the disreputable poor are periodically replenished on something approximating a mass basis, or how fractions of newcomers are selected to join them. These two related questions make up the topic of pauperization. The following answers are intended only to illustrate certain facets of the process, not to present a general theory of pauperization.

Pauperization is the process that results in disreputable poverty. That aspect of it by which the population is periodically replenished may be termed *massive generation;* that by which newcomers pass into the ranks of disreputable poverty may be termed *fractional selection.*

Massive Generation

Let us begin cautiously by guarding against two antithetical beliefs — both common — one connected with that hardy variety of humanitarian conservatism we now call "liberalism," the other associated with that harsh variety of economic liberalism we now call "conservatism." The first view all but denies the possibility of pauperization, claiming that the very category of disreputable poverty is a prejudice with no substantive foundation, and that pauperization is merely an unwarranted imputation. The second view assumes that pauperization occurs whenever the compulsion to work is relieved. This view was nicely summarized by Josephine Shaw Lowell. In 1884, she wrote, "human nature is so constituted that no man can receive as a gift what he should earn by his own labor without a moral deterioration."[89]

According to this view, the poor are readily susceptible to the immobilization and demoralization implicit in disreputable poverty and will succumb whenever they are given the slightest opportunity to do so. The view developed here is intermediate: Pauperization, in the form of massive genera-

---

[89] Josephine Shaw Lowell, *Public Relief and Private Charity* (New York: Putnam, 1884), p. 66.

tion, is always a possibility and occasionally occurs, but it requires extreme and special conditions. Pauperizing a significant part of a population is possible, but relatively difficult to accomplish. It must be worked at conscientiously, even if unwittingly.

The circumstances attending the early phases of industrialization in England offer a classic illustration of massive pauperization. As far as can be told, mass pauperization was not a necessary feature or by-product of industrialization or even of what Marx called primitive accumulation. Instead, it was probably an unanticipated consequence of purposive social action regarding the poor during the early phases of English industrialization.

Mass pauperization was implicit in the sequence of Poor Laws by which the harsh reform of 1834 was built on the indulgent and slovenly base provided by the Speenhamland system ("the decision of the Berkshire Justices at Speenhamland in 1795 to supplement wages from the [poor] rates on a sliding scale in accordance with the price of bread and the size of families concerned").[90] Neither the reform of 1834 nor the Speenhamland decision alone was sufficient to accomplish a massive generation of disreputable poverty, but together they achieved a major replenishing.

The principal consequence of the Speenhamland system was *potentially* to enlarge the ranks of the disreputable poor. This was accomplished through the moral confusion associated with a policy that in essence violated normal expectations regarding the relation between conscientious effort and economic reward.[91] Thus, one major aspect of the system was a peculiar type of outdoor relief in which "aid-in-wages" was regularly endorsed in such a way as to make independent laborers and paupers indistinguishable. The wage of the former was depressed,[92] while the lot of the latter was obviously improved.

> The poor-rate had become public spoil. . . . To obtain their share the brutal bullied the administrators, the profligate exhibited their bastards which must be fed, the idle folded their arms and waited till they got it; ignorant boys and girls married upon it; poachers, thieves, and prostitutes extorted it by intimidation; country justices lavished it for popularity and Guardians for convenience. This was the way the fund went.[93]

---

[90] Maurice Bruce, *The Coming of the Welfare State* (London: Batsford, 1961), pp. 41–42.
[91] This interpretation is based on, but departs somewhat from, that suggested in Karl Polanyi, *The Great Transformation,* p. 100. See also Maurice Bruce, *The Coming of the Welfare State,* pp. 41–42.
[92] Karl Polanyi, *The Great Transformation,* p. 280.
[93] *Ibid.,* p. 99.

Karl Polanyi has suggested the effect of this indiscriminate subsidy on the productivity of the labor force:

> Under Speenhamland . . . a man was relieved even if he was in employment, as long as his wages amounted to less than the family income granted him by the scale. Hence, no laborer had any material interest in satisfying his employer, his income being the same whatever wages he earned. . . . The employer could obtain labor at almost any wages; however little he paid, the subsidy from the rates brought the worker's income up to scale. Within a few years the productivity of labor began to sink to that of pauper labor, thus providing an added reason for employers not to raise wages above the scale. For once the intensity of labor, the care and efficiency with which it was performed, dropped below a definite level, it became indistinguishable from "boondoggling," or the semblance of work maintained for the sake of appearance.[94]

Though boondoggling and other forms of demotivation were implicit in the system, that in itself was probably not sufficient for the massive generation of paupers. Pauperization implies more than demotivation of effort; it also implies a general demoralization, the emergence of a view in which work is taken as a punishment or penalty. These features of pauperization both appeared in substantial, though obviously limited, sections of the amorphous mass of laborers and paupers, and both may perhaps be traced to an institution that was already apparent under the Speenhamland system and before, but came to full fruition only after the Poor Law reforms of 1834. Pauperization awaited an institution in which persistent poverty was *penalized* and in which the form of penalization was *coerced labor* administered on an *indoor* basis.

Under the Speenhamland system, the penalizing of poverty in the workhouse was a minor appendage to its major feature, indiscriminate outdoor relief. Under the reform of 1834, the penalization of poverty on an indoor basis became a major governmental policy in regulating the poor. Since this policy was pursued first side by side with, and subsequently in the wake of, a policy that confounded laborers with paupers, it was well suited to realize the enormous potential for massive pauperization implicit in that confounding. Penalizing poverty through the workhouse reinforced and established, inadvertently but effectively, whatever propensities in this direction resulted from the earlier system of indiscriminate outdoor relief. The indolence and boondoggling occasioned by the Speenhamland system created

---

[94] *Ibid.,* p. 79; also see Marcus Lee Hansen, *The Atlantic Migration, 1607–1860* (Cambridge, Mass.: Harvard University Press, 1940), p. 128.

the propensity for mass pauperization; but to be transformed into true paupers, those exhibiting indolence had to be stigmatized or defamed, work had to be reconstituted as penal sanction, and demoralization centralized under the roof of a facilitating institution. All this was accomplished by the workhouse system.

In the poorhouse, the ancient culture of paupers could now be transmitted to those who had been thrown together with them, and the potential for massive generation of disreputable poverty could be realized. Moreover, the confusion regarding the moral value of work could be compounded and finally resolved by the unmistakable lesson of the workhouse—that work is a penalty and thus to be avoided and resented.[95]

Collecting the indolent in an indoor setting was important for another reason. Persons receiving relief under the earlier system were not yet overwhelmingly concentrated in the urban slums we have come to associate with a tradition of disreputable poverty. Most were still distributed over chiefly agricultural areas.[96] Thus, the concentration that facilitates the formation of a subculture was aided by the poorhouse system. The poorhouses and workhouses served the same function for the disreputable poor that Marx assigned to the factories in the development of an industrial proletariat and that criminologists assigned to prisons in disseminating the standards and techniques of criminality. Each is a center for the collection of traits that can then be conveniently disseminated.

The defamation of character implicit in commitment to a workhouse is clearest after the Poor Law reform of 1834. This reform was a direct reaction to the Speenhamland system.[97] It was calculated to avoid the indulgence of indolence apparent in that system, but instead of undoing its effects, it compounded them. Penalizing poverty completed the historic process of pauperization begun by the moral confusion occasioned by this system. The abolition of the Speenhamland system was, in some respects, as Polanyi suggests, "the true birthday of the modern working classes" because it forced them to mobilize on their own behalf. But just as surely, the same abolition and the same enactment of the 1834 reform was the "true birthday of the modern disreputable poor," for it signaled the last phase of the pauperization process. If "Speenhamland was an automaton for demolishing the standards on which

---

[95] The moral confusion regarding the status of work occasioned by this dual aspect of the Speenhamland system is discussed by Reinhard Bendix, *Work and Authority in Industry* (New York: Harper, 1963), pp. 40–42.

[96] Neil J. Smelser, *Social Change in the Industrial Revolution* (Chicago: University of Chicago Press, 1959), p. 350.

[97] Sidney and Beatrice Webb, *English Poor Law History,* Vol. 8 of *English Local Government* (London: Longmans, 1929), pp. 14–15.

any kind of society could be based," then the reform was an instrument for institutionalizing the standards that replaced those "on which any kind of society could be based."

The reform of 1834 was designed to discourage the poor from going on relief by the stigma now attached to the workhouse and the conditions characterizing it.

> The new law provided that in the future no outdoor relief should be given. . . . Aid-in-wages was . . . discontinued. . . . It was now left to the applicant to decide whether he was so utterly destitute of all means that he would voluntarily repair to a shelter which was deliberately made a place of horror. The workhouse was invested with a stigma; and staying in it was made a psychological and moral torture. . . . the very burial of a pauper was made an act by which his fellow men renounced solidarity with him even in death.[98]

The effect of this change in the law was to reinstitute the distinction between independent laborer and pauper, after 40 years of confounding precisely that issue. Together the two policies (Speenhamland and the Reform Act) comprise the classic way of generating a mass population of paupers. Only America has done better.

Doubtless, pauperization is easier to accomplish when the population in question is a subjugated national or ethnic group rather than an indigenous group of subjects or citizens. Subjugated people are regarded as moral inferiors to begin with, capable of a variety of vices that typically include indolence and immorality. Pauperizing an indigenous population is more difficult, since national affinities limit, though without necessarily precluding, the possibilities of imputing subhuman stature. The English case is classic precisely because pauperizing some part of an indigenous population is difficult. But in that case too, the extent of indigenous pauperization is easily exaggerated, for many who were caught in the curious combination of indulgence followed by penalization were in fact not English but Irish. Some of the Irish in England were pauperized by the same circumstances that affected indigenous Englishmen, but many more were pauperized by a separate process, one that illustrates the pattern of extreme subjugation by which the poor among captive or conquered peoples are commonly pauperized. This second pattern of massive pauperization is of paramount importance in the United States because it perhaps produced the two major ethnic contributors to the tradition of disreputable poverty — the Irish and the blacks.[99]

---

[98] Karl Polanyi, *The Great Transformation*, pp. 101–02.

[99] For a general picture of the ways in which the Irish and blacks were at least some-

The great Irish famine was only the culmination of a long period of subjugated poverty which drove the Irish eastward to England and westward to America. Both before and during the famine it is likely that England, rather than America, received the most profoundly pauperized sections of the Irish poor,[100] if only because migration to nearby England was economically more feasible. Ireland was an impoverished colony before, during, and after its great famine, and perhaps, as travelers during the period suggested, impoverished to an extent unrivaled elsewhere in Europe.[101] Impoverishment, however, is not the same as pauperization. In the Irish experience, extreme economic impoverishment was combined with profound political subjugation. Just as penalization pauperizes an indigenous population, political subjugation of a captive or colonized people may transform the merely poor into paupers through the agency of oppression and degradation. The political subjugation experienced by the Irish was tantamount to the penalization of the entire island.

Beginning in 1695, the Irish were subjected to the infamous Penal Laws, which Edmund Burke aptly described as "a machine of wise and elaborate contrivance, and as well fitted for the oppression, impoverishment, and degradation of a people and the debasement in them of human nature itself, as ever proceeded from the perverted ingenuity of man." The effects of the Penal Laws are suggested by Woodham-Smith. She says:

> The material damage suffered through the penal laws was great; ruin was widespread, old families disappeared and old estates were broken up; but the most disastrous effects were moral. The Penal Laws brought lawlessness, dissimulation, and revenge in their train, and the Irish character, above all the character of the peasantry, did become in Burke's words degraded and debased. The upper classes were able to leave the country and many middle-class merchants contrived, with guile, to survive, but the poor Catholic peasant bore the full hardship. His religion made him an outlaw; in the Irish House of Commons he was described as "the common enemy," and whatever was inflicted on him, he must bear, for where could he look for redress? To his landlord? Almost invariably an alien conqueror. To the law? Not when every person connected with the law, from the jailer to the judge, was a Protestant who regarded him as "the common enemy."[102]

---

what different from other immigrant groups in America, see Nathan Glazer and Daniel P. Moynihan, *Beyond the Melting Pot* (Cambridge, Mass.: The M. I. T. Press and Harvard University Press, 1963).

[100] John A. Jackson, *The Irish in Britain* (London: Routledge, 1963), p. 9; also see Cecil Woodham-Smith, *The Great Hunger* (London: Hamish Hamilton, 1962), p. 270.

[101] Cecil Woodham-Smith, *The Great Hunger,* pp. 19–20.

[102] *Ibid.,* pp. 27–28.

The lingering effects of these laws were instrumental in creating the two traditions for which the Irish later became noted, terrorist rebellion and disreputable poverty.

The pauperization of the Irish peasantry was also facilitated by the Irish system of land tenure, characterized by absentee landlords whose holdings were managed largely by local agents. Under the policy of surrender and regrant of land, most Irish farmers had become rent-paying tenants.[103] Moreover, the land system, and especially the institution of "cant," seemed almost calculated to punish conscientious effort and reward slovenliness.

> The most calloused abuse by the landlord of his ownership was the practice of putting up farms for "cant" [or public auction] when leases expired. No matter how faithfully a tenant paid his rent, how dutifully he had observed regulations, or how well he had improved the property by his own labors, he was in constant danger of being outbid for his farm by the "grabber" upon the expiration of the lease. . . . Moreover, in the Catholic parts of Ireland . . . the tenant was not entitled to compensation for improvements brought by himself. . . . Hard experience had taught the tenant the penalties of improving the property he leased or hired and the self-interest of slovenliness. If he improved the property, his rent was raised! . . . progress and improvement, instead of being encouraged by the landlord for his own interests, were penalized. This upside-down system withered the character, destroyed the initiative, and squelched the ambition of the Irish tenant.[104]

A key factor in pauperization in Ireland, as in England, was the use of work as a negative sanction. In one instance, conscientious effort was punished; in the other it was used as a punishment. Either form of association of work with a negative sanction facilitates pauperization. Mere indolence is converted to an active antagonism to work. By the time the Irish began to emigrate to America, the combination of political subjugation and economic impoverishment had had its effect. A substantial proportion of the population had been pauperized though, almost certainly, it was nothing approaching a majority. So difficult is the process of pauperization that no more than a substantial minority are likely to succumb to it. Always counteracting the forces for degradation and demoralization are the stabilizing and moralizing forces of family, religion, and primary group solidarity; these are weakened but never obliterated.

In the years just before the famine and great emigration, the Irish poor were subjected to the workhouse system, which was instituted in the English

[103] Robert Ernst, *Immigrant Life in New York City, 1825–1863*, p. 5.
[104] George Potter, *To the Golden Door* (Boston: Little, Brown, 1960), p. 44.

Parliament as part of the Irish Poor Law Act of 1838. Thus, in Ireland the penalizing of poverty came in the wake of the political subjugation epitomized by the Penal Laws, whereas in the English case, the penalizing of poverty followed the indulgence of the Speenhamland system. The major effect of the Act was to spur "Assisted Emigration" from Ireland, mostly to America via Quebec.[105]

The penalization of poverty was the last phase in a long history of the English pauperization of the Irish poor. It occurred shortly before the great emigration to America. Thus, a substantial proportion of emigrants to America had experienced *both* the punishing of conscientious effort, as a result of the cant system, and the use of conscientious effort as punishment in the workhouse, along with political subjugation under the English. The disreputable poverty of the Irish immigrant in America is best understood in the context of this dubious legacy, and the subsequent tradition of disreputable poverty in urban America is best understood by stressing that our first massive immigration of the very poor was that of already pauperized Irish fleeing with English assistance from the great famine.[106]

In America, the Irish were almost immediately considered worthless paupers. This stigma was applied not only to those who were already truly pauperized but also to those who had somehow remained simply poor. Since the worthy poor were also frequently out of work, they were lumped together with their more disreputable brethren. George Potter summarizes their predicament:

The "indolent Irish" had been a characterization, fixed on the race by the English in Ireland, that America inherited. Superficial observation gave it currency in America for two major reasons. One was the frequent spells of unemployment the Irishman suffered from the nature of his manual work — inclement weather, cyclical depressions, and job competition. On this score the description was unjust because of the elements beyond the individual Irishman's control. The other [reason] was the shiftlessness of a ragtag and bobtail minority, noisy, dissolute, troublesome, gravitating to public relief, which unfairly settled a distorted reputation on the race in the minds of people often initially prejudiced.[107]

---

[105] Maurice Bruce, *The Coming of the Welfare State,* pp. 76–77; and Robert Ernst, *Immigrant Life in New York City, 1825–1863,* p. 5.

[106] Of course, there is another more familiar stream that feeds into this tradition in America and massively replenishes the population of disreputable poverty. It derives from the pauperization of substantial sections of the black population implicit in their enslavement and continued subjugation after formal emancipation. Suggestive in this respect is Stanley Elkins, *Slavery* (Chicago: University of Chicago Press, 1959).

[107] George Potter, *To the Golden Door,* pp. 84–85.

Fractional Selection

Fractional selection is the process whereby some fraction of newcomers pass into the ranks of disreputable poverty. It is the more normal, less dramatic process of pauperization, depending on existing traditions of disreputable poverty, which are only occasionally reinforced on a massive scale by newly generated cohorts. Given the relative infrequency of massive generation, the process of fractional selection is the major hindrance to the gradual attrition of disreputable poverty. The conversion of newcomers to dregs provides for the partial replacement of the pauperized individuals who somehow transcend their circumstance and pass into the reputable sections of society. Consequently, the survival of disreputable poverty has partly depended on barring newcomers from the normal routes of social mobility. Thus, the general conditions underlying fractional selection into the ranks of disreputable poverty are for the most part simply the reverse of those favoring social mobility. These general conditions need no special restatement; instead, we need to emphasize the temporal context of the circumstances favoring mobility.

Strong family organization, a cultural heritage stressing achievement, an expanding economy, an upgraded labor force, a favorable demographic situation, and other conditions generally favoring mobility, have their effect within a temporal context. Once a given period is over, these general circumstances favoring advancement are hampered by demoralization, first in the form of severe discouragement or immobilization and subsequently in the form of relaxed moral standards. Demoralization signals the culmination of the process by which some proportion of newcomers are selected for disreputable poverty.

The period during which newcomers enjoy relatively high morale is the temporal context within which the general factors favoring social mobility flourish. Its length varies, but the limits can be identified. Demoralization may be avoided until newcomers are reduced to dregs, and the reduction of newcomers to dregs occurs when the steady desertion of the area by mobile ethnic brethren is dramatically climaxed by an ecological invasion of new bands of ethnic or regional newcomers. When newcomers to the milieu of disreputable poverty predominate as neighbors and workmates, the remnants of earlier cohorts resentfully begin to notice what they have finally come to. They must now live and work with "them," and suddenly the previously obscured relation between their lot and that of their more fortunate or successful brethren from the original cohort is clear. They have become dregs, reduced to actually living and working with "niggers," or some other newcomers. Pauperization through fractional selection occurs, then, when newcomers take over the neighborhood and workplace. This kind of pauperization becomes more pronounced when the newcomers who have overtaken the dregs are themselves replaced by yet another cohort of newcomers. Thus, the milieu of disreputable poverty is temporally stratified: the older the vintage, the more thorough the pauperization.

The spiteful and condescending clucking of the now reputable segments of the original ethnic group is a main factor in demoralizing those who still live in a disreputable milieu. The attitudes of the reputable are illustrated by the comments of upper-lower-class Irish, reported by Warner and Srole:

"Maybe we haven't made a million dollars, but our house is paid for and out of honest wages, too," said Tim.

"Still, Tim, we haven't done so bad. The Flanagans came here when we did and what's happened to them? None of them is any good. Not one of them has moved out of the clam flats."

"You're right, Annie, we are a lot better than some. Old Pat Flanagan, what is he? He is worse than the clam diggers themselves. He has got ten or twelve kids—some of them born in wedlock, and with the blessings of the church, but some of them are from those women in the clam flats. He has no shame."

"His children," said Annie, "are growing into heathens. Two of them are in the reform school, and that oldest girl of his has had two or three babies without nobody admitting he was the father." [108]

However, rejection by significant members of one's ethnic community may be relatively unimportant, especially when compared to rejection by kinsmen. Rejection by kinsmen may be especially damaging and productive of apathy and demoralization. That it occurs even in close-knit families and extended kinship units is apparent. Powles describes the strong bonds that tie contemporary Appalachian migrants to their kinsmen, but points to a pertinent special situation in which certain members may be cut off or excluded.

The family of people into which the Appalachian workingman was born retains a particularly intense meaning for him throughout his life, emotionally sustaining him but also in a special way being a

---

[108] W. Lloyd Warner and Leo Srole, *The Social Systems of American Ethnic Groups* (New Haven: Yale University Press, 1945), pp. 12–13.

piece of social machinery of great personal assistance. . . . The wider or "extended" family is not a vital part of most city-dwellers' experience. But for the Appalachian migrant, its strengths, resources and ramifications play a crucial role. . . . He works his way into city-life [through] kinfolk who already have a toehold, however precarious, in the community. He negates his family ties only in one special case. This occurs when he begins to feel contempt for, and to cut himself off from, kinfolk whom he has bypassed on the urbanization ladder, who have gone to the devil, failed to make it, remained trash in the slums.[109]

We may conjecture that the closer the bonds of kinship, the greater the disparagement felt when cut off from them. Those who are thus excluded or left behind come eventually to live among yet another cohort of newcomers.

When they are forced to live and work with newcomers, the remnants need no longer overhear the disparaging comments of the reputable members of their ethnic brethren or extended kinship units. They disparage themselves. They know what they have come down to, for they share the wider social view that the newcomers are inferior and detestable. The irony here is that the demoralization of old ethnics and their subsequent transformation to dregs result partly from the provincialism that simultaneously maintains ethnic identity long after it has been partially obscured in other parts of society and manifests itself in pervasive prejudices perhaps unmatched elsewhere.[110] The measure in which the earlier arrivals are reduced to dregs depends partly on the extent to which they themselves denigrate newcomers. For now they become, in the eyes of significant others, and in that measure in their own eyes, "just like them." [111]

CONCLUSION

The disreputable poor are an immobilized segment of society located at a point in the social structure where poverty intersects with illicit pursuits.

---

[109] William E. Powles, "The Southern Appalachian Migrant: Country Boy Turned Blue-Collarite," pp. 275–76.

[110] See Seymour M. Lipset, "Working-Class Authoritarianism," in *Political Man* (New York: Doubleday, 1960), Chapter 4.

[111] The viciousness and bigotry with which the previous ethnic cohort treats newcomers is not just a consequence of their higher levels of provincialism and prejudice; what we regard as residential and occupational desegregation is to ethnic remnants a visible social indication of pauperization. Their intolerant response may be taken as an indication of the extent to which they wish to avoid the visible stigmata of pauperization.

They are, in the evocative words of Charles Brace, "the dangerous classes" who live in "regions of squalid want and wicked woe." [112] This stratum is replenished only rarely through massive generation, and it is difficult to assess whether any *recent innovations* in the American political economy foster the process of pauperization. Still, the tradition of disreputable poverty persists, partly because the legacy of the pauperized Irish immigrants has been continued in some measure by the fractional selection of subsequent newcomers, and partly because the internal situation of disreputable poverty persists. Moreover, it has persisted for a reason so brutally obvious as to be hardly touched on in this brief essay: The main victims of the uniquely American methods of pauperization—enslaved Africans, conquered Mexicans, subjugated and "concentrated" native Indians—have begun only recently to consciously mobilize and, thus, to undo the effects of the long-lasting dehumanization of substantial segments of each people. America has been at the very least, as perversely ingenious as Edmund Burke's England in instituting machines of "wise and elaborate contrivance . . . well fitted for the oppression, impoverishment and degradation of a people and the debasement in them of human nature itself." Indeed, my stress on the perverted ingenuity of the English is best understood as indicating that America possesses no monopoly on the capacity to oppress and debase the poor. Thus viewed, my relative neglect of the well-known American "peculiar institutions" for degrading, and pauperizing segments of the Afro-, Mexican-, and Native-American populations will, hopefully, not be confused with any belief on my part that such things did not happen. They did happen, and to some extent still do happen. Considerably more noteworthy, though, than the pauperization of many colored Americans—*a basic and central fact of American history* which should be familiar to even the most cursory student—is the actual possibility that the working descendants of that grim and long-standing oppression will now transcend the predicament left them in the most effective manner possible: by consciously taking history into their own hands.

If that should happen, the tradition of disreputable poverty will have used up its main capital and be reduced to squandering the interest drawn from fractional selection and its own internal situation—a fitting fate for so improvident an enterprise. No more than a possibility, the liberation of "the wretched of the earth" by their very own actions, through *consciously* struggling in their own behalf, is the only "policy recommendation" I wish to make. Any other would be a proposal made in bad faith. Fortunately— since *Contemporary Social Problems* is so long a text—my suggested "solution to the social question" is so unoriginal, so inherent in the worldwide

---

[112] Robert H. Bremner, *From the Depths,* p. 6.

movement beginning in the nineteenth century, it can be rendered with extreme brevity in slogan form: "All power to the people!"

That the meaning of that slogan has so frequently been vulgarized, misunderstood, distorted, abused, betrayed and even twisted beyond recognition during the twentieth century does *not* detract from the likely fact that a humane and democratic socialism is *still the* solution to the social question. Writing in 1970, the obvious question of whether such an eventuality is even worth considering no longer brings forth a sneering and certain negative reply. Instead, it yields the shriek of "law and order." The "natives" in America "are restless," as are a substantial segment of bourgeois youth. And even the working class, or proletariat — moribund since 1947 — may someday move. To update Marx, in the only way that seems immediately necessary, American workers, as much as they have, have *little* "to lose but their chains."

13

Community Disorganization and Conflict

JAMES S. COLEMAN

INTRODUCTION

One of the major developments in American society during the late 1960's was the growth of collective action by groups of people unified by a single issue. Fundamental to the civil rights movement of the early 1960's, this direct action soon spread to a wide variety of causes: demonstrations against the Vietnam war, actions against environmental pollution, rent and welfare strikes, support for black militants in prison, hippie "love-ins," actions by women's liberation groups, and a variety of other organized or mass actions.

At the same time, there were many other issues on which organized collective action might have taken place, but did not — issues that aroused individuals just as much as those described above but were not channeled into organized activity. For example, many aspects of life in black urban ghettos

This chapter is an extensive revision of a chapter titled "Community Disorganization" in the second edition of this textbook. I thank Arthur Stinchcombe and Jan Hajda for critical comments on the earlier version, and Robert Merton and Peter Rossi for advice and aid in both. My initial concern with community organization and disorganization stems from research in community conflict, begun in collaboration with Louis Kriesberg at the Bureau of Applied Social Research at Columbia University, and research on measurement of group properties that was initiated by Paul Lazarsfeld at Columbia University.

generated strong feelings. In many cities, however, these feelings were not harnessed to any effective community action, and they finally erupted into riots.

These cases of action and inaction represent community organization and disorganization—the ability or inability to engage in concerted action, and to achieve collectively ends that cannot be achieved alone. Since the beginning of societies men have combined to produce such ends and through collective action have been able to affect the future of their societies—so, too, the collective actions of the present are now determining the shape of tomorrow's society. These actions have often been based on residential propinquity—in villages, towns, and cities—and it is on this level that many of the problems of social organization continue to be felt. The questions we need to ask, then, are two: *First,* what are the processes through which social communities, and the ability to act as a community, are created; and *second,* what are the ways those processes fail and thus lead to disorganization of the community? Answers to these two questions can give some insight into contemporary social action in cities and outside them. Finally, this will lead to the examination of some contemporary conditions that lead to disorganization.

What Is a Community?

The term "community" concerns things held in common. Some of these may be tangible objects, such as the common property of a family or the common pasture lands held by a tribe. Others are less tangible: common ideas, beliefs, and values; common customs and norms held by all; and common or joint actions of a group as a whole. Furthermore, when we speak of a community, we ordinarily mean a set of people who have not just one element in common, but many.

There are numerous kinds of communities in the larger society: the adolescent community, the black community, the academic community—to name three. Yet in the past, the principal "communities" have been geographic or residential, so much so that sometimes the term is taken to mean geographically defined groups.

Modern society may currently be undergoing changes from geographic to other bases for community. Thus it is important to examine in general both the processes that create a community and some of the contemporary conditions that lead to disorganization of geographically defined communities: neighborhoods, villages, towns, cities, suburbs, farming communities, any geographic clustering of families. Some of these clusters, in fact, show hardly enough organization, hardly enough "commonness" among their members to be called communities. But this is precisely part of our inquiry. The geographic clustering that constitutes a village, town, or city ordinarily sets in motion certain processes that tend to make these localities into communities. But sometimes these natural processes are unsuccessful or are blocked, and a community fails to develop or falls apart.

What Is Community Disorganization?

Social organization is important for one reason alone: to enable the social unit to take action as a unit. If bridges are to be built, wars won, food grown, criminals caught, then there must be organization. Thus community disorganization concerns the community's inability to act as a community. If a community can act collectively toward the problems that face it, then it is well organized. If it cannot, then it is disorganized relative to these problems, though there may be a great amount of apparent organization.

Such inability to act can come about in one of two ways: through an absence of any collective effort, or through the existence of conflicting collective efforts that cancel each other out. That is, in some systems, there is no collective energy available for unitary action; in others, there is collective energy, but in mutual opposition, thereby setting up tension without action. The first can be likened to the wasting away of tissue in a body, the second to paralysis.

These have been the two elements of community disorganization pointed to by many authors. The first is often termed a decline in consensus, or a weakening of social norms and constraints. This will be called *disintegration* in the succeeding pages. The second concerns culture conflict, social conflict, or normative conflict. It will simply be called *conflict* in the succeeding pages.

SOCIAL PROCESSES THAT CREATE A COMMUNITY, AND THEIR MALFUNCTIONING

One of the elements of commonness composing a community is similarity of activities. In any community where people are engaged in similar activities and are subject to the same or similar events, the very similarity generates topics for conversation, leads people to enjoy one another's company, and creates bonds of mutual understanding. This is evident in such disparate situations as those indicated below:

1. In Harlem:

> All the Muslims now felt as though 125th Street was theirs. It used to belong to the hustlers and the slicksters. They're still there, but Seventh Avenue belongs to the Muslims. I think everybody knows this now. This group just came down and claimed it. They started setting up their stands and giving speeches. People started listening, and it just became known that if you wanted to hear a good antiwhite sermon on Saturday night, all you had to do was go to 125th Street and Seventh Avenue.
>
> It made everybody feel as though they had something. I suppose there were many people who had been mistreated by the white boss during the day. They could come out on Seventh Avenue and hear something that would be consoling . . . hear some of the "Buy Black" slogans and "hate the white devils" speeches.[1]

2. In a London slum:

> "My Mum comes around at about 3:15 – she comes round regularly at that time to spend the afternoon"; "Mum's always popping in here – 12 times a day I should say"; "Then my Mum and I collect Stephen from the school and go back to her place for tea"; "We usually have dinner round at her place"; "She's always popping in here"; "We've got four keys – one for each of us, one for Mum, and one for Mary. That's so they can come in any time they like." "Popping in" for a chat and a cup of tea is the routine of normal life.[2]

3. In a small southern community:

> The drug stores serve as social centers and are rarely empty. People come, not merely to buy a toothbrush or a cake of soap, but to linger over their Coca-Colas, which they take in small, leisurely sips interspersed with long drafts of gossip. The proprietor is always at hand and always ready with conversation. The habitués are mainly young women, clerks and stenographers from the courthouse, and "men about town," which may mean a lawyer, a county official, a planter from the country. Upon inquiring for the owner of a plantation ten or twelve miles away, one is told that he can be found any day at his favorite drug store.[3]

---

[1] Claude Brown, *Manchild in the Promised Land* (New York: Macmillan, 1965), p. 332.

[2] Michael Young and Peter Wilmott, *Family and Kinship in East London* (New York: Free Press, 1957), p. 31.

[3] Hortense Powdermaker, *After Freedom* (New York: Viking, 1939), p. 10.

The similar activities and experiences of these people in their respective communities are an important element in the development of a sense of community. It shapes similar attitudes and behavior, and it creates among people the sympathy, or mutual identification, that pulls them together. Though these in themselves give no cause for social organization, they do provide a basis from which organization may spring, and their absence takes this basis away, as the next section indicates.

Dependence of Activities on Common Events

There is more, of course, to the development of a community from a locality than mere similarity of activities and problems. Consider, for example, crime prevention. Almost everyone in society has the same interest in protecting himself from robbery, murder, and other criminal actions. But a resident of Los Angeles and a resident of Portland, Maine, have few *common* interests in crime prevention. Different criminals operate in the two places. Most actions that the residents of Portland might take to prevent crime would have no effect on criminal activity in Los Angeles.[4]

The matter is different, however, within a city and is even more striking within a neighborhood. Men's *similar* interests in self-protection become *common* interests, since safety is dependent upon the same events. A crime wave may set off neighborhood meetings, formation of vigilante groups, decisions of the town council to hire more policemen, grouping of neighbors when venturing out in the evening, and other such activities. A crime wave constitutes a common problem for those living close together, and by the very problem it creates, it spawns social organization.

Crime is but one of many matters in which similar interests become common interests for people who are in the same geographic locality. Air pollution is much the same. All persons have similar interests in protecting themselves and their possessions from pollution; but within a neighborhood, this becomes a common interest. The individual can hardly protect himself from polluted air as well as he and his neighbors can jointly protect themselves by means of concerted action. Thus air pollution, like crime, is a problem that requires and sometimes generates community organization. The quote below suggests the difficulty:

---

[4] Certain types of crime, of course, have nationwide networks, so that certain kinds of crime prevention (e.g., drug traffic) in one city have important repercussions for other cities.

In a large city in the Middle West . . . a nationally respected air pollution official concluded a disquisition on the nation's mounting smog problem by abruptly sweeping aside his sliderule, charts and tabulations and exclaiming:

"That's the official story. Now do you want to hear the truth?

"The truth is that the critical ingredient in smog simply is politics. By that I mean people and their instruments of government, and their attitudes about a community problem.

"We know how to cure smog. It's not unduly difficult or expensive. The problem is getting the people in the community to support a cleanup program.

"The most important part of a program is not technical expertise. It's having a wheeler-dealer who can put it across with the political establishment in a community. We've been long on engineering and short of wheeler-dealers. That's why our air is a mess.". . .

"Politically," the candid official continued, "air pollution is a far tougher can of worms than water pollution. With water pollution, the blame goes mainly to collective sources—municipalities and industries —and cleanup costs fall on them.

"A lot of air pollution goes back to individuals—their cars, their furnaces, their incinerators. When a cleanup program threatens to hit them directly, and change the way they're doing things, and cost a little bit, they back off." [5]

This comment on the difficulties of attacking air pollution shows some typical reasons for an inability to organize for action. However, it is not always inability to organize in the face of common problems that prevents concerted action; often the failure to act in concert is due to an attenuation of some of the basic common problems.

A study of a neighborhood in Tokyo discusses the decline in neighbor relations, and suggests they are in part due to the reduction of common problems:

In districts like Shitayama-cho the formal maintenance of neighbor relations still serves some important economic ends such as dealing with emergencies like death and illness, as well as being a means to the less calculable satisfactions of meeting smiling faces instead of blank stares as soon as one steps outside one's door. But these economic considerations are far less important than they are for the farmer whose livelihood depends on various forms of cooperation with his neighbors. Fire insurance, life insurance, and post-office savings schemes are widely employed; in the last resort there is always public assistance.[6]

---

[5] J. K. Hadden, L. H. Masotti, and C. J. Larson, eds., *Metropolis in Crisis* (Itasca, Ill.: Peacock, 1967), pp. 346–47.

[6] Ronald P. Dore, *City Life in Japan* (Berkeley: University of California Press, 1958), p. 258.

Thus one of the fundamental processes in the development of a community is the existence of common problems that can best be solved by joint action. If there are insurmountable barriers, or if there are formal structures established to solve them outside the community (such as fire insurance, government restrictions on air pollution, or federal financing for neighborhood rehabilitation), then no community action on these problems can take place and no perceptible strengthening of the community can occur as a consequence.

Interdependence of Dissimilar Activities

As the preceding section indicates, common dependence of activities upon the same events creates a common interest and a common goal. But any community is made up of a host of different activities, activities that may even have conflicting goals. Many of the activities of a community are complementary, involving an exchange of goods or services. The merchants in a city ghetto make their living from its residents; the merchants in a suburb are sustained by the commuters. A public schoolteacher is engaged in activities very different from those of a steelworker, but the schoolteacher must be paid from taxes, and the steelworker's children must be educated. That is, any geographic community in modern society contains specialists engaged in activities that are not similar but do depend upon one another.

A modern community, then, includes a great many relations of rational self-interest, in which the different parties to the relation have differing interests. This does not mean that community organization and community action cannot develop from such interdependent activities. But community organization does develop in somewhat different ways in this case than in the case of similar activities and common interests.

The question can be posed as before: How do these interdependent activities help create a community, and under what circumstances do they instead lead to conflict?

The matter is somewhat more complex here than in the case of similar activities with common dependence. *Similar* activities and problems, carried out in physical contiguity, often generate common dependence on the same events, and thus common interests. But interrelated and *different* activities generate interests that are sometimes conflicting, sometimes common. Such an alternation between the common and the conflicting is typical of these interdependent activities. In contrast to the similar activities that share a joint dependence, they cannot build up a strong bond of mutual identification. The common interests are soon supplanted by conflicting ones, and the initial impulses to identify with the other person are stifled. Hostility may develop when the activities generate conflicting interests over a period of time.

Within a geographic locality, these interdependent interests may often lead to community action. For example, in a city, political leaders, business-men, and ghetto residents all have a common interest in increasing the num-ber of resident black merchants in the ghetto: political leaders and business-men because of an anticipated reduction in antimerchant rioting, and thus a more peaceful city; ghetto residents because of the greater recycling of money within the ghetto itself. For some, as shopkeepers, it would mean direct money gains; for others, as customers, money gains would only be indirect, but in either case the increased racial identity would be a direct psychological gain.

Yet this is but one type of activity. During much of the time, these inter-dependent activities of worker and manager, customer and shopkeeper, politician and constituent, have conflicting interests. These conflicting in-terests do not lead to "common action," but to inaction or to community conflicts. Thus, the same interdependence of activities that, upon occasion, creates common goals and thus community action also upon occasion creates conflicting goals and thus community conflict or a failure to act.

Community Action Through Identification with Others or Through Self-Interest

In the processes examined above, community action occurs (if it occurs at all) through common interests or joint interests of the community members in a given course of action. The picture this gives of the community is that of independent persons, each set on personal goals that happen sometimes to coincide with others — either through common dependence of similar activ-ities on an event, or through interdependence of different activities. The coincidence of goals results in common action. In turn, interdependent activ-ities may have opposing goals, and community conflict rather than unitary action results. The view this gives of a community is, however, an incomplete one. Community action takes place through two fundamentally different mechanisms, as the example below illustrates.

Suppose there are some bricks loose in the cornice of a hotel, and I see them from my hotel room. These bricks could fall and injure or kill a passer-by on the sidewalk below. If action is to take place, I, out of concern for the passer-by or the hotel, must report this to the desk clerk, the desk clerk must report it to the manager, and the manager must call a bricklayer to have the loose bricks repaired. All this is no simple matter, for it requires a chain of organization: from me to the desk clerk to the manager to the repairman. Each person in this chain must be sufficiently motivated to carry out his particular action or there is effectively no organization. The bricklayer's motivation is simple: He is paid for the job he does. The manager's is somewhat more complex: If the hotel (and he as manager) will not be held liable for an accident to a passer-by, and if he has no sympathy with the passer-by, he may not be motivated to action. The desk clerk's motivation is even more problematic: He is not held liable for such accidents, and unless he has identification with the hotel or with the passer-by, he may not carry out his action. Finally, my motivation as a hotel guest is most problematic: I have little attachment to either the hotel or the unknown passer-by, and nothing to lose personally by failing to act.

The essence of the problem of organization for action in this instance is that the consequence of each person's action or inaction must somehow be felt by him. It takes effort to carry out the action, and to compensate for this effort there must be some reward or punishment to him, contingent upon his carrying out the action or failing to do so.

There are two very different mechanisms that can insure such motivation, the mechanisms outlined by Ferdinand Tönnies in his concepts of *Gemeinschaft* and *Gesellschaft,* and by Émile Durkheim in his distinction between repressive and restitutive law.[7] The mechanism of *Gemeinschaft* operates through a strong identification of each with all others. If each person in the chain of action is strongly identified with both the passer-by and the hotel, if he feels their fates as *his,* then he will carry out action to insure their well-being. Such a situation most nearly obtains in small, close communities, where all the members have known each other for a long time, and close bonds of identification with one another and with the institutions of the community have grown up. Even in large cities, such identification is present in some degree: The desk clerk usually feels some sense of identification with the hotel, and is thus motivated to see it fare well; and even though the hotel may be in a large city, all participants in the action-sequence may feel some slight identification with the passer-by who might be injured. But in modern,

[7] Durkheim's major concern was with the difference between the kind of solidarity that develops through mutual identification and that which develops through self-interests. His discussion of repressive law (resulting from community solidarity) and restitutive law (resulting from a network of self-interests) shows an important consequence of these different forms of organization. See his *Division of Labor* (New York: Free Press, 1947), Chapters 1–4; see also Ferdinand Tönnies, *Community and Society,* C. P. Loomis, trans. and ed. (East Lansing, Mich.: Michigan State University Press, 1957).

large, mobile society, such identification is slight indeed, and can hardly be counted on as sufficient motive-power for action.

The second mechanism that may furnish the force for action is that of *Gesellschaft*—the interdependence of self-interests. If my acting or failing to act can be made to have consequences for *me,* then I will act, and the same holds for the other participants in this chain of action. Such mechanisms are in force for a workman, who is not paid if he does a poor job, or a manager, who may lose his job if accidents occur. But in this example there are no such mechanisms in force for a desk clerk or a room occupant. The genius of social organization in *Gesellschaft* (where mutual identification is attenuated and is no longer a sufficient motive for community action) is the existence of such mechanisms. In factories, one example of such a mechanism is the suggestion box, with rewards for accepted suggestions. The large factory is not, generally, a *Gemeinschaft,* in which there is mutual identification and sympathy between worker and manager; thus the worker has little or no motivation to make suggestions that will aid the manager.[8] But if he is paid for accepted suggestions, there is potential benefit to him, not through the *Gemeinschaft* mechanism of identification with company goals, but through the self-interest mechanism of *Gesellschaft.* (The desire of some managers to operate their business like a "big happy family" shows their awareness that the self-interest mechanism of *Gesellschaft* is often not as efficient in insuring that the organization's interest is met as is the kind of identification involved in *Gemeinschaft.*)

Most complex actions in society depend upon both these mechanisms. Some institutions, however, depend more on one than on the other. The formally organized rational bureaucracy depends most fully upon relations involving self-interest, such as the reward-suggestion scheme mentioned above. Communities have traditionally included a higher component of sympathetic identification. But even a community often depends greatly upon actions that derive from pure self-interest.

The combination of identification-with-the-other and pure self-interest in a community is particularly well exemplified by the formalized neighbor-obligations that exist in Japan. This relation is called *giri,* and actions are said to be done from *giri* when they have the following characteristics:

1. They spring from a sense of obligation rather than from spontaneous inclination.

---

[8] Often, the interpersonal punishment he would receive from the foreman for making a suggestion in person would be sufficient to overcome whatever motivation he might have. The impersonal suggestion box reduces the possibility of such punishment.

2. The obligation is spoken of as an obligation *toward* a specific person or group of persons.
3. The immediate sanction that would attend nonfulfillment of the obligation is the displeasure or the distress of this specific person or group of persons.[9]

As point 3 indicates, the sanction upon which this action depends is the displeasure of the other person, the neighbor with whom many common actions have traditionally been carried out. With such a neighbor, bonds of identification have grown up, and the obligation of *giri* formalizes the actions that would spring from such identification. However, in examining the reduced observance of *giri*-obligation in present-day Tokyo, Dore notes that the action depends also upon self-interest:

> In the foregoing definition of a giri-relation it was said that the *immediate* sanction for the performance of a giri-act is the displeasure or distress of the person towards whom the obligation is felt. It is generally also the case that there is additionally the *ultimate* sanction of possible material disadvantage. . . . A clear appreciation of the economic implications of giri-relations was apparent in some of the replies to interview questions about giri-relations — "support and be supported," "live together, prosper together" were traditional phrases quoted as justifications for maintaining such relationships.[10]

The earlier discussion indicated how common interests and joint interests come about through the intersection of activities, so that the self-interest mechanism can operate to bring about community action. But the second mechanism for action, identification-with-the-other, does not derive so directly. It is necessary to ask how such identification comes about.

Identification and Hostility as a Residuum of Intersecting Interests

There is a crucial difference between similar activities and interdependent but dissimilar activities. Activities that are alike, and from which persons mutually derive benefit or loss, create similar and shared experiences in each participant. These experiences make it possible for each to identify

---

[9] Ronald P. Dore, *City Life in Japan*, p. 254.
[10] *Ibid.,* p. 257.

with the other, to feel the other's problems as if they were his own. Examples of this are abundant in times of stress. For example, during the Watts riot, a former Watts resident who had returned before the riot, a young man who had become a Rhodes scholar after being an All-American football player, experienced the riot this way:

> At the height of the violence, he found himself joyously speaking the nitty-gritty Negro argot he hadn't used since junior high school, and despite the horrors of the night, this morning he felt a strange pride in Watts. As a riot, he told me, "It was a masterful performance. I sense a change there now, a buzz, and it tickles. For the first time people in Watts feel a pride in being black. I remember, when I first went to Whittier, I worried that if I didn't make it there, if I was rejected, I wouldn't have a place to go back to. Now I can say 'I'm from Watts.'" [11]

This young man was experiencing the same events as others in Watts, events that allowed him to feel identification with them. He was drawn close by the experience, and a sense of identity emerged. Whether this identification would be strong enough to survive going back to Watts and living there with his former friends and neighbors is questionable. Yet the shared experience of that one night was strong enough to create identification that had been absent before.

Through this kind of mutual identification, each person in a sense "invests" a part of himself in the others, creating a solidary unit. Common interests leave a residuum, binding together the community, so that later events affecting one may be sympathetically felt and reacted to by all. In a community that confronts numerous problems together and successfully overcomes them, any hazardous condition—broken traffic lights or loose bricks that might fall on a passer-by—would immediately be reported and fixed, because every member of the community had invested a part of himself in every other, and any pain felt by the other would be sympathetically felt by him.

It is important to emphasize that such solidarity, which perhaps expresses the concept of community in its purest form, does not develop automatically. It develops through *time,* as a consequence of the *amount of shared activities* and *experiences* of the members of the community. Tönnies lists the following pairs of people as involved more or less in identification with others in communal relationships:

---

[11] *Life* (August 27, 1965).

More Identification	Less Identification
peasant	urbanite
those with families	those without families
natives	strangers
religious persons	free thinkers
inland dwellers	those dwelling by the sea
isolated persons	those living by the rivers
mountain people	valley people
religious leaders	worldly rulers
landed nobility	capitalistic leaders [12]

In most of the cases, the persons on the left differ from those on the right in having more prolonged and intensive relations with fewer people. Those on the right are involved—less intensively and less continuously—with a greater number. Thus bonds of mutual identification with any particular person have a smaller chance to build up.

One present-day community where such mutual identification grows is the military service, particularly during wartime. Soldiers share a multitude of experiences over a long, continuous stretch of time. They "go through hell together," as they are fond of saying; the bonds of mutual identity that grow among them are recorded in innumerable war stories. Paradoxically, a group of students occupying a college building in an antiwar demonstration generates similar bonds of mutual identity. Participants in such collective actions give reports of their experiences that sound strikingly similar to those of wartime comradeship and mutual bonds among soldiers.

However, when activities are interdependent but dissimilar, mutual identification is not the only sentiment that develops. Hostility can develop as well. It is paradoxical that close, continued contact, which can create strong solidarity, can also create strong hostility. Murder, the most violent of crimes, is the one crime most characteristic of small, stable communities. In the United States, murder rates are as high in rural areas as in urban areas, while most other crimes are far higher in urban areas (for example, the rate of robberies is about 3.5 times as high in urban areas as in rural).

How can the close association of small communities generate such intense hostility? When activities and experiences are dissimilar but highly interdependent in a community, this interdependence often leads to an opposition of interests. Though husband and wife may have common interests in raising the family, their interests are often opposed in specific action-situations:

[12] Ferdinand Tönnies, *Community and Society*, p. 276.

how to distribute work in the family, how to allocate finances, what interest the husband should have in other women, or with friends at the tavern, and so forth. If, when opposition of interests occurs, the relations are easy to break, they will be broken; on the other hand, there are usually other forces to hold them in place, so that the individuals tend to swallow their anger and keep it inside as a residue of mutual hostility.

A parenthetical note should be added here. The term "mutual" is used for convenience, but it should not be overlooked that there are certain social situations that lead to an asymmetric hostility; that is, in just one member of the relationship. Probably the most important case is that of power differential: If I can affect your destiny, but you cannot affect mine, and if my actions frustrate your goals, then hostility will build up in you, though not in me. In a society, the lower classes may build up hostility toward the upper classes who have power; meanwhile, the latter may be either totally unaware of the lower classes and their problems, or have mild sympathy for them so long as the lower classes do not themselves gain power. In a high school (which is one of the closest communities in American society), the members of the powerless out-cliques can often set down, in grim detail, the social structure of the school, while the members of the in-clique, which has power, are often unaware of the existence of other cliques, since these constitute no problem.

Many community conflicts take on this asymmetric character (as will be examined in more detail later), for they represent the outburst of an out-group against the administrative structure of the community toward which the out-group has built up hostility.

For the moment, considerations of such asymmetry may be put aside; our concern is with the general processes that build hostility within a community. As suggested earlier, interdependent activities often cause low levels of hostility — not enough to provoke disruption of the relation, but hostility nevertheless. Communities take action as communities; and whether that action is taken as the result of a town meeting, the city council vote, the city manager's decision, or a popular vote, it will seldom be an action favored by all. Merchants along one street may find themselves faced with an action to forbid parking on that street. They feel it will hurt their trade, as indeed it may. They cannot prevent the action, nor can they easily leave the community; but they can build up hostility toward those who are in favor of the action, or toward the community as a whole.

Such frustrations, stored up as unexpressed hostility, can create community disorganization in two ways: by building up to the point where the hostility becomes a basis for conflict in the community and by preventing common action when the need for it arises. Consider the latter first. Organization is necessary to carry out any community action. If there are barriers of hostility between the segments of the community that must cooperate, no action will be taken. Roads will not be built, school bonds will not pass, parks will not be cared for, simply because the hostility arising from frustrated goals erects a barrier to community action. The drift of responsibility for social action from towns and cities to the state and federal governments may be in part a result of such community paralysis-through-hostility,[13] itself a product of the social and economic polarities in the community.

The other consequence of this stored-up hostility is found in overt conflict. Particularly revealing is the community dominated by one group, with a separate, subjugated minority. In such a case, the subjugated minority, with no chance to win a dispute, may erupt in unorganized outbursts of violence. For example, Carle C. Zimmerman finds such behavior in the lower class in two rigidly dominated communities, one in Mississippi and one in Siam; and Everett C. Hughes finds this behavior among the English minority in French Canadian towns.[14]

In cases where the sides are more evenly split, hostility may lead to a real conflict and perhaps a realignment of community power. Many conflicts over the city-manager plan have been of this sort. Often, the city manager is not responsive to the electorate and sees his job as one purely of physical management of the community (in one study, 96 out of 112 city managers who had completed college had engineering degrees). As a consequence, the manager often aligns himself with business interests and alienates working-class members of the community. In one case (Mason City, Iowa) a letter to the editor appeared in the town newspaper from a carpenter complaining that the creek overflowed into his home. The existing antagonism to the city manager was so great that a controversy developed, resulting finally in abandonment of the city-manager plan.[15]

Thus interdependent activities, with their consequent conflicting goals alternating with the common ones, may produce not only identification of community members with one another—and thus the basis for community action—but also hostility and the basis for barriers to action.

---

[13] In part, of course, it is due to a different cause: community indifference resulting from the lack of common or interdependent activities at the local level.

[14] Carle C. Zimmerman, *The Changing Community* (New York: Harper, 1938) and Everett C. Hughes, *French Canada in Transition* (London: Kegan Paul, Trench, Trubner, 1946).

[15] Edwin K. Stene and George K. Floro, *Abandonment of the City-Manager Plan* (Lawrence, Kan.: University of Kansas Press, 1953).

Identification with or Hostility
toward the Community as a Whole

A special case of the processes discussed above occurs when the community as a unit takes some action. For example, when a community high school football team wins a game against another community, this is an action by the community *as* a community.[16] When a nation's armies make war, this is an action of the nation *as* a nation. Such actions tend to generate strong identification with the community or nation, not only among those who actually take part, but among those who participate only vicariously. A girl who attends every football game and cheers her team on to victory will, as a result, become identified with the team and school by her vicarious participation. A winning team will produce a sense of community identity, or increase that which exists. Thus, it has been said that Los Angeles became a city for the first time, rather than merely a collection of suburbs, when its Dodgers won the National League baseball pennant.

The same sort of thing can occur in reverse. When the police apprehend a man accused of a crime, a jury convicts him, and a judge sentences him, this may result in the man's hostility toward the community as a whole. Similar actions by other community officials may generate antagonism on the part of those adversely affected. For example, in some large cities, members of the black community develop hostility toward the police force, a hostility that sometimes generalizes to the city as a whole. A study carried out for the Kerner Commission Report showed that the most frequently expressed grievance of blacks in the cities surveyed concerned the police force.[17]

As a consequence of such processes, members of the community come to have feelings toward the community as a whole that are important in the development and maintenance of community organization. Such feelings are important elements in the preservation of the community itself, when threatened by an outside force or by disruptive conflict. In Table 1, on page 678, these feelings of identification or hostility are considered together with those feelings among community members themselves for the sake of simplicity, but it should be remembered that they constitute an important "extra" element in the organization or disorganization of the community.

---

[16] This is less true in modern suburban communities or in cities without distinct neighborhoods, for the school does not represent the community.

[17] *Report of the National Advisory Commission on Civil Disorders* (Washington, D. C.: U. S. Government Printing Office, 1968), p. 83.

Community Organization
as a Residuum of Past Action

Action toward community problems requires organization. Sometimes appropriate organization is not forthcoming, as in the example of air pollution cited earlier. Sometimes no organization of effort can solve the problem. This was the case, for example, in the dust storms of the 1930's for which farmers had no immediate solution, individual or collective. But when collective action does take place and the problem is solved, two types of residue are left. One is a residue of sentiments, either identification or hostility (or in many cases, both), as discussed above. The second is an organizational residue. The organization of effort that resulted in solution of the problem continues. Organizations, once in existence, tend to perpetuate themselves, as many sociologists have pointed out.[18] Even when these are informal organizations, as in the case of many community groups, the bonds between the members keep them in place.

One example illustrates this well. A new community was constructed during World War II for shipyard workers. Because of the contractor's malfeasance and wartime problems, the community was beset by problem after problem: Sidewalks caved in, electricity did not work, and so on. Because these problems involved similar interests, because they could only be solved by joint action, and because they were important and repetitive problems, they generated an extremely strong nucleus of community organization. After the problems were solved, the organizations became engaged in various social, civic, and other activities on which voluntary community groups subsist. But like a volunteer fire department, the groups also constituted standby organizations which could mobilize to meet problems as they arose. Robert K. Merton and associates, in studying this community at a later time, found that its rich community organization contrasted strikingly with the unorganized state of another development that had not been faced with such problems. The second development had been well constructed, was well managed, and offered no difficulties to be overcome. Its management, in

---

[18] An interesting present example at the societal level is the National Foundation for Infantile Paralysis that sponsors the March of Dimes. When polio vaccine was proved successful (in part through this organization's efforts), the foundation did not go out of existence, but searched about for a new goal. A part of that search included a survey of its facilities, reported by David L. Sills, *The Volunteers* (New York: Free Press, 1958).

fact, provided few opportunities for organizational activity to develop. Government was administered from above, not generated from below.[19]

A second example is even more striking than this one, because it concerns a community in the heart of a large city. This community's struggles in rebuilding itself are examined in graphic detail by Peter Rossi and Robert Dentler.[20] Hyde Park, in Chicago, found itself faced with sharp change: rapid decay of many of its buildings and a sudden influx of blacks. The prospect was one of quick transformation of a university community into a lower-class black ghetto, similar to much of the rest of Chicago's south side. But there existed in this community a high level of organization. This was true in part because men worked and lived in the same community (more than 90 percent of the faculty of the University of Chicago lived in the Hyde Park area or in areas immediately surrounding) and thus had many of their interests localized within the community. The community also subsisted on the talents and experience of many of its members in organized community activity. For these and other reasons, the grassroots organization, which took the form of block groups and a larger "Community Conference," as well as churches, neighborhood recreation centers, and other associations, played an important part in rebuilding the community, stabilizing the population, and preventing further decay. The community appears to have achieved that extremely rare condition in modern America: a stable racially integrated neighborhood. A most important factor in this achievement has been, as Rossi and Dentler show, the extremely high degree of community organization.

It may seem paradoxical that problems create community organization, but such is nevertheless the case. A community without common problems, as many modern bedroom suburbs tend to be today, has little cause for community organization; neither does a community that has been largely subject to the administration of persons outside the community. When community problems subsequently arise, there is then no latent structure of organization, no "fire brigade" that can become activated to meet the problem.

A new town, a budding community, is much like a child: If it faces no problems, if it is not challenged, it cannot grow. Each problem successfully met leaves its residue of sentiments and organization; without these sentiments and organization, future problems could not be solved.

---

[19] Robert K. Merton, Patricia S. West, and Marie Jahoda, *Patterns of Social Life: Explorations in the Sociology of Housing, 1948* (hectographed).

[20] Peter Rossi and Robert Dentler, *Rebuilding the City* (New York: Free Press, 1960).

Inability to Act and Rigid Organization

Despite the importance of organization-for-action, it can sometimes impede action and prevent a community from carrying out any positive plan. For instance, a legislature subject to highly organized pressure groups may find itself immobilized by them. The following example, relevant to the present plight of many cities, provides a good indication of the problem.

One of the most powerful reasons families have for moving from city to suburb is schools. A middle-class family finds itself able to choose between a school in a suburb with new buildings, small classes, highly paid teachers and the school its children presently attend, with old buildings, poorly paid teachers, large classes, and other obvious shortcomings reported daily by the children.[21]

Because schools are such an important determinant of residence for middle-class families, they constitute not only a reason for movement to the suburbs, but also a potential force for movement into the city. If a city had, in one or two of its neighborhoods, obviously better schools than those in any suburb, this fact alone would provide an important force to pull people into these neighborhoods. This would be a positive, powerful reason for families to move back into the city – a positive device for reconstituting city neighborhoods on the verge of decay. In other words, such an action would provide one means by which cities could combat the residential decay that most of them are undergoing with the flight of the middle class to the suburbs.

A related problem faced by many cities is neighborhood instability that comes about when blacks begin to move into white neighborhoods, making racially integrated neighborhoods almost impossible to maintain, except as a transitional stage. Again, if the city could make schools in such fringe areas strikingly better than others in the city and outside, this would serve as a powerful counterforce by helping to hold enough whites in the city to maintain an integrated neighborhood.

Yet such action is nearly impossible to take. A city cannot "unequalize" its schools, because of its very organization. In a city council, most of the members would be required to vote heavier taxes for their own districts, for the benefit of a district not their own. These members would face grave prob-

---

[21] This is not to say that the facilities of the suburban schools, *on the average,* are better than those of the city, for they may not be. But there is ordinarily more *variation* among them. In most places, the suburban schools are financed by the community itself, which can invest as much money in the schools as its members desire.

lems at the polls when their constituents could review such action. Nor would interest cleavage lie along racial lines. The interests of middle-class blacks in fringe areas would favor improving the schools in their neighborhoods; the interests of lower-class blacks, whose children are farthest behind, would favor improving those in the black core of the city.

Thus it is safe to say that such a policy of consciously unequalizing schools to pull suburbanites back into the city or to stabilize changing neighborhoods will not be carried out by any city.[22] This failure to act will not, of course, make American schools more nearly equal; the disparity will grow, and the process of city decay will reinforce and be reinforced by, the disparity between city and suburban schools. If school policies to halt the growth of disparity are to be introduced, it can only be by action at the state or national level.

This inability to act is not due to lack of social organization, but to organization inappropriate to solve the problem. Whether in this instance there could be organization appropriate to the problem, yet not grossly inappropriate for other problems, is questionable. Yet the important fact is that *organization* impedes action in this case. Paradoxically, in this instance organization itself helps bring about disorganization and disintegration of the city.

This example is not a special case, for the phenomenon is general. Organization must exist if an acting unit is to cope with its problems; yet it must not be so strong, so rigid, that it cannot meet a change in the problems created by its environment. The path of biological evolution is strewn with organisms whose activities became so rigidly organized that they could not survive in a modified environment. Business organizations face the same challenge. Automobile companies in early days faced problems of production and were accordingly organized to meet these problems. When the problems shifted from those of producing cars to those of selling cars, the Ford Motor Company's organization was not appropriate to cope with the new problems. The manufacturing department had too much power, the sales department had too little. It required a major reorganization of the company to regain its market and survive.[23]

---

[22] The policy of making schools unequal to compensate for cultural handicaps, however, has been and will increasingly be carried out in cities and towns. In this case, the political pressures toward equality are more than counterbalanced by the intensity of political action of black civil rights groups.

[23] I am indebted to Arthur Stinchcombe for bringing this example to my attention. See Philip Selznick, *Leadership in Administration* (Evanston, Ill.: Row, Peterson, 1957), pp. 109–10.

Similarly, many primitive tribes were so rigidly organized that they could not survive the coming of Westerners and their civilization. Other tribes were not so rigidly organized; they were able to withstand the onslaughts of civilization, and to continue their society by incorporating some aspects of civilization. For example, Tahitian society broke down quickly under white colonialism, and the population threatened to die out. In nearby Samoa, however, the society was able to survive, with the necessary changes of structure.

Social Processes and Their Consequences for Community Disorganization

The processes described above provide the bases for concerted community action, or for inaction and conflict — the basis for organization or disorganization. They all stem from the activities in which people engage, and the events which may befall them. Table 1 summarizes the processes as discussed in earlier sections, showing how they lead to certain types of actions, which in turn leave psychological and social residues to influence the subsequent path of the community.

The motives or springs for individuals to act in concert, in conflict, or separately lie in *interests* and *sentiments;* the residual *organization* (or lack of it) provides a further structuring of sentiments and interests to influence the community's future. The importance of these bases of action is evident in the preceding examples. In the case of the loose hotel bricks, strong bonds of identification would have resulted in action, though no immediate interests of the actors were involved; alternatively, a structure involving self-interest at every stage could result in action. Similarly, inaction, opposition, and conflict can arise either from presently opposed interests or from long-suppressed hostility.

Either community action or inaction may result from the distribution of these processes over time and also through the structure of the community. It is easy to see that these simple forces, operating with differing frequencies and in different social structures, can produce the most diverse forms of activity: mob action, violent conflict, dictatorial rule, apathy, states of tense inaction, and so on. Community disorganization in its various forms results from the recurrent operation of certain of the above processes to the exclusion of others. Thus the crucial question for present-day communities becomes, What conditions inhibit or encourage these varied processes?

CONTEMPORARY CONDITIONS LEADING TO DISORGANIZATION AND CONFLICT

There are three principal issues currently confronting the student of community organization and any policymaker who must make decisions that affect community and societal organization.

First is the issue of conscious creation – by government-sponsored social science or social work professionals – of community organization in conflict with established power structures.

Second is the issue of organizing communities based on homogeneity of race and social class versus organizing communities that reflect heterogeneity of race and class. This issue arises most frequently in relation to the desegregation of urban schools: decentralization and local control of the schools versus sufficient central control to prevent intolerance or exclusion of local minorities.

TABLE 1
The Processes Leading to Organization and Disorganization:
Summary of Preceding Sections

Intersection of Activities	Effects of Activities	Present Interests	Resulting Action	Residues: Sentiments and Organization
Similar activities dependent on same events	→ Action which benefits A benefits B	→ Common interests	→ Collective action	→ Identification and community organization
Dissimilar interdependent activities	→ Action which benefits A benefits B	→ Common interests	→ Collective action	Identification and community organization
	→ Action which benefits A hurts B	→ Opposed interests	→ { Conflict / Unilateral action / Inaction }	→ Hostility and organized cleavage
Independent activities	→ Action which benefits A does not affect B	→ Independent interests	→ Individual action	Indifference and mass

Third is the issue of what will be the building blocks of social organization in future society—will they be geographically compact residential communities that are functionally diffuse, or will they be geographically dispersed but functionally specialized?

Before examining in some detail historical trends in the third of these issues, it is useful to briefly discuss the first two.

Maximum Feasible Participation

Since the mid-1960's a new orientation to the social problems of urban poverty areas has evolved. It is based on community organization and community action; its advocates are professionals whose careers are tied to services for the poor or research on poverty; its resources are federal funds or foundation grants; its goals entail upsetting the power structure of the city. This new orientation has strong advocates [24] and just as strong opponents [25]; it excites intense passions. The views of its opponents are expressed in the pages of a journal entitled *The Public Interest;* those of its advocates appear in the pages of the journal, *Social Policy.*

The primary vehicles of this approach in the 1960's included the federal Office of Economic Opportunity, some Community Action Programs of OEO, Mobilization for Youth in New York, and the Ford Foundation-sponsored experiment in community control of some New York schools. These programs set up organizations that challenged local authorities by attempting to organize the poor against public and private services: welfare, housing, garbage services, schools, merchants. The ideological root of this challenge rests in participation and political control by the poor of those resources and activities that impinge upon them—a kind of reversal of the welfare state conception of benevolent paternalism.

These attempts by social service professionals to develop community organization using federal funds can fairly be said to have successfully challenged official authority structures, municipal governments; but they have been almost uniformly unsuccessful in establishing ongoing community organization with long-term benefits. In the words of a political scientist who has studied these programs at some length:

---

[24] Richard Cloward and Frances Fox Piven, "A Strategy to End Poverty," pp. 433–47 in J. K. Hadden, L. H. Masotti, and C. J. Larson, eds., *Metropolis in Crisis* (Itasca, Ill.: Peacock, 1967).

[25] Daniel P. Moynihan, *Maximum Feasible Misunderstanding* (New York: Free Press, 1969).

A recipe for violence: Promise a lot; deliver a little. Lead people to believe they will be much better off, but let there be no dramatic improvement. Try a variety of small programs, each interesting but marginal in impact and severely underfinanced. Avoid any attempted solution remotely comparable in size to the dimensions of the problem you are trying to solve. Have middle-class civil servants hire upper-class student radicals to use lower-class Negroes as a battering ram against the existing local political systems; then complain that people are going around disrupting things and chastise local politicians for not cooperating with those out to do them in. Get some poor people involved in local decision-making, only to discover that there is not enough at stake to be worth bothering about. Feel guilty about what has happened to black people; tell them you are surprised they have not revolted before; express shock and dismay when they follow your advice. Go in for a little force, just enough to anger, not enough to discourage. Feel guilty again; say you are surprised that worse has not happened. Alternate with a little suppression. Mix well, apply a match, and run. . . .[26]

It is clear that the idea of community organization of the poor to control their own futures has not been given a valid trial in the programs referred to above. The particular ingredients that made up Mobilization for Youth and similar activities did not create effective community organization; but some other attempts have been successful. Saul Alinsky, a former trade-union organizer, has implemented effective community organization in the Back of the Yards district and other areas of Chicago, in Rochester, and elsewhere; but he has done so with a different combination of elements. He does not expect to be supported by existing authority after he begins, and, therefore, obtains the necessary money from authorities before he begins. He creates an indigenous grassroots organization that is soon able to subsist independent of external financial support and of his own organizing skills. It is an old formula, long used in organizing trade unions and other conflict groups.

The growth of unions after the National Labor Relations Act of 1935 suggests that favorable federal legislation could change the rules of the game enough to spur the growth of effective continuing organization focused on services such as welfare and public housing. But there are two fundamental policy questions: Will community organization in poverty areas really augment the value of services designed to aid the poor? And, if so, how can such organization be developed? A careful study of the developments of the late 1960's could help in answering these questions.

---

[26] Aaron Wildavsky, in Daniel P. Moynihan, *Maximum Feasible Misunderstanding,* p. ii.

Homogeneity and Heterogeneity

The second principal issue has both academic and practical relevance. How socially homogeneous should local communities of the future be? The question may become irrelevant if a resident's investment of time and energy in the local area continues to decrease; but for now, the question certainly has a great deal of importance.

On one hand there is the present geographic structure of society with every major city largely black and poor at its center, still primarily black but less poor moving outward toward its periphery, and at its periphery, almost exclusively white with different income levels at different sectors of the periphery.

The other extreme is a society with economically and racially mixed neighborhoods — neighborhoods with both the tensions generated by such economic and racial diversity and the added potential that geographic propinquity produces for reducing those tensions. Many of the virtues and defects of these two modes of organization are known, but the questions remain more numerous than the answers. Which pattern is better for the growth of the individual? Which is better for the stability of the community? Which one strengthens the stability of the whole society? The Kerner Commission Report argues, with a great deal of evidence, that the stability of the whole society is best served by racially and economically heterogeneous communities.[27] But many questions remain to challenge the researcher and the policymaker.

Locality Specialization

The third principal current issue in community organizations is that of the building blocks of society as residential communities or other functional units. There has long been a trend toward functional specialization of localities. As the German sociologist, Georg Simmel, noted more than 50 years ago:

At first the individual sees himself in an environment which is relatively indifferent to his individuality, but which has implicated him in

---

[27] *Report of the National Advisory Commission on Civil Disorders,* Chapter 16.

a web of circumstances. These circumstances impose on him a close coexistence with those whom the accident of birth has placed next to him. . . . However, as the development of society progresses, each individual establishes for himself contacts with persons who stand outside this original group-affiliation, but who are "related" to him by virtue of an actual similarity of talents, inclinations, activities, and so on.[28]

This tendency of society to be less organized around communities in which one was born and more inclined toward specialized groups has produced a qualitative change in the structure of society, as Simmel goes on to note.[29] In the Middle Ages an individual was surrounded by a series of concentric groups, all based on the particular position into which he had been born. The development of specialized voluntary associations, each containing only a "part" of an individual, came about only slowly, and with difficulty. Earlier, the whole man was specialized (a soldier could not even marry, but was totally a soldier). The fragmentation of men into many roles, some dependent on purposive desires, was not common in the Middle Ages.

Such fragmentation, the result of affiliation with multiple groups transcending locality, has important implications for the organization of a community. Obviously, if all of a man's activities were contained within one community, the processes discussed earlier could operate without inhibition. Common, joint, and opposed interests would arise in abundance; mutual identification and hostility could grow unabated. Only when man broke out of this set of concentric circles did he become an individual through his particular combination of group affiliations. As he became an individual, his common activities and common interests were spread over a more and more diverse range of groups: Those persons with whom he shared one activity were not the same ones with whom he shared another. Thus, the processes that tend to make a *community* out of a *geographic locality* are interrupted and diverted.

The most recent development in this fragmentation into multiple group affiliations is physical mobility in and out of one's living-place. Modern transportation has made possible part-time residence in several localities. Not only is the community no longer a rigid circle confining men's activities totally within it; it is increasingly a less important and less permanent one of several circles of which the man is a part. At the same time, as geographic mobility becomes more frequent, communities more and more take on the character of purposive associations. Many men are now able to choose with a

---

[28] Georg Simmel, *Conflict* (New York: Free Press, 1955), pp. 127–28.
[29] *Ibid.,* p. 148.

considerable amount of freedom where they want to live and how much of themselves they invest in their living-place.

Locality Specialization and Kinds of Communities in Modern Society

As a consequence of mobility and fragmentation, there have come to be very specialized types of communities, specialized according to the kinds of activities they contain for their members.[30]

INDEPENDENT TOWNS AND CITIES—The most complete community is a type that is slowly vanishing in industrial society, except in its larger forms: the community that contains most of its members' activities—work, leisure, education, trade, and services. It was once true, when transportation was less developed, that all cities and towns were by necessity independent, with permanent members spending full time in the community. But now only large metropolitan areas and geographically isolated towns are even in part like this.

The very independence and isolation of such towns and cities create common problems. They must have police and fire protection, they must have water and sewage systems, they must educate their children, provide jobs for their members, regulate their drunkards, mend their roads, tend their sick, and bury their dead. If these communities were not physically set apart, isolated from other towns or cities, many such problems would not be community problems, but problems of the larger aggregate. But in independent

---

[30] There are, of course, many ways of classifying communities. The classification here is based upon the problem at hand: community disorganization. Because community organization depends intrinsically upon the activities of which the community consists, as indicated in earlier sections, the classification must be in terms of these activities. For other classifications, see Albert J. Reiss, Jr., "Functional Specialization of Cities," in A. J. Reiss and Paul K. Hatt, *Cities in Society,* 2nd ed. (New York: Free Press, 1957), pp. 555–75. Also, Otis Dudley Duncan and Albert J. Reiss, Jr., *Social Characteristics of Urban and Rural Communities* (New York: Wiley, 1956), p. 217. Chauncy D. Harris, "A Functional Classification of Cities in the United States," *Geographical Review,* Vol. 33 (January, 1943), pp. 86–96. Duncan and Reiss provide one important element used in the classification: the economic exports of goods and services from the community. Many people in the community make their living off their neighbors, but there must be some segment which provides the income of the community. This segment differs radically in different communities, as the classification below will indicate.

towns, each of these ordinary everyday activities of living creates problems that can ordinarily be best solved jointly, within this community. Recent controversies in many communities, large and small, over fluoridation of the water system suggest one such problem. Independent towns (unlike city suburbs) have their own water systems, so fluoridation is a matter that must be decided by the community. It thus poses a problem in these independent towns, and in some cases there is organization sufficient to solve it. In some cases, however, there is not, and an examination of such cases in a later section will suggest some of the causes.

Another problem of such independent towns and cities, in contrast to new forms of communities, is providing for the economic sustenance of their members. In one study of a community, the struggle toward this end occupied much of the attention of the community members during the period of the study. The community was faced with a prospective loss of its steel mills, a prospect it resisted at every turn. The mills finally did leave, but the high degree of organized effort resulted in new industries moving into town and old ones expanding. The community was thus able to survive in spite of an apparent death sentence.[31]

The major point, then, about independent towns is that their physical isolation and the consequent fact that they contain a large part of their members' activities create many community problems of importance to the members. These problems often generate a high degree of formal and informal community organization, through the processes discussed earlier. These communities need more organization than many others, and they tend to have more. If the town is small, the organization largely takes the form of informal norms, customs, and mores, and of loosely organized volunteer groups; if it is a large city, organization takes the form of laws, offices, and other aspects of bureaucracy.

All the remaining types of localities to be examined incorporate only some part of the life which is contained in an independent town or city. Although these localities are themselves sometimes parts of a larger metropolitan community, they may nevertheless face local community problems. It is thus important to examine them as communities in themselves, and not merely as parts of a metropolitan area community.

RESIDENTIAL COMMUNITIES THAT DAILY EXPORT WORKERS—City residential neighborhoods and suburbs outside a city have a very different character from independent towns and cities. They are living-places, where men live who work elsewhere. In the economy of these communities, the major export

---

[31] Charles Walker, *Steeltown* (New York: Harper, 1950).

is *people* — a daily export of people into factories or businesses outside the community. Such communities still contain a number of activities for their members, but many of these are tied to the central city, or to another community.[32] Police and fire protection are partly local, partly centralized in city or county departments. Water, sewage disposal, and other utilities are ordinarily provided by the central city. Roads are repaired by county, state, or city. Such communities have thus lost many of the activities that formerly made them close communities. The processes making for mutual identification and hostility have vanished with the common and interdependent activities on which they were based. Different segments of the community experience this process in varying degrees, and sometimes this variation itself creates further community disorganization.

In many such suburban towns, there are two very different groups of people: the commuters, who are daily exported to their places of work, and the local tradesmen, who provide the goods and services of living. The relative numbers of these two groups vary greatly, because these suburbs take on quite different forms. Some have industries of their own with consequent internal economic life.

In general, older suburbs tend to have a larger component of local tradespeople, and even some manufacturing or other concerns. Many of these suburbs began as independent towns, before transportation made feasible, and city growth made necessary, the daily mass movements into and out of the city. In such suburbs, with their own partial economic life, the bases for strife and conflict exist in abundance. For the commuters, many activities and interests are no longer interdependent with those of fellow community members, but are located in the larger metropolitan area. But the people whose economic and social life is bound up in the town have community problems which must be solved. When the commuters *do* become involved in some such problem, there are few bases of mutual identification and often no mechanism for expression of their desires, in order that divergent positions might be brought together.

For example, Yonkers, New York was in the past largely made up of lower-middle-class Catholics, many of them employed in local industries. Recently, new developments in East Yonkers have brought in white-collar commuters, mostly Jewish. The resulting problems in community organiza-

---

[32] Chauncy Harris suggests that there are two major types of modern suburbs: living-places and working-places. Thus some of the men who live in one suburb are commuters not to the central city, but to a neighboring suburb containing outlying industries. See Otis Dudley Duncan and Albert J. Reiss, Jr., *Social Characteristics,* p. 7, and Chauncy D. Harris, "Suburbs," *American Journal of Sociology,* Vol. 49 (July, 1943), pp. 1–13.

tion (largely centering about the schools) are great. The line that divides the "old nesters" on the West and the new "carpetbaggers" on the East is as difficult to cross as the superhighway that separates the two halves of the town.[33]

In the early 1950's, many conflicts in these communities arose as previously inactive, uninterested persons suddenly became aroused over issues of Communist subversion. In Scarsdale, New York, a commuter became actively involved in searching out Communist subversion in the school system as a result of personal experiences in New York City, which had persuaded him of such possibilities. His attacks upon the school library burst upon an unsuspecting superintendent and school board. He had previously been little involved in local community life; therefore, little had operated to bring his views into some correspondence with those of the rest of the community. Nor was he sufficiently identified with the community that norms or constraints could soften the intensity of his outburst.[34]

This kind of situation seems to have occurred frequently in suburban communities during the subversion scares of the 1950's. It was in the suburban fringes surrounding mushrooming cities (for example, Houston, Denver, Los Angeles, New York) that such cases were most frequently reported.[35]

Some young suburbs (for example, in the Chicago area, Park Forest, Flossmoor, Oak Lawn, and other southwestern suburbs) have little or no internal economic life, and are almost purely residential. Even local goods and services are provided by a few large shopping centers, whose owners and employees live elsewhere, thus keeping the suburb solely a living-place for commuters. This pure case represents a new type of wholly residential community, homogeneous in age, income level, and style of life. Disorganization in such communities takes the form of community disintegration, in the absence of common problems and common activities.

Such purely residential communities are not confined to suburban developments. New housing projects that have replaced slums in the center of many cities have often become solely places to live for their residents. One observer of such housing projects in New York City reports:

---

[33] Harrison Salisbury's series of articles in *The New York Times* on Yonkers' problems shows well the organizational difficulties of some of these communities. See Harrison E. Salisbury, Four Articles on Yonkers, N. Y., *The New York Times* (April 18–21, 1955).

[34] See James S. Coleman, *Community Conflict* (New York: Free Press, 1957), for a discussion of this case.

[35] See the several cases reported in "The Public School Crisis," *Saturday Review of Literature* (September 8, 1951), pp. 6–20.

Before East Harlem began to resound to the deadly plong of the wreckers' ball and the tattoo of new steel work it was a slum. But it had many institutions that gave stability. There were the Neapolitan blocks, the street fiestas, the interwoven relationship of stores and neighbors. Out it all went. In came the gangs.

The new project may permit a church to survive on a small island like St. Edward's. But an absence of churches and an absence of religious influence is notable among project youngsters. The Negro children seldom go to church. The same is true of the Puerto Ricans. The Irish and Italian gang youngsters are usually described by their priests as "bad Catholics," irregular in church observance.

The projects are political deserts. The precinct bosses have been wiped out with the slum. They do not seem to come back. No one cares whether the new residents vote or not. There is no basket at Thanksgiving. No boss to fix it up when Jerry gets into trouble with the police. The residents have no organization of their own and are discouraged from having any.

"We don't want none of them organizers in here," one manager of a project told me. "All they do is stir up trouble. Used to be some organizers around here. But we cleaned them out good. Lotsa Communists. That's what they were." [36]

In these ways, at least, the urban housing project and the suburban development are alike. They have become segmented, specialized parts of the adults' lives, devoid of many of the institutions that could make them complete communities. Though these dormitories may be in part the consequence of ill-conceived planning by developers, they also represent an advanced stage in the organizational structure of society — a movement away from total institutions in which a person is embedded, toward voluntary, specialized, segmental associations.

INDUSTRIAL AND TRADE CENTERS THAT DAILY IMPORT WORKERS — Central cities today are becoming more and more specialized, as places of work. Central cities are becoming less and less places to *live,* less and less places for retail trade, more and more places where people work, in manufacturing, wholesale trade, service, and governmental activities.[37] Though low-income

---

[36] Harrison E. Salisbury, *The Shook-Up Generation* (New York: Great Books, 1959), p. 67.

[37] See Otis Dudley Duncan and Albert J. Reiss, Jr., *Social Characteristics,* p. 229, for a tabulation of amount of wholesale and retail trade by size of place. Though there is no variation in mean per capita *retail* trade, *wholesale* trade in 1950 varied from a low of $667 per capita in the smallest urban places (10,000–25,000) to $3,450 in the largest (500,000 or more).

families continue to live close to the center of the city (many of them in their new purely residential housing projects), middle- and high-income families live farther and farther from the center, in suburbs. The difficulties in organization that this creates for the residential suburb were mentioned above; the difficulties it creates for the city are somewhat different. As the residences of upper-income families have moved outside the city, so have their interests and money. Their interests in and support of education and the physical improvement of the community are localized where they live. New York's or Chicago's northern suburbs, for example, have a concentration of business leaders and professional men whose absence from the city's educational and political affairs leaves a real vacuum. Similarly, school boards in suburbs of major cities include impressive arrays of legal and administrative talent, devoting their efforts to the small problems of a simple school system, while the far more complex problems of the city schools await solution.

Though the city has the formal organization for solving its problems, much of its informal support has been lost to the suburbs. It becomes more and more a purely economic center. It imports workers, and by so doing engages some of their interest on which organization can subsist; yet some of that interest remains in the residential communities that daily export these men to their jobs.

COMMUNITIES THAT IMPORT PEOPLE FOR LEISURE OR EDUCATION—Resort communities and college towns differ from all the communities described above. They differ because they contain two sets of people: those who *live* there and carry out most of their activities within the community; and those who *come* there for a special purpose: education, relaxation, or entertainment. As leisure becomes more important in our society, more and more communities are coming to have tourism or entertainment as their major export.[38] Whole states (for example, New Hampshire and Vermont) are undergoing a transition from an economy of subsistence farms and small manufacturing to one of resort and vacation communities.

The communities to which people come for leisure, education, or other activities have certain characteristic problems of organization. They contain both people whose activities are bound up within the community and those for whom the community is a temporary abode, fulfilling for them only one kind of function. This bifurcation of interests tends to split the community into two parts and has given rise to many conflicts: "town *vs.* gown" fights

---

[38] The term "export" used to describe tourism does not, of course, mean that these activities are physically exported. It means instead that this is the commodity that the community sells to the outside: it is the commodity that provides the income for the community.

in college towns, and "native *vs.* resorter" disputes in resort towns. There are usually few bases for community between these two groups, and many bases of cleavage. It is significant that after the Peekskill riots (between the natives and the resorters) several years ago, a measure of community integration was restored by one of the few interests both groups had in common: the volunteer fire department, which had previously included only natives, now added resorters to its ranks.[39]

AGE-SPECIALIZED COMMUNITIES—Some communities are tending toward a different functional character from those discussed above: They are becoming age-specific. In one type of community the matter works somewhat as follows: A couple with young children has no money for a substantial down payment on a house but can buy an inexpensive house with little or no down payment, and monthly payments lower than rent. Some new suburbs come to be filled with such people. But after a few years their income is higher and they have an equity in their house with which they can buy a more expensive one. They leave, and their place is taken by another couple with young children. Such communities have a continual influx and outflow of residents, tending to maintain their special character as communities of young families.

This age specialization of communities is not confined to the example cited above: Dormitory suburbs in general are not places for young unmarried persons or for retired persons. At the same time, other communities are becoming primarily retired persons' communities: Florida and California have a large number of such communities. These, in contrast to the dormitory suburb, contain a *large* part of their members' lives, but over a *short* period of time. They have their special problems of community organization, though little is known systematically about these problems. Such communities are a relatively new occurrence in society and represent another element in the vast reorganization that society is presently undergoing.

If we look at the family's life cycle, there seems to be developing a three- or four-stage pattern, with important implications for the age specialization of localities. The cycle is this: (1) early married life in a rented apartment in the central city; (2) the young-children stage in a suburb of inexpensive houses; (3) an optional third move, depending on the accumulation of capital, to a more expensive suburb; and (4) after children leave home, the return of the couple to the central city or the move to a community of retired people.[40]

---

[39] James Rorty and Winifred Raushenbusch, "The Lessons of the Peekskill Riots," *Commentary,* Vol. 10 (October, 1950), pp. 309–23.

[40] For further discussion, see Philip M. Hauser, *Population Perspective* (New Brunswick, N. J.: Rutgers University Press, 1961), Chapter 4.

Disorganizing Consequences of Locality Specialization

The consequence of locality specialization that is of major interest to us is the increasing attenuation of bonds to a particular community, with all the difficulties this creates for community organization. The problem is not due to any "evil" that can be exorcised; it is an historical process that must be recognized. Localities may ultimately cease to be political entities and may no longer have any form of organization involving the residents. As mobility becomes even greater and competition between communities increases, it is possible that the essential functions of a community will become incorporated as a business, whose "product" must be sold on the open market, and whose owner profits from their sales. Perhaps, in contrast, there will be an ever increasing transfer of functions from the local level to a central authority, so that community organization will become almost totally unnecessary.

Both these tendencies are evident today. The first occurs in large-scale suburban developments, in which the developer sells a "package" that includes not only a house, but also roads, sewage disposal, water, a community swimming pool, a country club, a shopping center, and sometimes even a school. The difficulty, of course, is that subsequent actions must be taken by the community. The developer is gone and the community members are left holding the bag of problems, so to speak, without any structure for solving them. An interesting variation upon this is the planned development by a single developer of small satellite cities, from 50,000 to 100,000 population, containing industry as well as the institutions found in suburbs.

The tendency toward central authority is evident in the increasing number of city and state functions taken on by the federal government. It is also evident in city housing projects. Many city housing projects constitute, in numbers, large communities (Fort Greene project, in New York City, has about 17,000 residents), but have no community organization other than the project administrator. This is little more organization than the even larger suburban developments whose developers have sold their package and left.

Through both tendencies, entrepreneurial activity and administration, community organization withers away. Local activity is still far from dead, but there is no sign that the historical trend is diminishing.

CHILDREN AND PARENTS—One special set of problems created by this historical trend toward community specialization has to do with children. Though suburban residential communities are only living-places for parents, they are total communities for their children. Thus there is a proliferation of community among the children,[41] as community among parents disintegrates.

One result of the highly developed adolescent community and minimal adult community is a relative powerlessness of adults to control their children. Because there is little communication among adults, there are no strong norms about hours for being in at night, frequency of dates, and use of cars. The adolescents have a powerful weapon when they say, "All the other kids do it; why can't I?" The parent simply does not know whether all the other kids do it or not. The "pluralistic ignorance" resulting from absence of an adult community often results in the children having their own way. Many authors have seen the greater freedom enjoyed by children as a consequence of greater permissiveness of the modern generation of parents.[42] While this may be so, it is also true that this greater permissiveness probably results from a lack of strong community organization. Such organization would give norms to the parent to reinforce his otherwise solitary and bewildered struggle in socializing his children.[43]

The formation of gangs in cities, and most recently in suburbs, is facilitated by the same lack of community among parents. The parents do not know what their children are doing, for two reasons: *First,* much of the parents' lives occurs outside the local community, while the children's lives take place almost totally within it; *second,* in a fully developed community, the network of relations gives every parent, in a sense, a community of sentries who can keep him informed of his child's activities. In modern living-places (city or suburban), where such a network is attenuated, he no longer has such sentries. He is a lone agent facing a highly organized community of adolescents.

---

[41] For example, in a study of ten high schools (two were suburban schools and the remainder were in independent towns and cities), in the upper-middle-class suburban school the students showed higher sensitivity to the adolescent social system and their position within it than in any of the other nine schools. In answer to a question about whether they would like to be in the "leading crowd" of adolescents (asked of all those who said they were not in the leading crowd), a higher proportion said "yes" in this school than in any of the other nine. Reported in James S. Coleman, "The Competition for Adolescent Energies," *Phi Delta Kappan,* Vol. 42, No. 6 (March, 1961), pp. 231–36.

[42] See, for example, David Riesman, *The Lonely Crowd* (New Haven: Yale University Press, 1952). Many of Riesman's observations about the current scene in modern society are undoubtedly consequences of the historical trends in social organization discussed here, rather than the consequence of personality changes.

[43] A few suburban communities (e.g., Palo Alto, California) have recently attempted to replace the now vanished norms of the community by a rational procedure: a formal code to govern teen-agers' behavior drawn up after a public opinion poll of parents and teen-agers.

GEOGRAPHIC MOBILITY, DEMOCRACY, AND SOCIAL ISOLATION — The consequences of this historical trend toward free choice of community and toward locality specialization exhibit peculiar twists. It is not easy to be "for" or "against" such changes when one examines their consequences. For example, a tightly knit community, which captures all a man's activities over his whole life, severely restricts his freedom. He is born into a particular position in the community and finds it difficult to change this position throughout his life. This was most pronounced in the closed communities of the Middle Ages, where a man's life was wholly determined by his birth; it also exists to a lesser degree in independent towns in American society. Some analysts of social stratification in American communities have pointed out that a working-class boy or girl's chances for status mobility lie almost wholly in leaving the community.[44]

Modern dormitory communities, on the other hand, do not entrap their residents by their social structure, for the structure is almost absent. And the freedom of choice of one's living-place means that any ensnarement that develops while one is young, in the highly organized adolescent community, can be easily shed.

Thus the historical trend brings freedom and a greater measure of democracy than could otherwise exist. The other side of this coin, however, is not so bright. Freedom and mobility cut away the bonds of mutual identification and solidarity before they can fully develop. The psychological sustenance provided by such bonds is withdrawn. The result is social isolation and anomie, with their attendant discomforts and debilitating effects.

THE LESSENING IMPORTANCE OF LOCAL INSTITUTIONS — One consequence of locality specialization and the mobility it implies is a decrease in the importance of local institutions. Churches in particular have always been at the core of community organization. They have played such an important part that many conflicts in communities have essentially been conflicts between two church groups in the community.

---

[44] This is well illustrated by A. B. Hollingshead's study of social classes and education in a midwestern town. See his *Elmtown's Youth* (New York: Wiley, 1949). A possibility of breaking out of one's position in the structure sometimes comes about through the local high school. For boys, athletics provide an avenue for mobility in the adolescent status system, and in the larger community as well. Such possibilities are not so great for girls, and probably as a consequence, girls are more anxious to leave the community than boys, and in fact do leave more frequently. For a documentation of the intent, see James S. Coleman, *The Adolescent Society* (New York: Free Press, 1961), p. 124. For a documentation of the different sex distribution of youth in cities and towns, see Otis Dudley Duncan and Albert J. Reiss, Jr., *Social Characteristics,* Chapter 3.

But the church is coming to mean less and less in modern society, and can serve less and less as a core of community organization. In a survey of community conflicts carried out in 1929, 9 out of 40 conflicts reported involved churches. In another survey of more than 40 community conflicts carried out in 1957, none of the conflicts involved churches.[45] Though these surveys are not representative samples of community conflicts at these two times, they suggest what the observer feels: the steady decline in importance of the church as a community institution.

Along with this general decline is the fact that the *local* church need no longer be the one a person attends. For example, with the mass migration of city-dwellers to the suburbs, many city churches are losing their neighborhood base. Some suburbanites continue to attend the city church, making it a collecting-point for persons who were once neighbors but are no longer. When the city church "moves out," as many have done, it again often becomes a collecting-point, rather than a neighborhood or community church. The church often moves to some location that will serve several suburban communities, for its former congregation is dispersed throughout them.

This tendency is not, of course, always followed; but the strain in this direction is evident, because of the dispersion of the congregation and its freedom to travel. Such free movement means that churches with dispersed congregations need not be temporary arrangements. Such a situation can persist, and as it does so, the church becomes less and less an institution of the local community.

LOCALS, COSMOPOLITANS, AND A PECULIAR INVERSION—A study of a community in New Jersey found two sets of influential individuals: those concerned with local community activities, to whom others turned for local problems, and those concerned with external affairs, who served as leaders of opinion in things cosmopolitan.[46] In subsequent studies, similar differences have been found between opinion leaders whose attention is focused inward and those whose attention is focused outward. The preceding examination of kinds of communities suggests that such a bifurcation of interests is becoming more pronounced. Many kinds of communities consist of persons whose activities are wholly local and those whose activities are largely outside the

[45] The Inquiry, *Community Conflict* (New York, 1929); and James S. Coleman, *Community Conflict.*

[46] Robert K. Merton, "Patterns of Influence: A Study of Interpersonal Influence and of Communications Behavior in a Local Community," in P. F. Lazarsfeld and Frank Stanton, eds., *Communications Research, 1948–49* (New York: Harper, 1949), pp. 180–219.

community. The former will ordinarily become the "locals" and the latter the "cosmopolitans."

In many such communities, those persons with segmentalized activities partly in and partly outside the community are more educated, of a higher socioeconomic level, and are by training more fitted for organizational leadership than those who are wholly contained within the community. They represent a later point in the historical trend of role specialization, just as suburban communities represent a later point in community specialization than do independent towns.

But paradoxically, these men who are best fitted by education and organizational experience for positions of local community leadership have the smallest amount of their interest and activities located there. Those who are *interested* in the community, because their own lives are bound up in it, are lower in status, have less education, and are ordinarily the men who would look to others for leadership. In such communities, then, there is a peculiar inversion that would seem to inhibit community organization. Often this inversion creates an inversion of power as well. In Montgomery County, Maryland, contiguous to Washington, the average per capita income is one of the highest in the nation, and the schools are among the highest in production of National Merit and other talent search winners. Both these facts are due to the very high proportion of cosmopolitans, professionals who run the federal government. But in 1963, the locals, though greatly outnumbered, were able to take over control of the school board and cut school budgets. Many of the cosmopolitans were not even registered to vote in that county; others were involved in affairs of national interest and failed to vote.

Thus again, as in the historical trend of community specialization, the prospect is not bright for community organization; the trend seems rather away from organization. This is of course neither bad nor good in itself; its consequences are mixed and only serve to emphasize that it is hardly possible to conceive a world which is the best of all possible worlds. A given change may have both good and bad consequences; and what may be a bad consequence for one community (e.g., a suburb) may be good for another (e.g., the nation).

Locality Specialization and the Difference between Social and Community Disorganization

The historical trend toward locality specialization has undermined community organization in all the ways suggested above. Yet in doing so it has not necessarily undermined social organization of the larger society. If social disorganization is seen as a deterioration of consensus and a weakening of the norms of society (as many have seen it), this is not a necessary consequence of locality specialization. To be sure, the consequences noted above involve a reduction of consensus and undermining of norms in the *local* community—but consensus and norms may be simultaneously strengthened, through this very locality specialization, in other associations within society.

There was at one time a confusion among students of society between personality disorganization and social disorganization. As long as society was composed of concentric circles surrounding its members, as in the Middle Ages, personalities were little more than reflections of these concentric circles. Thus, personality disorganization and social disorganization were not distinct, even in principle. Their separation came about only with the development of multiple-group affiliations in place of the concentric ones. Because such a highly articulated structure necessarily had points of inconsistency and strain, there could be personality disorganization in the face of strong social organization, or conversely, there could be a highly disorganized society filled with persons not especially afflicted with personality disorganization.[47]

In the same way today, locality specialization is beginning to separate community disorganization from social disorganization. Communities are becoming less and less the "building blocks" of which society is composed. So long as they were so, a deterioration of those building blocks meant a deterioration in the structure of society. But the present changes are of a different sort, changes to different kinds of building blocks for society. The new society emerging in the twentieth century may well have social organization without local community organization.

There has been much debate among social philosophers on precisely this point. Throughout American history, many intellectuals have held to the image of the rural community or continuously interacting groups of neighbors as the ideal building block of society. Thomas Jefferson, Alexis de Tocqueville, John Dewey and many others viewed the new social structure

---

[47] As a number of authors have pointed out, from W. I. Thomas and Florian Znaniecki (*The Polish Peasant in Europe and America* [New York: Dover, reissued 1958]) to Albert Cohen ("The Study of Social Disorganization and Deviant Behavior," in Robert K. Merton, L. Broom, L. S. Cottrell, Jr., eds., *Sociology Today* [New York: Basic Books, 1959]), social disorganization is distinct from personal disorganization, just as psychological conflict within an individual is distinct from social conflict. Similarly, societal disorganization is distinct from community disorganization, though in the past there has been empirical connection.

developing in cities with alarm because it was not based on the strong organization of small residential communities or neighborhoods.[48] They argued that the geographic community *is* the only building block for strong social organization. However, some authors regard the functional specialization of local areas developing in American cities as beneficial, even when these areas do not support the rich substructure of informal activities that makes for community life. This debate over the need for diffuse residential communities that serve a broad range of functions versus functionally specialized localities focuses on a fundamental question in the organization of future societies.

Invasion of the Community: Mass Communication

The historical trend examined above exhibits a greater and greater freeing of the individual from community bonds. He can choose his residence, and his residence, once chosen, contains only one segment of his life. But there is yet another special development in modern society that results in an invasion of the community by the larger society. This development is mass communication, which has culminated in television. With movies, radio, and television, communication has come to be used as mass entertainment and mass leisure. Into the community's life comes daily entertainment from without — entertainment unrelated to the life of the community and by its very existence supplanting that life. The ultimate effects of television and other mass media on individuals and on communities have yet to be assessed, but it is indisputable that the time spent consuming this entertainment is time subtracted from the potential life of the community.

This is evident in local bars and taverns, which have traditionally been the meeting place of friends and one of the wellsprings of solidarity among neighbors.[49] They have been invaded by television, and though the life of the tavern continues, it is attenuated by the omnipresent visitor from without who demands the attention of those present. Just as a child continually demands its parents' attention and reduces the time they have to themselves, the television set's demands reduce the time members of a family or a tavern

---

[48] This antiurban perspective is discussed by Morton and Lucia White, *The Intellectual vs. The City: From Jefferson to Frank Lloyd Wright* (Cambridge: Harvard University Press, 1962).

[49] See David Gottlieb, "The Neighborhood Tavern and the Cocktail Lounge: A Study of Class Differences," *American Journal of Sociology,* Vol. 62 (May, 1957), pp. 559–62, for a discussion of the role that neighborhood taverns play in the lives of their patrons.

or a community have to themselves. The result is a weakening of those relations of identification and hostility of which a community is composed.

Mass communication has a second effect as well, an effect upon the content of norms in the community. Norms in a community have always derived from the structure of activities in the community and have been of such a character to maintain these activities. For example, women have ordinarily been the upholders of norms governing sexual relationships and family responsibility in the community. Why? Georg Simmel explains it this way: Women, as the physically weaker sex, have always been subject to the exploitations and aggressions of men. Unable to protect themselves individually and unable to separate themselves into a distinct society, they have depended upon the customs and norms of the community for their protection. They have upheld these norms because it is in their interest to do so. They have most to lose by a disintegration of norms.[50]

Similarly, the laws governing protection of property in a community derive directly from the community's activities. They are made into laws through the efforts of those who have property and are most staunchly upheld by these same property owners. Most laws or norms in a community can be understood in the same way: as serving the interests either of all community members or of some faction having enough power to put them into effect. Norms about childbearing have been handed down by mothers of mothers—both by virtue of their authority in the family and by virtue of their experience. The norms they transmit are designed to uphold the existing structure of the community—they are essentially conservative.

But this is coming to be no longer true in an age of mass communication. Norms can now derive from the movies or the television set, rather than from the local community. Authority no longer rests with age, because of the rapidity of change. Mothers, fathers, and children receive, through mass communication, images of moral acceptability that may be very different from the existing norms of their community. Sometimes these norms are commensurate with those in the larger society, but sometimes they derive from the special needs of the medium of communication. The movies that feature sex and violence do so not because these attributes reflect norms of the larger society but because they sell movies. The television quiz shows that were "fixed" were so not because this reflected the existing norms of society, but because this made the shows more interesting, and thus more lucrative for the producers and sponsors. The frequency with which social drinking and requests for "bourbon and water" occur in a movie may reflect

---

[50] Georg Simmel, *Conflict,* pp. 95, 96. As Simmel points out, the emancipation of women in modern society may tend to invalidate this relationship.

less the normative structure of society than it does the success of the bourbon manufacturers' trade association in persuading the movie producer to help them sell bourbon. The prevalence in films of such ceremonial religions as Catholicism and Episcopalianism does not reflect their position in society; they simply make better subjects for visual presentation than do nonceremonial religions, in which a minister dresses like everyone else.

Although these things do not reflect the present structure of society, they do have an effect upon the future structure. They tend to set into operation norms, attitudes, and behavior in an irresponsible way. The community and the larger society have so little control over them that normative patterns can establish themselves in full opposition to the community's previous standards. The public clamor over the television quiz show fixes can be seen in these terms. People recognized that television was *setting* the norms of society, in this case undermining the norm of honesty in one's dealing with others. The public clamor may be seen as an outcry against such irresponsible toying with the traditional values of honesty.

There have, of course, always been changes in the basic activities in society that have produced changes in the norms of the society (often after rigid resistance). But there is a fundamental difference between those changes and the ones cited above. Previously, norms have developed (as they still do to a great extent) through interactions of people with one another. They thus bore a close relation to the basic activities of which society was composed, and supported that structure of activities. But with mass communication, norms may be created in a very different and highly irrelevant way, depending, for example, on which advertising agent is closest to a particular television producer.

Rapidity of Change and the Irrelevance of Existing Constraints

In a stable society, the authority of the elders in a community is well grounded. They have had more experience in life, and that experience can be a valuable aid to those younger than they. Part of that experience has been codified into customs, norms, mores, and laws. These guides and constraints are of utmost relevance to the problems that daily face members of a community.

But in a rapidly changing society, the change itself makes many of these guides and constraints irrelevant. They were relevant to the society in which they developed, and they helped preserve that society. But as that society undergoes change of any sort, they become irrelevant. New guides for action are needed, and these residua of past experience are of little help.

Such a reduction in the authority of elders is likely to occur whenever society is undergoing change, whatever the change may be. The old norms are no longer good guides for action, but before new ones can grow up, the old ones must be cut away. Before new community organization can develop appropriate to the changes (e.g., changes in technology or in population size), the old organization must give way. Thus it seems inevitable that change in the community must be accompanied by a certain amount of community disorganization, until new norms and new organization-for-action can become established.

Considerations like these are particularly relevant to the present. Society seems to be undergoing more than sporadic changes followed by stability; since the industrial revolution, new changes have followed quickly upon previous ones. Such continual change tends to keep community organization at a low level—for the existing norms, customs, and authority structure are undergoing continual erosion, as they become irrelevant for the new conditions.

Community Disorganization as a By-Product of Higher-Level Policy

All the preceding conditions leading to community disorganization have been a consequence of broad historical changes in society. Yet there are numerous other factors affecting disorganization that have little or nothing to do with historical trends. One of these is governmental policy of a state or nation.

The existence of governmental units above the level of the community, at the level of the state or nation, can have important implications for community disorganization.[51] Community government itself tends to be conservative with respect to its own structure, that is, to preserve the organization that presently exists. But supracommunity government is concerned with preserving the structure of the larger society. Its decisions and laws are made from this perspective.[52] Often this is consistent with maintenance of com-

---

[51] As in preceding sections, the "community" whose disorganization is in question may be a whole metropolitan area or, alternatively, one of its parts such as a suburb or central city.

[52] It is true that sectional and community interests often play a part in national legislative decisions. But the decision is a balance among these interests, along with others (business interests, union interests, etc.), and by this token seldom satisfies any particular community's interest.

munity organization, but sometimes it is not. In some cases, the by-product of these supracommunity decisions is a disorganizing tendency at the community level. Two examples of this will illustrate how it can come about.

GOVERNMENT FINANCING POLICY—It was once true that buying a house required a rather large sum of money for a down payment, a considerable fraction of the total cost of the house. However, after World War II, the federal government made available two loan programs, FHA and GI, that made very easy the purchase of a *new* house. These programs did not similarly increase the ease of purchasing an older house. Even more difficult has been the task of securing government-insured loans for extensive renewal of such older properties as apartment buildings.

This state of affairs has been a remarkable stimulus to new home construction; but it has meant at the same time a speeding-up of the deterioration of older neighborhoods. A house that would have been sold or rented as a single family dwelling, were it not for the discrepancy between its ease of purchase and that of a suburban house, can no longer be thus sold or rented. It can, however, be a good real estate investment if converted for multiple-family use, that is, converted into a tenement.

Because most new home construction lies outside city limits, this old-new disparity has accelerated the exodus from the city to the suburbs. The city has thus deteriorated, while the construction industry and the suburbs have been favored by the government policy. To be sure, prospective home-owners have benefited as well, but no more (certainly less, in fact) than if the policy had made it as easy to purchase or renovate older housing as to purchase a new house.

This is not to say that the policy has been "bad," for community disorganization is not in itself necessarily "bad," as the preceding sections have pointed out. The policy has had differential consequences for different social entities, and cities are one entity for which the consequences have been bad.

DESEGREGATION AND DISORGANIZATION OF SOUTHERN COMMUNITIES—This example will illustrate even more clearly the effect of a decision at the national level on community disorganization. It will illustrate as well that community disorganization is not inherently "bad."

Throughout the history of communities in the American South, the community organization included norms and patterns of behavior insuring racial inequality between blacks and whites. This inequality was enforced through various means, including laws (such as those requiring separate schools for blacks and whites), norms about interpersonal relations (such as deference of blacks to whites), and in rare occurrences, violence beyond the law (such as lynching of a black accused of some grossly improper behavior toward a white). This system as established formed a stable community organization, as have other systems based on inequality throughout history.

But one fundamental element in the organization of these communities was inconsistent with a value premise of the nation as a whole, expressed in the Constitution: equality among all, regardless of race. In 1954, the United States Supreme Court decreed that this inconsistency in access to education be resolved in favor of the Constitution.

But resolution of the inconsistency between local law and national Constitution did not *do away* with the inconsistency. It merely *shifted* the inconsistency to a different level, to within the community organization itself. In border-state communities, in communities with few blacks, or in large cities where blacks and whites interact little and only impersonally, the inconsistency is not great, for few elements of community organization are founded upon the premise of inequality. But in the deep South the inconsistency introduced by integrated schools occurs in almost all walks of life. In every case, a building block in the organization of the community has been pulled out, and the organization that remains is less firm. It may reorganize on a different basis after a period of time, but for the present it will certainly be weakened, because that structure of control has been based in considerable part upon the premise of black-white inequality.

Again it is evident that community disorganization is not necessarily a "bad" thing. It is disruptive or disintegrative of the local community, but this disruption may serve some other aim—in this case, maintenance of a value premise of equality, upon which the organization of the nation as a whole is based.

SPECIAL CONDITIONS LEADING TO CONFLICT

The preceding conditions leading to disorganization are those that lead primarily to disintegration of norms and consensus, and only secondarily to conflict. Beyond these conditions there are others that lead especially to conflict within a community. Some of these are discussed below.[53]

---

[53] For a more extended examination of community conflict and its dynamics, see James S. Coleman, *Community Conflict*. For a number of theoretical points in the sociology of conflict, see Georg Simmel, *Conflict*, and Lewis Coser, *The Functions of Social Conflict* (New York: Free Press, 1964). The present examination will be limited to certain conditions that lead to conflict.

Internally Generated and Externally
Generated Conflict

The interdependent activities of which a community is composed sometimes generate joint action and develop community norms, but they often do just the opposite, as discussed in earlier sections. Probably the best example of interdependent activities that often lead to opposed action are economic activities. Workers and managers have some common interests (for example, high import tariffs for substitutable goods), but many that are opposed (for example, wages per unit of goods produced). Since these interests are crucial ones to both parties, they sometimes lead to open conflict such as a strike. At other times, they generate mutual hostility, which may remain temporarily unexpressed, but which later provides the dynamics for industrial conflict.

In another quite different way, the system of interdependent activities may lead to conflict. When one person or group has control over an activity in which another is interested as well, antagonism is likely to build up in the other. He cannot express his interests in modifying the activity to his taste, so antagonism develops. This has been a partial source of some public school fights in recent years. In one (Pasadena, California), the school superintendent was unresponsive to community pressures from groups that had been heeded by the previous superintendent. Hostility built up in these groups and was fanned by nationalistic persons who had developed special hostility toward innovations in education. The final result was the removal of the superintendent and a return to the old system of easy accessibility to the administration by interested groups.[54]

Perhaps the best example of a power differential generating hostility and finally community conflict is that between blacks and whites in the South. The absence of a black's control over his destiny in the South has generated the latent hostility that can lead to conflict once the opportunity arises to gain partial control.

In general, community members' lack of control over activities that are of central interest to them creates hostility, which sometimes obtains its outlet through subsequent conflict. In any highly differentiated community, there are control differentials of this sort. Lower classes and newcomers to the community tend to be without control, in contrast to old, established families. Thus, the potential for conflict exists in the very structure of activities,

---

[54] See David Hurlburd, *This Happened in Pasadena* (New York: Macmillan, 1950).

giving some persons control over parts of others' lives and creating situations of opposing interests. Conflicts from such sources need no external event to set them in motion, for they are generated by the activities of the community itself.

Racial conflicts are largely produced by hostilities generated through the interdependent activities of the community itself. The example below illustrates how these hostilities may be responsible for conflict.

A young mathematician from England was at the University of Chicago for a short period in the late 1950's. When he was walking across the Midway, he was accosted by several Negro boys who demanded his wallet. He objected, one of them produced a knife, and they led him over toward bushes beside the walk. The ensuing conversation went something like this, according to his later account: One boy said, "Come on, now, give us your wallet, or we'll have to get tough with you." He replied, "Look here, I don't want to give up my wallet to you. Besides, I've just arrived here from England, and I don't think this is the way to treat someone who's a visitor here." The boys looked at one another, and then one said, "Oh. We thought you were one of those white guys," and they quickly went away.

To these black boys, "white guys" had nothing to do with skin color per se, for the English mathematician was white. "White guys" were their fellow community members, the whites from whom they felt alienated because there had been no processes to create common identity between them, only those creating hostility. The Englishman was not a "white guy" against whom a reserve force of hostility had been built up.

This incident illustrates more than a peculiar, localized abnormality. There was no less integration of blacks into the local community in the Hyde Park area of Chicago, where this incident occurred, than in other large cities. The absence of integration, the absence of any processes that produce a common bond of identity, is very likely an important source, not only of conflict, such as the Trumbull Park riots in Chicago, but also of the black crime that occurs in such areas. The flow of blacks and Puerto Ricans into large cities is great, and these migrants initially have no stake in the city, no reason for not committing crime other than the fear of getting caught. The existence of such a flow of migrants makes especially important those processes that generate mutual identification between whites and blacks and processes that generate identification of the new migrants with the community.

Such processes are all too few in modern cities, but they are not totally absent. What is more important, they need not be left to fate, but can consciously be instituted to combat the disorganizing tendencies of migration and other "natural processes" in society.

Controversies involving racial or ethnic cleavages ordinarily build up through internal processes of the sort implied above. But they also usually include components that are not developed within the community itself: different backgrounds, cultural values, and norms; and differences due to time of movement into the community (classical examples of migrations inducing conflict are Irish Catholics moving into East Coast cities and New England towns in the nineteenth century; "Okies" moving into Southern California during the 1930's; ex-city dwellers moving into established suburbs in the 1950's, often with a different age and income distribution from that of the existing population; and rural southerners, mostly black, moving into the center of cities in the 1950's and 1960's).

Some community conflicts, however, are precipitated by purely external events. A new highway coming through a town may cause social cleavage where no trace had existed before. The opposition of interests between those whose homes would be demolished and those who would profit by increased business may lead to conflict. Another external source of such cleavages exists in some modern suburbs: continuing value differences due to the residential character of the community. This may be illustrated by an example in the suburbs of New York City: in Port Washington, Long Island, there were continuing school controversies in the 1950's maintained by two groups with political values at polar opposites. The persons concerned were employed in New York in activities supporting, respectively, their left-wing and right-wing views. Without this external support, grounded in national organizations for which these men worked, such extremes could not have maintained themselves in the same community. But grounded in New York City as they were, these differences continued to provoke violent school conflicts for a long period of time.[55]

As this example indicates, modern dormitory suburbs allow a great diversity of values to be maintained, held in place by diverse jobs and associations in the city. This value diversity can then become, as it has in numerous instances of school controversies, the basis for an explosive conflict.

To summarize, conflict can arise from the activities of the community itself, from purely external sources, or from some conjunction of the two. The internally induced conflict depends on the structure of interdependent activities in the community, which can operate over time to generate cleavage between two groups or to generate alienation of one group that has little control over these interdependent activities.

---

[55] See Louis Engel, "Port Washington, N. Y.," in "The Public School Crisis," *Saturday Review,* Vol. 34 (September 8, 1951), pp. 6–20.

Locality Specialization, the Mass
Community, and Conflict

As we have seen, locality specialization has taken out of the hands of the local community many of the activities it once had, resulting, for example, in modern bedroom suburbs. In doing so, it has removed many of the interests of its residents into associations that cut across community bounds. Their interests and activities have become extensive, over a wide range of associations. Most of these associations have a special organizational structure: a large mass of members, who are only tangentially interested in the activities of the organization; and a small corps of officers, whose major interests and activities are bound up in the association, men for whom the organization may even be a livelihood. Voluntary associations of all sorts are like this. Unions are probably the best example; professional associations, such as the American Medical Association; political groups, such as the Americans for Democratic Action or the League of Women Voters; P.T.A.'s, consumer co-operatives, conservation leagues, and other similar groups, are other examples.[56]

The local community, fast becoming a specialized living-place, has begun to take on a form similar to that of these voluntary associations. It holds only a small part of the interests of most of its members, whose other interests have become fractionated into many parts, most of them outside the community. Only those few merchants and others whose livelihood is within the community, or who are part of its government, are centrally involved.

The community thus tends toward a "mass society," with a small organized elite and a large unorganized, undifferentiated mass. This is not, of course, to say that its members are a "mass" from the viewpoint of the larger society. They are members of many groups — occupational, recreational, political, professional, and other interest groups. But many of these are not local. Some have their locus in the central city, some spread over the nation, but so long as they are not within the local community, they contribute nothing to its organization. Their members are therefore *in effect* a mass,

---

[56] For a general discussion of the "mass society" structure of such organizations, see Bernard Barber, "Participation and Mass Apathy in Associations," in Alvin W. Gouldner, ed., *Studies in Leadership* (New York: Harper, 1950). For an examination of the organizational structure of a mass society, see William Kornhauser, *The Politics of Mass Society* (New York: Free Press, 1959).

not organized into interest groups and associations that play a role in community decisions. There are special consequences of such a structure, consequences which have much to do with conflict.

It is interesting to note that such a mass society structure can come about through two exactly opposite societal forms: the members' having no important associations outside the family and close friends, so that no interest groups mediate between individual and government; and the members' having all their associational ties in large associations that go beyond the bounds of the governmental unit (in this case, the community), and thus play no role in its decision-making. Though these associations can and do play a mediating role at the metropolitan, state, or national level, protecting and furthering their members' interests, they cannot do so at the community level.

The first of these two forms of mass society is exemplified by traditional societies like those of Central America, where the large mass of the populace is tied only to family and friends. The second is exemplified by modern suburban communities. Despite the apparent polar extremes that these two social entities exemplify, their mass society form gives rise to similar types of conflicts, as will be evident below.

Consequences of the Mass Community for Conflict

Trade unions and Latin-American countries having the elite mass structure described above show a characteristic political cycle: alternations between long periods of apathy and violent revolts. The administrative elite goes on for a long time making decisions that are unchallenged by the mass, but then at some point the mass does rise up and attempt to "throw the rascals out." Such a cyclical pattern of authority seems to be a quality of many voluntary associations that engage only a small part of their members' interest and attention. Until some special issue or a special leader comes along to capture a major part of their attention, they are inactive and let the "authorities" administer the affairs of the association. But then there are no regular political channels through which their intentions may be expressed, and the "normal" processes of government give way to conflict in which the outsiders use any means to gain their ends.

As communities come more and more to take on the form of mass communities, with a small interested elite and an uninterested (though often educated) mass, one might expect that their political processes would take on this apathy-revolt pattern. There are no systematic data to document this, but two kinds of recent controversies exhibit precisely the form of a "revolt of the masses." These are school controversies centering around school desegregation; and fluoridation controversies over the question of whether the water system should or should not be fluoridated.

Some fluoridation controversies show the pattern perfectly [57]: a town or city council will have considered the question of fluoridation of the water system, and passed favorably upon it, often voting the small sum necessary to install it. Before this action is taken, only a few voices have been raised in opposition through letters to the editor of the local newspaper; until after the action, no real opposition to the plan is evident. All organizations in town favor it: business, labor, the professional associations of doctors and dentists, and others; and all members of the interested elite favor it.

But after the action, sentiment begins to build up against the plan, based partly on the charge that fluoridation is dangerous, but partly on the belief that this was not something for the council to decide alone, but should be a decision of the community as a whole. Fluoridation is then put to a vote, and the revolt is accomplished, resulting (in a majority of cases which have so far come to a popular vote) in defeat of the plan.

The normal procedure of decision-making in these communities is one in which the uninterested mass plays no part at all, since the community is only a segmental part of their lives. Thus the council makes this decision as it does others. But the mass membership, aroused by a few dedicated opponents of fluoridation, does not consider this assumption of authority legitimate in this case, and arises to revolt against the decision-makers. There are no organizational channels through which these beliefs could be transmitted as political pressures *before* the decision; the normal process of decision-making does not include the mass of community membership. Only by using new channels, that is, popular revolt, spread by word of mouth and letters to the editor, do the community members take part. And by this time, their antagonism is directed against the "high-handed behavior" of the city council, so that the vote against fluoridation is in part a vote against the council itself.

In short, the mass society form of local community that is arising through locality specialization generates a special kind of community conflict, a "revolt of the masses" against the administrative elite who have been making decisions. These revolts sometimes explode into real conflicts, because the intermediary associations, through which opinions are both expressed and compromised, are largely missing. This particular form of community con-

---

[57] See James S. Coleman, *Community Conflict,* for a more detailed discussion of the pattern of fluoridation controversies.

flict is especially prevalent today and is particularly interesting, since it seems to be a consequence of social changes (which promise to become even more widespread) toward locality specialization.

In this, as in other processes of community disorganization, it is only possible to point to overall tendencies. The details of these processes, some given in references above, most of them yet to be found, provide the means by which community disorganization, and social organization as a whole, can be understood, and in some cases altered.

14

Violence

AMITAI ETZIONI

VIOLENCE AS A SOCIAL PROBLEM

Throughout history, violence—killing, maiming, and the willful destruction of property—occurs in all societies. Violence is not only common during wars but is part of everyday life. One American is murdered every 39 minutes; one forcibly raped every 17 minutes; one subject to aggravated assault every two minutes; and one robbed every two minutes.[1] Much of this daily violence is viewed as the result of deviant acts by criminals or the mentally ill, or of temporary escalations of conflicts among social groups, such as labor and management, blacks and whites.

Unlike this "routine" violence, there are periods in history and in contemporary societies in which violence rises sufficiently in scope and intensity to threaten the very organization of society. During the *violencia* in Colombia, for example, in the decade from 1949 to 1958, about 180,000 persons were killed out of a population of about 12 million.[2] For a while, this situation

---

[1] Federal Bureau of Investigation, *Uniform Crime Reports for the United States* (Washington, D. C.: U. S. Dept. of Justice, 1968), Chart No. 16, p. 29.

[2] German G. Campos, O. F. Borda, and E. U. Luna, *La Violencia en Colombia,* tomo 1 (Colombia: Ediciones Tercer Mundo, 1962), p. 292. U. S. Army, *Area Handbook for Colombia* (Washington, D. C.: U. S. Government Printing Office, 1964), pp. 52–53.

prevented safe passage, let alone government control, through large sections of Colombia. The economy was disrupted and people were preoccupied with their security rather than other activities—that is, the normal functioning of social life in the areas affected was seriously undermined. Even more extreme are genocides, in which attempts are made to wipe out a whole people, like the Armenians in Turkey, or the Jews in Europe during the Nazi period.

In still other periods, a threat to social organization is perceived, but not necessarily because violence has reached an explosive level but because: (1) It is perceived as rising to higher levels than previously, or (2) the society has become aware that it is more violent than some other societies, or because (3) the society seeks actively, as a matter of policy, to reduce the level of violence it is experiencing.

In the 1960's, the amount of all major forms of violence in the United States was high, rising, and perceived by many as threatening the social fabric. Riots in cities were common; campus unrest was unprecedentedly frequent; 588,840 violent crimes were reported in one year, 1968; serious crime was up about 100 percent from 1958. President John F. Kennedy, Reverend Martin Luther King, Jr., and Senator Robert Kennedy were victims of political assassination. The United States was involved in a war. By 1970, 42,000 American servicemen had been killed, beside 107,000 South Vietnamese and 643,000 North Vietnamese and Vietcong (these figures do not include civilians). Within the United States itself the rate of deaths by homicide was exceptionally high in comparison with other industrialized societies.

Deaths Due to Homicide (rate per 100,000 population)

United States	6.0 (1966)
Canada	1.3 (1966)
England and Wales	0.7 (1966)
Austria	1.1 (1966)
Australia	1.5 (1966)
Mexico	18.9 (1967)
Guinea	31.1 (1967)
Colombia	21.3 (1966)
Costa Rica	4.0 (1966)
Uruguay	4.5 (1966)

Sources: For data on developed countries see U. S. National Commission on the Causes and Prevention of Violence, *To Establish Justice to Insure Domestic Tranquility* (New York: Bantam Books, 1970), p. xxiv. For data on underdeveloped countries see *U. N. Demographic Yearbook, 1968,* 20th issue (New York: 1969), Table 20, pp. 416–27. The data from this last source are defined as including deaths due to "operations of war." Because none of the countries cited were involved in such operations at the time, their data are limited to deaths caused by homicide. Data on underdeveloped countries are often quite unreliable and tend to underestimate the problem.

The perspective one takes in regard to violence largely determines whether or not one sees it as a social problem and how serious a problem it is thought to be. For instance, although the homicide rate in the United States was higher than in many other Western countries (a matter of great concern to Americans at the end of the sixties), the rate was lower than in many underdeveloped countries.

If we take a longer perspective, violence has been rampant throughout American history. A report prepared for the National Commission on the Causes and Prevention of Violence, itself a response to recent alarm, noted that:

> The first and most obvious conclusion is that there has been a huge amount of it. It is not merely that violence has been mixed with the negative features of our history such as criminal activity, lynch mobs, and family feuds. On the contrary, violence has formed a seamless web with some of the noblest and most constructive chapters of American history: the birth of the nation (Revolutionary violence), the freeing of the slaves and the preservation of the Union (Civil War violence), the occupation of the land (Indian wars), the stabilization of frontier society (vigilante violence), the elevation of the farmer and the laborer (agrarian and labor violence), and the preservation of law and order (police violence).[3]

The 1970's began with widespread debate over the moral concepts and authority structures of the society. Part of the citizenry and the leadership felt it was a question of law and order. When a national sample of Americans were given a list of ten domestic problems in a 1970 Gallup survey and asked which three the government should concentrate on 56% of the respondents chose "reducing the amount of crime." A smaller number of Americans viewed the unresponsiveness of the societal structure to the needs and demands of the minorities, the young, and ultimately most Americans as inviting violent uprisings and crime.

Social thinkers and political philosophers tend to view violence as a social evil. Even when it is argued that violence is "justified," as when the oppressed rise against their violent oppressors, we usually mean that we are willing to accept the human sacrifice of an uprising to prevent further violence, and in order to advance other values such as social justice and freedom. And we see the "justified" violence in itself as demeaning, to both its victims

---

[3] H. D. Graham and T. D. Gurr, eds., *The History of Violence in America: A Report to the National Commission on the Causes and Prevention of Violence* (New York: Bantam, 1969), p. 75.

and the executioners. To make a human being an object of violence brutalizes not only him but also the violent actor. Concentration camp guards, hangmen, or totalitarian elites are not free, happy people.[4] Only a very few writers have depicted violent acts as indicating positive attributes such as virility or toughness, or being therapeutic and releasing inhibitions.[5] Most students of violence ask how it can be minimized and how other means of advancing one's goals can be followed instead.

THE CONCEPTS OF VIOLENCE

Without entering into a lengthy exposition of conceptual differences and definitions, two distinctions in the concept of violence ought to be noted because the terms used technically here differ significantly from some common usages.

First, we are dealing in this paper with physical violence, not with economic or psychic coercion. Some people argue that there is no difference between forcing a person to take a line he does not wish to by pointing a gun at him, by threatening the loss of his job, or by manipulating his symbols, such as those involved in excommunication. This view is especially argued by those who justify their acts of physical violence by the economic and psychic coercion of others. Social scientists must note the difference: While economic and psychic pressures can be very powerful indeed, except in limited conditions they leave the ultimate decision to the subject — the pressures reduce but do not eliminate his freedom. When physical force is used, however — when a person is jailed, gagged, or shot — under most conditions he has no choice left in the matter.

This difference may account for a corollary one. Most people find physical violence more alienating than economic or psychic pressures; they would rather be scolded or have their pay reduced than be beaten.[6] Hence, it does matter to those subject to pressure which means of social control are em-

---

[4] This point was eloquently made by Albert Camus, *The Myth of Sisyphus and Other Essays* (New York: Vintage, 1955).

[5] See Ernst Nolte, *Three Faces of Fascism* (New York: Holt, 1966), on the masculine view of violence. Georges Sorel attributed mystic rejuvenating power to mass violence. See his *Reflections on Violence* (London: Allen and Unwin, 1915). Frantz Fanon saw it in a personal therapeutic potential; see his *The Wretched of the Earth* (New York: Grove, 1965).

[6] For some evidence see Amitai Etzioni, *A Comparative Analysis of Complex Organizations* (New York: Free Press, 1961).

ployed, and it is not useful to cloud the issue semantically by referring to all acts of coercion as violence.

Second, violence and aggression are not to be confused. "Violence" is an act that causes damage, often to a person, sometimes only to property. "Aggression" refers to the entire range of "assertive, intrusive, and attacking behaviors. Aggression thus includes both overt and covert attacks, such defamatory acts as sarcasm, self-directed attacks, and dominance behavior." [7]

Aggression may lead to violence, but it may also find an outlet in business competition, a lawyer's powerful brief, and sports—all legitimate modes of conduct. Those who seek peace do not want a world, a society, or even a family free of aggressive feelings or conflicts—which may well be impossible and even undesirable. Peace does not mean the tranquility of inaction; it requires the advancement of one's positions and the solution or curbing of conflict by nonviolent means. Actually, developing and maintaining a nonviolent system may well require providing sufficient room for legitimate forms of conflict, the way keeping a bicycle upright requires pushing the pedals. Standing still, passivity, is not a prerequisite of a nonviolent world.

THE FORMS OF VIOLENCE

Violence takes many forms: the assassination of presidents; the murder of mafiosi; riots in which city blocks are burned down and shops looted; bombs planted in mail boxes, police headquarters, department stores; lynching of blacks by whites; police or National Guardsmen using excessive force in their legal capacity, or running beserk; war; genocide.

For the social scientist, behind this plethora of concrete forms are a few analytic dimensions that allow an order to emerge from this chaos. Violence may be defined according to the kind of actor involved, whether individuals, small groups, or collectivities, such as classes or regions; how organized it is, whether spontaneous or planned; its legitimacy, whether it is authorized by the society's institutions and sanctioned by its values or is condemned for seeking to evade these controls and values, or whether it is revolutionary, seeking to redefine society, in which case the use of violence may be considered legitimate.

These distinctions express a general concern with consequences rather than with motives. Thus individual or small group deviant violence does not

---

[7] Marshall F. Gilula and David N. Daniels, "Violence and Man's Struggle to Adapt," *Science,* No. 164 (April 25, 1969), p. 396.

tend to have societal consequences unless it rises to very high levels or is hysterically perceived, while violence by collectivities seeking to redefine the society tends to alter history, as civil wars and revolutions indicate. The form of violence, though, does not determine the consequences. These are more affected by the sources of violence and the ways they are faced.

SOURCES OF VIOLENCE: ALTERNATE THEORIES AND THEIR POLICY IMPLICATIONS

But why is there violence of any kind, personal or collective? What does an analysis of the sources of violence tell us about the opportunities to reduce or eliminate it?

There are competing answers, or at least theories, attempting to explain why man is violent. They are important for understanding the violence around and before us and for suggesting different policies to pursue if violence is to be curbed. Violence, say various schools of thought, is the result of man's biological nature, of "normal" psychic predispositions; the result of successfully learning violent norms; or is caused by the social structure itself. Each of these views deserves attention not only because they are still subscribed to but also because each contains an element out of which a full theory of violence may evolve.

Human Nature: The Biological Schools

One major view of violence sees its sources in man's biological, "animal," or instinctual foundation. Social philosophers, especially Hobbes, held man to be violent in his original state of nature, acquiring the means to solve conflicts peacefully only through considerable effort devoted to developing and maintaining civilization's constraints. The animal base, nevertheless, is constantly lurking in the background, threatening to break through in violent acts. Since man, in this view, is naturally violent, what requires explanation is not his violence but the conditions under which civil conduct (which some call a "social veneer," to stress its fragility), arises and is sustained.

Many theoretical works in psychology are based on a variant of this assumption: Man is born an animal, is inclined to serve his own needs, and is capable of violent conduct. Through the processes of education (or socialization) he acquires a measure of self-regulation and an emotional commitment to limit himself in conflicts with his fellow man to nonviolent means. He also learns to pursue shared and complementary goals and not only his immediate self-interest. The more salient these shared or complementary goals, the less likely they are to come into conflict, and conflicts that do occur are less likely to intensify to the point where men will fight. Citizens of one nation more often than not tend to share goals; citizens of different nations rarely do. This is one reason nations fight each other more often than do groups within a nation.

Recent works in psychology stress that socialization is not sufficient even when successfully completed. People must be continuously rewarded for their civilized conduct or punished for breaking the rules and using violence illegitimately. Moreover, even the combination of socialization and social control does not assure full adherence to the nonviolent procedures the society fosters.

Not all social philosophers or scientists share this view of man. Some, including Locke, saw the state of nature as peaceful, in which men had "perfect freedom to order their actions and dispose of their possessions and persons as they think fit, within the bounds of the law of nature, without asking leave, or depending upon the will of any other men." [8] This state of peace is undermined when a small minority of disruptive, rapacious men seeks to violate the rights of others and forces the majority to defend itself. From then on, conflict is endemic to society. Recently, students of animal societies report that such societies are more peaceful than human societies, and that intraspecies violence among animals is rare.[9] Violent intraspecies fights occur chiefly when one's turf (or domicile) is invaded or a territory becomes overcrowded. Animals prey on each other, but "predation should not come within the scope of aggressive activity . . . a hawk swooping on a small bird is no more aggressive than the family butcher engaged in his livelihood." [10] Otherwise, aggression among animals is rare and tends to be playful (as among dogs) or ritualistic (as among cocks), but "fighting to the death very rarely occurs in vertebrates, and it is doubtful whether it ever occurs in mammals under natural conditions." [11] Because of the rapid development of his brain and weapons man is said to have lost the natural inhibitions against fratricide and genocide that even carnivorous animals have.

Nikolaas Tinbergen sees the essence of the social life of animals as cooperation among members of a species. Mating, rearing offspring, association

---

[8] John Locke, *Of Civil Government* (London: Cassell and Co., Ltd., 1901), Chapter 2, Section 4.

[9] John D. Carthy and F. J. Ebling, eds., *The Natural History of Aggression* (London: Academic, 1964), p. 2.

[10] *Ibid.*, p. 2.

[11] *Ibid.* See also J. P. Scott, *Animal Behavior* (New York: Anchor, 1963).

between individual animals outside the family, and intraspecific fighting constitute the four basic areas of intraspecific cooperation, which "although not of use to the individuals, is highly useful to the species, however paradoxical this may sound." [12] Most fighting occurs during the breeding season ("reproductive fighting"), and the two animals involved rarely try to kill each other. Most fights "take the form of 'bluff' or threat. The effect of threat is much the same as that of actual fighting; it tends to space individuals out because they mutually repel each other." [13] This reproductive fighting insures each member of the species the "possession of some object, or a territory, which is indispensable for reproduction. It thus prevents individuals sharing such objects, which would in many cases be disastrous, or at least inefficient." [14] And "stimuli from the territory to which the animal reacts either innately or as an added result of conditioning, makes the animal confine its fighting to the territory." [15]

As men cannot return to their animal nature, reducing violence depends on providing alternative nondestructive outlets for man's aggression. Speaking of war, A. Storr calls for playing off aggression in alternative spheres: "There will always be plenty of ways in which countries can compete, whether it be in the space race, in education, in technology, or even in welfare. We ought to encourage competition in these fields as much as we possibly can." [16]

Frustration-Aggression Theory

We have discussed theories that find the root of violence in man's nature, in his biological substructure, and in his psychic superstructure. A second set of theories sees the source of violence in a person's relationship to his social environment; the most popular of these is known as the "frustration-aggression theory." It states that aggressive behavior (of which violent conduct is a major form) results when purposeful activity is interrupted. The classical proponents of this theory often cite an example of a boy being

---

[12] Nikolaas Tinbergen, *Social Behavior in Animals* (London: Methuen, 1953), p. 21.

[13] *Ibid.,* p. 58.

[14] *Ibid.,* p. 62.

[15] *Ibid.,* p. 64.

[16] A. Storr, "Possible substitutes for war," in John D. Carthy and F. J. Ebling, eds., *The Natural History of Aggression* (New York: Academic, 1964), p. 144. Similar suggestions have been made by Konrad Lorenz, *On Aggression* (New York: Bantam, 1966).

prevented by his mother from getting an ice cream cone after the ice cream vendor's bell has been heard and the boy is on his way to buy it.[17] The frustration-aggression theory is frequently criticized for not explaining under which circumstances frustration leads to aggression and under which it does not: Some children regress rather than aggress; for example, when toys are taken from them they wet their pants rather than attack other children. The theory does not differentiate between aggression that is violent and aggression that is not (which may take the form of personal insult rather than physical assault). And, it has been pointed out, aggression may be evoked other than by frustration, for example, by boredom or by disrupting physiological rather than purposeful activities, such as sleep.

Still, a considerable body of data in support of the theory has evolved. Studies do show which factors affect aggressive responses.[18] For example, aggression is more likely to occur if frustration is *arbitrary* rather than *explainable:* A commuter is less likely to react aggressively if a bus passing him by displays a clear sign that it has broken down and is on its way to the garage. Previous exposures are also a factor; studies show that during World War II people nearly missed by a bomb reacted more severely to a new bombing than those without such previous experience. In an experiment measuring the effect of differing degrees of frustration, a five-month-old baby was deprived of his bottle at varying lengths of time after he had started feeding. When the length of time before he started crying was measured, it was found that the less milk the child had consumed before he was interrupted, the quicker he responded by crying.[19] Thus the more frustrated (or less satiated) the child was, the greater the motivation for an aggressive response.

In a study investigating the differential effect of experiencing a series of frustrations rather than a single one, several pairs of college students exchanged written notes on two occasions arranged by the experimenters. The notes prepared by the students were intercepted and replaced with notes either friendly or hostile in tone. After two sessions, each student was asked to describe his partner, and these descriptions were scored according to the degree of hostility expressed. Students who received two unfriendly notes were found to be significantly more hostile in describing their partners than students who received only a single unfriendly note—indicating that

---

[17] The classical book is John Dollard, Leonard W. Doob, Neal E. Miller, O. H. Mowrer, and Robert R. Sears, *Frustration and Aggression* (New Haven: Yale University Press, 1939).

[18] For an overview see Leonard Berkowitz, *Aggression: A Social Psychological Analysis* (New York: McGraw-Hill, 1962).

[19] The studies report almost exclusively on work with children or students.

aggressive motivation may "accumulate" from earlier experience until an occasion for its expression arises.

The implications of this conception go far beyond the carefully designed experiments. This theory is often cited to suggest that if peoples' aspirations are kept from outpacing the opportunities available to them, violence will be less common than in our own frustrating world, where everyone is encouraged to strive for economic and social success but the avenues are not equally available to all.[20]

The Learning Theories

While the frustration-aggression theory sees violence as the result of "social and psychic failure" — disruption of purposeful activity, the absence of expected rewards, and inadequate maturity and development of "safe" outlets — learning theory views violence as the result of successful socialization and social control. Aggressive behavior in general, and violent behavior in particular, is learned just like other behavior, and can be triggered where "expected," even without frustration. Middle-class people, especially intellectuals, it is said, tend to view bloodshed with horror, but in other subcultures some forms of violence are considered normal or acquire a positive evaluation. In the frontier society, a fast gun was a source of prestige. The lower classes often associate using force (e.g., in a fist fight) with masculinity. And the same educated people who abhor violence in abstraction frequently approve of using it for one's nation or for some other "just" cause.

Thus under conditions in which violence is expected — soldiers at the front, teen-agers in a street gang — members of the subculture may learn to conform to the norms and behave violently because such conduct is presented to them as socially desirable. They may feel violence "is the thing to do," because they have been "brought up right," and they know they will win approval if they fight well and receive censure if they "chicken out."

What one learns is largely defined by one's culture and subculture. Hence one common explanation for why Americans are more violent than Europeans is that American culture is more approving of violence than most other Western cultures. Swedish movies set practically no limits on the sexual behavior filmed, but they censor violence; American movies used to be, and to some degree still are, sexually inhibited, but they are not violence-shy.

---

[20] Amitai Etzioni, "Making Riots Mandatory," *Psychiatry and Social Science Review,* Vol. 2, No. 5 (May, 1968), pp. 2–7.

Not only does violence appear—in westerns and war movies—in gory detail, but it tends to be romanticized—the war hero gets the girl, the war makes a man out of a timid boy, and so on. Our frontier experiences and the mixing of immigrants from widely varied backgrounds, sharing few "ultimate" values or bonds, are believed to have shaped American culture in this regard.

> The American character . . . was forged through an extraordinary 300-year process of settlement during which the Indians were driven back, the English, Spanish, and French were driven off, the Africans were involuntarily driven over, the Mexicans involuntarily annexed, and the immigrant minorities were thrust irrevocably into a vibrant competition both with a raw physical environment and with one another. That Americans often resorted to violence under such trying circumstances is no surprise. But more important today is the question of the pervasiveness of the legacy of nativism, vigilantism, and ethnic aggression that was an inevitable byproduct of the interaction of immigrant and open continent.[21]

Very recently, efforts have been made to disarm American culture. Television networks have begun to limit violence, especially in children's programs. Mothers demonstrated against war toys. By and large, little was changed; the culture of a free society is not given to ready guidance. The profit from "violent" movies or toys is considerable, and the demand for either item does not seem to subside.

Social scientists disagree considerably on the effect of violent-cultural items. Research conducted by R. H. Walters and his associates from 1962 to 1966 seems to indicate that viewing filmed violence stimulates aggressive behavior. College students were chosen as subjects; they were instructed to act as "teachers" in a learning experiment in which they punished the "learner" for his mistakes. After viewing a knife fighting scene from a film, the test subjects "showed a significant increase in the level of shock delivered to the learner when errors were made." [22] The authors conclude that:

> The pattern of data is consistent with the interpretation that filmed violence stimulated aggressive motivations or aggressive response tendencies and that this aroused aggressiveness was manifested in permissive aggression against another person.[23]

---

[21] H. D. Graham and T. D. Gurr, eds., *The History of Violence in America: A Report to the National Commission on the Causes and Prevention of Violence,* p. 102.

[22] Walter Weiss, "Effects of the Mass Media of Communication," in Gardner Lindzey and Elliot Aronson, *The Handbook of Social Psychology,* 2nd ed., Vol. 5 (Reading, Mass.: Addison-Wesley, 1969), p. 133.

[23] *Ibid.*

The work of O. I. Lovaas seems also to demonstrate the aggression-stimulating effect of viewing filmed aggression. In a series of experiments, preschool children viewed cartoons with a very high content of violence; the children's observed aggressive behavior seems to have been stimulated by the aggressive cartoons.[24] In contrast, other studies of the effects of media that convey violence (e.g., television, comic books) upon children frequently report the absence of a causal relationship between the amount of exposure to the media and antisocial behavior. One study of 263 New York City boys of average intelligence compared the behavior of the 25 boys most interested in comic books with the behavior of the 25 boys least interested in comic books. When the two groups were compared with regard to school attendance, school achievement, conduct, and tendencies toward delinquency, no significant differences were found.[25] Another study of 626 fifth- and sixth-grade children in a Boston suburb investigated the relationship between their interpersonal behavior and their choice of aggressive or nonaggressive material in television, movies, and comic books. While boys who tended to have unusual problems with interpersonal relations and also were highly exposed to pictorial media had a "particular preference" for aggressive media content, it was suggested that interpersonal problems were more nearly a cause than a consequence of the boys' concern with violent media content.[26]

An aggressive movie may release aggressive motivations rather than encourage hostile actions or violent behavior. It was found that preexposure psychological characteristics, such as a high number of interpersonal problems, affect the child's use of the mass media; they differentiate the content he prefers and how he perceives it and they determine how this content influences him.

> A boy with problems, extrapunitive leanings, and rebelliously independent tendencies who, mainly as a result of his social environment and his I.Q., is highly exposed, relies on the media for temporary solutions to difficulties; structures the content of the media in black-and-white terms around elements of aggression, threat, amoral views of crime and negative attitudes to existing law enforcement institutions; and draws on this structure in his judgments of people and in a projection of his own self-image.[27]

---

[24] *Ibid.,* p. 134.

[25] Herbert S. Lewin, "Facts and Fears about the Comics," *Nations Schools,* Vol. 52, pp. 46–48, in Joseph T. Klapper, *The Effects of Mass Communications* (New York: Free Press, 1960), p. 151.

[26] Walter Weiss, "Effects of the Mass Media of Communication," in Gardner Lindzey and Elliot Aronson, *The Handbook of Social Psychology,* 2nd ed., Vol. 5, p. 133.

[27] Lotte Bailyn, "Mass Media and Children: A Study of Exposure Habits and Cognitive Effects," *Psychological Monographs,* Vol. 73, No. 1 (1959), p. 36.

The Commission on the Causes and Prevention of Violence took a different position, referring to experimental studies showing that children exposed to filmed or televised violence may respond by imitating the aggressive behavior. In one study, nursery school children watched a film showing an adult striking an inflatable "knock-down" doll; later these children and others who had not seen the film were subjected to deliberate frustration and placed in a room with a "knock-down" doll and other toys. Children who had seen the film displayed significantly more hostility toward the doll than did the other children.[28]

In another study, one group of nursery school children saw a cartoon featuring aggressive action and a second group saw a cartoon containing relatively peaceful activity. Children from both groups were then permitted to play with two mechanical toys. Both were activated by a bar which, when pressed, in one toy caused a doll to strike another, and in the other toy led to more peaceful activity. While both groups made the same total number of responses to the toys, the children who had seen the violent cartoon used the aggressive toy significantly more frequently than the children who had seen the nonviolent cartoon.[29]

Possibly the issue is the difference between cultural *items* and *contexts*. If a war is reported in the news each day, and since killings occur often in the streets, and much violence is depicted in movies, novels, history books, and toys, removing a few such items will have little general effect and hence will not "show" in studies. Changing the whole context, however, disarming the culture, might well make a difference. While it is extremely difficult to disarm a culture, it might at least be possible to enrich it with strong antidotes—such as are now being provided against smoking—until slowly the violence-predisposing items are rendered less poisonous. The most important factor is probably not how much violence we see, but rather the framework in which it is reported and viewed—whether horrible or noble, a measure of last resort, or a shortcut to fame and fortune. Here is where "editing" and education may be comparatively useful.

---

[28] A. Bandura, D. Ross, and S. Ross, "Transmission of Aggression Through Imitation of Aggressive Models," *Journal of Abnormal and Social Psychology,* Vol. 63 (1961), pp. 575–82, in Leonard Berkowitz, *Aggression: A Social Psychological Analysis,* p. 236.

[29] Ivar Lovaas, "Effect of Exposure to Symbolic Aggression on Aggressive Behavior," *Child Development* 32, pp. 37–44, in Leonard Berkowitz, *Aggression: A Social Psychological Analysis,* p. 236.

TOWARD AN INTEGRATED THEORY OF VIOLENCE

The three sources of violence we have identified may well appear jointly, making it difficult to tell which source is at work. When a criminal shoots a storekeeper, he is surely biologically capable of violence; he may also be frustrated—perhaps he has just lost his job—and may have learned that "it's all right" to behave that way. Analytically, however, these theories are not compatible, and the policy-implications are not identical. Nor do the theories have the same explanatory power.

Analogies to animal societies are of limited value, since man and his society differ in so many ways from animal societies, and each difference affects the issue at hand. Members of human societies respond to rich and complex sets of symbols (culture) which may serve to curb, or to generate, a level of violence very different from the one man is biologically capable of; in contrast, the role of symbols in most animal societies is extremely limited. A genetically set division of labor and reflexes are the marks of animal nature; man is not governed by these. Some say that we would be "better off," less violent, if we were more bound by our reflexes, but we are not and cannot be so reconstituted. Even if humans, who are often provoked to armed conflict by considerations of status and ideology, followed the examples of animals and fought only when their territories are threatened or their physical existence endangered, the level of warfare would still be high, as in Europe when the Nazis fought for *lebensraum* (literally, "space to live").

Social scientists have been saying for years that man can find different outlets for his aggressive tendencies—the aggressive individual may become a lawyer, butcher, policeman, or criminal. But it is not clear why some people become one or the other, and even less clear to what extent we can redirect the factors that so assign people without radical transformation of the whole society. Human malleability may be smaller than had been expected. Aggressive children in kindergartens are given a doll to hit as a "substitute outlet" when they want to hit other children. But when a three-year-old in a nursery school says: "I want to hit something which makes . . . Ooh," he is saying, in effect, that substitutes have different attributes, are not so attractive, and hence do not replace the need for violent, antisocial behavior.

Both frustration and learning seem important factors in violent behavior. But these are not to be viewed as narrow personality concepts, determined merely by an individual's ability to learn, his maturity, or his previous experience. These factors are significantly affected by societal forces, and societal forces work directly on the aspirations a person has and the actual opportunities available to him. Their balance versus discrepancy is one significant factor determining the level of violence in a society. If aspirations are escalated—by the movies, televison, advertising, and modern secular education—while new jobs, income, and housing increase more slowly, violence will rise.

From a theoretical viewpoint, the societal aspects of learning and frustrations allow us to tie in these two distinct theories, and place the study of violence in a general framework that includes other deviant and innovative behavior.[30] The point is that culture offers both the goals members of society aspire to (e.g., material success) and the means they are expected to use in reaching these goals (e.g., hard work, saving). When the legitimate means are not available and the goals are accepted, some members of society are frustrated and under pressure to resort to illegitimate means—of which violence, as applied by the criminal, is a major example.

Learning becomes a chief factor, once a deviant, violence-approving subculture has been established, but learning does not explain how and why such a culture came about. An individual may well be violent because he grew up in a frontier or gangster community where violence was an approved mode of conduct, and he was successfully socialized into it. But collectives, such as classes or races, do not pick up at random violent cultural patterns, which are then "learned" by their individual members. By and large the more violent cultures seem to be those that are located in relatively deprived areas, such as southern United States and southern Italy. In the United States, violence as "part of life" seems more acceptable in the South than in most other parts of the country, more common in the cities than in the suburbs and in the poorer areas of the cities than in the richer ones.

The concepts of learning and frustration, especially if enlarged to include sociological concepts such as the content of culture and subculture, and the structure of aspirations and opportunities, are helpful in understanding the factors that determine the forms and level of violence. In searching for a more comprehensive theory of violence, a process far from complete, we turn next to *societal* sources, which affect the level and modes of violence directly as well as the motivational and cognitive processes just explored.

---

[30] On this framework see Robert K. Merton, *Social Theory and Social Structure,* enl. ed. (New York: Free Press, 1968), Chapters 6–7; Richard A. Cloward and Lloyd E. Ohlin, *Delinquency and Opportunity* (New York: Free Press, 1960); Marshall B. Clinard, ed., *Anomie and Deviant Behavior: A Discussion and a Critique* (New York: Free Press, 1964).

The single most significant insight for a sociopolitical theory of violence is, to paraphrase a famous saying, that violence is the continuation of normal societal processes by "other" means. To illustrate, workers may have grievances (a sign of social tension) and go on strike (by itself, a legitimate, nonviolent form of conflict), which may turn into a violent confrontation if demands are continually ignored or attempts are made to suppress the overt expression of the conflict (by use of police or strike breakers). Only if we understand the forces that cause tensions and conflicts in society will we ultimately be able to account for the level of violence. While these forces may be nonviolent, if they are ignored and not responded to, they will, under certain conditions, turn violent.

It is difficult to account fully for the level of tension and conflict in society and the conditions under which it escalates into violence, without going into considerable detail.[31] Three central concepts, though, can be briefly introduced and their relationships to violence explored. These are "societal bonds" (or "systems"), which refer to the extent to which a society is *glued* together or *integrated;* "societal structures," which indicate the shapes or patterns of the relationships among those bound together into one societal grouping (e.g., is there one subgroup which subjugates the others or is there a more egalitarian distribution of opportunities?); and *"societal processes,"* which are the mechanisms through which both societal bonds and societal structure can be changed. The processes may be effective and make structure and bonds responsive to the memberships, or ineffective and allow for great or growing discrepancies between the desires of the members and what the society provides for them. Major sociological conceptualizations of the societal sources of violence lie in these three concepts.

Societal Bonds (or Systems): The Extent of Societal Integration

The intricate webs of social bonds that tie individuals and groups to each other are of three major kinds: One is the values the members share, which they acquire at home, in school, from peers, and in church. For instance, they may share a belief in the "American way of life" or in "individualism." Shared beliefs allow groups with conflicting interests and viewpoints to work

---

[31] A theory on which we draw here is presented in detail in Amitai Etzioni, *The Active Society: A Theory of Societal and Political Processes* (New York: Free Press, 1968).

them out and, hence, to curb conflict, limiting it to nonviolent means. It is as if each participant says to himself, "Well, I don't really like this ("this" being whatever the conflict is all about), but there is something more important I and my adversary share; hence let me give in, at least part of the way, to keep the shared enterprise alive." When basic values are not shared by members of a society, as, for instance, among the tribes of some newborn nations such as Nigeria or in the United States before the Civil War, intergroup violence is more likely. This violence may take the form of tribal warfare, civil war, urban riot, or, most commonly, international war.

The second major societal bond is the economic exchanges that bind people and groups to each other not out of commitment to the same values but out of necessity. They trade with each other or use each other's facilities (e.g., ports) or own joint facilities (e.g., interstate railroads). The more exchanges occur, the more people or groups are bound to each other and the less likely are they to come into violent conflict.

A third bond, frequently not recognized as such, is the ability of an authority to speak for the unit (whatever unit is encompassed by the bonds) to keep the subunits "in line" (i.e., to continue within the system and not to threaten it) by disarming them, or at least by keeping their capacity to fight at clearly lower levels. It is something like a school yard: One reason the fourth graders do not fight each other, at least not much, is that some eighth graders (or teachers) are appointed to see that they do not. Both the superior power and the legitimacy of the "law and order" force are relevant: If the "peace-keeping" force is weak, it will invite a revolution; if it is itself unjust, not duly appointed, or discriminatory in its enforcement of nonviolence, it will encourage the "subjects" to seek means to rebel. In the process of nation-building, in which societal bonds are intensified, often the right to bear arms is shifted from individuals and local groups to a national authority such as the police or the army.

A brief look at the development of societal bonds in the United States is useful. Having grown out of colonies that were fairly separate entities, the United States only slowly evolved nationwide integrative forces of all three kinds, and this largely after the Civil War. Even today no nationwide school system teaches all children the same "civics" or otherwise introduces them to the same set of ultimate values, as in France or Israel. Even today segments of the country, especially the poorest ones, are left out of many of the economic exchanges. Even today the United States, unlike most Western countries, has no nationwide police force. These factors are a major reason the United States is more violent than most Western nations. They also help explain why in many underdeveloped nations, much less integrated than the United States, intergroup violence is considerably higher.

The three kinds of bonds are weakest *among* nations, and, hence, conflicts which arise among these entities are most likely to turn to violence that, once it erupts, is most difficult to curb. If one thinks about a nation divided by a civil war or large-scale intergroup violence, along racial or class lines, for example, as two or more "nations" not deeply bound together, we see how the same conception of bonds applies both to intra- and international conflicts.

So far, we have asked a "static" question: What bonds tie men together? Dynamically, we ask next: Under what conditions may groups heretofore not sufficiently tied to make a community that rules out large-scale intergroup violence come to fashion such bonds? We shall illustrate our answer by examples from situations in which bonds are weakest, among nations, but the same points apply to *intra*-national systems.

SYSTEM-BUILDING: AN INTERNATIONAL EXAMPLE—*Encapsulation, not conflict resolution:* Bonds provide a "capsule" that contains conflicts and prevents them from turning into violence. "Encapsulation" refers to the process by which conflicts are modified so that they become limited by rules (the "capsule"). The rules exclude some earlier modes of conflict, while they legitimate other modes. Encapsulated conflicts are not solved in the sense that the parties necessarily become pacified. But the use of arms, or at least some usage of some arms, is effectively ruled out. Where some observers may see only two alternatives—powers are basically either hostile or friendly—encapsulation points to a third kind of relationship. Here, some differences of belief or interests, even a mutually aggressive orientation, might well continue. But states agree to rule out some means and some modes of conflict, that is, armed ones, and set up the machinery necessary to enforce this agreement. Encapsulation is thus less demanding than pacification, since it does not require that the conflict be resolved or extinguished, only that the range of its expression be curbed.

Propelling forces, the limits of communication: How may bonds be built up to curb intergroup violence? Robert Ezra Park points out that conflict generates interaction between its parties (e.g., races); the parties come to know each other and communicate with each other, which in turn leads to the evolution of shared perspectives and relations, until the conflict turns into competition. (Park and many other sociologists use the term "competition" to refer to a conflict limited by a set of rules.) [32] Daniel Lerner reports that French businessmen who travel, read foreign magazines, and meet foreign visitors are more likely to favor the formation of a European com-

[32] Robert E. Park, *Human Communities* (New York: Free Press, 1952).

munity than those less exposed to foreigners. Among businessmen with much exposure, sentiment in favor of such a community is about six to one, while those who have had little contact with foreigners favor the community only by a ratio of two to one. The difference between these two groups might be related to factors other than exposure, but Lerner shows that variables such as age, birthplace, socioeconomic status, size of firm, and location of firm do not explain the difference.[33]

The theorem that increased communication between parties is the mechanism through which conflicts are encapsulated, and violence thus reduced, seems to hold more for parties with similar values and sentiments to begin with. Communication may make the participants aware of a latent consensus upon which they may draw to build agreed-upon procedures to further limit conflicts and to legitimate accommodation. But when the basic values, sentiments, and interests of the parties are not compatible, increased communication may only stir this incompatibility into conflict, make the parties more conscious of the deep cleavages that separate them, and increase the likelihood of violence. The larger the differences between the parties to a conflict, the smaller the degree of encapsulation that can be attained through increased communication.

The effect of power constellations: To encapsulate conflicts between hostile parties who lack shared values, the number of members in the system and the distribution of power among them seems to be more important for the system's integration than communication. The balance-of-power system seems to require at least four or five participants.[34] Systems with three participants tend to lead to coalitions, in which two gang up against the third.[35] Bipolar systems (i.e., with two participants) have been shown to be particularly difficult to pacify. Encapsulation seems to be enhanced by the transition from a relatively duopolistic (two party) system to a more pluralistic one.

International relations approximated a state of duopoly between 1946 and 1956. In this period, the height of the Cold War, there were two fairly monolithic camps, one directed from Moscow, the other from Washington. A number of countries were not aligned with either camp but their military and political weight was small. Such a duopolistic situation was highly unfavorable to encapsulation. The sides focused their attention on keeping their respective blocs integrated and trying to keep nonaligned countries from

---

[33] Daniel Lerner, "French Business Leaders Look at EDC: A Preliminary Report," *Public Opinion Quarterly,* Vol. 20 (1956), pp. 212–21.

[34] See Morton A. Kaplan, *System and Process in International Politics* (New York: Wiley, 1957), pp. 27, 34 ff.

[35] Georg Simmel, *Conflict* (New York: Free Press, 1955).

swelling the ranks of the opposite camp. Each bloc eyed the other, hoping for an opportunity to expand its respective area of influence while waiting for the other's collapse.

Between 1956 and 1964 a secondary power rebelled in each of the two major camps. Both France and China had been weak powers, forced to follow a foreign policy formulated in foreign capitals. Under reawakening nationalism and augmented national power, both, however, increasingly followed an independent foreign policy. The rebellion of the secondary powers in both camps pushed the two superpowers closer to each other. Seeking to maintain their superior status and fearing the consequences of conflicts generated by their rebelling client-states, the superpowers set out to formulate some rules binding on all parties. The treaty of the partial cessation of nuclear tests, which the United States and the Soviet Union tried to make binding on France and China as well, was a case in point. American-Russian efforts to stem proliferation of nuclear weapons was another. In this period Russia stopped whatever technical aid it was giving to Chinese nuclear research and development,[36] and the United States refused to help France develop its nuclear force. American-Soviet negotiations to agree on inspection of atomic plants, aimed mainly at insuring the use of atomic research for nonmilitary purposes in third countries, pointed in the same direction. The 1963–1964 *detente,* which isolated Communist China and France, and the Geneva disarmament negotiations in the same years, in which these two countries did not participate, were further reflections of this trend.

These measures have in common the important characteristic that they serve the more "narrow" needs of the superpowers while they advance the "general welfare" of the world; they can therefore be presented as universal values and implemented through world institutions (i.e., extend the "capsule"). For instance, the prime superpower motivation for the 1963 test treaty might well have been the desire of the United States and Russia to remain the only two great nuclear powers, but it also indirectly reduced the danger of nuclear war. It was presented as if the prime motive were to advance peace and disarmament and reduce fallout to protect human health. It is a familiar strategy of political interest groups to work out solutions among themselves and then clothe them in the values of the community at large. Indirectly, these values affect the course of action an interest group chooses to follow from among available alternatives and they provide a common basis upon which similar or compatible interests of divergent powers can be harmonized and the shared community broadened.

---

[36] G. F. Hudson, Richard Lowenthal, and Roderick MacFarquhar, *The Sino-Soviet Dispute* (New York: Praeger, 1961).

Consensus formation and "intermediary" bodies: Sociopolitical processes that reduce the differences of interest and viewpoint and build ties are conflict-reducing, violence-curbing processes, as well as community-building processes. Communities, especially if they have a government, require consensus that needs to be developed. To form an effective consensus-forming structure, it is essential to divide the processes into several levels of representation. Rather than attempting to reach consensus among all parties in one general assembly, the parties are best divided into subgroups that are more homogeneous than the community as a whole. These subgroups work out a compromise and are represented as if they were a single unit on the next level of the structure in which consensus is formed. To be effective such divisions may have to be repeated several times.[37]

Regional organizations, communities, and blocs might serve as "intermediary bodies" for the international community. It would, however, be a mistake to view every regional organization as a step toward a world community. Regional organizations that have only socially marginal roles, such as the European research organization on peaceful uses of nuclear energy (CERN), tend to have much less impact than those that pool the sovereignties of several nations, as the European Economic Community (EEC) has begun to do. Regional bodies intended to countervail other regional bodies, especially military alliances such as NATO and the Warsaw Treaty Organization, often retard rather than advance encapsulation of conflict; they tend to reflect, on a large scale, the features of nationalism. Regional bodies aimed at internal improvement, such as "welfare" communities (a foundation of the EEC) or development associations (e.g., in Central America) that stress rapid economic growth, are more likely to serve as intermediary layers in the process of building a world community.

Above all, only regional bodies that allow the process of "upward transfer" of loyalties are helpful in building a world community. Studies of social structures as different as the American federal government and the Southern Baptist Association have shown that once a center of authority is established, it tends to grow in the power, rights, and command of loyalties earlier com-

---

[37] In the American political system the primaries and the national conventions and, to a degree, postelection negotiations over participation in the cabinet provide such a multilayer consensus-formation structure. Thus, for instance, the struggle over the presidential and vice-presidential candidate is also a struggle over what policy the party is to face the electorate with. Once chosen, most segments of the party—liberal and conservative—tend, as a rule, to support the candidates and the policy. In the negotiations on participation in the cabinet, the party that lost the election is often given some indirect representation to enhance national support for what is a one-party administration.

manded by the units (as when states' rights declined and those of the federal government grew).[38] But a social unit can, by the use of ideological and political mechanisms, advance or retard this process. Only those units that encourage or at least allow the process to occur provide a sociopolitical foundation on which a world community might be erected.

Rules and enforcement: Another major process of community-building is the evolution of rules and of agencies for their enforcement. Here is much room for the application and further development of the sociology of law, which warns against relying excessively on legislation when there is only a narrow sociopolitical base. A premature and ineffectual world law might be worse than no law at all. Laws that are not backed by effective enforcement and adequate consensus, as illustrated by the abortive attempt to institute prohibition in the United States, breed contempt for the laws and their makers and nurture a whole range of previously unknown criminal interests. A premature world law on disarmament might well generate clandestine production of weapons and large profits to arms smugglers, and thereby lead to repeal of the law rather than to lasting disarmament.

The concern in the study of encapsulation is not so much with protecting the existing mechanism from erosion; it is, rather, with accelerating its extension and growth. Hence the importance of formalizing implicit and "understood" rules into explicit and enforced international laws becomes clear. This principle is neither obvious nor widely agreed upon. Many stress the value of implicit, unnegotiated understandings. For instance, after the Soviet Union removed its missiles from Cuba late in 1962, the United States removed its Thor and Jupiter missiles from Turkey and Italy in 1963, without such reciprocation ever being publicly discussed, let alone negotiated. (Even today, it is not clear that this was a deliberate act of reciprocation.)

There are several disadvantages in reaching agreement in this particular way, especially for community-building efforts. The danger of misunderstanding is larger, especially when matters are complex. When misunderstandings occur, they generate bitter feelings of betrayal and mistrust, which, in turn, stand in the way of future exchanges. Further, the community's institutions do not gain in experience and responsibility unless implicit understandings are codified and enforced by them. This is not to suggest that the path of implicit understanding should not be traveled, but only that unless an enlarging flow of such traffic is directed through world institutions, they will remain the dirt roads rather than the highways of international relations.

---

[38] Paul M. Harrison, *Authority and Power in the Free Church Tradition* (Princeton, New Jersey: Princeton University Press, 1959), especially the chapter on power and authority in the church.

When rules are formalized, effective verification and response machinery is necessary. The 1954 agreements to neutralize Laos and limit arms supplies for Vietnam were supervised by an understaffed, underfinanced, ill-equipped, and above all politically deadlocked commission. (Its members were India, Poland, and Canada.) In 1959 East and West accused each other of violating these agreements; the enforcement machinery provided neither a clear picture of who was the first to violate the agreements nor an appropriate response.

We have examined the ways societal bonds may be built up among previously less integrated societal units; we illustrated the factors by drawing upon the relations among nations, but similar statements about the role of increased communication, varying power constellations, the functions of intermediary bodies (or subgroupings) upon building consensus, and the role of developing shared laws all apply to the relations among the parts of an underdeveloped country or the races in one society. In all these systems, the more favorable these factors are, the more and stronger societal bonds we expect, and the more powerful these bonds — for reasons discussed earlier — the less intergroup violence is to be expected. But the potency of the societal bonds is not the only factor in determining the level of violence; the particular way members bound together relate to each other is another major factor in accounting both for group and personal violence.

Violence-Prone Structures

Each society can be viewed as a set of distributions. Society has economic assets, annual income, educational opportunities, prestige, power — but who gets what? Sociologists ask this question not in terms of individuals but for large groupings of people. For instance, the annual income of the United States is divided in such a way that the 20 percent of the population in the "lowest" end of the income distribution receives 5 percent of the total national income, while another 20 percent (the "highest") receives 45 percent.[39] While the distributions of various assets are not the same, and all change over time, those at the top of one distribution tend to get a very disproportionate share of most of what is to be had. And those at the bottom of one distribution tend to be at the bottom of most other distributions. If you look at higher education as an asset, among those families whose income is $15,000 or more, 87 percent of the children attend college, compared with 41 percent

---

[39] Paul A. Samuelson, *Economics: An Introductory Analysis,* 6th ed. (New York: McGraw-Hill, 1964), p. 115.

of the children in middle-income homes, and 20 percent in those earning less than $3,000 a year.[40]

Being given a disproportionately low share does not by itself cause much violence; it is a universal condition in which some groups in most, if not all, societies find themselves (although there are significant differences in degree). However, once a group—a class, a race, an age category—has become aware of its deprived status, and is mobilized to act on it, intergroup tension and conflicts mount. (Mobilization is frequently initiated by intellectuals and leaders who are not themselves members of the group, but anger soon is internalized and the conflict is taken over by those who are members.) The rise in tensions and conflicts may cause no violence if reallocation follows, or if some project that all groups will share in equally is advanced, such as opening up new territories or stimulating the economy into rapid growth.

But if the structure is rigid, and no reallocations occur after the society is faced with rising demands, tensions and conflicts are likely to escalate to a level where violence is highly probable. This does not mean that the demanded reallocations, or more generally, social justice, will follow. Those who have most of what there is may, despite the violence, use their power to keep the new demands at bay. Or some accommodations will be made to reduce, maybe only temporarily and partially, the new violence (say, riots in slums). Or those in power may be ousted in a revolution and a new disproportionate allocative pattern set up. Whatever the final accommodation, a rise in violence is the price of undue rigidity.

Processes: The Mechanisms of Change

The strength of the societal bonds and the "slant" of the societal structure affect the level of violence. So does the flexibility of the processes that allows for adaptation to changes in the environment and in the relations among the members constituting a society. Each society has a set of procedures and processes whose function is to keep adjusting the societal bonds and structure to the changing relations among the group members. These are mainly political processes, such as in lobbying, legislation, presidential action, and so on. Those processes differ in two ways: (1) their efficacy in keeping the societal bonds and structure responsive to new mobilized demands, even if it entails far-reaching transformation of both, and (2) the extent to which they themselves—by the way they operate—encourage or discourage escala-

---

[40] *Ibid.* The year referred to is 1962.

tion of conflicts to a violent level. For instance, in some Latin American societies the armed forces act like interest groups and the government is adjusted to reflect the changing relations among the Army, Navy, and Air Force, and the social groups they are allied with. The procedures in such adjustments are the renegotiation of cabinet membership and the marshaling of divisions by each service. Often this is very peaceful; at one point, it is told, the president of a Latin American republic sent a telegram to each of six commanders who were marching on the capital to ask whom they favored, and the future composition of the government was reflected in their answers. But violent clashes among the armed services occasionally do erupt. The ballot box is a less violence-prone mechanism, aside from the fact that it is much more participatory.

But voting, petitions, and the other means of democratic adjustment may not suffice for the vast social changes contemporary society must respond to. To illustrate response-producing processes and their effects on the level of violence, the author reports briefly one of his own studies of the newest one — that of demonstrations.

DEMONSTRATION DEMOCRACY: AN EXAMPLE—*Webster* defines a demonstration as "the act of making known or evident by visible or tangible means. . . a public display of group feeling." Demonstrations are thus public acts designed to express or call attention to a position. The specific features of demonstrations — from carrying placards to obstructionist acts — are intimately tied to this wish to make a position "visible or tangible," and this characteristic distinguishes demonstrations from more routine forms of expression, such as participation in a town meeting or party convention. In this sense demonstrations are still an extraordinary, not entirely institutionalized, means of political expression.

Each generation of Americans evolves its own procedures to sustain and reinforce democracy. Our generation is characterized by the evolution of new means of mass communication, notably television; by an increased political mobilization of underprivileged groups; and by increasingly complex bureaucratic structures — in government, education, religion, and other areas. Demonstrations are a particularly effective means of political expression, in an age of television, for underprivileged groups to advance their interests and, more generally, to prod stalemated bureaucracies into taking necessary actions. Indeed demonstrations are becoming part of the daily routine of contemporary democracy and may be its most distinctive mark.

Today's American citizen has available a number of alternative forms of political action during the long periods between elections and for dealing with the numerous "private governments" not directly responsible to the electorate, such as universities, hospitals, or churches. In addition to writing letters to his representatives, submitting petitions, advertising in the press, and supporting organized pressure groups, a citizen may demonstrate to make known his views when expression through other means has brought no, or only inadequate, redress. In this sense demonstrations are becoming for the citizen the avenue that strikes have become for the workers. Like strikes, demonstrations—especially in this early stage of their evolution—entail a danger: They may escalate into obstructionism or violence. For a democracy to function effectively, it is essential that the modes of political expression be both nonviolent and effective. That is, the inevitable differences of viewpoint, interest, and belief must be worked out peacefully and the legitimate needs of all the member groups of the society must be taken into account. To suppress all demonstrations because they are a volatile means of expression would be both impossible under our present form of government and inconsistent with the basic tenets of the democratic system, in that it would deprive the citizens—especially disadvantaged ones—of a political tool.

The number of participants in demonstrations seems to be increasing and includes an increasingly large proportion of the members of society. In one month chosen at random, 216 demonstrations were reported in the United States, or about seven per day. This figure is certainly an understatement of the actual number. It is very likely that many cases went unreported. Antiwar demonstrations in the United States, for example, have grown almost continuously since spring 1965, from approximately 100,000 participants in one-quarter of the year to about 280,000.[41] Students produced at least 221 demonstrations in 101 colleges between January 1 and June 15, 1968, involving 38,911 participants, according to a study conducted by the National Student Association.

Demonstrations are often viewed as the political tool of only a few dissenting groups, such as students and blacks. Actually, the number and variety of social groups resorting to this mechanism, at least on occasion, seem to be increasing. This is not to suggest that all social groups demonstrate with equal frequency. Blacks and students do demonstrate much more often than other groups. But members of such professional groups as teachers and social workers, who rarely took part in demonstrations a decade ago, now do so fairly frequently. A very large number of the antiwar demonstrators are white, middle-class citizens, as well as "respectable" professionals. Three hundred doctors, nurses, researchers, and others from the medical profession demonstrated against the war in Vietnam outside the Bellevue Hospital compound. Several hundred clergymen held a silent vigil near the Pentagon

---

[41] Jerome H. Skolnick, *The Politics of Protest* (New York: Ballantine, 1969), p. 32.

on May 12, 1965. Lawyers demonstrated against the invasion of Cambodia in May, 1970. Demonstrations have been extended to other issues also. On several Sundays in September and October, 1968, parishioners demonstrated near Catholic churches in Washington, D. C., to protest sanctions against priests who did not support the Pope's edict against artificial birth control. Even the staffs of law-enforcement agencies have not refrained from demonstrating; on October 1, 1968, about 100 "welfare patrolmen" picketed New York City's Social Services Department.

There are basically three kinds of demonstrations: Those which are entirely nonviolent and legal, such as a march following the issuance of a permit and in accord with its restrictions; obstructionist demonstrations, which entail, for example, blocking the traffic on a street, the entrance to a school, or the movement of construction equipment, and, as a rule, some degree of civil disobedience; and violent demonstrations, which may include the throwing of missiles, fist fights, beatings, arson, and even shooting—clearly illegal acts.

Contrary to the impression that seems to prevail in many quarters, the majority of demonstrations begin, are carried out, and end peacefully. Of the 216 incidents studied, 134 (or 62 percent) were reported to be peaceful, 7 (3 percent) involved an act of obstruction, and 75 (35 percent) were violent. Of the 75 incidents that included violence, the reporting of 11 incidents was not clear enough on this point to allow us to specify the initiator of the violence. The violence in 26 of the demonstrations was initiated not by the demonstrators but by other groups—either those opposed to the demonstrators or their cause (in 17 incidents) or the police (in nine cases). In 38 cases, violence seems to have been started by the demonstrators—in only 17.5 percent of the total number of demonstrations.

Wide segments of the public do not distinguish between peaceful demonstrations—which are a legal and constitutional means of political expression—and violent demonstrations or riots. And these segments of the public condemn demonstrations indiscriminately. For instance, 74 percent of the adults questioned in a poll in California expressed disapproval of the student demonstrations at Berkeley in 1964 although they were nonviolent up to that point. Asked explicitly about the right to engage in peaceful demonstrations —"against the war in Vietnam"—40 percent of the people sampled in both December, 1966, and July, 1967, felt that the citizenry had no such right. Fifty-eight percent were prepared to "accept" such demonstrations "as long as they are peaceful," showing a majority of the public to be unaware that such demonstrations have the same legal status as writing a letter to a congressman or participating in a town meeting.

The situation is somewhat similar to the first appearances of organized, peaceful labor strikes. Not only the owners and managers of industrial plants but also broad segments of the public at the beginning of the century did not recognize the rights of workers to strike if their grievances were unheeded, and to picket factories peacefully if such actions did not involve violating the rights of others (e.g., occupying the plant or physically preventing people from coming or going). Strikes are widely accepted now. According to a Harris Poll of March 27, 1967, "the majority (77 percent of those sampled) feels that the refusal to work is the ultimate and legitimate recourse for union members engaged in the process of collective bargaining." Gradually the public is likely to accept the legitimacy of peaceful demonstrations more completely.

It should be noted in this context that as more of the public learned to accept strikes, violent strikes became less frequent. Of course, other factors are in part responsible for the decrease in labor-management violence, the most important of which seems to have been the increased readiness to respond to the issues raised by the strikers rather than responding merely to the act of striking. It is to be expected that reactions to peaceful demonstrations will undergo similar transformations both in the public mind and in the relevant institutions. Thus demonstrations, especially peaceful ones, are one major new way societal structure and bonds may be made more responsive or kept responsive.

The function of demonstrations is *not* to "cool it," to provide an inauthentic solution, but to make the needed changes that will result in a reduction of tension. If the poor are rebelling because they are unable to earn a living, because welfare payments have been cut, because their schools do not educate, and their houses are falling apart, measures such as setting up a television set in public squares on hot nights and sending baseball heroes to tour the community do not constitute adaptive mechanisms. These measures may postpone the explosion, which may well be more violent when it finally erupts. Negotiating with the neighborhood about the construction of a housing project, which will employ men from the community, which will provide opportunities for training-on-the-job as well as an immediate rise in income and prestige, constitutes a much more meaningful and effective way of dealing with the tensions.

THE TECHNOLOGY OF VIOLENCE: CAUSE OR SYMPTOM?

We saw that man's nature permits violence and that his motivations and cognitions affect the level of violence he resorts to. We then enlarged our canvas and took in the broader societal context: the cohesion of society; its shape and its flexibility are all closely related to the level of violence. We close by looking at the tools of man, the technologies of violence. Do "wars start in the minds of men"? Or does the technology of violence command a force of its own? Seeking to curb violence, should we deal with arms or the "deeper" causes of conflict? Interestingly, this question is debated upon both international and intranational levels.

International Arms Races

Some people see the main source of danger in the very existence of arms, especially the new thermonuclear weapons. In this view, man can regain control of his fate by reasserting his control over the development of weapons. Arms races follow their own "logic." "The increase of armaments that is intended in each nation to produce consciousness of strength and a sense of security, does not produce these effects. On the contrary, it produces a consciousness of the strength of other nations and a sense of fear," wrote the British foreign secretary, Sir Edward Gray, at the outbreak of World War I.[42] Every nation that arms for its own security is simultaneously the "other nation." Arming for security often leads to arming for defense by the "other nation." The defensive intent of the arms built up by the other nation is rarely so regarded by the first nation. It rather sees in the other's new arms evidence of its hostile intent; the first nation often sees no alternative but a new rush of armaments—for security. Hence one major approach to the prevention of war is to reduce armaments. If the nuclear genie were somehow to be returned to the bottle, the main new danger of war would be erased. If military arms could be entirely eliminated, it is argued, there would be no war.

An opposing view suggests that arms are chiefly the symptoms of deep-seated conflicts. If there were no hostile motivations, people would not produce arms; even if there were triggers, they would not pull them. The people of Canada do not fear American nuclear bombardment. "War starts in the minds of men," says the charter of UNESCO. Curbing arms, it is said, is like treating only the symptoms of disease, without identifying and treating the illness. The treatment is unlikely to be successful, and if successful, other symptoms will soon break out elsewhere. Disarmament, if ever

---

[42] Lewis F. Richardson, *Arms and Insecurity* (Pittsburgh: Boxwood, 1960), p. 15.

achieved, will be followed not by peace, but by rearmament. What is needed is a treatment for the underlying conflicts of ideology and interest, the clash of powers.[43]

A third position seems more tenable. This one conceives of arms as both a symptom and a contributory cause that must be treated. The malaise that results in the arms race and war is a deep one; basically, it expresses man's willingness to treat his fellow man as an object rather than as an end in himself, to the point of turning him into a perishable utensil. The complete cure of this malaise requires providing the social foundations for a world community, since only members of a community treat each other as goals as well as means. If such a global community can be built at all, it will surely be a long process; meanwhile, mankind might destroy itself. The world society in the nuclear age is like a patient running a high fever: Until we determine and treat the sources of this fever, some measures must be taken to reduce the fever itself if the patient is to survive. But obviously, this treatment of the symptoms must be accompanied and followed by treatment of the disease itself.[44]

Furthermore, while the main causes of war seem to lie outside the propelling force and spell of armaments, the pressures of the military establishments are more than a symptom; they are a contributory cause. The military services, as a rule, demand larger defense budgets, not their curtailment[45]; the military's power, prestige, and—to a degree—income are affected by the size of these budgets. Most industries set up or extended to serve the military can turn elsewhere for their business, but the shift involves, at the least, the costs and pains of transition. Congressmen are known to lobby against closing military bases in their districts, and since each district has a congressman—and many at least one military installation—it is hard to sustain a broad reduction of arms without evoking some political resistance. This holds true not simply for missile sites or naval yards. The production of nuclear warheads in the United States was continued beyond the point of need, as estimated by most military experts, in part because congressmen whose states

---

[43] For both sides of this debate see John Burton, *Peace Theory* (New York: Knopf, 1962); Herbert C. Kelman, ed., *International Behavior* (New York: Holt, 1965); Evan Luard, *Peace and Opinion* (London: Oxford University Press, 1962); and Walter Millis, *An End to Arms* (New York: Atheneum, 1965).

[44] For a good review article of various approaches to the "symptoms and disease" question, see Philip Green, "Alternatives to Overkill: Dream and Reality," *Bulletin of the Atomic Scientists* (November, 1963), pp. 23–27.

[45] This holds for the Soviet Union as well. See, for instance, Colonel S. Kozlov, *Armed Forces Communist* (January, 1961), in *Survival* (July-August, 1961), p. 160.

had employment problems feared deeper unemployment.[46] Added to these extrinsic interests in the production of arms come the intrinsic pressures to expand the military system continually, for building one component generates a call for others. Bombers are of little use without runways. Runways are of little value if they are not protected from bombardment. The commanders of the bomber fleets have to be sheltered. Thus armed systems tend to produce some extrinsic and intrinsic pressures for their expansion. When a point is reached where the original reason for building up armaments might have declined or disappeared, special efforts are still required if arms are to be reduced. Simply treating the original causes will not suffice.

Finally, armaments contribute to the potential of war through psychological consequences. Arms build-ups express and magnify hostilities; arms reductions tend to indicate efforts to move toward an accommodation. Russia's abrupt resumption of the testing of thermonuclear bombs in 1961, after a three-year moratorium, was taken by the United States as a hostile and aggressive act. The 1963 Soviet-American agreement on partial cessation of thermonuclear tests, though of limited disarmament value, was hailed as heralding a new period in East-West relations. In other words, arms reductions can be used to create the atmosphere in which the "treatment" of the deeper causes of war can be better achieved, in much the way that reducing the fever of the patient enables him to survive long enough for antibiotics to take effect.

National Arms

A surprisingly similar issue exists in domestic politics. On the one hand, there are those who hold that the prevalence of guns, pistols, and other arms —there are an estimated 100 million—is a major reason that the United States has a higher rate of homicides, suicides, and fatal firearms accidents than most other industrialized countries. On the other hand, there are those who hold that arms are only a symptom, that individuals intent on murder or suicide will simply adopt other means if weapons are not available. Most specialists in the area are in the first category. The National Rifle Association, gun collectors, sportsmen, and gun manufacturers tend to be in the second group. Illustrating his view that there is no relationship between the availability of firearms and the occurrence of homicides, the N.R.A.'s

---

[46] James Reston, *The New York Times* (December 18, 1963), p. 40.

president told a visiting reporter that "there are twenty weapons in this office that I could use to kill you, and you won't find a single gun in the room. This dictating machine. The telephone. That picture frame—I could kill you with any of them if I wanted to badly enough."[47]

Much of the evidence suggests that effective domestic disarmament would save thousands of lives. A comparison of homicides committed by the use of guns in states with strong gun laws and those with weak ones supports the point. There are weak laws in Mississippi, Texas, and Florida; in these states guns were used, respectively, in 71, 69, and 66 percent of all murders during the four years ending in 1965. In three states with strong laws—New Jersey, Massachusetts, and New York—the comparable rates were 38, 35, and 32 percent.

The same point holds in cross-nation comparisons. Firearms control is strict in other nations. Britain requires a certificate from local police before a long gun can be purchased. There, guns account for 10 percent of all homicides, compared to 60 percent in the United States. France requires police permits for handguns and military rifle purchases; Canada requires registration of all handguns; in Sweden a need must be proved before gun ownership is allowed. In these nations homicide with handguns or long guns seldom occurs as against the high rates in the United States. As a very high proportion of homicides in the United States involves guns, their elimination would sharply reduce the total homicide rate. Much of the killing is done "in hot blood." Of the 13,650 homicides committed in 1968 in the United States, roughly 65 percent were relatives and acquaintances. Were weapons not so readily available, people would have more chance to calm down. When a knife is used, studies show that in four out of five instances the wound is not fatal.

Because of the vocal and powerful opposition to domestic disarmament, the national policy tends to focus instead on arms limitation and reduction. Various gun control measures enacted and under consideration impose only a set of restrictions, most of them not very consequential in reducing the actual availability of guns to the criminals, relatives, and acquaintances who do most of the killing. In short, firearms have an effect of their own; if they were seriously restricted, or, still better, removed, there would be a lot less killing.

The enormous costs of major societal reforms have encouraged societal planners to look for technological short cuts or "fixes." These are to provide a quick, low-cost, but effective way to reach the desired reforms, by using tools, machines, drugs, or some other nonsocial and nonpsychic procedure.

---

[47] *The New York Times* (June 8, 1968).

Examples of such "fixes" include the administration of drugs that terminate the desire for heroin, alcohol, or cigarettes, and the use of teaching machines to promote learning. In light of these applications, the question arises: Can violent crime also be treated in this way?

The answer depends in part on a more precise formulation of the question. If "treated" is taken to mean "eliminated," the answer is definitely negative. However, the answer is quite likely to be affirmative if the question is reformulated to ask: Can violent crime be reduced very significantly, say by more than one-half? The level of violent crime depends on a complex interaction among personal and societal pressures and on the tools that are available. Curbing the available instruments will reduce the fatalities caused by criminals, even if the motivational and the structured predispositions to engage in crime will remain untouched by these efforts.

Ultimately, the level of violence is affected by the interaction of motivational and cognitive, "psychological," forces; societal bonds, structures, and procedures; and the technologies available to the violent. Hence there is no isolated, basic treatment of violence. Surely one can guard presidents better, put more locks on one's doors against criminals, and be more tolerant of peaceful demonstrations. But only a just and cohesive society, responsive to new demands, satisfying old ones, providing a meaningful life to its members, would sharply reduce violence, and even such a society would not eliminate it. The single most effective short-run cure is to remove the weapons. The single most important long-run cure is to supply the needs of those who have been excluded from most of what society offers.

15

Youth
and Politics

SEYMOUR M. LIPSET

"Generation Gap" has been a misleading euphemism used to describe the
emergence of a serious division in the United States and many other countries
during the 1960's. That decade witnessed the revival of an intense commitment to politics, to the effort to change major aspects of society and the
polity. To a considerable degree, those who were most deeply involved in the
effort have been young—the confrontation style of political action practiced
by leftist university students has won the attention of the media and the
politicians. More often than not, the latter have seen the new forms of political action as representing a generation gap, as reflecting the different
interests and values of the young in comparison with older age groups. But
a careful examination of the available evidence clearly indicates that the
conflict that divides America most significantly is not primarily a matter of
age. The fundamental cracks in society can be seen most clearly by examin-

This chapter summarizes and includes much of what I have written elsewhere
concerning youth and student conflict. See especially S. M. Lipset and Earl Raab,
The Politics of Unreason: Right-Wing Extremism in America 1790–1970 (New York:
Harper, 1970), pp. 370–72, 418–20, 513–14; and S. M. Lipset, "The Dimensions of Stu-
dent Involvement," Part I, Chapters 1–7, in S. M. Lipset and Gerald Schaflander,
They Would Rather Be Left (Boston: Little, Brown, 1971). I am indebted to Bartley
Horwitz for assistance and The Salk Institute for providing the environment in which
this essay could be completed.

ing differences that exist *within* the younger generation rather than by looking at the variations between generations.

For example, in the election of 1968, millions of young people (under 30) rejected both Nixon and Humphrey because they were too "liberal" and voted for George Wallace; in the same election another group of youth turned away from Nixon and Humphrey because they were too "conservative."[1] They would have preferred to vote for Senator Eugene McCarthy, or a leftist fourth party candidate. The image of youth as radical, "bohemian," and wild in their personal styles also does not hold up when subject to empirical scrutiny.

Karl Mannheim suggested the concept of "generation-units" which have disparate identities or views within the same generation or temporal span. It is clear that there are significantly different generation-units among the youth of today. The views they hold are *not* new, for the most part. In a real sense, they are generation-units which maintain a continuity with certain generation-units of the past. That is to say, they continue certain singular perceptions and identities which cross age and generational lines.

It is true, however, that young people extend and dramatize the views which they foster because of certain qualities peculiar to youth. If behavior may be seen as a combination of impulse and restraint, then young people have been much more likely to press for the attainment of their goals without concern for the counterproductive consequences their actions may have. Aristotle pointed out the lack of youthful restraint 2500 years ago. Since then, Martin Luther, Karl Marx, Max Weber, and a multitude of others have stressed the propensity of youth to emphasize ideals—ends—rather than means, to err on the side of zeal, rather than of caution. The propensity of youth to zealously pursue an ideal can be seen as a direct outgrowth of the socialization process. Societies teach youth to adhere to the basic values of the social system in absolute terms. This emphasis on absolute values, on idealism, has understandable consequences for the beliefs of youth.

The real world, of course, necessarily deviates considerably from the ideal, and part of the process of maturing is to learn to function in a world of conflicting values, roles, interests, and demands. Compromises which are dictated by contradictory pressures and are justified in the eyes of many adults are viewed by idealistic youth as violations of basic morality. Young people tend to be committed to ideals rather than institutions. Hence events which point up the gap between ideals and reality often stimulate them to

---

[1] See S. M. Lipset and Earl Raab, *The Politics of Unreason: Right-Wing Extremism in America 1790–1970,* pp. 362–70, 393–94. Philip E. Converse, Warren E. Miller, Jerrold F. Rusk, and Arthur C. Wolfe, "Continuity and Change in American Politics: Parties and Issues in the 1968 Election," *American Political Science Review,* Vol. 63 (December, 1969), pp. 1103–04.

action, though cynicism and withdrawal occur as well if they see no appropriate way to act.

But commitment comes in many forms. Being patriotic is a form of altruistic behavior, as is being a committed antiwar pacifist who refuses to serve in the armed services. The youth of most churches tend to be more idealistic than the adults. Many denominations have had trouble with their young parishioners, who denounce the older members for not living up to the principles of the church. Political parties of all varieties have also had difficulty with their youth affiliates. Young conservatives, Republicans, or right-wingers have frequently attacked their older colleagues for their moderation, their willingness to conciliate liberals. Conversely, young liberals, Democrats, socialists, radicals also have demanded that their elders practice what they preach. Mussolini had trouble with his young followers who saw fascism in power as betraying the doctrinal objectives of the party. Mao turned to the youth for support, when he apparently sought in the late 1960's to return the Chinese Communist party to greater ideological purity.

RIGHT-WING YOUTH MOVEMENTS

Movements which seek to change social systems, whether defined as leftist or rightist, necessarily look to the youth on their side of the political spectrum for support. The Italian Fascist party glorified youth. Its anthem began *"Giovinezza, giovinezza, primavera di bellezza. . . ."* – "Youth, youth, springtime of beauty. . . ." Before its seizure of power, fascism was largely an anti-system youth party.[2] Few Fascist leaders, other than Mussolini, were over 30 years of age. The German Nazi party also worked hard at creating an image of itself as the party of youth which would end the reactionary system dominated by old men. Like Italian fascism, it had extensive support among university students and other groups of young people.[3]

The young Fascists and Nazis were mainly the children of right-wing nationalists or conservatives. They went further faster along the ideological road than their parents. Conversely, young socialist workers in Italy and Germany moved in the direction of the Communists, who also gained during

---

[2] Daniel Guerin, *Fascism and Big Business* (New York: Pioneer, 1939), pp. 47–50, 62–63.

[3] Daniel Guerin, *Fascism and Big Business,* pp. 48–50, 63; Karl Bracher, *Die Auflösung der Weimarer Republik* (Villengen, Schwarzwald: Ring Verlag, 1964), pp. 146–49.

the crises preceding the overthrow of democracy. One should not, therefore, speak of a generation gap between German or Italian youth and their parents, but rather of different generation-units.

This point may also be illustrated in reference to the United States in recent years. Although, as noted earlier, heavy attention has been given to the radical activities of college youth, another significant and identifiable generation-unit, which in tone resembles the Fascist supporters of earlier decades, has surfaced, revealing a yawning intrageneration gap. This less publicized generation-unit can be identified by examining the support which George Wallace received in 1968. Both the Gallup and Harris polls reported in a number of their preelection surveys that one-quarter of the younger voters (under 30) were for Wallace as compared with one-fifth of the older voters. This disproportion between the age groups occurred in both southern and nonsouthern states. Postelection surveys indicated that in the northern states there had been a 13 percent Wallace bite into the vote at the 21-to-25-year-old level, compared to 3 percent at the 50-plus level. This pattern held at all educational levels.[4] A higher proportion of younger voters were likely to have voted for Wallace, whether they were grade school, high school, or college graduates. Of course, an extremely small number of Wallace voters in general were college graduates. A poll taken a month before the election indicated that 25 percent of people 18 to 24 years old who were not in college expressed a preference for Wallace, in contrast to 7 percent of those who were in college. One of the social conditions of the intragenerational gap in America is already apparent.

To interpret Wallace's appeal to youth, it is necessary to recognize that it was more expressive of backlash than of racism. Backlash is the attempt to recover status which seems to be slipping away, which often uses racism or nativism as its ideological justification. Right-wing extremist movements in America have all risen against the background of economic and social changes which have resulted in the displacement of some population groups from former positions of dominance in values, status, or power terms.

The relations between the Wallace movement and the American workingman are a classic case in point. Much journalistic attention has been given to the sense of displacement which is felt by the working-class and lower-middle-class whites. There have been hard problems on the surface: inflation, taxes, crime, public disorder. But as *Newsweek* stated after its poll of White America: ". . . the Middle American malaise cuts much deeper — right to those fundamental questions of the sanctity of work and the stability

[4] S. M. Lipset and Earl Raab, *The Politics of Unreason: Right-Wing Extremism in America 1790–1970,* pp. 367–69, 371–72, 394.

of the family, of whether a rewarding middle-class life is still possible in modern America."⁵ Behind it all is a sense of powerlessness, of lessening influence with the "establishment," of diminishing social and political status. This disaffection has been felt no less, and in some ways more intensely, by the working-class youth. Sociologists William Simon, John H. Gagnon, and Donald Carns comment:

> Now, as the post-industrial society advances and changes, the possibilities for working class youth to recognize themselves in the emerging images of man have significantly lessened. They may well be looking to society for some sense of confirmation as to who they are and who they might become, and they may be looking increasingly in vain. Part of the problem has been the failure of the society's cultural middle men, its intellectuals, even to begin to recognize this population. . . . [These] anti-establishment intellectuals may be hard to distinguish from the establishment itself. . . . For working class populations, particularly the young, these anti-establishment groups have become the establishment, at least to the degree that they set the tone for the surface imagery of our times. And, for example, much is said of the crisis of the colleges and the ghetto schools, both apparently requiring growing investments of society's resources. Does anyone for a moment think that the quality of education in the working class schools in this country — both public and parochial — is any better? That the slaughter of human potential and sensibility is any less severe? Or that a crisis of identity equal in magnitude to that of the children of the affluent middle class or those of the ghettos is not going on among the youth of the working class? . . . For him [the working class youth] racial integration (and the disruption of community life that he feels, not without justification, must follow) is part of an organized effort within which agents of government, the mass media, and even the church are co-conspirators. Thus he too becomes anti-establishment, but for him it is a liberal establishment, and before it he feels increasingly powerless. . . .⁶

This was the generation-unit among the young from which Wallace drew such disproportionately youthful support. This support was particularly noticeable in the subgroups that gave him considerable backing, such as union members and the police. Various analysts and pollsters noted that older unionists tended to be for Humphrey and to recall the economic gains that they had achieved under previous Democratic administrations. Young

---

⁵ "The Troubled Americans: A Special Report on the White Majority," *Newsweek* (October 6, 1969), p. 29.
⁶ William Simon, John H. Gagnon, and Donald Carns, "Working Class Youth: Alienation Without an Image," *New Generation*, Vol. 51 (Spring, 1969), pp. 16–17.

workers, however, took trade unions and prosperity for granted, and were more prone to defect either to Nixon or Wallace on issues of taxes, integration, crime in the streets, and the like. A private national poll of union members conducted before the national conventions found considerable discontent with unions among young workers, and a heavy predilection to back Wallace.[7] The same pattern of youthful discontent moving in a Wallace direction was reported by a *New York Times* reporter among the police.

> "What we're seeing, I think," said a police lieutenant in Lower Manhattan, "are dissident youth on the police force—like around the universities. They're exploding. They're fighting back against what they consider an intolerable situation." Just as there's a New Left on the campuses, there seems to be a New Right among some younger men in the Police Department.
>
> The lieutenant and several other police officials who were interviewed . . . stated [the New Right] was largely composed of men in their 20s who feel—perhaps more strongly than older men—the frustrations of being a policeman: hostility from some segments of the community, overt attacks in slum neighborhoods, the belief that political leaders are preventing them from enforcing the law forcefully enough, a persistent conviction that the police are abused in the courts while criminals are "coddled."[8]

Another journalist's report on the emergence of a militant right-wing organization among New York police, the Law Enforcement Group (LEG), suggested that it symbolized "a strong swing to the Right among . . . young policemen in particular." LEG is largely composed of younger policemen (one-third of New York's force consists of men under 30 years of age) while the "traditionally conservative Patrolmen's Benevolent Association (PBA) . . . [is] dominated by older men. . . ." The journalist continued:

> This accent on youth has worked to produce a far different picture of police-leftist frictions and clashes than is generally accepted. Instead of a confrontation between generations, between young radical demonstrators on the one side and wide-beamed, middle-aged cops on the other, the emerging picture portrays a collison of contemporaries. In their own way, these young officers of the right have been as displeased with the current state of the republic as their opposite numbers in the New Left.[9]

---

[7] S. M. Lipset and Earl Raab, *The Politics of Unreason: Right-Wing Extremism in America 1790–1970*, p. 369.

[8] Sylvan Fox, "Many Police in City Leaning to the Right," *New York Times* (September 6, 1968), p. 49.

[9] Richard Dougherty, "Confrontation between New Left and New Right Emerges in N.Y.," *Boston Sunday Globe* (September 29, 1968), p. 16.

The white youth who want to maintain the traditional society, the promise of which they feel is being stripped away by liberal changes, are clearly a key generation-unit in America. They have been countered by another major unit, composed of those who want to change the traditional society just enough so that they can get into it for the first time. They include the majority of black youth. Whatever polls and studies one looks at, it is clear that at least three-quarters of the embittered black youth are angered not by the system, but by their failure to get into it. They want a materialistically rich American industrial society in which the distribution of money and power is drastically changed. They are supported by the ideologically radical students, both black and white, who see in the frustration of the black slum youth an opportunity to find a mass base outside of the university with which to change society in radical directions. But the frustrated black youth, in a curious sense, have been closer in their objectives to the Wallace youth: neither is concerned with basically overthrowing the system, but rather with bringing it closer to them—with gaining "more."

ANTISYSTEM TENDENCIES

Thus far we have seen two generation-units composed of those who are committed to keeping the existing social structure but who seek to maintain *or* change the reward system, perceived largely in terms of the particular position of different racial groups. There are, however, two other groups, the radicals and the "renunciators," both largely composed of university students and their campus fellow travelers, often dropouts or recent graduates. These two segments are frequently confused with each other because, on the surface, their behavior, their antiestablishment beliefs, their total rejection of the system often seem the same. Yet in a real sense, the radicals are closer to the Wallace white youth, or the militant blacks, since all three are basically concerned with *owning* Western society. The renunciators are essentially interested in *disowning* Western society. The term "renunciation" is clearly inadequate, yet it is useful, for it would certainly be a mistake to identify this tendency as "radical" or "revolutionary." In fact, in its rejection of much of the modern world, especially the use of large scale technology and urbanization, the renunciatory tendency is much closer in outlook to many classic conservative or reactionary doctrines. One reason for the difficulty in distinguishing the renunciatory tendency from the other forms of student protest is that there is, in fact, considerable overlap between the radicals and the renunciators. Many students move back and forth between them. Many radicals adopt renunciatory styles of dress and personal behavior. Most renunciators agree with the specific antisystem beliefs of the radicals.

The distinction between the radical and renunciatory tendencies among youth, or in society generally, is, of course, related to comparable distinctions drawn in other analyses. The sociologist David Matza has suggested that deviant behavior among youth may take one of three forms: delinquent, bohemian, or radical. All three are "specifically antibourgeois," that is, reject private property relations. Delinquency, however, "seems most pronounced among that section of youth which terminates its education during or at the end of high school. Radicalism and bohemianism, particularly in the United States, are apparently enmeshed within the system of higher education." The bohemians, as Matza uses the term—those who are "opposed to the mechanized, organized, centralized, and increasingly collectivized nature of modern capitalism"—come close to the concept of the renunciators.[10] The psychologist Kenneth Keniston has similarly differentiated between student deviants who are "alienated," apolitical, romantic, and esthetic in their orientation and those who are "activists," political, humanitarian and universalistic.[11]

More recently, another sociologist, Alvin Gouldner, has pointed to the emergence within the protest movement of a "Psychedelic Culture," which "differs profoundly from the protest movements and 'causes' of the 1930's, however politically radical, for Psychedelic Culture rejects the central values to which *all* variants of industrial society are committed. . . . [It] resists . . . routine economic roles whether high or low, inhibition of expression, repression of impulse, and all the other personal and social requisites of a society organized around the optimization of utility. Psychedelic Culture rejects the value of conforming usefulness, counterposing to it, as a standard, that each must 'do his thing.' In short, many, particularly among the young, are now orienting themselves increasingly to expressive rather than utilitarian standards, to expressive rather than instrumental politics. . . ."[12] Though it is possible to argue that the concepts of renunciators, bohemians, alienated, and psychedelic refer to somewhat different emphases, there is agreement among a number of observers that student rejection of the "system" involves two quite different social tendencies.

---

[10] David Matza, "Subterranean Traditions of Youth," *Annals of the American Academy of Political and Social Science,* Vol. 338 (November, 1961), p. 106, *passim.*

[11] Kenneth Keniston, "The Sources of Student Dissent," *Journal of Social Issues,* Vol. 23, No. 3 (1967), pp. 109–15.

[12] Alvin W. Gouldner, *The Coming Crisis of Western Sociology* (New York: Basic Books, 1970), p. 78.

PROTEST IN THE UNIVERSITY

The propensity of universities to be centers of radical and renunciatory behavior has long been noted. Thomas Hobbes, writing of the "Causes of the Civil Wars" in the mid-seventeenth century in his book *Behemoth,* stated unequivocally, "The Universities have been to this nation, as the wooden horse was to the Trojans. . . . The core of the rebellion, as you have seen by this, and read of other rebellions, are the Universities. . . ." The nineteenth century produced many similar comments concerning the inherently oppositional role of both students and scholars, even by relatively nonideological American observers. Thus a Yale graduate of the late 1830's, C. A. Bristed, who went on to study for five years at Cambridge University, during which time he also visited continental universities, concluded that the majority of students "under any government are opposed to the spirit in which that government is administered. Hasty and imperfect as the conclusion is, it certainly does hold good of many countries." He argued that the typical student "sees the defects in the government of his country; he exaggerates them with the ardor of youth, and takes that side which promises to remedy them, without reflecting at what cost the remedy may have to be purchased." [13] Numerous writers have suggested that the disposition of university youth to engage in antisystem activities is related to the fact that scholarship and other forms of creative intellectual work foster antagonism to dominant belief systems and institutions. Intellectuals, who are by role-definition concerned with creation or innovation and are partisans of the abstract or the ideal, are more disposed than others to sympathize and foster ideologies which reject the status quo in their particular society.[14] This thesis was expressed by an American intellectual, Whitelaw Reid, abolitionist and editor of the *New York Tribune,* as appropriate to this country, in addresses to various college audiences as early as 1873:

> Exceptional influences eliminated, the scholar is pretty sure to be opposed to the established. The universities of Germany contain the deadliest foes to the absolute authority of the Kaiser. The scholars of

[13] C. A. Bristed, *Five Years in an English University* (New York: Putnam, 1874), p. 61.
[14] I have discussed this general thesis and the evidence related to it in an article, "The Politics of Academia," in David C. Nichols, ed., *Perspectives on Campus Tensions* (Washington, D. C.: American Council on Education, 1970), pp. 85–118.

France prepared the way for the first Revolution, and were the most dangerous enemies of the imperial adventurer who betrayed the second. . . . While the prevailing parties in our country were progressive and radical, the temper of our colleges was to the last degree conservative. As our politics settled into the conservative tack, a fresh wind began to blow about the college seats, and literary men, at last, furnished inspiration for the splendid movement that swept slavery from the statute book. . . . Wise unrest will always be their [the scholars'] chief trait. We may set down . . . the very foremost function of the scholar in politics, *To oppose the established.*

. . . As for the scholar, the laws of his intellectual development may be trusted to fix his place. Free thought is necessarily aggressive and critical. The scholar, like the healthy redblooded young man, is an inherent, an organic, an inevitable radical. . . . And so we may set down, as a second function of the American scholar in politics, *An intellectual leadership of the radicals.*[15]

The histories of various universities and social movements have documented the activities of students engaged in deviant, avant-garde, or revolutionary behavior in a number of countries. Renunciatory personal styles, including long hair among men and short hair among women, colored spectacles, dirty clothes and life style, and a stress on obscene language have been reported among students in France, Germany, and Russia in the century before World War I. Political protest was also a common phenomenon among European students. The nineteenth-century Russian revolutionary movement was almost entirely based in the university.[16] Students played a major role in protest movements in the Germanic states in the first half of the same

---

[15] "The Scholar in Politics" (a Commencement Address delivered at Dartmouth and Amherst Colleges, and before the alumni of Miami University),*Scribner's Monthly,* Vol. 6 (1873), pp. 613–14. (Emphasis in original) Twenty-eight years later, speaking at Stanford in 1901, an older Reid saw the same behavior by American academics as bad. "It is a misfortune for the colleges, and no less for the country, when the trusted instructors are out of sympathy with its history, with its development, and with the men who made the one and are guiding the other." Whitelaw Reid, *American and English Studies,* Vol. I (New York: Scribner's, 1913), pp. 241–423.

[16] Bernard Pares, *Russia Between Reform and Revolution* (New York: Schocken, 1962), pp. 180–81, see generally pages 161–282; Anatole Leroy-Beaulieu, *The Empire of the Tsars and the Russians,* Part II, "The Institutions" (New York: Putnam, 1894), pp. 486–87; Gabor Kiss, *Die gesellschaftspolitische Rolle der Studentenbewegung im vorrevolutionären Russland* (Munich: Georg Heller Verlag, 1963); Franco Venturi, *Roots of Revolution* (New York: Knopf, 1960), "The Student Movement," pp. 220–31, *passim;* George Fischer, *Russian Liberalism* (Cambridge: Harvard University Press, 1958), pp. 53–56; Jacob Walkin, *The Rise of Democracy in Pre-Revolutionary Russia* (New York: Praeger, 1962), pp. 129–32, 188–89, *passim;* S. M. Lipset, "Students and Politics in Underdeveloped Countries," *Minerva* 3 (Autumn, 1964), pp. 23–26; Lewis S. Feuer, *The Conflict of Generations* (New York: Basic Books, 1969), pp. 88–172.

century. Engels described them as "the nucleus, the real strength, of the revolutionary force" in the Revolution of 1848 in Vienna.[17] A contemporary Marxist history of the Paris Commune reported that students had played a leading role in all of the preceding French revolts during the century.[18]

Students, as C. Wright Mills pointed out, have remained an important source of leadership and mass support for antisystem movements, both of the "left" and "right," during the twentieth century.[19] During the mid-fifties, they were important in revolts in Communist Poland and Hungary. They have demonstrated in opposition to the Communist regimes in China (1956), Czechoslovakia (1967), Yugoslavia (1968 and 1970), and Poland (1968). Student movements helped bring down governments of varying orientations elsewhere in the world. During 1968, they produced the first massive protests against the dominant party systems of De Gaulle in France and the PRI (Party of the Institutional Revolution) in Mexico.

There are many explanations offered for the special readiness of a segment of the university youth to oppose the system. Some point to the inherent need of youth to find their own outlook, but clearly university students are normally much more disposed than other groups of young people to engage in protest. Students are marginal, between roles; that is, between the security and status derived from their families and the obligation to find a status of their own. Like all marginal men, they suffer from special insecurities, and also have special capacities to see the imperfections of society. They have more freedom than other segments of youth, and adults as well, to act without concern for consequences.[20] They are foot-loose, without economic or social obligations to restrain them, and with considerable energies to use up. Whatever outlet any particular group of them chooses to use, the ecology of the university, the easy communication among people on a campus, makes it possible for those who hold similar views to find one another. Out of their new awareness as members of an intellectual community, out of their detached and advantaged position, students are better able than most to recog-

---

[17] Henry M. Christman, ed., *The American Journalism of Marx and Engels* (New York: New American Library, 1966), p. 40.

[18] Prosper Oliver Lissagaray, *History of the Commune of 1871* (New York: Monthly Review Press, 1967), p. 91.

[19] C. Wright Mills, *Power, Politics and People* (New York: Ballantine, 1963), pp. 256–59.

[20] Daniel and Gabriel Cohn-Bendit, *Obsolete Communism* (New York: McGraw-Hill, 1968), p. 47. "The student, at least, in the modern system of higher education, still preserves a considerable degree of personal freedom, if he chooses to exercise it. . . . He can, if he so chooses, take extreme political positions without any personal danger; in general, he is not subjected to formal sanctions or even reprimands."

nize the inconsistencies around them and to afford the expression of disaffection thus produced in them.[21] Sometimes their horizons are limited to the institutions that are close by, the universities themselves, as in much of the nineteenth century; in periods of broad social ferment, however, the world and its problems are their oyster.

A SHORT HISTORY
OF AMERICAN STUDENT UNREST

Although European students have traditionally played a vigorous role as political protestors, American academic history indicates that our own students have their own lengthy tradition of dissent. There are many reports of early dissent and social protest by American students, including involvement in anti-British activities from 1770 on.[22] For one-half century after the American Revolution, students recurrently engaged in protests, some of them quite violent in character and many directed against the colleges. Samuel Eliot Morison, in his study of Harvard, noted: "The typical student of the early 1790s was an atheist in religion, an experimentalist in morals, a rebel to authority." [23]

Student opposition to the dogmatically conservative and orthodox beliefs enunciated by many colleges, religious institutions, and other parts of the established society did not reflect a generational conflict as such. Rather, the undergraduate student rebels, especially those who fought for religious freedom, were allied with that portion of the adult world which demanded a completely voluntaristic religious system. Harry Bowes, studying the student rebellions of 1790–1830, comments that student behavior reflected "the growing liberalism of the age, a liberalism which was impatient with puritanical restraint and in some cases with religion itself." The universities, as well as other parts of the society, tried "to crush what they termed as irreligious, immoral, and disorderly behavior," but failed.[24]

During the period between 1830 and 1900 there were few conflicts over

---

[21] See Talcott Parsons, "Youth in the Context of American Society," in Erik H. Erikson, ed., *Youth: Change and Challenge* (New York: Basic Books, 1963), p. 117.

[22] Much of this historical discussion is drawn from a forthcoming publication, S. M. Lipset, *The Dimensions of Student Involvement,* Section I of S. M. Lipset and Gerald Schaflander, *They Would Rather Be Left,* Chapters 4 and 5.

[23] Samuel Eliot Morison, *Three Centuries of Harvard* (Cambridge: Harvard University Press, 1936), p. 185.

[24] Harry P. Bowes, "University and College Student Rebellion in Retrospect and Some Sociological Implications" (Ed. D. Thesis, School of Education, University of Colorado, 1964), pp. 104–05.

belief systems or politics, although some student protest developed in the direction of nonconformist dress and the organization of abolitionist clubs.[25] Instead, protest took the form of violent antagonism toward members of the faculty.[26] Almost all of the organized student protests from 1880 to 1900 were against the schools and centered on such issues as *loco parentis,* curriculum content, administrative power, due process, student self-government, and the like. Many college presidents were toppled by demonstrations.[27]

After 1900, responding to the growth of socialist, progressive, and populist concerns among intellectuals and in the polity generally, a small minority of students linked their protests to an involvement in socialist politics.[28] By 1912, over 2000 students out of a national population of 400,000 belonged to the 60 chapters of the Intercollegiate Socialist Society, located largely at major institutions. Even more students, approximately 15,000, wishing to apply their values to social betterment, engaged not in radical or antiwar politics, but rather in the rapidly growing Settlement House movement. They worked directly with the oppressed immigrant poor in urban slums.[29] American entry into World War I brought an end to this movement, but a new set of radical activities, in part stimulated by reactions to the Russian Revolution, occurred with the return of peace. Student groups and newspapers reacted to the severe postwar repression, to industrial ills, and to militarism. Antiwar, progressive, and socialist clubs, which invited controversial speakers to the campus, sprang up around the country. Free speech became a major controversial issue at many colleges. "Students demanded the right to hear all sides of every question; conservative alumni, trustees, and citizens objected to colleges becoming a forum for radical views."[30]

While various forms of student protest developed during the 1920's, the renunciatory style characteristic of some of today's youth first surfaced in America in a specific cultural aspect of the same period. Henry May describes this time as the ". . . decade when the fragmentation first became deep and obvious . . . a period in which common values and common beliefs were replaced

---

[25] Russell Nye, *Fettered Freedom: Civil Liberties and the Slavery Controversy* (East Lansing: Michigan State University Press, 1949), p. 93.

[26] Lawrence R. Vesey, "The Emergence of the University" (Ph.D. Thesis, Department of History, University of California, Berkeley, 1962), pp. 164–65.

[27] George E. Peterson, *The New England College in the Age of the University* (Amherst, Mass.: Amherst College Press, 1954), pp. 113–48; Lewis S. Feuer, *The Conflict of Generations,* pp. 332–36.

[28] David A. Shannon, *The Socialist Party of America* (Chicago: Quadrangle, 1967), pp. 55–56; Ira Kipnis, *The American Socialist Movement 1897–1912* (New York: Columbia University Press, 1952), pp. 259–60.

[29] George E. Peterson, *The New England College in the Age of the University,* pp. 179–84.

[30] Ernest Earnest, *Academic Procession* (Indianapolis: Bobbs-Merrill, 1953), p. 265.

by separate and conflicting values."[31] It is not surprising that the 1920's experienced a "vast dissolution of ancient habits," to borrow phrase from Walter Lippman.[32] The enormous changes which had been going on in America for over a century seemed to be coming to a visible head in the 1920's. The 1920 census was the first in which the urban population exceeded the rural one. The number of people engaged in manufacturing had doubled. The number of young people attending college shot up from 4 percent at the turn of the century to 12 percent by the end of the 1920's. Basic premises were brought into serious question by the new encounters between new groups of people and, perhaps most dramatically, by the trauma of World War I.

The dissolution of past values lent itself to a kind of disaffection, not only with the political situation but also with the total set of classical, rationalistic assumptions on which American and Western society rested. This disaffection found expression through an identifiable generation-unit of youth who sought new forms of personal behavior: in freer sexual relations than previously, in a disregard of legal restraints on the consumption of alcoholic beverages, and in a generally "high style" of life.[33] For the first time educated Americans became aware of the gap between the values of those belonging to different generations. As Malcolm Cowley noted with reference to the short stories of F. Scott Fitzgerald, "the elders were discredited in their [the younger generation's] eyes by the war, prohibition, by the Red Scare of 1919–1920, and by scandals like that of Teapot Dome."[34]

The renunciatory youth not only rejected the traditional mores of American society, they also rejected the rational discourse of modern politics. Many of them wrapped their social protest and a kind of pseudopolitics around a form of cultural and intellectual nihilism. George Santayana referred in 1922 to "their scandalous failure in expression, when expression is what they yearn for and demand at all costs,"[35] much as six years earlier a more sympathetic observer, Randolph Bourne, had complained that the college radical and socialist clubs were "full of the unfocused and unthinking," and suggested that they would be more effective "by being more fiercely and concen-

---

[31] Henry May, "Shifting Perspectives on the 1920's," *The Mississippi Valley Historical Review,* Vol. 43 (1956–1957), p. 425.

[32] William Leuchtenberg, *The Perils of Prosperity* (Chicago: University of Chicago Press, 1958), p. 176.

[33] Kinsey documented one aspect of the breakdown in traditional mores when he reported a large increase in the proportion of females with premarital sexual experiences in the 1920's. Alfred C. Kinsey et al., *Sexual Behavior in the Human Female* (Philadelphia: Saunders, 1953), pp. 298–302.

[34] Ernest Earnest, *Academic Procession,* p. 249.

[35] George Santayana, "America's Young Radicals," *The Forum,* Vol. 67 (May, 1922), pp. 373–74.

tratedly intellectual." [36] In opposition to these views, some students objected to the dehumanizing effect of modern technology and the inappropriateness of scientific rationalism. As the most widely circulated national voice of student dissent phrased it: "A certain scholarly, scientific attitude must go. The values for which we are searching do not seem susceptible of proof, of capture by the 'scientific spirit.'" [37] Student rejection of the educational situation was sufficiently intense and widespread to cause the *New York World* to editorialize in 1925 about the "revolt which is going on in colleges and universities all over the country," against ROTC, abridgement of free speech, stupid courses, official history, and the like.[38]

The renunciatory pattern of the college elite was deflected by the Great Depression of the 1930's. That traumatic event did, of course, stimulate radical political protest in the form of social rationalism. The largest single left-wing radical group among young people was the Communist party. But the party was bitterly opposed to all forms of cultural deviance or personal exhibitions of nonconformity. At best, the Communists saw renunciatory behavior as politically counterproductive or, as Lenin put it, as a form of "infantile leftism"; at worst, the Communists identified it with the romantic antisystem beliefs of the young fascists.

The Communists apart, cultural protest and innovation were also inhibited by the concern with economic failure, which made most students yearn for security. *Fortune* magazine, conducting a national survey of college students in 1936, found that the "family as such is no longer an object of derision, as it was in the early twenties. Fathers and mothers are listened to once more. . . ." [39] An unpublished report of this first national sample of college youth suggests that many supported drastic structural changes on the economic level. Over two-thirds indicated that they favored changes in the Constitution to enable people "to live comfortably . . . even if this means a revision in our attitude about property rights." Yet close to 90 percent indicated that they subscribed to the conventional American belief that "there are plenty of employers who will give you satisfactory promotion in due course if you work hard and learn your job well." [40] Paradoxically, these three indicators

---

[36] Randolph S. Bourne, "The Price of Radicalism," *The New Republic,* Vol. 6 (March 11, 1916), p. 161.

[37] D. P. H., "This Paper," *The New Student,* Vol. 3 (October 20, 1923), pp. 1–2.

[38] "The Students Buck the Drill-Master," *The New York World* (November 18, 1925), as reprinted in *The New Student,* Vol. 5 (December 9, 1925), p. 15.

[39] "Youth in College," *Fortune,* Vol. 13 (June, 1936), pp. 99–102, 155–62.

[40] (Unpublished report of 1936 national college student study prepared by Cherington, Roper, and Wood.) I would like to thank Burns Roper for making this report available to me.

reinforce *Fortune*'s assessment that students were primarily concerned with security—with family acceptance, material comfort, and approval from authority.

Fear of the aggressive power of monolithic communism played the same role during the late 1940's and 1950's that communism and the Great Depression played during the 1930's. The movements toward renunciation and political protest were curtailed. In order to resist the new totalitarian threat posed by Stalinism, liberals and non-Communist leftists adopted the united-front tactic of the American Communists and concentrated solely on defeating the expansionist enemy, even to the point of sharply reducing criticism of the status quo. A more common interpretation credits the absence of left-wing activism in the United States to the domination by Senator Joe McCarthy. However, much the same pattern of intellectual and campus quiescence occurred in Western Europe and Canada during the 1950's. In many European countries, socialist parties changed their programs to eliminate reference to the "class struggle" and the goal of a socialist society. Left-wing intellectuals in Europe joined with nonsocialist ones in anti-Communist united fronts, much as they had done in anti-Fascist ones earlier.

This period came to an end with de-Stalinization in the Communist world. The break with Stalinism destroyed the image of a monolithic communism and revealed the presence of liberal, as well as polycentric, forces culminating in the Sino-Soviet split. The concept of a unified, totalitarian, expansionist foe was considerably weakened, and with its decline came a return of substantive criticism of Western society by intellectuals and students.

THE REVIVAL OF PROTEST AND RENUNCIATION

This change in ideological climate, as well as the rather rapid escalation of protest from words to action, was facilitated in the United States by the struggle for civil rights which emerged in the years following the Supreme Court's school desegregation decision of 1954. This was the perfect issue around which to create a new student protest movement, since it confronted the principal aspect of American society in which the system's actions were at sharp variance with its manifest creed of equality and democracy. Most Americans, and the university system *in toto,* recognized that Negro inequality is evil, and in principle, approved all actions designed to reduce or eliminate it. Hence race was the best issue around which the new political criticism could mobilize. Fighting segregation, particularly in the South, was not a radical act, yet the struggle contributed greatly to radicalizing sections of the young. In this particular situation, the conservative or traditionalist forces introduced the tactics of civil disobedience, and even of violence; that is, the Southern segregationists refused to accept the law as laid down by the Supreme Court and Congress, and taught the advocates of civil rights, both the black community and white students, that the regular peaceful methods of democracy would not work. The confrontationist tactics of civil disobedience, which first emerged in the South, were then diffused by the American student movement to other parts of the country and the world, and to other issues both inside and outside the university.

The aggressive strategy of the civil rights movement was successful when judged by the criteria of government actions to outlaw discrimination and to foster economic and educational improvements. Whatever the profound limitations of these actions, the fact remains that more has been attempted by government to improve the situation of black people in recent years than in all the preceding years since Reconstruction. Many actions taken by the administrations from Eisenhower to Johnson, by Congress, and by local agencies could be credited as responses to political militancy or the fear of ghetto riots. But though these efforts attested to the value of political action, they did not result in any major visible change in the position of the majority of the blacks. They remained poor, segregated, and uneducated, getting only the leavings of the labor market. To each succeeding group of civil-rights-concerned youth who came to political consciousness during this period, the gap between what ought to be and what actually existed appeared to have increased rather than decreased. They took for granted the existing structure, including the changes which had been made, and reacted with outrage against the continued sources of deprivation of the blacks. Older liberals, on the other hand, often reacted with pleasure at the considerable progress that had been made within the past few years. Thus an inevitable age-related split occurred.

This division between the generations was particularly acute within the black community. To younger blacks, the gains made since the 1950's appeared empty compared to the continuing pattern of black social and economic inferiority. On the major campuses of the nation, the growing numbers of black students found themselves in a totally white dominated world that included few, if any, black faculty and a white student body which turned increasingly from involvement in civil rights to activity directed against the Vietnam war. The concern with black power—black control over their own communities, and particularly over civil rights organizations—won growing support from black college students. These students played a major role in confronting university administrations with demands for more black students and faculty, and for changes in the curriculum.[41] Black students were among the major forces initiating sit-ins at schools as diverse and separated as Cornell University, San Francisco State College, Columbia University, Boston University, Northwestern University, and many black schools as well.

The acceptable pace of reform also was influenced by events abroad, particularly in Cuba and Vietnam. The triumph of the Castro revolution, an event dominated by young men, produced an example of a regime seemingly uncontaminated by Stalinism. Cuban events helped generate the possibility of revolution as a desirable way to eliminate social evils. Again generational differences divided the liberal-left communities. The older members had learned from experience that revolutions could lead to totalitarianism, to new and more intense forms of exploitation, and to cynical betrayals of the revolutionary impetus. To many young people, raising such matters seemed only an excuse to justify inaction against the intolerable aspects of the status quo.

The opposition to the Vietnam war became the dominant political issue affecting student activism. To the older generation, including, at first, most liberals, the war in Vietnam was only the most recent episode in a two-decade-long struggle against Communist expansion. To the new generations on the left, largely the children of liberals and former and continuing radicals, the war became defined in terms which placed American actions at odds with certain basic American beliefs, those of anti-imperialism, of the right of politically weak peoples to self-determination. Given the existence of a polycentric, divided communism, it simply did not make sense to look upon Vietnamese communism as an extension of Russian or Chinese power. The very failure of the powerful United States to quickly defeat its small and poorer Vietnamese opponents was evidence of the oppressive character of the war, of its being a war in which a foreign power seeks to impose its will by force upon another people. The very values which led Americans to be suspicious of, and opposed to, the British, French, and Dutch empires were turned against the United States.

Much of the student activism which was involved in these political campaigns took classic rationalist forms, whether they were for black rights, liberal programs, social-democratic reforms, or Marxist revolution. In a sense, they produced student movements directly or indirectly affiliated with adult activities, from the Kennedy and McCarthy presidential campaigns to the Young Trotskyites active in the New Mobilization Against the War or

---

[41] See articles in James McEvoy and Abraham Miller, eds., *Black Power and Student Rebellion* (Belmont, California: Wadsworth, 1969), esp. pp. 222–306, 379–418.

the short-haired, nondrug-using members of the Progressive Labor (Maoist) party, who controlled the Worker-Student Alliance faction of the Students for a Democratic Society (SDS).

With the revival of political activism in America, it became clear that the same conditions that produced the renunciatory youth of the 1920's once more obtained. There were more intense stimuli to establish the continuity. The city, the machine—and now the computer—had been moving apace. To many students, the social evils—racism and Vietnam, napalm and "the bomb"—were ultimate symbols of a civilization botched by reason and science. And the same type of generation-unit which had emerged in the 1920's out of the affluent college population reemerged in the 1960's—with new force. Wealth had spectacularly piled up and had spread out, and so had education. In 1938, 14 percent of American college-age youth were in college; in 1948 the figure was 29 percent; by 1968 it was close to 45 percent. Among the black population, the proportion had grown from 3 percent or less in 1938 to close to 25 percent of the age group in 1968. These figures meant that a relatively small percentage of the total student group formed an impressive body of people. In 1920, one percent of the students equaled but 6000; in 1970, one percent of the students totaled 77,500.

The same confusing range of expressions from cultural nihilism to both political and antipolitical activities appeared in various shifting combinations. The groups of elite middle-class liberal-arts protestors divided between those who accepted the rational political mode, whether in the form of Kennedy-McCarthy liberal antiwar politics or Bolshevism—or among the blacks, racial militancy—and those committed to total renunciation of classical rationalism, most evident in the use of drugs which reduce contact with reality and the body politic.

In any case, it would be a mistake to invest the renunciatory group's "cultural baggage"—mores of bed, dress, or hair—with too much intrinsic significance. More often than not, they have not been the substance of some new vision, but merely the absence of some old vision. And through the loss of social controls, and the medium of the youth culture, they stretched across more than one generation-unit. At least for the purposes of this discussion, the characteristics of this renunciatory generation-unit are its counter-enlightenment bias against rationality, its disbelief in social reform, and its rejection of politics.

The proof that the renunciatory youth, themselves, recognized that their deviant behavior was politically counterproductive may be seen in the fact that whenever events moved them to temporarily return to politics, that is, to efforts to influence the general public or the political elite, some of them cleaned up, shaved, and became presentable in conventional terms. This phenomenon occurred during the 1968 primary campaign, again in New Haven in April and May 1970, when attempts were made by Yale students to reach the New Haven working class with the case for the Black Panther defendants up on a charge of murder, and in the efforts to press government officials or to elect antiwar candidates after the war spread to Cambodia in May, 1970.

The renunciatory youth would argue, of course, that their behavior, their rejection of the dominant mode of life, is a self-conscious political act, much like the anarchist's refusing to vote. It is their way of declaring that there is no way to work within the system, even as a political revolutionary, that will really change the repressive aspects of society. But since *they* are in contact with reality, they are willing occasionally to work in camouflage, to shave and clean up when they feel the necessity to achieve a pragmatic goal such as helping to free the Black Panthers.

Yet Sam Brown, the founder of the student campaign for a peace candidate which resulted in the McCarthy candidacy in 1968, and of the national antiwar Moratorium movement in 1969, has argued that many in the student antiwar movement have, in fact, helped to prolong the Vietnamese War by alienating "potential doves" among the adult nonuniversity population through pushing their special form of "counter-culture." As he put the argument:

> First, personal appearance, language, and life style have nothing to do with the substance or purity of one's political views. Behavior that is offensive to Middle America neither establishes nor identifies real political differences; it merely offends Middle America. . . .
> Middle America is still sexually Victorian on the whole, but politically pragmatic while students are politically absolutist and sexually situational. One could, as Richard Nixon has, drive a truck through the gap.[42]

And Brown cited Madame Nguyen Thi Binh, the foreign minister of the Provisional Government of South Vietnam, that is, of the NLF or Viet Cong, in support of his view that the emphasis on purity of personal ethos and innovative life styles of American student protestors has been counterproductive politically. She argued "that the confused assortment of political objectives on the left—from legalizing marijuana to overthrowing the government to providing free abortions—dilutes the political impact of the peace movement. The result . . . is that the Vietnamese people and American soldiers

---

[42] Sam Brown, "The Politics of Peace," *The Washington Monthly,* Vol. 2 (August, 1970), p. 31.

carry the burden of America's social problems. Insofar as unrelated issues are tied to the peace movement, weakening it, Vietnamese people and American soldiers die every day because the peace movement has exported America's social problems to Asia." [43]

THE CONFORMING MAJORITY

The emphasis on the generation-units of youth, which expressed different forms of protest or renunciatory behavior, may give a false impression concerning the extent of such activities during the past decade. Several studies of the attitudes and behavior of young people in America (and other countries) suggest that the bulk of them never diverged much from the mainstream in terms of politics or personal life styles. This large group has often been ignored both by social analysts and the press.

Thus national surveys of attitudes toward the Vietnam war reported that young people, aged 21–30, were less opposed to the war than older age groups. The Gallup Poll consistently found that the young were less likely to say the Vietnam war was a mistake, as the data in Table 1 indicate.

There is no question that young people turned against the war as the conflict continued, but so did older ones. And those 50 and over remained the most antiwar age group through the end of 1969. This "is even more surprising in view of the propensity of older people not to express opinions. Those under 30 averaged only about eight percent with no opinion on the question over the years, as compared with an average of 15 percent without opinions among the 50-and-over. This leaves positive war backing among youth even stronger than the table would indicate. . . ." [44]

The majority of college students, though less bellicose than their non-college age-mates, remained prowar until 1968. [45] A Gallup survey of student attitudes toward Vietnam in the spring of 1967 "showed 49 percent of students in favor of a policy of escalation compared to 35 percent who wanted

---

[43] *Ibid.,* p. 24.

[44] Hazel Erskine, "The Polls: Is War a Mistake?" *Public Opinion Quarterly,* Vol. 34 (Spring, 1970), p. 134.

[45] See S. M. Lipset and Philip Altbach, "Student Politics and Higher Education in the United States," in S. M. Lipset, ed., *Student Politics* (New York: Basic Books, 1967), pp. 231–32, for a summary of various national polls of student opinion on Vietnam in 1965 and 1966; see also Lipset, *The Dimensions of Student Involvement,* Chapter 2, for more recent summaries.

TABLE 1

Percent in Different Age Groups Who Consider American Intervention
in the Vietnam War a Mistake — 1966–1969

Nationwide Gallup Poll Results		21–29 Years	30–49 Years	50 Years and Over
		Percent Considering the Vietnam War a Mistake		
1966	March	21 percent	23 percent	30 percent
	May	29	32	42
	September	37	28	40
	November	21	30	36
1967	May	31	34	42
	July	32	37	50
	October	43	43	53
1968	February	40	46	48
	March	46	47	52
	April	38	46	54
	August	48	48	61
	October	44	49	64
1969	February	49	49	57
	October	58	54	83

Source: Hazel Erskine, "The Polls: Is War a Mistake?" *Public Opinion Quarterly,* Vol. 34 (Spring, 1970), p. 134.

military activity to be reduced." [46] In April–May 1968, one-half the students said that the United States had made a mistake getting involved in Vietnam.[47] At this time, 48 percent of the public, but only 38 percent of the total 21–30-year-old age group, gave the same response, suggesting a rather large opinion gap between college and noncollege youth. This difference between the two groups continued in succeeding years.

Opposition to the Vietnam War, the perception that it was a mistake, continued to grow once the bombing of North Vietnam stopped in April, 1968 and subsequent negotiations began in Paris. In effect, once the United States government gave up the goal of defeating the Communists on the battlefield, it became impossible to prevent a steady erosion of support for the war, particularly, though obviously far from exclusively, on campus. Two Gallup samples of students taken two and one-half years apart dramatically point up the change in opinion.

Yet, though most students opposed the war, the survey data suggested

---

[46] "Results of a New Gallup Survey of College Students," *The Gallup Opinion Index,* Report No. 55 (January, 1970), p. 16.

[47] "Special Survey of College Students," Gallup Poll Release (June 29, 1968).

TABLE 2

Percentage of Students Identifying Themselves as "Hawks" [a] or "Doves," 1967 and 1969

	Spring, 1967	Fall, 1969
Dove	35	69
Hawk	49	20
No Opinion	16	11

Source: Gallup Poll Release (December 21, 1969).
[a] In response to the question: "People are called 'hawks' if they want to step up our military effort in Vietnam. They are called 'doves' if they want to reduce our military effort in Vietnam. How would you describe yourself — as a 'hawk' or as a 'dove'?"

that a majority accepted the new Nixon administration's policy of Vietnamization as a means of getting out. The administration was able to coopt some of the campus opposition. Thus a Gallup survey of college students taken in May, 1969, reported that when asked: "Do you approve or disapprove of the way Nixon is handling his job as President?" 57 percent approved, 27 percent disapproved, and 16 percent had no opinion.[48] A second 1969 Gallup national student poll taken in the Fall found that students were seemingly losing interest in protest, though they remained against the war. *Newsweek,* in reporting the survey, concluded, "the mood of the American campus is apparently undergoing a striking change: militancy and violence are in good measure giving way to passivity and personal introspection, and the revolutionary impulse seems—for a while, at least—to have largely spent itself." [49] When asked specifically what they thought "of the way President Nixon is handling the situation in Vietnam," more students (50 percent) approved than objected (44 percent).[50] The interviewing for this survey was done in October at a time when organized efforts to mobilize campus opposition to the war were at a height, that is, between the October 15 Moratorium demonstrations and the November 15 Mobilization that culminated in a massive Washington March, the goals of which were heavily supported by the same students (69 percent).[51]

The reaction against the May, 1970, Cambodian incursion produced the largest and most extensive student protest movement the United States

[48] "Special Report on the Attitudes of College Students," *The Gallup Opinion Index,* Report No. 48 (June, 1969), p. 42.
[49] "The New Mood on Campus," *Newsweek* (December 29, 1969), p. 42.
[50] "Results of a New Gallup Survey of College Students," *The Gallup Opinion Index.*
[51] Gilbert Marketing Group, National Gilbert Youth Poll, "Young Hawks on Decrease" (December 12, 1969).

has ever experienced. It involved more students at more campuses than in earlier years. And the survey data documented the extent of participation (over 50 percent according to Harris), as well as the fact that the attitudes of students in general moved to the left, not only with respect to the war itself, but on other issues as well. A Harris survey taken late in May caught the full flush of this discontent. With respect to the war, Harris found that 54 percent now favored stopping the fighting and bringing the boys back home, as compared with 34 percent for a phased withdrawal, and 9 percent who wanted to expand the war.[52] This finding may be contrasted with the results of a 1965 survey of students conducted for *Playboy,* which reported that 6 percent were for immediate withdrawal, 35 percent supported continued fighting in South Vietnam, and 56 percent wanted to escalate by invading North Vietnam.[53]

The antagonism to the Cambodian events naturally led to a drastic decline in student approval of the way President Nixon was handling the war. Fifty-nine percent gave him a rating of "poor," 17 percent said fair, and only 22 percent would say pretty good or excellent.[54] Only 27 percent of the students interviewed thought the President was right in ordering troops into Cambodia.[55] And 60 percent said the action had increased their opposition to American policy in Indochina.[56]

Though there is no question of the shift to the left among the students during 1970, it is curious that researchers have agreed since 1968 that only about 10 percent of the students are alienated or politically radical, and of these, perhaps one-third have revolutionary views. Thus in 1968, Samuel Lubell classified students on the basis of their responses to 10 items and concluded that with "only one in every 10 students interviewed did these 10 items link up to a pattern of general revolt or 'alienation.' "[57] A Roper Research Associates' study in the Winter of 1968–1969 asked students to evaluate four basic institutions: the political system, administration of justice, business and industry, and higher education. It found that "9% of the seniors are *very* critical of our basic institutions generally; 18% are *very* favorable," and while large majorities thought all four were "basically sound," the same majorities

---

[52] *Report of the Harris Survey of Students* (May 20–28, 1970), p. 49.

[53] *Playboy* Student Poll news release (November, 1965); for a more recent survey conducted for *Playboy,* which reiterated Harris' findings, see "Playboy's Student Survey," *Playboy,* Vol. 17 (September, 1970), p. 182.

[54] *Report of the Harris 1970 Survey of Students,* p. 20.

[55] *Ibid.,* p. 35.

[56] *Ibid.,* p. 51.

[57] Samuel Lubell, "Unresolved Crises Causes Youth Dissension," *Boston Globe* (October 9, 1968).

thought they "need improvement." [58] The percentages saying "basically sound" for the political system were 82 percent, for the system of justice 74, for business and industry 87, and for higher education 75. Conversely, the percentiles replying "basically unsound" for these four institutions were 2, 3, 3, and 4 respectively. [59] When asked to rate their "confidence in leaders for their ability to make real contributions to our society," the proportions giving the negative response "not much confidence" were 13 percent for political leaders, 11 percent for business leaders, and 7 percent for leaders in education. [60]

A sociologist, Jeffrey Hadden, also queried a national sample of 2000 seniors in 1969 for the magazine *Psychology Today*. His results similarly challenged the assumption that widespread opposition to the Vietnam war or support of various specific measures of social reform, particularly in the civil rights area, implied a fundamentally rebellious campus population. Thus Hadden reported that 67 percent of the seniors agreed with the statement that "those who knock free-enterprise misunderstood what made this a great nation." About three-fifths (61 percent) agreed that "the free-enterprise system is the single system compatible with the requirements of personal freedom and constitutional government." [61] Over one-half the students (54 percent) still put the blame for poverty on the poor themselves. They agreed that "most people who live in poverty could do something about it if they really wanted." [62]

The Yankelovich market research organization polled 4000 youth, one-half of them college students, in March and April, 1969. They reported that the college students as a group were much more alienated and radical than a sample of youth aged 17 to 23 who were not in college. [63] This survey, however, also found that the bulk of the students favored working within the democratic system. Though the large majority of white students agreed that America is to some degree a "racist nation," only 21 percent would welcome "more vigorous protests by blacks." Fifty-nine percent of the students said they would reject such protests. Eighty-eight percent of the white students

---

[58] *A Study of the Beliefs and Attitudes of Male College Seniors, Freshmen and Alumni* (New York: Roper Research Associates, May, 1969), p. 5.

[59] *Ibid.*, pp. 56–67.

[60] *Ibid.*, pp. 103–06.

[61] Jeffrey K. Hadden, "The Private Generation," *Psychology Today* (October, 1969), Special Publication giving "Complete Report on CRM's national study of college seniors. . . ." See 13th and 14th unnumbered pages, responses to questions 41 and 67.

[62] *Ibid.*, 12th unnumbered page, response to question 27.

[63] Daniel Yankelovich, Inc., *Profile of a Generation* (Multilith report of a survey prepared for CBS News, April, 1969).

believed that the "American system can respond effectively" to the need for change. Eighty-nine percent of the white students agreed that the radical left is as much a threat as the radical right. The majority of all college students "believe that competition encourages excellence" (72 percent), "that hard work will always pay off" (56 percent), and "that the right to private property is sacred" (75 percent).

The Yankelovich study also agreed with the other national surveys taken in 1969 that at most 10 to 15 percent of the student population were alienated from the body politic, and that possibly only one-third of these backed the extreme left. Essentially, these studies reported that the dominant political mood on campus during 1968–1969 was liberal, pro-McCarthy and Kennedy, antiwar, and sympathetic to civil rights demands. But their results indicated that the students as a stratum were far from being radical.[64] National surveys of college students taken in the Spring of 1970 before the demonstrations against the Cambodian incursion also suggested that the "alienated" were still a minority. The Gilbert Youth Poll reported that 60 percent agreed the United States form of government is "just about right."[65] Only 16 percent stated that they thought equal rights for minority groups could not be achieved under our present form of government.[66] Two-thirds were opposed to control over business profits; about the same proportion rejected paying for medical bills through public taxation; 60 percent were against a government guaranteed minimum income.[67] A study completed by Gallup in late April inquired as to whether "you think people who are successful get ahead largely because of their luck or largely because of their ability." Only 9 percent of the students said "luck," fully 88 percent thought that success is a result of "ability." And in spite of the widespread endorsements of the legalization of marijuana, only one-half the students interviewed thought that the "use of marijuana should be made legal."[68]

A third set of 1970 polls of college students, limited to those on 18 campuses in Illinois, Ohio, Indiana, Michigan, and Kentucky, yielded comparable results to the national ones by Harris, Gilbert, and Gallup. The University

---

[64] James A. Foley and Robert K. Foley, *The College Scene* (New York: Cowles, 1969), esp. pp. 19, 36, 128, 132; and "Results of a New Gallup Survey of College Students," *The Gallup Opinion Index*, p. 16.

[65] Gilbert Marketing Group, *Omnibus Youth Survey* (February, 1970), Table 22.

[66] *Ibid.*, Table 31.

[67] *Ibid.*, Tables 24–25.

[68] "The Student Revolution," *The Gallup Opinion Index*, pp. 22–23; see also "Playboy's Student Survey," *Playboy*, p. 238.

Index found overwhelming opposition to the war and to Nixon's "handling of his job" before the Cambodian incursion, among this regional group. Yet only 19 percent gave an "unfavorable" rating to the "competitive free enterprise system . . . in comparison with alternative economic systems." Three-quarters of them said they did *not* "feel that a person's disagreement with a particular law justified his disobedience to it." [69]

The obvious question arises to what extent the events surrounding the Cambodian incursion, the killings at Kent State and Jackson State, and the mass involvement in the various forms of protest during May and June, 1970, increased the long-term alienation of students from the American political system. Clearly, no study made during those events could have answered this question, since in the heat of the reaction to these occurrences, students and others made angry judgements about the President and the operation of the national political system. Some of the questions asked students by the Harris Poll during this period produced much larger proportions endorsing the need for fundamental changes (75 percent) than in previous surveys. A large number also believed that demonstrations are an effective form of protest (58 percent), and felt that social progress is more likely to come through radical pressure (44 percent), as many as thought through institutional reforms (45 percent). Most students (67 percent) believed that student protest would speed up needed changes, although close to four-fifths of them (79 percent) thought that radical pressures would have their greatest impact through institutional changes rather than through efforts to overthrow the system (10 percent). [70] Similar results were reported for a large sample survey conducted for *Playboy* at the same time. [71]

Yet if the responses to these questions point up the extensive academic reaction to the Cambodian events, some other replies suggest that even at the height of the greatest antiwar protests in American history, student reaction expressed much less than total alienation. In spite of the increased hostility to the military and the war, only 25 percent of the Harris respondents were in favor of not having ROTC on campus. Thirty-seven percent favored continuing it as a credit course, while another 33 percent supported an on-campus noncredit ROTC. Only 30 percent said that individual professors should not "be allowed to undertake research projects for the military,"

---

[69] Daniel C. Beggs and Henry A. Copeland, "The Student in 1970: Social Issues and the Generation Gap," *The University Index* (July 16, 1970), pp. 2–3; "The Student and Politics: 1970," *ibid.* (July 30, 1970), pp. 1–2.

[70] *Report of the Harris 1970 Survey of Students*, p. 88.

[71] "Playboy's Student Survey," *Playboy*, p. 184.

as contrasted with 62 percent who supported their right to do so.[72] Demonstrations against companies doing defense business recruiting on campus were frequent from 1968 on. Yet even in late May, 1970, only 22 percent opposed such activities, while almost three-quarters (72 percent) said that companies engaged in defense work should be "permitted to recruit at college."[73] When asked *after* the Kent State killings who had been more responsible for the violence at college protests, the demonstrators or the authorities, only 17 percent replied the "authorities," an equal proportion blamed the "demonstrators," while 64 percent said "both."[74] The large majority of students (69 percent) thought that "school authorities are right to ask the police for help when students threaten violence," as compared with 21 percent who considered it wrong to do so. While most students (52 percent) believed that it was wrong to seek help from the National Guard in such situations, almost as many (42 percent) said that the "National Guard has acted responsibly in most cases" as said they acted irresponsibly (46 percent).[75] Again the data from the *Playboy* survey strongly supports these findings.[76]

In examining the results of various national surveys of students from 1965 to 1970, it is difficult to come to any definitive conclusions concerning the depth and enduring quality of the grievances felt by American students, or what this may portend in terms of continued tension between a significant number of them and the government. The approximately 10 percent who show up as "radical," "alienated," or "dissident," in the surveys completed from 1968 to 1970 may be contrasted with those who identified "socialism" (24 percent) or "communism" (6 percent) as positive terms in the 1936 Roper national student survey.[77] And in a Harris survey taken in November, 1970 the self-identified radicals have declined to 7 percent from a May height of 11 percent.

At the other end of the spectrum, Harris reported that in 1969 and May, 1970 the percentages of students who identified their politics as "conservative" were 16 and 15, figures which are identical with the 15 percent who told Roper in a 1936 survey that they felt positive about the term "conservatism."[78]

---

[72] *Report of the Harris 1970 Survey of Students,* pp. 110, 112.
[73] *Ibid.,* p. 114.
[74] *Ibid.,* p. 163.
[75] *Ibid.,* pp. 165, 167, 171.
[76] "Playboy's Student Survey," *Playboy,* p. 184.
[77] A report on this study was published as "Youth in College," *Fortune;* the data reported here, however, are from the unpublished report prepared by Roper, Cherington, and Wood.
[78] *Harris 1970 Survey of Students,* p. 3. It rose to 19 percent in November, 1970.

THE OVERESTIMATION OF THE DRAMATIC

The evidence presented here from the various national opinion surveys, while documenting the increased opposition to the Vietnam War and the concomitant growth in radical and critical sentiments toward social institutions, generally indicates that the alienated include a relatively small proportion of the student population (10 to 15 percent). The state of opinion on campus cannot be gauged from observing demonstrations, or even through securing estimates of such opinion from campus leaders, whether these be university administrators, student body officers, or any other set of authorities. Informants have a strong tendency to overestimate the extent of support for highly visible forms of behavior.

The general point may be illustrated with respect to the proportions involved in drug-taking on American campuses during the first six years of the campus cultural revolt (1965–1970). A Gilbert national survey of youth asked respondents to estimate the percentage of their own age group who have tried drugs. Among college students in the sample (1005), close to two-thirds (65 percent) guessed 50 percent or more have tried drugs, and 34 percent thought 70 percent or more have. The same survey found that only one-third of the college student respondents reported that they had ever had any experience with a drug, marijuana or other. The proportion who were involved in regular use of drugs was, of course, much smaller, just under 10 percent.[79]

This study points up the extent to which students themselves overestimate the extent to which their fellows have engaged in a form of well-publicized illicit behavior, much as students and others have exaggerated the propensity of *others* to violate middle-class sexual morality. Given the resistance to acceptance of these data among many interested in the campus scene, it may be worth documenting their credibility by reference to other studies from this period. In an earlier review of the literature on drug use, Kenneth Keniston concluded that such behavior was limited to a small minority of the campus population. Extensive use of drugs was then found primarily in a small group of schools, generally the elite colleges and universities which admit the brightest students, many from liberal intellectual

---

[79] Gilbert Marketing Group, *Omnibus Youth Survey* (February, 1970), Tables 20 A and 27 A.

family backgrounds.[80] Different national surveys completed in 1969 yielded results in line with Keniston and Gilbert. Roper reported that 76 percent of the college seniors said that they had never tried marijuana, and that 96 percent had never used LSD. Only 2 percent said they use it occasionally.[81] The Gallup Survey of students in all classes in November found results very comparable to those of Roper. In response to an anonymous secret ballot, 68 percent stated they had never tried marijuana, 88 percent had not taken barbiturates, and 92 percent had never used LSD.[82] The College Poll found that 62 percent denied ever taking "drugs, such as marijuana or LSD." [83] It was not until the *Playboy* survey of mid-1970 that over 40 percent of the students reported taking marijuana or other drugs. But only a small minority (13 percent) acknowledged using marijuana "frequently"; 34 percent reported "occasionally." Although many in the older generation have an image of college students as slovenly, bearded, and long-haired, this stereotype does not agree with the impression which Gallup interviewers formed of the national sample which they interviewed in April, 1969. Only 6 percent of the men had beards, and 10 percent were reported to be dressed in sloppy clothes. The interviewers judged that 81 percent of the male students and 94 percent of the female had "generally neat appearances." [84] The Yankelovich survey reported that only 38 percent of the college youth verbally "reject the idea of conforming in dress and grooming." A majority (59 percent) "would welcome more emphasis on respect for authority." [85]

Since the results of these surveys are so much at variance with the conceptions of student attitudes and behavior presented by the media and held by many students, particularly the more activist among them, and by college administrators, some may question their accuracy. The best argument for their reliability and validity is that five different national survey organizations, varying in their methods (anonymous questionnaires using different questions, or personal interview), and necessarily dealing with different samples of institutions, produce a high degree of consensus. It may be argued that the more left-disposed students were underrepresented since SDS and

[80] Kenneth Keniston, "Heads and Seekers," *The American Scholar,* Vol. 38 (Winter, 1968–1969), pp. 97–112.
[81] Roper Research Associates, *A Study of the Beliefs and Attitudes of Male College Seniors, Freshmen and Alumni,* p. 198.
[82] "The New Mood on Campus," *Newsweek.*
[83] James A. Foley and Robert K. Foley, *The College Scene,* p. 66.
[84] "Special Report on the Attitudes of College Students," *The Gallup Opinion Index,* p. 26.
[85] Daniel Yankelovich, Inc., *Profile of a Generation,* pp. 74, 77.

other extreme left groups and publications began in 1969 to attack survey studies of student attitudes as serving the interests of the academic establishment. It is curious, therefore, that some of these surveys would seem to have overestimated the membership of SDS. For example, the Yankelovich study suggested that 4 percent of the 1969 student sample claimed membership in SDS. Given a total student population of over seven million in 1968–1969, this implied an SDS membership of about 280,000. Before SDS split at its 1969 convention, its leaders never claimed a national dues-paying membership of more than 7000, with another 30,000 reported involved in local chapter activities. It would seem that either the sample was drawn from institutions in which SDS is disproportionately strong, or that some sympathetic nonmembers claim membership. The argument that some who engaged in formally illicit behavior such as smoking marijuana would not admit it to interviewers, thus resulting in an underestimation of those involved, may have some validity, but the findings of studies using anonymous questionnaires have not been very different from those based on personal interviews.

WHO ARE THE ACTIVISTS?

The opinion surveys of American students indicated that the large majority have not been sympathetic with radical doctrines and tactics. Yet the activist elements, both liberals and leftists, dominated the political tone of many campuses and played a major role in influencing American politics in the 1960's. Given the fact that the activists are a relatively small minority, the questions may be raised as to who they are, and what are the factors which contribute to activist strength.

The major conclusion to be drawn from a large number of studies (particularly those of Kenneth Keniston and Richard Flacks), in the United States and other countries, is that leftist students are largely the children of leftist or liberal parents.[86] The Harris survey of participants in the largest example

[86] Richard Flacks, "The Liberated Generation: An Explanation of the Roots of Student Protest," *Journal of Social Issues,* Vol. 23, No. 3 (1967), pp. 66, 68. Kenneth Keniston, "Notes on Young Radicals," *Change,* Vol. 1 (November–December, 1969), p. 29. For a summary of various studies bearing on this point see also Richard G. Braungart, *Family Status,* "Socialization and Student Politics: A Multivariate Analysis" (Ph.D. Thesis, Department of Sociology, Pennsylvania State University, 1969), p. 61; Kenneth Keniston, "The Fire Outside," *The Journal,* Vol. 9 (September–October, 1970), pp. 9–10.

of student activism in American history, the 1970 protest against the Cambodian incursion, basically found the same strong relationship between parent and student orientations. In the United States, where left-wing radical parties or consistently liberal programs have relatively little support among the less educated and poorer strata of society, liberal or radical sentiments have found backing among a well-educated segment of the affluent population engaged in intellectual pursuits and among members of traditionally progressive religious groups, particularly the liberal Protestant denominations and the Jews.[87] In other countries, in which socialist and Communist parties have heavy backing from workers, leftist students are more likely to come from working-class families, or class origins do not differentiate among those of varying political persuasions.[88] The leaders, and core groups of activists, however, as a recent French study has shown, have similar backgrounds to those of American activists (e.g., the children of well-to-do leftists, of academics, and Jews). Conversely, studies of those active in conservative student groups, such as the Goldwater Young Americans for Freedom (YAF), indicate that they are largely from conservative backgrounds, much more likely to come from upward striving working-class families or from Republican business and professional groups, both heavily white Protestant.[89]

[87] Richard Flacks, "Who Protests: The Social Bases of the Student Movement," in Julian Foster and Durwood Long, eds., *Protest: Student Activism in America* (New York: Morrow, 1970), pp. 147–52, and S. M. Lipset, *Political Man* (New York: Doubleday, 1960), pp. 109–10, 285–94. On the Jewish contribution to activism see Nathan Glazer, "The New Left and the Jews," *The Jewish Journal of Sociology,* Vol. 11 (December, 1969), pp. 122, 127–31; Richard Flacks, *ibid.,* p. 65; Nathan Glazer, "The Jewish Role in Student Activism," *Fortune,* Vol. 79 (January, 1969), pp. 112–13, 126–29; S. M. Lipset, *Revolution and Counterrevolution,* rev. ed. (New York: Doubleday-Anchor, 1970), pp. 375–400.

[88] Michiya Shimbori, "Zengakuren: A Japanese Case Study of a Student Movement," *Sociology of Education,* Vol. 37 (Spring, 1964), pp. 232–33; C. J. Lammers, *Student Unionism in the Netherlands* (Leyden: Institute of Sociology, University of Leyden, 1970, mimeographed), pp. 25–26, 31; Frank Bonilla and Myron Glazer, *Student Politics in Chile* (New York: Basic Books, 1970); Ted Goertzel, "Political Attitudes of Brazilian Youth" (Paper presented at Session on "Politics of Students and Young Workers," VIIth World Congress of Sociology, Varna, Bulgaria, September, 1970), p. 3; Klaus R. Allerbeck, "Alternative Explanations of Participation in Student Movements" (Paper prepared for the VIIIth World Congress of International Political Science Association, Munich, September, 1970), pp. 13–14; Tessa Blackstone, Kathleen Gales, Roger Hadley, and Wyn Lewis, *Students in Conflict* (London: Weidenfeld and Nicolson, 1970), p. 200.

[89] Reports on the membership of the YAF may be found in David L. Westby and Richard G. Braungart, "Class and Politics in the Family Backgrounds of Student Political Activists," *American Sociological Review,* Vol. 31 (October, 1966), pp. 690–92; Richard G. Braungart (Ph.D. Thesis), p. 142; David L. Westby and Richard G. Braun-

Intellectuals, academics, writers, musicians, and so forth tend as a group to be disproportionately on the left. For the most part they are liberal Democrats, or supporters of left-wing minor parties.[90] Various surveys indicate that students who are intellectually oriented, who identify as "intellectuals," or who aspire to intellectual pursuits after graduation are also much more prone to be on the left and favorable to activism than those inclined to business and professional occupations.[91]

Among both faculty and students, there are clear-cut correlations between disciplines and political orientations. On the whole those involved in the social sciences and humanities, or in the more theoretical fields of science, in that order, are more likely to be on the left than those in the more practical, applied, or experimental fields.[92] Such variations, however, would appear to be more a product of selective entrance into different disciplines than of the effects of the content of the fields on those pursuing them as students or practitioners. Thus studies of entering freshmen have reported similar relationships between intended college major and political attitudes as found among seniors, graduate students, and faculty.[93] Morris Rosenberg, who conducted a panel study (repeat interviews with the same people two years apart) of students, reported that political orientation proved to be a major determinant of shifts in undergraduate major.[94] A large proportion of the minority of conservatives who chose liberal (in political terms) majors as freshmen changed to subjects studied by most conservatives, while many

---

gart, "The Alienation of Generations and Status Politics: Alternative Explanations of Student Political Activism," in Roberta S. Sigel, ed., *Learning About Politics* (New York: Random House, 1970), pp. 476–88; David G. Jansen, Bob B. Winborn, and William D. Martinson, "Characteristics Associated with Campus Social-political Action Leadership," *Journal of Counseling Psychology*, Vol. 15 (November, 1968), pp. 552–62.

[90] See S. M. Lipset, *Political Man*, pp. 310–43.

[91] Roger Kahn and William Bowers, "The Social Context of the Rank-and-File Student Activist: A Test of Four Hypotheses," *Sociology of Education*, Vol. 43 (Winter, 1970), pp. 39, 45–47, 48–49; Richard G. Braungart (Ph.D. Thesis), pp. 61–62; Richard Flacks, "The Liberated Generation: An Explanation of the Roots of Social Protest," *Journal of Social Issues*, pp. 69–70.

[92] Kenneth A. Feldman and Theodore M. Newcomb, *The Impact of College on Students* (San Francisco: Jossey-Bass, 1969), Vol. I, p. 161.

[93] Hanan Selvin and Warren Hagstrom, "Determinants of Support for Civil Liberties," in S. M. Lipset and S. S. Wolin, eds., *The Berkeley Student Revolt* (New York: Doubleday-Anchor Books, 1965), p. 513.

[94] Morris Rosenberg, *Occupations and Values* (New York: Free Press, 1957), pp. 19–22; see also James A. Davis, *Undergraduate Career Patterns* (Chicago: Aldine, 1965), pp. 52–53.

liberals who had selected conservative majors tended to shift to fields which were presumably more congenial with their political outlook.

The relationships between academic fields and political sympathies are also linked to the finding that the leftist activists within American universities tend to come from relatively well-to-do backgrounds as compared to the student population generally. A comparison by Westby and Braungart of the delegates to conventions of SDS and YAF also indicated that the left-wingers come from somewhat more affluent backgrounds than the rightists. The majority of the latter were the children of conservative businessmen and professionals, but they included a significant proportion, one-fifth, from working-class origins, a group almost unrepresented among the SDS delegates.[95] In general, studies of the social backgrounds of students in different disciplines suggest that those who major in the liberal arts and have an intellectual or scholarly bent have well-educated parents, while first-generation college students of working-class origins tend to be vocationally oriented in a narrow sense. They are more likely to be found among those preparing to become engineers, businessmen, and the like. They come disproportionately from that segment of the less well-to-do which is strongly oriented toward upward mobility and the values of the privileged. Their strong concentration on professional objectives, plus the need of many of them to hold a job during school term, also results in these students being less available for political activities than those from more affluent families. These findings may help to explain the fact that colleges attended by large numbers of less well-to-do students, apart from blacks, were less likely to be strongholds of left-wing groups during the 1960's than those which educated the scions of the upper-middle class.

Not surprisingly, the black student activists do not resemble either the white militants or renunciators in their social background and aspirations. As suggested earlier, their principal objectives are not to change the fundamental character of the society or to engage in expressive personal protest, but rather to improve the position of the blacks within the larger society generally and inside the university in particular. Although to achieve their objectives they often find it necessary to engage in militant, sometimes violent forms of protest, their goals are similar to the instrumental ones of the less privileged, sometimes racist white youth. They want a better life, more money, a job with higher status, social dignity. The black student activists are less aspiring for personal advantages than other black youth,

[95] David L. Westby and Richard G. Braungart, "Class and Politics in the Family Backgrounds of Student Political Activists," *American Sociological Review*, Vol. 31, pp. 690–92; Richard G. Braungart (Ph.D. Thesis), pp. 326–30.

seeing themselves as leaders of their people, but they clearly differ from the white activists. A study of 264 black student activists in 15 colleges and universities in 1969 indicated that the blacks came from much poorer families than the whites. Only 11 percent had college graduate parents. While most white activists are undecided about future careers, 76 percent of the black militants "said they were fairly certain"![96]

The political character of different schools may be linked to sources of selective recruitment and the resultant political orientation of their students. Those with a large number of well-to-do Jewish students — or, with the rise of black militancy, of black students — tended to be centers of activism. High-level liberal arts colleges with an intellectual aura attract students oriented to becoming intellectuals. This may account for the pattern of support for radical student protest at schools like Reed, Swarthmore, Antioch, and others. The best state universities, as judged in terms of the scholarly prominence of their faculties, for example, the universities of California, Michigan, and Wisconsin, have also been identified as important centers of confrontationist politics. These schools attract a disproportionate number of intellectually oriented students.

The proposition that the likelihood of a given university to sustain protest is largely a function of the type of students who attend it rather than of the policies or structural characteristics of the institution was first argued in detail by Alexander Astin. Astin gathered data from a sample of 35,000 students in 246 schools. His analyses were designed to estimate the relative importance of student and institutional variables. He concluded:

> The proportion of students who participate in demonstrations against either the war in Vietnam or racial discrimination can be predicted with substantial accuracy solely from a knowledge of the characteristics of the students who enter the institution. . . . Environmental factors seem to be somewhat more important with respect to protests against the administrative policies of the college, although student input characteristics still appear to carry much more weight than environmental characteristics in determining whether or not such protests will occur.[97]

[96] Charles V. Hamilton, "Minority Groups," in Robert H. Connery, *The Corporation and the Campus,* Vol. 30, No. 1, of The Proceedings of the Academy of Political Sciences, pp. 20–21.

[97] Alexander W. Astin, "Personal and Environmental Determinants of Student Activism," *Measurement and Evaluation in Guidance,* Vol. 1 (Fall, 1968), pp. 161–62. Another study of the characteristics of schools which had protests in 1969 indicated that those "with student bodies that had high scholastic aptitudes were more likely to face protests than other schools." Urban Research Corporation, *Student Protests 1969 Summary* (Chicago: 1970), p. 14. Alexander W. Astin and Alan E. Bayer, "Antecedent

Since completing his original research, which was based on 1966–1967 data, Astin has continued his investigations, and most recently suggests that while these basic conclusions hold up for subsequent years, there is some indication that given the same type of student characteristics, large and/or more bureaucratic institutions are more likely to have demonstrations than small and/or more student-oriented colleges. More recent studies of the demonstrations against the Cambodian incursion also support this conclusion. These findings, in part, reflect the fact that demonstrations require a given number of people to occur, and that the same percentage of students disposed toward activism will provide the critical mass in a large university, but may be too few in a small college.

The thesis that the bureaucratic characteristics of a university are causally related to demonstrations received confirmation in a survey of over 1000 schools, conducted by Peter Blau and Ellen Slaughter during the academic year 1967–1968. They found, in addition to student intellectualism and university size, that the university's use of computers for administrative purposes (an index of impersonality), its capacity for intellectual innovation (indicated by new fields of learning), and its willingness to allow students to evaluate teacher performance are each independently associated with student protest. Schools that do not use computers, that are intellectually innovative, and that permit student-evaluations of faculty are less likely to experience serious protests. However, the correlations with these measures of "counterbureaucratization," or greater flexibility, are each smaller than those with university size or student intellectualism.[98] The small difference between Blau-Slaughter and Astin-Bayer may reflect the latter's concern with political and racial demonstrations while Blau-Slaughter dealt with these together with protests against university policies. Blau and Slaughter may also have underestimated the importance of student characteristics in determining the protest potential of institutions. They use only one such

---

and Consequences of Disruptive Campus Protesters," *Measurement and Evaluation in Guidance* (in press, 1971); see also Urban Research Corporation, *ibid.,* p. 13; Joseph W. Scott and Mohamed El-Assal, "Multiversity, University Size, University Quality and Student Protest: An Empirical Study," *American Sociological Review,* Vol. 34 (October, 1969), pp. 702–09; Harold Hodgkinson, "Student Protest—An Institutional and National Profile," *The Record,* Vol. 71 (May, 1970), pp. 547–48; Garth Buchanan and Joan Brackett, *Summary Results of the Survey for the President's Commission on Campus Unrest* (Washington, D. C.: The Urban Institute, 1970), pp. 18–21; Richard Peterson, "Cambodia, Kent, Jackson and the Campus Aftermath" (mimeographed, Berkeley: Carnegie Commission on Higher Education, October, 1970), p. 4; Peter Blau and Ellen Slaughter, "Institutional Conditions and Student Demonstrations" (mimeographed, New York: Department of Sociology, Columbia University, Fall, 1970), p. 2.

[98] Peter Blau and Ellen Slaughter, *ibid.,* Table 1 and *passim.*

indicator, student intellectualism, while Astin and his colleagues, who had questionnaire data, correlated demonstrations with a large number of measures derived from students in different schools.

The conclusion that dissent within the American university system stems more from the privileged than from the poor, and occurs in the more elite or intellectually oriented schools, has been reported for many periods of academic history. Samuel Eliot Morison, chronicler of Harvard, in describing the rather violent clashes at the beginning of the nineteenth century, states: "If the college atmosphere seemed oppressive to young scions of rich mercantile families, it was Elysium to boys . . . who came to Cambridge from poor or provincial surroundings after a hard struggle to qualify." [99] The last two decades of the century were also characterized by a revived wave of undergraduate protest against many aspects of the colleges. Then as now, according to Lewis Feuer, they occurred "not in universities where students were from the lower classes but in the schools of the more well-to-do, not in the universities where the sciences and the practical arts were pursued but in the colleges of the liberal arts." [100] And Feuer goes on to suggest that the less affluent students of the 1890's did not protest because they often had to work their way through college, and studied hard in courses designed to get a good job after graduation. The backgrounds of the students who staffed the settlement houses of the pre-World War I era have been described as "from families that were moderately well-to-do . . . [with] many of the parents . . . actively involved in reform or concerned with aiding the poor." [101] The radical young intellectuals of the same period, recent alumni of the campus socialist movement, "came from secure upper-middle class families, and for this reason were eager to like and admire the poor, especially, the urban poor, especially the recent immigrants. . . ." [102]

The campus political protest of the 1930's stimulated the growth of the Communist party, which according to studies of its membership largely recruited from those of college age, 18 to 23. It seems clear that "the proportion of party members who have been to college is very high." [103] The family background of these young Communists resembled those reported for New Left activists more recently. "They have been brought up, in general,

[99] Samuel Eliot Morison, *Three Centuries of Harvard*, pp. 179–80.

[100] Lewis S. Feuer, *The Conflict of Generations*, p. 327.

[101] Allen F. Davis, *Spearheads for Reform: The Social Settlements and the Progressive Movement 1890–1914* (New York: Oxford University Press, 1967), pp. 35–36.

[102] Henry F. May, *The End of American Innocence: A Study of the First Years of Our Own Time 1912–1917* (Chicago: Quadrangle, 1964), p. 281.

[103] Morris L. Ernst and David Loth, *Report on the American Communist* (New York: Holt, 1953), pp. 3–4.

in comfort and often in luxury. They are the children of professional men or more than usually successful businessmen, bankers and ministers." [104] Academically conducted attitude surveys during the 1930's which sought to locate the correlates of liberal-left to conservative beliefs reported that the more liberal students tended to come from relatively well-educated professional families, disproportionately Jewish or irreligious, and that they were majoring in the social sciences. [105] "A linkage with father's and mother's political attitudes was established, not supporting the view that student radicalism is primarily a protest against parental conservatism. . . ." [106]

In stressing that involvement in student activism has been a function of the general political orientation which students bring to the university, one should not imply that changes in attitude do not occur, or even that conversions do not take place. Universities clearly do have a liberalizing effect so that there is a gradual shift to the left. A significant number of students in the late 1960's have been much more radical in their actions and opinions than earlier postwar generations of American students, or than their parents. The larger events which created a basis for a renewed radical movement have influenced many students to shift from the orientation in which they were reared. Many students of liberal parents have felt called upon to act out the moral imperatives implicit in the seemingly "academic" liberalism of the older generation. Political events, combined with various elements in the individual situation of students, impelled a number of liberal students to become active radicals.

Kenneth Keniston and William Cowdry indicate that students "most likely to hold radical beliefs *and* act on them" are those whose fathers have similar social and political values. Those who hold radical beliefs, but are not active politically, are much more likely to report that their fathers are very unlike themselves. [107]

However, if we hold preuniversity orientation constant, it obviously will make a difference which university a student attends, what subjects he

---

[104] *Ibid.,* p. 3.

[105] Gardner Murphy and Rensis Likert, *Public Opinion and the Individual* (New York: Harper, 1938), pp. 68–87.

[106] *Ibid.,* pp. 110–11.

[107] Kenneth Keniston, "Notes on Young Radicals," *Change,* pp. 31–32; R. William Cowdry and Kenneth Keniston, "The War and Military Obligation: Attitudes, Actions and Their Consistency" (mimeographed paper, Department of Psychiatry, Yale University, 1969), pp. 22, 26–27, 30; Jeanne H. Block, Norma Haan, and M. Brewster Smith, "Socialization Correlates of Student Activism," *The Journal of Social Issues,* Vol. 25, No. 4 (1969).

decides to major in, who his friends are on the campus, what his relations are with his teachers of varying political persuasions, what particular extracurricular activities he happens to get involved in, and the like. The relationships between the orientations which students form before university and the choices they make after entering which help maintain their general political stances are only correlations; many students necessarily behave differently from the way these relationships would predict.

Clearly, conversions, drastic changes in belief, in political identity, do occur among university students, as among other groups. During a period in which events shift the larger political climate to the left or right, young people, with fewer ties to the past, are undoubtedly more likely to change than older ones. There is also a special aspect of university life that enhances the possibility that certain groups of students will find satisfaction from intense political activity. Various studies suggest that mobility, particularly geographic mobility in which one becomes a stranger confronted by an unfamiliar social context, tends to make individuals available for causes which demand intense commitment.

Thus new students, or recent transfers, are more likely to be politically active than those who have been in the social system for longer periods.[108] Local students, or those relatively close to home, are less likely to be active than those who are a considerable distance from their home communities. In Berkeley, Madison, and other university centers, the activists have come disproportionately from the ranks of the migrants.

PSYCHOLOGICAL RESEARCH

Some psychologists have sought through an examination of personality traits to account for varying political orientations and degrees of involvement. Several of the studies by psychologists have reported that left-activists tend to be the offspring of permissive families characterized by a dominant mother.[109] Conversely, conservative activists tend to come from authoritarian families in which the father is dominant. Other studies have found a

---

[108] Glen Lyonns, "The Police Car Demonstration: A Survey of Participants," in S. M. Lipset and S. S. Wolin, eds., *The Berkeley Student Revolt*, p. 521.

[109] Richard Flacks, "The Liberated Generation: An Explanation of the Roots of Student Protest," *Journal of Social Issues;* David L. Westby and Richard G. Braungart, "Class and Politics in the Family Backgrounds of Student Political Activists," *American Sociological Review.*

correlation between "cause orientation" and activism,[110] and still others have found a correlation with training for independence.[111]

It is difficult to evaluate these studies since many of these reported differences between leftist and conservative activists correspond to the variations reported in analyses of Jewish and Protestant families, and the samples of left activists tend to include heavy Jewish representation (or those who report themselves as of "no religion," many of whom appear to be of Jewish parentage), while those of active campus rightists are largely Protestant, many from smaller communities. It is, therefore, difficult to conclude that socialization experiences, as such, have an independent causal effect, that is, independent of family values which bear rather directly on politics. Thus Kenneth Keniston, in summing up the recent evidence bearing on an earlier critique of mine which raised this question, concluded:

... The issue cannot be settled with only the evidence at hand. In all probability, several interacting factors are involved. On the one hand, it seems clear that *if* children are brought up in upper-middle-class professional families with humanitarian, expressive and intellectual values, and *if* the techniques of discipline emphasize independence and reasoning, and *if* the parents are themselves politically liberal and politically active, then the chances of the child's being an activist are greatly increased, regardless of factors like religion. But it is also clear that these conditions are fulfilled most often in Jewish families. And there may be still other factors associated with social class and religion that independently promote activism; for example, being in a Jewish minority group that has preserved its culture in the face of opposing community pressures for centuries may in some way prepare or permit the individual to take controversial positions as a student.[112]

The distinction between the politically radical and the culturally renunciatory protestors suggested in this chapter has not been made in most of

---

[110] Lamar E. Thomas, "Family Congruence in Political Orientations of Politically Active Parents and Their College-Age Children" (Ph.D. Thesis, Committee on Human Development, University of Chicago, 1968), p. 46. Liberal parents were much more "cause-oriented" than conservatives. Whether the children of the former were activist or not correlated strongly with degree of cause orientation rather than childrearing practices.

[111] Jeanne H. Block *et al.*, "Socialization Correlates of Student Activism," *The Journal of Social Issues,* pp. 163–64 and Table 7.

[112] Kenneth Keniston, "Notes on Young Radicals," *Change,* p. 31; Jeanne H. Block *et al.*, attempted to control for the effect of religion but it is not clear from the report whether the investigators inquired as to respondents' religion or that of their parents. Left-oriented people tend to say "none" for their own religion. Hence, unless family religious background is probed, many of the "none" turn out to in fact come from Jewish backgrounds. The statistical differences were also quite small.

the research literature on student activism. Some psychologists, however, have attempted to isolate differences between "hippies," "nihilists," habitual drug-users, and political radicals which are somewhat close to the renunciatory-radical distinction. These indicate that the renunciatory group is involved in some sort of generational conflict, of rejection of traditional or conservative views of their parents, while the political radicals come from liberal-left family backgrounds. Both groups, of course, share a radical rejection of the conventional society. As Kenneth Keniston has described the difference,

> [The political radical tends to follow] the pathway of identification. Both father and son are described as expressive, humanitarian, and idealistic. The son identified with his father, although the son is usually more radical. Such sons are very likely be be radicals in action as well as in theory. . . . There is, however, clearly a second pathway to radical beliefs, though less often to radical actions: the pathway of rejection of identification. Such students describe themselves as expressive, idealistic, and humanitarian, but describe their fathers as distinctly *not* any of these things. They are rather less likely to be politically active, more likely to adopt an apolitical or "hippie" style of dissent, and, if they become involved in political action, more likely to fall within the "nihilist" group.[113]

Jeanne Block and her colleagues have pursued similar differentiations between "activists"—those disillusioned with the status quo, involved in antiestablishment protest *and* supporting programs and policies designed to do something about "pain and poverty and injustice"—and "dissenters"—those who are also involved in antiestablishment protests, but who do not seek to change the policies and institutions they object to through positive action. Activists differ from dissenters in evaluating their relationships with their parents more positively. The dissenters tend to describe a "conflicted, unsatisfying parental relationship," one which presumably precipitated or justified a break with family social values.[114]

Studies of committed drug users among students also indicate that they differ from those who express their antagonisms to society more through organized political activities than through expressive forms of personal deviance in ways similar to those reported above. Richard Blum concluded that "families with greater divergency of opinion, more distant relationships to

[113] Kenneth Keniston, "Notes on Young Radicals," *Change*, p. 32.
[114] Jeanne H. Block *et al.*, "Socialization Correlates of Student Activism," *The Journal of Social Sciences*, pp. 146–47, 163–65.

the children, and more unresolved parent-child interpersonal crises seem to be those which generate the drug explorers." [115]

But if the psychological research does suggest that those engaged in renunciatory activities are disproportionately recruited from the ranks of individuals with histories of family conflict and personal difficulties, a number of analysts of left-wing political activists report that "the findings on activists are reasonably consistent in showing that, on the average, they are good students, are psychologically 'healthy.' . . . They can also be close to their families rather than rebellious and can reflect intellectual, humanistic, and democratic ideals fostered in the home." [116] As one study summed up its findings, "few college students in general can match the positive development of these personality characteristics that distinguish student activists from their college contemporaries." [117] Many writers and researchers dealing with the background and values of student activists have continued — up until 1971, at least — to elaborate on these supposedly positive traits of the active protestors.

These reports on the psychological "health" of left-wing militants pose an interesting problem in the sociology of knowledge, for a number of other studies and evaluations of the research literature have pointed for many years to the fact that almost all the analyses of student activism which conclude that the left-wing militants exhibit "superior" attributes are based on comparisons with the student body as a whole, rather than with activists of other ideological persuasions. A 1966 review of the extant studies pointed to the evidence that conservative activists, as well as those involved in student government affairs, possessed some of the psychologically healthy traits assigned to the campus militants. [118]

More recent efforts to systematically compare various groups of involved students refute the thesis that leftist activists are the noblemen of the campus. The psychologist Larry Kerpelman explicitly set out to analyze the

---

[115] Richard Blum, "Epilogue: Students and Drugs," in Richard Blum and Associates, *Students and Drugs: Drugs II* (San Francisco: Jossey-Bass, 1969), p. 366.

[116] Richard Blum, "Prologue: Students and Drugs," in *ibid.*, p. 8.

[117] James W. Trent and Judith L. Craise," Commitment and Conformity in the American College," *Journal of Social Issues,* Vol. 23 (1967), p. 39.

[118] S. M. Lipset and P. G. Altbach, "Student Politics and Higher Education in the United States," *Comparative Education Review,* Vol. 10 (June, 1966), pp. 320–49. The review of the literature is on pages 331–34. This article was reprinted and updated in S. M. Lipset, ed., *Student Politics,* pp. 222–24. See also David L. Westby and Richard G. Braungart, "Class and Politics in the Family Background of Student Political Activists," *American Sociological Review,* pp. 331–32, and Larry C. Kerpelman, "Student Political Activism and Ideology: Comparative Characteristics of Activists and Nonactivists," *Journal of Counseling Psychology,* Vol. 16 (1969), pp. 8–13.

psychological traits of six groups of students on a number of campuses: "left activists, middle-of-the-road activists, right activists, left nonactivists, middle-of-the-road nonactivists, and right nonactivists." He concluded that "characteristics that have been identified with left activists . . . characterize the involved generally. . . . All student activists, no matter what their ideology, are less needful of support and nurturance, value leadership more, are more socially ascendant and assertive, and are more sociable than students who are not politically active." [119]

A somewhat different study designed to test the assumption that "militant radicals" were psychologically healthier than moderates and nonmilitant conservatives also found it necessary to reject the assumption that radical students are psychologically "healthier."

> [T]here were statistically significant differences between the student types on four of the six personality measures: Authoritarianism, Dogmatism, Paranoia and Personal Efficacy. Militant radicals were the least authoritarian and the least dogmatic while non-militant conservatives were the most authoritarian and the most dogmatic. These findings supported the view of student radicals as "healthy" personalities. On the other hand, militant radicals were most paranoid and least efficacious. Clearly, if one assumes that it is more desirable to be lower on paranoia and higher on efficacy, these findings do not fit the "healthy" personality thesis.[120]

Similar conclusions with respect to consistency of political action and ideology were reported by Cowdry and Keniston in their study of a random sample of 1968 Yale seniors. They found, when comparing the characteristics of students who were for or against the Vietnam war, that those whose actions were consistent with their beliefs about the war, whether "pro" or "con," were more like each other than either resembled the "inconsistent" group.[121]

Various early surveys suggested that left-wing activists were superior academically to other students. This finding also has been challenged since a comparison of various analyses indicates that the alleged superiority of the leftists is based on "*self-reported* grade-point averages," but that surveys

---

[119] Larry C. Kerpelman, *Student Activism and Ideology in Higher Education Institutions* (Washington, D. C.: Bureau of Research, Office of Research, U. S. Department of Health, Education and Welfare, March, 1970), pp. xv, 79, 85.

[120] Roy E. Miller and David H. Everson, "Personality and Ideology: The Case of Student Power" (Paper presented at the Midwest Political Science Association, April 30–May 2, 1970 – Public Affairs Research Bureau and Department of Government, Southern Illinois University), p. 36.

[121] R. William Cowdry and Kenneth Keniston, "The War and Military Obligation: Attitudes, Action and Their Consistency" (mimeographed), pp. 21–23.

which compare the *"actual"* grades reveal no differences.[122] Left activists seemingly have a propensity to "perceive themselves as ranking higher . . . than they are in reality."[123] Another study attempted to further test a suggestion of mine that the reason that left activists showed up as having positive traits in some studies is that "their ideologies rather than their true sentiments . . . are dictating the answers, . . . [that] leftists who have demonstrated intolerance and authoritarian behavior traits in practice may still give voice or pencil to liberal values in principle."[124] Miller and Everson report that their findings show "a remarkable fit with the Lipset thesis (and understandably somewhat disconcerting to the authors of this paper). We cannot reject the Lipset model. In fact, it provides the best fit of any model tested."[125]

Given the sharp divergences among researchers, the fact that so many social scientists have chosen to ignore studies that criticize the methodology of the research that concludes that left activists have healthier personalities and are academically superior raises the obvious question as to why this occurs. Curiously, one of the most insightful explanations for the bias has been suggested by an investigator, Richard Blum, who himself has given expression to the positive stereotype. Blum points out that there is a correspondence of interests and values between the intellectual community and the protesting students.

> The importance of adjustment, of curiosity, of social criticism, and of "progressive" sociopolitical doctrine, as well as an emphasis on . . . spontaneity in relationships, and on being antagonistic toward traditional authority, are likely to be found in the social sciences and mind-studying trades, or espoused by their members, as well as by the liberal students. Consequently, when these scientists and clinicians undertake to evaluate today's left and/or drug-using students, they are often looking at people much like themselves. . . . [Their] "liking" reactions [for these students] probably reflect preferences for people acting more as . . . [they] thought people ought to act. . . . The danger is that the evaluation may be positive only because of the charm of the young peo-

---

[122] Larry C. Kerpelman, "Student Political Activism and Ideology: Comparative Characteristics of Activists and Nonactivists," *Journal of Counseling Psychology,* pp. 5–6, 42, 80.

[123] *Ibid.,* p. 80; see also S. M. Lipset and P. G. Altbach, "Student Politics and Higher Education in the United States," *Comparative Education Review,* pp. 333–34.

[124] Enunciated as a possibility in S. M. Lipset, "The Activists: A Profile," in Daniel Bell and Irving Kristol, eds., *Confrontation: The Student Rebellion and the Universities* (New York: Basic Books, 1968), p. 56.

[125] Roy E. Miller and David H. Everson, "Personality and Ideology: The Case of Student Power" (paper), pp. 35, 38–39.

ple without the investigators' recognizing the grounds for their reactions and without coming to grips with either fundaments or implications of student behavior. We are posing the problem of investigator
identification with his subjects, of "countertransference," in which it
may be — as some of the students contend — that the young are admired
because they act out the fantasies of their frustrated elders. The corollary danger is also acute and is commonplace. When conservative
people offer their more negative evaluations . . . many university
and professionally based people reject outright what the "reaction-
aries" have to say.[126]

Studies that concentrate primarily on activists in their efforts to distinguish among the social and pyschological traits of students of different
persuasions also present special analytical problems inherent in the fact
that whether or not students direct their extracurricular energies into
politics is strongly linked to political orientations. Studies of student bodies in
different countries indicate that those on the left (as well as the group on the
extreme right) generally view politics as an appropriate and even necessary
university activity. Committed morally to the need for major social changes,
leftists feel that the university should be an agency for social change — that
both they and their professors should devote a considerable portion of their
activities to politics.

Conversely, however, the less leftist students are, the more likely they
are to disagree with this view, the more prone they will be to feel that the
university should be an apolitical "house of study." Liberals and leftists,
therefore, are much more likely to be politically active than moderates and
conservatives. A relatively strong conservative stance will not be reflected
in membership or activity in a conservative political club. This means that on
any given campus or in any country, the visible forms of student politics
will suggest that the student population as a whole is more liberal or radical
leftist than it actually is. Since conservative academic ideology fosters campus political passivity, one should not expect to find much conservative
activity.

Presumably it takes a lower threshold of political interest or concern to
activate a liberal or leftist than a conservative. One would deduce, therefore,
that the average conservative student activist should be more of an extremist
within his ideological tendency than the average liberal. Hence a comparison
of campus activists of different persuasions should contain a greater share of
extremists among the rightists than among the leftists.

---

[126] Richard Blum, "Epilogue: Students and Drugs," in Richard Blum and Associates,
Students and Drugs: Drugs II, p. 377.

THE CONFLICT CONTINUES

No society should find it remarkable that a visible proportion of its student population is actively involved in politics. The psychic security that derives from membership in a "privileged" group is among the factors which make their activism possible. It can also be argued that a politically inactive student population is a cause for greater misgivings than an active one. The fact remains, however, that a large part of the group of self-identified "radicals" in the American movement which began in the mid-sixties have been close to total alienation from the rational and the political world. The overwhelming majority of them do *not* belong to any of the numerous "small c" communist groups which dominate the organized New Left and maintain some links (though often very nebulous) to philosophical and tactical doctrines of Marxism-Leninism. They belong, in fact, to the renunciatory rather than the radical tendency. The anarchist Paul Goodman, whose writings were a basic text for many of the Berkeley activists of 1964–1965, and who was invited to teach at San Francisco State with the students voluntarily paying the bill, wrote at the end of the decade with troubled concern about the future of the movement with which he once almost totally identified. As he pointed out, many student radicals had isolated themselves from any ability to communicate about reality.

> There was no knowledge, but only the sociology of knowledge. They had so well learned that physical and sociological research is subsidized and conducted for the benefit of the ruling class that they did not believe there was such a thing as simple truth. To be required to learn something was a trap by which the young were put down and co-opted. . . .[127]

---

[127] Paul Goodman, "The New Reformation," *New York Times Magazine,* September 14, 1969, pp. 33, 143, 144. Similar criticisms have been advanced by Norman Birnbaum, the Amherst sociologist, who was a founding editor of the *New Left Review* in London, and who is both an identified Marxist scholar and a disciple of C. Wright Mills:

> The ahistoricism and pragmatism of American thought has found a parody in the disdain for political thinking exhibited by most of the militants of the American student left. An unreflected doctrine of immediacy, an explicit fear of academicism (and an implicit incapacity, engendered by a defective university system, for sustained thought), a considerable ignorance of nearly everything and

The young dissidents whose behavior so disturbed Paul Goodman, and many older radicals as well, were engaging in renunciatory activity. Radicals, as we have seen, are political; that is, they want to make changes in public institutions. The renunciators reject that aspect of Western society which emphasizes public rather than private experience. To understand this aspect of contemporary youth protest, it is necessary to recall that modern Western society was born in a burst of individualism, which was later subverted, in its own name, partly by political liberalism. The break with medieval society was a break with the tight, regulatory group life which oppressed the individual. But, as he was being freed from these rigid, deindividualizing social forms, Western man began to be caught up in larger, differently rigid, differently deindividualizing social forms. Technology and political ideology, instruments of his freedom, became more devious instruments for capturing him again. Depending on one's view of history, this can be seen as a terrible mistake that man made, or one of man's painful, staged moves toward the messianic era, or merely the existential acting-out of one of the eternal tensions of man's earthly condition. But the least common denominator is the constant tension between the individual and society, which has been endlessly celebrated by poets on the one hand, sociologists on the other, and psychoanalysts in between. And it is to that tension that the renunciators address themselves, again, at this appropriate time.

There is often confusion in distinguishing between the renunciatory youth and the radical youth — especially the ideologues among them — partly because so many of these youth are themselves confused and shuttle back and forth between these two incompatible positions — and partly because on the surface the slogans are the same, as are the identifiable enemies. But in fact, the renunciation tendency is a conservative tendency in that it wants to protect the individual and the individual imagination against the crush of the economically expanding, collectivist industrial society, committed ideally to greater equalitarianism, and the renunciation youth must be counted as significantly *conservative* (antimodern) in impulse.

Indeed, there could even be a confusion at times between the radical youth and the backlash youth, because, on the surface again, the slogans and the identifiable enemies in the establishment are often the same. A leaflet of the overtly racist and anti-Semitic National Youth Alliance, headed "Lost

---

especially of the history of socialism, combine in the jargon, the slogans, and the bewilderment of the *avant-garde* of the new American left.

Norman Birnbaum and Marjorie Childers, "The American Student Movement," in Julien Nagel, ed., *Student Power* (London: Merlin Press, 1969), p. 139.

and Alone," said to college students in terms reminiscent of the seminal Free Speech Movement of Berkeley: ". . . You are no longer the individual you thought you were; but are now a mere number in a file. . . . Your English professor hardly shows up for class." Several years ago in the mid-1960's in Boston, the SDS and the John Birch Society both campaigned in a white working-class area against a social reformist attempt to replace old housing with new apartments. Birch Society members of the police department actually contributed to the bail bond funds of SDS members arrested in civil disobedience campaigns in the area.

Ironically, the logic of the problem suggests that the only genuine link is between the generation-unit tendencies that are most likely to end up in mortal combat: the revisionist youth (black and radical) and the rightist backlash youth. They are both committed to the rationalistic, modern Western society and its fruits. The first wants to seize power he never had; the second wants to secure power he is no longer confident of. They both are poised to fight against an inimical establishment. They both feel that the establishment belongs to the other, or is in danger of so belonging. In fact, if the establishment belongs to anybody, it is to the parents of the renunciatory youth, among others; and while the renunciatory youth also abhor the establishment, it is as part of a larger complex which must include the radical and backlash youth, and those things they savor.

In other words, there are two major gaps, or axes of polarization, among American youth. One is a value-oriented axis, one of whose poles is renunciation, the other acceptance. Both the backlash youth and the radical youth, including a substantial part of the black youth, sit on the latter pole together. The other axis is an interest-oriented axis, that is, an orientation toward the distribution of power and rewards. On one pole of that axis sits the backlash youth; on the other, the radical and black militant youth.

This analysis has, for the most part, ignored the large numbers of young people, in total a majority, who accept the system and seek only to find a comfortable niche in it. They do not fall clearly into any of these camps: renunciatory, radical (including black militant), or backlash. But any stress on a purely statistical assessment would create a possibly erroneous illusion of prospective stability. The various conflicting tendencies are strongly present among those segments of American youth who will provide a substantial segment of tomorrow's adult leadership. There is general agreement among sociologists that maturation and responsibility generally contribute to modifying radical or violent tendencies. Most juvenile delinquents become law-abiding job-holders. Most college radicals are absorbed in the demands of family and career after they leave campus. Whether the efforts among the radical and renunciatory youth of the 1970's to sustain their own antiestablishment communities which negate the pulls of the adult structures succeed remain to be seen. Past experience argues against them.

From their various vantage points, and at their outer edges, the renunciation youth, the backlash youth, the black youth, and the radical youth have been brewing a common political mode: moralistic, nonnegotiable — and therefore possibly violent. It is important because it involves more than just youthful temper: These generation-units of American youth have strong and legitimate differences to negotiate. And they will negotiate them with each other — not with the older generation.

epilogue

Social Problems
and Sociological Theory

ROBERT K. MERTON

In sociology, as in the other sciences, there is an intellectual division of labor
rather than an all-or-nothing commitment to either pure or applied science.
Some men, both by temperament and capacity, are no doubt better suited to
the exclusive pursuit of one of these paths of inquiry; some may move back
and forth between both; and a few may manage to tread a path bordered on
one side by the theoretical and on the other by the practical or applied. In
the main, this is the path that has been followed in the chapters of this book.
By personal commitment rather than by express consent, the authors of this
book exhibit in their chapters agreement with the position set forth by
Whitehead:

> Science is a river with two sources, the practical source and the
> theoretical source. The practical source is the desire to direct our
> actions to achieve predetermined ends. . . . The theoretical source is
> the desire to understand. I most emphatically state that I do not con-
> sider one source as in any sense nobler than the other, or intrinsically
> more interesting. I cannot see why it is nobler to strive to understand
> than to busy oneself with the right ordering of one's actions. Both

—

I am indebted to Aron Halberstam for aid and comfort in revising this chapter.

have their bad sides; there are evil ends directing actions, and there are ignoble curiosities of the understanding.[1]

All the chapters in this book have drawn upon both theoretical and practical sources of sociological knowledge. This does not mean that they have uniformly made use of a single comprehensive theory of social problems —of social disorganization and deviant behavior—for there is, in truth, no such overarching theory to draw upon. No qualified sociologist holds that the discipline has evolved a single, strictly formulated theory that fully encompasses the wide range of social problems, such as those treated in this book, and so enables us to account for every significant aspect of all these problems. That sort of claim must be reserved to those cryptosociologists who turn up in quantity whenever trouble is brewing in society and announce their quickly designed cures for everything that ails us socially. Yet in matters so complex and obscure as much of social organization and human behavior, we are wise to be on our guard against "explanations" that profess to account for every facet of that organization and behavior. For, as the ancients knew, he who tries to prove too much proves next to nothing. In no sphere of systematic knowledge—whether it be mechanics, biology, linguistics or sociology—do specialists go on the fool's errand of explaining every aspect of concrete phenomena. Instead, particular aspects, structures, and processes of the phenomena are singled out, under the guidance of some general ideas, and methodically investigated, while other aspects are conscientiously neglected as no part of the problem in hand. This responsible, well-attested, and effective frame of mind has become so definitely established in the older scientific disciplines that it is soon taken over by novices as a firm implication of their training; it is seldom taught in explicit and didactic fashion. But the need for dealing with selected aspects of concrete events is not so widely or immediately sensed in the newer social sciences, particularly, perhaps, in psychology and sociology (since every man considers himself a psychologist by virtue of his being human and a sociologist by virtue of living his life in society). The heavy didactic emphases in these fields upon methodology and the role of theory can be understood in part as a collective effort to keep their practitioners from falling into the trap of explaining little by trying to explain too much. Tidy and seemingly complete explanations of every aspect of human behavior and organization include unrelated and specially concocted assumptions that are rigidly forced into each distinct aspect of the complex whole under study.

---

[1] Alfred North Whitehead, *The Aims of Education* (New York: New American Library, 1951), p. 107.

But if there is nothing remotely resembling a single, rigorous, all-encompassing theory of social problems, there is a general theoretical orientation toward social problems widely current among sociologists and largely reflected in the pages of this book. Similar sociological ideas and similar procedures of sociological analysis are put to work in chapter after chapter that deal with the most varied kinds of social problems. If there is no one theory unifying all the significant questions that can be raised about social problems, there is a sociological perspective from which similar kinds of questions have been raised and, in some cases and in some degree, tentatively answered. The rest of this chapter will consider a few — far from most — of the theoretical questions to be kept in mind when examining social problems.

SOCIOLOGICAL THEORY OF SOCIAL PROBLEMS: CURRENTS AND CROSSCURRENTS

The decade since the first edition of this book has witnessed a deepening interest in the sociological theory of social problems. In the course of this growth, theorists of one persuasion or another have occasionally developed selective perceptions of what other theorists have said, with the result that sociological orientations which are entirely compatible are treated as though they were at odds. In its criticism of the theory being advanced here, a recent text on social problems provides us with a case in point.[2] A short review of that criticism will serve the double purpose of introducing the reader to our theoretical orientation and to alert him to basic agreements among superficially opposed orientations.

In the generally thoughtful introduction to their book, Skolnick and Currie suggest that our theoretical "approach" has three principal limitations. *First,* it provides a basis for "evaluating and criticizing particular policies and structures within a *presumably consensual society* whose basic values and directions are not seen as problematic."[3] To emphasize the point,

---

[2] Jerome H. Skolnick and Elliott Currie, eds., *Crisis in American Institutions,* Introduction (Boston: Little, Brown, 1970, italics inserted), pp. 10–16. Their discussion refers throughout to the first edition of Merton and Nisbet, published back in 1961, rather than to the more accessible second edition published in 1966. This does not much matter since the theoretical position, though specified and extended, remains basically the same in both editions. My own quotations are from the more widely available second edition.

[3] *Ibid.,* p. 11.

they repeatedly assert that the conception of social problems set out here ultimately rests "on some notion of social consensus." *Second,* the conception presumably does not raise the "question of the adequacy of social life." And *third,* it allegedly assigns the role of technician to the social scientist, rather than the more fitting role of social critic.

Without entering into polemics, it must be said that the theoretical formulations imputed to me contrast strangely with those actually set out in earlier editions of this book (and retained in this one). Compare first the imputation of the notion of a "consensual society" with the basic theoretical assumption to the contrary reiterated throughout the chapter:

> Even otherwise differing "schools of sociological thought" are agreed on the theoretical conception that all societies are differentiated into a variety of structurally connected social statuses. This is *universally* the case although societies vary, of course, in the degree of structural differentiation. Furthermore, people occupying different positions in the social structure tend to have *distinctive interests and values* (as well as sharing some interests and values with others).
>
> .   .   .
>
> In short, full or substantial consensus in a complex, differentiated society exists for *only a limited number of* values, interests, and derived standards for conduct.
>
> .   .   .
>
> . . . the structural circumstances, which we have previously noted, of status groups and social strata having *not only different but incompatible values and interests.* This circumstance enlarges the potential for social disorganization . . .
>
> .   .   .
>
> The extent of agreement on norms within the group or society may vary . . .
>
> .   .   .
>
> . . . as we have noted, various groups and strata in the structure of a society have *distinctive interests and values as well as in some degree sharing other interests and values.* To the extent that this *diversity, and sometimes this conflict, of values and interests is distributed among statuses in the society* . . .[4]

In the light of these repeated formulations, it is difficult to see the basis for imputing the notion of a "consensual society" to functional analysis. It is as though an intellectual stereotype had taken charge, as though it were mandatory for a functional orientation to social problems to adopt the as-

---

[4] Robert K. Merton and Robert A. Nisbet, eds., *Contemporary Social Problems* (1966), pp. 785–86, 802, 812, 819. That social conflict is not mere happenstance but has a basis in social structure is a continuing functional premise in Robert K. Merton, *Social Theory and Social Structure* (New York: Free Press, 1968), pp. 424–25.

sumption of full consensus, and so one need look no further to learn whether this is really so. What makes this even more perplexing is that the critics of our position themselves focus on social institutions and would propose changes in them; presumably, then, they must assume, just as the functional orientation does, *some* degree of consensus among *some* people who share their moral criticism with them. It begins to appear that the critics may be engaging in moral rhetoric rather than in analyzing theoretical substance.

This holds also for the second criticism leveled against the functional perspective which, it is said, does not raise the "question of the adequacy of social life." What makes this criticism surprising is that it is precisely the functional orientation, with its theoretical commitment to the assessment of consequences, that invites such appraisals. Thus it is noted in *Contemporary Social Problems* that

> not all conditions and processes of society *inimical to the values of men* are recognized as such by them. It is the function of the sociologist to discover and to report *the human consequences of holding to certain values and practices just as it is his function to discover and to report the human consequences of departing from these values and practices.*[5]

Symptomatically, the theoretical perspective set out by Skolnick and Currie says nothing at all about how "the question of the adequacy of social life" is to be assessed. Once again, it seems to substitute moral rhetoric exhorting us to engage in "critical analysis" without providing a theoretical apparatus for doing so.

This brings us to the third criticism, which maintains that the functional orientation assigns the role of mere technician to the social scientist rather than leading him to examine "critically the basic institutions and processes of society," recognizing all the while that "institutions exist to serve man, and must therefore be *accountable* to men." Skolnick and Currie go on to observe that

> to speak of something as a "problem" is to bring it out of the realm of the inevitable or the tacitly accepted, take away its "sacred" character, and suggest that it need not be the way it is. To focus on institutions in this way is to open them to public scrutiny and to insist on the responsibility for change. More generally, *such an approach holds those in positions of authority, power and influence accountable for their actions.*[6]

---

[5] *Ibid.,* p. 788.
[6] Jerome H. Skolnick and Elliott Currie, eds., *Crisis in American Institutions,* pp. 15–16.

With this statement, the critics of functional analysis have come full circle to reaffirm the theoretical orientation that they are ostensibly disparaging. For in emphasizing that their own "approach holds those in positions of authority, power and influence *accountable* for their actions," they adopt almost the very language of functional analysis as set out in *Contemporary Social Problems:*

> . . . Through its successive uncovering of latent social problems and through its clarification of manifest social problems, sociological inquiry does make *men increasingly accountable for the outcome of their collective and institutionalized actions.*[7]

This brief confrontation between the criticism and the theory being criticized would seem to have one result: that moral rhetoric can for a time obscure but not transform the import of a theoretical orientation to social problems.

THE SOCIOLOGICAL DIAGNOSIS OF SOCIAL PROBLEMS

Just about everyone has at least a gross conception of "social problems." Unsought but undeniable troubles in society, social conflicts and confusions usually described as the "social crisis of our time," the victimizing of-people by social institutions that put them at a disadvantage in life, crime, presently curable but uncured disease, the socially unauthorized use of violence – all these and more are caught up in what most of us ordinarily mean by the term "social problems." Nor is this general understanding far removed from the technical sense in which the sociologist employs the term. But since the popular and the technical senses of social problems are not identical, although they overlap, it will be useful to consider what enters into the sociologist's diagnosis of a social problem. In considering this, we must recognize that sociologists do not all agree on the conception of a social problem; but, as can be seen throughout the pages of this book, there is enough agreement to provide a working basis.

---

[7] *Contemporary Social Problems* (1966), p. 790. For more on *ways in which* functional analysis makes for accountability, see *ibid.*, p. 789, where, after noting a variety of cases in point, it is noted: "In this sense and in this way, sociological knowledge eventually presses policy-makers to justify their social policies to their constituencies and the larger community." On the critical and "moral dimension" of social research, see Robert K. Merton, *Mass Persuasion* (New York: Harper, 1946), pp. 185–89; T. S. Simey, *Social Science and Social Purpose* (London: Constable, 1968), pp. 59–62, 178–84.

In examining the sociological notion of a social problem, we must treat at least six connected questions: (1) the central criterion of a social problem: a significant discrepancy between social standards and social actuality; (2) the sense in which social problems have social origins; (3) the judges of social problems, those people who in fact principally define the great problems in a society; (4) manifest and latent social problems; (5) the social perception of social problems; and finally (6) the ways in which belief in the corrigibility of unwanted social situations enters into the definition of social problems.

Social Standards and Social Actuality

The first and basic ingredient of a social problem consists of a substantial discrepancy between widely shared social standards and actual conditions of social life. Such discrepancies vary in extent and in degree of importance assigned them so that social problems are regarded as differing in magnitude as well as kind. In referring to social standards, we do not mean to imply that they are uniformly shared throughout the sectors of a society. Quite the contrary. As we shall see when we turn to "the judges of social problems," these standards and their implementation differ among the several social strata and social segments. Nevertheless, we can begin by considering certain aspects of the gap between social standards and social actuality, for this provides a useful way of thinking about widely diversified kinds of social problems.

The extent of the disparity between what is and what people think ought to be varies from time to time in the same society and from place to place among societies. But it is difficult to devise acceptable measures of this disjunction between social standards and social reality. I do not refer here to the notorious inadequacies in the statistics officially registering the frequency of various types of deviant behavior and symptoms of social disorganization, for many of our chapters have paused to consider in detail these defects in official statistics. All sociological authorities agree that the statistics of mental illness and suicide, of crime and juvenile delinquency, or prostitution and divorce are subject to all manner of bias owing to difficulties in obtaining a thorough count of comparable units. (It is ironic that the most nearly faultless and most informative social statistics available in American society deal with performance in professional baseball and football, indeed, in sports generally; among statistics dealing with social problems, those of traffic accidents and casualties are perhaps the most reliable.) Beyond the technical shortcomings of the statistics of social troubles lie further difficulties in devising apt measures of the extent of the discrepancy between social standards and social actuality.

In dealing with extremely simplified cases of social casualties — as Bredemeier and Toby describe the people who signally fail to meet social standards [8] — we can adopt simple measures that serve, up to a point. One such measure would be provided, for example, by a full record of the number of homicides in a society, thus indicating the extent of the gap between the norm forbidding murder and the way things actually are in this respect. But even in this seemingly simplest of instances, instructive ambiguities remain. Some, indeed many, moralities hold every human life to be sacred. For people subscribing to this value, the sheer number of homicides would be the appropriate indicator of the extent of this particular social problem. Since each unlawful killing violates the value placed on human life, the absolute number of homicides becomes central, entirely apart from the differing probabilities of homicides in populations of widely differing size. For other observers, intent on making standardized comparisons of the scale of the problem among different societies, the absolute number of homicides no longer holds as a measure. Instead, they would use standardized rates of homicide — say, homicides per 100,000 of the population or per 100,000 of the adult population. (For the specimen case of homicide, any other form of deviant behavior can be substituted without change in the logic of the argument: For people holding fast to a value, it is the *absolute numbers* of violations of that value that register the scale of the problems; for the sociological investigator, intent on ferreting out the sources and consequences of social problems, it will ordinarily be the *relative numbers* — the rates or proportions — that are used to estimate the magnitude of the problem.)

Furthermore, the frequency of deviant acts — whether counted in absolute or relative numbers — is of course not enough to measure the social significance of the discrepancy between standards and behavior. Social values and their associated standards differ greatly in the importance people assign to them. They are not all of a kind. Everyone knows that petty theft — the very term includes an evaluation of significance — differs in its moral and social significance from homicide, this difference being partly registered in the currently [9] different punishments meted out to the two classes of offenders.

---

[8] Harry C. Bredemeier and Jackson Toby, *Social Problems in America* (New York: Wiley, 1960).

[9] "Currently" because it was not, of course, always so. What is now defined as petty larceny and subject to mild sanctions was in other times and places defined as a capital offense. In sixteenth- and seventeenth-century England, for example, thieves were savagely punished, with many of them included among the 72,000 estimated to have been executed during the reign of Henry VIII alone. See Jerome Hall, *Theft, Law, and Society* (Boston: Little, Brown, 1935), pp. 84–85.

But how are these two classes of deviant behavior to be compared in terms of their ranking as social problems? Is one homicide to be equated with 10 petty thefts? 100? 1000? We sense that these are incommensurables and so *feel* that the question of comparing their magnitude is a nonsense question. Yet this feeling is only a prelude to recognizing the more general fact that we have no strict common denominator for social problems and so have no workable procedures for comparing the scale of different problems, even when the task is simplified by dealing with two kinds of criminal acts.

When we try to compare the magnitude of very different kinds of social problems, the issue of course becomes all the more difficult to resolve. Shall we conclude that the approximately 9000 murders in 1969 represent about one-fifth as great a social problem in the United States as the approximately 56,700 deaths from vehicular accidents in that year? And, in turn, how are these to be compared in order of magnitude with the three million un-employed Americans in that same year, the nearly 500,000 patients in mental hospitals, or the unnumbered millions who are seriously alienated from their jobs, who find little joy and small purpose in them and at best resign them-selves to using only part of their capacities in work that is for them little more than a necessary evil?

In short, there are no agreed-upon bases for rigorously appraising the comparative magnitude of different social problems. In the end, it is the values held by people occupying different positions in society that provide the rough bases for the relative importance assigned to social problems and, as we shall see later in this chapter, this sometimes leads to badly distorted impressions of the social consequences of various problems, even when these are judged in the light of reigning values.

Social Origins of Social Problems

It is sometimes said that social problems must have social origins. It is not always clear whether this statement is offered as a partial definition or an empirically testable proposition, as a criterion or a hypothesis. In one sense, the requirement of social origins is redundant. For, as we have just seen, a social problem formally involves a discrepancy, judged unacceptable, be-tween social standards and social actuality.

But more than this is ordinarily meant by the proposal that only the problems that originate in social conditions or processes can usefully be regarded as social problems. It is often proposed that society itself, rather than its public definitions is the substantive *cause* of social problems. According to this version of the idea, crime and suicide and family disorganization constitute social problems because they result from identifiable social circumstances. In this view, socially disruptive events that are not man-made but nature-made would be excluded from consideration. Earthquakes, tornadoes, cyclones, hurricanes, eruptions of volcanoes, floods, perhaps famines and epidemics—these and all other nature-caused events that greatly affect the lives of men in society would be ruled out.

Like other investigators, sociologists are of course free to limit the range of their inquiry. They are free to state the criteria of the phenomena to be investigated. But in proposing particular criteria, sociologists, like other investigators, are required to show that these criteria are theoretically useful, if the proposal is to be taken seriously by others. Freedom to define does not mean license to exclude. And until now, no satisfactory case has been made for confining the scope of social problems to only those problems that are in their origin social in the sense that the events precipitating them are initiated by men in society. Rather, it is proposed that, whatever the precipitating events, they become part of a social problem whenever they give rise to significant discrepancies between social standards and social actuality. For whether the forces disrupting patterns of social life are nature-made or man-made, they will, in the end, confront members of the society with the task of responding to them, and the nature of that response is, in sociological principle, greatly affected by the structure of the society, by its institutions, and its values.[10]

Perhaps later inquiry will find distinct patterns of social problems according to whether they are social both in origin and consequences or are precipitated by nonsocial events that have socially disruptive consequences. But this would only mean the working out of further discriminations. It would not mean scrapping the conception that social problems are defined by their consequences, whatever their origins.

The Judges of Social Problems

We have noted the difficulty of assessing the scale of diverse social problems and the sense in which the unwanted discrepancy between social standards and social actuality makes for a social problem, irrespective of the character of the precipitating events that help create the discrepancy. A third ingredi-

---

[10] This conception is developed and documented in the first edition of this book in Charles Fritz's chapter dealing with disasters and catastrophes, pp. 682–94.

ent entering into the diagnosis of social problems requires us to consider the people who judge that the discrepancy exists and that it matters. Sociologists often say that "many people" or a "functionally significant number of people" or even that "a majority of people" in a society must regard a social circumstance as departing from their standards in order for this circumstance to qualify as a social problem. As a first rough approximation, this formulation can serve for many cases. When social norms are a matter of overwhelming consensus, as usually with the norms proscribing murder or rape or kidnapping, a more exacting formulation is not required. But for many other kinds of social behavior and social conditions, this merely numerical criterion is no longer adequate. It becomes necessary to distinguish among "the many" who define certain recurrent events or a social condition as a problem.

Social definitions of social problems have this in common with other processes in society: Those occupying strategic positions of authority and power of course carry more weight than others in deciding social policy and therefore, among other things, in identifying for the rest what are to be taken as significant departures from social standards. There is not a plebiscitary democracy of judgment in which every man's appraisal is assigned the same voting power in defining a condition as a social problem. It is a mistaken, atomistic notion that each member of society sets about to define social problems for himself and that it is the aggregate of these independent judgments that decides the array of problems in the society and the comparative importance of each problem in the array. Even otherwise differing "schools of sociological thought" are agreed on the theoretical conception that all societies are differentiated into a variety of structurally connected social statuses. This is universally the case although societies vary, of course, in the degree of structural differentiation. Furthermore, people occupying different positions in the social structure tend to have distinctive interests and values (as well as sharing some interests and values with others). As a result, not all social standards are evenly distributed among diverse social positions. It follows logically and is found empirically that to the extent that these standards differ among social positions and groups within a society, the same circumstances will be variously evaluated as being at odds with the standards held by some and as consistent with standards held by others. Thus one group's problem will be another group's asset.

Societies that are highly differentiated into a great variety of social statuses, with their characteristic interests and values, will tend to have correspondingly different, and often strongly conflicting, judgments of what constitute particular social problems. Abortion, for example, is defined as a social problem by many whose religiously based or otherwise legitimized values are violated by it. Others define abortion as a means of preventing a personal problem—having an unwanted child, whether legitimate or illegitimate—which, aggregated for many cases, could become a serious social problem.[11] Thus some American states largely forbid abortion, others do not. Or again, to take a stale and therefore at once evident example, free and easy access to alcoholic drink was defined by many Americans, two generations ago, as the source of an important social problem; therefore, for a time, such access was prohibited by legislation. For a good many others—who also defined alcohol*ism* as a problem—the would-be social cure was worse than the ailment: Prohibition was held to violate standards by entering the private lives of Americans to regulate what they regarded as altogether personal decisions.

In short, full or overwhelming consensus in a complex, differentiated society exists for only a limited number of values, interests, and derived standards for conduct. We must therefore be prepared to find that the same social conditions and behaviors will be defined by some as a social problem and by others as an agreeable and fitting state of affairs. For the latter, indeed, the situation may begin to become a problem only when the presumed remedy is introduced by the former. What is loosely described as "socialized medicine," for example, was defined as a social remedy by Walter Reuther and many others in his constituency of the AFL-CIO just as it was defined as a social problem by the successive presidents of the AMA and many others in their constituency. In the eyes of some, unemployment benefits help solve a problem by providing aid to people for their work in the past and for willingness to work in the present; for others, whose secure positions in society help them sustain the belief, these benefits are at best a dole, morally suspect and socially undesirable. For some, the widespread acceptance of things as they are registers the social problem of public apathy; for others, the problem begins with the appearance of organized social protest. Thus Kenneth B. Clark observes that

> Continuing evidence of the pervasive moral apathy and political cynicism in the American mass culture is a significant negative in weighing the possibilities for social democracy. If constructive change were to depend on the chance of profound moral conversion, there might be cause for pessimism. Negroes must convince the majority, who are white, that continued oppression of the Negro minority hurts

---

[11] Edwin M. Schur, *Crimes without Victims: Deviant Behavior and Public Policy: Abortion, Homosexuality, and Drug Addiction* (Englewood Cliffs, N. J.: Prentice-Hall, 1965). On changing definitions of crime as these relate to major interest groups and strata, see Richard Quinney, *The Social Reality of Crime* (Boston: Little, Brown, 1970) and Austin T. Turk, "Conflict and Criminality," *American Sociological Review*, Vol. 31 (June, 1966), pp. 338–52.

the white majority too. Nor is it sophistry to argue that this is indeed the case. If it were not the case, the Negro cause would be hopeless. Certainly the Negro cannot hope to argue his case primarily in terms of ethical concerns, for these historically have had only sentimental and verbal significance in themselves. They have never been the chief source of power for that social change which involves significant alteration of status between privileged versus unprivileged groups. Child labor legislation was not the direct result of a moral indignation against the exploitation of children in factories, mines, mills, but rather reflected a growing manpower shortage and the new rise of the labor unions. The value of ethical appeals is to be found only when they can be harnessed to more concrete appeals such as economic, political, or other power advantages to be derived from those with the power to facilitate or inhibit change. Ethical and moral appeal can be used to give theoretical support for a program of action, or in some cases to obscure and make the pragmatic aspects of that program more palatable to conscience. If moral force opposes economic or political ends, the goal of moral force may be postponed. The reverse may also be true. But where moral force and practical advantage are united, their momentum is hard to deny.[12]

What has been stated here concerning the situation of American blacks and whites as a social problem, holds for all manner of other discrepancies between widespread social values and actual social situations. The gap between values and actuality is defined by those who perceive the gap as a problem confronting society. It must be closed by bringing social situations closer to social values, not by accommodating values to currently existing situations. But the judges of the problem who also wield power and authority will succeed in inaugurating the change only to the degree that other forces in society work in the same direction as the moral mandate. When we speak of the times "being ripe for a designated social change" we are referring metaphorically to the convergence of moral and social system imperatives.

The fact that the conflicting values and interests of differentiated groups in a complex society result in disparate conceptions of the principal problems of society would at first seem to dissolve the concept of social problems in the acid of extreme relativism. But this is only apparently so. Sociologists need not and do not limit the scope of social problems to those expressly defined by the people they are studying and trying to understand. Fortunately, they have an alternative to the doctrine of extreme philosophical idealism, which holds that nothing is either a social problem or a social asset but thinking makes it so. They need not become separated from good sense by imprisoning

---

[12] Kenneth B. Clark, *Dark Ghetto: Dilemmas of Social Power* (New York: Harper, 1965), p. 204.

themselves in the set of logically impregnable premises that only those situations constitute social problems which are so defined by the people involved in them. For *social problems are not only subjective states of mind; they are also objective states of affairs.*

Manifest and Latent Social Problems

The sociologist assumes that social problems, along with other facets of human society, have both their subjective aspect, this appearing in the perceptions and evaluations of people in society who affirm or deny that something is a social problem, and their objective aspect, this appearing in the actual conditions that are being appraised.[13] For the sociologist to confine himself only to the conditions in society that a majority of people regard as undesirable would be to exclude study of all manner of other conditions that are in fact at odds with the declared values of those who accept these conditions. Such a limitation would require the sociologist to subscribe to an extreme subjectivism, under the self-deceiving guise of retaining the objectivity of the scientific observer. But it is possible to escape this heedless subjectivism that in effect abandons definition of the scope of sociological inquiry to the decisions of the men and groups under study. For not all conditions and processes of society inimical to the values of men are recognized as such by them. It is the function of the sociologist to discover and to report the human consequences of holding to certain values and practices just as it is his function to discover and to report the human consequences of departing from these values and practices.

Apart from manifest social problems—those objective social conditions identified by problem-definers as at odds with social values—are latent social problems, conditions that are also at odds with values current in the society but are not generally recognized as being so. The sociologist does not impose his values upon others when he undertakes to supply knowledge about latent social problems. When the demographer Kingsley Davis, for example, identifies the social, economic, and cultural consequences of rapidly growing popu-

---

[13] This double aspect of social problems has been recognized for some time, as in the seminal paper by Richard C. Fuller and Richard R. Myers, "Some Aspects of a Theory of Social Problems." But they blur the objective aspect when they say that "social problems are what people think they are." F. James Davis deliberately limits his purview to manifest social problems on the grounds that only problems identified by the public are defined by their values and beliefs rather than by those of the sociologist. F. James Davis, *Social Problems* (New York: Free Press, 1970).

lations in diverse kinds of society, he in effect calls the advocates of alternative population policies to account for the results of one or another policy. They can no longer evade responsibility for the social consequences of policy by claiming these to be fundamentally unforeseeable. Or again, the sociologists who demonstrate the "wastage of talent" that results from marked inequalities of opportunity for the training and exercise of socially prized talent bring to a focus what was experienced by the diffuse many as only a personal problem rather than a problem of society. Or yet again, as our knowledge, still notoriously sparse, of the social, economic, and psychological consequences of racial discrimination is enlarged — consequences for the dominant majority as well as for the subordinate minority — advocates of alternative policies will be brought increasingly to account for their distinctive positions. Or, for a final important example, the development of "technology assessment" — a sort of early-warning system for anticipating and assessing the major social and ecological consequences of proposed technological innovations — is a similar thrust toward accountability in essentially social decisions and represents another recent change in social policy which is altogether congruent with functional perspectives on latent social problems.[14] In this way, sociological knowledge eventually presses policymakers to justify their social policies to their constituencies and the larger community.

SOCIAL VALUES AND SOCIOLOGICAL ANALYSIS — We should pause to take note of what is *not* involved in the analytical process of making latent social problems manifest. Otherwise, it will be easily mistaken for another version of extreme and untenable sociological rationalism. Sociologists do not claim that knowledge of the consequences attendant on current social beliefs and practices will automatically lead people to abandon the beliefs and practices that frustrate their own basic values. Man-in-society is not as strictly rational a creature as all that. The sociological truth does not instantly make men free. It does not induce a sudden rupture with demonstrably dysfunctional arrangements in society. But by discovering consequences of accepted practices and by making these known, the sociologist engaged in the study of social problems provides a basis for substantial reappraisals of these practices in the long run, if not necessarily at once. It might be asked, of course, why we should be interested in the long run since, as John Maynard

---

[14] For an exacting overview of the prospects and problems of technology assessment, see the Report of the National Academy of Sciences, *Technology: Processes of Assessment and Choice* (Washington, D. C.: U. S. House of Representatives Committee on Science and Astronautics, July, 1969).

Keynes emphatically reminded us, in the long run we are all dead. The reply is as thoroughly evident as the question: because, contrary to our egoistic faith, the world does not die with us.

In other words, there is a degree of pragmatism in the sociological outlook, as there is in every other scientific outlook. But it is not pragmatism run riot. New objective knowledge of the probable consequences of action need not lead men to act at once in the light of this knowledge. Sociology need not make men wise or even prudent. But, through its successive uncovering of latent social problems and through its clarification of manifest social problems, sociological inquiry does make men increasingly accountable for the outcome of their collective and institutionalized actions.

There is a further use of this distinction between manifest and latent social problems, between the social conditions currently judged by various categories of men in society to be deeply objectionable and the social conditions that would be so judged, were their multifarious consequences known. Among other things, the distinction helps sociologists themselves recognize how they can move beyond prevalent social beliefs, practices, and judgments without entering upon the misplaced career of trying to impose their own values upon others.[15] Through his work, the sociologist does not remain aloof from social controversy, but in his capacity as sociologist—rather than as citizen—he takes a distinctive and limited part in it. He introduces pertinent sociological truths so that the substantive morality and the social policy governing the issues at stake can take account of these truths. It does not follow, however, that these truths will shape morality and policy in their every aspect. In his capacity as sociologist, emphatically not in his capacity as citizen, the student of social problems neither exhorts nor denounces, neither advocates nor re-

---

[15] As the debate over the place of values in sociological inquiry becomes ever more polarized, it invites increasingly extravagant statements of one's own position and stereotyped distortions of the other's position, as is generally the case when social conflict is substituted for intellectual disagreement. (On the process of conflict, see Robert K. Merton, "Social Conflict over Styles of Sociological Work," *Transactions* (Fourth World Congress of Sociology, III, 1959), pp. 21–44, esp. p. 29 ff.) For a muscular statement of the place of values in social science that in effect claims to destroy and bury all other formulations but his own, see Alvin W. Gouldner, *The Coming Crisis of Western Sociology* (New York: Basic Books, 1970). For a recent statement intellectually congenial to the position set forth here, see Robert M. Solow, "Science and Ideology in Economics," *The Public Interest*, Vol. 21 (Fall, 1970), pp. 94–107. Another position is the one set forth by Gunnar Myrdal in several places, most recently in his book, *Objectivity in Social Research* (New York: Pantheon, 1969). For still other shades of opinion, see Ralf Dahrendorf, *Essays in the Theory of Society* (Stanford: Stanford University Press, 1968), esp. Chapters 1, 2, 10 and Gideon Sjoberg, ed., *Ethics, Politics and Social Research* (Cambridge: Schenkman, 1967).

jects. It is enough that he uncover to others the great price they sometimes pay for their settled but insufficiently examined convictions and their established but inflexible practices.

Above all, this view of the sociologist's role avoids the opposite and equal errors of assuming that in any society, "whatever is, is right" and that "whatever is, is wrong." It discards the perspectives of both the complacent old men and the angry young men. It repudiates the extravagant optimism that sees everything in society as bound to turn out all right in the end just as it repudiates the extravagant pessimism that sees nothing but catastrophe ahead. Nor does it assume that the middle way is everywhere and always the right way: The disparaging connotations of the word *mediocrity,* the condition of being intermediate between extremes, should be enough to ward us off that bland and simple-minded assumption. Rather, this sociological outlook has us examine each set of social conditions in terms of its diverse and progressively discovered consequences for the condition of men, including all those consequences that bear upon the values held by men in the particular society. In following this path, we avoid both forms of that insolent ignorance that would have us pretend to know that society is bound to move in the one direction of cumulative improvement or in the other of continuing decline. Not least, this sociological perspective has the scientifically extraneous but humanly solid merit of leaving a substantial place for men-making-their-future-history while avoiding the utopianism-that-beguiles by recognizing that the degrees of freedom men have in that task are variously and sometimes severely limited by the objective conditions set by nature, society, and culture.[16]

To some degree, then, the distinction between manifest and latent social

---

[16] This conception of deliberate social change being forced to operate within the constraints set not only by nature (modified through technology) but also by the existing structure of society and culture is found in a variety of sociological theories of notably differing ideological origins. We have encountered it in Kenneth B. Clark's discussion of the black-white problem in the United States. It is central to functional analysis in sociology, principally in the form of the concept of structural context (or structural constraint). See, for example, Robert K. Merton, *Social Theory and Social Structure,* enl. ed., pp. 106-7, 126-27, *passim.* It was also central to Marx's theories of social change (although not necessarily to the work of all those who profess to find the source of their ideas in Marx); see the summary in *ibid.,* pp. 93-95. It is also basic to the theory of sociologists who see themselves as altogether at odds with Marxist theory; to take only one example, the penetrating paper by Willard Waller, "Social Problems and the Mores," *American Sociological Review,* Vol. 1 (December, 1936), pp. 922-33. In short, the conception of structural constraints on social change is one that transcends many, though not all, theoretical and ideological differences in sociology.

problems crystallizes ideas governing the range of matters selected for sociological inquiry and the role of values in such inquiry. The distinction maintains that to confine the study of social problems to only those circumstances
that are expressly defined as problems in the society is arbitrarily to ignore
other conditions that are also dysfunctional to values held by people in that
society. To adopt this course is to hamstring sociological analysis by setting
unnecessary limits on the selection of problems for investigation. Under the
conception intrinsic to the distinction between manifest and latent social
problems, the sociologist neither abdicates his intellectual and professional
responsibilities nor usurps the position of sitting in moral judgment on his
fellow men.

The Social Perception of Social Problems

Linked with the distinction between manifest and latent social problems is
the variability in the degree of public attention accorded diverse manifest
problems. We cannot take for granted a reasonably correct public image of
social problems: of their scale, distribution, causation, consequences, and
persistence or change. Public images are often egregiously mistaken, for
reasons we are beginning to understand. Some, such as those of mental illness, are walled off and substantially denied for a time; others, such as "crime
waves" and drug addiction, become a focus of popular attention to be regarded as of far greater magnitude and consequence than investigation
finds them to be.[17]

A familiar and comparatively simple kind of episode brings out the
socio-psychological processes that make for a disparity between the objective
magnitude of events (even when this is gauged by the express values of those
perceiving them) and the social perceptions of them. Many more people are

---

[17] For cases in point of public misperceptions of various social problems, see the foregoing chapters. See also Gerald Gurin, Joseph Veroff, and Sheila Feld, *Americans View
Their Mental Health* (New York: Basic Books, 1960); and Daniel Bell, "The Myth of
Crime Waves," in his *The End of Ideology* (New York: Free Press, 1960), Chapter 8.
An ingenious study of the reporting of crime news in four Colorado newspapers bears
directly on this matter of the social perception of social problems. The amount of crime
news varied independently of the amount of crime in the state. Moreover, a public
opinion survey found that the public perception of violent crimes and theft reflected
trends in the amount of crime *news* rather than actual crime *rates*. F. James Davis,
"Crime News in Colorado Newspapers," *American Journal of Sociology,* Vol. 57 (1952),
pp. 325–30.

killed each year in the United States by automobile accidents than by air-plane accidents. The number of deaths occasioned by the two are of entirely different orders of magnitude: In 1969 for example, about 56,700 Americans were put to death by automobiles and 1546 by planes. Yet the intensity of public attention accorded a dramatic airplane accident in newspapers, radio, and television far outruns that accorded the cumulatively greater number of deaths in automobile accidents. The dramatic collision of two planes in mid-air late in 1960, for instance, aroused nationwide interest — assuredly in the nation's press, radio, and television, with even the conservative *New York Times* devoting some ten pages to the event, and probably also in uncounted millions of conversations. Yet during the days that this disaster, with its toll of 137 killed, remained in the forefront of public attention, several hundred more people had been killed by automobiles.

The particular instance of marked disparity between the objective magnitude of human tragedies and the popular perceptions of them only highlights the general point (the very familiarity of the case testifying to the generality of the pattern). Popular perceptions are no safe guide to the actual magnitude of a social problem. Ill-understood but partly known processes of social perception [18] involve the patterned omitting, supplementing, and organizing of what is selectively perceived as the social reality. In the case just under review, perception seems affected by what we are better able to describe than to explain: the dramatic quality of unitary events that evoke popular interest. The airplane disaster is perceived as a *single* event, although it is of course compounded of many occurrences that eventuated in the victims going to their death. In contrast, the hundreds of automobile accidents occurring on the same day, with their, say, 200 dead, comprise a compound event that can be detected only through the aggregation of cold and impersonal numbers. [19] The import of this kind of thing is clear. Pervasive social problems that seldom have dramatic and conspicuous manifestations are apt to arouse smaller public attention than problems, less serious even when judged by the beholder's own values, that erupt in the spotlight of public drama. This is another reason that the sociologist need not order the importance of social problems in the same way as the man in the street. For, as we have noted before, even when we take, as we do, the values of the people we are observ-

---

[18] For a comprehensive overview of the subject, see Henri Tajfel, "Social and Cultural Factors in Perception," in Gardner Lindzey and Elliot Aronson, *The Handbook of Social Psychology* (Reading, Mass.: Addison-Wesley, 1969), 2nd ed., Vol. 3, Chapter 22.

[19] For a psychological theory of what makes things seem to belong together and so to comprise an event or unit, see Fritz Heider, "Social Perception and Phenomenal Causality, *Psychological Review,* Vol. 51 (1954), pp. 358–74; also F. Heider, *The Psychology of Interpersonal Relations* (New York: Wiley, 1958), pp. 60–64.

ing as one basis for assessing social problems—in the present case, the sanctity of life and the tragedy of premature death—the public's perception of these problems is often found to be badly distorted.

The perception of social problems is affected by the structure of social relations between people. A generation ago, Pitirim Sorokin found experimentally that the greater the social distance between victims of catastrophe and the people made aware of it, the less are these people motivated to perceive it as a problem calling for effective action and sympathy.[20] Millions of victims of famine in India or China elicit less effective sympathy from Americans than do scores of victims of castastrophes within their own national borders. Further inquiry is needed to find out whether all kinds of social problems are apt to be perceived as less significant the greater the social distance between the observer and the people most directly and visibly affected by the problem.

Related to this fact is the apparently great disparity in people's concern with public and private troubles. This disparity has been depicted in a prototypical instance by the scientist, civil servant, and novelist C. P. Snow. In his novel, *The New Men*,[21] he has his protagonist, Lewis Eliot, muse on the morning after the bomb had been dropped on Hiroshima:

> I went straight off to sleep, woke before four, and did not get to sleep again. It was not a bad test of how public and private worries compare in depth, I thought, when I remembered the nights I had lain awake because of private trouble. Public trouble—how many such nights of insomnia had *that* given me? The answer was, just one. On the night after Munich, I had lain sleepless—and perhaps, as I went through the early hours of August 7th [1945], I could fairly count another half.

What the novelist Snow observed of his emblematic and thinly disguised fictional civil servant Eliot, the sociologist Stouffer found to be true for Americans generally. Stouffer's study [22] was conducted during the summer of 1954, better described as the time when the Army-Joseph McCarthy hearings were in full swing and were being avidly watched over television by millions of Americans. During this time of public troubles, less than one percent in two matched national samples of Americans reported that "they were worried either about the threat of Communists in the United States or about civil liberties." No more than 8 percent mentioned the danger of war or other

---

[20] Pitirim A. Sorokin *et al.*, "An Experimental Study of Efficiency of Work under Various Conditions," *American Journal of Sociology,* Vol. 35 (May, 1930), pp. 765–82.

[21] London: Macmillan, 1954, p. 188.

[22] Samuel A. Stouffer, *Communism, Conformity, and Civil Liberties* (New York: Doubleday, 1955), pp. 59–74, reports the findings summarized here.

forms of international conflict as a source of anxiety. Even when interviewers directed attention to public concerns by asking whether there are "other problems you worry about or are concerned about, especially political or world problems," as many as 52 percent had nothing to add to their previous account. The number referring to problems of civil liberties doubled, rising from the unimpressive total of one percent to the no more impressive total of 2 percent. When asked to report the kinds of problems they had discussed with friends during the preceding week or so, one-half of these representative Americans said they had talked about personal or family problems only. Evidently, there was something less than a burning preoccupation with some of the most demanding public troubles of the time. These seemed remote, crowded out by the personal problems in family and place of work that turn up in the day-by-day round of social life. This research, then, provides another indication that the judgments of individual members of the society afford anything but a secure guide to the objective saliency of social problems, even for themselves. The connections between public and private troubles are difficult to detect, and it cannot be assumed that they are perceived by most people as they live out their lives.

Chronic victims of collective suffering have on occasion sensed that their problems are invisible to many in the society and have taken dramatic steps to call public attention to their situation. Boycotts, picketing, sit-ins, teach-ins and all manner of public demonstrations are designed to increase the visibility of problems that are otherwise largely ignored because, being chronic and widespread, they tend to be taken for granted. These expedients are rough functional equivalents for providing the high visibility that automatically comes, in this day of nearly instantaneous communication, from sudden mass disasters.[23] Whatever their other purposes and consequences, such demonstrations aim and sometimes succeed in shaking people loose from the tacit conviction that whatever is, is inevitable, and so might as well be ignored.

---

[23] For an instructive analysis of the differences in social response to large-scale chronic suffering and to sudden and acute episodes of collective stress, see Allen Barton, *Communities in Disaster: A Sociological Analysis of Collective Stress Situations* (New York: Doubleday, 1969), pp. 208, 232–38. For a general formulation of how visibility and observability enter into social processes, see Robert K. Merton, *Social Theory and Social Structure*, pp. 373–76, 390–411. On the functions of violence and mass demonstrations in focusing public attention on otherwise chronic suffering, see Lewis Coser, *Continuities in the Study of Social Conflict* (New York: Free Press, 1967), Chapter 4. For historical analysis of the changing functions of collective violence, see Charles Tilly, "Collective Violence in European Perspective," in Hugh D. Graham and Ted R. Gurr, eds., *Violence in America* (New York: New American Library, 1969), pp. 4–42.

Value Systems and Corrigibility of Social Problems

Functionally considered, unwanted discrepancies between social standards and social reality qualify as manifest social problems only when people believe that they can do something about them. The discrepancies must be perceived as corrigible. It must be thought possible to cope with the problem, to reduce its scale if not to eliminate it altogether. The most completely manifest social problems encompass those frustrations of human purpose on the large scale that are being subjected to active efforts at prevention or control.

From this it is evident that the value orientations in a society toward the preventability or controllability of unwanted social conditions will affect the perceptions of social problems. At one extreme are the societies appreciably committed to fatalism, a system of beliefs that holds everything to have its appointed outcome, not to be avoided or modified by foreknowledge or by effort. Among those holding to such fatalistic beliefs, there will of course be little sense of social problems: rampant morbidities, high death rates, widespread poverty, and all the rest in the calendar of troubles are simply taken as inevitable. In such a society, the social problems are chiefly or altogether latent. Only the informed observer, exempt from this philosophy of resignation and quietism, sees the possibility of reducing or eliminating these frustrating conditions.

At the other extreme are societies largely committed to an activist philosophy of life that takes just about everything in society as being in principle subject to human control. Such a society, in fact coping with many of its problems — reducing death rates, curbing diseases, trying to eliminate acute poverty — may have many manifest social problems though fewer problems altogether. The active, dissatisfied society will have the more manifest problems, for people in it not only focus on the discrepancies between what they want and what they have, but try to do something about these discrepancies. The fatalistic society, on the other hand, may have a greater complement of social problems altogether — both manifest and latent — because they are not moved to do much about the disparity between what exists and what they would like to exist since they identify what exists with what is inevitable.

This relation between fatalism and social problems is not merely a matter of definition but, empirically, is one of mutual reinforcement. As many have noted, fatalism tends to develop among those living under conditions of extreme stress or rigorous arbitrary rule. Philosophy and conditions of life interact and reinforce one another: men are apt to think fatalistically under depressed conditions and they are apt to remain under these conditions because they think fatalistically. This fatalistic acceptance of things as they are develops among the extremely deprived social stratum described by Karl Marx as the *Lumpenproletariat* (the aggregate of demoralized workers), by Lloyd Warner as the lower-lower class and by many others, in the recent past, as the underclass. As this has been put by A. Eustace Haydon:

> For the social process the importance of fatalism lies in the ease with which it may serve as a way of escape from responsibility for social maladjustments. Conditions of unresolved wretchedness are fertile soil for the fatalistic attitude. In many cases the anaesthesia of fatalism combines with the rigidity of long established patterns of social behavior and the interests of privileged classes to produce the quietistic resignation which results in toleration of social wrongs and incapacity for experimental change.[24]

The contrast between fatalist and activist value systems and the societies or social strata in which they occur has been deliberately exaggerated in order to point up the theoretical idea. In concrete reality, few societies have maintained a wholly passive and fatalistic outlook on all their conditions of life, just as few societies have succeeded in maintaining a wholly active and voluntaristic outlook on all their unapproved conditions of life. Strands of active rebellion against fate are found in dominantly fatalistic societies and social strata just as strands of resignation and retreatism are found in dominantly activist societies and social strata. Yet if these extremes are seldom encountered in all their detailed contrast, they have nevertheless been approximated. As Max Weber and Karl Mannheim,[25] among others, have pointed out, the ethic of fatalism has often been replaced by the ethic of responsibility, in which knowledge of the sources of social problems and efforts to control them become defined as a moral obligation.

To the extent that the ethic of responsibility spreads in a society, social problems tend to become manifest rather than remaining latent. But even within such a society, largely oriented toward directed social change, countervailing processes make for the continued latency of certain social problems. One of these processes has been described by the German jurist,

[24] A. Eustace Haydon, "Fatalism," *Encyclopedia of the Social Sciences* (New York: Macmillan, 1931), Vol. 6, p. 147.

[25] Max Weber, *Essays in Sociology,* trans. and ed. by H. H. Gerth and C. W. Mills (New York: Oxford University Press, 1946), pp. 120–25. Karl Mannheim, *Ideology and Utopia,* trans. by Louis Wirth and E. A. Shils (New York: Harcourt Brace Jovanovich, 1936), pp. 170–71.

Georg Jellinek, as "the normative force of the actual." [26] By this phrase he refers to the tendency, of unknown scope and prevalence, for social practices, whatever their origins, to become converted into normatively prescribed practices. Such legitimatizing of much that exists in society tends to militate against the perception of conditions that are in fact opposed to major values held by many in the society.

Associated with this tendency to *legitimatize the existent* is another that makes for tacit acceptance of the existent, if not for its moral legitimacy. According to this attitude, unwanted conditions that are not deliberately intended but are by-products of other sought-for developments rank low in the scale of social problems. These unanticipated and undesired consequences of purposive action may become a focus of attention, but they are less apt to mobilize pressure for preventive or remedial measures than those problems that violate a prevailing morality.[27] Since the problem is unintended by those whose actions in the aggregate lead to it, moral sentiments are less often activated by the unfortunate outcome. Widespread states of anxiety in a population, the wastage of talent resulting from economic inequities of access to opportunity for the development of talent, the choking of transportation in tangled traffic—these are for a long time widely considered to be among the costs of a complex society even by many who pay these costs, partly because, objectionable as they are, they are not the result of deliberate intent. In contrast, the purposed behavior that is directly at odds with socially shared norms is at once defined as a problem of society. Crime is generally regarded as a social problem; widespread alienation from the job is not. In other words, people are less apt to experience social disorganization as a social problem than they are deviant behavior.

This observation on the contrasting public saliency of social disorganization and deviant behavior is of course only a first, loose approximation. It is scarcely true that popular concern with evidences of social disorganization

---

[26] Georg Jellinek, *Das Recht des modernen Staates* (Berlin, 1900). William G. Sumner made substantially the same observation, in his classic work, *Folkways* (Boston: Ginn, 1906), when he noted that "the notion of right is in the folkways." In much the same vein, Robert S. Lynd observed that "man's inveterate need to feel pride and rightness in his achievements has prompted him to honor the accidents of his past after the fact by describing them as 'ordained by God' or as arising from the 'inner genius' of his race, culture or nation." *Knowledge For What?* (Princeton, N. J.: Princeton University Press, 1939), p. 64. And finally, N. S. Timasheff has incorporated the notion of the normative force of the actual in his *Introduction to the Sociology of Law* (Cambridge: Harvard University Committee on Research in the Social Sciences, 1939).

[27] For the context of this statement, see Robert K. Merton, "The Unanticipated Consequences of Purposive Social Action," *American Sociological Review,* Vol. 1 (December, 1936), pp. 894–904.

is absent. After all, much organized effort is devoted to the replacing of slum housing by public housing; increasing effort is mounted to rescue talent from disuse; the city-planning movement aims to bring under control the unplanned sprawl and self-defeating traffic found in the great urban centers. But this enlarged concern with problems of social disorganization as distinct from problems of deviant behavior is itself a major social change. It is, in large part, the result of an accumulating social technology, just as other social changes are in large part the result of an accumulating physical technology. Whereas deviant behavior at once attracts the indignant notice of people whose norms and values have been violated by it, social disorganization tends not to (except as it eventuates in deviant behavior). Technical specialists, unattached intellectuals, and social critics play a central role in trying to alert greater numbers of people to what they take to be the greater immorality—living complacently under conditions of social disorganization that in principle can be brought under at least partial control. Under the progressive division of social labor it becomes the office of these specialists to try to design ways of coping with social disorganization. That the social change in this direction is far from complete can be inferred from the uniform complaints by these specialists about public apathy and misunderstanding of the problems with which they deal.

Social problems have been identified here as the substantial, unwanted discrepancies between what exists in a society and what a functionally significant collectivity within that society seriously (rather than in fantasy) wants to exist in it. The scale of these discrepancies is affected in either or both of two ways: by a raising of standards and by a deterioration of social conditions. There is no paradox, then, in finding that some complex, industrial societies, having a comparatively high plane of material life and rapid advancement of cultural values, may nevertheless be regarded by their members as more problem-ridden than other societies with substantially less material wealth and cultural achievement. Nor is there any longer a paradox in finding that as conditions improve in a society (as gauged by widespread values), popular satisfaction may nevertheless decline. Tocqueville noted this pattern more than a century ago:

> It was precisely in those parts of France [in the reign of Louis XVI] where there had been most improvements that popular discontent ran highest. . . . For it is not always when things are going from bad to worse that revolutions break out. On the contrary, it oftener happens that when a people which has put up with an oppressive rule over a long period without protest suddenly finds the government relaxing its pressure, it takes up arms against it. Thus the social order overthrown by a revolution is almost always better than the one immedi-

ately preceding it, and experience teaches us that, generally speaking, the most perilous moment for a bad government is one when it seeks to mend its ways. . . . For the mere fact that certain abuses have been remedied draws attention to the others and they now appear more galling; people may suffer less, but their sensibility is exacerbated.[28]

In short, the tide of expectations often rises disproportionately to each advance toward realizing collective values in practice. There develops an inflationary spiral of expectation, which makes for anomie and multitudinous expressions of discontent in a comparatively opulent society; what Tocqueville described in the other of his momentous books as restlessness amid prosperity.[29] These observations remind us once again of a principal theme in our theoretical orientation: Like everything else in social life, the discrepancies between socially shared standards and actual social conditions, which we call social problems, have both subjective and objective components.

SOCIAL DISORGANIZATION
AND DEVIANT BEHAVIOR

We are now ready to take systematic note of the idea, central to the plan of this book, that social problems can be usefully divided into two broad classes, the one described as "social disorganization," the other, as "deviant behavior." Even before we examine the theoretical basis for distinguishing

---

[28] Alexis de Tocqueville, *The Old Régime and the French Revolution*, trans. by Stuart Gilbert from the French ed. of 1858 (Garden City, N. Y.: Doubleday, 1955), pp. 176–77.

[29] The concept of rising expectations implied by Tocqueville is the dynamic counterpart to the concept of relative deprivation introduced by Samuel Stouffer and incorporated into the theory of reference groups by Merton and Rossi. See Alexis de Tocqueville, *Democracy in America*, Vol. II, esp. Book I (New York: Knopf, 1945; based on the Henry Reeve text of 1840), Chapter 8, "How Equality Suggests to the Americans the Idea of the Indefinite Perfectibility of Man" and Book II, Chapter 13, "Why the Americans Are So Restless in the Midst of their Prosperity." For a deep analysis of Tocqueville's ideas, see Robert A. Nisbet, *The Sociological Tradition* (New York: Basic Books, 1966), Chapter 1, *passim*. On relative deprivation, see Herbert H. Hyman and Eleanor Singer, eds. *Readings in Reference Group Theory and Research* (New York: Free Press, 1968); Robert K. Merton and Alice S. Rossi, "Contributions to the Theory of Reference Group Behavior," in Robert K. Merton, *Social Theory and Social Structure*, pp. 279–334, esp. pp. 281–90; Thomas J. Crawford and Murray Naditch, "Relative Deprivation, Powerlessness, and Militancy: The Psychology of Social Protest," *Psychiatry*, 33 (May, 1970), pp. 208–23.

these two classes of social problems, we can be reasonably sure that the two concepts are analytical, not depictive; abstract, not concrete. That is to say, they do not describe classes of events in all their actual complexity but refer only to selected aspects of them. That is why we find in each of the concrete social problems examined in this book—for instance, family disorganization, criminal behavior, and community conflict—evidence of both social disorganization and deviant behavior, though in differing compounds. Nevertheless, it is useful to distinguish in each social problem the components and aspects that are matters of disorganization and those that are matters of deviant behavior, recognizing that the two interact and, under certain conditions, tend to reinforce each other.

Social Disorganization

No single conception of social disorganization is employed by sociologists today, any more than yesterday.[30] But within the diversity of usage, there is appreciable agreement. And since nothing resembling an official nomenclature exists in sociology, just as there was none in chemistry before Lavoisier set to work, the conception of social disorganization as it is reviewed here cannot claim to be uniformly accepted by sociologists. Nevertheless, it does approximate a good deal of current usage, being much like most and not much unlike any.

Social disorganization refers to inadequacies or failures in a social system

---

[30] The range of variation in usage is roughly bounded by the formulation by Thomas and Znaniecki in 1927 and the formulation by A. K. Cohen in 1959 (although there were numerous accounts before the first of these and even a few since the second). See William I. Thomas and Florian Znaniecki, *The Polish Peasant in Europe and America* (New York: Knopf, 1927), Vol. 2, pp. 1127–33. A. K. Cohen, "The Study of Social Disorganization and Deviant Behavior," in Robert K. Merton, L. Broom, and L. S. Cottrell, Jr., eds., *Sociology Today* (New York: Basic Books, 1959), pp. 461–84. Many textbooks have subjected the concept to critical reexamination; for examples, Jessie Bernard, *Social Problems at Midcentury* (New York: Holt, 1957); Marshall B. Clinard, *Sociology of Deviant Behavior,* 3rd ed. (New York: Holt, 1968); S. N. Eisenstadt, ed., *Comparative Social Problems* (New York: Free Press, 1964); Earl Raab and Gertrude Jaeger Selznick, *Major Social Problems,* 2nd ed. (New York: Harper, 1964); Bernard Rosenberg, Israel Gerver, and F. William Howton, *Mass Society in Crisis* (New York: Macmillan, 1964); Howard S. Becker, ed., *Social Problems* (New York: Wiley, 1967), Introduction; Jerome H. Skolnick and Elliott Currie, eds., *Crisis in American Institutions* (Boston: Little, Brown, 1970), Introduction; Walter M. Gerson, ed., *Social Problems in a Changing World* (New York: Crowell, 1969).

of interrelated statuses and roles such that the collective purposes and individual objectives of its members are less fully realized than they could be in an alternative workable system. Social disorganization is relative and a matter of degree. It is not tied to an absolute standard located in some Platonic empyrean but to a standard of what, so far as we know, could be accomplished under attainable conditions. When we say that a particular group or organization or community or society is disorganized in some degree, we mean that the structure of statuses and roles is not as effectively organized as it, then and there, might be. This type of statement, then, amounts to *a technical judgment about the workings of a social system*. And each case requires the sociological judge to supply competent evidence that the actual organization of social life can, under attainable conditions, be technically improved to make for the more substantial realization of collective and individual purposes. To find such evidence is no easy task. That is why, perhaps, diagnoses of social disorganization are often little more than moral judgments rather than confirmable technical judgments about the workings of a social system.

The composite of faults in the normative and relational structure of a social system described as social disorganization can be thought of as representing inadequacies in meeting one or more of the functional requirements of the system. Social patterns of behavior fail to be maintained (possibly as a result of inadequate socialization of members of the group, though not only because of this). Or, personal tensions generated by life within the system are insufficiently controlled, canalized, or siphoned off by social processes so that, for example, anxieties accumulate and get out of hand. Or, the social system is inadequately related to its environment, neither controlling it nor adapted to it. Or, the structure of the system does not allow sufficiently for its members to attain the goals that are its *raison d'être*. Or, finally in this list of functional imperatives of a social system, the relations between its members do not maintain the indispensable minimum of social cohesion needed to carry on both instrumental and intrinsically valued activities. Social disorganization exists in the degree to which patterned activities fail to meet one or more of these functional requirements of the system, whether this be an organization or an institution, a comparatively large and complex group or a small and slightly differentiated one.[31]

---

[31] This account draws upon the list of functional imperatives set forth by Parsons and Bales. See Talcott Parsons, R. F. Bales, and E. A. Shils, *Working Papers in the Theory of Action* (New York: Free Press, 1953), pp. 180–90. For a concise and clear summary of this list, see H. M. Johnson, *Sociology: A Systematic Introduction* (New York: Harcourt Brace Jovanovich, 1960), pp. 51–63; and for a detailed analysis of it,

Rigorous and demonstrably valid measures of the degree of social disorganization have yet to be developed. Even good rough estimates are difficult to come by. It would be no small task, for example, to arrive at a sound comparison of the extent of social disorganization in the United States and in the Soviet Union. Somewhat better results can be achieved in comparing formal organizations within the same sphere of activity in the same society. But even in advance of reasonably precise, reliable, and valid measures of social disorganization, we can identify some of the conditions making for disorganization and some of the forms in which it finds visible expression.

Contributing to social disorganization are inadequacies or partial breakdowns in channels of effective communication between people in a social system — whether a national society, local community, or purposive association — who are reciprocally dependent for doing what they are socially supposed to do and what they individually want to do. By turning to them first, we do not imply, of course, that inadequate avenues of functionally relevant communication comprise the single most consequential source of social disorganization. But as many experimental and observational inquiries have found, faulty communication has led to disorganization even in the absence of opposed interests and values among those in a group.

Superimposed on clogged lines of communication and often contributing to lapses of communication is the structural circumstance, which we have previously noted, of status groups and social strata having not only different but incompatible values and interests. This circumstance enlarges the potential for social disorganization, as can be seen in Chapter 13 concerning community disorganization. *People may thus work at cross-purposes, even*

---

see Chandler Morse, "The Functional Imperatives," in Max Black, ed., *The Social Theories of Talcott Parsons* (Englewood Cliffs, N. J.: Prentice-Hall, 1961), pp. 100–52. Whether this list of functional requirements or another is employed need not be at issue. What is theoretically decisive is the notion that social disorganization results from the inadequate meeting of one or more such requirements, and that this implication is followed in practice even by theorists of social disorganization who explicitly disavow a functional orientation in sociology.

Even the early formulations by Thomas and Znaniecki, which practically equate disorganization and deviant behavior, are based on a comparable, though implicit, assumption. They elect to focus on disorganization as a failure in maintaining social patterns of behavior, when they define it as "a decrease of the influence of existing social rules of behavior upon individual members of the group." By the same logic, disorganization stems also from failure to meet other functional requirements of the social system — such as a culturally validated degree of goal attainment (William I. Thomas and Florian Znaniecki, *The Polish Peasant in Europe and America*, Vol. 2, Chapter 1).

though, or precisely because they are living up to the requirements and norms of their respective positions in society. When the social organization of an economy, for example, does not provide for ways of settling the clash between the often opposed interests of, say, workers, management, and owners (stockholders), a degree of disorganization results, with interest groups having only the alternative of acting in terms of their own interests. Conflicts of interests dispose toward disorganization, without entailing it.

Defects in the processes of socialization — the acquisition of attitudes and values, of skills and knowledge needed to fulfill social roles — are another prominent source of disorganization. Not infrequently, for example, rapid social mobility occurs without adequate socialization of the mobile individuals. As a result, these mobile people simply do not know how to behave in their newly acquired statuses. Not knowing the informal limits on the exercise of his formally designated authority, the new boss may "throw his weight around," making demands that, though they are well within the scope of his formal authority, are far beyond the limits of the normative expectations held by the workers of what the boss may legitimately exact of them. The effectiveness of organized effort declines and problems of disorganization ensue.[32]

Disorganization stems also from faulty arrangements of competing social demands upon people who inevitably occupy a variety of statuses in society. This often gives rise to the familiar clash of the multiple statuses that call for contradictory behavior. Statuses pull in different directions. When the social system fails to provide for a widely shared priority among these potentially conflicting obligations, the individuals subject to them experience strains, with their behavior often becoming unpredictable and socially disruptive. The obligations of work and home, of local mores and national law, of religious commitment and scientific outlook, of the particularistic expecta-

---

[32] The theoretical basis for the substance of this paragraph was formulated by Chester I. Barnard, *The Functions of the Executive* (Cambridge: Harvard University Press, 1938), especially in his important Chapter 12, "The Theory of Authority." Further theoretical implications have been drawn by Talcott Parsons, *The Social System* (New York: Free Press, 1951), Chapter 6. An imaginative experiment with groups of children found that effective "leadership" was constrained by being required to operate within group norms: F. Merei, "Group Leadership and Institutionalization," *Human Relations,* Vol. 2 (1949), pp. 23–39. For summaries of many researches that have since come to the same results, see Cecil A. Gibb, "Leadership," in Gardner Lindzey and Elliot Aronson, eds., *The Handbook of Social Psychology,* Vol. 4, Chapter 31. For complementary sociological perspectives, see Peter M. Blau, *Exchange and Power in Social Life* (New York: Wiley, 1967), esp. Chapter 8 and Victor A. Thompson, *Modern Organization: A General Theory* (New York: Knopf, 1961), esp. Chapter 4.

tions of friends and the universalistic requirements of bureaucracy—these and many other sorts of patterned occasions for conflicting obligations make for disorganization in the degree that the regulatory system fails to establish shared priorities of obligation. The fault—in the objective, almost geological rather than moral, sense—lies in the inept organization of potentially conflicting obligations, not in the ineptitude of the people confronted with these conflicts.

Put in general terms, then, *the type of social problem involved in disorganization arises not from people failing to live up to the requirements of their social statuses, as is the case with deviant behavior, but from the faulty organization of these statuses into a reasonably coherent social system.* Rather than role-conformity leading to people's realizing their several and collective purposes, it leads to their getting in one another's way.

Seen in proper time perspective, some recurrent social situations might better be described as involving a lack of organization than as being instances of disorganization. They are cases of un-organization, in which a system of social relations has not yet taken shape, rather than cases of disorganization, in which an acute disruption has occurred in a once more or less effective system of social relations. The difference is a little like the difference between an apartment about to be occupied by new tenants, with furniture still scattered almost at random, lacking structural arrangement and functional order—this situation being un-organization—and an apartment, long lived in, but now a shambles after a knock-down and drag-out fight among its occupants, this, needless to say, being the analogue to disorganization. The latter is a case of disarray; the former, a case of not yet having an array. In society, instances of the first kind are approximated under conditions where the rules themselves and the organization of statuses are vague or still unformulated, as when people find themselves in a sudden and previously unexperienced kind of catastrophe; instances of the second kind are approximated by a complex of statuses that are ill-assorted, incompatible, or so linked as to provide little effective integration among them.

In a word, the kind of social problem that is dominated by social disorganization results from instrumental or technical flaws in the social system. The system comes to operate less effectively than it realistically might, owing to defects in meeting one or more of its functional requirements. The sources of social disorganization are many and diverse, and we still have much to learn about them. But whatever the source, disorganization means that even when people conform to their roles within the system they behave at cross-purposes so that the outcome is substantially different from what they severally or collectively expected and wished for.

Deviant Behavior

Deviant behavior on a sizable scale represents quite another kind of social problem. Whereas social disorganization refers to faults in the arrangement and working of social statuses and roles, deviant behavior refers to conduct that departs significantly from the norms set for people in their social statuses. The same behavior may be construed as deviant or conforming, depending upon the social statuses of the people exhibiting the behavior. This fact is simply a corollary of the sociological notion that each social status involves its own set of normative obligations (although many statuses may share some of the same obligations). When a man acts "like a child" or a layman acts "like a physician," he engages in deviant behavior. But as these allusive phrases imply, the same behavior by children and by physicians would of course be in accord with normative expectations. That is why deviant behavior cannot be described in the abstract but must be related to the norms that are socially defined as appropriate and morally binding for people occupying various statuses.

As used by the sociologist, the term "deviant behavior" is thus a technical rather than a moralizing one. But as the term has entered into the vernacular, its morally neutral denotation has become overladen with the connotation of moral censure. The reasons for this are understandable and theoretically interesting. Moralistic responses to deviant behavior have one or another, or both, of two sources, depending upon the distance of people from that behavior. For associates who are in direct social interaction with a person, his sustained deviant behavior is apt to be disruptive. His failure to live up to socially defined expectations makes life difficult or miserable for them. They cannot safely count on him, although in fact they must. Whatever the intent, deviant behavior interferes, at the least, with the measure of predictability required by social relations and thus results in a punishing experience for the associates of the deviating person. They respond in turn by a familiar and important kind of social control. Through spontaneous expression of their injured feelings or by more deliberate sanctioning behavior, role-partners of the deviating person act in such a way as to bring him back into line with their normative expectations, if only so that they can go about their usual business. This, then, is one source of response to deviant behavior.

Much the same type of response to observed deviant behavior occurs among members of a social system even when they are not *directly* engaged in immediate social relations with the deviating person. In such cases, their hostile responses can be described as disinterested. They themselves have little or nothing to lose by the deviating person's departures from norms; their situation is not damaged by his behavior. Nevertheless, they too respond with hostility. For, having internalized the moral content of the norms that are being violated, they experience the deviant behavior as threatening or repudiating the social validity of norms that they hold to be right and important. Reprisals of various kinds can be described as stemming from moral indignation,[33] a disinterested attack on people who depart from norms of the group, even when the deviation does not interfere with the performance of one's own roles since one is not socially connected with the persons engaging in the deviant act. The pattern of moral indignation has been exemplified in recent times by attacks of American construction workers ("hardhats") on radical students or on those who resemble these students in mere outward appearance.

DEVIANT BEHAVIOR AND SOCIAL RESPONSE — When we say that deviant behavior departs from norms set for given statuses, we do not wish to imply that social responses to such deviation occur uniformly and without respect of person (or to use the sociologist Max Weber's favored phrase, *sine ira et studio* — "without anger or partiality"). On the contrary. We have noted throughout the pages of this book, and especially in the chapter on crime and juvenile delinquency, that social sanctions are not evenly applied to all those who have violated social rules, with the race, ethnicity, class, sex, and age of violators being only among the more conspicuous bases for differentials.

If it were not already evident to most sociologists, the existence of such differentials in imposing sanctions would alert them to the necessity of having the theory of deviant behavior handle two distinct though related problems: (1) how to account for varying rates of rule-violating behavior in various groups, social strata and other social systems; and (2) how to account for differences in the societal reactions to such behavior, depending in part on the social characteristics of those exhibiting that behavior and of those judging it.

---

[33] The *locus classicus* of the theory of moral indignation is in Svend Ranulf, *Moral Indignation and Middle Class Psychology* (Copenhagen: Levin & Munksgaard, 1938). As Ranulf emphasizes, his work develops the fundamental theory set out by Émile Durkheim. The earlier monograph on the subject by Ranulf can also be profitably consulted in *The Jealousy of the Gods and Criminal Law at Athens: A Contribution to the Sociology of Moral Indignation* (London: Williams & Norgate, 1933).

The theory of anomie-and-opportunity-structure [34] addresses itself primarily to the first of these problems. In brief, it states that varying rates of particular kinds of deviant behavior result from socially patterned discrepancies between culturally induced aspirations and differentials in access to the opportunity structure for moving toward those aspirations by use of legitimate means. Since the theory is discussed elsewhere in this book (for example, in the chapter by A. K. Cohen and J. F. Short), it need not be considered further here.

More recently, another orientation to deviant behavior has been evolving, that, variously known as the "labeling theory" or "societal reactions approach," centers on reactions to behavior by the official agents in society. The chief exponents of this theoretical orientation are Edwin Lemert, Howard S. Becker, Kai T. Erikson, John I. Kitsuse and Aaron V. Cicourel.[35] The chief ingredients of this interesting theoretical orientation can be set out in the language of one of its chief exponents:

> Deviance . . . is created by society. I do not mean this in the way it is ordinarily understood, in which the causes of deviance are located in the social situation of the deviant. . . . I mean, rather, that *social*

---

[34] Robert K. Merton, "Social Structure and Anomie," *American Sociological Review,* Vol. III (October, 1938), pp. 672–83, further developed in Merton, *Social Theory and Social Structure,* pp. 184–248. For extended discussions, see Marshall B. Clinard, ed., *Anomie and Deviant Behavior* (New York: Free Press, 1964) which includes an annotated inventory by Stephen Cole and Harriet Zuckerman of nearly 200 empirical and theoretical studies of anomie-and-deviant-behavior. During the past five years, almost as many more empirical studies and empirical extensions have critically examined the theory. See Richard Cloward and Lloyd Ohlin, *Delinquency and Opportunity* (New York: Free Press, 1960); Albert K. Cohen, *Deviance and Control* (Englewood Cliffs, N. J.: Prentice-Hall, 1966); Marshall B. Clinard, *Sociology of Deviant Behavior,* 3rd ed. (New York: Holt, 1968), pp. 154–61; David Matza, *Becoming Deviant* (Englewood Cliffs, N. J.: Prentice-Hall, 1969), pp. 57–62, 96–99, who manages to be emphatically opposed to the functional analysis of social patterns by persistently ignoring the focus on *multiple consequences* for different groups and strata in the system. For a theoretical orientation like that adopted here, see William A. Rushing, ed., *Deviant Behavior and Social Process* (Chicago: Rand McNally, 1969), esp. pp. 11–15; Mark Lefton, James K. Skipper, Jr. and C. H. McCaghy, eds., *Approaches to Deviance* (New York: Appleton-Century-Crofts, 1968).

[35] Edwin M. Lemert, *Social Pathology* (New York: McGraw-Hill, 1951) and *Human Deviance, Social Problems and Social Control* (Englewood Cliffs, N. J.: Prentice-Hall, 1967); Howard S. Becker, ed., *The Other Side: Perspectives on Deviance* (New York: Free Press, 1964) which includes the paper by John I. Kitsuse, "Notes on the Sociology of Deviance," pp. 9–21; Howard S. Becker, *Outsiders* (New York: Free Press, 1964); John I. Kitsuse and Aaron V. Cicourel, "A Note on the Use of Official Statistics," *Social Problems,* Vol. 11 (Fall, 1963), pp. 131–39; Aaron V. Cicourel, *The Social Organization of Juvenile Justice* (New York: Wiley, 1968).

groups create deviance by making the rules whose infraction consti-
tutes deviance, and by applying those rules to particular people and
labeling them as outsiders. From this point of view, deviance is *not*
a quality of the act the person commits, but rather a consequence of the
application by others of rules and sanctions to an "offender." The
deviant is one to whom that label has successfully been applied;
deviant behavior is behavior that people so label.[36]

This passage puts forward a variety of theoretical claims. The first, which
it shares with every other theory of deviance, is blatantly true and trivial:
namely, the statement that behavior cannot be considered "deviant" unless
there are social norms from which that behavior departs. It seems banal and
safe to stipulate: no rule, no rule-violating behavior.

But evidently, much more is intended by the claim that society or social
groups "create" deviance; or by the equally strong claim, on the part of
Kitsuse and Cicourel, that "rates of deviant behavior *are produced by* the
actions taken by persons in the social system which define, classify and
record certain behaviors as deviant." [37] This directs our attention away from
the question of the social structures and processes which generate differing
rates of rule-breaking behavior to the question of how this behavior is
identified and responded to by official agencies of social control. In a word,
it abandons the sociological question of the sources of rule-violating behavior
and proposes to substitute an entirely different sociological question: How is
this behavior detected and how is it variously defined by official agencies
depending on the status of those engaging in it? As many recent critics of
this theoretical position have noted, by merging rule-violating acts and
official reaction to them, the labeling school of thought altogether abandons
basic questions of a theory of deviant behavior, namely: [38] (1) Why rates of

---

[36] Howard S. Becker, *Outsiders,* pp. 8–9.

[37] John I. Kitsuse and Aaron V. Cicourel, "A Note on the Use of Official Statistics,"
Social Problems, p. 135.

[38] This is drawn from the incisive but sympathetic critique of labeling theory by
Jack P. Gibbs, "Conceptions of Deviant Behavior: The Old and the New," *Pacific
Sociological Review,* Vol. 9 (Spring, 1966), 9–14. For other pointed yet appreciative
criticisms, see Rodolfo Alvarez, "Informal Reactions to Deviance in Simulated Work
Organizations," *American Sociological Review,* Vol. 33 (December, 1968), pp. 895–912,
esp. pp. 900–02. For an empirical appraisal of the labeling perspective on mental ill-
ness, see Walter R. Gove, "Societal Reaction as an Explanation of Mental Illness: An
Evaluation," *American Sociological Review,* Vol. 35 (October, 1970), pp. 873–84. In an
overview of such criticisms, Schur has rightly suggested that the labeling perspective
complements rather than supplants alternative theories of deviant behavior: Edwin
M. Schur, "Reactions to Deviance: A Critical Assessment," *American Journal of
Sociology,* Vol. 75 (November, 1969), pp. 309–22. In a pointed formulation, Akers indi-

particular acts vary from one population to another; (2) why certain persons engage in these acts while others do not; and (3) why the act is considered deviant in some societies and not in others. In effect, this approach no longer deals with the etiology of behavior that may or may not be tagged as deviant, but confines itself to the alternative question of the processes making for different evaluations of that behavior. This theoretical decision, as Gibbs and others have indicated, results in certain theoretical contradictions. For example, "if deviant behavior is defined in terms of reactions to it, then Becker cannot speak properly of 'secret deviance' [as he emphatically and usefully does]. . . . To be consistent, Becker, Kitsuse, and Erikson would have to insist that behavior which is contrary to a norm is not deviant unless it is discovered and there is a particular kind of reaction to it." [39]

By distinguishing between deviant behavior and the responses to it, rather than merging them as the labeling perspective would have us do, we can deal with the interaction between them. Thus to put it somewhat parochially, the sociologist does not typically respond to deviant actions as the social system does. The sociologist is trained to distinguish between deviant behavior and the people engaged in such behavior.[40] In contrast, conforming members of social systems tend to identify the *persons* apprehended in deviant conduct as deviant social types (i.e., chronically devoted to rule-breaking behavior): a criminal, a delinquent, an ex-con, a pervert, renegade, or traitor. By doing so, representatives of the social system may help to confirm people in a *career* as deviants through the social process of the self-fulfilling prophecy, as both Becker and Erikson, among others, have noted:

> Treating a person as though he were generally rather than specifically deviant produces a self-fulfilling prophecy. It sets in motion several mechanisms which conspire to shape the person in the image people have of him. . . . One tends to be cut off, after being identified as deviant, from participation in more conventional groups. . . . When . . . caught, one is treated in accordance with the popular diagnosis of why

---

cates that the theory of deviance must deal with *both* the sources and the social definition of deviant acts: Ronald L. Akers, "Problems in the Sociology of Deviance: Social Definitions and Behavior," *Social Forces,* Vol. 46 (June, 1968), pp. 455–65.

[39] Jack P. Gibbs, "Conceptions of Deviant Behavior: The Old and the New," *Pacific Sociological Review,* p. 13.

[40] For an example in the era of the 1930's, note the observation that the typology of deviant behaviors refers "to role adjustments in specific situations, not to personality *in toto.*" Robert K. Merton, "Social Structure and Anomie," *American Sociological Review,* p. 676.

one is that way, and the treatment itself may likewise produce increasing deviance.[41]

That is the essential process of the self-fulfilling prophecy: Widespread beliefs help to bring about a social environment that so constrains the range of options for the people who are the object of those beliefs that their subsequent behavior can only seem to confirm the beliefs.[42]

Among the labeling theorists, it is primarily Erikson who has recognized all along that they have been writing the prose of structural and functional analysis while trying their hands at labelist prose. For in focusing on the range, intensity, and distribution of societal responses to rule-breaking behavior, they have continued a line of theory stemming from Émile Durkheim's early work on the same problem.[43] And to do so effectively, that theory must, as Gibbs puts it, "identify deviant acts by reference to norms, and treat reaction to deviation as a contingent property."[44] Only so, can one investigate the interaction between rates of norm-breaking behavior and societal responses to it in a system of feedback loops which intensify or dampen the rates of both deviant behavior and patterns of response.

NONCONFORMING AND ABERRANT BEHAVIOR—As a first approximation, all substantial departures of behavior from social norms can be caught up in the single concept and associated term, deviant behavior. But first approximations are useful to the degree that they are recognized for what they are: rough discriminations to be progressively replaced by more exacting ones. And so it is with the concept of deviant behavior. Since departures from established norms differ greatly in both character and social consequences, they should not be indiscriminately grouped together.

Two major varieties of deviant behavior can be usefully distinguished on the basis of their structure and their consequences for social systems. The first can be called "nonconforming behavior"; the second, "aberrant behavior." Both types retain the technical conception of deviant behavior in sociological analysis; the distinction does not smuggle in moral judgments through the back door of connotative language. It only helps us to identify

---

[41] Howard S. Becker, *Outsiders,* p. 34; also Kai T. Erikson, "Notes on the Sociology of Deviance," in Howard S. Becker, ed., *The Other Side: Perspectives on Deviance,* p. 17; Kai T. Erikson, *Wayward Puritans: A Study in the Sociology of Deviance* (New York: Wiley, 1966), p. 17 ff.

[42] On the general process of the self-fulfilling prophecy, see Robert K. Merton, *Social Theory and Social Structure,* Chapter 13.

[43] Émile Durkheim, "Deux lois de l'évolution pénale," *L'Année Sociologique,* Vol. 4 (1899–1900), pp. 65–95.

[44] Jack P. Gibbs, "Conception of Deviant Behavior: The Old and the New," *Pacific Sociological Review,* p. 14.

systematic differences in kinds of deviant behavior that are alike only in that they move away from what is prescribed by specifiable social norms. These types of nonconforming behavior and aberrant behavior differ in several conjoint respects. *First,* the nonconformer announces his dissent publicly; unlike the aberrant, he does not try to hide his departures from social norms. The political or religious dissenter insists on making his dissent known to as many as will look or listen; the aberrant criminal seeks to avoid the limelight of public scrutiny. Contrast the pacifist who burns his draft card in public with the draft dodger who tries to escape into obscurity. This patterned attitude toward visibility links up with a *second* basic difference between the two kinds of deviants. The nonconformer challenges the legitimacy of the social norms he rejects or at least challenges their applicability to certain kinds of situations. Organized "sit-in" campaigns designed to attack local norms of racial segregation in restaurants and schools afford a recent example of this aspect of nonconforming behavior. The aberrant, in contrast, acknowledges the legitimacy of the norms he violates: It is only that he finds it expedient or expressive of his state of mind to violate them. He may try to justify his own behavior, but he does not argue that theft is right and murder virtuous.

Third and correlatively, the nonconformer aims to change the norms he is denying in practice. He wants to replace what he believes to be morally suspect norms with ones having a sound moral basis. The aberrant, in contrast, tries primarily to escape the sanctioning force of existing norms, without proposing substitutes for them. When subject to social sanction, the nonconformer typically appeals to a higher morality; except as an instrumental device, the aberrant does not; at most he appeals to extenuating circumstances.

Fourth, and possibly as a result of the preceding components of his behavior, the nonconformer is acknowledged, however reluctantly, by conventional members of the social system to depart from prevailing norms for disinterested purposes and not for what he personally can get out of it. Again in contrast, the aberrant is generally assumed to be deviating from the norms in order to serve his own interests. Although the law of the land may not make the formal distinction between the nonconformer and the aberrant in this respect, many members of society do. Whatever the generic concept of deviant behavior might seem to pronounce to the contrary, the two types of social deviants are widely acknowledged as having far different social consequences. Those courageous highwaymen of seventeenth-century England, John Nevinson and his much advertised successor, Dick Turpin, were not of a sociological piece with that courageous nonconformist of their time, Oliver Cromwell. And in the event that one's political or religious sympathies, as well as the detachment made easy by historical distance, serve to make this observation self-evident, one should reexamine those judgements that once made Trotsky or Nehru little more than criminals heading up sizable gangs of followers.

Fifth, and for present purposes finally, the nonconformer, with his appeal to an allegedly higher morality, can in historically propitious circumstances lay claim to legitimacy by drawing upon the ultimate values, rather than the particular norms, of the society. He is trying to make justice a social reality rather than an institutionalized fiction. He is for genuine freedom of speech rather than its everyday pretense. He would rearrange the social structure to provide actual equality of opportunity for all men to develop prized talents and not allow the social simulacra of equality to be mistaken for the real thing. In these ways, his nonconformity can appeal to the moral values that are in some measure being denied in social practice while being reaffirmed in ideological doctrine. The nonconformer can appeal to the tacit recognition by others of discrepancies between the prized values and the social reality.[45] He thus has at least the prospect of obtaining the assent of other, initially less critical and venturesome, members of society whose ambivalence toward the current social structure can be drawn upon for some degree of support. Nonconformity is not a private dereliction but a thrust toward a new morality or a promise of restoring a morality held to have been put aside in social practice. In this respect again, the nonconformer is far removed from the other major type of social deviant, the aberrant, who has nothing new to propose and nothing old to restore, but seeks only to satisfy his private interests or to express his private cravings.[46]

Although sociologists continue to lavish more attention on the form of deviant behavior we have described as aberrant, they have begun systematic investigations of what we have described as nonconforming behavior. As a result, the third edition of this book can examine such matters as the rebellious youth culture and collective forms of social protest as well as the principal kinds of aberrant behavior—crime, alcoholism, drug addiction, and so forth. As Francis Bacon put it, "Books must follow sciences, and not

[45] Talcott Parsons has long ago noted the important point that patterns of social deviation differ significantly according to whether or not they lay claim to legitimation. See *The Social System,* pp. 291–97.

[46] The foregoing account of nonconforming behavior develops somewhat the pattern of behavior identified as "rebellion" in the typology set forth in "Social Structure and Anomie." In that same typology, innovation, ritualism, and retreatism would comprise forms of aberrant behavior. And, as has been indicated in the text, nonconforming and aberrant behavior together compose deviant behavior. See Robert K. Merton, *Social Theory and Social Structure,* p. 194.

sciences, books." As the body of sociological investigation of still other kinds of nonconforming behavior develops, the shape of qualified books on social problems will change even more in this direction.

Future investigations into nonconformity will need to take care that they do not move from an unthinking orthodoxy to an equally unthinking heterodoxy by valuing nonconformity for its own sake. We must remember that what is nonconformity to the norms of one group is often conformity to the norms of another group. There is no merit in escaping the error of taking heterodoxy to be inevitably false or ugly or sinister only to be caught up in the opposite error of thinking heterodoxy to be inevitably true or beautiful or altogether excellent. Put in so many words, this is a commonplace. Yet people alienated from the world about them often do take heterodoxy as a good in itself, whatever its character. And others, perhaps in reaction to the cases, familiar in every age, of true merit being neglected or punished because it is unorthodox, are quick to value heterodoxy or countercyclicalism, all apart from their substance. In every time, apparently, shrewd men have recognized that an appropriate kind of seeming heterodoxy appeals greatly even to the more orthodox members of society. As British lecturers to American audiences have evidently known for a long period, and as "radical" American lecturers to civic clubs, literary societies, and businessmen's associations know now: there is no better way to win their audiences' hearts than by attacking part of what they stand for while intimating that they are not beyond redemption.[47] These and other expressions of specious nonconformity have long been recognized, particularly by some of the most notable nonconformers of their time. It has been said of Marx, for example, that "all his life [he] detested two phenomena with peculiar passion: disorderly life and histrionic display. It seemed to him that Bohemianism and deliberate flouting of conventions was but inverted Philistinism, emphasizing and paying homage to the very same false values by exaggerated protest against them, and exhibiting therefore the same fundamental vulgarity."[48]

ATTRIBUTES OF SOCIAL NORMS AND DEVIANT BEHAVIOR—Concepts such as conformity, nonconformity, and aberrant behavior must be kept under theoretical control if they are not to become misleading. To begin with, these concepts suggest that one can readily identify behavior that represents

[47] This paragraph is based on Robert K. Merton, "Recognition and Excellence: Instructive Ambiguities," in *Recognition of Excellence: Working Papers* (New York: Free Press, 1960), pp. 297–328, especially pp. 321–22.

[48] Isaiah Berlin, *Karl Marx* (London: Oxford University Press, 1960), p. 79.

compliance with a norm or departure from it. But while such clarity can be achieved on the conceptual plane it is difficult to achieve in social practice. Law courts provide an abundance of examples testifying how difficult it is to find out whether a particular act was deviant by trying to match up the act with pertinent norms embodied in the law. It becomes even more difficult to compare acts with kinds of norms, such as folkways and mores, that are less carefully formulated than legal norms.

In terms of sociological theory, we can identify several dimensions of social norms. *First,* norms vary in their location in the *spectrum of normative control.* This location can be roughly gauged by the "4 P's": Norms may *prescribe* behavior or *proscribe* it; they may only indicate what behavior is *preferred* or simply *permitted. Second,* norms differ in the *extent of agreement* they gain within the group or society. The range is from almost full consensus, as in most societies regarding the norm that proscribes the kidnapping of children, to limited agreement confined to a small sector, as, in some societies, with norms governing the payment of taxes upon income. *Third,* norms differ in the intensity of *affective or moral commitment to them.* They may engage deepseated values or only superficial support among those who subscribe to them. *Fourth,* norms differ in the *social structure of control* associated with them. These control structures range from agencies formally and specifically charged with responsibility for imposing social sanctions upon deviants to altogether diffuse, informal, and spontaneous sanctions resulting from the punitive responses of people who directly suffer from these deviations. *Fifth,* norms differ in the *kind of adherence* they require: only overt behavioral conformity, only inner assent, or both. *Sixth* and finally in this short listing, norms differ in the extent of their *elasticity,* sometimes requiring close adherence to a form of behavior or belief, sometimes allowing much leeway before behavior or belief is defined as significantly deviant.[49]

This last attribute of norms, their degree of elasticity, is particularly important in the study of deviant behavior. It reminds us that strict and continued compliance with rigorously defined norms is only a mental con-

---

[49] For an application of this list of attributes of social norms, see Aaron Rosenblatt, "The Application of Role Concepts to the Intake Process," *Social Casework,* Vol. 43 (January, 1961), pp. 8–14. On the elasticity of norms, see Lewis A. Coser, "Some Functions of Deviant Behavior and Normative Flexibility," *American Journal of Sociology,* Vol. 68 (September, 1962), pp. 172–81. See also Richard T. Morris, "A Typology of Norms," *American Sociological Review,* Vol. 21 (October, 1956), pp. 610–13.

The interest of ethnomethodology in discovering the tacit norms in social interaction—the "logic-in-use" in contrast to "reconstructed logic"—apparently concerns the attribute of elasticity or flexibility in norms. In effect, ethnomethodologists try to track down the implicit rules involved in particular social interactions; see Aaron V. Cicourel, *The Social Organization of Juvenile Justice* (New York: Wiley, 1968).

struct, at most only approximated for brief occasions in social life (as on highly ceremonial occasions). For the most part, social norms provide for a range of behavior that is judged admissible even though it departs from the strict letter of the norms. The extent of this range differs among norms and for the same norm under differing social conditions. For example, when it is widely felt that the group or society is in grave danger — as under conditions of war or after a great catastrophe — this range of permissiveness contracts, as exemplified by martial law. Much remains to be discovered about the social processes affecting the extent of patterned leeway for compliance with norms required by a group. Until this general knowledge of regularities grows considerably larger, variations in expected compliance must be empirically investigated in each case.

INSTITUTIONALIZED EVASIONS OF INSTITUTIONAL RULES — Apart from the elasticity of norms that provides for degrees of socially acceptable conformity is another pattern that provides for systematic nonconformity to them. This has been described as the pattern of "institutionalized evasions of institutional rules." [50]

Evasions of institutional rules are themselves institutionalized when they are (1) patterned in fairly well-defined types; (2) adopted by substantial numbers of people rather than being scattered subterfuges independently and privately arrived at; (3) organized in the form of a fairly elaborate social machinery made up of tacitly cooperating participants, including those who are socially charged with implementing the rules; and (4) rarely punished and when they are, punished in largely symbolic forms that serve primarily to reaffirm the sanctity of the rules. [51]

These social patterns of evasion develop when practical exigencies confronting a collectivity require goal-oriented or adaptive behavior that is at

[50] The analysis of institutionalized evasions was developed in lectures at Harvard in the late 1930's, with part of it first seeing print in Robert K. Merton, "Discrimination and the American Creed," in R. M. MacIver, ed., *Discrimination and National Welfare* (New York: Harper, 1949), pp. 99–126, and in Merton, *Social Theory and Social Structure,* pp. 371–72, 397–400. For a variety of institutionalized evasions in various institutional spheres, see Wilbert E. Moore, *Industrial Relations and the Social Order,* rev. ed. (New York: Macmillan, 1951), p. 114; Kingsley Davis, *Human Society* (New York: Macmillan, 1949), pp. 263–64; Robin M. Williams, Jr., *American Society* (New York: Knopf, 1951), Chapter 10; Charles P. and Zona K. Loomis, *Modern Social Theories* (Princeton, N. J.: Van Nostrand, 1961), pp. 156–57, 270–71, 529–30, 553–54, 615–16; Joseph R. Gusfield, *Symbolic Crusade* (Urbana: University of Illinois Press, 1963), pp. 112–17; Rex Lucas, *Men in Crisis: A Study of a Mine Disaster* (New York: Basic Books, 1969), Chapter 5.

[51] Robert K. Merton in Hubert J. O'Gorman, *Lawyers and Matrimonial Cases: A Study of Informal Pressures in Private Professional Practice* (New York: Free Press, 1963), pp. ix–xi; Robin M. Williams, Jr., *American Society,* p. 356.

odds with long-established norms or when newly formulated norms (most clearly in the form of new legislation) are at odds with long-established social practices and sentiments. Such evasions on the large scale are signs of malintegration between norms and widespread, socially induced needs. When there is a gross discrepancy between newly instituted legal norms and local mores, all manner of procedures for evading the full force of the norms will be adopted: nullification, circumvention, subterfuge, connivance, and legal fictions. Even such crude qualitative knowledge (as distinct from precise quantitative knowledge) of the conditions making for institutionalized evasions can serve to forecast the occurrence of evasions on a substantial scale. Thus it was possible to anticipate, a half-dozen years before, the broad outlines of response to a decision such as that taken unanimously by the Supreme Court on May 17, 1954, which declared unconstitutional the separate-but-equal doctrine (Plessy v. Ferguson) that had enabled communities to exclude Negro children from public schools maintained for white children. One such forecast read as follows:

> In an unfavorable cultural climate—and this does not necessarily exclude the benign regions of the Far South—the immediate resort will probably have to be that of working through legal and administrative federal controls over extreme discrimination, with full recognition that, in all probability, these regulations will be systematically evaded for some time to come. In such cultural regions, we may expect nullification of the law as the common practice, perhaps as common as was the case in the nation at large with respect to the Eighteenth Amendment, often with the connivance of local officers of the law. The large gap between the new law and local mores will not *at once* produce significant change of prevailing practices: token punishments of violations will probably be more common than effective control. At best, one may assume that significant change will be fitful, and excruciatingly slow. But secular changes in the economy may in due course lend support to the new legal framework of control over discrimination. As the economic shoe pinches because the illiberals do not fully mobilize the resources of industrial manpower nor extend their local markets through equitable wage-payments, they may slowly abandon some discriminatory practices as they come to find that these do not always pay—even the discriminator.[52]

Another instance of the pattern of institutionalized evasions is provided by widespread social response to the law governing divorce in the state of New York. Here we see the law lagging behind the changing interests,

[52] Robert K. Merton, "Discrimination and the American Creed," p. 120. See also Lyle G. Warner and Rutledge M. Dennis, "Prejudice versus Discrimination: An Empirical Example and Theoretical Extension," *Social Forces*, Vol. 48 (June, 1970), pp. 473–84.

values, and wants of a substantial part of the population. This lag has given rise to a social machinery built up of tacitly collaborating clients, lawyers, judges, trained connivers, and specialized inventors of make-believe evidence of adultery. A grand jury investigating the matter "confirmed what had long been suspected: fraud, perjury, collusion, and connivance pervade matrimonial actions of every type." They discovered "a wholesale system of fabricating evidence for a divorce, the service of a correspondent and witness being supplied for a fee." The institutionalized though ostensibly proscribed evasions are thoroughly known to officers of the court. As one lawyer summed it up: "Ninety percent of the undefended matrimonials are based on perjury. They are all arranged. The raids are made with the consent of the defendant. We all know this. The judges know it. It's embarrassing to go [to court]." [53]

We see in this particular case the dynamics of institutionalized evasions. A legal rule is experienced as excessively restrictive by a substantial number of people whose status in the community is otherwise "respectable" and conforming. This goes far toward subverting the legitimacy of the rule. A system of evasive practices develops to close the gap between the law and the socially legitimatized though illegal wants of many people. The law is maintained on the books, not as a result of "inertia" but in response to certain interested groups in the community that are sufficiently powerful to have their way. But they are not powerful enough to prevent the circumvention of the law by other "respectable" segments of the community who find it unduly cramping and who deny its legitimacy. During the interim of this social conflict, the social system evolves a pattern of institutionalized evasions in which the rules remain nominally intact while devices for neutralizing them evolve. Such institutionalized evasions give rise to institutional change—in this case, the change of the law governing divorce—when the balance of power between contending sectors of the "respectable" community shifts in favor of those who have made the evasions in the first place. [54]

Historical instances of institutionalized evasions that have run their full course bring out the connections between the pattern of regularized evasion

---

[53] Hubert J. O'Gorman, *Lawyers and Matrimonial Cases*, pp. 23, 33.

[54] For a recent analysis of the interaction between law and morality within a context of social stratification, see Troy Duster, *The Legislation of Morality* (New York: Free Press, 1970). Reiss suggests that it is theoretically useful to distinguish patterned evasions in which individuals deviate with a measure of social support from evasions which implicate an entire organizational system. Albert Reiss, "The Study of Deviant Behavior," *Ohio Valley Sociologist*, Vol. 32 (Autumn, 1966), pp. 1–12, reprinted in Mark Lefton *et al.*, *Approaches to Deviance* (New York: Appleton-Century-Crofts, 1968), pp. 55–66.

and subsequent institutional change. A meticulously analyzed case is that of the eighteenth-century criminal law in England. The punishments for certain crimes then prescribed by law were so severe as to be at great variance with sentiments and values widely held in the society. As a result, the law was ridden with "absurd technicalities" that were designed to give "a criminal undue chances of escape from conviction by the practical revolt of jurymen against the immorality of penalties out of all proportion to moral guilt, and by the constant commutation of capital for some lighter punishment." [55] In due course, simple theft was no longer treated as a capital crime after generations in which "juries, judges, prosecutors, and complainants collaborated" to evade the full force of the extremely punitive law.[56] Once again we see that the social functionaries charged with administering the widely rejected norms are the best situated to evade their literal force and that they do precisely that. To some extent, all this was recognized by observers of human society long ago. From the time of the ancient Roman adage—*Quid leges sine moribus?* to what avail are laws without support of the mores?—down to the present, men have recognized that legal norms will be evaded on the large scale when they are substantially opposed to other norms or values or to what can be practically carried into effect.

The pattern of institutionalized evasions is not at all peculiar to complex literate societies. It has been amply identified in nonliterate societies by such anthropologists as Malinowski, Radcliffe-Brown, Firth, and others, the gist of their observations being admirably set forth by Alexander Macbeath, as

---

[55] A. V. Dicey, *Lectures on the Relation Between Law and Public Opinion in England During the Nineteenth Century* (London: Macmillan, 1905), pp. 79–80. This classic is chock-full of historical materials bearing on the emergence of institutionalized evasions of institutional rules. Another classic, published just about a century ago, Henry Sumner Maine's *Ancient Law,* 5th ed. (New York: Holt, 1887) also sets forth apposite materials in the second chapter.

[56] Hall, *Theft, Law, and Society,* p. 87. Jerome Hall has given us a remarkably analytical account of the process through which the evasion of institutional rules has led to a new body of rules, especially in his Chapter 3, significantly entitled "The Function of Technicality and Discretion in Criminal Law Administration," pp. 68–121.

Oliver Wendell Holmes, like Roscoe Pound and Benjamin Cardozo after him, has argued that law is inevitably subject to social and cultural lag. He writes: "It cannot be helped, it is as it should be, that the law is behind the times. . . . As law embodies beliefs that have triumphed in the battle of ideas and then have translated themselves into action, while there still is doubt, while opposite convictions still keep a battle front against each other, the time for law has not yet come; the notion destined to prevail is not yet entitled to the field." What we note here is that institutionalized evasions emerge to take up the slack during this interim of changing social interests and lagging legal norms. Holmes, *Collected Legal Papers* (Boston: Little, Brown, 1920), pp. 290, 294.

when he notes that "even the most rigid rules, those which have a super-natural sanction, can be evaded or circumvented not only with the conniv-ance but with the backing of public opinion and legalized usage, when the exceptions are in conformity with the people's sense of what is right." [57]

Since the persistence of institutionalized evasions tends to make for changes in the structure of social norms, actions that were at one time deviant behavior later become conforming behavior. This, then, reminds us of what we already know: Not only is deviant behavior relative to the norms of a designated group, so that it can simultaneously be described as deviation from one set of norms and conformance with another, but it is also relative to changing norms, so that what is regarded in one generation as deviation is in the next a self-evident kind of conformity. [58]

SOCIAL PROBLEMS AND SOCIAL DYSFUNCTIONS

As has been noted many times before, the investigation of social problems has a distinct intellectual interest altogether apart from its possible use in ultimately helping men to cope with the social troubles that confront them. One such point of theoretical interest is that the study of social problems requires sociologists to attend to the dysfunctions of patterns of behavior, belief, and organization rather than focusing primarily or exclusively on their functions. It thus curbs any inadvertent or deliberate tendency in functional sociology to reinstitute the philosophy that everything in society works for "harmony" and "the good." [59]

---

[57] Alexander Macbeath, *Experiments in Living* (London: Macmillan, 1952), pp. 144–47. For some of the factual bases of this summary statement, see B. Malinowski, *Crime and Custom in Savage Society* (New York: Harcourt Brace Jovanovich, 1931), pp. 80–81; A. R. Radcliffe-Brown, "The Social Organization of Australian Tribes," *Oceania*, Vol. 1, Nos. 1–4 (1930–1931), pp. 34–63; 206–46; 322–41; 426–56; Raymond Firth, *We, the Tikopia* (London: Allen & Unwin, 1936), p. 129; Edward Norbeck, "African Rituals of Conflict," *American Anthropologist*, Vol. 65 (December, 1963), pp. 1254–79.

[58] As has been recently noted by Joseph R. Gusfield: "What is attacked as criminal today may be seen as sick next year and fought over as possibly legitimate by the next generation." "Moral Passage: The Symbolic Process in Public Designations of Deviance," *Social Problems*, Vol. 15 (Fall, 1967), pp. 175–88.

[59] Without considering the question of the extent to which current functional sociology has exhibited this tendency—a question that would take us far afield—we might note the claim that such a tendency has been expressed in physiology, especially in that part of physiology heavily influenced by Walter B. Cannon's notion of *homeostasis* (the maintenance of steady states in the organism). For Cannon's ideas

The theoretical relation of social dysfunctions to social disorganization can be briefly stated. Social disorganization, it will be remembered, refers to the composite of faults in the operation of a social system that interferes with the fulfillment of its functional requirements. Social dysfunction refers to the particular inadequacies of a particular part of the system for a designated requirement.[60] Social disorganization can be thought of as the resultant of multiple social dysfunctions.

    1. The first point essential to using the concept of social dysfunction for the analysis of social problems can stand repetitive emphasis if only because the point has so often been blunted in the course of usage. A social dysfunction refers to a *designated* set of consequences of a *designated* pattern of behavior, belief, or organization that interfere with a *designated* functional requirement of a *designated* social system. Otherwise, the term social dysfunction becomes little more than an epithet of disparagement or a largely vacuous expression of attitude. To say, for example, that a high rate of social mobility is "functional" or "dysfunctional," without indicating the particular consequences it has for particular attributes of a designated social system, is to say little. But it is quite another thing to say, as has been said,[61] that a

---

were also influential in the recent resurgence of a functional outlook in sociology. The criticism is set forth, in sufficiently nontechnical fashion that even those without a thorough grounding in physiology may learn as they read, by the physician and physiologist, Dickinson W. Richards (who was later to become a Nobel laureate for his work on catheterization of the heart). See his account of "The Stupidity of the Body," designed as a complement to rather than a substitute for Cannon's "The Wisdom of the Body," in his paper, "Homeostasis *versus* Hyperexis," *The Scientific Monthly,* Vol. 77 (December, 1953), pp. 289–94, reprinted in his *Medical Priesthoods and other essays* (Connecticut Printers, 1970), pp. 46–57.

    [60] A more exact formal statement is provided by Ernest Nagel, "A Formalization of Functionalism," in his *Logic Without Metaphysics* (New York: Free Press, 1956), especially p. 269.

    [61] This hypothesis was in effect adopted not long ago by a branch of the Labour Party in Birmingham; that is, by people who were, of course, ideologically and in the abstract, staunch supporters of enlarging opportunity for social mobility. Nevertheless, they officially stated that "from Labour's point of view, the objection to the grammar school system was that it had the effect of taking the brightest children of the working class and in effect de-classing them by separation from children in the modern [essentially vocational] schools. Eventually, they get white-collar jobs and upon marriage go to live in the outer suburbs and vote Tory." Substantially, the same hypothesis about the dysfunctions of rapid and large-scale mobility for maintaining the solidarity and effective goal attainment of a working class was set forth by such ideologically opposed theorists as Karl Marx and Vilfredo Pareto. See Marx, *Capital* (Chicago: Kerr, 1906), pp. 648–49; Pareto, *The Mind and Society* (New York: Harcourt Brace Jovanovich, 1935), Vol. 3, pp. 1419–32; Vol. 4, pp. 1836–'6. For an analysis of this

high rate of social mobility from the working class into the middle class is dysfunctional for effective attainment of its goals by a solidary working class, since mobility involves exporting talent from that class and a consequent depletion of its potential leadership. This type of statement is at the least and in principle a testable hypothesis about a dysfunction of social mobility, whatever the practical difficulties in putting it to decisive test. Easy imputations of social dysfunction in the abstract are no more defensible than easy imputations of social causation in the abstract. Like social causes, social dysfunctions must be discovered through inquiry. And it is no more to be expected that inquiry will promptly discover previously unknown dysfunctions of social patterns than it is that inquiry will promptly discover previously unknown causes of these same patterns.

2. It must be noted, secondly, that the same social pattern can be dysfunctional for some parts of a social system and functional for other parts. This arises from a characteristic of social structure that has been repeatedly called to our attention in the pages of this book: *Social patterns have multiple consequences, and, in a differentiated society, these consequences will tend to differ for individuals, groups, and social strata variously situated in the structure of the society.*

The continued persistence of a social pattern makes it improbable, not impossible, that it is uniformly dysfunctional for all groups. Thus relatively free access to higher education, irrespective of racial and other origin, is dysfunctional for maintaining a relatively fixed system of caste. Extended popular education militates against the fixing of caste position or resigned acceptance to it. But of course to the very same degree that higher education of the socially subordinate is dysfunctional for maintaining a caste system, it is functional for the enlarged attainment of culturally induced goals by those formerly excluded from higher education.

All this is something more than a paraphrase of Lucretius' adage that one man's meat is another man's poison. The general idea that serves as a begin-

---

pattern of "cognitive agreement and value disagreement," see Robert K. Merton, "Social Conflict Over Styles of Sociological Work," *Transactions* (Fourth World Congress of Sociology, 1959), Vol. 3, pp. 21–46, especially pp. 39–40. Most recently, the same ambivalence toward social mobility among a disadvantaged population is found among "the masses of lower-class Negroes [who] regard this movement up the ladder with mixed feelings, both proud and resentful of the success of 'one of their own.' " (Kenneth B. Clark, *Dark Ghetto: Dilemmas of Social Power,* pp. 57–58.) In the same ambivalent fashion, the collective efforts to have many more black scholars appointed to the faculties of major universities and colleges is now being described as "the black brain drain to white colleges" (*New York Times,* February 6, 1969), p. 34.

ning for the analysis of functions and dysfunctions of the same social pattern is, as we have noted, that various groups and strata in the structure of a society have *distinctive* interests and values and also *shared* interests and values. To the extent that this diversity, and sometimes this conflict, of values and interests is so distributed among statuses in the society, we should naturally be prepared to find social patterns serving the interests or values of some and interfering with the interests or values of other groups differently located in the society. This structural condition is one of the principal reasons why the periodically popular notion of a society in which everything works together for good is literally utopian, and describes an engaging utopia at that. But to forgo this image of a society entirely free of imperfections does not require us to assume that nothing can be done, through deliberate plan, to reduce the extent to which obsolescent institutions and disorganization work against the realization of values that men respect. Quite the contrary: it is precisely by discovering such dysfunctional social formations that functional analysis in sociology links up with critical morality as opposed to conventional morality.[62]

3. Not only is the same pattern sometimes functional for some groups and dysfunctional for others but it can also serve some and defeat other functional requirements of the *same* group. The reason for this is of the same general sort as the reason for cases in which the pattern is variously consequential for *different* groups. A group has diverse functional requirements: to take only one thoroughly investigated example, the group's need for enough social cohesion to provide a sense of group identity in contrast with the need to work toward group goals, to get a job done. It is not unusual, therefore, that activities functional for one of these requirements proves to be dysfunctional for the other. When this is true to a substantial degree, the group confronts an organizational problem.

This example of composite function-and-dysfunction for distinct properties of the same group can be profitably considered in a little more detail in order to bring out the general idea it exemplifies. In the main, sociologists have found that social cohesion facilitates the productivity of a group. This is what one might expect from everyday experience: In cohesive groups, people feel at one with each other and so are the better prepared to work together for joint ends. But this mutually reinforcing relation between social cohesion and productivity holds only under certain conditions. A functional imbalance can develop between the activity that serves chiefly to maintain co-

---

[62] Ralph Ross, *Obligation: A Social Theory* (Ann Arbor: University of Michigan Press, 1970), esp. Chapter 5, "Critical Morality" and Chapters 8, 9.

hesion and the activity that results chiefly in getting work done. Great social cohesion can restrict intragroup competition in performance; [63] members of a highly cohesive group may become reciprocally indulgent to the degree that they do not hold one another to exacting standards of performance; or a large part of the social interaction in the group may be devoted to expressing and reinforcing group cohesiveness at the expense of time and energy for getting the job done.[64] When such functional imbalances obtain, the problem confronting the group is one of establishing or of reestablishing a balance in the distribution of activities such that an optimal combination of the two properties of cohesion and goal attainment is approximated.[65]

It cannot be assumed, of course, that an optimal balance is one that maximizes both social cohesion and productivity. We do not yet know enough to say whether such simultaneous maxima may turn out to be incompatible. The optimal balance depends upon the comparative value set upon social cohesion and productivity by members of the group, with their being prepared to reduce the one in order to enlarge the other. This is a prototype of the value decisions that must be made in social systems of all kinds. Morale and productivity, compassion and efficiency, personal ties and impersonal tasks — these are familiar enough pairs of values not simultaneously realiz-

---

[63] Indeed, this conception that activities directed toward instrumental and system-maintenance functions are antithetical is basic to the functional analysis of social problems. This is one of the several respects in which, contrary to much superficial opinion, the assumption of structural and functional *conflict* is inherent in functional sociology. Considerable observational and experimental work bears on this example of composite function-and-dysfunction; for a summary of this one finding, see James G. March and Herbert A. Simon, *Organizations* (New York: Wiley, 1958), pp. 60–61.

[64] For a few of the many studies to this effect, see A. B. Horsfall and C. M. Arensberg, "Teamwork and Productivity in a Shoe Factory," *Human Organization,* Vol. 8 (1949), pp. 13–25; J. G. Darley, Neal Gross, and W. E. Martin, "Studies of Group Behavior: Factors Associated with the Productivity of Groups," *Journal of Applied Psychology,* Vol. 36 (1952), pp. 396–403; N. Babchuk and W. J. Goode, "Work Incentives in a Self-Determined Group," *American Sociological Review,* Vol. 16 (1951), pp. 679–87.

[65] On the conception of the net balance of an aggregate of social consequences, see Robert K. Merton, *Social Theory and Social Structure,* pp. 105–8; Ralph M. Stogdill, *Individual Behavior and Group Achievement* (New York: Oxford University Press, 1959), pp. 222 ff. Melvin Tumin has indicated that the difficult problem of measuring this net balance has not yet been solved. That is the case. But it should also be noted that this problem, which has at least been identified in functional sociology as a focus of inquiry and analysis, is of course implicit in other sociological analyses of social disorganization and deviant behavior. In short, the same analytical difficulty is there, whether recognized or implicit. See Melvin Tumin, "The Functionalist Approach to Social Problems," *Social Problems,* Vol. 12 (Spring, 1965), pp. 379–88.

able to the fullest extent.[66] All this comprises a sociological near-equivalent to the economist's conception of opportunity costs, which means, in effect, as Scott Greer has indicated, that under certain conditions one commitment reduces the opportunities to make other commitments. By recognizing the composite of function-and-dysfunction we guard against that form of utopian thinking that neglects the social constraints upon pursuit of certain objectives that result from commitment to other, differing objectives. Neglect of these constraints leads to the false assumption that all values can be simultaneously maximized in society. But as the preceding chapters variously indicate, cost-free social action is only a sociological chimera.

4. It must be emphasized, above all, that the concept of social dysfunction does not harbor an implied moral judgment. Social dysfunction is not a term substituting for immorality, unethical practice, or the socially undesirable. It is an objective concept, not a morally evaluating one. Whether one judges a particular social dysfunction as good or bad, as desirable or regrettable, depends, not on the sociological analysis of the consequences for a particular social system, but upon the further and entirely independent judgment of the moral worth of that system. When we noted, for example, that enlarged opportunities for higher education are dysfunctional for the persistence of a caste system, we did not imply, let alone say, that the dysfunction was being judged as evil or undesirable. Or when it is observed that the extremely authoritarian character of the Nazi bureaucracy proved to be dysfunctional for the work of the bureaucracy by excessively restricting lines of communication among its several echelons, it is not to deplore that circumstance. Or when sociologists specify the functions of social conflict and,

---

[66] *Cf.* Robert K. Merton and Elinor Barber, "Sociological Ambivalence," in Edward A. Tiryakian, ed., *Sociological Theory, Values, and Social Change*, pp. 91–120. A rough analogy with the dysfunctional associates of functional genes does not of course supply evidence for the sociological parallel but does provide a sense that this combination is not confined to the plane of human society. Note, for example, the observation by the biochemist and geneticist, Caryl P. Haskins: ". . . the genes . . . do not assort completely independently in inheritance, but are associated into linkage groups. . . . These linked genes are inherited together, though each group as a whole assorts independently of other groups. This means that genetic characteristics which are disadvantageous or are of neutral value to the organism may be firmly linked to other characteristics which are of predominant survival value. Thus shielded by them in evolution, as it were, they may persist for very long periods merely by virtue of the fact that, under normal circumstances, they are inseparable from the benefactor genes and the damage which they cause the organism is much less serious than the evolutionary advantages conferred by their partners." *Of Societies and Men* (New York: Norton, 1951), pp. 113–14.

more specifically, the functions of racial conflict, they are engaged in socio-logical analysis, not in making moral judgments.[67] Sociological analyses of function and dysfunction are in a different universe of discourse from that of moral judgments; they are not merely different expressions for the same thing.[68]

All this would not need emphasis were it not for the frequently made assumption that nonconforming and other kinds of deviant behavior are necessarily dysfunctional to a social system and that social dysfunction, in turn, necessarily violates an ethical code. In the history of every society, one supposes, some of its culture heroes eventually come to be regarded as heroic in part because they are held to have had the courage and the vision to challenge the beliefs and routines of their society. The rebel, revolutionary, nonconformist, heretic, or renegade of an earlier day is often the culture hero of today. The distinction we have drawn between nonconforming and aber-rant behavior was in part designed to capture the basic differences in forms of deviant behavior. As has been noted before:

> If sociology does not systematically develop the distinctions between the social structure and functions of these diverse forms of deviant behavior, it will in effect . . . place a premium on the value to the group of conformity to its prevailing standards and imply that noncon-formity is necessarily dysfunctional to the group. Yet, as has been emphasized at several places in this book, it is not infrequently the case that the nonconforming minority in a society represents the interests and ultimate values of the society more effectively than the conforming majority. This, it should be repeated, is not a moral but a functional judgment, not a statement in ethical theory but a statement in sociological theory.[69]

Moreover, the accumulation of dysfunctions in a social system is often the prelude to concerted social change that may bring the system closer to the

---

[67] Dorothy Emmet, *Function, Purpose, and Powers* (London: Macmillan, 1958), pp. 78–82.

[68] Lewis A. Coser, *The Functions of Social Conflict* (New York: Free Press, 1956); Joseph S. Himes, "The Functions of Racial Conflict," *Social Forces,* Vol. 45 (September, 1966), pp. 1–10; Robert A. Dentler and Kai T. Erikson, "The Functions of Deviance in Groups," *Social Problems,* Vol. 7 (1959), pp. 98–107. See also the implications of theories affirming the value of lower-class social life as these are drawn by Lewis A. Coser, "Unanticipated Conservative Consequences of Liberal Theorizing," *Social Problems,* Vol. 16 (Winter, 1969), pp. 263–72.

[69] Robert K. Merton, *Social Theory and Social Structure,* pp. 107, 428 and Alvin Boskoff, "Social Indecision: A Dysfunctional Focus of Transitional Society," *Social Forces,* Vol. 37 (1959), pp. 305–11.

values that enjoy the respect of members of the society. For reasons of this kind, we end this section as we began it: The concept of social dysfunction is not based on ethical premises for it refers to how things work in society and not to their ethical worth.

The sociological art of drawing practical conclusions from theoretical premises and empirical investigation is of course still in the making. But then, so are all the other arts and sciences, no matter how advanced. At least, for the sake of their practitioners, one must hope so. It would be a sad thing if any branch of knowledge and its application had finished growing, with nothing left to be done. The pages of this book give some indication of how things now stand with the unfinished sociology of social problems.

Name Index

Bandura, A., 720n
Banfield, Edward, 9n, 13n
Barbash, Jack, 588n
Barber, Bernard, 705n
Barber, Elinor, 843n
Barber, Mary R., 237n
Barchha, R., 260n
Barnard, Chester I., 822n
Barnett, James H., 488n
Barton, Allen, 813n
Bateson, Gregory, 59n
Battacchi, M. W., 456n
Baxter, James C., 519n
Bayer, Alan E., 777n
Beach, Frank A., 332n, 353n, 357n
Beardslee, David C., 575n
Bechhofer, F., 394n
Becker, Howard S., 206, 206n, 207, 208,
   495n,513n,597n,819n,826,826n,827n,
   828, 829n
Becker, Joseph, 519n
Beebe, Gilbert, 42n
Beegle, J. Allan, 293n
Beers, Clifford, 66, 67
Beggs, Daniel C., 767n
Beigel, Hugo G., 316n
Beisser, Arnold, 519n
Belknap, Ivan, 74n, 79n
Bell, Daniel, 169n, 518n, 786n, 810n
Bell, Gerald, 596n
Bell, Norman W., 519n
Bell, Robert R., 333n
Bendix, Reinhard, 647n
Benedict, Ruth, 284, 284n
Benjamin, Harry, 341n, 358n
Bennis, Warren G., 518n
Bentham, Jeremy, 5, 6, 6n
Berelson, Bernard, 402n
Berger, Morroe, 384n
Berger, Peter L., 550n, 551n
Berkowitz, Leonard, 717n, 721n
Berlew, David E., 581n
Berlin, Isaiah, 832n
Bernard, Jessie, 495n, 496n, 526n, 532n,
   819n
Bettelheim, Bruno, 455n
Betz, George W., 372n
Bewley, T. H., 205n
Bienstock, Herbert, 577n
Biernacki, Patrick, 213n
Biesanz, J., 447n
Birch, Herbert G., 43n
Bird, Caroline, 532n
Birnbaum, Norman, 788n, 789n
Birren, James E., 60n

Bixby, F. Lovell, 142n
Blacker, C. P., 634n, 635n
Black, Hugo L., 420n
Black, Max, 820n
Blackstone, Tessa, 774n
Blackwell, Gordon, 616n
Blake, Judith, 315n, 392n, 476n, 616n
Blauner, Robert, 581n, 583n
Blau, Peter M., 574n, 575n, 579n, 778,
   778n, 822n
Blaustein, Albert P., 416n
Bloch, Herbert A., 150, 150n
Block, Jeanne H., 780n, 782n, 783, 783n
Bloomberg, Warner, Jr., 582n
Blumer, Herbert, 201n, 210, 210n
Blum, Richard, 783n, 784n, 786, 787n
Bodme, George E., 103n
Bogoras, Waldemar, 281n, 284n
Bogue, Donald J., 249n, 639n
Bond, Julian, 428n
Bonilla, Frank, 774n
Booth, Charles, 633n
Borda, O. F., 709n
Bordua, David J., 154n
Borgstrom, George, 388n
Borinski, E., 238n
Borkenstein, R. F., 245n
Borow, Henry, 595n
Boskoff, Alvin, 844n
Boulding, Elise, 515n
Boulding, Kenneth, 628n, 631n
Bourne, Randolph S., 756, 757n
Bowen, Howard R., 557n, 562n, 563n,
   567n, 570n
Bowers, William, 775n
Bowes, Harry P., 754, 754n
Brace, Charles, 655n
Bracher, Karl, 745n
Brackett, James W., 386n
Brackett, Joan, 778n
Bradley, Thomas, 429
Braly, K. W., 456n
Brandeis, Louis, 23
Braungart, Richard G.,773n,774n,775n,
   776, 776n, 781n, 784n
Brazer, Harvey, 613n
Breckenridge, M. B., 239n
Bredemeier, Harry C., 800, 800n
Breed, Warren, 295n
Bremner, Robert H., 624n, 628n, 630n,
   655n
Bright, James R., 557n, 562n, 564, 564n,
   565n
Brill, Norman O., 42n
Brimmer, Andrew, 436n

Mayhew, Leon, 421, 421n
Mays, John B., 153n
Means, R. L., 229n
Mechanic, David, 85n
Menninger, Karl A., 273n, 280n
Merei, F., 822n
Merrill, Francis E., 302, 302n
Merton, Robert K., 1, 11, 12, 12n, 20,
119n, 127n, 130, 155, 155n, 302n, 450n,
578n, 607n, 657n, 673, 674n, 693n, 695n,
723n, 793–845
Messinger, Sheldon L., 519n
Metzger, Walter, 556n, 578n
Meyer, Philip, 465n
Michael, Stanley T., 56n
Midelfort, Christian F., 519n
Miller, Abraham, 760n
Miller, Delbert C., 577n, 588n, 595n
Miller, Henry, 633n
Miller, Herman, 603n, 607, 607n
Miller, Neal E., 717n
Miller, Roy E., 785n, 786n
Miller, S. M., 576n, 606n, 630, 630n
Miller, Walter B., 111n, 130, 131, 131n,
156n, 606n
Miller, Warren E., 744n
Millet, Kate, 532n
Millis, Walter, 738n
Mills, C. Wright, 12, 581n, 593, 593n,
642n, 753, 753n, 788n, 815n
Mills, Enid, 47n
Milton, John, 479
Minard, R. D., 448n
Miner, John Rice, 282n, 290n
Mischler, Elliot G., 59n
Mitchell, Howard E., 506
Mitchell, John N., 221
Monahan, Thomas P., 112n, 495n, 496n,
497n, 498n, 499n
Moore, Wilbert E., 596n, 834n
Morgan, James, 613n
Morgan, Theodore, 372n, 374n
Morison, Samuel Eliot, 754, 754n, 779,
779n
Morreale, Ben, 599n
Morris, R., 432n
Morris, Richard T., 833n
Morse, Chandler, 820n
Morselli, Henry, 287n, 294n
Morse, Mary, 335n
Morse, Nancy C., 571n
Morton, R. S., 338n, 339n, 340n
Moss, M. K., 261n
Mowrer, Ernest R., 273n, 302, 302n, 495n
Mowrer, O. H., 717n

Moynihan, Daniel P., 436n, 437n, 610,
649n, 679n, 680n
Mudd, Emily H., 506n
Mugge, Robert, 614, 614n
Mulford, Harold A., 236n
Mullen, Joseph P., 643n
Mulvihill, Donald, 133n
Muñoz, Laura, 204n
Munsey, Frank, 18
Murchison, Carl, 121n
Murdock, George P., 323, 323n, 353n,
473n
Murphy, Gardner, 780n
Murphy, G. E., 216, 216n, 239n
Murphy, John P., 392n
Murtagh, John M., 342n, 347n, 349n
Mussolini, Benito, 745
Myers, Jerome K., 76n, 518n
Myers, Richard R., 806n
Myrdal, Gunnar, 808n

Naditch, Murray, 818n
Nagel, Ernest, 839n
Nass, Gilbert, 334n
Nehru, Jawaharlal, 831
Nevinson, John, 830
Newcomb, Theodore M., 775n
Nichols, David C., 751n
Niederhoffer, Arthur, 150, 150n
Nimkoff, Myer F., 526n
Nisbet, Robert, 1–25, 796n, 818n
Nixon, Richard M., 744, 748, 762, 765,
766, 769
Nolte, Ernst, 712n
Noonan, John T., 393n
Norbeck, Edward, 838n
Nosow, Sigmund, 568n, 577n, 598n
Nunnally, Jum C., 45n
Nye, F. Ivan, 111n
Nye, Russell, 755n

O'Connor, Richard, 631n
O'Donnell, John A., 214n, 215n
O'Dowd, Donald B., 575n
O'Gorman, Hubert J., 834n, 836n
Ohlin, Goran, 372n, 723n
Ohlin, Lloyd E., 130, 130n, 143, 152n,
154n, 155, 156n, 826n
Oliver, Ward L., 340n
Olson, V. J., 111n
O'Neill, William L., 532n
Opler, Marvin, 52n
Orbach, Harold, 640n

Westoff, Charles F., 392n
West, Patricia S., 446n, 674n
Wheelis, Allen, 597n
Whelpton, Pascal K., 392n
White, Edward, 418
Whitehead, Alfred North, 793, 794n
White, Lucia, 696n
White, Morton, 696n
White, R. W., 450n
Whitlow, Alana, 545n
Whitney, Eli, 413
Whyte, William Foote, 552n, 562n, 572n
Whyte, William H., Jr., 594–95, 596n
Wilcock, Richard C., 561n
Wildavsky, Aaron, 680n
Wilensky, Harold L., 596, 596n
Wilkins, Caroll, 448n
Williams, J. E. Hall, 353n
Williams, J. R., 238n
Williams, Richard H., 84n
Williams, Robin M., Jr., 448n, 834n
Wilmott, Peter, 660n
Wilner, D. M., 446n
Wilson, C. W. M., 205n
Wilson, Robert N., 62n
Winborn, Bob B., 775n
Winograd, Barry, 203, 203n
Winter, Ella, 348n
Wirth, Louis, 815n
Wirth, P. H. A., 189n
Wirtz, W. Willard, 589n
Wise, John M., 111n

Wittenborn, J. R., 188n, 195n, 196n, 204n, 218n, 220n, 226n
Wolfe, Arthur C., 744n
Wolfgang, Marvin, 104n, 112, 112n, 132, 132n, 133, 146n
Wolin, S. S., 775n, 781n
Woodham-Smith, Cecil, 649, 649n
Wood, Robert C., 353n, 384n
Woodward, C. Vann, 415, 415n
Wooton, Barbara, 633n
Works, E., 446n
Wynne, Lyman C., 59n, 519n

Yablonsky, Lewis, 142n, 151n, 156n, 225n
Yang, C. K., 490
Yarrow, Leon, 57n
Yarrow, Marian R., 46n
Yarrow, Penny R., 448n
Yorty, Samuel, 429
Young, Michael, 660n

Zilboorg, Gregory, 277, 277n, 280n, 281n
Zimmerman, Carle C., 292n, 671, 671n
Zimmern, Alfred, 343n
Znaniecki, Florian, 14, 20, 629, 630n, 695n, 819n, 821n
Zola, Émile, 18
Zubin, Joseph, 44n
Zuckerman, Harriet, 826n
Zuta, Jack, 348

Subject Index

Aberrant behavior, distinguished from nonconforming behavior, 829–32
Abortion, 107, 226, 327, 328, 332, 336, 337–38, 390, 391, 401, 402, 803–04; illegal, 328, 401
Abstinence syndrome, in drug addiction, 190, 192, 193, 198, 214
Accountability, 815–16
Activist value systems, 814–15
Activists, student, 758–61, 773–81, 783–87
Adolescence, 242; behavior disorders of, 35; and conflict with parents, 527, 529, 691; and drinking, 240–43, 258; and drug use, 201, 224, 243; organized community of, 691, 692; peer groups in, 209, 243, 528; see also Delinquency; Youth
Adultery, 326–29, 351
Affluent society, 15, 436, 569, 570
Africa: divorce rates in, 484; illegitimacy in, 474, 475; population growth in, 367; suicide rates in, 291
Age: alcohol use and, 236, 237; crime and delinquency rates by, 105, *106*, 107; employment status by, *548*, 549; of populations, 363, 375–79, 542; suicide rates by, 290, *291*, 303; see also Aging
Aggression, 716–17, 720, 722; distinguished from violence, 713

Aging: and disreputable poverty, 640–41; and family, 61, 538–44; marital adjustments and, 543–44; mental disorders and, 36, 39–41, 60–62, 85; social care of, 542–43; social roles and, 61; see also Retirement
Agrarian countries: child labor in, 375; consequences of population change in, 371–79, 380–81; economic development of, 372–78; family size in, 375, 378; land distribution schemes in, 378; political instability in, 377–78, 381; poverty in, 373, 374; unemployment in, 375–77; youthful populations in, 375–78, 381; see also Underdeveloped countries
Agriculture: mechanization of, 557; population shift out of, 378–79
Aid to Families with Dependent Children (AFDC), 495, 496, 560, 606, 613, 614, 616; and chiseling, 618–24; eligibility for, by states, *620–21*; and recipient rates, by place of residence, 614; recipients found ineligible, listed by states, 622–23; and status of fathers, 617
Aid to the Blind, 613
Air pollution, 384, 661–62
Albania, 368

31; student, 762–63; *see also* Subcultures

Courtship, 323, 327; anomie and conflict in, 334–36; for remarriage, 524

Crime, 8, 9, 10, 15, 89, 661, 810; by age groups, 105, *106*, 107; amateur, 163; anomie theory of, 127–28, 129; biological theories of, 139–40; causation of, 114–18, 132–34; concept of, 90–91; corruption and, 162–63, 165, 168–70, 175–76, 180–83, 348–49; data sources, 103; deterrence of, 135, 136, 137; and differential association, 126–27, 128, 142; distribution of, 102, 105, *106*, 107–14; drug use and, 214–15; ecological differences in, 111–14; effects of, on criminal-justice system, 97–98; functional necessity of, 3–4; "hidden," 110; and homosexuality, 358, 359; legal approach to reducing, 144–45; lower-class, 131; macrosociology of, 116, 127, 132; microsociology of, 115, 132–33, 144; multiple-factor theories of, 116–18; opportunity-structure theories of, 140–41, 143; organized, 147–58; *see also* Syndicated crime; "permissive," 182; and poverty, 181; professional, 158–63; psychiatric theories of, 122–23, 140; psychobiological theories of, 118–20; psychometric approaches to, 120–22; punishment of, 90, 101, 136; by race and ethnicity, 108–10; rates of, 15, 104–05, *106*, 107, 108; reduction of, 741; by sex, *106*, 107–08; social control of, *see* Social control of crime and delinquency; and social problems, 98–99; sociological perspectives on motivation in, 123–25; statistics, computation of, 102–04, 800; syndicated, *see* Syndicated crime; training for, 160–62; trends, 104–05; white-collar, 96, 102, 104, 107; working groups in, 158–63; *see also* Criminal-justice system; Criminology; Delinquency; Law; Police; Prison; Violence

Criminal-justice system, 90, 91, 93; effects of crime on, 97–98; and extralegal order, 94–96; humanitarianism and, 8; outputs of, 99–102; *see also* Crime; Criminology; Delinquency; Law; Police; Prison

Criminal law, 90, 91, 92, 148

Criminology, 97–98, 135; cultural-transmission theory in, 126, 141–42; and dif-

ferential association, 126; interactional framework for theory of, 114–16; *see also* Crime; Criminal-justice system; Delinquency; Law; Police; Prison

Cuba, *287*, *289*, 730, 760

Cultural-transmission theory, in criminology, 126, 141–42

Current Population Survey, 547, 550, 556

Cyprus, 370

Czechoslovakia, *287*, *289*, 753

Darwinism, Social, 413–14, 418

Death: adjustment to bereavement and divorce compared, 512–15, 522–24; rituals of, 513; *see also* Suicide

Death rates, 9, 328, 355, 364; from alcoholism, 256; decline of, 368–71, 373, 390; history of, *391*; and population problem, 389–90; suicidal, *see* Suicide rates; in underdeveloped countries, 366, 373

Delinquency, 67, 89, 750; by age groups, 105, *106*, 107; anomie theory of, 127–28, 129; biological theories of, 139–40; concept of, 91–94; distribution of, 102, 105, *106*, 107–14; ecological differences in, 111–14; education level and, 750; by ethnicity and race, 108–10; friendship groups, 148; gangs, 104, 130–31, 133–34, 149–50, 152–58; "hidden," 110, 112; legal approach to, 93–94, 144–45; life styles, 152, 156–68; macrosociology of, 127–32; microsociology of, 133–34, 144; multiple-factor theories of, 116–18; opportunity-structure and, 130–31, 140–41, 143, 177–83; organization in, 147–58; and poverty, 181; psychiatric theories of, 122–23, 140; psychobiological theories of, 118–20; psychometric approaches to, 120–22; rates of, 104, 105, *106*, 107, 108, 112, 113; rehabilitation and, 92, 93, 136; by sex, *106*, 107–08; and social class, 110–11, 128–31; social control of, *see* Social control of crime and delinquency; and sociological perspectives on motivation, 123–25; sources of data on, 103; statistics on, official, 102–04; subcultures in, 128–31, 141–43, 154–58; and syndicated crime, 175–83; trends, 104–05; violence in, 130, 132–34; working groups, 153–54; *see also* Crime; Criminal-justice system; Criminology; Law; Police; Prison

subcultures of, 150, 152, 155, 208–14, 216; types of, 210–11; *see also* Drug addiction; Drugs; specific drugs
Drugs: defined, 188–89; effects of, 188–98; "over-the-counter," 200; prescription, 189, 199, 200, 202; psychotropic, legal use of, 199–200; and public policy, 218–26; tolerance for, 190, 191, 192, 197; traffic in, 216–18; tranquilizing, 81–82, 84, 200, 208, 209; *see also* Drug addiction; Drug use; specific drugs
Duopoly, in international politics, 727
Dysfunctions, social, 838–45

Economic development, and population, 368–69, 372–78, 396–97
Economic trends, in race relations, 434–39
Education, 761; of blacks, 414, 420, 439–44, 461, 576, 761; impersonalization problem in, 444; integrated, 442; for occupation, 437, 574–80; and proneness to divorce, relationship between, 492–93; and race relations, 439–44; segregated, 414, 419, 420, 440–44, 461; *see also* Student unrest
Egalitarianism: divorce and, 489–90; and recognition of social problems, 6–9
Ego, in psychoanalytic theory, 122
Egypt, 331, 374, 378; Aswan Dam in, 374; death rate in, 373; divorce rates in, 482; population growth in, 367–68, 373, 374
Emancipation Proclamation, 415, 416
Employment: by age, *548*, 549; alcohol use and, 258; and automation, 561–68; of civilian noninstitutional population, *548*; and government educational programs, 438–39; mechanization and, 616, *617*; by race, *548*, 549, 554–56; and race relations, 419, 421–22, 434–39; by sex, *548*, 549, 552–54; welfare poor, 616, *617*; *see also* Automation; Labor; Labor unions; Occupation(s); Unemployment; Work
Encapsulated conflict, 726, 727, 729
Encounter groups, 595
England, 4, 65, 83, 189, 413, 541, 629, 800; abortion in, 338; Brock Committee in, 633–34, 635; common law of, 92; crime ratio in, male-female, 108; criminals of, Elizabethan period, 158; divorce rates in, 484; drug addiction in, 205;

drunken driving in, 246; eighteenth-century criminal law in, 837; firearms control in, 740; homosexuality in, 353; illegitimacy in, 338, *474*; infant mortality in, 337; Irish in, 648, 649; pauperization and, 645–51; police system in, 94; Poor Laws in, 559, 645, 646, 647; premarital intercourse in, 335; prostitution in, 350; race relations in, 395, 411–12; Speenhamland system in, 645, 646, 647, 648, 651; suicide in, *272*, *287*, 288, 289, 294, 302, 304; syphilis in, 339, 340; wartime stress in, and mental illness, 57
Epidemiology, 49–63
Ethnic groups: alcohol use and, 234–35, 237–39, 253–55; crime rates among, 108–10; labor discrimination, 589; occupational attainment of, 573–74; norms of, 12–14; poverty and, 611–12, 631–39, 652–54; race conflicts, 702–04; *see also* Minorities
Ethnomethodology, 833
Evasion, institutionalized, *see* Rules, evasions of
Externalization function of prejudice, 450, 452
Extramarital sex relations, 322, 326, 327

Fair Housing Act (1968), 431, 434
Family, 10, 404; adjustment of, to crises, 512–24; and aging, 61, 538–44; in agrarian countries, 378; and alcohol use, 258–60; disorganization of, *see* Family disorganization; empty-shell, 469, 470, 510–12; and mental disorders, impact of, 46–47, 83–84, 517–22; problem, 626; of schizophrenic patients, 57, 59–60; sex regulation and, 319–27; system, 470–72; uncompleted, 469, 472–79; and women's liberation movement, 532–38; *see also* Children; Family planning; Marriage
Family disorganization, 9, 467–544; of disreputable poor, 634–35; ghetto, and syndicated crime, 177; and larger society, 470–72; and parent-youth conflict, 469, 527–32; types of, 468–70; of welfare poor, 616–17; *see also* specific aspects
Family planning, 393, 399–402, 403; *see also* Birth control
Fascism, 745, 746, 757

Narcotics, *see* Drugs

National Advisory Commission on Civil Disorders, 176, 177

National Commission on the Causes and Prevention of Violence, 711, 721

National Housing Act, 431

National Institute of Mental Health, 36, 69, 70, 71, 75, 80, 263, 267

National Labor Relations Act (1935), 680

National Mental Health Act, 69

National Opinion Research Center, 44, 456

National Rifle Association, 739

National Student Association, 734

National Youth Alliance, 789

Nationalism, 729

NATO, 729

Nazis, 451, 722, 745–46, 843

Negative income tax, 439

Negroes, *see* Blacks

Netherlands, 277, *287*, *289*, 293, *295*

Neuroses, 35, 36, 41–42, 85; etiology of, 62–63

New Haven study of mental illness, 53–54

New Left, 748, 779, 788; *see also* Radicals, student; Student unrest

New Mobilization Against War, 760

New York City, 449, 465, 550, 636, 686, 720; anti-Negro riots in, before Civil War, 414; Hell's Kitchen in, 631, 632; heroin addiction in, 214, 216; housing projects in, 686–87; housing trends in, 432; mental illness in, 54–55, 56; Mobilization for Youth in, 679; Negro population of, 424; Patrolmen's Benevolent Association in, 748; population of, 382; syndicated crime in, 180

New York State, 448; abortion in, 338; antidiscrimination employment law in, 449; civil rights legislation in, 421; divorce law in, institutionalized evasions of, 835–36; gun law in, 740; hospitalization for mental illness in, 52; legal age in, for drinking, 241, 243; welfare programs in, 614

New Zealand, suicide in, 278, *287*, 288, *289*, *295*, 296, 304, 311

Nicaragua, *287*, *289*, 290

Nigeria, 368

Nihilism, 756, 761, 783

Nonconforming behavior: and aberrant behavior compared, 829–32; drug use and, 187, 201, 211

Normative reference groups, 125

Norms: of aging, 539, 541; attributes of, and deviant behavior, 832–34; discrepancies between actuality and, 799–801, 802–06; and divorce attitudes, 487–88, 506–07; institutionalized evasion of rules and, 834–38; mass communication and, 697–98; moral status of law and, 94–95; mores and, 3; sex, *see* Sex norms; situational, and discrimination, 447–50; suicide and weakness of, 273–74; variability of, 12–14

Norway, 394; abortion in, 338; courtship in, 323; drunken driving in, 246; illegitimacy in, 338; infant mortality in, 337; suicide in, 276, 287, *289*, *299*

Nosology, 34

"Numbers" racket, 157–58, 174, 175–77

Numerical-control machines, 565

Obsessive-compulsive reaction, 41

Occupation(s): of AFDC fathers and employed men, 617, *618*; and divorce, *492*; employed persons in major, *553*, *554*, *555*; ethnicity and, 435, 437, 554–56, 573–74; professional and managerial, 595–600; and schooling, 437, 574–80; by sex, 552–54, *553*; suicide rates by, 293–94; trends in, 550–61; *see also* Automation; Employment; Labor Unions; Unemployment; Work

Office of Economic Opportunity, 679

Old age, *see* Aging

Old-Age Assistance, 613

Ontario, 267, 268

Opiates, 185–93, 199, 205, 214, 219

Opium, 185, 191, 218, 219

Opportunity-structure in crime and delinquency, 130–31, 140–41, 143, 177–83, 826

Oregon, 414

Orientals (U. S.), 109, 291, 292, 307

Outpatient services, for mental illness, 75–77, 78, 84

Overpopulation, *see* Population growth

Pakistan, 399, 602

Palestine, 394, 395

Panopticon, 6

Paranoia, 39

Paranoid schizophrenia, 30, 39

Parent-youth conflict, 469, 527–32

Renaissance, 7, 64
Renunciatory youth, 749–52, 756–57, 761–62, 783, 788–91
Residual deviance, 48
Responsibility, ethic of, 815–16
Retardation, mental, 43, 121, 469, 520–21
Retirement, 61, 542, 549, 572, 582, 596–97; see also Aging
Retreatism, 131, 152, 155
Right-wing youth movements, 745–49, 790
Role(s): aging and, 540; in conflict gangs, 150–51; criminality and, 124–25; in family conflicts, 469, 489–90, 504, 505, 516, 517–22; mental illness and, 47–48, 519–22; racial, 459–61; schizophrenia, and conflict of, 60; self-definition and, 124–25; and women's liberation movement, 532–38
ROTC, 757, 769
Rules, evasions of, 89–90; crime as, 90–91; deviant behavior and, 825–38; institutionalized, 834–38
Rural-urban migration, 378–79, 380–81
Russell Sage Foundation, 631
Russia, 189, 752; see also Soviet Union
Rwanda, 368

Samoa, 677
San Francisco: drug use in, 202, 203; homosexuality in, 359; mental illness of aged in, 61; Negro population of, 424
Satellite cities, 690
Scandinavia: abortion in, 328, 337–38; birth rates in, 403; drug addiction in, 205; drunken driving in, 246; illegitimacy in, 474; premarital intercourse in, 327, 331, 475; see also specific countries
Schizophrenia, 36, 51, 53, 80, 84; case description of, 30–32; etiology of, 58–59, 60; and family relationships, 57, 59–60; genetic predisposition in, 58–59, 60; and social relations, 58–60; subtypes of, 39; symptomatic manifestations of, 38–39
Schooling, see Education
Science: and population problem, 387, 389, 397–98
Segregation, 416–19, 758, 759; de facto, 422, 423, 440, 441; de jure, 419, 420,

422–23, 441; educational, 414, 419, 420, 440–44, 461; in housing, 430–34; roots of, 415–16; Social Darwinism and, 418; see also Desegregation
Self: components of, 123; defined in role terms, 124–25; value and meaning of, 125
Self-fulfilling prophecy, 829
Self-help, ethic of, 45–49
Senility, see Aging
Separation, marital dissolution by, 469, 479, 481, 491, 494, 495, 617
Separatism, black, 462, 464, 465
Sex: alcoholism rates by, 238–39, 252; crime rates by, 106, 107–08; employment by, 548, 549, 552–54; income by, 552–54; suicide rates by, 276, 288, 289, 290, 291
Sex drive, 316, 323, 329; as object of regulation, 316–17; see also Sexual behavior
Sex norms: enforcement of, 317–18, 329; gradation of, 318, 323; homosexuality and, 351–55; keys to, 319–22; theory of, 314–22; for youth, conflict over, 329
Sexual behavior: aging and, 543–44; alcohol use and, 241, 252, 253; anarchic position on, 313–14, 324–25, 328–29; authoritarian position on, 313; contraception and, 328, 332, 337; deviant, 35; double standard of, 326–27, 331; family disorganization and, 504, 505, 506; homosexuality, 351–60; venereal disease and, 328, 336, 338–40, 341, 358, 359; premarital, 319, 320, 323, 327, 330–40, 475–76, 477; prostitution, 341–51; regulation of, 314, 316–22; social change and, 327–30; see also Illegitimacy; Sex drive; Sex norms
Shoplifting, 147–49, 159–62
Singapore, 399–400, 405
Slavery, 408, 411–14, 545; and free Negroes, 414–15
Slums, 631–39
Smoking, 189, 200, 202–03, 226
Social action, and social policy, 22–25
Social change: authority and, 698–99; divorce rates as indices of, 484–85; mechanisms of, 732–36; parent-youth conflict and, 529–30; population control and, 402–05; right-wing movements and, 745–79; and sex behavior in advanced countries, 327–30
Social class: delinquency and, 110–11, 128–31; humanitarianism and, 6–9;

Social class (cont.)

marriage stability and, 483–84, 491–503; mental illness and, 52–56, 59; norms and, 12–13; occupational education and, 574–80; sex regulation and, 321–22; *see also* specific classes

Social control of crime and delinquency, 134–45, 183; behavior theories in, 139–45; functions of, 136–39; and group and individual treatment, 138, 140, 142–43; and institutionalization, 138; levels of intervention in, 138; strategies for, 139–45; and structural change in community, 138–39, 143

Social Darwinism, 413–14, 418

Social disorganization, 86, 87, 272, 695, 819–23; and deviant behavior, 818–38; and homosexuality, 358; and social dysfunctions, relationship between, 839; and suicide, 272–74, 302–03; *see also* Community disorganization

Social dysfunctions, 838–45

Social perception, 5–9, 810–13

Social policy: on alcoholism, 265–68; and deliquency and crime, 134–45; and mental disorder, 63–70; and social action, 22–25

Social problem(s): approaches to, 16–19; comparative study of, 14–16; corrigibility of, 10–11, 22–25, 814–18; and crime, 98–99; cultural base of, 9–14; definition of, 1–2, 798–813; and discrepancy between social standards and social actuality, 799–801; drug use as, 186–88; functional analysis of, 795–98; judges of, 802–06; and law, 17, 144–45; manifest and latent, 806–10; modern recognition of, 5–9; objective aspect of, 1, 12; population growth as, 365; poverty as, 2, 601–55; relativity of, 2–5; and social dysfunctions, 838–45; social origins of, 801–02; social perception of, 5–9, 810–13; and sociology, 19–21, 793–845; study of, 1–25; subjective aspect of, 1, 12; suicide as, 271–75, 310–12; variability, historical, of, 12–14

Social standards, *see* Norms

Social structure: consensus formation and, 729–30; divorce and, 487–90; violence-prone, 731–32

Social visibility, 624–25, 813

Socialization, disorganization and, 822

Socialism, 656, 745, 755, 756, 758

Socioeconomic strata, *see* Social classes

Sociology, 11; comparative, 3; and crime, 123–25; defined, 2; history of, 21; of law, 730; and social problems, 19–21, 793–845; of suicide, 275–79, 284–86, 310–12

South Africa, 395, 412, 444, 456

South Korea, 368, 399, 400

Soviet Union, 24, 728, 730, 738, 739, 821; abortion in, 328; drinking in, 257; exclusionist policy of, 395; population growth in, 381, *382*; prostitution in, 348; views of, on overpopulation, 385–87, 389, 393, 396; *see also* Russia

Spain, *287*, *289*, 411, 480

Speenhamland system, 645, 646, 647, 648, 651

Stalinism, 758, 760

Standard metropolitan statistical areas, 430

Statistics, computation of: on crime and delinquency, 102–04, 800; on diseases associated with cigarette smoking, 226; on suicide, 276–78

Status: of father in AFDC families, *617*; and integration, 308, 309; and mental health, 52–56, 59; middle-class criteria of, 129; in organized crime, 147, 159–60, 163; and reference groups, 125; social disorganization and, 823; and suicide, *198*, 306–09; and working class, 129, 584

Stereotypes, prejudice and, 455–59, 637–39

Stimulus-object approach to race relations, *409*, 410

Stirling County (Canada) study of mental illness, 56

Street clubs, juvenile, 150–54

Street corner groups, *see* Gangs, delinquent

Stress: alcoholism and, 250–55, 259; criminality as response to, 122; and mental illness, 56–57

Strikes, 546, 590–92, 724, 735–36

Students, college: activists, 758–61, 773–81, 783–87; alienation, 766–67, 769–73; antisystem movements supported by, 751–54; backgrounds and politics of, 773–84; black, 759–60, 776–77; conforming, 763–70; conservative politics and, 746, 774; cultural protests by, 754–58, 771–73; dissenters, 783; drug use and, 771–72, 783, *see also* Drug use; life style, 761–63, 771–73; protests, 751–63; psychological research on, 781–87;